OXFORD
PRIVATE INTERNATIONAL LAW
SERIES

GENERAL EDITOR: JAMES J FAWCETT
Professor of Law
University of Nottingham

INTERNATIONAL SALE OF GOODS IN THE CONFLICT OF LAWS

OXFORD PRIVATE INTERNATIONAL LAW SERIES

General Editor: James J Fawcett

The aim of the series is to publish works of quality and originality in a number of important areas of private international law. The series is intended for both scholarly and practitioner readers.

INTERNATIONAL SALE OF GOODS IN THE CONFLICT OF LAWS

JAMES J FAWCETT
Professor of Law
University of Nottingham

JONATHAN M HARRIS
Professor of International Commercial Law
University of Birmingham

MICHAEL BRIDGE
Professor of Commercial Law
and
Dean of the Faculty of Laws,
University College London
Director of Legal Research, Norton Rose

OXFORD
UNIVERSITY PRESS

OXFORD

UNIVERSITY PRESS

Great Clarendon Street, Oxford OX2 6DP

Oxford University Press is a department of the University of Oxford.
It furthers the University's objective of excellence in research, scholarship,
and education by publishing worldwide in

Oxford New York

Auckland Cape Town Dar es Salaam Hong Kong Karachi
Kuala Lumpur Madrid Melbourne Mexico City Nairobi
New Delhi Shanghai Taipei Toronto

With offices in

Argentina Austria Brazil Chile Czech Republic France Greece
Guatemala Hungary Italy Japan South Korea Poland Portugal
Singapore Switzerland Thailand Turkey Ukraine Vietnam

Oxford is a registered trade mark of Oxford University Press
in the UK and in certain other countries

Published in the United States
by Oxford University Press Inc., New York

British Library Cataloguing in Publication Data

Data available

Library of Congress Cataloging in Publication Data

Data available

ISBN 0–19–924469–3

1 3 5 7 9 10 8 6 4 2

Typeset by RefineCatch Limited, Bungay, Suffolk
Printed in Great Britain by
Antony Rowe Ltd, Chippenham

Preface

It is difficult to think of a more common or more important contract in any domestic legal system than the contract for the sale of goods. Contracts of sale with a cross-border element are an everyday occurrence and one which is becoming ever more common with the advent of modern communications technology: from the traditional standard form contract for the purchase of grain to the purchase of software over the internet. Of course, conflict of laws (private international law) rules exist in England to deal with international contracts and much of that law is of central importance to the contract for the international sale of goods. However, the application of general principles and rules of the conflict of laws to international sale of goods cases raises many problems on which the learning is sparse. There are also some special conflict of laws rules which deal specifically with contracts for the sale of goods; these merit a more detailed examination than has hitherto been given to them. The aim of the book is to fill this gap in the literature. At the same time, the process of applying general principles and rules of the conflict of laws to a specific area can reveal much about the strengths and weaknesses of those principles and rules.

The book is divided up into sections to reflect the classic issues in the conflict of laws: jurisdiction; choice of law; and recognition and enforcement of foreign judgments. Few sales specific problems arise in relation to recognition and enforcement and so this section is brief. Most of the book is concerned with jurisdiction and choice of law. Within these two sections, there are chapters to reflect the major actions that can arise out of a contract for the international sale of goods: actions in contract between the buyer and seller; actions in tort; restitutionary claims and claims arising out of proprietary matters. Multi-party claims are commonplace in international sale of goods cases and raise particular questions in the jurisdictional context which deserve separate treatment. Concurrent claims raise particular problems in the choice of law context and these too deserve separate treatment. Choice of law problems also arise in cases where the Vienna Convention or the Hague Convention on the Law Applicable to International Sale of Goods of 1955 is applicable and these have to be considered. Finally, in cases where the contract for the international sale of goods involves use of the internet, this can give rise to any of the actions mentioned above. The application of conflict of laws rules to actions arising out of the international sale of goods becomes doubly difficult in internet cases. There are therefore lengthy chapters on jurisdiction and choice of law in cases of electronic commerce.

The emphasis in the book is on the conflict of laws rather than on international sale of goods law. Nonetheless, in order to understand how conflict of laws problems arise and are solved, some knowledge of the substantive law background is at times necessary and is provided. For example, jurisdictional rules concerned with the contractual obligation in question make little sense unless the reader is aware of the basic obligations of the seller and buyer. Likewise, jurisdiction and choice of law rules for torts require the elements of the tort in question to be identified. The book is aimed at practitioners as well as academics. This means that an outline of the basic conflict of laws rules has to be given before moving on to the heart of the book, the application of these rules to international sale of goods cases.

James Fawcett has written Chapters 1–10 of the book. Jonathan Harris has written chapters 11, 12, 13, 14, 15, 17, 19, 20 and 21. Michael Bridge has written Chapters 16 and 18. A number of chapters contain inserts explaining the substantive law background in England, under the Vienna Convention and in other jurisdictions to the conflict of laws issues that are discussed in that chapter. Michael Bridge has written the majority of these. All of the authors have read and commented upon all chapters in the book and take joint responsibility for the entirety of the book.

We have relied upon the help and guidance of friends and colleagues in preparing this book and would like particularly to thank: Howard Bennett, Jean-Paul Béraudo, Stephen Girvin, Sarah Green, Myriam Hunter-Henin, Frank Meisel, Horton Rogers, Craig Rotherham, Stephen Todd.

Any errors are, of course, our own responsibility.

The law is stated as at 1 June 2004.

James Fawcett
Jonathan Harris
Michael Bridge
Nottingham, Birmingham and London

Summary Contents

Contents

PART II RECOGNITION AND ENFORCEMENT
OF FOREIGN JUDGMENTS

Chapter 11 THE RECOGNITION AND ENFORCEMENT OF FOREIGN
JUDGMENTS

PART III CHOICE OF LAW

Contents

Table of Cases

UNITED KINGDOM

AUSTRALIA

AUSTRIA

BELGIUM

CANADA

DENMARK

GERMANY

HONG KONG

NEW ZEALAND

RUSSIA

SINGAPORE

SWITZERLAND

UNITED STATES

ICC COURT OF ARBITRATION

ECJ DECISIONS

Table of Legislation

NATIONAL LEGISLATION

UK Statutes

UK Statutory Instruments

Australia

Abbreviations

Glossary

C&F	cost and freight
CIF	cost, insurance and freight
DES	delivery ex ship
ECJ	European Court of Justice
FAS	free alongside ship
FOB	free on board
FOR	free on rail
FOSFA	Federation of Oils, Seeds and Fats Associations Ltd
FOT	free on truck
GAFTA	Grain and Feed Trade Association
ICC	International Chamber of Commerce
UNCITRAL	United Nations Commission on International Trade Law

Instruments cited in abbreviated form

Brussels I Regulation	Council Regulation (EC) No 44/2001 of 22 December 2000 on Jurisdiction and the Recognition and Enforcement of Judgments in Civil and Commercial Matters [2001] OJ L12/1
CISG	UN Convention on the International Sale of Goods (Vienna Convention)
CPR	Civil Procedure Rules
E-Commerce Directive	Directive (EC) 2000/31 of the European Parliament and Council, 8 June 2000, on Certain Legal Aspects of Information Society Services, in particular Electronic Commerce [2000] OJ L178/1
E-Commerce Regulations	Electronic Commerce (EC Directive) Regulations 2002, SI 2002/2013
Rome Convention	EC Convention on the Law Applicable to Contractual Obligations 1980
RSC	Rules of the Supreme Court
ULF	Uniform Law on the Formation of Contracts for the International Sale of Goods
ULIS	Uniform Law on the International Sale of Goods
Vienna Convention	UN Convention on the International Sale of Goods (CISG)

Books cited in abbreviated form

Benjamin	A Guest (ed), *Benjamin's Sale of Goods* (6th edn, London: Sweet & Maxwell, 2002)
Bridge, *The International Sale of Goods*	M Bridge, *The International Sale of Goods: Law and Practice* (Oxford: OUP, 1999)
Bridge, *The Sale of Goods*	M Bridge, *The Sale of Goods* (Oxford: Clarendon, 1997)
Briggs and Rees	A Briggs and P Rees, *Civil Jurisdiction and Judgments* (3rd edn, London: LLP, 2002)
Cheshire and North	P North and J Fawcett (eds), *Cheshire and North's Private International Law* (13th edn, London: Butterworths, 1999)
Dicey and Morris	L Collins et al (eds), *Dicey and Morris on the Conflict of Laws* (13th edn, London: Sweet & Maxwell, 2000)
Fawcett and Torremans	J Fawcett and P Torremans, *Intellectual Property and Private International Law* (Oxford: OUP, 1998)
Gaskell	N Gaskell, R Asariotis and Y Baatz, *Bills of Lading: Law and Contracts* (London: LLP, 2000)
O'Malley and Layton	S O'Malley and A Layton, *European Civil Practice* (London: Sweet & Maxwell, 1989)
R Plender and M Wilderspin	*The European Contracts Convention* (2nd edn, London: Sweet and Maxwell, 2001)
Schlechtriem	P Schlechtriem (ed) (trans Thomas), *Commentary on the UN Convention on the International Sale of Goods* (2nd edn, Oxford: Clarendon, 1998)

1

Introduction

I. IMPORTANCE OF THE INTERNATIONAL SALE OF GOODS

It is sometimes said that God must have loved shipowners because he **1.01** covered two-thirds of the Earth's surface with water and located raw materials and minerals in the places and continents where they were not needed. Large quantities of grain, oil, coal, phosphates and bauxite and other ores are bought, sold and shipped across the world. The volume of trade is enormous. In addition to such raw materials, there is the trade in manufactured items which, in the years since the Second World War, has proliferated, almost from a standstill in the case of the emergent Far Eastern economies. The importance of sale of goods in the world economy is close to being self-evident, even as world trade in services and construction assumes ever-greater importance.

The importance of sale is recognized too by the prominent position it **1.02** occupies in the vanguard of the uniform law movement, whether it is a matter of uniform choice of law rules or of uniform substantive law. Techniques and principles that appear in sale instruments are adopted elsewhere. In this regard, attention should be drawn to the intellectual and practical force of the UN Convention on the International Sale of Goods (CISG) 1980, which is the linchpin of modern attempts, descriptive and prescriptive, to recreate the mediaeval *lex mercatoria*.

II. SCOPE OF THE BOOK

1.03 This book is concerned with the application of the principles and rules of the conflict of laws to claims arising out of the international sale of goods. A little needs to be said about what is meant by 'international sale of goods' for the purposes of this book, the sort of claims that arise out of the international sale of goods, and the principles and rules of the conflict of laws.

1. INTERNATIONAL SALE OF GOODS

The Different 'Definitions'

1.04 It is important to consider at the outset what we mean for the purposes of this book by 'the international sale of goods'. There is no single universally accepted definition of this concept. However, guidance on the meaning of this concept can be found in the CISG, often referred to in conflict of laws cases as the Vienna Convention, and in the Hague Conventions on the Law Applicable to International Sale of Goods of 1955 and 1986, although none of these provides a positive definition of 'international sale of goods'. What is clear is that these three Conventions differ on the meaning of 'international', 'sale' and 'goods'. There is, though, a definition of 'sale of goods' under English law. This means something different from sale of goods under the Vienna and Hague Sales Conventions of 1955 and 1986. We will now consider in brief the meaning of these terms under the Vienna Convention, the Hague Sales Conventions of 1955 and 1986 and English law, highlighting some of the differences between them. A fuller treatment will follow later when the scope of these Conventions is examined in detail.[1]

The Vienna Convention

1.05 **International** Article 1(1) of the Vienna Convention starts off by stating that: 'This Convention applies to contracts of sale of goods between parties whose places of business are in different States . . .'. It goes on to require for the application of the Convention that the states (where the parties have their respective places of business) are Contracting States to the Convention or that the rules of private international law lead to the application of the law of a Contracting State.[2]

---

[1] For a detailed examination of the meaning of 'international sale of goods' under the Vienna Convention see paras 16.16–95, and under the Hague Sales Conventions 1955 and 1986 see paras 15.11–20. See also paras 12.18–20.

[2] Art 1(a) and (b). The UK is not a Contracting State.

Sale The Vienna Convention does not define 'sale'. However, it does **1.06** specifically exclude certain types of sale, such as judicial sales and sales by auction.[3] Article 3(2) of the Convention also excludes contracts where the 'preponderant' part of the supplier's obligation is the provision of labour or services. In contrast, Article 3(1) makes it clear that contracts for the supply of goods to be manufactured or produced are to be considered sales 'unless the party who orders the goods undertakes to supply a substantial part of the materials necessary for such manufacture or production'.

Goods The Vienna Convention also provides no definition of 'goods'. **1.07** However, it does set out some specific exclusions, such as stocks, shares, securities, negotiable instruments and money.[4] It excludes goods that are purchased for personal, family or household use.[5] It also excludes the sale of ships and aircraft[6] and the sale of electricity.[7] More generally, the fact that the Vienna Convention contains specific exclusions but no positive definition of 'goods' would suggest that this concept should be given a broad meaning. This might include minerals and crops.[8]

The Hague Sales Conventions 1955 and 1986

Article 1 of the 1955 Convention states that the Convention applies to **1.08** 'international sales of goods'. The title of the 1986 Convention uses the same phrase, as does its preamble.

International The 1955 Convention applies only to 'international' **1.09** sales contracts. This is not defined in a positive way, but the Convention does state what would be insufficient to render a contract 'international' for these purposes. Article 1(4) provides that: 'A mere declaration by the parties relative to the application of a law or the jurisdiction of a judge or arbitrator is not sufficient to confer upon the sale international character . . .'. Article 1 of the 1986 Convention, which is concerned with its scope, refers merely to 'contracts of sale of goods'. Nonetheless, Article 1 makes it clear that the 1986 Convention requires for its application an 'international' sale of goods contract. This Article provides that the Convention will only apply to sale of goods contracts (a) where the parties have their places of business in different states; (b) in all other cases involving a choice between the laws of different states, unless such a choice arises solely from a stipulation by the parties as to the applicable law, even if accompanied by a choice of court or arbitration.

---

[3] Art 2(b) and (c).   [4] Art 2(d).   [5] Art 2(a).   [6] Art 2(e).   [7] Art 2(f).
[8] According to Art 3(1), the Convention applies to goods which are 'produced'.

1.10 Sale The 1955 Convention fails to explain what the word 'sale' means. Doubtless this is referring to property passing from the buyer to the seller. However, it does provide an answer where the contract is for the delivery of goods which first have to be manufactured or produced: namely that the contract still falls within the scope of the Convention as long as the party who is to deliver the goods is to provide the raw materials for the manufacture or production.[9] A similar provision is to be found in the 1986 Convention.[10] The 1986 Convention also makes express provision for contracts involving the supply of labour or other services. These will not be treated as contracts of sale if the provision of labour or other services is the preponderant part of the obligations of the party who furnishes the goods.[11] This adopts the same wording as that found in the Vienna Convention.[12]

1.11 Goods When it comes to the meaning of 'goods', under the 1955 Convention the same pattern as in the Vienna Convention of specific exclusions, rather than a positive definition, is to be found. Sales of securities, as well as sales of ships, registered boats and aircraft are excluded from the scope of the 1955 Convention.[13] Also excluded are 'sales upon judicial order or by way of execution'.[14] There is one positive inclusion. This provides that the Convention applies to sales based on documents.[15] Beyond that, it is unclear what 'goods' are. There is, for example, no express exclusion of certain types of contract expressly excluded in the Vienna Convention, such as the sale of stocks, shares, negotiable instruments and money.[16]

1.12 The 1986 Convention is more helpful on the meaning of goods in two respects. First, it contains a much more extensive list of exclusions than the 1955 Convention. This list draws upon the exclusions in the 1955 Convention and the Vienna Convention, but is not identical to either. Involuntary sales by way of execution or by authority of law are excluded,[17] as under the 1955 Convention. The 1986 Convention also excludes sales of 'stocks, shares, investment securities, negotiable instruments or money . . .'.[18] Finally, it excludes goods bought 'for personal,

---

[9] Art 1(3).
[10] Art 4(1) states that contracts for the supply of goods to be manufactured or produced shall still be treated as contracts of sale unless the *buyer* undertakes to supply a substantial part of the materials for manufacture or production.
[11] Art 4(2).   [12] Art 3(2).   [13] Art 1(2).   [14] ibid.   [15] Art 1(2)
[16] Art 2(d) of the Vienna Convention. Contracts for the sale of electricity are also excluded from the Vienna Convention: Art 2(f).
[17] Art 2(a) of the 1986 Convention.
[18] Art 2(b) of the 1986 Convention.

family or household use'.[19] Second, and more positively, the 1986 Convention does expressly state that certain matters do fall within the definition of goods. So, a sale of goods based on documents will fall within the Convention,[20] as do sales of 'ships, vessels, boats and aircraft'.[21] The 1986 Convention also extends to the sale of electricity,[22] which is excluded from the Vienna Convention.[23]

Sale of goods under English law

The Sale of Goods Act 1979 defines a contract of sale as comprising 'an **1.13** agreement to sell' and 'a sale'.[24] Section 2(1) describes a 'sale' as the process by which 'the seller transfers or agrees to transfer the property in the goods for money consideration called the price'. This excludes contracts of exchange of goods or consideration through the provision of services.[25] Although there is a distinction in English law between work and materials contracts and sale of goods contracts,[26] this distinction is of little importance because the law governing sale and work and materials has become more or less identical.[27]

In English law, the term 'goods' is defined in s 61 of the Sale of Goods Act **1.14** 1979 as including 'all personal chattels other than things in action and money', in particular 'emblements, industrial growing crops, and things attached to or forming part of the land which are agreed to be severed before sale of under the contract of sale'.[28] Gas and electricity may also be considered to be goods.[29] Unlike the Vienna Convention, the Act does cover the sale of ships and aircraft.[30]

Different 'Definitions' for Different Purposes

Each of these different 'definitions' will become important at different **1.15** points of discussion in the book. Thus in Chapter 3 (jurisdiction under the EC rules), when it comes to defining the meaning of sale of goods for the purposes of Article 5(1)(b) of the Brussels I Regulation it is the meaning under the Vienna Convention to which we should turn.[31] In contrast, in

---

[19] Art 2(c). The Convention does, however, apply if the seller at the time of the conclusion of the contract neither knew nor ought to have known that the goods were bought for any such use.

[20] Art 2(b). [21] Art 3(a). [22] Art 3(b) of the 1986 Convention.

[23] Art 2(f) of the Vienna Convention.

[24] ss 2(1),(4) and (5). Discussed in Bridge, *The Sale of Goods*, 36–38.

[25] See ibid, 46–49 for a discussion of works and materials contracts.

[26] ibid, 46–49. [27] ibid. [28] ibid, Ch 2.

[29] See the Sale of Goods Act 1979, s 61(1); Benjamin, 25–004.

[30] See further Bridge, *The Sale of Goods*, 21–31.

[31] See below, paras 3.147–148.

Chapter 13 (choice of law in contract and the international sale of goods), when it comes to deciding whether the Unfair Contract Terms Act 1977 applies, it is to the English substantive law concept of a sale of goods that we must turn.[32] Chapter 16 deals specifically with the question whether the Vienna Convention contains choice of law rules.[33] In that chapter we are concerned with the meaning of 'international sale of goods' as set out in the Vienna Convention and this will necessitate a very detailed discussion. Similarly, Chapter 15, which discusses the Hague Sales Conventions of 1955 and 1986, is concerned with the meaning of the 'international sale of goods' as set out in those Conventions.[34] Again this will necessitate a detailed discussion.

'International' Sale of Goods and the Scope of the Book

1.16 The scope of this book is not and should not be limited to cases of 'international' sale of goods within the narrow meaning of the Vienna Convention or the Hague Sales Conventions of 1955 and 1986. What we are concerned with in this book are conflict of laws problems that arise in international sale of goods cases. Conflict of laws problems arise in cases where there is a foreign element. Reference to the 'international' sale of goods naturally connotes a foreign element. But, as has been seen, under the Vienna and Hague Sales Conventions the 'international' requirement for the operation of those Conventions is a specific and narrow one that is not satisfied merely by showing a foreign element. A number of examples can be given to illustrate the difference.

1.17 In the first example, a contract is made between two parties whose places of business are both in France. But under the contract delivery takes place in England. A contractual dispute arises between the parties and the claimant wishes to sue the defendant in England. This falls outside the scope of the Vienna Convention because this only applies to contracts of sale of goods between parties whose places of business are in different states.[35] In such a case, there is obviously a foreign element. Technically these facts raise a jurisdictional problem falling within the scope of the Brussels I Regulation. The latter does not require that the parties are domiciled in different Member States. According to its title,[36] the Regulation is concerned, *inter alia*, with 'jurisdiction'. This should be read as referring to 'international' jurisdiction.[37] Normally, no such problem is

---

[32] See below, para 13.302   [33] See below, paras 16.24–26.
[34] See below, paras 15.11–20.   [35] Art 1(1).
[36] Council Regulation (EC) No 44/2001 of 22 December 2000 on jurisdiction and the recognition and enforcement of judgments in civil and commercial matters [2001] OJ L12/1
[37] This was spelt out in the Preamble to the earlier Brussels Convention.

raised where the parties are domiciled in the same Member State.[38] But it is different if the facts trigger the application of a basis of jurisdiction (other than jurisdiction based on the domicile of the defendant).[39] In the above example, jurisdiction is allocated to England under the Regulation by virtue of the delivery there,[40] as well as to France. The application of the Regulation also requires that there is a civil and commercial matter, which there is. This example raises a conflict of laws problem in relation to jurisdiction, and is properly a matter for discussion in this book. This example also raises a conflict of laws problem in relation to the law applicable to the sales contract. The EC Convention on the law applicable to contractual obligations of 1980 (the Rome Convention) applies where there is a choice between the laws of different countries. This requirement can be met even where the parties have their place of business in the same country.[41]

The second example is where one of the parties has its place of business in **1.18** the United Kingdom, the other in France, and the law applicable to the sale of goods contract is that of England. It will be recalled that the Vienna Convention requires that the different states (where the parties have their respective places of business) are Contracting States to the Convention or that the rules of private international law lead to the application of the law of a Contracting State.[42] The United Kingdom is not a Contracting State. It follows that the Vienna Convention will not apply. Yet such a case clearly raises a jurisdictional problem which should be discussed in this book.

The third example is where A, a seller resident in France, contracts to sell **1.19** goods to B, a buyer resident in France, and the goods are to be delivered from Paris to Marseilles. The contract is clearly a domestic one. The contract contains a clause stating that it shall be subject to the law of England. Under the Hague Sales Convention 1955 it is expressly provided that the mere choice of a foreign law by the parties does not render the contract 'international'.[43] However, it appears that under the Rome Convention, this is enough to bring the matter within its scope as creating a choice between the laws of different countries within the meaning of Article 1(1).[44] This example raises a question of the law applicable to a sale of goods contract and is properly a matter for discussion in this book.

---

[38] See the Jenard Report [1979] OJ C59/8, accompanying the Brussels Convention
[39] See O'Malley and Layton, 13.11.
[40] Under Art 5(1). Even if delivery took place in France, the English courts could have jurisdiction by virtue of a clause providing for the jurisdiction of the English courts.
[41] See Cheshire and North, 544–545.
[42] Art 1(a) and (b).
[43] Art 1(4).
[44] See Art 3(3) of the Rome Convention, on which see below, paras 13.99–102.

Specific Issues and the Scope of the Book

1.20 The Hague Sales Conventions of 1955 and 1986 expressly exclude certain
contractual issues from their scope. For example, both exclude the issue of
capacity to contract.[45] The 1955 Convention excludes the issue of formal
validity.[46] The Vienna Convention is expressly stated not to be concerned
with the validity of the contract.[47] Yet these issues can raise choice of law
problems and are properly dealt with in this book. Similarly, the Hague
Convention of 1955 excludes the effect of the sale on third parties[48] and the
1986 Convention excludes issues relating to the transfer of ownership.[49]
The 1986 Convention goes on to make clear that the effect of the sale in
respect of third parties is outside the scope of the Convention.[50] The
Vienna Convention excludes 'the effect which the contract may have on
the property in the goods sold'.[51] But claims relating to the ownership
of the goods sold can raise conflict of laws problems. Such claims arise
out of the sale of goods contract, more on which is said below, and are,
accordingly within the scope of this book. The upshot is that the scope of
this book is not limited to issues that fall within the scope of the Vienna
Convention, or the Hague Sales Conventions of 1955 or 1986.

Transfer of Contractual Rights and Obligations

1.21 Closely associated with the contract for the international sale of goods
are the contracts for the carriage, insurance and payment of the goods.
The application of the principles and rules of the conflict of laws to
claims arising out of the contract of carriage is a subject that merits a monograph of its own. The same is true of claims arising out of the contract of
insurance.[52] Documentary credits in the conflict of laws is likewise a very
large topic. Such coverage would not be appropriate for a book that focuses
on the contract for the international sale of goods. There is, therefore, no
separate discrete coverage of the conflict of laws problems in relation to
the contract of carriage, insurance and payment by documentary credit.
However, the contract of carriage and of insurance cannot be ignored
entirely. They are rooted in the performance of the contract of sale and to
that extent they have to be considered. In particular, there is one issue
involving the contract of carriage and of insurance of goods that must be
addressed. This is the issue of the transfer of contractual rights and obligations between the seller and the buyer. With a CIF sales contract, the buyer

---

[45] Art 5(1) of the 1955 Convention, Art 5(a) of the 1986 Convention.
[46] Art 5(2).   [47] Art 4(a).   [48] Art 5(4).   [49] Art 5(c).   [50] Art 5(c).
[51] Art 4(b).
[52] There is now such a book, see F Seatzu, *Insurance in Private International Law: A European
Perspective* (Oxford: Hart Publishing, 2003).

acquires rights and duties under the contract of carriage made between the seller and the carrier, giving the buyer, as holder of the bill of lading, the right, at least under English law, to sue the carrier if, for example, the goods delivered to him by the carrier are damaged. Conflict of laws problems, both jurisdictional and as to the applicable law, can arise out of this transfer of contractual rights and obligations between the seller and buyer and are discussed in detail in separate chapters in this book.

E-Commerce

Goods are increasingly being sold over the internet. Electronic commerce **1.22** presents the international sales lawyer with numerous problems. For example, are digitized products, such as software, which are then transferred over the internet, goods for the purposes of the Vienna Convention? Are such products sold or merely transferred under a licensing agreement? The answer to these questions is of considerable interest to the conflicts lawyer, who will have to decide whether the special jurisdictional rule, that applies 'in the case of the sale of goods', will come into play where there are digitized products. It is argued below that digitized products transferred over the internet should be regarded as goods for the purposes of this rule.[53] There is then the problem under this jurisdictional rule of identifying where these goods were delivered to. Is it where the digitized product was uploaded by the seller or downloaded by the customer? Electronic commerce does not just produce jurisdictional problems. The interaction of the substantive law of electronic commerce, contained in the E-Commerce Directive, and the conflicts rules on the law applicable to contractual obligations is a matter of considerable complexity. The latter rules are not easy to apply in cases of contracts made and performed over the internet. So far, mention only has been made of contractual disputes arising out of electronic commerce, but there can also be tortious, restitutionary and proprietary disputes. The fact that, for instance, a tort is committed over the internet, adds an extra layer of complexity when applying the principles and rules of the conflict of laws. For all of these reasons it has been felt necessary to give a very detailed treatment to the topic of electronic commerce and two chapters are devoted to it.

The Omission of Consumer Contracts

This book does not deal with consumer contracts. Both international sale **1.23** of goods and conflict of laws considerations have led to this omission. As

---

[53] See below, paras 10.46–49.

regards the substantive law of international sale of goods, it has been seen that the Vienna Convention largely excludes such contracts from its scope by providing that the Convention does not apply to sales 'of goods bought for personal, family or household use, unless the seller, at any time before or at the conclusion of the contract, neither knew nor ought to have known that the goods were bought for any such use'.[54] When it comes to conflict of laws considerations, there are special jurisdictional and choice of law rules for consumer contracts.[55] These rules are very different from those applying for commercial contracts, reflecting very different policy concerns. Consumer contracts in private international law is a major topic in its own right and one deserving of a monograph.[56]

2. Claims Arising out of the International Sale of Goods

1.24 We are concerned with claims arising out of the international sale of goods. This goes wider than claims in relation to the sale of goods contract itself, although such claims are the starting point for our discussion. The most obvious claim that can arise from this contract is one in contract between the buyer and the seller. Most commonly the claim will be based on a breach by one of the parties of an obligation under the contract for the international sale of goods. Alternatively, or in addition, there may be a claim in tort arising out of this contract. In particular, there may be a claim for conversion, for negligent misstatement, negligent or fraudulent misrepresentation, for a refusal to sell (under French law), for inducement of breach of contract, or for negligence. These are the most common torts that can arise out of a contract for the international sale of goods. The claim may be as between the seller and the buyer or it may be between one of the contracting parties and a third party. There may be a dispute where what are at issue are property rights arising under, and in connection with, the sales transaction, in particular a dispute over the passing of property and the transfer of title. For example, there may be a claim for a declaration as to ownership. This may arise on its own or be sought in addition to a claim for damages for conversion, the price of goods, a proprietary remedy following the process of tracing, or a declaration that the defendant holds goods as a constructive trustee. A claimant may seek a restitutionary remedy such as return of money paid in advance. For example, the buyer seeks the return of money he paid under a contract for

---

[54] Art 2(a). Thus if a consumer sells his car to a garage the Convention will apply, but in the converse situation, normally it will not do so.

[55] See Section 4 of the Brussels I Regulation and Art 5 of the Rome Convention.

[56] By a happy coincidence, a distinguished author is writing such a book for the Oxford Private International Law Series.

the international sale of goods, which is void *ab initio*, or the recovery of money that he overpaid after being overcharged. Multiple party claims are a common feature of international sale of goods cases. There can be multi-defendant claims in contract and in tort. Multi-defendant claims can arise where the claim against one defendant is in contract and the other defendant is in tort. There are also numerous examples of third party claims being brought in international sale of goods cases. Counter-claims also feature in the international sale of goods context. For example, a manufacturer may bring a claim for payment against a retailer to whom the goods have been delivered, the latter counter-claims for costs and damage to reputation arising because of problem deliveries. Multi-party claims is very much a jurisdictional topic. Indeed, there are special jurisdictional rules for such claims. There is, therefore, a chapter in the jurisdictional section of the book dealing with these claims, but no corresponding choice of law chapter. In contrast, an important issue that arises in the context of choice of law but not, at least to the same extent, in the context of jurisdiction is that of concurrent claims. Arising out of an international sales contract, the claimant may have claims available to him in contract and tort, in contract and in restitution, or in tort and restitution. The claims may constitute distinct causes of action, alternative claims or parallel claims. There is a separate chapter in the choice of law section of the book dealing with the issue of concurrent claims.[57] This seeks to set out a coherent approach towards such claims which is capable of application more generally than in the context of the international sale of goods. There is no corresponding chapter in the section on jurisdiction, although at times the chapters on jurisdiction do address this issue.

3. THE PRINCIPLES AND RULES OF THE CONFLICT OF LAWS

The principles and rules of conflict of laws that we are concerned with are **1.25** the classic ones of jurisdiction, choice of law and the recognition and enforcement of foreign judgments that go to make up this subject. They can be found in any of the leading textbooks on the conflict of laws. How jurisdiction and choice of law problems arise in international sale of goods cases and the principles and rules that must be applied to solve these problems will be the subject-matter of the ensuing chapters. A brief mention will also be made of the recognition and enforcement of foreign judgments problems that arise in international sale of goods cases. This is one of the shorter chapters in the book because there are few sales specific recognition and enforcement problems.

---

[57] Ch 20.

PART I
JURISDICTION

2

Preliminary Remarks

I. JURISDICTION UNDER THE EUROPEAN AND TRADITIONAL ENGLISH RULES

In a case involving a foreign element, the first thing that a court has to **2.01** decide is whether it has jurisdiction. This refers to 'the question of whether an English court will hear and determine an issue upon which its decision is sought'.[1] The jurisdiction of the English courts is complicated by the fact that there are two very different regimes of jurisdiction rules. The first is the European regime, which comprises rules contained in: the Brussels I Regulation (the EC rules);[2] the Brussels Convention;[3] and the Lugano Convention.[4] Following on from the European regime there

---

[1] Cheshire and North, 179.

[2] Council Regulation (EC) No 44/2001 of 22 December 2000 on jurisdiction and the recognition and enforcement of judgments in civil and commercial matters [2001] OJ L12/1. This is sometimes and best referred to as 'Brussels I', so as to avoid confusing it with 'Brussels II', i.e. Council Regulation (EC) No 1347/2000 of 29 May 2000 on jurisdiction and the recognition and enforcement of judgments in matrimonial matters and in matters of parental responsibility for children of both spouses [2000] OJ L160/19; to be replaced by Council Regulation (EC) No 2201/2003 of 27 November 2003 concerning jurisdiction and the recognition and enforcement of judgments in matrimonial matters and the matters of parental responsibility [2003] OJ L338/1 (Brussels II *bis*). See generally on the relationship between the Brussels I Regulation and the Brussels and Lugano Conventions, Briggs and Rees, 1.02–1.11.

[3] The Brussels Convention of 1968, which was entered into by the original six Member States of the EEC, was amended by four subsequent Accession Conventions; i.e. the Danish, Irish and UK Accession Convention of 1978; the Greek Accession Convention of 1982; the Portuguese and Spanish Accession Convention of 1989; the Austrian, Finnish and Swedish Accession Convention of 1996. A consolidated version of the 1968 Convention and 1971 Protocol, as amended by the four Accession Conventions, is set out in [1998] OJ C27/1. The latest text also appears in SI 2000/1824. See generally on the Brussels Convention, Cheshire and North, Ch 11.

[4] [1988] OJ L391/9. See generally Cheshire and North, 278–283.

is the Modified Regulation[5] which allocates jurisdiction within the United Kingdom. The second regime is the traditional English rules on jurisdiction. In this book, we will be concentrating on the EC rules in the Brussels I Regulation and the traditional English rules.[6]

1. The European Regime

The Brussels I Regulation (EC Rules)

2.02 The Brussels I Regulation replaces and updates the Brussels Convention.[7] The rules on jurisdiction contained in the Brussels I Regulation apply where the following conditions have been met. First, the Brussels I Regulation is doubtless only concerned with the international jurisdiction of EC Member States, and will not apply where there is no foreign element. The position was clearer under the Brussels Convention, the preamble to which expressly referred to 'international' jurisdiction. The recitals to the Regulation do not contain this word. Nonetheless, given that the Regulation closely corresponds to the Convention, taking over its essential structure and most of its fundamental principles, it is doubtful that any change in this respect was intended. Certainly, the Explanatory Memorandum from the Commission does not mention this as one of the changes brought about by the Regulation. Second, the matter is within the scope of the Regulation, i.e. a civil and commercial matter.[8] Third, when it comes to bases of jurisdiction,[9] the defendant is domiciled in an EC Member State.[10] This does not include Denmark. Even if the defendant is not, jurisdiction may be allocated to the courts of an EC Member State (other than Denmark) by virtue of Article 22 (exclusive jurisdiction) or Article 23 (an

---

[5] Sch 4 to the Civil Jurisdiction and Judgments Act 1982, as substituted by the Civil Jurisdiction and Judgments Order 2001, SI 2001/3929, Sch 2, Part II, para 4.

[6] At times differences between the different sets of rules that go to make up the European regime will be pointed out.

[7] The legal basis for this is Title IV of the EC Treaty, in particular Art 65; see generally P Beaumont, 'European Court of Justice and Jurisdiction and Enforcement of Judgments in Civil and Commercial Matters' (1999) 48 ICLQ 225 and 'The Brussels Convention becomes a Regulation: Implications for Legal Basis, External Competence, and Contract Jurisdiction', Ch 1 in J Fawcett (ed), *Reform and Development of Private International Law* (Oxford: OUP, 2002) 12–15.

[8] Art 1; see Cheshire and North, 190–195, for the meaning of this concept under the Brussels Convention.

[9] Other provisions on jurisdiction contained in Sections 8 (examination as to jurisdiction and admissibility) and 9 (*lis pendens* and related actions) will apply even though the defendant is not domiciled in an EC Member State (this does not include Denmark).

[10] Austria, Belgium, Finland, France, Germany, Greece, Ireland, Italy, Luxembourg, Netherlands, Portugal, Spain, Sweden, UK. As from 1 May 2004 there are ten new Member States: Cyprus, the Czech Republic, Estonia, Hungary, Latvia, Lithuania, Malta, Poland, Slovakia, Slovenia.

agreement conferring jurisdiction on the courts of an EC Member State) of the Regulation.[11]

The Brussels I Regulation does not prejudice the application of provisions **2.03** governing jurisdiction and the recognition and enforcement of judgments in specific matters which are contained in Community instruments or in national legislation harmonized pursuant to such instruments.[12] Neither does the Regulation affect any conventions to which the Member States are parties and which, in relation to particular matters, govern jurisdiction or the recognition or enforcement of judgments.[13]

The Brussels Convention

Denmark did not participate in the adoption of the Brussels I Regulation,[14] **2.04** and the Brussels Convention[15] continues to apply between Denmark and the EC Member States bound by the Brussels I Regulation.[16] It is intended that the Brussels Convention will be amended so that its terms are brought into line with those contained in the Brussels I Regulation.[17] But in the meantime it continues to apply some rules that are materially different from those contained in the Brussels I Regulation.[18]

The rules on jurisdiction contained in the Brussels Convention[19] are **2.05** applied in the United Kingdom, and in the other Member States bound by the Brussels I Regulation, where the following conditions are met. First, it is a matter concerning the international jurisdiction of Contracting States.[20] Second, the matter is within the scope of the Brussels Convention, i.e. a civil and commercial matter. Third, when it comes to

[11] In cases of submission under Art 24 it is arguable that the defendant does not have to be domiciled in a Member State, see Briggs and Rees, 2.08, 2.179. But compare Cheshire and North, 246.

[12] Art 67.

[13] Art 71(1). This preserves existing conventions but Member States are unable to enter into any new conventions.

[14] See Recital 21 of the Brussels I Regulation. Denmark has an opt out Protocol from Title IV of the EC Treaty and cannot selectively opt in, see Beaumont, in Fawcett (ed), n 7 above, at 13. In contrast, the UK and Ireland can opt in, which they have done.

[15] See generally, Cheshire and North, 183–273; Dicey and Morris, 337–384, 264–281; Briggs and Rees, 3.01–3.17.

[16] Recital 22 of the Brussels I Regulation. At the moment this is just the original 15 EC Member States. There will need to be negotiations for the accession of the ten new EC Member States to the Convention.

[17] Once a new Brussels Convention has been concluded it will need to be ratified by the Contracting States.

[18] One important difference for sales cases is that Art 5 (special jurisdiction in matters relating to a contract) is differently worded, see below, paras 3.143 and 3.247.

[19] The ECJ has jurisdiction to interpret these rules.

[20] See the Preamble.

bases of jurisdiction[21] the defendant is domiciled in Denmark. Even if the defendant is not, jurisdiction may be allocated to the Danish courts under Articles 16 (exclusive jurisdiction) or 17 (an agreement conferring jurisdiction on the Danish courts) of the Brussels Convention.[22]

2.06 The Brussels Convention does not affect any conventions to which the Contracting States are or will be parties and which, in relation to particular matters, govern jurisdiction or the recognition or enforcement of judgments.[23] Neither does the Convention affect the application of provisions which, in relation to particular matters, govern jurisdiction or the recognition or enforcement of judgments and which are or will be contained in acts of the institutions of the European Communities or in national laws harmonized in implementation of such acts.[24]

The Lugano Convention

2.07 This is a parallel Convention to the Brussels Convention and applies as between the EC countries[25] and the EFTA countries.[26] Its rules[27] are based on, but not identical with, those contained in the Brussels Convention,[28] rather than the Brussels I Regulation. However, it is intended that the Lugano Convention will be amended so that its terms are brought into line with those contained in the Brussels I Regulation.[29] But in the meantime it continues to apply some rules that are materially different from

---

[21] Other provisions on jurisdiction contained in Sections 7 (examination as to jurisdiction and admissibility) and 8 (*lis pendens* and related actions) will apply even though the defendant is not domiciled in Denmark.

[22] In cases of submission under Art 18, it is arguable that the defendant does not have to be domiciled in Denmark, see n 11 above.

[23] Art 57(1). Under this provision Contracting States are able to enter into new conventions. Contrast the position under Art 71(1) of the Brussels I Regulation, discussed at n 13 above.   [24] Art 57(3).

[25] At the moment this is just the original 15 EC Member States. As regards the ten new EC Member States, Poland is a third state party to the Lugano Convention. The remaining nine new EU Member States will in due course accede to the Convention.

[26] Iceland, Norway and Switzerland.

[27] See Cheshire and North, 278–283; Briggs and Rees, 3.01–3.17. The ECJ has no jurisdiction to interpret the rules contained in the Lugano Convention.

[28] For differences between the Lugano and Brussels Conventions see Cheshire and North, 281–282.

[29] The EFTA States were consulted on the substantive changes to be made to the Brussels Convention with a view to a future new Lugano Convention which would be in the same terms as the Convention. However, as a result of the Convention becoming a Regulation, the EFTA States have had to wait until the Brussels I Regulation has come into force and new negotiations are now necessary. There is a problem as to who is competent to conduct these negotiations. See generally Beaumont, n 14 above, at 13–14. The Council of the European Union has sought an Opinion (Opinion 1/03 [2003] OJ C101/1) from the ECJ as to whether the conclusion of the new Lugano Convention is a matter for the Community's exclusive competence or shared between the Community and Member States. Once a new Lugano Convention has been concluded it will need to be ratified by the Contracting States.

those contained in the Brussels I Regulation[30] and, indeed, those contained in the Brussels Convention.[31]

The rules on jurisdiction contained in the Lugano Convention are **2.08** applied in the United Kingdom and in other European Community States (including Denmark) where the following conditions are met. First, it is a matter concerning the international jurisdiction of Contracting States.[32] Second, the matter is within the scope of the Convention, i.e. a civil and commercial matter. Third, when it comes to bases of jurisdiction,[33] the defendant is domiciled in an EFTA State. Even if the defendant is not, jurisdiction may be allocated to the courts of an EFTA State under Articles 16 or 17 of that Convention.[34]

The Lugano Convention does not affect any conventions to which the **2.09** Contracting States are or will be parties and which, in relation to particular matters, govern jurisdiction or the recognition or enforcement of judgments.[35]

2. THE MODIFIED REGULATION

The Modified Regulation allocates jurisdiction within the United **2.10** Kingdom. This is necessary for two reasons. First, the Brussels I Regulation (or Brussels or Lugano Conventions) may have allocated jurisdiction to the courts of the United Kingdom as the Member (Contracting) State to the Regulation (Convention). The parties will then need to know which part of the United Kingdom has jurisdiction. Second, there are internal United Kingdom cases where, for example, a Scotsman sues an English company for breach of a sales contract, the goods having been delivered from England to Scotland. The terms of the Modified Regulation are by and large based on those in the Brussels I Regulation.[36] The Modified

---

[30] One important difference for sales cases is that Art 5 (special jurisdiction in matters relating to a contract) is differently worded, see below, paras 3.143 and 3.247.

[31] See, e.g. Art 16(1)(b) of Lugano which is different from Art 22(1) of the Brussels I Regulation and from Art 16(1)(b) of the Brussels Convention (which is also different from the Brussels I Regulation).   [32] See the Preamble.

[33] Other provisions on jurisdiction contained in Sections 7 (examination as to jurisdiction and admissibility) and 8 (*lis pendens* and related actions) will apply even though the defendant is not domiciled in an EFTA State.

[34] In cases of submission under Art 18, it is arguable that the defendant does not have to be domiciled in an EFTA State.   [35] Art 57(1).

[36] One important difference for sales cases is that in matters relating to a contract, the Modified Regulation does not follow Art 5(1) of the Brussels I Regulation, but instead retains the Brussels Convention wording, see Sch 4, r 3(a), of the Civil Jurisdiction and Judgments Act 1982, as substituted by the Civil Jurisdiction and Judgments Order 2001, Sch 2, Part II, para 4. See further on this difference, below, paras 3.143 and 3.247. One other important difference between the Modified Regulation and the Brussels I Regulation is that the ECJ has no jurisdiction to interpret the former, see Case C-346/93 *Kleinwort Benson Ltd v Glasgow City Council* [1995] ECR I-615.

Regulation will apply where (a) the subject-matter of the proceedings is within the scope of the Regulation as determined by Article 1 of the Regulation (whether or not the Regulation has effect in relation to the proceedings); and (b) the defendant is domiciled in the United Kingdom or the proceedings are of a kind mentioned in Article 22 of the Regulation (exclusive jurisdiction regardless of domicile).[37]

3. THE TRADITIONAL ENGLISH RULES

2.11 The traditional English rules will apply in cases outside the scope of the Brussels I Regulation, Brussels Convention and Lugano Convention.[38] Let us assume however that the case falls within the scope of the Brussels I Regulation. If the defendant is not domiciled in a Member State (this does not include Denmark) and jurisdiction is not allocated to courts of a Member State under Articles 22 or 23, then the Regulation provides that the jurisdiction of the courts of each Member State is determined by the traditional national rules of jurisdiction of that Member State.[39] A similar provision is to be found in the Brussels and Lugano Conventions.[40]

2.12 Under the traditional rules, jurisdiction is based on service of a claim form on the defendant. In certain circumstances, it is possible to effect service within the jurisdiction. Where this is not possible, service has to be effected out of the jurisdiction using r 6.20 of the Civil Procedure Rules.

---

[37] s 16 of the Civil Jurisdiction and Judgments Act 1982, as amended by the Civil Jurisdiction and Judgments Order 2001, Sch 2, Part II, para 3.

[38] If the case does not concern international jurisdiction there will presumably be no jurisdictional problem for the traditional rules to solve. As has been seen, Conventions to which Member States/Contracting States are parties and which, in relation to particular matters, govern jurisdiction will continue to apply.

[39] Art 4.

[40] Art 4 of the Brussels and Lugano Conventions provides that: 'If the defendant is not domiciled in a Contracting State, the jurisdiction of the courts of each Contracting State shall, subject to the provisions of Article 16 [exclusive jurisdiction], be determined by the law of that State'.

3

An Action in Contract Between the Buyer and Seller: Jurisdiction under the EC Rules

I. INTRODUCTION

In this chapter, the law of jurisdiction under the EC rules and its applica- **3.01** tion to actions in contract between the buyer and seller under a contract for the international sale of goods will be examined.

II. WHEN WILL THE EC RULES APPLY?

1. A CIVIL AND COMMERCIAL MATTER

3.02 Article 1 of the Brussels I Regulation[1] states that: 'This Regulation shall apply in civil and commercial matters'.[2] An action in contract between a buyer and seller of goods clearly comes within this concept. However, the Regulation expressly excludes a number of matters from its scope, even though they are civil and commercial matters. These exclusions will now be considered to see whether they will operate in the context of a contract for the international sale of goods.

The Exclusion of Arbitration

3.03 The Regulation excludes from its scope, 'arbitration'.[3] The subject-matter of the dispute may fall within this exclusion. It is important therefore to look briefly at precisely what does and does not fall within the arbitration exclusion.[4] As will be seen, contracts for the international sale of goods commonly contain arbitration clauses and so this question of the scope of the arbitration exclusion is one of real practical importance when discussing this type of contract.

Arbitration clauses in contracts for the international sale of goods

3.04 Standard form contracts used for the international sale of goods very commonly include an arbitration clause.[5] For example, contract no 20 of the Federation of Oils, Seeds and Fats Associations Ltd (FOSFA) provides that the contracts should be governed by English law; that any dispute in connection therewith, should be referred to arbitration in London; and that no action or other legal proceedings should be brought by one party against the other in respect of any such dispute until the dispute had been heard and determined by arbitration under the FOSFA rules of arbitration and appeal. This standard form may well be adopted by parties, neither of whom is English.[6] FOSFA 53 provides that 'any dispute arising out of

---

[1] [2001] OJ L12/1.

[2] Art 1(1). See generally Cheshire and North, 190–195; Dicey and Morris, 269–273; Briggs and Rees, 2.23–2.27.

[3] Art 1(2)(d).

[4] See generally, Cheshire and North, 193–195; Dicey and Morris, 271–273; Briggs and Rees, 2.27.

[5] These are even more common than jurisdiction clauses, which are discussed below, para 3.28. The contract may contain both, see, eg, GAFTA Form 100, cll 31 and 32.

[6] See, e.g., *Tracomin SA v Sudan Oil Seeds Co Ltd* [1983] 1 WLR 1026—Sudanese sellers of ground nuts and Swiss buyers.

[this contract] or in connection therewith shall be submitted to arbitration in accordance with the Rules of the Federation',[7] arbitration to be held in London.[8] Similarly, the Grain and Feed Trade Association (GAFTA) Form 100 provides that: 'Any dispute arising out of or under the contract shall be settled by arbitration in accordance with the Arbitration Rules, No. 125, of The Grain and Feed Trade Association . . .'.[9] It goes on to provide that: 'Neither party hereto, nor any persons claiming under either of them shall bring any action or other legal proceedings against the other of them in respect of any such dispute until such dispute shall first have been heard and determined by arbitrator(s) . . .'.[10] Again, this standard form may well be adopted by parties, neither of whom is English.[11] The standard terms of the contract issued by the Dried Fruit Association of California include a clause providing for arbitration in California, except for determination of shortage of weight or disputes over quality, grade, size and condition, which are to be determined at the port of discharge. This form of contract has been adopted by parties neither of whom is Californian.[12]

In the oil trade, it is the standard terms of individual companies (and **3.05** not of a trade association) that dominate. They may be used by a party other than the company itself, as where parties down a contractual string use the terms of the operator of the oil terminal.[13] BP terms (February 1994 edition)[14] call in clause 20(2) for 'arbitration under the rules of conciliation and arbitration of the London Court of International Arbitration' with the arbitration conducted in London.[15] The clause[16] in BP Crude Oil CFR, CIF & EX SHIP (Single Shipment) (August 1994 edition) is the same, as is that in BP Oil International *General* Terms and Conditions for Sales and Purchases of Crude Oil 2000.[17] Again, Norwegian State Oil Co (Den norske stats oljeselskap a.s.) Conditions of Sale Applicable to Terminal Crude Oil Sales FOB/FIP (January 1999), provide for arbitration in London.[18] Shell terms (1 November 1992 edition) for C and F[19]/CIF also call for arbitration in London.[20] BP's 'Standard Terms and Conditions for the Purchase and Sale of Crude Oil FOB Port of Loading' contain a term providing for arbitration in England. This standard form contract is not

---

[7] cl 27.   [8] cl 29.   [9] cl 32(a).   [10] cl 32(b).

[11] See, e.g. *Toepfer International GmbH v Société Cargill France* [1998] 1 Lloyd's Rep 379, CA; discussed below.

[12] See *Gill and Duffus Landauer Ltd v London Export Corp GmbH* [1982] 2 Lloyd's Rep 627.

[13] See *Phibro Energy Inc v Coastal Bermuda Ltd (The Aragon (1987))* [1991] 1 Lloyd's Rep 61: BP terms.

[14] e.g. Crude Oil FOB (Single Shipment).

[15] In contrast with most of the rest of the contract form, cl 20(2) is all capitalized.

[16] cl 21(2).   [17] cl 38.2.   [18] cl XXIV.   [19] Which is the same as CFR.

[20] cl 13.

simply used by BP for their transactions but is adopted as well by other oil companies which are foreign.[21]

3.06   As for the ICC, the ICC Model International Sale Contract (Manufactured Goods Intended for Resale) calls for arbitration in accordance with the Rules of Conciliation and Arbitration of the International Chamber of Commerce.[22]

The scope of the arbitration exclusion

3.07   *Marc Rich & Co v Società Italiana Impianti PA*[23] is a classic example of how a sale of goods contract can raise questions in relation to the scope of the arbitration exclusion. The dispute arose out of a contract for the sale of oil (fob) where the buyers, a Swiss company, claimed against the sellers, an Italian company, alleging that the cargo was seriously contaminated. The defendants commenced proceedings in Italy for a declaration that they were not liable to the plaintiffs. The plaintiffs alleged that there was an arbitration clause in the contract and commenced arbitration in London. The defendants failed to appoint an arbitrator and the plaintiffs asked an English court to appoint one. The defendants argued that the contract did not contain an arbitration clause and that, since the dispute came within the Brussels Convention, the Italian courts had jurisdiction. The plaintiffs argued that the dispute was excluded from the scope of the Convention by virtue of the arbitration exclusion. The English Court of Appeal[24] referred to the European Court of Justice the question whether the present dispute fell within the arbitration exception. The European Court of Justice held that arbitration is excluded in its entirety, including proceedings brought for the appointment of an arbitrator. This was unaffected by the fact that the existence or validity of the arbitration agreement was raised as a preliminary matter. That Court has also held that the Brussels Convention does not apply to proceedings and decisions concerning applications for the revocation, amendment, recognition and enforcement of arbitration awards.[25]

3.08   More generally, proceedings that are ancillary to the arbitration proceedings are excluded.[26] This includes not only proceedings for the appointment of an arbitrator, but also those for his dismissal, the fixing of

---

[21] See, e.g. *Sohio Supply Co v Gatoil (USA) Inc* [1989] 1 Lloyd's Rep 588, CA.
[22] Art 14.   [23] Case C-190/89 [1991] ECR I-3855.
[24] *Marc Rich & Co AG v Società Italiana Impianti PA (The Atlantic Emperor)* [1989] 1 Lloyd's Rep 548, CA.
[25] Case C-391/95 *Van Uden Maritime BV (t/a Van Uden Africa Line) v Kommanditgesellschaft in Firma Deco-Line* [1998] ECR I-7091.
[26] ibid.

the place of arbitration or the extension of the time limit for making awards.[27] The English courts have referred to the exclusion of judicial proceedings that are integral to the arbitration process,[28] and of proceedings directed to the regulation and support of arbitration proceedings and awards,[29] such as for security for the costs of an arbitration.[30] Proceedings in relation to the existence or validity of the arbitration agreement raise particular problems. If this issue arises as a preliminary one to an issue which is itself outside the scope of the Convention, there is authority to the effect that this preliminary issue is also excluded.[31] Where the issue of the existence or validity arises on its own, rather than as a preliminary issue, this is also probably excluded.[32] It is unclear whether proceedings for the enforcement of the arbitration agreement (by way of a declaration that a party must refer a dispute to arbitration and/or an injunction restraining the commencement or continuance of proceedings abroad) are excluded.[33]

The Exclusion of the Status or Legal Capacity of Natural Persons, etc.

The Regulation also excludes from its scope 'the status or legal capacity of **3.09** natural persons . . .'.[34] The issue of legal capacity could arise in the context of a contract for the international sale of goods. For example, an 18-year-old buyer from Utopia agrees to buy whisky from an English seller. By the law of Utopia the buyer lacks capacity to contract, the age for entering

[27] ibid.

[28] *Toepfer v Molino Boschi* [1996] 1 Lloyd's Rep 510, 513; *The Lake Avery* [1997] 1 Lloyd's Rep 540, 549.

[29] *Lexmar v Nordisk* [1997] 1 Lloyd's Rep 289, 292. The arbitration exclusion does not extend to proceedings involving persons who are not parties to the arbitration, *Vale Do Rio Doce Navegacao SA v Shanghai Bao Steel Ocean Shipping Co Ltd* [2000] 2 Lloyd's Rep 1.

[30] The *Lexmar* case, n 29 above.

[31] See AG Darmon's opinion in the *Marc Rich* case, n 24 above, 3875–3876.

[32] See the opinion of AG Darmon in the *Marc Rich* case, n 24 above, 3876. See also the *Van Uden* case, n 25 above, where the ECJ said that the Convention does not apply to judgments determining whether an arbitration agreement is valid or not or, because it is invalid, ordering the parties not to continue the arbitration proceedings; *Navigation Maritime Bulgare v Rustal Trading Ltd (The Ivan Zagubanski)* [2002] 1 Lloyd's Rep 106.

[33] Compare (excluded) *Toepfer v Cargill* [1997] 2 Lloyd's Rep 98, 102–105, *The Ivan Zagubanski*, n 32 above, and *Through Transport Mutual Insurance Association (Eurasia) Ltd v New India Assurance Co Ltd* [2003] EWHC 3158 (Comm) at [24], [2004] 1 Lloyd's Rep 206 with (not excluded) *Toepfer v Molino Boschi* [1996] 1 Lloyd's Rep 510, 512–513 and *Charterers Mutual Assurance Association Ltd v British and Foreign* [1998] IL Pr 838, 854–855. This question was referred to the ECJ by the Court of Appeal in *Toepfer v Cargill* [1998] 1 Lloyd's Rep 379 but the action was subsequently settled. The better view is that such proceedings should be regarded as being excluded, see Briggs and Rees, 2.27.

[34] Art 1(2)(a). This provision also excludes 'rights in property arising out of a matrimonial relationship, wills and succession'. This exclusion does not concern us.

into a contract being 21. The English seller fails to deliver the whisky, alleging that he is not contractually bound to do so because of the buyer's lack of capacity. The buyer brings proceedings in England for breach of contract. Does this fall within the exclusion? The exclusion will only operate if status or capacity is the principal object of the proceedings.[35] It appears to be the principal issue that arises in the case and therefore it should fall within the exclusion.[36]

The Exclusion of Bankruptcy, etc.

3.10 The Regulation excludes from its scope: 'Bankruptcy, proceedings relating to the winding-up of insolvent companies or other legal persons, judicial arrangements, compositions and analogous proceedings'.[37] Would a claim for payment brought by an insolvent seller against the buyer of goods, or one brought for breach of contract by a buyer against an insolvent seller, fall outside the scope of the Regulation? The test for determining whether proceedings fall within the bankruptcy exclusion is as follows: is bankruptcy the principal subject-matter of the proceedings?[38] The mere fact that the claimant happens to be a trustee in bankruptcy is not sufficient to bring the proceedings within the exception.[39] A claim by a trustee in bankruptcy to recover from a third party assets said to belong to the bankrupt's estate did not have bankruptcy as its principal subject-matter, and thus fell outside the bankruptcy exclusion.[40] Similarly, proceedings brought by a trustee in bankruptcy for an order for the sale of a bankrupt person's villa with vacant possession and directions for the completion of sale to be conducted by the trustee fell outside the bankruptcy exclusion because it did not have bankruptcy as its principal subject-matter.[41] In neither case was the issue as to bankruptcy law.[42] A claim for payment brought by an insolvent seller against the buyer of goods, or one brought for breach of contract by a buyer against an insolvent seller, does not have bankruptcy as its principal subject-matter and therefore would not fall within the bankruptcy exclusion. Accordingly, it would come within the scope of the Brussels I Regulation.

---

[35] See generally the Jenard Report [1979] OJ C59/8, the authoritative report accompanying the original version of the Brussels Convention, 10.

[36] See also Dicey and Morris, 269, which says that this exclusion should operate where the proceedings deal directly with the matter, rather than incidentally.

[37] Art 1(2)(b). Also excluded is social security: Art 1(2)(c). But this does not concern us.

[38] *Ashurst v Pollard* [2001] Ch 595, 602, CA; *Re Hayward* [1997] Ch 45, 53–55.

[39] The *Ashurst* case, n 38 above.

[40] *Re Hayward*, n 38 above, at 53–55.

[41] The *Ashurst* case, n 38 above.

[42] Compare Case 133/78 *Gourdain v Nadler* [1979] ECR 733.

2. WHETHER THE DEFENDANT IS DOMICILED IN A MEMBER STATE

In the situation where the defendant is domiciled in a Member State, **3.11** the bases of jurisdiction under the Regulation will apply and not the traditional national rules of jurisdiction of the forum.[43] Where the defendant is not domiciled in a Member State, in general, the traditional national rules of jurisdiction of the forum will apply.[44] As exceptions to this, Articles 22 (exclusive jurisdiction) and 23 (an agreement on jurisdiction) will apply to defendants, even though they are not domiciled in a Member State.[45]

III. A SPECIAL DEFINITION OF DOMICILE

The Regulation makes extensive use of the concept of domicile for the **3.12** purposes of deciding when the Regulation applies and, where it does, of allocating jurisdiction to particular Member States. However, this important concept is only partially defined under the Regulation. Article 59 of the Regulation deals with the question of which Member State's definition of domicile is to be used. The first paragraph provides that in 'order to determine whether a party is domiciled in the Member State whose courts are seised of a matter, the court shall apply its internal law'. The second paragraph goes on to provide that, in 'order to determine whether the party is domiciled in another Member State, the court shall apply the law of that Member State'. Thus if a court in the United Kingdom, having decided (using the UK definition of domicile) that a party is not domiciled in the United Kingdom, wants to know whether a defendant is domiciled in Germany, it must apply the German definition of domicile.

As far as the United Kingdom is concerned, there are special provisions **3.13** on the meaning of domicile for the purposes of the Regulation[46] with separate definitions for each of the contexts in which an individual's domicile has to be ascertained.[47] For most of these purposes,[48] domicile is equated with the state where (a) an individual is resident and (b) the nature and circumstances of his residence indicate that he has a

---

[43] Art 3.   [44] Art 4(1).   [45] ibid.

[46] See the Civil Jurisdiction and Judgments Order 2001, SI 2001/3929, Sch 1, para 9.

[47] The rules state when an individual is domiciled: (i) in the UK, (ii) in a particular part of the UK, (iii) in a particular place in the UK and (iv) in a state other than a Regulation State.

[48] But not when domicile in a particular place in the UK is being ascertained, see para 9(4).

substantial connection with it. Showing a substantial connection is made easier by the use of a presumption (based on residence for the last three months or more), which is available under some of these definitions but not others.[49]

3.14 The Regulation does, however, provide a definition of the domicile of a company. Article 60(1) provides that a company or other legal person or association of natural or legal persons is domiciled at the place where it has its: (a) statutory seat, or (b) central administration, or (c) principal place of business.[50] For the purposes of the United Kingdom and Ireland, 'statutory seat' means the registered office or, where there is no such office anywhere, the place of incorporation or, where there is no such place anywhere, the place under the law of which the formation took place.[51] It follows from the fact that the domicile of a company is defined in terms of a series of alternatives that a company may be domiciled in more than one Member State.

IV. BASES OF JURISDICTION

3.15 The first seven sections of Chapter II set out the bases of jurisdiction under the Brussels I Regulation. The Regulation provides for: (i) general jurisdiction (Section 1, Articles 2–4); (ii) special jurisdiction (Section 2, Articles 5–7); (iii) jurisdiction in matters relating to insurance (Section 3, Articles 8–14); (iv) jurisdiction over consumer contracts (Section 4, 15–17); (v) jurisdiction over individual contracts of employment (Section 5, Articles 18–21); (vi) exclusive jurisdiction (Section 6, Article 22); (vii) prorogation of jurisdiction (Section 7, Articles 23–24). In some situations, the plaintiff will have to sue the defendant in the courts of the Member State which has been allocated jurisdiction under the Regulation. In other situations, the courts of more than one Member State will have jurisdiction and the plaintiff will be able to choose the Member State in which to sue the defendant. There is a hierarchy of rules of jurisdiction with one rule taking priority over another.[52] At the top there is Article 22. If the courts of a Member State are allocated jurisdiction under this provision, those courts

---

[49] The presumption is contained in para 9(6). It can be used for the purposes of sub-paras (2) (domicile in the UK) and (3) (domicile in a particular part of the UK), but not sub-paras (4) (domicile in a particular place in the UK) and (7) (domicile in a state other than a Regulation State).

[50] *King v Crown Energy Trading AG* [2003] EWCA 163 (Comm), [2003] IL Pr 28; *The Rewia* [1991] 2 Lloyd's Rep 325; *Latchin (t/a Dinkha Latchin Associates) v General Mediterranean Holdings SA* [2002] CLC 330, 337–339.

[51] Art 60(2).

[52] See Briggs and Rees, 2.08.

have exclusive jurisdiction and the courts of no other Member State have jurisdiction. There follows Article 24. If the defendant has entered an appearance before a court of a Member State, that court has jurisdiction. Then comes jurisdiction in matters relating to insurance, consumer contracts and individual contracts of employment. In such cases, jurisdiction is allocated under the rules contained in Sections 3, 4 or 5 and no other courts have jurisdiction. Next comes Article 23. If the parties have agreed that a court or courts of a Member State are to have jurisdiction that courts or courts shall have exclusive jurisdiction, unless the parties have agreed otherwise. Next comes jurisdiction under Article 2. A person domiciled in a Member State can be sued in the courts of that Member State. Finally, there is special jurisdiction under Articles 5–7, according to which, a person sued in a Member State may be sued in another Member State in certain specified circumstances, including in matters relating to a contract and in disputes arising out of the operations of a branch, agency or other establishment.

International sale of goods cases will not involve exclusive jurisdiction **3.16** under Article 22. Neither are we concerned with jurisdiction in matters relating to insurance.[53] Our discussion will therefore start with jurisdiction based on the entry of an appearance under Article 24, look at the definitions of consumer contracts and individual contracts of employment, move on to an agreement on jurisdiction under Article 23, then turn to general jurisdiction based on the defendant's domicile under Article 2 and will conclude with special jurisdiction under Article 5 in matters relating to a contract (Article 5(1)) and in disputes arising out of the operations of a branch, agency or other establishment (Article 5(5)). Special jurisdiction under Article 6, which is concerned with multi-defendant actions, third party actions and counter-claims, will be considered separately in Chapter 9.

1. ARTICLE 24

This provides that 'a court of a Member State before which a defendant **3.17** enters an appearance shall have jurisdiction'. This rule does not apply where appearance was entered to contest the jurisdiction, or where another court has exclusive jurisdiction by virtue of Article 22.[54] There are no special problems in applying this provision to actions in contract between the buyer and seller of goods.

---

[53] However, insurance serves as an illustration in relation to the transfer of rights and obligations, see below, para 5.13.
[54] Art 24.

2. Section 4: Jurisdiction over Consumer Contracts

3.18 Section 4 of the Brussels I Regulation contains special jurisdiction rules for consumer contracts. Such contracts are omitted from the scope of this book, which is only concerned with commercial contracts.[55] However, consumer contracts may be contracts of sale. The reader needs to be aware of the definition under the Regulation of consumer contracts so that they will be able to identify such contracts. They will then have to turn to other works for detailed coverage of this topic.[56]

3.19 Article 15 defines a consumer contract as one:

concluded by a person, the consumer, for a purpose which can be regarded as being outside his trade or profession[57] . . ., if:
  (a) it is a contract for the sale of goods on instalment credit terms; or
  (b) it is a contract for a loan repayable by instalments, or for any other form of credit, made to finance the sale of goods; or
  (c) in all other cases, the contract has been concluded with a person who pursues commercial or professional activities in the Member State of the consumer's domicile or, by any means, directs such activities to that Member State or to several States including that Member State, and the contract falls within the scope of such activities.

This definition follows that contained in the Brussels Convention with the exception of alternative (c). Article 15(1)(c) involves two major changes from its predecessor.[58] The first is to introduce the concept of activities pursued in, or directed towards a Member State. This replaces the requirement that in the state of the consumer's domicile, the conclusion of the contract was preceded by a specific invitation addressed to him or by advertising.[59] The new provision is much more general, merely referring to 'activities', without specifying what these are, pursued in or directed towards a Member State. Directing activities towards a Member State can be 'by any means'. The second major change is to get rid of the requirement[60] that the consumer must have taken the steps necessary for the conclusion of the contract in his home state. Both changes are designed to make clear that point (c) applies to consumer contracts con-

---

[55] The reasons for this are explained above, para 1.23.
[56] For discussion of consumer contracts, see generally: Dicey and Morris, 370–374; Briggs and Rees, 2.73–2.78.
[57] See Case C-269/95 *Benincasa v Dentalkit Srl* [1997] ECR I-3767; Case C-89/91 *Shearson Lehman Hutton Inc v TVB* [1993] ECR I-139.
[58] Art 13(3) of the Brussels Convention.
[59] See Art 13(3)(a) of the Brussels Convention.
[60] In Art 13(3)(b) of the Brussels Convention.

cluded via an interactive website accessible in the state of the consumer's domicile.[61]

Section 4 is a protective provision, designed to protect the consumer who **3.20** is regarded as being in a weaker position than the business with which he contracts. Protection is provided by allowing the consumer to sue either in the defendant's domicile or in his own.[62] In contrast, proceedings against the consumer have to be brought in the Member State in which the consumer is domiciled.[63]

3. SECTION 5: JURISDICTION OVER INDIVIDUAL CONTRACTS OF EMPLOYMENT

Section 5 of the Brussels I Regulation contains special jurisdiction rules **3.21** for individual contracts of employment.[64] A sale of goods contract may also require the seller to perform a service for the buyer. For example, the contract may be for the sale and installation of a machine. The service element does not constitute an individual contract of employment.[65] The special rules in Section 5 will therefore not apply. The Regulation does not define such a contract. However, the decision of the European Court of Justice in *Shenavai v Kreischer*[66] provides guidance. The case concerned a claim by an architect for fees in connection with the drawing up of plans for the building of houses. The European Court of Justice held that this was not a contract of employment for the purposes of the Brussels Convention. Such contracts had certain peculiarities: they created a lasting bond bringing the worker to some extent within the organizational framework of the business of the employer; 'they are linked to the place where the activities are pursued, which determines the application of mandatory rules and collective agreements'. The relationship of the parties to a contract of employment has also been described as one of subordination of the employee to the employer.[67] These criteria

---

[61] See the Explanatory Memorandum in the Proposal for a Council Regulation COM (1999) 348 final, 16.

[62] Art 16(1) of the Brussels I Regulation. This can be departed from by an agreement on jurisdiction, provided that one of a series of alternatives is met, Art 17.

[63] Art 16(2). This can be departed from by an agreement on jurisdiction, provided that one of a series of alternatives is met, Art 17.

[64] The employer may be sued in the Member State where he is domiciled or in the place where the employee habitually carries out his work (Art 19). The employer may only sue in the Member State in which the employee is domiciled (Art 20(1)). These provisions can be departed from by an agreement on jurisdiction, provided that one of two alternatives is met (Art 21).

[65] The question whether a contract for sale and installation is one for the sale of goods under Art 5(1)(b) of the Brussels I Regulation is examined below, paras 3.151–156.

[66] Case 266/85 [1987] ECR 239.

[67] Jenard and Moller Report [1990] OJ C189/57, at 73.

are clearly not met where there is a contract for the sale and installation of goods.

4. ARTICLE 23

The Provision

3.22 Article 23 is concerned with the situation where the parties 'have agreed that a court or the courts of a Member State are to have jurisdiction to settle any disputes which have arisen or which may arise in connection with a particular legal relationship'. If one or more of the parties is domiciled in a Member State, the effect of such an agreement is to give exclusive jurisdiction to the court or courts of the Member State agreed upon, unless the parties have agreed otherwise.[68] For an agreement to come within Article 23 it must satisfy certain requirements as to form. The agreement must be:

(a) in writing or evidenced in writing; or

(b) in a form which accords with practices which the parties have established between themselves; or

(c) in international trade or commerce, in a form which accords with a usage of which the parties are or ought to have been aware and which in such trade or commerce is widely known to, and regularly observed by, parties to contracts of the type involved in the particular trade or commerce concerned.

Any communication by electronic means which provides a durable record of the agreement is regarded as equivalent to 'writing'.[69]

3.23 A claimant who seeks to establish the jurisdiction of the English courts under Article 23 must show a good arguable case that its terms have been met, which suggests that one side has the better argument on the material available.[70] However, if the defendant claims that an English court, which would otherwise have jurisdiction, has no jurisdiction because of a

---

[68] i.e. a non-exclusive jurisdiction clause is given non-exclusive effect and does not preclude trial in another Member State. Under the less clearly worded Lugano Convention (at the moment based still on the Brussels Convention, rather than Regulation) the position is less obvious. However, it has been held in the context of the Brussels Convention that a non-exclusive English jurisdiction clause gives the English courts jurisdiction (*Kurz v Stella Musical Veranstaltungs GmbH* [1992] Ch 196). It has also been held in the context of the Lugano Convention that a foreign non-exclusive jurisdiction clause gives the courts of that foreign Contracting State jurisdiction but does not preclude jurisdiction in another Contracting State (*Insured Financial Structures Ltd v Elektrocieplownia Tychy SA* [2003] EWCA Civ 110, [2003] 2 WLR 656). See generally on non-exclusive jurisdiction clauses, J Fawcett, 'Non-exclusive jurisdiction agreements in private international law' [2001] LMCLQ 234.

[69] Art 23(2).

[70] *Bank of Tokyo-Mitsubishi Ltd v Baskan Gida Sanayi Ve Pazalarma AS* [2004] EWHC 945 (Ch) at [194].

foreign exclusive jurisdiction clause, seemingly, the burden lies on the defendant.[71]

Whilst it is undeniable that the parties must have 'agreed' that the courts **3.24** of a Member State are to have jurisdiction, the relationship between this requirement and the formal requirement has been a matter of some confusion. This has arisen because the European Court of Justice has held that the purpose of the requirement as to form is to ensure that the consensus of the parties is in fact established,[72] which can lead to the impression that satisfaction of the requirement of form also establishes the agreement between the parties. Yet clearly the two are separate requirements. This is apparent from the wording of Article 23 and has been acknowledged recently by the European Court of Justice, which has held that the words 'have agreed', in the first paragraph of Article 17 of the Brussels Convention, cannot be interpreted as meaning that it is necessary for a jurisdiction clause to be formulated in such a way that the competent court can be determined on its wording alone.[73] This decision was not guided by the formal requirements under Article 17. Indeed, the Court appears to have accepted that the purpose of Article 17 was to protect the wishes of the parties. When it comes to the English courts, they have regarded the requirement as to form as a separate requirement from the requirement that the parties have agreed that a court or the courts of a Member State are to have jurisdiction.[74]

This leads on to a separate but related question of how the material **3.25** validity of the 'agreement' is to be determined. Material validity encompasses issues of formation of the agreement and consent to the

---

[71] See the judgment of David Steel J in *Knauf UK GmbH v British Gypsum Ltd* [2001] EWCA Civ 1570 at [41], [2002] 1 Lloyd's Rep 199—the Court of Appeal did not comment on whether this was correct; *Bank of Tokyo-Mitsubishi Ltd v Baskan Gida Sanayi Ve Pazalarma AS* [2004] EWHC 945 (Ch) at [193]. But compare *Provimi Ltd v Roche Products Ltd* [2003] EWHC 961 (Comm) at [55], [2003] 2 All ER (Comm) 683.

[72] Case 24/76 *Colzani v RUWA* [1976] ECR 1831, para 7; Case 25/76 *Segoura v Bonakdarian* [1976] ECR 1851, para 6; Case C-106/95 *MSG v Gravières Rhénanes* [1997] ECR I-911, para 15.

[73] Case C-387/98 *Coreck Maritime GmbH v Handelsveem BV* [2000] ECR I-9337, para 15. It is sufficient that the clause state the objective factors on the basis of which the parties have agreed to choose the court or the courts to which they wish to submit disputes which have arisen or may arise between them.

[74] *Dresser UK Ltd v Falcongate Ltd* [1992] 1 QB 502 at 511 (*per* Bingham LJ); *IP Metal Ltd v Ruote OZ SpA (No 2)* [1994] 2 Lloyd's Rep 560 at 566 (*per* Saville LJ); *Credit Suisse Financial Products v Société Générale d'Entreprises* [1997] IL Pr 165, CA; *AIG Europe (UK) Ltd v The Ethniki* [2002] 2 All ER 566 at 576 (*per* Evans LJ); *Bank of Tokyo-Mitsubishi Ltd v Baskan Gida Sanayi Ve Pazalarma AS* [2004] EWHC 945 (Ch) at [192]; *Provimi Ltd v Roche Products Ltd* [2003] EWHC 961 (Comm), [2003] All ER (Comm) 683. See also *Erich Gasser GmbH v Misat SRL* (Case 4 r 41/02i) [2002] IL Pr 11 at [24], Oberlandesgericht, Innsbruck. The latter case referred to the ECJ the question of the relationship between agreements on jurisdiction and the first seised rule under Art 21 of the Brussels Convention, see below, para 3.328.

agreement.[75] For example, there may be a jurisdiction clause in writing but it is alleged that this is not incorporated into the contract between the parties. It might be alleged that, as a result of mistake, misrepresentation, duress or undue influence, there was no consent to the clause. Is the material validity of the 'agreement' (i.e. the jurisdiction clause) to be determined by reference to national substantive law as identified by the relevant private international law rules for determining the applicable law, or by giving the concept of an 'agreement' an autonomous Community meaning?[76] It is submitted that the former view is the better one in terms of principle. It would seem wrong not to test the validity of this term (i.e. the jurisdiction agreement) by the law governing the contract, just as one would test the material validity of other terms of the contract by that law. There is one decision of the European Court of Justice which, by providing that national law does have a role to play in determining whether the terms of Article 17 have been met, gives support to this interpretation,[77] and there is an English first instance decision,[78] French decisions[79] and a German decision[80] which have applied national substantive law to the issue of material validity of the jurisdiction agreement. However, the authorities are split on this. There are comments in two other decisions of the European Court of Justice that give support to an autonomous Community definition.[81] Moreover, in the one case coming

---

[75] This is how material validity is defined under Art 8 of the Rome Convention on the law applicable to contractual obligations of 1980, discussed below, paras 13.143–149. The latest version of the Convention is contained in [1998] OJ C27/34.

[76] The Schlosser Report, [1979] OJ C59/71, 125. See generally: Briggs and Rees, 2.97; Hill, 116–117.

[77] Case C-214/89 *Powell Duffryn v Petereit* [1992] ECR I-1745, paras 32–33—the questions whether the dispute arose out of the legal relationship in connection with which the jurisdiction agreement was made and whether the scope of the clause applied to the dispute are both a matter for the national court applying national laws. However, the Court at para 14 also said that the concept of an agreement conferring jurisdiction must be regarded as an independent one, and see *Provimi Ltd v Roche Products Ltd* [2003] EWHC 961 (Comm) at [83], [2003] 2 All ER (Comm) 683.

[78] *Lafi Office and International Business SL v Meriden Animal Health Ltd* [2001] 1 All ER (Comm) 54. The High Court considered that it should test the incorporation of a jurisdiction clause by reference to English law, no other law having been pleaded. But it clearly thought that there was a question to be referred to the governing law as to the clause's incorporation.

[79] *ISEA Industrie SpA v SA LU* [1997] IL Pr 823, Court of Appeal, Paris, discussed below, para 3.38; *Les Verreries de Saint-Gobain SA v Martinswerk GmbH* [1999] IL Pr 296, Cour de cassation, discussed below, para 3.39.

[80] *Re a Wood-Cutting Machine* [1995] IL Pr 191, Oberlandesgericht, Dusseldorf.

[81] Case C-269/95 *Benincasa v Dentalkit Srl* [1997] ECR I-3767, para 25, criticized by Harris, (1998) 23 ELR 279; Case C-159/97 *Transporti Castelletti Spedizioni Internazionali SpA v Hugo Trumpy SpA* [1999] ECR I-1597, paras 49 and 51. See also Case 25/76 *Galeries Segoura Sprl v Bonakdarian* [1976] ECR 1851 at 1860. See also the Giuliano and Lagarde Report accompanying the Rome Convention on the law applicable to contractual obligations of 1980, [1980] OJ C282/11, A5.13–A5.14. Even if the requirements of Art 23 cannot be supplemented by substantive requirements of national law, they are always subject to the requirements of

before the European Court of Justice where this question has been fully discussed, Advocate General Lenz came to the conclusion that Article 17 of the Brussels Convention provided an exhaustive definition of the requirements with regard to substantive consensus and the forms for guaranteeing those requirements.[82] Once it was decided that there was a validly concluded jurisdiction clause under Article 17, there was no room for a further examination in the light of national substantive rules of the applicable law of the question whether the jurisdiction clause was validly incorporated into the contract.[83] There are also English first instance decisions applying these principles.[84]

It is possible to have an incorporation of a jurisdiction clause by reference. **3.26** Both the European Court of Justice and the English courts provide guidance as to the principles to be applied in determining whether the incorporation by reference is effective for the purposes of Article 23.[85] Community law recognizes the validity of this, provided that the body of terms to be incorporated is clearly identified. However, in the absence of specific language the court may not be able to conclude that the parties have demonstrated clearly and precisely the existence of a consensus to incorporate clauses, such as a jurisdiction clause, that are ancillary to the subject-matter of the contract. The commercial background has to be taken into account but cannot always be relied upon to make good deficiencies in the language that the parties have chosen to use. In England, the question of whether there has been an incorporation of a

---

European law. So a jurisdiction clause must not, for example, infringe the Unfair Terms in Consumer Contract Regulations 1999, SI 1999/3159; D Staudenmayer, 'The Directive on the Sale of Consumer Goods and Associated Guarantees—A Milestone in European Consumer and Private Law' (2000) 8 European Rev of Private Law 547. See also the discussion below, para 13.56.

[82] Case C-288/92 *Custom Made Commercial Ltd v Stawa Metallbau GmbH* [1994] ECR I-2913, 2946–2947.

[83] ibid at 2948.

[84] *Knauf UK GmbH v British Gypsum Ltd* [2001] 2 All ER (Comm) 332, David Steel J found that as a matter of German law, a jurisdiction clause was not incorporated into the contract. Nonetheless, there was a good arguable case that, if the clause complied with Art 17 of the Brussels Convention, it was effective. There was no appeal on this point and the Court of Appeal left this point open: [2001] EWCA Civ 1570 at [61], [2002] 1 Lloyd's Rep 199. The problem under German law appeared to relate to whether German was one of the languages of the relevant contracts. The defect therefore could arguably be described as one relating to formalities. It is not surprising therefore that David Steel J held that German law could not supplement the requirements under Art 17. It was not concerned with the more difficult situation where, for example, there is a dispute over which parties' terms of contracting apply (and hence whether a jurisdiction clause is incorporated). See also *Provimi Ltd v Roche Products Ltd* [2003] EWHC 961 (Comm) at [82], [2003] 2 All ER (Comm) 683.

[85] Case 24/76 *Colzani v RUWA* [1976] ECR 1831; *AIG v Ethniki* [1998] 4 All ER 301, [2000] 2 All ER 566, CA; *AIG v QBE International Insurance Ltd* [2001] 2 Lloyd's Rep 268; *Siboti K/S v BP France SA* [2003] 2 Lloyd's Rep 364; *Prifti on behalf of Lloyd's Syndicates v Musini Sociedad Anónima de Seguros y Reaseguros* [2003] EWHC 2796 (Comm).

jurisdiction clause by reference has arisen, not in the context of the international sale of goods, but in the context of reinsurance contracts, where the issue has been whether they incorporate the terms of an insurance contract, and of bills of lading, where the issue has been whether they incorporate the terms of a charterparty.

3.27 The parties must have agreed that a court or courts of a Member State are to have jurisdiction 'to settle any disputes which have arisen or which may arise in connection with a particular legal relationship'. A question of construction may arise as to whether the jurisdiction agreement is worded in such a way as to encompass the dispute that arises. For example the claim may be in tort. This question should be determined by the application of the law governing the jurisdiction agreement, rather than the contract as a whole.[86]

Application to Contracts for the International Sale of Goods

The parties have agreed that a court or the courts of a Member State are to have jurisdiction

3.28 **Choice of jurisdiction clauses in contracts for the international sale of goods**   An agreement that a court or courts of a Member State are to have jurisdiction will normally take the form of a choice of jurisdiction clause. Any party, advised by a City firm for a big, one-shot contract, invariably will have incorporated into the contract a jurisdiction clause. When it comes to routine contracts where clauses are included in invoices, manufacturers' standard terms, etc., it is very likely that a jurisdiction clause will be found. There is no standard practice concerning the location of small print as to whether it is to be found in an order form (which could be a buyer's or seller's standard order form), confirmation of order, invoice, delivery note or general conditions of sale. It may be located in more than one of these, for example in both the seller's confirmation of order and invoices. Invoices in many cases refer to the manufacturer's standard conditions. As for standard form contracts, jurisdiction clauses are commonplace, indeed universal. For example, clause 31 in GAFTA 100 provides that 'the Courts of England or arbitrators appointed in England, as the case may be, shall . . . have exclusive jurisdiction over all disputes which may arise under this contract'.

3.29 **Have the parties agreed on jurisdiction?**   The mere fact that the contractual documentation contains a choice of jurisdiction clause does not necessarily mean that the parties have actually agreed that this clause is to govern any disputes between them. As with any other type of contract,

---

[86] See the discussion below, paras 6.02–06.

the jurisdiction agreement in a contract for the international sale of goods may have been inserted as a result of mistake, misrepresentation or duress. The better view is that the material validity of the jurisdiction agreement should be determined by reference to the law governing the international sale of goods contract.[87]

The problems of mistake and so on are no more likely to arise with an **3.30** international sale of goods case than with any other type of contract. The problem that frequently does arise in cases of the international sale of goods is whether a jurisdiction clause has been incorporated into the contract, or sometimes which party's jurisdiction clause has been incorporated into the contract. The jurisdiction clause may not have been incorporated into the contract, having been introduced after the contract was formed. Moreover, each party may attempt to insert its own choice of jurisdiction clause into the contract.[88] The question will then arise of which jurisdiction clause, if any, has been incorporated into the contract. It is necessary therefore, when considering whether the parties have agreed on jurisdiction, to determine when the contract was formed. This then raises the question of how the rules on formation of the contract are to be determined. Are these rules to be determined by a reference to the national law that governs the contract for the international sale of goods or by reference to an autonomous Community definition of when such a contract is formed for the purposes of Article 23? This is all part and parcel of the question considered earlier[89] of whether the agreement for the purposes of Article 23 is to be determined by a reference to the governing law or by giving this concept an autonomous Community meaning. The better view is that the formation of the contract should be determined by a reference to the applicable national law. But the position if, contrary to what is argued here, it were to be decided that formation should be determined by reference to an autonomous community definition, will also be considered.

Formation of the contract: a reference to the applicable national law

Identification of the applicable law In order to identify the relevant applic- **3.31** able law, it is necessary to apply the choice of law rules in relation to contracts for the international sale of goods. In the case of the United Kingdom these rules are contained in the Rome Convention on the law

---

[87] See above, para 3.25. The alternative is to give the concept of an 'agreement' an autonomous community meaning.

[88] See generally G Dannemann, 'The "Battle of the Forms" and the Conflict of Laws' in Rose (ed), *Lex Mercatoria—Essays on International Commercial Law in Honour of Francis Reynolds* (London: LLP, 2000), Ch 11; see also the discussion below, paras 13.57–61.

[89] Above, para 3.25.

applicable to contractual obligations of 1980.[90] Thus in *Egon Oldendorff v Libera Corp*,[91] one of the issues that arose was whether an arbitration clause had been incorporated into the contract. Mance J applied Article 8 of the Rome Convention, which deals with the issue of material validity, to determine this issue. It was for the law governing the contract to determine whether the arbitration clause had been validly incorporated into the contract. Mance J regarded the question of the incorporation of the clause as coming within the question of the material validity of the contract.[92]

3.32   In most other EC Member States,[93] the position is the same as that in England. These Member States will apply the Rome Convention to cases of international sale of goods. However, a significant number of EC Member States have adopted the 1955 Hague Convention on the law applicable to international sale of goods.[94] In these Member States, when faced with

---

[90]   Discussed below, paras 13.43–264.

[91]   [1995] 2 Lloyd's Rep 64 where Mance J had to determine whether there was a good arguable case that English law governed for the purposes of service out of the jurisdiction. Subsequently Clarke J in *Egon Oldendorff v Libera Corp* [1996] 1 Lloyd's Rep 380 had to determine whether English law really did govern, by which time it was accepted that, regardless of whether English or Japanese law governed, the arbitration clause was incorporated into the contract. See also *Welex AG v Rosa Maritime Limited (The Epsilon Rosa) (No 1)* [2002] EWHC 762 (Comm), [2002] Lloyd's Rep 81; *Welex AG v Rosa Maritime Limited (The Epsilon Rosa) (No 2)* [2002] EWHC 2033 (Comm), [2002] 2 Lloyd's Rep 701. An unsuccessful appeal was made to the Court of Appeal [2003] EWCA Civ 938, [2003] 2 Lloyd's Rep 509 against both decisions (the first concerned the incorporation of the arbitration clause, the second an anti-suit injunction) but this did not challenge the first instance decision that English law governed by virtue of Art 8 of the Rome Convention.

[92]   On the facts there was a separate issue as to whether any contract was ever validly made. The issue of the incorporation of an arbitration clause or choice of jurisdiction clause into a contract could, in theory, be regarded as an issue of material validity of that clause. This issue should be determined by traditional national choice of law rules, rather than by the Rome Convention (Art 1(2)(d) of which excludes arbitration agreements and agreements on the choice of court from its scope). Under English law, in the great majority of cases the same country's law will be applicable, regardless of which set of rules is applied. This is because a choice of jurisdiction clause may well be accompanied by a choice of law clause. Even if it is not, the jurisdiction clause is a strong indication of an implied choice both under the Convention and at common law, see below, paras 13.50–52.

[93]   Austria, Belgium, Cyprus, Czech Republic, Estonia, Germany, Greece, Hungary, Ireland, Latvia, Lithuania, Luxembourg, Malta, Netherlands, Poland, Portugal, Slovakia, Slovenia and Spain. There will need to be an Accession Convention of the ten new Member States (Cyprus, Czech Republic, Estonia, Hungary, Latvia, Lithuania, Malta, Poland, Slovakia and Slovenia) to the Rome Convention.

[94]   Discussed below, paras 15.10–64. The 1955 Convention has entered into force in Denmark, Finland, France, Italy, and Sweden (Belgium adopted the Convention but subsequently denounced it. Luxembourg, the Netherlands and Spain signed the Convention but never brought it into force. The Convention has entered into force in the EFTA countries of Norway and Switzerland but not in Iceland). The 1986 Convention has not yet entered into force. Of the 25 EC Member States only the Czech Republic, the Netherlands and Slovakia have signed it (but not ratified it).

an international sale of goods case, recourse will be had to this Convention, rather than the Rome Convention.[95]

In cases involving the international sale of goods, it will often happen that **3.33** the substantive law will be the same, regardless of the applicable law and it will therefore be unnecessary to have recourse to choice of law rules. This is because many countries throughout the world, including 12 of the original 15 EC Member States,[96] have enacted the Vienna Convention. If, on the facts of the case, all the relevant connecting factors point to countries that have enacted the Vienna Convention there can be no question but that the relevant substantive law is contained in that Convention, provided of course that the instant case comes within the sphere of application of the Vienna Convention.[97] This can be illustrated by two French decisions involving the question of whether Article 17 of the Brussels Convention applied. The first of these is *ISEA Industrie SpA v SA LU*,[98] a decision of the Cour d'appel, Paris. The French plaintiffs sued an Italian supplier and its Italian insurer in relation to a delivery of defective packaging. All the connections were with France or Italy, both of which have enacted the Vienna Convention. After checking that the case came with the scope of application of that Convention (it did because the parties had places of business in different states when those were Contracting States), the Court went on to apply the provisions in the Vienna Convention on formation of the contract in order to determine whether a choice of jurisdiction clause was agreed upon by the parties. The second illustration is *Les Verreries de Saint-Gobain SA v Martinswerk GmbH*, a decision of the French Cour de cassation (French Supreme Court).[99] In this case, all the connections were with France or Germany. Again, both countries had enacted the Vienna Convention and the applicable substantive law on formation of the contract was accepted as being contained in the Convention and no recourse was made to choice of law rules.

The substantive law on the formation of contracts for the international sale of **3.34**
goods Articles 14–24 of the Vienna Convention deal with standard issues

---

[95] Art 21 of the Rome Convention provides that, in cases coming within the scope of the 1955 Hague Convention, that Convention will apply instead of the Rome Convention, see the discussion on the Hague Conventions, below at para 15.05. The 1955 Hague Convention does not expressly exclude from its scope agreements on arbitration or on choice of court. Compare Art 5(e) of the 1986 Hague Convention on the law applicable to contracts for the international sale of goods.

[96] All of the 25 EC Member States have brought the Vienna Convention into effect with the exception of the UK, Cyprus, Ireland, Malta and Portugal. The three EFTA States (Iceland, Norway and Switzerland) have also brought the Convention into effect.

[97] See Arts 1–6 of the Vienna Convention; discussed in outline above, at paras 1.04–07 and in detail below, at paras 16.16–95.

[98] [1997] IL Pr 823, Court of Appeal, Paris.　　　　　　　　　　　　　　[99] [1999] IL Pr 296.

of formation:[100] what is an offer as opposed to an invitation to treat?[101] When does an offer become effective as an offer?[102] And until when is revocation effective?[103] And what effect does rejection have on an offer?[104] And when is an offer irrevocable?[105] What is the duration of an offer?[106] And when may a late acceptance be effective?[107] What form may an acceptance take?[108] And when does that acceptance take effect?[109] And when may it be retracted?[110] What is a counter-offer so as to constitute a rejection of offer?[111] When is a contract concluded?[112] When does an offer, acceptance, etc. 'reach' the other party?[113] There is no rule on open-ended offers lapsing through effluxion of time.[114] In addition, there are no rules concerning consideration (or its civil law counterpart of cause).[115] This is why a promise to keep an offer open results in an offer being irrevocable.[116] There are no separate rules on contractual certainty; for example, agreements to agree and agreements to negotiate.[117]

3.35 As for English law, the obvious differences are as follows.[118] First, promises to keep an offer open are not binding in the absence of consideration.[119] Second, the postal rule of acceptance applies, and hence a posted acceptance cannot be retracted by a faster method of communication.[120] Third, contracts cannot in English law be concluded where there is discrepancy between offer and acceptance.[121] Fourth, late acceptances are never effective in English law.[122]

---

[100] See also in relation to formation, Art 8 which lays down a compromise on subjectivity/objectivity in the matter of a party's statements, and Art 11 (no form requirements), which is subject to reservation under Art 96.

[101] Art 14.   [102] Art 15.   [103] Art 16(1).   [104] Art 17.   [105] Art 16(2).

[106] Art 20.   [107] Art 21.   [108] Art 18(1): concerns statements, conduct and silence.

[109] Art 18(2), (3).   [110] Art 22.   [111] Art 19.

[112] Art 23 (but there is no rule as to where a contract is concluded).

[113] Art 24.

[114] Does this mean that such an offer always remains open until it is retracted?

[115] Indeed, Art 29(1) on modification of contracts makes it clear that variation can occur by mere agreement.

[116] Art 16(2)(a), which uses the tamer language of an offer 'indicating' that it will remain open for a stated time.

[117] But see the requirement of an offer (in Art 14(1)), requiring provision to be made for the price, and note the inconsistency with Art 55, which deals with contracts 'validly concluded' where no provision has been made for the price.

[118] For detailed differences see Bridge, *The International Sale of Goods*, Ch 3, 71–79.

[119] *A fortiori*, the keeping open of an offer where there is simple reliance on it being kept open.

[120] Any difference between the Vienna Convention and English law is diminished by the rule that a contract will be concluded if the rejection reaches the offeree after he has dispatched an acceptance (Art 16(1)).

[121] cf. Art 19(2), (3).

[122] Any difference between the Vienna Convention and English law is magnified by the former's rejection of the postal rule.

Formation of the contract and the agreement of the parties as to jurisdic- **3.36**
tion   The way in which the agreement of the parties as to jurisdiction is
determined by the application of the relevant substantive law on the
formation of the contract for the international sale of goods is illustrated
by an English decision, which involved the application of English
substantive law, and by two decisions of the French courts mentioned
above,[123] which involved the application of the Vienna Convention.

In *Lafi Office and International Business SL v Meriden Animal Health Ltd*,[124] **3.37**
the buyer's terms and conditions, one of which was a clause which provided that the seller submitted to the non-exclusive jurisdiction of the
English courts, were set out on the reverse of the order that it addressed to
the seller. This order was accepted by the seller. The seller thereafter acted
upon that order and supplied the chemical which the buyer ordered. The
buyer argued that its terms and conditions were not incorporated into
the contract. It was not suggested that the judge should apply anything
other than English law to determine this question and no other law was
pleaded. Christopher Symons QC, sitting as a Deputy Judge of the High
Court, held that the buyer's terms and conditions were incorporated
into the contract.[125] He said that where a party has itself sent the terms
and conditions, which it wished to have included as part of the contract, it
cannot raise the argument that these were not sufficiently brought to its
attention to be incorporated into the contract or that it had not consented
to the terms and conditions that it had sent.[126] He went on to say that the
position might have been different if the seller had not accepted the order
or part of the order. This indicates that the conclusion was reached after an
application of the English rules on offer and acceptance.[127]

We can now turn to look at the two French cases that involved the applica- **3.38**
tion of the Vienna Convention. In the *ISEA* case,[128] the buyer placed an
order for packaging with the Italian seller. The buyer's general purchasing
conditions, which included a clause conferring jurisdiction on the Tribunal de commerce, Paris, were printed on the back of the order form. The
seller returned this, signed by its representative and with the words
'accepted by the supplier'. This was received by the buyer on 5 April 1991.
On 23 April 1991, the seller sent the buyer an order confirmation form, on
the back of which were the words: 'We thank you for your order, which
we have accepted in accordance with our conditions of sale'. These conditions, which appeared on the reverse, included a clause conferring
jurisdiction on the court of Tortona. The buyer brought an action against

---

[123] See also *Re a Wood-Cutting Machine* [1995] IL Pr 191, Oberlandesgericht, Dusseldorf.
[124] [2001] 1 All ER (Comm) 54.
[125] ibid at 65.   [126] ibid.   [127] ibid.   [128] n 98 above.

the seller before the Tribunal de commerce, Paris. Both Italy and France are parties to the Vienna Convention and the instant case came within the sphere of application of that Convention.[129] According to Article 18(2) of that Convention the contract for the international sale of goods was formed at the moment when the indication of assent reaches the offeror. This was when the order form was returned by the seller to the buyer, i.e. 5 April 1991. The order confirmation of 23 April 1991 was subsequent to the date of the formation of the contract. It was not a counter-offer within the meaning of the Convention.[130] The upshot was that the Tortona jurisdiction clause did not fulfil the requirements of Article 17 of the Brussels Convention.[131]

3.39 In the *Les Verreries* case,[132] the French courts had to decide whether they had jurisdiction in a dispute between a French buyer and a German seller over the quality of goods delivered. The buyer's order form contained a jurisdiction clause conferring jurisdiction on the Tribunal de commerce, Orleans. However, the confirmation of order dispatched by the seller conferred jurisdiction on the courts of its seat, Germany. The applicable substantive law was contained in the Vienna Convention, Article 19 of which provides that a reply to an offer which purports to be an acceptance but which contains modifications that materially alter the terms of the offer is a rejection of the offer and constitutes a counter-offer. The same Article goes on to provide that different terms relating to the settlement of disputes are considered to alter the terms of the offer materially.[133] Accordingly, the Cour de cassation held that the French buyer could not rely on the jurisdiction clause providing for trial in France with the result that the French courts lacked jurisdiction.

3.40 Formation of the contract: an autonomous Community definition   If, contrary to what is argued here, it were to be decided that formation should be determined by reference to an autonomous community definition of the concept of an 'agreement', this raises the question of how this definition is to be reached. In arriving at an autonomous Community definition, it is necessary to look at the objectives and scheme of the Regulation and at the 'the general principles which stem from the corpus

---

[129]   Art 1(1) requires that the parties have places of business in different states, when the states are Contracting States to the Convention or when the rules of private international law lead to the application of the law of a Contracting State, see in outline above, para 1.05 and in detail below, paras 16.12–41.

[130]   See Art 19(1) which provides that a counter-offer is a reply to an offer which purports to be an acceptance but which contains modifications.

[131]   The French jurisdiction clause failed to meet the formal requirements, see below, para 3.45.

[132]   [1999] IL Pr 296.   [133]   Art 19(3).

of the national legal systems'.[134] The Vienna Convention, which it will be recalled has been adopted in 12 of the original 15 EC Member States, can be regarded as setting out the general principles which stem from the corpus of the national legal systems. Its provisions on formation could be adopted verbatim as the autonomous community definition of the agreement. If the community definition is the same as that in the Vienna Convention, this will mean that in practical terms it is often not going to make any difference whether the rules on formation of the contract are determined by a reference to the applicable national law or by reference to an autonomous Community definition since both paths will lead to the Vienna Convention. But there are still three of the original 15 Member States which have not enacted the Vienna Convention and in so far as their national laws contain rules on formation which are different from those contained in the Convention, it is going to matter which approach towards determining the rules on formation is adopted.

An agreement as to jurisdiction in an associated contract We are con- **3.41** cerned here with the situation where the contract for the international sale of goods itself does not contain an agreement as to jurisdiction but a closely related contract does contain such an agreement. This raises the question whether the parties can be assumed to have also intended that this agreement should apply to the international sales contract. The best example of a contract that is closely related to an international sale of goods contract is that of an exclusive distribution (or concession) agreement.[135] The latter contract is the main one, but flowing from this will be a number of contracts for the international sale of goods. The relationship between these different contracts and the effect that this has on the operation of Article 17 of the Brussels Convention was examined by the Dutch courts in *Hacker Kuchen GmbH v Bosma Huygen Meubelimpex BV*.[136] In this case, the Dutch Court of Appeal was faced with the converse of the situation that we are now concerned with, namely whether, in an action for breach of an exclusive distribution agreement, an agreement on jurisdiction could be assumed from the fact that the parties had entered into an agreement on jurisdiction in the related sales agreement. The Dutch Court of Appeal held that it could not and the Dutch Supreme Court (the Hoge Raad) held that that this did not disclose any erroneous view of the law. The position would doubtless be the same in the converse situation and the parties cannot be assumed to have intended to apply the jurisdiction

---

[134] Case C-172/91 *Sonntag v Waidmann* [1993] ECR I-1963.
[135] See below, para 16.95.
[136] [1992] IL Pr 379. See also *Printed Forms Equipments Ltd v Société Matériel Auxiliaire d'Informatique* [2000] IL Pr 597, Cour d'appel, Paris.

agreement in the exclusive distribution contract to the international sales contract.

3.42 A contract for the carriage of goods or one for marine insurance may be closely related to a contract for the international sale of goods. This is most apparent where there is a CIF contract; the seller is under an obligation to procure a contract of carriage by sea and to arrange for insurance. The position in such a case should be no different from that where there is an exclusive distribution agreement and the parties to the sales contract cannot be assumed to have intended to apply the agreement as to jurisdiction in the carriage or insurance contract to that contract. Indeed, it is even harder to make such an assumption in these types of related contract than it is with an exclusive distribution agreement. The parties to the distribution agreement will be the same as to the sales agreement, whereas the parties to the carriage or insurance agreement will, of course, not be the same as those to the sales agreement. Contracts involving a method of payment for the goods sold, such as by a letter of credit, are likewise related to the international sale of goods contract but should be treated in the present context in the same way as an exclusive distribution agreement, a carriage contract or an insurance contract.

Formal requirements

3.43 Article 23(1) of the Brussels I Regulation sets out three different forms, one of which the agreement must take in order to satisfy the requirement as to form. The purpose of the formal requirements is to ensure that the consensus between the parties is in fact established.[137] Problems in relation to the formal requirements have arisen most commonly in relation to contracts for the international sale of goods. This is partly because of the large number of such contracts but also because of the fact that standard form contracts are the norm, and it is particularly hard to establish the consensus of the parties when there is such a contract. These three different alternative forms will now be examined.

In writing or evidenced in writing

3.44 *In writing*   In *Colzani v RUWA*,[138] the European Court of Justice held that, where a clause conferring jurisdiction is included among the general conditions of sale of one of the parties, printed on the back of a contract, the requirement of writing under Article 17 of the Brussels Convention is fulfilled only if the contract signed by both parties contains an express reference to those general conditions. A German seller brought proceedings in Germany against an Italian firm for failure to perform a

---

[137] Case 24/76 *Colzani v RUWA* [1976] ECR 1831.   [138] Case 24/76 [1976] ECR 1831.

contract for the supply of machines and sought to rely on a choice of jurisdiction clause providing for trial in Germany. The sale was agreed in a contract written on the business notepaper of the seller and signed by the parties, printed on the reverse of which were the German plaintiff's general conditions of sale. The text of the contract did not refer to the conditions of sale expressly and, accordingly, the requirement of writing would not be met.

The problem posed by conditions, including a choice of jurisdiction **3.45** clause, on the back of the sales contract came before the Cour d'appel, Paris, in the *ISEA* case.[139] It will be recalled that the contract was formed by acceptance of an order form, on the back of which were printed the buyer's general purchasing conditions, including a choice of jurisdiction clause providing for trial in France. The court held that, as there was no express reference on the front of the order form to the general conditions on the back, the seller could not be deemed to have accepted them.[140]

The European Court of Justice in the *Colzani* case went on to hold that, **3.46** in the case of a contract concluded by reference to earlier offers, which were themselves made with reference to the general conditions of one of the parties including a clause conferring jurisdiction, the requirement of writing is satisfied only if the reference is express and can therefore be checked by a party exercising reasonable care.[141] It must also be established that the general conditions, including the clause conferring jurisdiction, have in fact been communicated to the other contracting party with the offer to which reference is made. Applying this principle, the Bundesgerichtshof held that, since the text of the contract referred to previous offers made by the German plaintiff, which contained an express reference to those general conditions of sale, the Italian defendant could immediately acquaint itself with the plaintiff's general conditions of business and therefore with the jurisdiction clause. The upshot was that the German courts had jurisdiction.[142]

There is one situation though where terms and conditions set out on the **3.47** reverse of a contractual document, with no reference to these on the front, will nevertheless satisfy the requirement of writing. This is where a party, which has itself sent the terms and conditions that it wished to have included as part of the contract, argues that it has not consented to these

---

[139] *ISEA Industrie SpA v SA LU* [1997] IL Pr 823, Court of Appeal, Paris; discussed above, para 3.38.
[140] ibid at 827.
[141] n 138 above, para 13.
[142] Judgment of 4 May 1977—VIII Z R 14/75, RIW 1977, 649; D Series I-17.1.2—B 9.

terms and conditions. It has been held that this party cannot raise this argument.[143]

3.48 The interpretation of the requirement of writing adopted in *Colzani* was a very strict one. The effect of the decision was that not only must the choice of jurisdiction clause be in writing but also the consensus on its application must also be writing. But later decisions of the European Court of Justice have adopted a more liberal view towards the requirement of writing.[144] However, these later cases did not involve the sale of goods and the problem found with sales of standard form contracts with conditions on the back. *Colzani* remains the definitive decision on this situation.

3.49 *Evidenced in writing*   This alternative is concerned with the situation where an oral agreement is confirmed in writing. What is needed to satisfy this requirement was considered by the European Court of Justice in *Galeries Segoura SPRL v Rahim Bonakdarian*.[145] The German seller of a consignment of carpets brought proceedings in Germany against the Belgian buyer for payment of the balance of the purchase price. The contract was concluded orally between the parties. However, on handing over the goods, the seller delivered to the buyer a document described as 'Confirmation of order and invoice', which stated that the sale and delivery had taken place 'subject to the conditions stated on the reverse'. The conditions printed on the reverse of this document included a choice of jurisdiction clause stipulating that all disputes were to be decided exclusively by the Hamburg courts. This document was not confirmed by the buyer. The European Court of Justice held that the requirements as to form under the Brussels Convention are satisfied only if the seller's confirmation in writing, accompanied by notification of the general conditions of sale, has been accepted in writing by the buyer. It makes no difference if, at the conclusion of the oral contract, the seller has stated that he wishes to rely on his general conditions of sale and then confirms the contract in writing. The confirmation in writing accompanied by the general conditions of sale must be accepted in writing by the buyer. For, even if the buyer agrees to abide by the seller's general conditions, he cannot be deemed to have agreed on a jurisdiction clause which might appear in those conditions. The problem with this is that it is incompatible

---

[143] *Lafi Office and International Business SL v Meriden Animal Health Ltd* [2001] 1 All ER (Comm) 54.
[144] See Case 313/85 *Iveco Fiat SpA v Van Hool NV* [1986] ECR 3337; Case C-214/89 *Powell Duffryn plc v Petereit* [1992] ECR I-1745. See generally Briggs and Rees, 2.86.
[145] Case 25/76 [1976] ECR 1851.

with practices in international trade.[146] In the situation where the oral contract is concluded, without any reference being made to the seller's general conditions, it is clear that the jurisdiction clause does not form part of the contract orally concluded between the parties. What is needed again is that the confirmation in writing, accompanied by the general conditions of sale, is accepted in writing by the buyer. Moreover, the fact that the buyer does not raise any objections against a confirmation issued unilaterally by the other party does not amount to an acceptance on his part of the jurisdiction clause, unless the oral agreement comes within the framework of a continuing trading relationship between the parties which is based on the general conditions of one of them, and those conditions contain a clause conferring jurisdiction.

When it comes to the development of the law, the same pattern emerges as with Colzani. The *Segoura* case adopted a strict interpretation of the concept of evidenced in writing. Later decisions of the European Court of Justice have adopted a more liberal line.[147] But these are not cases on the sale of goods with the use of standard form contracts with conditions on the back. *Segoura* remains the definitive case on this situation. Nevertheless, this liberal attitude has been adopted by an English judge in a first instance decision involving sale of goods.[148] Judge Dean QC said that: **3.50**

> if a party who is willing to supply goods presents a document which contains either on the face of the document or by reference to documents which the other party already has, offering to supply goods on particular terms, including a jurisdiction clause, and the party to whom that document is proffered orders the goods and takes delivery of the goods upon that basis, that is the clearest evidence that he is agreeing to the written terms, and in my judgment that is sufficient to satisfy art 17(a) as constituting evidence in writing.[149]

It is common in relation to the purchase of metal for terms to be negotiated over the telephone. However, not every term will be agreed on in this way since some of the terms will be regarded as being obvious. There will then be a confirmation of these terms by telex.[150] This was what happened in *IP Metal v Ruote*.[151] The seller sent a fax to the buyer offering to sell it aluminium. At the end of the fax it stated 'competent forum London'. **3.51**

---

[146] See the Schlosser Report, n 76 above, para 179. Hence the introduction of alternative (c) based on trade practices.

[147] Case 71/83 *Partenreederei MS Tilly Russ and Co AG v Haven and Vervaebedriff* [1985] QB 931; Case 221/84 *F Berghoefer GmbH v ASA SA* [1985] ECR 2699. See generally Briggs and Rees, 2.86.

[148] *Middle East Tankers & Freighters Bunker Services SA v Abu Dhabi Container Lines PJSC* [2002] EWHC 957 (Comm), [2002] 2 Lloyd's Rep 643.

[149] ibid at 651.

[150] See, eg, the *IP Metal* case, n 151 below.   [151] [1993] 2 Lloyd's Rep 60.

This led to a number of orders from the buyer, with seven contracts being concluded orally. The seller confirmed the contracts by telexes to the buyer, which contained an express term that the competent forum was London. In an action in relation to six of the contracts, Waller J held that there was an oral agreement between the parties that the English courts should have jurisdiction and that this was then evidenced in writing. Accordingly, Article 17 applied. Waller J reached the same conclusion in a separate action for breach of the seventh contract and the Court of Appeal upheld this decision.[152]

3.52   In a form which accords with practices which the parties have established between themselves   This alternative originates from an addition made to the Brussels Convention by the Spanish/Portuguese Accession Convention. It incorporated into the Brussels Convention certain principles enunciated by the European Court of Justice in, *inter alia*, the *Segoura* case.[153] In that case, it was held that the consensus between the parties can be shown where an oral agreement forms part of a continuing trading relationship between them which was subject to the general conditions containing the jurisdiction clause.[154] The question whether the agreement is in a form that accords with practices which the parties have established between themselves is one of fact[155] and is to be determined by reference to all the material circumstances.[156] 'Practices' requires a long-standing business relationship of some intensity.[157] It presupposes a certain length of time, so that a party may rely on a particular form as customary between the parties.[158] The operation of alternative (b) in the context of a contract for the international sale of goods is illustrated by the *IP Metal* case.[159] Waller J looked at the contractual history of the parties and noted that, prior to the contracts of 1990, which were the subject of the

---

[152] *IP Metal v Ruote (No 2)* [1994] 2 Lloyd's Rep 560, CA.

[153] Case 25/76 *Segoura v Bonakdarian* [1976] ECR 1851. See also Case 71/83 *Partenreederei MS Tilly Russ v Haven and Vervaebedriff* [1985] QB 931.

[154] n 153 above, para 11.

[155] *OT Africa Line Ltd v Hijazy (The Kribi)* [2001] 1 Lloyd's Rep 76 at [56].

[156] *Erich Gasser GmbH v Misat SRL* (Case 4 r 41/02i) [2002] IL Pr 11 at [24], Oberlandesgericht, Innsbruck. The latter case referred to the ECJ the question of the relationship between agreements on jurisdiction and the first seised rule under Art 21 of the Brussels Convention, see below, para 3.328.

[157] ibid.   [158] ibid.

[159] [1993] 2 Lloyd's Rep 60; aff'd [1994] 2 Lloyd's Rep 560, CA. See also *SSQ Europe SA v Johann & Backes OHG* [2002] 1 Lloyd's Rep 465—a good arguable case established that the defendant had traded for a long period (with 672 invoices) in the knowledge that the claimant was only willing to deliver on its standard terms and the defendant knew the content of these terms and never once objected to them. For other international sales case see: *Middle East Tankers & Freighters Bunker Services SA v Abu Dhabi Container Lines PJSC* [2002] EWHC 957 (Comm), [2002] 2 Lloyd's Rep 643, 652; *Clare Taverns v Charles Gill* [2000] ILRM 98, 109.

present proceedings, the parties had entered into three oral contracts in 1987 and a further oral contract in 1989, all of which included confirmation by the seller by telex which contained an express term providing for trial in England. Furthermore, during 1988 the seller confirmed certain contracts with an associated company of the buyer, sending the confirmations to the person who negotiated on behalf of the buyer. The confirmations again contained a choice of jurisdiction clause providing for trial in England. Having looked at this history, Waller J gave as an alternative ground for satisfying the formal requirement under Article 17 of the Brussels Convention, that the oral agreement on the jurisdiction of the English courts was in a form which accorded with the practices which the parties had established between themselves.

In international trade or commerce, in a form which accords with a **3.53**
usage of which the parties are or ought to have been aware   This alternative was added to the Brussels Convention by the 1978 United Kingdom, Denmark and Ireland Accession Convention.[160] The incorporation of contract terms by reference, commercial custom or trade practice is a phenomenon very much more familiar in the common law than in the civil law world.[161] There are many examples concerning times and dates of port activity and place of delivery in port. Payment issues could also arise in respect of local banking hours.[162] The consensus of the parties to the choice of jurisdiction clause is presumed to exist where commercial usages in the relevant branch of international trade or commerce exist in this regard of which the parties are or ought to have been aware.[163] A trade practice can be used to surmount what would otherwise amount to a lack of consensus. Thus if the language of general conditions of business, including a choice of jurisdiction clause, attached to a commercial letter of confirmation, is different from the language in which the contract was concluded and the negotiations were conducted, it cannot be said that the

---

[160] [1978] OJ L304/1. See the Schlosser Report, n 76 above, para 179.

[161] *Dresser UK Ltd v Falcongate Ltd* [1992] 1 QB 502, 511 (*per* Bingham LJ).

[162] Examples of incorporation of usage etc, especially foreign usage, include: *Kum v Wah Tat Bank Ltd* [1971] 1 Lloyd's Rep 439 (mate's receipt recognized as a document of title when issued in Singapore because it would be so recognized in Singapore though not under English law); *Total Transport Corp v Arcadia Petroleum Ltd (The Eurus)* [1998] CLC 90 (bill of lading validly dated 31 January, though relating to loading in the hours before 8 am on 1 February, because the custom of the loading port in Nigeria permitted the bill to be dated 31 January in such circumstances). Although arising in the context of a contract of affreightment, the local meaning of delivery 'alongside' a ship could affect a sale of goods contract on FAS (free alongside ship) terms, see *Palgrave Brown & Sons v SS Turid* [1922] 1 AC 397. Domestic case law also furnishes examples, eg, *Steels & Busks Ltd v Bleeker Bik & Co Ltd* [1956] 1 Lloyd's Rep 228 (meaning of 'pale crepe rubber'); *Peter Darlington and Partners Ltd v Gosho Co Ltd* [1964] 1 Lloyd's Rep 149 (meaning of 'pure' in 'canary seed on pure basis').

[163] Case C-106/95 *Mainschiffahrts-Genossenschaft eG (MSG) v Les Gravières Rhénanes Sarl* [1997] ECR I-911.

other party is given adequate notice of the jurisdiction clause and actual consensus would be absent.[164] However, it would be different if a trade practice authorized a language to be used different from the one in which the contract was drawn up and the negotiations were conducted.[165] Similarly, the fact that one of the parties repeatedly paid, without objection, invoices issued by the other party containing a jurisdiction clause, may be deemed to constitute consent to the jurisdiction clause in issue, provided that such conduct is consistent with a practice in force in the area of international trade or commerce in which the parties in question are operating and the parties are or ought to have been aware of the practice.[166]

3.54 The conditions imposed by alternative (c) and their operation in a case of the international sale of goods were discussed in detail by Advocate General Lenz in *Custom Made Commercial Ltd v Stawa Metallbau GmbH*.[167] The German plaintiff brought proceedings in Germany for payment for doors and windows of its manufacture from an English buyer. The contract, which was the first one made between the parties, was concluded orally in London. The plaintiff confirmed the conclusion of the contract by a letter. Confirmation was described as being 'subject to our terms of sale'. This letter was accompanied for the first time by the plaintiff's general business conditions, which provided for jurisdiction in Germany. The seller argued that there was a commercial practice that an absence of response to a letter of confirmation has to be regarded as assent to a jurisdiction clause. Were the conditions required by (c) satisfied in such circumstances?

3.55 First, the transactions at issue must relate to *international trade or commerce*. It is for the national court to determine whether the contract in question comes under the head of international trade or commerce.[168] However, the European Court of Justice has said that it should indicate the objective evidence needed in order to make such a determination.[169] In *Custom Made*, the transaction covered by the jurisdiction clause was international in character since it involved a contract of sale relating to the supply of goods from one Contracting State to another, the parties to which were established as commercial companies in those States.[170] Moreover, since

---

[164] AG Lenz in the *Custom Made* case, n 167 below, at 2946.   [165] ibid.
[166] The *MSG* case, n 163 above, para 25; the *Erich Gasser* case, n 156 above, at [26].
[167] Case C-288/92 [1994] ECR I-2913. For the application of this provision to a bill of lading see Case C-159/97 *Trasporti Castelletti Spedizioni Internazionali SpA v Hugo Trumpy SpA* [1999] ECR I-1597; *The Kribi*, n 155 above.
[168] See the *MSG* case, n 163 above, para 21.   [169] ibid.
[170] But there could be more difficult cases where, e.g. the only foreign element is that the currency of the contract is foreign. It should be regarded as *international* where there is any relevant foreign connection.

the parties were commercial companies and both were acting in their own sector of business, there was no doubt that the transactions at issue related to commerce or trade.

Second, the jurisdiction clause has to be concluded in a *form which accords* **3.56** *with practices in the trade or commerce*. Advocate General Lenz gave his opinion that, as regards a particular method of reaching consensus, a commercial or trade practice means a de facto usage which is generally and continuously followed and regularly observed by the circles concerned in commercial transactions corresponding, objectively and from the point of view of their localization, to the commercial transaction at issue, and which warrants the conclusion that the conduct concerned embodies an agreement (or consent on the part of the party concerned).[171] This means that, in a case involving the manufacture and sale of windows, reliance cannot be placed on practices in relation to the sale of cars, and, in a case of Anglo-German trade, reliance cannot be placed on practices in relation to Franco-German trade.[172] Article 17 confers legal effect on such a usage. The existence of a relevant commercial practice has to be proved.[173]

Third, the practice must be one *of which the parties are or ought to have been* **3.57** *aware*. In the instant case, the buyer was unaware of the trade practice that was sought to be relied upon. Ought the buyer to have been aware of such a usage? Advocate General Lenz gave his opinion that the question should be answered in the negative if no such practice existed at the place at which that party (in this case the buyer) has its head office and it was the first time that that party did business with a party adopting such a usage.[174] The European Court of Justice, having come to the conclusion that the German courts would have jurisdiction by virtue of Article 5(1) of the Brussels Convention, did not find it necessary to go into Article 17.

Fourth, there is an additional requirement that this usage must be both **3.58** *widely known to, and regularly observed by, parties to the contracts of the type involved in the particular trade or commerce concerned*. This was introduced by the 1989 Spanish/Portuguese Accession Convention to the Brussels Convention.[175] What is striking about its terminology is that it is virtually identical with that found in Article 9(2) of the Vienna Convention, which deals with the question of when, as a matter of substantive law, parties are

---

[171] See also the *MSG* case, n 163 above, para 23. It is for the national court to determine whether there is such a usage, ibid, para 21.
[172] AG Lenz in the *Custom Made* case, n 167 above, at 2942.
[173] ibid at 2939 and 2944.   [174] ibid at 2945.   [175] [1989] OJ L285/1.

bound by a trade usage. This is no coincidence and represents a deliberate policy of ensuring that the former accords with the latter.[176]

3.59 The decision on whether the conditions under (c) have been satisfied does not always receive as systematic treatment as this. The answer may indeed be regarded as obvious. Thus in the *IP Metal* case, Waller J, after referring to the fact that in contracts for the purchase of metal it is common form for the terms to be negotiated over the telephone, concluded that the oral agreement on the jurisdiction of the English courts was in a form which accords with the usage of the trade in the purchasing of aluminium.[177]

5. GENERAL JURISDICTION: ARTICLE 2

3.60 Article 2 of the Brussels I Regulation provides that: 'Subject to this Regulation,[178] persons domiciled in a Member State shall, whatever their nationality, be sued in the courts of that Member State'. The expectation under the Regulation is that, normally, persons should be sued in the courts of the Member State where they are domiciled.[179] When trial takes place in England, a claimant, who seeks to rely on this provision, has to establish a good arguable case that the defendant is domiciled within the jurisdiction.[180] There are no special difficulties in applying Article 2 to contracts for the international sale of goods. The effect of Article 2 is that a plaintiff, rather than suing in his home state, will have to pursue the defendant abroad in the Member State where the defendant is domiciled. However, a plaintiff who wishes to sue in his home state may be able to do so by invoking the special jurisdiction under Article 5.

6. SPECIAL JURISDICTION: ARTICLE 5(1)

3.61 Jurisdiction under Article 5 is special in that it allows for trial in the courts of a Member State other than the one in which the defendant is domiciled. The plaintiff is therefore given a choice of fora. He can sue either in the courts of the Member State where the defendant is domiciled or in courts of the Member State allocated jurisdiction under Article 5. Article 5 of the

---

[176] See the Almeida Cruz, Desantes Real and Jenard Report, [1990] OJ C189/06, para 26; the Jenard and Moller Report, [1990] OJ C189/57, 77.

[177] n 151 above, at 67. The other alternative ways of satisfying the requirement as to form were also satisfied.

[178] This is referring to the hierarchy of rules under the Regulation. For example, Arts 22 and 23 take priority over Art 2, see above, para 3.15.

[179] For the definition of domicile see above, paras 3.12–14.

[180] *Latchin (t/a Dinkha Latchin Associates) v General Mediterranean Holdings SA* [2002] CLC 330, 336–337.

Brussels Regulation provides that a person domiciled in a Member State may, in another Member State, be sued:

(1) (a) in matters relating to a contract, in the courts for the place of performance of the obligation in question;

  (b) for the purpose of this provision and unless otherwise agreed, the place of performance of the obligation in question shall be:
    — in the case of the sale of goods, the place in a Member State where, under the contract, the goods were delivered or should have been delivered,
    — in the case of the provision of services, the place in a Member State where, under the contract, the services were provided or should have been provided,

  (c) if sub-paragraph (b) does not apply then sub-paragraph (a) applies;

When trial takes place in England, a claimant, who seeks to rely on this provision, has to establish a good arguable case that its terms have been met.[181] For the purposes of analysis this rule can be divided into three elements: matters relating to a contract; the obligation in question; the place of performance of the obligation in question. The first element is concerned with the scope of Article 5(1) and the other elements go to make up the rule allocating jurisdiction.

Matters Relating to a Contract

In order for Article 5(1) to apply there must be a matter relating to a **3.62** contract. The European Court of Justice has given an independent community meaning to this concept, rather than applying the classification adopted under the national law of a Member State.[182]

A contractual relationship

There must be a contractual relationship between the parties.[183] In certain **3.63** circumstances, this can present a problem, with no consensus under the substantive law of the Member States over this, and the European Court of Justice has had to resolve the question. Thus the Court has had to consider the relationship between: an association and its members;[184]

---

[181] *Canada Trust Co v Stolzenburg (No 2)* [1998] 1 WLR 547, 553–559, aff'd [2002] 1 AC 1, 13 (*per* Lord Steyn). See also *Bank of Tokyo-Mitsubishi Ltd v Baskan Gida Sanayi Ve Pazalarma AS* [2004] EWHC 945 (Ch) at [174].

[182] Case 34/82 *Peters v Zuid Nederlandsee Aannemers Vereniging* [1983] ECR 987; Case C-26/91 *Jakob Handte & Co GmbH v Traitements Mecano-Chimiques des Surfaces SA (TMCS)* [1992] ECR I-3967.

[183] Case C-51/97 *Réunion Européenne SA v Spliethoff's Bevrachtingskantoor BV* [1998] ECR I-6511.

[184] The *Peters* case, n 182 above.

a manufacturer and a sub-buyer who brings a claim in respect of damage to the product itself;[185] a consignee and the carrier of goods.[186] However, it is uncontroversial that the relationship between the buyer and seller where there is a contract for the international sale of goods is contractual. There is unanimity in the substantive law of the Member States over this.

An obligation that is freely assumed

3.64 There must be an obligation freely assumed by one party towards another.[187] According to the European Court of Justice in *Fonderie Officine Meccaniche Tacconi SpA v Heinrich Wagner Sinto Maschinenfabrik GmbH (HWS)*,[188] this is to be contrasted with an obligation derived from rules of law. An example of the latter is the obligation, that arose in the case itself, to make good the damage allegedly caused by the unjustified breaking off of negotiations, in particular the rule which requires the parties to act in good faith in negotiations with a view to the formation of a contract.[189] The phrase 'matters relating to a contract' does not cover such a case and Article 5(1) will not apply.[190] Another example of where this requirement was not met was a case where, although there was no direct contractual relationship between a sub-buyer and the manufacturer, under French law the sub-buyer had a contractual claim against the manufacturer.[191] The European Court of Justice said that the manufacturer 'undertakes no contractual obligation to that [sub]buyer whose identity and domicile may legitimately be unknown to him'.[192] Neither was this requirement met where a guarantor (A), who paid customs duties under a guarantee

---

[185] Case C-26/91 *Jakob Handte & Co GmbH v Traitements Mécano-Chimiques des Surfaces SA (TMCS)* [1992] ECR I-3967; discussed further below, paras 5.22–26.

[186] Case C-51/97 *Réunion Européenne SA v Spliethoff's Bevrachtingskantoor BV* [1998] ECR I-6511; discussed further below, paras 5.28, 14.06 and 17.157–162.

[187] The *Jakob Handte* case, n 185 above, 3994, para 15; Case C-51/97 *Réunion Européenne SA v Spliethoff's Bevrachtingskantoor BV* [1998] ECR I-6511, paras 17 and 19, [2000] QB 690; Case C-334/00 *Fonderie Officine Meccaniche Tacconi SpA v Heinrich Wagner Sinto Maschinenfabrik GmbH (HWS)* [2002] ECR I-7357, para 23; Case C-265/02 *Frahuil SA v Assitalia SPA* [2004] IL Pr 11. For the problems raised by this requirement in the case of restitutionary claims, see below, paras 8.28–30 and in the case of the transfer of rights and obligations, see below, paras 5.24–26.

[188] Case C-334/00 *Fonderie Officine Meccaniche Tacconi SpA v Heinrich Wagner Sinto Maschinenfabrik GmbH (HWS)* [2002] ECR I-7357.

[189] ibid, paras 24–25.

[190] ibid. However, this pre-contractual liability will come within Art 5(3), discussed below, para 6.11.

[191] The *Jakob Handte* case, n 185 above. This is based on the theory that the intermediate supplier transmits to the sub-buyer his contractual rights against the manufacturer (or against a previous intermediary) as an accessory of the goods.

[192] ibid, para 20.

obtained by the forwarding agent (V), sought reimbursement from the owner of goods (F), who was not a party to the contract of guarantee. It would however be met if F authorized the conclusion of the contract of guarantee.[193]

If we turn now to the situation where a contract has been concluded and **3.65** there is a direct contractual relationship between the parties, contractual obligations will arise both by virtue of the terms of the contract and under the general law. Contractual obligations arising by virtue of the terms of the contract are undeniably freely assumed by one party towards another. It can also be said that the obligations that arise by virtue of the general law are freely assumed. This is on the basis that by voluntarily entering into a contract the parties freely assume the legal incidents of the contract.[194] This avoids having to identify and distinguish the precise source of the obligation, something which Lord Woolf has described as being 'unattractive'.[195] He said this in the House of Lords in *Agnew v Lansforsak-ringsbolagens AB*.[196] In this case, the House of Lords held that it had jurisdiction under Article 5(1) of the Lugano Convention to grant a declaration that the plaintiffs were entitled to avoid (i.e. rescind) insurance contracts on the basis of misrepresentations and non-disclosure. It was held that the source of the obligation (which on the facts could variously be described as being to make a fair representation of the risk, not to misrepresent the risk, or to disclose facts material to the risk), whether it was the general law or the express terms of the contract, did not matter.[197]

When it comes to contracts for the international sale of goods, many obli- **3.66** gations are imposed by law, rather than being contained expressly in the contract. However, these obligations could and sometimes are spelt out in the contract. In the light of the *Agnew* case, it can be said that a claim based on these obligations, whether these are spelt out in the contract or not, will fall within Article 5(1). It would be absurd if this were not the case.[198] Even if the source of the obligation were to be crucial and Article 5(1) were to be confined to cases where the source of the obligation is the terms of the contract, in sale of goods cases it may be possible to say that the obligations imposed by law are implied terms of the contract,[199] as is

---

[193] Case C-265/02 *Frahuil SA v Assitalia SPA* [2004] IL Pr 11.
[194] *Agnew v Lansforsakringsbolagens AB* [2001] 1 AC 223, 264 (*per* Lord Millett).
[195] ibid at 241.
[196] [2001] 1 AC 223.
[197] ibid, at 240–244 (*per* Lord Woolf), 233–234 (*per* Lord Nicholls), 253 (*per* Lord Hope), 264 (*per* Lord Millett).
[198] See generally, Briggs and Rees, 2.119.
[199] This would have to be determined by the law applicable to the contract.

the case under the English law of sale of goods.[200] The source then becomes the contract itself, rather than a rule of law.

Contractual obligations and the nature of the claim

3.67 Even though the parties have a contractual relationship, this does not necessarily mean that the matter relates to a contract. In *Kleinwort Benson Ltd v Glasgow City Council*,[201] a majority of the House of Lords, influenced by the allocation of jurisdiction to the place of performance of the obligation in question, adopted a principle that a claim can only come within Article 5(1) of the Modified Convention, allocating jurisdiction within the United Kingdom,[202] if it is based on a particular contractual obligation, i.e. the obligation whose performance is sought in the judicial proceedings.[203] Although this was a decision on the interpretation of the Modified Convention, it is, nonetheless, highly authoritative and persuasive in relation to the interpretation of the essentially identically worded provision in the Brussels Convention.[204] It also appears from their Lordships' judgments that these would have been exactly the same if it had been a case on the Brussels Convention.

3.68 Subsequently, a differently constituted House of Lords in *Agnew v Lansforsakringsbolagens AB*[205] confirmed that there must be a contractual obligation that can be identified.[206] It was also held that there must be a place of performance that can be identified.[207] These were regarded by the majority[208] as requirements for the application of Article 5(1) that are separate from the requirement that there be a matter relating to a contract. This is a change in position from that taken in the *Kleinwort Benson* case where the need for the claim to be based on a particular contractual

---

[200] The *Agnew* case, n 196 above, at 264 (*per* Lord Millett). See also at 253 (*per* Lord Hope). See Lord Cooke at 246 who regarded a pre-contractual obligation imposed by law to make a fair presentation of a risk, not to misrepresent a risk, or to disclose material facts as a condition precedent to the formation of a contract.

[201] [1999] 1 AC 153.

[202] Now modified Regulation, see Sch 4 to the Civil Jurisdiction and Judgments Act 1982, as substituted by SI 2001/3929, Sch 2, Part II, para 4.

[203] At 167–171 (*per* Lord Goff), 181 (*per* Lord Clyde), 189 (*per* Lord Hutton). Lords Nicholls and Mustill dissented.

[204] *Eddie v Alpa Srl* 2000 SLT 1062, 1068.   [205] [2001] 1 AC 223.

[206] ibid, at 240 (*per* Lord Woolf), 246 (*per* Lord Cooke—an obligation so intimately connected with contract that it falls within Art 5(1)), 250 (*per* Lord Hope), 262–266 (*per* Lord Millett), 233–234 (*per* Lord Nicholls). The case concerned Art 5(1) of the Lugano Convention.

[207] ibid, at 240 (*per* Lord Woolf), 246 (*per* Lord Cooke), 250 (*per* Lord Hope), 233–234 (*per* Lord Nicholls). The ECJ has held that a single place of performance for the obligation in question must be identified: Case C-256/00 *Besix SA v Wasserreinigungsbau Alfred Kretzschmar GmbH & Co KG (WABAG)* [2002] ECR I-1699; discussed below, para 3.206.

[208] [2001] 1 AC 223, 240 (*per* Lord Woolf), 246 (*per* Lord Cooke), 250 (*per* Lord Hope), 262–266. Lord Millett (262–266) accepted these requirements but regarded them as falling within the concept of matters relating to a contract, as, seemingly, did Lord Nicholls (233–234).

obligation was seen as coming within the ambit of the requirement of a matter relating to a contract. The European Court of Justice has recently said that 'while Article 5(1) of the Brussels Convention does not require a contract to have been concluded, it is nevertheless essential, for that provision to apply, to identify an obligation, since the jurisdiction of the national court is determined, in matters relating to a contract, by the place of performance of the obligation in question'.[209]

It is therefore necessary to look at the nature of the claim brought by the plaintiff and determine what it is based on. **3.69**

A claim based on the performance of a contractual obligation Typically a dispute between the buyer and seller of goods will be about the performance of a contractual obligation. For example, a seller will commonly be seeking to enforce the performance of the buyer's obligation to pay for the goods. A buyer will commonly be in dispute about the performance of the seller's obligation to deliver goods in conformity with the contract. In such circumstances, there will be a matter relating to a contract under Article 5(1) of the Brussels I Regulation. **3.70**

Parallel claims in tort/delict and contract We are concerned here with the situation where there is concurrent liability in contract and tort and parallel claims are brought based on the same facts.[210] A party to a sale of goods contract may choose to bring parallel claims based on a tortious obligation and a contractual obligation. This is illustrated by the facts of the German case of *Re a Consignment of Italian Wine*.[211] The plaintiffs alleged that the defendants were not only in breach of their contractual obligation to deliver wine in conformity with the contract but also had negligently infringed wine regulations on the minimum alcohol content, in specifying the alcohol content in accompanying documents and in the illegal addition of sugar. Presumably the wine did not conform with the contract because, allegedly, it was not of the minimum alcoholic strength permitted and also because raw cane sugar had been added. The Bundesgerichtshof accepted, and this was not in issue in the case, that the claims arose from the same facts and were concurrent claims. **3.71**

Article 5(3) of the Brussels I Regulation deals with jurisdiction in matters relating to tort, delict or quasi-delict. The European Court of Justice has held that Articles 5(1) and 5(3) are mutually exclusive.[212] Accordingly, a **3.72**

---

[209] The *Fonderie* case, n 188 above, para 22.
[210] See generally in relation to concurrent claims, below, paras 20.07–10 and 20.14.
[211] Judgment of 24 September 1986-VIII ZR 320/85; BGHZ Vol 98, 263; IPRax 1988, 159, Note: Hausmann, 140; KTS 1987, 230; MDR 1987, 228; NJW 1987, 592; RIW 1986, 991; ZZP 1987, 435, Note: Schack; [1988] EEC 159; D Series I-5.3—B 18; [1988] ECC 159.
[212] Case 189/87 *Kalfelis v Schroder* [1988] ECR 5565.

matter may relate to contract or to tort but not to both.[213] The plaintiff is not able to choose which it is. If a party to a sale of goods contract bases his claim on tort and contract, rather than just contract, is this a matter relating to tort, contract, or neither? Essentially the same question arose before the Court of Appeal in *Source Ltd v TUV Rheinland Holding AG*,[214] where there were allegations of breach of contract and of breach of a duty of care in failing to exercise reasonable skill and care in the preparation and supply of reports as to the quality of goods purchased by the plaintiffs. The Court of Appeal held that both causes of action were excluded from the scope of Article 5(3) because both related to a contract within Article 5(1).[215] Does the fact that the claim in tort cannot be brought within Article 5(3) automatically mean that it will be channelled within Article 5(1)? The *Source* case suggests that it will. After all, the reason why Article 5(3) did not apply was because the tort claim was said to relate to a contract. However, this was before the *Kleinwort Benson* case was decided by the House of Lords, with its requirement that the dispute must be about the performance of a contractual obligation, thereby giving a narrow interpretation to Article 5(1). It is unclear how this affects the principle adopted in the *Source* case. It has been suggested that the *Source* case is no longer good law.[216] A claim based on a tortious obligation is self evidently not based on the performance of a contractual obligation and would therefore not come within the scope of Article 5(1). Neither can it be said that the whole of the action can be channelled into the Member State with contract jurisdiction.[217] The upshot is that, in a concurrent action based on tort and contract, it may well be that the tort claim falls not only outside Article 5(3) but also outside 5(1). An alternative view is that the tort claim would come within Article 5(3).[218] But what then happens to the contract claim? This is not a matter relating to tort.[219] Neither, presumably, can it be automatically be channelled within Article 5(3). The court cannot split the claims[220] because this would breach the basic principle that Articles 5(1)

---

[213] In *Re a Consignment of Italian Wine*, n 211 above, the Bundesgerichtshof allowed the two claims to be split with Art 5(1) applying to the contract claim and Art 5(3) to the tort claim. This was decided before the *Kalfelis* case and must now be regarded as a wrong decision.

[214] [1998] QB 54.

[215] At 63 (*per* Staughton LJ, Waite and Aldous LJJ concurring).

[216] *RZB v NBG* [1999] 1 Lloyd's Rep 408, 411 (obiter dicta by Tuckey J). But compare *Rayner v Davies* [2003] IL Pr 14 at [18]–[19] (obiter dicta by Morison J who considered that *Source* had to be followed as a matter of precedent and also was correct), aff'd by the Court of Appeal without discussion of this point [2002] EWCA Civ 1880; [2003] IL Pr 15. Morison J does not discuss the difficulty caused by the requirement that the claim must be based on the performance of a contractual obligation.

[217] See the *Kalfelis* case, n 212 above, at 5586, paras 19 and 20; the *Kleinwort Benson* case, n 201 above, at 166–167 (*per* Lord Goff), 183–184 (*per* Lord Clyde).

[218] See *RZB v NBG*, n 216 above, at 414.   [219] See the *Kalfelis* case, n 212 above.

[220] This is what Tuckey J did in *RZB v NBG*, n 216 above.

and 5(3) are mutually exclusive. It follows that the contract claim would fall outside both Article 5(1) and 5(3).

Separate claims in contract and tort/delict Under English law, in certain **3.73** circumstances separate claims (i.e. they are not parallel claims) in tort and contract may be brought in the same action.[221] The claims may not only not be parallel, but they may also be premised on opposite lines of argument. This is what happened in *Domicrest v Swiss Bank Corp*,[222] where the claim in contract was based on the argument that payment was due from the defendant bank under a payment order; whereas the claim in tort was based on the argument that an employee of the bank was wrong to tell the plaintiff that a payment order was as good as cash. In this situation, there are in effect two matters, a matter relating to contract and a separate matter relating to tort. The two claims would have to be treated separately and Article 5(1) would apply to the contract claim and Article 5(3) to the tort/delict claim. Similarly in *RZB v NBG*,[223] the defendant bank gave a warranty in a letter that there was no default under a loan agreement. This was untrue. The plaintiff brought an action for breach of contract and/or negligent misrepresentation. Tuckey J said obiter that the contractual obligation relied upon was not identical to the obligation in tort. The warranty was an absolute obligation and did not involve the exercise of reasonable care and skill which was the basis of the tort claim.[224] He went on to consider the claims under Article 5(1) and 5(3) separately.[225]

A number of examples can be given of separate claims in contract and **3.74** tort/delict that have arisen out of a contract for the international sale of goods. The first example can be found in *Viskase Ltd v Paul Kiefel GmbH*.[226] The writ sought damages: first, for breach of contract on the basis that machines supplied were not fit for their purpose; and, second, for misrepresentations that the machines were capable of processing certain types of films. These are not parallel claims, being based as they are on different facts. In the Court of Appeal, Chadwick LJ said that it was not clear to him from the pleadings whether the claim was just in contract or in addition in tort for misrepresentations inducing the contract. But he went on to say that, if there were a claim in tort, the relevant jurisdiction

---

[221] It is unclear whether the question whether there are separate claims or parallel claims is one for the law of the forum or for the applicable law (and should this be the law applicable to the tort or the law applicable to the contract?) or whether these concepts should be given an autonomous definition. See the discussion below, paras 20.28–52.

[222] [1999] QB 548.   [223] [1999] 1 Lloyd's Rep 408.   [224] ibid at 411.

[225] But this was on the basis that the *Source* case was no longer good law, rather than because the two claims were separate.

[226] [1999] 1 WLR 1305, CA.

was that conferred by Article 5(3).[227] This was obiter because counsel for the plaintiffs clarified that they were not making a claim in tort. The second example also involves an action brought by the buyer against the seller, namely where the seller fails to deliver goods and the buyer claims damages for breach of contract and conversion.[228] The third and rather different example can be found in *Tesam Distribution Ltd v Schuh Mode Team GmbH and Commerzbank AG*,[229] where the plaintiff buyer brought an action for breach of contract for failure to deliver shoes against the second defendant, a bank, arguing that the bank, which it was alleged was the owner of the shoes or had a charge over them, was a party to the contract of sale. This was accompanied by an alternative claim in tort to the effect that, if the bank was not a party to the sales contract, it had induced the first defendant, the supplier of the shoes, to breach this contract. The Court of Appeal treated the two claims as being separate and held that they fell squarely within the Community concepts of a contract and a tort respectively.[230] The fourth example is where a plaintiff was sold negligently and in breach of contract a 1989 model of a piling rig rather than a 1991 model as specified.[231] The fifth and final example can be seen in a Dutch case[232] where a Liechtenstein plaintiff bought goods from an Italian defendant. The goods were intended for a third party, a Dutch company, and were delivered to the Netherlands. The goods were defective and the plaintiff claimed rescission of the contract and damages. The plaintiff also pleaded a claim in tort, which had been assigned to it by the third party. The Gerechtshof held that it had jurisdiction over the contract claim by virtue of Article 5(1) and over the tort claim by virtue of Article 5(3).

3.75 **A claim solely in tort/delict**   Although concurrent liability exists, a party to an international sale of goods contract may bring a claim against the other party to the contract based solely on tort/delict. For example, the buyer brings a claim solely for negligence, ignoring a possible claim for breach of contract arising from the same facts. In the *Source* case, claims

---

[227] At 1320. In *Casey v Ingersoll-Rand Sales Co Ltd* [1996] 2 ILRM 456 Shanley J did not find it necessary to decide whether negligent misstatement can exist separately as a tort which is not related to a contract in the situation where the buyer is suing the seller for breach of contract. If it was a tort within Art 5(3), on the facts that rule did not allocate jurisdiction to Ireland, see below, paras 6.14–16.

[228] *Glencore International v Metro* [1999] 2 All ER (Comm) 899. Jurisdiction was not based on Art 5.

[229] [1990] IL Pr 149, CA.   [230] ibid at 155–156.

[231] See the *Casey* case, n 227 above. On the facts, statements made after the contract was concluded could not be used to support a separate cause of action in negligence and this claim failed.

[232] Judgment of 27 March 1979, *Bombardieri v Esta Trust Reg* AAe 1981, 193, Note: De Boer; NJ 1980, No 512; D Series I-5.1.2—B 24.

were brought in tort and contract but it seems that the position would have been exactly the same if the action had only been pleaded in tort.[233] The matter relates to contract because the parties have a contractual relationship and the claim could have been brought in contract. But since then the correctness of the *Source* case has been thrown into doubt by the decision of the House of Lords in the *Kleinwort Benson* case. A tort claim cannot be regarded as being based on a particular contractual obligation and is therefore not a matter relating to contract. Arguably then Article 5(3) should apply.

As regards torts arising out of the international sale of goods, such as **3.76** negligent misrepresentation inducing a contract, the fact that the parties have a contractual relationship does cause a problem when it comes to the application of Article 5(3). This will be considered in Chapter 6, where this tort, and others arising out of the international sale of goods, are considered in detail.[234]

A claim in restitution The most difficult situation of all to deal with is **3.77** where a claim is brought in restitution. In the *Kleinwort Benson* case, a majority of the House of Lords held that a claim based on the concept of unjust enrichment, rather than on a particular contractual obligation, fell outside the scope of Article 5(1) of the Modified Convention. In contrast, a restitutionary claim that is based on a contractual obligation will fall within the scope of this provision. Where a buyer, relying on the Vienna Convention, avoids the contract on the basis of a defect in the goods and seeks restitution of the purchase price,[235] this would appear to be a restitutionary claim based on a contractual obligation and accordingly constitutes a matter relating to a contract.[236] The application of this distinction drawn in *Kleinwort Benson* to the sort of restitutionary claims that can arise in the context of contracts for the international sale of goods will be considered in detail in Chapter 8.

Alternative claims in contract/restitution We are concerned here with **3.78** the following type of situation. A buyer of goods makes a part payment in advance of delivery. The seller subsequently denies the existence of the contract and refuses to deliver the goods or to return the payment in advance. On the one hand, if the buyer sues solely for breach of contract, this is seeking to enforce the performance of a contractual obligation and, accordingly, would be a matter relating to a contract. On the other hand, if the buyer sues solely for return of the payment in advance, accepting that the contract is a nullity, this would be a claim based on unjust enrichment

---

[233] [1998] QB 54, 63–64.   [234] See below, paras 6.78–82.   [235] Art 81(2).
[236] See Schlechtriem, 373 and the discussion below, paras 8.20–21.

and, accordingly, would not be a matter relating to a contract. But what if the buyer brings an action for breach of contract but adds on an alternative claim for return of the payment in advance should the court hold the contract to be null and void? Does the court with jurisdiction in relation to the contractual claim also have jurisdiction over the restitutionary claim? Lord Nicholls in his dissenting judgment in the *Kleinwort Benson* case[237] thought that it should, and that it should make no difference that the restitutionary claim was put first with the claim in contract as the alternative coming second in the order of pleading. In his view the restitutionary relief is no more than a part of the effective determination of a dispute relating to a contract. The *Kleinwort Benson* case did not involve an alternative claim for breach of contract and the majority did not discuss this situation. However, the majority were influenced by the need to give Article 5(1) a restrictive interpretation as a derogation from Article 2 of the Convention.[238] Moreover, the European Court of Justice in *Kalfelis v Schroder*, which involved claims in contract, tort and restitution, seemingly rejected the idea put forward by Advocate General Darmon in that case, that different claims should be channelled into the state with contract jurisdiction under Article 5(1).[239]

A dispute over the existence of the agreement

3.79 The European Court of Justice in *Effer SpA v Kantner*[240] has held that jurisdiction under Article 5(1) may be invoked by the plaintiff even where there is a dispute between the parties over the existence of the contract on which the claim is based. This principle was applied by the Court of Appeal in *Tesam Distribution Ltd v Schuh Mode Team GmbH and Commerzbank AG*,[241] a case involving the international sale of goods. The plaintiff claimed that the defendants were in breach of contract in not delivering shoes. The second defendant, a bank, argued that it had not entered into any contract with the plaintiff. The real subject-matter of the dispute was as to the existence of this contract. If the parties had entered into such a contract, it was clear that the English courts would have had jurisdiction under Article 5(1) of the Brussels Convention. The Court of Appeal held that there was a serious question to be tried on the merits as to whether there was such a contract. Accordingly, it had jurisdiction to determine the dispute. These two cases involved actions for the enforcement of a contractual obligation, during the course of which was raised the question

---

[237] n 201 above, at 175.
[238] The plaintiff can always bring an action in the courts where the defendant is domiciled as an alternative to suing in the courts of another Member State under Art 5(1).
[239] n 212 above, at 5586, paras 19 and 20; see also the *Kleinwort Benson* case, n 201 above, at 166–167 (*per* Lord Goff), 183–184 (*per* Lord Clyde).
[240] Case 38/81 [1982] ECR 825.   [241] [1990] IL Pr 149, CA.

of the existence of the contract. The position as regards whether Article 5(1) can apply is much less certain where the question of the existence of the contract is the only matter in issue between the parties.[242] Nonetheless, it is submitted that this is still a matter 'relating' to a contract.

Pre-contractual liability

Cases involving pre-contractual liability raise the question of whether **3.80** there is an obligation that is freely assumed. Both the *Fonderie*[243] and *Agnew*[244] cases involved this type of liability. It has already been seen[245] that, in the former case, this requirement was not met; whereas, in the latter case, it was. In the former case, no contract was ever concluded and so any obligation must be derived from rules of law. In the latter case, a contract was concluded and by entering into the contract the parties freely assumed the legal incidents of the contract. The source of the legal obligation (whether under the general law or the express terms of the contract) does not matter.

The two further requirements for the operation of Article 5(1), namely that **3.81** there is a contractual obligation and a place of performance that can be identified, also raise difficulties. According to the *Agnew* case, a contractual obligation can include a pre-contractual obligation, which, if not fulfilled, gives rise to a contractual remedy such as damages.[246] It followed that, on the facts of the case there was a contractual obligation. In contrast, in the *Fonderie* case, there was no contractual obligation.[247] No contract was ever concluded in that case. The form of liability that arose in that case was one that followed from failure to conclude a contract.

The question whether these two further requirements have been met **3.82** is more difficult to answer where there is a claim for rescission for misrepresentation, duress, undue influence or mistake inducing a contract. Rescission is more appropriately dealt with when discussing restitutionary claims, at which point the difficulties raised by these two further requirements will be examined.[248]

The Obligation in Question

Article 5(1) allocates jurisdiction to the courts for the place of performance **3.83** of the obligation in question. The 'obligation in question' will now be

---

[242] See the *Agnew* case, n 205 above, at 264 (*per* Lord Millett); the *Kleinwort Benson* case, n 201 above, at 170 (*per* Lord Goff who had serious doubts whether Art 5(1) could apply).
[243] n 188 above.   [244] n 205 above.   [245] See above, para 3.64.
[246] See the *Agnew* case, n 205 above.
[247] However, Art 5(3) of the Brussels Convention applied, see below, para 6.11.
[248] See below, paras 8.24–26.

examined. After which, attention will turn to 'the place of performance of the obligation in question'.

The obligation in question: general principles

3.84 Which obligation is being referred to?   The European Court of Justice has held that this is referring not to any obligation under the contract but to the contractual obligation forming the basis of the legal proceedings, the one which the contract imposes on the defendant, the non-performance of which is relied upon by the plaintiff.[249] What has to be identified is the obligation of which performance is sought, rather than the obligation which characterizes the contract.[250] In order to identify the obligation on which the claim is based it is necessary to examine the plaintiff's pleaded case.[251] In an English action, this means looking at the particulars of claim.

3.85 Claims based on several different contractual obligations   The plaintiff may make several claims involving different contractual obligations to be performed in different states. In *Shenavai v Kreischer*,[252] the European Court of Justice held that in this situation the judge dealing with the case is to identify the principal obligation on which the plaintiff's action is based, and jurisdiction is to be determined in accordance with the maxim *accessorium sequitur principale*. In other words, the court with jurisdiction in relation to the principal obligation also has jurisdiction in relation to the other obligations. This has the effect of concentrating the claims before one court. However, the European Court of Justice has also held that, in the situation where the action is founded on two obligations of equal rank arising from the same contract, one obligation to be performed in one Member State and the other in another Member State, the same court does not have jurisdiction to hear the whole of an action.[253] For the purposes of

---

[249] Case 14/76 *De Bloos v Bouyer* [1976] ECR 1497; Case C-266/85 *Shenavai v Kreischer* [1987] ECR 239; Case C-288/92 *Custom Made Commercial Ltd v Stawa Metallbau GmbH* [1994] ECR I-2913, 2957. See also *Kleinwort Benson Ltd v Glasgow City Council* [1997] 3 WLR 923, 929–930 (*per* Lord Goff).

[250] The *Shenavai* case, n 249 above, at 256, paras 17 and 18. The ECJ refused to follow their earlier decision in Case 133/81 *Ivenel v Schwab* [1982] ECR 1891, where the ECJ had looked for the obligation which characterized the contract rather than the one on which the claim is based (as set out in the *De Bloos* case). The former approach was to be confined to contracts of employment. It follows that what has to be characterized is the contractual obligation founding the claim rather than the nature of the contract, see *MBM Fabri-Clad Ltd v Eisen-Und Huttenwerke Thale AG* [2000] IL Pr 505, 514 (*per* Ward LJ), CA. Contrast the position under Art 4(2) of the Rome Convention, discussed below, paras 13.114–116.

[251] *Viskase Ltd v Paul Kiefel GmbH* [1999] 1 WLR 1305, 1318 (*per* Chadwick LJ), 1316 (*per* Morritt LJ).

[252] Case 266/85 [1987] ECR 239. Applied in England in, eg, *Union Transport plc v Continental Lines SA* [1992] 1 WLR 15, HL; *AIG Europe (UK) Ltd v The Ethniki* [2000] 2 All ER 566.

[253] Case C-420/97 *Leathertex Divisione Sinetici SpA v Bodetex BVBA* [1999] ECR I-6747, para 36.

Article 5(1) the claims are split up and tried before the courts of different Member States. The plaintiff can, though, avoid this by bringing the whole of the action in the Member State where the defendant is domiciled, using Article 2 of the Brussels I Regulation.

A claim for compensation The European Court of Justice in *De Bloos v* **3.86** *Bouyer*[254] held that: 'In the case of actions for payment of compensation by way of damages, it is for the national court to ascertain whether under the law applicable to the contract, an independent contractual obligation or an obligation replacing the unperformed contractual obligation is involved'.[255] Article 5(1) would apply to the former obligation but not to the latter, although obviously it would apply to the unperformed contractual obligation itself. Another way of looking at it is to say that the obligation which is relevant is the substantive obligation under the contract which gives the claimant his cause of action, not the mere procedural remedy which the claimant is invoking.[256] An example under English law of an independent contractual obligation to pay damages, not merely one imposed by the courts as a remedy, could be that of paying liquidated damages as required under a contractual provision in the event of certain breaches or failure to perform by the defendant.[257] Where a mere remedy is being sought or a right to terminate the contract is being alleged, the relevant obligation is that which has been broken by the defendant and is alleged to give rise to such right of termination. In a case where compensation is sought in lieu of notice, the obligation in question is that of giving notice.[258]

Application to contracts for the international sale of goods

Typical obligations under the substantive law The obligations of the **3.87** parties to a contract for the sale of goods are laid down in their contract.[259] Obligations are also imposed by the law applicable to the contract. Set out below are typical obligations laid down by the substantive law or by the parties in their contract.

The seller's obligation to deliver the goods Article 30 of the Vienna Conven- **3.88** tion obliges the seller to deliver the goods and hand over any documents

---

[254] Case 14/76 [1976] ECR 1497.
[255] ibid, para 17. There is a paradox that this independent obligation may be governed by a different law from that governing the contract.
[256] *Medway Packaging Ltd v Meurer Maschinen GmbH & Co KG* [1990] 1 Lloyd's Rep 383, 387. See, eg, *Pil-Pak v Crowson Fabrics Ltd* [2002] UfR 424, [2003] IL Pr 437, Danish Maritime and Commercial Court—compensation sought for termination of a supply of goods contract, obligation in question was that of supplying the goods.
[257] The *Medway* case, n 256 above, at 388.
[258] *Leathertex Divisione Sintetici SPA v Bodetex BVBA*, n 253 above.
[259] The applicable law has to allow the parties to agree on their contractual obligations, which it will almost certainly do.

relating to them 'as required by the Contract and this Convention'. The Convention does not deal at all with the different types of shipping term, a characteristic that it shares with the UK Sale of Goods Act 1979.

3.89 There are numerous well-known shipping terms employed in international sale transactions.[260] Many are defined in English law; others are defined according to the standard terms issued by the International Chamber of Commerce known in their current edition as Incoterms 2000. These terms may not impose quite the same obligations on the parties as their equivalents would under English law.[261] Moreover, the identifying label of a delivery term may differ under English law and Incoterms 2000.[262] In addition, Incoterms 2000 apply only if expressly chosen by the parties and not as a matter of presumptive intention: the Paris-based International Chamber of Commerce is a private body. It is common for them to be adopted in oil contracts governed by English law but they are not to be found in the case of dry commodities such as wheat and soya beans.

3.90 Delivery in an international sale can physically range from any point between the seller's and the buyer's premises. For example, an FOB contract will require the seller to clear customs and cause the goods actually to be loaded on board ship and not merely delivered to the ship for loading. The failure of the Vienna Convention to deal in any detail at all with shipping terms can give rise to difficulties in interpreting the Convention. For example, Article 31 provides that, in the case of carriage, the seller completes delivery by handing over the goods to the first carrier (in those cases where more than one carrier is employed). If an FOB seller employs an inland carrier to take the goods down to the docks, Article 31 thus suggests that the seller has completed delivery on handing over the goods to that carrier. To avoid that result, it either has to be argued (very plausibly) that an admitted exception to this delivery rule exists in that the seller has undertaken to deliver the goods at some 'other particular place', namely on board ship. Alternatively and less satisfactorily, it would have to be argued that the parties have impliedly departed form the rule in Article 31, as Article 6 in general terms permits them to do with any Vienna Convention provision.

---

[260] For example, ex works, FAS (free alongside ship), FOB (free on board), ex ship, ex quay, delivered at frontier (franco frontier), CIF (cost insurance and freight) and C&F (cost and freight).

[261] Incoterms 2000 states categorically that it is the FOB seller's duty to provide an export licence. English law takes a more nuanced approach, treating the matter as one of contractual construction, with the consequence that in some cases the buyer may have the duty to apply for an export licence. See *HO Brandt & Co v HN Morris & Co Ltd* [1917] 2 KB 784.

[262] For example, ex ship, ex quay and C&F under English law are, respectively, DES, DEQ and CFR under Incoterms 2000.

The Vienna Convention, in Article 32, contains obligations relating to the **3.91** marking of goods by the seller and to the making of ancillary contracts relating to the sale of goods, such as contracts of carriage and insurance.

Apart from physical delivery terms such as FOB, a common form of **3.92** delivery term is CIF, by which the seller's duty of physical delivery, whether directly to the buyer or to some other person such as a carrier, is commuted into a duty to enter into contracts of carriage and insurance and provide by means of documents the means whereby the buyer can succeed to the seller's contractual position as regards the carrier and the insurance company.[263] A similar term, without insurance, is the C&F (or, under Incoterms 2000, the CFR) term.

Broadly, the delivery terms in English law and under the Vienna **3.93** Convention are the same. English law provides that, unless otherwise agreed, delivery and payment are mutual and concurrent conditions,[264] a position reached by the Vienna Convention in a less straightforward way.[265] While Article 31(b) calls for delivery at the place where an identified bulk (or 'specific stock') is located, no such rule or anything to contrary effect is to be found in English law. In some respects the Vienna Convention states what would be implied under English law. For example, Article 32(2) requires the seller to specify the goods for the buyer's benefit where the goods are handed over to a carrier and are not clearly marked.

The seller's obligation to hand over any documents relating to them The basic **3.94** delivery duty in Article 30 relates to documents as well as goods. In Article 34, the Convention contains provisions relating in general terms to the time, manner and place of documentary delivery.[266] A notable feature of the Convention is that it descends to no detail at all in relation to documents, leaving it to the parties themselves to agree the documents that the seller must provide. Subject to what follows, the Vienna Convention and English law are alike in the documentary obligations they impose on the seller. In one respect, however, they may be significantly different. Article 34 allows a seller to cure any lack of conformity in the documents if this does not cause unreasonable inconvenience to the buyer in those cases (surely rare) where documentary delivery takes place before the agreed time. The form of cure is unstated but, to the extent that it might take the form of a visible correction of a bill of lading, or involve the reissue of an original bill, it would appear to infringe English law

---

[263] See below, para 5.01.   [264] Sale of Goods Act 1979, s 28.
[265] Art 58(1).   [266] Schlechtriem, 271, para 3a.

rules requiring documents to be 'clean'[267] and to be issued at the point and time of loading.[268]

3.95 *The seller's obligation to transfer the property in the goods*   Article 30 of the Vienna Convention requires the seller to transfer the property in the goods as required by the contract and the Convention. The Convention does not define 'property' but it would seem to signify what passes for ownership in English law. It does not state *when*, if the contract itself is silent on the matter (which must very frequently be the case), the seller should pass the property in the goods to the buyer. The Convention goes on to provide that the goods delivered must be free of third party claims, whether of an intellectual or industrial property kind or more generally. It should be noted that the Convention contains no rules determining when property passes under the contract:[269] this was left to be determined by the forum's choice of law rules.[270]

3.96 English law, in contrast, is not at all clear on the seller's *duty* to pass the property in goods. The Sale of Goods Act 1979 contains provisions dealing with the extent of the property rights that the seller must possess, as well as the time *when* the property passes. But it falls short of enunciating a duty on a resistant seller actually to transfer the property in the goods. The provision corresponding broadly to Article 30, s 27 of the Sale of Goods Act, merely recites a duty on the seller to deliver the goods. There are no signs that this deficiency in English law has actually caused any difficulties in practice. The express language of buying and selling used by the parties would determine the existence of a duty to pass the property but it would not as such affect *when* this should be done. Since the passing of property is, to the extent that the goods have been ascertained or a bulk containing them been ascertained, a matter of dual party intention, a resistant seller could delay the passing of property indefinitely, unless a court were to find an implied term that the seller should give his consent to the property passing when he has been paid and has no legitimate interest in continuing to reserve the property in the goods.

3.97 *The seller's obligation to deliver goods in conformity with the contract*   Section II of the Vienna Convention lists 'conformity of goods' under the obligations of the seller and Article 35(1) states that: 'The seller must deliver goods which are of the quantity, quality and description required by the contract and which are contained or packaged in the manner required by

---

[267] *SIAT di del Ferro v Tradax Overseas SA* [1980] 1 Lloyd's Rep 53.
[268] *Hansson v Hamel & Horley Ltd* [1922] 2 AC 36.
[269] Art 4(b).
[270] On which, see below, paras 13.01–321, 15.10–64.

the contract'. This provision would include express statements relating to quantity, quality and description. There is no justification for giving the word 'description', which has a very technical and narrow meaning in English law, anything other than a broad commercial interpretation. Express warranties in English would therefore fall within Article 35(1), though it is doubtful that the words of the provision would extend to misrepresentations, for that would be to beg the question whether the contents of a misrepresentation are 'required by the contract'.[271]

Article 35(2) goes on to provide that: 'Except where the parties have **3.98** agreed otherwise, the goods do not conform with the contract unless they: (a) are for the purposes for which goods of the same description would ordinarily be used . . .'. It then requires in sub-paragraph (b) that the seller supply goods fit for the buyer's particular purpose at the time of conclusion of the contract, unless the buyer unreasonably relies or does not rely upon the seller's skill and judgment. Sub-paragraph (c) requires the goods to correspond to any sample or model provided and sub-paragraph (d) calls for the usual packaging or a method of packaging that is sufficient to protect and preserve the goods. According to Article 35(3), the seller's liability under the previous provisions of Article 35 ceases if the buyer was aware, or could not have been unaware, of any lack of conformity in the goods at the contract date.

English law has similar provisions. Section 14(3) of the Sale of Goods Act **3.99** 1979 lays down an implied obligation relating to the buyer's particular purpose that is more or less identical to Article 35(2)(b) and s 15 lays down an obligation relating to samples (but not models) that is similar to its equivalent in Article 35(2)(c). The packaging obligations of the seller in Article 35(2)(d) are not expressly recited in the Sale of Goods Act but would doubtless be treated as an unspecified aspect of the various obligations in s 14. Although the Vienna Convention does not contain a provision that the goods shall be of satisfactory (or merchantable) quality, it does require the goods to be fit for the purposes for which they would ordinarily be used. This is similar to an element of satisfactory quality in s 14, which, however, limits this fitness for a multiplicity of purposes to 'appropriate cases'. The exclusion of the seller's liability in the case of the buyer's knowledge of non-conformity extends in s 14 only to actual and not imputed knowledge. Moreover, the exclusion is confined to the satisfactory quality provision in s 14(2) and does not extend to the fitness for purpose provision in s 14(3). Nevertheless, in this latter provision, the examination exclusion would be no doubt recognized in the transposed

---

[271] See below, paras 16.71, 16.82.

form of unreasonable reliance on the seller's skill or judgment or the absence of reliance.

3.100 *The seller's obligation to deliver goods which are free from any right or claim of a third party*   This is laid down in general terms by Article 41 of the Vienna Convention which requires the seller to deliver the goods free from any right or claim by a third party unless the buyer agrees to take the goods subject to such a claim. This provision is therefore similar to s 12 of the Sale of Goods Act 1979, which states that the seller must have a 'right to sell' the goods, an obligation that goes beyond matters pertaining to the strength of the seller's title. Likewise, s 12 also permits a so-called limited title sale, though a careful distinction needs to be drawn between a limited title sale as such and an exclusion of the seller's duty in relation to the right to sell, which even in the case of business sales is void under s 6(1)(a) of the Unfair Contract Terms Act 1977. The Vienna Convention in Article 6 permits derogation from the terms of the Convention and contains no regulatory material restricting or preventing the exclusion or limitation of the seller's liability.

3.101 Article 42 imposes on the seller a duty to deliver goods free from industrial or intellectual rights or claims of third parties. The seller's duty is not broken unless the seller knew or could not have been unaware of the third party claim or right. A similar duty arises under s 12(2) of the Sale of Goods Act, except that the seller's duty is expressed in the broader terms of a charge or encumbrance on the goods and this duty can be breached by the seller even if excusably unaware of the third party claim or right.[272] The seller under the Sale of Goods Act is also the guarantor of the buyer's quiet possession, a matter that has no direct equivalent under the Vienna Convention and arguably is not needed since it covers cases where a third party claims a superior property right in the goods or asserts an intellectual or industrial property claim.

3.102 Article 42 provides that the seller will not be liable if the seller's liability would otherwise flow from compliance with the buyer's specifications or technical drawings (which has no Sale of Goods Act equivalent). Unlike the Sale of Goods Act, the seller is not liable where the buyer knew or could not have been unaware of the third party right or claim.

3.103 *The buyer's obligation to pay the price*   The buyer's duty to pay the price is laid down in Article 53 of the Vienna Convention. That duty is expressed by Article 54 to extend to taking steps and complying with forms laid down by the contract and by laws and regulations. This reference to laws and regulations is odd in that it does not indicate which country's laws

---

[272] *Microbeads AG v Vinhurst Road Markings Ltd* [1975] 1 WLR 218.

and regulations are relevant. It is best understood as meaning that, if a buyer chooses to take steps to pay in one country then the buyer should abide by that country's laws and regulations. The same compliance, moreover, should extend to the laws and regulations of any (other) country where payment of the seller actually takes effect.

The default place of payment is under Article 57 the seller's place of **3.104** business or, instead, the place where goods are handed over if the contract calls for payment against delivery. Under Article 58, the seller is allowed, in the language of English law, to reserve the right of disposal to the goods until paid by the buyer, who presumptively pays when the goods are handed over but only after having had a chance to examine the goods. The buyer's duty to pay is, under Article 59, fixed by or determinable from the contract, while Article 55 imposes an obligation to pay the price generally charged for such goods when the contract is silent as to the actual price.[273]

Most of this accords with English law. Section 27 of the Sale of Goods Act **3.105** recites the buyer's duty. Thereafter, apart from asserting in s 28 the presumptive concurrency of the seller's duty of delivery and the buyer's duties of taking delivery and payment, the Act says nothing more about the duty to pay the price, except that the buyer's right of examination of the goods presupposes the exercise of this right prior to taking delivery in the presumptive s 28 case.[274] The place of payment would most likely be the place of delivery, however, in the presumptive s 28 case,[275] for how otherwise might mutual and concurrent performance be arranged? Otherwise, the place of payment will be the seller's residence or place of business.

The Vienna Convention and Sale of Goods Act alike make no provision **3.106** regarding currency matters and payment instruments. So far as they might be relevant,[276] the Unidroit Principles of International Commercial Contracts make quite extensive provision for these matters.[277]

The buyer's obligation to take delivery This duty is recited in Article 53 **3.107** of the Vienna Convention, along with the buyer's duty to pay. The

---

[273] This Article is difficult to reconcile with Art 14 which requires, for the existence of a contractual offer, that it expressly or impliedly fix or make provision for determining the price.

[274] The Sale of Goods Act, in s 8(2), like Art 55 of the Vienna Convention permits a contract to be enforced where there is no stated price or machinery for determining the price. A reasonable price is exacted.

[275] Delivery in the case of CIF documents would therefore take place where the documents are to be presented, since cash on delivery is the usual rule. Where payment takes place by means of a documentary letter of credit, payment would therefore take place in the usual case where a confirming bank takes up the seller's documents.

[276] See below, para 16.84.   [277] See Arts 6.1.7–10.

Convention says nothing more since the buyer's duty is necessarily further defined by the detail already given concerning the seller's delivery. The same can be said for the buyer's duty to take delivery under s 27 of the Sale of Goods Act.

3.108 *The buyer's obligation to place orders*   Neither the Vienna Convention nor the Sale of Goods Act deals explicitly with the duty resting upon the buyer to place orders with the seller for the delivery of goods on an instalment basis. This is a matter of express contract.

3.109 **Identification of the obligation in question for the purposes of Article 5(1)**   Normally, it will be clear what the obligation in question is. For example, if a claim is brought for payment of the purchase price, the obligation in question for the purposes of Article 5(1) will be the buyer's obligation to pay the price. Nevertheless, there is a problem in identifying the obligation in question in the following situations: first, where the goods do not conform with the contract; second, where the seller has to supply and deliver goods; third, where the obligation is capable of being re-labelled; fourth, where claims are based on several different obligations; fifth, where there is a claim for compensation; sixth, where the right to other remedies is exercised; seventh, where there is a claim for repayment of the purchase price. These situations will now be considered in more detail.

3.110 *The goods do not conform with the contract*   The difficulty here is that an obligation presupposes that a party is required to do something and, whilst liability is undoubtedly imposed on the seller in the situation where the goods sold are not in conformity with the contract, it is by no means clear what precisely the seller has failed to do. In *Tessili v Dunlop*,[278] Advocate General Mayras gave his Opinion that, where a claim is brought on the basis that the goods are not in conformity with the contract, the seller is to be regarded as having failed to perform his obligation to deliver the goods.[279] He based this view on the substantive law background which the drafters of the Brussels Convention had in their minds, namely the Uniform Law on the International Sale of Goods.[280] This provides that, where goods do not conform with the contract, the seller is regarded as having failed to fulfil his obligation to deliver the goods.[281] As has been seen, Article 35(1) of the Vienna Convention is to the same effect, requiring the seller 'to deliver' goods in conformity with the contract. If

---

[278] Case 12/76 [1976] ECR 1473.   [279] ibid, at 1492.
[280] The Hague Convention of 1964 on the Uniform Law on the International Sale of Goods was introduced into English law by the Uniform Laws on International Sales Act 1967. This also introduces the Hague Convention of 1964 on the Uniform Law on Formation.
[281] Art 33.

this is the obligation, it is easy to identify the place of performance; it is the place of delivery of the goods.

Morritt LJ in the Court of Appeal in *Viskase Ltd v Paul Kiefel GmbH*[282] has **3.111** likewise focused on the obligation to deliver goods. The obligation on which the proceedings were based was to supply a machine which was reasonably fit for the known purpose. Morritt LJ said that it was not appropriate to analyse this obligation in isolation from the other terms of the contract.[283] This was one of the terms of a contract for the sale and *delivery* of machinery. By clarifying the nature of the obligation in this way, it becomes clear where the place of performance is, namely the place of delivery.[284] It was unsuccessfully argued that the warranty as to fitness for purpose continued after delivery, in the sense that the seller continued to have obligations to perform, which would have been performed in a different country from that where the delivery took place. However, there was nothing in the contractual documentation to justify the conclusion that the defendant undertook to guarantee future performance.

Supply and delivery of goods Once one starts referring to supply and **3.112** delivery, the question arises of whether these are two different obligations, which could have different places of performance, or all part of one obligation. This question arose in *MBM Fabri-Clad Ltd v Eisen-Und Huttenwerke Thale AG.*[285] The parties entered into a contract for the supply and delivery of goods, where the supplier was also responsible for the design and manufacture of the goods. This meant that potentially there could be up to three different obligations: to supply; to deliver; and to manufacture. The goods were defective through a design or manufacturing fault. The plaintiffs, an English subsidiary of a German company, brought an action for damages in England against the German domiciled defendants on the basis that this was the place of performance of the obligation in question under Article 5(1) of the Brussels Convention. The defendants argued that there were two separate obligations under the contract: an obligation to supply in the sense of to make available, which involves design and manufacture; and an obligation to deliver. In support of this they pointed out that the plaintiffs' purchase order had added to it in handwriting the words 'To supply & deliver' the goods. They went on to argue that the principal obligation was to supply, the place of performance of which was in Germany. The Court of Appeal held that the obligation in question was to supply goods in conformity with the contract but

---

[282] [1999] 1 WLR 1305, CA. [283] At 1317.

[284] Chadwick LJ, at 1317–1323, reached the same conclusion as to the place of performance but by a different route which concentrated on the time at which the obligation to supply must be carried out, see below, para 3.265. Evans LJ dissented.

[285] [2000] IL Pr 505, CA.

this was to supply by delivery in England.[286] Aldous LJ referred to this as the principal obligation. He pointed out that if the contract was for the supply of goods in Germany this would mean that the property passed there, yet the contract specifically provided that the property passed on delivery. Pill LJ appeared to accept that the obligation to deliver was a separate obligation but the emphasis in the contract remained on the supply. In contrast, Ward LJ described supply and delivery as being separate parts of a composite obligation.[287] It is composite because, if there has been no delivery at all, then the goods cannot have been supplied. The defendants argued in the alternative that, even if the contract was for the supply of goods in England, the principal obligation was to manufacture the goods in an appropriate way. This argument was also rejected. The obligation forming the basis of the legal proceedings was the obligation to supply goods conforming with the contractual specification. The place of performance of that obligation was England. It was immaterial that the acts and omissions which led to the failure to supply appropriate goods in England occurred in Germany.[288] That confused what the defendant was in breach of with the reasons for the breach.[289] The contract was for the supply in England and it mattered not to the plaintiffs how the goods came to be defective.[290]

3.113 *The obligation is capable of being re-labelled*   National courts have been known to reach some rather surprising conclusions on the obligation in question by re-labelling it. Thus in *Re Yarn Sales*,[291] the Bundesgerichtshof had to determine the nature of the obligation when one party refuses to accept delivery of goods on the basis that there is no contract. The court held that the obligation in question for the purposes of Article 5(1) of the Brussels Convention was the obligation to pay for the goods, and went on to determine where this obligation was to be performed. But one could rather more convincingly say that the obligation in question was simply that of accepting the goods, the place of performance of which would be readily identifiable as being where delivery was to be effected.

3.114 *Claims based on several different contractual obligations*   In a sale of goods case, it is not unusual for a plaintiff to bring several claims based on different contractual obligations. In such cases, it is necessary to identify the principal obligation. For example, in the Scots case of *Ferguson Shipbuilders Ltd v Voith Hydro GmbH & Co KG*,[292] a Scottish shipbuilding company brought an action for damages against a marine engineering

---

[286] At 511 (*per* Pill LJ); at 513 (*per* Aldous LJ).   [287] At 513 (*per* Ward LJ).
[288] At 511 (*per* Pill LJ).   [289] At 514 (*per* Ward LJ).   [290] At 513 (*per* Aldous LJ).
[291] Case VIII ZR 185/92 [1995] IL Pr 180.   [292] 2000 SLT 229.

company domiciled in Germany. This involved claims in respect of the breach by the defendant of two separate obligations: first, to deliver to Port Glasgow manufactured goods conforming to contractual specification and guaranteed quality within agreed times; and, second, to indemnify the plaintiffs against all and any loss, damage and expense suffered by them in consequence of negligence or breach of duty by the defendant, and in particular loss and damage arising as a result of contractual delay caused by the defendant's faulty design of the propulsion unit.[293] Lord Penrose in the Outer House of the Court of Session held that the first of these obligations was the principal one. It was held that Scotland was the place of performance of the principal obligation. Applying the maxim *accessorium sequitur principale* meant that Scotland also had jurisdiction over subordinate or accessory matters, i.e. the claim based on the obligation to indemnify.

To take another example, this time concerned with the obligations of the buyer, in *SA Etablissement Legrand v SA Cebelor*,[294] the legal proceedings were based on several obligations: the obligation to pay the price; interest; and a contractual penalty. The Cour d'appel, Brussels, held that the main obligation was to pay the price of the goods, the other obligations being merely ancillary in nature. **3.115**

It is a matter for the law governing the contract to determine what the principal obligation is. This is illustrated by the *Ferguson Shipbuilders* case. Lord Penrose at the outset of the case determined that Scots law governed the contract. He pointed out that, if German law had governed the contract, the main obligation would have been that of manufacture and the payment, indemnification and delivery obligations would have been ancillary to this main obligation. Germany was the place of performance of the obligation to manufacture and the German courts would have had jurisdiction under Article 5(1) of the Brussels Convention over the claims in respect of all the obligations. **3.116**

The maxim *accessorium sequitur principale* only applies where there is a claim in respect of more than one obligation under the *same* contract. Thus it will not apply to give jurisdiction in relation to a claim based on the breach of a distribution agreement to a Member State which has jurisdiction in relation to a claim based on the breach of a sales agreement made in pursuance of the distribution agreement.[295] The obligations which have been broken arise under separate contracts. **3.117**

---

[293] This obligation presumably referred back to standard contractual terms laying down 'penalties' and liquidated damages.
[294] Judgment of 30 June 1987, RGDC 1988, 557, Note: Barnich; D Series I-5.1.1—B 26.
[295] *Eddie v Alpa Srl* 2000 SLT 1062, Outer House.

A claim for compensation

3.118 THE SUBSTANTIVE LAW   The Vienna Convention states, in Article 45, the existence of a right to damages accruing to the buyer for breaches of contract by the seller, and in Article 61, a seller's right to damages for breaches of contract by the buyer. The further details of these damages rights are to be found in Articles 74–77.

3.119 Article 74 deals with the necessary factual link that must be established between the breach of contract and the damages claimed. It goes on to lay down a rule of remoteness of damage based upon reasonable foreseeability, which on its face depends upon a lower order of probability than the equivalent rule in English law. Like English law, the foreseeability of the loss is established at the contract date. Article 74 explicitly includes loss of profit, which is implicitly covered by the English rule. It could therefore apply to a buyer's claim for lost profits when a profit-earning chattel is supplied that fails to perform at the level impliedly or expressly promised under the contract. Like the Sale of Goods Act, the Vienna Convention does not deal specifically with the consequences of late delivery, so that the general rule of recovery would have to be brought into play in such a case.

3.120 Articles 75 and 76 deal with specific cases that arise in the event of avoidance of the contract for breach, which correspond in their function to ss 50–51 of the Sale of Goods Act. Article 75 deals economically with two cases which are divided between ss 50 and 51 of the Sale of Goods Act. The first case concerns the seller who, having avoided the contract for the buyer's breach, resells the goods. The second case is the buyer who, having avoided the contract for the seller's breach, purchases substitute goods from another source. The rule in Article 74 is that the price realized or paid, as the case may be, is compared with the contract price and, in the event that the substitute transaction is on less favourable terms than the original transaction, the plaintiff recovers the difference between the two prices. The substitute transaction must take place within a reasonable time and in a reasonable manner if damages are to be assessed in this way.

3.121 Where Article 75 does not apply, because no qualifying substitute transaction has been concluded, damages will be awarded to the seller or buyer, as the case may be, according to the difference between the current price and the contract price prevailing at the time of avoidance. For the time of avoidance is substituted the time of taking over the goods, where a buyer avoids the contract after the goods have been handed over. The current price is that prevailing at the place of delivery or, if no such price can be determined, at a reasonable substitute place.

English law, as expressed in ss 50–51 of the Sale of Goods Act, differs **3.122**
significantly from Articles 75 and 76. First of all, it bases the assessment of
damages on a comparison between the contract price and the market
price. It disregards substitute transactions. The current price in the Vienna
Convention and the market price may broadly be treated as the same.
Secondly, English law is committed to looking at the market price at the
date of delivery, which in the case of a delivery period will be the last
date in that period. This is sometimes referred to, a little misleadingly, as
the 'breach date rule'. Damages are not calculated according to the date
of contractual termination: one party, by an act of unilateral waiver of the
delivery date prior to termination, cannot thereby alter the date of
assessment.

Article 77 of the Vienna Convention lays down a 'duty' to mitigate loss. **3.123**
Its primary role would appear to be to limit claims for consequential
damages under Article 74. This is because the need to take prompt action,
whether it is a case of a seller reselling goods or of a buyer in effecting a
'cover' or substitute purchase, is already built into the rules in Articles 75–
76. It is an uncertain matter whether the duty to mitigate would prevent a
party from 'requiring performance' (the Convention's broad equivalent to
specific performance in English law), which a party is entitled to pursue
as of right under Articles 46 and 62. The better view, since the sanction
for a failure to mitigate is a reduction in the claimant's damages, is that
a claimant's right to require performance is not qualified by Article 77.
English law likewise requires a claim for damages to be mitigated in
circumstances similar to those provided for in Article 77. Indeed, the
operation of the market rule in ss 50–51 of the Sale of Goods Act is often
explained in terms of mitigation, since the claimant must enter the market
promptly, sometimes impossibly promptly. The better view, however, is
that the claimant's damages right crystallizes in terms of the market position prevailing on the delivery date, so that any later transaction is a
private speculation of the damages claimant. If the market improves after
the delivery date, the claimant keeps the gain; if the market deteriorates,
the claimant cannot charge the loss against the contract-breaker. The
claimant is entitled to damages whether he enters the market or not: any
loss he suffers is crystallized in terms of the market as it stands on the
delivery date.

A final point under this heading concerns Article 50 of the Vienna Con **3.124**
vention, which provides a self-help remedy to a buyer who receives non-
conforming goods. A buyer who retains the goods may abate the purchase
price to the extent of the non-conformity. This is not as such a damages
remedy. It is not clear whether a buyer could elect instead to pursue a
claim for damages under Article 74. The common law counterpart of

Article 50 is a damages remedy under s 53 of the Sale of Goods Act, which measures the non-conformity according to the market at the delivery date. The outcome under s 53 will be a reduction of the purchase price that is similar to the abatement in Article 50, but in volatile market conditions the amounts yielded under the two provisions will not be the same.

3.125 WHAT IS THE OBLIGATION IN QUESTION FOR THE PURPOSES OF ARTICLE 5(1)?   The Court of Appeal, applying English law, has repeatedly held, without argument, in cases where a claim has been brought for damages for breach of contract following the delivery of defective goods, that the obligation in question was that of delivering goods in conformity with the contract.[296] The Scots courts, applying Scots law, have reached the same conclusion.[297] There was no question in any of these cases of the right to damages being an independent contractual obligation. Where damages were sought for breach of contract, what the court was concerned with was the obligation under the contract which had allegedly been breached.[298]

3.126 What if the applicable law is that of a country which has adopted the Vienna Convention? Is the obligation to compensate under Articles 45 and 74 of that Convention an independent contractual obligation or an obligation replacing the unperformed contractual obligation?

3.127 The fact that the Vienna Convention does not lay down a place of performance for the obligation to compensate[299] would suggest that this is not an independent obligation. If compensation is merely a remedy that applies where the seller fails to perform any of his obligations under the contract or the Vienna Convention, it is to those obligations that one must turn to identify the obligation in question. Thus, if damages are sought on the basis that the seller is in breach of his obligation to deliver goods in conformity with the contract, or of his obligation to deliver goods which are free from any right or claim of a third party, the obligation in question is that of delivering goods in conformity with the contract or delivering goods which are free from any right or claim of a third party.

3.128 This view is supported by two decisions of the Bundesgerichtshof, in both of which the governing law was that of a country which applied the

---

[296] See *Viskase Ltd v Paul Kiefel GmbH* [1999] 1 WLR 1305, CA; *MBM Fabri-Clad v Eisen-Und Huttenwerke Thale AG* [2000] IL Pr 505, CA.

[297] *Ferguson Shipbuilders Ltd v Voith Hydro GmbH & Co KG* 2000 SLT 229, Outer House; *Eddie v Alpa Srl* 2000 SLT 1062, Outer House.

[298] The *Eddie* case, n 297 above, at 1063.

[299] In *Re a Wood Cutting Machine* [1995] IL Pr 191, Oberlandesgericht, Dusseldorf, it was said that the place results from the general principles of the Convention, to which reference is made under Art 7(2) and then looked at the place of performance under the Convention of the obligation to pay.

Uniform Law on the International Sale of Goods, which predates the Vienna Convention and in many respects is the same as that Convention. The first of these cases was *Re a Consignment of Italian Wine*, decided in 1986.[300] The German buyers of wine, which it alleged contravened EEC wine regulations as being not of the minimum alcoholic strength permitted and as having had raw cane sugar added, brought a claim, *inter alia*, for contractual damages in Germany against a wine trading company established in Italy and its director. The Court held that such a claim depended on the place where the broken obligation, which in this case was the delivery of goods in conformity with the contract, should have been fulfilled. The second case, decided in 1994, is *Re Yarn Sales*.[301] The Bundesgerichtshof said that, if the plaintiff is claiming damages for breach by the other party, reference must be made to the obligation the non-fulfilment of which gives rise to the claim for damages. However, the Court went on to hold that, in the present case, which involved the seller claiming damages from the buyer who had refused to accept delivery of goods on the basis that there was no contract, this was the obligation to pay the purchase price of the goods.[302] The Court went on to determine where this obligation was to be performed in the light of the applicable law.[303] The decision is to be welcomed as not treating a claim for compensation as an independent obligation, but its identification of the underlying unperformed obligation as being that of payment of the purchase price is not entirely convincing. The underlying unperformed obligation is better regarded as that of accepting delivery of the goods.

However, against these cases there is the 1993 decision of the Oberlandes- **3.129** gericht, Dusseldorf, in *Re a Wood-Cutting Machine*,[304] which specifically deals with the Vienna Convention. The Court treated a claim to compensation under the Vienna Convention as an independent contractual obligation. It then had to solve the problem of identifying the place of performance of this obligation to compensate. The Vienna Convention does not specify a place of performance for this. However, the Court held that such a claim is aimed at obtaining the payment of money and then applied the provision in the Convention which sets out where the obligation to pay the purchase price is to be performed. The decision in *Re a Wood-Cutting Machine* has been rightly criticized as being incorrect.[305]

[300] Judgment of 24 September 1986-VIII ZR 320/85; BGHZ Vol 98, 263; IPRax 1988, 159, Note: Hausmann, 140; KTS 1987, 230; MDR 1987, 228; NJW 1987, 592; RIW 1986, 991; ZZP 1987, 435, Note: Schack; [1988] EEC 159; D Series I-5.3—B 18; [1988] ECC 159.
[301] Case VIII ZR 185/92 [1995] IL Pr 180.
[302] See below, para 3.281.
[303] German law, which applied the Uniform Law on the International Sale of Goods of 1973, governed.
[304] [1995] IL Pr 191.
[305] Schlechtriem, 373.

Exercising the right to other remedies

3.130 THE SUBSTANTIVE LAW   The other principal remedy in the Vienna Convention is the right to require performance, available under Articles 46 and 61 to buyer and seller alike in appropriate cases. As stated above, there is no inhibition or restriction on the award of the remedy, save for Article 46(2) which prevents the buyer from requiring the delivery of substitute goods when the seller's breach is not a fundamental one under Article 25. There is no specific provision in the Vienna Convention for injunctive relief, but a court assisting a claimant who is requiring performance will draw upon its own domestic powers.

3.131 The approach of the Vienna Convention is very different from the position taken in the Sale of Goods Act. The Act in s 52 deals with specific performance only in respect of the seller's breach to deliver specific or ascertained goods. In practice, the exercise of the court's discretion is confined to specific goods and is exercised by the court only in rare cases. The broad equivalent of specific performance, however, may be exercised in the form of a mandatory injunction binding the seller, at least on an interim basis, to deliver pursuant to a contract for unascertained goods.[306] There is little scope for an action by the seller for specific performance of a contract for the sale of goods. First, the Act does not provide for it. Second, if such a decree could be granted, it would be only in the rarest of circumstances, pursuant to the doctrine of mutuality, in the sense that the decree would have been available against the buyer had circumstances been the other way round. Third, and more significantly, a seller's action for specific performance has in effect been displaced by a very similar action, namely the seller's action for the price. Although such an action if successful would not compel the buyer to take delivery, the buyer would have every incentive to do so having been required to pay for the goods.

3.132 Subject to one very rare exception, a seller may recover the price under s 49 of the Sale of Goods Act only where the property in the goods has passed to the buyer, an event that normally occurs upon delivery, unless the buyer is given credit and the seller has the protection of a reservation of title clause. Unlike the case of specific performance, the action for the price does not depend upon the discretion of the court. It is in relatively rare circumstances that a seller under the Sale of Goods Act will be successful in an action for the price; the Vienna Convention is significantly more accommodating to sellers who are requiring the buyer to do one or both of taking delivery and paying the price.

---

[306] *Sky Petroleum Ltd v VIP Petroleum Ltd* [1974] 1 WLR 576.

The position stated above in relation to the Vienna Convention and **3.133**
requiring performance needs to be glossed by referring to Article 28, a
provision that was inserted in the Convention to deal with difficulties that
common law courts might have in translating the requiring of performance into a domestic decree of specific performance.[307] Article 28 provides
that a court is not bound to enter a judgment for specific performance
unless it would enter such a judgment under its own law in respect of
similar contracts not governed by the Vienna Convention. The limits of
this dispensation should be noted. It is confined to specific performance
cases and should not apply where a seller is suing for the price and would
not recover the price in respect of a similar sale contract governed by the
domestic law administered by the court. Moreover, it should not apply
to Article 75 cases where seller or buyer, as the case may be, crystallizes
its loss according to the terms of a substitute transaction by way of resale
or cover, even though such action by the seller or buyer might be seen in
some legal systems as a type of direct execution or performance of the
contract conducted on behalf of the contract-breaker.

Avoidance of the contract, or termination, is a type of remedy, but it is a **3.134**
self-help remedy. Both the Vienna Convention and the Sale of Goods Act
have adopted the view that a claimant should not have to go to court to
seek the remedy. Under the Sale of Goods Act, termination is more
broadly available than the equivalent remedy of avoidance under the
Vienna Convention. Termination is available for any breach of condition,
as well as for factually serious breaches that go to the root of the contract.
Avoidance under the Convention requires there to be a fundamental
breach of contract as defined by Article 25, a test that is less stringent than
the test for a breach going to the root of the contract in English law. In
addition to fundamental breach, the Vienna Convention permits avoidance where buyer (under Article 47) or seller (under Article 63) has served
a notice requiring performance within a reasonable time and no such
performance has been forthcoming. There is less need for a similar process of making time of the essence in English law in that the time of
performance of commercial sale obligations is routinely treated even
without such notices as being of the essence of the contract (despite the
somewhat inconsistent language of s 10 of the Sale of Goods Act).

The remedy of termination under the Sale of Goods Act may be more **3.135**
freely available than avoidance under the Vienna Convention but it is
more easily lost by the effluxion of time and other events. The Sale of
Goods Act does not contemplate mutual restitution between buyer and
seller of the kind that might be needed if a contract were to be unwound

---

[307] See below, paras 16.142–145.

some considerable time after delivery and payment. The buyer's right to reject goods in the event of a terminating breach has to be exercised within a reasonable time, which is conventionally interpreted as a very brief period that is unlikely to exceed two weeks or so. The performance by the buyer of an act inconsistent with the seller's ownership (such as delivery of the goods under a subsale) also precludes rejection.

3.136 The Vienna Convention, on the other hand, whilst in principle requiring restitution of the goods if the contract is to be avoided, carves out major exceptions to this position in Article 82(2). Avoidance will be allowed, for example, where the impossibility of making restitution of the goods in the condition in which the buyer received them is not due to the behaviour of the buyer, and will also be allowed where the goods have been used, consumed, transformed or sold on to a sub-buyer before the buyer could reasonably have discovered them to be non-conforming. The passage of time is not as such a bar to avoidance.

3.137 What is the obligation in question for the purposes of Article 5(1)?   The position is analogous to that where a claim for compensation is brought and this would suggest that there is no independent obligation where the right to remedies other than compensation is sought. It follows that the obligation in question for the purposes of Article 5(1) is the obligation that the seller or buyer has failed to perform and which gives rise to the remedy now being sought.

3.138 *A claim for repayment of the purchase price*   In the event of avoidance, Article 81(2) of the Vienna Convention gives the seller a restitutionary claim for the recovery of the price if paid. In cases where the buyer also has to return goods, the restitutionary obligations of buyer and seller have to be performed concurrently. This duty of mutual restitution extends also to the fruits of the price or goods received by buyer and seller from each other. Given the limited temporal availability of rejection of the goods and ensuing termination of the contract under the Sale of Goods Act, it is not surprising that the Act makes no provision for mutual restitution of the fruits generated by the goods and the purchasde price. So far as a buyer effectively rejecting the goods has a right to recover the purchase price, this will be effected outside the Sale of Goods Act by a restitutionary action for money had and received. The revesting of the property in the goods in the seller will take effect pursuant to a term of the contract implied at common law.[308]

3.139 Is this a matter relating to a contract?   As has been seen, where a buyer, relying on the Vienna Convention, avoids the contract on the basis

---

[308] *RV Ward Ltd v Bignall* [1967] 1 QB 534.

of a defect in the goods and seeks restitution of the purchase price, this would appear to be a restitutionary claim based on a contractual obligation and accordingly constitutes a matter relating to a contract.

WHAT IS THE OBLIGATION IN QUESTION FOR THE PURPOSES OF ARTICLE **3.140** 5(1)? The obligation in question under Article 5(1) is the contractual obligation to deliver goods in conformity with the contact. The buyer is therefore able to bring his restitutionary claim in the place of performance of this obligation. If the right to reclaim the purchase price is based on some independent non-contractual obligation, then this would be a restitutionary obligation and thus outside Article 5(1).

Conclusion on the process of determining the obligation in question

The determination of the obligation in question is not an exact science **3.141** for courts. Judges clearly have considerable leeway when it comes to analysing the nature of the obligation, determining whether there is one obligation or more than one obligation, and in the latter eventuality determining what the principal obligation is.

The Place of Performance of the Obligation in Question

In this section we will start by examining the special rule in Article 5(1)(b) **3.142** for identifying the place of performance of the obligation in question in the case of the sale of goods. We will then examine the position in sale of goods cases where this special rule does not apply. Finally, brief mention will be made of the special rule in Article 5(1)(b) for the provision of services.[309]

The special rule for sale of goods

Article 5(1)(b) of the Brussels I Regulation[310] provides that: **3.143**

for the purpose of this provision and unless otherwise agreed, the place of performance of the obligation in question shall be:
— in the case of the sale of goods, the place in a Member State where, under the contract, the goods were delivered or should have been delivered

---

[309] See below, paras 3.298–301.
[310] See K Takahashi, 'Jurisdiction in Matters Relating to Contract: Art 5(1) of the Brussels Convention and Regulation' [2002] ELR 530; Forner, 'Special Jurisdiction in Commercial Contracts: From the 1968 Brussels Convention to Brussels-One Regulation' [2002] ICCLR 131. Art 5(1) of the Brussels and Lugano Conventions does not contain this special rule introduced by the Brussels I Regulation, neither does the Modified Regulation, see r 3(a) of the Modified Regulaton contained in Sch 4 to the Civil Jurisdiction and Judgments Act 1982, as substituted by Sch 2, para 4 of SI 2001/3929.

3.144   The background to Article 5(1)(b)   Article 5(1) of the Brussels Convention contained no autonomous definition of the place of performance of the obligation in question. Neither was the European Court of Justice prepared to provide such a definition. Instead, the national court before which the matter was brought had to determine in accordance with its own rules of conflict of laws what was the law applicable to the legal relationship in question and define in accordance with that law the place of performance of the contractual obligation in question.[311] This approach came in for considerable criticism both from academics[312] and from Advocates General Leger,[313] Lenz[314] and Ruiz-Jarabo Colomer.[315] Its shortcomings have been said to be as follows. First, it leads to a lack of harmonisation in the law of jurisdiction.[316] Second, the definition of the place of performance under the substantive law is arrived at by taking into account considerations, such as, in the case of the obligation to pay, the distribution of risks and charges connected with the transfer of money, different from those under the Brussels Convention.[317] Third, neither does a reference to substantive law fit in with the justification of Article 5(1) in terms of there being a close connection between the dispute and the court called upon to deal with it.[318] Fourth, the applicable law approach is partly responsible for the multiplicity of places of performance,[319] i.e. different obligations can, according to the applicable substantive law, have different places of performance. Fifth, more generally the objectives of the Convention in terms of enabling the parties to foresee which courts have jurisdiction, providing legal certainty and equality of treatment[320] are not met.[321] The process that has to be gone through is undeniably complex

---

[311] Case 12/76 *Industrie Tessili Italiana Como v Dunlop AG* [1976] ECR 1473; the *Custom Made* case, n 249 above; Case C-440/97 *GIE Groupe Concorde v Master of the Vessel Suhadiwarno Panjan* [1999] ECR I-6307; the *Leathertex* case, n 253 above, also explicitly accepted the correctness of these three cases, although the reference in that case was on a different point; Case C-256/00 *Besix SA v Wasserreinigungsbau Alfred Kretzschmar GmbH & Co KG (WABAG)* [2002] ECR I-1699. The principle is discussed further below, paras 3.241–247. For the arguments in favour of this rule see the *Tesssili* case, para 14; the *GIE* case, paras 23, 24, 28, 29.

[312] See W Kennett, 'Place of Performance and Predictability' [1995] Ybk of European Law 193; AE Anton and PR Beaumont, *Private International Law* (2nd edn, Edinburgh: Green, 1990) 101; J Hill, 'Jurisdiction in Matters Relating to a Contract under the Brussels Convention' [1995] ICLQ 591, 618. But for a robust defence of the rule see Briggs and Rees, 2.129.

[313] In the *Leathertex* case, n 253 above.

[314] In the *Custom Made* case, n 249 above.

[315] In the *GIE* case, n 311 above.

[316] AG Leger in the *Leathertex* case, n 253 above, para 128.

[317] AG Leger in the *Leathertex* case, n 253 above, para 114 and Lenz AG in Case C-288/92 *Custom Made Commercial Ltd v Stawa Metallbau GmbH* [1994] ECR I-2913, para 21.

[318] AG Leger in the *Leathertex* case, n 253 above, paras 115–116.

[319] ibid, para 86.   [320] The *GIE* case, n 311 above, para 15.

[321] This was the argument of the German and UK Governments and the Commission in the *GIE* case, ibid.

and difficult to apply.[322] Sixth, the content of the substantive law, at least in cases of international sales, often leads to the allocation of jurisdiction to the state of the plaintiff's domicile or the defendant's domicile.[323] Seventh, in cases where the obligation in question was the payment of money it led to the allocation of jurisdiction to the place of payment and this was regarded by some as only a minor connection between the dispute and the courts taking jurisdiction.[324]

The special rule in Article 5(1)(b) of the Brussels I Regulation giving an **3.145** autonomous definition to this place was introduced to remedy the shortcomings in Article 5(1) of the Brussels Convention.[325] It does not attempt to define the place of performance for every contractual obligation.[326] Instead, it concentrates on the place of performance for certain commonly encountered types of contract, namely sale of goods and the provision of services, rather than for particular obligations, and when giving an autonomous definition for these contracts it applies the same definition regardless of the obligation on which the claim is based. Its introduction was a compromise.[327] Some Member States favoured retention of the status quo, others the abolition of Article 5(1) altogether, and yet others a

---

[322] See AG Ruiz-Jarabo Colomer in the *GIE* case, n 311 above, at 874–875. This has led to resistance from national courts, particularly in France, to applying the *Tessili* approach, see G Droz, '*Delendum est forum contractus?* (vingt ans après les arrêts *De Bloos* et *Tessili* interprétant l'article 5.1 de la Convention de Bruxelles du 27 septembre 1968)' [1997] Recueil Dalloz 351; AG Ruiz-Jarabo Colomer in the *GIE* case, n 311 above, at 878.

[323] AG Ruiz-Jarabo Colomer in the *GIE* case, n 311 above, at 879–880. This particularly concerned Luxembourg, which typically was faced with Luxembourg buyers purchasing goods from Belgian sellers, who generally stipulated that an FOB clause be put in the contract. This would mean that the place of performance of the obligation in question would be the State of the seller's domicile. This led to a special provision in the Brussels Convention for the benefit of Luxembourg according to which a person domiciled in Luxembourg and sued in a court of another Contracting State pursuant to Art 5(1) may refuse to submit to the jurisdiction of that court (Art 1 of the Protocol annexed to the Brussels Convention, on which see the Jenard Report, 109). The special provision is replaced by a more limited provision contained in Art 63 of the Brussels I Regulation. For differences between the old and new provisions, see Forner, n 310 above, at 136–137.

[324] See P Beaumont, 'The Brussels Convention becomes a Regulation: Implications for Legal Basis, External Competence, and Contract Jurisdiction', Ch 1 in J Fawcett (ed), *Reform and Development of Private International Law* (Oxford: OUP, 2002) 10, 16.

[325] See the Explanatory Memorandum in the Proposal for a Council Regulation COM (1999) 348 final, 14.

[326] For the objections to an autonomous definition for each obligation see AG Leger in the *Leathertex* case, n 253 above, paras 93–96, 119; AG Ruiz-Jarabo Colomer in the *GIE* case, n 311 above, at 879–881, paras 50–58; the *GIE* case, paras 25–27, ECJ.

It is particularly difficult to find an autonomous definition of the place of performance of the obligation to pay because of the lack of agreement amongst Member States as to whether, in the absence of agreement, this is the creditor's domicile or the debtor's, see AG Leger in the *Leathertex* case, n 253 above, para 92.

[327] See Beaumont, n 324 above, 15 et seq.

solution based on the concept of the place of performance of the characteristic obligation.[328]

3.146 **The scope of the special rule for sale of goods**   There are two clear
limitations on the scope of the special rule for the sale of goods contained
in Article 5(1)(b). First, it is explicitly provided that the case must be one
of 'sale of goods'. Second, it is implicit from that part of Article 5(1)(b)
allocating jurisdiction that the goods were delivered or should have been
delivered to *a place in a Member State*. There are, though, three further
possible limitations on the scope of Article 5(1)(b). The first of these is
where the displacement rule operates. The second of these is that there is
an agreed place of delivery. The third is that there is delivery to just one
place in one Member State. At the same time, the scope of this provision
is given width by the fact that it applies regardless of the obligation in
question. These definite and possible limitations, as well as the widening
out of this provision, will now be examined.

3.147 *Sale of goods*   Article 5(1) (b) only applies in 'the case of the sale of goods'.
This concept is not defined in the Regulation and, accordingly, raises a
definitional problem.[329] It is easier to say what this does not cover than
what it does. What we know from other provisions in the Regulation is
that 'sale of goods' does not cover insurance contracts, individual contracts of employment and, most importantly, consumer contracts, which
are dealt with separately under Sections 3, 4 and 5 of the Regulation.
Interestingly, the term 'sale of goods' appears in Section 4. In this section,
a consumer contract is defined so as to include 'a contract for the sale
of goods on instalment credit terms'. A Scots court has held that 'sale of
goods' in that context does not include unit trusts.[330] Nor does the concept
cover the provision of services, which Article 5(1)(b) subjects to a separate
special rule identifying the place of performance of the obligation in
question. Article 5(1)(b) refers to the 'sale' of goods, rather than to the
'supply' of goods.[331] The latter is a wider concept which includes not just
sales but 'possibly, any contract which makes provision for the supply of

---

[328] For the concept of characteristic performance in the context of contract choice of law
see Art 4(2) of the Rome Convention, discussed below, paras 13.114–116.

[329] See Takahashi, n 310 above, 532–534.

[330] *Waverley Asset Management v Saha* 1989 SLT 87, Sh Ct, a case on the Modified
Convention.

[331] The latter phrase is used in Art 6 of the Hague Conference on Private International
Law Preliminary Draft Convention on Jurisdiction and Foreign Judgments in Civil and
Commercial Matters adopted by the Special Commission on 30 October 1999. A second
version is contained in the First Part of the Diplomatic Conference 6–20 June 2001 Interim
Text. A third much narrower text concerned with Choice of Court Agreements has been
prepared, see Prel Doc No 8 March 2003.

goods, such as sub-contracting, lettings, leases, etc.'.[332] However, under the Vienna Convention contracts for the supply of goods to be manufactured or produced are to be considered sales unless the party ordering the goods undertakes to supply a substantial part of the necessary materials.[333] Article 5(1)(b) also requires that the contract is for the sale of 'goods' and so it does not cover things which cannot be described as 'goods'.

When it comes to defining what 'the sale of goods' does cover, something **3.148** needs to be said about the process of interpreting the Regulation. It has been suggested that the fact that the law of jurisdiction is now contained in a regulation, rather than in a Convention, means that, when it comes to interpreting the rules, this is more open to EC law influences than was hitherto the case.[334] Interpretation must also be determined in accordance with the decisions and principles laid down by the European Court of Justice. There are as yet no decisions from the Court interpreting the Regulation. Nor have there been any decisions of that Court defining 'sale of goods' either in the context of Article 5(1) of the Brussels Convention or in that of Section 4 of that Convention. However, the European Court of Justice has developed a number of principles to be applied when interpreting the Brussels Convention. These principles will continue to apply to the interpretation of the Regulation. Normally an autonomous community meaning has been given to the terms used in the Brussels Convention, rather than defining them by reference to a particular national system. In determining what this definition should be, it is necessary to look at the objectives and scheme of the Convention and at 'the general principles which stem from the corpus of the national legal systems'.[335] Given that the overwhelming majority of the EC Member States have adopted the Vienna Convention, this Convention, and, more particularly, the concept of sale of goods to be found within it,[336] can be said to represent the corpus of most of the national legal

---

[332] See the Report of the Special Commission on the future Hague Judgments Convention drawn up by Nygh and Pocar, Prel Doc No 11, at 49. This Report relates to the 30 October 1999 version of the draft Convention.

[333] Art 3(1); Bridge, *The International Sale of Goods*, 2.15. For the position under the 1955 Hague Convention on the Law Applicable to International Sales of Goods, see Art 1 and the discussion below, para 15.16. For the position under the 1986 Hague Convention on the Law Applicable to Contracts for the International Sale of Goods, see Art 4(1) and the discussion below, para 15.74.

[334] See JJ Forner Delaygua, 'Internet Jurisdiction in "Business to Business" On-Line Performed Contracts: Lessons From the Hague?' in JJ Barcelo and KM Clermont (eds), *A Global Law of Jurisdiction and Judgments: Lessons from the Hague* (The Hague/London: Kluwer Law, 2002).

[335] Case 79/26 *LTU v Eurocontrol* [1976] ECR 1541.

[336] Discussed in outline above, paras 1.06–07, and in detail below, paras 16.16–95.

systems.[337] Indeed, this Convention represents the substantive law back-ground to many of the cases decided under Article 5(1) of the Brussels Convention. Admittedly, Article 5(1)(b) refers to the sale of goods rather than the 'international' sale of goods, which is what the Vienna Convention is concerned with. However, Article 5(1)(b) is contained in an EC regulation that is concerned with 'conflict of jurisdiction' and is therefore inevitably dealing with the *international* sale of goods.

3.149 SALE OF GOODS UNDER THE VIENNA CONVENTION   Turning then to the Vienna Convention for the meaning of 'sale of goods',[338] this is particu-larly helpful in determining whether a contract for the supply of goods to be manufactured is one for the 'sale' of goods,[339] and in determining whether a contract for the provision of goods plus services is one for the sale of goods.[340] It is also useful in determining the meaning of 'goods'. It has been argued earlier that this concept should be given a broad meaning that might include minerals and crops.[341] The list of exclusions in the Vienna Convention also makes clear that certain sales are not of goods.[342] It could be argued that, just because an item is excluded from being 'goods' for the purposes of the Vienna Convention, should not necessarily mean that it should also be excluded from the scope of Article 5(1)(b) of the Brussels I Regulation. The purpose of this provision, namely to remedy the shortcomings in Article 5(1)(a), might be better served by giving a wider scope to the meaning of goods than under the Vienna Convention so as to include at least some of these excluded items.[343] One obvious candidate is the sale of ships. There is some controversy over whether this should have been excluded from the scope of the Vienna Convention in the first place.[344] This is very much a borderline case on the meaning of 'goods'.[345] However, to depart from the meaning of goods

[337] One other possible source of a definition of 'sale' and 'goods' is the 1955 Hague Con-vention on the law applicable to international sale of goods, discussed below paras 15.12–16. However, this is concerned with choice of law rules and is therefore not part of the substan-tive law background.

[338] See in outline above, paras 1.06–07, and in detail below, paras 16.16–95.

[339] This is to be considered a sale 'unless the party who orders the goods undertakes to supply a substantial part of the materials necessary for such manufacture or production': Art 3(1) of the Vienna Convention.

[340] The Convention does not apply to contracts 'in which the preponderant part of the obligations of the party who furnishes the goods consists in the supply of labour or other services': Art 3(2).

[341] See in outline above, para 1.07, and in detail below, paras 16.86–88.

[342] See Art 2(a), (d), (e) and (f) of the Vienna Convention.

[343] This consideration means that there is no case for excluding from the scope of Art 5(1)(b) items that are goods under Vienna.

[344] See below, para 16.88.

[345] It is excluded from the1955 Hague Sales Convention but expressly included within the 1986 Convention.

under the Vienna Convention in the case of the sale of ships would lead to uncertainty in other cases of exclusions. Why not then depart from Vienna on the meaning of sales as well, so as to allow in matters that are not sales under that Convention? The better view is that the meaning of 'sale of goods' under the Vienna Convention should be adopted, without widening this out by introducing exceptions to the Vienna Convention meaning.

DOCUMENTARY SALES With a CIF contract the seller's obligation to **3.150** deliver the goods themselves is replaced by an obligation to deliver to the buyer a number of documents (the bill of lading, the insurance document and a commercial invoice).[346] Is this a contract for the sale of goods for the purposes of Article 5(1)? It is submitted that it is. The Vienna Convention applies to such a transaction, because the goods themselves are purchased, rather than the documents.[347]

MIXED SALES AND OTHER CONTRACTUAL OBLIGATIONS One particular **3.151** problem of scope that is likely to arise frequently is where a single contract involves several obligations, some of which relate to the sale of goods, others of which do not. These other obligations will frequently involve the provision of services but could involve obligations which cannot be so regarded. This type of problem is graphically illustrated by the facts of a German case decided by the Oberlandesgericht, Koblenz.[348] A German manufacturer of spectacles supplied frames to the defendant in the Netherlands who acted as distributor for their frames to opticians in that country. On termination of their business relationship, the plaintiff manufacturer sought payment for alleged unpaid deliveries of goods for resale and damages for failure to return samples provided on loan. Another example is that of a contract to design, manufacture, deliver and set up ready for operation a machine; the obligation to set up being regarded as one which was separately enforceable.[349] A final example is where there is a contract to supply oil plus technical assistance to enable the buyer to blend and produce lubricating oils.[350]

Under the Brussels Convention, such a case was easily dealt with by **3.152** identifying the principal obligation on which the plaintiff's action was

---

[346] Bridge, *The International Sale of Goods*, 1.07.

[347] Schlechtriem, 23. Art 1 of the Hague Convention of 1955 on the Law Applicable to International Sale of Goods states that it applies 'to sales based on documents', as does Art 2(b) of the Hague Convention of 1986 on the Law Applicable to Contracts for the International Sale of Goods.

[348] Judgment of 24 May 1985–2U 1259/83, Oberlandesgericht, Koblenz, IPRax 1986, 105, Note: Geimer, 85: RIW 1986, 459.

[349] *NV Siersteenfabriek Heylen v BV Machinefabriek Esmil Hubert & Co* Judgment of 24 May 1983, Hof van beroep, Antwerp, D Series I–5.1.1—B 19.

[350] See *Shell International Petroleum Co Ltd v Coral Oil Co Ltd* [1999] 1 Lloyd's Rep 72.

based.[351] Thus in the German case referred to above, the Oberlandes-gericht, Koblenz, held that the focus of the dealer's contract was the sale of goods supplied for resale and not the samples provided free of charge, which only assisted such sales. Payment had to be made at the seller's place of business in Germany and, accordingly, the German courts had jurisdiction over both the payment claim and the damages claim.

3.153 The position is more complicated under the Brussels I Regulation because of the introduction in Article 5(1)(b) of the special rules for determining the place of performance of the obligation in question in the case of the sale of goods and the provision of services. The type of contract assumes a new significance because this will determine the rule for determining the place of performance of the obligation in question.

3.154 There are three possible approaches to solving this problem of mixed obligations. The first, and best approach, is to classify the contract by having recourse to the meaning of sale of goods contained in the Vienna Convention. As has been mentioned, this excludes from the scope of the Vienna Convention 'contracts in which the predominant part of the obligations of the party who furnishes the goods consists in the supply of labour or other services'.[352] If the predominant part of the obligations of the party who furnishes the goods is the provision of services, then the contract should be regarded as one for the provision of services and the special rule in Article 5(1)(b) for such contracts should apply. However, if the predominant part of the obligations of the party who furnishes the goods is not the provision of services, the exclusion does not apply and the contract is one for the sale of goods and the special rule in Article 5(1)(b) for such contracts should apply. This solution is consistent with what was proposed under the draft Hague Judgments Convention.[353] This had a jurisdiction rule for matters relating to the supply of goods and a separate jurisdiction rule for matters relating to the provision of services.[354] It then had a third rule for matters relating both to the supply of goods and the provision of services.[355] This allocated jurisdiction to the

---

[351] Case 266/85 *Shenavai v Kreischer* [1987] ECR 239, discussed above, para 3.85; Case 9/87 *Arcado SPRL v SA Haviland* [1988] ECR 1539.

[352] Art 3(2); discussed below, para 16.93.

[353] See the Hague Conference on Private International Law Preliminary Draft Convention on Jurisdiction and Foreign Judgments in Civil and Commercial Matters adopted by the Special Commission on 30 October 1999. A second version is contained in the First Part of the Diplomatic Conference 6–20 June 2001 Interim Text. A third much narrower text concerned with Choice of Court Agreements has been prepared, see Prel Doc No 8 March 2003.

[354] Art 6 (a) and (b) of the 30 October 1999 version of the draft Convention. This was repeated in the 2001 Interim Text.

[355] Art 6(c) of the 30 October 1999 version of the draft Convention. This was repeated in the 2001 Interim Text.

courts of the state in which performance of the principal obligation took place.[356]

The second possible approach involves focusing on the obligations *on* **3.155** *which the action is based* and identifying the principal obligation.[357] If this is an obligation arising under the contract of sale, then the special rule for this type of contract set out in Article 5(1)(b) should be used, and it should be used to identify the place of performance of all the obligations under the contract, even the obligations that do not stem from the sale of goods contract. This approach can be justified on the basis that the search under Article 5(1) is ultimately to identify the place of performance of the obliga- tion in question, i.e. the obligation the non-performance of which is relied upon by the plaintiff. It is therefore appropriate to solve the problem posed by mixed obligations and identification of the type of contract for the purposes of Article 5(1)(b), by focusing on the obligation in question. However, against this approach is the fact that it does not actually involve classifying *the contract*, which is what Article 5(1)(b) presupposes will happen. Instead, it is concerned with classifying the obligation.

The third possible approach is to say that Article 5(1)(b) presupposes **3.156** that all the obligations are sales obligations (or that all the obligations are service obligations) and, accordingly, has no application in a case of mixed sales and other obligations. What will then happen is that Article 5(1)(a) will apply and it will be necessary to determine the place of performance of the obligation in question, without the assistance of the special rule in Article 5(1)(b). The court will have to determine what the principal obligation is (this may be the sales obligation or it may be some other obligation), and then where it is to be performed. The court with jurisdiction in relation to the principal obligation will also have jurisdic- tion in respect of the other obligations. This approach will in practice greatly limit the use of Article 5(1)(b), the introduction of which was so as to avoid the drawbacks inherent in the use of Article 5(1)(a).

THE SALES CONTRACT IS SUPERSEDED   Contracts involving mixed obliga- **3.157** tions must be distinguished from a sales contract which is superseded by another type of contract. For example, if goods that have been sold are unsuitable for the purpose for which they have been supplied, the parties may negotiate a repair contract.[358] If the repairs are inadequate and

---

[356] See also Art 4(2) of the Hague Convention on the Law Applicable to Contracts for the International Sale of Goods 1986, which provides that contracts in which the preponderant part of the obligations of the party who furnishes goods consists of the supply of labour or other services are not to be considered contracts of sale.

[357] See Takahashi, n 310 above, at 533, in relation to contracts for the sale of goods and the provision of services.

[358] *WH Martin v Feldbinder Speziaffahrzeugwerke GMBH* [1998] IL Pr 794, CA.

the claimant sues for damages, the obligation in question will be that under the repair contract and its place of performance will have to be ascertained under Article 5(1)(a) rather than 5(1)(b).

3.158 DISTRIBUTION AGREEMENTS   An exclusive distribution (or concession) agreement is closely related to an international sale of goods contract. It is a complex arrangement involving both elements of service and sales. It has been argued that such an arrangement should fall outside the scope of Article 5(1)(b).[359] However, this is to give up too easily. It is possible to separate out the different contracts involved and apply Article 5(1)(b) to them.[360] The typical arrangement is as follows.[361] The distribution agreement itself will give one party (A) the right, which may be an exclusive right, to distribute goods supplied by the other party (B), at an agreed price. A will then resell the goods to customers (C). As and when A finds customers, it places orders with B, who supplies the goods to A. Thus the distribution agreement is implemented by a series of individual contracts of sale.[362] Another way of putting it is to say that the distribution agreement is the main or framework contract but flowing from this will be a number of individual contracts for the international sale of goods.[363]

3.159 Let us assume that an action is brought for breach of the distribution agreement. For example, A complains that B has been supplying goods to another distributor and therefore his exclusive right of distribution has been broken. Or A may explicitly claim damages for termination of the distribution agreement.[364] Or B complains that A has been distributing the goods of another supplier in breach of the exclusive arrangement. Or B seeks a declaration that no exclusivity exists or, if it does, that the distribution agreement has been terminated by notice.[365] Should the distribution agreement be regarded as a contract for the provision of services, and thus within the special provision for such contracts set out in Article 5(1)(b),[366]

---

[359] See Briggs, 2.128; Beaumont, n 324 above, at 20.

[360] For splitting up of these contracts for the purposes of Art 5(1) of the Brussels Convention see *Bio-Medical Research v Delatex SA* [2001] ILRM 51, Irish Supreme Court.

[361] See the analysis in *Print Concept GmbH v GEW (EC) Limited* [2001] EWCA Civ 352, [2002] CLC 382, CA.

[362] In some cases, it may be possible to regard the individual purchase as an instalment. In this situation, the framework agreement should be regarded as a contract for the sale of goods.

[363] The relationship between these different contracts and the effect that this has on the operation of Art 17 of the Brussels Convention was examined by the Dutch courts in *Hacker Kuchen GmbH v Bosma Huygen Meubelimpex BV* [1992] IL Pr 379 and by the Irish Supreme Court in the *Bio-Medical Research* case, n 360 above.

[364] See, e.g. *Meyer v La Société Charles Wednesbury Limited* [1996] IL Pr 299, Cour d'appel, Paris—the obligation in question for the purposes of Art 5(1) of the Brussels Convention was said to be the obligation of the distributor to supply the distributee with its products.

[365] See the *Bio-Medical Research* case, n 360 above.

[366] See below, paras 3.298–301.

or as one for the sale of goods, and thus within the separate special provision for such contracts also set out in Article 5(1)(b)? The distribution agreement may be interpreted as containing an implied agreement by B to supply goods as and when required by A,[367] as well as obligations by both A and B in relation to distribution. Indeed, it is this element of supply that constitutes the characteristic performance of the contract for choice of law purposes.[368] However, an agreement by B to supply as and when required in the future by A is not a contract for the sale of goods.[369] A distributorship agreement lacks the characteristics of a true sale contract, such as terms relating to delivery and (often) quantity. It is for this reason that it is argued later on[370] that such an agreement falls outside the concept of the sale of goods for the purposes of the Vienna Convention.[371] The distribution agreement as a whole looks more like a contract for the provision of services. It is submitted therefore that the special rule in Article 5(1)(b) that applies 'in the case of the provision of services' should be applied to actions for breach of the distribution agreement.

Now let us assume that an action is brought for breach of one of the sales **3.160** contracts that flow from the distribution agreement. For example, A places an order for goods and then complains that the goods delivered are not of the requisite quality and seeks damages from B. Alternatively, B may complain that A has not paid for the goods delivered and seeks payment from him. Both examples would clearly come within the special rule in Article 5(1)(b) that applies 'in the case of the sale of goods'.

The position is further complicated by the fact that it is not always clear **3.161** whether an action is being brought, on the one hand, for breach of the sales agreement, or, on the other hand, for breach of the distribution agreement. Take the situation where the gist of A's complaint is that B has failed to deliver goods.[372] This may be because B regards the distribution agreement as being at an end. Is this an action based on a breach of the distribution agreement or on a breach of the sales agreement? In order for it to be the latter it will be necessary to show that an individual contract for the sale of goods has been entered into.[373] In other words, an order for goods has been placed and accepted by the distributor. In such a case, an action for failure to deliver is based on a breach of the sales agreement. An

---

[367] The *Print Concept* case, n 361 above, at [25] (*per* Longmore LJ).

[368] ibid, at [34] (*per* Longmore LJ); discussed below, para 13.124.

[369] See above, para 3.158.   [370] See below, para 16.95.

[371] Even if a different approach is adopted and distributorship obligations are weighed against sales obligations it is likely that sales obligations will be outweighed by distributorship obligations.

[372] See *SIPAL Rexons Società Italiana Prodotti Auto E Locomozione SpA v Sprl Gold's Products* [1990] IL Pr 386, Cour d'appel, Mons, a case on Art 5(1) of the Brussels Convention.

[373] ibid.

even more difficult situation is where A alleges that there is a defect in the quality of the goods and seeks damages. At first sight, this would appear to be based on the sales contract. But what if A explicitly bases this claim on a breach of the distribution agreement, i.e. alleges that there is a term of the distribution agreement that goods of a certain quality will be supplied when ordered? If there is such an express or implied term, it is not clear whether, for the purposes of the application of Article 5(1)(b), the plaintiff should be allowed to choose which contract to base the claim on in this way. However, as far as jurisdiction is concerned, it will probably not make any difference whether the contract is regarded as one for the provision of services or as one for the sale of goods since the place where services are provided (for the purposes of the special rule under Article 5(1)(b) dealing with contracts for the provision of services) is likely to be the same place as that where goods are delivered (for the purposes of the special rule under Article 5(1)(b) dealing with contracts for the sale of goods).

3.162 A claim for a declaration that the exclusive distribution agreement has been terminated by notice is clearly based on the distribution agreement.[374] It is submitted that the position would be no different if B claims the right to terminate the distribution agreement on the ground that A has not paid promptly for the goods delivered under individual sales contracts and that this constitutes a breach of a term (express or implied) of the distribution agreement.

3.163 THE SALE OF DIGITIZED PRODUCTS   The question whether the sale of digitized products, such as software, over the internet, is a contract for the sale of goods under Article 5(1)(b) raises particular difficulties which are considered in Chapter 10 on electronic commerce and jurisdiction.[375]

3.164 *Delivery to a place in a Member State*   There is another limitation on the scope of this provision. It only applies in cases where, under the contract, the goods were delivered or should have been delivered to a place in a Member State. Where the effect of the autonomous definition is to designate a court in a non-Member State, rule (a) will apply rather than rule (b).[376] It follows that if delivery has taken place, or should have taken place, in say New York, Article 5(1)(b) will not apply.

3.165 What if delivery has taken place, or should have taken place, partly in New York and partly in an EC Member State? It is submitted that the part which has been or should be delivered to a place in a Member State

---

[374] See the *Bio-Medical Research* case, n 360 above.   [375] See below, paras 10.46–49.
[376] See the Explanatory Memorandum, n 325 above, 14.

should be distinguished from that other part which has been or should be delivered to a place outside a Member State. This would be consistent with the treatment, suggested below,[377] of cases of part delivery involving delivery to more than one place within the EC. Article 5(1)(b) would apply to that part of the goods which has been or should be delivered to a place in a Member State. Article 5(1)(a) would apply to that part of the goods which has been or should be delivered to a place in a non-Member State, provided that under that rule the place of performance of the obligation in question is in a Member State.

The displacement rule According to Article 5(1)(b), the special rule deter- **3.166** mining the place of performance of the obligation in question can be displaced.[378] The special rule allocating jurisdiction to the place where, under the contract, the goods were delivered or should have been delivered only applies 'unless otherwise agreed'. It is unclear what part this displacement rule contained in Article 5(1)(b) plays in the scope of that provision. It has been suggested that Article 5(1)(b) does not apply at all in cases where the displacement rule operates and, accordingly, recourse will have to be had to subparagraph (a) to identify the place of performance of the obligation in question.[379] The alternative view is that, in cases where the displacement rule operates, jurisdiction is implicitly allocated to the place of performance of the obligation in question agreed by the parties. This allocation is effected by Article 5(1)(b) itself and recourse is not to be had to Article 5(1)(a). It is submitted that this second view is the better one. It fits in better with the language of Article 5(1)(b) and minimizes the number of sale of goods cases where recourse has to be had to Article 5(1)(a) with all the problems that poses. In practical terms, the result is going to be the same, regardless of which approach is adopted, since under the applicable substantive law (the Article 5(1)(a) approach) effect will be given to the parties' intentions.

Problems still remain over the displacement rule and the requirement of **3.167** delivery to a place in a Member State. The place of delivery under the contract may be in a non-Member State but the parties have agreed that the place of performance of the obligation in question (for example the obligation to pay) is in a Member State. Does one say that Article 5(1)(b) does not apply because delivery under the contract is not to a place in a Member State and therefore one never gets on to the displacement rule?[380] Article 5(1)(a) would then apply and it would be necessary to determine

---

[377] See below, paras 3.205–211, in particular the discussion of the second scenario.
[378] The operation of this provision is considered further below, paras 3.227–235.
[379] Forner, n 310 above, at 136; Beaumont, n 324 above, at 20.
[380] Advocated by Takahashi, n 310 above, at 540.

the place of performance of the obligation in question under that provision. Or does one say that Article 5(1)(b) does apply on the basis that it allows the parties to agree the place of performance in question? They have agreed on a place in a Member State and therefore that state has jurisdiction by virtue of Article 5(1)(b). Under the first alternative the place of performance is determined by application of the applicable substantive law. Under the second alternative it is determined by the agreement of the parties. In practice, the two will produce the same result because the relevant substantive law will take account of any agreement of the parties. In principle, though, it is submitted that the first approach is the better one in terms of logic. It is impossible to displace a rule that does not apply in the first place.

3.168 The converse situation can also arise. The place of delivery under the contract may be in a Member State but the parties have agreed that the place of performance of the obligation in question (for example to pay) is in a non-Member State. The special rule under Article 5(1)(b) will apply. But can it be displaced by an agreement that the place of performance of the obligation in question is in a non-Member State? In the situation where the displacement rule operates, the place of performance of the obligation in question is, *by virtue of Article 5(1)(b)*, the place agreed by the parties. But Article 5(1)(b) cannot allocate jurisdiction to the courts of a place in a non-Member State. The displacement rule must therefore be referring to an agreement on the place of performance of the obligation in question *in a Member State*.[381] It follows, that where the parties have agreed that the place of performance of the obligation in question is in a non-Member State, the displacement rule cannot operate. The rule that allocates jurisdiction to the place in a Member State where the goods were delivered or should have been delivered will continue to apply.

3.169 *No agreed place of delivery?*   There is a further possible limitation on the scope of Article 5(1)(b). Jurisdiction is allocated to the place in a Member State where, 'under the contract', the goods were delivered or should have been delivered. But what if 'under the contract'[382] the parties have not agreed on the place of delivery? It is arguable that, in this situation, Article 5(1)(b) will not apply.[383] However, it is possible to interpret this provision in such a way that it can still operate in this situation[384] and it may well be that the courts will prefer this course of action to that of

---

[381] This fits in with Art 5(1)(a). This is referring to the place of performance of the obligation in question in a Member State.

[382] See further below, paras 3.176–178.

[383] See B Ancel, 'The Brussels I Regulation: Comment' (2001) III Ybk of Private Intl Law 101, 109.

[384] See below, paras 3.192–198.

excluding this situation altogether from the scope of Article 5(1)(b). Hence the description of this as merely a 'possible' limitation on scope. This situation, and the problems it poses will be further examined below.

Delivery to just one place in one Member State? Article 5(1)(b) refers to 'the **3.170** place' in 'a' Member 'State'. In other words, it is phrased in the singular. It assumes that goods are delivered to just one place in one Member State. If there is delivery to two or more places in a single Member State or to places in two or more Member States, it is at least arguable that Article 5(1)(b) will not apply. However, it is unlikely that the European Court of Justice would adopt such a literal approach. An analogous problem arose with Article 17 of the Brussels Convention. Although this refers to an agreement that the courts of a Contracting State (in the singular) are to have jurisdiction, an agreement giving jurisdiction to the courts of two Contracting States has been held by the European Court of Justice to come within this provision.[385] This still leaves a problem, which will be examined later,[386] of how jurisdiction is to be allocated under Article 5(1)(b) in a case of delivery to two or more places.

Regardless of the obligation in question One final point that should be made **3.171** about the scope of Article 5(1)(b) relates to its width. It 'applies regardless of the obligation in question, even where this obligation is the payment of the financial consideration for the contract. It also applies where the claim relates to several obligations'.[387] The width of the rule can be justified on the basis that delivery characterizes the contract.[388] Moreover, a place of delivery rule will normally designate the courts of the place where the goods are located which makes it easy to furnish proof and enforce the decisions of the courts.[389] This does not work an injustice in cases of non-payment because this is often the result of a complaint in respect of delivery, including delivery of defective goods[390] and it is questionable

---

[385] Case 23/78 *Meeth v Glacetal Sarl* [1978] ECR 2133.

[386] See below, paras 3.205–211.

[387] See the Explanatory Memorandum, n 325 above, 14. See also Ancel, n 383 above, at 109. But compare Forner, n 310 above, at 136 who argues that Art 5(1)(b) could be narrowly interpreted just to encompass the obligation to deliver. The wording of the provision does not support this, and the intention of the Commission was to the contrary.

[388] AG Mayras in Case 12/76 *Industrie Tessili Italiana Como v Dunlop AG* [1976] ECR 1473; Takahashi, n 310 above, at 534; Ancel, n 383 above, at 109; R Moura Ramos, 'The New EC Rules on Jurisdiction and the Recognition and Enforcement of Judgments' in J Nafziger and S Symeonides (eds), *Law and Justice in a Multistate World: Essays in Honor of Arthur T von Mehren* (New York: Transnational Publishers Inc, 2002).

[389] See the expert meeting on Electronic Commerce and International Jurisdiction organized by the Hague Conference on Private International Law held in Ottawa, 28 February to 1 March 2000, Summary of Discussions in Prel Doc No 12 of August 2000.

[390] See generally AG Leger in Case C-420/97 *Leathertex Divisione Sinetici SpA v Bodetex BVBA* [1999] ECR I-6747, para 152. See also AG Ruiz-Jarabo Colomer in Case C-440/97 *GIE Groupe Concorde v Master of the Vessel Suhadiwarno Panjan* [1999] ECR I-6307, para 65.

whether jurisdiction should be allocated to the state where payment is made since this is not the most important factual connection.[391] If, for reasons of simplicity, one connecting factor is to be applied to all obligations, the place of delivery has the biggest claim to recognition. The width of the rule also has the advantage that, in a sale of goods case where the plaintiff is suing in relation to two obligations of equal standing (whose places of performance are in different Member States), the action is concentrated in one Member State. This is the one where, under the contract, the goods were delivered or should have been delivered. Under the old rule in Article 5(1) of the Brussels Convention, the action had to be split between the courts of two different Member States.[392]

3.172 **Is it still necessary to determine the obligation in question?** The fact that Article 5(1)(b) applies, regardless of the obligation in question, raises the question of whether it is necessary in the case of the sale of goods to determine what the obligation in question actually is. It also raises the question whether, in a case involving a number of claims based on different obligations, it is necessary to determine the principal obligation since this is only necessary in cases where the different obligations have different places of performance. At first glance this would not appear to be necessary. However, it is submitted that for two reasons it is still important to identify the obligation in question even in the case of sale of goods.

3.173 The first is the ever present possibility of displacement of the general rule. This will happen in the situation where agreement has been reached on the place of performance of the obligation in question and this place is other than the place in a Member State where under the contract the goods were delivered or should have been delivered. In order to determine whether the displacement rule will operate, it is necessary to identify the obligation in question. This is neatly illustrated by the facts of *Re Yarn Sales*,[393] a decision of the German Bundesgerichtshof. The plaintiff sued the defendant for refusal to take delivery. What was the obligation in question for the purposes of Article 5(1) of the Brussels Convention? Was it the obligation to accept delivery or was it the obligation to pay? The Bundesgerichtshof held that it was the obligation to pay. When it comes to applying Article 5(1)(b) of the Brussels Convention to a case involving this obligation, if the parties agree a place of payment and this is different from the place of delivery then the displacement rule will operate.[394] However, if the obligation in question is held to be that of

---

[391] See Beaumont, n 324 above, at 16, who describes the place of payment as a minor factual connection. But where the claim is for payment it would appear to be highly relevant.
[392] See Beaumont, n 324 above, at 16.
[393] [1995] IL Pr 180.   [394] See below, para 3.227.

delivery the displacement rule will not operate. If all the obligations under the contract have to be performed in the same Member State and this is the same State as that where delivery is made or should have been made then it would not appear to be necessary for the purposes of Article 5(1) to determine what the precise obligation in question is.

The second reason why it is necessary to identify the obligation in **3.174** question, even in the case of the sale of goods, is because a single contract can involve, for example, not only obligations in relation to the sale of goods but also other obligations, for example in relation to the loan of goods. Whether Article 5(1)(b) applies may then depend, at least on one view, on the identification and separation of the different obligations.

The place in a Member State where, under the contract, the goods were 3.175 delivered or should have been delivered The special rule that applies in the case of the sale of goods states that the place of performance of the obligation in question shall be 'the place in a Member State where, under the contract, the goods were delivered or should have been delivered'. This rule is said to provide a 'pragmatic determination of the place of enforcement'.[395] The process of ascertaining the place where, under the contract, the goods were delivered etc. will now be examined. Then attention will be turned to the allocation of jurisdiction to the place where the goods were delivered or *should have been delivered*. Finally, problems in determining the place of delivery will be considered.

Ascertaining the place 'under the contract' In a case of non-delivery, the **3.176** place where goods should have been delivered is by no means self-evident. In other words, reference has to be made to something other than what has actually happened, such as to the contract or the applicable substantive law, in order to ascertain this place. Even where goods have undoubtedly actually been delivered, the place where this took place is not always clear. This is particularly so where the goods are transported by a carrier. For example, the seller/manufacturer is domiciled in France, the goods are transported from France to England, where the buyer is domiciled, by a carrier. Delivery has undoubtedly occurred, but is the place where the goods were delivered in France or in England?[396] To be sure, there are cases where the place where the goods were delivered is self-evident. For example, the goods may be situated in England at the time they are sold to the English buyer by the foreign seller. The goods come into the possession of the buyer in England. In such a case, there can be no doubt that the place where the goods were delivered is in England.

---

[395] See the Explanatory Memorandum, n 325 above, at 14.
[396] See the discussion below, paras 3.178–198.

However, this is not necessarily the place allocated jurisdiction under Article 5(1)(b). It may be that the goods should have been delivered in France, but there has been a mis-delivery. If so, France will be the place allocated jurisdiction under Article 5(1)(b).[397] This means that even where the goods have been delivered and it is clear where this took place, the contract should be examined to check whether there has been mis-delivery. And this place is not self-evident. This all sounds rather complicated. In practice, what may well happen is that the parties do not refer to the contract at all. In a case where the goods have actually been delivered (they have been received by the buyer in a Member State), this will simply be accepted by the parties as the place with jurisdiction under Article 5(1)(b).[398] The implications of the goods being carried from one Member State to another or of it being a case of mis-delivery are ignored.

3.177 Article 5(1)(b) provides an answer as to how the place of delivery is to be ascertained. It allocates jurisdiction to the place where, 'under the contract', the goods were delivered or should have been delivered. Although it is not entirely clear precisely what these words mean, it is submitted that their effect is clear. They ensure that, when ascertaining this place, recourse must be had to the terms of the contract.[399] This has an important negative effect in ensuring that recourse cannot be had to the applicable national substantive law. Nor can an autonomous community definition of the concept of the place where the goods were delivered or of the concept of the place where the goods should have been delivered be adopted.[400] Without this wording there would have been the danger of one or other of these approaches being adopted. The parties are therefore allowed to choose the place of delivery and, indirectly, the place that is allocated jurisdiction under Article 5(1)(b). A reference to the terms of the contract must be to the terms as agreed by the parties and not to terms laid down by the applicable substantive law,[401] for the latter would merely reintroduce what Article 5(1)(b) was designed to get away from.

3.178 Normally the parties will expressly agree on the place of delivery of goods. This is done by specifying the place of delivery in the contract. The parties are effectively choosing the place to be allocated jurisdiction. Nonetheless there is no requirement that the formalities under Article 23

---

[397] The problem raised by mis-delivery is discussed further below, paras 3.201–203.

[398] See, eg, *Comet Group PLC v Unika Computer SA* [2004] IL Pr 1 at [11].

[399] See Forner, n 310 above, at 136. The words 'under the contract' also have significance when it comes to the allocation of jurisdiction in cases of mis-delivery, see below, paras 3.201–203.

[400] But see the situation where examination of the contract does not provide an answer, below, paras 3.192–198.

[401] See the discussion below, paras 3.192–198, of the problem posed where there is no agreement by the parties on the place of delivery.

have to be met.[402] However, it is not unknown for the parties not to so provide in the contract.[403] Indeed, the substantive law of international sale of goods makes provision for this eventuality.[404] In the absence of such an express agreement by the parties on the place of delivery, it may be possible to imply an agreement from the terms of the contract. In the absence of an express or implied agreement as to the place of delivery, there is considerable uncertainty as to whether Article 5(1)(b) applies at all and, if it does, of how the place where the goods were delivered or should have been delivered is to be identified. We will now examine in more detail: an express agreement on the place of delivery; an implied agreement; and what happens where there is no agreement.

An express agreement on the place of delivery Normally the parties will **3.179** specify the place of delivery in the contract. Special trade terms that deal with delivery and the passing of risk in the case of the international sale of goods have been developed over the years. Definitional problems can be avoided by the use of standard trade terms, such as INCOTERMS,[405] which are internationally recognized. Some of the most common trade terms found in contracts for the international sale of goods[406] will now be examined and from this we can identify the place where, under the contract, the goods were delivered or should have been delivered.

Ex works etc In the case of a contract ex works, ex factory, ex ware- **3.180** house or ex store, the seller must place the goods at the disposal of the buyer at the point of delivery named, i.e. at the seller's works, factory, warehouse or store. The buyer must take delivery of the goods as soon as they are placed at his disposal at the point of delivery named. The place where, under the contract, the goods were delivered for the purposes of Article 5(1)(b) is probably best regarded as being the place where goods were placed at the disposal of the buyer, i.e. at the seller's works, factory, warehouse or stores. If the goods were not in fact placed at the disposal of the buyer at this place, this will be the place where, under the contract, the goods should have been delivered.[407]

The operation of Article 5(1)(b) in the case of a contract ex works etc. can **3.181** be illustrated by a practical example. An English claimant enters into

---

[402] See Case 129/83 *Zelger v Salinitri (No 2)* [1984] ECR 2397.
[403] See *Mode Jeune Diffusion SA v Maglificio il Falco di Tiziana Goti* [1998] IL Pr 812, French Cour de cassation; *Bulk Trading Corp Ltd v Zenziper Grains and Feed Stuffs* [2001] 1 Lloyd's Rep 357, CA.
[404] See Art 31 of the Vienna Convention.
[405] These are sponsored by the International Chamber of Commerce. The latest version is INCOTERMS 2000, ICC No 560.
[406] See generally the excellent description in Schmitthoff, *Export Trade*, Ch 2.
[407] Cases of non-delivery and mis-delivery are discussed further below, paras 3.199–203.

seven contracts for the supply and delivery of machines by a German manufacturer. The defendant's confirmation of order includes the following statement: 'Terms of prices: Our quoted prices are ex works, unpacked, . . .'. There are also invoices that record 'delivery ex works'.[408] After taking delivery of the seven machines in Germany, the buyer claims that they are not fit for their purpose. The place in a Member State where, under the contract, the goods were delivered would be in Germany and the English courts would not have jurisdiction under Article 5(1) of the Brussels I Regulation. The facts are taken from *Viskase Ltd v Paul Kiefel GmbH*,[409] a case decided under Article 5(1) of the Brussels Convention. The result was the same under the old law, although the process by which it was reached was different. The place of performance of the obligation to deliver was in Germany and, accordingly, the English courts lacked jurisdiction under Article 5(1) of the Brussels Convention. In the *Viskase* case, there was in fact an eighth contract in relation to which the position was different. The machine was being used for demonstration purposes at the National Exhibition Centre Birmingham, where the contract was made. The place where, under the contract, this machine was delivered would clearly be in England and the English courts would now have jurisdiction under Article 5(1) of the Brussels I Regulation, unless it is shown that the goods should have been delivered to a place in another Member State. This is most unlikely. The same result was reached under Article 5(1) of the Brussels Convention in the *Viskase* case. As far as this eighth contract was concerned, the English courts had jurisdiction in England, this being the place of performance of the obligation to deliver.

3.182 **FAS** In such a contract, the seller must clear customs and deliver the goods alongside the vessel at the loading berth named by the buyer, at the named port of shipment. If the goods have been so delivered at this port, this will be the place where, under the contract, the goods were delivered. If they have not been so delivered, this will be the place where, under the contract, the goods should have been delivered.

3.183 **FOB** In such a contract, the seller must clear customs and deliver on board the vessel named by the buyer, at the named port of shipment. If the goods have been so delivered at this port this will be the place where, under the contract, the goods were delivered. If they have not been so delivered this will be the place where, under the contract, the goods should have been delivered.

---

[408] See also *Soc. Leybold-Heraeus and Leybold-Heraeus Sogev SI v Seima* RIW 1978, 271; D Series I-6—B 3.
[409] [1999] 1 WLR 1305, CA.

FOT   In such a contract, the seller's obligation is to deliver, not to a ship **3.184** but to a truck at some named point.[410] An equivalent, involving railway transport, is FOR. Neither shipment term is much used in English mercantile practice, nor are they to be found in Incoterms 2000. They are more common in North American practice and, like the similar so-called FOB destination contract (where the expression does not necessarily signify the use of a ship), may be used just to identify an inland carrier engaged to take the goods on the final leg far removed from the start of the transit. It is not clear whether the seller's duty is performed when the goods are delivered to the carrier operating the truck or railway, given that US practice treats an FOB contract as being performed when the goods are taken in charge by the carrier, or only when they are loaded into the truck or rail conveyance. If the goods have been so delivered at this place, this will be the place where, under the contract, the goods were delivered. If they have not been so delivered, this will be the place where, under the contract, the goods should have been delivered.

CIF   In such a contract, the seller must enter into or adopt a contract of **3.185** carriage by sea under which the goods will be transported to the destination contemplated by the CIF contract (a named port of destination).[411] The essential feature of a CIF contract is that shipping documents are transferred to the buyer, as a result of which a contractual relationship is established between the buyer, on the one hand, and the insurer and carrier on the other hand.[412] Payment of the price of the goods becomes due when these documents are tendered. Under a CIF contract, the seller never delivers the goods to the buyer or even to the buyer's agent. Since the documents stand in for the goods, the place where the goods were delivered or should have been delivered must refer to the place where the documents were transferred or should have been transferred. This is so even though a documentary sale is a sale of goods and not of documents.[413] There are a number of variants of the CIF contract, such as the C&F (or CFR) contract and, more rarely, the CIF and C contract, the CIF and E contract, and the CIF and C and I contract. All of these involve different obligations from the normal CIF contract, but in none of them is the parties' agreement as to delivery any different and the position under Article 5(1)(b) will be the same as that for a CIF contract.

---

[410] See *Bulk Trading Corp Ltd v Zenziper Grains and Feedstuffs* [2001] 1 Lloyd's Rep 357.

[411] Delivery at the named port does not mean that the goods under the law prevailing at that port are capable of being discharged from the ship: *Congimex Cia Geral SARL v Tradax Export SA* [1983] 1 Lloyd's Rep 250. But the parties may stipulate that the contract is performed only if the goods are unloaded, which is commonly done in oil trading.

[412] See further Ch 5 below on the transfer of rights and obligations.

[413] As has been seen above, para 3.150, a documentary sale is a contract for the sale of goods because what is purchased is the goods not the documents.

3.186 Ex SHIP (OR DES)　In such a contract, the seller has to cause delivery to be made to the buyer from a ship which has arrived at the named port of delivery. If the goods have been so delivered at this port, this will be the place where, under the contract, the goods were delivered. If they have not been so delivered, this will be the place where, under the contract, the goods should have been delivered.

3.187 Ex QUAY (OR DEQ)　In such a contract, the seller's obligation in relation to delivery is the same as with the ex ship term and the above analysis in relation to that contract is equally applicable to a contract ex quay.

3.188 DELIVERED AT FRONTIER (FRANCO FRONTIER)　'This term is frequently used in the Continental export trade where no sea or air carriage is involved.'[414] The seller must deliver the goods at the specified frontier at the named place of delivery. For example, the contract may say 'Delivered at Franco-Italian frontier (Mondane)'. If the goods have been so delivered at this named place this will be the place where, under the contract, the goods were delivered. If they have not been so delivered, this will be the place where, under the contract, the goods should have been delivered.

3.189 DELIVERED FREE DUTY PAID (FRANCO DOMICILE OR FREE DELIVERY)　In such a contract, the seller must deliver the goods at the named place of destination (the buyer's address). If the goods have been so delivered at this named place this will be the place where, under the contract, the goods were delivered. If they have not been so delivered, this will be the place where, under the contract, the goods should have been delivered. The operation of Article 5(1)(b) in the case of such a contract can be illustrated by a practical example. English buyers enter into a contract with a German company for the supply of goods. The buyer's purchase order states the point of delivery of the goods, giving an address in England. The goods prove to be defective on delivery. The English courts have jurisdiction under Article 5(1)(b) on the basis that the place in a Member State where, under the contract, the goods were delivered is in England. The facts are taken from *MBM Fabri-Clad Ltd v Eisen-Und Huttenwerke Thale AG*,[415] a case decided under Article 5(1) of the Brussels Convention. The result was the same under the old law, although the process by which it was reached was different. The place of performance of the obligation to deliver was in England and, accordingly, the English courts had jurisdiction under Article 5(1) of the Brussels Convention. To take another illustration, the English courts would have jurisdiction under Article

---

[414] Schmitthoff, *Export Trade*, 2–044.
[415] [2000] IL Pr 505, CA; discussed further below, para 3.239.

5(1)(b) if the parties had agreed on delivery 'free London'.[416] To take a final example, if goods are ordered from a German company and invoiced as delivered to the Belgian buyer's factory (franco de fabriek van Conforma) in Belgium, the Belgian courts have jurisdiction under Article 5(1)(b) of the Brussels I Regulation. The facts are taken from *NV Conforma v Giulini Chemie GmbH*,[417] a decision of the Hof van beroep, Ghent, decided under Article 5(1) of the Brussels Convention.

An implied agreement on the place of delivery In the absence of such an express agreement by the parties on the place of delivery, is it permissible, as a matter of principle, to imply an agreement from the terms of the contract? This would undoubtedly be a place where, 'under the contract', the goods were delivered or should have been delivered. It is therefore submitted that this should be permissible.[418] The implied agreement should have to be demonstrated with reasonable certainty.[419] However, it is as yet unclear which terms of the contract would allow such an implication to be drawn.[420] Can an intention be implied from the circumstances of the case, for example from the fact that the parties have contracted before on a number of occasions and delivery has always been to one particular place? In such a case, the place of delivery is not identified 'under the contract'. It is identified by virtue of earlier contracts. Despite this, it should be permissible to imply an intention from the circumstances of the case.[421] What we should be concerned with is finding a clearly identifiable place of delivery and an examination of the circumstances of the case may reveal this. Another example where an intention can be implied from the circumstances is that given earlier of a self-evident place of delivery. For example, the goods are situated in England at the time they are sold to the English buyer by the foreign seller. The goods come into the possession of

3.190

---

[416] See *Tesam Distribution Ltd v Schuh Mode Team GmbH and Commerzbank AG* [1990] IL Pr 149, CA—a case decided under Art 5(1) of the Brussels Convention.

[417] Judgment of 23 June 1983, D Series I-5.1.2—B 41.

[418] There is an argument against allowing an implied choice in that Art 31 of the Vienna Convention, which is the substantive law background in most EC Member States, has no such category. It has a specified place of delivery and an allocated place in the absence of this, see Schlechtriem, 223. Forner, n 310 above, at 136, says the place of delivery must be 'stated' in the contract itself.

[419] This is by analogy with Art 3(1) of the Rome Convention, discussed below, para 13.44.

[420] Compare the position as to an implied choice of the governing law, see below, paras 13.44–53. The terms which would allow an inference to be drawn should not be ascertained by reference to the applicable law since this would defeat the purpose of Art 5(1)(b).

[421] AG Mayras in *Tessili v Dunlop*, n 388 above, at 1495; Takahashi, n 310 above, at 537. German courts have inferred an intention as to the place of payment from the circumstances of the case, see Judgment of 12 February 1981–10 U 195/80, Oberlandesgericht Stuttgart, NJW 1982, 529; RIW 1982, 591; VersR 1982, 378; D Series I-5.1.2—B 35; discussed below, para 3.283.

the buyer in England. In such a case, there can be no doubt that the place where the goods were delivered is in England. It can legitimately be said, in such circumstances, that this was the intention of the parties. There was no mis-delivery.

3.191 The problem with the concept of an implied agreement is that there is considerable scope for a judge to impose his idea of where the goods were delivered or should have been delivered and then dress this up as being what the parties intended. Finding an intention where there is in reality no such intention is a rather dubious exercise and some judges may be reluctant to go down this road.[422]

3.192 *No agreement on the place of delivery*   In the absence of an express or implied agreement by the parties as to the place of delivery, there are two alternative approaches that could be adopted.

3.193 The first is to say that Article 5(1)(b) does not apply. This is on the basis that there is no place of delivery 'under the contract'. This is to treat these words as operating as a limitation on the scope of Article 5(1)(b). If sub-paragraph (b) does not apply then subparagraph (a) applies.[423] It would then be necessary to identify the place of performance of the obligation in question without the benefit of the special rule for sale of goods. The place of performance of the obligation in question would be identified by application of the applicable national substantive law. The process of identifying this place will be more complex than if Article 5(1)(b) were to apply. Depending on what the obligation in question is, a place in a different Member State may be identified from that which would have been identified under Article 5(1)(b).[424] An overeagerness to withdraw matters from the scope of Article 5(1)(b) rather defeats the purpose of that provision. However, leaving it to a national court to identify the place of performance may well appeal to the European Court of Justice.[425]

3.194 The second possible approach is to say that Article 5(1)(b) will still apply. This is to regard the words 'under the contract' as having been inserted solely to explain how the place where goods have been delivered or should have been delivered is to be identified, rather than as a limitation on the scope of this provision. This leaves the problem of ascertaining the place where, under the contract, the goods were delivered or should have been delivered when there is no agreed place of delivery.[426] There is an

---

[422] When ascertaining the proper law of the contract some English judges were much less willing than others to infer a choice by the parties.

[423] Art 5(1)(c).

[424] See below, paras 3.255–297.   [425] See the *GIE* case, n 390 above.

[426] In some cases it may be possible to identify the place where the goods were delivered, see above, para 3.176, but not where they were delivered *under the contract*.

obvious temptation to ascertain this place by reference to the applicable substantive law. But this place must be identified by looking at where, 'under the contract', the goods were delivered or should have been delivered. The insertion of the words 'under the contract' makes it clear that this place is not to be ascertained by reference to the applicable substantive law. Moreover, a reference to the applicable substantive law would merely reintroduce what Article 5(1)(b) was designed to get away from.

Under this second approach, an autonomous community definition could **3.195** be given to the concept of the place where the goods were delivered and to the concept of the place where goods should have been delivered. This would apply in the absence of an agreement by the parties as to this place. Admittedly, if an autonomous community definition were to be adopted it cannot be said that the place has been identified by looking at where, 'under the contract', the goods were provided or should have been provided. Moreover, there would be the problem of deciding what this definition should be. The European Court of Justice would have to determine this. However, that Court would not be required to define the place of performance for every obligation that can arise, something which it has been very unwilling to do in the past, but merely for the one obligation which characterizes a contract for the sale of goods, namely that of delivery.

An autonomous community definition would be in keeping with the **3.196** spirit of the special rule in Article 5(1)(b) which aims to give an autonomous definition to the concept of the place of performance of the obligation in question in sale of goods cases. It is for this reason that, it is submitted, the second approach should be adopted and, in the absence of agreement by the parties, an autonomous community definition should be given to the concept of the place where the goods were delivered and to the concept of the place where goods should have been delivered. Moreover, it is particularly important to allow the opportunity for the development of an autonomous community definition because of cases of business to business e-commerce. In cases of performance online, if, in the absence of agreement on the place of delivery, recourse is had to substantive domestic law by virtue of Article 5(1)(a) this may not provide an answer.[427]

THE ALTERNATIVES FOR AN AUTONOMOUS COMMUNITY DEFINITION When **3.197** it comes to what this autonomous community definition should be there are two possibilities. The first is derived from the fact that the aim of a

---

[427] See below, paras 10.57–58.

sales contract is to ensure that goods are supplied by the seller to the buyer. Accordingly, the place where goods have been delivered or should have been delivered should be regarded as being the place where the goods are ultimately supplied to the buyer, irrespective of which party bears the risk of conveying the goods to that place. This place will normally be where the buyer is domiciled. There is support for such an approach from Advocate General Lenz in the *Custom Made case*,[428] who gave his opinion that where there is a claim for payment, the place of performance of the obligation in question under Article 5(1) of the Brussels Convention should be regarded as the place agreed in the contract at which the goods are intended to be supplied, irrespective as to which of the parties has to bear the risk of conveying the goods to that place.[429] Whilst no longer useful in relation to the obligation to pay, this idea could still be useful when it comes to defining the place of delivery.

3.198 The second possible answer is derived from the common core of the substantive law in the Member States. Given that 20 out of the 25 EC Member States have adopted the Vienna Convention this could form the basis of this common core. Article 31 of the Vienna Convention provides that:

> If the seller is not bound to deliver the goods at any other particular place, his obligation to deliver consists:
>   (a) if the contract of sale involves carriage of the goods—in handing the goods over to the first carrier for transmission to the buyer;
>   (b) if, in cases not within the preceding sub-paragraph, the contract relates to specific goods, or unidentified goods to be drawn from a specific stock or to be manufactured or produced, and at the time of the conclusion of the contract the parties knew that the goods were at, or were to be manufactured or produced at, a particular place—in placing the goods at the buyer's disposal at that place;
>   (c) in other cases—in placing the goods at the buyer's disposal at the place where the seller had his place of business at the time of the conclusion of the contract.

In the absence of agreement (express or implied) by the parties, (a), (b) and (c) would apply. Against a solution based on this substantive law rule, it has to be pointed out that the substantive law is concerned with risk in relation to carriage. This is a very different consideration from the considerations that should guide the allocation of jurisdiction under the Brussels I Regulation.

3.199 *Allocation of jurisdiction to the place where the goods were delivered or should have been delivered*   Article 5(1)(b) allocates jurisdiction to the place where

---

[428]   Case C-288/92 *Custom Made Commercial Ltd v Stawa Metallbau GmbH* [1994] ECR I-2913.
[429]   ibid, para 80.

the goods were delivered or *should have been delivered*. The latter deals with cases of non-delivery or mis-delivery.

NON-DELIVERY   Recourse to the place where the goods were delivered is **3.200** impossible in a case of non-delivery. In such a case, the place of perform-ance of the obligation in question is that where, under the contract, the goods should have been delivered. The process for ascertaining this place has already been discussed.[430]

MIS-DELIVERY   In a case of mis-delivery, the place of performance of the **3.201** obligation in question is that where, under the contract, the goods should have been delivered, rather than the place where they were delivered. To take a simple example, if goods are delivered to France when, under the contract, they should have been delivered to Germany, the place of per-formance of the obligation in question under Article 5(1)(b) will be Ger-many, rather than France. The argument may be raised that on a literal reading of Article 5(1)(b) the plaintiff has a choice of suing either in France (the place where the goods were delivered) or in Germany (the place where the goods should have been delivered). However, such an argu-ment is misplaced[431] since France is not the place where, 'under the con-tract', the goods were delivered. A problem could arise where goods should have been delivered to Germany but this has become impossible. In this situation, the law applicable to the sales contract allows the seller to deliver to France, which he does. The delivery to France is not 'under the contract'. This should be treated as a case of mis-delivery and the place of performance of the obligation in question is that where, under the con-tract, the goods should have been delivered, i.e. Germany.

The fact that the place where the goods *should* have been delivered **3.202** trumps the place where the goods *were* delivered, means that in every case of actual delivery there is the possibility of this place turning out not to have jurisdiction because the goods should have been delivered in some other place.

So far the discussion has proceeded on the basis that the mis-delivery has **3.203** not been accepted by the buyer. If it has been, this raises a separate prob-lem, which will be considered later,[432] of whether such an agreement should have any effect on the identification of the place where the goods were delivered or should have been delivered, given that the agreement has been entered into after the sales contract was made.

Problems in determining the place of delivery   Application of the place of **3.204** delivery rule to a number of concrete situations that can arise in relation to

---

[430] See above, paras 3.176–198.   [431] See Forner, n 310 above, at 136.
[432] See below, paras 3.221–224.

the delivery of goods shows that this rule is not without its difficulties and uncertainties.

3.205 DELIVERY TO MORE THAN ONE PLACE What happens if goods are delivered to more than one place and these are in different Member States? It is helpful to consider four different scenarios. The first is where there is one contract and one obligation to deliver the goods but this obligation is to be performed in two or more different Member States. For example, there is a contract for the sale of 100,000 tons of oil, 30,000 tons to be delivered to England and 70,000 tons to France. All 100,000 tons are rendered defective by contact with a previous cargo. The plaintiff wishes to sue in one Member State in respect of the whole 100,000 tons. The rule proposed in the preliminary draft Hague Judgments Convention would appear to allow this. Article 6 of this provided that a plaintiff may bring an action in contract in a state in which goods were supplied 'in whole or in part'. This necessarily means that more than one state will have jurisdiction. Moreover, it appears that this would allow each state to have jurisdiction over the whole of the goods (the whole 100,000 tons in our example).[433]

3.206 However, it is submitted that Article 5(1)(b) of the Brussels I Regulation should not operate in this situation to give jurisdiction in respect of the whole 100,000 tons to both England and France, thereby giving the plaintiff a choice of fora. In *Besix SA v Wasserreinigungsbau Alfred Kretzschmar GmbH & Co KG (WABAG)*,[434] the European Court of Justice held that Article 5(1) of the Brusssels Convention had to be interpreted as meaning that, in the event that the relevant contractual obligation, has been, or is to be performed in a number of places, jurisdiction to hear and determine the case cannot be conferred on the court within whose jurisdiction any one of those places of performance happens to be located.[435] Instead, jurisdiction has to be based on Article 2. It was clear from the wording of the provision, which is in the singular (the place of performance) that a single place of performance for the obligation in question must be identified.[436] The Court was concerned to avoid a multiplicity of competent courts and the risk that the plaintiff is able to choose the place of performance which he judges to be most favourable to his interests. The case concerned the situation where the place of performance of the obligation in question could not be determined because it consisted of an undertaking by the defendants not to do something (not to commit themselves to other partners) which is not subject to any geographical limit and was therefore characterized by a multiplicity of places of its performance. The

---

[433] See the Nygh and Pocar Report, n 332 above, at 49–50.
[434] Case C-256/00 [2003] 1 WLR 327.   [435] ibid, at [28].   [436] ibid, at [29], [32].

place of performance, in effect, was in any place in the world, including all the Contracting States. In our example, the choice is more limited, just referring to two Member States. However, this is just a question of degree. There is still no single place of performance. There is still the risk of a multiplicity of competent courts and the plaintiff being able to choose between two different Member States. In such a case, Article 2 must be used as the basis of jurisdiction.

This risk of a multiplicity of competent courts could be avoided by allo- **3.207** cating jurisdiction to the principal place of delivery, by analogy with the position where there are two or more obligations.[437] However, such an approach is incompatible with *Besix*, which makes it clear that Article 5(1) requires and is limited to cases where there is a single place of performance. This was said to be dictated by the text of the provision as well as the objectives of the Brussels Convention. In contrast, the principal place of delivery concept accepts that there is more than one place of performance.

The second scenario is the same as the first, but now the plaintiff wishes to **3.208** sue in England for merely the 30,000 tons delivered there. It is submitted that the English courts would probably have jurisdiction in relation to the 30,000 tons.[438] It is arguable that this does not fall foul of the spirit of the *Besix* case. There is not a multiplicity of competent fora in respect of the whole 100,000 tons. Neither does the plaintiff have a choice of bringing the action for the whole 100,000 tons in two different fora. To get round the requirement that a contractual obligation has to have a single place of performance, it would have to be argued that there are two differ-ent obligations; an obligation to deliver 30,000 tons to England and an obligation to deliver 70,000 tons to France. The plaintiff would be suing in respect of one obligation, with one place of delivery.[439] Not only would the *Besix* case have to be got round, but it would also be necessary to adopt a rule that part delivery would be enough to allocate jurisdiction over that part to the state where that part is delivered.

Giving the English (or any Member State's) courts jurisdiction in this **3.209** situation is consistent with the approach adopted by the European Court of Justice in *Shevill v Pressse Alliance SA*.[440] This was a case of multi-state defamation in which it was held that each Contracting State in which a defamatory publication was distributed and in which the victim claimed to have suffered injury to his reputation in that state only had jurisdiction under Article 5(3) of the Brussels Convention to rule on the injury caused

---

[437] See Takahashi, n 310 above, at 539.   [438] But see Takahashi, n 310 above, at 538–539.
[439] See Beaumont, n 324 above, at 21–22.   [440] Case C-68/93 [1995] 2 AC 18.

in that state to the victim's reputation in that state. The Court justified this rule in terms of the sound administration of justice. It was said that 'the courts of each Contracting State in which the defamatory publication was distributed and in which the victim claims to have suffered injury to his reputation are territorially the best placed to assess the libel committed in the state and to determine the extent of the corresponding damage'. Whether the English courts should have jurisdiction in this situation is a different matter and depends on the extent to which one likes or dislikes the approach adopted in the *Shevill* case. It has to be admitted that this approach can lead to splitting of the litigation between different Member States. The plaintiff may not be prevented from suing in England for the 30,000 tons delivered there and then suing in France for the remaining 70,000 tons.[441] It has also been objected that the *Shevill* case provides opportunities for forum shopping by the plaintiff.[442] The risk of forum shopping must not be exaggerated because what the plaintiff wants is a choice of fora in which he can sue for the whole damage, which is what *Shevill* prevents. The state of injury only had jurisdiction under Article 5(3) of the Brussels Convention to rule on the injury caused in that state to the victim's reputation in that state.

3.210 The third scenario is really a gloss on the second. This is where the arrangement between the parties is construed as a series of separate obligations, each of which may have a separate place of delivery. This would mean in our example that there is an obligation to deliver 30,000 in England and a separate obligation to deliver 70,000 tons in France. In such a case, the principal obligation should be regarded as being to deliver in France and the French courts would have jurisdiction over the whole 100,000 tons. However, it is highly artificial to regard there as being two obligations in such a case. The reality is that there is just one obligation to deliver.

3.211 The fourth scenario is where the arrangement between the parties is construed as a series of separate contracts, each of which may have a separate place of delivery. This is what happened in *Viskase Ltd v Paul Kiefel GmbH*.[443] The plaintiffs, English manufacturers, entered into eight contracts between 1989 and 1992 for the supply and delivery by the defendant, a German company, of machines. Under seven of the contracts delivery was to be ex works in Germany and this was therefore held to be

---

[441] Art 27 of the Regulation, discussed below, paras 3.313–329, will not apply because the subject-matter of the two sets of proceedings is different. Quaere whether the proceedings are related under Art 28, discussed below, paras 3.330–338.

[442] See A Reed and TP Kennedy, 'International Torts and *Shevill*: The Ghost of Forum-Shopping Yet to Come' [1996] LMCLQ 108.

[443] [1999] 1 WLR 1305.

the place of performance of the obligation in question. Accordingly, the English courts had no jurisdiction under Article 5(1) of the Brussels Convention in so far as the plaintiff's claim related to these contracts. However, they did have jurisdiction in so far as the claim related to delivery of the eighth machine, which fell to be delivered in England. There is no part delivery in such a case. Each contract involves an obligation to deliver in full in a single Member State.

DELIVERY TO ALTERNATIVE PLACES   It is not unknown for a contract to **3.212** provide that goods are to be delivered, at the option of the seller, in State A or State B. Let us assume that the seller fails to deliver the goods to either state. Where should the goods have been delivered for the purposes of this Article? One answer would be to say that the goods should have been delivered in either state and accordingly the plaintiff can designate either state as the place of delivery. In effect, the plaintiff would be able to choose the place of performance of the obligation in question. However, this would fall foul of the principle set out in the *Besix* case[444] that there must be a single place of performance. An alternative way of answering the question would be to say that Article 5(1)(b) is unworkable in this situation.[445] Recourse would then have to be had to Article 5(1)(a). The European Court of Justice has been prepared to say that if an Article in the Brussels Convention is unworkable in particular circumstances it cannot be used. Thus in the different context of Article 5(3) of that Convention, the European Court has acknowledged that it may be difficult or impossible to determine the place where the event giving rise to the damage occurred and in such circumstances the plaintiff will be unable to rely on this basis of jurisdiction.[446]

What if the seller exercises this option to deliver in alternative places (in **3.213** State A or State B) and delivers the goods in State A? At first sight, this would appear to be the place of delivery for the purposes of Article 5(1)(b). However, it has to be asked whether this too would fall foul of the principle set out in the *Besix* case, that there must be a single place of performance. It could be argued that once the seller exercises the option there is then a single place of performance. But if the plaintiff is the seller, he is effectively being given a choice of fora, which was a concern in the *Besix* case. In the light of this uncertainty, the alternative solution of saying that Article 5(1)(b) is unworkable may well be adopted.

[444] Case C-256/00 *Besix SA v Wasserreinigungsbau Alfred Kretzschmar GmbH & Co KG (WABAG)* [2002] ECR I-1699.
[445] Under the traditional English rules on jurisdiction the breach ground for service out of the jurisdiction is not satisfied in this situation, see below, para 4.86.
[446] Case C-51/97 *Réunion Européenne SA v Spliethoff's Bevrachtingskantoor BV* [1998] ECR I-6511.

3.214 A FICTITIOUS PLACE OF DELIVERY   What happens if the contract provides for delivery in a place when this is designed not to determine where delivery will actually take place, but solely to establish that the courts of a particular place have jurisdiction? That this is the aim can be shown by the fact that a place of delivery has been designated which has no connection with the reality of the contract and the obligations under the contract, obligations which, because of their very nature or because of geographical fact, can only be performed in some other country.[447] Goods may then be delivered to this other country (Member State A), rather than to the fictitious place of delivery (Member State B). Alternatively, faced with the impossibility of delivering in the fictitious place of delivery (Member State B), there may have been no delivery to any place. In either eventuality, an attempt may be made to bring an action in the fictitious place of delivery (Member State B) on the basis that, under the contract, goods 'should have been delivered' there, reliance being placed on the fact that Article 5(1)(b) fixes the place of performance by reference to the place where 'the goods were delivered or should have been delivered'. The European Court of Justice has held that where there is a fictitious place of performance this is governed not by Article 5(1) of the Brussels Convention but by Article 17 (now Article 23 of the Brussels I Regulation) and the requirements of that provision must be met.[448] In other words, the fictitious place of performance is treated as an attempted jurisdiction clause. The same approach should be adopted towards a fictitious place of delivery, bearing in mind that the place of delivery rule is being used to determine the place of performance of the obligation in question.

3.215 A DEEMED PLACE OF DELIVERY   An example of this phenomenon can be found in clause 31 of the Grain and Feed Trade Association Form 100, which states that: 'Buyers and Sellers agree that for the purpose of proceedings either legal or by arbitration this contract shall be deemed to have been made in England and to be performed there any correspondence in reference to the offer, the acceptance, the place of payment or otherwise notwithstanding . . .'. This form is used by parties from different EC States.[449]

3.216 In some circumstances, the deemed place of delivery will be a fictitious place of delivery and reference should be made to what is said above in relation to a fictitious place of delivery. However, there can be a deemed delivery which does not involve a fictitious place of delivery. The latter

---

[447] Case C-106/95 *MSG v Gravières Rhénanes* [1997] ECR I-911. Compare the earlier case of *Re the Supply of Wooden Panels* [1998] IL Pr 100, in which the District Court, Stuttgart, adopted a wider test for a fictitious place of performance.
[448] Case C-106/95 *MSG v Gravières Rhénanes* [1997] ECR I-911.
[449] *Toepfer International GmbH v Société Cargill France* [1998] 1 Lloyd's Rep 379, CA.

concept is fairly narrowly defined. It requires that the contract can only be performed in some state other than the one specified in the contract as the place of delivery. It is also concerned with motives, with the fact that a place of delivery is chosen so as to obtain jurisdiction. It finally requires that the place chosen has no connection with the reality of the contract. If we revert back to the example given earlier of a deemed place of delivery, it may be that the contract could be performed in England, the deemed place of delivery. It may be that England has some connection with the reality of the agreement. There is no fictitious place of performance but there remains the problem of a deemed place of delivery.

If England is the deemed place of delivery but the grain is actually **3.217** delivered to France, then is the place where, under the contract, the goods were delivered or should have been delivered England or France?[450] It is arguable that the place where 'under the contract' the goods were delivered or should have been delivered is England, because the contract provides that the goods were deemed to have been delivered there. In other words, effect should be given to the deemed delivery. But the better view is that a deemed place of delivery involves a degree of artificiality and, even if it does not fall within the technical definition of a fictitious place of delivery, is sufficiently close to this to merit being treated in the same way. Thus the requirements of Article 23 should have to be met.

CONSTRUCTIVE DELIVERY Does delivery for the purposes of Article **3.218** 5(1)(b) include the concept of constructive delivery? The essence of this concept is that the law permits a change of possession without any change of the actual custody of the goods.[451] English law allows constructive delivery in a number of situations, including that of a sale and leaseback of goods. Under this arrangement a seller in possession of goods sold acknowledges that he is holding the goods on account of the buyer in circumstances where he recognizes the purchaser's right to possess as owner and that his continuing possession is as a bailee with possession derived from that right. This amounts to delivery to the buyer immediately followed by redelivery to the seller as bailee. The fact that this concept is to be found in the English law of sales does not, of course, mean that it necessarily will fall within the concept of 'delivery' for the purposes of Article 5(1)(b). This concept should be given an autonomous community definition. Whether constructive delivery will fall within this community definition will depend on whether it can be said to be a

---

[450] If the goods are not delivered, is the place where they should have been delivered the deemed place of delivery or is it the place identified by the normal process that applies where there has been no delivery, as outlined above, para 3.200?

[451] See generally *Michael Gerson (Leasing) Ltd v Wilkinson* [2001] 1 All ER 148, CA.

general principle to be found in other national legal systems. If other national legal systems do not regard the arrangement under a sale and leaseback as constituting a delivery then a constructive delivery under English law will fall outside the community definition of a 'delivery'.[452] If the common core of the substantive law of international sale of goods is regarded as being contained in the Vienna Convention then the position is as follows. The Vienna Convention does not formally recognize the concept of constructive delivery: care was taken in drafting the Convention to avoid the complexities thrown up by delivery.[453] This is why the Convention speaks blandly of goods being handed over. There is no reason to see this omission, however, as a rejection of constructive delivery. The examples of delivery in Article 31 are hardly comprehensive. Rather, the lack of reference to constructive delivery is a gap in the coverage of the Convention to be filled in the usual way by invoking under Article 7(2) the general principles on which the Convention is based. In the straightforward drafting of the Convention, one can see the eschewal of technicalities and a full commitment to the autonomy of the parties. If a form of constructive delivery suits the parties, then a court or tribunal should see this as a form of delivery.

3.219 If one accepts, for the sake of argument, that 'delivery' encompasses the concept of constructive delivery, this leaves the problem of identifying the place where such a delivery occurs given that there is no change in the custody of the goods. It has not been necessary under English law to identify a moment, and hence the place, at which delivery takes place in cases of constructive delivery.[454] Nonetheless, under the English concept of constructive delivery the position would appear to be clear. The moment of delivery is the moment when the seller in possession acknowledges that he is holding the goods on account of the buyer. The rule in English law (to which documents of title at common law are an exception) is that, where there is a change of bailor and the bailee undertakes to hold the goods for the new bailor, this undertaking must be made in the form of an attornment by the bailee to the new bailor. From this it should follow that the seller, assuming the responsibility of a bailee, must acknowledge this to the buyer as bailor. This is an argument that the constructive delivery takes place where the seller's attornment is received by the

---

[452] Under German and Austrian law it is very common to have this type of deemed delivery (*constitutio possessorium*) for the purpose of passing of property. The rule in these systems is that the goods must physically be delivered (the French system is radically different). Sale and leaseback transactions are widely recognized across Europe. Given the passing of property rules in France—based upon the conclusion of the contract—there is no need actually to find a delivery.

[453] The notion of délivrance having given rise to great difficulty with ULIS.

[454] The *Michael Gerson* case, n 451 above, at 158 (*per* Clarke LJ).

buyer. Nevertheless, since constructive delivery is an artificial concept and the goods will normally be located in the place where the acknowledgement is made, there is a compelling argument that the substance of the constructive delivery occurs in the place where this acknowledgement is made.[455] The place of delivery would therefore be the place where this acknowledgement is made. The acknowledgement will normally be made in the Member State in which the seller has its seat.

A FLOATING PLACE OF DELIVERY There is a phenomenon of a floating **3.220** place of payment. A letter of credit may provide that 'we shall pay you as per your instructions'. There is no identifiable place of payment as at the time the contract is concluded but there is a mechanism for identifying this place and this place will crystallize later on when the beneficiary gives his instructions. Similarly, the sales contract could stipulate that 'delivery shall be as per your (the buyer's) instructions'. This would be a floating place of delivery. Effect has been given by the Court of Appeal to a floating place of payment in a letter of credit for the purposes of identifying the place of performance of the obligation in question under Article 5(1) of the Brussels Convention.[456] Arguably the same should happen with a floating place of delivery when applying Article 5(1)(b) of the Brussels I Regulation. This would mean that once the buyer has nominated the place of delivery, this would be the place where, under the contract, the goods were delivered (in cases where the goods were delivered to that place) or should have been delivered (in cases where the goods were not delivered to that place). Setting up a mechanism for identifying the place of delivery means that there is a place of delivery 'under the contract'. However, if the buyer nominating the place of delivery is the plaintiff, he is effectively being given a choice of fora, which was a concern in the *Besix* case. The present situation is very similar to that where the contract provides for delivery to alternative places and the seller exercises his option and delivers to State A. In that situation, it has been suggested[457] that, arguably, Article 5(1)(b) is unworkable in the light of the *Besix* case. The same argument can be made in the present situation.

AN AGREEMENT ON THE PLACE OF DELIVERY ENTERED INTO AFTER THE SALES **3.221** CONTRACT IS MADE We are concerned here with the scenario where the parties originally agree a place of delivery but after the sales contract is made they agree a different place of delivery. This situation raises difficulties not only in relation to the place of delivery rule but also in relation to the displacement of that rule.

---

[455] But would this be a place where 'under the contract' the goods were delivered? This would presumably depend on what the contract says about acknowledgement.
[456] *Credit Agricole Indosuez v Chailease Finance Corp* [2000] IL Pr 776, CA.
[457] Above, paras 3.212–213.

3.222 The difficulty when applying the place of delivery rule to a case where the parties have agreed a place of delivery after the sales contract was made is whether the delivery can then be said to be 'under the contract'. Looking at the context in which it appears, this phrase seems to be referring to the sales contract, and, accordingly, any agreement by the parties on the place of delivery must be under the sales contract. Is the subsequent agreement under the sales contract? It can only be said to be so if it is accepted that the subsequent agreement alters the original agreement (contained in the sales contract) in respect of the obligation to deliver.

3.223 There is then a separate problem. Can you have an implied agreement that alters the original agreement? The original agreement on the place of delivery can be implied from the terms of the contract and arguably even from the circumstances of the case.[458] Likewise, it should be possible to imply a subsequent agreement from the terms of the agreement and argu-ably even from the circumstances of the case. An example of where a subsequent agreement was implied from the circumstances of the case is *Manheim & Zoon BV v Tasselli*,[459] a case decided under Article 5(1) of the Brussels Convention. One of the invoices issued in relation to the goods bore the words 'franco frontiera italiana'. Nonetheless, Amsterdam was held to have been agreed by the parties as the place of performance of the obligation in question within the meaning of Article 5(1) of the Brussels Convention on the basis that the goods ordered through the defendant's Amsterdam agents had been transported to Amsterdam. It is submitted that if the same facts were to arise now, Amsterdam should be regarded as the place where, under the contract, the goods were delivered for the purposes of Article 5(1)(b).

3.224 Seemingly, an agreement on the place of performance of the obligation in question that is entered into after the sales contract was made can displace the place of delivery under the sales contract as the place of performance of the obligation in question. However, as will be seen later,[460] if what appears to be the view of the Commission, that the agreement must be explicit, is accepted, this would preclude the sort of agreement, that is implied from the circumstances of the case, that arose in the *Manheim* case.

3.225 A REFUSAL TO ACCEPT DELIVERY   What happens if the buyer refuses to accept delivery of the goods, claiming, for example, that the goods are defective? Can it be said that the goods have been delivered in that place for the purposes of Article 5(1)(b)? If the seller has discharged his obliga-tion to deliver the goods there can be no question but that the goods have

---

[458] See above, paras 3.178–191.
[459] Judgment of 6 July 1977, D Series I-5.1.2—B 14.   [460] See below, para 3.229.

been delivered. Whether the seller has discharged his obligation to deliver is a matter for the substantive law of international sale of goods, as determined by the rules on the applicable law. Under the Vienna Convention, in certain circumstances the obligation to deliver consists in handing goods over to a carrier.[461] This would be the moment of delivery and the fact that a buyer subsequently refuses to collect the goods from the carrier would be irrelevant. If the seller is prevented from discharging his obligation to deliver the goods owing to the refusal of the buyer to accept delivery, as might happen for example where an FOB buyer refuses or fails to nominate a ship or refuses to accept a tender of CIF documents, then the seller should still be able to rely on Article 5(1)(b) to found jurisdiction in the place where the goods should have been delivered. A refusal to accept delivery by the buyer should not operate to deprive a seller of the option of using Article 5(1)(b) to found jurisdiction.

3.226 THE PLACE OF DELIVERY IN CASES OF E-COMMERCE   This topic is dealt with in detail in Chapter 10.[462]

3.227 **Displacement Where It is Otherwise Agreed**   The special rule is subject to the caveat that it applies 'unless otherwise agreed'. This displacement rule ameliorates to some extent the weakness in Article 5(1)(b) whereby it subjects all obligations, not just the obligation to deliver, to the place of delivery rule, which can in turn mean a lack of connection between the obligation that the plaintiff is suing on and the place with jurisdiction.[463] For example, if goods have been delivered in France but it has been agreed that payment shall be made in England,[464] the place of performance of the obligation to pay will be England by virtue of the displacement rule. The displacement rule can be seen to give direct effect to the intentions of the parties as to the place of performance of the obligation in question. That is not to say that the place of delivery rule ignores the parties' intentions. After all the place of delivery is determined by looking at the parties' intentions as regards this place. For the displacement rule to operate, what is required is that there is: (i) an agreement; (ii) on the place of performance in question; (iii) this place is somewhere other than where the goods were delivered or should have been delivered. These three requirements will now be examined. Finally, the question of what happens when the displacement rule operates will be examined.

---

[461] Art 31; discussed below, para 3.198.   [462] See below, paras 10.55–74.

[463] See the criticism of Art 5(1)(b) by Beaumont, n 324 above, at 20–21.

[464] It has been suggested that the agreement may not only take the form that payment for the goods is to be made in X but also a more general form that confers jurisdiction in X for any dispute over payment under the contract, see Beaumont, n 324 above, at 21, n 28. However, in the latter situation it could be argued that Art 23 of the Regulation would apply.

3.228   *An agreement*   The Explanatory Memorandum accompanying the Brussels I Regulation states that the place of delivery rule 'may, however, be "displaced" by an explicit agreement on the place of performance'. Article 5(1)(b) does not lay down any formalities in relation to the agreement. However, the substantive law applicable to the agreement may require that certain formalities are satisfied.[465] It is submitted that, in principle, these should be applicable. In *SPRL Creations Davos v Katag Gruppe top Textil AG*,[466] the Tribunal de commerce, Brussels, held that since Article 5(1) of the Brussels Convention did not prescribe any formalities for a contractual agreement on the place of performance, the matter was governed by the law applicable to the contract. This was Belgian law and under that law the parties could agree on a place of performance seemingly without any formalities. This reasoning would equally apply to Article 5(1)(b), given that this too does not lay down any formalities in relation to the agreement on the place of delivery. This contrasts with the position under Article 23 of the Regulation. The European Court of Justice has held that formalities under national law did not apply in relation to an agreement on jurisdiction under Article 17 of the Brussels Convention, given that this provision itself laid down certain formalities.[467] To require a plaintiff to satisfy both this requirement and any formalities laid by the applicable law would impose an undue burden on the parties that would interfere with normal commercial practices.

3.229   The Explanatory Memorandum appears to require that the agreement is 'explicit'. An 'explicit' agreement will normally be in writing or at least evidenced in writing. But, in principle, there is nothing to stop it being oral, although there may be problems of proof in respect of such an agreement. However, it would rule out the possibility of inferring an agreement from the conduct of the parties, as happened in the *Manheim* case,[468] where it will be recalled that Amsterdam was held to have been agreed by the parties as the place of performance of the obligation in question following the transportation of goods to there. Neither would it be possible to infer an agreement on the place of performance from a previous course of dealing between the parties or from a trade practice. It is hard to see why, as a matter of principle, an implicit agreement should not be recognized for these purposes. The essential requirement should be that the agreement on the place of performance is clear and, if it is, it should not matter that it is implicit, rather than explicit. The Explanatory

---

[465] This would be identified by the application of Art 9 of the Rome Convention, discussed below, paras 13.256–258.
[466] Judgment of 13 June 1977, D Series I-5.1.2—B 12.
[467] cf. Case 150/80 *Elefanten Schuh GmbH v Jacqmain* [1981] ECR 1671.
[468] See above, para 3.223.

Memorandum only states the views of the Commission and in this instance its view should be ignored.

Normally, you would expect to find the agreement on the place of per- **3.230** formance in the contractual documentation. For example, sales invoices will often contain a provision on the place where payment is to be made.[469] However, seemingly, there is nothing to stop agreement being reached after the sale of goods contract has been made. The agreement could be contained in a separate contract. There is no requirement that the agreement on the place of performance is 'under the contract', i.e. under the sale of goods contract.[470] Provided this agreement on the place of performance is clear, the displacement rule should operate. This would be consistent with the position under Article 5(1) of the Brussels Convention, in relation to which an agreement on the place of performance of the obligation in question could be contained in a separate agreement from the sales agreement.[471] The agreement must be valid according to the law applicable to it.[472] There is nothing to stop the parties agreeing on a place of performance which is different from the place laid down by the applicable substantive law.[473]

On the place of performance of the obligation in question   It is important to **3.231** identify what the obligation in question is because the parties may have agreed a place of performance for some obligations but not for others. The agreement must be 'on the place of performance'. But it does not actually have to use this wording. Where, for example, a claim is brought for payment of goods it would be enough to show that the parties have explicitly agreed that payment is to be made in a particular Member State.[474] This was the position under Article 5(1) of the Brussels Convention. For example, in *SPRL Creations Davos v Katag Gruppe top Textil AG*,[475] invoices stated that the price of goods was payable in Brussels. The Tribunal de commerce, Brussels, held that, as a result of this agreement,

[469] See, e.g. the *SPRL Creations Davos* case, n 466 above; *SA Etablissement Legrand v SA Cebelor* RGDC 1988, 557, Note: Barnich; D Series I-5.1.1—B 26.

[470] Compare the position in relation to the place where the goods were delivered or should have been delivered, discussed above.

[471] Judgment of 25 June 1975, *Cartonnagefabriek NV v Les Editions René Touret* Gerechtshof, Arnhem, NJ 1977, No 304; D Series I-5.1.2—B 2.

[472] See Art 8(1) of the Rome Convention, discussed below, paras 13.143–149.

[473] The *SPRL Creations Davos* case, n 466 above. The two will seldom be different. In EC countries the place of performance laid down by the substantive law is subject to any contrary agreement by the parties.

[474] But compare Takahashi, n 310 above, at 537–538, who interprets the displacement rule as requiring the parties to agree that Art 5(1)(b) will not apply. This does not square with the wording of the provision, fails to give effect to the intentions of the parties in any meaningful way and would require the parties to have knowledge of the law.

[475] n 466 above. See also *SA Etablissement Legrand v SA Cebelor*, n 469 above.

Belgium was the place of performance of the obligation to pay and that, accordingly, the Belgian courts had jurisdiction. Doubtless, the result would be the same under Article 5(1)(b) of the Brussels I Regulation.

3.232 A problem can arise over whether the parties, who have undoubtedly reached agreement on various aspects of payment of the price, have actually agreed on the *place* of payment. This is illustrated by *Re The Cross-Border Dyeing of Clothes*, a case on Article 5(1) of the Brussels Convention.[476] The contract provided for payment of cash on collection of goods (in the place of collection). The Oberlandesgericht, Schleswig-Holstein, held that this was not an agreement on the place of performance as regards payment but only on a remittance obligation. Nevertheless, it is common for the parties to reach an agreement on the place of payment of the price, which means that the displacement rule will frequently operate, at least in cases where the obligation in question is that of payment. The problem of the parties agreeing on a fictitious place of performance has already been mentioned[477] and it has been seen that in such a case the agreement is governed not by Article 5(1) but by Article 23 of the Brussels I Regulation.

3.233 There is also a problem where the parties agree on a place of performance of the obligation in question in a non-Member State. For example, the place where, under the contract, the goods were delivered or should have been delivered is in Germany but the parties have agreed that payment is to be made in New York. The plaintiff is suing for payment. It has been argued earlier[478] that in this situation the displacement rule should not operate and that jurisdiction should be allocated to Germany by virtue of Article 5(1)(b).

3.234 *This place is somewhere other than where the goods were delivered or should have been delivered*   The displacement rule involves the displacement of the place of performance of the obligation in question, as identified by the place of delivery rule, by a *different* place of performance, as agreed by the parties. It follows that, in a case where an action is brought for the payment of goods, which are delivered in France, but the parties have agreed on payment in France, that will be the place of performance of the obligation in question by virtue of the place of delivery rule, rather than the displacement rule.

The displacement rule is unlikely to operate in cases where the obligation in question is that of delivery of the goods, including the obligation to deliver goods in conformity with the contract. The place of performance

---

[476] Case 2 U 78/91 [1994] IL Pr 202.   [477] See above, para 3.214.
[478] Above, para 3.168.

of this obligation is determined by looking at the place of delivery[479] and will therefore normally be in the same place as that where the goods were delivered under the contract as provided in the rule set out in Article 5(1)(b). Accordingly, the displacement rule will not operate. The displacement rule is most likely to operate in cases involving an obligation other than that of delivery, the most obvious example being the obligation to pay, this being an obligation in respect of which the parties will normally have agreed on the place of performance.

What happens when the displacement rule operates? All that Article 5(1)(b) **3.235** expressly tells us is that the place of performance of the obligation in question is not the place in a Member State where, under the contract, the goods were delivered or should have been delivered. Where then is the place of performance of the obligation in question? How is this to be identified? It has been argued earlier[480] that, in cases where the displacement rule operates, jurisdiction is implicitly allocated to the place of performance of the obligation in question agreed by the parties. This allocation is effected by Article 5(1)(b) itself and recourse is not to be had to Article 5(1)(a). The alternative, which is not supported by the authors of this book, is to treat this situation as falling outside the scope of Article 5(1)(b) and recourse must therefore be had to Article 5(1)(a).[481]

Sale of goods cases falling outside the special rule

Article 5(1)(c) of the Brussels I Regulation provides that if Article 5(1)(b) **3.236** does not apply then Article 5(1)(a) applies. Article 5(1)(b) does not apply to cases falling outside the scope of that provision.[482] In such cases, Article 5(1)(a) applies. A few words need to be said about what the effect of this is. Then attention will be turned to the process of identifying the place of performance of the obligation in question under Article 5(1)(a).

The effect of the application of Article 5(1)(a) It is important to note **3.237** that application of the rule in Article 5(1)(a) will not necessarily result in jurisdiction being allocated to the courts of a Member State. It will only do so if the place of performance of the obligation in question is in a Member State. In sale of goods cases falling outside the scope of Article

---

[479] See the *Viskase* case, n 443 above; *Boss Group Ltd v Boss France SA* [1997] 1 WLR 351, CA; *Mode Jeune Diffusion SA v Maglificio il Falco di Tiziana Goti* [1998] IL Pr 812, French Cour de cassation.

[480] See above, para 3.168.

[481] If the traditional approach towards identification of the place of performance of the obligation in question is adopted for the purposes of Art 5(1)(a), see below, paras 3.254–297, there would not appear to be any practical difference in an allocation effected under this provision as opposed to one under Art 5(1)(b).

[482] See above, paras 3.146–171. The Brussels and Lugano Conventions and the Modified Regulation have no equivalent of Art 5(1)(b). The identification of the place of performance of the obligation in question in these cases is discussed below, para 3.247.

5(1)(b), it can well happen that the place of performance of the obligation in question is in a non-Member State. The obvious example of a sale of goods case falling outside the scope of Article 5(1)(b) is where the goods were delivered or should have been delivered to a place in a non-Member State.[483] Article 5(1)(a) will apply but, if the obligation in question is that of delivery, the place of performance of this obligation under Article 5(1)(a) will be in that same non-Member State. Accordingly, Article 5(1) will not operate to provide a forum for trial in a Member State and the plaintiff will have to sue in the Member State where the defendant is domiciled. However, if the obligation in question is not one of delivery but instead, for example, the obligation to pay, the place of performance could be in a Member State. For example, a New York seller sues a buyer, domiciled in France, for the price of goods delivered in New York ex factory, the price being payable in England. This case falls outside the scope of Article 5(1)(b) because the place of delivery under the contract is in a non-Member State.[484] Article 5(1)(a) will apply and the place of performance of the obligation to pay is in England. The upshot is that the plaintiff has the option of suing the defendant either in France, by virtue of Article 2, or in England, by virtue of Article 5(1)(a).

3.238   The other possible example of a sale of goods case falling outside the scope of Article 5(1)(b) is where the parties have not agreed on any place of delivery. If the argument is accepted that this situation is outside the scope of Article 5(1)(b)[485] then Article 5(1)(a) will apply. Let us assume that the seller has his place of business in France and that the applicable substantive law is contained in the Vienna Convention. According to Article 31(c) of the Vienna Convention, the place of delivery is in France. This will be the place of performance of the obligation in question for the purposes of Article 5(1)(a) of the Brussels I Regulation and the French courts will have jurisdiction under this provision.

3.239   **The importance of identifying the obligation in question**   It has been seen that, in cases coming within the scope of Article 5(1)(b), the significance of identifying the obligation in question has been reduced considerably by the fact that the place of delivery rule applies, regardless of the obligation. But in cases falling outside the scope of this provision, and

---

[483] It is argued above, paras 3.164–165, that this is the only clear example. Obviously Art 5(1)(b) will also not apply if it is not a sale of goods case.

[484] See the discussion above, paras 3.166–168, where it is argued that the displacement rule under Art 5(1)(b) cannot operate because there is no special rule to displace.

[485] See the discussion, above, para 3.169. If it is accepted that this situation is *within* the scope of Art 5(1)(b) of the Brussels I Regulation then there is the practical problem, discussed above, paras 3.192–198, of identifying the place where, under the contract, the goods were delivered or should have been delivered.

accordingly within Article 5(1)(a), it is vital to identify the obligation in question[486] because different obligations may have different places of performance. Indeed, the parties may argue over what the obligation in question is because of the effect that this has on the place of performance. *MBM Fabri-Clad Ltd v Eisen-Ud Huttenwerke Thale AG*[487] is a good illustration of this. It will be recalled that the plaintiff argued that the obligation in question was to supply goods of the required specification at the place of delivery in England. The place of performance of this obligation would undeniably be England and the English courts would accordingly have jurisdiction under Article 5(1) of the Brussels Convention. The defendants argued that the obligation was to supply goods and that this was a separate obligation from that of delivery. This led on to the argument that the place of performance of the obligation to supply (ie make available) involving design and manufacture was Germany where the goods were designed and manufactured. The defendants argued in the alternative that the obligation was to manufacture the goods in an appropriate way; the place of performance of that obligation would undeniably be in Germany where the defendants manufactured the goods. The Court of Appeal held that the obligation in question was to supply goods in conformity with the contract but this was to supply by delivery in England.[488]

Even more fundamentally, the identification of the obligation in question **3.240** can determine whether any Member State has jurisdiction under Article 5(1)(a). For example, if the obligation is to deliver goods, and this will encompass cases where the goods are defective, the place of performance of the obligation will be in the state where delivery takes place.[489] It follows, that if delivery takes place in New York, a plaintiff will be unable to bring an action in any Member State on the basis of Article 5(1)(a). In contrast, if the obligation in question is to pay for the goods and payment is to be made in France, this will be the place of performance of the obligation in question. The French courts will then have jurisdiction under Article 5(1)(a).

Identification of the place of performance of the obligation in 3.241 question   We will start with an examination of the approach adopted by the European Court of Justice for the identification of the place of performance of the obligation in question under Article 5(1) of the Brussels Convention (the traditional approach) and then discuss its continued use under the Brussels and Lugano Conventions and the Modified Regulation

[486] The concept of the obligation in question is discussed above, paras 3.83–141.
[487] [2000] IL Pr 505, CA; discussed above, para 3.112; Beaumont, n 324 above, at 23–24.
[488] At 511 (*per* Pill LJ); at 513 (*per* Aldous LJ).
[489] See the *Viskase* case, n 443 above; the *Boss* case, n 479 above; the *Mode Jeune* case, n 479 above.

and, more importantly, whether this approach should be applied to Article 5(1)(a) of the Brussels I Regulation.

3.242 *The traditional approach*   The European Court of Justice held repeatedly in relation to the place of performance under Article 5(1) of the Brussels Convention that the national court before which the matter is brought 'must determine in accordance with own rules of conflict of laws what is the law applicable to the legal relationship in question and define in accordance with that law the place of performance of the contractual obligation in question'.[490] It is open to the parties to specify the place of performance by means of a clause which is valid under the law applicable to the contract and the formalities of Article 17 (now Article 23) do not have to be complied with.[491] This assumes that the applicable substantive law allows the parties to agree on the place of performance, which in practice it will do.[492]

3.243 The first decision of the European Court of Justice to set out this approach was *Tessili v Dunlop*,[493] which was an international sale of goods case. The buyer brought an action for annulment of a contract for the sale of ski suits against the seller claiming defects in the suits. The European Court of Justice, after setting out the relevant principles, sent the case back to the German courts to apply them to the facts of the case. The Oberlandesgericht, Frankfurt am Main, held that, according to German substantive law,[494] where claims were made for rescission the place of performance would be the buyer's place of business, where in accordance with the contract the goods to be returned were situated.[495] The German courts therefore had jurisdiction. Of the three subsequent cases confirming this approach, the first one was concerned with the international sale of goods.[496] This was *Custom Made Commercial Ltd v Stawa Metallbau GmbH*,[497] where the Bundesgerichtshof referred to the European Court of Justice the question whether the normal rule, whereby the place of performance under Article 5(1) of the Brussels Convention is determined pursuant to the substantive law applicable to the obligation in issue under

---

[490] Case 12/76 *IndustrieTessili Italiana Como v Dunlop AG* [1976] ECR 1473, 1485; Case C-288/92 *Custom Made Commercial Ltd v Stawa Metallbau GmbH* [1994] ECR I-2913; Case C-440/97 *GIE Groupe Concorde v Master of the Vessel Suhadiwarno Panjan* [1999] ECR I-6307; Case C-420/97 *Leathertex Divisione Sinetici SpA v Bodetex BVBA* 1999] ECR I-6747.

[491] Case C 56/79 *Zelger v Salinitri* [1980] ECR 89; The *GIE* case, n 490 above.

[492] Kennett, n 312 above, at 193 et seq.

[493] n 490 above.

[494] This was the applicable law according to German private international law.

[495] Judgment of 23 March 1977–21 U 158/74, D Series I-5.1.2—B 9.

[496] The *GIE* case, n 490 above, involved an action by an insurer against a carrier; the *Leathertex* case, n 490 above, involved claims for commission and compensation in lieu of notice following the termination of a commercial agency agreement.

[497] Case C-288/92 [1994] ECR I-2913.

the conflicts rules of the court hearing the case, should be departed from in a case concerning a claim for payment of the price brought by the supplier against the customer under a contract for manufacture and supply. According to the conflicts rules of the court hearing the case, that contract was governed by the Uniform Law on the International Sale of Goods, annexed to the Hague Convention of 1 July 1964. Article 59(1) of this Uniform Law provides that the place of performance of the obligation on the buyer to pay the price to the seller is the seller's place of business or, if he does not have a place of business, his habitual residence, subject only to the proviso that the parties to the contract have not stipulated a different place for the performance of that obligation under Article 3 of that law.

In this situation, two arguments can be made for departing from the nor- **3.244** mal rule for determining the place of performance of the obligation in question. The first is that it can in certain circumstances lead to jurisdiction being allocated to the courts of a state that has no connection with the dispute. This was a matter of concern to Advocate General Lenz, who said that Article 59(1) is 'not able to confer jurisdiction on a court which is physically proximate to the relationship in issue'.[498] The place of performance of the buyer's obligation to pay is independent of the seller's reciprocal obligation to supply goods, the defective performance of which is generally the cause of the dispute about payment. Consequently, the Advocate General proposed a rule for cases to which the first part of Article 59(1) of the Uniform Law on the International Sale of Goods is applicable whereby the place of performance within the meaning of Article 5(1) of the Brussels Convention is the place agreed in the contract at which the goods are intended to be supplied, irrespective of which of the parties has to bear the risk of conveying the goods to that place.[499] However, the European Court of Justice rejected this suggestion. The Court accepted that a defendant may be sued in the courts for the place of performance of the obligation in question even where the court thus designated is not that which has the closest connection with the dispute.[500] The Court pointed out that the use of criteria other than the place of performance might jeopardize the possibility of foreseeing which court will have jurisdiction and for that reason would be incompatible with the aim of the Convention. If one used as the sole criterion the existence of a connecting factor between the facts at issue in a dispute and a particular court this would involve looking at the pleas relied on by the defendant and would render Article 5(1) nugatory.[501]

---

[498] At 2932. [499] At 2934, para 82. [500] At 2957, para 21.
[501] At 2956–2957, paras 18 and 19.

3.245 The second argument, which was considered but then rejected by Advocate General Lenz is that application of Article 59(1) of the Uniform Law results in jurisdiction being allocated to the courts of the plaintiff's domicile.[502]

3.246 The Court concluded that Article 5(1) of the Brussels Convention must be interpreted as meaning that the place of performance of the obligation to pay the price is to be determined pursuant to the substantive law governing the obligation in dispute under the conflicts rules of the court seised, even where those rules refer to the application to the contract of provisions such as those of the Uniform Law on the International Sale of Goods, annexed to the Hague Convention of 1 July 1964.

3.247 *The traditional approach and the Brussels and Lugano Conventions and the Modified Regulation*   In the situation where the Brussels or Lugano Convention applies,[503] one is faced with a differently worded Article 5(1) from that contained in the Brussels I Regulation. Article 5(1) of these two Conventions simply provides that, in matters relating to a contract, jurisdiction is allocated to 'the courts for the place of performance of the obligation in question'. There is no autonomous definition of this place for contracts for the sale of goods or the provision of services. The traditional approach was developed so as to identify the place of performance in question for the purpose of Article 5(1) of the Brussels Convention and will continue to be applied in cases coming under either this Convention or the Lugano Convention until such time as these two Conventions are amended to bring them into line with the Brussels I Regulation.[504] The traditional approach will also continue to apply to the interpretation of the contract provision of the Modified Regulation that allocates jurisdiction within the United Kingdom. Although this by and large adopts the terminology of the Brussels I Regulation, one notable exception is the contract provision[505] which keeps the old terminology based on the Brussels Convention, rather than adopting the autonomous definition of the place of performance of the obligation in question for contracts for the sale of goods or the provision of services.

3.248 *Should the traditional approach be applied to Article 5(1)(a) of the Brussels I Regulation?*   The intention of the EC Commission when putting forward

---

[502] AG Lenz, at 2922, para 32, denied that there was any such antipathy when interpreting the Convention.

[503] See above, paras 2.04–09.

[504] The question will then arise under the Conventions, as it does under the Brussels I Regulation, of whether the traditional approach should be adopted for cases falling outside Art 5(1)(b).

[505] Sch 4, para 3(a) of the Civil Jurisdiction and Judgments Act 1982, as substtuted by SI 2001/3929, Sch 2, Part II, para 4.

the proposed new Article 5(1) was that where rule (a) applies: 'Jurisdiction will lie with the court designated by the rules of private international law of the state seised as the court for the place of performance of the obligation in question'.[506] In other words, the traditional approach used in relation to the Brussels Convention should apply.[507]

There is, though, an alternative approach that could be adopted. The **3.249** European Court of Justice could introduce an autonomous definition or definitions for the place of performance of the obligation in question. This would avoid reference to the applicable national substantive law with all its drawbacks. It might also be argued that this would be more in keeping with the autonomous approach under the place of delivery rule under Article 5(1)(b). Such an argument is not entirely convincing. As regards contracts for the sale of goods, it is true that the drafters of the Brussels I Regulation clearly intended to alter the approach towards identifying the place of performance of the obligation in question. But the only thing intended to be altered was sale of goods cases coming within the scope of the special rule, not sale of goods cases coming outside the scope of that rule. We are concerned with a situation where Article 5(1)(a) applies unaffected by Article 5(1)(b) and Article 5(1)(a) deliberately maintains the Brussels Convention rule regarding contractual obligations.

Moreover, none of the obvious possibilities for an autonomous definition **3.250** is likely to be attractive to the European Court of Justice. There are three obvious possibilities for such a definition. First, it would be possible in sale of goods cases falling outside the scope of Article 5(1)(b) to seek an autonomous definition by looking for the obligation that characterizes the sale of goods contract.[508] According to Advocate General Mayras in the *Tessili* case,[509] this is the obligation to deliver the goods, the place of performance of which is the place of delivery. But the case falls outside the special rule in Article 5(1)(b) in the first place because there is no place of delivery in an EC Member State. In other words, this is a definition which would necessarily deprive the EC Member States of jurisdiction.

Second, a more complicated alternative would be to provide an autono- **3.251** mous definition of the place of performance for the particular obligation in question.[510] This approach was criticized by Advocate General Lenz and Advocate General Colomer in the context of reform of Article 5(1) of

---

[506] See the Explanatory Memorandum, n 325 above, 14.
[507] Takahashi, n 310 above, at 531 and Forner, n 310 above, at 135 presume without authority or discussion that this is the case.
[508] See the opinion of AG Ruiz-Jarabo Colomer in the *GIE* case, n 490 above, at 893.
[509] n 493 above, at 1494–1495.
[510] See the observations of the Commission and the UK and German Governments in the *GIE* case, n 490 above.

the Brussels Convention: it would create legal uncertainty;[511] with some obligations, such as the obligation to pay, it would lead to a definition derived from national law that would not fit in with the principles under the Convention;[512] with the obligation to pay there is no obvious place of performance, Member States being evenly divided as to whether the place in question is the debtor's domicile or the creditor's, so that whichever definition from national law is adopted, some Member States would be forced to adopt a definition which is contrary to their own.[513]

3.252 Third, the European Court of Justice could seek to establish, having regard to the nature of the relationship creating the obligation and the circumstances of the case, the place where performance actually took place or should have taken place. The question of whether this approach should be adopted in relation to Article 5(1) of the Brussels Convention was referred to the European Court of Justice in the *GIE Group Concorde* case, which rejected the use of such an approach.[514]

3.253 In conclusion, it is submitted that the place of performance of the obligation in question under Article 5(1)(a) of the Brussels I Regulation should be ascertained by applying the traditional approach adopted in relation to Article 5(1) of the Brussels Convention.

3.254 **Application of the traditional approach to contracts for the international sale of goods: applying rules on the applicable law**   As has been seen, it is necessary to apply conflict of law rules so as to identify the applicable substantive law. In a case of sale of goods, the rules in the United Kingdom for determining the applicable substantive law are to be found in the Rome Convention on the law applicable to contractual obligations of 1980.[515] However, as has been seen,[516] a number of EC Member States have adopted the 1955 Hague Convention on the law applicable to international sale of goods.[517] In these Member States

---

[511] AG Leger in the *Leathertex* case, n 490 above, para 119.

[512] If the creditor's domicile is adopted this will allow the plaintiff to sue in the Member State in which he is domiciled; if the debtor's domicile is adopted this will be the same as the defendant's domicile and the plaintiff will be denied an alternative forum in which to bring his action under Art 5(1), AG Leger in the *Leathertex* case, n 490 above, paras 93–96. See also AG Ruiz-Jarabo Colomer in the *GIE* case, n 490 above, at 879–881, paras 50–58.

[513] AG Leger in the *Leathertex* case, n 490 above, para 92. But see the opinion of AG Lenz in the *Custom Made* case, n 490 above, 2934, para 82 who said that an autonomous definition in terms of the place at which the goods are intended to be supplied should be adopted.

[514] In Case C-125/92 *Mulox IBC Ltd v Geels* [1993] ECR I-4075, an autonomous definition was adopted, for the purposes of Art 5(1) of the Brussels Convention, in matters relating to individual contracts of employment. This was based on the objectives and scheme of the Convention. This looks to be a different approach from that discussed in the *GIE* case.

[515] *Ferguson Shipbuilders Ltd v Voith Hydro GmbH & Co KG* 2000 SLT 229. The Rome Convention is discussed below, paras 13.01–321.

[516] Above, para 3.32.   [517] Discussed in detail below, paras 15.10–64.

recourse will be had to this Convention,[518] provided, of course, that the matter falls within its scope,[519] rather than to the Rome Convention.[520]

Application of the traditional approach to contracts for the inter- 3.255 national sale of goods: the place of performance according to the relevant substantive law Having identified the applicable substantive law, it is necessary to examine this so as to determine the place of performance of the obligation in question. One common theme to be found in the substantive law, and this is regardless of the obligation in question and regardless of which Member State's law is being applied, is that the parties are able to agree on the place of performance of an obligation.[521] One consequence of this is that it is commonplace for national courts to look directly at the parties' agreed place of performance without bothering first to identify the relevant applicable law.[522] It is a matter for the applicable substantive law of international sales to say whether it is possible to have an implied agreement as to the place of performance. There are several examples of national courts inferring an agreement on the place of performance of the obligation in question from the conduct of the parties.

In the situation where there is no agreement by the parties, the substan- 3.256 tive law has to allocate a place of performance to a particular obligation. Legislation on the international sale of goods defines the place of performance for some obligations, although different substantive laws will sometimes disagree on where this place is located. However, it does not do so for all obligations and in such cases identification of the place of performance becomes very problematic.[523] The place of performance (in the absence of agreement by the parties) of various obligations that arise out of a contract for the international sale of goods will now be examined.

The place of performance of the seller's obligation to deliver the goods In its 3.257 starkest form, the failure to perform the obligation to deliver goods involves a simple failure to deliver the goods at all.[524] However, it can go

---

[518] See, e.g.: for France, *San Carlo Gruppo Alimentaire SpA v SNC Vico* [1996] IL Pr 493, French Cour de cassation; for the Netherlands, The Hof's-Hertogenbosch, decision of 27 March 1979, NJ 1980, 512 and the court of Arnhem, 21 February 1980, Asser 12.225, both considered by Boele-Woelki in 'Convention sur la Loi Applicable aux Ventes a Caractere International d'Objets Mobiliers Corporels, du 15 Juin 1955' in *Les Nouvelles Conventions de la Haye*, 15–17.
[519] On which see below, paras 15.11–18.
[520] Art 21 of the Rome Convention. [521] See Kennett, n 492 above.
[522] *Tesam Distribution Ltd v Schuh Mode Team GmbH and Commerzbank AG* [1990] II Pr 149, CA. But see *Anton Huber GmbH and Co v Polyspace SA* [2003] IL Pr 10 at 203, where the French Cour de cassation held that the appeal court was in error in not referring to the Vienna Convention when this was the applicable law.
[523] cf. AG Ruiz-Jarabo Colomer in the *GIE* case, n 490 above, at 881.
[524] See, e.g. *Tesam Distribution Ltd v Schuh Mode Team GmbH and Commerzbank AG* [1990] IL Pr 149, CA.

wider than this. In *Tessili v Dunlop*,[525] Advocate General Mayras gave his opinion that, where the seller is at fault as regards the terms and conditions of delivery of the goods (ie the date and place of delivery), he is regarded as having failed to perform his obligation to deliver the goods.[526] The place of performance of this obligation is the place of delivery of the goods.[527] The courts have frequently had to ascertain the place of delivery when applying Article 5(1) of the Brussels Convention. When identifying this place, it has been accepted that the terms in the contract referring to delivery are decisive.[528] The place of delivery under various national laws will now be considered, starting with that in Member States which apply the Vienna Convention.

3.258 THE VIENNA CONVENTION   As has been seen, Article 31 of the Vienna Convention deals not only with the obligation to deliver but also with the place of delivery. It allows the parties to stipulate the place of delivery. Normally the parties will agree on a place of delivery. They will insert a trade term in their contract specifying that it is for example a contract ex works or franco frontier or, in cases of carriage of goods by sea, that it is an FOB or CIF contract.[529] However, in cases where the parties have failed to specify the place of delivery, Article 31 provides an answer.[530] The operation of this provision in the absence of a stipulated place of delivery is illustrated by the decision of the French Cour de cassation in *Mode Jeune Diffusion SA v Maglificio il Falco di Tiziana Goti*,[531] a case on Article 5(1) of the Brussels Convention. The obligation in question for the purposes of this Article was that of delivery as the dispute related to defects in the goods. In order to identify the place of performance of this obligation, the Court had to ascertain the place of delivery. According to French rules of private international law, French substantive law applied. This meant that reference had to be made to the Vienna Convention. Applying Article 31 it was held as a matter of law that in the absence of an express term this was where goods were handed over to the first carrier, i.e. Italy. If the same facts were to arise now this would raise the problem of whether Article 5(1)(b) of the Brussels I Regulation would apply, given that there is no agreement on the place of delivery. If, as is arguable, it does not do so, Article 5(1)(a) will apply and, applying the traditional approach, the place

---

[525] n 490 above.   [526] ibid at 1492.

[527] ibid at 1493; the *Tesam* case, n 524 above, at 156 (*per* Nicholls LJ) and 165 (*per* Stocker LJ).

[528] AG Mayras in *Tessili v Dunlop*, n 490 above, at 1495, who was referring to the determination of the place of delivery.

[529] ibid.   [530] This is set out at para 3.198 above.

[531] [1998] IL Pr 812, French Cour de cassation. See also *Les Verreries de Saint-Gobain SA v Martinswerk GmbH* [1999] IL Pr 296, French Cour de cassation. See also in relation to the earlier International Sale of Goods Convention 1964, *SIPAL Rexons Società Italiana Prodotti Auto E Locomozione SpA v Sprl Gold's Products* [1990] IL Pr 386, Cour d'appel, Mons.

of performance of the obligation in question will be in Italy. The Italian courts will therefore have jurisdiction under Article 5(1)(a).

ENGLISH LAW   The question of the place of performance of the seller's **3.259** obligation to deliver the goods has arisen under the traditional rules on jurisdiction in cases of service out of the jurisdiction. These cases are discussed in detail below[532] and are equally relevant in the present context as setting out the English substantive law on the place of performance of this particular obligation. In brief, the position under English law is very similar to that under the Vienna Convention. Delivery to a carrier for the purposes of transmission to the carrier is, *prima facie*, deemed to be a delivery of the goods to the buyer.[533] It follows that, in cases where the applicable substantive law is that of England, the result would be the same as under Article 31 of the Vienna Convention.

The place of performance of the obligation to deliver the goods is not **3.260** affected by the fact that in a CIF contract documents must be delivered to a different place in this sense. The seller must first deliver the goods to the carrier in order to procure the documents, notably the bill of lading, that stand in for the goods and whose delivery to the buyer is a constructive form of the delivery of the goods themselves. Under English and Scots law the obligation to deliver goods is a separate obligation from that of the obligation to deliver documents, and, accordingly, the two may have different places of performance.[534] This principle was applied in the context of the Brussels Convention by the Scots case of *Eddie v Alpa Srl*.[535] Contracts of sale were made ex works in Italy. It was accepted by counsel for the plaintiff that, under this arrangement, the place of performance of the obligation to deliver the goods was not in Scotland. However, it was argued that the position was altered by the fact that under a new arrangement in relation to the terms of payment, with cash against documents, the seller was under an obligation to deliver bills of lading in Scotland, and that this constituted a symbolic delivery in Scotland. This argument was rejected by Lord Eassie in the Outer House, who pointed out that the obligation to deliver documents was a separate obligation from that of delivering the goods and could therefore have a separate place of performance. The plaintiff was unable to show that the place of performance was in Scotland, with the result that the Scots courts lacked jurisdiction under Article 5(1) of the Brussels Convention.

---

[532] See 3 below, paras 4.74–76.   [533] Sale of Goods Act 1979, s 32.

[534] *Johnson v Taylor Bros & Co Ltd* [1920] AC 144; *Kwei Tek Chao v British Traders & Shippers Ltd* [1954] 2 QB 459.

[535] 2000 SLT 1062. The case concerned the obligation to deliver goods in conformity with the contract, discussed below, but treated this for the purposes of the place of performance of the obligation in question as an obligation to deliver.

3.261   *The place of performance of the seller's obligation to deliver goods in conformity with the contract*   There is a conceptual problem in ascribing a place of performance to an obligation that by its very nature does not involve an act of performance by one of the parties, but is rather the acceptance of responsibility on the occurrence or non-occurrence of an event.[536] We can see how this problem has been solved in cases where the applicable law was: the ULIS, the Vienna Convention, and English law.

3.262   ULIS   In *Tessili v Dunlop*,[537] Advocate General Mayras, after giving his opinion that, where a claim was brought on the basis that the goods were not in conformity with the contract, the seller was to be regarded as having failed to perform his obligation to deliver the goods,[538] held that the place of performance of this obligation was the place of delivery of the goods.[539] In *Re a Consignment of Italian Wine*,[540] the Bundesgerichtshof held that the obligation to deliver goods in conformity with the contract, to which the Uniform Law on International Sales applied, was to be performed at the place of delivery stipulated by the parties.

3.263   THE VIENNA CONVENTION   Where is the place of performance of the obligation under Article 35 of the Vienna Convention to deliver goods in conformity with the contract? The Vienna Convention does not say, at least not in direct terms. However, the Cour d'appel, Paris, in cases concerning Article 5(1) of the Brussels Convention, has held, on more than one occasion,[541] that Article 35(1) and 35(2)(a) of the Vienna Convention associates the obligation of conformity with the delivery of goods and, accordingly, these corresponding obligations are or ought to be fulfilled at one and the same place. Subsequently, the French Cour de cassation in a dispute over the quality of goods to which the Vienna Convention applied, determined whether the French courts had jurisdiction under Article 5(1) of the Brussels Convention by reference to the obligation of delivery of the goods and the place where this obligation was to be performed.[542]

3.264   Once the obligation to deliver goods in conformity with the contract is classified[543] as one simply of delivery of goods, then the position is exactly

---

[536]   *Viskase Ltd v Paul Kiefel GmbH* [1999] 1 WLR 1305, 1314 (*per* Evans LJ).
[537]   n 490 above.   [538]   See Art 33 ULIS.
[539]   n 490 above, at 1494–1495.   [540]   See above, para 3.128.
[541]   *ISEA Industrie SpA v SA LU* [1997] IL Pr 823; *Société Laborall v SA Matis* [1999] IL Pr 4.
[542]   *Les Verreries de Saint-Gobain SA v Martinswerk GmbH* [1999] IL Pr 296. The same principle was applied in *Anton Huber GmbH and Co v Polyspace SA* [2003] IL Pr 10 at 203, Cour de cassation. See also *SpA OMV Officine Meccaniche Ventura v Prometal SA* [1990] IL Pr 184, Tribunale (District Court), Monza (In Plenary Sesssion)—applying the French substantive law of sales.
[543]   Autonomously based on the substantive law background the drafters of the Brussels Convention had in mind.

the same as that described above when the place of performance of the obligation to deliver goods was discussed.

ENGLISH LAW   The question of the place of performance of the seller's **3.265** obligation to deliver goods in conformity with the contract has arisen under the traditional rules on jurisdiction in cases of service out of the jurisdiction. These cases are discussed in detail below[544] and are equally relevant in the present context as setting out the English substantive law on the place of performance of this particular obligation. The question of the place of performance of the obligation under s 14(3) of the Sale of Goods Act 1979 to supply goods which are reasonably fit for the known purpose arose in England, in the context of Article 5(1) of the Brussels Convention, in *Viskase Ltd v Paul Kiefel GmbH*.[545] Both Morritt LJ and Chadwick LJ were in agreement that the place of performance must be the place of delivery. However, they reached this conclusion by different routes. Morritt LJ reached this conclusion by clarifying the nature of the obligation as being one to sell and deliver goods in accordance with contractual provisions; this denoted the place of performance, i.e. the place of delivery.[546] Chadwick LJ reached this conclusion by looking at *when* the obligation has to be performed, namely at the time when the machine was supplied. The place *where* the obligation has to be performed is therefore the place of delivery under the contract.[547] This process of reasoning is not only different from that of Morritt LJ but also from that of the French courts, in relation to the place of performance of the obligation of conformity under the Vienna Convention, in that it seems to treat the obligation to supply a machine which is reasonably fit for the known purpose as one that is independent of the obligation to deliver. Nonetheless, by concentrating on the time at which the obligation has to be performed it produces the same result as that arrived at by Morritt LJ and as that reached in the French decisions. In relation to the machines supplied under seven of the eight contracts, delivery was to take place at the defendant's factory in Germany and the English Court had no jurisdiction under Article 5(1) of the Brussels Convention. However, it did have jurisdiction in relation to the remaining contract which concerned a machine that was to be delivered in England.

The close relationship between supply and delivery also comes out in the **3.266** decision of the Court of Appeal in *MBM Fabri-Clad Limited v Eisen-Und Huttenwerke Thale AG*.[548] This case concerned a contract, governed by

---

[544] See below, paras 4.77–79.   [545] [1999] 1 WLR 1305, CA.

[546] Questions of durability and conformity of goods should be gauged according to the state of the goods at the time of delivery.

[547] At 1321 and 1323.   [548] [2000] IL Pr 505, CA.

English law, which expressly provided that goods supplied should correspond with samples. The goods supplied did not conform to the contractual specification. After much argument on what the obligation in question was,[549] Pill LJ simply held, without any argument or reference to the *Viskase* case, that the place of performance of the obligation to supply goods conforming with the contractual specification was England. This was because England was specified as the place of delivery under the contract. The link between supply and delivery comes across strongly in the judgment of Pill LJ, who described the contract as being one for supply *by* delivery in England.[550] Ward LJ reasoned that with a contract to supply and deliver to the purchaser's place of business, the contract is not performed unless and until the delivery has taken place, and the breach of the performance occurs in England. Looking at it another way, the plaintiff was complaining that the goods delivered to it (in England) were defective and therefore the breach of performance occurred in England. Although the judges in the Court of Appeal were clearly influenced by the close relationship in the case between supply and delivery, as has been seen,[551] they were not agreed on the precise relationship between the supply and delivery and, in particular, over whether, on the one hand, there was a separate obligation to deliver or, on the other hand, supply and delivery are separate parts of a composite obligation.

3.267 The close link between supply and delivery raises a question of where the place of performance of the obligation to supply is if there is no obligation by the supplier to deliver to the buyer. Ward LJ said that such a contract is performed by furnishing the goods and making them available at the supplier's place of business.[552] This would be the place of performance of the obligation to supply. This points to the same place of performance as in the case of a contract which specifies that delivery is ex works, which must be right.

3.268 Would the place of performance be any different if the place where the goods are delivered is in Member State A, the state of the seller's domicile, but the lack of conformity is only discovered when they are examined in Member State B, the state of the buyer's domicile? The obligation in question remains that of delivery of goods in conformity with the contract and so the place of performance should remain the same. It must be admitted though that the place of performance of the obligation to deliver looks to have less of a claim (in terms of the connections between the dispute and the forum) to have jurisdiction under Article 5(1) of the Brussels I Regulation in such a case.

---

[549] Above, para 3.112.   [550] n 548 above, at 511. See also at 513 (*per* Aldous LJ).
[551] Above, para 3.112.   [552] n 548 above, at 513.

One final important point in relation to the position under English law **3.269** is that, as has already been seen,[553] allocating jurisdiction to the place of delivery means that, normally, Article 5(1)(a) will not apply.

SCOTS LAW   The *Viskase* case was followed in Scotland in *Ferguson* **3.270** *Shipbuilders Ltd v Voith Hydro GmbH & Co KG*.[554] The claim was brought for breach, *inter alia*, of the obligation to ensure that manufactured goods conformed to contractual specification and guaranteed quality within agreed times. Scots law governed the contract. Delivery of the completed machinery to the purchaser's yard in Scotland was specifically provided for in the contract. Lord Penrose in the Outer House held that this was one of the seller's obligations and that it was in Scotland, and in Scotland alone, that the seller performed its contractual obligations. It was there that the specification had to be satisfied. The analogy was drawn with the position in the *Viskase* case in relation to the one contract which involved delivery of a single machine to England, and in respect of which the English courts therefore had jurisdiction. However, Lord Penrose regarded the *Ferguson* case as an even stronger one for saying that the forum was the place of performance of the obligation of conformity because it did not involve, as in the *Viskase* case, a free-standing machine. It involved a propeller which had no integrity until it was delivered for incorporation into the vessel being built by the buyer. It was in Scotland alone that due performance of the contractual stipulations as to performance and quality could be ascertained once the goods were incorporated into the ship. The end result was that the Scots courts had jurisdiction under Article 5(1) of the Brussels Convention.

The subsequent Scots case of *Eddie v Alpa Srl*[555] involved the manufacture **3.271** and supply of furniture, i.e. goods which had their own integrity as free-standing items, and so was more like the *Viskase* case. The obligation in question was that of delivery in conformity with the contract. It was accepted without argument that the place of performance of this obligation was the contractual place of delivery. It was accepted by counsel for the plaintiff that the place of delivery was not in Scotland and the Scots courts lacked jurisdiction.

The place of performance of the seller's obligation to hand over any documents relating to the goods

THE VIENNA CONVENTION   Article 34 of the Vienna Convention provides **3.272** that, if the seller is bound to hand over documents relating to the goods, he must hand them over at the time and place and in the form required by the contract. The obligation to hand over documents is a separate

---

[553] Above, para 3.237.   [554] 2000 SLT 229.   [555] [2000] IL Pr 1062.

obligation from that of delivery of the goods and the parties may agree on different places of performance for these obligations. This means that, unlike in cases where the obligation is that of delivery of the goods, Article 5(1)(a) could well apply in cases involving this obligation. For example, the parties may have agreed under the contract that the goods are to be delivered FOB in New York but that the bill of lading retained by the seller until payment is to be handed over in England, the buyer's place of business. Article 5(1)(b) will not apply and therefore Article 5(1)(a) applies. The English courts will have jurisdiction in an action against the seller for breach of the obligation to hand over documents relating to the goods on the basis that the place of performance of the obligation in question is in England. In the situation where the parties have not expressly agreed on the place where the documents are to be handed over, this can be ascertained by looking at the method of payment. For example, if the parties have agreed on cash against documents with payment to be made by a bank, the place of handing over the documents is the place of business of the bank.[556] If cash against documents has been agreed without any reference to a bank, this means that the seller must present the documents at the latter's place of business.[557]

3.273 ENGLISH LAW   The question of the place of performance of the seller's obligation to hand over any documents in relation to the goods has not arisen so far in the context of the Brussels Convention or Brussels I Regulation. However, it has arisen under the traditional rules on jurisdiction in cases of service out of the jurisdiction. These cases are discussed in detail below[558] and are equally relevant in the present context as setting out the English substantive law on the place of performance of this particular obligation. There is no clear law on the place of tender of documents in English law. The documents will normally be sent to the seller's agent, often a bank, to be forwarded to the buyer. There seems to be a weak presumption that the documents must be delivered at the residence of the buyer or of an agent such as a bank.[559]

The place of performance of the seller's obligation to transfer the property in the goods

3.274 THE VIENNA CONVENTION   The Vienna Convention does not define the place where the property is to be transferred. It has been argued that: 'In so far as the transfer of property is conditional on the goods being handed over (as is the case in German law and in numerous other legal systems),

---

[556] See Schlechtriem, 270–271, paras 3 and 3a.   [557] ibid.
[558] See below, paras 4.80–82.   [559] Bridge, *The International Sale of Goods*, 5.133.

the seller fulfils his obligation to perform that transfer if he effects "delivery" within the meaning of Article 31'.[560] The difficulty with this view is that it presupposes rules of passing of property based upon delivery that are not to be found in the Vienna Convention and that are by no means common to the substantive laws of all Vienna Contracting States. Let us assume though that this view is accepted. It means that the place of performance of the obligation to transfer the property in the goods is the same place as the place of performance of the obligation to deliver the goods. What has been said above in relation to the place of performance of the latter obligation will be equally applicable to the place of performance of the former obligation.

ENGLISH LAW   As stated above, the Sale of Goods Act does not impose a **3.275** statutory obligation on the seller to transfer to the buyer the property in goods, though such a duty should be implied from the express language ('sell' etc) of the contract. The place of performance of such a duty is a matter of first impression and, so far as performance depends upon acts in relation to the goods that effect a passing of property under the rules of the Sale of Goods Act, such as the unconditional appropriation of the goods to the contract, it is submitted that this is where the seller performs his duty. The place of performance is likely to track the delivery terms, so that an FOB seller performs on shipping the goods, unless payment is deferred, whereupon performance should occur at the place of documentary tender. An ex works seller would perform upon making the goods available to the buyer.

The place of performance of the seller's obligation to deliver goods which are free from any right or claim of a third party

THE VIENNA CONVENTION   This does not state where the seller's obliga- **3.276** tion under Article 41 to deliver goods which are free from any right or claim of a third party is to be performed. Neither do there appear to be any national decisions which have had to decide this for the purposes of Article 5(1) of the Brussels Convention. However, one approach is to apply the analogy of the obligation to deliver goods in conformity with the contract and to regard the obligation as being one of delivery of the goods. If this is done then the position is exactly the same as that described above when the place of performance of the obligation to deliver goods was discussed. This answer, again, is open to criticism in that it assumes the existence of delivery-based rules for the passing of property, which under Article 4(b) is a subject that falls outside the scope of the Convention. It is not easy to see, nevertheless, any plausible alternative.

---

[560] Schlechtriem, 219, para 7.

3.277 ENGLISH LAW   In principle, the seller's duty to supply the goods free from encumbrances ought to to be performed at the place where the seller performs his duty to pass the property in the goods to the buyer, which will usually be the place of delivery (of the goods or the documents as the case may be). The seller's duty to guarantee quiet possession is different in that it is a continuing obligation broken only when an actual interference takes place. In principle, the place of performance should be where the interference takes place.

3.278 *The place of performance of the seller's obligation to indemnify*   In *Ferguson Shipbuilders Ltd v Voith Hydro GmbH & Co KG,*[561] the buyer brought an action for breach not only of the obligation to ensure that manufactured goods conformed to contractual specification and guaranteed quality within agreed times but also of the obligation of the seller to indemnify it. This was against all and any loss, damage and expense suffered by it in consequence of any negligence or breach of duty by the seller, and in particular loss and damage arising as a result of contractual delay caused by the seller's faulty design of propeller systems. Lord Penrose in the Outer House, after holding that Scots law governed the contract, described the obligation to indemnify as an obligation to make payment, which was to be performed in Scotland, which was seemingly the place of performance of the obligation to pay for the goods. This was obiter because the principal obligation on which the action was based, namely to deliver goods to Scotland which conformed with the contract, had its place of performance in Scotland. Scotland therefore had jurisdiction in relation to the subordinate matter of the indemnity.

3.279 The Oberlandesgericht, Dusseldorf, in *Re a Wood-Cutting Machine*[562] reached the same result but by a less direct process of reasoning. The applicable law for determining the place of performance was that of a country which had adopted the Vienna Convention. The Court held that: 'A claim to an indemnity is in principle to be satisfied at the place where a claim for damages seeking payment of money would have to be satisfied; for that is the place where the consequent indemnification must take place'.[563] The case involved a claim for damages as well as an indemnity. As has been seen,[564] the place of performance of the claim for damages was in Germany where the creditor had its seat.[565] It followed that the place of performance in respect of an indemnity was also in Germany.

3.280 *The place of performance of the buyer's obligation to pay the price*   In an action for payment for goods delivered under a sales contract, the courts with jurisdiction under Article 5(1) of the Brussels Convention are those for the

---

[561] 2000 SLT 229.   [562] [1995] IL Pr 191.   [563] ibid at 196.
[564] See above, para 3.129.   [565] See Art 57(1)(a) of the Vienna Convention.

place where payment was to be made.[566] This place will depend on the applicable substantive law. The most likely laws to be applied in the EC context will now be examined.

ULIS   As has been mentioned, Article 59(1) of the Uniform Law on the **3.281** International Sale of Goods, annexed to the Hague Convention of 1 July 1964, stipulates that the place of performance of the buyer's obligation to pay the price is the seller's place of business or, if he does not have a place of business, his habitual residence, subject to the parties stipulating a different place of performance under Article 3 of that law. The Bundes-gerichtshof has applied this rule on a number of occasions.[567] In the *Custom Made Commercial* case,[568] application of this rule to the facts of the case, which involved an action by a German company against an English company for payment of part of the price agreed under a contract for the supply of windows and doors to be manufactured by Stawa, resulted in the German courts having jurisdiction under Article 5(1) of the Brussels Convention.

THE VIENNA CONVENTION   Article 57 of the Vienna Convention essen- **3.282** tially reproduces Article 59(1) of the Uniform Law on the International Sale of Goods. It states that:

(1) If the buyer is not bound to pay the price at any other particular place, he must pay it to the seller;
  (a) at the seller's place of business; or
  (b) if the payment is to be made against the handing over of the goods or of the documents, at the place where the handing over takes place.

This provision contains three parts. The first is concerned with the agree-ment of the parties, the second with the seller's place of business, and the third with the place where the goods or documents are handed over.

Article 57(1) gives priority to the agreement of the parties that the buyer is **3.283** bound to pay the price at a particular place. Can an agreement be inferred or must it be expressed? This is by no means a theoretical question. A German court has taken jurisdiction under Article 5(1) of the Brussels Convention after inferring from the circumstances, in particular the nature of the obligation, that Germany was the place of performance of the obligation to pay.[569] The case involved reciprocal obligations to be performed simultaneously. Germany was the place of performance of

---

[566] *Société Alususse France v Société Rodwer* [19990] IL Pr 102, Cour d'appel, Paris.
[567] See, e.g. *Re Yarn Sales* [1995] IL Pr 180 (a claim for compensation case).
[568] See above, para 3.54.
[569] Judgment of 12 February 1981–10 U 195/80, Oberlandesgericht, Stuttgart, NJW 1982, 529; RIW 1982, 591; VersR 1982, 378; D Series I-5.1.2—B 35.

both parties since it was there that the consideration typical of the contract, namely the delivery of goods, was to be provided. German law prior to the Vienna Convention taking effect allowed a place of performance to be inferred from the circumstances of the case. If an agreement can be inferred, from what can it be inferred? We know it can be inferred from the circumstances of the case. No doubt it can also be inferred from the terms of the contract. Presumably it can be inferred from the conduct of the parties, for example by delivering goods to a particular country. The parties' agreement only takes priority in so far as it designates a place of payment 'other' than the place designated under paragraph (a) or (b). It follows that if the parties agree on payment at the buyer's place of business, this will be the place of payment under Article 57(1) by virtue of the parties' agreement. The courts of the buyer's place of business will then have jurisdiction under Article 5(1) of the Brussels I Regulation.[570] If the parties agree on payment at the seller's place of business again this will be the place of performance, but this time it will be by virtue of Article 57(1)(a), not by virtue of the parties' agreement.

3.284 The Italian Supreme Court applied Article 57(1)(a) of the Vienna Convention in *Jeumont-Schneider SA v Gruppo Industriale Ercole Marelli SpA*,[571] which concerned a claim for payment of the price of electric motors brought by the Italian seller against the French buyer. Italian substantive law was applicable. The Vienna Convention has been adopted under Italian law and, accordingly, reference was made to Article 57 of that Convention. Italy was the place of performance of the obligation to pay and the Italian courts had jurisdiction under Article 5(1) of the Brussels Convention.

3.285 Article 57(1)(b) was considered by the Swiss Federal Supreme Court in *Re the Supply of Equipment for the Purification of Waste Gases*.[572] A Swiss company entered into a contract with an Italian company for the supply of equipment. After it was delivered and installed, the buyer made a number of complaints and said that it was avoiding the contract. The Swiss company commenced proceedings in Switzerland for the payment of the purchase price. The Italian defendant argued that this was a case where payment was to be made against the handing over of the goods within the meaning of Article 57(1)(b) and, accordingly, the place of performance of the obligation to pay was the place where the handing over took place,

---

[570] See Judgment of 22 January 1979 *SpA CICA v SA Vepel*, Cour d'appel, Paris, Gaz Pal 1980, Somm., 92; D Series I-5.1.2—B 21, a case decided under Art 5(1) of the Brussels Convention applying the French law prior to adoption of the Vienna Convention.

[571] [1994] IL Pr 12, Italian Supreme Court. See also *Re a Wood-Cutting Machine* [1995] IL Pr 191, Oberlandesgericht, Dusseldorf; discussed below, para 3.296.

[572] [1998] IL Pr 77, Swiss Federal Supreme Court.

Italy. Was this a transaction where payment was to be made against the handing over of the goods? This raised a point of interpretation of the Vienna Convention. The Court held that the special characteristic of such a transaction was that neither party was obliged to make performance in advance of the other. What is being referred to is payment against delivery contracts in which it is important that consideration and counter-consideration are due to be performed at the same time so that one party can immediately ascertain whether the other party is in fact fulfilling his obligation at that time and can make use of his right to withhold per-formance of his own obligation until the other party makes performance. At no point in the development of the performance of the contract, which involved a mutual credit arrangement with payment to be made in stages, did the (part) performance of one party have to take place simultaneously with that of the other. It followed that this was not a payment against delivery transaction and Article 57(1)(b) did not apply. Instead, Article 57(1)(a) applied. The obligation to pay was to be performed at the seller's place of business, Switzerland, and the Swiss courts had jurisdiction under Article 5(1) of the Lugano Convention.

EXCLUSION OF THE VIENNA CONVENTION   It is possible for the parties to **3.286** exclude the application of the Vienna Convention.[573] This opens up the possibility of manipulating the place of performance of the obligation in question and hence the Member State in which a party can bring an action by virtue of Article 5(1) of the Brussels I Regulation. This is illustrated by *Re the Supply of Wooden Panels*,[574] a decision of the District Court, Stuttgart, in relation to Article 5(1) of the Brussels Convention. A German seller sued in Germany a Swiss buyer for payment on a number of sales invoices. German law was applicable to the contract. Germany has adopted the Vienna Convention. However, the parties' contract excluded the application of this Convention. Instead of Article 57 applying, para-graph 269 of the German Civil Code applied, according to which the place of performance of the buyer's alleged obligations to pay was said to lie in Germany.[575] It seems from what the Court said that application of Article 57 would have produced a different result.[576]

---

[573] Art 6 of the Vienna Convention. This invariably happens in the case of GAFTA and similar dry commodity trading forms as well as in the trading forms used by the major oil companies. The rules of the Vienna Convention, geared to keeping contracts alive, are widely regarded as unsuitable in contracts susceptible to market fluctuations.

[574] [1998] IL Pr 100, District Court of Stuttgart.

[575] It is not clear how the Court came to this conclusion since para 269 of the German Civil Code provides that an obligation is to be performed at the place where the person liable resides at the time when the obligation comes into being, in so far as no other place is designated by the parties or may be inferred from the circumstances.

[576] This too is a bit of puzzling since Art 57(1)(a) points to the seller's place of business, which was Germany.

3.287 NATIONAL LAWS IN EC MEMBER STATES   We must consider the position in Member States that have not adopted the Vienna Convention, and in those cases where, although a Member State has adopted this Convention, it does not apply. National laws in Member States are fairly evenly divided on whether the place of performance of the obligation to pay should be at the creditor's domicile or the debtor's domicile. The United Kingdom has not adopted the Vienna Convention. Under English law, if the sale of goods contract is silent on the question of the due place of payment, the normal rule that is applied is that, in the absence of contrary implication, the debtor must seek out his creditor.[577] The question of the place of performance of the buyer's obligation to pay the price of the goods has arisen under the traditional rules on jurisdiction in cases of service out of the jurisdiction. These cases are discussed in detail below[578] and are equally relevant in the present context as setting out the English substantive law on the place of performance of this particular obligation. The same principle, namely that the payment obligation should be fulfilled at the creditor's domicile, is adopted in Denmark, Greece, Ireland, the Netherlands, Finland and Sweden.[579] In contrast, Belgium, Germany, Spain, France and Luxembourg consider that payment obligations should in principle be fulfilled at the debtor's domicile.[580]

The place of performance of the buyer's obligation to take delivery

3.288 THE VIENNA CONVENTION   Article 60 of the Vienna Convention provides that:

the buyer's obligation to take delivery consists:
   (a) in doing all the acts which could reasonably be expected of him in order to enable the seller to make delivery; and
   (b) in taking over the goods.

Taking delivery involves two different elements.[581] First the acts referred to in (a), and second in taking over the goods under (b). The acts referred to in (a) will normally be set out in the parties' contract. Thus, in an FOB

---

[577] *Crédit Agricole Indosuez v Chailease Finance Corp* [2000] 1 All ER (Comm) 399, 410, CA.
[578] See below, paras 4.83–86.
[579] Case C-420/97 *Leathertex Divisione Sinetici SPA v Bodetex BVBA* [1999] ECR I-6747, para 94 (AG Leger). See also AG Ruiz-Jarabo Colomer in Case C-440/97 *GIE Groupe Concorde v Master of the Vessel Suhadiwarno Panjan* [1999] ECR I-6307, para 879.
[580] ibid. See also the *Crédit Agricole Indosuez* case, n 577 above. For Luxembourg see Judgment of 7 June 1978, *Gondert v Pultz* cour superieure de justice, Pas Lux 1978–168; D Series I-5.1.2—B 17. For Germany see para 269 of the German Civil Code; see Judgment of 12 February 1981–10 U 195/80, n 569 above; *Definitely Maybe (Touring) Ltd v Marek Lieberberg Konzertagentur GmbH* [2001] IL Pr 30. For France see *San Carlo Gruppo Alimentaire SpA v SNC Vico* [1996] IL Pr 493, Cour de cassation.
[581] See generally the discussion in Schlechtriem, 477–479.

contract involving liner shipping, the buyer must, unless the seller has undertaken responsibility for booking space, give the seller due notice of the name, loading berth and delivery dates to the vessel chartered by the buyer, or on which the buyer has reserved the necessary space. It is by no means clear where the place of performance is in the situation where the obligation is that of giving information by the buyer to the seller. Is it where the information is sent from, which will normally be where the buyer has its domicile, or where the information arrives, which will normally be where the seller has its domicile? Suppose the buyer sends information to the seller but that the information goes astray in the course of transmission, as might happen where a courier fails to deliver it or it is lost in the post. In such a case, has the buyer in fact given due notice? If he has, then the place of performance of this obligation is at the place of sending. If he has not, then the place of performance is in the place of arrival. The Vienna Convention supplies no direct answer so an answer must be sought so far as possible from general principles underpinning the Convention. In the case of contract formation, it requires under Article 18(2) that an acceptance reach the offeror. In Article 26, it states that a declaration of avoidance of the contract is effective only if notice is given to the other party. These provisions—the last in particular—point to actual communication rather than the emission of information as required in performance of information obligations under the Convention.

Taking over the goods under (b) is referring to the buyer physically **3.289** accepting the goods. This occurs immediately after delivery of the goods. Accordingly, it is submitted that the place in which the goods are accepted is the same place as that where they are delivered.[582]

There is no difficulty in identifying the place of performance of the **3.290** buyer's obligation to take delivery if the place of performance is the same for each of the two elements which make up this obligation. But what happens if they are not the same? For example, the place where notice is given (under Article 60(a)) is in France but the place of taking over the goods (under Article 60(b)) is in England. In cases where notice has been given and the action is based on a failure to take over the goods, it would be possible simply to ground jurisdiction on the place of performance of the obligation to take over the goods. But this still leaves a problem in cases where the action is based on both elements which go to make up the buyer's obligation to take delivery. There are two possible solutions that could be adopted for such cases. The first is to accept that it is impossible to identify the place of performance of the obligation in question and,

---

[582] ibid at p 478, para 2a.

then, following the case law of the European Court of Justice,[583] to say that therefore jurisdiction cannot be based on Article 5(1)(a). The second is to regard each element under Article 60 as a separate obligation. In accordance with the case law of the European Court of Justice,[584] it would then be necessary to identify the principal obligation; the place of performance of the principal obligation would then have jurisdiction in relation to both obligations. One solution that is not available is to treat the buyer's obligation to take delivery as one obligation which has in effect two places of performance. The European Court of Justice has held that a single place of performance for the obligation in question must be identified.[585]

3.291 ENGLISH LAW   So far as information has to be given in English law, the obligation to do so is not the subject of specific provision in the Sale of Goods Act. In view of the treatment over time of the postal rule of acceptance as an exception to the normal rule that declarations of intention must reach the other party, it is scarcely arguable that a notice would be effectively given if it did not reach the other party. As for the buyer's taking delivery, English law treats delivery as a seamless transfer of possession by seller to buyer (the 'voluntary transfer of possession', according to s 61(1) of the Sale of Goods Act) so that there is no hiatus in possession. The place of taking delivery would therefore necessarily be the place where the seller makes delivery.

3.292 *The place of performance of the buyer's obligation to place orders*   This is an obligation that is not imposed by law in some statute or Convention but where it arises, instead derives from the parties' agreement. If the parties have gone on to agree, either expressly or impliedly, on the place of performance of this obligation, there can be no doubt that the courts of Member States will give effect to this. But if there is no such agreement, what happens then? The courts could presumably invent a rule ascribing a place of performance for this obligation. However, the Irish Supreme Court was not prepared to do this in *Handbridge Services Ltd v Aerospace Communications Limited*.[586] The Irish plaintiff had contracted with the UK defendants to manufacture and sell to them 8,000 computers in accordance with a sample. The plaintiff sought to sue in Ireland, relying on Article 5(1) of the Brussels Convention on the basis that the obligation in question was to order computers in the numbers alleged and that this

---

[583] *Réunion Européenne v Spliethoff's Bevrachtingskantoor BV* [1998] ECR I-6511, a case on Art 5(3) of the Brussels Convention.

[584] Case 266/85 *Shenavai v Kreischer* [1987] ECR 239.

[585] Case C-256/00 *Besix SA v Wasserreinigungsbau Alfred Kretzschmar GmbH & Co KG (WABAG)* [2002] ECR I-1699, paras 29, 32.

[586] [1993] IL Pr 778.

obligation was to be performed in Ireland. The Irish Supreme Court accepted that this was indeed the obligation in question but that there was not evidence before the trial judge that justified the conclusion that there was an act to be performed by the defendant in Ireland in the placing of orders. The trial judge accepted that the obligation in question was performed by the defendants communicating their order to the plaintiff at Shannon in Ireland. But the Supreme Court held that this did not necessarily and unambiguously mean that the obligation to place these orders was to be performed in Ireland. Finlay CJ pointed to the difficulty in determining whether an order is placed when it is sent in writing or by fax from England or when it arrives in Ireland.

Rather than invent a rule for the place of performance of this particular **3.293** obligation, the place of performance was simply treated as a matter of evidence. The question of the onus of proof then becomes vital. The Court pointed out that the onus is on the plaintiff to show that it is entitled to sue in some Member State other than the defendant's domicile. In this case the plaintiff had simply not satisfied the onus placed on him. This is very much a common lawyer's response to the situation where it is difficult to identify the place of performance of the obligation in question. Nevertheless, it is compatible with the case law of the European Court of Justice. In *Réunion Européenne v Spliethoff's Bevrachtingskantoor BV*,[587] the Court acknowledged that in certain cases it may be difficult or indeed impossible to determine the place where the event giving rise to the damage occurred for the purposes of Article 5(3) of the Brussels Convention. In such circumstances, the plaintiff cannot base jurisdiction on this place. When it comes to Article 5(1) of the Brussels Convention, there is House of Lords authority stating that there must be a place of performance that can be identified.[588]

The Dutch courts have also had to consider where the obligation to place **3.294** orders is to be performed. In *Rapido Nederland BV v Rapido Warmetechnik GmbH*,[589] the President of the Arrondissementsrechtbank, Roermond, held that, taken by itself, the clause in the parties' contract to the effect that boilers were to be delivered 'ex works Tegelen' did not mean that the obligation, under an exclusive distribution agreement, to purchase a certain number of boilers from the plaintiff each month was to be performed

---

[587] [1998] ECR I-6511.

[588] *Agnew v Lansforsakringsbolagens AB* [2001] 1 AC 223, 240–244 (*per* Lord Woolf), 233–234 (*per* Lord Nicholls), 253 (*per* Lord Hope), 264 (*per* Lord Millett); *Kleinwort Benson Ltd v Glasgow City Council* [1999] 1 AC 153, 184 (*per* Lord Clyde). See also *Bank of Scotland v Investment Management Regulatory Organisation Ltd* 1989 SLT 432, 445, in relation to Sch 8 to the Civil Jurisdiction and Judgments Act 1982.

[589] Judgment of 18 May 1982, KG 1982, No 90, D Series I-2.1—B 2.

in the Netherlands and that the dispute should therefore be brought before the Dutch courts under Article 5(1) of the Brussels Convention. This tells us where the place of performance of the obligation is not, rather than where it is. The plaintiff supplier was a Dutch company. Seemingly, it was not argued before the Dutch Court that the place of performance of the obligation was in the Netherlands on the basis that orders should have been placed with the supplier in the Netherlands.

The place of performance in the situation where the buyer/seller exercises its right to claim damages

3.295 THE VIENNA CONVENTION   This does not state where the place of performance is for a claim for compensation under Articles 45 and 74 of the Vienna Convention. The crucial question is what the obligation in question is in such a case. It will be recalled that the better view is that the obligation in question is the underlying unperformed contractual obligation. Thus, in *Re a Consignment of Italian Wine*,[590] the Bundesgerichtshof held that, where contractual damages were sought by the buyers of wine which allegedly contravened EEC wine regulations as being not of the minimum alcoholic strength permitted and having had raw cane sugar added, the obligation broken was that of delivery of the goods in conformity with the contract. The contract contained a clause providing for delivery in Turin (franco partenza torino). Furthermore, the parties had agreed that the goods were to be collected in Turin from the vendor by a freight company engaged by the buyer. It followed from the applicable law[591] that the place of performance of the obligation in question was in Italy. Accordingly, there was no question of the German courts having jurisdiction under Article 5(1) of the Brussels Convention. Similarly, in *Re Yarn Sales*,[592] it will be recalled that, where the seller claimed damages from the buyer who had refused to accept delivery of goods on the basis that there was no contract, the obligation, the non-fulfilment of which gives rise to the claim for damages, was held to be that of paying the purchase price of goods. The law governing the contract was German and Germany had adopted the Uniform Law on the International Sale of Goods, which applied in this case. According to Article 59(1)(a) of ULIS, the place of performance of the obligation to pay the purchase price under the contract was at the place of business of the seller, that was in Germany.

---

[590] Judgment of 24 September 1986-VIII ZR 320/85; BGHZ Vol 98, 263; IPRax 1988, 159, Note: Hausmann, 140; KTS 1987, 230; MDR 1987, 228; NJW 1987, 592; RIW 1986, 991; ZZP 1987, 435, Note: Schack; [1988] EEC 159; D Series I-5.3—B 18; [1988] ECC 159; discussed above, para 3.128.

[591] ULIS, Arts 19(1), (2) and (38).   [592] [1995] IL Pr 180; discussed above, para 3.128.

The alternative view, which should be regarded as being incorrect, is that **3.296** the obligation in question where a buyer/seller exercises the right to claim damages is an independent contractual obligation aimed at the payment of money. In *Re a Wood-Cutting Machine*,[593] as has already been seen, the Oberlandesgericht, Dusseldorf, whilst acknowledging that the place of performance for claims for compensation is not dealt with in the Vienna Convention, said that the place of performance results from the general principles of the Convention. Such a claim is aimed at the payment of money. According to Article 57(1)(a) of the Vienna Convention, the place of performance of the obligation to pay the purchase price is the creditor's place of business. This is to be regarded as a general principle for the performance of any obligation to pay under the Vienna Convention. Accordingly, the claim is to be subjected to the place where the creditor (plaintiff) has its seat, which in the instant case was in Germany. The upshot was that the German courts had jurisdiction under Article 5(1) of the Brussels Convention.

ENGLISH LAW It will also be recalled[594] that the Court of Appeal, apply- **3.297** ing English law, has repeatedly held in cases where a claim has been brought for damages for breach of contract following the delivery of defective goods that the obligation in question was that of delivering goods in conformity with the contact. Where damages are sought for breach of contract, what the court is concerned with is the obligation under the contract which has allegedly been breached.

The special rule for the provision of services

Article 5(1)(b) of the Brussels I Regulation[595] is concerned not only with **3.298** contracts for the sale of goods but also with contracts for the provision of services. As far as the latter are concerned it provides that:

for the purpose of this provision and unless otherwise agreed, the place of performance of the obligation in question shall be:

— in the case of the provision of services, the place in a Member State where, under the contract, the services were provided or should have been provided

We are concerned in this chapter with actions in contract between the **3.299** buyer and seller. This contract will be for the sale of goods, rather than for the provision of services.[596] It is when one looks at contracts closely associated with the sales contract that the question of whether the contract

---

[593] [1995] IL Pr 191; discussed above, para 3.279.   [594] See above, paras 3.111–112.
[595] See Takahashi, n 310 above; Forner, n 310 above.
[596] The question whether a contract for the purchase of a digitized product, such as software, transferred over the internet is one for the sale of goods, provision of services or neither is discussed below, paras 10.46–49.

is one for the provision of services arises. An obvious example is an exclusive distributorship agreement. There is the main contract, flowing from which will be a number of contracts for the international sale of goods. There are also the contracts made between the buyer or seller and a third party, namely those of carriage of goods and the separate autonomous contracts under a letter of credit. Another example of a contract that is closely associated with the sales contract is where the buyer enters into a contract with a third party for the inspection of the goods to check that they are of the requisite quality.[597] It is worth looking briefly at the definition of 'provision of services' to see whether such contracts fall within this concept.

3.300   The concept of the provision of services is not defined in the Brussels I Regulation and there is no explanation of its meaning in the Explanatory Memorandum from the EC Commission, which accompanied the proposal for a Regulation on jurisdiction and the recognition and enforcement of judgments in civil and commercial matters.[598] We know from other provisions in the Regulation that this concept does not cover insurance contracts, consumer contracts and individual contracts of employment. Neither does it cover sale of goods. The concept of 'the provision of services' should be given an independent community meaning. A number of EC instruments refer to this concept and it is to these that we should turn for guidance on the meaning of the provision of services in the context of the Brussels I Regulation. The phrase 'the provision of services' is found in the EC Directive 93/13 on Unfair Terms in Consumer Contracts but is unfortunately not defined.[599] More significantly, the draft Council Directive on the liability of suppliers of services,[600] having regard to, inter alia, the diversity of services adopts a broad definition of service, namely 'any transaction carried out on a commercial basis or by way of a public service and in an independent manner, whether or not in return for payment, which does not have as its direct and exclusive object the manufacture of movable property or the transfer of rights *in rem* or intellectual property rights'.[601] There is the EEC

---

[597] See, eg, *Source Ltd v TUV Rheinland Holding AG* [1998] QB 54; *Rayner v Davies* [2003] IL Pr 14.

[598] Proposal for a Council Regulation COM (1999) 348 final, 14.

[599] [1993] OJ L95/29.

[600] COM (90) 482 final-SYN 308 submitted by the Commission on 9 November 1990 [1991] OJ C12/8. The Commission was forced to withdraw the proposal after it encountered resistance.

[601] Art 2. This would exclude an assignment of intellectual property rights but seemingly not a licensing agreement. Nonetheless a licensing agreement should not be regarded as the provision of services because it involves only a one-off act of granting the licence, rather than a continuing act. Art 2 goes on to exclude packet travel and waste services which would otherwise come within the definition of service.

Regulation on maritime cabotage of 1992,[602] which applies the principle of freedom to provide services to maritime transport. For the purposes of this Regulation, 'maritime transport services' is defined as including 'the carriage of passengers or goods by sea'.[603] Such a contract should also be regarded as one for the provision of services for the purposes of Article 5(1)(b) of the Brussels I Regulation. A Council Decision establishing a programme for the development of European statistics on services[604] includes within the concept of 'services' 'financial services (including insurance)'.[605] One other factor that should be taken into account when giving an independent community meaning to the concept of 'services' is the objectives and scheme of the Regulation and the objectives of the provision in question and how this relates to other provisions in the Regulation.[606] The purpose of giving an autonomous definition to the place of performance of the obligation in question in the case of the sale of goods and the provision of services is that this remedies the shortcomings of applying the rules of private international law of the state whose courts are seised.[607] In order to give effect to this objective, the concept of the provision of services should be given its natural broad meaning,[608] which would encompass the carriage of goods by sea,[609] distribution agreements, the separate autonomous contracts under a letter of credit[610] and contracts

---

[602] Council Regulation (EEC) No 3577/92 of 7 December 1992 applying the principle of freedom to provide services to maritime transport within Member States (maritime cabotage) [1992] OJ L364/7.

[603] Art 2.

[604] 92/326/EEC: Council Decision of 18 June 1992 establishing a two-year programme (1992 to 1993) for the development of European statistics on services [1992] OJ L179/131.

[605] Annex (c). Insurance cannot be a contract for the provision of services for the purposes of Art 5(1)(b) of the Brussels I Regulation because of Section 3 of the Regulation.

[606] Case 33/78 *Somafer v Saar-Ferngas* [1978] ECR 2183.

[607] See the Explanatory Memorandum in the Proposal for a Council Regulation COM (1999) 348 final, 14.

[608] See generally MBM Loos, 'Towards a European Law of Service Contracts' (2001) European Rev of Private Law 565. As an illustration of the natural broad meaning of services there are indications that Mance J in *Bank of Baroda v Vysya Bank Ltd* [1994] 2 Lloyd's Rep 87 at 91, speaking in the context of ascertaining the applicable law under the Rome Convention, regarded the concept of services as encompassing 'transport, insurance, banking, operations of security, etc.'. Insurance cannot be a contract for the provision of services for the purposes of Art 5(1)(b) of the Brussels I Regulation because of Section 3 of the Regulation. But compare Beaumont, n 324 above, at 22–23, who gives a narrow interpretation to 'the provision of services' excluding letters of credit, commercial agency and reinsurance contracts.

[609] One commonly used standard form of bill of lading defines carriage as 'operations and services undertaken by the carrier', see P&O Nedlloyd Bill, cl 1. See also the views of the Commission, the German and UK governments in the *GIE* case, n 579 above; Takahashi, n 310 above, at 533.

[610] But compare Beaumont, n 324 above, at 22–23 who argues that it is not helpful to characterize a contract of payment under a letter of credit as a service. He says it is one party providing a financial guarantee to another. This does not explain why it should not be regarded as a service.

for the inspection of goods. One possible limitation on the width of the concept of 'services' is that it is envisaged that it is possible to identify the place where, under the contract, the services were provided or should have been provided. If the nature of the alleged service is such that it is not possible to identify this place, this raises a question over whether it can be regarded as a service in the first place.[611] There does not appear to be any such impossibility with the contracts mentioned above.

3.301 When it comes to identification of the place in a Member State where, under the contract, the services were provided or should have been provided, the situation is analogous to that of identification of the place in a Member State where, under the contract, the goods were delivered or should have been delivered and reference should be made to what was said above. Ditto for the operation of the displacement rule and for the position where it is a contract for the provision of services that falls outside the scope of Article 5(1)(b).

7. Special Jurisdiction: Article 5(5)
The Provision

3.302 Article 5(5) states that a defendant domiciled in one Member State may be sued in another Member State 'as regards a dispute arising out of the operations of a branch, agency or other establishment, in the courts for the place in which the branch, agency or other establishment is situated'.

3.303 There are two requirements under this provision. First, the defendant domiciled in a Member State must have a 'branch, agency or other establishment' in another Member State. The European Court of Justice[612] has defined a 'branch, agency or other establishment' in terms of a number of characteristics. The branch etc must: (i) have a fixed permanent place of business; (ii) be subject to the direction and control of the parent: (iii) have a certain autonomy; and (iv) act on behalf of and bind the parent.

3.304 Second, the dispute must arise out of the operations of the branch etc. According to the European Court of Justice in *Somafer v Saar-Ferngas*

---

[611] An analogous argument was applied by the House of Lords in *Kleinwort Benson Ltd v Glasgow City Council* [1999] 1 AC 153 where the majority of the Law Lords, in deciding upon the scope of matters relating to a contract under Art 5(1) of the Brussels Convention and matters relating to tort under Art 5(3), was influenced by the rule in these provisions that allocates jurisdiction to the place of performance of the obligation in question and to the place of the harmful event respectively.

[612] Case 14/76 *De Bloos v Bouyer* [1976] ECR 1497; Case 33/78 *Somafer v Saar-Ferngas* [1978] ECR 2183; Case 139/80 *Blanckaert and Willems v Trost* [1981] ECR 819; Case 218/86 *Sar Schotte GmbH v Parfums Rothschild SARL* [1987] ECR 4905; Case C-439 *Lloyd's Register of Shipping v Société Campenon Bernard* [1995] ECR I-961.

AG,[613] the concept of 'operations' comprises 'actions relating to undertakings which have been entered into at the . . . place of business [of the branch etc] in the name of the parent body . . .'.[614] The Court went on to hold in *Lloyd's Register of Shipping v Societe Campenon Bernard*[615] that there does not necessarily have to be a close link between the entity with which a customer conducts negotiations and places an order and the place where the order will be performed, and that undertakings may form part of the operations of a branch etc. even though they are to be performed outside the Contracting State where it is situated, possibly by another branch etc.[616] According to the Court of Appeal in *Anton Durbeck GmbH v Den Norske Bank Asa*,[617] what this case demonstrates is that there must be such nexus between the branch etc. and the dispute as to render it natural to describe the dispute as one that has arisen out of the activities of the branch.[618] Where the claim is in contract, that nexus can be derived from the negotiations between the claimant and the branch etc which give rise to the contractual obligation, the alleged breach of which is the subject of the dispute.[619] This would include a case where the branch etc. conducts all the negotiations but the final contract is signed by the parent.[620]

Application to Cases of the International Sale of Goods

A branch, agency or other establishment

This is a useful provision in actions in contract between the buyer and **3.305** seller of goods. In practice, whether the plaintiff will be able to base jurisdiction on this provision is going to depend on the method of carrying on business abroad that has been adopted by the defendant. If a seller, domiciled in one Member State, opens a branch office in another Member State to sell its goods, this will normally mean that it becomes subject to jurisdiction in that Member State by virtue of Article 5(5). The branch is likely to have the characteristics laid down by the European Court of Justice when defining a branch etc. for the purposes of Article 5(5). Indeed, these characteristics are those of a typical branch office. However, opening a branch does involve incurring considerable expense. If the seller merely

---

[613] Case 33/78 [1978] ECR 2183.

[614] ibid at 2194. See *Latchin (t/a Dinkha Latchin Associates) v General Mediterranean Holdings SA* [2002] CLC 330, 341.

[615] Case C-439/93 [1995] ECR I-961.   [616] ibid at 981, para 20.

[617] [2003] EWCA Civ 147, [2003] 2 WLR 1296. An appeal is being made to the House of Lords on the question of a stay of the English proceedings.

[618] ibid at [40].   [619] ibid.

[620] But compare the opinion of AG Slynn in Case 218/86 *SAR Schotte GmbH v Parfums Rothschild SARL* [1987] ECR 4905 at 4914. However, this was a case decided before the *Lloyd's Register* case with its wide view of the requirement that the dispute arises out of the operations of the branch etc. Moreover, AG Slynn would have preferred to interpret the requirement widely to encompass this situation.

uses a sales representative this will be much cheaper. What will then be raised are questions over whether the alleged branch etc. has a fixed permanent place of business and whether the sales representative has the power to act on behalf of and bind the parent.[621]

3.306 Goods are commonly sold in Europe by means of a commercial agent.[622] Indeed, with commodities it is usual to use the services of a broker. This again will be cheaper than opening a branch office. This method of selling goods abroad will raise the question whether the agent is subject to the direction and control of the parent. A commercial agent which is free to arrange its own work, is not prevented from representing several other firms competing in the same sector, and transmits orders to the parent without being involved in their terms or execution, will not have the character of a branch, agency or other establishment.[623] It is also common to use an exclusive distributor to market goods elsewhere in Europe.[624] This will also raise the question of whether the grantee is under the direction and control of the parent.

3.307 Finally, a seller may set up a foreign subsidiary to market its goods. This will have a separate legal identity from that of the parent company and typically will act for itself and not on behalf of the parent. Accordingly, it will fall outside the definition of an establishment for the purposes of Article 5(5). A rare instance where this did not happen arose in *SAR Schotte GmbH v Parfums Rothschild SARL*,[625] which is the only decision of the European Court of Justice on the interpretation of Article 5(5) of the Brussels Convention involving an action in contract between the buyer and seller of goods. A German seller of atomizers sued the French buyer (French Rothschild), which claimed that the goods did not meet its requirements for the price. The plaintiff sought to bring the action in Germany on the basis that the defendant's parent company (German Rothschild), which was situated in Germany, constituted an establishment of French Rothschild. The European Court of Justice held that Article 5(5) would apply, even though under company law German Rothschild was an independent company with a separate legal personality. This was because German Rothschild acted in effect as if it were a branch of French Rothschild. German Rothschild and French Rothschild had the same name and identical management, and German Rothschild negotiated and conducted business in the name of French

---

[621] See the *Somafer* case, n 606 above.

[622] See, e.g. the *Blanckaert* case, n 612 above. The action, however, was brought by a commercial agent against the manufacturer for payment of commission and agent's fees.

[623] ibid.

[624] See, e.g. the *De Bloos* case, n 612 above. The action, however, was brought by the grantee of the exclusive distribution rights against the grantor.

[625] Case C-218/86 [1987] ECR 4905.

Rothschild, which used German Rothschild as an extension of itself and would appear as such to third parties.

When does a sale of goods dispute arise out of the operations of a branch etc?

It is enough that the branch etc., acting on behalf of the seller, merely **3.308** entered into the sale of goods contract with the buyer.[626] In such a case, undertakings have been entered into at the place of business of the branch etc in the name of the parent body. It does not matter that the branch etc takes no part in the performance of these obligations. The argument that the branch had to take part in the performance, and that therefore the undertakings had to be performed in the Contracting State where the branch was situated, was rejected by the European Court of Justice in the *Lloyd's Register* case.[627] It is also enough if the branch merely negotiated the sale of goods contract, even if the final contract was signed by the parent. This liberal interpretation has much to commend it in principle. Without it, the application of Article 5(5) would be very limited.

The fact that undertakings do not have to be performed in the Member **3.309** State where the branch etc. is situated means that if, for example, a contract is signed or negotiated by the German branch in Germany and the goods are delivered in France the operations requirement will still be met and the defendant parent can be sued in Germany.

Of course, in many cases the branch etc. will be involved not only in the **3.310** formation of the contract but also in the performance of the undertaking. This is what happened in the *Sar Schotte* case. No specific question was raised as to whether the dispute arose out of the operations of the branch etc. and the Court of Justice did not discuss the matter. The alleged establishment in Germany took part in the negotiations and in the conclusion of the contract but was also responsible, during the performance of the contract, for ensuring that the deliveries contracted for were made and that invoices were paid. It is perhaps not surprising, in such circumstances, that it was, seemingly, accepted by the parties that there was no question but that the dispute arose out of the operations of the branch etc.

If the branch in France enters into obligations which are to be performed **3.311** by a sister branch in Spain, do the Spanish courts have jurisdiction by virtue of Article 5(5)? The undertakings have not been entered into at the place of business of the Spanish branch and, accordingly, the definition laid down in the *Somafer* case is not satisfied. Under this definition, it

---

[626] It is submitted that it does not also have to negotiate the contract. But compare the comments of Lawrence Collins QC in *Saab v Saudi American Bank* [1999] 1 WLR 1861, 1866, CA; discussed below, para 4.10.

[627] n 615 above.

would be necessary to find some undertaking that is given at the place of business of the Spanish branch. However, as has been seen the English Court of Appeal in the *Anton Durbeck* case[628] has adopted a wide view of the operations requirement, justifying this in the light of the *Lloyd's Register* case.[629] If merely negotiating the contract (the undertakings being given by the parent when signing the contract) can demonstrate a sufficient nexus between the branch and the dispute, it is arguable that being concerned with the performance of the contractual obligation giving rise to the dispute can equally demonstrate a sufficient nexus. Entering into or negotiating the contract, on the one hand, and being concerned with its performance, on the other hand, should be regarded as being alternatives. The branch may not have entered into or negotiated the contract. Nonetheless, it is submitted that it should be enough if the branch is concerned in the performance of the undertaking or is substantially so concerned. However, it would not be enough if it was only partly so concerned.[630]

3.312   Neither does the dispute arise out of the operations of a branch in the situation where a seller sues for payment for goods and the buyer claims a set-off relating to payment made by the buyer to the branch of a company jointly owned by the seller and buyer.[631] The dispute does not relate to undertakings entered into by the branch in the name of the parent.

V DECLINING JURISDICTION AND RESTRAINING FOREIGN PROCEEDINGS

1. Declining Jurisdiction Under the Brussels I Regulation

(a) *Lis Pendens*

3.313   Article 27 of the Brussels I Regulation states that:

1. Where proceedings involving the same cause of action and between the same parties are brought in the courts of different Member States, any court other than the court first seised shall of its own motion stay its proceedings until such time as the jurisdiction of the court first seised is established.
2. Where the jurisdiction of the court first seised is established, any court other than the court first seised shall decline jurisdiction in favour of that court.

---

[628] n 617 above.   [629] n 615 above.   [630] See the discussion below, para 4.10.
[631] *Société des Etablissements J Verdier v Jose Oliveira Da Silva (Liquidator of Moutinho LMD SA)* [2001] IL Pr 34, Cour de cassation.

A court is deemed to be seised at the time when the document instituting the proceedings or an equivalent document is lodged with the court, provided that the plaintiff has not subsequently failed to take the steps he was required to take to have service effected on the defendant.[632]

For Article 27 to apply, there must be proceedings in the courts of dif- **3.314** ferent Member States. This causes no particular problem in actions in contract between the buyer and seller of goods. More problematical are the requirements in relation to the cause of action and the parties.

The same cause of action

The meaning of the phrase   For Article 27 to apply, the two sets of **3.315** proceedings must involve 'the same cause of action'. This single expression comprises two concepts, both of which have to be satisfied: the same cause and the same 'objet' (subject-matter).[633] Actions have the same cause if they have the same facts and rule of law as their basis.[634] Actions have the same 'objet' if they have the same end in view.[635] There is no problem if one party brings the same claim against the defendant in two different Member States. More commonly perhaps, one party is seeking to assert liability in one state and the other is seeking to deny liability in another state. The issue is essentially the same and the two claims are essentially mirror images of one another and Article 27 will apply.[636] In contrast, if the same claimant is suing the same defendant on different bases giving rise to different issues and different financial consequences, and where liability on one claim does not involve liability (or non-liability) on the other, then Article 27 will not apply.[637] Although the cause is the same and there is some overlap in the claims and issues, different claims may

---

[632] Art 30(1). If the document has to be served before being lodged with the court, a court is deemed to be seised at the time when it is received by the authority responsible for service, provided that the plaintiff has not subsequently failed to take the steps he was required to take to have the document lodged with the court.

[633] Case C-406/92 *The Maciej Rataj* [1994] ECR I-5439 at 5475, para 38; Case 144/86 *Gubisch Maschinenfabrik KG v Palumbo* [1987] ECR 4861, paras 14–17. The French version refers to 'la meme objet et la meme cause'. See also *Haji-Ioannou v Frangos* [1999] 2 Lloyd's Rep 337 at 348–351 (*per* Bingham CJ), CA; *Glencore International AG v Shell International Trading and Shipping Co Ltd and Metro Oil Corp* [1999] 2 Lloyd's Rep 692.

[634] *The Maciej Rataj*, n 633 above, at 5475, para 39.

[635] ibid at 5475, para 41. In determining whether claims have the same subject-matter, account should be taken only of the claims of the respective applicants, not of defence submissions, in particular of set-off: Case C-111/01 *Gantner Electronic GmbH v Basch Exploitatie Maatschappij BV* [2003] ECR I-4207.

[636] *Glencore International AG v Shell International Trading and Shipping Co Ltd and Metro Oil Corp* [1999] 2 Lloyd's Rep 692 at 697. See also the *Gubisch* case, n 633 above, and *The Maciej Rataj*, n 633 above.

[637] *Glencore*, ibid at 692 at 697. See *Sarrio SA v Kuwait Investment Authority* [1999] 1 AC 32.

raise sufficiently different issues of sufficient importance in the overall litigation for it to be concluded that the 'objet' differs.[638]

Application to contracts for the international sale of goods

3.316 *Situations where the cause of action is the same*   In contracts for the international sale of goods, concurrent litigation, and hence the question whether the cause of action is the same in two different sets of proceedings, has arisen in a number of different situations. The first is where a seller seeks payment for goods and the buyer disputes the validity of the contract of sale. The second is where, again, the seller seeks payment for goods, but this time the buyer disputes the quality of the goods delivered and seeks a price reduction. The third is where one party seeks damages for breach of the sales contract and the other party seeks a negative declaration. In all of these situations, although the claims naturally differ, the issue between them is essentially the same, the claims being essentially mirror images of one another and Article 27 will apply.

3.317 This first situation arose in *Gubisch Maschinenfabrik KG v Palumbo*,[639] which was the first case in which the European Court of Justice examined the meaning of 'the same cause of action'. The German seller of a machine brought an action in Germany against the Italian buyer to enforce performance of the latter's obligation under the contract to pay for the goods. Subsequently, the buyer brought proceedings in Italy for a declaration that the contract was inoperative on the ground that his order had been revoked before it reached the seller for acceptance. In the alternative, the buyer claimed that the contract should be set aside for lack of consent or, in the further alternative, that it should be discharged on the ground that the seller had not complied with the time limit for delivery. The European Court of Justice held that the two sets of proceedings were based on the same cause, that is the same contractual relationship. It was also held that the two actions had the same subject-matter. The Court said that it was apparent that the action to enforce the contract was aimed at giving effect to it, and that the action for its rescission or discharge was aimed precisely at depriving it of any effect. The question of whether the contract was binding lay at the heart of the two actions. Indeed, the subsequent action for discharge might even be regarded as simply a defence against the first action,[640] brought in the form of independent proceedings before a court in another Contracting State. The Court went on to say that the concept

---

[638] *Glencore*, ibid at 697; the *Haji-Ioannou* case, n 633 above.

[639] Case 144/86 [1987] ECR 4861.

[640] For the significance of defences when ascertaining whether the subject-matter of the two sets of proceedings is the same, see the *Gantner* case, n 635 above.

of the same subject-matter cannot be restricted so as to mean two claims which are entirely identical.

The *Gubisch* case was followed by the German Bundesgerichtshof in *Re A* **3.318** *Sale of Shares*,[641] where the issue of the validity of the contract of sale arose in proceedings in two different Member States in a rather different context. The plaintiff buyer of shares paid part of their price but then refused to pay the rest, rescinding the contract for misrepresentation and mistake. The plaintiff sought a declaration in Italy that the contract was invalid and restitution of the part of the price already paid. Subsequently the plaintiff brought an action in Germany for restitution of the price already paid. The Bundesgerichtshof held that the German courts were obliged to decline jurisdiction because of Article 21 of the Brussels Convention. The validity or invalidity of the contract was said to be the central issue in both sets of proceedings.

The second situation has arisen before national courts in Italy. In *SpA* **3.319** *Silpol v Pears Plastics Belgium NV*,[642] the Corte d'appello, Milan was faced with a case where an Italian buyer of goods commenced an action in Italy for, inter alia, reduction of the purchase price, claiming that the goods supplied by the seller under previous contracts between the parties were defective. This was followed by the seller commencing an action in Belgium for payment of the purchase price. The Court was clear that the proceedings involved the same cause of action since one action was for payment and the other for reduction of the purchase price. One action may be for payment and the other for damages for breach of contract, the buyer alleging that the goods are defective.[643] Nonetheless, the two sets of proceedings are based on the same contractual relationship and the subject-matter is also the same. The question of the quality of the goods lies at the heart of both actions.

The third situation arose before national courts in Germany in *Re a Cloth-* **3.320** *ing Sale Contract*.[644] The buyer commenced proceedings in Germany for breach of a contract for the delivery of clothing, claiming damages or, alternatively, restitution on the grounds of unjust enrichment. Before this action was started the defendant had begun proceedings for a declaration of non-liability before an Italian court in respect of the same claims. The Oberlandesgericht, Munchen, held that both sets of proceedings involved

---

[641] Case VIII ZR 14/94 [1996] IL Pr 292.

[642] Judgment of 26 September 1978, Foro pad 1978, I, 394, Note: Pesce; Riv dir int priv proc 1978, 843, D Series I-21—B 4.

[643] See, eg, the Canadian case of *Sydney Steel Corp v Canadian National Railway Co* (1998) 164 DLR (4th) 747, Novia Scotia CA.

[644] Case 7 W 2919/93 [1995] IL Pr 172, Oberlandesgericht Munich.

the same subject-matter. The Court pointed out that a successful application for a negative declaration establishes that a claim does not exist; a successful action for payment or performance by contrast establishes that there is a claim on the relevant grounds. Conflicting judgments are therefore possible. Similarly in *IP Metal Ltd v Ruote OZ SpA (No 2)*,[645] it appears to have been common ground amongst counsel that, where the plaintiff buyers brought proceedings for breach of contract in relation to the seventh of seven contracts for the sale of aluminium and the defendant sellers brought proceedings in Italy seeking a declaration that they were under no liability to the plaintiffs in relation to this contract, the cause of action was the same in both sets of proceedings.

3.321 We now in fact have authority from the European Court of Justice that negative declarations come within the *lis pendens* provisions. It has held that an action seeking to have the defendant held liable for causing loss and ordered to pay damages has the same cause of action and the same object as earlier proceedings brought by that defendant seeking a declaration that he is not liable for that loss.[646] If the action for a negative declaration is brought promptly in a Member State in which trials are notoriously slow, such as Italy, this will have the effect of blocking the claimant's action for breach of contract.[647]

3.322 *Examples where the cause of action is not the same* A simple example of where the cause of action was not the same, which arose in the context of the international sale of goods is *IP Metal Ltd v Ruote OZ SpA*.[648] The plaintiff sellers brought proceedings in England for breach of contract in relation to six out of seven contracts for the sale of aluminium. The defendant buyers brought proceedings in Italy seeking a declaration that they were under no liability to the plaintiffs in relation to the seventh contract. It was common ground amongst counsel that it was not seriously arguable that the Italian proceedings involved the same cause of action as the English proceedings.[649] A further simple example is provided by *Lafi Office and International Business SL v Meriden Animal Health Ltd*.[650] The plaintiff seller, a company domiciled in Spain, brought proceedings against the defendant buyer, a company domiciled in England, for the unpaid price of the goods sold and delivered. The defendant had

---

[645] [1994] 2 Lloyd's Rep 560. The case was concerned with the issue of consensus under Art 17 of the Brussels Convention and this aspect is discussed above, para 3.25

[646] *The Maciej Rataj*, n 633 above, para 45.

[647] See, e.g. *Re Lifting A Stay of Proceedings* (Case 7W 1461/98) [1999] IL Pr 291—the Oberlandesgericht, Munich, refused to lift the stay of German proceedings even though there had been a complete standstill for two years of Italian proceedings that had lasted six years so far.

[648] [1993] 2 Lloyd's Rep 60.   [649] ibid at 61.   [650] [2001] 1 All ER (Comm) 54.

previously issued a petition in the Spanish courts against certain named individuals associated with the plaintiff company. The Spanish proceedings were parasitic upon criminal proceedings and were essentially for compensation in relation to damage caused by the allegedly fraudulent conduct of these named individuals. Christopher Symons QC, siting as a Deputy Judge of the High Court, held that there was no specific claim being made by the defendant in the Spanish proceedings relating, in terms, to the specific contract, and it followed that the English action did not involve the same cause of action as the Spanish proceedings.[651] The English court was therefore unable to decline jurisdiction under Article 21 of the Brussels Convention.[652]

A more complex example, which arose out of the storage of goods, rather **3.323** than their sale, is *Glencore International AG v Shell International Trading and Shipping Co Ltd and Metro Oil Corp*.[653] Metro, the operator of an oil storage system used by many large oil companies, went into receivership and this led to complex multi-party litigation over who was entitled to oil remaining in storage or which had been sold prior to the collapse. One of the claimants (Banque Trad) brought an action against Shell in Paris, based on an alleged assignment to it by Metro. Subsequently Shell, faced with numerous claims in respect of the same debt, brought a claim for interpleader relief against Banque Trad and other claimants in London. The effect of Shell's interpleader summons was to invoke Banque Trad's claim against itself in the English proceedings. Rix J had to decide whether the two sets of proceedings involved the same cause of action. He held that if the relevant English proceedings were taken as being the action by Banque Trad which was generated by Shell's application for interpleader relief then the cause was the same as that in the Paris proceedings.[654] If, on the other hand, the relevant English proceedings were taken as being the application for interpleader relief then the cause was not the same because the claim by Banque Trad against Shell in England was a mere incident of the overall application.[655] When it came to the question whether the proceedings had the same 'objet', it was necessary to consider the application for interpleader relief as a whole. The essential issue in Banque Trad's claim against Shell in Paris was whether Shell was liable to it for the price of two cargoes bought from Metro. But the essential issue in Shell's application against Banque Trad in England was not Shell's liability to Banque Trad, for that was not even disputed, but whether Banque Trad's claim was superior to that of the other

---

[651] ibid at 70–71.
[652] It was also held that the Spanish court was not first seised, ibid at 70.
[653] [1999] 2 Lloyd's Rep 692.   [654] ibid at 698.   [655] ibid.

claimants.[656] Even if Banque Trad's claim against Shell, as generated by Shell's application, had to be considered as the relevant second set of proceedings, the 'objet' of the two sets of proceedings was not the same. The claim in France stood by itself and the issue was Shell's liability. The 'objet' of the claim in England was the raising of the issue whether Shell's liability to Banque Trad, which was not in dispute, was subject to a better title possessed by another claimant.[657]

3.324 Finally, the Court of Appeal in *Toepfer v Société Cargill*[658] left unresolved the question whether a challenge to the jurisdiction of the French courts based on an arbitration clause (the challenge being made in the course of French proceedings for a substantive claim for damages for breach of sale contracts) involved the same cause of action as English proceedings for an anti-suit injunction based on a breach of the arbitration agreement.[659] The principal issue was the same, namely the existence of a binding arbitration agreement. So was the 'objet' of each proceeding, namely the restraint of the substantive hearing before the French court. However, because the existing case law of the European Court of Justice did not provide a clear answer, this question was referred to that Court for a decision. No such decision was given, the action being settled.

3.325 *One cause of action or several?* This question arose in *Kloeckner & Co AG v Gatoil Overseas Inc*,[660] which involved a complex contractual situation. The parties entered into a basic agreement which provided the framework for the making of sale 'contracts', purchase 'contracts' and book-out 'contracts' in respect of oil. A very large number of such 'contracts' were entered into by the parties. The plaintiffs instituted proceedings in England for damages in relation to these 'contracts'. The defendants instituted proceedings in Germany for a negative declaration in relation to just three of these contracts, a tiny proportion of those entered into. Was the cause of action the same in the two sets of proceedings? The defendants argued that they were on the ground that the German proceedings were founded on the basic agreement, and it was this that constituted the cause of action for the present purposes. The plaintiffs, on the other hand, argued that the proper approach was to scrutinize each individual cause of action. It followed that the proceedings were only identical in so far as the English proceedings concerned claims relating to the three contracts which were the subject of the German proceedings, and the English proceedings raised a whole host of different causes of action based on

---

[656] ibid at 698–699.   [657] ibid at 699.   [658] [1998] 1 Lloyd's Rep 379, CA.
[659] The Court of Appeal, [1998] 1 Lloyd's Rep 379 at 387–388, raised the question of what would have happened if there had been no challenge to the jurisdiction of the French courts. It was said that commencing proceedings in the second seised court in order to challenge the jurisdiction of the first seised court was against the scheme of the Brussels Convention.
[660] [1990] 1 Lloyd's Rep 177.

different contracts which were not the subject of the German proceedings. Hirst J accepted the plaintiffs' argument[661] and held that every claim on each 'contract' was itself technically a separate cause of action and could not be bundled together into one composite cause of action just because they were all foreshadowed by the basic agreement. He said obiter that had the German court been the court first seised he would have declined jurisdiction only to the extent that the English proceedings related to the three 'contracts' which were the subject of the German proceedings.

The same parties

The meaning of the phrase The two sets of proceedings must also be **3.326** between the same parties. Multi-party cases, which are common in the context of litigation arising out of the international sale of goods, have raised the question whether this requirement has been met. The European Court of Justice in *The Maciej Rataj*[662] has held that 'the second court seised is required to decline jurisdiction only to the extent to which the parties to the proceedings before it are also parties to the action previously commenced; it does not prevent the proceedings from continuing between the other parties'.[663]

Application to contracts for the international sale of goods The *Lafi* **3.327** *Office* case[664] is a simple example of where the requirement that the parties must be the same was not met, the claimant company in the English action not being a party to the Spanish proceedings. The defendant to the English proceedings tried to get round this obvious difficulty by arguing that the individuals associated with the claimant company as its principals, who were parties to the Spanish proceedings, were in effect the same as the claimant company. In other words, the judge was being urged to remove the corporate veil. This he declined to do.

First seised

The meaning of the phrase A court is deemed to be seised of **3.328** proceedings:

at the time when the document instituting the proceedings or an equivalent document is lodged with the court, provided that the plaintiff has not

---

[661] An analogous approach was subsequently adopted by the ECJ in *The Maciej Rataj*, n 633 above, in relation to the question of whether the parties were the same, see below, para 3.326.
[662] n 633 above.
[663] ibid at 5474. Applied in *Glencore*, n 636 above, at 694. However, it is possible to look beyond the formal identities of the parties. Thus an insurer and insured are the same parties where their interests are the same, such as where the insurer, by virtue of its right of subrogation, brings or defends an action in the name of the insured: Case C-351/96 *Drouot Assurances SA v Consolidated Metallurgical Industries* [1998] ECR I-3075.
[664] n 650 above.

subsequently failed to take the steps he was required to take to have service effected on the defendant, or if the document has to be served before being lodged with the court, at the time when it is received by the authority responsible for service, provided that the plaintiff has not subsequently failed to take the steps he was required to take to have the document lodged with the court.[665]

A court second seised whose jurisdiction has been claimed under an agreement conferring jurisdiction has to stay proceedings of its own motion until the jurisdiction of the court first seised has been established and, where it has been so established, has to decline jurisdiction in favour of the latter.[666] It is for the court first seised to pronounce as to its jurisdiction in the light of the jurisdiction clause before it.[667] If the court first seised declares it has no jurisdiction then the court second seised will lift its stay of the proceedings. This means that Article 27 takes priority over Article 23.[668] The first seised rule is to be applied even though the duration of proceedings before that court is excessively long.

3.329 Application to contracts for the international sale of goods   Although English jurisdiction clauses are prevalent in contracts for the international sale of goods, the English courts are going to have to stay proceedings of their own motion in favour of courts in other Member States which are first seised.

Related Actions
A stay of proceedings

3.330 Article 28(1) of the Brussels I Regulation states that:

> Where related actions are pending in the courts of different Member States, any court other than the court first seised may stay its proceedings.

This provision deals with situations that fall outside the scope of Article 27 because the cause of action and subject-matter, or the parties, or even both, are not the same.

---

[665] Art 30.

[666] Case C-116/02 *Erich Gasser GmbH v Misat Srl* [2004] IL Pr 7. The reference from the Oberlandesgericht, Innsbruck, is reported in (Case 4 r 41/02i) [2003] IL Pr 11. The *Gasser* case overrules the decision of the English Court of Appeal in *Continental Bank NA v Aeakos Compañía Naviera SA* [1994] 1 WLR 588.

[667] The *Continental Bank* case has been criticized on the basis that it was the English court second seised that was pronouncing on the jurisdiction of the Greek court first seised, see Cheshire and North, 256.

[668] When it comes to recognition and enforcement of foreign judgments the Regulation provides no defence based on breach of an exclusive jurisdiction clause, see below, paras 11.09–15.

According to Article 28(3), 'actions are deemed to be related where **3.331** they are so closely connected that it is expedient to hear and determine them together to avoid the risk of irreconcilable judgments resulting from separate proceedings'. Lord Saville in *Sarrio SA v Kuwait Investment Authority*[669] has said that 'there should be a broad commonsense approach to the question whether the actions in question are related, bearing in mind the objective of the article, applying the simple wide test set out in Article 22 and refraining from an over-sophisticated analysis of the matter'.[670] It seems to be implicit from the part of the definition of related actions that refers to it being expedient to hear the two actions together that the court first seised must be able to try both actions together. It has been held that where this is not the case, the use of Article 28 is wholly inappropriate and the action should not be stayed on that ground.[671]

Any court other than the court first seised *may*, rather than must, stay its **3.332** proceedings. This gives a discretion, in exercising which 'regard may be had to the question of which court is in the best position to decide a given question'.[672] In exercising this discretion, there is a strong presumption in favour of granting a stay so as to avoid the risk of irreconcilable judgments.[673]

Application to contracts for the international sale of goods

Are the actions related? National decisions on this tend to regard the **3.333** answer to this question as being self evident and give little explanation for their decision. Thus, applying the commonsense approach of Lord Saville in *Sarrio*,[674] it was held in the *Lafi Office* case[675] that where an English action was for the price of goods sold and delivered and Spanish proceedings were parasitic upon criminal proceedings and were essentially for compensation in relation to damage caused by the allegedly fraudulent conduct of certain named individuals, the actions were obviously not related. Furthermore, the actions could not be heard together.[676] The civil proceedings in Spain had no independent existence of their own and were therefore not capable of being heard with other civil proceedings.[677] Finally, it was said that, whilst it may be that the Spanish courts would have to consider certain issues which would also become relevant in the

---

[669] [1999] 1 AC 32; criticized in a note by J Harris, 'Related Actions and the Brussels Convention' [1998] LMCLQ 145.

[670] ibid at 41.

[671] *Haji-Ioannou v Frangos* [1999] 2 Lloyd's Rep 337 at 352, CA; *Lafi Office and International Business SL v Meriden Animal Health Ltd* [2001] 1 All ER (Comm) 54 at 71.

[672] See the opinion of AG Lenz in Case C-129/92 *Owens Bank Ltd v Bracco (No 2)* [1994] QB 509 at 542; [1994] ECR I-117.

[673] [1994] QB 509 at 541.   [674] n 669 above.   [675] n 671 above.   [676] ibid at 71.

[677] ibid. See also *Haji-Ioannou v Frangos* [1999] 2 Lloyd's Rep 337 at 352, CA.

English proceedings, it could never be expedient for the two proceedings to be heard together.

3.334 *In IP Metal Ltd v Ruote OZ SpA,*[678] it was common ground that the proceedings in England, for breach of contract in relation to six out of the seven contracts between the parties, and the proceedings in Italy, for a declaration that they were under no liability to the plaintiffs in relation to the seventh contract, were related for the purposes of Article 22 of the Brussels Convention.[679] This case neatly illustrates the usefulness of the related actions provision (in what is now Article 28) in dealing with cases falling outside the *lis pendens* provision (in what is now Article 27), in this case because the cause of action was not the same in the two sets of proceedings.[680]

3.335 The usefulness of Article 28 in encompassing cases that fall outside Article 27 is also shown by a decision of the French Cour de cassation which concerned proceedings in the Netherlands and in France. In the Dutch proceedings, a Dutch plaintiff sued a French company for the balance of the purchase price of equipment for processing waste paper. In the French proceedings, the French company sued the Dutch company for damages for injury suffered by reason of defects in the equipment and for an order that it was entitled to keep the balance of the purchase price, for which it was being sued in the Dutch courts, as part of the damages.[681] It was held that the two sets of proceedings were related. The only explanation given for this was that the French company's resistance to paying the balance of the price of the equipment was not unconnected with the incidents relating to its operation nor with the resulting loss.

3.336 The above cases can be contrasted with the decision of the Court of Appeal in *Miles Platt Limited v Townroe Limited.*[682] Proceedings in France, whereby S, the buyer of electrical coils, sought a declaration that the seller and a component manufacturer (MP) were responsible for the economic damage it had suffered when television sets containing the coils caught fire and were liable to make good the loss, were held not to be related to proceedings in England brought by MP against a supplier (T) for breach of contract and/or negligence. The French proceedings were not likely to go beyond the question of whether pins in the electrical coils were defective. Whereas the English proceedings would examine how they came to be defective, for example whether this was due to storage by MP or the electro-plating process used by T.

---

[678] [1993] 2 Lloyd's Rep 60.   [679] ibid at 61.   [680] See above, para 3.322.
[681] *SA Des Papeteries De L'AA v Machinefabriek BOA BV* [1993] IL Pr 392, Cour de cassation.
[682] [2003] IL Pr 746.

The exercise of the discretion to stay There are no special circumstances that **3.337** arise when it comes to contracts for the international sale of goods.

Declining jurisdiction

Article 28(2) goes on to state that: **3.338**

> Where these actions are pending at first instance, any court other than the court first seised may also, on the application of one of the parties, decline jurisdiction if the court first seised has jurisdiction over the actions in question and its law permits the consolidation thereof.

Under this provision, a court may decline jurisdiction, as opposed to merely staying its proceedings.

2. DECLINING JURISDICTION USING THE DOCTRINE OF *FORUM NON CONVENIENS*

The Brussels I Regulation contains no general discretionary power to **3.339** decline jurisdiction on the basis of *forum non conveniens*.[683] Nonetheless, the Court of Appeal in *Re Harrods (Buenos Aires) Ltd*[684] held, in the situation where a basis of jurisdiction under the Brussels Convention applied,[685] that an English court still had the power to stay its own proceedings on this basis, provided that the alternative forum for trial was a non-Contracting State to the Brussels Convention, in the instant case Argentina. It was accepted though that there was no such power where the alternative forum was a Contracting State. This decision has been approved by the Court of Appeal on a number of occasions.[686] It has however been subject to strong academic criticism[687] and Lord Bingham has held that the law in this area is not clear.[688] The recent decision of the Court of Appeal in *Owusu v Jackson*[689] to refer to the European Court of

---

[683] This doctrine is considered below, paras 4.156–163.

[684] [1992] Ch 72.

[685] The English court's jurisdiction was based on Art 2 of the Convention. For the situation where Art 4 of the Convention (and now the Regulation) applies and the basis of jurisdiction is not one set out in the Convention (now Regulation) but is instead under the traditional English rules of jurisdiction, see Cheshire and North, 264–266.

[686] *Haji-Ioannou v Frangos* [1999] 2 Lloyd's Rep 337, CA; *ACE Insurance SA v Zurich Insurance Co* [2001] 1 Lloyd's Rep 618, CA.

[687] See Cheshire and North, 263–266; Briggs and Rees, 2.216. Compare the note by Collins, 'Forum Non Conveniens and the Brussels Convention' (1990) 106 LQR 535.

[688] *Lubbe v Cape plc* [2000] 1 WLR 1545, HL.

[689] [2002] EWCA Civ 877, [2002] IL Pr 45, CA. See also *American Motorists Insurance Co (Amico) v Cellstar Corp* [2003] EWCA Civ 206, [2003] IL Pr 22, where the Court of Appeal referred the same question to the ECJ as in *Owusu* with a view to it being combined with the reference in that case.

Justice[690] the correctness of the principle in *Re Harrods* is therefore to be welcomed.[691] The correctness of this principle is also due to be considered by the House of Lords in the context of the Lugano Convention.[692]

3. Restraining Foreign Proceedings

3.340 The English courts also have a discretionary power, in certain limited circumstances,[693] to issue an injunction restraining a party from commencing or continuing as plaintiff with foreign proceedings. This power has been used in relation to proceedings in other Member States.[694] However, the Brussels I Regulation contains no such discretionary power. The House of Lords in *Turner v Grovit*[695] referred to the European Court of Justice[696] the question whether it is inconsistent with the Brussels Convention 'to grant restraining orders against defendants who are threatening to commence or continue legal proceedings in another Convention country when those defendants are acting in bad faith with the intent and purpose of frustrating or obstructing proceedings properly brought before the English courts?'. The European Court of Justice held that the Brussels Convention precludes the grant of an injunction whereby a court of a Contracting State prohibits a party to proceedings pending before it from commencing or continuing legal proceedings before a court of another Contracting State, even where that party is acting in bad faith with a view to frustrating the existing proceedings.[697] The Court said that such an injunction constituted an interference with the jurisdiction of the foreign court which, as such, was incompatible with the system of the Conven-

---

[690] Case C-281/02.

[691] Until there is a decision of the ECJ or the House of Lords overruling it the *Re Harrods* principle still applies: *Chellaram v Chellaram No 2* [2002] EWHC 632 (Ch) 17 at [132], [2002] 3 All ER 17. AG Ruiz-Jarabo Colomer in Case C-159/02 *Turner v Grovit* [2004] 1 Lloyd's Rep 216, para 35 has criticized the use of *forum non conveniens* in the EC context. This was in a case where he gave his Opinion that the Brussels Convention precludes the judicial authorities of a Contracting State from issuing orders to litigants restraining them from commencing or continuing proceedings before judicial authorities of other Contracting States. He described the effect of restraining orders as being similar to those produced by application of the doctrine of *forum non conveniens*. The ECJ has followed his Opinion but without mentioning *forum non conveniens*.

[692] *Anton Durbeck GmbH v Den Norske Bank Asa*. The decision of the Court of Appeal is reported at [2003] EWCA Civ 147, [2003] 2 WLR 1296.

[693] Discussed below, paras 4.172–188. Of particular importance in sale of goods cases is the granting of an injunction where there has been a breach of an exclusive jurisdiction or arbitration clause, see below, paras 4.173–180.

[694] See *Continental Bank NA v Aeakos Compañía Naviera SA* [1994] 1 WLR 588, CA; *The Angelic Grace* [1995] 1 Lloyd's Rep 87, CA.

[695] [2001] UKHL 65, [2002] 1 WLR 107, HL.

[696] Case C-159/02 [2004] 1 Lloyd's Rep 216.

[697] para 32.

tion.[698] The European Court of Justice in another case has held that a court seised second whose jurisdiction has been claimed under an agreement conferring jurisdiction has nevertheless to stay proceedings until the court first seised has declared that it has no jurisdiction.[699] It is for the court first seised to pronounce as to its jurisdiction in the light of the jurisdiction clause.[700] In such circumstances, an English court second seised cannot claim that there has been a breach of an exclusive jurisdiction clause providing for trial in England and is therefore unable to restrain on this basis the foreign proceedings in the Member State first seised.

---

[698] para 27.

[699] Case C-116/02 *Erich Gasser GmbH v Misat Srl* [2003] ECR I-4207. The reference from the Austrian Oberlandesgericht (Case 4 r 41/02i) is reported in [2003] IL Pr 11.

[700] The *Gasser* case, n 699 above.

4

An Action in Contract Between the Buyer and Seller: Jurisdiction under the Traditional English Rules

I. INTRODUCTION

In cases where the European regime of rules,[1] outlined in Chapters 2 and   **4.01**
3, do not apply, recourse must be had to the traditional English rules
on jurisdiction.[2] The process is in one respect more complicated than that

---

[1] i.e. the Brussels I Regulation, the Brussels Convention and the Lugano Convention.

[2] More positively, Art 4 of the Brussels I Regulation directs that the jurisdiction of the courts of each Member State shall be determined by the law of that State in cases where the defendant is not domiciled in a Member State (subject to Arts 22 and 23).

when operating the European regime of rules. It is not simply a question of finding a basis of jurisdiction in respect of a foreign defendant, it also has to be asked whether the English court will exercise its discretionary powers to stay the action. However, in another respect the process is simpler in that there are not the problems of classification[3] that arise under the European regime of rules.

II. BASES OF JURISDICTION

1. Service of a Claim Form Within the Jurisdiction

The Rules

Individuals

4.02 An individual who is present in England and has been duly served with a claim form is subject to the jurisdiction of the English courts.[4] Part 6 of the Civil Procedure Rules sets out rules on the method of service within the jurisdiction. It provides[5] that a document may be served by any of the following methods: (a) personal service; (b) first class post; (c) leaving the document at a place specified in r 6.5; (d) through a document exchange; (e) by fax or other means of electronic communication. The court may make an order permitting service by an alternative method.[6] The court will serve a document which it has issued or prepared, subject to a number of exceptions.[7] Where the court is to serve a document, it is for the court to decide which of the methods of service specified above is to be used.[8]

4.03 It is worth looking at personal service and at service at a place specified in r 6.5 in a little more detail. A document is served personally on an individual by leaving it with that individual.[9] The position therefore remains the same as at common law in that a defendant who is transiently present in England, rather than being resident in England, and who is served in England will be subject to the jurisdiction of the English courts. The only difference now under the Civil Procedure Rules is the court will normally decide on the method of service. However, there is an exception

---

[3] Under the traditional rules the English courts will not use an autonomous community definition to determine whether a claim is made in contract or tort. Compare the problems in determining whether a matter relates to contract or tort under the Brussels I Regulation, see above, para 3.62.

[4] *John Russell & Co Ltd v Cayzer, Irvine & Co Ltd* [1916] 2 AC 298 at 302, HL. The defendant may be merely transiently present, *Maharanee of Baroda v Wildenstein* [1972] 2 QB 283. See generally Dicey and Morris, 291–295.

[5] r 6.2(1) CPR.   [6] r 6.8.   [7] r 6.3(1).   [8] r 6.3(2).   [9] r 6.4(3).

to this where the party on whose behalf the document is to be served notifies the court that he wishes to serve it himself.[10]

As regards the method of service by leaving the document at a place **4.04** specified in r 6.5, this provides that, except for cases of service out of the jurisdiction, a document must be served within the jurisdiction.[11] A party must give an address for service within the jurisdiction.[12] Where a party does not give the business address of his solicitor as his address for service, and resides or carries on business within the jurisdiction, he must give his residence or place of business as his address for service.[13] Where no solicitor is acting for the party to be served and the party has not given an address for service, the document must be sent or transmitted to, or left at, the place shown in a table. In the case of an individual, this is the usual or last known residence. In the case of the proprietor of a business, it is the usual or last known residence, or place of business or last known place of business. In the case of an individual who is suing or being sued in the name of a firm, it is the usual or last known residence, or the principal or last known place of business of the firm.

Companies

There are two sets of rules dealing with the question whether a foreign **4.05** company is subject to the jurisdiction of the English courts. The first set is contained in the Companies Act 1985, the second in the more recently introduced Civil Procedure Rules, Part 6. The latter contains alternative methods of service on a foreign company. The law on service on a foreign company using the Companies Act 1985 is well settled, whereas, in contrast, it is as yet not entirely clear what Part 6 does and does not allow. It follows that, where a case falls clearly within the Companies Act 1985, this is the set of rules that should be used. However, in cases falling outside this Act, recourse should be had to Part 6, which may allow service on the foreign company.

The Companies Act 1985

A company registered in England If a company is registered in England **4.06** under the Companies Act 1985, service of a claim form can be effected by sending it to the registered office of the company.[14]

---

[10] r 6.3(1)(b).
[11] r 6.5(1) CPR. Does this mean that in a case where service within the jurisdiction is problematic, a claimant who goes straight for service out of the jurisdiction may fall foul of this provision?
[12] r 6.5(2) CPR.   [13] r 6.5(3) CPR.
[14] Companies Act 1985, s 725(1). This is unaffected by the fact that the CPR have introduced methods of service. These different methods of service are alternatives: see r 6.2(2) CPR; *Murphy v Staples UK Ltd* [2003] EWCA Civ 656, [2003] 1 WLR 2441.

4.07 *A foreign company which has a branch in Great Britain*   A limited company which is incorporated outside the United Kingdom and Gibraltar, and has a branch[15] in Great Britain is required to register with the registrar of companies the names and addresses of all persons resident in Great Britain authorized to accept on the company's behalf service of process in respect of the business of the branch.[16] Process in respect of the carrying on of the business of a branch is sufficiently served if addressed to any such person and is left at or sent by post to that address.[17] Where a company fails to comply with its statutory obligations to so register, or if all the persons named are dead or have ceased to reside in Great Britain, or refuse to accept service on the company's behalf, or for any other reason cannot be served, a document may be served on the company in respect of the carrying on of the business of the branch by leaving it at, or sending it by post to, any place of business established by the company in Great Britain.[18]

4.08 For these provisions to come into play the claimant must establish a good arguable case that: first, the foreign company has a branch in Great Britain; and second, the process that is served on the foreign company is in respect of the carrying on of the business of the branch.[19]

4.09 As regards the meaning of a 'branch',[20] in *Saab v Saudi American Bank*[21] it was common ground that a branch is a more permanent establishment than a mere place of business.[22] However, guidance on the meaning of a 'branch' cannot be gained from the decisions of the European Court of Justice on the interpretation of a branch, agency or other establishment under Article 5(5) of the Brussels Convention.[23] A branch is different from a subsidiary company in that it has no separate legal identity and for the same reason is different from an independent commercial agent.

4.10 When is process served in respect of the carrying on of the business of a branch? To answer this one must turn to the decision of the Court of Appeal in the leading case of *Saab v Saudi American Bank*.[24] The plaintiffs engaged the defendant, a Saudi Arabian bank, to market shares in a development company throughout the world, including the United

---

[15] For the interpretation of branch see Sch 21A, para 13.
[16] s 690A and Sch 21A, 3(e).   [17] s 694A(2).   [18] s 694A(3).
[19] *Saab v Saudi American Bank* [1999] 1 WLR 1861 at 1873 (*per* Clarke LJ). He was referring to the standard of proof in relation to the second requirement but would doubtless apply the same standard to the first requirement.
[20] See generally Cheshire and North, 290–291.
[21] [1999] 1 WLR 1861.
[22] ibid, at 1868.
[23] See *Saab v Saudi American Bank* [1999] 1 WLR 1861, CA; discussed below, para 4.10.
[24] [1999] 1 WLR 1861, CA.

Kingdom. The plaintiffs brought an action against the bank for breach of contract, negligence and misrepresentation, alleging that the bank had represented that it had the ability and resources to market the shares on a global basis and that its London branch would be actively involved in the marketing. The Court of Appeal held that process would be 'in respect of the carrying on of the business' of the branch if it is in part in respect of the carrying on of the business, unless the connection between the process and the carrying on of the business is *de minimis*, that is of so little significance that it should be disregarded.[25] It affirmed the decision of Tuckey J at first instance that the process in this particular case was in respect of the carrying on of the business of the bank's London branch since it was partly in respect of that business. The Court rejected the argument of counsel for the bank that Article 5(5) of the Brussels Convention provided the closest analogy for the question of statutory interpretation with which the court was concerned and that useful guidance was to be obtained from the judgments of the European Court of Justice interpreting that Article, which have given a narrow interpretation to the concept of a dispute arising out of the operations of a branch, agency or other establishment.

A foreign company which has established a place of business, which is not a **4.11** *branch, in Great Britain* A company incorporated elsewhere than in Great Britain which establishes a place of business in Great Britain (this does not include a limited company which is incorporated outside the United Kingdom and Gibraltar, and has a branch in the United Kingdom[26]) is required to file with the registrar of companies the names and addresses of some one or more persons resident in Great Britain authorized to accept service of process on its behalf.[27] If a company fails to comply with its statutory obligations, or if the persons on the register are dead or no longer resident here, or refuse to accept service on the company's behalf, or for any reason cannot be served, the claim form may be served on the company by leaving it at, or sending it by post to, 'any place of business established by the company in Great Britain'.[28]

The question may well arise as to what constitutes the establishment of **4.12** a place of business, other than a branch. We know that this is referring to a less permanent establishment than a branch.[29] Ultimately it is a question of fact whether a place of business has been established in Great Britain.[30]

---

[25] ibid, at 1872.   [26] Companies Act 1985, s 690B.
[27] ibid, s 691.   [28] ibid, s 695.   [29] The *Saab* case, n 24 above, at 1868.
[30] *Rakusens Limited (A Company) v Baser Ambalaj Plastik Sanayi Ticaret As* [2001] EWCA Civ 1820, [2002] 1 BCLC 104. See also *Reuben v Time Inc* [2003] EWHC 1430 (QB) at [33].

Prior to 1992, the Companies Act did not contain a separate provision for branches and the only question was whether a place of business had been established. There are cases determining this question which can be still used as guidance now, with the proviso that some of them may in fact have involved a branch.[31] These cases indicate that it is relevant to see whether the business is carried on from a fixed and definite place and whether the company uses an agent that can bind it contractually.[32] Indeed, the latter factor should be regarded as being a powerful one, albeit not determinative.[33] There is no requirement that the dispute has to relate to the activities of the business carried on at the place of business which has been established in Great Britain. This stands in marked contrast to the position in respect of branches where, as has been seen, the provisions on service are dealing with service *in respect of the carrying on of the business of the branch*. It is hard to see in policy terms why there should be such a distinction.

4.13 Part 6 of the Civil Procedure Rules   As has been seen, the Companies Act 1985 sets out methods of service in relation to oversea companies. However, as an alternative to these methods of service a company may be served by any method permitted under Part 6 of the Civil Procedure Rules.[34] The argument that Part 6 is *ultra vires* in providing these alternative methods of service has been rejected by Longmore J in *Sea Assets Ltd v PT Garuda Indonesia*.[35] After looking at these alternative methods of service, three related questions have to be addressed in relation to service under Part 6. What is the relationship between Part 6 and the Companies Act 1985? Which foreign companies can be served using these alternative methods of service under Part 6? What are the advantages in using these alternative methods?

4.14 *The alternative methods of service*   One of these is leaving the document at a specified place. The obligation of a party to give an address for service applies equally to companies as it does to individuals. Where a company does not give the business address of its solicitor as its address for service and carries on business within the jurisdiction it must give its place of

---

[31] See *South India Shipping Corp Ltd v Import-Export Bank of Korea* [1985] 1 WLR 585, CA; *Re Oriel Ltd* [1985] 1 WLR 180, CA; *Adams v Cape Industries plc* [1990] Ch 433 at 530–531; *Cleveland Museum of Art v Capricorn Art International SA* [1990] 2 Lloyd's Rep 166. See generally Cheshire and North, 292–295.

[32] The *Rakusens* case, n 30 above, at [17] (*per* Buxton LJ), [39] (*per* Arden LJ).

[33] The *Adams* case, n 31 above, at 531; followed by Arden LJ in the *Rakusens* case, n 30 above, at [40], [41] and in *Reuben v Time Inc* [2003] EWHC 1430 (QB) at [40], [41].

[34] r 6.2(2) CPR. See *Murphy v Staples UK Ltd* [2003] EWCA Civ 656, [2003] 1 WLR 2441.

[35] [2000] 4 All ER 371.

business as its address for service.[36] Where no solicitor is acting for the party to be served and the party has not given an address for service the document must be sent or transmitted to, or left at, the place shown in the table set out in r 6.5(6).[37] For a company registered in England and Wales,[38] the specified place of service is the principal office of the company, or any place of business of the company within the jurisdiction which has a real connection with the claim. For any other company it is any place of business of the company within the jurisdiction.

Another method is that of personal service. A document is served per- **4.15** sonally on a company or other corporation by leaving it with a person holding a senior position within the company or corporation,[39] such as a director. There is some uncertainty over whether this provision can be used in relation to a foreign company. The accompanying Practice Direction[40] is phrased in narrower terms than the rule itself. It states that personal service on a 'registered company or corporation' is effected by leaving a document with a person holding a senior position. When it defines what is meant by a person holding a senior position it again refers to a 'registered company or corporation'.[41] The intention is clearly that this method of service cannot be used with a foreign company. It would be absurd if service on a director of a foreign company (which may have no branch or other established place of business or even carry on business in England) who happens to be transiently present in England were to regarded as being effective service on that company. This has never been the position under English law. However, Gray J was, seemingly, prepared to use personal service in respect of a foreign company, not one registered in England.[42] This is a weak authority because this point was not raised by counsel. Moreover, on the facts of the case personal service was not effective because it was not made on a senior officer of the

---

[36] r 6.5(3). This rule does not distinguish between individuals and companies. Thus it refers to a party and then to his residing or carrying on business within the jurisdiction. The former term seems designed just to cover individuals since a company cannot literally be resident anywhere and can only have an artificial residence. If a company is given an artificial residence, at common law this was where it carried on business, see generally J Fawcett, 'A New Approach to Jurisdiction over Companies in Private International Law' (1988) 37 ICLQ 645. It follows that in the case of a company the term reside appears to add nothing to that of carrying on business.

[37] r 6.5(6).

[38] This does not include an overseas company which has obtained a branch registration certificate, see the *Sea Assets* case, n 35 above; discussed below, para 4.20.

[39] r 6.4 CPR. See 6PD.6.2 for the definition of 'a person holding a senior position'.

[40] 6PD.6.1.

[41] It does though have a definition of such a person in respect of a 'corporation which is not a registered company', 6PD.6.2(2).

[42] *Lakah Group v Al Jazeera Satellite Channel* [2003] EWHC 1231 (QB) at [27]–[33]; aff'd [2003] EWCA (Civ) 1781.

defendant company. The Court of Appeal affirmed the decision of Gray J.[43] This specific point was not discussed but it was said more generally that Gray J had applied the correct tests.[44]

4.16 *What is the relationship between Part 6 and the Companies Act 1985?* The relationship between the Companies Act 1985 and the methods of service under Part 6 of the Civil Procedure Rules is by no means clear. Two cases discussing Part 6 have assumed that this is an alternative basis of jurisdiction to the Companies Act 1985.[45] More significantly, one of the few cases specifically discussing the point has adopted this view.[46] Under this wide view of the role of Part 6, compliance with the methods of service under Part 6 provides the basis of jurisdiction. However, it could be argued that the methods of service in Part 6 are precisely that, just methods of service, and are not as such bases of jurisdiction against foreign companies. Under this narrow view of the role of Part 6, the question of which foreign companies can be served is dealt with under the Companies Act 1985 and this requires the foreign company to have a branch or an established place of business other than a branch in England. Only if this requirement is met are you entitled to go on to the next stage which is the method of service. This appears to be the view adopted in the two other cases to specifically address the point.[47] In one of these cases, it was said that 'the wording of the CPR does not enable one to by-pass the need to demonstrate that a place of business has been established within this jurisdiction'.[48] The argument in favour of this narrow view and against the wide view is that the latter would widen the jurisdiction of English courts considerably and the provisions in the Companies Act 1985 dealing with jurisdiction against foreign companies would become largely redundant. It is hard to believe that either of these consequences was intended when Part 6 was introduced. This narrow interpretation of Part 6 is further supported by a decision in relation to service on an individual using Part 6[49] where it was held that, although this contained general rules about service, it had not swept away the general principle that a defendant could only be served within the jurisdiction if he were present in the jurisdiction at the time of

---

[43] [2003] EWCA (Civ) 1781.   [44] ibid, at [8].

[45] *Sea Assets Ltd v PT Garuda Indonesia* [2000] 4 All ER 371; the *Saab* case, n 24 above, at 324–325 (*per* Clarke LJ).

[46] *Lakah Group v Al Jazeera Satellite Channel* [2003] EWHC 1231 at [39]–[41]; aff'd [2003] EWCA (Civ) 1781. However, *Harrods Limited v Dow Jones & Company Inc* [2003] EWHC 1162 (QB) and *Reuben v Time Inc* [2003] EWHC 1430 (QB) took a different view, discussed below.

[47] *Harrods*, ibid and *Reuben*, ibid.

[48] *Harrods*, n 46 above, at [33]. This view has been expressly adopted and applied by another High Court judge in the first instance decision in *Reuben*, n 46 above, at [30], [31].

[49] The case concerned service by first class post at the usual or last known residence under r 6.5(6) CPR.

service.[50] The same could be said to be true of companies and whether a company is present is determined by the Companies Act 1985.

Which foreign companies can be served using these alternative methods?

COMPANIES THAT HAVE REGISTERED AS AN OVERSEAS COMPANY OR SHOULD **4.17** HAVE REGISTERED UNDER THE 1985 COMPANIES ACT According to *Sea Assets Ltd v PT Garuda Indonesia*,[51] if a company has obtained a branch registration certificate under the Companies Act, service can be effected under the method set out in that act or by any of the methods set out in Part 6 of the Civil Procedure Rules. But what of a foreign company that has not so registered either in respect of a branch or an established place of business other than a branch? If the company has a branch or an established place of business other than a branch in England within the meaning of the Companies Act, again service can be effected under the methods set out in that Act or, as an alternative, by any of the methods set out in Part 6. This is uncontroversial. Even under the narrow view of the role of Part 6, it is clear that the alternative methods of service in Part 6 can be used in this situation.

FOREIGN COMPANIES THAT HAVE A PLACE OF BUSINESS WITHIN THE **4.18** JURISDICTION Under r 6.5(6) of the Civil Procedure Rules service has to be effected at any place of business[52] within the jurisdiction. This presupposes that the foreign company has a place of business within the jurisdiction. Whether service on such a company using the methods set out in Part 6 forms a basis of jurisdiction depends on whether the wide view of the role of Part 6 is adopted or the narrow.

What are the advantages in using these alternative methods? There are two **4.19** advantages in using Part 6 of the Civil Procedure Rules (as widely interpreted), rather than the Companies Act 1985. First, there is no requirement that service is in respect of the carrying on of the business of the branch. Second, service can be effected on a foreign company which merely has a place of business within the jurisdiction.

NO REQUIREMENT THAT SERVICE IS IN RESPECT OF THE CARRYING ON OF **4.20** THE BUSINESS OF THE BRANCH In *Saab v Saudi American Bank*,[53] Clarke LJ discussed obiter the position where the method of service is that of leaving the document at a place specified under r 6.5(6) of the Civil Procedure Rules. He said that 'it appears . . . that process can be served on a foreign company with a place of business in, say, London without the

---

[50] *Chellaram v Chellaram (No 2)* [2002] EWHC 632 (Ch) at [47], [2002] 2 All ER 17.
[51] n 45 above.
[52] The meaning of this is examined below, para 4.22. [53] n 24 above.

necessity for establishing any link between the process and the business being conducted in London'.[54] This dictum was applied by Longmore J in *Sea Assets Ltd v PT Garuda Indonesia*.[55] In this case, the claim form was served at the branch office of a company incorporated in Indonesia, which had obtained a branch registration certificate under the Companies Act. The dispute did not relate to the carrying on of the business of the defendant's London branch. Accordingly, it was not possible to rely on service under s 694A of the Companies Act 1985. Instead the claimant sought to rely on service under Part 6 of the Civil Procedure Rules, arguing that service was effected at 'any place of business of the company within the jurisdiction' under r 6.5(6) of the Civil Procedure Rules. Longmore J held that the claim form had been validly served under this provision. The argument that Part 6 of the Civil Procedure Rules was *ultra vires* in providing alternative methods of service to those contained in the Companies Act 1985 was rejected. Also rejected was the argument that for the purposes of r 6.5(6) the defendant was a company registered in England and Wales by virtue of its obtaining a branch registration certificate under the Companies Act. It was a company whose essence was overseas. If this argument had succeeded then the service would not have been valid. It will be recalled that with a company registered in England and Wales the place of service is the principal office of the company or any place of business of the company within the jurisdiction which has a real connection with the claim. The branch office at which the process was served did not fall within either of these two categories.

4.21 If the narrow view of the role of Part 6 is adopted this raises a question over the correctness of the decision in the *Sea Assets* case. The requirement in the Companies Act 1985 that, in the case of a branch, the document served must be in respect of the carrying on of the business of the branch, whilst admittedly appearing in the sections of the Act dealing with service, does not appear to be concerned with the method of service. It is not concerned with how and where the process is served. It looks to be a substantive requirement. If you look at Article 5(5) of the Brussels I Regulation this contains two substantive requirements, namely that there is a branch etc and that the dispute arises out of the operations of the branch etc. The position is arguably the same under the Companies Act 1985. If you accept that this is a substantive requirement, it should then apply regardless of the method of service. Accordingly, it would apply even where the method employed is one set out in Part 6 of the Civil Procedure Rules.

---

[54] ibid, at 324–325.   [55] [2000] 4 All ER 371.

SERVICE ON A FOREIGN COMPANY WHICH HAS A PLACE OF BUSINESS WITHIN **4.22**
THE JURISDICTION   There is an obvious difference between the wording
of the Companies Act 1985, which requires that the foreign company
has 'established' a place of business and r 6.5(6) of the Civil Procedure
Rules which merely requires that a foreign company has a place of business within the jurisdiction. 'Establishing' a place of business within the
meaning of the Companies Act 1985 'connotes a degree of formality and
permanence of location which is not required by Part 6.5(6)'.[56] However,
the requirement of a 'place of business' remains under the Civil Procedure
Rules.[57] That means that service on an address with which the company
has no more than a transient or irregular connection will not be valid.[58] It
must be the defendant's place of business; what is needed is evidence of
actual business activity on the part of the defendant. Business activity on
the part of an associated company is not enough.[59] Nevertheless, if the
wide view of the role of Part 6 is adopted, it is going to be easier to use
r 6.5(6) as the basis of jurisdiction than the Companies Act 1985. Some
situations will come within the former but fall outside the latter. It follows
that, if a foreign company has not registered as an overseas company
under the 1985 Act, recourse should be had to Part 6, rather than trying
to show that it should have registered under the 1985 Act (i.e. that it has a
branch or has established a place of business other than a branch). In
contrast, if the narrow view of the role of Part 6 is adopted, it would
be necessary to show that the foreign company not only has a place of
business within the jurisdiction (to satisfy r 6.5(6)) but also has a branch
or has established a place of business other than a branch within the
meaning of the 1985 Act.

Application to Contracts for the International Sale of Goods

In general, there are no particular problems in applying the rules on ser- **4.23**
vice within the jurisdiction to a claim based on a contract for the international sale of goods. The one exception to this is where a foreign company has a branch in England and the method of service is that set out in
s 694A of the Companies Act 1985, with its requirement that process is in

---

[56] *Lakah Group v Al Jazeera Satellite Channel* [2003] EWHC 1231 at [40]; the Court of Appeal
in affirming the decision at first instance said it was unnecessary to discuss this point [2003]
EWCA (Civ) 1781 at [8].
[57] ibid, at [41]; aff'd [2003] EWCA (Civ) 1781. Rule 6.5(6) CPR refers also to service where a
corporation 'carries on its activities'. According to the Court of Appeal at [8], the test for this
is the same as for any place of business. It therefore does not matter whether the defendant is
a corporation or a company and in the *Lakah* case there was no attempt to say which it was.
[58] *Lakah Group v Al Jazeera Satellite Channel* [2003] EWCA (Civ) 1781 at [8].
[59] *Lakah Group v Al Jazeera Satellite Channel* [2003] EWHC 1231 at [48]; aff'd without discussion of this point [2003] EWCA (Civ) 1781.

respect of the carrying on of the business of the branch. It is submitted that this requirement would be met in two situations. The first is where the branch, acting on behalf of the seller, entered into the contract of sale of goods with the buyer.[60] It should be enough also if the branch has merely negotiated the contract but has not actually entered into it on behalf of the seller.[61] The second is where the obligation on which the claim was principally based was required to be performed by the branch or substantially so performed. For example, a claim is made in relation to non-delivery and the branch is responsible for ensuring that deliveries are made or the claim is for non-payment and the branch is responsible for ensuring that invoices are paid. Earlier on,[62] it was suggested that, in these two situations, the requirement under Article 5(5) of the Brussels I Regulation, that the dispute arises out of the operations of a branch, agency or other establishment, would be met. Given that the Court of Appeal in the *Saab* case has given a wider interpretation to the requirement under s 694A than to that under Article 5(5), it would be surprising if contract cases coming within the latter did not also come within the former. Indeed, counsel for the bank in the *Saab* case,[63] who argued unsuccessfully that a narrow interpretation should be given to the s 694A requirement, along the lines of the narrow interpretation given by the European Court of Justice to the Article 5(5) requirement, mentioned these two situations as ones where the s 694A requirement, as narrowly interpreted, would be met in contract cases.[64]

4.24 It is submitted that the s 694A requirement would also be met in the situation where the performance of the obligation on which the claim is principally based was to be performed in part by the branch. The effect of the *Saab* case is that the s 694A requirement is to be given a wider interpretation than the Article 5(5) requirement so that, when it comes to the former requirement, process can be partly in respect of the carrying on of the business of the branch. So to what situations would this wide interpretation extend? One such situation would be where the performance of the obligation on which the claim is principally based was to be performed in part by the branch. This would doubtless fall outside the Article 5(5) requirement but squarely within the more widely interpreted s 694A requirement.

4.25 All this difficulty over the requirement that the document served on the company must be in respect of the carrying on of the business of the branch can be avoided if service is effected by one of the methods set out

---

[60] It should not be required that the branch also negotiated the contract. But compare the example given by Lawrence Collins QC in the *Saab* case, n 24 above, at 1866.
[61] This is the position under Art 5(5) of the Brussels I Regulation, discussed above, para 3.304.   [62] See above, paras 3.308–312.   [63] [1999] 1 WLR 1861.   [64] ibid, at 1866.

in Part 6 of the Civil Procedure Rules, at least if the wide view of its effect is accepted.

2. SERVICE OF A CLAIM FORM OUT OF THE JURISDICTION

A judge faced with an application for leave to serve a claim form out of the **4.26** jurisdiction under r 6.20 of the Civil Procedure Rules has to be satisfied: first, that there is a good arguable case that one of the grounds (paragraphs) of r 6.20 is satisfied; second, that there is a reasonable prospect of success (a serious issue to be tried on the merits); third, that the discretion should be exercised to permit service out of the jurisdiction.[65] These three requirements and their application in international sale of goods cases will now be examined.

The Grounds of Rule 6.20

General grounds

Rule 6.20 sets out a number of general grounds of jurisdiction, namely **4.27** that a claim is made for a remedy against a person domiciled within the jurisdiction,[66] a claim is made for an injunction ordering the defendant to do or refrain from doing an act within the jurisdiction,[67] or that a claim is made in a multi-defendant case.[68] A claim in contract brought by the buyer against the seller, or vice versa, may come within one of these general grounds. Indeed, the last of these general grounds is commonly employed in international sales cases and is discussed in detail in Chapter 9. Be that as it may, the most common ground to use in an international sale of goods case is one of the three grounds specifically dealing with the situation where a claim is made in relation to a contract.

Claims in relation to contracts

Rule 6.20(5)   Rule 6.20(5) of the Civil Procedure Rules states that a claim **4.28** form may be served out of the jurisdiction with the permission of the court if:

a claim is made in respect of a contract where the contract—
   (a) was made within the jurisdiction;

---

[65] The court will not give permission to serve a claim form out of the jurisdiction unless satisfied that England and Wales is the proper place in which to bring the claim, r 6.21(2A) CPR. For the written evidence needed in support of service out of the jurisdiction see r 6.21(1) RSC. See generally on what the claimant has to establish for service out, *Seaconsar Far East Ltd v Bank Markazi Jomhouri Islami Iran* [1993] 3 WLR 756 at 767 (*per* Lord Goff).

[66] r 6.20(1). In most cases where the defendant is domiciled in England, the Brussels I Regulation will apply. It will not do so though if the matter is outside the scope of that Regulation.

[67] r 6.20(2).   [68] r 6.20(3).

(b) was made by or through an agent trading or residing within the jurisdiction;
(c) is governed by English law; or
(d) contains a term to the effect that the court shall have jurisdiction to determine any claim in respect of the contract.

4.29 *A claim is made in respect of a contract*   Rule 6.20(5) in effect sets out four
separate grounds, each of which requires that a claim is made in respect of
a contract. This wide but rather vague wording contrasts with the much
more detailed wording in the predecessor of r 6.20(5), namely Order 11,
r 1(1)(d) of the Rules of the Supreme Court. This required that 'the claim
is brought to enforce, rescind, dissolve, annul or otherwise affect a contract, or to recover damages or obtain any other remedy in respect of
the breach of a contract'.[69] It is unlikely that this drafting change was
intended to have any substantive effect on the court's powers.[70] It follows that cases that fell within the detailed requirement under Order 11,
r 1(1)(d) may well provide some guidance as what falls within the new
wording.[71] Thus, for example, a claim for damages for breach of contract
would fall within the scope of the new wording, as it did within the
old.[72] Inevitably, the change in wording is likely to lead to an argument
that the new provision is wider than its predecessor and therefore
should encompass certain claims that fell outside the old wording.
However, the temptation to squeeze claims that naturally fall outside
this ground within the new wording should be avoided. For example, a
claim for damages for fraudulent misrepresentation inducing the claimant to enter a contract did not fall within the predecessor provision and
should not fall within the new wording.[73] What is clear is that a claim in
respect of a contract does not encompass a claim for a declaration that
no contract exists since a new ground for service out of the jurisdiction
has been added to the list of grounds to cover such a claim.[74] Neither
does it encompass a claim for interpleader relief since this involves a
claim to be released from proceedings, not a claim for a substantive
right.[75]

---

[69] It is clear that a number of drafting changes were made in order to produce a
list of grounds for service out of the jurisdiction which is clearer and simpler, see
the Lord Chancellor's Department Consultation Paper on the CPR, *Service of Court
Process Abroad*, para 23. This particular drafting change probably stems from this same
objective.
[70] ibid.
[71] Compare Dicey and Morris, *Third Supplement to the Thirteenth Edition* (2003), 53.
[72] But see the position in relation to quasi-contract, discussed below, paras 8.64–67.
[73] *Arab Business Consortium International Finance and Investment Co v Banque Franco-
Tunisienne* [1996] 1 Lloyd's Rep 485 at 492. The use of the tort ground in cases of misrepresentation is discussed below, paras 6.96–114.
[74] r 6.20(7); discussed below, paras 4.90–93.
[75] *Cool Carriers AB v HSBC Bank USA* [2001] 2 Lloyd's Rep 22.

The Court of Appeal has held in relation to a predecessor of r 6.20(5) of the **4.30** Civil Procedure Rules[76] that it is necessary to assert that there is a contract and that the cause of action is based upon this contract.[77] In determining whether there is a cause of action based on a contract, regard has to be paid to the applicable law. If the law governing the contract imposes no liability there is no cause of action based on the contract. Moreover, there would be no serious issue to be tried on the merits and accordingly service out of the jurisdiction would not be permissible.

Finally, it should be noted that as far as classification of claims is **4.31** concerned what we are dealing with here is the English concept of a 'contractual' claim.[78] It follows that, where there is a cause of action under English law but this is in tort (there being no contract under English law), this should not be classified for jurisdictional purposes as being contractual, even if the foreign law applicable to the cause of action classifies it as contractual.[79] Liability is imposed by the applicable law but this is not what English law would regard as contractual liability.

Where the contract was made within the jurisdiction The determination of **4.32** the place where a contract was made presents no problem if the contract was negotiated and signed in a single country.[80] But with contracts for the international sale of goods this will not always be the case. Sometimes, contracts may be concluded between brokers resident in the same country but representing seller and buyer in different countries. In other cases, however, where seller and buyer deal with each other across national frontiers, they will do so by a variety of means, ranging from electronic forms of communication to paper-based forms that can for example take the form of telex messages, standard correspondence, transmission of order forms and fax messages. There is no standard method of concluding an international sales contract.

The place where a contract is made is a connecting factor and the rule **4.33** is well established that English law, as the law of the forum, is applied to determine the meaning of any connecting factor. It follows that the

---

[76] Ord 11, r 1(1)(d) RSC.

[77] *DVA v Voest Alpine* [1997] 2 Lloyd's Rep 279 at 287 (*per* Hobhouse LJ), 291 (*per* Morritt LJ), CA.

[78] *Youell v Kara Mara Shipping Co* [2000] 2 Lloyd's Rep 102. Compare the position under Art 5(1) of the Brussels I Regulation, above, para 3.62.

[79] This is the situation that arose in the EC context in Case C-26/91 *Jakob Handte v Société Traitements Mécano-Chimiques des Surfaces (TMCS)* [1992] ECR I-139.

[80] In principle, it is possible to have a contract made in more than one country: *Apple Corps Ltd v Apple Computer Inc* [2004] EWHC 768 (Ch)—where the parties deliberately signed separate copies in different countries so as to avoid giving the other party an advantage in terms of where the contract was finalized.

English rules on formation of a contract must be applied in order to determine whether the contract was made within the jurisdiction. The leading case is the decision of the House of Lords in *Brinkibon Ltd v Stahag Stahl und Stahlwarenhandelsgesellschaft GmbH*,[81] which concerned a contact for the international sale of goods. The plaintiff buyers in England, by a telex dated 26 April 1979, offered to buy from the defendant sellers in Austria, 20,000 tonnes of steel bars, C & F liner out of Alexandria. On 3 May 1979, by telex the sellers accepted the buyers' offer subject to certain amendments. In particular, the sellers were only prepared to supply a performance bond of 3 per cent. On 4 May 1979 the buyers procured instructions to their bank in London to open the letter of credit and by a telex of the same date the sellers were informed that a letter of credit had been opened. By a telex dated 21 May 1979, the sellers purported to withdraw from the contract. The sellers did not open a performance bond nor did they deliver any steel. The buyers claimed damages, seeking to ground jurisdiction under Order 11, r 1(1) of the Rules of the Supreme Court on the basis that the contract had been made in England. The question of which country's rules on the formation of a contract should be applied was not in issue between the parties and the House of Lords simply applied the English domestic law on formation without any discussion of this question. The House of Lords held that the general principle is that a contract is formed where the acceptance is communicated to the offeror and that this principle will apply equally to instantaneous forms of communication, such as by telephone, as to *inter praesentes*. The well known exception to this is where communication is by letter or telegram. As far as communication by telex is concerned this should be treated as an instantaneous form of communication. It followed that the contract (if any) was made when and where the acceptance was received. This was in Vienna. The sellers telex of 3 May amounted to a counter-offer and the acceptance of this was contained in the telex from the buyers in London to the sellers in Vienna dated 4 May. An alternative argument was raised that there was acceptance by conduct in that the buyers gave instructions in England for the opening of a letter of credit. This argument was rejected on the basis that the letter of credit was not opened in England and that giving instructions to agents could not amount to an acceptance. This would only take place when the correspondent bank in Vienna notified the seller, which happened in Vienna. The *Brinkibon* case has beeen followed in Canada where communication by facsimile has been treated as an instantaneous form of communication.[82]

---

[81] [1983] 2 AC 34.
[82] *Eastern Power Ltd v Azienda Comunale Energia E Ambiente* [2001] IL Pr 6, Ontario CA.

Neither was the contract made in England in *Gill and Duffus Landauer Ltd v* **4.34**
London Export Corp GmbH,[83] which concerned a contract made by telephone for the sale of 20 tons of shelled almonds FAS California. Robert
Goff J analyzed the case in terms of the English law on formation of a
contract.[84] The plaintiffs, English sellers, authorized brokers (Afrika) to
offer almonds for sale at a certain price. Afrika, as agents for the sellers
offered the goods to the German defendants, who made a counter-offer.
Afrika communicated this to their principals. The plaintiffs, having
renegotiated the commission payable by them to Afrika, authorized
Afrika as their agents to accept this counter-offer. This Afrika did by
communicating the acceptance to the buyers in Frankfurt. The contract,
being made by telephone, was made when and where the acceptance was
communicated to the defendants. This was in Germany.

One point that has not yet been addressed by the courts is whether effect **4.35**
will be given to an express stipulation by the parties as to where the
contract is made. Such a choice is to be found in clause 31 of the Grain and
Feed Trade Association (GAFTA) Form 100.[85] This states that: 'Buyers
and Sellers agree that for the purpose of proceedings either legal or by
arbitration this contract shall be deemed to have been made in England
and to be performed there any correspondence in relation to the offer,
the acceptance, the place of payment or otherwise notwithstanding'.
Similarly, clause 18 of the Federation of Oils, Seeds and Fats Associations
Ltd (FOSFA) contract no 20 states that: 'This contract shall be deemed
to have been made in England . . .'. There is no problem in giving effect to
such provisions in cases where, according to the English rules on formation of a contract, the contract is also made in England. But what if,
according to these rules, it is made in, say, New York? Should effect be
given to a deemed place of making of the contract in such circumstances?
The parties are free to choose the applicable law[86] and the place of trial
and this will have the effect of satisfying r 6.20(5)(c) or (d) as the case may
be. It is hard to see why, as a matter of principle, they should not also be
able to satisfy r 6.20(5)(a) by virtue of an agreement, in this case, as to the
place where the contract was made.[87] Of course, satisfying a ground of
r 6.20 is not the end of the matter. The court must exercise its discretion
to permit service out of the jurisdiction[88] and it is at that stage when
operating the doctrine of *forum conveniens* that the court can take into

---

[83] [1982] 2 Lloyd's Rep 627. [84] ibid, at 631.
[85] See also Bylaw 200 of the Liverpool Cotton Association.
[86] The limitations on this right are discussed below, paras 13.99–102.
[87] Compare the position under Art 5(1) of the Brussels I Regulation, see above,
paras 3.175–179.
[88] See below, paras 4.101–153.

account the fact that the place where the contract is made is a deemed one, rather than the one in which it was actually made, and this will affect the weight to be attached to this factor.

4.36 Should there be a ground of jurisdiction based on the mere fact that a contract was made in England? Hawkins J in the Ontario Court of Justice in *Bailey and Company Inc v Laser Medical Technology Inc*[89] said in relation to this ground for service out of the jurisdiction that: 'The international aspects of commerce, the mobility of businessmen and modern technology all point to the inappropriateness today of narrow technical rules'. The place where the contract was made rule is undoubtedly a narrow technical rule and the modern conditions that Hawkins J referred to mean that the place where a contract was made, as ascertained by the application of the rules on formation of a contract adopted in the forum, is increasingly likely to be a matter of pure chance and to have nothing to do with the parties, the contract and its obligations or the law governing the contract. Hawkins J gave an example of an Ontario businessman who, whilst on business in Tokyo, faxed an offer to a Delaware company carrying on business in California to raise money for it (the money to be delivered to California), and received the acceptance there. He then asked the following question: 'would anyone seriously argue that the contract was made in Japan, could be sued upon in Japan and would be subject to the laws of Japan?'.[90] Whatever reservations Hawkins J might have, the position under English law is clear. The contract was undoubtedly made in Japan and if the facts were altered so that England is substituted for Japan it would have undoubtedly have been made in England and a ground for service out of the jurisdiction would have been established. Of course, the English courts can exercise their discretion so as to refuse to grant permission for service out of the jurisdiction.[91] But that is no answer. The litigation should not get to the discretionary stage in the first place unless there is a sufficient connection with England on which to base a ground for service out of the jurisdiction. The problem of identifying the place where a contract is made and of a lack of connection with that place is even more acute where a contract is made over the internet. This will be discussed below in Chapter 10.[92]

4.37 *Where the contract was made by or through an agent trading or residing within the jurisdiction*   The Court of Appeal in *National Mortgage and Agency Co of New Zealand Ltd v Gosselin*[93] held that a contract is made *by* an agent if the agent has authority to bind his principal. If an agent, who has no such

---

[89] [1994] IL Pr 444.   [90] ibid, at 446.
[91] This is what Hawkins J did in the *Bailey* case.
[92] At paras 10.99–100.   [93] (1922) 38 TLR 832, CA.

authority, negotiates the terms of the contract, it can be said that the contract was made *through* an agent. This provision therefore covers the situation where a foreigner carries on business abroad but has an agent in England whose duty is to obtain orders, although he has no authority to accept them.[94] This is what happened in *National Mortgage and Agency Co of New Zealand Ltd v Gosselin*, in which the sale of goods case was made through an agent in London. Similarly, in the *Gill and Duffus Landauer* case,[95] the sale of goods contract was made *through* an agent, Afrika, rather than *by* an agent. It has previously been mentioned[96] that the counter-offer by the defendants was communicated by Afrika to its principal, the plaintiffs, and it was only after Afrika was authorized by its principal to do so that it communicated the plaintiff's acceptance to the defendants. A contract can be made *through* an agent trading or residing within the jurisdiction, even though the contract is not made until an offer is accepted by the principal outside the jurisdiction.

The predecessor of this provision contained extra wording, omitted from **4.38** the current version, which required that the contract was made by or through an agent 'on behalf of a principal trading or residing out of the jurisdiction'. This latter requirement was not met in the *Gill and Duffus Landauer* case, and, accordingly, fell outside the agent sub-paragraph head of Order 11, r 1 of the Rules of the Supreme Court. The problem in that case was that the agent was at all times acting on behalf of the English plaintiffs and so was not acting on behalf of a principal trading or residing out of the jurisdiction. To have satisfied this requirement it would have had to be shown that the agent was acting on behalf of the German defendants. What would happen if the same facts were to arise now? It is submitted that the result should be the same. The old wording should be regarded as being implicitly incorporated into r 6.20(5)(b). This provision makes no sense unless the agent is acting on behalf of the foreign defendant who is the principal. The agent must have a connection with England, namely that he is trading or residing within the jurisdiction. What is then needed is a connection between the foreign defendant and England which justifies the English court's assertion of jurisdiction over a defendant who is out of the jurisdiction. This would appear to be another of the drafting changes made by r 6.20 of the Civil Procedure Rules to the rules in Order 11, r 1(1) of the Rules of the Supreme Court so as to produce a list which was clearer and simpler; it was not intended that these changes should have any substantive effect on the court's powers.[97]

---

[94] ibid, at 833.   [95] n 83 above.   [96] Above, para 4.34.
[97] See the Lord Chancellor's Department Consultation Paper on the CPR, *Service of Court Process Abroad*, para 23. A number of drafting changes are mentioned but not this particular one.

4.39 The usefulness of this provision in international sale of goods cases depends on the extent to which there is a practice in such cases for parties to make contracts by or through an agent. In the *Gosselin* case, the contract was made through an agent acting on behalf of the defendant sellers of barbed wire. In the *Gill and Duffus Landauer* case, the contract for the sale of almonds was made through an agent but this agent only acted on behalf of the plaintiff sellers. The defendant buyers did not contract by or through an agent and so this provision was not satisfied. There are only a relatively few reported cases discussing this provision and most of these are concerned with contracts other than ones for the sale of goods, such as insurance,[98] reinsurance,[99] letters of credit[100] and royalty agreements.[101] Nonetheless, in the commodities trade (dry and oil) it is very common for parties to make contracts by or through an agent and so this provision is potentially very useful.

4.40 *Where the contract is governed by English law*   The law governing a contract for the international sale of goods is determined by the application of the rules contained in the Rome Convention of 1980.[102] These rules are considered in detail in Chapter 13 and reference should be made to what is said there in order to decide whether such a contract is governed by English law. Under the Rome Convention it is possible for different laws to govern different parts of the contract.[103] If the dispute only relates to part of the contract it should be enough that this part of the contract is governed by English law.[104] It must be stressed that for the purposes of service out of the jurisdiction all that has to be shown, at least in cases involving any factual investigation or a mixture of fact and law, is a good arguable case that the contract is governed by English law.[105]

4.41 STANDARD FORM CONTRACTS FOR THE INTERNATIONAL SALE OF GOODS   It is very common practice to have an applicable law clause in a sales contract. Importers and exporters use the advisory services of trade associations and their standard form contracts normally will contain such a clause. In oil and dry commodities, it is very common indeed for the

---

[98] See *Gibbon v Commerz und Creditbank Aktiengesellschaft* [1958] 2 Lloyd's List 113, CA.

[99] *Citadel Insurance Co v Atlantic Union Insurance Co SA* [1982] Lloyd's Rep 543, CA.

[100] *Bank of Baroda v Vysya Bank Ltd* [1994] 2 Lloyd's Rep 87.

[101] *BHP Petroleum Pty Ltd v Oil Basins Ltd* [1985] VR 725.

[102] See Cheshire and North, 304—rejecting the view that the traditional common law choice of law rules should apply in this context.

[103] Art 3(1).   [104] Cheshire and North, 304.

[105] *Marubeni Hong Kong and South China Ltd v Mongolian Government* [2002] 2 All ER (Comm) 873. If, for the purposes of determining whether it has jurisdiction, the court has to decide issues involving only law or interpretation of a document, it will definitively decide the issue or point of interpretation at the jurisdictional stage and not come back to it later on at the trial of the merits. See also *Chellaram v Chellaram (No 2)* [2002] EWHC 632 (Ch) at [136], [2002] 2 All ER 17.

applicable law clause to favour English law. For example, clause 31 of GAFTA Form 100 states that 'all disputes which may arise under this contract . . . shall be settled according to the law of England, whatever the domicile, residence or place of business of the parties to this contract may be or become'. Likewise, clause 18 of FOSFA contract no 20 provides that '. . . the construction, validity and performance . . . [of this contract] shall be governed in all respects by English law'. There are well known instances of both forms of contract being adopted by parties, neither of whom is English.[106] Two foreign parties may also specifically negotiate and agree on English law to govern the contract.[107] Contracts for the sale and purchase of cargoes of North Sea crude oil on 15 day terms invariably contain English law and English jurisdiction clauses.[108] Bylaw 200 of the Liverpool Cotton Association, which governs a large number of US cotton deals, likewise contains an English law clause.[109] In the case of manufactured goods, normally the applicable law will be the seller's law. With an English seller of such goods there is therefore likely to be a clause providing for English law to govern.

Nonetheless, there are examples of standard form sales contracts which **4.42** do not contain a choice of law clause. For example, the standard terms of the contract issued by the Dried Fruit Association of California contain no such clause. Forms designed by American trading associations, largely for US internal trade, may well lack such a clause.[110] In the eventuality of the parties adopting such terms, the applicable law has to be ascertained in the light of any implied choice by the parties. Most difficult of all is the ascertainment of the applicable law in the absence of any choice by the parties. The Rome Convention provides that the contract shall be governed by the law of the country with which it is most closely connected.[111] It then provides a presumption based on the concept of characteristic performance.[112] This is one of the most controversial features of the

---

[106] See in relation to GAFTA 100, *Toepfer International GmbH v Société Cargill France* [1998] 1 Lloyd's Rep 379, CA—German sellers and French buyers. See in relation to FOSFA no 20, *Tracomin SA v Sudan Oil Seeds Co Ltd* [1983] 1 WLR 1026, CA—Sudanese sellers and Swiss buyers.

[107] See, e.g. *Sohio Supply Co v Gatoil (USA) Inc* [1989] 1 Lloyd's Rep 588, CA—two Delaware registered companies entering into a contract for the sale of Brent crude oil FOB Sullom Voe.

[108] *Kloeckner & Co AG v Gatoil Overseas Inc* [1990] 1 Lloyd's Rep 177 at 206.

[109] See Lisa Bernstein, 'Private Commercial Law in the Cotton Industry: Creating Co-operation through Rules, Norms and Institutions', University of Chicago, John M Olin Law & Economics Working Paper No 133 (2nd Series) (www.law.uchicago.edu/Lawecon).

[110] The form may contain a jurisdiction clause. Choice of law is seen as less of a problem because of the harmonisation of the substantive law by the Uniform Commercial Code.

[111] Art 4(1).

[112] Art 4(2). The presumption is to be disregarded if it appears from the circumstances as whole that the contract is more closely connected with another country, Art 4(5).

Convention.[113] The relationship between this presumption and the most closely connected test is a matter on which courts in different Member States have taken very different views.[114] Even within England there is a lack of consistency of approach on this.

4.43 IS THE CHOICE OF LAW CLAUSE INCORPORATED INTO THE SALES CON-TRACT?   The question may arise of whether a choice of law clause is incorporated into the contract between the parties. The existence and validity of a contract, or of any term of a contract, is determined by the law which would govern it under the Rome Convention if the contract or term were valid.[115] This means that, if a question arises as to whether a clause providing that English law governs the contract is incorporated into the contract, English law will be applied to determine this.[116] Thus parties are able to pull themselves up by their own bootstraps. In a sales contract, the way in which the question of incorporation of a choice of law clause into the contract may well arise is in the wider context of whether the sales contract was concluded on the basis of the conditions of sale, which include a choice of law clause, of one of the parties to the con-tract.[117] The law which would govern the contract if the contract were valid will determine this issue.[118]

4.44 A PREVIOUS COURSE OF DEALING   A choice of law clause may be incorpor-ated into the contract by virtue of a previous course of dealing between the parties. This is illustrated by *Banque Paribas v Cargill International SA*.[119] The parties agreed on the sale and purchase of 6,000 tonnes of gas oil FOB storage Amsterdam. The sale contract contained no choice of law or choice of jurisdiction clause. The plaintiffs[120] argued that English law was applicable by virtue of the pattern of trading between the parties in which all previous contracts had provided for English law and jurisdiction. The defendants, whilst accepting this, argued that all previous contracts had been on CIF terms whereas the present sale contract was on FOB barge terms and that, in such market, choice of law clauses were not included, it being understood that Dutch law governed. The Court of Appeal held

---

[113] See Cheshire and North, 569–571.   [114] See below, paras 13.127–133.
[115] Art 8(1) of the Rome Convention.
[116] This assumes that if the term (i.e. the English choice of law clause) were valid then effect would be given to the parties' choice as to the applicable law. In the vast majority of cases this is, indeed, what will happen. There are, however, some limitations on the parties' choice of the applicable law, see below, paras 13.99–102.
[117] But see the discussion at paras 13.155 and 19.25–29 of the argument that the choice of law clause is separate from the contract and can survive its invalidity.
[118] *Thierry Morin v Bonhams & Brooks Limited and Bonhams & Brooks SAM* [2003] EWHC 467 (Comm) at [23]–[25]; the Court of Appeal [2003] EWCA Civ 1802, [2004] IL Pr 24 upheld the finding at first instance that Monegasque law governed the tort.
[119] [1992] 2 Lloyd's Rep 19, CA; the choice of law aspect is discussed below, para 13.47.
[120] Assignees of the rights of the original sellers.

that the plaintiffs had made out a sufficiently arguable case to justify service out of the jurisdiction.[121]

Where the contract contains a term to the effect that the court shall have jurisdic- **4.45** *tion to determine any claim in respect of the contract* An English exporter will normally contract on terms that include an English jurisdiction and choice of law clause. However, such a clause may well also be used in cases where neither party is English. It is important to distinguish these two situations when it comes to deciding whether Article 23 of the Brussels I Regulation will apply.

WILL ARTICLE 23 OF THE BRUSSELS I REGULATION APPLY? In cases where **4.46** there is a choice of jurisdiction clause providing for trial in England, normally Article 23 of the Brussels I Regulation will apply. However, this provision will not operate if the formalities required under it have not been met. Moreover, if neither party is domiciled in an EC Member State the Regulation does not give jurisdiction to the court or courts of the Member State selected by the parties. Instead this court will apply its national rules of jurisdiction and will decide whether it has jurisdiction under those rules.[122] The courts of other Member States have no juris-diction under their national rules unless the court or courts chosen have declined jurisdiction.[123]

STANDARD FORM CONTRACTS FOR THE INTERNATIONAL SALE OF **4.47** GOODS Standard form contracts will very commonly contain a choice of jurisdiction clause. This will not necessarily provide for trial in England. Nonetheless, probably the most famous and commonly used of all trading forms is GAFTA Form 100, clause 31 of which does provide for trial in England.[124] As has previously been mentioned,[125] GAFTA Form 100 may well be adopted by parties, neither of whom is English, and this could include two parties who are domiciled outside the EC. Similarly, parties, neither of whom is English, may specifically negotiate and agree upon the insertion in the sales contract of an exclusive jurisdiction clause providing for trial in England.[126] This may be because they think that there are posi-tive advantages in having trial before the English courts or they just want to choose a neutral forum.[127] If the parties have chosen English law to govern the contract they may think that England is the best place for

---

[121] n 119 above, at 24–25. A ground for service out was already established under Ord 11, r 1(1)(e), discussed below, para 4.83. The applicable law was still relevant when it came to the exercise of the forum conveniens discretion.

[122] See Art 4 of the Brussels I Regulation. [123] Art 23(3).

[124] This is set out above, para 3.198. [125] See above, para 3.04.

[126] See, eg, *Sohio Supply Co v Gatoil (USA) Inc* [1989] 1 Lloyd's Rep 588, CA; discussed below, para 4.180.

[127] ibid, at 592.

English law to be applied. In the situation where there is the sale of manufactured goods, the sale is more likely to be on the seller's terms than the buyer's. If the seller is English, the contract is then likely to provide for trial in England.

4.48 IS THE CHOICE OF JURISDICTION CLAUSE INCORPORATED INTO THE SALES CONTRACT?   It has already been seen[128] that, in cases of the international sale of goods, the problem will frequently arise of whether a jurisdiction clause has been incorporated into the contract, or sometimes which party's jurisdiction clause has been incorporated into the contract. It is necessary to determine when the contract was formed. The law governing the contract for the international sale of goods will determine which country's rules on the formation of the contract for the international sale of goods will apply. This law is ascertained by the application of English choice of law rules contained in the Rome Convention.[129] The issue of incorporation of a clause has been regarded as one of material validity of *the contract*. In contrast, if the issue arises of material validity of *the jurisdiction clause* this will be determined by the application of traditional English choice of law rules, rather than the Rome Convention.[130]

4.49 *Harvey v Ventilatorenfabrik Oelde GmbH*[131] is a good example of how problems of incorporation can arise in the context of the international sale of goods. The English plaintiff entered into an oral contract with the German sellers for the supply of two machines. The oral contract was confirmed in writing, the plaintiff having been sent two sets of acknowledgements of his orders. He signed one of the sets and returned it to the defendants. This contained in German printed conditions on the back, including a choice of jurisdiction clause stating that any disputes would be settled by a court in Germany and the governing law would be German. The other set, which had nothing at all printed on the back, was retained by the plaintiff. There was no reference to the clause in the oral discussions and there was no reference on the face of the documents to the printed terms and conditions on the back of one set. Leave was granted for service of a writ out of the jurisdiction. The defendants sought to have this set aside, relying on the German jurisdiction clause. But had the plaintiff assented to its incorporation into the sales contract? The Court of Appeal held that, viewed objectively, a reasonable person in the position of the plaintiff could naturally conclude that the printed material on the back could be regarded as irrelevant. The court could draw the inference

---

[128] See above, para 3.30.

[129] See *Egon Oldendorff v Libera Corp* [1995] 2 Lloyd's Rep 64; discussed above, para 3.31.

[130] Art 1(2)(d) of the Rome Convention excludes arbitration agreements and agreements on the choice of court from its scope.

[131] [1989] Trading L Rep 138, CA.

that the plaintiff was misled by the difference between the two sets of documents and did not in reality assent to the incorporation of the jurisdiction clause. The case was decided before the Brussels Convention or the Rome Convention came into force. If the same facts arose now the question would be whether the jurisdiction clause was incorporated into the contract for the purposes of the application of Article 23 of the Brussels I Regulation.[132]

A NON-EXCLUSIVE JURISDICTION CLAUSE   A clause providing for the **4.50** exclusive jurisdiction of the English courts is clearly a term to the effect that the English court shall have jurisdiction. So too is a clause providing for the non-exclusive jurisdiction of the English courts.[133] The fact that the parties are not precluded from commencing proceedings abroad does not alter this.

Rule 6.20(6)   Rule 6.20(6) states that a claim form may be served out of **4.51** the jurisdiction with the permission of the court if a claim is made in respect of a breach of contract committed within the jurisdiction.

Many of the reported cases on this ground[134] involve contracts for the **4.52** international sale of goods. It has been commonly invoked in two situations: first, and often unsuccessfully, where an English buyer brings a claim against a foreign seller alleging non-delivery or delivery of faulty goods; second, and usually successfully, where an English seller brings a claim against a foreign buyer alleging non-payment. The two elements of this ground, i.e. a claim made in respect of a breach of contract and the breach is committed within the jurisdiction, will now be considered.

A claim is made in respect of a breach of contract   A claim must be made in **4.53** respect of a breach of contract. It is understandable that the scope of this ground should be restricted to claims made in respect of a breach of contract, given that it allocates jurisdiction to England in cases where a breach was committed within the jurisdiction.

The claimant must establish a good arguable case that there was a breach **4.54** of contract. It is unclear what role, if any, the applicable law plays in establishing this. The question does not appear to have arisen before the courts. Nonetheless, it could arise. For example, the facts may involve what English law regards as an anticipatory breach of contract but the applicable law has no such doctrine. Another example would be where

---

[132] See above, para 3.30.
[133] *Gulf Bank KSC v Mitsubishi Heavy Industries Ltd* [1994] 1 Lloyd's Rep 323; *Standard Steamship Owners' Protection and Indemnity v Gann* [1992] 2 Lloyd's Rep 528; J Fawcett, 'Non-exclusive Jurisdiction Agreements in Private International Law' [2001] LMCLQ 234, 244–245.
[134] See Dicey and Morris, 324–328.

under English law there is a breach of a particular obligation, whereas under the foreign applicable law there is no such obligation and therefore no breach, or vice versa.

4.55 No requirement has been laid down that the claimant must establish a good arguable case that there was a breach according to the law applicable to the contract. The case law on this ground has adopted the English concept of a breach. However, in most of these cases, English law was in fact applicable to the contract. As will be seen, in a few cases a foreign law was applicable to the contract but this law may not have been pleaded and proved with the result that the foreign law was assumed to be the same as English law. It follows that uncertainty remains in the situation where a foreign law is applicable to the contract and this law is proven to be different from English.

4.56 It is arguable that, even in this situation, a 'breach' of contract is referring to what the English domestic law of contract means by this word. This is on the basis that the place where a breach of contract is committed is a connecting factor and, accordingly, it is for English law to determine the meaning of all the elements of this connecting factor. This would mean that the breach ground would be satisfied in the situation where English law provides that there is a breach but under the foreign applicable law there is no breach. However, there would be no serious issue to be tried on the merits and permission for service out of the jurisdiction should be refused or, if previously granted, set aside. It would also mean that the breach ground would not be satisfied in the situation where under English law there is no breach but the foreign applicable law provides that there is a breach. This is a much more difficult situation. It looks to be unfair to the claimant if, in this situation, he is denied recourse to the breach ground. Faced with this situation, a judge may decide that identification of the breach should be a matter for the law applicable to the contract.

4.57 We can now turn to look at the different ways that a breach can be committed under English law and at the case law applying this law. Under English law a breach can be committed by repudiation of the contract or by non-performance of the contract. Repudiation consists of a general refusal to be bound by the contract. It may occur when the obligations of the party in breach have accrued or, instead, it may take place by anticipation, in which latter case it has long been settled that the breach is to be regarded as a present breach. Not all anticipatory breaches are anticipatory repudiations giving rise to a right to terminate the contract. An anticipatory breach can present itself in the form of a renunciation, which is a wilful refusal to be bound, but it can also be seen in the form of prospective incapacity, which deals with the case of the disabled party who has no defence to an impending failure to perform. Apart from repudiation, a contract can be breached in myriad ways by non-performance of one or more of its several duties. The tendency in English law is to speak in terms of breach rather than non-performance, though the terminology of non-performance is gaining currency by virtue of its use in international conventions, such as the Vienna Convention, and in international instruments, such as the Unidroit Principles of International Commercial Contracts 1994.

REPUDIATION   It is a well established principle of English law, that where **4.58** a contract is to be performed on a future date or is dependent on a contingency, and one of the parties to the contract repudiates it and shows by word or act that he does not intend to perform it or cannot perform it, the other party is entitled to sue him for breach of the contract without waiting for the arrival of the time fixed for performance, or the happening of the contingency on which the contract is dependent, and is himself absolved from the further performance of his part of the contract.[135] But the repudiation of a contract by one of the parties to it does not of itself discharge the contract.[136] It only gives to the other party the option of either treating the contract as at an end, or of waiting until the stipulated time has arrived or the contingency upon which the performance of the contract was dependent has happened.[137] We will start by looking at the application of r 6.20(6) in the situation where the repudiation is accepted and then turn to examine the situation where it has not been accepted.

A REPUDIATION THAT IS ACCEPTED   For the purposes of r 6.20(6), with an **4.59** anticipatory breach of contract, the breach is the repudiatory act or conduct, i.e. the act or conduct indicating an intention not to proceed with the contract.[138] What is needed is some overt act, rather than the decision of the party in default not to perform the contract.[139]

A REPUDIATION THAT HAS NOT BEEN ACCEPTED   If the innocent party **4.60** opts to wait until the time stipulated arises he can then sue for non-performance of the contract.[140] It is entirely possible that, if the anticipatory breach is accepted, r 6.20(6) will not apply (because this breach

---

[135] *Martin v Stout* [1923] AC 359 at 364, PC.   [136] ibid.   [137] ibid.
[138] *Safran v Chani* [1970] 1 NSWLR 70, CA; *Mutzenbecher v La Aseguradora Espanola* [1906] 1 KB 254 at 259, CA.
[139] *Harvey v Ventilatorenfabrik Oelde GmbH* [1989] Trading L Rep 138, 149, CA. See also *Oppenheimer v Louis Rosenthal & Co AG* [1937] All ER 23, CA.
[140] The *Brinkibon* case, n 81 above, at 49–50 (*per* Lord Brandon). Waiting until the time stipulated would not amount to a waiver of performance as of the time when performance falls due. The non-accepting party may in turn be sued for a present breach if he is unable to perform on the due date: *Fercometal SARL v Mediterranean Shipping Co SA* [1989] AC 788.

occurred out of the jurisdiction) whereas, if it is not, a claim for non-performance may come within this ground (because there is a breach of an obligation that should have been performed in England) or vice versa.

4.61 What may well happen is that the contract has been repudiated by one party but a claim is not brought until after the time for performance has passed by. In such circumstances, it is very important, because of its implications for the application of r 6.20(6), to ascertain whether the claim is based on repudiation (this having been accepted by the other party) or on non-performance (the repudiation not having been accepted by the other party). This can be ascertained by looking at the way the claim is pleaded and at whether there is any evidence of acceptance. This is illustrated by the *Brinkibon* case.[141] The House of Lords regarded the breach by the seller as being non-performance of the contract, namely the failure to open a performance bond and to deliver steel.[142] This was on the basis that this is what was pleaded by the plaintiff[143] and also on the basis that there was no evidence of acceptance of the repudiation.[144] In so deciding, the House of Lords expressly[145] overruled the Court of Appeal,[146] which had held that the sellers were in breach of contract by repudiating the contract. This made no difference to the result, as regards the application of the breach head, on the facts of the case since not only was the failure to perform the relevant acts located abroad but so also was the act of repudiation. But in other cases it can make a difference.

4.62 If the foreign applicable law does not have a doctrine of anticipatory breach it is unclear whether the breach ground is satisfied. However, this does not really matter. There is no serious issue to be tried on the merits and permission for service out of the jurisdiction should be refused or, if previously granted, set aside.

4.63 Non-performance   In order to determine whether there has been a breach of an obligation to perform, it is first necessary to identify what the obligations of the parties are under the contract. Are these the obligations as laid down by English law, on the basis that we are concerned with the English concept of a 'breach' of contract, or as laid down by the law applicable to the sales contract, which may, of course be a foreign law? This question does not appear to have been discussed in any of the reported cases on this ground. The courts have automatically looked at English law in order to define the obligation on which the claim is based. In many of these cases, doubtless the applicable law was English law.

---

[141] n 81 above.   [142] ibid, at 43 (*per* Lord Wilberforce), 49–50 (*per* Lord Brandon).
[143] ibid.   [144] *per* Lord Brandon at 49.
[145] *per* Lord Brandon at 49.   [146] [1980] 2 Lloyd's Rep 556.

More interesting therefore are those cases where English law has defined the obligation, even though it was clear that a foreign law governed the sales contract. *Cordova Land Co Ltd v Victor Brothers Inc*[147] is an example. The question that arose was whether the vendors of skins CIF Hull were in breach of contract when the goods on discharge in Hull were found to have deteriorated. Winn J held that there was no implied warranty in the sale contracts that the skins would be of contract description and quality on arrival in Hull. What he appears to have been concerned with was whether under English law there was such an implied warranty, even though he had earlier held that the sales contracts were not governed by English law. Accordingly, there was no breach of contract within the jurisdiction under the predecessor of r 6.20(6).[148] *Cuban Atlantic Sugar Sales Corp v Compañía De Vapores San Elefterio Limitada*[149] is to the same effect. The contract of carriage was governed by a foreign law but when it came to the operation of the breach ground for service out of the jurisdiction the obligations under this contract were identified without reference to this law. Finally, there is *Gill and Dufus v London Export*.[150] Robert Goff J held that Californian law governed the sales contract. But he then went on to identify the obligation that had been breached without any reference to that law. Although these three cases provide implicit support for the idea that the obligation is referring to the obligation as laid down by English law on the basis that we are concerned with the English concept of a 'breach' of contract, they cannot be regarded as conclusive on this point. A possible explanation of all three cases is that English law was simply applied by virtue of the principle that, unless one of the parties pleads and proves foreign law, English law will be assumed to be the same as that law. It must be admitted though that there was no reference to this principle.

The upshot is that uncertainty remains in the situation where a foreign **4.64** law is applicable and this is proven to be different from English law as regards obligation and breach. If under the foreign applicable law there has been no breach but under English there has been a breach (the obligation imposed being different) it is unclear whether the breach ground is satisfied. However, this does not really matter. There is no serious issue to be tried on the merits and permission for service out of the jurisdiction should be refused or, if previously granted, set aside. More difficult is the converse situation, namely where under the foreign applicable law there has been a breach but under English there has been no breach (the

---

[147] [1966] 1 WLR 793.
[148] There was a separate action brought against the ship-owners for fraudulent misrepresentation. Jurisdiction in relation to such action is discussed below, paras 6.96–113.
[149] [1960] 1 QB 187, CA.   [150] [1982] 2 Lloyd's Rep 627.

obligation imposed being different). In this situation, a judge could decide that identification of the breach should be a matter for the law applicable to the contract.

4.65 Different obligations with different places of performance   There is no requirement that the whole of the contract has to be performed within the jurisdiction. 'It is sufficient if some part of it is to be performed within the jurisdiction, and if there is a breach of that part of it within the jurisdiction.'[151] Thus if, for example, all the duties of the buyer have to be performed abroad, except for the duty of payment, the breach ground can be used in a claim for non-payment.[152] The position has long been clear in cases where there are distinguishable and independent obligations, some of which have a place of performance within the jurisdiction and others of which have a place of performance outside the jurisdiction. But what if the obligations are not independent of each other? If one of these occurs in England and the other abroad, do the English courts have jurisdiction under r 6.20(6)?

4.66 This problem arose in relation to one of the predecessors of this rule in *Johnson v Taylor Bros & Co Ltd*.[153] Swedish sellers failed to ship goods that they had sold to English buyers under a contract CIF Leeds. The shippers failed both to deliver the shipping documents and to ship the goods. The former breach occurred in England but the latter occurred in Stockholm. The House of Lords refused permission for service of process out of the jurisdiction[154] on the basis that, although the failure to deliver the shipping documents represented a breach in England, the substantial breach was the non-shipment of the goods at Stockholm. If the goods have not been shipped, the shipping documents will never have come into existence. The wording of the breach head of Order 11 was subsequently altered to ensure that such a case would come within it. This was done by adding to Order 11, r 1(1)(e) of the Rules of the Supreme Court the words 'and irrespective of the fact, if such be the case, that the breach was preceded or accompanied by a breach committed out of the jurisdiction that rendered impossible the performance of so much of the contract as ought to have been performed within the jurisdiction'. Rule 6.20(6) of the Civil Procedure Rules has deliberately omitted this wording and what we now have is wording that is similar to that at the time when the *Johnson*

---

[151] *Rein v Stein* [1892] 1 QB 753 at 757 (*per* Lindley LJ), CA. See also *Robey v Snaefell Mining Co* (1887) 20 QBD 152; *The Eider* [1893] P 119 at 126 (*per* The President, Sir Francis H Jeune), at 126.

[152] See the *Rein* case, n 151 above.   [153] [1920] AC 144.

[154] Under Ord 11, r 1(e) RSC, which required that: 'The action is founded on any breach within the jurisdiction of any contract wherever made, which, according to the terms thereof, ought to be performed within the jurisdiction'.

case was decided. Nonetheless, it is submitted that this omission should not be regarded as reflecting any intention to go back to the position under the *Johnson* case. Rule 6.20 of the Civil Procedure Rules made a number of drafting changes to the rules in Order 11, r 1(1) of the Rules of the Supreme Court so as to produce a list which was clearer and simpler; it was not intended that these changes should have any substantive effect on the court's powers.[155] As regards the breach provision, it was considered unnecessary to retain the wording specifying that this provision applied irrespective of whether some other breach was committed out of the jurisdiction.[156] It follows that, if facts such as those in the *Johnson* case were to arise now, then the courts should be regarded as having jurisdiction under r 6.20(6)of the Civil Procedure Rules on the basis that the shippers failed to deliver the shipping documents to England. Having obtained jurisdiction in relation to this breach, the claimants presumably cannot add on a separate claim for the separate breach which arose out of the failure to ship the goods and in respect of which there was no jurisdiction under r 6.20(6).

Committed within the jurisdiction   The claimant must establish a good **4.67** arguable case that the breach of contract was committed within the jurisdiction. The place where a breach was committed is clearly a connecting factor. The determination of this place is therefore a matter for English law, as the law of the forum, rather than for the law governing the contract. Similarly, the place where a tort was committed for the purposes of service out of the jurisdiction was also a matter for English law.[157] Identification of the place where the breach was committed, according to English law, has been made easier by the fact that, in the reported cases at least, the breach has also been identified by reference to English law. If the breach were to be identified by reference to a foreign applicable law, as might happen where there is no breach by English law but there is a breach by the foreign governing law, it would be by no means easy for the English courts, applying English law, to ascribe a place to the commission of this breach. There would then be a case for also applying the foreign applicable law to identify the place where the breach was committed. What is important is that the same law should identify the breach and the place where this is committed.[158]

---

[155] See the Lord Chancellor's Department Consultation Paper on the CPR, *Service of Court Process Abroad*, para 23.

[156] ibid.

[157] See, e.g. *George Monro v American Cyanamid* [1944] KB 432, CA.

[158] See above, paras 3.254–297, the rule that applies under the Brussels I Regulation (in cases falling outside the special rule in Art 5(1)(b)) whereby the place of performance of an obligation is to be determined according to the law applicable to the contract.

4.68 In determining where a breach of contract is committed it is important to look separately at the different forms of breach.

4.69 WHERE IS A REPUDIATION COMMITTED?   A long line of authority going back to the nineteenth century,[159] including a decision of the Privy Council,[160] establishes that where repudiation is claimed to have been effected by the posting of a letter or the sending of a cable or telegram or telex, the place of posting or sending is the place where the act of repudiation took place and hence where the breach of contract occurred. The receipt of the communication in another state furnishes the claimant with the evidence that the defendant has repudiated the contract.[161] But the act of repudiation takes place in the place of posting or sending. To treat the place of receipt as being the place where the anticipatory breach was committed would be inconsistent with the nature of repudiation.[162] It follows that where the posting or sending took place abroad and receipt was in England there is no breach committed within the jurisdiction.[163] In contrast, if the posting or sending takes place in England there is a breach committed within the jurisdiction,[164] even if the letter is received abroad.[165] The same principle applies where communication of the repudiation is made by a phone call. The breach occurs where the overt act of repudiation takes place, that is where the words are spoken by the party in default, rather than where they are heard in another state.[166]

4.70 Many of these authorities arose in the context of breach of a promise to marry or dismissal of an employee or agent. In one such case, the agent was concerned with the sale of the goods of the party in default.[167] These principles were applied by the Court of Appeal in the *Brinkibon* case to the anticipatory breach of a contract for the international sale of goods. As has been seen, the breach was regarded by that Court as being the repudiation of the contract by the sellers. According to Templeman LJ,[168] the act of repudiation was that of the sellers in Austria in determining to repudiate

---

[159] *Cherry v Thompson* (1872) LR 7 QB 573; *Holland v Bennett* [1902] 1 KB 867, CA; *Mutzenbecher v La Aseguradora Espanola* [1906] 1 KB 254, CA; the *Oppenheimer* case, n 139 above; *Atlantic Underwriting Agencies Ltd v Compagnia di Assicurazione di Milano SPA* [1979] 2 Lloyd's Rep 240; the *Safran* case, n 138 above; *Stanley Kerr Holdings Pty Ltd v Gibor Textile Enterprises Ltd* [1978] 2 NSWLR 372.

[160] *Martin v Stout*, n 135 above.

[161] *Cherry v Thompson*, n 159 above, at 579 (*per* Blackburn J).

[162] The *Safran* case, n 138 above, at 148.

[163] See the *Cherry, Holland, Atlantic Underwriting, Stanley Kerr* and *Safran* cases.

[164] See the *Mutzenbecher* and *Oppenheimer* cases, in both of which the letter was also received in England.

[165] The *Martin* case, n 135 above.

[166] The *Safran* case, n 138 above, at 150.

[167] *Stanley Kerr Holdings Pty Ltd v Gibor Textile Enterprises Ltd* [1978] 2 NSWLR 372.

[168] n 81 above, at 564–565.

and in sending the telex of repudiation dated 21 May 1979. The breach of contract occurred in Austria where the sellers determined to repudiate and where they took effective steps to communicate that determination to the buyers.[169] Strictly speaking, in such a case, it is the taking of the steps to communicate that constitutes the relevant act and not the determination to repudiate. Thus, in a case where the decision to repudiate was made in Germany but the letter communicating this was posted in London, the Court of Appeal held that the breach was committed in London.[170] Stephenson LJ in the *Brinkibon* case held that the breach of contract was constituted by the telex message, which evinced an intention not to be bound[171] and where the act of repudiation is done by telex this is committed where the party who sets the telex in motion is.[172] The House of Lords took a different view as to what constituted the breach of contract. The breach of contract pleaded was simply a failure by the sellers to perform the contract by opening a performance bond and delivering the steel. In the light of this, it was held that the breach was the failure by the sellers to perform any part of their obligations under the contract, rather than any alleged anticipatory repudiation of the contract.[173]

WHERE IS A NON-PERFORMANCE OF THE CONTRACT COMMITTED? Having **4.71** identified the obligation that has been breached it is necessary to ask where it should have been performed. A failure to perform an obligation is located in the same place.[174] For the purposes of r 6.20(6) the place of performance of contractual obligations is a matter for English law, as the law of the forum, to determine, rather than for the law applicable to the contract. This is because the place where a breach occurs is a connecting factor.[175]

It is possible to have an obligation which should have been performed **4.72** partly in England and partly abroad. For example, payment is to be made partly in England and partly abroad. If a claim is partly within this ground and partly outside it the judge may still give permission for service out of the jurisdiction.[176] At one time this problem was dealt with by an undertaking by the plaintiff that jurisdiction would not be taken in

---

[169] The place where the decision was made was the same as that from where the telex was sent. In the rare situation where they are different, the breach is committed where the telex is sent from, see the *Safran* case, n 138 above.

[170] The *Oppenheimer* case, n 139 above. See also the *Safran* case, n 138 above, at 149.

[171] [1980] 2 Lloyd's 556 at 562, CA.

[172] ibid, at 563. This assumes he is in the place from where the telex is sent. If he is not, the breach is committed in the place from where the telex is sent.

[173] [1983] 2 AC 34 at 49–50 (*per* Lord Brandon).

[174] ibid, at 43 (*per* Lord Wilberforce).

[175] See the discussion at para 4.67 above.

[176] *Bremer Oeltransport GmbH v Drewry* [1933] 1 KB 753 at 765 (*per* Slesser LJ), CA.

respect of breaches which were not committed within the jurisdiction, i.e. the payments to be made abroad.[177] However, the introduction of such an undertaking into the order of the judge granting permission for service out of the jurisdiction has been described as being undesirable.[178] Instead the fact that the payment is to be made partly in England and partly abroad is a matter to be considered by the judge when exercising his discretion to permit service out of the jurisdiction.[179] If a claim is brought in respect of the whole payment (i.e. the payment that should have been made abroad as well as the payment that should have been made in England) this runs the risk of permission not being granted for service out of the jurisdiction.

4.73   To illustrate this process of identification, according to English law, of the place of performance we can look at various obligations under a contract for the international sale of goods, the breach of which most commonly leads to a claim for breach of contract. There has been some criticism of the breach ground in the context of a case where the obligation of an investment banking company was to raise money and it was exceptionally difficult to ascertain where the contract was to be performed.[180] As will be seen no such problem arises with contracts for the international sale of goods.

4.74   A BREACH OF THE SELLER'S OBLIGATION TO DELIVER   The House of Lords in *Johnson v Taylor Bros & Co Ltd*[181] held that, in an ordinary contract for the sale of goods on CIF terms, the seller is under an obligation to ship goods on board a ship bound to the contract destination. The case involved a Swedish seller and the goods were to be shipped from a Swedish port. It was held that this was not a contract to be performed within the jurisdiction. The upshot was that the English buyer of the goods was unable to found jurisdiction against the Swedish defendant on the breach ground. The case has considerable implications for any English buyer who has bought goods on CIF terms with shipment from a foreign port and wants to bring a claim for simple non-delivery. One device that can be used to get round the jurisdictional problem is to base the claim not on a breach of the obligation to deliver the goods but on a breach of the seller's obligation to hand over documents relating to the goods. In contrast, if the purchase of the goods is on FOB terms with specified delivery in England

---

[177]   *Malik v Narodni Banka Ceskoslovenska* (1947) 176 LT 136, CA.
[178]   *Vitkovice Horni A Hutni Tezirstvo v Korner* [1951] AC 869 at 881 (*per* Lord Simonds), 891 (*per* Lord Tucker), at 887 (*per* Lord Radcliffe).
[179]   ibid, at 887 (*per* Lord Radcliffe).
[180]   Hawkins J in *Bailey and Co Inc v Laser Medical Technology Inc* [1994] IL Pr 444 at 446–447.
[181]   n 153 above.

there is no problem in bringing a simple case of non-delivery within the breach head.

In the *Brinkibon* case, the plaintiff sought to base jurisdiction on a breach **4.75** of contract committed in England, as an alternative to basing it on the contract being made in England. The breach of contract pleaded by the plaintiff buyers was the sellers' failure to open a performance bond and to deliver any steel. It was held that each of these acts should have been performed outside the jurisdiction and the failure to perform them must be similarly located outside the jurisdiction.[182] Indeed, it had never been suggested that any part of the contract was to be performed by the sellers anywhere except outside the jurisdiction.[183] The steel was to be delivered C & F Alexandria on liner terms. It is less clear from the reported facts where the performance bond was to be opened. Given that this was an Austrian seller presumably this would be in Austria. Perhaps more to the point, there was no evidence that this should have been performed by the Austrian seller in England.

If delivery is to take place partly in England and partly abroad the **4.76** position is dealt with above[184] where we considered the situation where there is an obligation which should have been performed partly in England and partly abroad.

A BREACH OF THE SELLER'S OBLIGATION TO DELIVER GOODS IN CONFORMITY **4.77** WITH THE CONTRACT   When it comes to the operation of the breach head, the position is exactly the same in cases of a breach of the obligation to deliver goods in conformity with the contract as it is in cases of a breach of the obligation to deliver the goods.[185] It will be recalled[186] that the two obligations are treated the same for the purposes of jurisdiction under Article 5(1) of the Brussels I Regulation and it is right and proper that the same should happen in the present context.

If the parties contract on CIF terms the breach consists in not shipping **4.78** goods in accordance with the quality stipulated for in the contract. The time and place of the delivery are the time when and place where the seller delivers the goods on board ship. If this is at a foreign port the result is that the breach head cannot be used as the ground for service out of the jurisdiction.[187] This has obvious implications in the common situation

---

[182] n 173 above, at 43 (*per* Lord Wilberforce).
[183] ibid, at 50 (*per* Lord Brandon). The other Law Lords concurred with both Lords Wilberforce and Brandon.
[184] Above, para 4.66.
[185] *Crozier, Stephens & Co v Auerbach* [1908] 2 KB 161 at 165 (*per* Vaughan Williams LJ), 167 (*per* Farwell LJ) CA.
[186] Above, para 3.110.
[187] The *Crozier* case, n 185 above; the *Cordova* case, n 147 above, at 796.

where an English buyer of goods wishes to sue a foreign seller after delivery of goods which do not conform with the contract. It was this basic inability to come within the breach ground in this situation that led to the failed attempt to get round this in the *Cordova* case[188] by arguing that the sale contract contained a warranty that the goods would be of contract description and quality on arrival in England.

4.79 The *Harvey* case[189] is a simple example where the terms of the breach head were met. It was not in issue between the parties that the terms of this ground were satisfied in circumstances where the plaintiff alleged that the machines manufactured by the defendants and erected at the plaintiff's factory in England did not comply with warranties given by the defendants in relation to their performance, were not of merchantable quality, and were unfit for the purpose for which he required them.[190]

4.80 A BREACH OF THE SELLER'S OBLIGATION TO HAND OVER ANY DOCUMENTS RELATING TO THE GOODS   It is necessary to distinguish between 'genuine' cases of a breach of the seller's obligation to hand over documents and 'spurious' cases. A genuine case arises where the goods have been delivered and, accordingly, there has been no breach of the obligation to deliver, but the documents relating to the goods have not been handed over. A spurious case arises where the goods have not been delivered and the claim for breach of the seller's obligation to hand over any documents relating to the goods is a mere device to bring the case within the breach ground.

4.81 In a 'genuine' case, the position is entirely straightforward. Lord Atkinson in the *Johnson* case[191] held that, where the buyer and seller enter into a CIF contract, the seller, in the absence of a provision to the contrary, is bound, inter alia, with all reasonable despatch to send forward and tender to the buyer the shipping documents, delivery of which to the buyer is symbolical of delivery of the goods purchased.[192] A place may be named in the CIF contract for tender of the shipping documents. If no such place is named, the shipping documents must, *prima facie*, be tendered at the residence or place of business of the buyer.[193] This means in a case where an English buyer was buying from a foreign seller there would be a breach committed within the jurisdiction for the purposes of the breach head.

4.82 In a spurious case, the position is more complicated. The *Johnson* case itself involved a 'spurious' claim for breach of the obligation to tender documents, which was added to the claim for non-delivery of the goods. As has been seen, having decided that the essential breach was the failure to

---

[188] n 147 above.   [189] n 131 above.   [190] ibid, at 139–140.
[191] n 153 above.   [192] ibid, at 156.   [193] ibid. See also Lord Birkenhead at 149.

deliver the goods, the House of Lords held that it was not possible to base the breach ground on the breach of the obligation to tender the shipping documents, documents which in fact never came into existence. But it has also been seen[194] that the wording of the breach ground was subsequently amended to allow this. The position now is therefore that, if facts such as those in the *Johnson* case were to arise, the courts should be regarded as having jurisdiction under r 6.20(6) of the Civil Procedure Rules on the basis that the shippers failed to deliver the shipping documents to England.

A BREACH OF THE BUYER'S OBLIGATION TO PAY   When does the buyer's **4.83** obligation to pay arise in an international sale of goods case? The sales contract may expressly provide for payment against shipping documents. Where there is a CIF contract, in the absence of such an express stipulation, the rule applies that a seller is entitled to payment upon his shipping the goods and tendering the documents.[195] The seller is entitled to tender the bill of lading at any reasonable time and does not have to wait till the ship has arrived. The parties may well expressly stipulate in the sales contract the place where payment is to be made.[196] In *Banque Paribas v Cargill International SA*,[197] the express stipulation took a rather indirect form. There was a contractual provision for the payment of net cash into the seller's bank account by telegraphic transfer prompt upon receipt of the telex invoice. All the telex invoices specified the seller's bank account with a bank in London and stated the number of that account. The Court of Appeal held that, on receipt of the invoice, there was a contractual obligation to pay promptly by telegraphic transfer into the seller's bank account in London.[198] On the question of where the payment was to be made, it was true that the buyers were aware of other bank accounts of the seller in Geneva but, the seller having nominated a particular account in London, the buyer was obliged to pay into this account, rather than into any other account of which he was aware. Accordingly, there had been a breach of the sales contract within the jurisdiction and the court had jurisdiction to permit service out of the jurisdiction.[199]

However, in perhaps a surprising number of reported cases there is no **4.84** express stipulation as to the place of payment. The breach head does not require there to be an express provision.[200] It is enough if it appears, from a consideration of the terms of the contract and the facts existing when the

---

[194] Above, para 4.66.   [195] *E Clemens Horst Company v Biddell Brothers* [1912] AC 18.
[196] For a summary of the English law on the place of payment see Law Com No 109 and Scot Law Com No 66 (1981), *Private International Law: Council of Europe Conventions on Foreign Money Liabilities (1967) and on the Place of Payment of Money Liabilities (1972)*, 23–31.
[197] [1992] 2 Lloyd's Rep 19, CA.   [198] ibid, at 23.   [199] ibid.
[200] *Reynolds v Coleman* (1887) 36 Ch D 464, CA; *Robey & Co v Snaefell Mining Company, Limited* (1887) 20 QBD 152; *Bell & Co v Antwerp, London and Brazil Line* [1891] 1 QB 103; *Rein v Stein* [1892] 1 QB 753, CA; *Charles Duval & Co, Limited v Gans* [1904] 2 KB 685, CA.

contract was made,[201] that it was intended to be performed within the jurisdiction.[202] In other words, it may be possible to infer[203] or imply[204] an agreement by the parties as to the place of payment. This involves looking at the terms of the contract and the surrounding circumstances.[205] The Court must look at the contract and construe it according to the normal rules of construction of a contract and determine whether upon the terms of the contract so construed it appears to be one to be performed within the jurisdiction.[206] A contract made in England to transfer shares in an English company to a person resident in England has been held to be a contract which, according to its terms, ought to be performed within the jurisdiction.[207] If it appears that, according to the course of business in similar sales transactions between the claimant and the defendant, such payment would be made in England, then the breach ground is satisfied.[208] The mode of payment may clearly indicate the place of payment. In *Comber v Leyland*,[209] it was expressly agreed that payment for the goods was to be made by remitting the amount payable in first class bank bills on England, not exceeding 90 days sight. It was held that the contract was to be performed by putting into the post office abroad a letter containing such bank bills. Accordingly, payment was not to be made in England and therefore the breach ground was not satisfied. The fact that payment was made in English money has been used to support the inference that payment was to be made in England.[210] The fact that payment was to be made against documents and those documents were to be handed over in Italy has been used to support the inference that payment was to be made in Italy.[211] Drawing inferences in this way is by no means an easy exercise. The case may involve a number of circumstances which point towards different places of payment. This is illustrated by the case of *Fry v Raggio*[212] where one judge drew his inference as to the place of payment from the fact that payment was in English currency[213] and another drew his inference from the fact that documents were to be handed over in Italy.[214]

---

[201] But see the *Rein* case, n 200 above, at 758, where Lindley LJ looked at the course of business between the parties since the contract was made.

[202] The *Reynolds* case, n 200 above.

[203] The *Rein* case, n 200 above, at 758 (*per* Lindley LJ).

[204] The *Duval* case, n 200 above, at 692 (*per* Mathew LJ). See also *Earthworks and Quarries Ltd v FT Eastment & Sons Pty Ltd* [1966] VR 24; *BP Australia Limited v Wales* [1982] Qd R 386; *Shallay Holdings Pty Ltd v Griffith Co-operative Society Ltd* [1983] VR 760.

[205] The *Bell* case, n 200 above, at 109 (*per* Kay LJ).

[206] The *Bell* case, ibid, at 108 (*per* Lord Esher MR), 109 (*per* Kay LJ), CA.

[207] The *Reynolds* case, n 200 above.   [208] *Rein v Stein*, n 200 above.

[209] [1898] AC 524.

[210] *Fry v Raggio* (1891) 40 WR 120, see the judgment of Coleridge CJ.

[211] ibid, see the judgment of Mathew J.   [212] ibid.

[213] ibid, at 121 (*per* Coleridge CJ).   [214] ibid, at 121 (*per* Mathew J).

In identifying the place of breach, the courts have often invoked the rule **4.85** that the debtor must follow his creditor and must pay where his creditor is, i.e. has his residence or place of business[215] at the time the contract was concluded.[216] This rule should be regarded as coming into play in the absence of any intention, express or implied[217] and by its very nature automatically identifies the place of payment. Nonetheless, the courts seem to be unwilling to get away from the language of an inferred choice. Thus the rule has been described as allowing an inference to be drawn as to the place of payment from the residence of the creditor.[218] It has also been held that an intention may be inferred that the payment should be to a creditor company where its office is situated.[219] At the end of the day, whether the rule identifies the place of payment automatically or by way of an inference does not matter. What does matter is that this rule has considerable implications in the common scenario facing the courts of an English seller of goods suing a foreign buyer for non-payment of the price. Such a case will fall within the breach ground.[220] In the situation where a debtor is bound to pay his creditor on demand, which can happen in sales cases,[221] the creditor need not demand his debt at the debtor's place of business, he may demand payment from his debtor wherever he may find him.[222] Wherever he finds the debtor and demands his debt, the debtor is bound to pay him then and there. Payment of the debt has not to be made in any specified place, but may be anywhere.

---

[215] The *Robey* case, n 200 above; The *Bell* case, n 200 above; the *Rein* case, n 200 above, at 758 (*per* Kay LJ); The *Eider* [1893] P 119 at 128 (*per* the President), 131 (*per* Lord Esher MR), CA; the *Bremer Oeltransport* case, n 176 above, at 765–766 (*per* Slesser LJ), CA; *Drexel v Drexel* [1916] 1 Ch 251 at 260. But not where the creditor moves abroad after the contract is made, see *The Eider*, ibid, at 131 (*per* Lord Esher MR); *Fessard v Mugnier* 18 CB (NS) 286.

[216] In the context of service out of the jurisdiction, the position seems to be clear, see the *Rein*, *Duval* and *Drexel* cases. In other contexts, there are various alternatives that could be used to answer the question of the precise moment at which one is concerned with the creditor's residence or place of business, see Law Com No 109, 27–28.

[217] See *Crédit Agricole Indosuez v Chailease Finance Corp* [2000] IL Pr 776 at 789, CA; *The Eider*, n 215 above, at 136 (*per* Bowen LJ). The alternative is to regard the rule as applying in the absence of an express choice: see Lord Esher MR in the same case (this is based on the idea that the rule itself allows an inference to be drawn from the residence of the creditor); *Bank of Scotland v Seitz* 1990 SLT 584 at 591–592.

[218] *The Eider*, n 215 above, at 128 (*per* Lord Esher MR). See also the *Drexel* case, n 215 above.

[219] The *Duval* case, n 200 above, at 692 (*per* Mathew LJ). See also the *Earthworks* case, n 204 above; the *Shallay* case, n 204 above.

[220] See, e.g. the *Robey* case, n 200 above; the *Duval* case, n 200 above.

[221] s 28 of the Sale of Goods Act 1978 sets out a presumptive rule that payment and delivery are mutual and concurrent conditions. To that extent a tender of delivery amounts to a request for payment on demand. And if the contract requires payment by means of a sight draft [bill of exchange], then that too is payment on demand.

[222] The *Bell* case, n 200 above, at 107.

4.86 If the contract provides that payment can be made either in England or abroad the terms of the breach ground are not satisfied.[223] There has to be a breach committed within the jurisdiction and a breach that merely may be so committed is not enough. If payment is to be made both in England and abroad the position has already been discussed[224] when we considered the situation where there is an obligation which should have been performed partly in England and partly abroad.

4.87 THE BUYER'S OBLIGATION TO ACCEPT THE DOCUMENTS RELATING TO THE GOODS   It is not always clear whether the relevant breach should be regarded as one of a failure to pay or as one of a failure to accept the documents relating to the goods.[225] In *Gill and Duffus Landauer Ltd v London Export Corp GmbH*,[226] the German buyers rejected documents covering shipment tendered by the English sellers on the ground that, by reason of the quality specified in the Dried Fruit Association of California inspection certificate, these documents were not in accordance with the contract and refused to pay for the goods. Robert Goff J held that the relevant breach was the non-acceptance of the documents, which took place in Frankfurt, rather than the failure to pay the purchase price.[227] The reason for this appears to be his earlier comment that the dispute between the parties was as to whether the defendants were entitled in the circumstances to reject the documents. On the facts it would not have made any difference if failure to pay had been regarded as the relevant breach of contract because the price was payable in New York and not in England.[228] However, in other cases it may well happen that the non-acceptance of the documents may take place in England, whilst the place of payment may be abroad. This shows the importance of identifying what the obligation is that has been breached. This process of identifying the obligation is not a precise science and, as a result, gives the courts some flexibility when deciding whether to subject a foreign defendant to jurisdiction in England. But to ensure predictability the test of 'what is the dispute really about?' should be applied in order to determine whether the relevant breach should be regarded as one of a failure to pay or as one of a failure to accept the documents relating to the goods.

---

[223] *The Eider*, n 215 above, at 132 (*per* Lord Esher MR); the *Bell* case, n 200 above.

[224] See above, paras 4.65–66.

[225] A refusal to accept shipping documents is a clear case of breach (see, eg, *Berger v Gill & Duffus* [1984] AC 225). This should be treated as a breach of condition: ibid. If the refusal to accept is announced in advance, then it is anticipatory. But in CIF and similar contracts, documentary delivery *is* contractual performance, as opposed to a harbinger of performance. In this respect, it is to be distinguished from the giving of a notice of appropriation (GAFTA 100, cl 10) which is a form of pre-tender protocol (see *The Vladimir Ilich* [1975] 1 Lloyd's Rep 322).

[226] [1982] 2 Lloyd's Rep 627.   [227] ibid, at 629–630.   [228] ibid.

AN OBLIGATION THAT CAN BE PERFORMED IN ENGLAND OR ABROAD It has **4.88**
already been seen that, if the contract provides that payment can be made
either in England or abroad, the terms of the breach ground are not satisfied. The position is the same in relation to any other obligations which
can be performed either in England or abroad.[229] For example, the sales
contract may provide for delivery of goods in England or Scotland at the
option of the buyer. The buyer complains of non-delivery. The breach
ground will not be satisfied. That this is so is clear from *Cuban Atlantic
Sugar Sales Corp v Compañía De Vapores San Elefterio Limitada*,[230] a case
involving the obligation to deliver under a bill of lading. The Costa Rican
defendant shipowners undertook to deliver sugar to one safe port in
the United Kingdom at the plaintiff's option, to be declared 120 hours
before the ship arrived off Land's End. The ship sank shortly after sailing,
before the option could be declared. The Court of Appeal held that, as the
contract could be performed in Scotland, or Northern Ireland, as well as in
England, until a port had been nominated, it could not be said that it was
to be performed within the jurisdiction.

Does it matter where the contract was made? The predecessor of r 6.20(6) **4.89**
spelt out that the breach head applied to a contract 'made within or out
of the jurisdiction'. This wording was deliberately omitted from r 6.20(6).
Nonetheless, it is submitted that this ground should apply regardless of
whether the contract was made within or out of the jurisdiction. It will be
recalled that certain drafting changes introduced by the Civil Procedure
Rules in relation to service of process out of the jurisdiction were not
intended to have any substantive effect on the court's powers.[231] As far
as the breach head was concerned, it was considered unnecessary to retain
the previous provision specifying that this applies irrespective of where
the contract was made.[232]

Rule 6.20(7) Rule 6.20(7) states that a claim form may be served out of **4.90**
the jurisdiction with the permission of the court if a claim is made for a
declaration that no contract exists where, if the contract was found to
exist, it would comply with the conditions set out in paragraph (5).[233]

This is a new ground of jurisdiction, added by the Civil Procedure Rules, **4.91**
which makes it clear that r 20.6(5) applies where there is a claim for a

---

[229] The language used by Lord Esher MR in *The Eider*, n 215 above, at 132 would support
this.
[230] [1960] 1 QB 187, CA. [231] See above, para 4.29.
[232] See the Lord Chancellor's Department Consultation Paper on the CPR, *Service of Court
Process Abroad*, para 23.
[233] Discussed above, para 4.28.

negative declaration that no contract exists.[234] This ensures that the position under the traditional rules on jurisdiction[235] is the same as that under the Brussels I Regulation.[236] It is important to note that r 6.20(7) does not cover a claim made for a declaration of non-liability.

4.92 It is not uncommon for a party to a contract for the international sale of goods to seek a declaration that no such contract exists. For example, a buyer of goods who has paid part of the price may wish to obtain a declaration that no contract exists and then restitution of the money paid.[237] Another example is where a buyer of goods, who claims his order was revoked before being accepted by the seller but is being pressed by the seller for payment and fears that legal proceedings will be commenced against him abroad, decides to strike first and seek a negative declaration in his home state that no contract exists.[238] Now there is a basis of jurisdiction under the traditional rules which enables him to bring such a claim in England against a foreign defendant. There is, of course, a great tactical advantage in making such a pre-emptive strike, at least in cases where the alternative forum is another EC Member State.[239] If the English court is first seised then the second seised courts of other EC Member States must decline jurisdiction in relation to proceedings brought before them involving the same cause of action and the same parties.[240]

4.93 This ground only covers a declaration that no contract 'exists'. The validity of a contract is different from its existence[241] and therefore a declaration in relation to the former, for example that a contract is formally invalid, would, if a literal interpretation is taken, fall outside this provision. However, there does not appear to be any good policy reason for excluding validity from the scope of r 6.20(7) and the courts may well take a wide view of this provision and bring this issue within it. The 'existence' of a contract will cover the question of whether a contract ever

---

[234] See the Lord Chancellor's Department Consultation Paper on the CPR, *Service of Court Process Abroad*, para 21.

[235] The position previously was unclear. Compare *Finnish Marine Insurance Co Ltd v Protective National Insurance Co* [1990] 1 QB 1078—not within the contract head, with *DR Insurance Co v Central National Insurance Co* [1996] 1 Lloyd's Rep 74—within the head if agreement entered into with intent to create legal relations.

[236] For the use of Art 5(1) of the Brussels Convention to take jurisdiction to grant a negative declaration that no contract existed see *Boss Group Ltd v Boss France SA* [1997] 1 WLR 351, CA.

[237] See, e.g. *Re A Sale of Shares* (Case VIII ZR 14/94) [1996] IL Pr 292, discussed above, para 3.318. Jurisdiction for claims for unjust enrichment is discussed in Ch 8 below.

[238] See, e.g. Case 144/86 *Gubisch Maschinenfabrik AG v Palumbo* [1987] ECR 4861, discussed above, para 3.317

[239] Or an EFTA State.

[240] Art 27 of the Brussels I Regulation, discussed above, paras 3.313–329

[241] See Art 8(1) of the Rome Convention, which refers to the 'existence and validity of a contract'.

came into being. Will it also cover the question of whether a contract is still in existence? For example, there is a dispute between the parties as to whether the contract has been frustrated by supervening illegality. A claim is brought for a declaration that the contract has been frustrated. Another example would be where a buyer claims lawfully to have terminated an instalment contract. The seller denies this and then tenders a future instalment falling due after the buyer has said that the contract has come to an end. The buyer may then seek a declaration that no contract exists. In both examples, the question will arise as to what the claim for a declaration is really concerned with. In the first example, it could be argued that the claim for a declaration looks to be more about frustration of the contract than its existence and should therefore fall outside r 6.20(7). A similar argument could be made in relation to the second example, i.e. the claim for a declaration is more about termination of the contract than about its existence. Nonetheless, the purpose of this new rule is to allow service out of the jurisdiction in cases where negative declarations are sought and it would be wrong to interpret the scope of the provision too restrictively. It is submitted therefore that it should cover cases where the issue is whether the contract is still in existence.

Claims about property within the jurisdiction

A claim form may be served out of the jurisdiction with the permission of **4.94** the court if the whole subject-matter of a claim relates to property located within the jurisdiction.[242] This ground has been widely interpreted so that it would encompass a claim for damages for breach of contract relating to goods located within the jurisdiction.[243] The claim must 'relate' to the property located within the jurisdiction. If, for example, a buyer sues a seller for breach of contract alleging that the goods are defective, it can be said with some confidence that this requirement will be met. This is because compensation is sought for damage to that property.[244] In contrast, if the seller sues the buyer for payment for the goods and their quality is not in issue it cannot be said that the claim relates to the property (ie the goods). However, if the reason for non-payment is that the buyer alleges that the goods are defective, the real issue is as to the quality of the goods and such a dispute should be regarded as relating to the property. The claim must relate to property 'located within the jurisdiction'. If the dispute relates to goods in Texas to be delivered to England (but which have not been delivered) this requirement would not be met. But if it relates to goods in England to be delivered to Texas (but which have not been delivered) it would.

---

[242] r 6.20(10) CPR.   [243] r 6.20(10) is discussed in more detail below, paras 7.27–38.
[244] See below, para 7.31.

A Reasonable Prospect of Success (Serious Isssue on the Merits)

4.95 An application for permission to serve a claim form out of the jurisdiction under r 6.20 must be supported by written evidence stating that the claimant believes that his claim has a reasonable prospect of success.[245] This is synonymous with 'a real prospect of success'.[246] 'Real is to be contrasted with fanciful or imaginary.'[247] The test is the same or substantially the same as that previously laid down by the House of Lords in *Seaconsar Far East Ltd v Bank Markazi Jomhouri Islami Iran*[248] in relation to service out of the jurisdiction under Order 11, r 1(1) of the Rules of the Supreme Court, the predecessor of r 6.20.[249] In that case, the House of Lords held that the claimant has to establish that there is a serious issue to be tried in that there is 'a substantial question of fact or law or both, arising on the facts disclosed by the affidavits, which the [claimant] . . . bona fide desires to try . . .'.[250] An issue that is imaginary or fanciful is not a serious issue to be tried.[251]

To what extent is it necessary to make a separate enquiry into the merits?

4.96 When considering the merits of the claimant's claim the standard of proof is that of merely a serious issue. In contrast, the standard of proof applicable when the claimant has to establish that one of the grounds of r 6.20 is satisfied is that of a good arguable case, a higher standard. This is subject to the rider that where jurisdiction depends on a question of law or construction, the court will decide it rather than apply the good arguable case test.[252] The position is then complicated by the fact that with some grounds it is necessary to go into the merits of the case in order to establish that the terms of that ground have been satisfied. In such circumstances, the claimant has to show a good arguable case on the merits, and the merits will not be gone into again at this jurisdictional

---

[245] r 6.21(1)(b) CPR.

[246] *Swiss Reinsurance Company Ltd v United India Insurance Company* [2002] EWHC 741 (Comm) at [27], [2004] IL Pr 4 at 62. The wording 'real prospect of success' is to be found in CPR Parts 3 and 24.

[247] The *Swiss Reinsurance Company* case, ibid.   [248] [1994] 1 AC 438.

[249] The *Swiss Reinsurance Company* case, n 246 above (the same or substantially the same); *Navigators Insurance Company v Atlantic Methanol Production Company* [2003] EWHC 1706 (Comm) at [33] (treated as the same); *BAS Capital Funding Corp v Medfinco Ltd* [2003] EWHC 1798 at [153] (no reason to believe differs in any material way)), [2004] IL Pr 16; *MRG (Japan) Limited v Engelhard Metals Japan Limited* [2003] EWHC 3418 (Comm), [2004] 1 Lloyd's Rep 731 at [7]–[10] (the same). See also *De Molestina v Ponton* [2002] 1 Lloyd's Rep 271 at 281—the merits threshold under r 6.20 should not differ in substance from that of summary judgment under r 24.2 CPR. In other words, the court should not subject a foreign defendant to proceedings which the defendant would be entitled to have summarily dismissed.

[250] *Seaconsar Far East Ltd v Bank Markazi Jomhouri Islami Iran* [1994] 1 AC 438 at 452 (*per* Lord Goff), HL.

[251] The *Swiss Reinsurance Company* case, n 246 above.

[252] *Chellaram v Chellaram (No 2)* [2002] EWHC 632 (Ch) at [136], [2002] 2 All ER 17.

stage of the action. In contrast, in cases where it is not necessary to go into the merits in order to establish that the terms of the ground have been satisfied, the examination of the merits will arise as a separate enquiry after the terms of the ground have been satisfied but the claimant will only have to establish that there is a serious issue to be tried on the merits.[253] The contract grounds, which are the ones most commonly used to found jurisdiction in the case of contracts for the international sale of goods, will now be examined to ascertain the extent to which with these particular grounds it is necessary to make a separate enquiry into the merits of the case.

Rule 6.20(5) The position with regard to this ground is complex.[254] The **4.97** claimant has to establish a good arguable case that the terms of the particular sub-paragraph have been met. Thus with sub-paragraph (a) the claimant has to establish a good arguable case that there was a contract and that this contract was made within the jurisdiction. In order to come within sub-paragraphs (b), (c) or (d) the claimant must establish a good arguable case that the contract exists. With sub-paragraph (b) the claimant must also establish that this contract was made by or through an agent trading or residing within the jurisdiction, with (c) that the contract was governed by English law[255] and with (d) that the contract contains a term to the effect that the court shall have jurisdiction to determine any claim in respect of the contract. But once these terms of the sub-paragraph have been established, a separate issue arises as to the merits of the claimant's claim in relation to the contract. The lower standard of proof applies to this.[256] So, for example, if the claim is for breach of contract, the claimant has to establish that there is a serious issue to be tried in relation to this breach.[257] But he has already established that a contract exists and so no separate enquiry is needed as to this.[258]

Rule 6.20(6): a breach of contract committed within the jurisdic- **4.98** **tion** The position with regard to this ground is more straightforward. In

---

[253] This can raise questions as to the applicable law, see *Metall und Rohstoff AG v Donaldson Lufkin and Jenrette Inc* [1990] 1 QB 391, CA, overruled on a different point in *Lonhro plc v Fayed* [1992] 1 AC 448, HL.

[254] The *Seaconsar* case, n 250 above, at 454–455.

[255] It must be established that the contract is governed by English law, rather than that there is a good arguable case that this is so: the *Chellaram* case, n 252 above, at [136].

[256] The *Seaconsar* case, n 250 above, at 454–455. See, e.g. *DR Insurance Co v Central National Insurance* [1996] 1 Lloyd's Rep 74 at 80.

[257] This can raise questions as to the applicable law, see n 253 above.

[258] But this should be subject to the rider that the question of whether a contract exists for the purposes of establishing r 6.20(5) is looking at the meaning of this concept according to the law of the forum whereas establishing the merits can raise questions as to the applicable law. If this is a foreign law then a separate enquiry as to the merits may be necessary, see below, para 4.100.

order to come within this ground, the claimant must establish a good arguable case in relation to the three elements of contract, breach and place of breach. Establishing a breach of contract involves going into the merits of the case. Once the terms of the head have been established, no separate issue will arise at the jurisdictional stage as to the merits of the claimant's case, to which a lower standard of proof is applied.[259]

4.99 **Rule 6.20(7): a negative declaration**   In order to come within this ground, the claimant must establish a good arguable case that no contract exists and that the terms of the sub-paragraph of r 6.20(5) being relied upon have been met. Once a good arguable case has been established that no contract exists, no separate enquiry as to the merits of the claimant's case will be necessary at the jurisdictional stage.

Establishing liability

4.100 Any enquiry as to the merits can raise questions regarding the applicable law even at the jurisdictional stage of the action.[260] Thus when determining whether there was a contract and whether there was a breach of this contract this means a contract according to the applicable law and a breach according to the applicable law. If a foreign law is applicable to the contract this means that a separate enquiry should be made into the questions of the existence of the contract and its breach. This is because, although these questions may have been considered when establishing one of the contract heads, this will have been in the context of whether there was a contract and a breach according to the law of the forum, rather than according to the governing law.

The Exercise of the Discretion to Permit Service Out of the Jurisdiction

The principles to be applied when exercising the forum conveniens discretion

4.101 Rule 6.20 is a discretionary form of jurisdiction. The courts *may*, rather than must, give permission for service of a claim form out of the jurisdiction. They will not do so unless satisfied that England and Wales is the proper place in which to bring the claim.[261] The criterion for the exercise of

---

[259] The *Seaconsar* case, n 250 above, at 453–454. See also *Agrafax Public Relations Ltd v United Scottish Society Inc* [1995] IL Pr 753. But this should be subject to the rider that the question of breach for the purposes of establishing the breach ground is looking at the meaning of this concept according to the law of the forum whereas establishing the merits can raise questions as to the applicable law. If this is a foreign law then a separate enquiry as to the merits may be necessary, see below, para 4.100.

[260] See *Metall und Rohstoff AG v Donaldson Lufkin and Jenrette Inc* [1990] 1 QB 391, CA, overruled on a different point in *Lonhro plc v Fayed* [1992] 1 AC 448, HL.

[261] r 6.21(2A) CPR.

this discretion is that of *forum conveniens*.[262] The principles to be applied when exercising this discretion were set out by Lord Goff in the House of Lords in *Spiliada Maritime Corp v Cansulex Ltd*.[263] The basic principle is that the court has 'to identify the forum in which the case can be suitably tried for the interests of all the parties and for the ends of justice'.[264] This involves identifying the appropriate forum for trial and examining whether justice will be obtained in the alternative forum abroad. The same basic principle underlies the exercise of the discretion to stay English proceedings on the ground of forum non conveniens,[265] and cases decided in that context are of assistance in the present context.

An alternative forum abroad   The exercise of the *forum conveniens* dis- **4.102** cretion presupposes that there is an obvious alternative forum abroad. If not,[266] it is proper to allow service of the claim form out of the jurisdiction. This does not mean that it is always necessary to ascertain whether there is an alternative forum abroad. It is possible to identify England as the clearly appropriate forum for trial without ever going into this question.

The appropriate forum   The burden of proof is on the claimant to show **4.103** that England is the appropriate forum for trial, and that this is clearly so.[267] This is sometimes referred to as the natural forum, that with which the action has the most real and substantial connection. The concern is with connecting factors. 'The court must take into account the nature of the dispute, the legal and practical issues involved, such questions as local knowledge, availability of witnesses and their evidence and expense.'[268] The inconvenience to witnesses of having to travel to England to give evidence is a less potent factor nowadays because of the increasing use of video links.[269] Some of the more important other factors commonly taken into account are listed below.

The applicable law   Another consideration is the question of the applicable **4.104** law. The fact that English law governs the contract is, in some cases, of

---

[262] This criterion is not affected by the introduction of the CPR. The 'proper place' for trial is synonymous with the *forum conveniens*, see *Swiss Reinsurance Company Ltd v United India Insurance Company* [2002] EWHC 741 (Comm) at [27], [2004] IL Pr 4 at 61.

[263] [1987] AC 460.   [264] ibid, at 480.   [265] See below, para 4.156.

[266] This may be because the injustice abroad would be so great, see *Konamaneni v Rolls-Royce Industrial Power (India) Limited* [2002] IL Pr 40 at [59]. See also on the question of whether there is another 'available' forum, *Mohammed v Bank of Kuwait and the Middle East KSC* [1996] 1 WLR 1483, CA; criticized in Cheshire and North, 336–337; *Lubbe v Cape Plc* [2000] 1 WLR 1545 at [48], HL—alternative forum in South Africa available because the defendant had undertaken to submit to the jurisdiction of the courts of that country.

[267] The *Spiliada* case, n 263 above, at 481.

[268] *Amin Rasheed Corp v Kuwait Insurance Co* [1984] AC 50 at 72 (*per* Lord Wilberforce).

[269] *The Prestrioka* [2002] EWCA Civ 1132, [2003] 2 Lloyd's Rep 327 at 336 and in the Court of Appeal at [76]—the fact that evidence can be given by a video link was described as a minor factor in the overall equation.

very great importance, and, in others, of little importance. It all depends on the circumstances of the case. In the *Spiliada* case, the fact that English law governed was said to be by no means an insignificant factor since the dispute was, *inter alia*, as to the nature of the obligation under the contract. The fact that the parties have chosen English law is a factor of importance, in particular, where there is some distinction or some arguable distinction between the law of the two competing jurisdictions.[270] But where there is no such evidence it is important not to attach too much weight to this factor.[271] A choice of law is not to be equated with a choice of forum.[272] Again, the applicable law factor is important in cases where the parties can be treated as having agreed not only on the application of English law but also on trial in England, a legal centre in a neutral country familiar with the resolution of such disputes as the one in question[273] and in cases raising the issue of English public policy[274]

4.105 *A foreign exclusive jurisdiction clause* It is also important to consider whether the parties have agreed to trial abroad. The parties should be kept to their agreement and it takes a strong cause to permit the court to ignore a foreign exclusive jurisdiction clause.[275] When the question is whether to give leave for service out of the jurisdiction, rather than to stay otherwise well founded proceedings, there is an even heavier burden to discharge upon the applicant who asks the court not to enforce a foreign jurisdiction clause.[276]

4.106 *An English exclusive jurisdiction clause* In cases involving an exclusive jurisdiction clause providing for trial in England, 'the Court has a discretion [whether to allow service out of the jurisdiction or not], but it is a discretion which, in the ordinary way and in the absence of strong reason to the contrary, will be exercised in favour of holding parties to their bargain'.[277] The normal principle established in *Spiliada*, namely that the

---

[270] *Macsteel Commercial Holdings (Pty) Ltd v Thermasteel V (Canada) Inc* [1996] CLC 1403 at 1407, CA.

[271] ibid. See also *Navigators Insurance Company v Atlantic Methanol Production Company* [2003] EWHC 1706 (Comm) at [48].

[272] The *Macsteel* case, n 270 above, at 1408 (*per* Millett LJ); the *Navigators Insurance Company* case, n 271 above. But when it comes to choice of law a choice of forum is often equated with a choice of law, see below, para 13.50.

[273] The *Macsteel* case, n 270 above, at 1408. See also *Egon Oldendorff v Libera Corp* [1995] 2 Lloyd's Rep 64 (Mance J).

[274] *Mitsubishi Corp v Aristidis I Alafouzos* [1988] 1 Lloyd's Rep 191; *Du Pont v Agnew* [1987] 2 Lloyd's Rep 585, CA.

[275] *Sinochem International Oil (London) Ltd v Mobil Sales and Supply Corp Ltd (Sinochem International Oil Co Ltd, third party) (No 2)* [2000] 1 All ER (Comm) 758 at 766. Foreign choice of jurisdiction clauses are also important when it comes to stays of action, discussed below, para 4.164.

[276] The *Sinochem* case, ibid, at 767.

[277] *Unterweser Reederei GmbH v Zapata Off-Shore Company (The Chaparral)* [1968] 2 Lloyd's Rep 158 at 163 (*per* Willmer LJ).

burden of proof is on the claimant to satisfy the court that England is clearly and distinctly the appropriate forum for trial, is replaced in cases where there is an agreement as to jurisdiction.[278] This means that the court will give effect to the submission to jurisdiction, although still retaining a discretion to grant a stay if the defendant can show strong reasons against holding the parties to their bargain. This can be justified on the basis that the parties, by agreeing that the English courts shall have exclusive jurisdiction, are also implicitly agreeing that England is the clearly appropriate forum for trial. A good reason for not granting permission may be some factor that could not have been foreseen at the time that the contract was made.[279] When it comes to a stay of English proceedings on *forum non conveniens* grounds in a case where the parties have agreed on the exclusive jurisdiction of the English courts, it has been held that, when it comes to showing the strong cause needed for a stay, this must go beyond matters of mere convenience and must enter into the interests of justice itself.[280]

An English non-exclusive jurisdiction clause   The position is less certain in **4.107** cases where the parties have agreed on the non-exclusive jurisdiction of the English courts.[281] There are cases where the same principle has been applied as in cases involving an exclusive jurisdiction clause.[282] However, other cases have correctly regarded a non-exclusive jurisdiction clause differently from an exclusive one[283] and the Court of Appeal has applied the normal principle in the *Spiliada* case to a non-exclusive jurisdiction clause.[284] When applying this principle it is relevant to take into account the fact that the parties have implicitly agreed that England is *an* appropriate forum for trial.[285] However, they are not agreeing that it is *the* appropriate forum.

---

[278] *Standard Steamship Owners' Protection and Indemnity Association (Bermuda) Ltd v Gann* [1992] 2 Lloyd's Rep 528. See also *Insurance Company 'Ingosstrakh' Ltd v Latvian Shipping Company* [2000] IL Pr 164, CA; *Citi-March Ltd v Neptune Orient Lines Ltd* [1997] 1 Lloyd's Rep 72.

[279] *Marubeni Hong Kong and South China Ltd v Mongolian Government* [2002] 2 All ER (Comm) 873 at [43].

[280] The *Sinochem* case, n 275 above, at 772.

[281] See generally J Fawcett, 'Non-exclusive Jurisdiction Agreements in Private International Law' [2001] LMCLQ 234, 245–248. For the identification of a clause as being non-exclusive see Fawcett, ibid, at 235–241.

[282] The *Standard Steamship Owners* case, n 278 above; *Gulf Bank KSC v Mitsubishi Heavy Industries Ltd* [1994] 1 Lloyd's Rep 323.

[283] *Evans Marshall & Co v Bertola SA* [1973] 1 WLR 349 at 361 (Kerr J); *Sinochem v Mobil (No 2)* [2000] 1 All ER (Comm) 758.

[284] *Colonia Versicherung AG v Amoco Oil, (The Wind Star)* 1993 unreported.

[285] *S & W Berisford PLC and NGI Precious Metals Inc v New Hampshire Insurance Co* [1990] 1 Lloyd's Rep 454 at 463.

4.108 *An arbitration agreement*   If a claim lies within an agreement to arbitrate and a mandatory stay of the proceedings would be granted under the Arbitration Act 1996[286] if the action were allowed to proceed, permission for service out of the jurisdiction should not be granted.[287]

4.109 *A multiplicity of proceedings*   One final important consideration is the question whether trial in England will lead to a multiplicity of proceedings with concurrent actions, involving the same parties and issues, taking place in England and abroad (which would suggest that the discretion should be exercised against granting permission for service out of the jurisdiction).[288]

4.110 Injustice abroad   If substantial justice will not be done abroad, the court may well exercise its discretion in favour of allowing service out of the jurisdiction even though there are strong connections with the alternative forum abroad. If England is not otherwise shown to be the more appropriate forum, then the onus remains on the claimant to show circumstances by reason of which justice cannot be done abroad if there is to be any basis for invoking the English jurisdiction.[289] It is not easy to show that there will be positive injustice abroad. What is easier to show is that the trial abroad will deprive the claimant of some advantage that would be obtained from trial in England. However, the advantage to the claimant has been downgraded in importance by the *Spiliada* case, where Lord Goff said that the court should not be deterred from refusing leave in cases of service out of the jurisdiction simply because the claimant will be deprived of an advantage, such as higher damages or a more generous limitation period, provided that the court is satisfied that substantial justice will be done in the available appropriate forum abroad.[290]

4.111 The significance of the particular ground under r 6.20   The different grounds vary greatly in the extent of the connection with England that is required. This may affect the willingness of the court to exercise the discretion to permit service of the claim form out of the jurisdiction. It is important, therefore, to examine the attitude of the courts towards the exercise of the discretion in relation to the different contract grounds. At the same time it is important to note that all the circumstances of the particular case have to be considered. It follows that even in cases

---

[286] Discussed below, para 4.169.

[287] *A and B v C and D* [1982] 1 Lloyd's Rep 166, aff'd sub nom *Qatar Petroleum v Shell International Petroleum* [1983] 2 Lloyd's Rep 35, CA—a case decided with reference to the Arbitration Act 1975.

[288] See, e.g. *New Hampshire Insurance Co v Strabag Bau AG* [1992] 1 Lloyd's Rep 361, CA.

[289] *Bank of Baroda v Vysya Bank Ltd* [1994] 2 Lloyd's Rep 87, 96. See also the *Konamaneni* case, n 266 above.

[290] The *Spiliada* case, n 263 above, at 482–484.

involving the same contract ground the willingness or otherwise to permit service out of the jurisdiction in that particular case may be very different.

A contract made within the jurisdiction   In the light of the difficulties that **4.112** can sometimes arise in ascertaining where the contract is made and the fact that this place can be fortuitous[291] it is suggested that there should be a cautious attitude towards the exercise of the discretion in cases where this ground is being used.

A contract made by or through an agent   At first glance, the fact that a **4.113** foreign defendant has an agent trading or residing in England and the contract was made by or through this agent, although a relevant factor,[292] would not appear to constitute a particularly strong connection with England and, accordingly, there should be a cautious attitude towards the exercise of the discretion in cases where this ground is being used. Nonetheless, there is an argument that can be made on policy grounds that there should be a willingness to allow service out of the jurisdiction with this sub-head. If a foreign company uses an agent in England, which enters into contracts on its behalf, it may well be possible to say that the company has established a place of business (other than a branch) in England, with the result that the company can be served within the jurisdiction as of right.[293] If, on the other hand, the foreign defendant is not a company but an individual, who has an agent in England trading or residing in England and the contract was made by or through this agent, there is no such possibility of service within the jurisdiction. Instead, permission will be needed for service out of the jurisdiction and the obvious ground to use is the agency ground. If the courts showed a willingness to grant permission under this ground it would go some way to closing the gap between the position where there is a corporate defendant and that where it is an individual defendant who carries on business in the same way.[294]

A contract governed by English Law   Lord Goff in the *Spiliada* case has said **4.114** that the importance to be attached to any particular head may vary from case to case.[295] This is particularly so where the head in question is this one. As has been seen,[296] the fact that English law governs the contract is,

---

[291] See above, paras 4.32–36. Moreover, the applicable law may regard the contract as having been made abroad.

[292] *Citadel Insurance Co v Atlantic Union Insurance Co SA* [1982] Lloyd's Rep 543, 549, CA.

[293] See above, paras 4.11–12.

[294] For a concern in the context of enforcement of foreign judgments at common law to bring the position where there is an individual defendant into line with that where there is a corporate defendant see *Blohn v Desser* [1962] 2 QB 116.

[295] n 263 above, at 481.   [296] See above, para 4.104.

in some cases, of very great importance, and in others of little importance. It all depends on the circumstances of the case, and, in particular, on the sort of circumstances mentioned above.

4.115 *An English jurisdiction clause* The attitude towards the exercise of the discretion under this head is different from that in relation to any of the other contract heads. As has been seen,[297] the normal principles of *forum conveniens* are departed from and, in the absence of strong reason to the contrary, the discretion will be exercised in favour of holding the parties to their bargain.

4.116 *A breach of contract committed within the jurisdiction* The fact that a breach of contract was committed within the jurisdiction constitutes a substantial connection with England, particularly when it is remembered that this ground is concerned with claims for breach of contract. Moreover, the place where the breach was committed will not normally be fortuitous.[298] In the case of a breach by non-performance, the place of performance, and hence the place of breach, will generally have been agreed by the parties. The attitude of the courts towards the exercise of the discretion when jurisdiction is based on this ground should therefore in general not be one of a reluctance to exercise the discretion. The qualification introduced by the words 'in general' takes account of those cases where the fact that the breach was committed in England is of little significance on the facts of the particular case. An example would be where a claim is brought for non-payment but the reason for this was a complaint by the buyer about the quality of the goods. The fact that payment should have been made in England should be regarded as being of less significance than the location of the evidence as to the quality of the goods.

4.117 *A declaration that no contract exists* There is, as yet, no case law on the exercise of the discretion on this ground. In so far as this ground involves the use of one of the sub-paragraphs under r 6.20(5), it could be argued that the attitude towards the exercise of the discretion should be the same as that where that particular sub-paragraph is being used. Thus, for example, if sub-paragraph (a)—if a contract was found to exist this con-tract was made within the jurisdiction—is being used, caution is called for. However, it is submitted that much more important than this is the evidence on whether a contract actually does exist and where this is located. This will be the live issue at any ultimate trial. There is then one important additional factor that needs to be taken into account when exercising the discretion under r 6.20(7). This is the attitude of the courts

---

[297] See above, para 4.106.
[298] An example of where it would be fortuitous would be where a repudiation is sent from abroad by the defendant whilst on a business trip.

towards the grant of a negative declaration.[299] In the past, the jurisdiction to grant such a declaration has been exercised with caution and most of the cases where a negative declaration has been sought, albeit not under this particular ground, have been held not to be proper ones for service out of the jurisdiction.[300] It has been said that if the possibility exists that the claimant in the English proceedings will be sued by the defendant in an alternative forum abroad, the English court must be particularly careful to ensure that the negative declaration is sought for a valid and valuable purpose and not in an illegitimate attempt to pre-empt the jurisdiction in which the dispute between the parties is to be resolved.[301] However, this factor is not an absolute bar to such service.[302] More recently though the Court of Appeal has softened its attitude towards negative declarations. In *Messier-Dowty v Sabena SA (No 2)*,[303] it has been said that: 'The deployment of negative declarations should be scrutinized and their use rejected where it would serve no useful purpose. However, where a negative declaration would help to ensure that the aims of justice are achieved the courts should not be reluctant to grant such declarations. They can and do assist in achieving justice.'[304] No valid reason could be seen for taking an adverse view of negative declaratory relief.[305] But even under this softer line permission for service out of the jurisdiction of a claim for a negative declaration may be refused on the basis of the normal *forum conveniens* factors.[306]

Jurisdiction based on more than one ground   It is common in contract cases **4.118** to base jurisdiction on a number of the different contract grounds. This raises an interesting, and as yet unanswered, question when it comes to the exercise of the *forum conveniens* discretion. If, for example, jurisdiction is based both on the contract being made in England (in respect

---

[299] See generally Cheshire and North, 318; Dicey and Morris, 402–403; A Bell, *Forum Shopping and Venue in Transnational Litigation* (Oxford: OUP, 2003) 246–263.

[300] *Insurance Corp of Ireland v Strombus International Insurance Co* [1985] 2 Lloyd's Rep 138 at 144, CA; *The Volvox Hollandia* [1988] 2 Lloyd's Rep 361, CA; *DR Insurance Co v Central National Insurance Co* [1996] 1 Lloyd's Rep 74 at 83 et seq; *New Hampshire Insurance Co v Aerospace Finance Ltd* [1998] 2 Lloyd's Rep 539. See also *Akai Pty Ltd v People's Insurance Co Ltd* [1998] 1 Lloyd's Rep 90 at 106.

[301] *New Hampshire Insurance Co v Phillips Electronics North America Corp* [1998] IL Pr 256, CA.

[302] *HIB v Guardian Insurance* [1997] 1 Lloyd's Rep 412.

[303] [2000] 1 WLR 2040, CA; followed in *Chase v Ram Technical Services Ltd* [2000] 2 Lloyd's Rep 418; *Swiss Reinsurance Company Ltd v United India Insurance Company* [2002] EWHC 741 (Comm) at [27], [2004] IL Pr 4 (a case on service out of the jurisdiction). The *Chase* case provides an example of where the grant of a negative declaration would serve no useful purpose, see 420–421.

[304] The *Messier-Dowty* case, n 303 above, at 2050.

[305] ibid, at 2049.

[306] *Chase v Ram Technical Services Ltd* [2000] 2 Lloyd's Rep 418, 421–422.

of which caution should be exercised when deciding whether to grant permission for service out of the jurisdiction) and the fact that the contract is governed by English law (in respect of which there is not this need for caution), what should the court's attitude be towards the exercise of the discretion? Should it be to take the most favourable attitude, the least favourable attitude, or a broadly neutral view? If jurisdiction could be based solely on the fact that English law governs the contract, it would seem wrong to adopt the least favourable attitude towards the exercise of the discretion which applies for that ground just because the claimant has invoked, as an alternative, the fact that the contract is made in England, in respect of which a less favourable attitude prevails.

Application to contracts for the international sale of goods

4.119 The appropriate forum   We will now consider the typical considerations that arise, irrespective of the ground used under r 6.20 of the Civil Procedure Rules, in cases involving the international sale of goods.

4.120 *The place of delivery of the goods*   One obvious connecting factor is the place where an agreement is to be performed.[307] In the case of a contract for the international sale of goods, this means looking at the place of delivery of the goods. This has long been regarded as a relevant factor.[308] For example, in *Aaronson Bros Ltd v Maderera Del Tropico SA*[309] English sellers contracted to sell wood veneers to Mexican buyers, subject to a Mexican import licence being obtained by the buyers. The buyers did not obtain an import licence and did not take delivery of the goods. The sellers sought damages for alleged breach of contract. The contract was made in England and therefore service of process out of the jurisdiction was permissible. Was England the *forum conveniens*? The Court of Appeal held that it was, on the basis that this was 'an English contract made in England in the English language for the goods to be delivered FOB an English port and to be governed by English law'.[310] This was despite the fact that the only issue in the case was whether the buyer had used due diligence to obtain the import licence, and evidence for this would have to obtained from Mexican officials. Similarly, in *Crane Accessories Ltd v Lim Swee Hee*[311] Smellie J in the High Court in Auckland took into account the fact that contract goods were delivered in Singapore when deciding that Singapore was the natural forum for trial and granted a stay of the New Zealand proceedings.

---

[307] See *Saab v Saudi American Bank* [1999] 1 WLR 1861 at 1881–1883, CA.
[308] The importance of this factor when determining the applicable law, in the absence of choice by the parties, is discussed below, paras 13.134–136.
[309] [1967] 2 Lloyd's Rep 159, CA.
[310] ibid, at 161 (*per* Lord Denning MR).   [311] [1989] 1 NZLR 221.

HOW MUCH WEIGHT IS TO BE GIVEN TO THE PLACE OF DELIVERY FACTOR? In **4.121**
the *Aaronson* case, it was merely one of five factors pointing towards
England, one of which was that English law governed the sales contract.
As will be seen, the governing law can be an important factor. In the *Crane
Accessories* case, this was but one of seven factors mentioned by Smellie J
as pointing towards Singapore as the natural forum. The question of the
applicable law was not important in this case since the relevant law of
Singapore was said to be substantially the same as New Zealand law. The
place of delivery is best regarded as a factor whose importance will vary
with the facts of the case. More weight should be attached to it in cases
where the claim relates to the obligation to deliver the goods, for example
a claim for damages for non-delivery. This includes not only the obligation
to deliver itself but also the obligation to deliver goods in conformity with
the contract and the obligation to deliver goods free from any right or
claim of a third party. It can even be argued that a claim for non-payment,
where this is due to an alleged breach of the obligation to deliver goods in
conformity with the contract, relates to the obligation to deliver the goods.
In a case where the claim does not relate to a breach of the obligation to
deliver (for example, a claim for simple non-payment where there is no
alleged breach of the obligation to deliver goods in conformity with the
contract), the place of delivery factor should not be regarded as being as
important as the applicable law factor when it is at its most important.[312]
Thus where the place of delivery is in State A, and in the circumstances
this is not a very significant factor, but the applicable law is that of State B
and in the circumstances of the case this is a very significant factor, the
forum conveniens is likely to be State B, rather than State A.

This is illustrated by the decision of the Supreme Court of South Australia **4.122**
in *FF Seeley v El AR Initiations*.[313] The plaintiff, a company incorporated
in South Australia, entered into a contract with the first defendant, a UK
company, for the sale and delivery of air conditioners to be delivered to
Greece. The plaintiff alleged that the defendant made default in payment
for these. The plaintiff brought proceedings in South Australia in respect
of this contract and in respect of a supplementary contract entered into by
the parties dealing with the title to the air conditioners and the terms of
payment. The Supreme Court of South Australia held that the principal,
if not the decisive consideration, was that of the applicable law. If the law
of South Australia was the law which governed the contracts, then there
was a very strong argument of convenience in favour of trial before the
South Australian courts.[314] This was a simple case of non-payment, ie

---

[312] The applicable law factor can vary in importance with the circumstances of the case.
[313] (1990) 53 SASR 302.   [314] ibid, at 305–306.

there is no alleged breach of the obligation to deliver goods in conformity with the contract. If non-payment had been due to an alleged breach of the obligation to deliver goods in conformity with the contract then more weight should have been given to the place of delivery factor.

4.123 Similarly, in *Mitsubishi Corp v Aristidis I Alafouzos*,[315] when deciding that England was the *forum conveniens* in relation to a claim under a performance guarantee, Steyn J regarded the fact that English law governed the guarantee and the shipbuilding contract to which the guarantee related as being of very great importance. The fact that the shipbuilding contract involved delivery of the ship to Greece was not even mentioned by Steyn J as a relevant factor.

4.124 It is submitted that this was not the right approach to adopt in relation to this factor. The place of delivery should still be regarded as being a relevant factor, even in cases where the claim does not concern the obligation to deliver, as widely defined, albeit of reduced weight when compared with cases where the claim does concern this obligation. This can be justified on the basis that the delivery of goods characterizes the contract for the international sale of goods. It is this feature that distinguishes it from other contracts. The importance of the place of delivery is recognized by the 1986 Hague Convention on the law applicable to international sale of goods, which provides that in the absence of choice by the parties the contract is governed by the law of the state where the buyer has his place of business at the time of the conclusion of the contract, if, *inter alia*, the contract provides expressly that the seller must perform his obligation to deliver the goods in that state.[316] Moreover, when it comes to jurisdiction under the EC rules the importance of the place of delivery has been recognized by Article 5(1)(b) of the Brussels I Regulation with its special rule for sale of goods that, in such cases, the place of performance of the obligation in question is the place where, under the contract, the goods were delivered or should have been delivered.[317] Finally, under the Rome Convention when it comes to determining the applicable law in the absence of choice by the parties, the place of delivery is the most important factor.[318]

4.125 THE DEFINITIONAL PROBLEM   There is an obvious definitional problem over what is meant by the place of delivery. In the present context, ultimately the concern is with identifying the forum with which there is the most real and substantial connection and definitional problems are best avoided so far as is possible. In terms of relevant connections, it is

---

[315] [1988] 1 Lloyd's Rep 191.   [316] Art 8(2)(b), discussed below, paras 15.90–92.
[317] Discussed above, para 3.143.
[318] See the discussion of Art 4(5) of the Rome Convention below, para 13.127.

submitted that what one is concerned with is the place where the goods were actually delivered.[319] Recourse may well have to be made to the terms of the contract, for example whether it is an FOB or CIF contract, to ascertain where this is. In a case of non-delivery, one is concerned with where under the contract the goods should have been delivered. In a case where there has been an alleged mis-delivery with goods delivered to State A when the contract required them to be delivered to State B, there can be said to be connections with both State A and State B. However, more weight should be given to the connection with State B since this is where the goods should have been delivered. In such a case, there may, though, be other factors pointing towards State A, such as the fact that this is the place of inspection of the goods.

However, to put the definitional problem into perspective, it is not of the **4.126** order of magnitude that arises when determining the place of delivery under Article 5(1)(b) of the Brussels I Regulation.[320] Thus in cases involving delivery to more than one place, there is a connection with each of the places where delivery occurs. In cases where the contract provides for delivery to alternative places and there has been no delivery to either place, there is a connection with each place specified in the contract. There is a connection with the place of fictitious delivery as specified in the contract but, unless you regard this as being an attempt to allocate juris-diction to a state and therefore akin to a jurisdiction clause, the weight given to this connection should be small. This takes into account the fact that this place has no connection with the reality of the contract and the contractual obligations can only be performed in some other country. In a case where the parties have agreed that delivery should be deemed to have taken place in country A but the goods have in fact been delivered in country B, there are connections with both countries and little weight can be given to the place of delivery factor; in other words it provides little connection with either A or B. In a case of constructive delivery, the crucial point is that the goods physically do not move into the custody of the buyer but remain in the custody of the seller. In a case of a refusal to accept delivery, there is still a connection with the place where the goods were to be delivered under the contract. If the contract specifies delivery in State A but the parties subsequently agree on delivery in State B after the contract was made, there can be said to be a connection with both states. However, the stronger connection should be regarded as being with State B, where the delivery actually took place. If no place of delivery is agreed by the parties, there is, nonetheless, a connection with the place

---

[319] For problems in relation to digitized products, see below, paras 10.55–58.
[320] See above, paras 3.175–226.

where delivery actually takes place. But what if not only is there no agreed place of delivery but also there is no actual delivery? It is always possible to work out where the delivery should have taken place according to the applicable substantive law. However, this complicates matters by requiring identification of the applicable law and then proof of the content of this law. It is arguable that it is better simply to say that, in such circumstances, the place of delivery factor should be regarded as being of no significance.[321]

4.127 A DIFFERENT APPROACH   A much simpler approach than looking at the place of delivery with its definitional problems is simply to look at where the goods were shipped from and where they were consigned to. This approach has been adopted when determining the objective proper law of a sales contract[322] and could be adopted in the present context when looking for the natural forum for the purposes of *forum conveniens*. The place where goods are to be supplied is as a general rule nearer to the facts than the place from which they were sent.[323]

4.128 *The place of payment for the goods*   Arguably this should be a relevant factor even in cases where the claim does not concern the obligation to pay. This can be justified on the basis that payment is the basic obligation of the buyer. However, it is submitted that the payment factor should not be given as much weight as the place of delivery factor. If you ask what characterizes an international sale of goods contract, it is the delivery of the goods, rather than the payment for them, since payment is the common feature of many types of contract. This has been recognized in the context of the determination of the applicable law, where the characteristic performance of a contract is the performance other than that of payment,[324] and the same should apply in the present context.

4.129 The place of payment should be given more importance in cases where the claim is brought by the seller for payment for the goods. This is recognized by Article 5(1)(b) of the Brussels I Regulation which has the effect that in a case of a claim for payment where the parties have agreed that this place is other than the place of delivery, the place of performance of the obligation in question will be in the place of payment rather than that of delivery. But even in cases where the claim is for payment it has to be remembered that a dispute over payment will normally arise because

---

[321] The difficulty of ascertaining the place of delivery of digitized products, such as software or music, transferred over the internet is discussed below, paras 10.55–58.
[322] See *Gill and Duffus Landauer Ltd v London Export Corp GmbH* [1982] 2 Lloyd's Rep 627.
[323] See *AG Lenz* in Case C-288/92 *Custom Made Commercial Ltd v Stawa Metallbau GmbH* [1994] ECR I–2913, para 80.
[324] See Art 4(2) of the Rome Convention, discussed below, paras 13.114–115.

defective goods have been delivered and so the place of payment should still be less important than the place of delivery. It should be asked therefore what underlies the dispute over payment. If it is truly a dispute over payment, for example the issue is whether payment was in fact made, the place of payment should be given more weight than if it is basically a dispute as to the quality of the goods.

In this connection, it is worth looking again at the *Crane Accessories*[325] and **4.130** *Seeley*[326] cases. In the former case, the action was one brought by the seller for payment. In listing the connections with Singapore, no mention was made of the allegation of the defendant that payment had in fact been made by it in Singapore to the plaintiff's agent. Presumably this was because this payment was denied by the plaintiff. But the question whether payment had been made was at the heart of the dispute between the parties and so the fact that this was alleged to have occurred in Singapore was surely of some significance. No significance appears to have been attached either to the fact that payment under the contract was, seemingly, to be made in New Zealand. This should have been taken into account, given that it was a true dispute over payment, not one for payment raising the issue of the quality of the goods. This is not to say though that it should have outweighed the many connections with Singapore that existed in that case. Similarly, in the *Seeley* case, no mention was made by the Court of where payment was to be made under the supply contract or the supplementary contract. It is submitted that this is a factor that should have been taken into account, and in attaching weight to this factor it should have been noted that this was truly a dispute as to payment, rather than a dispute as to the quality of the goods.

These two cases can be contrasted with an English case, *Banque Paribas v* **4.131** *Cargill International SA*,[327] where the place of payment factor was given its correct importance. The case concerned non-payment under a sales contract. The defendants contended that they were entitled to set off against the amounts claimed by the plaintiffs certain damages they had suffered as a result of the seller's repudiation of a separate contract (the Lavera contract) between the buyer and seller. Webster J held that England was the forum conveniens, a decision that was affirmed by the Court of Appeal. One of the five factors he relied upon in coming to this conclusion was the fact that payment under the sales contract would have been made in England if payment had been made.

As has been seen,[328] the place of payment will normally be stipulated in **4.132** the contract of sale. In those rare cases where there is no such provision

---

[325] n 311 above.   [326] n 313 above.   [327] [1992] 2 Lloyd's Rep 19, CA.
[328] See above, para 4.83.

and no payment has actually been made, recourse could be had to the law applicable to the sales contract, which will state where payment is to be made in the absence of agreement by the parties. But the same argument can be made here as was made above[329] in relation to cases where there is no specified place of delivery and no delivery has taken place, namely that it is better to say simply that, in such circumstances involving a definitional difficulty, the place of payment factor should be regarded as being of no significance.

4.133 *The place of performance of an obligation under the sales contract (other than to deliver or pay for the goods)* Most international sales of goods disputes concern the buyer's obligation to pay or the seller's obligation to deliver (this includes not only the obligation to deliver itself but also the obligation to deliver goods in conformity with the contract and the obligation to deliver goods free from any right or claim of a third party). However, there could be a claim which is not based on either the obligation to pay or to deliver. For example, the claim could be based on the seller's failure to hand over documents or to transfer the property in the goods or on the buyer's obligation to take delivery of the goods. In such a case, the place of performance of the obligation to hand over documents or to transfer the property or to take delivery should be regarded as a relevant factor. The same weight should be attached to this factor as is attached to the place of delivery in cases where the claim relates to the performance of this obligation. However, in cases where the dispute does not relate to the handing over of documents or to the transfer of the property or to taking delivery, it is submitted that these factors should not be regarded as being relevant. This is to treat the handing over of documents, transfer of the property and taking delivery factors differently from the place of delivery and place of payment factors, which should always be regarded as being relevant, even where the dispute does not relate to delivery or payment.

4.134 The place of performance of the obligation to hand over documents may be different from the place of delivery of the goods. Thus in an FOB contract, where the seller reserves the right of disposal and then payment is to be made against the bill of lading through the banking system, it will very often be the case that the delivery of the bill of lading and the shipment of the goods (which is delivery to the buyer in an FOB contract) will take place in different countries.[330] In contrast, in practice the place of performance of the buyer's obligation to take delivery is going to be the same as the place of performance of the seller's obligation to deliver. In

---

[329] See above, para 4.126.
[330] With a CIF contract there is no obligation to deliver the goods to the buyer. There is a duty to deliver the goods to the ship, see *Johnson v Taylor Bros & Co Ltd* [1920] AC 144.

order to avoid a hiatus in possession, the two acts of making and taking delivery will occur simultaneously and therefore in the same place. But if the complaint is that the buyer failed to give information to the seller to enable him to make delivery, the place where the information should have been given may be different from the place where the goods were to be delivered. For example, the information should have been given to the seller in the seller's residence, whereas the goods should have been delivered in the buyer's residence. The place of performance of the obligation to transfer property is arguably the same as the place of performance of the obligation to deliver.[331]

The situs of the goods The present *situs* of the goods is a particularly **4.135** important factor in cases where the court orders the seller to transfer property in the goods. This is because the order may have to be enforced in the state in which the goods are situated. In a case where the court does order the seller to transfer property in the goods, the present *situs* factor should be regarded as an even more important one than the state to which the seller was supposed to transfer property under the contract. In contrast, if damages are sought for failure to transfer the property then the place of performance of this obligation should be regarded as being much more important than the present *situs* of the goods.

The place where the sales contract was made This is potentially a relevant **4.136** consideration in all contract cases. The determination of this place in cases of the international sale of goods has already been examined in the context of the discussion of r 6.20(5)(a) of the Civil Procedure Rules.[332] Inevitably there will be cases where the evidence is equivocal as to where the contract is made, as happened in the *Crane Accessories* case,[333] where it was disputed whether the contract had been made orally with an agent of the plaintiff in Singapore, and, in such a case, no significance should be attached to this factor. The same approach was adopted in England in *Bank of Baroda v Vysya Bank Ltd*.[334] Mance J, whilst coming to the clear conclusion that the discretion should be exercised in favour of permitting service out of the jurisdiction, said that, in the context of the case in front of him, he did not regard it as particularly significant whether the contract was in law made within the jurisdiction or not.[335] The context that Mance J was referring to was that of a contract where it was by no means easy to ascertain how and when the contract was made. Mance J came to the conclusion that the contract was not made over the phone in India but by conduct in England by accepting requests from the defendant bank which it received by acting in accordance with them and confirming the credit.

---

[331] See above, paras 3.274–275.   [332] See above, paras 4.32–36.   [333] n 311 above.
[334] [1994] 2 Lloyd's Rep 87.   [335] ibid, at 96.

4.137   In cases where the place where the contract was made is not in dispute, this is clearly a relevant factor. This is illustrated by the *Aaronson* case,[336] where the contract was made orally in England and this was listed as one of the factors pointing to England as the forum conveniens. But what weight should be given to this factor? In the *Seeley* case,[337] this was regarded as an important consideration, albeit not as important as the applicable law, which was the principal, if not the decisive, consideration. At one point King CJ said that 'if it emerges that the supply agreement was a contract made within the jurisdiction, or that it is governed by the law of South Australia ... then the South Australian court is clearly the convenient forum for the resolution of the issues between the parties'.[338] However, it is submitted that, in principle, the mere fact that a contract was made in a particular state does not in itself constitute much of a connection with that state. After all, the state where a contract was made may well be fortuitous and represent no real connection with the parties, the contract and its obligations, or the subject-matter of the litigation, as the example given by Hawkins J in the *Bailey* case[339] graphically illustrates. However, the connection is greater if the contract was made by the parties face to face and is greater still if it was also negotiated in that state. The modern conditions that have cast doubt on the place where a contract was made as a connecting factor raise similar problems for the place where negotiations took place. 'If people talk back and forth with telephones, computers and fax machines across internal or international borders, where are the negotiations "taking place"? Obviously, either in two places or in no place.'[340] However, if negotiations are carried out face to face the position is different and it is easy to identify the place where the negotiations took place.[341] The subject-matter of the litigation is also very relevant. Thus if the live issue in the case is as to the formation of the contract, the place where it was made assumes an importance that it would not have if the issue is as to discharge of the contract.

4.138   In cases where the parties have agreed that the contract is deemed to have been made in country A but, according to the English rules on formation of a contract, it was made in country B,[342] there is connection with both A and B but little weight can be given to the place where the contract was made factor. In other words it provides little connection with either A or B. This is by analogy with the position where there is a deemed place of delivery.[343]

---

[336] n 309 above.   [337] n 313 above.   [338] ibid, at 305.
[339] *Bailey and Co Inc v Laser Medical Technology Inc* [1994] IL Pr 444 2nd see para 4.36.
[340] Hawkins J in the *Bailey* case, ibid, at 447.
[341] ibid.   [342] See above, para 4.35.   [343] See above, para 4.126.

The law applicable to the sales contract The identification of the law applic- **4.139** able to a contract for the international sale of goods has been mentioned already in this chapter[344] and is considered in detail in Chapter 13. The relevance of this factor is illustrated by the *Banque Paribas* case,[345] where Webster J used the fact that the central question in the case was the validity of a no set-off clause contained in a sales contract, which was arguably subject to English law, as one of the five factors pointing to England as the forum conveniens. In the *Cordova* case,[346] the fact that a foreign law governed the sales contract was one of the factors indicating that permission for service out of the jurisdiction should not be granted.[347]

How important is this factor in international sale of goods cases? In such **4.140** cases, the substantive law in Commonwealth States will often be sub- stantially the same and, where this is so, the applicable law factor is fairly unimportant. It will be recalled that this was the case in *Crane Accessories*, where the sale of goods law of Singapore was said to be substantially the same as that of New Zealand. This can be contrasted with the *Aaronson* case, where this factor was clearly relevant in reaching the conclusion that England was the *forum conveniens*. The precise weight attached to this factor was not discussed but, in such a case, the fact that the international sales law of Mexico was presumably different from that of England meant that this factor should be regarded as a significant one. In the *Seeley* case, the applicable law was the principal, if not the decisive, consideration. Greek law was presumably different from South Australian on the matters in dispute, which included the validity of the alleged supple- mentary agreement. It was alleged that this was entered into as a result of duress and that it was made in breach of the Australian Trade Practices Act 1974.

An agreement providing for trial in England The common practice, even **4.141** where both parties are foreign, of inserting exclusive jurisdiction clauses providing for trial in England[348] in contracts for the international sale of goods means that this will be a frequently encountered consideration in cases concerning such contracts. The fact that, in the absence of strong reason to the contrary, the discretion will be exercised in favour of holding parties to their bargain means that this must be regarded as the dominant consideration when exercising the discretion. Where, as com- monly occurs in sales contracts, there is also an English choice of law clause, leave for service out of the jurisdiction is regarded as presenting no

---

[344] See above, para 4.40.   [345] [1992] 2 Lloyd's Rep 19, CA.
[346] [1966] 1 WLR 793.   [347] ibid, at 796–797.
[348] For the position where the contract provides for the jurisdiction of a foreign court, see above, para 4.105 and below, paras 4.164–167.

problem.[349] If a clause providing for the non-exclusive of the English courts is inserted in the sales contract it is relevant to take into account the fact that the parties have implicitly agreed that England is *an* appropriate forum for trial.[350]

4.142   *The availability of witnesses*   In many international sale of goods cases, the dispute between the parties will be as to the quality of the goods delivered. The location of the witnesses in relation to this will depend very much on the particular facts of the case. If the contract is one for manufacture and supply, witnesses as to the process of manufacture may be necessary and these will normally be located in the place of manufacture.[351] In other cases though, there can be real problems in locating witnesses. *Chevron International Oil Co Ltd v A/S Sea Team (The TS Havprins)* illustrates the point.[352] There was a dispute over the quality of bunker fuel, which it was alleged caused trouble to a ship's engines. The fuel was sold by the plaintiff English company, but physically supplied by a US company, to the defendant Norwegian company, the charterers of a ship. Staughton J held that the evidence for the defendants would be that of ship's witnesses (who were itinerant, although based in Norway), administrators in Norway, and one or more experts. The evidence of the plaintiff as to the nature of the fuel supplied was likely to be for the most part in the United States. This suggested that it was a truly international dispute and gave no clear pointer to the forum conveniens.[353] The decisive factors were the English jurisdiction clause and choice of law clause in the sales contract. *Roneleigh Ltd v MII Exports Inc* is another good illustration.[354] The plaintiff English company entered into a contract with the defendant New Jersey company to buy scrap steel to be delivered FOB New York for export direct to Turkey and paid the purchase price to the defendant. The plaintiff claimed that when the goods arrived in New York they did not comply with their description. The real question therefore was: what was the condition of the goods when taken on board ship in New York? Sir Neil Lawson at first instance, whose decision permitting service out of the jurisdiction was affirmed by the Court of Appeal,[355] held that it would be necessary to have evidence from the United States about the condition

---

[349] *Bastone & Firminger Ltd v Nasima Enterprises (Nigeria) Ltd* [1996] CLC 1902 at 1905 (sales of chemical and polymer products); *Chevron International Oil Co Ltd v A/S Sea Team (The TS Havprins)* [1983] 2 Lloyd's Rep 356 (sale of bunker fuel).

[350] *S & W Berisford PLC and NGI Precious Metals Inc v New Hampshire Insurance Co* [1990] 1 Lloyd's Rep 454 at 463.

[351] See, e.g. *Applied Processes Inc v Crane Co* [1994] IL Pr 209, Mackenzie J, Ontario Court of Justice (General Division).

[352] [1983] 2 Lloyd's Rep 356.   [353] ibid, at 363.   [354] [1989] 1 WLR 619, CA.

[355] The major consideration in the case was that substantial justice would not be done if trial was held in New Jersey, see below, para 4.153.

of the steel when it was shipped and evidence from Turkey as to its condition when it arrived. The distances that witnesses will have to travel is an important consideration. This assumes, of course, that oral evidence will be needed, on which evidence is required.[356] Witnesses as to quality will often be located in the loading port because of the practice of binding certificates of inspection.[357] However, in some cases[358] there will be a certificate issued at the discharge port. Witnesses as to documents will be located at the place of tender.

When it comes to payment, the witnesses will be located in the state **4.143** where payment is made. Thus, in the *Crane Accessories* case, the witnesses as to whether the Singapore defendants paid the plaintiff's agent in Singapore would be from Singapore, although this was not mentioned as a consideration by Smellie J. In the *Aaronson* case, the witnesses as to whether the Mexican buyers had exercised due diligence in seeking a Mexican import licence would be Mexican officials. This was not seen as presenting a major problem, it being assumed that they could give evidence by affidavit.[359] In the *Seeley* case too, the witnesses factor was not treated as being of importance. The case involved disputes over when and where the supply contract was made and the validity of the supplementary agreement. There was inconvenience for the defendants in bringing witnesses to South Australia but a trial overseas would equally involve inconvenience to the South Australian plaintiff in taking witnesses abroad.[360] If payment is dispatched from State A to State B and never arrives, the relevant witnesses as to dispatch will be in State A.

Witnesses may also be required as to the formation of the sales contract. In **4.144** *The TS Havprins*,[361] one of the issues that arose was whether there was a contract between the parties. It was held that evidence as to the formation of the contract would come partly from England and partly from Norway, again suggesting that this was a truly international dispute.[362] In such a case, the place where the contract was made is also a material factor.

The residence of the parties In cases of the international sale of goods, the **4.145** residence[363] of the parties is a relevant consideration as it is with any other type of dispute. In the *Crane Accessories* case, one of the factors that pointed to Singapore as the natural forum was said to be that the defendants resided and worked in Singapore and had no connection with

---

[356] n 354 above, at 624 (*per* Nourse LJ).
[357] See Bridge, *The International Sale of Goods*, Ch 1. See also the FOSFA and GAFTA forms.
[358] See *Gill & Duffus SA v Berger & Co Inc* [1984] AC 382.
[359] n 311 above, at 160. [360] n 313 above, at 305. [361] n 349 above.
[362] ibid, at 363.
[363] Residence is the usual common law connecting factor in commercial cases, rather than domicile.

Singapore. In contrast, the plaintiff company's managing director, although a New Zealander, went to Singapore regularly and, according to Smellie J, this meant that there should be no great hardship for him in conducting the litigation there.[364] What can be said though about international sale of goods cases is that they involve genuine international disputes, ie normally both parties will be from different states, and so the residence of the parties is unlikely to be of any real significance.[365] Indeed, Sir Neil Lawson in the *Roneleigh* case went so far as to say that this was 'a case of international trade and the nationality and domicile of the parties and the national law is fortuitous'.[366] The lack of significance to be attached to the residence of the parties for the purposes of forum conveniens contrasts with the significance attached to the seller's residence at the choice of law stage.[367]

4.146 *A multiplicity of proceedings*   Examples of how the problem of *lis pendens* can arise in the context of the international sale of goods have been given earlier when discussing Article 27 of the Brussels I Regulation.[368] In cases where the multiplicity of proceedings is in the United Kingdom and in another Member State, Article 27 (*lis pendens*) may well apply. There is also Article 28 (related actions) which is there to cover cases that do not fall within the technical definition of *lis pendens* (for example the parties are not the same in the two sets of proceedings but there is a risk of irreconcilable judgments if there are separate proceedings). Neither of these provisions requires that jurisdiction in the two sets of proceedings is founded on the bases of jurisdiction contained in the EC rules. In both sets of proceedings, it could be based on traditional national rules of jurisdiction. Nonetheless, Articles 27 and 28 will still apply. However, if the multiplicity of proceedings is in England and a non-EC Member State,[369] such as New York or Japan, these Articles will not apply. Instead, traditional English rules will apply to solve the problem.

4.147 Under these traditional English rules, *lis pendens* is regarded as merely a facet, albeit an important one, of the doctrine of *forum conveniens* and *forum non conveniens*.[370] This flexible approach means that the law can deal with any problem of parallel proceedings, even where the case is technically not one of *lis pendens* because the parties or the cause of action or both are not the same in the two sets of proceedings.

---

[364] n 311 above, at 232.
[365] But see for the significance of the residence of the seller under the Rome Convention, below, para 13.116.
[366] n 354 above, at 622.
[367] See Art 4(2) of the Rome Convention, discussed below, para 13.116.
[368] See above, paras 3.316–327.   [369] Or EFTA State.
[370] See generally J Fawcett, *Declining Jurisdiction in Private International Law* (Oxford: Clarendon Press, 1995) 27–46.

The normal principles that apply in cases involving a multiplicity of **4.148** proceedings[371] apply equally to cases involving the international sale of goods. It is relevant whether it is a case of the same claimant starting proceedings in two different states or a case where the claimant in one jurisdiction is the defendant in another jurisdiction and vice versa. In the former case, the claimant will generally be forced to elect the country in which he wants trial.[372] This is neatly illustrated in the context of the international sale of goods by *Hing Fat Plastic Manufacturing Co Ltd v Advanced Technology Products (HK) Ltd*,[373] a decision of Keith J in the High Court in Hong Kong. The plaintiff Hong Kong company commenced proceedings in the People's Republic of China against another Hong Kong company for the price of goods sold and delivered. A month later the plaintiff commenced identical proceedings against the same defendant in the High Court in Hong Kong. The plaintiff alleged that only by suing in both jurisdictions would it be able to effect execution on all the defendant's known assets. Keith J held that this was not sufficient to justify the continuance of both sets of proceedings. The plaintiff was required to elect the country in which he wanted trial. Having elected for trial in Hong Kong, the plaintiff was restrained from continuing the proceedings in the People's Republic of China. If the plaintiff had elected for trial in the latter country doubtless a stay would have been granted of the Hong Kong proceedings.

Associated contracts The courts will not only take into account what the **4.149** law governing the sales contract is but also the law governing other related contracts. Thus, in the *Banque Paribas* case,[374] Webster J took into account the fact that the Lavera contract, damages in relation to the repudiation of which were sought to be set off against payment under the sales contract, was governed by English law. Moreover, the plaintiffs were assignees of the sellers under the sales contract and the fact that these assignments were governed by English law was also held to point towards England as the *forum conveniens*. The contract that is perhaps most closely connected with the contract for the international sale of goods is that for the carriage of the goods contained in or evidenced by a bill of lading. The law governing the latter[375] should be taken into account when determining the appropriate forum for trial in relation to the sales contract. Going beyond this, the bill of lading will have connections with particular states[376] and these too should be taken into account. What

---

[371] See Cheshire and North, 347–350; Dicey and Morris, 400–401.
[372] See *Australian Commercial Research and Development Ltd v ANZ McCaughan Merchant Bank Ltd* [1989] 3 All ER 65 at 70.
[373] [1992] 2 HKLR 350.   [374] n 327 above.   [375] See below, paras 14.09–37.
[376] For *forum conveniens* factors in relation to bills of lading, see below, para 5.55.

weight should be given to these associated contract considerations? Normally, these should be regarded as part of the surrounding circumstances and therefore not as much weight should be accorded to such considerations as those directly linked to the international sale of goods contract itself. However, if one of the parties to the sales contract is likely to be involved in litigation in relation to the associated contract much more weight should be attached to the associated contract factors. It is very desirable that all the litigation is tried in the same state and this is a way of trying to ensure that this happens.[377]

4.150 *Other considerations*   The above is not a complete list of the considerations that can apply in cases involving the international sale of goods. The particular circumstances of the case may throw up other considerations. *Charm Maritime Inc v Minas Xenophon Kyriakou and David John Mathias*[378] serves as an illustration. The first defendant entered into a declaration of trust with the second defendant, whereby the former declared that he held shares on trust for the latter and would transfer them as the latter directed. The second defendant entered into an agreement of sale of the shares with the plaintiffs. The plaintiffs began proceedings against the first defendant in Greece for delivery of the shares. This action was dismissed. Subsequently the plaintiffs began proceedings in England against the first defendant for, *inter alia*, the delivery of the shares and for a declaration that the first defendant held the shares on trust. The buyer claimed in the alternative against the second defendant for breach of warranty or misrepresentation. One important factor pointing towards trial in Greece was the estoppel factor, that is the question whether the Greek judgment was a final one on the merits, thereby giving rise to a cause of action estoppel. This would involve a great deal of evidence from Greek lawyers. However, this was outweighed by the factors pointing towards trial in England. One important factor was the fact that the English courts were familiar with the concept of a trust on which the plaintiff's case depended, whereas the Greek courts were not. Another was the fact that the second defendant was a party to the English proceedings but probably could not be sued by the plaintiffs in Greece. In the light of these considerations, the appeal against the decision refusing a stay was affirmed by the Court of Appeal.

4.151 In the *Cordova* case,[379] which involved goods shipped CIF Hull, Winn J took into account the US origin of the goods and the fact that the handling of them prior to shipment also took place in the United States.[380]

---

[377] The factor of consolidation of litigation in multi-party cases is considered below, para 4.166
[378] [1987] 1 Lloyd's Rep 433.   [379] [1966] 1 WLR 793.   [380] ibid, at 796–797.

Injustice abroad The question of whether there would be injustice in **4.152** trial abroad has to be considered in cases of the international sale of goods as with any other case. In the *Crane Accessories* case, Smellie J satisfied himself that there was no suggestion that the plaintiff would not obtain a just hearing in the Singapore courts. The scenario that concerned Lord Goff in *Spiliada* of a plaintiff seeking trial in England because of the advantage of higher damages is much more likely to arise in the context of a tort action for personal injury than in one for damages for breach of an international sales contract. If trial is held in England, the English courts will apply the law applicable to the sales contract to the issue of assessment of damages in so far as this raises questions of law.[381] The alternative forum abroad may apply its own law as the law of the forum to matters of assessment of damages for breach of contract. This could result in different laws being applicable to this issue.[382] But whichever law is applicable this is unlikely to lead to a much lower figure.

One of the best examples of injustice abroad arose in the context of the **4.153** international sale of goods is the *Roneleigh* case.[383] The fact that the plaintiff would recover his costs in English proceedings but would have to pay them in proceedings in New Jersey meant that substantial justice was not likely to be done in the foreign forum and that this was a sufficient factor against proceedings in New Jersey, which was the more appropriate forum for trial. The question of costs is going to be relevant whatever the type of action. Another example of injustice abroad is where an English court would uphold an arbitration agreement whereas the foreign court might not.[384] This is a much more interesting example because it is particularly likely to occur in cases of the international sale of goods. Arbitration clauses are common place in contracts for the international sale of goods. The problem may well arise of an alternative forum abroad which does not recognize such a clause. There are no obvious examples of injustice abroad which will only arise in the context of the international sale of goods. To that extent it can be said that such cases do not raise any special points when it comes to operating this aspect of the doctrine of forum conveniens.

---

[381] Art 10(1)(c) of the Rome Convention, discussed below, paras 13.205–239.

[382] The law applicable to the sales contract may be that of the alternative forum and then it will be irrelevant where the trial occurs, at least as regards the issue of assessment of damages.

[383] *Roneleigh Ltd v MII Exports Inc* [1989] 1 WLR 619 at 623.

[384] *Union de Remorquage et de Sauvetage SA v Lake Avery Inc (The Lake Avery)* [1997] 1 Lloyd's Rep 540—a salvage case.

III. DECLINING JURISDICTION AND RESTRAINING FOREIGN PROCEEDINGS

1. DECLINING JURISDICTION

4.154 An English court, even though it has jurisdiction following the service of a claim form on the defendant, can decline to exercise that jurisdiction by granting a stay of the English proceedings. A stay will be granted in three different situations: where the doctrine of *forum non conveniens* applies; where there is a foreign jurisdiction clause; and where there is an agreement on arbitration.

4.155 Before turning to examine each of these situations, it is important to recall that Articles 27 and 28 of the Brussels I Regulation[385] apply to cases of concurrent litigation in two EC States, even though the jurisdiction in both of these States is based on traditional national rules on jurisdiction. If the requirements of Article 27 or 28 are met, jurisdiction will be declined under this provision. In rare cases, there will be concurrent litigation in two EC States, with jurisdiction based on traditional national rules, which does not satisfy the requirements of either of these two Articles, for example the cause of action is not the same in the two actions and they are not related.[386] In this situation, recourse can be had to the traditional English doctrine of *forum non conveniens*, despite the fact that there is concurrent litigation in another EC Member State.[387]

Forum Non Conveniens

The principles to be applied when exercising the discretion

4.156 Lord Goff in *Spiliada Maritime Corp v Cansulex Ltd*[388] set out the basic principle that:

> a stay will only be granted on the ground of *forum non conveniens* where the court is satisfied that there is some other available forum, having competent jurisdiction, which is the appropriate forum for trial of the action, i.e. in which the case may be tried more suitably for the interests of all the parties and the ends of justice.[389]

This involves a two stage process: first, determination of whether there

---

[385] Discussed above, paras 3.313–338. See also Arts 21 and 22 of the Lugano Convention.

[386] This situation will seldom arise because of the wide interpretation given to Art 28. See *Sarrio SA v Kuwait Investment Authority* [1999] 1 AC 32, HL.

[387] The *Sarrio* case in the Court of Appeal, [1997] IL Pr 481; reversed by the House of Lords without discussion of this point, n 386 above.

[388] [1987] AC 460; followed in *Connelly v RTZ Corp Plc* [1998] AC 854, HL and *Lubbe v Cape Plc* [2000] 1 WLR 1545, HL.   [389] The *Spiliada* case, n 388 above, at 476.

is a clearly more appropriate forum abroad; second, consideration of the requirements of justice.

A clearly more appropriate forum abroad The burden of proof is on the **4.157** defendant to show that there is another available forum which is clearly or distinctly more appropriate than the English forum.[390] It is not enough to show that England is a clearly inappropriate forum[391] or not the natural forum. In cases where there is no clearly more appropriate forum abroad, i.e. there is no country which is the natural forum or England is the natural forum, the courts will ordinarily refuse a stay of proceedings.[392] If it is shown that there is another available forum which is clearly or distinctly more appropriate than the English forum, the court will move on to the second stage, which is to consider the requirements of justice. In order to establish that there is a clearly more appropriate forum abroad, the defendant has to show two things: first, that there is another available forum abroad; second, that this is clearly or distinctly more appropriate than the English forum.

Another available forum It is impossible to establish that there is a clearly **4.158** more appropriate forum for trial abroad in the absence of an alternative forum abroad.[393]

Which is clearly more appropriate than the English forum When determining **4.159** whether the foreign forum is clearly more appropriate than the English forum, the same considerations apply as are applied when exercising the *forum conveniens* discretion in cases of service out of the jurisdiction under r 6.20 of the Civil Procedure Rules.[394]

The requirements of justice If there is some other available forum **4.160** which, *prima facie*, is clearly more appropriate for the trial of the action, the court will, ordinarily, grant a stay unless there are circumstances by reason of which justice requires that a stay should nevertheless not be granted.[395] Once it has been shown that there is a clearly more appropriate forum for trial abroad, the burden of proof shifts to the claimant to justify coming to England.[396] In *Connelly v RTZ Corp Ltd*,[397] Lord Goff elaborated on this second stage. He said that there was a general principle that:

if a clearly more appropriate forum overseas has been identified, generally

---

[390] ibid, at 474.
[391] Compare *Voth v Manildra Flour Mills Pty Ltd* (1991) 171 CLR 538, HC of Australia.
[392] The *Spiliada* case, n 388 above, at 478.
[393] See *Konamaneni v Rolls-Royce Industrial Power (India) Limited* [2002] IL Pr 40 at [59]; *Mohammed v Bank of Kuwait and the Middle East KSC* [1996] 1 WLR 1483, CA; *Lubbe v Cape Plc* [2000] 1 WLR 1545 at [48], HL; *Gheewala v Hindocha* [2003] UKPC 77.
[394] See above, paras 4.103–109.   [395] The *Spiliada* case, n 388 above, at 478.
[396] ibid, at 476.   [397] [1998] AC 854, HL.

speaking the plaintiff will have to take that forum as he finds it, even if it is in certain respects less advantageous to him than the English forum. He may, for example, have to accept lower damages, or do without the more generous English system of discovery. The same must apply to the system of court procedure, including the rules of evidence, applicable in the foreign forum . . . Only if the plaintiff can establish that substantial justice cannot be done in the appropriate forum, will the courts refuse to grant a stay.[398]

Application to contracts for the international sale of goods

4.161   **A clearly more appropriate forum abroad**   The typical considerations in an international sale of goods case (the place of delivery of the goods, the place of payment for the goods, the place where the sales contract was made, the law applicable to the sales contract, an agreement as to jurisdiction, the availability of witnesses, the residence of the parties, a multiplicity of proceedings) have already been examined and what has already been said[399] about them does not need to be repeated.

4.162   **The requirements of justice**   Examples have earlier been given of injustice abroad that have arisen in other contexts but could also arise in the context of the international sale of goods, such as the inability to recover costs abroad. There are though recent examples of injustice abroad which cannot by their very nature arise in the commercial context of the international sale of goods. The English courts have been faced with a series of actions brought before them by foreign plaintiffs who have suffered personal injury abroad. The clearly appropriate forum was abroad but the English courts have refused to stay the English proceedings because of the requirements of justice. In the *Connelly* case,[400] this was because the nature and complexity of the case was such that it could not be tried at all without the benefit of financial assistance in the form of legal aid and, although available in England, this was unavailable in Namibia, the natural forum. Similarly in *Lubbe v Cape Plc*,[401] if the proceedings had been stayed in favour of the more appropriate forum, South Africa, this would have been a denial of justice. The probability is that the plaintiffs would have had no means of obtaining the professional representation and the expert evidence which would have been essential if these claims were to have been justly decided.[402]

4.163   One important reason in sales cases why trial may be sought in England, despite the fact that the natural forum is abroad, is that the English judges in the Commercial Court are very experienced. However, this cannot be

---

[398] ibid, at 872; the *Lubbe* case, n 388 above, at [16].   [399] Above, paras 4.120–151.
[400] [1998] AC 854, HL.   [401] [2000] 1 WLR 1545, HL.
[402] ibid, at [27] (*per* Lord Bingham, with whom the other Law Lords concurred).

used to justify trial in England.[403] The English courts will not enter into comparisons of the quality of justice obtained in England and abroad.[404]

Foreign Jurisdiction Clauses

The principles to be applied when exercising the discretion

Lord Bingham in the House of Lords in *Donohue v Armco Inc*[405] sum- **4.164** marized the principles that apply when exercising the discretion to stay English proceedings brought in breach of a foreign exclusive jurisdiction clause.[406] The case concerned an injunction sought to restrain proceedings brought abroad in breach of an English exclusive jurisdiction clause. But Lord Bingham widened the discussion to refer more generally to the principles that apply where there has been a breach of an exclusive juris-diction clause, which includes the situation where proceedings are brought in England in breach of a foreign jurisdiction clause.

If contracting parties agree to give a particular court exclusive jurisdiction to rule on claims between those parties, and a claim falling within the scope of the agreement is made in proceedings in a forum other than that which the parties have agreed, the English court will ordinarily[407] exercise its discretion (whether by granting a stay of proceedings in England, or by restraining the prosecution of proceedings in the non-contractual forum abroad, or by such other procedural order as is appropriate in the circumstances) to secure compliance with the con-tractual bargain, unless the party suing in the non-contractual forum (the burden being on him) can show strong reasons for suing in that forum.[408]

Whether a party can show strong reasons, sufficient to displace the other party's prima facie entitlement to enforce the contractual bargain, will depend on all the facts and circumstances of the particular case.[409] The House of Lords approved[410] the judgment of Brandon J in *The Eleftheria*,[411] a case on the stay of English proceedings brought in breach of a foreign exclusive jurisdiction clause which has been repeatedly cited and approved over the years.[412] Brandon J listed some of the matters which

---

[403] *The Abidin Daver* [1984] AC 398 at 424–425.

[404] *Amin Rasheed Shipping Corp v Kuwait Insurance Co* [1984] AC 50 at 67; *The Abidin Daver* [1984] AC 398 at 410.

[405] [2001] UKHL 64, [2002] 1 All ER 749.

[406] Lords Mackay at [40] and Nicholls at [41] concurred with the judgment of Lord Bingham. The other two Law Lords (Lords Hobhouse and Scott) delivered judgments coming to the same conclusion as Lord Bingham and agreed that these were the principles to be applied.

[407] This recognizes that it is a discretion. Also a party may lose his claim to equitable relief by dilatoriness or other unconscionable conduct, n 405 above at [24].

[408] n 405 above, at [24].   [409] ibid.   [410] ibid.   [411] [1970] P 94.

[412] Most importantly, *The Eleftheria* was affirmed by the Court of Appeal in the *El Amria* [1981] 2 Lloyd's Rep 119, and by the Privy Council in *The Pioneer Container* [1994] 2 AC 324, PC.

might properly be regarded by the court when exercising its discretion.[413] These were as follows:

(a) In what country the evidence on the issues of fact is situated, or more readily available, and the effect of that on the relative convenience and expense of trial as between the English and foreign courts.

(b) Whether the law of the foreign court applies and, if so, whether it differs from English law in any material respects.

(c) With what country either party is connected, and how closely.

(d) Whether the defendants genuinely desire trial in the foreign country, or are only seeking procedural advantages.

(e) Whether the plaintiffs would be prejudiced by having to sue in the foreign court because they would:
  (i) be deprived of security for their claim;
  (ii) be unable to enforce any judgment obtained;
  (iii) be faced with a time bar not applicable in England; or
  (iv) for political, racial, religious or other reasons be unlikely to get a fair trial.

However, this list was not intended to be comprehensive.[414]

4.165 The matters listed by Brandon J are the same factors of appropriateness and justice as are considered under the doctrine of *forum non conveniens*. Nonetheless, there is a vital difference between these two discretionary grounds for a stay of English proceedings. In cases involving a foreign jurisdiction clause, the burden is on the claimant to show why a stay should not be granted. In cases of *forum non conveniens*, it is the other way round and the defendant must show that the clearly appropriate forum is abroad. The result is that the principles in respect of the former discretionary power are loaded in favour of a stay; under the latter discretionary power they are loaded in favour of trial continuing in England.

4.166 The authorities show that where the dispute is between two contracting parties and the claim falls within the exclusive jurisdiction clause in the contract, and the interests of other parties are not involved, effect will in all probability be given to the clause.[415] In contrast, the English court may well decline to grant an injunction or a stay, as the case may be, where the interests of parties other than the parties bound by the exclusive jurisdiction clause are involved or grounds of claim not the

---

[413] [1970] P 94 at 99–100.

[414] The *Donohue* case, n 405 above, at [24] (*per* Lord Bingham).

[415] The *Donohue* case, n 405 above, at [25], where the authorities that support this statement are cited by Lord Bingham.

subject of the clause are part of the relevant dispute so that there is a risk of parallel proceedings and inconsistent decisions.[416]

So far we have been discussing foreign exclusive jurisdiction clauses. **4.167** If the foreign jurisdiction clause is non-exclusive the position is very different. There is no breach of agreement in commencing proceedings in England and a stay of the English proceedings will not be granted on this basis. Instead the principles on the grant of a stay on the ground of *forum non conveniens* will be applied.[417]

Application to contracts for the international sale of goods

The great majority of the reported cases on foreign choice of jurisdiction **4.168** clauses involve bills of lading.[418] However, the principles that apply where there is a foreign jurisdiction clause apply equally to cases involving a contract for the international sale of goods. An example is *A/S Nyborg Plast v Lameque Quality Group Ltd*.[419] The New Brunswick buyer of plastic bags sued a Danish seller in New Brunswick, alleging that the bags were not fit for their purpose. The seller's confirmation of order form contained a clause providing for trial in Denmark. The New Brunswick Court of Appeal, applying the principles in *The Eleftheria*, held that, if the clause was binding on the plaintiff, the court would have to give effect to it unless the plaintiff was able to meet the heavy burden described in *The Eleftheria*. The fact that New Brunswick might be a more convenient forum was not a sufficient ground to exercise its discretion against a stay. An example going the other way is *Carvalho v Hull Blyth (Angola) Ltd*,[420] a case involving the sale of shares in a group of Angolan companies. It was agreed in a choice of jurisdiction clause that, in the case of litigation, the courts of Luanda were the sole competent courts to the exclusion of all others. Nevertheless, the Court of Appeal held that strong cause was shown for the English court to exercise its discretion and to refuse a stay in that the court named, although it still existed after Angola became an independent state, was not the same court to which the parties had agreed to refer all disputes. Alternatively, it could be said that, as a matter of construction, the jurisdiction clause was no longer applicable.

---

[416] ibid, at [27], where the authorities that support this statement are cited by Lord Bingham.

[417] See *The Rothnie* [1996] 2 Lloyd's Rep 206; Fawcett, n 133 above, at 253–255. But compare *Import-Export Metro Ltd v Compañía Sud Americana De Vapores SA* [2003] EWHC 11 (Comm), [2003] 1 Lloyd's Rep 405.

[418] This is because many carriers will be foreign and their standard terms and conditions will provide for trial in their home state. The cargo insurers may well be English and will want trial in England.

[419] (2001) 213 DLR (4th) 301, New Brunswick CA.

[420] [1979] 1 WLR 1228, CA.

Arbitration Agreements

The rules

4.169 A party to an arbitration agreement against whom legal proceedings are brought (whether by way of claim or counter-claim) in respect of a matter which under the agreement is to be referred to arbitration may (upon notice to the other parties to the proceedings) apply to the court in which the proceedings have been brought to stay the proceedings so far as they concern that matter.[421] The staying of the proceedings is mandatory unless the court is satisfied that the arbitration agreement is null and void, inoperative, or incapable of being performed.[422]

Application to contracts for the international sale of goods

4.170 As has been seen,[423] standard form contracts used for contracts for the international sale of goods very often include an arbitration clause. In cases where the sales contract contains such a clause, a mandatory stay of proceedings will be granted. The arbitration agreement can also affect related proceedings. Thus a stay will be granted of an action in tort against a third party who acted as advisor in relation to the sale of a business pending the outcome of arbitration proceedings commenced against the seller of the business.[424]

4.171 The question will frequently arise of whether an arbitration clause has been incorporated into the contract for the international sale of goods. It is necessary to determine when the contract was formed. The law governing the contract for the international sale of goods will determine which country's rules on the formation of the contract for the international sale of goods will apply.[425] As far as England is concerned, this law is ascertained by the application of English choice of law rules contained in the Rome Convention.[426]

---

[421] Arbitration Act 1996, s 9(1).   [422] ibid, s 9(4).   [423] See above, para 3.04.
[424] *Reichold Norway ASA v Goldman Sachs International* [1999] CLC 486.
[425] *Egon Oldendorff v Liberia Corp* [1995] 2 Lloyd's Rep 64 (applying Art 8 of the Rome Convention); discussed above, para 3.31. See also *OTM Ltd v Hydronautics* [1981] 2 Lloyd's Rep 211 and *Astro Venturoso Compañía Naviera v Hellenic Shipyards SA (The Mariannina)* [1983] 1 Lloyd's Rep 12 at 14, CA—both cases were decided at common law prior to the introduction of the Rome Convention. But compare *Marc Rich & Co AG v Società Italiana Impianti PA (The Atlantic Emperor)* [1989] 1 Lloyd's Rep 548 (the headnote refers to the law governing the arbitration agreement, whilst the judgment at 554 seems to suggest that the law governing the contract as a whole should be applied); the case was referred to the ECJ on a different point.
[426] Art 8, discussed below, paras 13.143–155. If incorporation were a matter for the law governing the arbitration agreement this would be determined according to traditional common law contract choice of law rules—on which see Dicey and Morris at 1209—since arbitration is excluded from the scope of the Rome Convention.

2. RESTRAINING FOREIGN PROCEEDINGS

An English court has a discretionary power, in certain limited circum- **4.172** stances, to issue an injunction restraining a party from commencing or continuing as plaintiff with foreign proceedings.[427] The jurisdiction is to be exercised when the ends of justice require it.[428] The order is directed not against the foreign court but against a party.[429] An injunction will only be granted against a party who is amenable to the jurisdiction of the English courts.[430] The power to make the order is dependent upon there being wrongful conduct of the party to be restrained of which the applicant is entitled to complain and has a legitimate interest in seeking to prevent.[431] The conduct in question should fall within the description of being unconscionable.[432] This power must be exercised with caution because of the obvious comity problems inherent in its use.[433] There are three different categories where this power has been exercised: where the bringing of the proceedings abroad would be in breach of an agreement; where the pursuit of the proceedings abroad would be vexatious or oppressive; where the bringing of the proceedings abroad would be unconscionable for some other reason.[434] These categories and their application in cases of the international sale of goods will now be considered.

Where the Bringing of the Proceedings Abroad would be in Breach of an Agreement

The principles to be applied when exercising the discretion

Breach of an exclusive choice of jurisdiction clause   The English courts **4.173** have a discretionary power to restrain by injunction the prosecution abroad of proceedings brought in breach of an exclusive jurisdiction clause providing for trial in England. The principles to be applied when exercising this discretion were summarized by Lord Bingham in the House

---

[427] See Cheshire and North, 359–373; Dicey and Morris, 414–422, 445–450. The issue of principle raised where an injunction is sought restraining proceedings in another EC Member State is discussed above, para 3.340.

[428] *Donohue v Armco Inc* [2001] UKHL 64 at [19], [2002] 1 All ER 749; *Turner v Grovit* [2001] UKHL 65 at [24] (*per* Lord Hobhouse), [2002] 1 WLR 107; *Société Nationale Industrielle Aerospatiale v Lee Kui Jak* [1987] AC 871 at 892, PC.

[429] The *Donohue* case, n 428 above; the *Turner* case, n 428 above, at [23]; the *Société Nationale Industrielle* case, n 428 above.

[430] ibid.   [431] The *Turner* case, n 428 above, at [24].

[432] *British Airways v Laker Airways* [1985] AC 58 at 81 (*per* Lord Diplock); *Turner v Grovit* [2002] IL PR 28 at [24], [25] and [27] (*per* Lord Hobhouse), HL.

[433] The *Donohue* case, n 428 above; the *Turner* case, n 428 above, at [24]; the *Société Nationale Industrielle* case, n 428 above.

[434] *Turner v Grovit*, n 432 above; *Airbus Industrie GIE v Patel* [1999] 1 AC 119. In the latter case, this third category was recognized but it appears to have been regarded as a separate category rather than as encompassing the first two categories.

of Lords in *Donohue v Armco Inc.*[435] The case concerned an injunction sought to restrain proceedings brought in New York in breach of English exclusive jurisdiction clauses contained in agreements relating to the sale of shares. As has already been seen, Lord Bingham widened the discussion to refer more generally to the principles that apply where there has been a breach of an exclusive jurisdiction clause, which includes the situation where proceedings are brought in England in breach of a foreign jurisdiction clause. These common principles that apply in both the contexts of an injunction restraining foreign proceedings and a stay of English proceedings have already been examined in the latter context[436] and reference should be made to what is said there. Where the applicant is relying upon a contractual right not to be sued in the foreign country then, absent some special circumstance, he has by reason of his contract a legitimate interest in enforcing that right against the other party to the contract.[437] The applicant does not have to show that the contractual forum is more appropriate than any other; the parties' contractual agreement does that for him.[438] On the facts of the *Donohue* case, the defendants in the English proceedings were able to show the requisite strong reasons, sufficient to displace the claimant's *prima facie* entitlement to enforce the contractual bargain, and an injunction restraining the proceedings in New York was refused. There were other defendants in the New York proceedings who were potential co-claimants in the English proceedings (PCCs),[439] some of whom were not parties to the exclusive jurisdiction clauses. The strong reasons lay in the prospect, if the injunction were to be granted, of litigation between the defendants on the one side and the claimant and the PCCs on the other continuing partly in England and partly in New York.[440] The interests of justice were best served by the submission of the whole suit to a single tribunal which could adjudicate on all the matters in issue, namely the New York courts.[441]

4.174 The principles governing the grant of injunctions and stays are not entirely the same, a point acknowledged by Lord Bingham in the *Donohue* case,[442] in that considerations of comity arise in the former case but not in the latter. However, a concern with comity has not been evident in cases where the ground for an injunction is that of a breach of an agree-

---

[435] [2001] UKHL 64, [2002] 1 All ER 749.   [436] Above, paras 4.164–167.

[437] The *Turner* case, n 428 above, at [27] (*per* Lord Hobhouse).

[438] ibid, at [25] (*per* Lord Hobhouse).

[439] They could not be joined to the English action as claimants because they had no cause of action entitling them to an anti-suit injunction on the ground of vexation or oppression, ibid, at [17]–[22] (*per* Lord Bingham) and [45] (*per* Lord Hobhouse).

[440] ibid, at [33] (*per* Lord Bingham) and [75] (*per* Lord Scott).

[441] ibid, at [34].

[442] ibid, at [24].

ment.[443] Indeed, Lord Bingham did not think that this difference in the principles governing the grant of injunctions and stays needed to be explored in the instant case (one where there was a breach of an exclusive jurisdiction agreement).[444] And the Court of Appeal has said that there is no reason in principle why comity should stand in the way of granting an injunction where proceedings are brought in breach of an English exclusive jurisdiction clause.[445]

Where the agreement provides for the non-exclusive jurisdiction of the **4.175** English courts there is no breach of agreement in bringing proceedings abroad and therefore an injunction will not be granted on the basis of breach of an agreement.[446] However, if one party seeks an injunction abroad whereby the other party will be permanently restrained from making any demand under a contract in the hope of preventing the latter from starting proceedings in England this is a breach of contract and vexatious.[447] An injunction restraining that first party from continuing the proceedings abroad will then be granted.[448]

Breach of an arbitration agreement Where there is an agreement valid **4.176** under its governing law to arbitrate and foreign court proceedings are pending, the English courts have an inherent power to restrain the parties from bringing or continuing the foreign proceedings, for that would constitute a breach of contract.[449] In such cases, the court need feel no diffidence in granting the injunction, provided that it is sought promptly and before the foreign proceedings are too far advanced.[450] There has often been said to be no difference in principle between an injunction to restrain proceedings in breach of an arbitration clause and one to restrain proceedings in breach of an exclusive jurisdiction clause.[451] The justification for the grant of an injunction in either case is that, without it, the claimant will be deprived of his contractual rights in a situation in which

[443] Lord Goff in *Airbus Industrie GIE v Patel* when discussing comity stressed that he was not discussing cases where the choice of forum was the subject of an agreement between the parties, n 434 above, at 138.

[444] n 435 above at [24].

[445] *National Westminster Bank v Utrecht-America Finance Company* [2001] EWCA Civ 658, [2001] 3 All ER 733.

[446] *Royal Bank of Canada v Coopérative Centrale Raiffeisen-Boerenleenbank BA* [2004] EWCA Civ 7, [2004] 1 Lloyd's Rep 471; *Continental Bank v Aeakos* [1994] 1 WLR 588, CA; *A/S Svendborg v Wansa* [1997] 2 Lloyd's Rep 183, CA; Fawcett, n 133 above, at 255–257.

[447] *Sabah Shipyard (Pakistan) Ltd v Islamic Republic of Pakistan* [2002] EWCA Civ 1643, [2003] 2 Lloyd's Rep 571, CA. Distinguished in *Royal Bank of Canada v Coopérative Centrale Raiffeisen-Boerenleenbank BA* [2004] EWCA Civ 7, [2004] 1 Lloyd's Rep 471.

[448] The *Sabah* case, ibid.

[449] See *Aggeliki Charis Compañía Maritima SA v Pagnan SpA (The Angelic Grace)* [1995] 1 Lloyd's Rep 87, CA.

[450] ibid, at 96 (*per* Millett LJ).

[451] ibid. See also the *Natwest Bank* case, n 445 above, at [32].

damages are manifestly an inadequate remedy.[452] The ground for granting the injunction to restrain the foreign proceedings is the clear and simple one that the defendant has promised not to bring them.[453] Moreover, the principles in the *Donohue* case[454] (a case concerned with exclusive jurisdiction clauses) have been applied where an injunction was sought to restrain proceedings brought in breach of a clause providing for arbitration in England.[455]

Application to contracts for the international sale of goods

4.177   The fact that international sale of goods contracts will commonly contain an exclusive jurisdiction clause providing for trial in England or an arbitration clause means that the restraint of foreign proceedings on the ground that the bringing of the proceedings abroad is in breach of the parties' agreement is a common occurrence with this type of contract. *Toepfer International GmbH v Société Cargill France*[456] is an example. The plaintiffs by three contracts sold to the defendant buyers soya bean meal pellets CIF Montair. The contracts incorporated the provisions of GAFTA 100 and 125 including the arbitration clause, which provided, *inter alia*, that all disputes arising out of or under the contract were to be settled by arbitration in accordance with the GAFTA rules. It was further provided that no legal proceedings would be brought until such dispute had first been determined by arbitration. The defendants became concerned about the condition of the cargo and rejected 5,000 tonnes. The defendants commenced proceedings in the French courts for damages for breach of contract. Colman J at first instance granted the plaintiffs an injunction restraining the defendants from continuing with the French proceedings.[457] The Court of Appeal upheld the grant of this injunction. Colman J had not erred in the exercise of the discretion to grant an injunction.

---

[452]   *The Angelic Grace*, n 449 above.

[453]   *Toepfer International GmbH v Société Cargill France* [1998] 1 Lloyd's Rep 379 at 384, CA.

[454]   n 435 above and text accompanying.

[455]   *Welex AG v Rosa Maritime Limited* [2003] EWCA Civ 938 at [47]–[52], [2003] 2 Lloyd's Rep 509; followed in *Through Transport Mutual Insurance Association (Eurasia) Ltd v New India Assurance Co Ltd* [2003] EWHC 3158 (Comm), [2004] 1 Lloyd's Rep 206. Compare *Toepfer International GmbH v Société Cargill France* [1997] 2 Lloyd's Rep 98 at 110, where Colman J held that, when it comes to exercising the discretion to grant an injunction in the case of a breach of an arbitration agreement, little or no weight should be given to *forum non conveniens* criteria or to the risk of inconsistent judgments. This was on the basis that such considerations play no part in the New York Convention scheme as regards stays of action. The Court of Appeal at [1998] 1 Lloyd's Rep 379, without discussing this specific point, held, at 386, that Colman J did not err in principle in the exercise of his discretion.

[456]   [1998] 1 Lloyd's Rep 379, CA.

[457]   This raises the issue of principle whether an injunction can be granted restraining proceedings in another EC Member State. The ECJ has subsequently held that it cannot, see above, para 3.340.

This was perhaps the easiest of the several points raised on the appeal. **4.178**
Some of these were concerned with the Brussels Convention and have
already been discussed.[458] One further point was concerned with the rela-
tionship between the arbitration clause set out in clause 32 of GAFTA
Form 100[459] and the exclusive jurisdiction clause set out in clause 31.[460]
Colman J held that the effect of these provisions was to share between the
English court and the arbitrators exclusive jurisdiction over all disputes.
There would be a split with disputes as to substance falling within
the exclusive jurisdiction of the arbitrators and disputes as to ancillary
matters falling within the exclusive jurisdiction of the English courts.
However, the Court of Appeal disagreed and held that clause 31 provides
alternative jurisdictional regimes applicable to all disputes covered by
that clause. Clause 31 is designed to apply where the contract provides
for arbitration and where it does not. Where the contract, as in the present
case, includes clause 32, the alternative provisions in clause 31 for
exclusive jurisdiction of the English court do not take effect. Thus proceedings to enforce the arbitration clause by way of injunction were not
subject to the exclusive jurisdiction of the English court.

The Court of Appeal has also exercised its discretion to grant an injunc- **4.179**
tion restraining Swiss buyers from continuing with proceedings in
Switzerland for damages against Sudanese sellers in a case where the
contracts were as per FOSFA contract no 20, with its provision for arbitration in London.[461]

The two examples given so far involved a breach of an agreement on **4.180**
arbitration contained in a contract for the international sale of goods. *Sohio
Supply Co v Gatoil (USA) Inc*[462] is a simple example involving the breach of
an exclusive jurisdiction clause contained in such a contract. The Court
of Appeal affirmed the first instance decision to grant Delaware registered
sellers an injunction restraining Delaware registered, but carrying on
business in Texas, buyers of barrels of Brent crude oil FOB Sullom Voe
from proceeding in the Texan courts in breach of an exclusive jurisdiction
clause providing for trial in England. This was one of the earlier cases of
the English courts granting an injunction restraining foreign proceedings.

---

[458] The case raised a number of points in relation to the Brussels Convention, namely in
relation to the arbitration exclusion in Art 1(4) (discussed above, para 3.03) and *lis pendens*
under Art 21 (discussed above, para 3.324). It was also held that the present proceedings for
injunctive relief to enforce the arbitration clause fell outside the scope of an English exclusive
jurisdiction clause in the contract.

[459] This is quoted above, para 3.04.

[460] This is quoted above, para 3.28.

[461] *Tracomin SA v Sudan Oil Seeds Co Ltd* [1983] 1 WLR 1026, CA.

[462] [1989] 1 Lloyd's Rep 588, CA.

Where the Pursuit of the Proceedings Abroad would be Vexatious or Oppressive

The principles to be applied when exercising the discretion

4.181 The grant of an injunction on this ground is a particular application of the broad principle underlying the jurisdiction to grant an injunction restraining foreign proceedings, namely that this is to be exercised where the ends of justice require it.[463] When discussing the grant of an injunction on this ground it is important to distinguish two different situations. The first is where there are two or more available fora for trial, one of which is England. The second is where trial is available in alternative fora abroad, but not in England.

4.182 **There are two or more available fora for trial (one of which is England)** The leading authority on this situation is the decision of the Privy Council in *Société Nationale Industrielle Aerospatiale v Lee Kui Jak*,[464] which was approved by the House of Lords in the *Donohue* case.[465] Lord Goff in the *SNIA* case, said that 'in a case such as the present where a remedy for a particular wrong is available both in the English court and in a foreign court, the English . . . court will, generally speaking, only restrain the plaintiff from pursuing proceedings in the foreign court if such pursuit would be vexatious or oppressive'.[466]

4.183 An example of *prima facie* oppression is where the claimant brings an action in a clearly inappropriate forum in circumstances where there are two appropriate fora for trial.[467] Requiring the defendant to fight in two different jurisdictions can amount to substantial injustice.[468] Other examples of substantial injustice are where: a party is prevented from properly presenting his case; the foreign court is misled; a party is forced to incur expense not apparently connected with the case;[469] and where a claim abroad is brought in bad faith, or is doomed to fail.[470] The vexation or oppression test generally presupposes that the English court has first concluded that it provides the natural forum for trial.[471]

4.184 **Trial is available in alternative fora abroad (but not in England)** This was the situation that arose in *Airbus Industrie GIE v Patel*,[472] where the House of Lords held that the grant of an injunction in such circumstances

---

[463] The *Airbus Industrie* case, n 434 above, at 133; the *Turner* case, n 428 above, at [24].
[464] [1987] AC 871.   [465] n 435 above, at [19]–[21].
[466] The *SNIA* case, n 464 above, at 896.
[467] *Airbus Industrie GIE v Patel* [1997] 2 Lloyd's Rep 8, CA; reversed by the House of Lords but not on this point.
[468] *SCOR v Eras EIL (No 2)* [1995] 2 All ER 278.
[469] *FMC Corp v Russell* 1999 SLT 99 at 102.   [470] The *SCOR* case, n 468 above.
[471] The *Société Aerospatiale* case, n 464 above, at 896.   [472] [1999] 1 AC 119.

is inconsistent with comity. The English courts had no interest in, or connection with, the matter in question to justify such interference. This was despite the fact that the natural forum for trial was India, the courts of which were unable to grant effective relief in respect of the English defendants, whereas the English courts could grant effective relief to prevent the pursuit of proceedings in Texas which might properly be regarded as oppressive.

Application to contracts for the international sale of goods

There are two or more available fora for trial (one of which is England)   **4.185** When an English court is ascertaining whether England is the natural forum for trial the typical considerations in an international sale of goods case (the place of delivery of the goods, the place of payment for the goods, the place where the sales contract was made, the law applicable to the sales contract, the availability of witnesses, the residence of the parties, a multiplicity of proceedings)[473] will apply. When it comes to the central issue of whether the pursuit of proceedings abroad would be vexatious or oppressive it is going to be as difficult to show this in a case involving the international sale of goods as in any other case.

Trial is available in alternative fora abroad (but not in England)   The **4.186** position is the same for contracts for the international sale of goods as for any other type of contract and no special comment is needed.

Where the Bringing of the Proceedings Abroad would be Unconscionable for Some Other Reason

The principles to be applied when exercising the discretion

The English courts can grant an injunction restraining foreign pro-   **4.187** ceedings 'if the bringing of the suit in the foreign court is in the circumstances so unconscionable that in accordance with our principles of a "wide and flexible" equity it can be seen to be an infringement of an equitable right of the applicant'.[474] Lord Hobhouse in *Turner v Grovit* regarded this as the umbrella category that embraced the two categories that have already been described.[475] There is therefore a residual category where the bringing of the proceedings abroad is unconscionable for some other reason than a breach of an agreement or vexation or oppression. There are very few reported cases where it has been possible to show this.[476] One instance is where the effect of the unconscionable conduct is to

---

[473] Discussed above, paras 4.120–150.

[474] *British Airways Board v Laker Airways Ltd* [1985] AC 58 at 95. See also *South Carolina Insurance Co v Assurantie NV* [1987] AC 24.

[475] n 428 above at [24], [25] and [27].

[476] There is *Midland Bank plc v Laker Airways Ltd* [1986] QB 689, CA.

create an abuse of process.[477] This will be so where the defendants have in bad faith commenced and propose to prosecute proceedings against the applicant in another jurisdiction for the purpose of frustrating or obstructing the proceedings in England.[478] Caution is said to be necessary in cases where the court is being asked to restrain the proceedings in the only state in which the claimant can obtain a remedy.

Application to contracts for the international sale of goods

4.188 There is no reported case of unconscionability that has arisen in the context of the international sale of goods. In *Toepfer v Société Cargill*,[479] Phillips LJ in the Court of Appeal said that the defendants had done nothing intrinsically unconscionable in commencing proceedings in France.[480] The only ground on which objection could be made to their conduct was that it conflicted with the defendants' contractual agreement to arbitrate.[481]

---

[477] The *Turner* case, n 428 above, at [24] (*per* Lord Hobhouse).
[478] The *Turner* case, n 428 above.   [479] n 456 above.   [480] ibid, at 384.   [481] ibid.

5

Transfer of Contractual Rights and Obligations: Jurisdiction

I. INTRODUCTION

We are concerned in this chapter with jurisdictional problems arising out **5.01** of the transfer of contractual rights and obligations between the seller and buyer. The best example of this is with a CIF contract.[1] This is a documentary sale, which means that the seller undertakes no duty physically to deliver to the buyer or buyer's agent.[2] Nor does the seller normally

---

[1] On which see generally Bridge, *The International Sale of Goods* Ch 5.

[2] Which the seller in an FOB contract does, the carrier being presumptively the buyer's agent.

guarantee that the goods will be delivered at destination or the buyer undertake to pay conditionally on this event. Instead, the seller tenders to the buyer a bill of lading (or other transport document) and insurance policy (or other insurance document). The purpose of the bill of lading is, when transferred to the buyer, to give the buyer the documentary equivalent of the goods themselves.[3] The bill also provides evidentiary assurance that the seller has complied with his documentary responsibilities under a CIF contract[4] and with his statutory duty to enter into a reasonable contract of carriage.[5] It is a document of title.[6] This means that the holder may demand the goods from the carrier without the carrier, as other bailees could do, being able to say that its duty is to deliver to someone else. Under English law, the transfer of the bill also serves to transfer contractual rights under the contract of carriage to the buyer. It is also instrumental in transferring duties.[7] Again under a CIF contract, the seller transfers the insurance policy to the buyer. Under English law the transfer is effected under the Marine Insurance Act 1906 and operates as a type of statutory assignment. CIF contracts are unworkable without these arrangements.

5.02 Let us assume that the bill of lading has been transferred to the buyer, who has subsequently taken delivery of the goods from the carrier. There has been short delivery or the goods have been damaged. The buyer wishes to sue the carrier under the contract of carriage. Let us also assume that this raises a jurisdictional problem, for example the carrier is domiciled in a different state from the buyer.[8] This is to be solved by the application of the EC rules contained in the Brussels I Regulation[9] or the traditional English rules on jurisdiction.[10] When applying these rules, what jurisdictional problems are raised by the fact that the buyer is a third party to the original contract of carriage made between the seller and the carrier? This chapter will set out to answer this question.[11]

---

[3] See *Sanders Bros v Maclean & Co* (1883) 11 QBD 327, 341.

[4] *Soon Hua Geng Co Ltd v Glencore Grain Co Ltd* [1996] 1 Lloyd's Rep 398.

[5] Sale of Goods Act 1979, s 32(2).

[6] It is perhaps more accurate to describe it as a *potential* document of title. If certain requirements as to form are not fulfilled the bill of lading cannot be transferred (e.g. if it is a 'straight' bill). See generally *The Rafaela S* [2003] 2 Lloyd's Rep 113, CA (on appeal to HL); G Treitel, 'The Legal Status of Straight Bills of Lading' (2003) 119 LQR 608.

[7] See the Carriage of Goods by Sea Act 1992, s 2(1).

[8] The question of when a jurisdictional problem arises is discussed above, paras 1.17–1.18.

[9] The question of when the EC rules are applied is discussed above, paras 2.02–03. For application generally of these rules to bills of lading see Gaskell, 20.23–20.195. The Brussels Convention may apply in the case of a defendant domiciled in Denmark and the Lugano Convention in the case of a defendant domiciled in an EFTA State.

[10] The question of when the traditional English rules of jurisdiction are applied is discussed above, para 2.11. For application generally of these rules to bills of lading see Gaskell, 20.196–20.251.

[11] Multi-defendant actions arising out of carriage are considered below, paras 9.07–08.

II. THE EC RULES

The third party (i.e. the buyer to whom rights and obligations have been **5.03** transferred by the seller) is able to sue the carrier in the Member State in which he is domiciled by virtue of Article 2 of the Brussels I Regulation or by virtue of Article 5(5) in a Member State in which the carrier has a branch etc. The fact that the plaintiff was a third party to the original contract of carriage made between the seller and the carrier does not create any difficulty in using these particular bases of jurisdiction. However, this does create a problem if the third party wishes to rely under Article 23 on a choice of jurisdiction clause in the bill of lading, or indeed if the carrier wishes to rely on such a clause to avoid being sued by the third party in a particular Member State. It also creates a problem in cases where there is no choice of jurisdiction agreement under Article 23 of the Regulation and the third party seeks to rely on Article 5(1) so as to be able to sue in a Member State other than the one in which the defendant was domiciled. Attention will therefore focus on the application of Articles 23 and 5(1).

1. DIFFICULTIES FOR THE PARTIES IN RELYING ON CHOICE OF JURISDICTION AGREEMENTS

Jurisdiction Clauses in Bills of Lading Generally

Bills of lading will almost invariably contain a choice of jurisdiction **5.04** clause.[12] The bill of lading normally will be issued by the carrier,[13] signed by the ship's master or agent, and will contain the standard terms and conditions laid down by the carrier. The choice of jurisdiction clause will therefore provide for trial in the carrier's home state. The clause may be worded in terms that: 'Any dispute arising under this bill of lading shall be decided in the country where the carrier has his principal place of business'. This is the wording used in the Conlinebill,[14] which is in regular use by carriers contracting on liner terms. Essentially the same wording is

---

[12] See for a rare example of where there was no foreign or English jurisdiction clause, *The Polessk and Akademik Iosif Orbeli* [1996] 2 Lloyd's Rep 40.

[13] The 'carrier' could be the actual registered shipowner, the charterer (time charterer or voyage charterer)—in which case it is customary to refer to him as the disponent owner. Equally the 'carrier' may be the demise charterer. There are many cases where the bill of lading is issued not by the shipowner but by charterers, pursuant to their right to do so under a given charterparty. On the question whether the bill is an owners' or a charterers' bill see *The Starsin* [2003] UKHL 12, [2004] AC 715; discussed below, para 14.38.

[14] cl 3. This and many other standard form jurisdiction clauses are set out in Gaskell, 589–592.

also to be found in Combiconbill (as revised 1995).[15] The use of the term 'principal place of business' raises a definitional problem but we have authority in the context of ascertaining the domicile of a company on the meaning of this phrase.[16] Alternatively the carrier may directly name a country where disputes are to be tried. This will be the country where the carrier is based (has its seat, principal place of business or is managed). Thus an English carrier will provide that disputes shall be 'determined by the High Court of Justice in London',[17] a Japanese carrier for trial 'before the Tokyo District Court in Japan',[18] a German carrier for trial before the Hamburg courts[19] and so on.

5.05 The question of whether an agreement on jurisdiction contained in a bill of lading satisfied the requirements of the predecessor of Article 23 of the Brussels I Regulation (Article 17 of the Brussels Convention) came before both the European Court of Justice and national courts on a number of occasions. In particular, questions have arisen as to whether the formal requirement under Article 17 of the Brussels Convention had been met.[20] As interesting as these questions are, what this chapter is primarily concerned with is the position of a third party holder of the bill of lading (i.e. the buyer under a CIF contract), which is what will now be considered.

The Position of a Third Party Holder of the Bill of Lading

Is a third party holding the bill of lading bound by the jurisdiction clause?
Can the third party rely on the jurisdiction clause?

5.06 This question commonly arises because of the practice whereby a bill of lading entered into by the shipper (seller) and carrier and containing a valid choice of jurisdiction clause is subsequently transferred to a consignee or indorsee. In such a case, the bill of lading, initially evidence of the contract of carriage between shipper and carrier,[21] becomes conclusive evidence of that contract as between carrier and subsequent holder of the bill.[22] Let us assume that this third party to the original contract between the shipper and carrier, who is now the holder of the bill of lading, wishes

---

[15] cl 5.

[16] See above, paras 3.12–14. The Court of Appeal in *The Rewia* [1991] 2 Lloyd's Rep 325 assumed that the same definition would apply in the context of a jurisdiction clause using this term as under Art 2. Difficult questions of fact may then arise as to whether the definition is satisfied, see *The Blue Wave* [1982] 1 Lloyd's Rep 151.

[17] Ellerman, cl 24(2).

[18] The 'K' Line Bill of Lading, cl 3.   [19] The Hapag-Lloyd Bill of Lading 1996, cl 25.

[20] Case 71/83 *Partenreederei ms Tilly Russ v Haven & Vervoerbedrijf Nova* [1984] ECR 2417, [1985] QB 931; Case C-159/97 *Trasporti Castelletti Spedizioni Internazionali SpA v Hugo Trumpy SpA* [1999] ECR I-1597. For an English decision see *OT Africa Line Ltd v Hijazy (The Kribi)* [2001] 1 Lloyd's Rep 76. The formal requirement under Art 23 of the Brussels I Regulation is discussed above, paras 3.43–59.

[21] *The Ardennes* [1951] 1 KB 55.   [22] *Leduc v Ward* (1888) 20 QBD 475.

to sue the carrier for short delivery or for damage in respect of the goods delivered in his (the third party's) home state, using Article 5(1) of the Brussels I Regulation. However, the bill of lading, as is very commonly the case, is on carrier's terms and contains a choice of jurisdiction clause providing for trial exclusively in the carrier's home state. Is the third party holding the bill of lading bound by the jurisdiction clause and thus precluded from suing in his home state? Alternatively, and this is going to be rarer, it is the third party who wishes to rely on the jurisdiction clause so as to found jurisdiction. For example, the original contract of carriage unusually was made on the shipper's terms and provides for trial in the shipper's home state and the third party also comes from this state. Can the third party holding the bill of lading rely on the jurisdiction clause?

The European Court of Justice in *Partenreederei ms Tilly Russ v Haven &* **5.07** *Vervoerbedrijf Nova*[23] held that the conditions laid down by Article 17 of the Brussels Convention were satisfied if the jurisdiction clause had been adjudged valid as between the carrier and the shipper and if, by virtue of the relevant national law, the third party, upon acquiring the bill of lading, succeeded to the shipper's rights and obligations.[24] The need for the third party to succeed by virtue of the relevant national law to the shipper's rights and obligations was confirmed by the European Court of Justice in *Coreck Maritime GmbH v Handelsveem BV*,[25] where one of the questions referred to the Court was whether a jurisdiction clause which has been agreed between a carrier and a shipper and appears in a bill of lading is valid as against any third party bearer of the bill of lading, or whether it is only valid as against a third party bearer of the bill of lading who succeeded by virtue of the applicable national law to the shipper's rights and obligations when he acquired the bill of lading. The Court answered this in favour of the second alternative. If the third party bearer of the bill of lading succeeded by virtue of the applicable law to the shipper's rights and obligations when he acquired the bill of lading there is no need to ascertain whether he accepted the jurisdiction clause in the original contract.[26] The third party becomes vested with all the rights and obligations mentioned in the bill of lading including those relating to the agreement on jurisdiction.[27]

---

[23] n 20 above.

[24] Compare the position for choice of law clauses, see below, paras 14.60–63.

[25] Case C-387/98 [2000] ECR I-9337. See also *Siboti K/S v BP France SA* [2003] 2 Lloyd's Rep 364—application of this principle to a jurisdiction clause incorporated into a bill of lading by reference to a charterparty.

[26] The *Coreck* case, n 25 above, para 25. Compare the attitude of the ECJ towards the use of Art 5(1) of the Brussels Convention, see below, paras 5.21–26. Contrast the choice of law position, see below, paras 14.60–67.

[27] The *Coreck* case, n 25 above.

5.08   However, if, under the applicable national law, the party not privy to the original contract did not succeed to the rights and obligations of one of the original parties, the court seised must ascertain, having regard to the requirements laid down in the first paragraph of what is now Article 23, whether he actually accepted the jurisdiction clause relied on against him.[28] The question whether a party not privy to the original contract has succeeded to the rights and obligations of one of the original parties must be determined according to the applicable national law.[29] According to the European Court of Justice, the question of which national law is applicable is not one of interpretation of the Brussels Convention; it falls within the jurisdiction of the national court which must apply its rules of private international law to determine the applicable national law.[30] The Court refused to say what rules of substantive law apply in the event that the applicable national law provides no solution as to whether the third party upon acquiring the bill of lading succeeds to the shipper's rights and obligations, this not being a question of interpretation of the Convention.[31] The Court also pointed out that this was a hypothetical question. English law provides a solution in the Carriage of Goods by Sea Act 1992, s 2 (1) of which provides that a person who is the lawful holder of a bill of lading, the identified consignee in a sea waybill, or the person entitled to delivery of goods to which a delivery order relates, has the right to sue the carrier under the contract of carriage[32] 'as if he had been a party to that contract'. The lawful holder[33] of a bill of lading will succeed to the rights and liabilities of the shipper and will therefore be bound by a choice of jurisdiction clause in the bill of lading.[34] Under English law insurers may also succeed to the rights and liabilities of the shippers and they too will then take the benefit and burden of all the contract terms including the jurisdiction clause.[35]

5.09   In both the *Tilly Russ* and *Coreck* cases, the question on the facts was whether the plaintiff third party was bound by a jurisdiction clause in a contract to which he was not a party. As will very commonly be the case, it was the carrier who sought to rely on the clause to avoid trial in the plaintiff's preferred forum. What was involved therefore was the transfer

---

[28] ibid, para 26; *Hapag Lloyd Container Line GmbH v La Réunion Européenne* [2003] IL Pr 51, French Cour de cassation. Regard must be had to the formalities under Art 23(1) of the Brussels I Regulation. In *Astilleros Zamakona SA v MacKinnons* 2002 SLT 1206, Lord Macfadyen held that there was no need to seek direct evidence of consensus in the situation where the third party evinced consent by seeking to rely on the exclusive jurisdiction clause in a shipbuilding contract and the pursuers (a party to the original contract) consented to the clause and to its application to any further agreement that became part of the original contract.
[29] [2000] ECR I-9337, para 24.   [30] ibid, para 30.   [31] ibid, para 31.
[32] i.e. it is a contractual claim.   [33] On which see *The Berge Sisar* [2002] 2 AC 205, HL.
[34] *The Kribi*, n 20 above, at 90.   [35] ibid.

to the third party of the shipper's obligation of being subject to trial in the forum agreed in the contract of carriage. However, the European Court of Justice made no distinction between the transfer of rights and obligations. The Court referred to the third party bearer of the bill of lading who has succeeded by virtue of the applicable law to the shipper's rights and obligations. If a case were to arise where the third party seeks to rely on a jurisdiction clause the principles set out in the *Tilly Russ* and *Coreck* cases would apply equally to the facts of the case.[36]

Validity of the jurisdiction agreement and third parties

One of the requirements for the operation of Article 23 as a basis of juris- **5.10** diction is that one or more of the parties is domiciled in a Member State.[37] If either the shipper or carrier is so domiciled and the dispute is as between these two contracting parties then clearly this requirement is met. But the position is more complicated if the dispute is between the third party holder of the bill of lading and the carrier. The European Court of Justice in the *Coreck* case held that 'the validity of a jurisdiction clause under Article 17 of the [Brussels] Convention must be assessed by reference to the relationship between the parties to the original contract'.[38] This means that at least one of the parties to the original contract must be domiciled in a Member State.[39] It follows that, provided that the shipper or carrier is domiciled in a Member State, this requirement has been met and it does not matter that the third party holder of the bill of lading, who has succeeded to the shipper's rights and obligations, is not so domiciled.[40] Conversely, where neither the shipper nor the carrier is domiciled in a Member State this domicile requirement has not been met, even though the third party holder of the bill of lading, who has succeeded to the shipper's rights and obligations, is domiciled in a Member State.[41]

---

[36] In the situation where, under the applicable national law, the party not privy to the original contract did not succeed to rights and obligations, the consensus of the third party can be shown by the fact that it seeks to rely on the jurisdiction clause: see *Astilleros Zamakona SA v MacKinnons* 2002 SLT 1206.

[37] Where the agreement is concluded by parties, none of whom is domiciled in a Member State, the courts of other Member States shall have no jurisdiction over their disputes unless the court or courts chosen have declined jurisdiction: Art 23(3).

[38] n 25 above, para 20. This follows the *Tilly Russ* case, n 20 above, para 24 and the *Trumpy* case, n 20 above, paras 41–42.

[39] The *Coreck* case, n 25 above, para 21. This is supported by Art 23(3) of the Brussels I Regulation which refers to parties to the [jurisdiction] agreement none of whom is domiciled in a Member State.

[40] See also North, [1985] LMCLQ 177 at 179.

[41] See also the opinion of AG Slynn in *The Tilly Russ*, n 20 above, at 2440; North, ibid, at 179. Contrast the position as regards choice of law, see the discussion of Art 3(3) of the Rome Convention, below, paras 13.99–102.

The wording of the clause

5.11 Article 23 requires the parties to 'have agreed' that a court or the courts of a Member State are to have jurisdiction. There is a risk that the third party, who does not need to have consented to the agreement on jurisdiction, will be unable to identify the court having jurisdiction from the wording alone. Indeed, there is doubtless more of a risk of this with a third party than there is of the shipper being unable to identify this court. This raises the question of how precise the wording of the jurisdiction clause must be, which is a different question from that of whether there is consent. Must the jurisdiction clause be formulated in such a way that it is possible to identify the court having jurisdiction on its wording alone? This was essentially one of the questions referred to the European Court of Justice in the *Coreck* case, which concerned an action between the third party holder of the bill of lading and the carrier. In that case, the jurisdiction clause in the bill of lading provided for trial in the country 'where the carrier has his principal place of business'. Such wording could be said to be imprecise in two respects. First, it refers to the principal place of business. There are however, numerous decisions of the European Court of Justice where this formulation has been used and not held to be invalid on the ground of imprecision.[42] Second, it refers to the carrier. As is well known, it is sometimes difficult to determine the identity of the carrier.[43] The legal carrier is the person with whom the contract of carriage is concluded but the actual carrier may be different from the legal carrier.[44] In the *Coreck* case, the Rechtbank Rotterdam took the view that there were two possible carriers,[45] hence the need to decide the question of how precise the wording of the jurisdiction clause must be. The European Court of Justice held that it was not necessary for the jurisdiction clause to be formulated in such a way that it is possible to identify the court having jurisdiction on its wording alone.

It is sufficient that the clause state the objective factors on the basis of which the parties have agreed to choose a court or the courts to which they wish to submit disputes which have arisen or which may arise between them. Those factors, which must be sufficiently precise to enable the court seised to ascertain whether it

---

[42] See, e.g. Case 784/79 *Porta-Leasing GmbH v Prestige International SA* [1980] ECR 1517; Case 201/82 *Gerling Konzern Speziale v Amministrazione Del Tesoro Dello Stato* [1983] ECR 2503; Case 48/84 *Spitzley v Sommer Exploitation SA* [1985] ECR 787; Case 22/85 *Anterist v Crédit Lyonnais* [1986] ECR 1951; Case C-214/89 *Powell Duffryn PLC v Petereit* [1992] ECR I-1745.

[43] See Schmitthoff, 15–051; S Boyd, A Burrows and D Foxton (eds), *Scrutton on Charterparties and Bills of Lading* (20th edn, London: Sweet & Maxwell, 1996), 80. See also the discussion above, para 5.04, and in detail below, paras 14.38–45.

[44] ibid.

[45] An approach rejected by the House of Lords in *The Starsin* [2003] UKHL 12, [2004] AC 715.

has jurisdiction, may, where appropriate, be determined by the particular circumstances of the case.[46]

A clause conferring jurisdiction on the court 'most familiar with maritime law' would be invalid because of its imprecise nature, the criterion being subjective.[47] What happens in the situation where there are two carriers, as, for example, where there is a contracting carrier and a performing carrier? Advocate General Alber said that:

it is for the national court to establish whether it is clear from the bill of lading[48] who, for the purposes of the bill of lading . . . is to be deemed the carrier. If that cannot be determined or if there is more than one carrier for the purposes of the bill of lading, the clause must indeed be regarded as invalid.[49]

Formalities

It has been seen that if the third party bearer of the bill of lading has **5.12** succeeded by virtue of the applicable law to the shipper's rights and obligations when he acquired the bill of lading there is no need to ascertain whether he accepted the jurisdiction clause in the original contract.[50] What of the formal requirement under Article 23? It may be that the contract of carriage between the shipper and the carrier satisfies this formal requirement because it is in a form which accords with practices which the parties have established between themselves or there are usages in international trade or commerce known to the parties etc. In contrast, the contractual relationship between the third party holder of the bill of lading and the carrier does not satisfy the formal requirement since they have not established any such practices. It is more difficult to say whether there are any such usages known to the parties within Article 23(1)(c). It is arguable that the indorsement and delivery of the carrier's bill to the subsequent holder would come within this provision. In other words, this is an implied agreement in a form which accords with a usage of which the parties are or ought to have been aware and which in such trade or commerce is widely known to, and regularly observed by, the parties to this type of agreement. Does the fact that the formal requirement has been satisfied under the contract between the shipper and carrier mean that it is also automatically satisfied as between third party, who in acquiring the bill of lading has succeeded to the rights and obligations of the shipper, and carrier? In *Trasporti Castelletti Spedizioni*

---

[46] n 25 above, para 15.   [47] n 25 above, para A33 (*per* AG Alber).
[48] Art 10(1)(a) of the Rome Convention, discussed below, paras 13.157–158, provides that interpretation of a contract is governed by the law applicable to the contract. See also below, paras 14.38–44.
[49] The *Coreck* case, n 25 above, para A35 (*per* AG Alber).   [50] ibid.

Internazionali SpA v Hugo Trumpy SpA,[51] Advocate General Leger answered this question in the affirmative.[52] This is consistent with the position whereby the third party does not need to have accepted the jurisdiction clause in the bill of lading contract.

5.13 The same question has arisen in the context of an insurance contract and has also been answered in the affirmative. According to the European Court of Justice in *Gerling Konzern Speziale Kreditversicherung AG v Amministrazione del Tesoro dello Stato,*[53] a third party beneficiary is entitled to rely on a choice of jurisdiction clause inserted for his benefit in a contract, which satisfied the requirement as to form, between an insurer and a policyholder, even though the third party had not satisfied the requirement as to form. The Court pointed out that the provisions on insurance were designed to protect the policy holder. It would be pointless to require a third party to go through these formalities;[54] and in those cases where the beneficiary was not told of the jurisdiction clause, impossible for him to do so.

The Position of a Shipowner Whose Ship has been Chartered

5.14 The question can arise of whether a shipowner whose ship has been chartered can rely on/is bound by a jurisdiction clause in the bill of lading. This is a situation where there is no transfer of rights and duties under national substantive law and so forms an interesting contrast with the situation in the previous section.

5.15 In order to answer the question of whether a shipowner whose ship has been chartered can rely on/is bound by a jurisdiction clause in the bill of lading, two further questions arise. First, is the shipowner a party to the bills of lading? In other words, is he the contracting carrier?[55] Under English law this is a difficult question to answer, although a degree of certainty has been achieved on this matter.[56] The answer depends on whether the bills of lading are charterers' bills, evidencing a contract solely between the cargo-owners and the charterers, or owners' bills, evidencing a contract between the cargo-owners and the shipowner.[57]

---

[51] Case C-159/97 [1999] ECR I-1597.

[52] The case dealt with the situation where neither party was privy to the contract of carriage and is discussed below, para 5.18.

[53] Case 201/82 [1983] ECR 2503.

[54] Contrast the discussion of formal validity in relation to choice of law, below, para 14.88.

[55] See above, para 5.04.

[56] By the House of Lords decision in *The Starsin* [2003] UKHL 12, [2004] AC 715; noted by s Girvin, 'Contracting Carriers, Himalaya Clauses and Tort in the House of Lords' [2003] LMCLQ 311.

[57] The leading case on whether the bill of lading is a charterers' bill or an owners' bill is *The Starsin*, ibid.

Moreover, the law in other EC Member States on this matter can be different from the English law. This is illustrated by *The Rewia*,[58] where under English law the shipowners were the carriers.[59] However, under German law the sub-charterers were the carriers.[60] This choice of law problem should be answered by the application of the law governing the contract of carriage contained in or evidenced by the bills of lading.[61] If the shipowner is indeed a party to the contract contained in or evidenced by the bills of lading then clearly he can rely upon/is bound by a jurisdiction clause in those bills of lading.

The second question is concerned with the situation where the shipowner **5.16** is not a party to the bills of lading. In this situation, can he nevertheless still rely on/be bound by the jurisdiction clause? This raises an issue of privity of contract, which is for the law applicable to the bill of lading contract to determine.[62] It follows that in order to rely upon the jurisdiction clause in a bill of lading, the shipowners who are not a party to that contract, have to establish that under the law governing the bill of lading[63] they have an enforceable right to invoke that clause.[64] This reference to the relevant national law is consistent with the European Court of Justice's reference to that law when it considered the analogous position of a third party holder of the bill of lading.[65] English law, in certain circumstances, gives a shipowner who is not a party to the bill of lading contract the right to invoke a jurisdiction clause contained therein. The cases on this have arisen in the context of the traditional rules on jurisdiction in the situation where a stay of English proceedings has been sought on the basis that there is a foreign exclusive jurisdiction clause and will be examined later on in this chapter.[66]

The Position of a Shipowner Sub-Contractor

An analogous problem is that of whether a defendant shipowner, who is **5.17** a sub-contractor, can rely on a jurisdiction clause in its bill of lading contract with a carrier as against a claimant cargo-owner who entered into a

---

[58] [1991] 2 Lloyd's Rep 325, CA.

[59] ibid, at 335. There was no jurisdiction in England against the German shipowners (carriers) under Art 6 of the Brussels Convention, discussed generally below, para 9.11, because there was no good arguable claim against the English sub-charterers.

[60] ibid. Under German law the shipowners would be under a potential liability in delict.

[61] For determination of the law governing the contract of carriage see Dicey and Morris, 1401–1418; Gaskell, Ch 19; below, paras 14.09–37.

[62] See below, paras 14.77–80.   [63] ibid.

[64] The position is the same under the traditional English rules on jurisdiction, see *The Forum Craftsman* [1985] 1 Lloyd's Rep 291, CA, discussed below, para 5.63.

[65] See above, paras 5.07–08.   [66] See below, paras 5.59–68.

bill of lading contract with the carrier not the sub-contractor.[67] Under English law the position is clear. There is no contractual relationship between the sub-contractor and the cargo-owner.[68] The question then arises of whether, despite this, the sub-contractor can still rely on the jurisdiction clause. As in cases where a ship has been chartered and the shipowner wishes to rely on a jurisdiction clause in a bill of lading contract to which he is not a party, this raises an issue of privity of contract. This issue is for the law applicable to the bill of lading contract to determine. It follows that in order to rely upon the jurisdiction clause in a bill of lading contract as against a cargo-owner who is not a party to that contract, the shipowners have to establish that under the law governing that contract they have an enforceable right to invoke that clause against the cargo-owner.

Neither Party is Privy to the Original Contract of Carriage

5.18 An example would be where the dispute is between the third party holder of the bill of lading and the agent of the ship and of the carrier. This is the situation that arose in *Trasporti Castelletti Spedizioni Internazionali SpA v Hugo Trumpy SpA*,[69] where the jurisdiction clause was agreed between an Argentinian shipper and a Danish carrier but the dispute was between two parties not privy to the original contract, the third party holder of the bill of lading and the agent of the ship and of the carrier.[70] Advocate General Leger gave his opinion that the fact that both parties were not privy to the original contract did not change the basic outcome as indicated by the *Tilly Russ* case.[71] 'Article 17 of the Convention applies where the jurisdiction clause was adjudged to be valid between the shipper and the carrier, and, under the applicable national law, the third party bearer, in acquiring the bill of lading, and the agent, by virtue of his capacity, succeeded to the rights and obligations of the shipper and the carrier respectively.'[72] This involves a two stage process. First, it must be shown that the original contracting parties, i.e. the shipper and carrier, consented

---

[67] This was the issue in the case that arose under the traditional English rules of jurisdiction, *The Pioneer Container* [1994] 2 AC 324, PC; discussed below, para 5.65.

[68] ibid, at 334. That is unless it were clear, in some way, that the sub-contractor were intended to be a party. However, under the Contracts (Rights of Third Parties) Act 1999, contracts of carriage are excluded (see s 6(5)) from the ambit of s 1 (with two exceptions); see below, paras 14.116–120.

[69] Case C-159/97 [1999] ECR I-1597.

[70] As regards the agent, AG Leger said, at 1617, n 51, that it is likely that the agent is considered by the national court to be the carrier's agent and in this situation cannot be considered to be a third party to the bill of lading. It is for the applicable law to determine whether a person is a third party or not, ibid, at 1615, n 44.

[71] ibid, at 1617, para 79.   [72] ibid, at 1617–1618, para 85.

to the clause.[73] In the situation where, in order to comply with the requirement as to form, reliance is placed on 'usages in international trade or commerce' known to the parties etc, the parties can be presumed to have consented to the clause.[74] The parties whose awareness of the usage is required are those having originally concluded the clause.[75] 'Such a requirement cannot apply to each successor, of which there may be many, since a bill of lading can pass from hand to hand.'[76] Second, it must be shown that, under the applicable national law, the third party bearer, in acquiring the bill of lading, succeeded to the rights and obligations of the shipper and the agent, by virtue of his capacity, succeeded to the rights and obligations of the carrier.[77]

2. THE DIFFICULTY IN USING ARTICLE 5(1) OF THE BRUSSELS I REGULATION

Is There a Matter Relating to a Contract?

Article 5(1) of the Brussels I Regulation applies 'in matters relating to **5.19** a contract'. This requires that there is a contractual relationship freely entered into by the parties.[78] There is no difficulty in establishing this where the action in contract is between the shipper and the carrier. There is difficulty though in cases where the action is between the third party holder of the bill of lading and the carrier. There is even more difficulty in cases where the action is between a consignee and a sub-carrier. These three situations will now be examined.

An action between the shipper and carrier

In the situation where the dispute is between the shipper and the carrier, **5.20** there are no particular difficulties in establishing that there is a matter relating to a contract within the meaning of Article 5(1) of the Brussels I Regulation. In this situation, there is a contractual relationship freely entered into by the parties. There is a separate requirement that the claim is based on a particular contractual obligation, i.e. the obligation whose performance is sought in the judicial proceedings.[79] The nature of the claim will have to be examined to ensure that this is the case. Normally a dispute between the shipper and carrier will be about the

---

[73] ibid, at 1617, para 81.　　　　　　　　　　　　　　　[74] See above, para 5.12.
[75] The *Trumpy* case, n 20 above, at 1655, para 45.
[76] ibid, at 1627, para 137 (*per* Leger AG).　　　　　　　[77] See also para 14.81.
[78] Case C-51/97 *Réunion Européenne SA v Spliethoff's Bevrachtingskantoor BV* [1998] ECR I-6511. See generally above, para 3.64.
[79] See above, para 3.67.

performance of a contractual obligation. For example, typically a carrier will be seeking to enforce the performance of the shipper's obligation to pay freight charges.[80] A shipper typically will be seeking to enforce the performance of the carrier's obligations in relation to the safety of the goods entrusted to his care, such as the obligation to deliver goods to the port of destination without damage. Advocate General Colomer has accepted that a claim in relation to the latter obligation involves a matter relating to a contract.[81] Similarly, the Italian Supreme Court has accepted that a carrier's liability to the shipper in the carriage of goods by sea for the loss of those goods is contractual in nature.[82] On the other hand, Advocate Colomer went on to say that a claim by the consignee of the goods against the ship's master lay in tort.[83]

An action between the third party holder of the bill of lading and the carrier

5.21 Let assume that under the applicable national law the third party holder of the bill of lading has succeeded to the rights and obligations of the shipper.[84] One of the rights to which the third party has succeeded is the right to sue the carrier in contract in circumstances where the shipper would have had this right.[85] Similarly, because the third party has succeeded to the obligations of the shipper, the third party can be sued by the carrier in circumstances where the shipper could have been. Let us assume that the third party or the carrier wishes to base jurisdiction on Article 5(1) of the Brussels I Regulation. Does such a case come within the scope of that provision? Our discussion will begin with an examination of the relationship between the carrier and the third party holder.

5.22 **No direct contractual relationship** There is no direct contractual relationship between the carrier and the holder. English law provides that a person who is the lawful holder of a bill of lading has rights transferred to and vested in him to sue the carrier under the contract of carriage 'as if he

---

[80] Unless there is a freight pre-paid type of freight charge, which would have to be paid usually when the ship leaves the loading port.

[81] Case C-440/97 *GIE Groupe Concorde v Master of the Vessel Suhadiwarno Panjan* [1999] ECR I-6307, at 638, para 34.

[82] *Gracechurch Container Line Ltd v SpA Assicurazioni Generali* [1994] IL Pr 206, Italian Supreme Court.

[83] The *GIE* case, n 81 above, at 638, para 34. Under English law the Himalaya clause (see the discussion below, paras 14.104–115, and *Adler v Dickson* [1955] 1 QB 158) was invented to protect the master and crew from tort actions. See generally on the position of masters and other agents under English law, *Scrutton on Charterparties*, n 43 above, 44–58.

[84] For example, where a bill of lading, in negotiable form, has been endorsed to him.

[85] i.e. under the Carriage of Goods by Sea Act 1992. Such rights of suit were not transferable at common law and were only transferred with great difficulty under the Bills of Lading Act 1855.

had been a party to that contract'.[86] This accepts that the third party holder is not a party to the contract of carriage but nevertheless is to be treated as if he were. The third party also has burdens imposed on him. The arrangement under the Carriage of Goods by Sea Act 1992 is hard to classify.[87] In some respects, it looks like a novation (i.e. a new contract replacing the earlier contract). As between the shipper and the carrier, the bill of lading is merely evidence of the contract of carriage, but as between the third party holder and the carrier the bill of lading is the contract of carriage. Moreover, the terms may have altered. There appears therefore to be a new contract. But it is not precisely the same as a novation because the earlier contract does not disappear completely.[88] It is somewhat similar to an assignment. However, it is not precisely the same in that the burdens of a contract cannot be assigned. Yet the 1992 Act allows for burdens to be transferred. It is perhaps best regarded as being *sui generis*. But clearly what it is not is the creation of a direct contractual relationship between the carrier and holder. Similarly there was no direct contractual relationship between a sub-buyer of a product[89] and the manufacturer in *Jakob Handte et Cie GmbH v SA Traitements Mécano-Chimiques des Surfaces*, a decision of the European Court of Justice.[90] This was so even though, according to the French law of the forum, the sub-buyer has a contractual claim against the manufacturer which is based on the theory that the intermediate supplier transmits to the sub-buyer his contractual rights against the manufacturer (or against a previous intermediary) as an accessory of the goods.[91]

As will be seen, where there is no direct contractual relationship between **5.23** the carrier and the holder, it will be difficult, if not downright impossible, to meet the requirement for the application of Article 5(1) that there is an obligation freely assumed by one party towards another. Moreover, there may be difficulty in showing that the nature of the liability involved is contractual. If it is not, Article 5(1) will not apply.

Is there an obligation freely assumed by one party towards 5.24 another? Admittedly, the rights of suit transferred to the third party

---

[86] See s 2(1) of the Carriage of Goods by Sea Act 1992. For the way in which the contents of that contract are defined see *Leduc v Ward* (1888) 20 QBD 475.

[87] On the important implications of this classification for choice of law purposes, see below, paras 14.49–59.

[88] This is because s 3(3) of the Carriage of Goods by Sea Act 1992 provides that the liabilities imposed under s 3 on the person in whom rights are vested under s 2(1) (the holder of the bill of lading etc.) 'shall be without prejudice to the liabilities under the contract of any person as an original party to the contract'.

[89] Who was suing for defects in the product itself.

[90] Case C-26/91 [1992] ECR I-3967, paras 16 and 20. See also the opinion of AG Jacobs at para 39.

[91] See the opinion of AG Jacobs at para 20.

holder under English law are rights of suit in contract. But the difficulty that arises, regardless of how the arrangement under the 1992 Act is classified, is over the requirement that there is an obligation freely assumed by one party towards another.[92] It would appear that this requirement has not been met. This is because the carrier has not undertaken any contractual obligation towards the third party.[93] There is no direct contractual relationship between these two.[94] Any obligation that arises comes about by operation of law,[95] rather than being freely assumed by one party towards another.[96] Again it is instructive to look at the *Jakob Handte* case, which introduced the requirement that there must be an obligation that is freely entered into by one party to another. The European Court of Justice pointed out that the manufacturer 'undertakes no contractual obligation to that [sub] buyer, whose identity and domicile may legitimately be unknown to him'.[97] Accordingly, Article 5(1) of the Brussels Convention did not apply to such a case. In cases where there are successive sales of the goods being shipped, the carrier will not know, at least at the outset (i.e. at the moment of entering into the contract with the shipper), the identity and domicile of the third party holder of the bill of lading. Accordingly, the carrier undertakes no contractual obligation towards the third party holder.

5.25 Despite this, there is an argument that can be made for regarding a carrier as having freely assumed an obligation towards the third party, thereby bringing claims as between the carrier and the third party holder of a bill of lading within Article 5(1).[98] This argument is based on the mischief at which the requirement, that there be an obligation freely assumed by one party towards another, was directed. Underlying this requirement was a

---

[92] See generally on this requirement, above, paras 3.64–66. See specifically in relation to carriage, Briggs and Rees, 2.118. There is no such requirement in relation to a contractual obligation for the purposes of choice of law under the Rome Convention, see, below, paras 14.03–05.

[93] It is not sufficient to show that the shipper freely entered into a contractual relationship with the carrier. This is different from the position taken by the ECJ in relation to choice of jurisdiction agreements whereby the third party who succeeds to rights and obligations under the applicable national law does not need to have accepted a jurisdiction clause, see above, para 5.07. There, it is enough that the shipper accepted it.

[94] It cannot therefore be argued that by voluntarily entering into a contract the parties freely assume the legal incidents of the contract.

[95] Under the terms of a CIF contract in English law, the buyer must accept a transfer of a bill of lading when it and the remainder of the documents are in conformity with the contract and will have to present the bill of lading to recover the goods from the carrier.

[96] See Case C-334/00 *Fonderie Officine Meccaniche Tacconi SpA v Heinrich Wagner Sinto Maschinenfabrik GmbH (HWS)* [2002] ECR I-7357.

[97] At para 20.

[98] There would have to be an exception which would bring the carrier/third party holder situation within the freely assumed requirement, even though the carrier undertakes no contractual obligation towards the third party holder.

concern with foreseeability. Article 5(1) had to be interpreted in such a way as to enable a normally well-informed defendant to make a reasonable prediction as to the court in which he may be sued.[99] An action brought by a sub-buyer against a manufacturer was not foreseeable to the latter and was therefore incompatible with the principle of legal certainty.[100] However, a carrier does foresee vis-à-vis a third party considerably more than a manufacturer usually foresees. A carrier will contemplate from the outset that delivery will be made to a third party holder since the bill of lading will provide for delivery 'to [consignee] or order'. Moreover, normally the carrier will know from the outset the place of delivery. This will be the port of discharge named in the carriage contract. Advocate General Jacobs in the *Jakob Handte* case said that the position in that case 'might be different [and Article 5(1) would apply] if the manufacturer had known that the dealer intended to resell the goods to an end user in France and it would certainly be different if the manufacturer agreed to deliver the goods directly to the sub-buyer'.[101] In the former instance, the manufacturer would at least know where the goods would end up and therefore would be able to make a reasonable prediction that he might be sued there under Article 5(1). In the latter instance, the manufacturer would know from the outset the identity and domicile of the third party. When it comes to an action between the carrier and the third party holder of the bill of lading, the carrier will not know from the outset the identity and domicile of the third party. But *normally* the carrier will know from the outset where the goods will end up, i.e. the named port of discharge. This will be the place in a Member State that is allocated jurisdiction under Article 5(1)(b),[102] assuming that Article 5(1) is applicable. The carrier would be able to make a reasonable prediction that he might be sued in that place under Article 5(1). It is arguable that, in such circumstances, the carrier should be regarded as having freely assumed an obligation towards the third party, thus bringing the case within Article 5(1). However, when it comes to what the carrier foresees, the word *normally* is important. In the oil trade, a range of destinations is often chosen instead of a named place. The carriage contract may say, for example, 'CIF Gibraltar for orders'. This contemplates orders for an alternative destination. In such a case, there is no argument for treating the case any differently from a standard one involving a manufacturer and a sub-buyer and Article 5(1) should not apply.

[99] The *Jakob Handte* case, n 90 above, para 18.
[100] ibid, para 19.
[101] At para 29 of his opinion.
[102] Under Art 5(1)(b), in the case of the provision of services, jurisdiction is allocated to the place where, under the contract, the services were provided or should have been provided. The meaning of 'services' is discussed above, paras 3.298–300.

5.26 A principle of foreseeability can be regarded as underlying the decision of the European Court of Justice in the most recent case to discuss the freely assumed requirement, *Frahuil SA v Assitalia SPA*.[103] A guarantor (A), paid customs duties under a guarantee obtained by the forwarding agent (V). It sought reimbursement from the owner of goods (F), relying on provisions under the Italian Civil Code which gave A, as guarantor, a right of subrogation to the rights of the customs authorities and a right of recourse against the third party debtor (F). F argued that these rights were derived from rules of law and not from the guarantee. A argued that the action was contractual since the rights under these Italian provisions were the natural consequence of the contract of guarantee. The European Court of Justice pointed out that F was not a party to the contract of guarantee.[104] In this situation, there was no matter relating to a contract if F did not authorize the conclusion of the contract of guarantee.[105] In other words, the Court accepted that, even though F was not a party to the contract of guarantee, there would still be a matter relating to a contract if F authorized the conclusion of the contract of guarantee. On the facts it appeared that F instructed V to carry out the formalities of customs clearance. It was a matter for the referring court to examine the legal relationship between F and V in order to establish whether that relationship permitted V, on behalf of F, to enter into a contract such as the contract of guarantee.[106] If F authorizes the conclusion of the contract of guarantee it is going to foresee the possibility of a claim being brought against it by the guarantor.[107]

5.27 **Liability in contract**   The nature of the liability involved must also be examined. Although the nature of the liability of the carrier towards the third party holder of the bill of lading under English law should be regarded as being contractual this is not enough on its own to justify a contractual classification for the purposes of Article 5(1). What needs to be shown is that there is contractual liability under the law of the majority of Member States. It may be that in the majority of Member States there is no liability at all, whether contractual or otherwise. If this is the case, Article 5(1) should not apply. Again it is instructive to look at the *Jakob Handte* case. An additional reason given for the non-application of Article 5(1) was that, in the overwhelming majority of Contracting States, the liability of a manufacturer towards a sub-buyer for defects in the goods sold is not regarded as being of a contractual nature.[108] It was not enough that it was so regarded in France (the forum) and Belgium and Luxembourg. A

---

[103] Case C-265/02 [2004] IL Pr 11.
[104] ibid, para 25.   [105] ibid, para 26.   [106] ibid, para 25.
[107] A much narrower interpretation would be to say that the reference to V, *on behalf of F*, entering into a contract is referring to a principle of agency.
[108] See the decision of the ECJ, n 90 above, para 20.

comparative survey showed that most Contracting States did not recognize a claim at all in this situation.[109]

An action between a consignee and a sub-carrier

This situation forms an interesting contrast with that of an action between **5.28**
the third party holder of the bill of lading and the carrier in that now there
is an action involving a third party but there has been no transfer of rights
and duties. An action between a consignee and a sub-carrier raises starkly
the question whether there is a contractual relationship freely entered
into by the parties. This question was examined by the European Court of
Justice in *Réunion Européenne SA v Spliethoff's Bevrachtingskantoor BV*.[110]
Brambi, a French company, was the consignee of goods found to be damaged on completion of a transport operation by sea and land. The plaintiffs, Reunion, were insurers, who were subrogated to the rights of
Brambi, and sought compensation for the damage suffered from three
defendants:[111] RCC, a company with its registered office in Australia
which issued the bill of lading; Spliethoff's, the actual carrier of the goods
by sea (despite not being mentioned in the bill of lading), a company
whose registered office was in the Netherlands; and the master of the ship
on which the goods were carried. The plaintiffs sought to rely on the bill
of lading in their claim against not only the first defendant but also the
second and third defendants. The contractual relationships between
the various parties were by no means clear but the only relationship that
was relevant for the present purposes was that between Brambi and
Spliethoff's. According to Spliethoff's and the ship's master, the dispute
was a matter relating to a contract since the action against them was based
on the bill of lading, the document containing the transport contract. This
argument was rejected by the European Court of Justice. The Court said
that it was clear that the bearer bill of lading issued by RCC covered the
carriage of the goods by sea to Rotterdam, the port of discharge and
delivery, that it specified Brambi as the person to whom the arrival of the
goods must be notified and that it indicated that the goods were to be
carried aboard a particular ship. Spliethoff's were not mentioned in the
bill of lading. 'It must therefore be held that the bill of lading discloses no
contractual relationship freely entered into between Brambi on the one
hand and, on the other, Spliethoff's and the [ship's] master ... who,
according to the plaintiffs, were the actual maritime carriers of the
goods.'[112] In other words, Spliethoff's and the master would be third
parties in relation to any contract of transport between RCC and Brambi.

---

[109] See the opinion of AG Jacobs at para 21.   [110] Case C-51/97 [1998] ECR I-6511.
[111] The multi-defendant aspects of the case are dealt with below, paras 9.07 and 9.17.
[112] n 110 above, at 1234, para 19.

This meant that there was an absence of the contractual link required between the plaintiff and defendants. However, given that the action against Spliethoff's and the master did not fall within matters relating to a contract 'in those circumstances, it must be held that such an action is a matter relating to a tort, delict or quasi-delict within the meaning of Article 5(3) of the [Brussels] Convention'.[113]

The Place of Performance of the Obligation in Question

An action under the carriage contract

5.29   Let us assume that there is an action between the shipper and the carrier or one between the carrier and the holder of the bill of lading which, as is arguably the case, should be regarded as falling within the scope of Article 5(1). Where, under this Article, is the place of performance of the obligation in question? It has previously been argued that the concept of 'services' should be given its natural broad meaning which would encompass the carriage of goods by sea.[114] Article 5(1)(b) would therefore apply and jurisdiction would be allocated to 'the place in a Member State where, under the contract, the services were provided or should have been provided'. It is submitted that the place where, under the carriage contract, the services by the carrier were provided is the place where the goods were delivered by the carrier, ie the port of discharge named in the carriage contract.

An action under the sales contract

5.30   In the present context of the transfer of rights and obligations, there could be an action brought by the buyer against the seller for breach of the latter's obligation under a CIF sales contract to hand over the documents relating to the goods, i.e. the bill of lading and insurance policy.[115] In such a case, there is a contract for the sale of goods because what is sold are the goods rather than the documents.[116] Accordingly, Article 5(1)(b) of the Brussels I Regulation will apply.[117] It will be recalled[118] that this allocates jurisdiction to the courts for the place in a Member State where, under the contract, the goods were delivered or should have been delivered. Under a CIF contract, the seller never delivers the goods to the buyer or even to

---

[113] ibid, at 1235, para 24. The tortious aspect of the case is discussed further below, para 6.160.

[114] See above, para 3.300.   [115] See above, para 3.94.   [116] See above, para 3.150.

[117] This is subject to the fact that certain cases will fall outside the scope of Art 5(1)(b). For example, cases where the place where the goods are delivered is in a non-Member State. In such cases, Art 5(1)(a) will apply. The application of that provision to cases where the obligation is a failure to hand over documents under a CIF contract is discussed above, paras 3.272–273.

[118] See above, paras 3.176–178.

the buyer's agent. It is the carrier that delivers the goods. What the CIF seller does is to transfer the documents to the buyer. Since the documents stand in for the goods, the place where the goods were delivered or should have been delivered must refer to the place where the documents were transferred or should have been transferred.[119]

III. THE TRADITIONAL ENGLISH RULES

1. ESTABLISHING A BASIS OF JURISDICTION

The third party (i.e. the buyer to whom rights and obligations have been **5.31** transferred by the seller) is able to sue the carrier in England if he is able to serve him within the jurisdiction. The fact that the claimant was a third party to the original contract of carriage made between the seller and the carrier does not create any difficulty in using this particular basis of jurisdiction. However, this does create a problem if the third party is unable to serve within the jurisdiction and instead has to rely on service out of the jurisdiction. There are difficulties in using two of the most commonly used grounds for service out of the jurisdiction under the Civil Procedure Rules, namely where a claim is made in respect of a contract under r 6.20(5) and where a claim is made in respect of a breach of a contract committed within the jurisdiction under r 6.20(6). These difficulties will now be examined, after which something needs to be said about the relationship between establishing a contract ground for service out of the jurisdiction[120] and the need to establish that there is a reasonable prospect of success (a serious issue to be tried on the merits).

Establishing a Ground for Service Out of the Jurisdiction

The difficulties in using r 6.20(5)

The difficulties in using r 6.20(5) relate not only to establishing that the **5.32** 'claim is made in respect of a contract' but also to establishing that the contract is governed by English law or that it contains a term to the effect that the court shall have jurisdiction to determine any claim in respect of the contract.

Is the claim made in respect of a bill of lading contract? It will be **5.33** recalled[121] that, for service of a claim form out of the jurisdiction under r 6.20(5) of the Civil Procedure Rules, there is a requirement that 'a claim is made in respect of a contract'. As far as classification of claims is

---

[119] See above, para 3.185.   [120] r 6.20(5)(6) and (7) CPR.   [121] See above, para 4.29.

concerned we are dealing with the English concept of a contract.[122] A 'contract' for the purposes of r 6.20(5) of the Civil Procedure Rules does not require that there is a contractual relationship freely entered into by the parties.[123] The Court of Appeal has held in relation to a predecessor of r 6.20(5) of the Civil Procedure Rules[124] that it is necessary to assert that there is a contract and that the cause of action is based upon this contract.[125] In determining whether there is a cause of action based on a contract, regard has to be paid to the applicable law. If the law governing the contract imposes no liability there is no cause of action based on the contract.[126] Moreover, there would be no serious issue to be tried on the merits and accordingly service out of the jurisdiction would not be permissible.

5.34 A bill of lading contract is clearly a 'contract' for these purposes.[127] In contrast, a claim for non-contractual bailment on the terms of the bills of lading arising out of the same facts as a contractual claim will fall outside this provision.[128] Saville J said that it was clearly unsatisfactory that the bailment claim could not be pursued alongside other claims, particularly when this was a secondary claim and the primary claim in contract (i.e. for breach of the bill of lading contract) fell within the contract head, but, nonetheless, service out of the jurisdiction in relation to a particular claim was not permissible unless it fell within one of the listed grounds.[129]

5.35 In determining whether a claim is made in respect of a contract of carriage, it is important to pay attention to the question of who is bringing the claim and against whom it is brought.

5.36 *An action between the shipper and the carrier* The shipper and carrier are the original contracting parties and, accordingly there is no problem if the shipper brings a claim against the carrier based on the contract of carriage. This is a claim made in respect of a contract for the purposes of r 6.20(5). It is very common for a bill of lading to be signed by someone other than the shipowner, such as the master (acting as his agent) or some other shore-based agent, on the shipowner's behalf.[130] In this situation, the question may then arise of whether the shipowner is a party to the bill of

---

[122] *Youell v Kara Mara Shipping Co Ltd* [2000] 2 Lloyd's Rep 102, 116.
[123] Compare the position under Art 5(1) of the Brussels I Regulation, examined above.
[124] Ord 11, r 1(1)(d) RSC.
[125] *DVA v Voest Alpine* [1997] 2 Lloyd's Rep 279 at 287 (*per* Hobhouse LJ), 291 (*per* Morritt LJ), CA.
[126] See the discussion below, para 5.41.
[127] *Compañía Continental del Perú SA v Evelpis Shipping Corp (The Agia Skepi)* [1992] 2 Lloyd's Rep 467; *Enichem Anic SpA v Ampelos Shipping Co Ltd (The Delfini)* [1988] 2 Lloyd's Rep 599, aff'd [1990] 1 Lloyd's Rep 252, CA.
[128] *The Agia Skepi*, ibid, at 470.   [129] ibid, at 471.   [130] ibid.

lading. All that the shipowner claimant has to show for the purposes of service out of the jurisdiction is a good arguable case that he is a party to the bill of lading.[131] The court is not required to come to a final conclusion on this issue. The shipowner can show this by evidence that the person who signed was authorized to sign on the shipowner's behalf, together with the probability that it described the true state of affairs.[132]

An action by the third party against the carrier

THE POSITION OF THIRD PARTIES GENERALLY   The Court of Appeal[133] has **5.37** held that an assignee who is asserting an assigned right under a contract can obtain leave for service out of the jurisdiction relying on a predecessor of r 6.20(5) of the Civil Procedure Rules,[134] as can a transferee of liabilities who has sought relief which would have a direct effect on his liability.[135] Service out of the jurisdiction under this contract ground can be permitted where the effect of the assignment or transfer is to create contractual rights and liabilities directly between the parties to the action.[136] Following this decision, a predecessor to r 6.20(5) has also been applied to a case where the claimant had not become a party to insurance policies by a mechanism of statutory novation[137] or of statutory assignment but nonetheless had rights conferred on it by a Louisiana Direct Action Statute that were contractual.[138] The Statute conferred a statutory right to make a claim on a contract to which the claimant was not a party. It is submitted that the position would be the same if the claimant is subrogated to the position of one of the parties.

A THIRD PARTY WHO HAS THE RIGHT TO SUE UNDER THE CONTRACT OF **5.38** CARRIAGE   Under English law the third party holder of a bill of lading is not a party to the (original) contract of carriage. Nonetheless, he may still have the right to sue the carrier for breach of contract. As has previously been mentioned, s 2(1) of the Carriage of Goods by Sea Act 1992 provides that a person who is the lawful holder of a bill of lading, the identified

---

[131] *Ilyssia Compañía Naviera SA v Ahmed Abdul-Qawi Bamaodah (The Elli 2)* [1985] 1 Lloyd's Rep 107, CA.

[132] ibid, at 111.

[133] *DVA v Voest Alpine* [1997] 2 Lloyd's Rep 279 at 287 (*per* Hobhouse LJ), 291 (*per* Morritt LJ), CA.

[134] Ord 11, r 1(1)(d) RSC.

[135] The *DVA* case, n 133 above. But compare *Baytur SA v Finagro Holding SA* [1992] QB 610, CA (equitable assignee of buyer's cause of action could not automatically take advantage of an arbitration clause in an original contract of sale governed by English law, but could if it gave notice of the assignment to the seller and submitted to the arbitrator's jurisdiction).

[136] See *DR Insurance Co v Central National Insurance Co* [1996] 1 Lloyd's Rep 74 at 78, approved in the *DVA* case, n 133 above, at 287.

[137] See, e.g. the English Third Parties (Rights against Insurers) Act 1930, s 1(1).

[138] *Youell v Kara Mara Shipping Co Ltd* [2000] 2 Lloyd's Rep 102, 117. Service out of the jurisdiction was sought in relation to a claim for an anti-suit injunction.

consignee in a sea waybill, or the person entitled to delivery of goods to which a delivery order relates, has the right to sue the carrier under the contract of carriage 'as if he had been a party to that contract'.[139] The effect of the statute is to create contractual rights and liabilities directly between the parties to the action. This too is a situation where a statute confers a statutory right to make a claim on a contract to which the claimant was not a party. It follows that a claim by the third party, who has succeeded to the rights of the shipper, against the carrier should be regarded as falling within the scope of r 6.20(5).

5.39 This is confirmed by *The Agia Skepi*.[140] The plaintiffs, cargo owners and consignees, brought a claim against shipowners following short and damaged delivery of the cargo. They claimed that, by virtue of s 1 of the Bills of Lading Act 1855 (the predecessor of s 2(1) of the Carriage of Goods by Sea Act 1992), they were a party to the contracts contained in or evidenced by the bill of lading issued in respect of the cargo. Saville J held that this claim for breach of a bill of lading contract fell within the more detailed wording of Order 11, r 1(1)(d) of the Rules of the Supreme Court,[141] the predecessor of r 6.20(5). Given that the new wording is not intended to have any effect on the court's powers,[142] the position would be the same under the new wording. The plaintiffs also claimed in the alternative that, by presenting the bills of lading and taking delivery thereunder, they contracted with the defendant shipowners on the terms of the bills of lading (ie a *Brandt v Liverpool*[143] type of contract, implied where the shipowner delivered goods to a person without presentation of the bill of lading). It was held that this claim also fell within the predecessor of r 6.20(5).[144]

5.40 A THIRD PARTY WHO HAS NO RIGHT TO SUE UNDER THE CONTRACT OF CARRIAGE   The corollary to this is that, if a third party claimant is not entitled to sue the carrier, the claim cannot be brought within r 6.20(5). This is illustrated by *The Delfini*.[145] Vanol BV bought Algerian oil from S of Algeria and then sold it on to the second plaintiffs, Enichem SpA,which then sold it to the first plaintiffs, Enichem Anic SpA. Vanol BV entered into a charterparty with the defendant shipowner, a Liberian company,

---

[139] This replaces s 1 of the Bills of Lading Act 1855, which transferred the right to sue to the consignee or indorsee but was more restrictive in that it required property to have passed and that this was 'upon or by reason of' consignment or endorsement.

[140] n 127 above.

[141] It was common ground between the parties that this was so.

[142] See above, para 4.29.

[143] *Brandt v Liverpool Brazil and River Plate Steam Navigation Co Ltd* [1924] 1 KB 175. See also below, paras 14.124–125.

[144] This follows the earlier decision of the Court of Appeal in 131 *The Elli 2*, n 131 above.

[145] *Enichem Anic SpA v Ampelos Shipping Co Ltd (The Delfini)* [1990] 1 Lloyd's Rep 252, CA.

for the carriage of the oil from Bejaia in Algeria to Gela in Italy. The charterparty was governed by English law. A bill of lading was issued naming the shipper as S and the consignee as 'to order'. Phillips J, at first instance, held that the bill of lading contract was governed by English law.[146] The oil was discharged at the port of destination after an indemnity had been given to the defendant. The second plaintiffs paid Vanol BV for the oil and the first plaintiffs paid the second plaintiffs. At that time, the original bills of lading were in the hands of S and had not been delivered to Vanol BV. The shipping documents, including the bills of lading, which were generally endorsed, were subsequently sent to the second plaintiffs. The plaintiffs alleged that there was a short delivery of the oil and brought proceedings for breach of the bill of lading contract against the defendant shipowner. The case was important because it raised a common scenario: a string of buyers and sellers of bulk cargo, a short sea journey, the cargo arrives at the port of discharge before any of the shipping documents, including the original bills of lading, an indemnity is issued to enable the cargo to be discharged, the ultimate buyer wants recourse under the contract of carriage against the shipowner for short delivery or damage to the goods in transit, and the ultimate buyer is not a party to the contract of carriage.[147] The Court of Appeal affirmed the decision of Phillips J setting aside service out of the jurisdiction.[148] The plaintiffs sought to establish the right to sue as endorsees of the bills of lading under s 1 of the Bills of Lading Act 1855. This argument was rejected on the basis that the property in the cargo passed under the provisions of the sales contract and not by reason of the endorsement of the bill of lading. Accordingly, it could not be shown that property passed 'upon or by reason of' consignment or endorsement as required by this provision. Would the result be any different now that the 1855 Act has been replaced by the Carriage of Goods by Sea Act 1992, which widens the circumstances in which a third party is given the right to sue the carrier?[149] This no longer requires the property to have passed, let alone that it passed 'upon or by reason of consignment or endorsement'. What would have to be shown though would be that the plaintiffs were lawful holders of bills of lading, the persons to whom the goods were to be delivered under the terms of a sea waybill or the persons entitled to delivery of the goods under the terms of a delivery order.[150] The Court of Appeal also discussed the possibility of

---

[146] [1988] 2 Lloyd's Rep 599 at 604–605.

[147] *The Delfini*, n 145 above, at 257, CA.

[148] [1988] 2 Lloyd's Rep 599. The question of whether a third party had the right to sue in contract on essentially the same facts arose before Phillips J in *The Sirina* [1988] 2 Lloyd's Rep 613, which was decided in the light of his decision in *The Delfini*, n 145 above.

[149] This was one of the reasons why the 1992 Act was passed. See Law Com No 196 (1991), *Rights of Suit in Respect of Carriage of Goods by Sea*.

[150] s 2(1) of the 1992 Act.

an action in tort arising from the short delivery. However, this will require the claimant to have property in the oil at the time the tort is committed.[151] The Court came to the conclusion that this was not the case on the facts.[152] The tort was presumably committed at the moment of discharge of the oil[153] and at that time the claimants (technically plaintiffs as they were then known as) did not own the oil.

5.41 Saville J in *The Agia Skepi* and Phillips J and the Court of Appeal in *The Delfini* relied on English law and not that of some other state with which the facts were connected in determining whether the third party had a right to sue under the bill of lading. In both of these cases, the law applicable to the contract of carriage was English law. What would happen in a case where a foreign law is applicable to the contract of carriage and under this law the third party has no right to sue the third party but under English law he has such a right? In such a case, it cannot be shown that there is a cause of action based on a contract and therefore r 6.20(5) would not apply.[154] Moreover, there would be no serious issue to be tried on the merits and accordingly service out of the jurisdiction would not be permissible. However, if the foreign applicable law gives the third party a right to sue but does not, as English law does, classify this as contractual, this should not matter. It should still be possible to use r 6.20(5). For the purposes of service out of the jurisdiction we are concerned with the English concept of a contract.[155]

5.42 *An action by the carrier against the third party*   We are concerned here with an action brought by the carrier not against the original contracting party to the contract of carriage, the shipper, but against the third party holder of the bill of lading. The third party may not only have the right to sue under the contract of carriage but may also assume liabilities under this contract, including the liability to pay freight and demurrage. Under English law, s 3 of the Carriage of Goods by Sea Act 1992 provides that a person who is the lawful holder of a bill of lading, the identified consignee in a sea waybill, or the person entitled to delivery of goods to which a delivery order relates assumes liability when he: (a) takes or demands delivery from the carrier of any of the goods to which the document relates; (b) makes a claim under the contract of carriage against the carrier in respect of any of those goods; or (c) is a person who, at a time before those rights were vested in him, took or demanded delivery from the carrier of any of those goods.

---

[151] n 145 above, at 263.   [152] ibid.   [153] See *The Sirina*, n 148 above, at 616.
[154] *DVA v Voest Alpine* [1997] 2 Lloyd's Rep 279 at 287 (*per* Hobhouse LJ), 291 (*per* Morritt LJ), CA.
[155] *Youell v Kara Mara Shipping Co Ltd* [2000] 2 Lloyd's Rep 102, 116.

A claim based on the contract of carriage brought by the carrier against a **5.43** third party, who, according to the applicable law, has assumed liability under the contract of carriage, should be regarded as being a claim made in respect of a contract for the purposes of service out of the jurisdiction. This principle is supported by the decision of the Court of Appeal in *The Elli 2*,[156] where it was held, in the context of service out of the jurisdiction under the predecessor of r 6.20(5), that there was a good arguable case that there was a contract between a shipowner and a third party holder of the bills of lading, against whom the shipowner was claiming demurrage under the contract of carriage.[157] The contract in question was of the *Brandt v Liverpool* type.[158] This principle is also consistent with the stance adopted by the courts in the situation where the third party is claiming under the contract of carriage against the carrier.[159]

The contract is governed by English law or contains a term to the effect 5.44 that the court shall have jurisdiction It will be recalled that, in order to come within r 6.20(5), one of four alternatives must be shown. There is no particular problem in showing the first two of these, namely that the contract was made within the jurisdiction or that it was made by or through an agent trading or residing within the jurisdiction. It is when one comes to the third and fourth possibilities, namely that the contract is governed by English law or that it contains a term to the effect that the court shall have jurisdiction to determine any claim in respect of the contract, that problems arise.

The contract of carriage is governed by English law It is not uncommon **5.45** to find a contract of carriage governed by English law,[160] even though neither party is English and neither the port of loading nor the port of destination are English.[161] This can come about because of an express choice of English law as the governing law or because of an inferred choice of English law,[162] for example the bill of lading incorporates a charter party which provides that the contract is governed by English law[163]or provides for arbitration in England.[164] As will be seen later, the English courts will give effect to the parties' choice of the applicable law, subject to certain limitations on the right to choose.[165]

---

[156] n 131 above.   [157] See also *The Captain Gregos No 2* [1990] 2 Lloyd's Rep 395, CA.
[158] There are clear limitations on the use of such devices: see *The Gudermes* [1993] 1 Lloyd's Rep 311, CA.
[159] See above, paras 5.38–39.
[160] For determination of the law governing the contract of carriage see Dicey and Morris, 1401–1418; Gaskell, Ch 19; below, paras 14.09–37.
[161] See, eg, *The Agia Skepi*, n 127 above; *The Delfini*, n 145 above, the facts are given above at para 5.40.
[162] See generally below, paras 14.11–14.   [163] *The Delfini*, n 145 above, at 604–605.
[164] *The Agia Skepi*, n 127 above.   [165] See below, paras 13.99–102.

5.46 As regards the express choice of English law, many commonly used standard form bills of lading contain a clause that not only provides for jurisdiction but also for the applicable law.[166] The two provisions are linked so that the state whose law governs will also be the state whose courts have jurisdiction. For example, the Cunard Ellerman Mediterranean Container Service Bill provides that 'this Bill of lading shall be governed by English law and determined by the High Court of Justice'.[167] The Conlinebill provides that: 'Any dispute arising under this Bill of Lading shall be decided in the country where the carrier has his principal place of business, and the law of such country shall apply except as provided elsewhere herein'.[168] If the carrier has his principal place of business in England then according to this clause English law will govern the contract. In these cases where there is both an English jurisdiction clause and an English choice of law clause in the bill of lading, service out of the jurisdiction can be based on the jurisdiction clause as an alternative to the choice of law clause. Indeed, it is better to use the former because of the court's more positive attitude towards exercising the discretion to permit service out of the jurisdiction on this basis than that which is evident when the basis is that the contract is governed by English law.[169] There are, though, standard form bills of lading which contain an English choice of law clause but no jurisdiction clause.[170] In such cases, service out of the jurisdiction will have to be based on the fact that English law governs the contract.

5.47 If the contract of carriage contains an English choice of law clause can a third party holder of the bill of lading rely on this clause in order to found jurisdiction? Can a carrier rely on such a clause where his claim is against a third party holder of the bill of lading? The same two questions arise in relation to a clause in the contract of carriage providing for the jurisdiction of the English courts. This whole topic is best examined in the latter context.[171]

5.48 *The contract of carriage contains a term to the effect that the court shall have jurisdiction to determine any claim in respect of the contract* As has been seen, jurisdiction clauses providing for trial in England are not uncommon in bills of lading and are to be found where the carrier is English. However, many carriers are foreign and so any jurisdiction clause con-

---

[166] Cunard Ellerman Mediterranean Container Services Bill, cl 26; Conlinebill, cl 3; Combiconbill (as revised 1995); ANL Tranztas Bill of Lading, cl 28; Combidoc, cl 5; Hapag-Lloyd Europe—North America Services Bill, cl 27; Hapag-Lloyd Bill of Lading 1996, cl 25; P&O Containers Bill, cl 24; P&O Nedlloyd Bill, cl 24; 'K' Line Bill of Lading, cl 3; Mitsui OSK Lines Combined Transport Bill 1993, cl 25.

[167] cl 26.   [168] cl 3.   [169] See above, para 4.106.

[170] See, e.g. Shell Bill of Lading, cl 10.(A); Ellerman East Africa/Mauritius Service Bill, cl 24.

[171] See below, paras 14.60–67.

tained in a bill of lading will reflect this and provide for trial abroad in the state where the carrier is based.[172] As has been mentioned, although a bill of lading does not itself contain an English jurisdiction clause, it may purport to incorporate a charterparty which contains such a clause into the bill of lading. The question of whether a choice of jurisdiction clause has been incorporated into the bill of lading is more easily answered under the traditional rules than it is under the Brussels I Regulation. The law governing the bill of lading contract will determine whether a choice of jurisdiction clause is incorporated into the bill of lading.[173]

IS A THIRD PARTY BOUND BY AN ENGLISH JURISDICTION CLAUSE? CAN A **5.49** THIRD PARTY RELY UPON AN ENGLISH JURISDICTION CLAUSE? This former question would arise in the situation where the carrier seeks to rely on such a clause in his action brought against a third party, who would prefer trial abroad. The latter situation would arise where a third party seeks to rely on such a clause in his action brought against a carrier, who would prefer trial abroad. The latter situation is less common because carriage will normally be on carrier's terms so it will be the carrier who seeks to rely on the jurisdiction clause. It is submitted that, if under the applicable law the third party succeeds to the shipper's rights and obligations, he should be able to rely on and should be bound by an English jurisdiction clause in the original contract of carriage. In other words, the rights and obligations that the third party succeeds to include the right and obligation to sue and to be sued in an agreed state. It is well established that a jurisdiction clause imposes mutual rights and obligations;[174] this is illustrated by the fact that a person who is sued in breach of an exclusive jurisdiction clause can claim damages for this breach. As has been seen, the same principle based on succession to rights and duties under the applicable law has been applied by the European Court of Justice to this question when it has arisen in the context of the Brussels I Regulation. There is much to be said for aligning the traditional rules with the EC rules where this is possible. Moreover, the English courts have already effectively adopted this principle when deciding whether there is a claim in respect of a contract of carriage. There would then be consistency of principle in relation to different requirements for service out of the jurisdiction under r 6.20(5). It is submitted that no distinction should be drawn between a third party taking the benefit of a jurisdiction clause and having the burden of such a clause imposed on him.[175] It might

---

[172] Foreign jurisdiction clauses are discussed below, paras 5.58–64.

[173] See *Egon Oldendorff v Libera Corp* [1995] 2 Lloyd's Rep 64. The issue of incorporation in was regarded as one of material validity of the *contract* and therefore Art 8 of the Rome Convention, discussed below, paras 13.143–155, was applied.

[174] *The Mahkutai* [1996] AC 650, 666, PC.

[175] But compare the position in relation to choice of law, see below, paras 14.66–67.

be argued that, in principle, whilst the former is acceptable the latter is not. But if the applicable national law on carriage does not draw a distinction between the two, as is the case under the English law contained in the Carriage of Goods by Sea Act 1992, it is hard to justify drawing such a distinction for jurisdictional purposes.[176] Moreover, it has been seen that the European Court of Justice has made no such distinction under the EC rules.

5.50 SIGNATURE ON BEHALF OF THE SHIPOWNER   A shipowner defendant, who is being sued in England by plaintiff cargo owners or endorsees of bills of lading and who wishes not to be bound by an English choice of jurisdiction clause in the bills of lading, may claim that sub-time charterers or their agents who signed the bills of lading for the master had no authority to sign bills for the master so as to bind them (the shipowners).[177] The court will then examine whether there is such authority. In the *Vikfrost*,[178] the Court of Appeal, applying English law,[179] held that the contract contained in or evidenced by the bills of lading purported to be a contract between the shippers and the shipowners and not between the shippers and the charterers. Moreover, by implication the head charter, entered into by the charterers and the shipowners, authorized the charterers to authorize the sub-charterer to require the master to sign bills of lading or to sign them himself. This authority necessarily included authority for the sub-charterers to sign by agents.

5.51 NEITHER PARTY IS PRIVY TO THE CONTRACT OF CARRIAGE   Neither party may be privy to the original contract of carriage. For example, the dispute could be between an agent of the ship and of the carrier and a third party holder of the bill of lading. It is submitted that, in this situation, an English jurisdiction clause should bind both parties if under the applicable national law,[180] the third party, in acquiring the bill of lading succeeded to the rights and obligations of the shipper and the agent, by virtue of his capacity, succeeded to the rights and obligations of the carrier. This principle is based on that adopted by the European Court of

---

[176] See more generally Briggs and Rees, 2.89. If the applicable substantive law of carriage merely transfers rights to the third party, including the right to rely on a jurisdiction clause, there would be no objection to this. There would be no authority under such an applicable law for transferring the burden of such a clause. It is hard to envisage a national law of carriage only transferring burdens. If it did so there is an argument for saying it should not transfer the obligation to be bound by a jurisdiction clause.

[177] *W & R Fletcher (New Zealand) Ltd v Sigurd Haavik Aksjeselskap (The Vikfrost)* [1980] 1 Lloyd's Rep 560, CA.

[178] ibid.

[179] There was no discussion as to what law should be applied. However, English law expressly governed the contract contained in or evidenced by the bills of lading in question.

[180] As determined by application of the Rome Convention, discussed below in Ch 13.

Justice when faced with this situation in the context of the Brussels Convention.[181]

The difficulties in using r 6.20(6)

Rule 6.20(6) requires that 'a claim is made in respect of a breach of contract **5.52** committed within the jurisdiction'. In so far as this requires that a claim is made in respect of a contract, everything said about this concept when discussing r 6.20(5) is equally applicable to r 6.20(6). What is also required is a breach of contract committed within the jurisdiction. It has earlier been seen[182] that the breach in question may be a breach of the seller's obligation to hand over documents relating to the goods.[183] A place may be named in the CIF contract for tender of the shipping documents. If no such place is named, they must, prima facie, be tendered at the residence or place of business of the buyer.[184]

Establishing that there is a Reasonable Prospect of Success (A Serious Issue to be Tried on the Merits)

In the situation where the claimant is a third party to the contract of **5.53** carriage and does not have the right to sue the carrier,[185] there is no serious issue on the merits to be tried.[186] The claimant has no cause of action in contract. However, in principle no separate enquiry as to this aspect of the merits should be necessary because this matter should already have been raised earlier on at the stage when the claimant is trying to establish that one of the contract grounds under r 6.20 is established.[187] In this situation, there is no claim made in respect of a contract under r 6.20(5).[188] Neither is there a breach of a *contract* committed within the jurisdiction under r 6.20(6). Conversely, if the third party claimant can establish that there is a claim in contract on the basis that statutory provisions give him the right to sue, it is undeniable that he has a cause of action in contract. There is a contract but obviously there may have to be a separate enquiry into the merits in relation to this contract in order to ascertain, for example,

---

[181] See above, para 5.18.

[182] See above, para 4.74.

[183] *Johnson v Taylor Bros & Company Limited* [1920] AC 144 at 156 (*per* Lord Atkinson).

[184] ibid. See also Lord Birkenhead at 149.

[185] This may be because the applicable law does not give this right or does not give it to this particular claimant.

[186] See generally on this requirement, above, para 4.95.

[187] See, however, *The Agia Skepi*, n 127 above, where Saville J when discussing whether there was a *Brandt v Liverpool* type contract seemed to regard this as going to the merits, blurring the distinction between establishing the heads of Ord 11, r 1(1) RSC and going into the merits. However, this case was decided before *Seaconsar Far East Ltd v Bank Markarzi Jomhouri Islami Iran* [1994] 1 AC 438, HL, which made the distinction an important one.

[188] See *The Delfini*, n 145 above; discussed at para 5.40.

whether there has been a breach of this contract. Thus where the claimant is claiming short delivery of cargo then he has to establish a serious issue on the merits that there was indeed short delivery.[189]

5.54 The contract in relation to which the enquiry as to whether there is a good cause of action is made may not be the bill of lading but rather a contract on the terms of the bill of lading (i.e. a *Brandt v Liverpool* type contract). In *The Agia Skepi*,[190] the second of the plaintiffs' alternative claims was for the breach of this type of contract. It was argued by the defendants that there was nothing in the dealings between the plaintiffs and defendants to indicate that by conduct or otherwise the parties had struck a bargain to take delivery of the goods on the terms of the bills of lading, since everything that they did was wholly explicable on the basis that they were respectively performing their obligations under other contracts. Saville J rejected this argument, saying that:

> The law on what is required to create a *Brandt v Liverpool* type contract is far from clear-and since the plaintiffs have produced material to suggest that they owned the goods before the ship arrived; that they presented the bills of lading and took delivery of the goods although it was their bank and not they that were named as consignees; and that they paid for the stevedoring and taxes and dues on the cargo, it seems to me that this claim cannot be categorized as frivolous or vexatious. On the contrary, it seems to me to be a proper and serious alternative to the plaintiffs' primary claim.[191]

Forum Conveniens

5.55 The normal principles on which the discretion to permit service out of the jurisdiction is exercised, set out by the House of Lords in *Spiliada Maritime Corp v Cansulex Ltd*,[192] apply to cases of carriage of goods by sea. Indeed, the *Spiliada* case on its facts concerned a claim for breach of a contract of carriage contained in or evidenced by bills of lading. Typical factors of appropriateness that can arise in cases involving a bill of lading are as follows: the presence of a closely related contract;[193] the presence of related proceedings involving similar issues in which experience had been gained by lawyers and expert witnesses;[194] the law applicable to the

---

[189] *The Delfini*, n 127 above, at 601–602, affirmed by the Court of Appeal, n 145 above, before whom this matter was not raised; *The Sirina*, n 148 above.

[190] n 127 above.

[191] ibid, at 470.

[192] [1987] AC 460, HL; discussed above, paras 4.101–110.

[193] *The Delfini* [1988] 2 Lloyd's Rep 599—a charterparty, the terms and conditions of which applied to the bill of lading contract.

[194] The *Spiliada* case, n 192 above, at 485–486. This was referred to as the *Cambridgeshire* factor.

contract of carriage;[195] the involvement of insurers;[196] a jurisdiction agreement;[197] the availability of witnesses;[198] time bars;[199] consolidation of litigation;[200] a claim for contribution.[201]

In cases where there has been a transfer of rights and obligations to a third **5.56** party and the latter sues the carrier, or vice versa, a question arises when exercising the *forum conveniens* discretion of the weight to be attached to connections under the original contract between the carrier and the shipper. For example, what weight should be given to the fact that the shipper is resident in a particular state when he is not a party to the action between the third party and the carrier? It is submitted that the shipper's residence should be regarded as being a relevant factor. However, this factor should not be accorded much weight and certainly should not have as much weight attached to it as is attached to the third party's residence. The issue may arise of whether the third party has had rights and obligations transferred to it under the Carriage of Goods by Sea Act 1992. This is a complex area of English law which should be dealt with by an English court. It follows that, where this is the issue, the fact that English law governs the contract of carriage should be given particular weight in favour of England being the clearly appropriate forum for trial.[202]

2. DECLINING JURISDICTION

Forum Non Conveniens

There are relatively few reported cases applying the doctrine of *forum* **5.57** *non conveniens* in carriage cases.[203] This is because such cases very frequently involve a foreign jurisdiction clause and this will constitute the ground on which a stay is sought. Of course, if for some reason a foreign

---

[195] *The Spiliada* case, ibid, at 486; *The Delfini*, n 193 above.

[196] *The Spiliada* case, ibid, at 486 (*per* Lord Goff). Lord Goff referred to *Société du Gaz de Paris v Société Anonyme de Navigation (Les Armateurs Francais)* 1926 SC (HL) 13, 20.

[197] *W & R Fletcher (New Zealand) Ltd v Sigurd Haavik Aksjeselskap (The Vikfrost)* [1980] 1 Lloyd's Rep 560, CA.

[198] *Citi-March Ltd v Neptune Orient Lines Ltd* [1996] 2 All ER 545; the *Spiliada*, n 192 above, at 484–485.

[199] The *Spiliada* case, n 192 above, at 483–484.

[200] *The Citi-March* case, n 198 above; The *Spiliada* case, n 192 above, at 485. For another example of where this factor was a dominant consideration see *Aratra Potato Co Ltd v Egyptian Navigation Co (The El Amria)* [1981] 2 Lloyd's Rep 119; discussed below.

[201] See, eg, *Petroleo Brasiliero SA v Mellitus Shipping Inc (The Baltic Flame)* [2001] EWCA Civ 418 at [41], [2001] 2 Lloyd's Rep 203.

[202] See *The Elli 2* [1985] 1 Lloyd's Rep 107, 113 (*per* Ackner LJ), 119 (affirming the decision of Staughton J at first instance).

[203] See for a rare example of where there was no foreign or English jurisdiction clause, *The Polessk and Akademik Iosif Orbeli* [1996] 2 Lloyd's Rep 40.

jurisdiction clause is ineffective, for example because the shipowner who wishes to rely on it is not a party to the contract in which it is contained[204] or because it is struck out by a statutory provision,[205] then the stay will have to be on the basis of *forum non conveniens*. The normal principles on *forum non conveniens* apply in carriage cases.[206] Indeed, the leading case on *forum non conveniens*, the *Spiliada* case, was a carriage case. The typical factors of appropriateness that arise in cases involving a bill of lading have already been examined in the context of *forum conveniens* and will apply equally in the context of *forum non conveniens*. It is important to note that the defendant can neutralize possible objections to trial abroad by giving undertakings that, for example, the plaintiffs can have the same security for their claim regardless of whether the claim is heard abroad or in England, that there should be an extension of time for bringing proceedings abroad so that there will be no time bar defence available to them there, and/or that the foreign court should apply English law relating to limitation of liability including the monetary limit under that law.[207]

Foreign Choice of Jurisdiction Agreements

5.58 It has already been seen that bills of lading will almost invariably contain a choice of jurisdiction clause.[208] The English courts will very commonly be faced with a foreign exclusive jurisdiction clause. This is because many carriers will be foreign and their standard terms and conditions will provide for trial in their home state. However, cargo insurers may well be English and will want trial in England. In the situation where a third party (i.e. the buyer to whom rights and obligations have been transferred by the seller) is suing the carrier in England and has established a basis of jurisdiction, the carrier may seek a stay of the English proceedings on the ground that there is foreign choice of jurisdiction agreement. Equally it may be a case where the carrier is suing the third party in England and it is the latter who seeks a stay of the English proceedings on this ground. Both cases raise the question of who can rely on/is bound by a foreign jurisdiction agreement.

Who can rely on/is bound by a foreign jurisdiction agreement?

5.59 **A shipowner who has a direct contractual relationship with the cargo-owner** If a shipowner has a direct contractual relationship with the

---

[204] See *The Forum Craftsman* [1985] 1 Lloyd's Rep 291, CA; discussed below, para 5.63.
[205] See *The Hollandia* [1983] AC 565.
[206] See *The Polessk and Akademik Iosif Orbeli*, n 203 above.
[207] ibid, at 44.   [208] See above, para 5.04.

cargo owner, for example the cargo owner shipped goods under bills of lading signed on behalf of the shipowner, there is no question but that the shipowner can rely on a foreign choice of jurisdiction clause contained in the bills of lading[209] and is also bound by such a clause. That is assuming that it is a valid clause.

A third party holder of the bill of lading The question whether a third **5.60** party holder of a bill of lading is bound by/can rely on an English juris- diction clause has already been examined.[210] The same question arises in relation to a foreign jurisdiction clause and should be answered in the same way. If under the law applicable to the contract of carriage the third party succeeds to the shipper's rights and obligations he should be bound by and should be able to rely on a foreign jurisdiction clause contained in the original contract of carriage.[211] No distinction should be drawn between the situation where the third party seeks to rely on a foreign jurisdiction clause and that where the third party is being bound by such a clause.[212]

The position in England can be contrasted with that in France where the **5.61** Cour de cassation has held that the fact that a jurisdiction clause had been accepted by a shipper was not enough to make it possible for the carrier to rely on a foreign exclusive jurisdiction clause against a consignee who had not himself accepted it.[213]

A shipowner whose ship has been chartered This is a situation where **5.62** there is no transfer of rights and duties under national substantive law and so forms an interesting contrast with the situation of a third party holder of a bill of lading. The question of whether a shipowner whose ship has been chartered can rely on/is bound by a choice of jurisdiction clause in the bill of lading contract made between the cargo-owners and the charterer is a familiar one and has been discussed in relation to the Brussels I Regulation. This issue has actually been given far more

---

[209] *The Pioneer Container* [1994] 2 AC 324 at 333, PC.

[210] See above, paras 5.48–49.

[211] *The Blue Wave* [1982] 1 Lloyd's Rep 151 at 154. In this case, no evidence was adduced as to the content of the foreign applicable law and the normal assumption was made that it was the same as English law. See also *Standard Chartered Bank v Pakistan National Shipping Corp* [1995] 2 Lloyd's Rep 365, 371–372.

[212] See the arguments, above, para 5.49, in relation to not making this distinction where there is an English jurisdiction clause.

[213] *Insurance Company of North America v Société Intramar* [1999] IL Pr 315. It is not clear from the report whether the consignee had succeeded to the rights and obligations of the shipper so that too much should not be made of this case. The position can also be contrasted with that in relation to choice of law, see below, paras 14.66–67.

attention in the present context of the traditional rules on jurisdiction than in the EC context.[214] Two questions arise. First, is the shipowner a party to the bill of lading contract? Second, if not, can the shipowner nevertheless still rely on/be bound by the jurisdiction clause?

5.63 *Is the shipowner a party to the bill of lading contract?*   The first question that arises is whether the shipowner is a party to the bill of lading contract containing the exclusive jurisdiction clause, a question that is difficult to answer but on which a degree of certainty has been achieved under English law[215] and which may be given a different answer if a foreign law is applied.[216] It is for the law governing the bill of lading contract to determine whether the shipowner is a party to the bill of lading contract containing the exclusive jurisdiction clause. This is illustrated by *The Forum Craftsman*.[217] The plaintiff cargo-owners entered into a bill of lading contract, containing a foreign exclusive jurisdiction clause, with charterers who had chartered a ship belonging to the defendant shipowners. The defendant sought a stay of the English proceedings, relying on the foreign jurisdiction clause. The Court of Appeal turned to Japanese law, which governed the bills of lading containing the exclusive jurisdiction clause, to determine whether the shipowner was a party to this contract. It was common ground that under Japanese law these were charterers' bills and not owners' bills, evidencing a contract solely between the cargo-owners and the charterers.[218]

5.64 *Can a shipowner who is not a party to the bill of lading contract nevertheless still rely on/be bound by the jurisdiction clause?*   But what if the shipowner is not a party to the bill of lading contract? This raises the second question, can the shipowner nevertheless still rely on/be bound by the jurisdiction clause? This raises an issue of privity of contract, which is for the law applicable to the bill of lading contract to determine. It follows that, in order to rely upon the exclusive jurisdiction clause in a bill of lading, the shipowners who are not a party to that document, have to establish that under the law governing the bill of lading they have an enforceable right to invoke that clause. Thus, in *The Forum Craftsman*,[219] the shipowners were unable to rely on a Japanese exclusive jurisdiction clause in circumstances where Japanese law governed the bill of lading and under Japanese law the terms of a bill of lading, including any choice of jurisdiction clause, cannot be invoked to protect shipowners, who under Japanese

---

[214] *The Mahkutai* [1996] AC 650; *The Forum Craftsman* [1985] 1 Lloyd's Rep 291.
[215] See *The Starsin* [2003] UKHL 12, [2003] 1 Lloyd's Rep 571, HL.
[216] See *The Rewia* [1991] 2 Lloyd's Rep 325, CA; discussed above, para 5.15.
[217] [1985] 1 Lloyd's Rep 291, CA.   [218] ibid, at 295.   [219] ibid.

law are not parties to the bill, in a claim in tort brought against them by the buyers.[220]

GETTING ROUND THE PROBLEM OF PRIVITY   Let us assume that English law **5.65** governs the bill of lading contract. The doctrine of privity has proved to be so commercially inconvenient that the English courts have had to find various ways of getting round it. This has had considerable implications when it comes to who can rely on/is bound by a foreign jurisdiction clause. The Privy Council in *The Pioneer Container*,[221] applying English law,[222] used the law of bailment to get round the privity of contract problem. The plaintiff cargo-owners contracted with carriers who in turn sub-contracted with the defendant shipowners and it was the bill of lading in relation to this second contract that contained the foreign exclusive jurisdiction clause. The contract between the plaintiff cargo-owners and the carriers gave the latter authority to sub-contract the whole or part of the carriage on any terms. The Privy Council held that where goods had been sub-bailed with the authority of the owner, the obligation of the sub-bailee towards the owner was that of a bailee for reward and the owner could proceed directly against the sub-bailee under the law of bailment without having to rely on the contract of sub-bailment between the bailee and sub-bailee. A sub-bailee (the shipowners) could only invoke terms of the sub-bailment qualifying their responsibility to the owner if the owner had expressly or impliedly consented to those terms and the consent given by the plaintiffs to their carriers to sub-contract the carriage on any terms was wide enough to embrace consent to an exclusive jurisdiction clause, the incorporation of which would have been in accordance with reasonable commercial expectations. *The Forum Craftsman* was distinguished on the basis that it was a case in which the owners of the goods were seeking to enforce against the sub-bailees an exclusive jurisdiction clause in their contract (the bill of lading contract) with the bailees (the charterers), a contract to which the sub-bailees (the shipowners) were not a party, and to which they had never consented.[223] The upshot was that the shipowner could rely on the foreign exclusive

---

[220] There was an attempt to show a contract between the shipowner and the plaintiff on the terms of the Japanese bill of lading, which would include the Japanese choice of jurisdiction clause. However, this was unsuccessful because it was held that the goods were received on board the ship subject to the shipowners' terms, not the terms contained in the Japanese bill of lading that was subsequently issued.

[221] n 209 above. The case is also discussed in the context of choice of law, see below, paras 14.121–123.

[222] It is unclear whether in fact English law or Hong Kong law was being applied, n 209 above, at 335. These were regarded as being the same. Moreover, it is unclear why either law was applied when the bill of lading containing the foreign jurisdiction clause was governed by Chinese law.

[223] n 209 above, at 346–347.

jurisdiction clause and accordingly the Hong Kong Court of Appeal had been entitled to stay the Hong Kong proceedings. There are strong policy reasons, which were not lost on the Privy Council,[224] for upholding exclusive jurisdiction clauses in shipowners' standard bills of lading and allowing the shipowner to rely on these. If a ship is lost, particularly where it is a container ship, there may be numerous cargo claims brought in different countries by the different cargo-owners. This can lead to chaos, with much unnecessary expense to the parties. Exclusive jurisdiction clauses in shipowners' standard bills of lading ensure uniformity of treatment for each claim as regards the place of trial. This is commercially convenient.

5.66   Under English law another way of getting round the doctrine of privity that has been adopted in carriage cases is the insertion of a Himalaya clause[225] into the bill of lading. The clause will serve to give servants, agents and independent contractors of the carrier the benefit of exceptions and limitations in the bill of lading contract. Upon performance of the relevant duties for which they have been engaged by the carrier to act, the third parties accept the offer of exemption or limitation of liability contained in the clause. Does such a clause enable the shipowner to rely on a foreign exclusive jurisdiction clause? In *The Mahkutai*,[226] the Himalaya clause provided that sub-contractors, among others, shall have the benefit of 'all exceptions, limitations, provisions, conditions and liberties herein benefiting the carrier as if such provisions were expressly made for their benefit'. The Privy Council held that an exclusive jurisdiction clause did not fall within the scope of this clause. Lord Goff said that 'Such a clause [an exclusive jurisdiction clause] can be distinguished from terms such as exceptions and limitations in that it does not benefit only one party, but embodies a mutual agreement under which both parties agree with each other as to the relevant jurisdiction for the resolution of disputes. It is therefore a clause which creates mutual rights and obligations.'[227] The exclusive jurisdiction clause was not an exception, limitation, condition or liberty, nor was it a 'provision' since this related to provisions in the bill of lading which were for the carrier's benefit and protection, and not to a mutual agreement such as an exclusive jurisdiction clause. Neither could a bailment on terms be shown.[228] A bailment on terms including an express choice of jurisdiction clause would be contrary to express terms of the bill of lading, which included a Himalaya

---

[224] ibid, at 334–335.

[225] Named after *Adler v Dickson* [1955] 1 QB 158, CA—where the ship was the *Himalaya*—and recognized in a series of Privy Council cases. See *The Eurymedon* [1975] AC 154, PC.

[226] [1996] AC 650, PC. English law was applied even though the bill of lading was governed by Indonesian law. There was no explanation in the case of this.

[227] ibid, at 666.   [228] ibid, at 668.

clause which did not encompass a choice of jurisdiction clause. The result was that the shipowners, not being parties to the bill of lading containing the foreign jurisdiction clause, were not entitled to invoke that clause as against the cargo-owners. In the absence of that clause, the cargo-owners were entitled to bring their action against the shipowners in Hong Kong and the stay had properly been set aside in that country.

To what extent does the result in *The Mahkutai* depend on the wording of **5.67** the particular Himalaya clause used in that case? The Court of Appeal in *Bouygues Offshore SA v Caspian Shipping Company*[229] was faced with a differently worded Himalaya clause.[230] However, this made no difference. According to Hobhouse LJ: 'The judgment of the Privy Council did not depend upon a linguistic analysis . . . Lord Goff [in *The Mahkutai*] was clearly distinguishing between the effect of a Himalaya clause and the character of a jurisdiction clause . . . of its nature, a jurisdiction clause does not come within the scope of a Himalaya clause.'[231] He acknowledged[232] that it would be possible to draft a Himalaya clause which possibly had the effect of enabling a third party to rely on a jurisdiction clause but a conventional Himalaya clause as in the instant case was clearly covered by the decision in *The Mahkutai*.[233]

A shipowner sub-contractor   The same question arises as was examined **5.68** under the Brussels I Regulation of whether a defendant shipowner who is a sub-contractor can rely on a jurisdiction clause in its bill of lading contract with a carrier as against a claimant cargo-owner who entered into a bill of lading contract with the carrier not the sub-contractor. As has been seen, under English law there is no contractual relationship between the sub-contractor and the cargo-owner.[234] In order to rely upon an exclusive jurisdiction clause in a bill of lading contract as against a cargo-owner who is not a party to that contract, the shipowners would have to establish that under the law governing that contract they have an enforceable right to invoke that clause against the cargo-owner. *The Pioneer Container*[235] shows that, if English law governs the bill of lading contract, the shipowners may have such a right by virtue of the law of bailment.[236] It may also be possible, although not easy, to draft a Himalaya clause to provide this right.

---

[229] [1997] IL Pr 472, CA.
[230] It stated that 'all exceptions, exemptions, defences, immunities, limitations of liability, indemnities, privileges and conditions granted or provided by this Agreement shall apply to and for the benefit of all parties performing services within the scope of this Agreement'.
[231] n 229 above, at 476.   [232] ibid.
[233] See further the discussion of choice of law clauses below, paras 14.104–115.
[234] *The Pioneer Container*, n 209 above, at 334.   [235] ibid.
[236] See *The Starsin* [2003] UKHL 12 at [132]–[136] (*per* Lord Hobhouse), [2004] AC 715. Also *East West v Utaniko* [2003] QB 1509, CA.

3. RESTRAINING FOREIGN PROCEEDINGS

5.69   The question of who can rely on/is bound by a jurisdiction agreement can arise in the context of restraining foreign proceedings. One of the grounds for the grant of an injunction restraining a party from commencing or continuing proceedings abroad is that this would constitute a breach of an exclusive jurisdiction agreement providing for trial in England.[237] If a third party holder of a bill of lading seeks the injunction against the carrier the question will arise of whether he can rely on an English exclusive jurisdiction clause in the original contract of carriage. The answer is the same in this context as it is in the context of whether a third party holder of a bill of lading can rely on an English jurisdiction clause for the purpose of serving a claim form out of the jurisdiction.[238] Another ground for the grant of such an injunction is that there is a breach of an arbitration clause.[239] The original contract of carriage may contain such a clause. The question will then arise of whether a third party holder of a bill of lading can rely on the arbitration clause.[240] The answer to this is the same as the answer to the question whether the third party can rely on the breach of an exclusive jurisdiction clause providing for trial in England where this is the ground for the grant of the injunction.

IV. CONCLUSION

5.70   There are difficulties in applying both the EC and the traditional English jurisdiction rules in the situation where a buyer, to whom rights and obligations have been transferred under national law, wishes to sue the carrier in contract, even though he is not a party to the original contract of carriage. The first difficulty is whether the buyer can rely on/is bound by a choice of jurisdiction clause in the original contract of carriage. The second is whether there is a matter relating to a contract/a claim in

---

[237] See above, paras 4.173–175.   [238] Discussed above, para 5.49.

[239] See above, para 4.176.

[240] See *Through Transport Mutual Insurance Association (Eurasia) Ltd v New India Assurance Co Ltd* [2003] EWHC 3158 (Comm), [2004] 1 Lloyd's Rep 206—the question of whether a claimant bringing a claim against the insurer of carrier B was bound by an arbitration clause contained in the original contract of insurance between carrier B and its insurers hinged on the nature of the right provided by a Finnish statute which allowed a direct action against carrier B's insurer when carrier B was insolvent. This was not an independent right of action, rather it enabled an injured party who has a claim against the insolvent insured to bring proceedings directly against the insurer to obtain the benefit that the insured would have been entitled to obtain under the contract of insurance. It followed that the claimant was bound by the arbitration clause. This then led to the grant of an injunction restraining the claimant from continuing proceedings abroad.

contract. As regards the EC rules on jurisdiction, the first difficulty has been surmounted by the European Court of Justice which has given proper effect to the transfer of rights and obligations by holding that if the third party bearer of the bill of lading has succeeded by virtue of the applicable law to the shipper's rights and obligations this will include those relating to the agreement on jurisdiction. In contrast, when it comes to whether there is a matter relating to a contract, it is uncertain whether effect can be given to the transfer of rights and obligations. The fact that there is no direct contractual relationship between the third party buyer and the carrier means that there is a problem in satisfying the requirement, for the application of Article 5(1), that there is an obligation freely entered into by one party to the other. If Article 5(1) does not apply, the approach towards, on the one hand, choice of jurisdiction agreements and, on the other hand, the issue of whether there is a matter relating to a contract, is inconsistent. It would be much better if effect could be given to the transfer of rights and obligations in both contexts. This, seemingly, is the position under the traditional English rules on jurisdiction. Under these rules, the position as regards choice of jurisdiction agreements lacks authority but is probably the same as that under the EC rules. What is clear is that a transfer of rights and obligations is given effect to under these rules which ensures that there is a claim in contract.

6

Torts Arising out of the International Sale of Goods: Jurisdiction

I. INTRODUCTION

6.01 In this chapter, we are concerned with the torts that arise out of the international sale of goods, in the sense that they arise directly out of the relationship between the buyer and seller. The most obvious examples of such torts are: conversion; negligent misstatement; and negligent and fraudulent misrepresentation. It is commonplace for the buyer under an international sale of goods contract to bring a claim against the seller based on one of these torts and, accordingly, there can be no question but that these are torts that arise out of the international sale of goods. A less well known example is the delict under French law which imposes liability on a 'seller' of goods for failure to sell them to the 'buyer'. It is important also to examine the tort of inducement of breach of contract. A buyer/seller under an international sale of goods contract is unlikely to bring an action against the seller/buyer for inducement of breach of contract, but he may well bring such an action against a third party. Finally, it is necessary to look at the tort of negligence. There may, for example, be a case of negligent assembly of goods by the seller which causes the buyer economic loss. Various other torts can arise following the international sale of goods. For example, if the goods cause injury there may be a claim in product liability against the producer, and, if false allegations are made in the course of trade about goods that have been sold, there may be a claim for unfair competition or even defamation. However, in none of these instances can the tort be said to arise directly out of the relationship between the buyer and seller of goods. The torts of conversion, negligent misstatement and negligent and fraudulent misrepresentation, failure to sell, inducement of breach of contract and negligence, will therefore be the ones considered in this chapter. Before examining these torts and the application of the jurisdictional rules to them, something needs to be said about jurisdiction in tort cases generally.

II. JURISDICTION IN TORT CASES GENERALLY

1. The EC Rules

Non-Specific Bases of Jurisdiction

Article 23

Sometimes the parties to the tort action will have a contractual relation- **6.02** ship. This will be the case whenever the buyer sues the seller or vice versa. If the parties have agreed that the court or courts of a Member State are to have jurisdiction to settle any disputes which have arisen or which may arise in connection with a particular legal relationship, that court or courts will have exclusive jurisdiction[1] under Article 23 of the Brussels I Regulation,[2] provided that the requirements as to form set out in that Article are met. One major question that will arise is whether the jurisdiction clause is wide enough to encompass a claim in tort. This involves a question of construction of the clause.[3] The European Court of Justice has held that 'it is for the national court to interpret the clause conferring jurisdiction invoked before it in order to determine which disputes fall within its scope'.[4] However, different countries have different rules of construction of jurisdiction clauses and so a choice of law question arises as to which country's rules of construction are to be applied. An English court should answer this question by applying the law governing the jurisdiction agreement,[5] rather than the contract as a whole.[6] Against this, it might be argued that since the claim is in tort the law applicable to the tort should determine which country's rules of construction are to be applied.[7] But this ignores the fact that the jurisdiction clause is an agreement and this has its own applicable law.

---

[1] Unless the parties have agreed otherwise, i.e. there is a non-exclusive jurisdiction clause.

[2] Art 23 is discussed above, paras 3.22–59.

[3] See generally the discussion in J Hill, *The Law Relating to International Commercial Disputes* (2nd edn, London: LLP, 1998) 5.3.43 and 5.3.44. This question also arises in the context of choice of law, see below, paras 17.82–84 and 20.22–26.

[4] Case C-214/89 *Powell Duffryn Plc v Petereit* [1992] ECR I-17745, 1778, para 37; Case C-269/95 *Benincasa v Dentalkit Srl* [1997] ECR I-3767, 3798–3799, para 31.

[5] This will be determined under traditional common law rules; Art 1(2)(d) of the Rome Convention excludes agreements on jurisdiction from its scope.

[6] *Evialis SA v SIAT* [2003] EWHC 863 at [60]–[61], [2003] 2 Lloyd's Rep 377 and *Provimi Ltd v Roche Products Ltd* [2003] EWHC 961 (Comm), [2003] All ER (Comm) 683 support the law governing the contract approach. For the analogous question of construction as to whether a jurisdiction agreement is exclusive or not see Cheshire and North, 239.

[7] Complex questions arise at the choice of law stage of the effect of a choice of law clause in a contract between the parties on the law applicable to the tort, see below, paras 17.82–84 and 20.22–26.

6.03 The practice of the English courts is to give exclusive jurisdiction clauses, as between the parties to them, a generous interpretation.[8] The Court of Appeal in *Kitechnology BV v Unicor GmbH Rahn Plastmaschinen*,[9] had to determine whether a jurisdiction clause which stated that 'the parties hereto thereby submit to the exclusive jurisdiction of the English courts' was wide enough to cover an action for breach of confidence based on contractual and non-contractual duties of confidentiality. There was no definition of the kinds of dispute agreed to be so referred. Evans LJ, giving the unanimous judgment of the Court of Appeal said that: 'The sole question, in my judgment, is whether the clause on its true construction does include the claims or causes of action upon which the plaintiff relies'.[10] He then came to the conclusion that:

the express jurisdiction clauses in the present case include not only claims for breach of the relevant contract, but also other claims which are so closely connected with them that the parties can properly be taken to have intended that they should be decided by the same tribunal . . . But all such claims must be connected with the contract, rather than with any 'legal relationship' between the parties other than the relationship established by the contract itself.[11]

Applying this test it was decided that the English courts had exclusive jurisdiction over claims alleging misuse of confidential information obtained during a visit pursuant to a Look-See Agreement, regardless of whether the claims were formulated in contract or otherwise. The claims were based on the existence of both contractual and non-contractual duties of confidentiality. It is unclear what would have happened if the claim had been formulated solely in terms of non-contractual liability. The question would presumably still have been whether the claim was so closely connected with the contract that the parties can properly be taken to have intended that this claim should be decided by the same tribunal that would decide any claim in contract that might be brought. It should not matter that the claim in contract has not actually been brought. A jurisdiction clause may be more explicit in its coverage of tortious disputes than the one in the *Kitechnology* case and this would resolve any uncertainty in cases where the claim is brought solely in tort.

6.04 We can now turn to some of the torts that arise out of the international sale of goods. Where there are claims for breach of contract and in tort for negligent or fraudulent misrepresentation inducing the contract, it can be said that the latter claims are so closely connected with the former claims that the parties can properly be taken to have intended that they should

---

[8] *Donohue v Armco Inc* [2001] UKHL 64 at [14], [2002] 1 All ER 749. This is assuming that English law governs the jurisdiction agreement. For a case involving a foreign applicable law and foreign principles of construction see *Provimi*, n 6 above.
[9] [1994] IL Pr 560, Ch D 568.   [10] ibid, at 575.   [11] ibid, at 576.

be decided by the same tribunal.[12] If the claim is brought solely for negligent or fraudulent misrepresentation then again it can be said that this claim is so closely connected with the contract that the parties can properly be taken to have intended that this claim should be decided by the same tribunal that would decide any claim in contract that might be brought.[13]

The *Kitechnology* case[14] involved possible further claims for inducement of **6.05** breach of contract, namely that the first and second defendants procured breaches by others, or by each other, of contractual duties owed to the plaintiffs under other contracts. Thus the second defendant who was alleged to have broken a Visitors Agreement was also alleged to have induced a breach of a Look-See Agreement contract, to which he was not a party, by the first defendant. The first defendant, who was alleged to have broken the Look-See Agreement, was also alleged to have induced a breach of the Visitors Agreement, to which it was a party, by the second defendant. As far as each tort claim was concerned, the contract which it was alleged was broken was not one to which the defendant, against whom the allegation was made, was a party. Nevertheless, according to Evans LJ 'it might be argued that when two contracts are directly related to each other, then a claim in tort alleging procurement of a breach of one contract is connected with the other'.[15] Thus it might be argued that the tortious claim against the second defendant, for inducement of the breach of the Look-See Agreement by the first defendant, was connected with the contractual claim against the second defendant for breach of the Visitors Agreement (containing a jurisdiction clause). It seems to have been assumed that the two contracts, the Visitors Agreement and the Look-See Agreement, were directly related to each other. This must be right. The first of these contracts was entered into with one of the companies in the plaintiff group by an individual, the second defendant, who was interested in acquiring the right to manufacture for his company, the first defendant. This was followed a few months later, after further negotiation by the second defendant signing on behalf of the first defendant, by the Look-See Agreement with the plaintiffs.[16]

---

[12] See *Clare Taverns v Charles Gill* [2000] 2 ILRM 98 at 111—a case where English law was applicable to the contract; distinguished in *Bio-Medical Research Ltd v Delatex SA* [2001] 2 ILRM 51 at 62–64, Supreme Court of Ireland.

[13] See *Donohue v Armco Inc* [2000] 1 Lloyd's Rep 579 at 593 (*per* Stuart-Smith LJ), 600 (*per* Sedley LJ), CA; this point was not in issue in the House of Lords [2001] UKHL 64 at [14], [2002] 1 All ER 749; discussed below, para 6.114. See also *Capital Trust Investments Ltd v Radio Design TJ AB* [2002] EWCA Civ 135 at [50]–[51], [2002] CLC 787.

[14] n 9 above.

[15] ibid, at 578.

[16] It is not clear from the report which company in the plaintiff group of companies entered into the contract and this did not seem to be material.

Article 2

6.06 In the absence of exclusive jurisdiction being allocated to the courts of a Member State under Article 23, the plaintiff can always commence proceedings in tort in the Member State in which the defendant is domiciled by virtue of Article 2 of the Brussels I Regulation. This has the inherent disadvantage for the plaintiff of having to pursue the defendant abroad.

Article 5(1)

6.07 As has been seen,[17] in order for a claim to come within this provision there must be a matter relating to a contract. In the situation where the plaintiff and defendant do not have a contractual relationship, a claim brought solely in tort will fall outside this provision. The position is more complicated if the parties to the tort claim have a contractual relationship and the plaintiff brings parallel claims in contract and tort.[18] In this situation, it is not possible simply to channel the tort claim into the courts of the Member State with contract jurisdiction under Article 5(1).[19] The separate question of whether the plaintiff is also precluded from basing jurisdiction in relation to the tort claim on Article 5(3) of the Brussels I Regulation, which is concerned with jurisdiction in matters relating to tort, delict or quasi-delict, is considered below.[20]

Article 5(5)

6.08 As in a contract case, a plaintiff who brings a claim in tort may be able to sue the defendant in a place in a Member State other than the one in which the defendant is domiciled by virtue of Article 5(5). Turning to the requirements under this provision, there are no particular difficulties in tort cases in showing that the defendant has a branch, agency or other establishment in a particular Member State and what has been said earlier on this[21] need not be repeated.

6.09 However, the second requirement, namely that the dispute arises out of the operations of a branch, agency or other establishment, may cause more of a difficulty in tort cases. The European Court of Justice has held that this concept encompasses non-contractual obligations arising from the activities in which the branch etc. has engaged at the place in which it is established on behalf of the parent body.[22] However, the Court of

---

[17] See above, paras 3.62–82.
[18] See generally, above, paras 3.71–72. See also the discussion below, paras 20.07–11, dealing with choice of law aspects of concurrent claims.
[19] Case 189/87 *Kalfelis v Schroder* [1988] ECR 5565 at 5586, paras 19 and 20; *Kleinwort Benson Ltd v Glasgow City Council* [1999] 1 AC 153 at 166–167 (*per* Lord Goff), 183–184 (*per* Lord Clyde).
[20] At para 6.161.   [21] See above, paras 3.302–304.
[22] Case 33/78 *Etablissements Somafer SA v Saar-Ferngas* [1978] ECR 2183 at 2192–2193.

Appeal has denied that there is any such geographical limit, i.e. the activities in which the branch etc. has engaged do not have to be carried out at the place in which the branch etc. is established.[23] Instead what is required is 'such nexus between the branch and the dispute as to render it natural to describe the dispute as one which has arisen out of the activities of the branch'.[24] It was not thought by the Court of Appeal to be desirable to formulate any test to determine whether a tortious dispute has arisen out of the activities of a branch.[25] The answer must depend on the facts of the individual case. Turning to the torts with which we are concerned in this chapter, if, in an action for negligent or fraudulent misrepresentation, the misrepresentation was made by the branch manager or some other branch employee at the place where the branch is established, or even in some other state, then the tortious obligation can be said to arise from the activities of the intermediary. The same can be said in an action for conversion, if the act of conversion was committed by the branch manager or some other branch employee at the place where the branch is established, or even in some other state. In an action under French law for refusal to sell goods, if the act of refusing to sell is committed by the branch manager or some other branch employee at the place where the branch is established, or even in some other state, this too would meet the requirement.

Specific Jurisdiction in Tort: Article 5(3) of the Brussels I Regulation

Article 5(3) of the Brussels I Regulation provides that a person domiciled **6.10** in a Member State may, in another Member State, be sued:

in matters relating to tort, *delict* or *quasi-delict*, in the courts for the place where the harmful event occurred or may occur.

Matters relating to tort, delict or quasi-delict

The European Court of Justice has held that the concept of 'matters **6.11** relating to tort, *delict* or *quasi-delict*' must be given a community definition.[26] What is less clear is how widely or narrowly this concept is to be interpreted. The European Court of Justice in *Kalfelis v Schroder*[27] held that matters relating to tort, delict or quasi-delict 'must be regarded as an independent concept covering all actions which seek to establish the liability of a defendant and which are not related to a "contract" within

---

[23] *Anton Durbeck GmbH v Den Norske Bank ASA* [2003] EWCA 147 at [40], [2003] 2 WLR 1296. This was in the light of Case C-439/93 *Lloyd's Register of Shipping v Societe Campenon Bernard* [1995] ECR I-961.
[24] The *Anton Durbeck* case, n 23 above, at [40].   [25] ibid, at [41].
[26] Case 189/87 *Kalfelis v Schroder* [1988] ECR 5565.   [27] ibid.

the meaning of Article 5(1)'.[28] This statement has been approved in numerous subsequent decisions of that Court[29] and has been followed in national courts.[30] The European Court of Justice has interpreted this statement as setting out the scope of Article 5(3), and that this is wide.[31] The Court has not enquired into whether there was a tort in the strict sense.[32] This is shown most graphically in the recent decision in *Fonderie Officine Meccaniche Tacconi SpA v Heinrich Wagner Sinto Maschinenfabrik GmbH (HWS)*.[33] The European Court of Justice held that a claim based on pre-contractual liability under Article 1337 of the Italian Civil Code, which provides that, in the context of the negotiation and formation of a contract, the parties must act in good faith, did not relate to a contract and in the light of this was a matter relating to tort, delict or quasi-delict within Article 5(3) of the Brussels Convention. Article 1337 sets out a non-contractual obligation which is not regarded under Italian or presumably other natural laws as delictual.[34] This means that other non-contractual obligations which are not characterized as tortious, the most obvious one being that of unjust enrichment, should be regarded as falling within the scope of Article 5(3).[35]

6.12 Unfortunately, the House of Lords in *Kleinwort Benson Ltd v Glasgow City Council*[36] has given a narrow interpretation to Article 5(3), holding unanimously that a claim for restitution based on unjust enrichment did

---

[28] ibid, at 5585, para 17.

[29] Case C-261/90 *Reichert v Dresdner Bank (No 2)* [1992] ECR I-2149; AG Darmon in Case C-89/91 *Shearson Lehman Hutton Inc v TVB* [1993] ECR I-139 at 178; AG Jacobs in Case C-26/91 *Jakob Handte & Co GmbH v Société Traitements Mécano-Chimiques des Surfaces SA (TCMS)* [1992] ECR I-3967 at 3984–3985; Case C-51/97 *Réunion Européenne v Spliethoff's Bevrachtingskantoor BV* [1998] ECR I-6511; Case C-96/00 *Gabriel v Schlanck & Schick GmbH* [2002] ECR I-6367, [2002] IL Pr 36 at [33]; Case C-167/00 *Verein Fur Konsumenteninformation v KH Henkel* [2002] ECR I-8111, para 36; Case C-334/00 *Fonderie Officine Meccaniche Tacconi SpA v Heinrich Wagner Sinto Maschinenfabrik GmbH (HWS)* [2002] ECR I-7357, para 21; Case C-18/02 *DFDS Torline v SEKO* [2004] IL Pr 10, para 30 of the opinion of AG Jacobs.

[30] See, e.g. *Re Mail Order Promise of Win in a Draw* [2003] IL Pr 46, Bundesgerichtshof.

[31] See the *Réunion Européenne, Verein, Gabriel* and *DFDS* cases, n 29 above.

[32] See the *Réunion Européenne* case—having decided that the liability in that case did not fall within Art 5(1) the ECJ said that: 'In those circumstances, it must be held that such an action is a matter relating to tort, delict or quasi-delict'. See also the *Verein* case, n 29 above, paras 40–41. See too the technique adopted in the *Gabriel* case—in determining whether the circumstances came within Art 5(3), the first question to be asked was whether the action was contractual in nature (see para 34), the assumption being that if it was not it would fall within Art 5(3).

[33] Case C-334/00 [2002] ECR I-7357.

[34] F Benatti, *La Responsabilità Precontracttuale* (Milan: 1963) 133 et seq.

[35] See the Opinion of AG Darmon in Case C-89/91 *Shearson Lehman Hutton Inc v TVB* [1993] ECR I-139, para 102. See also the decision of the Austrian Supreme Court in *Re Concurrent Claims (Royalties)* (Case 4 Ob 66/01) [2003] IL Pr 30—a non-contractual claim based on 'any conceivable legal ground' held to fall within Art 5(3).

[36] [1999] 1 AC 153.

not fall within this provision.[37] Reliance was placed on another passage in the *Kalfelis* case[38] which states that 'a court which has jurisdiction under Article 5(3) over an action in so far as it is based on tort or delict does not have jurisdiction over that action in so far as it is not so based'. The House of Lords interpreted the first key passage, which has been relied upon so much by the European Court of Justice, as merely being concerned with whether an independent meaning should be given to the term 'tort', not with the question of scope which in their Lordships view was dealt with in the second passage.[39] This may have been a tenable interpretation at the time the *Kleinwort* case was decided but it cannot be reconciled with the decision of the European Court of Justice in the *Fonderie* case, nor with other decisions of that Court which have not asked whether there is a tort in the strict sense.[40] This leaves English judges, particularly when faced with cases of unjust enrichment,[41] in a quandary over conflicting authorities. Ultimately, the European Court of Justice trumps the House of Lords on questions of interpretation of the Brussels I Regulation and the English courts should follow the former. It follows that matters relating to tort, delict or quasi-delict 'must be regarded as an independent concept covering all actions which seek to establish the liability of a defendant and which are not related to a "contract" within the meaning of Article 5(1)'.

To come within Article 5(3) the action must seek to establish the liability **6.13** of a defendant.[42] In *Reichert v Dresdner Bank (No 2)*,[43] the European Court of Justice held that an action whereby a creditor sought to set aside a gift of property made by a debtor, which allegedly defrauded him of his rights (an action paulienne under French law) did not seek to establish the liability of a defendant in the sense understood in Article 5(3).

---

[37] ibid, at 172 (*per* Lord Goff), 185 (*per* Lord Clyde), 196 (*per* Lord Hutton), 172 (*per* Lord Mustill), 177 (*per* Lord Nicholls). But see *Casio Computer Co Ltd v Sayo* [2001] IL PR 164, where the Court of Appeal held that a constructive trust claim based on dishonest assistance fell within Art 5(3), distinguishing *Kleinwort Benson* on the basis that, in the case in front of them, there was a harmful event whereas there is, apart from in exceptional circumstances, no such event in the case of a claim based on unjust enrichment. But this ignores the narow interpretation of the *Kalfelis* case adopted by the House of Lords.

[38] n 26 above, at 5585, para 19.

[39] n 36 above, at 196 (*per* Lord Hutton). The more obvious explanation for the second passage is that it is dealing with concurrent actions in tort and contract (as well as unjust enrichment), i.e. the situation that actually arose in the *Kalfelis* case, see Cheshire and North, 213.

[40] See the *Réunion Européenne*, *Verein* and *Gabriel* cases, n 29 above.

[41] Unjust enrichment is discussed further below, paras 8.12–30. In cases other than unjust enrichment the courts may find a way out by distinguishing the *Kleinwort Benson* case, see the *Casio* case, n 37 above.

[42] For the difficulties caused by this requirement see Briggs and Rees, 2.138.

[43] Case C-261/90 [1992] ECR I-2149.

The place where the harmful event occurred

6.14 The European Court of Justice has held that Article 5(3) of the Brussels Convention is intended to cover both the place where the damage occurred and the place of the event giving rise to it, where the two are not identical.[44] The plaintiff therefore has the option of suing in either place. The European Court of Justice justified this wide interpretation by pointing out, *inter alia*, that Article 5(3) allocates jurisdiction to a Contracting State with which the dispute has a particularly close relationship, 'with a view to the efficacious conduct of the proceedings'.[45] Article 5(3) of the Brussels I Regulation should be interpreted in the light of this. Both the place of the event giving rise to the damage and the place where the damage occurred are appropriate places for trial.

6.15 **The place of the event giving rise to the damage**   The European Court of Justice has given a community definition to the place of the event giving rise to damage.[46] This is consistent with it giving the concepts of a matter relating to tort, delict or quasi-delict[47] and a matter relating to a contract[48] a community meaning. This means that the elements of the tort should be identified, not by looking at the law of the state which is actually applicable in the instant case or at the law of the forum, but more generally by looking at the common core of the national legal systems in relation to that tort. The objectives and scheme of the Regulation and the objectives of Article 5(3) and how it fits in with other provisions should also be considered.

6.16 **The place where the damage occurred**   The place of damage under Article 5(3) of the Brussels Convention has been interpreted by the European Court of Justice as referring to the place where direct damage has occurred and does not allow jurisdiction where indirect damage has occurred.[49] This principle applies even more strongly to the situation where there is financial damage which has simultaneous and co-extensive consequences in a Member State (X), where the victim was domiciled and his assets were concentrated, other than that in which it arises and is suffered by the victim.[50] There is no jurisdiction in Member State X. The place of damage also does not encompass the place where the victim claimed to have suffered financial loss consequential upon initial damage arising and suffered by him in another Contracting State.[51] Two principles

---

[44] Case 21/76 *Bier BV v Mines de Potasse d'Alsace SA* [1976] ECR 1735; Case C-68/93 *Shevill v Presse Alliance SA* [1995] 2 AC 18.

[45] The *Bier* case, n 44 above, at 1746.   [46] See the *Shevill* case, n 44 above.

[47] See the *Kalfelis* case, n 26 above.   [48] See above, paras 3.62–83.

[49] Case C-220/88 *Dumez France v Hessische Landesbank (Heleba)* [1990] ECR I-49.

[50] Case C-168/02 *Kronhofer v Maier*, ECJ.

[51] Case C-364/93 *Marinari v Lloyds Bank plc (Zubaidi Trading Co intervener)* [1995] ECR I-2719.

underlie this interpretation. First, the European Court of Justice has been concerned to keep Article 5(3) within certain bounds so as to avoid the multiplication of competent fora.[52] Second, the Court has also wanted to avoid the situation where the claimant is able to sue in the place in which he is domiciled.[53] This is because the Brussels Convention adopted the principle that, in general, persons should be sued in the Contracting State in which they are domiciled.

2. THE TRADITIONAL ENGLISH RULES

Non-Specific Bases of Jurisdiction

Service within the jurisdiction

There are, in general, no particular problems in applying the normal rules **6.17** on service within the jurisdiction[54] to tort cases. The only matter which must be mentioned is the requirement that applies where the method of service adopted is that set out in s 694A of the Companies Act 1985 (service of documents on companies incorporated outside the United Kingdom and Gibraltar and having a branch in Great Britain), namely that the document that is served on the company must be in respect of the carrying on of the business of the branch. How does this requirement operate in tort cases, in particular in the case of the torts that arise out of international sales?

To answer this one must turn once again to the decision of the Court of **6.18** Appeal in *Saab v Saudi American Bank*.[55] It will be recalled,[56] that the case involved not only a claim for breach of contract but also a claim in tort for negligence and misrepresentation. The claims in contract and tort were not separated out, as they are when considering Article 5(5), but were all looked at together in the round.[57] Thus the Court of Appeal's statement, that process would be in respect of the carrying on of the business of the branch if it is in part in respect of the carrying on of the business,[58] applies regardless of whether the claim is in tort, or contract, or both.

Let us turn to some obvious examples of situations involving tort claims **6.19** which would satisfy the requirement that the document served on the company must be in respect of the carrying on of the business of the branch. It is submitted that this would be so where the tort was

---

[52] ibid. [53] ibid. [54] Discussed above, paras 4.02–25.
[55] [1999] 1 WLR 1861, CA. [56] See above, para 4.10.
[57] See Tuckey J in the first instance decision at [1998] 1 WLR 937 at 941. Compare the position under Art 5(5) of the Brussels I Regulation where what has to be shown to satisfy the requirement that the dispute has arisen out of the operations of the branch etc. is different for contract (see above, para 3.304) and tort (see above, para 6.09).
[58] The *Saab* case, n 55 above, at 330 (*per* Clarke LJ).

committed by one of the branch officers, for example the acts of conversion or misrepresentations are made by the branch manager, or it is the branch manager or other branch officer that refuses to sell the goods. Earlier on,[59] it has been suggested that these examples would satisfy the requirement under Article 5(5) of the Brussels I Regulation that the dispute arises out of the operations of a branch, agency or other establishment. Given that the Court of Appeal has given a wider interpretation to the requirement under s 694A of the Companies Act 1985 than to that under Article 5(5), it would be surprising if tort cases coming within the latter did not also come within the former.

6.20 All of this difficulty over the requirement that the document served on the company must be in respect of the carrying on of the business of the branch can be avoided. It will be recalled[60] that, as an alternative to service by the method set out in s 694A, it is possible to effect service by any method permitted under Part 6 of the Civil Procedure Rules and it has been held that, where this is the method adopted, there is no such requirement.[61]

Service out of the jurisdiction

6.21 It may be possible to bring a claim in tort within one of the general grounds set out in r 6.20 of the Civil Procedure Rules, that is r 6.20(1), (2) or (3).[62] It is not possible to bring a claim in tort within grounds (5), (6) or (7), which are concerned with claims in relation to contracts.[63] In the situation where the parties have a contractual relationship and parallel claims are brought in contract and tort, the position is much more straightforward than that under the Brussels I Regulation.[64] There is no question of the claimant being precluded from using the tort ground under r 6.20(8). The claims can be split and the contract claim brought within one of the contract grounds and the tort head within the tort ground. If service out of the jurisdiction is permissible under one of the contract heads, the claim being in contract, the claimant is not allowed to add on a claim for breach of a non-contractual obligation when leave to serve the claim form out of the jurisdiction would not have been given for this.[65] Finally, it is sometimes possible to bring claims in relation to certain torts, such as conversion, within the property ground contained in r 6.20(10).

---

[59] See above, para 6.09.   [60] See above, paras 4.13–22.
[61] *Sea Assets Ltd v PT Garuda Indonesia* [2000] 4 All ER 371. But for criticism of the correctness of this decision see above, paras 4.20–21.
[62] These grounds are discussed above, para 4.27.
[63] These grounds are discussed above, paras 4.28–93.   [64] See above, para 6.07.
[65] *Waterhouse v Reid* [1938] 1 KB 743; *The Siskina* [1979] AC 210. See also *Donohue v Armco Inc* [2001] UKHL 64 at [21], [2002] 1 All ER 749.

Specific Jurisdiction in Tort: Rule 6.20(8) of the Civil Procedure Rules

Rule 6.20(8) of the Civil Procedure Rules provides that a claim form may **6.22**
be served out of the jurisdiction with the permission of the court if:

a claim is made in tort where—
(a) damage was sustained within the jurisdiction; or
(b) the damage sustained resulted from an act committed within the
    jurisdiction

The almost identically worded predecessor of this provision, Order 11,
r 1 (1)(f) of the Rules of the Supreme Court, was designed to bring service
out of the jurisdiction in tort cases under the traditional rules into line
with jurisdiction under Article 5(3) of the Brussels Convention. This has
considerable significance when it comes to the interpretation of r 6.20(8)
of the Civil Procedure Rules.

A claim is made in tort

This ground requires that 'a claim is made in tort'. A claim is 'made' in tort **6.23**
when it is founded on a tort,[66] i.e. based on a tort. The predecessor of
this ground[67] explicitly required that 'the claim is founded on a tort'.
This is another one of the drafting changes introduced by the Civil
Procedure Rules when replacing the old Order 11, r 1(1) of the Rules of
the Supreme Court with r 6.20 of the Civil Procedure Rules, seemingly,
so as to produce a list which is clearer and simpler. It was not intended
that these changes should have any substantive effect on the court's
powers.[68]

We are not concerned here with a Community definition of 'a claim made **6.24**
in tort', but rather with whether the English courts classify the claim as
being one made in tort for the purposes of service out of the jurisdiction.
Normally this will not present a problem. If the claim is founded on what
is, in English law, a tort then clearly it should be classified as tortious for
jurisdictional purposes.[69] The notion of a claim being founded on what is,
under English law, a tort covers two situations. The first is where the claim
is founded on the English law of tort. The second is where it is founded on
a foreign law but the cause of action under that law is one that is known to
English law and is classified as tortious under the English domestic law of

---

[66] See Dicey and Morris, *Third Supplement to the Thirteenth Edition* (2003), 64–65.
[67] Ord 11, r 1(1)(f) RSC; formerly Ord 11, r 1(1)(h).
[68] See the Lord Chancellor's Department Consultation Paper on the CPR, *Service of Court
Process Abroad*, para 22 which lists these changes, although it does not mention the tort
ground.
[69] See *Metall und Rohstoff AG v Donaldson Lufkin and Jenrette Inc* [1990] 1 QB 391 at 449, CA;
overruled on a different point in *Lonrho plc v Fayed* [1992] 1 AC 448.

tort, for example a claim for negligence under New York law. In either eventuality, the claim should be classified as tortious for jurisdictional purposes. There is a problem, though, where the claimant relies upon a foreign cause of action that is unknown to English law, such as a claim based on the failure to sell goods under French law. If this is classified as a delict under the French domestic law of delict then this should be persuasive evidence of its classification for jurisdictional purposes. Even more so, if other countries which have this cause of action classify it as tortious. It is also very relevant to see how this cause of action has been classified for the purposes of jurisdiction under Article 5(3) of the Brussels I Regulation or earlier Brussels Convention.

6.25 Claims based on contract do not fall within r 6.20(8). Neither do claims to equitable restitutionary remedies for breach of trust or fiduciary duty. Such claims must be brought within some other paragraph of r 6.20.[70]

An act committed within the jurisdiction

6.26 The damage may have resulted from a series of acts, some of which were committed within the jurisdiction and others outside the jurisdiction. It is not necessary that all the acts were committed within the jurisdiction. On the other hand, jurisdiction cannot be assumed on the basis of some relatively minor or insignificant act having been committed in England. It is enough that 'substantial and efficacious acts' were committed within the jurisdiction, whether or not other substantial and efficacious acts were committed outside the jurisdiction.[71] When identifying the relevant act it is important to remember that r 6.20(8) allows service out of the jurisdiction on the alternative basis that damage was sustained within the jurisdiction.

6.27 As will be seen, the English courts have identified the relevant act for a number of torts. In the absence of any such authority, is there any other source from which guidance on identifying this place can be sought? One possible source is the case law on the pre-1987 tort head of Order 11, r 1 of the Rules of the Supreme Court,[72] for the purposes of which it had to be determined whether a tort had been committed within the jurisdiction. In determining this, the English courts asked the question: where in substance did the cause of action arise?[73] However, the change in wording

---

[70] *ISC Technologies Ltd v James Howard Guerin* [1992] 2 Lloyd's Rep 430.

[71] The *Metall und Rohstoff* case, n 69 above.

[72] Ord 11, r 1(1)(h) RSC. This was reworded and became Ord 11, r 1(1)(f) RSC in 1987 when the Brussels Convention, as amended, came into force in the UK.

[73] *Distillers Co (Biochemicals) Ltd v Thompson* [1971] AC 458; *Castree v ER Squibb & Sons Ltd* [1980] 1 WLR 1248, CA.

to that found in r 6.20(8), allowing jurisdiction if either the damage or the act from which the damage resulted was committed within the jurisdiction, would suggest that these earlier cases are now of minimal relevance in the present context.[74] The other possible source of authority is the case law identifying the place of the event giving rise to the damage for the purpose of Article 5(3) of the Brussels I Regulation or the earlier Brussels Convention. In various areas of private international law, it can be observed that where a traditional rule is based on an EC rule, the former has been interpreted in the light of decisions interpreting the latter.[75] The same should happen in this context.[76] However, whilst such cases are relevant, a degree of caution is needed when they are being considered. The English courts have been known to interpret the English tort provision more widely than the Brussels I Regulation equivalent. Thus the Court of Appeal appears to contemplate that there could be a case where there are substantial and efficacious acts committed in two different countries.[77] Logically it follows that if either of these acts takes place in England then there is an act committed within the jurisdiction. This has the potential for making it easier to come within this provision than it is to come within the concept of the place of the event giving rise to the damage under Article 5(3) of the Brussels I Regulation, which contemplates that there is only one such place. One further reason for caution is that, in the situation where it is hard to identify this place, the response of the European Court of Justice is to say simply that jurisdiction cannot be based on the place of the event giving rise to the damage,[78] whereas an English court is unlikely just to give up in this way.

[74] In Art 5(3) cases, the English courts have refused to follow these traditional English cases because of the difference in the test, see *Domicrest Ltd v Swiss Bank Corp* [1999] QB 548 at 567, and *Minster Investments Ltd v Hyundai Precision and Industry Co Ltd* [1988] 2 Lloyd's Rep 621 at 623. These cases are, however, relevant when it comes to determining where a misstatement/misrepresentation is made once it is decided that this should be regarded as the relevant act in misstatement/misrepresentation cases, see below, paras 6.97–102. These traditional cases are still relevant when determining the natural forum for *forum conveniens* purposes, see below, paras 6.30–32.

[75] See in relation to 'the same parties' under s 34 of the Civil Jurisdiction and Judgments Act 1982, *Republic of India v India Steamship Co Ltd (No 2)* [1998] AC 878, and in relation to 'damage' for the purposes of Ord 11, r 1(1)(f) RSC, *Bastone & Firminger Ltd v Nasima Enterprises (Nigeria) Ltd* [1996] CLC 1902, discussed below, para 6.106. See generally J Fawcett, 'Cross-Fertilisation in Private International Law' [2000] CLP 303 at 308–309.

[76] See *ABCI (Formerly Arab Business Consortium International Finance and Investment Co) v Banque Franco-Tunisienne* [2003] EWCA Civ 205 at [41], [2003] 2 Lloyd's Rep 146.

[77] It may be difficult to persuade the courts that a claim for a particular tort actually involves two sets of substantial and efficacious acts, see, e.g. *Arab Business Consortium International Finance and Investment Co v Banque Franco-Tunisienne* [1996] 1 Lloyd's Rep 485; discussed below, para 6.98.

[78] Compare Case C-51/97 *Réunion Europeenne v Spliethoff's Bevrachtingskantoor BV* [1998] ECR I-6511 where the ECJ refused to apply Art 5(3) in a case where it was difficult, or indeed impossible, to identify the place of the event giving rise to the damage.

Damage was sustained within the jurisdiction

6.28 It is not necessary that all the damage has been sustained within the jurisdiction. It is 'enough if some significant damage has been sustained in England'.[79] The better view is that damage refers to the direct damage sounding in monetary terms which the wrongful act produced upon the claimant.[80] This is the same definition of damage as that applied by the European Court for the purposes of Article 5(3) of the Brussels Convention. The adoption of this EC definition for the purposes of service out of the jurisdiction[81] acknowledges the fact that the tort ground for service out of the jurisdiction was reworded to align with Article 5(3).[82] However, it has to be remembered that the principles of interpretation adopted by the European Court of Justice are very different from the principles adopted by the English courts when interpreting traditional rules. There is, for example, not the need to avoid the multiplication of courts of competent jurisdiction under the latter. This suggests that caution is necessary when borrowing from the decisions of the European Court of Justice.

A reasonable prospect of success (a serious issue to be tried on the merits)

6.29 As with any other case of service out of the jurisdiction, the claimant has to establish that there is a reasonable prospect of success (a serious issue to be tried on the merits).[83] A separate enquiry as to this is needed. It is accepted that the standard of proof for establishing negligence is a lesser one than that for establishing that negligence occurred within the jurisdiction (which goes to establishing the terms of the ground).[84] Establishing a serious issue on the merits can raise choice of law questions at this jurisdictional stage of the proceedings.[85]

---

[79] The *Metall und Rohstoff* case, n 69 above, at 437.

[80] *ABCI (Formerly Arab Business Consortium International Finance and Investment Co) v Banque Franco-Tunisienne* [2003] EWCA Civ 205 at [44], [2003] 2 Lloyd's Rep 146; *Beecham Group plc v Norton Healthcare Ltd* [1997] FSR 81 at 97–98; *Bastone & Firminger Ltd v Nasima Enterprises (Nigeria) Ltd* [1996] CLC 1902. There is also Canadian authority in favour of a direct damage rule in *National Bank of Canada v Clifford Chance* (1996) 30 OR (3d) 746. But compare *Barings plc v Coopers & Lybrand (a firm)* [1997] IL Pr 12 at 24–25, aff'd by CA, [1997] IL Pr 576 at 585.

[81] The *ABCI* case, n 80 above, at [44]. See also Rix J in the *Bastone* case, n 75 above, at 1912, who quoted in support of the direct damage principle a decision of the ECJ on the meaning of damage for the purposes of Art 5(3) of the Brussels Convention.

[82] The *ABCI* case, n 80 above, at [43].

[83] See the discussion above, para 4.95.

[84] *Seaconsar Far East Ltd v Bank Markazi Jomhouri Islami Iran* [1994] 1 AC 438, 455; approving the judgment of Lord Tucker in *Vitkovice Horni a Hutni Tezirstvro v Korner* [1951] AC 869 at 889, HL. See also *Barings plc v Coopers & Lybrand (a firm)* [1997] IL Pr 12 at 25–26, aff'd by CA, [1997] IL Pr 576 at 585.

[85] See the *Metall und Rohstoff* case, n 69 above.

Forum conveniens

The courts have shown a distinct willingness to exercise their discretion **6.30**
to allow service out of the jurisdiction under the predecessor of r 6.20(8),
that is Order 11, r 1(1)(f) of the Rules of the Supreme Court. The House of
Lords in *Berezovsky v Michaels*[86] has confirmed that the burden is on the
claimant to show that England is clearly the appropriate forum in which
the case should be tried in the interests of all the parties and the ends of
justice but that, consistently with that test, regard is to be had to the
principle that the jurisdiction in which a tort was committed is, prima
facie, the natural forum for the dispute.

This natural forum principle was introduced at the time when service out **6.31**
of the jurisdiction in tort cases was based on the commission of a tort
within the jurisdiction.[87] It makes less sense now that service out of the
jurisdiction is no longer based on this test. Sensibly, the present tort
ground does not seek to find a single place which is where the tort was
committed but, instead, looks at both the place of damage and the place
where the act from which the damage resulted was committed. Nonetheless, this natural form principle can still be justified in cases of defamation
because, when it comes to the question of the law applicable to this particular tort, this is determined under the common law rules.[88] According
to these rules, the place of the tort is to be determined by asking 'where in
substance did this cause of action arise?'.[89] So in defamation cases the
forum conveniens principle can be justified on the ground that it is based
on the applicable law.[90] However, with torts other than defamation the
applicable law is now ascertained by statutory choice of law rules which
do not concern themselves with where in substance the cause of action
arose/where the tort was committed.[91] The risk when exercising the
forum conveniens discretion in tort cases is that there will be argument
over where the tort was committed and this place will have to be ascertained,
even though it is not relevant either for establishing that the tort ground

---

[86] [2000] 1 WLR 1004. See also *Dow Jones & Company Inc v Gutnick* (2002) 210 CLR 575, HC
of Australia; discussed below, paras 10.168–169.
[87] *Cordoba Shipping Co Ltd v National State Bank, Elizabeth, New Jersey (The Albaforth)* [1984]
2 Lloyd's Rep 91, CA.
[88] Discussed below, para 17.11.
[89] The *Metall und Rohstoff* case, n 69 above, at 446.
[90] It has been seen that this question of the applicable law may arise at the jurisdictional
stage as part of the enquiry into whether the claimant can establish that there is a serious
issue to be tried on the merits. Having already decided where in substance the cause of
action arose (i.e. where the tort was committed) it is easy to apply a principle based on this
concept when operating the *forum conveniens* discretion. This is what happened in the
Metall und Rohstoff case, ibid. This case applied the common law tort choice of law rules,
being decided prior to the introduction of statutory tort choice of law rules.
[91] See below, paras 17.14–51.

under r 6.20(8) is satisfied or for choice of law purposes. Furthermore, whilst it is easy enough to state and apply the rule as to where the tort of defamation is committed, namely where the defamation is published,[92] it is by no means always easy to state or apply the rule as to where many other torts are committed.[93] The identification of the place where a tort is committed when this has occurred over the internet is particularly problematic, even for defamation.[94]

6.32 We would be better off not having a principle that the jurisdiction in which a tort was committed is, prima facie, the natural forum for the dispute. Such a presumption can no longer be justified for the reasons stated in the previous paragraph. Instead, what we should look at in tort cases is the law applicable to the tort, which is after all the idea underlying the presumption. If the law applicable to the tort is English law this should be recognized as strong evidence in favour of England clearly being the appropriate forum for trial.[95] It must be recalled that, in tort cases, in order to establish that there is a serious issue to be tried on the merits, it may be necessary to identify the applicable law at this jurisdictional stage.[96] The importance already attached at the jurisdictional stage to the applicable law in tort cases justifies giving the applicable law factor strong weight when exercising the *forum conveniens* discretion in such cases.

III CONVERSION

1. THE SUBSTANTIVE LAW BACKGROUND

The Common Law Tort of Conversion

The use of conversion in international sale of goods cases

6.33 Under English law the tort of conversion protects an owner's property rights in chattels and documentary intangibles, for example cheques.[97]

---

[92] On the facts of the *Berezovsky* case, all the constituent elements of the tort were said to have occurred in England, *per* Lord Steyn at 1013, and so there was no difficulty over where the tort was committed.

[93] See, e.g. the discussion below, paras 6.110–113, in relation to negligent misstatements and negligent and fraudulent misrepresentations. For an attempt to find a principle explaining many of the cases (involving different torts) on the identification of the place where a tort was committed see *Base Metal Trading Limited v Ruslan Borisovich Shamurin* [2002] CLC 322, [2003] EWHC 2419 (Comm) at [37], [2004] IL Pr 5, [2004] EWCA Civ 1316, CA—the 'notion of looking to see whether conduct abroad was directed against persons in the forum jurisdiction, in the sense of being intended to be acted upon in that forum and likely to cause damage there to those who in consequence place reliance on it'.

[94] See below, paras 10.168–169.

[95] See *Voth v Manildra Flour Mills Pty Ltd* (1990) 171 CLR 538, 566, HC of Australia.

[96] See the *Metall und Rohstoff* case, n 69 above.

[97] See generally M Bridge, *Personal Property Law* (3rd edn, Oxford: OUP, 2002) Ch 3.

This is why damages normally represent the value of the chattel at the date of the act of conversion. The remedy amounts to a forced judicial sale of the chattel to the defendant.[98] But mere ownership (the general property) does not give a claimant standing to sue. The claimant must have either possession or the right to immediate possession[99] at the date of the act of conversion. The latter fits the case of the owner out of possession and is necessary where another wrongdoer or a term bailee intrudes in the possessory chain between claimant and defendant.[100] A thief technically may sue in conversion. To deal with multiple claimants and defendants, there are rules for consolidated proceedings and the avoidance of unjust enrichment in the Torts (Interference with Goods) Act 1977.

In the case of sale, a buyer to whom the property has passed may sue **6.34** the seller in possession only where the buyer has the right to immediate possession, which will not be the case where the seller is exercising a lien.[101] In such a case, the buyer does not have standing to sue a third party converter.[102]

Cases where a buyer may wish to sue a seller include: (a) the seller who **6.35** falsely asserts a lien over x chattel for non-payment for a chattel supplied under a separate contract; (b) the unlawful sale by a seller to a third party which act terminates the unpaid seller's lien;[103] (c) the situation that arose in *The Playa Larga*:[104] the Cuban seller instructed the Cuban carrier, after property and constructive possession had passed to the CIF buyer receiving the bill of lading against payment, not to unload goods in the destination port in Chile in 1973.

An action for conversion brought against a seller by a buyer who is able to **6.36** show that the goods sold are still in the possession of the seller is likely to be combined with a separate action against the seller for breach of contract. If the buyer is claiming that goods sold and delivered to a third party were his (the buyer's) property, it is possible to bring an action in conversion against this third party. Such a claim may well be combined with a separate claim against the seller for breach of contract. In other words, the claimant will bring a multi-defendant claim.[105]

---

[98] *Brinsmead v Harrison* (1872) LR 7 CP 547; s 5(1) of the Torts (Interference with Goods) Act 1977.

[99] For trespass to chattels the latter does not suffice.

[100] There is, for owners who do not qualify for a conversion action, a similar action for damage done to a reversionary interest.

[101] Technically, a lien where property has passed to B, otherwise a right of retention.

[102] *Lord v Price* (1874) LR 9 Ex 54. See generally Bridge, *The Sale of Goods*, 37, n 108.

[103] But the buyer may not sue a third party in conversion where the third party is a thief and the seller had a lien at the time of the theft.

[104] [1983] 2 Lloyd's Rep 171.

[105] There is an additional basis of jurisdiction in such cases. This is discussed in Ch 9 below.

6.37 It is also possible in certain circumstances for a consignee of goods to sue a carrier in conversion. This can be done where the carrier (a) delivers to someone who is not the holder of a bill of lading,[106] except where the carrier may be required in special cases to deliver;[107] (b) delivers to the holder of a forged bill of lading. But the carrier will not be liable for delivering to the person presenting an original bill of lading from a set of (usually) three originals, where that bill has been avoided by the earlier transfer of another original to a bank or buyer.[108]

The elements of the tort

6.38 Conversion can occur in so many different circumstances that framing a precise definition of universal application has been described as well nigh impossible.[109] Nonetheless, it has been described as 'an act of deliberate dealing with a chattel in a manner inconsistent with another's right whereby that other is deprived of the use and possession of it'.[110] In general it encapsulates three basic ingredients.[111]

First, the defendant's conduct was inconsistent with the rights of the owner (or other person entitled to possession). Second, the conduct was deliberate, not accidental. Third, the conduct was so extensive an encroachment on the rights of the owner as to exclude him from use and possession of the goods. The contrast is with lesser acts of interference. If they cause damage they may give rise to claims for trespass or in negligence, but they do not constitute conversion.[112]

The requisite act can be committed in a wide variety of different ways: by unauthorized taking; detaining; misusing; disposing; or receiving goods.[113] The concept of 'depriving' the owner of possession does not mean that the wrongdoer must himself actually take the goods from the possession of the owner, although this will often be the case.[114] Whether the owner is excluded from possession may sometimes depend upon whether the wrongdoer exercised dominion over the goods.[115] Then the intention with which acts were done may be material. Mere unauthorized

---

[106] A carrier may be willing, or bound under a charterparty, to deliver against a letter of indemnity.

[107] *The Sormovskiy 3068* [1994] 2 Lloyd's Rep 266.

[108] *Glyn Mills Currie & Co v East & West India Docks Co* (1882) 7 App Cas 591.

[109] *Kuwait Airways Corp v Iraqi Airways Co (Nos 4 and 5)* [2002] 2 AC 883, 1084 (*per* Lord Nicholls), HL.

[110] MR Brazier (ed), *Clerk and Lindsell on Torts* (17th edn, London: Sweet & Maxwell, 1995) 636, para 13–12 (see now 18th edn, 2000); approved in the *Kuwait Airways* case, ibid.

[111] ibid. See also *Marcq v Christie Manson and Woods Ltd (t/a Christie's)* [2004] QB 286.

[112] The *Kuwait Airways* case, n 109 above, at 1084 (*per* Lord Nicholls).

[113] Sees S Todd, *The Law of Torts in New Zealand* (3rd edn, Wellingdon: Brookers, 2001) 572–587, para 11.3.2.

[114] The *Kuwait Airways* case, n 109 above, at 1084 (*per* Lord Nicholls).

[115] ibid.

retention of another's goods is not conversion of them.[116] Mere possession of another's goods without title is not necessarily inconsistent with rights of the owner.[117] To constitute conversion detention must be adverse to the owner, excluding him from the goods.[118] It must be accompanied by an intention to keep the goods.[119] Whether this intention can properly be inferred depends on the circumstances of the case. A demand and refusal to deliver up the goods are the usual way of proving an intention to keep goods adverse to the owner, although this is not the only way.[120] The elements of the tort do not require that the claimant suffers damage. However, the normal remedy for conversion will be damages.[121] The 'loss suffered by the person whose goods have been converted must be compensated by an award of money which represents the value of the goods'.[122]

Revendication in Civil Law States

The common law is unusual in treating claims for interference with prop- **6.39**
erty rights as part of the law of tort (delict). Countries in the civil law tradition, following the Roman law and its vindication, treat the matter as part of the law of property. Hence a claimant seeks revendication rather than damages. Such an action to recover possession from a third party acquirer is defeated in France by the rule that possession is tantamount to ownership. This is the possession vaut titre principle in Article 2279, al 1 of the Code civil. That third party will have bought from someone in possession. This rule is subject to the following qualification contained in Article 2279 al 2. In the case of loss or theft, the owner can recover the thing within three years from any person in whose hands he finds the thing.[123] Even within the three year period, the bona fide acquirer, directly or indirectly from a finder or thief, having to surrender the thing is entitled to be repaid by the revendicating owner the price he paid to acquire the thing if it was bought in a fair or market place or in a public sale or from a dealer in such things.[124] The possession vaut titre principle in Article 2279 al 1 means that a French owner who voluntarily entrusts possession to another, for example, the seller in possession, buyer in possession or mercantile agent, may not revendicate at all from a third

---

[116] ibid.   [117] ibid.   [118] ibid, at 1084–1085.   [119] ibid, at 1085   [120] ibid
[121] In certain circumstances, specific restitution of the goods will be available, see Todd, n 113 above, at 594.
[122] Todd, n 113 above, at 590, citing *Furness v Adrium Industries Pty Ltd* [1966] 1 VR 668.
[123] But the finder or the thief still in possession is always liable to surrender the thing to the owner in a revendication action.
[124] C civ Art 2280 al 1. cf J Bell, S Boyron and S Whittaker, *Principles of French Law* (Oxford: Clarendon 1998), 289.

party acquirer.[125] The owner who trusts another bears the risk of that other's dishonesty. This is because the qualification in Article 2279 al 2 applies only to cases of involuntary dispossession of the original owner (loss and theft). Hence the French substantive law of title transfer prevents from arising many of the cases that in English law would give rise to liability in conversion and allows equivalent French law to be cast as pure property law as opposed to delict.

6.40 The position in German law appears to be somewhat similar to the French.[126] There are liberal rules on the transfer of title. Someone buying in good faith and without notice from someone in possession with the consent of the owner, and taking delivery from that person, acquires good title.[127] The former owner's title is expunged. But this rule does not apply where the thing is stolen or otherwise forcibly taken from the owner[128] for then the title of the owner persists even if the thing is disposed of down a title chain. In the case of an owner who lends the thing, his recourse is against the borrower.[129] He can claim the proceeds of sale in the hands of the wrongful transferor on the ground of unjust enrichment.[130]

Fault Based Interference with Goods Under German Law

6.41 Markesinis[131] notes that, where there is fault, interference with the substance of a thing can give rise to delictual liability under BGB §823 I. The example given is of the plaintiff's ring dropped in the river. In the absence of fault, the rules on property in book 3 of the BGB come into play: under §985, there is a real action for dispossession, and in §1004 a remedy for interferences falling short of dispossession.[132] Markesinis[133] also observes that §823 I supplies a remedy for interference with possession as well as with ownership provided the possessor is in a position similar to that of an owner.

---

[125] J Carbonnier, *Droit Civil, Tome 3, Les biens (Monnaie, immeubles, meubles)* (16th edn, Presses Universitaires de France, 1995) 398, para 228.
[126] See N Horn, H Kötz and HG Leser (trans Weir), *German Private and Commercial Law: An Introduction* (Oxford: Clarendon, 1982) 176.
[127] BGB §932.   [128] BGB §935.
[129] Hand wahre Hand: the original owner looks to his bailee.
[130] BGB §816.
[131] *The German Law of Obligations, Volume II The Law of Torts: A Comparative Introduction* (3rd edn, Oxford: Clarendon, 1994) (reprinted with same pagination 'with corrections and additions' 1997).
[132] These rules apply to movables and immovables alike, but are more likely to be seen at work in the case of the latter.
[133] Citing Medicus.

2. APPLICATION OF JURISDICTIONAL PROVISIONS

The EC Rules: Article 5(3) of the Brussels I Regulation

Is an action for revendication or conversion or fault based interference with goods within the scope of Article 5(3)?

The fundamental differences between the common law concept of con- **6.42** version and the civil law concept of revendication make it particularly difficult to answer this question. This can only be done by looking carefully at the basis of the claim. This means looking separately at: an action for revendication; an action based on the English law of conversion; an action for fault based dispossession under German law; and claims in tort and contract. There is also a lack of direct authority from the European Court of Justice and from national courts in relation to such claims, so what is said below must be rather tentative.

An action for revendication Applying the wide definition of the scope **6.43** of Article 5(3) adopted by the European Court of Justice,[134] an action for revendication will fall within this provision if it is one which seeks to establish the liability of a defendant and which is not related to a 'contract' within the meaning of Article 5(1). An action for revendication is not a matter relating to a contract within the meaning of Article 5(1). It is a matter of property. Does such an action seek to establish the liability of a defendant? 'Liability' has been widely defined to encompass types of legal liability other than the obligation to make financial reparation, such as refraining from certain types of unlawful conduct.[135] Thus a plaintiff may seek to establish liability not just by claiming compensation. He could equally do so by seeking an injunction to prevent damage[136] or by seeking a declaration that certain conduct is unlawful as an essential precursor to an action for damages.[137] Each of these has been held to come within the scope of Article 5(3). The liability can be in respect of a non-contractual obligation, i.e. one that is not in a strict sense tortious or delictual.[138]

Even so, it is doubtful whether an action for revendication can be said to **6.44** seek to establish the liability of a defendant. In *Reichert v Dresdner Bank*

---

[134] See above, paras 6.11–12.
[135] Case C-167/00 *Verein Fur Konsumenteninformation v KH Henkel* [2002] ECR I-8111, para 36 of the opinion of AG Jacobs. See also AG Geelhoed in the *Fonderie* case, [2002] ECR I-7357, at para 76 of his opinion who said that Art 5(3) covered a 'failure to comply with a legal rule regulating conduct'. The statement by the Bundesgerichtshof in *Re Mail Order Promise of Win in a Draw* [2003] IL Pr 46, that Art 5(3) relates to actions asserting the defendant is liable in damages, must be regarded as incorrect.
[136] As in the *Verein* case, n 135 above.
[137] Case C-18/02 *DFDS v SEKO* [2004] IL Pr 10 at [19]–[28].
[138] The *Fonderie* case, n 135 above.

(No 2),[139] the European Court of Justice held that an action whereby a creditor sought to set aside a gift of property made by a debtor, which allegedly defrauded him of his rights (an action paulienne under French law) did not seek to establish the liability of a defendant in the sense understood in Article 5(3). The Court explained that:

> The object of such an action is not to compel the debtor to make good the damage he has caused the creditor by his fraudulent act, but to set aside, as against the creditor, the effects of the disposition by the debtor. It is directed not only against the debtor but also against the beneficiary of the disposition, viz a third party in relation to the debtor's obligation to the creditor, even if, where the disposition is by way of gift, the debtor does not commit a wrongful act.[140]

Indeed, the action can take effect against a bona fide third party who has not committed a wrongful act. There are obvious parallels between an action paulienne and an action for revendication. The object of an action for revendication is not to compel the defendant to make good the damage he has caused the plaintiff by his unlawful act but to recover possession. It may also be directed against a bona fide third party acquirer of the property. The upshot is that an action for revendication probably should not be regarded as falling within the scope of Article 5(3).

6.45   There is another potential reason why an action for revendication might fall outside the scope of Article 5(3) which should briefly be examined. This is if there were no harmful event.[141] This is a wide concept and with regard to consumer protection it covers situations other than where an individual has personally suffered damage.[142] As will be seen, with an action for revendication, it is possible to identify a harmful event, both in terms of damage and an event giving rise to the damage.

6.46   **An action based on the English law of conversion**   Under English law, and also that of Ireland, an action for conversion is classified as a tort. However, the question we have to ask is whether such an action is a tort, delict or quasi-delict within the meaning of Article 5(3) of the Brussels I Regulation. In other words, is it one which seeks to establish the liability

---

[139] Case C-261/90 [1992] ECR I-2149.

[140] ibid, para 19.

[141] As required by *Kleinwort Benson Ltd v Glasgow City Council* [1999] 1 AC 153 at 172 (*per* Lord Goff), 185 (*per* Lord Clyde), 196 (*per* Lord Hutton), 172 (*per* Lord Mustill), 177 (*per* Lord Nicholls).

[142] The *Verein* case, n 135 above, para 42. In the instant case, the concept of a 'harmful event' covered the undermining of legal stability by the use of unfair terms which it was the task of associations such as the Consumers' Association to prevent. This was an action to prevent damage and it was held that Art 5(3) of the Brussels Convention encompasses this. Art 5(3) of the Brussels I Regulation expressly allocates jurisdiction to the place where the harmful event may occur.

of a defendant and which is not related to a 'contract' within the meaning of Article 5(1)? An action for conversion is not a matter relating to a contract within the meaning of Article 5(1). The action is tortious according to English and Irish law. The European Court could conceivably take the view that it is a matter of property, on the basis that in other EC Member States whose law is based on the civil law tradition, the nearest equivalent law is cast as pure property law as opposed to delict.[143] This, though, would still mean that it is not a contractual matter. If damages are sought for conversion this is also an action which seeks to establish the liability of a defendant.[144] It is an action to compel the defendant to make good the damage he has caused the plaintiff by his unlawful act.[145] It is not directed against a bona fide third party who has not committed a wrongful act.[146] However, the position is more difficult if specific restitution of the goods is sought.[147] It could be argued that this is not an action which seeks to establish the liability of a defendant.[148] However, against this it has been pointed out that under English law there has been a wrongful act (a denial of title) and damages are available for this.[149] Moreover, Morison J in *Cronos Containers NV v Palatin*,[150] held that a claim for proprietary restitution of money based on conversion did seek to establish the liability of a defendant. Turning to the separate requirement that there is a harmful event, an action for conversion, like one for revendication, can be analysed in terms of a harmful event, both in terms of damage and an event giving rise to the damage.[151] This is so not only where damages are sought but also where what is sought is specific restitution of the goods.[152] The upshot is that an action for conversion should be regarded as falling within the scope of Article 5(3). In *Bank of Tokyo-Mitsubishi Ltd v*

---

[143] When it comes to classifying the action what matters is not how English law classifies it, even though the action is based on English law, but how Member States generally classify it: Case C-26/91 *Jakob Handte & Co GmbH v Traitements Mécano-Chimiques des Surfaces (TMCS)* [1992] ECR I-3967—a case concerned with the meaning of matters relating to a contract for the purposes of Art 5(1), discussed above, para 3.63.

[144] See *Cronos Containers NV v Palatin* [2002] EWHC 2819 (Comm) at [16] and [18], [2003] 2 Lloyd's Rep 489. This was a conversion case where what was sought was proprietary restitution of money. This is a more difficult situation than one where damages are sought. Nonetheless, Morison J held that the claim was one to establish the liability of the defendant for the purposes of Art 5(3).

[145] Compare *Reichert v Dresdner Bank (No 2)*, n 139 above, and accompanying discussion; distinguished in the *Cronos* case, n 144 above, at [15]

[146] ibid.

[147] In certain circumstances, specific restitution of the goods will be available, see Todd, n 113 above, at 594. Proprietary restitution based on the law of property or on unjust enrichment is discussed below, paras 8.107–121.

[148] See generally the discussion in Briggs and Rees, 2.138.

[149] ibid.   [150] [2003] 2 Lloyd's Rep 489 at [15].

[151] See below, paras 6.52–54.   [152] See the *Cronos* case, n 144 above, at [18].

Baskan Gida Sanayi Ve Pazarlama AS,[153] Lawrence Collins J accepted that it did so fall. However, this was not a point at issue between the parties.

6.47 **An action for fault based interference with goods under German law**   It is submitted that the analysis of such an action is essentially the same as that for an action for conversion under English law. This is not a matter relating to a contract within the meaning of Article 5(1). A fault based dispossession under German law gives rise to delictual liability under BGB §823 I. However, the European Court of Justice could conceivably classify such an action as being a matter of property. This, though, would still mean that it is not a contractual matter. It is also an action which seeks to establish the liability of a defendant. Moreover, with such an action there is a harmful event. The upshot is that an action for fault based dispossession under German law should be regarded as falling within the scope of Article 5(3).

6.48 **Claims in tort and contract**   The fact that a claimant bringing the action for conversion adds this onto a separate claim for breach of contract does not stop the action for conversion from involving a matter relating to tort etc. In this situation the claims are separate, i.e. they are based on different facts, and will accordingly be treated separately for the purpose of Article 5 of the Brussels I Regulation.[154] Likewise, the fact that a claimant bringing the action solely for conversion has a contractual relationship with the defendant, i.e. they are buyer and seller,[155] will not prevent the action from being regarded as a matter relating to tort etc.[156] It worth noting though that where the parties to the action for conversion have a contractual relationship there is always the possibility of their contract containing a jurisdiction clause. The issue will then arise of whether this clause is wide enough in scope to encompass a claim in conversion.[157]

The place where the harmful event occurred

6.49 **An action for revendication**   If, contrary to what is argued above, an action for revendication based on French or German law falls within the scope of Article 5(3), it is necessary to identify the place of the event giving rise to the damage and the place where the damage occurred. Identification of these places involves looking at the elements of the 'tort, delict or quasi-delict'. A practical problem with this is that there is no such thing as a common European concept of revendication. The European Court of Justice would want to define these places in such a way that they

---

[153]   [2004] EWHC 945 (Ch) at [218].   [154]   See above, para 3.73.
[155]   See, e.g. *Glencore International AG v Metro Trading International Inc (No 2)* [2001] 1 Lloyd's Rep 284. The case raised the question of the effect of a choice of law clause on the law applicable to tort of conversion and is examined below, paras 17.76–81 and 20.25.
[156]   See above, para 3.73.   [157]   See generally the discussion above, paras 6.03–05.

operate, regardless of on which Member State's law the action is based.[158] But it is difficult to see how this can be done with this particular 'tort, delict or quasi-delict', given the lack of common ground between civil law revendication and the common law concept of conversion. The only practicable solution is to look at the common elements of revendication as laid down by French and German law. Any definition of these places for the purposes of revendication would only apply in relation to actions based on French or German law.

The place of the event giving rise to the damage   The identification of this **6.50** place can be illustrated by a simple example. Goods are stolen in Belgium by B from the owner, A, who is domiciled in Belgium, and taken to France where B sells them to an innocent third party, C, who is domiciled in England. B disappears with the proceeds of sale and cannot be found. A brings an action in France against C for revendication of the goods. It is submitted that the damage suffered by A is the loss of the possession of the goods. The event giving rise to this is the acquisition of the goods by C. This takes place in France and therefore the French courts have jurisdiction under Article 5(3). The more obvious act which leads to the loss of possession of the goods by A is their theft. But this is an act committed by B and should not be regarded as the relevant event when the action is against C. The act by C which leads to the continuing loss of possession by A is his (C's) acquisition of the goods.

The place where the damage occurred   It is submitted that the damage **6.51** suffered by A is the loss of the possession of the goods. In the above example, where the action is brought against C, this occurs in France when C acquires possession of the goods. The place where the event giving rise to the harmful event and the place where the damage occurred are both in the same Member State.

An action for conversion   If, as is argued above, a claim for conversion **6.52** based on English law falls within the scope of Article 5(3), it is necessary to identify the place of the event giving rise to the damage and the place where the damage occurred. When identifying these places the same practical problem arises as with an action for revendication in that there is no such thing as a common European concept of conversion. It is therefore difficult to see how one can define these places in such a way that they operate, regardless of on which Member State's law the action is based. The only practicable solution is to look at the elements of conversion as

---

[158] Case C-68/93 *Shevill v Presse Alliance SA* [1995] 2 WLR 499—in cases of multi-state defamation, the definition of the place of the harmful event adopted by the ECJ will apply regardless of whether it is a defamation case brought under the French law of defamation or under the different English law.

laid down by English and Irish law. Any definition of these places for the purposes of conversion would only apply in relation to claims based on English or Irish law.

6.53 *The place of the event giving rise to the damage*   It is submitted that with the tort of conversion the event giving rise to the damage is the act, such as the unauthorized receiving of goods, which this tort requires. This was the view of Lawrence Collins J in *Bank of Tokyo-Mitsubishi Ltd v Baskan Gida Sanayi Ve Pazarlama AS.*[159] The position is analogous to that under the traditional rules.[160] It is perhaps inevitable that this should be so since in the latter context we are concerned, as we are in the present context, with the elements of the tort as laid down by English law. The act of conversion does not have to be communicated to the plaintiff for the cause of action to arise.[161] With tangible goods there is normally no problem in identifying the place where this act occurred.[162] For example, if the act is the unauthorized receiving of goods, it takes place in the Member State in which the goods were received, i.e. in which they were delivered. Thus in the *Cronos* case,[163] the act of conversion was diverting money from a bank account abroad to a bank account in England. It was held that the harmful act for the purposes of Article 5(3) took place in England.[164] In *Bank of Tokyo-Mitsubishi Ltd v Baskan Gida Sanayi Ve Pazarlama AS*[165] the act of conversion by the defendants appears to have been receiving hazelnuts pledged to the claimant bank. Lawrence Collins J, after pointing out that these goods were released in Turkey and delivered to the defendant companies in Turkey or Italy, France and Germany, held that neither the act of conversion nor the damage (the loss of security) took place in England.[166] If the act is the use of goods involving transformation, it takes place in the Member State in which the goods were used. If the act is the unauthorized detention of goods, it takes place in the Member State in which the goods were detained. If the act is a refusal to deliver to the true owner, it takes place in the Member State in which delivery should have been made. However, the position is more difficult if the act is the disposal of the goods to someone else. This takes place in the Member State in which the disposal was effected. The determination of this place requires identification of the precise act of disposal. If this is the sale and delivery to another person, disposal should be regarded as being effected in the place where the goods were delivered. However, if, as is arguably the case, the mere offer to sell to another is regarded as a sufficient act for the purposes

---

[159] [2004] EWHC 945 (Ch) at [218].   [160] See below, paras 6.59–61.

[161] See Webb, PRH, and North, PM, 'Thoughts on the place of commission of a non-statutory tort' (1965) 14 ICLQ 1314, 1346.

[162] For problems in relation to digitized products see below, para 10.192.

[163] n 144 above.   [164] ibid, at [18].

[165] [2004] EWHC 945 (Ch).   [166] ibid, at [218].

of conversion then disposal should be regarded as being effected where the offer is made. The fact that conversion can be committed in many different ways means that potentially the plaintiff may be given a choice of fora under the place of the event rule. There is nothing to prevent the claimant from choosing the particular act of conversion that suits his jurisdictional (or choice of law) purposes. In particular, there is no rule that would amalgamate a defendant's several acts of conversion so as to locate the centre of gravity of the defendant's tortious misconduct.[167]

The place where the damage occurred   The fact that under the English law of **6.54** conversion proof of damage is not one of the elements of the tort does not preclude the use of Article 5(3).[168] The *direct* damage to the plaintiff, and this is what Article 5(3) is referring to, is normally the loss of the goods.[169] In *Bank of Tokyo-Mitsubishi Ltd v Baskan Gida Sanayi Ve Pazarlama AS,*[170] where the goods converted by the defendants by receiving them were pledged to the claimant bank, it was the loss of security.[171] Again the position is analogous to that under the traditional rules. Let us assume that this loss has occurred abroad. The English courts will have no jurisdiction under the damage limb. If the plaintiff is an English company this loss can have financial consequences in England. Nevertheless, the English courts will still lack jurisdiction under the damage limb of Article 5(3). The financial consequences in England are a form of indirect damage and accordingly do not give the English courts jurisdiction under the damage limb of Article 5(3).[172]

An action for fault based interference with goods under German 6.55 law   It is submitted that, when it comes to the identification of the place where the harmful event occurred, the position in an action for fault based dispossession under German law is essentially the same as for a claim based on the English law of conversion. Thus the event giving rise to the damage is the act of fault based dispossession which this tort requires. The *direct* damage to the plaintiff is the loss of the goods.

---

[167] Compare the position in contract under Art 5(1) of the Brussels I Regulation. Where a claim is based on several obligations, the principal obligation is identified, Case 266/85 *Shenavai v Kreischer* [1987] ECR 239.

[168] The European Court of Justice in the *Shevill* case, n 158 above, held that the fact that under national law damage is presumed in cases of libel did not preclude the application of Art 5(3).

[169] In some circumstances, specific restitution of the goods will be available, see Todd, n 113 above, at 594. But compare the *Cronos* case, n 144 above, at [18] where it was held that the damage occurred both when the money diverted from a bank account abroad was paid into the bank account in England and when it was removed and used to pay for improvements to a house in England.

[170] [2004] EWHC 945 (Ch).   [171] ibid, at [218].

[172] See Case C-364/93 *Marinari v Lloyds Bank plc (Zubaidi Trading Co intervener)* [1995] ECR I-2719.

Proprietary matters

6.56 One of the elements of the tort of conversion under English law is that the defendant's conduct was inconsistent with the rights of the owner or other person entitled to possession. There may be no dispute between the parties over this particular issue. However, in practice the question of who owns the property or is entitled to possession will not uncommonly come into issue. This presents no problem if there is jurisdiction over the defendant by virtue of Article 2 of the Brussels I Regulation, for this is not concerned with the matter before the court. But does the court with juris-diction over the tort claim for conversion by virtue of Article 5(3) also have jurisdiction in relation to the dispute over the issue of ownership/possession? This is a matter of some complexity because of the different ways in which the dispute over ownership can be raised before the court. It will be examined in Chapter 7 which deals with jurisdiction in relation to proprietary matters.[173]

The Traditional English Rules: Rule 6.20(8) of the Civil Procedure Rules

6.57 In a claim for conversion brought under the traditional rules, it may be possible to serve a claim form within the jurisdiction. This is what happened in the House of Lords case of *Kuwait Airways Corp v Iraq Airways Co*[174] where service was made at the defendant's London office and this was held to be good service. There are no particular problems of service within the jurisdiction in conversion cases. The same would be true if an action were to be brought in England for revendication based on French or German law. The more interesting question is how the tort ground for service out of the jurisdiction, r 6.20(8) of the Civil Procedure Rules, operates in such cases.

Is a claim for conversion or revendication made in tort?

6.58 A claim for wrongful interference with goods, such as for conversion, is founded on what is, in English law, a tort and, accordingly should be regarded as being made in tort for the purpose of jurisdiction under r 6.20(8) of the Civil Procedure Rules. This point was accepted without argument by Rix J in *Bastone & Firminger Ltd v Nasima Enterprises (Nigeria) Ltd*[175] and by Jacob J in *Beecham Group plc v Norton Healthcare Ltd*.[176] An

---

[173] See below, paras 7.12–18.
[174] n 109 above.
[175] [1996] CLC 1902. Conversion has been accepted as a tort for choice of law purposes, see *Glencore International AG v MetroTrading International Inc (No 2)* [2001] 1 Lloyd's Rep 284; discussed below, paras 17.76–81.
[176] [1997] FSR 81.

action for fault based dispossession under German law gives rise to delictual liability under BGB §823 I and should therefore also be regarded as coming within r 6.20(8). In contrast, an action for revendication cannot be classified as a tort (in a strict sense).[177] It is founded on the law of property, and, accordingly, should not be regarded as being made in tort for the purpose of jurisdiction under r 6.20(8). The rest of the discussion will therefore concentrate on actions for conversion.[178]

An act of conversion committed within the jurisdiction

It is submitted that the act of conversion in question is the act of dealing **6.59** with a chattel in a manner inconsistent with another's rights. This act does not have to be communicated to the plaintiff for the cause of action to arise.[179] In the *Bastone* case, counsel for the plaintiff accepted that the relevant acts constituting the torts of conversion or wrongful interference with goods took place in Nigeria and therefore jurisdiction could not be founded on this first alternative under Order 11, r 1(1)(f).[180] This was undoubtedly correct. The plaintiff English sellers sold consignments of chemical products to a Nigerian company (Nasima) and the goods were shipped to Nigeria. Payment was to be made under bills of exchange. The defendant Nigerian bank (Ecobank) was appointed as collecting bank and was instructed to warehouse the goods on arrival and to release the shipping documents upon acceptance by Nasima of the relevant bills of exchange. The plaintiff was never paid for the goods, which were released from custody. The plaintiff brought an action against Ecobank in tort for conversion or wrongful interference with the consignments or documents sent out to Nigeria. The act of conversion or wrongful interference was presumably the release of the goods from the warehouse and the release of the documents when these should have been retained until proper acceptance or payment of the bills.

It has previously seen that conversion can be committed in many different **6.60** ways. Take the case of a buyer who buys from someone without title. Buying and taking delivery can be conversion. Use involving wear and

---

[177] Compare the wide definition of a tort, delict or quasi-delict for the purposes of Art 5(3) of the Brussels I Regulation, discussed above, paras 6.11–12.

[178] An action for fault based dispossession under German law is perhaps unlikely to be brought in England. If it were to be, it would be necessary to look at the elements of this tort under German law to work out whether the damage was sustained in England or the act from which the damage resulted was committed in England.

[179] See Webb, PRH, and North, PM, n 161 above, at 1346.

[180] n 175 above, at 1910. An attempt to base jurisdiction on the multi-defendant head also failed, see below, para 9.36.

tear, certainly transformation, can be conversion. A refusal to deliver to the true owner can be conversion. A disposition to someone else can be conversion. There is nothing to prevent the claimant from choosing the particular act of conversion that suits his jurisdictional (or choice of law) purposes. The position is the same as under the EC rules in that there is no rule that would amalgamate a defendant's several acts of conversion so as to locate the centre of gravity of the defendant's tortious misconduct.

6.61 There will usually be no difficulty in ascertaining the place where this act of conversion was committed and thus whether it was committed within the jurisdiction. For example, in a case where the act is that of receiving goods (where this amounts to an assertion of dominion over the goods which is inconsistent with owner's rights), this will be committed in England if the goods are received there, i.e. they are delivered there. If the act is the use of goods involving transformation, it is committed in England if this is where the goods were used. If the act is the unauthorized detention of goods, it is committed in England if this is where the goods were detained. If the act is a refusal to deliver to the true owner, it is committed in England if this is where delivery should have been made. If the act is the disposal of the goods to someone else, this is committed in England if this is where the disposal was effected. The determination of this place requires identification of the precise act of disposal. If this is the sale and delivery to another person, disposal should be regarded as being effected in England if this is where the goods were delivered. However, if the mere offer to sell to another is a sufficient act for the purposes of conversion then disposal should be regarded as being effected in England if this is where the offer was made. This in turn raises the problem of where an offer is made. The offer may be contained in a letter/fax/telex/email sent from country A to someone in country B. Is this act committed when and where the offer is sent or when and where it is received? The analogy can be applied with the torts of negligent misstatement and negligent and fraudulent misrepresentation.[181] In cases where an instantaneous form of communication has been used, such as by fax/telex/email, the act of making an offer is probably best regarded as being committed where the offer is received. However, where the offer is contained in a letter it is arguable that the act is committed when and where the letter is posted.[182] If the act of conversion consists of giving an order the same problem arises of identifying where an order is made and the same solution should be adopted as for offers.

---

[181] See below, paras 6.101–102.
[182] ibid.

Damage resulting from the act of conversion was sustained within the jurisdiction

Nor in the *Bastone* case was damage sustained within the jurisdiction. **6.62**
Rix J held that the damage was sustained in Nigeria.[183] It was there that
documents and goods were lost to the plaintiff. It was only the financial
consequences that were felt in England, the plaintiff being an English
company, and this was not enough to found jurisdiction.[184] Admittedly,
if the goods and documents had not already been lost in Nigeria, the
documents might have been returned to England and the goods disposed
of. But by then both had already been lost and the damage sustained.

The *Bastone* case was followed by Jacob J in *Beecham Group plc v Norton* **6.63**
Healthcare Ltd.[185] The case concerned the manufacture in Slovenia of an
antibiotic drug for importation into the United Kingdom. It was argued
that this manufacture would cause the plaintiff, which had patents over a
strain which it was alleged was contained in the drug, direct damage in
England. Jacob J rejected this argument. He held that the direct damage to
the plaintiff was caused by the sale in England of the finished product
by the first defendant, the English importer, not the use of the strain (the
wrongful interference) by the second defendant, the Slovenian manufacturer and supplier. The mere effect on the plaintiff's financial position
in England was not enough. The result was that the case did not fall
within Order 11, r 1(1)(f).[186]

Proprietary matters

In conversion cases, the question of who owns the property or is entitled **6.64**
to possession will not uncommonly come into issue. There is no problem
if service has been effected within the jurisdiction because this is not
concerned with the nature of the claim. But does the English court which
has jurisdiction over the tort claim for conversion by virtue of r 6.20(8)
also have jurisdiction over the dispute as to the issue of ownership/
possession? Is a claim made in tort? This is a matter of some complexity
because of the different ways in which the dispute over ownership can be
raised before the court. It will be examined in Chapter 7 which deals with
jurisdiction in relation to proprietary matters.[187]

Forum conveniens

It is necessary to determine where the tort of conversion was committed **6.65**
so as to apply the principle that the jurisdiction in which a tort was

---

[183] n 175 above, at 1912.   [184] ibid.   [185] n 176 above.
[186] However, it did fall within the multi-defendant head of Ord 11, r 1(1). This head is
discussed below, paras 9.26–30.
[187] See below, paras 7.12–18. See also the discussion of r 6.20(10) CPR at para 6.66.

committed is, *prima facie*, the natural forum for trial. This means looking at where in substance this tort was committed. This does not present as much of a problem as arises with some other torts because the essential elements of the tort of conversion (an act inconsistent with the rights of an owner, a deliberate act, conduct so extensive an encroachment on the rights of the owner as to exclude him from use and possession of the goods) are likely to be committed in the same state. Thus the act of conversion is likely to be committed in the same state as that where the owner is excluded from use and possession of the goods since it is that act which excludes the owner from use and possession. However, it is possible to envisage a case where the conversion consists of the giving of orders in one country which results in goods being transferred in another country. Is the substance of the tort committed where the order is given or where the goods are transferred? No help is to be obtained from looking at other torts. With some torts the courts have opted for one of the last elements in the sequence of elements that go to make up the tort,[188] with other torts the courts have opted for one of the first elements.[189] The essence of the tort of conversion is 'the denial by the defendant of the possessory interest or title of the plaintiff in the goods'. In other words it is an act. It is submitted therefore that the tort of conversion should be regarded as having in substance been committed in the state where the act of conversion took place.[190] Thus in a case where the act of conversion consists of receiving goods and this act took place in England (the goods having been received, ie delivered, there) the tort should be regarded as having in substance been committed in England.

The Traditional English Rules: Rule 6.20(10) of the Civil Procedure Rules

6.66 A claim form may be served out of the jurisdiction with the permission of the court if the whole subject-matter of a claim relates to property located within the jurisdiction. This ground has been widely interpreted so that it would encompass a claim for damages arising from a tort relating to property located within the jurisdiction.[191] An obvious example of this would be a claim for damages for conversion of goods located within the jurisdiction. The claim for damages relates to the property in that it seeks

---

[188] See the discussion of misstatement, below, paras 6.110–113, and inducement of breach of contract, below, para 6.146.

[189] See the discussion of negligence, below, para 6.172.

[190] Webb and North, n 161 above, 1345–1347, citing *Rourk v Wiedenbach* (1901) 1 OLR 581. For identification of this place, see above, paras 6.59–61. See also the discussion below, para 17.73.

[191] r 6.20(10) CPR is discussed in more detail below, paras 7.27–45.

to compensate the claimant for the loss suffered from being deprived of the use and possession of the property. Similarly, an action for fault based dispossession under German law, even though it gives rise to delictual liability under BGB §823 I, would come within this provision This ground for service out of the jurisdiction could also be used if a claim were to be brought in England for revendication based on French or German law. The fact that such a claim is based on the law of property means that it would be uncontroversial that it would come within this ground, provided, of course, that the property was located within the jurisdiction.

IV. NEGLIGENT MISSTATEMENT, NEGLIGENT AND FRAUDULENT MISREPRESENTATION

1. THE SUBSTANTIVE LAW BACKGROUND

English Law

Under English law, where a party has been induced to enter a contract by **6.67** a misrepresentation he has a choice of remedies.[192] He may seek to rescind the contract. This is a contractual remedy or in, some circumstances, a restitutionary remedy.[193] Alternatively, he may decide to sue for damages.[194] First of all, there is the common law tort of negligent misstatement, exemplified by *Hedley Byrne v Heller*,[195] which is capable of arising in a precontractual setting in cases of a special relationship (one party reposing trust in the other to exercise care and that other undertaking responsibility). Negligent misstatement has the following ingredients: (a) the defendant must have negligently made an incorrect statement; (b) the claimant must have reasonably relied on this; (c) the claimant must have thereby incurred loss.[196] Second, there is the additional statutory tort of negligent misrepresentation in s 2(1) of the Misrepresentation Act 1967. The Act does not apply where the parties did not enter into a contract or the representation was made by a person not a party to the contract.[197]

---

[192] *Agnew v Lansforsakringsbolagens AB* [2001] 1 AC 223, 252–253 (*per* Lord Hope).

[193] See below, paras 8.24–25.

[194] The *Agnew* case, n 192 above, at 246 (*per* Lord Cooke). The claim form may set out the alternatives of rescission or damages, see *Thierry Morin v Bonhams & Brooks Limited and Bonhams & Brooks SAM* [2003] EWHC 467 (Comm), [2003] IL Pr 25; aff'd [2003] EWCA 1802, [2004] IL Pr 24.

[195] [1964] AC 465.

[196] *Thierry Morin v Bonhams & Brooks Limited and Bonhams & Brooks SAM* [2003] EWCA 1802, [2004] IL Pr 24 at [14]. See generally WVH Rogers (ed), *Winfield and Jolowicz on Tort* (16th edn, London: Sweet & Maxwell, 2002) 381–399.

[197] AM Dugdale (ed), *Clerk and Lindsell on Torts* (18th edn, London: Sweet & Maxwell, 2000) 15–44.

Third, there is the non-negligent misrepresentation that sounds in damages where the court exercises its discretion not to allow rescission (s 2(2) of the 1967 Act).[198] This is hard to classify: it is probably best regarded as a remedial alternative to the exercise of a contractual remedy, rescission, and so it should be classified as either contractual or pro-cedural, but not tortious. In *William Sindall plc v Cambridgeshire County Council*,[199] Hoffmann LJ stated that damages under s 2(2) should never exceed damages for breach of warranty in contract. Fourth, there is the tort of fraudulent misrepresentation or, as it is often called, deceit.[200] Fraud is the making of a statement without belief in its truth; there must be at least recklessness,[201] though there need not be an intent to injure the claimant.

6.68 Where a contract of sale ensues, it is far better for a claimant to rely on s 2(1) of the 1967 Act than on negligent misstatement. This is because of: (a) the presumption of negligence in s 2(1); and (b) the rules on damages arising out of the fiction of fraud in s 2(1). According to *Royscot Trust Ltd v Anderson*,[202] the measure of damages under s 2(1) is the measure granted in the tort of deceit and not the measure in the tort of negligence. Hence damages will be granted for all losses arising out of entry into the contract and not just for losses that were foreseeable, provided they are not other-wise too remote.[203] The House of Lords in *Smith New Court Securities Ltd v Citibank NA*,[204] stated that direct losses caused by entry into the contract,[205] even if unforeseeable, could be recovered in deceit. Direct losses arising out of entry into the contract include losses sustained on a post-contract falling market. Hence the reference to fraud in s 2(1) has a considerable impact.

6.69 A claim under *Hedley Byrne* can coexist with a claim for breach of a contractual duty to take care, so as to leave the claimant a free choice.[206] A claim under s 2(1) similarly should coexist with a claim for breach of warranty (this seems to follow from s 1(a) of the Misrepresentation Act 1967 which preserves the right to rescind for misrepresentation although the misrepresentation has become a term of the contract). A claimant can sue a seller for breach of contract and a third party, for example a manu-facturer, for negligent misstatement.

---

[198] The claim may refer in the alternative to all three of these bases for damages.
[199] [1994] 1 WLR 1016.
[200] *Clerk and Lindsell on Torts*, n 197 above, Ch 15; *Winfield and Jolowicz on Tort*, n 196 above, 369–381.
[201] *Derry v Peek* (1889) 14 App Cas 337.   [202] [1991] 3 WLR 57, CA.
[203] In the sense, seemingly, of the chain of causation being broken by a *novus actus*.
[204] [1997] AC 254, HL.   [205] Note: not caused by the fraud.
[206] *Henderson v Merrett Syndicates Ltd* [1995] 2 AC 145—thus permitting a tort claim under the Latent Damage Act 1986, which does not apply to contract claims.

In the situation where there is no contractual relationship between the **6.70** parties, negligent misstatement has to be used, rather than s 2(1). A common example arising out of a contract for the international sale of goods is where the buyer of goods which do not conform with the contract brings a claim for negligent misstatement against a company which has certified that the goods did conform with the contract in terms of quantity and quality, acting in reliance on which the buyer paid for the goods. This claim may well be combined with a separate claim against the seller for breach of contract.

A claim for negligent misstatement, or negligent or fraudulent misrepre- **6.71** sentation may arise out of the carriage of the goods. Thus a carrier who issues a clean bill of lading, attesting to the goods being received in apparent good order and condition when they manifestly are not, is guilty of fraud and for that reason cannot enforce an indemnity promised by the consignor (shipper) for a clean bill.[207] At common law, the carrier is also conclusively estopped by the statement in the event of proceedings brought by the consignee under the contract of carriage. Where it is the consignor bringing proceedings, the carrier's statement is, *prima facie*, evidence of the condition of the goods on shipment. The same is true under the Hague-Visby Rules.[208]

French and German Law

As far as French substantive law is concerned, the rules on delict govern **6.72** the negotiation process[209] since the Code civil has no contract formation rules outside the vices du consentement.[210] There is a principle of 'loyal [i.e. fair] and good faith negotiating',[211] with liability for breach of negotiations when the other party would expect a contract to be concluded.[212]

In the case of French law, when it comes to the question of overlap **6.73** between contract and delict, the first point to note is the doctrine of non-cumul which prevents at least two types of conduct: (a) combining features of delict and contract to enhance liability; and (b) selecting delict where the parties' relationship is governed by contract.[213] If there is a valid contract and a contractual obligation extends to the operative facts, for example fault arising out of the performance of the contract, then the

---

[207] *Brown Jenkinson & Co Ltd v Percy Dalton Ltd* [1957] 2 QB 621.
[208] Art III, r 4.
[209] See E Hondius, *Precontractual Liability* (Deventer: Kluwer, 1991), Schmidt-Szalewski, the French Reporter Ch 9, 148.
[210] ibid, at 147.   [211] ibid, at 150.   [212] Com 20 mars 1972.
[213] See J Carbonnier, *Droit Civil, Tome 4, Les obligations* (19th edn, Presses Universitaires de France, 1995) 459, para 292.

claimant may not sue in delict. But there do appear to be exceptions to non-cumul.[214] An exclusion clause in the contract is one such exception. This may block a claim in contract but leave open a subsidiary claim in delict. Another example is the claimant suing for delictual fault under Article 1382 of the Code civil, liability under the latter being of a public policy nature.[215] But if the obligation breached is precontractual and remains outside the contract, as in the case of fraud (*dol*) or in the abusive withdrawal of a contractual offer, then liability exists in delict.[216] Hence the commercial section of the Cour de cassation has held that the availability of avoidance (nullity) for *dol* does not prevent a claim for damages for fraudulent behaviour under Article 1382.[217] Further, if a contract is avoided for mistake (*erreur*), in cases where one party's mistake was induced by the fault of the other, the latter will be liable for damages in delict under Article 1382 of the Code civil.

6.74 German law subscribes to the principle of *culpa in contrahendo* whereby liability can arise as a result of pre-contractual fault. The classic case of *culpa in contrahendo* in German law is the person who is physically injured prior to buying linoleum[218] where there is 'a kind of proleptic contractual effect'.[219] This approach avoids delictual rules, including the restrictive rules on vicarious liability. There are various other advantages in German law of contract rules over delict rules.[220] One that deserves special mention is that they allow economic loss whereas the German rules on economic loss in the case of fault and delict[221] permit it only where it is consequent upon physical loss. There is the possibility of *culpa in contrahendo* in the following instances, inter alia:[222] reliance damages to the other party if the declarant of intention rescinds the declaration for mistake;[223] the offeror who neglects to inform the offeree as soon as possible that his acceptance, forwarded in the normal way, has been delayed in transit and thus has arrived out of time: a contract is deemed to be concluded;[224] and liability for wilfully damaging another, *contra bonos mores*, by breaking off negotiations,[225] though there is no decision on this point.[226]

---

[214] Carbonnier, ibid, at 459, para 292, and 290, para 176.
[215] On the public policy point, see Civ 2e, 17 févr 955, D 1956, 17 (note Esmein).
[216] See Carbonnier, n 213 above, at 458, para 292.
[217] Com 18 oct 1994.   [218] Reichsgerichtshof RGZ78, 239.
[219] Horn, Kötz and Leser, n 126 above, 108.
[220] See Markesinis, n 131 above, 777.   [221] BGB §823 I.
[222] See Hondius, n 209 above, Lorenz, the German Reporter, Ch 10.
[223] BGB §122.   [224] BGB §149.   [225] BGB §826.
[226] Lorenz in Hondius, n 222 above, describes this as 'astonishing'.

2. APPLICATION OF JURISDICTIONAL PROVISIONS

The EC Rules: Article 5(3) of the Brussels I Regulation

Is the action within the scope of Article 5(3)?

Differences between English law and that in other Member States in cases **6.75** of pre-contractual liability make it important to look closely at the basis of the action.

An action based on pre-contractual liability under civil law The **6.76** European Court of Justice in *Fonderie Officine Meccaniche Tacconi SpA v Heinrich Wagner Sinto Maschinenfabrik GmbH (HWS)*[227] held that a claim based on pre-contractual liability under Article 1337 of the Italian Civil Code, which provides that, in the context of the negotiations with a view to the formation of a contract, the parties must act in good faith, was a matter relating to tort, delict or quasi-delict within Article 5(3) of the Brussels Convention. The European Court of Justice adopted the wide view of Article 5(3), namely that it covers all actions which seek to establish the liability of a defendant and which are not related to a contract within the meaning of Article 5(1). The liability in question could not be contractual. First, there was no obligation for the purposes of Article 5(1).[228] In other words, there was no contractual obligation.[229] Second, there was no obligation *freely assumed by the defendant towards the plaintiff*.[230] The obligation to make good the damage allegedly caused by the unjustified breaking off of negotiations could derive only from breach of rules of law, in particular the rule which requires the parties to act in good faith in negotiations with a view to the formation of the contract.[231] In the light of this, it was a matter relating to tort etc.

An action for negligent misstatement, negligent or fraudulent mis- **6.77** **representation** There can be no doubt that an action for negligent misstatement comes within the scope of Article 5(3). This is not a matter relating to a contract within the meaning of Article 5(1). It is also an action which seeks to establish the liability of a defendant. Accordingly, it falls within the wide definition of the scope of Article 5(3) adopted by the

---

[227] Case C-334/00 [2002] ECR I-7357.   [228] ibid, para 22.
[229] Compare the decision in the *Agnew* case, n 192 above, where it was held that a pre-contractual obligation, which if not fulfilled provides the right to set aside a contract, can constitute a contractual obligation under Art 5(1); discussed above, paras 3.80–82.
[230] Case C-334/00 *Fonderie Officine Meccaniche Tacconi SpA v Heinrich Wagner Sinto Maschinenfabrik GmbH (HWS)* [2002] ECR I-7357, para 24. No contract was concluded between the parties. The liability followed on from the failure to conclude a contract. Compare the *Agnew* case, n 192 above, which involved liability in respect of a pre-contractual obligation where a contract was concluded. See generally on the requirement of an obligation freely assumed by one party towards the other, above, paras 3.64–66.
[231] The *Fonderie* case, ibid, para 25.

European Court of Justice.[232] Moreover, in a series of English national decisions, Article 5(3) of the Brussels Convention has been accepted as applying to such cases.[233] There is also English authority that a claim for negligent misrepresentation under Greek law[234] falls within Article 5(3).[235] As regards fraud, there are obiter dicta in the House of Lords[236] and there is also first instance authority that this too comes within Article 5(3).[237] There is likewise first instance authority that a claim for negligent misrepresentation under s 2(1) of the Misrepresentation Act 1967 falls within Article 5(3).[238] In contrast, a claim under s 2(2) of the Misrepresentation Act 1967, because it is best regarded as not being tortious, may well be treated by an English court as falling outside Article 5(3).[239] However, applying the wide definition of tort, delict or quasi-delict adopted by the European Court of Justice, the crucial question is whether this is a matter relating to a contract within the meaning of Article 5(1). If it is, it cannot fall within Article 5(3). As will be seen, rescission is regarded as a matter relating to a contract. A claim under s 2(2) is best regarded as a remedial alternative to rescission and therefore arguably should also be regarded as a matter relating to a contract. If, contrary to what has been suggested earlier in this chapter, s 2(2) is regarded as being procedural it could be said to be a procedural rule relating to a contract. It would therefore fall outside Article 5(3).

6.78 What if the parties have a contractual relationship?   We are concerned here with the scenario where the plaintiff is induced to enter into a contract with the defendant because of a misstatement/misrepresentation by the defendant. The plaintiff then brings an action in tort for negligent

---

[232] Moreover, since, as a matter of substantive law, such an action is classified in common law jurisdictions as a tort it would also no doubt be regarded by an English court as falling within the narrow definition adopted by the House of Lords in *Kleinwort Benson* case. But if you look at the classification adopted by other Member States in cases of pre-contractual liability should it really be regarded as tortious in the strict sense?

[233] *Minster Investments Ltd v Hyundai Precision & Industry Co Ltd* [1988] 2 Lloyd's Rep 621; *Domicrest Ltd v Swiss Bank Corp* [1999] QB 548; *Alfred Dunhill Ltd v Diffusion Internationale de Maroquinerie de Prestige* [2002] IL Pr 13. See also the obiter dicta by Chadwick LJ in *Viskase Ltd v Paul Kiefel GmbH* [1999] 1 WLR 1305 at 1320, CA, and Mance LJ in *ABCI v Banque Franco-Tunisienne* [2003] EWCA Civ 205 at [41], [2003] 2 Lloyd's Rep 146.

[234] ss 197 and 198 of the Greek Civil Code.

[235] *RZB v NGB* [1999] 1 Lloyd's Rep 408.

[236] *Agnew v Lansforsakringsbolagens AB* [2001] 1 AC 223, 259 and 252–253 (*per* Lord Hope).

[237] *Raiffeisen Zentral Bank Osterreich AG v Alexander Tranos* [2001] IL Pr 9 (the claim was based on fraudulent or negligent misrepresentations); *Bank of Tokyo-Mitsubishi Ltd v Baskan Gida Sanayi Ve Pazarlama AS* [2004] EWHC 945 (Ch) at [223] (a claim based on deceit and what was sometimes described as negligent misstatement and at other times as negligent misrepresentation).

[238] The *Alfred Dunhill* case, n 233 above; discussed below, para 6.82.

[239] Applying the narrow definition of the scope of Art 5(3) adopted by the House of Lords in the *Kleinwort Benson* case.

misstatement or negligent or fraudulent misrepresentation under English law. Is this a matter relating to tort, delict or quasi-delict under Article 5(3)? It cannot be so regarded if it is a matter relating to a contract within the meaning of Article 5(1). Although the parties have a contractual relationship there are serious questions over whether Article 5(1) can apply in the present situation.

First, Article 5(1) requires that there must be a *contractual obligation* freely **6.79** assumed by one party towards another.[240] Is there a contractual obligation in the present situation? Lord Millett in the House of Lords in the *Agnew* case[241] has said that under English law 'there is no contractual obligation not innocently to misrepresent the facts during contractual negotiations'. He pointed out though that this may give rise to an action in tort for damages for fraud. Lord Woolf in the same case appears to have had some doubts along the same lines, referring to: 'If it would be appropriate to refer to an obligation not to . . . induce a contract by mistake as relating to a contact . . .'.[242]

Second, is there an obligation *freely assumed by one party towards another*? **6.80** Let us assume for the sake of argument that there is a contractual obliga-tion not to misrepresent. It is submitted that this contractual obligation is freely assumed by one party towards another.[243] The parties have a direct contractual relationship. By voluntarily entering into a contract the parties freely assume the legal incidents of the contract.[244] Thus it would not matter whether that contractual obligation arose by operation of law as opposed to being a term of the contract.

Third, is there an identifiable place of performance of this contractual **6.81** obligation? Lord Woolf found another reason why it may not be possible to rely on Article 5(1) where a contract has been induced by mistake. This is because there could be no place for performance of such a negative obligation. The obligation not to misrepresent is likewise a negative obligation and likewise shares the same absence of a place of performance.

---

[240] Case C-26/91 *Société Jakob Handte et Cie GmbH v Société Traitements Mécano-Chimiques des Surfaces (TMCS)* [1992] ECR I-3967, 3994, para 15; Case C-51/97 *Réunion Européenne SA v Spliethoff's Bevrachtingskantoor BV* [1998] ECR I-6511, paras 17 and 19, [2000] QB 690; Case C-334/00 *Fonderie Officine Meccaniche Tacconi SpA v Heinrich Wagner Sinto Maschinenfabrik GmbH (HWS)* [2002] ECR I-7357, para 23. This requirement is discussed in detail above, paras 3.64–66.
[241] n 236 above, at 265.   [242] ibid, at 241.
[243] See generally Briggs and Rees, 2.121, who argue that liability for tortious misstatement falls within Art 5(1). But what of the need for a contractual obligation and an identifiable place of performance? For classification for choice of law purposes see below, paras 17.90–97.
[244] See Lord Millett in the *Agnew* case, n 236 above, at 264.

6.82   In conclusion, in the situation where the plaintiff is induced to enter into a contract with the defendant because of a misstatement/misrepresentation by the defendant, an action in tort for negligent misstatement or negligent or fraudulent misrepresentation under English law should not be regarded as a matter relating to a contract. What little authority there is supports this conclusion. It has been held that a claim for damages for alleged misrepresentation said to have induced the representee to enter into a contract with the representor was not a matter relating to a contract within the meaning of Article 5(1) of the Brussels Convention and that it fell squarely within Article 5(3).[245] Reliance was placed on obiter dicta by Lord Hope in the *Agnew* case,[246] where it was said that 'a liability in tort may arise in some circumstances where there has been a breach of duty in the formation of a contract, for example if the breach can be said to have been fraudulent. In that situation, it will be open to the injured party to claim damages, and jurisdiction may then be founded on the special rule in Article 5(3).'

6.83   **Claims in tort and contract**   We are concerned here with the situation where, for example, the plaintiff has been fraudulently induced to enter into a sale of goods contract because of a fraudulent misrepresentation that the goods (a machine) are ready for immediate use. As a result of this, the plaintiff suffers weeks of delay in preparing the machine for use and wishes to recover damages for this in tort. Moreover, the machine is not worth what the plaintiff paid for it because of certain defects. The fact that the claimant bringing the action for fraudulent misrepresentation inducing a contract adds this onto a separate claim for breach of the sales contract, does not stop the former action from being a matter relating to tort etc. In this situation, the claims are based on different facts and should be regarded as being separate claims, and, accordingly, should be treated separately for the purposes of Article 5 of the Brussels I Regulation.[247]

6.84   **An action for rescission**   We are concerned here with the situation where the plaintiff, as an alternative to claiming damages, seeks to rescind the contract. The House of Lords in *Agnew v Lansforsakringsbolagens AB*[248] held that a claim for a declaration that the plaintiffs were entitled to rescind contracts on the basis of misrepresentations and non-disclosure fell within the scope of Article 5(1) of the Lugano Convention.[249] It followed that the

---

[245] *Alfred Dunhill Ltd v Diffusion Internationale de Maroquinerie de Prestige* [2002] IL Pr 13 at [75]–[76].

[246] n 236 above, at 259.

[247] See in relation to separate claims and Art 5, above, para 3.73.

[248] n 236 above. The case is discussed in detail below, paras 8.24–25.

[249] The case concerned rescission as a contractual remedy. For the use of rescission as a restitutionary remedy see below, para 8.25.

claim fell outside the scope of Article 5(3) since the two articles are mutually exclusive.[250]

Alternative claims for rescission or damages in tort We are concerned **6.85** with the situation here where the claimant claims in the alternative for rescission or for damages in tort, whether under s 2(1) of the Misrepresentation Act 1967 or for negligent misstatement or for tortious misrepresentation under some foreign law.[251] The rescission claim is a separate one from the tortious claim for damages and should be treated as such under the Brussels I Regulation. The former claim will come within the scope of Article 5(1) and the latter one within Article 5(3).

The place where the harmful event occurred

The place of the event giving rise to the damage It is particularly dif- **6.86** ficult to identify this place in cases of misstatement/misrepresentation. This is because misstatement/misrepresentation will often involve a series of events that take place in different Member States. There is no decision of the European Court of Justice on the application of Article 5(3) in such cases. However, there are English first instance decisions on this. Unfortunately, the first of these to define the place of the event giving rise to damage in cases of misstatement/misrepresentation went off on the wrong path.

This was *Minster Investments Ltd v Hyundai Precision and Industry Co Ltd.*[252] **6.87** This is typical of the sort of case that can arise out of the international sale of goods. It involved English buyers of goods suing for negligent misstatement two defendants: the South Korean sellers and a company, based in France with an office in Korea, which in accordance with their contract with the first defendants had certified that the goods complied with the contractual specification. Steyn J said that, on the facts of the case, the event giving rise to the liability could be regarded as being either negligent work of certification of goods, which was performed in France and Korea, or, equally, the receipt of the relevant certificates in England, reliance thereon, and the instructions given from England to pay the Korean sellers of the goods. In such circumstances, Steyn J thought that the test in the *Bier* case[253] was not particularly helpful. Instead he returned to the wording of Article 5(3) itself and in the search for the place where the harmful event occurred was guided by a traditional English formula which asks 'where in substance the cause of action in tort arises, or what

---

[250] Case 189/87 *Kalfelis v Schroder* [1988] ECR 5565 the *Agnew* case, n 236 above, at 244–245 (*per* Lord Woolf), 233 (*per* Lord Nicholls), 267 (*per* Lord Millett).
[251] Claims for rescission and restitution of money paid are discussed below, para 8.25.
[252] [1988] 2 Lloyd's Rep 621.   [253] n 44 above and text accompanying.

place the tort is most closely connected with'.[254] The essence of the action was held to be a negligent misstatement, or negligent advice, and reliance on it, and not the historical carelessness which led to the misstatement or the wrong advice. The harmful event accordingly occurred in England where the advice by way of the negligently produced certificates was received and relied upon, and the English courts had jurisdiction against the French defendants under Article 5(3) of the Brussels Convention.

6.88 Subsequent cases have adopted a more orthodox approach, which accords with the decisions of the European Court of Justice. The first of these was *Domicrest Ltd v Swiss Bank Corp*,[255] which also involved an action for negligent misstatement arising out of the international sale of goods. The plaintiff English seller alleged that it released goods prior to payment on the strength of the defendant Swiss bank's representations that payment would be made for the goods and contrary to the plaintiff's trading policy. The plaintiff alleged that the bank represented that the transmission of a copy payment order by the bank to the plaintiff constituted an assurance by the bank that payment would be made for the amount referred to in the order and that such payment was guaranteed by the bank. The bank refused to pay three copy payment orders in respect of goods which had been released from store in Switzerland and Italy. The plaintiff brought an action in England against the bank alleging negligent misstatement as to the effect of a payment order. Did the English court have jurisdiction under Article 5(3) of the Brussels Convention?

6.89 Rix J refused to apply the 'substance' test, pointing out that it 'does not reflect either the wording or the philosophy of the [Brussels] Convention as laid down in the European Court's decisions'.[256] As regards the latter, it is important to note that, subsequent to the *Hyundai* case, the European Court of Justice had applied the *Bier* test in numerous other cases,[257] including one which involved the complex situation of multi-state defamation.[258] Moreover, the substance test as used in the *Hyundai* case denies the plaintiff the alternative option of suing in the place of damage.[259] Applying the structured approach adopted by the European

---

[254] This was the test used in cases of service out of the jurisdiction under the old tort head of Ord 11, RSC, as it was phrased prior to 1987 when it was brought into line with Art 5(3) of the Brussels Convention. See *Distillers Co (Biochemicals) Ltd v Thompson* [1971] AC 458.

[255] [1999] QB 548.   [256] ibid, at 566–567.

[257] Case C-220/88 *Dumez France v Hessische Landesbank (Heleba)* [1990] ECR I-49; Case C-364/93 *Marinari v Lloyds Bank plc (Zubaidi Trading Co intervener)* [1995] ECR I-2719; Case C-68/93 *Shevill v Presse Alliance SA* [1995] 2 WLR 449; the *Reunion Europeenne* case, n 240 above; Case C-167/00 *Verein for Konsumenteninformation v KH Henkel* [2002] ECR I-8111.

[258] The *Shevill* case, ibid.

[259] But for a case which uses the substance test plus the alternative of suing in the place where damage occurred see *Modus Vivendi Ltd v British Products Sanmex Co Ltd* [1996] FSR 790—a passing off case.

Court of Justice, which requires the determination of the place where the harmful event giving rise to the damage occurs, Rix J held that, in a case of negligent misstatement, this place is, by analogy with defamation, where the misstatement originates, rather than where it is received and relied upon. It is there that the negligence is likely to take place. The place where the misstatement is received and relied upon is likely to be in the state where the plaintiff is domiciled,[260] and thus overly favours the plaintiff, contrary to the wishes of the European Court of Justice.[261] Moreover, to prefer receipt and reliance was to ignore the fact that the plaintiff also has the option of suing in the courts of the place where the damage occurs, which is quite likely to be at the place of receipt and reliance.[262] There is no difference for these purposes between a written document and oral or other instantaneous communications.[263] In the case of instantaneous communications, and, in particular, of a telephone conversation between persons in different countries, the misstatement originates where the words constituting the misstatement are spoken, rather than where they were heard. In the instant case, the words were spoken in Switzerland and heard in England. The result was that the English courts lacked jurisdiction under Article 5(3) of the Brussels Convention.

In *Raiffeisen Zentral Bank Osterreich AG v National Bank of Greece*,[264] a **6.90** negligent misrepresentation case, Tuckey J found it unnecessary to have to choose between the approaches in the *Hyundai* and *Domicrest* cases[265] and deliberately refrained from expressing a view on which was the correct approach.[266] However, in the subsequent case of *Raiffeisen Zentral Bank Osterreich AG v Alexander Tranos*,[267] which involved a claim for fraudulent misrepresentation, Longmore J unhesitatingly followed the case law of the European Court of Justice and the *Domicrest* case and held that one must look to the place where the event which gave rise to the damage occurred and to the place where loss was suffered. As far as the former was concerned he also appears to have accepted the view of Rix J that this is the place where the misstatement originates.

---

[260] But not in cases where the plaintiff operates through a subsidiary company as in the *Dumez* case, n 257 above.

[261] The *Marinari* case, n 257 above.

[262] The *Domicrest* case, n 255 above, at 567–568. However, in the instant case the damage was held to have occurred in Switzerland and Italy, see below, para 6.94, rather than in England which was the place of receipt and reliance.

[263] The position in relation to communications via the internet is discussed below, paras 10.174–176.

[264] [1999] 1 Lloyd's Rep 408.

[265] It was possible to found jurisdiction on the basis that damage occurred in England, see below, para 6.93.

[266] n 264 above, at 414.   [267] [2001] IL Pr 9.

6.91 In *Alfred Dunhill Ltd v Diffusion Internationale De Maroquinerie De Prestige*,[268] Kenneth Rokison QC expressly adopted the approach in *Domicrest*, in preference to that in *Hyundai*.[269] The case is an interesting example of how a claim for negligent misstatement can arise in the context of the international sale of goods. The claimant entered into contracts for the first two defendants (French companies) to manufacture and supply travel goods to be distributed under the claimant's brand name. These defendants sub-contracted part of the work to the third defendant, an Italian company, which supplied fabric. The claimant sued the third defendant, *inter alia*, for negligent misstatement, alleging that in reliance on the alleged misstatements the claimant instructed the first and second defendants to contract with the third defendant, which it did.[270] Alleged misstatements as to the quality of the fabric were made by telephone or fax from Italy or France and received in England (with one face-to-face meeting in Italy). As a result, orders were placed for the supply of the fabric to France, where it was tested and found deficient. It was held, following *Domicrest*, that the place where the harmful event giving rise to the damage occurred was where the misstatement originated, rather than where it was received and relied upon, and that this was not in England.[271]

6.92 The final seal of approval of the reasoning and conclusion of Rix J in *Domicrest* over that of Steyn J in the *Hyundai* case is to be found in dicta of Mance LJ in the Court of Appeal in *ABCI (Formerly Arab Business Consortium International Finance and Investment Co) v Banque Franco-Tunisienne*.[272] It can be said with confidence now that the *Domicrest* approach is the right one to apply.[273]

6.93 **The place where the damage occurred** In many misstatement/misrepresentation cases, the place where the damage occurred will be obvious. Thus in the *Hyundai* case, the place where the damage occurred would appear to have been England.[274] This was where the price of the containers was released by the English buyers and where at that time the loss was felt. Similarly in *Raiffeisen Zentral Bank Osterreich AG v National Bank of Greece*,[275] the plaintiff's London branch made a bridging loan to H, to be repayable after a drawdown under a loan agreement under which

---

[268] [2002] IL Pr 13.   [269] ibid, at [31].
[270] There were also claims based on negligent misrepresentation under the Misrepresentation Act 1967 and on negligent misstatement resulting in a contract between the claimant and the third defendant.
[271] n 268 above, at [32].   [272] [2003] 2 Lloyd's Rep 146 at [41].
[273] But see the comments of Lawrence Collins J in *Bank of Tokyo-Mitsubishi Ltd v Baskan Gida Sanayi Ve Pazarlama AS* [2004] EWHC 945 (Ch), who said at [223] that it was not necessary to decide whether *Domicrest* applied to fraudulent misrepresentation, or whether it was rightly decided. See also at [185].
[274] See the *Domicrest* case, n 255 above, at 566.   [275] [1999] 1 Lloyd's Rep 408.

the defendant Greek bank agreed to lend money to a subsidiary company of H to finance the completion of the construction of a ship. Drawdown and repayment of the bridging loan were to take place in London and drawdown was subject to a condition precedent of an undertaking from the defendant bank to pay US $4.2 million to the plaintiff and confirmation that no breach of the loan agreement had taken place. This sum of money was never repaid to the plaintiff. The plaintiff claimed against the defendant bank, *inter alia*, in tort on the basis of fraudulent misrepresentation.[276] Counsel for the defendant bank did not dispute the fact that direct damage was suffered by the plaintiff in England, either when they permitted H to draw down the plaintiff's loan or when H failed to repay it which they were obliged to do in England.[277] Tuckey J said that counsel was right not to dispute this. In *Bank of Tokyo-Mitsubishi Ltd v Baskan Gida Sanayi Ve Pazarlama AS*,[278] the claimant alleged that, acting in reliance on fraudulent misrepresentations, banks entered into in England a facility agreement and made advances in England, from where the banks' resources were diminished.[279] Lawrence Collins J held that there was a good arguable case that the damage occurred in England.

In the *Hyundai* case, the place where the damage occurred coincided **6.94** with the place where there was receipt and reliance on the misstatement/ misrepresentation or negligent advice.[280] This is quite likely to happen.[281] However, this will not always be so. In the *Domicrest* case,[282] the place of receipt and reliance on the negligent misstatement was England. However, Rix J held that the damage suffered by the plaintiff occurred in Switzerland and Italy, where the goods, which were stored in those two countries, were released without prior payment.[283] It was by reference to the loss of those goods that the damages in the case were primarily pleaded. Moreover, the remedy in cases of negligent misstatement is concerned with putting the plaintiff in the position he would have been in if the negligent misstatement had not been made. The goods would have not been released before payment and were thus lost to the plaintiff. This was said by Rix J to be consistent with the case law of the European Court of Justice on the meaning of damage.[284] The argument that the damage occurred in England on the basis that this was where the economic loss to

---

[276] There was a separate claim for breach of contract. This aspect of the case, and the problems it raised in relation to using Art 5(3) is discussed above, para 6.83.

[277] n 275 above, at 414.

[278] [2004] EWHC 945 (Ch). [279] ibid, at [223].

[280] In the *RZB v NGB* case, it was not necessary to identify the place where the event giving rise to the damage occurred and so there was no identification of the place of origin or of receipt and reliance.

[281] The *Domicrest* case, n 255 above, at 568. [282] n 255 above.

[283] ibid, at 568. [284] ibid, at 568, referring to the *Marinari* case, n 257 above.

the plaintiff was suffered, for this was where the plaintiff maintained its bank account, received and acted upon the assurances, and where its commercial operations were based, was rejected. Similarly in the *Dunhill* case, receipt and reliance took place in England when the claimant took the decision to choose the third defendant's fabric and instructed the French defendants to place orders with the third defendant. However, the damage was suffered in France. This did not occur and certainly did not manifest itself until the samples of fabric were delivered in France, tested and found to be defective.[285] Moreover, the loss of profit to the claimant resulted from delays in production of the range of luggage in France, which was where the cost of obtaining alternative fabric and other costs were no doubt incurred.[286] The fact that the ultimate financial loss would be suffered in England where the claimant had its bank accounts did not constitute damage in England for the purposes of Article 5(3).[287]

6.95 There are misstatement/misrepresentation cases where the identification of the place where the damage occurred poses a very real difficulty. This is illustrated by *Raiffeisen Zentral Bank Osterreich AG v Alexander Tranos*,[288] in which the place of initial damage was by no means obvious. The claimant Austrian bank extended credit to the defendant, who was domiciled in Greece, via its London branch. The initial request for credit, involving misrepresentations, was made in Greece to an employee of the bank without authority to conclude an agreement with the defendant. The request required the approval of the board of the bank in Austria. The employee compiled a request to the board, which was also signed by the general manager of the bank in London. On receiving approval, the credit facility was arranged in London. Longmore J held that the initial damage occurred when reliance on the defendant's representations resulted in some concrete transaction that gave rise to the loss, rather than when the representation was made to any officer of the bank. The initial damage therefore occurred in London where the credit facility was arranged, rather than in Greece or Austria where the representation was received and given approval for further action.

The Traditional English Rules: Rule 6.20(8) of the Civil Procedure Rules

Is a claim made in tort?

6.96 A claim for negligent misstatement, negligent or fraudulent misrepresentation is founded on what is, in English law, a tort and, accordingly, should be regarded as being made in tort for the purpose of jurisdiction

---

[285] n 268 above, at [53].   [286] ibid, at [54].   [287] ibid, at [55].   [288] [2001] IL Pr 85.

under r 6.20(8) of the Civil Procedure Rules.[289] Numerous cases, including several decided by the Court of Appeal have adopted a tortious classification to claims for fraudulent misrepresentation and negligent misstatement for the purpose of service of process out of the jurisdiction under predecessors of r 6.20(8).[290] The same classification has been adopted under r 6.20(8) itself.[291] A claim in tort for misrepresentation under the law of Monaco has also been held to come within this ground.[292] All of this is consistent with the classification that has been adopted in relation to such claims for the purpose of jurisdiction under Article 5(3) of the Brussels Convention.[293] Doubtless, a claim for negligent misrepresentation under s 2(1) of the Misrepresentation Act 1967 would also be regarded as tortious. In contrast, a claim under s 2(2) of the Misrepresentation Act 1967, because it is best regarded as not being tortious, should be treated by an English court as falling outside r 6.20(8).

An act committed within the jurisdiction

Where the representation is made   In two first instance decisions, it **6.97** has been held that an act of misrepresentation is committed within the jurisdiction if the misrepresentation is made in England. The first of these cases is *ISC Technologies Ltd v James Howard Guerin*.[294] The plaintiffs, English companies which were subsidiaries of an English holding company (ISC), claimed that a director of ISC, Mr Pindell, who was also a

---

[289] Briggs and Rees, 2.39, argue that in order to establish that a claim is made in tort it may be necessary to show that there is a cause of action in tort, which requires recourse to the tort choice of law rules. The decision of the Court of Appeal in *Metall und Rohstoff AG v Donaldson Lufkin & Jenrette Inc* [1990] 1 QB 391 is cited as authority for this. Although this is one interpretation that could be put on the decision (see at 437), it is by no means clear that it actually established this. The discussion of the tort choice of law rules in that case appears to have been in the context of determining whether a good arguable case had been established on the merits (see at 438), rather than in establishing the terms of the tort head. Moreover, Slade LJ (at 449) giving the judgment of the Court of Appeal, when concluding that, as regards a claim for inducement of a breach of contract, the requirements of the tort head were also satisfied, said that: 'The claim is founded on what is, in English law, a tort'.

[290] For fraudulent misrepresentation, see in relation to Ord 11, r 1(1)(f) RSC: *ISC Technologies Ltd v James Howard Guerin* [1992] 2 Lloyd's Rep 430; *Arab Business Consortium International Finance and Investment Co v Banque Franco-Tunisienne* [1997] 1 Lloyd's Rep 531, CA. Again for fraudulent misrepresentation, see in relation to its predecessor, Ord 11, r 1(1)(h) RSC: *Cordova Land Co Ltd v Victor Brothers Inc* [1966] 1 WLR 793; *Diamond v Bank of London and Montreal Ltd* [1979] QB 333, CA. In *Armagas Ltd v Mundogas SA* [1986] AC 717 at 783, fraudulent misrepresentation was regarded by the House of Lords as a tort for choice of law purposes. For negligent misstatement, see in relation to Ord 11, r 1(1)(h) RSC *Cordoba Shipping Co Ltd v National State Bank, Elizabeth, New Jersey (The Albaforth)* [1984] 2 Lloyd's Rep 91, CA.

[291] See *Credit Agricole Indosuez v Unicof Ltd* [2003] EWHC 2676 (Comm), [2004] 1 Lloyd's Rep 196.

[292] *Thierry Morin v Bonhams & Brooks Limited and Bonhams & Brooks SAM* [2003] EWHC 467 (Comm), [2003] IL Pr 25; aff'd [2003] EWCA 1802, [2004] IL Pr 24.

[293] See above, para 6.77.   [294] [1992] 2 Lloyd's Rep 430.

director of the second plaintiff company, in collaboration with others knowingly participated in a fraudulent misrepresentation that a contract had been concluded when there was in fact no such contract. It was also claimed that this defendant participated in the pretence that goods and services were being ordered to enable the plaintiffs to perform the contract and gave English auditors a false version of a genuine contract that had been made by ISC. In consequence of these false representations, the plaintiffs acted upon them by authorizing the payment of money for the fictitious purchases and other expenses. Much of this money was diverted abroad for the use of another defendant and his associates. The plaintiffs sought leave for service upon the defendant out of the jurisdiction in Pennsylvania. Hoffmann J held that there was no doubt that the claim for damages for fraudulent misrepresentation fell within the tort head of Order 11, r 1(1) of the Rules of the Supreme Court. An act of misrepresentation was committed within the jurisdiction because representations were made to the plaintiffs' boards, auditors, lawyers and bankers in England.[295] However, the relief sought in claims against Mr Pindell included not only damages for fraud but also an account and restitution of the money paid out and an account of profits. Hoffmann J held that claims to equitable restitutionary remedies for breach of trust or fiduciary duty fell outside the tort head of Order 11, r 1(1).[296] However, it was possible to litigate the whole of the plaintiffs' case against Mr Pindell in England by using the multi-defendant head of Order 11, r 1(1).[297]

6.98 The second case is *Arab Business Consortium International Finance and Investment Co v Banque Franco-Tunisienne*,[298] in which Waller J held that there was no wrongful act committed by the defendant within the jurisdiction in the situation where the fraudulent misrepresentations were made abroad which induced the plaintiff, a company, to pay for shares in the defendant Tunisian company. The Court of Appeal held that it would be wrong to interfere with this decision, without going into detail on this point.[299] The misrepresentations were contained in the defendant's accounts for 1980, which were handed over in Tunisia. Waller J went on to say that it would have been different if the accounts had been sent to London. There would then have been an act committed within the jurisdiction. The plaintiff's argument, that a substantial and efficacious act was committed in England in that the plaintiff company through an individual, presumably one of its officers, was in London acting on the misrepresentations by being induced in London to agree to buy the shares and by accepting in London the defendant's contractual offer to sell the

---

[295] ibid, at 432.   [296] ibid.   [297] See below, paras 9.25–36.
[298] [1996] 1 Lloyd's Rep 485.   [299] [1997] 1 Lloyd's Rep 531, CA.

shares, was rejected in favour of looking at where the misrepresentations were made. A substantial and efficacious act does not include the fact of the misrepresentations being acted upon.

Where is a misstatement/misrepresentation made? In many cases, the **6.99** answer is obvious. Thus in the *Agnew* case,[300] it was made in the course of the brokers' presentation of the risk to the reinsurers in their office or underwriting boxes in London.[301] In *Saab v Saudi American Bank*,[302] the misrepresentations were made in London where negotiations were held, during which representations were made as to the bank's ability to market shares globally etc. These representations were also relied upon in London and it was common ground that the tort head of Order 11 was satisfied on the basis that there was an act committed in England.[303] Similarly in the *Arab Business Consortium* case, the answer was obvious, the accounts were handed over to the plaintiff in Tunisia and, accordingly, the misrepresentation was made there. But what if the accounts had been sent from Tunisia to England? Would the misrepresentation have been made in Tunisia, from where the accounts were sent, or in England, where the accounts would have been received by the plaintiff? Waller J referred to the situation where the accounts are sent to England and said, obiter, that in such a case there would have been an act committed within the jurisdiction. It follows that what matters is the receipt of the accounts in England. This is where the misrepresentation is made. Jurisdiction in England could also be justified under r 6.20(8) on the basis that there is a substantial and efficacious act in England, ie the receipt of the accounts.

The significance of the method of communication   Waller J does not **6.100** mention in his hypothetical example how the misrepresentation was communicated. Was he contemplating the situation where, for example, the accounts were sent to London by post or the situation where they were sent by an instantaneous method, such as by fax? Does this make a difference as to where the misrepresentation was made?

If the misstatement/misrepresentation is communicated by an instant- **6.101** aneous form of communication, such as a telex message, a telephone message, a fax or email then it can be asserted with some confidence that the misstatement/misrepresentation is made where it is communicated, ie received. This is supported by the *Bastone* case.[304] Prior to the claim for conversion or wrongful interference with goods, the plaintiff had brought a claim against Ecobank in tort based on negligent misrepresentations as

---

[300] n 236 above and text accompanying.   [301] ibid, at 247 (*per* Lord Cooke).
[302] [1999] 1 WLR 1861, CA.   [303] ibid, at 1865–1866.
[304] *Bastone & Firminger Ltd v Nasima Enterprises (Nigeria) Ltd* [1996] CLC 1902.

to the creditworthiness of the buyer, Nasima, and the custody of the goods. These misrepresentations were contained in two telexes. Acting in reliance on these representations, the plaintiff shipped further consignments to Nasima. Leave for service out of the jurisdiction under the first of the alternatives under Order 11, r 1(1)(f) was granted on the basis that the telexes were received in England.[305] This is also supported by *Diamond v Bank of London and Montreal Ltd*,[306] a case decided under the predecessor of Order 11, r 1(1)(f), Order 11, r 1(1)(h). Lord Denning in the Court of Appeal said that where a communication is made by telephone or by telex the misrepresentation was made at the point where it was received and where it was acted upon.[307] The position was the same as where a letter was sent by hand or a message sent by word of mouth by a messenger to the recipient.[308]

6.102 In contrast, if the message is contained in a letter sent through the post the position is less clear. It is at least arguable that the misstatement/misrepresentation is made in the country where the letter is posted and not in the country where it is received. This was the view of Lord Denning in the *Diamond* case.[309] He referred to an earlier case[310] dealing with the analogous situation where the master of a ship issued clean bills of lading and then handed them over to the shipper in Boston. Later on these bills of lading were indorsed to the plaintiff buyers in England. On arrival the goods were found to be badly damaged. Lord Denning said that the misrepresentation was made in Boston, USA.[311] He adopted the analogy of the rule that is applied when ascertaining where a contract is made.[312] But against this, as a matter of English domestic law the torts of negligent misstatement, negligent or fraudulent misrepresentation are not complete until the misstatement/misrepresentation has been received and acted upon.[313] This would suggest that the misrepresentation should be regarded as being made where it is received, and that the method of communication is irrelevant. Moreover, a Canadian judge in a jurisdiction case has taken the view that a representation is not made until it is communicated.[314] Finally, the fact that Waller J in the *Arab Business Consortium*

---

[305] ibid, at 1905.   [306] [1979] 1 QB 333, CA.

[307] This is where the tort was committed for the purposes of Ord 11, r 1(1)(h) RSC.

[308] *Original Blouse Co Ltd v Bruck Mills Ltd* (1963) 42 DLR (2d) 174 at 182; the *Diamond* case, n 306 above, at 346.

[309] n 306 above, at 346.

[310] *Cordova Land Co Ltd v Victor Brothers Inc* [1966] 1 WLR 793.

[311] This is where the tort was committed for the purposes of Ord 11, r 1(1)(h). For a discussion of the distinction made in these early cases between instantaneous and written communications see Rix J in the *Domicrest* case, n 255 above, at 567.

[312] See above, paras 4.32–36.

[313] *per* Stephenson LJ in the *Diamond* case, n 306 above, at 349.

[314] See Aikins J in the *Original Blouse* case, n 308 above, at 182.

case did not mention any method of communication of the message to London might suggest that he did not regard this as being relevant.

A continuing representation In *Thierry Morin v Bonhams & Brooks* **6.103** *Limited and Bonhams & Brooks SAM*,[315] the representation was first made in London when the English first defendant sent an auction catalogue, printed in England and prepared for the second defendant, a Monegasque subsidiary of the first defendant, to the claimant in London. This representation continued right up to the time that a contract was made at an auction in Monaco where the claimant bought a classic car. Jonathan Hirst QC, sitting as a deputy High Court Judge, held that the claimant's tort claim under the law of Monaco[316] fell within the second part of r 6.20(8) on the basis that the damage resulted (in part) from an act committed within the jurisdiction, that is the delivery of the catalogue.[317]

Damage was sustained within the jurisdiction

In both the *ISC* case[318] and the *Arab Business Consortium* case,[319] it was held **6.104** that damage was sustained where the plaintiffs, as a consequence of the misrepresentations, paid out money.[320] Thus in the *ISC* case, the English plaintiffs, in consequence of the false representations, acted upon them within the jurisdiction by authorizing the payment of money for the fictitious purchases and other expenses.[321] Hoffmann J held that the damage was suffered by the plaintiffs in England. Adopting the same principle, Waller J, in the *Arab Business Consortium* case,[322] held that damage had not been sustained in England in circumstances where there was little, if any, evidence as to where the plaintiff's commercial heart lay and the plaintiff paid money from an account in Switzerland and received shares in a Tunisian company.[323]

The Court of Appeal agreed with his conclusion on this point, adding that **6.105** there 'was no evidence before the judge of any actual loss within the jurisdiction. The money was paid from an account in Switzerland.'[324]

---

[315] [2003] EWHC 467 (Comm), [2003] IL Pr 25; aff'd [2003] EWCA 1802, [2004] IL Pr 24.

[316] The law applicable to the tort was held to be that of Monaco. The finding on this issue was upheld by the Court of Appeal [2003] EWCA 1802, [2004] IL Pr 24. See the discussion below paras 17.110–111.

[317] [2003] EWHC 467 (Comm) at [62], [2003] IL Pr 25; aff'd by the Court of Appeal [2003] EWCA 1802, [2004] IL Pr 24, which did not discuss this point.

[318] n 294 above.

[319] [1997] 1 Lloyd's Rep 531, 536, CA.

[320] See also *Crédit Agricole Indosuez v Unicof Ltd* [2003] EWHC 2676 (Comm) at [20], [2004] 1 Lloyd's Rep 196—damage sustained in England where loans advanced to the defendant.

[321] n 294 above, at 432.　　　　　　　　　　　　　　[322] n 298 above.

[323] ibid, at 493.　　　　　　　　　　[324] [1997] 1 Lloyd's Rep 531, 536, CA.

6.106 In the *Bastone* case, it was accepted that jurisdiction could alternatively be founded on the basis that damage resulting from the negligent misrepresentations was sustained in England.[325] There was no explanation of what this damage consisted and why it was sustained in England. Presumably, the damage was the loss of the consignments shipped to the buyer following the misrepresentations made by Ecobank and this was sustained in England because this was where the goods were shipped from.

6.107 In the *Thierry Morin* case,[326] the vast bulk of the damage was held to have been sustained by the claimant in Monaco by purchasing a car for a price that, in the light of the misrepresentation, was excessive. However, there were incidental expenses, trivial in comparison, sustained later in England. These fell within the damage part of r 6.20(8).[327]

6.108 A New Zealand court has held that damage was sustained in New Zealand in the situation where funds were raised in that country from a New Zealand bank and secured over assets in New Zealand, even though the purchase price for a group of companies was paid in the United Kingdom.[328]

A reasonable prospect of success (a serious issue to be tried on the merits)

6.109 As with any other case of service out of the jurisdiction, the claimant has to establish that there is a reasonable prospect of success (a serious issue to be tried on the merits). This requirement will not be met in circumstances where a claim is brought for rescission of a contract on the basis of misrepresentation or for damages under s 2(1) or 2(2) of the Misrepresentation Act 1967 but it turns out that there is no contract between the claimant and the defendant. This was what happened in the *Thierry Morin* case,[329] which involved as well as service out of the jurisdiction on the second defendant, a foreign company, a claim brought against the first defendant, an English company, which was served within the jurisdiction. This company merely delivered the auction catalogue containing the misrepresentation to the claimant. There was no contract between the claimant and the first defendant and, accordingly, the claim for rescission of the contract and for damages under s 2 of the 1967 Act had no reason-

---

[325] n 304 above, at 1905.
[326] [2003] EWHC 467 (Comm), [2003] IL Pr 25; aff'd [2003] EWCA 1802, [2004] IL Pr 24.
[327] [2003] EWHC 467 (Comm) at [62], [2003] IL Pr 25; aff'd [2003] EWCA 1802, [2004] IL Pr 24, which did not discuss this point.
[328] *Baxter v RMC Group plc* [2003] 1 NZLR 305 at [45].
[329] [2003] EWHC 467 (Comm) at [40]-[43], [2003] IL Pr 25; aff'd [2003] EWCA 1802, [2004] IL Pr 24, which did not discuss this point.

able prospect of success.[330] However, that still leaves the possibility of a claim for negligent misstatement, provided that the requirements for this tort are met. In particular, there must be a serious issue on the merits that a duty of care was owed by the defendant to the claimant.[331]

Forum conveniens

The natural forum principle The principle that the jurisdiction in **6.110** which a tort has been committed is prima facie the natural forum for the determination of the dispute was introduced in a case of negligent misstatement, *Cordoba Shipping Co Ltd v National State Bank, Elizabeth, New Jersey (The Albaforth)*,[332] where the Court of Appeal had to ascertain whether the tort of negligent misstatement was committed within the jurisdiction for the purposes of satisfying the terms of the then current tort head for service out of the jurisdiction.[333] The question of where this particular tort (and negligent and fraudulent misrepresentation) is committed is one of considerable difficulty.[334] A misstatement/misrepresentation may have originated in country A, been sent from country B, received in country C, acted on in country D, leading to damage in country E. Is the substance of the cause of action the misstatement/misrepresentation originating, the sending of the misstatement/misrepresentation, the subsequent receipt, the acting on this misstatement/misrepresentation or the ensuing damage? In the *Albaforth*, the Court of Appeal followed the *Diamond* case[335] in holding that the tort of negligent misstatement is committed where the misrepresentation is received and acted upon.[336] The negligent misstatement was contained in a telex sent from abroad to London, where it was received and relied upon. It followed that the tort was committed within the jurisdiction. England was therefore the natural forum for the determination of this dispute and service out of the jurisdiction was permitted. This leaves open the question of what would happen if the misstatement/misrepresentation is received in one state but then acted on in another state. It is submitted that in this situation the tort should be regarded as having been committed in the state in which it was

---

[330] Which meant that service within the jurisdiction was set aside.

[331] This was not shown in the *Thierry Morin* case, [2003] EWHC 467 (Comm) at [44]–[46], [2003] IL Pr 25; aff'd [2003] EWCA 1802, [2004] IL Pr 24, which did not discuss this point. But see the comments of the Court of Appeal at [26] about the possible liability of the first defendant as a joint tortfeasor.

[332] [1984] 2 Lloyd's Rep 91, CA.

[333] Ord 11, r 1(1)(h) RSC.

[334] See generally Law Commission Working Paper No 87, *Private International Law Choice of Law in Tort and Delict* (1984) 5.26–5.29.

[335] n 306 above.

[336] n 332 above, at 93.

received.[337] The place where it was acted on may have no connection at all with the place where the statement was initiated or where it was completed and the place where it was acted on may be entirely fortuitous.[338] Moreover, after sending the misstatement/misrepresentation the defendant has done everything required of him to incur tortious liability; what happens subsequently, ie the claimant acting on it, is beyond his control.

6.111 This natural forum principle was applied in the context of fraudulent misrepresentation in the *ISC* case.[339] Hoffmann J held that the alleged fraud was committed in England.[340] It will be recalled that most of the representations were made to the plaintiffs' boards, auditors, lawyers and bankers in England and the damage was suffered by the plaintiffs in England. This therefore was uncontroversial. Hoffmann J, in the light of his finding as to where the tort was committed, concluded that England was the appropriate forum for the trial of the proceedings.[341]

6.112 In the old cases where the courts had to decide whether a tort was committed within the jurisdiction for the purposes of satisfying the terms of the then current tort head for service out of the jurisdiction,[342] the result differed depending on whether there had been a written communication as distinct from some instantaneous form of communication.[343] In the former case, the tort was committed where it was put into circulation[344] (i.e. it was handed over to a third party by posting it or where a ship's master hands over bills of lading to the shipper).[345] In the latter case, it was committed where it was received and acted upon.[346] This distinction would no doubt still be applied.

---

[337] *Voth v Manildra Flour Mills Proprietary Limited* (1990) 171 CLR 538 at 568 (*per* Mason CJ, Deane, Dawson and Gaudron JJ), 578 (*per* Brennan J), HC of Australia. See also *Ennstone Building Products Ltd v Stanger Ltd* [2002] EWCA 916 at [48] 'Where the tort consists in essence of the giving of negligent advice, that tort is committed where the advice is received' (referring to the *Diamond* case), [2002] 2 All ER (Comm) 479. But compare *Base Metal Trading Limited v Ruslan Borisovich Shamurin* [2002] CLC 322, [2003] EWHC 2419 (Comm) at [37]; [2004] IL Pr 5, [2004] EWCA Civ 1316, CA, where Tomlinson J put the emphasis on where the misrepresentation is acted upon, and *Baxter v RMC Group plc* [2003] 1 NZLR 305 at [54]—substance of cause of action in deceit arose in England where reliance took place, rather than New Zealand where information was received.

[338] The *Voth* case, n 337 above, at 568 (*per* Mason CJ, Deane, Dawson and Gaudron JJ).

[339] n 294 above.   [340] ibid, at 435.   [341] ibid.   [342] Under Ord 11, r 1(1)(h) RSC.

[343] See Rix J in *Domicrest Ltd v Swiss Bank Corp* [1999] QB 548 at 567.   [344] ibid.

[345] See the *Cordova* case, n 310 above (Winn J looked to where the misrepresentation was made and this was in the USA where the ship's master handed over the bills of lading); the *Diamond* case, n 306 above, at 346.

[346] See Rix J in the *Domicrest* case, n 343 above, at 567. See also the *Diamond* case, n 306 above; the *Albaforth* case, n 332 above; *National Bank of Canada v Clifford Chance* (1996) 30 OR (3d) 746.

In the *Thierry Morin* case, Jonathan Hirst QC did not mention the principle **6.113** that the jurisdiction in which a tort has been committed is prima facie the natural forum for the determination of the dispute, despite the fact that he was concerned with a claim in tort. It was held that England was not the appropriate forum for trial.[347] Overall the case had much closer connections with Monaco than with England. In so deciding, he did, however, take into account the fact that the law applicable to the tort was that of Monaco.[348] Interestingly he also took into account the connections that the contract had with Monaco, such as that it was governed by the law of Monaco, sale by auction was carried out in Monaco, and the car was delivered and paid for in Monaco. Given that the case was concerned with a representation that induced the claimant to enter into the contract these are relevant connections. Surprisingly, he did not refer to the connections that the representation had with England and Monaco.

An exclusive jurisdiction clause   In the situation where the claimant **6.114** has been induced to enter into a contract with the defendant by a misrepresentation made by the defendant, it may be that the contract contains a clause providing for the exclusive jurisdiction of the English courts or a foreign court. A clause providing for the exclusive jurisdiction of the English courts will normally lead to the conclusion that England is the clearly appropriate forum for trial;[349] a clause providing for the exclusive jurisdiction of a foreign court normally to the conclusion that it is not.[350] Let us assume that the contract contains a jurisdiction clause providing for the exclusive jurisdiction of a foreign court. Let us also assume that the claimant wishes to bring an action in England against the defendant for damages for negligent misrepresentation under the Misrepresentation Act 1967 or for negligent misstatement at common law. The question that will then arise will be whether the wording of the clause is wide enough to encompass such a claim. For example, the clause may be limited to claims that 'arise out of or in connection with' the contract. Would this cover claims in tort for misrepresentations/misstatements inducing the contract? It has been held that it would.[351] It is submitted that this is

---

[347] [2003] EWHC 467 (Comm) at [64], [2003] IL Pr 25; aff'd [2003] EWCA 1802, [2004] IL Pr 24.

[348] This finding was upheld by the Court of Appeal [2003] EWCA 1802.

[349] *Unterweser Reederei GmbH v Zapata Off-Shore Company (The Chaparral)* [1968] 2 Lloyd's Rep 158 at 163 (*per* Willmer LJ). See also the discussion above, para 4.106.

[350] *Sinochem International Oil (London) Ltd v Mobil Sales and Supply Corp Ltd (Sinochem International Oil Co Ltd, third party) (No 2)* [2000] 1 All ER (Comm) 758 at 766–767. See also the discussion above, para 4.105.

[351] See *Donohue v Armco Inc* [2000] 1 Lloyd's Rep 579 at 593 (*per* Stuart-Smith LJ), 600 (*per* Sedley LJ), CA; this point was not in issue in the House of Lords [2001] UKHL 64 at [14], [2002] 1 All ER 749.

correct. If the English rules on construction of the clause are applicable,[352] it can be said that this claim is so closely connected with the contract that the parties can properly be taken to have intended that it should be decided by the same tribunal that would decide any claim in contract that might be brought.[353]

V. A FAILURE TO SELL

6.115 The sort of cross-border situation where this tort comes into play is illustrated by the facts of *Max Mara SA and Manifatture Del Nord SpA v Galerie Kleber SA*,[354] where the French Cour de cassation had to decide whether the French courts had jurisdiction in respect of a claim for refusal to sell goods. The appellants, two companies, one of which had its seat in France, the other of which had its seat in Italy, had entered into contracts for the supply of garments with the respondent, a company which ran two clothing businesses at Strasbourg and Mulhouse. The appellants refused to supply a particular range of garments on the basis that the franchise for that range for Strasbourg had been given to a third party. The respondent brought proceedings in Mulhouse against the appellants for compensation for this refusal of sale.

1. The Substantive Law Background

6.116 As seen above, someone who makes an offer and then withdraws it commits a delictual fault under Article 1382 of the Code civil. This Article also embraces various forms of commercial misconduct embraced under the heading 'concurrence déloyale'. Literally, this means unfair competition but the congeries of cases under the heading is wider than this.[355]

2. Application of Jurisdictional Provisions

The EC Rules: Article 5(3) of the Brussels I Regulation

Is an action for failure to sell within the scope of Article 5(3)?

6.117 The French Cour de cassation in the *Max Mara* case[356] held that a refusal to sell is an act of such a kind as to result in tortious, rather than contractual,

---

[352] See above, para 6.02.   [353] See for the use of this test, above, para 6.03.
[354] [1996] IL Pr 629, French Cour de cassation.
[355] See, generally, Bell, Boyron and Whittaker, n 124 above, 370–371 (observing that liability extends to a wide range of business conduct that can be stigmatized as unfair, including inducing breach of contract).
[356] n 354 above.

liability, and accordingly fell within the scope of Article 5(3) of the Brussels Convention. This was the assumption made in the earlier decision of the same Court in *Schimmel Pianofortefabrik GmbH v Hubert Bion*,[357] although the law report contains no discussion of this point. It follows that an action for failure to sell falls not only within the wide definition of the scope of Article 5(3) adopted by the European Court of Justice, i.e. an action which seeks to establish the liability of a defendant and which is not related to a 'contract' within the meaning of Article 5(1), but also within the narrow definition, ie a tort in the strict sense, adopted by the House of Lords in the *Kleinwort Benson* case.

The fact that the plaintiff bringing the action for failure to sell has a **6.118** contractual relationship with the defendant will not prevent the action from being regarded as a matter relating to tort, delict or quasi-delict. In the situation where reliance is placed on French substantive law, it is important to note that this does not allow cumulative actions in tort and contract and, accordingly, there is no question of the matter being regarded as one relating to a contract under Article 5(1), thereby preventing it being regarded as one relating to tort, delict or quasi-delict under Article 5(3).

The place where the harmful event occurred

The place of the event giving rise to the damage In the *Schimmel* case,[358] **6.119** the French 'buyer' sued the defendant German 'seller' before the French courts for refusing the offer to market in France the pianos made by the defendant. The Amiens Court of Appeal held that the alleged refusal to sell occurred at the actual moment—and therefore at the place—at which the decision to refuse the offer was made, namely at the seat in Germany of the defendant company. The Cour de cassation did not dissent from this view. However, as will be seen the French courts still had jurisdiction on the basis that the damage occurred in France, this being the state in which the goods were destined for resale. This solution has the advantage that the plaintiff is not given an excessively wide choice of fora. The place of the event giving rise to the damage will normally coincide with the defendant's domicile. This will mean that the plaintiff will have a choice of bringing his action in either the Member State of the defendant's domicile, under Article 2 or in the Member State where the damage occurred, under Article 5(3). Such a choice is compatible with the decision of the European Court of Justice in the *Bier* case. That Court envisaged that, normally, the place of the event giving rise to the damage will be the

---

[357] [1992] IL Pr 199.   [358] ibid.

same as that of the defendant's domicile, hence the need for the use of the place of damage rule as an alternative.[359]

6.120 The alternative to a rule based on the place where the decision to refuse to sell was made is to say that the place of the event giving rise to the damage is where the refusal is communicated to the 'buyer'.[360] On the facts of the *Schimmel* case, this would be in France. There are though two strong objections to such a rule. The first is that it does not accord with the substantive law on refusal to sell. A 'seller' who refuses to sell may be liable, *whether or not he communicates that refusal to the 'buyer'*. Communication is not a necessary ingredient of the tort. The second objection is more practical. The defendant may not communicate the decision not to sell to the customer. It may simply fail to enter into a contract. In this situation, it is impossible to identify the place where the refusal to sell is communicated to the 'buyer'. In contrast, faced with these facts it would be possible to identify the place where the decision to refuse to sell was made. For these reasons it is submitted that the French courts are right to regard the refusal to sell as having been made at the place where the decision to refuse to sell was made.

6.121 **The place where the damage occurred**   In the *Max Mara* case, the French Cour de cassation held that the damage resulting from a refusal to sell occurs at the place or places where resale of the items in question was anticipated. This was at Strasbourg and Mulhouse where the respondent 'buyer' had its businesses and where the designs in question were destined for resale. It followed that the Mulhouse courts had jurisdiction and the decision of the Cour d'appel, Colmar, to this effect was upheld. This is consistent with the same Court's earlier decision in the *Schimmel* case where it was held that the harm occurred in France. There is no explanation in the law report of why it occurred there but it is clear that this was where the French 'buyer' was offering to market the goods. One problem with a place of resale rule is that it may have been anticipated that the goods would be resold in more than one Member State. The European Court of Justice would not be in favour of allowing the plaintiff a choice of fora under the place of damage limb of Article 5(3). It might

---

[359] Case 21/76 *Bier BV v Mines de Potasse d'Alsace SA* [1976] ECR 1735 at 1746.

[360] In *Bus Berzelius Umwelt-Service AG v Chemconserve BV, Reakt Ltd* (C99/245HR) [2004] IL Pr 9, the Hoge Raad held that, with the tort of breaking off contract negotiations, the event giving rise to the damage was the receipt of the letter notifying the plaintiff of this. The method of communication would be relevant when ascertaining this place. See the discussion in relation to negligent misstatement, negligent and fraudulent misrepresentation, above, paras 6.88–92.

decide that the damage limb cannot be used at all in this situation.[361] Alternatively, it could territorially limit the notion of damage[362] so that, if it was contemplated that goods would be resold in France and the Netherlands, the plaintiff could only found jurisdiction in France in relation to the goods to be resold there and not in relation to the goods to be resold in the Netherlands. Another problem with a place of resale rule is that the 'buyer' may not have intended to resell the goods. In such a case, damage presumably occurs in the place where the use of the goods by the 'buyer' was anticipated.

The Traditional English Rules: Rule 6.20(8) of the Civil Procedure Rules

A claim based on a failure to sell under French law is more likely to arise **6.122** under the Brussels I Regulation than under the traditional rules. Nonetheless, it could arise in the situation where, for example, an English retailer contracts with a New York manufacturer for the supply of clothes for the former's outlets in France and the latter refuses to supply a certain line of clothing for these outlets. The English retailer brings an action in England against the New York manufacturer and seeks to base this on the French law of refusal to sell, arguing that French law governs the tort.

Is a claim for failure to sell made in tort?

A claim for failure to sell is not founded on what is, in English law, a tort, **6.123** and therefore its classification is particularly difficult. Nonetheless, it is suggested that such a claim should be classified as one made in tort. The fact that the French courts have classified a claim for failure to sell as one in delict for the purposes of jurisdiction under Article 5(3) of the Brussels Convention would suggest that the same classification should be adopted for jurisdictional purposes under r 6.20(8).

An act committed within the jurisdiction

There is not only a problem of classification where a cause of action, like **6.124** that of a failure to sell, is unknown to English law, there is also a problem in identifying the acts that go to make up that tort in order to ascertain whether a substantial and efficacious act has been committed in England. If reliance is placed on the French law of refusal to sell it is going to be necessary to focus on the ingredients of the tort as laid down by French

---

[361] See the analogous problem in relation to Art 5(1) that arose in Case C-256/00 *Besix SA v Wasserreinigungsbau Alfred Kretzschmar GmbH & Co KG (WABAG)* [2002] ECR I-1699. The ECJ held that a single place of performance for the obligation in question must be identified.

[362] This is what happened in the multi-state defamation case C-68/93 *Shevill v Presse Alliance SA* [1995] 2 WLR 499.

law. In determining which of these ingredients constitutes a substantial and efficacious act, which would then allow the English courts to assume jurisdiction once it had been shown that this act was committed in England, guidance can be found in the French decisions determining the place of the event giving rise to the damage for the purposes of jurisdiction under Article 5(3) of the Brussels Convention. This would mean that an English courts could assume jurisdiction under the first alternative under r 6.20(8) if the decision to refuse to sell was made in England. In the above example of a New York manufacturer refusing to sell to an English retailer, it is most unlikely that this could be shown since such a decision will normally be made where the manufacturer is based, ie New York.

6.125 The alternative approach is to say that the act of refusal to sell is committed where the refusal is communicated to the 'buyer'. It is submitted that this approach should be rejected for the reasons stated above when discussing its use in the context of Article 5(3) of the Brussels I Regulation.[363] These reasons are as follows: first, this approach does not accord with the substantive law on refusal to sell; and, second, it is impossible to use in cases where the 'seller' does not communicate the decision not to sell to the 'buyer'.

Damage was sustained within the jurisdiction

6.126 In determining whether damage was sustained within the jurisdiction, guidance can be found in the French decisions determining the place of damage for the purpose of Article 5(3) of the Brussels Convention. Thus an English court could assume jurisdiction if resale of the item in question was anticipated in England. In the above example, the goods would have been resold in France and therefore no jurisdiction would have been available under r 6.20(8). One difficulty with a place of resale rule is that it may have been anticipated that the goods would be resold in more than one state. However, this does not present the problem under the traditional rules that it presents under Article 5(3) of the Brussels I Regulation. Under r 6.20(8) it is not necessary that all the damage has been sustained in England. It is 'enough that some significant damage has been sustained in England'.[364] If resale of a significant part of the goods was anticipated in England this should suffice to satisfy this requirement and it should not matter that the rest of the goods were to be resold abroad. Another difficulty with a place of resale rule is that the 'buyer' may not have intended to resell the goods. In such a case, damage

---

[363] See above, para 6.120.
[364] *Metall und Rohstoff AG v Donaldson Lufkin & Jenrette Inc* [1990] 1 QB 391 at 437, CA.

presumably occurs in the place where the use of the goods by the 'buyer' was anticipated.

A reasonable prospect of success (a serious issue on the merits)

If English law is applicable there is no cause of action for a failure to sell **6.127** and therefore no reasonable prospect of success (no serious issue to be tried on the merits). In order to establish this, it is going to be necessary for French law, or that of some other state with a similar provision on failure to sell, to apply.

Forum conveniens

The principle that the jurisdiction in which a tort has been committed is, **6.128** prima facie, the natural forum for the determination of the dispute will doubtless apply to the tort of a failure to sell. But unlike the other torts considered in this chapter there is no case law providing guidance as to where this tort is committed. The obvious alternatives are the place where the act of refusal to sell was committed and the place where the damage occurred. It is submitted that the first of these alternatives is to be preferred to the second. The act of refusal to sell represents the essence of the tort. Once the 'seller' has refused to sell, he has committed all the acts or omissions necessary to render him liable. Moreover, if one focuses on the damage, this is defined in terms of the place where resale of the goods was anticipated. It has previously been seen that there are difficulties, albeit not insurmountable, with this definition in the situations where sale was anticipated in more than one state and where the 'buyer' did not intend to resell the goods. The place where the act of refusal to sell is committed should be defined in terms of the place where the decision not to sell was made, rather than where it was communicated to the 'buyer'.[365]

VI. INDUCEMENT OF BREACH OF CONTRACT

The facts of *Tesam Distribution Ltd v Schuh Mode Team GmbH and Com-* **6.129** *merzbank AG*[366] serve as a good illustration of how an action for the tort of inducement of breach of contract can arise out of an international sale of goods contract. The English plaintiff buyer brought an action for breach of contract against two German defendants, the supplier and a bank, which it was alleged was a party to the sales contract, for failure to deliver

---

[365] See above, paras 6.124–125. See also the discussion below, paras 17.129–131.
[366] [1990] IL Pr 149, CA. See for a similar example, *Astro Exito Navegacion SA v WT Hsu (The Messiniaki Tolmi)* [1983] 1 Lloyd's Rep 666, [1984] 1 Lloyd's Rep 266.

shoes. The plaintiff argued in the alternative that if the bank was not a party to the sales contract, it was liable in tort for inducing the breach of the sales contract by the supplier.

1. THE SUBSTANTIVE LAW BACKGROUND

English Law

6.130 English law does not have a general tort of unfair competition but rather promotes fair competition by various criminal, contractual and tortious means. One leading work refers to civil liability arising out of Articles 81–82 (formerly Articles 85–86) of the EC Treaty and speculates about the likelihood of liability issuing out of similar provisions in the domestic Competition Act 1998.[367]

6.131 One of the most prominent torts in the field of fair competition is the tort of interference with contractual relations, also referred to as inducement of breach of contract, or, as it is sometimes called, procurement of breach of contract. This tort has three ingredients.[368] First, intentional acts of inducement. Second, a breach or breaches of contract caused by that inducement. Third, resulting damage to the innocent party whose contract is broken.

6.132 Supposing a contract to exist between A (the promisor) and B (the promisee), a third party, C, will be guilty of the tort if, without justification,[369] either by persuasion or physical interference he prevents A from performing the contract. Persuasion can include advice.[370] Similarly, by entering into a contract with A that is inconsistent with due performance by A of his contract with B, C may commit the tort, as where C bought from A a car the subject-matter of the A-B contract.[371] Physical interference with a contract may take place by direct or indirect means. The potential width of liability for indirect interference is restrained by the requirement that C must employ unlawful means in order to be liable.[372] Liability for interference with contractual relations does not arise because C has been negligent. C must both know of the A-B contract[373] and intend[374] to bring

---

[367] *Winfield and Jolowicz on Tort*, n 196 above, 626.
[368] See *Metall und Rohstoff AG v Donaldson Lufkin & Jenrette Inc* [1990] 1 QB 391 at 447, CA. See also *Winfield and Jolowicz on Tort*, ibid, 627–634.
[369] *Brimelow v Casson* [1924] 1 Ch 302.
[370] *JT Stratford & Co Ltd v Lindley* [1965] AC 269, 333 (*per* Lord Pearce).
[371] *BMTA v Salvadori* [1949] Ch 556.
[372] *DC Thomson & Co Ltd v Deakin* [1952] Ch 646; *Merkur Island Shipping Corp v Laughton* [1983] 2 AC 581.
[373] Though not necessarily of its precise terms: *Emerald Construction Co Ltd v Lowthian* [1966] 1 WLR 691; *Merkur Island Shipping Corp v Laughton* [1983] 2 AC 581.
[374] A question of some difficulty: *Miller v Bassey* [1994] EMLR 44.

about its non-performance. B must also suffer damage.[375] A's failure to perform need not amount to an actionable breach of contract: A may for example be protected from liability to B by an exclusion clause that extends to the circumstances of C's interference.[376]

There are other forms of liability that are akin to the tort of interference **6.133** with contractual relations, for example, intimidation and interference with trade by unlawful means.

French and German Law

Under French law inducement of breach of contract is an example of **6.134** 'concurrence déloyale' under Article 1382 of the Code civil, which is concerned with delictual liability.[377] According to one author,[378] the defendant must actually know of the existence of the contract in question.

In Germany,[379] instead of one single general principle of delictual liability, **6.135** there are three separate principles: (a) §823 I BGB—liability for injury caused in an unlawful and culpable (intentional or negligent) manner to a protected interest of the victim (life, body, health, freedom, ownership and 'other right', the last not being so wide as to embrace all of a victim's material or financial interests); (b) §823 II BGB—liability where a statute designed to protect another is culpably contravened (namely all the rules of public and private law, especially criminal law); and (c) §826 BGB— liability in the event of intentional injury *contra bonos mores*. This third head of liability catches interference with contract, for example the case of the third party knowing that goods have been sold to the buyer but persuading the vendor to deliver the goods to him; the enticement of someone else's employee. German delict does not protect extensively pure economic loss negligently caused.

2. APPLICATION OF JURISDICTIONAL PROVISIONS

The EC Rules: Article 5(3) of the Brussels I Regulation
Is an action for inducement of breach of contract within the scope of Article 5(3)?

It can be said with some confidence that an action for inducement of **6.136** breach of contract is a matter relating to tort, delict or quasi-delict under

---

[375] *Winfield and Jolowicz on Tort*, n 196 above, 632–633.
[376] *Torquay Hotel Co Ltd v Cousins* [1969] 2 Ch 106.
[377] See above, para 6.116.
[378] Viney cited in Bell, Boyron and Whittaker, n 124 above, at 370.
[379] See K Zweigert and H Kötz (trans Weir), *An Introduction to Comparative Law* (2nd edn, Oxford: Clarendon, 1987) 292–299.

Article 5(3) of the Brussels I Regulation. Both principle and precedent support this conclusion. Such an action is one in tort under English (and Irish) law. Under French and German law inducement of breach of contract is encompassed within provisions imposing delictual liability. It follows that an action for inducement of breach of contract falls not only within the wide definition of the scope of Article 5(3) adopted by the European Court of Justice, i.e. an action which seeks to establish the liability of a defendant and which is not related to a 'contract' within the meaning of Article 5(1), but also within the narrow definition, i.e. a tort in the strict sense, adopted by the House of Lords in the *Kleinwort Benson* case. As regards precedent, Nicholls LJ in the Court of Appeal in the *Tesam* case[380] accepted that an action for inducement of breach of contract would fall within Article 5(3) of the Brussels Convention.

6.137   In the *Tesam* case, the alternative claim against the second defendant for inducement of breach of contract was based on the assumption that there was no contractual relationship between the parties. Accordingly, there was none of the potential difficulty in using Article 5(3) that arises where the parties have such a relationship. In theory though, there could be an action brought against two defendants where the claim against the second defendant is for breach of the sales contract and inducing the first defendant to breach the sales contract. In such a case, the claims against the second defendant are based on separate facts and should be regarded as separate claims. It follows[381] that the two claims should be treated separately for the purposes of Article 5(3) and Article 5(1) of the Brussels I Regulation.

The place where the harmful event occurred

6.138   When it comes to determining whether an action falls within the scope of Article 5(3) it is not necessary to determine precisely what the 'tort, delict or quasi-delict' in question is.[382] It is enough that the action is one which seeks to establish the liability of a defendant and which is not related to a 'contract' within the meaning of Article 5(1). However, when it comes to ascertaining the place of the event giving rise to the damage and the place where the damage occurred, it is hard to see how this can be done without identifying what the 'tort, delict or quasi-delict' for the purposes of Article 5(3) actually is. There is then the problem that the action could be based on the specific English tort of inducement of breach of contract or on the wide French principle of 'concurrence deloyale' (or on the wide German

---

[380] n 366 above, at 161–162.   [381] See above, para 3.73.
[382] Case C-51/97 *Réunion Européenne SA v Spliethoff's Bevrachtingskantoor BV* [1998] ECR I-6511; discussed below, para 6.160.

principle under 826 BGB) taking the form of inducement of breach of contract.[383] The elements of these torts may be different. However, the European Court of Justice would want to define the place where the harmful event occurred in such a way that it operates, regardless of the Member State's law on which the action is based.[384] There is enough common ground between the English tort of inducement of breach of contract and the wide French principle of *concurrence deloyale* (or the wide German principle under 826 BGB) where this takes the form of inducement of breach of contract to achieve this.[385]

The place of the event giving rise to the damage   It is submitted that, in **6.139** a case of inducement of breach of contract, whether based on English law or on its Continental equivalent, the event giving rise to the damage is the act of inducement by the defendant. It cannot be the breach of contract because this is an act committed by one of the contracting parties, not by the defendant third party. If you take the simple example of a third party knowing that goods have been sold to the buyer but persuading the vendor to deliver the goods to him, the act of inducement is persuading the vendor to deliver to him. Where is this act committed? If the third party and the vendor meet face to face this will be at the place where the meeting is held. If the third party writes to or telephones the vendor the position is more complicated. It is submitted that it is relevant to look at the method of communication. With an instantaneous form of communication, such as by a telex message, a telephone message, or a fax, the act of inducement would take place where it is received. But with communication through the post it is arguable that the act of inducement would take place where the letter is posted, rather than where it is received.

The place where the damage occurred   In principle, the damage could **6.140** be referring either to the breach of contract or to the direct loss to the plaintiff that flows from this. Under English law the breach of contract is regarded as a separate element of the tort from the damage. The act of inducement and the breach are the events leading up to the damage. It

---

[383] The courts should look at the form which 'concurrence deloyale' or liability under 826 BGB takes. The position is analogous to that of unfair competition, which under national laws can be committed in a wide variety of different ways, such as by passing off or by spreading false and disparaging rumours. National courts, for the purposes of Art 5(3), have concentrated on the particular way in which the competition is unfair, see Fawcett and Torremans, 411.

[384] Case C-68/93 *Shevill v Presse Alliance SA* [1995] 2 WLR 499—in cases of multi-state defamation, the definition of the place of the harmful event adopted by the ECJ will apply regardless of whether it is a defamation case brought under the French law of defamation or under the different English law.

[385] Compare the position in relation to the common law concept of conversion and the civil law concept of revendication, discussed above, paras 6.38–40.

is submitted that the damage should be regarded as the direct loss to the plaintiff that flows from the breach of contract. In a sale of goods case where the defendant third party, knowing that goods have been sold to the plaintiff buyer, has induced the vendor to deliver the goods to him, the loss to the plaintiff is not receiving the goods. This loss will be felt in the state in which the goods should have been received, ie the place where the goods should have been delivered under the sales contract. This rule will be difficult to apply in cases where the goods should have been delivered to places in more than one Member State. The European Court of Justice will not want to give the plaintiff a choice of fora under this damage limb of Article 5(3). It might decide that the damage limb cannot be used at all in this situation.[386] Alternatively, it could territorially limit the notion of damage[387] so that, if the goods would have been delivered in France and the Netherlands, the plaintiff could only found jurisdiction in France in relation to the goods to be delivered there and not in relation to the goods to be delivered in the Netherlands. The loss to the plaintiff in not receiving the goods may give rise to economic losses that are felt in some other state or states. For example, as a result of a failure to deliver in State A, the plaintiff is unable to sell the goods on in State B. Equally, the plaintiff is unable to incorporate the goods into a manufactured product which would have sold in State B. That economic loss will be felt in State B. However, the loss felt in State B is indirect damage and the damage limb of Article 5(3) does not allow jurisdiction where this occurs.[388]

The Traditional English Rules: Rule 6.20(8) of the Civil Procedure Rules

Is a claim for inducement of breach of contract made in tort?

6.141   In *Metall und Rohstoff AG v Donaldson Lufkin & Jenrette Inc*,[389] the Court of Appeal held that a claim for inducement of breach of contract was founded on what is, in English law, a tort and, accordingly, fell within the scope of the tort head of Order 11 of the Rules of the Supreme Court.[390] The same will be true now under r 6.20(8).

An act committed within the jurisdiction

6.142   The Court of Appeal in the *Metall und Rohstoff* case regarded the relevant act for the purposes of jurisdiction under Order 11, r 1(1)(f) as being the

---

[386] See the analogous problem in relation to Art 5(1) that arose in Case C-256/00 *Besix SA v Wasserreinigungsbau Alfred Kretzschmar GmbH & Co KG (WABAG)* [2002] ECR I-1699. The ECJ held that a single place of performance for the obligation in question must be identified.

[387] This is what happened in the multi-state defamation case C-68/93 *Shevill v Presse Alliance SA* [1995] 2 WLR 499.

[388] Case C-364/93 *Marinari v Lloyds Bank plc (Zubaidi Trading Co intervener)* [1995] ECR I-2719.

[389] n 368 above.   [390] ibid, at 449.

act of inducement of the breach of contract. There is subsequently the act of committing a breach of contract but the nature of the tort is such that this is committed by someone other than the defendant who has committed the acts of inducement of the breach of contract. The acts to be considered must be those of the putative defendant, because the question at issue is whether the links between him and the English forum are such as to justify his being brought to England to answer the claim.[391]

The facts of the case were complicated. The plaintiff traded on the London **6.143** Metal Exchange through a company called AML. Employees of AML assisted in fraudulent trading. AML, in order to protect its position, closed out the plaintiff's accounts on the exchange and seized a number of the plaintiff's warrants. AML became insolvent. The plaintiff brought proceedings against the two defendants, AML's American parent company (ACLI) and American holding company (DLJ), which knew about the fraudulent trading, claiming damages, *inter alia*, for inducement of breach of contract. The Court of Appeal held that the acts of inducement by the defendants took place largely, if not wholly, in New York. There were a series of meetings in New York attended by the defendant American companies and representatives of AML at which the inducement took place. The first breaches of contract by AML took place in New York when the plaintiff was told that AML would not pay the ledger credit due to the plaintiff and would retain the plaintiff's metal warrants. These were repudiations of the trading contracts. There then followed further breaches in London when AML took the action threatened in New York. It was the action taken by AML in London in breach of the trading contracts, not the action taken in New York, which really injured the plaintiff. Damage was then suffered in London.[392] This last element was enough to satisfy Order 11, r 1(1)(f). The Court of Appeal pointed out that it was not necessary for the plaintiff to show that the damage was caused by tortious acts committed by the defendants within the jurisdiction. But the Court went on to add that, if it were necessary, the plaintiff would not have been able to do so.[393]

In the *Metall und Rohstoff* case, it was easy to identify where the acts of **6.144** inducement were committed. These were committed at meetings and these were held in New York. However, the inducement may take place in a letter, or in an instantaneous form of communication such as a telex, fax, telephone message or email. Let us assume that the communication was sent from New York to London. In such a case, the Court of Appeal in *Metall und Rohstoff* seem to suggest that the act of inducement would have

---

[391] ibid, at 437.   [392] See further below, para 6.145   [393] n 368, above, at 449.

taken place in London.[394] No mention was made of the method of communication except to say that no inducing letters, telephone calls or telexes were pleaded. However, it is submitted that it is relevant to look at the method of communication. With an instantaneous form of communication, such as by a telex message, a telephone message, or a fax, the act of inducement would take place where it is received. But with communication through the post it is arguable that the act of inducement would take place where the letter is posted, rather than where it is received.

Damage was sustained within the jurisdiction

6.145 In the *Metall und Rohstoff* case, the Court of Appeal held that the damage which the plaintiff suffered as a result of the trading contract breaches was not receiving the ledger credit payment which should have been made, not receiving the warrants which should have been delivered and the detrimental closing out of their accounts. This damage was suffered in London. The plaintiff did not receive the ledger credit payment which should have been made in London, did not receive the warrants which should have been delivered in London and suffered the detrimental closing out of their accounts in London.[395] Similarly, the damage caused to the plaintiff by the breach of a compromise agreement was suffered in London since security which should have been available to the plaintiff in London was, it was said, wrongly charged in London and paid out of London.[396] In some cases, there may be damage not only in England but also in some other state. This does not present any real difficulty. Under r 6.20(8) it is not necessary that all the damage has been sustained in England. It is 'enough that some significant damage has been sustained in England'.[397]

Forum conveniens

6.146 In the *Metall und Rohstoff* case, the Court of Appeal held that as a matter of substance the torts were committed in London.[398] If the acts of inducement were viewed in isolation the torts alleged would properly be regarded as being in substance committed in New York. But in determining where as a matter of substance the tort was committed the matter had to be looked at more broadly, taking account of the breaches (particularly the effective breaches) induced and the effective damage.[399] Accordingly, England was, *prima facie*, the natural forum for the determination of the

---

[394] ibid, at 448.　　　[395] ibid, at 449.　　　[396] ibid.　　　[397] ibid, at 437.

[398] This had to be determined for the purposes of ascertaining the governing law under the common law rules that applied at that time.

[399] n 368 above, at 449. In the earlier case of *Atlantic v Milano* [1979] 2 Lloyd's Rep 240, Lloyd J held that this tort was committed where the breach occurred, which was in Italy where a telex was sent to the plaintiff's lawyers terminating the agreement.

dispute.[400] In determining the appropriate forum the usual factors will apply. In addition, it is relevant to take into account the law applicable to the sales contract that has been breached.[401]

VII. NEGLIGENCE

1. THE SUBSTANTIVE LAW BACKGROUND

The Common Law Tort of Negligence

The elements of the tort

Negligence in the common law is one of a series of separate civil wrongs **6.147** that make up a law of torts, rather than tort, though in terms of incidence and impact it is overwhelmingly the dominant tort. Although the English law of torts does not as such follow the German system of categorizing protected interests, it should be recognized that liability in negligence does not consist of a lack of due care that can be taken indifferently from a range of situations giving rise to different types of loss. For example, negligence is not an appropriate vehicle for dealing with harm in the nature of distress, psychological disturbance and anxiety.

The common law has also set its face against liability in negligence for **6.148** pure economic loss, with the exception of cases where such loss flows from advice or words,[402] where liability is constrained in various ways. To be recoverable in other cases, economic loss should be directly consequential upon physical loss.[403] The prospect of a more expansionist approach to liability for pure economic loss has been displayed in the past,[404] but judicial retrenchment in the last 20 years indicates that such liability is unlikely now. The effect of this retrenchment means that a loss of value inherent in goods because of a fault in their manufacture which leads to those goods damaging themselves will be treated as pure economic loss and will therefore not be recoverable.[405] All told, the common law does not accept the generalist approach to liability in negligence exemplified by Article 1382 of the French Code civil. It may fairly be described as falling somewhere between French and German law.

As a consequence of this abandonment of a general principle of liability, **6.149** the common law no longer subscribes to the view, if ever in fact it did so,

---

[400] ibid, at 484.   [401] *The Messiniaki Tolmi*, n 366 above, at 671–672.
[402] *Hedley Byrne & Co v Heller & Partners Ltd* [1964] AC 465.
[403] *Spartan Steel & Alloys Ltd v Martin & Co (Contractors) Ltd* [1973] 2 QB 27; *Candlewood Navigation Corp Ltd v Mitsui OSK Lines Ltd* [1986] AC 1.
[404] *Junior Books Ltd v Veitchi Co Ltd* [1983] 1 AC 520; *Lambert v Lewis* [1982] AC 225.
[405] See *Murphy v Brentwood District Council* [1991] 1 AC 398.

that a relationship of proximity based upon the principle of neighbour-hood was a sufficient ground for the establishment of a duty of care in negligence. This view had been put forward by Lord Atkin in *Donoghue v Stevenson*,[406] the ground-breaking decision of the House of Lords that established the liability of manufacturers for physical harm caused to the ultimate consumers of their goods. The concept of duty of care is a control device on the expansion of civil liability in negligence and a vehicle for the carrying out of policy debates on the case for an expansion of liability.[407] In particular, an English court is unlikely to allow tort to be used to establish civil liability just because there has been a breakdown in con-tractual mechanisms that could have advanced the defendant's liability in contract.[408]

6.150 Similarly to other legal systems, English law defines negligence in fact according to an objective standard of care, that of the reasonable man, that is varied according to professional and expert context (the reasonable manufacturer, the reasonable surgeon and so on).[409] In addition to estab-lishing a duty of care and its breach in this way, the claimant must also establish a factual causal link between the breach of duty and the injury. The injury, furthermore, must pass a test of remoteness of damage, which operates as a secondary control device that operates at a more detailed level than the duty of care. According to the remoteness rule, the injury must be of a type that could reasonably have been foreseen at the time of the negligent conduct as a consequence of that negligence.[410] The tort-feasor takes his victim as he finds him, so that a victim whose vulner-ability means that he suffers greater injury than would have been suffered by a normal person in his position—the so-called 'thin skull' victim—will recover in full. This rule has now been extended to victims whose aggra-vated vulnerability is of a financial as opposed to a physical kind.[411]

The use of negligence in international sale of goods cases

6.151 Claims in negligence as between buyer and seller are not common in domestic sales, given the general strictness of liability in contract. How-ever, there may be liability for a failure to warn in those cases where a problem comes to light after delivery but the goods may also have been unfit/ unsatisfactory at the time of delivery. Again, if they are not treated as part of the goods, which arguably they should be, there may be liability

---

[406] [1932] AC 562.   [407] See *White v Jones* [1995] 2 AC 207.
[408] See *Leigh and Sillivan Ltd v Aliakmon Shipping Co Ltd* [1985] AC 210.
[409] See *Wilsher v Essex Area Health Authority* [1987] QB 730.
[410] *Overseas Tankship (UK) Ltd v Morts Dock & Engineering Co Ltd (The Wagon Mound)* [1961] AC 388.
[411] *Lagden v O'Connor* [2004] 1 All ER 277, HL.

in respect of defective instructions accompanying the goods. And if the seller takes on a collateral obligation to install or assemble the goods, this may give rise to negligence liability or liability for a negligent breach of contract. If the seller holds the goods as a bailee for the buyer, his liability in negligence would remain despite risk being on the buyer.[412] And if the buyer acts as bailee,[413] he will owe duties in tort to the seller.

A buyer of goods under the international sale of goods contract, who is **6.152** also the consignee under the contract of carriage, is able, in certain circumstances, to bring an action in negligence against the carrier if the goods have been damaged during delivery. The negligence arises out of the carriage of the goods, which in turn arises out of the sale of the goods. Admittedly, the negligence does not arise directly out of the sale of goods contract, which is the focus of this chapter, but the lack of authority on negligence claims arising directly out of the sales contract means that it is useful to consider negligence claims arising in this indirect way, on which there is authority. When it comes to considering the issue of owners' bills or charterers' bills, the question is who is the other party to the contract of carriage. The consignee's right to sue in contract depends upon the terms of s 2 of the Carriage of Goods by Sea Act 1992. That Act applies only in the case of bills of lading, whether in the form of received for shipment or on board (i.e. marine) bills, sea waybills, which are non-negotiable (i.e. non-transferable) documents, and delivery orders, which are issued by the ship on surrender of a bill of lading to facilitate the breaking of bulk and dealings with parcels of that bulk. In appropriate cases, the holder of the bill, the person to whom delivery is to be made under the sea waybill or the holder of the delivery order, acquires rights and/or incurs obligations under the contract of carriage. The Act makes no mention of rights of suit in tort, and specifically does not prevent their exercise because the claimant has or has not a contractual right. Nevertheless, there is no obvious point in suing the carrier in tort because the defences and limits of liability in the Hague-Visby Rules (scheduled to the Carriage of Goods by Sea Act 1971) apply to actions for damage to or loss of goods whether the claim is brought in contract or tort.[414] However, tort will be a possibility where the claimant wishes to sue servants or agents of the carrier, though the limits and defences available to the carrier apply here too,[415] or those to whom the carrier has delegated performance, though an English court will be astute to incorporate the carrier's protection in any sub-bailment. In the case of an owner's bill where a charterer, under a

---

[412] Sale of Goods Act 1979, s 20.
[413] Which initially he did in *Leigh and Sillivan Ltd v Aliakmon Shipping Co Ltd (The Aliakmon)* [1986] AC 785—taking delivery from the carrier as the seller's agent.
[414] Art IV *bis* (1).   [415] Art IV *bis* (2).

time charterparty has issued orders to the owner, for example under the employment and agency clause in Baltime 1939 (cl 9) or NYPE 93 (cl 8), perhaps to proceed into a certain port, there is the possibility of an action by consignor or consignee against the charterer in negligence. The argument could be made that, for example, 'You should have realized that Haiphong was not a safe port'. The charterer in such a case is not the carrier under the Hague-Visby Rules[416] and so is not protected by those rules. Nor is the charterer a sub-bailee.

6.153   Tort may also be a possibility where, upon the transfer of a bill of lading, a consignor's contractual rights have been divested on transfer of rights to the consignee and that consignee, in, for example, an unusual case where the consignor remains on risk, has no wish to exercise its right[417] to sue the carrier for substantial damages for the account of the consignor. Again, the 1992 Act does not apply where goods have been received under a mate's receipt and no bill of lading was ever issued, or the bill of lading has been lost before rights under the contract of carriage can be transferred. A consignee/owner in this last case can sue only in tort, if able to demonstrate ownership of the cargo at the time of the carrier's negligence, or else on the basis of the highly fictitious *Brandt v Liverpool*[418] contract, ie an implied contract based upon the request to surrender the cargo, possibly against an indemnity.

French and German Law

French law

6.154   The French law relating to liability for negligence presents an appearance that is quite different from English law and German law.[419] The dominant characteristics of delictual liability in French law are the absence of nominate delicts, which contrasts French law with English law, and the failure to subscribe to a list of protected interests, which contrasts French law with German law. This is not to deny that there are gaps in the scheme of liability or to assert that all interests are protected by French law with equal vigour.[420]

6.155   Liability for negligence comes under Article 1382 of the Code civil, which in the broadest terms requires a person through whose fault another was injured to compensate that injured person. There is also liability for omissions according to Article 1383, but this provision does not have the

---

[416] Art I(a).   [417] Under s 2(4) of the Carriage of Goods by Sea Act 1992.
[418] From *Brandt v Liverpool, Brazil and River Plate Steam Navigation Co* [1924] 1 KB 575.
[419] See the excellent coverage given to delictual liability in French law in Bell, Boyron and Whittaker, n 124 above, 854–897.
[420] See generally Zweigert and Kötz, n 379 above Ch 17.

wide scope that a literal reading of it might suggest. Unlike English law, French law does not have a concept of duty of care that can be used as a matter of policy to restrict and filter instances of fault. Nevertheless, there is a requirement in practice that the harm caused by a defendant's behaviour be 'direct', 'certain' and 'licit'. These headings apply to economic loss as much as they do to physical loss but have perhaps a particular power to control the broad spread of liability for economic loss. When these heads have been satisfied in a given case, then the operative principle is that there should be compensation in full (*réparation intégrale*). Nevertheless, trial judges (*juges du fond*) have a significant amount of discretion in applying the further requirement that there be a causal link in fact between the fault and the injury.

Fault in French law, undefined in the Code civil, is established objectively **6.156** by reference to the *bon père de famille* but it is important to add the gloss that the commission of a criminal offence, even one of strict liability, is treated as an instance of fault and can be the subject of a civil claim arising out of the conduct of a criminal prosecution (*action civile*). Fault is a much more general concept than any principle underpinning tortious liability in English law: it includes for example abuse of rights (*abus de droit*) and unfair trading activity (*concurrence déloyale*).

No account of liability for 'negligence' in French law would be complete if **6.157** it failed to take account of the extraordinary judge-made creation of strict liability under Article 1384 al 1, which gives rise to a presumption of liability on the part of the custodian[421] of a 'thing'[422] that has injured another.[423] This provision has been used to create strict liability—the presumption of responsibility in that provision is not discharged by the custodian proving the absence of fault[424]—on the basis of the risk created by the thing, whether it is risk in the sense that the custodian benefits from the operation of the thing (*risque-profit*) or in the sense that the very operation of the thing creates a risk that heretofore did not exist (*risque créé*). Article 1384 al 1 can therefore be used as the basis for strict liability in car accidents, where liability in negligence would be the norm in England, but, since it requires the thing to be in the custody of the defendant at the time of the accident, it cannot serve to inject strict liability into the field of product liability. That function is served instead by contract law, so that for example the purchaser of a defective car can maintain

---

[421] Or guardian; namely, someone with the physical disposition of it.
[422] A word that includes every corporeal object, whether in motion or not, as long as it plays an active role in the occurrence of the harm.
[423] See the decision of the Chambres réunies of the Cour de cassation in the *Jand'heur* case (S 1930.1.121).
[424] But a defence exist for '*cas fortuity*' or '*force majeure*'.

a warranty claim (on the basis of the *'garantie'* against *'vices cachés'*)[425] against the manufacturer despite the absence of privity of contract between them.[426]

German law

6.158 The categorical nature of tortious (or delictual) liability in German law has already been noted. German law does not have a single general principle of liability for harm caused by unlawful acts. The claimant has to bring himself within one of the specific heads of liability in the BGB, namely, §§823 I and II and 826. According to §826, a person incurs delictual liability who intentionally inflicts harm *contra bonos mores*. Article 823 II is concerned with liability for breach of statutory provisions that are intended for the protection of others, such civil liability being conditional on the presence of fault even if this element of fault is not laid down in the statutory provision itself. This leaves §823 I which deals with the equivalent of liability in the tort of negligence in English law.

6.159 According to §823 I, there is liability for the intentional or negligent infliction of injury contrary to law. Negligence is defined in §276 II so as to catch behaviour that is contrary to the standard of care in ordinary life. If a claimant can show a defect concerning a product arising in the manufacturing process, then the manufacturer is required by §831 to show the absence of fault on the part of himself and of persons in his establishment. It is not enough to show fault or benefit from its presumption for a claim to be made successfully under §823 I. The claimant's injury has to be found in the closed list of interests contained therein. This means that the defendant's wrongdoing must injure the claimant's life, body, health, freedom, property or 'other right'. Because they are not recognized as falling on the list, German law allows no recovery for solatium, bereavement or other forms of pain and suffering consequent on the death of another.[427] Liability for psychiatric injury can arise under §823 I but the injury must be of a serious and extraordinary character.[428] German courts will not grant recovery under §823 I in respect of pure economic loss, but they will allow recovery for economic loss that is immediately consequential upon physical loss. This is the type of approach that is familiar to English courts. For example, an interruption to a power supply may damage raw materials or machinery and may also cause a loss of profit in

---

[425] Code civil, Art 1641.

[426] As discussed in Case C-26/91 *Jakob Handte & Co GmbH v Traitements Mécano-Chimiques des Surfaces SA (TMCS)* [1992] ECR I-3967; see further above, para 5.22.

[427] See BGB §§844–46.

[428] See Bundesgerichtshof of 11 May 1971, BGHZ 56, 163 (Case no 1 in B Markesinis and H Unberath, *The German Law of Torts* (4th edn, Oxford: Hart 2002)).

respect of the production cycle thus disrupted.[429] Somewhat controversially, German courts have recognized as property damage a type of
loss that in other jurisdictions might be characterized as economic: it concerns inherently flawed movables that damage themselves.[430]

2. APPLICATION OF JURISDICTIONAL PROVISIONS

The EC Rules: Article 5(3) of the Brussels I Regulation

Is there a matter relating to tort, delict or quasi-delict?

The leading case is *Réunion Européenne SA v Spliethoff's Bevrachtingskantoor* **6.160**
BV, a decision of the European Court of Justice.[431] The consignee (buyer)
of a consignment of pears carrried by sea from Australia to Rotterdam
and then by road to France, on finding on arrival that they were overripe
owing to a breakdown in the cooling system during the voyage, brought
proceedings[432] in France against three defendants: the Australian company which issued the bill of lading; the Dutch company (an alleged sub-
contractor) which actually carried the goods by sea, although was not
mentioned in the bill of lading; and the master of the ship which carried
the consignment. The European Court of Justice held that the bill of lading
disclosed no contractual relationship freely entered into between the
plaintiff and the second and third defendants. 'In those circumstances, it
must be held that such an action is a matter relating to tort, delict or quasi-
delict within the meaning Article 5(3) of the [Brussels] Convention'.[433]
This adopts the wide view of the scope of this provision consistently taken
by the European Court of Justice as 'covering all actions which seek to
establish the liability of a defendant and which are not related to a "contract" within the meaning of Article 5(1)'.[434] The Court did not specify
what the 'tort, delict or quasi-delict' for the purposes of this provision
actually was. It was not necessary for it to do so since, under this wide
definition, Article 5(3) encompasses non-contractual actions generally
including ones which, in a strict sense, are not tortious at all. Moreover, in
civil law systems liability in such a case is based not on a specific tort
of negligence but on a wider concept. In England, it has been accepted

---

[429] See BGHZ 41, 123.
[430] See Bundesgerichtshof of 24 November 1976, BGHZ 67, 359.
[431] Case C-51/97 [1998] ECR I-6511, [2000] 3 WLR 1213.
[432] The proceedings were actually brought by insurers who compensated the consignee
and were subrogated to its rights.
[433] n 431 above, at 1235, para 24.
[434] ibid, at 1235, para 22. This follows Case 189/87 *Kalfelis v Bankhaus Schroder, Munchmeyer, Hengst & Co* [1988] ECR 5565, 5585, para 18. The question of how widely or narrowly
the scope of Art 5(3) is to be interpreted is discussed above, paras 6.11–12.

without argument that an action for negligence fell within Article 5(3) of the Brussels Convention.[435]

6.161 **What if the parties have a contractual relationship?**   In the *Réunion Européenne* case, the plaintiff and the actual carrier of the goods did not have a contractual relationship. In the situation where they do have such a relationship and a claim is brought in negligence the question has to be asked whether there is concurrent liability in tort and contract. If parallel claims, that is based on the same facts, are brought in contract and tort, there is authority to the effect that the claim in tort is excluded from the scope of Article 5(3).[436] The same authority says that where there is concurrent liability in contract and tort the result would be the same even if the only claim is in tort.[437] If the consignee brings an action against the shipper for breach of contract and in negligence for failing to exercise reasonable care in the loading or stowage or loading the claims would appear to be based on the same facts. However, if there are separate claims in contract and tort, that is they are based on different facts, then each of them can be treated separately for the purposes of Article 5(3) and 5(1) of the Brussels I Regulation.[438] An example would be where the carrier promises to carry cargo below deck and breaks this promise by carrying it on deck. At the same time the carrier is negligent in not lashing down the cargo properly whilst it is on deck.

6.162 A sale of goods example of where the parties to a negligence action have a contractual relationship arising in the context of the sale of goods would be where the seller agrees to manufacture and install a machine in the buyer's factory. The installation is carried out negligently and the factory burns down. The buyer sues in negligence for the loss of the factory. In this example there would appear to be concurrent liability in contract and tort. The result, according to the above authority, is that the claim in tort is excluded from the scope of Article 5(3).

The place where the harmful event occurred

6.163 In the *Réunion Européenne* case, this place was particularly difficult to ascertain because there was a series of successive carriers.

6.164 **The place of the event giving rise to the damage**   The European Court of Justice in the *Réunion Européenne* case went on to hold that, in an international transport operation of this kind, the place where the event giving

---

[435] *Watson v First Choice Holidays* [2001] EWCA Civ 972 at [26], [2002] IL Pr 1. See also *Rayner v Davies* [2003] IL Pr 14 at [17]—negligently carrying out a survey which failed to pick up a number of defects; aff'd by the Court of Appeal without discussion of this specific point [2002] EWCA Civ 1880, [2003] IL Pr 15.
[436] *Source Ltd v TUV Rheinland Holding AG* [1998] QB 54; discussed above, para 3.72.
[437] See above, para 3.72.   [438] See above, para 3.73.

rise to the damage occurred may be difficult or indeed impossible to determine.[439] In such circumstances, jurisdiction cannot be based on this first alternative under Article 5(3).[440] The plaintiff will, however, still be able to bring proceedings in the place where the damage occurred. In other cases, though, it may be possible to identify the place of the event. For example, in a case of an allegation that a survey was carried out negligently it is place where the survey was carried out.[441] In the case of a failure to warn of a defect that existed at the time of delivery, this warning should have been made at the time of delivery in the place of delivery.[442] If the seller negligently assembles or installs goods, the place of the event giving rise to the damage is the place where the goods were assembled or installed.

The place where the damage occurred   The European Court of Justice in **6.165** the *Réunion Européenne* case held that the place where the damage arose in the case of an international transport operation of the kind at issue in the main proceedings can only be the place where the actual maritime carrier (the second defendant) was to deliver the goods.[443] The second defendant was in charge of the goods up to that point. That place meets the requirements of foreseeability and certainty and displays a particularly close connecting factor with the dispute in main proceedings. It cannot be either the place of final delivery (i.e. the place where the first defendant as initial carrier had to deliver the goods to the consignee), which the second defendant as a subsequent carrier may be unaware of and which can be changed in mid-voyage, or the place where the damage was ascertained, which, when there are successive carriers, could be at a variety of different places all of which would be unforeseeable to the defendant.[444] Moreover, to allow the consignee to bring proceedings in either of these places would in most cases mean attributing jurisdiction to the courts for the place of the plaintiff's domicile.[445]

If we turn to the example of the negligent assembly or installation of **6.166** goods, the direct damage, and that is what we are concerned with under Article 5(3), occurs in the Member State in which the assembly or installation took place. This is clearly so if the plaintiff is suing for damage to the goods themselves caused by the negligent installation or assembly. But

---

[439] The harmful conduct may have lasted for the entire voyage as the ship sailed through numerous places.

[440] n 431 above, at 1236, at [33].

[441] See *Rayner v Davies*, n 435 above, at [17], aff'd by the Court of Appeal, n 435 above, without discussion of this specific point.

[442] For identification of the place where goods were delivered see above, paras 3.175–189.

[443] n 431 above, at 1237, at [35].

[444] ibid, at 1236–1237, at [33]. See also AG Cosmas, ibid, at 1226–1227, at [55]–[56].

[445] ibid, at 1237, at [34].

the answer should be the same even if the plaintiff sues for consequent economic loss from being unable to use the damaged goods. The direct damage still occurs in the Member State in which the assembly or installation occurred. What if the plaintiff simply seeks compensation for the cost of having to hire another person to assemble or install the goods properly? It is arguable that the direct damage to the plaintiff occurs where this cost was incurred. This may be in a different Member State from that where the damage to the goods occurred.

The Traditional English Rules: Rule 6.20(8) of the Civil Procedure Rules

Is a claim for negligence made in tort?

6.167   A claim for negligence is founded on what is, in English law, a tort and, accordingly, should be regarded as being made in tort for the purposes of jurisdiction under r 6.20(8) of the Civil Procedure Rules. Moreover, numerous cases, including several decided by the Court of Appeal, have adopted a tortious classification for such claims for the purposes of service of process out of the jurisdiction under predecessors of r 6.20(8).[446] Further, the Privy Council adopted this classification for the New South Wales equivalent of this provision.[447]

An act committed within the jurisdiction

6.168   The English courts will have jurisdiction if substantial and efficacious acts of negligence were committed within the jurisdiction, whether or not substantial and efficacious acts were committed outside the jurisdiction. If the act of negligence by the carrier consists of negligent unloading of the cargo or its negligent stowage and this act takes place in England, the English courts will have jurisdiction under this provision. With such acts of negligence it is easy enough to ascertain whether they have been committed in England. Where the act of negligence consists of failing to provide a proper refrigeration system during the sea voyage as the result of which the cargo has deteriorated the position is more difficult. If it could be shown that the cooling system broke down in English territorial waters or, with a voyage ending at an English port, at some point not far from there, there would then be substantial and efficacious acts committed in England. However, it is unlikely that the place where the refrigeration system failed can be identified with this degree of accuracy. Indeed, as the *Réunion Européenne* case illustrates, it will probably be impossible to identify the point at which the refrigeration system broke

---

[446] See in relation to Ord 11, r 1(1)(h) RSC: *Monro (George) Ltd v American Cyanamid and Chemical Corp* [1944] KB 432, CA; *Castree v ER Squibb & Sons Ltd* [1980] 1 WLR 1248, CA.
[447] *Distillers Co (Biochemicals) Ltd v Thompson* [1971] AC 458.

down. All that is known is that the goods carried have on arrival been found to have deteriorated due to a failure in the refrigeration system. The act of negligence may have lasted for the entire voyage. At the very least, unless the claimant can establish that the act of negligence was confined to England, it will have to be assumed to have lasted for part of the voyage, including part outside English territorial waters. There is a continuing act of negligence which happens in a succession of places as the ship passes through the territorial waters of various countries and perhaps calls in at various ports on the way. In such circumstances, the claimant cannot establish a good arguable case that 'substantial and efficacious' acts of negligence have been committed in England. Whilst there are acts of negligence committed in England, as the ship passes through English territorial waters, these would not appear to be significant in the context of a lengthy sea voyage.

We can now turn to examples of negligence in the sale of goods context. In the case of an allegation that a survey of the goods was carried out negligently, the act resulting in the damage sustained is carrying out the survey. The terms of r 6.20(8)(b) will therefore be satisfied if the survey was carried out in England. In the case of a failure to warn of a defect that existed at the time of delivery, this warning should have been made at the time of delivery in the place of delivery.[448] It follows that if the goods were delivered in England then the terms of r 6.20(8)(b) will again be satisfied. If the seller negligently assembles or installs goods, the relevant act is the assembly or installation of the goods. If the place where this act was committed was England the terms of r 6.20(8)(b) will again be satisfied. **6.169**

Damage was sustained within the jurisdiction

In many cases where a claim is brought against the carrier in negligence, the place where damage was sustained will be the same place as where the negligent act was committed. This will be so in cases of negligent unloading or stowage of the cargo. Thus, if the cargo is negligently stowed or unloaded in England, the damage will be sustained in England, which is where the negligent act was committed. Again, the position is more difficult in cases where the negligent act is the failure to provide a proper refrigeration system during a sea voyage. If this act is committed in English territorial waters, it is clear that the damage is also sustained in England. But what of the situation where it is impossible to identify the point during the voyage when the refrigeration system broke down? The refrigeration system may have failed for the entire sea voyage. At the very least, unless the claimant can establish that the damage occurred in **6.170**

---

[448] For identification of the place where goods were delivered see above, paras 3.175–189.

England it will have to be assumed that it started during the voyage prior to arrival in English territorial waters. In either eventuality, the goods will have suffered a gradual deterioration, the cumulative effect of which is only discovered on arrival of the goods. In such circumstances the claimant cannot establish a good arguable case that some significant damage has been sustained in England, not when the length of the entire voyage is taken into consideration. However, this would mean that, in such a case, the claimant would not be able to use r 6.20(8) at all, being unable to bring the claim within either of the alternatives contained therein. The English courts may not be prepared to go this far and could avoid this by giving an artificial meaning to the concept of damage in cases of cumulative damage to the goods caused by the negligence of the carrier. One solution would be to say that damage is sustained in England if this is where the carrier is to deliver the goods. This is the solution that was adopted by the European Court of Justice in the *Réunion Européenne* case[449] and can be justified, as it was in that case, on the basis that the carrier is in charge of the goods up until this point

6.171   We can now turn to an example of negligence in the sale of goods context. In the case of the negligent assembly or installation of goods, the direct damage sounding in monetary terms which the wrongful act produced upon the claimant, and the better view is that is what we are concerned with under r 6.20(8)(a),[450] is sustained in the place in which the assembly or installation occurred. This is clearly so if the claimant is suing for damage to the goods themselves caused by the negligent installation or assembly. But the answer should be the same even if the claimant sues for consequent economic loss from being unable to use the damaged goods. The direct damage was still sustained in the place in which the assembly or installation occurred. What if the claimant simply seeks compensation for the cost of having to hire another person to assemble or install the goods properly? It is arguable that the direct damage to the claimant is sustained where this cost was incurred. This may be in a different place from that where the damage to the goods occurred. In all of these scenarios, if the relevant place was within the jurisdiction the terms of r 6.20(8)(a) are satisfied.

---

[449] n 431 above; discussed above, para 5.165.

[450] *ABCI (Formerly Arab Business Consortium International Finance and Investment Co) v Banque Franco-Tunisienne* [2003] EWCA Civ 205 at [44], [2003] 2 Lloyd's Rep 146; *Beecham Group plc v Norton Healthcare Ltd* [1997] FSR 81 at 97–98; *Bastone & Firminger Ltd v Nasima Enterprises (Nigeria) Ltd* [1996] CLC 1902. There is also Canadian authority in favour of a direct damage rule in *National Bank of Canada v Clifford Chance* (1996) 30 OR (3d) 746. But compare *Barings plc v Coopers & Lybrand (a firm)* [1997] IL Pr 12 at 24–25, aff'd by CA, [1997] IL Pr 576 at 585.

Forum conveniens

There can be no doubt that, if the act of negligence and the damage occur **6.172**
in the same state, this is the place where the tort of negligence was committed. If this place is England then England is, *prima facie*, the natural
forum for trial. In cases where the essential ingredients of the wrongful
act and the ensuing damage occurred in different countries, the tort of
negligence has been regarded for the purposes of service out of the jurisdiction under a former tort head for service out of the jurisdiction[451] as
having been committed in the country where the wrongful act was
committed, rather than the place where damage occurred.[452] Thus in the
situation where the defendant has negligently assembled goods and the
claimant sues in negligence for compensation to reflect the cost of hiring
another person to re-assemble the goods, the tort should be regarded as
being committed in the state where the negligent assembly took place.
The natural forum presumption does not have the same force in cases
where a tort is committed by a member of the crew or a passenger whilst a
ship is passing through territorial waters or an aircraft is flying through
airspace, at least where there is no connection between, on the one hand,
the tortfeasor and the ship/aircraft and, on the other hand, the place
where the tort was committed. The presumption that the jurisdiction in
which a tort has been committed is, *prima facie*, the natural forum is easily
rebutted in such cases.[453]

---

[451] Ord 11, r 1(1)(h) RSC.

[452] See the *Monro* case, n 446 above; the *Castree* case, n 446 above; the *Distillers* case, n 447
above. In the case of defective products causing personal injury the wrongful act has
been regarded as a failure to warn. Where the tort consists in giving negligent advice this is
treated the same as negligent misrepresentation for the purposes of ascertaining where the
tort was committed, see *Ennstone Building Products Ltd v Stanger Ltd* [2002] EWCA 916 at [48].
For the place where negligent trading (entering into certain contracts) is committed see *Base
Metal Trading Ltd v Shamurin* [2002] CLC 322 (Moore-Bick J), [2003] EWHC 2419 (Comm),
[2004] IL Pr 5, [2004] EWCA Civ 1316, CA—some of the acts of entering into the contracts
and the damage occurred in the same country.

[453] *The Forum Craftsman* [1985] 1 Lloyd's Rep 291 at 297, CA.

7

Property Matters Arising out of the International Sale of Goods: Jurisdiction

I. INTRODUCTION

This chapter is concerned with jurisdiction in relation to disputes where **7.01** what are at issue are property rights arising under and in connection with sales transactions. It is concerned in particular with disputes over the passing of property as between seller and buyer and the transfer of title, where third parties are also involved. Before turning to look at the jurisdiction rules that apply to such disputes, we need to look briefly at how property disputes arise and then at how jurisdictional problems arise in relation to such disputes.

II. HOW PROPERTY DISPUTES ARISE

1. The Importance of Passing of Property and of Transfer of Title

7.02 The passing of property, first of all, is important for a number of reasons in or connected with the law of sale, the principal one being insolvency. To the extent that the property has passed to the buyer, the goods do not form part of the estate of an insolvent seller available for distribution to that seller's creditors, even if the goods remain in the seller's possession. Where the goods are in the buyer's possession but yet the property has not passed, they do not form part of the estate of an insolvent buyer available to satisfy the claims of his creditors. Property is important too for other reasons. The passing of property to the buyer is almost always necessary if the seller is to be able in the event of non-payment to sue the buyer for the price,[1] instead of simply for damages for non-acceptance.[2] There is a presumptive attachment of the passing of property to the transfer of risk,[3] though the attachment is quite easily broken and indeed is routinely broken in certain types of international sale. The passing of property is an element too in the entitlement of a buyer to sue in the tort of conversion, whether the defendant is a third party or the seller himself, in the sense that the passing of property is factored into the question whether the buyer out of possession has the necessary immediate right to have standing to sue in the tort.[4] A buyer to whom the property has not passed is unlikely to have the right to immediate possession that a claimant out of possession needs to mount an action in conversion. A right to immediate possession is not to be found merely in a contractual right to demand delivery that a buyer might have who has been extended credit.[5] If the property has passed but the contract is not on credit terms, so that the seller is entitled to resist delivery unless and until the buyer pays, then the buyer will not have a right to immediate possession short of tendering payment in accordance with the contract.[6]

7.03 It is common for loose statements to be made about the transfer of title from seller to buyer. It is preferable to use the expression 'property' in seller-buyer relations and to confine the use of 'title', as does the Sale of Goods Act itself, to disputes over the ownership of goods. As far as English law is concerned, the Sale of Goods Act goes beyond the bilateral

---

[1] Sale of Goods Act 1979, s 49.   [2] ibid, s 50.   [3] ibid, s 20(1).
[4] See the discussion of conversion above, para 6.38.
[5] *Jarvis v Williams* [1955] 1 WLR 71.
[6] *Lord v Price* (1874) LR 9 Ex 54 (no credit extended); *Chinery v Viall* (1860) 5 H & N 288 (credit extended).

relations of buyer and seller and uses the language of transfer of title to deal with three-party proprietary issues where disputes arise. To reduce such cases to their basic expression, A is the owner of goods from whom B acquires possession of, but not the property in, those goods by consensual means or otherwise. B then disposes of those goods to C, a third party. A dispute can then arise as to who has title to the goods. Such disputes often arise in the context of sale agreements. The Act, for example, deals with sellers remaining in possession of goods, when the property has passed to the buyer, who then goes on to sell the goods to a second buyer.[7] This creates a title conflict between the two buyers, in the same way as a buyer in possession of goods, where the property remains in the seller, may sell the goods to a sub-buyer and create a title conflict between the seller and the sub-buyer.[8]

Whether, in a given case, a dispute arises out of the passing of property **7.04** between seller and buyer, or is connected to a transfer of title involving third parties, the tort of conversion, which protects claimants who are either in possession at the time of the wrong or who have a right to immediate possession, will be the means by which property rights will be asserted. For the remainder of this chapter, therefore, there is no further need to segregate passing of property and transfer of title.

2. Who Sues Who and for What?

Tate & Lyle Industries Ltd v Cia Usina Bulhoes and Cargill Inc,[9] where a seller **7.05** was alleged to have sold the same goods to two different buyers,[10] serves as an example of how a simple situation raising the question of the ownership of goods can give rise to a whole range of different actions against different persons. On the facts, as presented in proceedings concerning an application to extend an *ex parte* injunction granted earlier in the same day, A, a company domiciled in England, contracted with B, a Brazilian company, to purchase goods yet to be produced by B. B produced the goods but sold them to C, a company domiciled in Minnesota, and received money for them. A alleged that the effect of an ownership clause in the contract was that A was the owner of the goods as soon as they were produced by B.[11] B denied that A was the owner of the goods. According to Hobhouse LJ's account of the arguments advanced before him, A could

---

[7] Sale of Goods Act 1979, s 24. [8] ibid, s 25.
[9] [1997] 1 Lloyd's Rep 355 (Hobhouse LJ). The decision was an interlocutory one so that the presentation of facts and issues was not as clear as would otherwise have been the case.
[10] For another example, see *Glencore International AG v Metro Trading International Inc (No 1)* [1999] 2 Lloyd's Rep 632.
[11] On the law governing this issue, see Ch 18 and [1997] 1 Lloyd's Rep 355, 358.

proceed against B in various ways.[12] First, A might bring an action for damages for breach of contract or debt against B. Neither action would depend upon a finding as to ownership. The unexplained reference to a debt action seems to relate to an action for money had and received in respect of moneys in the hands of B and received from C, A having waived B's tort (conversion) arising out of the sale by B of A's property to C. Second, A could bring an action in conversion against B which necessarily raises the question of the passing of property between B and A, such being necessary to raise in A a right to immediate possession. The case is unclear on whether A had paid for the goods,[13] which is a matter of some importance. If A had paid, then A would certainly have had the right to immediate possession of the goods by the time when they were sold by B to C. If A had not paid, then A would have to make the rather more difficult argument that, at the moment of the sale of the goods to C, B surrendered the lien over the goods that B had against A. At the moment of that sale, therefore, A would thus have the right to immediate possession and the right to sue B for unlawfully disposing of the goods. Third, A could seek a proprietary remedy against B whereby A asserts rights to the money received by B from C as a fund identified with the sugar. As unclear as the argument is, it would seem to depend upon whether A was the owner of the goods so that A could trace into the money fund. This proprietary way of putting the money claim would not depend upon a waiver of the tort of conversion committed by B.

7.06 On the facts as presented, A would also have a conversion claim sounding in damages against C since C apparently had onsold the goods to D. This action would depend upon A's right to immediate possession, flowing from the effect of the ownership clause in the contract of sale.[14] Hobhouse LJ could not see the proprietary basis for a claim against C, though the only difference between A's third claim against B and A's claim against C seems to have been that B knew that the sale to C was wrongful whereas C had no such knowledge in relation to its sale of the sugar to D. This distinction ought to make no difference to the proprietary character or not of A's claims against B and C. The various claims, proprietary or otherwise, in a three- or four-party case like the present will turn out to be complex in even the most evidently straightforward case and the expeditious character of *ex parte* proceedings will serve badly the cause of unwinding these complexities.

---

[12] The plaintiff could use a combination of these, see the *Glencore* case, n 10 above, where the buyer sued for conversion and breach of contract.

[13] At [1997] 1 Lloyd's Rep 355, 357, Hobhouse LJ refers to the dispute as one that 'relates to the ownership of the cargo which has not been paid for by [B]'. This passage can only make sense if, for B the seller, there is substituted A the buyer.

[14] [1997] 1 Lloyd's Rep 355, 358.

3. CLAIMS RAISING THE ISSUE OF OWNERSHIP

As has been seen, certain claims will by their very nature raise the issue **7.07** of ownership of goods. For example, a claim for damages for conversion where a buyer out of possession needs to show an entitlement to immediate possession or a claim for the price of goods. In this way, the buyer demonstrates his right to sue in a tort that proceeds like a conventional tort remedy, until the point is reached when the damages remedy is levied against the defendant, upon satisfaction of which the claimant's property rights are vested in the defendant in consequence of what amounts to a forced judicial sale.[15] However, the issue of ownership may be raised more directly by way of a claim for a declaration that the claimant owns goods. In an action brought by the receiver of an insolvent buyer against the seller this may be the sole relief sought by the claimant.[16] More commonly though a declaration as to ownership will be sought in addition to damages for conversion,[17] the price of goods, a proprietary remedy,[18] or a declaration that the defendant holds goods as a constructive trustee.[19]

III. HOW JURISDICTIONAL PROBLEMS ARISE

1. THE SHORTAGE OF JURISDICTION CASES

Although there are cases, albeit not very many, discussing the choice **7.08** of law aspects of passing of property and transfer of title, there is very little authority on the question of jurisdiction.[20] One reason for this is, doubtless, because in most of these cases the defendant is English and the English courts have jurisdiction in such cases.[21] Furthermore, the incidence of conversion cases in domestic law is much less than that of negligence or breach of contract cases. It is quite possible that many conversion disputes are settled at the interlocutory stage before the issue of liability ever comes to trial. A typical scenario is that of valuable works of art stolen abroad and after being sold on ending up for auction through

---

[15] *Brinsmead v Harrison* (1872) LR 7 CP 547; Torts (Interference with Goods) Act 1977, s 5(1).
[16] See *Armour v Thyssen Edelstahlwerke AG* 1986 SLT 94; 1989 SLT 182; discussed below, para 7.09.
[17] See *Winkworth v Christie Manson and Woods Ltd* [1980] Ch 496. The declaration that the property had at all times been the plaintiff's was sought by a plaintiff not in possession so as to establish the immediate right to possession.
[18] See the *Tate & Lyle* case, n 9 above.
[19] See *International Credit and Investment Co (Overseas) Ltd v Adham* [1994] 1 BCLC 66.
[20] For this reason, the range of property issues canvassed in Ch 18 on choice of law is greater.
[21] There is though the possibility of the English court then declining jurisdiction on the basis of *forum non conveniens*.

one of the leading London auction houses. The original owner or a subsequent purchaser may bring an action in England against the English
auction house[22] or an English purchaser or the English police[23] who have
seized the works of art as stolen goods. More prosaically, it can be cars
stolen abroad that end up in England.[24] Not all of the transfer of title
choice of law cases involve the theft of goods. In one of the leading choice
of law cases on the transfer of title, goods were sold in Russia, auctioned
in Norway and then, having been shipped to England, sold in England to
an English buyer, the defendant.[25] All of these cases raise a choice of law
problem but not one of jurisdiction.

2. Examples Where Jurisdictional Problems Arise

7.09 The *Tate & Lyle Industries* case,[26] which involved defendants from Brazil
and Minnesota, is a good example of how jurisdictional problems can
arise in the context of disputes over the passing of property and the transfer of title. Moreover, some of the cases that discuss choice of law did in
fact raise, at least potentially, jurisdictional problems, although this aspect
was not mentioned in the report. The facts of these cases serve equally as
good illustrations of how jurisdictional problems can arise. One such case,
which was concerned with the passing of property, is *Armour v Thyssen
Edelstahlwerke AG*.[27] A German company sold and delivered a quantity
of steel to a Scottish company. Before payment, the buyers went into
receivership. The receivers sought from the Scots courts a declaration as
against the sellers that ownership of the steel had passed to the buyers on
delivery. This would mean that the goods would form part of the estate of
the buyer available to satisfy the claims of its creditors. The sellers relied
on a retention of title clause in the contract, the effect of which, according
to the sellers, was that ownership did not pass until the goods had been
paid for. The defendant was a German company and therefore there was a
question of whether the Scots courts had jurisdiction.[28]

---

[22] See the *Winkworth* case, n 17 above; *Gotha City v Sotheby's (No 2)* (9 September 1998).

[23] *Bumper Corp v Commissioner of Police of the Metropolis* [1991] 1 WLR 1362, CA.

[24] See *R Cruickshank Ltd v Chief Constable of Kent County Constabulary* (13 December 2002,
CA).

[25] *Cammell v Sewell* (1858) 3 H & N 617; aff'd 5 H & N 728.

[26] n 9 above.

[27] 1986 SLT 94; 1989 SLT 182.

[28] The case was decided before the Brussels Convention came into force in the UK and so
at that time jurisdiction would have to be taken under traditional Scots rules of jurisdiction.
There is no mention in the report of what the basis of jurisdiction was. The question
now would be whether the Scots courts have jurisdiction under the Brussels I Regulation. If
the unpaid foreign seller seeks a declaration of ownership against the Scottish buyer and
its receivers, subject to *forum non conveniens*, there is no problem of jurisdiction, see,
e.g., *Zahnrad Fabrik Passau GmbH v Terex Ltd* 1986 SLT 84.

Another choice of law case, concerned this time with transfer of title, **7.10** that raised a problem of jurisdiction is *Winkworth v Christie Manson and Woods Ltd.*[29] Works of art were stolen from the plaintiff in England and subsequently taken to Italy. They were sold in Italy to the second defendant, who it seems was Italian. The second defendant delivered these works of art to the first defendants, who were auctioneers, in England for sale. The plaintiff sought: a declaration that these works of art had at all material times been his property; an injunction restraining the first defendants from paying to the second defendant any part of the proceeds of sale of these works of art and an injunction restraining the second defendant from receiving any part of such proceeds of sale or disposing of any of the works of art in his possession; an order for the return of the works of art, or their value and damages for detinue or alternatively damages for conversion. The second defendant pleaded that he had acquired a good title to the works of art under Italian law. There is a problem in asserting jurisdiction against the second defendant, an Italian.[30]

IV. THE EC RULES

1. BASES OF JURISDICTION

No Specific Provision for Matters Relating to Movable Property

Property claims arising out of the international sale of goods are not **7.11** well served by the Brussels I Regulation. International sale of goods is a mixture of contract and property elements. The contractual aspects are well served by Article 5(1) but there is no specific provision dealing with matters relating to movable property.[31] Recourse can be had to Article 23 provided that there is an agreement by the parties as to jurisdiction. In cases where the buyer or seller is suing a third party, or vice versa, there is no contractual relationship between the parties and this provision will not apply. On the other hand, in cases where the buyer is suing the seller or vice versa, there is a contractual relationship between the parties and this provision may come into play. If there is an agreement as to jurisdiction the question then will arise as to whether the scope of the agreement conferring jurisdiction on the courts of a Member State is wide enough to

---

[29] [1980] Ch 496.

[30] The case was decided before the Brussels Convention came into force in the UK. There is no discussion in the law report of jurisdiction under the traditional rules.

[31] As regards immovable property see Art 22(1).

cover disputes in respect of proprietary matters.[32] In the absence of an agreement conferring jurisdiction, the plaintiff will have to sue the defendant in the Member State in which the latter is domiciled, with the possibility of suing in another Member State in which the defendant has a branch, agency or other establishment using Article 5(5) of the Regulation. This leaves the question whether it is possible to sue in a Member State other than the defendant's domicile on the basis of Article 5(1) or Article 5(3). The fact that proprietary matters will often arise in the context of contractual or tortious claims means that these Articles will frequently come into play.

Proprietary Matters and Conversion

7.12 Very often a dispute as to the passing of property in goods will arise in the context of a claim for damages for conversion. A conversion claim may be presented against a defendant in possession of goods. Alternatively, it can be presented against someone in a disposition chain who has onsold the goods, or against an agent who assisted in the disposal of goods. A claim against a defendant who is no longer, or who has never been, in possession of goods can only be regarded as a matter relating to tort, delict or quasi-delict for the purpose of Article 5(3) of the Brussels I Regulation.[33] Conversion imposes upon such parties tortious liability of a very strict character and is not used as a means of extricating the claimant's property from the defendant. Even against a defendant in possession, the paucity of occasions whereby the remedy of specific delivery is levied against the defendant, so as to require him to surrender the goods, ought to lead to the conclusion that Article 5(3) also applies to conversion claims against defendants in possession too. A claim in respect of the negligent infliction of damage on the claimant's property could, just like a conversion claim, require the claimant to demonstrate his property rights as a condition of bringing suit.[34] It should follow from this that the courts of the place where the harmful event occurred, which are allocated jurisdiction under Article 5(3), also have jurisdiction in relation to any dispute between the parties as to related issues of ownership/entitlement to possession of the goods. However, in determining whether Article 5(3) applies it is important to separate out the different ways in which the related issues of ownership/entitlement to possession of the goods may be raised before the courts.

---

[32] See the analogous discussion above, paras 6.02–05, on the scope of jurisdiction agreements and whether they cover tort actions.

[33] An action for conversion based on English law should be regarded as a matter relating to tort, delict or quasi-delict, see above, para 6.46.

[34] See *The Winkfield* [1902] P 42.

The different ways in which the related issues of ownership/entitlement to possession can arise in the context of a claim for conversion

A claim solely for a declaration   The plaintiff may seek solely a declara- **7.13** tion as to ownership. If this is the only relief sought by the plaintiff, it is submitted that Article 5(3) cannot apply. This is not a matter relating to tort, delict or quasi-delict. This is because it is not an action that seeks to establish the liability of a defendant.[35] Neither is there a harmful event.[36] The claim may be made as a precursor to a subsequent action for damages for conversion. Nonetheless this should make no difference. After all, once the declaration is granted it could be used for various purposes, including purposes which have nothing to do with the claim for damages for conversion. Alternatively, the plaintiff may seek a declaration that he has an immediate right to possession. But this too would be based on a finding that the buyer is the owner of the goods. It should therefore be treated no differently from a declaration as to ownership.

As part of the plantiff's claim for conversion   One of the elements of the **7.14** tort of conversion under English law is that the claimant must have actual possession or an immediate right to possession of the goods. If a buyer who does not have possession seeks to rely on an immediate right to possession then, for practical purposes, he will have to show that the property in the goods has passed to him so that he is now their owner. This is something that the defendant may well dispute.[37] The dispute as to ownership is all part and parcel of the claim. It follows that the court with jurisdiction under Article 5(3) over the claim for damages for conversion necessarily has jurisdiction in relation to any dispute over this ownership aspect of the claim.

The plaintiff seeks a declaration and damages in conversion   We are **7.15** concerned here with the situation where the plaintiff seeks in the same action a declaration as to ownership or immediate right to possession alongside damages for conversion. This situation, which is not uncommon,[38] is more difficult. If the declaration is looked at in isolation it is arguably not a form of relief based on tort, delict or quasi-delict. However, the declaration should not be looked at in isolation; it is after all sought alongside the damages for conversion. In this situation, a number of arguments can be made in favour of giving the court with jurisdiction under Article 5(3) in relation to the relief sought by way of damages for conversion an automatic additional jurisdiction in relation to the relief

---

[35] See the discussion above, para 6.13.   [36] See the discussion above, paras 6.14–16.

[37] This what happened in *Kuwait Airways Corp v Iraq Airways Co* [2002] 2 AC 883, HL, a case involving the seizure of goods.

[38] See, eg, the *Winkworth* case, n 29 above.

sought by way of a declaration. This would require the declaration to be treated as being based on tort. First, above all the declaration is probably concerned with establishing one of the elements of the tort of conversion. According to the declaration, the claimant will or will not have possession or the right to immediate possession at the time of the wrong. If so, the position is essentially no different from cases where the issues of owner-ship/immediate right to possession arise as part of the claim for damages for conversion. Second, it is highly desirable that all issues raised by the conversion litigation should be tried by the same court in the same Member State, rather than possibly being split up between different courts in different Member States.

7.16 It is submitted therefore that, where the plaintiff seeks relief by way of a declaration that he owns or has an immediate right to possession of goods, which is sought alongside relief by way of damages for con-version, the court with jurisdiction by virtue of Article 5(3) in relation to the latter should also have jurisdiction over the former. The proviso to this is that the declaration should be concerned with establishing the claim for conversion. If it is concerned with some other independent objective, then the court with jurisdiction under Article 5(3) should not have jurisdiction by virtue of that Article to grant the declaration sought. An example would be where relief sought by way of damages for con-version is based on the plaintiff's undisputed possession of the goods, so that any declaration of ownership would serve only some independent purpose not connected with a claim based upon the infliction of the wrong in the present case.

7.17 What if the declaration sought is concerned with two different matters: first, establishing one of the elements of the tort of conversion; and second, some other matter, such as a restitutionary claim in respect of fruits of the converted goods? It is submitted that in this situation, it is necessary to ask what the declaration is principally concerned with.[39] If it is the former, then the court with jurisdiction in relation to the relief by way of damages for conversion should also have jurisdiction to grant the declaration. If it is the latter, then an independent basis of jurisdiction should be needed in order to grant the declaration.

What if the parties have a contractual relationship?

7.18 The action for conversion may be brought by the buyer against the seller. The fact that the parties have a contractual relationship can, in certain

---

[39] This is by way of analogy with Art 22 of the Brussels I Regulation which is concerned with claims which are principally concerned with the matters listed in that Article, see Art 25.

circumstances, mean that the matter is not one relating to tort, delict or quasi-delict, even though the claim is pleaded as one in tort.[40] However, any claim that might arise between the parties by virtue of their contractual relationship would be an entirely separate one from the claim brought for conversion. A claim that the seller had not transferred the property in the goods, as required by the contract, would be a contractual claim. If the property in the goods had been transferred, and then the seller had wilfully destroyed or consumed the goods, it would be most artificial to conclude that the seller's liability was for non-delivery of the goods. His ensuing failure to deliver followed on from his earlier tortious misbehaviour in relation to the goods. On these facts, there is no alternative description in contract for behaviour that is tortious. We are not concerned here with parallel claims based on the same line of argument.[41] It follows that any contractual claim would, for the purposes of Article 5, have to be treated separately from the claim for conversion and would not affect the application of Article 5(3) in relation to the latter claim.

Proprietary Matters and Matters Relating to a Contract

Article 5(1) requires that the parties have a contractual relationship[42] **7.19** and that the claim be based on a particular contractual obligation, i.e. the obligation whose performance is sought in the judicial proceedings.[43] Furthermore, there is a requirement that the obligation is freely assumed by one party to the other.[44] These requirements will now be applied to two examples where the issue of the passing of property is raised in the context of a sales contract.

Insolvency and administration

Suppose that goods are in the hands of a corporate buyer, that the buyer **7.20** has granted security over his assets to a creditor and the creditor appoints

---

[40] See above, paras 3.71–73.
[41] See Cheshire and North, 214–215.
[42] Case C-26/91 *Jakob Handte & Co GmbH v Traitements Mécano-Chimiques des Surfaces SA (TMCS)* [1992] ECR I-3967; Case C-51/97 *Réunion Européenne SA v Spliethoff's Bevrachting-skantoor BV* [1998] ECR I-6511. See also the discussion above, para 3.63.
[43] *Kleinwort Benson Ltd v Glasgow City Council* [1999] 1 AC 153, 167–171 (*per* Lord Goff), 181 (*per* Lord Clyde), 189 (*per* Lord Hutton); discussed above, para 3.67.
[44] See the *Jakob Handte* case, n 42 above, at 3994; the *Réunion Européenne* case, n 42 above; Case C-334/00 *Fonderie Officine Meccaniche Tacconi SpA v Heinrich Wagner Sinto Maschinenfabrik GmbH (HWS)* [2002] ECR I-7357. See also the discussion in paras 3.64–66 above.

an administrator out of court (prior to the Enterprise Act 2002, a receiver) to realize its security.[45]

7.21 This leads us into the first example, which is the situation that occurred in the *Armour* case.[46] Is there a contractual relationship between the plaintiff out of court administrator of the buyers' business and the defendant sellers in a case of that kind? The out of court administrator acts as agent for the buyers in performing the mandate of paying down the debt and managing the buyers' business. But, in relation to the contract of sale previously concluded, the out of court administrator does not stand in a contractual relationship with the sellers. The contract between sellers and buyers remains and, so far as the sellers consider it worthwhile to proceed against the buyers in receivership, can be the subject of claims for breach of contract while the buyers are in receivership. The out of court administrator would have certain powers in relation to the affairs of the buyers, concerning for example the conduct of litigation, and, in exercising those powers, would act in the name of the buyers. The sellers would be at liberty to proceed against the buyers and the receiver would defend those proceedings in his representative capacity. To that extent, there would be a contractual relationship between the parties to the litigation. Accepting this, is the claim for a declaration against the sellers, that ownership of the steel had passed to the buyers on delivery, based on a particular contractual obligation? Under English law once the seller expressly undertakes to 'sell' the goods to the buyer, this undertaking will be treated as importing an obligation on the part of the seller, not merely to deliver the goods to the buyer against payment of the price, but also to transfer to the buyer the general property, the timing of which is then determined by the parties' intention. In so far as it is the buyers' claim that the property has passed, then they are making a proprietary and not a contractual claim. Suppose however that the buyers, through the receiver, are asserting that the sellers have in fact been paid. To the extent that any further action or consent on the part of the sellers were needed to pass the property in the goods to the buyers, then the buyers' claim would be a contractual one. Putting it another way, if the buyers' claim is descriptive, it is proprietary; if it is prescriptive, it is contractual. But would any such

---

[45] Further to Sch B1 to the Insolvency Act 1986, as added by the Enterprise Act 2002. If the buyers are in liquidation, then the sellers' position against the liquidators is largely the same for present purposes as it is against the out of court administrator. The onset of liquidation does not engage the personal liability of the liquidator on pre-liquidation contracts. However, the liquidator has power under Sch 4 to the Insolvency Act 1986, to bring or defend proceedings in the name of the company that is being wound up. The sanction of the court, though, will be needed if proceedings are to be brought against a company in liquidation (Insolvency Act 1986, s 130(2)).

[46] n 27 above and text accompanying.

contractual obligation be freely assumed by one party to the other? The
seller freely assumes obligations in relation to the buyer and this is what
matters in the current situation where the out of court administrator of the
buyer's business is acting in a representative capacity.[47]

An action for the payment of the price

The second example is where a claim is brought by the seller against the **7.22**
non-paying buyer for the price of goods, rather than for damages for non-
acceptance. Under English law at least, the seller is almost always going to
have to show that the property has passed to the buyer.[48] In this situation,
the parties have a contractual relationship, it is an action brought by the
seller against the buyer. Moreover, the claim is based on a particular contractual obligation. The obligation whose performance is sought in the
proceedings is the obligation to pay for the goods. This obligation is freely
assumed by one party to the other. The claim for payment of the price will
fall within the scope of Article 5(1) but what of the issue of the passing of
property that is raised by this claim? It is important to separate out the
different contexts in which the issue of the passing of property can arise.

A claim for a declaration as to ownership   If this the only relief sought **7.23**
by the plaintiff it is submitted that Article 5(1) cannot apply.[49] This is not a
matter relating to a contract, even if the action is brought as a precursor to
a subsequent action for payment of the price of the goods.

As part of the claim for payment   During the course of the claim for **7.24**
payment of the price the question of the ownership of the goods will
inevitably arise, at least if English law is applicable. This is something that
the seller is going to have to establish in order to justify his claim for
payment of the purchase price. It is part and parcel of his claim. It follows
that the court with jurisdiction under Article 5(1) over the claim for payment of the price necessarily has jurisdiction in relation to any dispute
over this ownership aspect of the claim.[50]

The plaintiff seeks a declaration as to ownership and payment of the **7.25**
price   This is a more difficult situation. Suppose that the buyer purports

---

[47] This is very different from the situation in the *Jakob Handte* case, n 42 above, where the
requirement that the obligation was freely assumed was introduced, see the discussion
above, paras 3.64–66.

[48] Sale of Goods Act 1979, s 49

[49] See by way of analogy the position where the sole issue is the validity of the contract,
the *Kleinwort Benson* case, n 43 above, at 170 (*per* Lord Goff who regarded this as falling
outside Art 5(1)), Cheshire and North, 203–204.

[50] Again the analogy can be drawn with the situation where the question of the existence
of a contract arises during the course of an action for the performance of a contractual
obligation and therefore comes within Art 5(1), the *Kleinwort Benson* case, n 43 above, at 182
(*per* Lord Clyde), 170 (*per* Lord Goff). See also Cheshire and North, 204.

to have terminated the contract, on the ground that the seller's right to sell (or ownership) is encumbered and the seller is therefore in breach of the implied condition that he has a right to sell. The seller, beside claiming the price, seeks a declaration that his ownership rights are unencumbered. It is submitted that the place which has jurisdiction under Article 5(1) in relation to the payment of the price should also have jurisdiction in relation to the declaration as to ownership when the latter is raised as a form of relief alongside the former. The proviso to this is that the declaration must be concerned with establishing the right to payment of the price. If it is concerned with some other independent matter, then the court with jurisdiction under Article 5(1) should not have jurisdiction by virtue of that Article to grant the declaration. An example of this would be where the buyer under an instalment sale, having refused to pay for an instalment delivered, also refuses to open in the seller's state a letter of credit for future instalments, and the seller seeks a declaration as to its entitlement to such credit. An independent basis of jurisdiction should be needed in order to grant the declaration. In the situation where the declaration sought is concerned with more than one matter, it is necessary to ask what it is principally concerned with.[51] If the declaration is principally concerned with establishing the right to payment of the price then the court with jurisdiction in relation to the relief by way of the price of the goods should also have jurisdiction to grant the declaration. If it is principally concerned with something other than this then an independent basis of jurisdiction should be needed in order to grant it.

V. THE TRADITIONAL ENGLISH RULES

1. A Basis of Jurisdiction: Service Out of the Jurisdiction

7.26 If service can be effected within the jurisdiction there are no special concerns arising from the fact that the dispute relates to property rights.[52] On the other hand, if recourse has to be had to service out of the jurisdiction the position is more complex. Unlike the EC rules, the traditional English rules (on service out of the jurisdiction) contain a special provision dealing with claims relating to property. This provision will be examined first, after which the question will be considered of whether such claims

---

[51] See above, para 7.17.
[52] See, e.g. the *Kuwait Airways Corp* case, n 37 above. Jurisdiction was taken on the basis that the defendant had a branch office in England.

can be brought within other provisions on service out of the jurisdiction, namely those concerned with torts, contracts and constructive trusts.

Claims Relating to Property Within the Jurisdiction

Rule 6.20(10) of the Civil Procedure Rules[53] provides that a claim form **7.27** may be served out of the jurisdiction with the permission of the court if:

(10) the whole subject-matter of a claim relates to property located within the jurisdiction.

This is a wholly new formulation, the purpose of which is to lay down a single rule in place of three earlier rules.[54] It embraces and extends beyond the contents of those rules.[55] The elements of this ground for service out of the jurisdiction will now be examined, after which its application in situations where the claim in relation to property arises in the context of a sales contract will be considered.

The elements of 6.20(10)

A claim This provision extends to any claim for relief, whether for dam- **7.28** ages or otherwise, so long as it is related to property located within the jurisdiction.[56] The relief sought could be that of a declaration that ownership of the goods had passed to the buyers on delivery.[57] Equally the relief sought could be damages. The rule cannot be construed as being confined to claims relating to the ownership or possession of property,[58] although these will commonly be the sort of claims where this ground will be invoked. Thus this provision was applicable in *Banca Carige v BNC*,[59] where the claimant creditor of the first defendant company sought: (i) a declaration that a transfer of shares by the first defendant to the second defendant constituted a transaction at an undervalue within the meaning of the Insolvency Act 1986; (ii) a declaration that the transfer was entered into for the purpose of putting assets beyond the reach of creditors; (iii) and an order that the value of the shares at the date of the transfer be paid

---

[53] See generally, Dicey and Morris, *Third Supplement to the Thirteenth edition* (2003) 68–69.

[54] *Banca Carige v BNC* [2001] 2 Lloyd's Rep 147, 157. The case is also reported as *In re Banco Nacional de Cuba* [2001] 1 WLR 2039. The three earlier rules are Ord 11, r 1(1)(g), (h), (i) RSC. These provided as follows: (g) the whole subject-matter of the action is land situate within the jurisdiction (with or without rents or profits) or the perpetuation of testimony relating to land so situate; (h) the claim is brought to construe, rectify, set aside or enforce an act, deed, will, contract, obligation or liability affecting land situate within the jurisdiction; (i) the claim is made for a debt secured on immovable property or is made to assert, declare or determine proprietary or possessory rights, or rights of security, in or over movable property, or to obtain authority to dispose of movable property, situate within the jurisdiction.

[55] The *Banca Carige* case, n 54 above, at 157.   [56] ibid.

[57] See the *Armour* case, n 27 above; discussed above, para 7.09.

[58] The *Banca Carige* case, n 54 above, at 157.   [59] n 54 above.

by the second defendant to the first defendant or to the claimant. The claimant had argued that it is enough that the claim relate to a transaction affecting the property. The defendants on the other hand had argued that it is necessary that the claim is as to the property or some interest therein. Lightman J accepted the claimant's argument. This has considerable implications for the use of this ground. It means that, in principle, it can extend to, for example, a claim for damages arising from a breach of contract or a tort relating to property located within the jurisdiction.

7.29 This extension makes r 6.20(10) a very useful provision. Not only can it be used where there is a claim solely for damages but it also can be used for a claim which seeks a variety of different forms of relief. *Winkworth v Christie Manson and Woods Ltd*[60] is a good example. It will be recalled that the plaintiff sought a declaration that he had title to the goods, injunctions in respect of the proceeds of sale and damages, inter alia, for conversion. The whole of the relief sought would fall within this one ground provided that the goods are located within the jurisdiction. In contrast, if recourse were to be had to the tort ground this would cover the relief sought in the form of damages for conversion. This would clearly be a claim made in tort. But what of the declaration as to title and the injunctions? The question whether these forms of relief can be brought within the tort ground is a difficult one to answer and is considered in detail later on.[61]

7.30 **The whole subject-matter of a claim** The claimant has to establish a good arguable case that the 'whole subject-matter' of a claim relates to property located within the jurisdiction. If the subject-matter of the claim relates to property in England and also to property abroad it cannot be said that the whole subject-matter of the claim relates to property within the jurisdiction. The whole subject-matter of the claim relates to property within the jurisdiction and to property outside the jurisdiction. On the other hand, if the claim is made solely in relation to that part of the property located in England then the ground will be satisfied.

7.31 **Relates to** In the *Carige* case, the property was the shares and the claim, set out above, was held to relate to this property.[62] This must be so when declarations are sought about the disposition of the shares. A wide interpretation was given to the concept of 'relates to'. A narrow construction would have meant that the action would have to have a direct effect on the property itself, its possession or title.[63] Lightman J refused to limit the ground in this way and accepted that a claim for damages could fall

---

[60] n 29 above.   [61] See below, paras 7.46–55.   [62] n 54 above, at 158.
[63] This is the position in South Australia, *Saltram Wine Estates Pty Ltd v Independent Stave Co* (1992) 57 SASR 156, 160–162.

within it.[64] If, for example, a buyer sues the seller for damages for breach of contract alleging that the goods situated in England are defective, it can be said with some confidence that the claim 'relates to' property located within the jurisdiction.[65] This is because compensation is sought in respect of the diminished value of that property arising out of its defective state. It would be different if the claim was for consequential damages arising out of losses caused by the defective goods, for example, damage caused to the buyer's machinery as a result of the supply of defective raw materials.

Property This provision is not limited to land,[66] but extends to personal **7.32** property.[67] In conflict of laws terminology, this is not limited to immovable property but extends to movable property. As far as movable property is concerned, this could be tangible movable property, such as physical goods, or intangible movable property, such as shares.[68] The *Carige* case was an example of where the property in question was shares in a company.

Does the concept of 'property' encompass digitized products, such as **7.33** software, music or a book, that is delivered over the internet? The nature of such a product is considered further in Chapter 10 which is concerned with electronic commerce and jurisdiction. There it is argued that digitized products are a form of property but intangible property, rather than tangible.[69]

Located within the jurisdiction With movable property there is the **7.34** obvious point that the property may be moved from one country to another. This raises the question: at what moment must the property be located in England? In principle, this should be at an early moment so as to avoid the risk of a defendant removing goods out of the jurisdiction so as to avoid service under r 6.20. It is submitted that we should be concerned with location at the time of the commencement of the proceedings, which should be regarded as being the moment when permission is sought for service out of the jurisdiction.[70]

---

[64] n 54 above, at 158.

[65] This is essentially what happened in the South Australian *Saltram* case, n 63 above. The case fell outside the South Australian equivalent of r 6.20(10), which was narrowly construed, but, according to Lightman J in the *Banca Carige* case, n 54 above at 158, would fall within the English ground, which he construed widely.

[66] Compare the earlier Ord 11, r 1(1)(g) RSC. However, the earlier r 1(1)(i) expressly encompassed movable property.

[67] The *Carige* case, n 54 above, at 157.

[68] ibid.

[69] See below, para 10.61.

[70] We are concerned with domicile as at the moment of the issue of proceedings, rather than the subsequent service on the defendant, *Canada Trust Co v Stolzenberg (No 2)* [2002] 1 AC 1, HL. Compare the choice of law position where the focus is on the time of the last transaction, see below, para 18.102.

7.35 *Tangible movable property*   There is normally no difficulty in fixing the location of tangible movable property. For example, if there is a dispute over the ownership of a cargo of oil that has been delivered to a port in England, the property is undeniably located within the jurisdiction.[71]

7.36 *Intangible movable property*   There is however some difficulty in fixing the location of intangible movable property. Shares and digitized products are commonly sold and are good examples of the difficulty involved.

7.37 SHARES   The situs of shares has variously been described as the place where the company is incorporated, where the share register is kept or in the case of shares which are negotiable the place where the actual documents are at the time of transfer.[72] In the *Carige* case, Lightman J held that the shares in question were situated in England.[73] This was because the share register was situated there.[74]

7.38 DIGITIZED PRODUCTS   A digitized product, such as software, sold and delivered over the internet should be regarded as being intangible property.[75] But where is it located? This question is best left to be answered in Chapter 10 on jurisdiction in cases of e-commerce, where the particular problems involved in the application of r 6.20(10) to such cases is considered in detail.[76]

Application of r 6.20(10)

7.39 Rule 6.20(10) will now be applied to a number of familiar situations where the issue of the passing of property or transfer of title is raised in the context of a sales contract.

7.40 **Insolvency and administration**   Let us assume that a factual variant of the *Armour* case[77] arises so that now it is an English buyer of the steel and the seller is domiciled in New York. The receiver of the buyer company seeks in his representative capacity a declaration from the English courts as against the sellers that ownership of the steel had passed to the buyers on delivery. There is a 'claim' for the purpose of r 6.20(10). This concept is widely defined and would include a declaration. There is property, namely the steel. The steel is located in England and the whole subject-matter of the claim relates to this property. It follows that a claim form may be served out of the jurisdiction under r 6.20(10).

---

[71] On the question whether ships and aircraft, whose ownership is recorded on an assets register, have an artificial situs in the place where the register is kept, see below, para 18.67.

[72] *Macmillan Inc v Bishopsgate Investment Trust plc (No 3)* [1996] 1 WLR 387, CA. See generally Cheshire and North, 970.

[73] n 54 above, at 158.   [74] ibid, at 152.   [75] See below, para 10.21.

[76] See below, para 10.225.   [77] n 27 above and text accompanying.

A claim for damages for conversion   If the goods in respect of which **7.41**
the claim for damages for conversion is brought are located in England
then there is property located within the jurisdiction. A 'claim' extends to
damages and the elements to be established for the tort of conversion
mean that a claim for damages for conversion 'relates to' this property. In
the situation where an English court has jurisdiction in relation to a claim
for damages for conversion by virtue of r 6.20(10) it can also consider any
dispute as to the ownership/immediate right to possession of the goods
which arises in the context of that claim, regardless of how this dispute
comes before the court. This can be seen by examining the different ways
in which this can happen.

A claim solely for a declaration   A claim solely for a declaration as to owner- **7.42**
ship or immediate right to possession which is brought as a precursor to
a subsequent action for damages for conversion would come within
r 6.20(10), provided that the goods are located in England. The whole
subject-matter of the *claim*, i.e. the declaration, relates to property located
within the jurisdiction.

As part of the claim for damages for conversion   We must now turn to the **7.43**
situation where the dispute as to ownership/immediate right to possession arises during the course of the claimant's attempt to establish his
claim for damages for conversion. If service out of the jurisdiction can
be effected in relation to this claim by virtue of r 6.20(10) the English
court will necessarily have jurisdiction over the dispute as to ownership/
immediate right to possession.[78]

The claimant seeks a declaration and damages for conversion   In the situation **7.44**
where the claimant seeks two forms of relief, a declaration as to ownership or immediate right to possession and damages for conversion, is
there just one 'claim' for the purposes of r 6.20 or two 'claims'? This is a
matter of some complexity which will be examined below.[79] However, in
this present context of r 6.20(10) it actually does not make any difference
whether there is one claim or two; the result is the same in either eventuality. If one regards the declaration as being a separate claim,[80] then the
position is the same as in a claim solely for a declaration and r 6.20(10)
would apply so that an English court would be able to permit service out
of the jurisdiction, provided that the goods are located in England. If one
treats the case as just raising one claim then the position would be the

---

[78] Even if one were to regard the claim as being the dispute as to ownership/entitlement
to possession, r 6.20(10) would apply to this 'claim', provided that the goods are located in
England.
[79] At paras 7.49–55.   [80] This will normally be the position, see below, para 7.51.

same as if it were part of the claim for damages for conversion and r 6.20(10) would still apply.

7.45 **A claim for the payment of the price** We are concerned here with situation where a claim is brought by the seller against the non-paying buyer, who is domiciled outside the EC or the EFTA countries, for the price of goods, rather than for damages for non-acceptance. If the goods are situated in England there is property located within the jurisdiction. A 'claim' covers any relief and therefore could include a claim for the price of the goods. Does the claim 'relate to' this property? Under English law at least, the seller is almost always going to have to show the property has passed to the buyer. It follows that even if 'relates to' is narrowly construed, so as to require that the action have a direct effect on the property itself, its possession or title, the claim can be said to relate to the property. Moreover, even if this narrow definition was not satisfied, a claim for the price of goods would fall within the wide construction of 'relates to' adopted by Lightman J in the *Carige* case. This wide construction covers a claim for damages and would presumably also cover a claim for the price of the goods.

Proprietary Matters and Claims in Conversion

7.46 As has been seen, in conversion cases the question of who owns the property/immediate right to possession will not uncommonly be disputed by the parties.[81] If service out of the jurisdiction can be effected in relation to the tort claim for damages for conversion under r 6.20(8), can the English court also adjudicate on the dispute as to ownership/immediate right to possession? Is a claim made in tort? In answering these question, it is important to separate out the different ways in which this dispute can arise before the English court.

A claim solely for a declaration

7.47 If the only relief sought by the claimant is a declaration as to ownership or a declaration as to immediate right to possession it is submitted that r 6.20(8) cannot apply. A claim is not made in tort, even if the action is brought as a precursor to a subsequent action for conversion. The claim is based on a separate cause of action and if this is so it cannot be brought within the tort ground.[82]

---

[81] See above, para 7.12 and more generally on conversion, above, para 6.64.
[82] See Cheshire and North, 311–312.

As part of the claim for conversion

A claim for damages for conversion is undeniably one made in tort. **7.48**
During the course of this claim, the question of the ownership/immediate
right to possession of the goods will inevitably arise, at least if English law
is applicable. This is something that the seller is going to have to establish
in order to prove his claim and something that the defendant may well
dispute.[83] It follows that, if service out of the jurisdiction can be effected
in relation to the tort claim for damages for conversion under r 6.20(8),
the English court can also adjudicate on the dispute as to ownership/
immediate right to possession. It has to be admitted though that this
is not compatible with the position in respect of the applicable law. In
Kuwait Airways Corp v Iraq Airways Co,[84] there was a claim for damages
for conversion. The ownership of the property was disputed by the
defendants. Property choice of law rules were applied to this issue.[85] Iraqi
law was the law of the situs. However, an Iraqi resolution that purported
to transfer ownership of the property to the defendants was not regarded
as being effective on grounds of public policy. Tort choice of law rules
were then applied, on the footing that the transfer of title was to be
disregarded.[86]

The claimant seeks a declaration and damages for conversion

This is a more difficult situation, which raises starkly the question of **7.49**
whether there is just one 'claim' for the purposes of r 6.20, albeit what
is sought are two different forms of relief, or two claims, i.e. one for a
declaration as to ownership or immediate right to possession and one
for damages for conversion? In answering this question, it is important
to distinguish between, on the one hand, cases where the declaration is
concerned solely with establishing one of the elements of the tort of conversion and, on the other hand, cases where the declaration is concerned
with some other matter.[87]

**The declaration is concerned solely with establishing one of the
elements of the tort**

One claim It is arguable that, where the declaration is concerned solely **7.50**
with establishing one of the elements of the tort, although two forms

---

[83] This what happened in *Kuwait Airways Corp v Iraq Airways Co*, n 37 above.
[84] n 37 above. The case is also discussed in the context of choice of law in paras 17.85–87
and 18.56.
[85] *per* Lord Nicholls at [13]–[14], *per* Lord Hope at [135]–[136], [148], *per* Lord Hoffmann at
[125]. Compare Lord Steyn at [111] and Lord Scott at [175]–[176].
[86] *per* Lord Nicholls at [37], *per* Lord Hope at [160]–[161], *per* Lord Hoffmann at [125].
It followed that the acts in question were actionable as usurpation under Iraqi law.
[87] If the declaration is concerned with more than one matter it should be asked: what is it
principally concerned with?

of relief are sought, there is only one claim, the one for damages for conversion. This claim is one made in tort. If service out of the jurisdiction can be effected in relation to the tort claim for damages for conversion under r 6.20(8), the English court can also adjudicate on the relief sought by way of the declaration as to ownership or immediate right to possession, which is just part of that claim.

7.51   *Two claims*   There is an alternative way of analyzing this scenario of a declaration which is concerned solely with establishing one of the elements of the tort of conversion. This is that there are two claims,[88] one for a declaration and another for damages for conversion, but that, in this scenario, if service out of the jurisdiction can be effected in relation to the tort claim for damages for conversion under r 6.20(8), the English court should also be able to adjudicate in relation to the claim for a declaration. The following arguments can be made in favour of giving this extended jurisdiction. First, by seeking the declaration the claimant is merely establishing one of the elements of the tort of conversion. The position is essentially no different from cases where the question of ownership/immediate right to possession arises as part of the claim for damages for conversion.[89] Second, it is highly desirable that all issues raised by the conversion action should be tried by the one court in England, rather than possibly being split up between different courts in different states.

7.52   In addition to these arguments of principle there is an English authority under the traditional rules on jurisdiction which supports this approach. This is *International Credit and Investment Co (Overseas) Ltd v Adham*.[90] The claimant sought a declaration that it was the owner of shares and that three of the defendants held these on constructive trust. It is necessary to establish the former in order to satisfy the latter. Harman J held that the claims fell within the constructive trust ground for service out of the jurisdiction.[91] The constructive trust claim clearly fell within this ground and there was no suggestion that the claim for a declaration would not also do so. The position should be the same where there is an action for damages for conversion.

7.53   The one argument against this approach is that as far as choice of law is concerned the court doubtless will apply the property choice of law rule, ie the law of the situs rule, to the declaration as to ownership even though this claim is sought alongside the claim for damages for conversion.[92]

---

[88] See *International Credit and Investment Co (Overseas) Ltd v Adham* [1994] 1 BCLC 66.
[89] See above, para 7.48.   [90] [1994] 1 BCLC 66.   [91] ibid, at 70.
[92] See the *Kuwait Airways Corp* case, n 37 above and text accompanying. See also the *Winkworth* case, n 29 above, where the declaration was sought alongside a claim for damages for conversion. But arguably in the latter case the property choice of law rules were applied because the issue of ownership was tried as a preliminary issue.

The declaration is concerned with some other matter A declaration **7.54**
may be concerned with some other matter than establishing one of the
elements of the tort. This would happen if the claimant sought as against
the defendant a declaration of ownership concerning one item of property
and damages for conversion in respect of another. The claim for a
declaration is not one made in tort and accordingly falls outside the scope
of r 6.20(8). The English court may have power to serve out of the jurisdiction in relation to the claim for damages for conversion, by virtue of
that rule but this is not a situation where the English court should thereby
be able to adjudicate in relation to the declaration as to ownership.
Recourse should be had to some other ground before permission can be
granted for service out of the jurisdiction in relation to the claim for the
declaration. However, it may be possible to use the property ground
under r 6.20(10) as the basis for service out of the jurisdiction in relation to
this claim.[93]

The declaration is concerned with more than one matter We must now **7.55**
look at the situation where the declaration as to ownership or immediate
right to possession is concerned with more than one matter: first, establishing one of the elements of the tort of conversion; and second, some
other matter. It is submitted that, in this situation, it is necessary to ask
what the declaration is principally concerned with.[94] As far as the first
situation is concerned, if service out of the jurisdiction can be effected in
relation to the relief by way of damages for conversion under r 6.20(8), the
English court should also have jurisdiction to grant the declaration.
In contrast, in the second situation, an independent basis of jurisdiction
should be needed in order to grant the declaration.

Proprietary Matters and Claims in Relation to Contracts

Rule 6.20(5) of the Civil Procedure Rules requires that a claim is made **7.56**
in respect of a contract. Guidance on the meaning of this requirement in
the context of a dispute over the ownership of property can be gained
from *Esal (Commodities) Ltd v Mahendra Pujara*,[95] a case concerned with the
differently worded predecessor contract head, Order 11, r 1(1)(f) of the
Rules of the Supreme Court.[96] The plaintiff alleged that he had provided
payment for a consortium for the purchase of shares. The defendant

---

[93] See above, para 7.27.
[94] This is by way of analogy with s 30(1) of the Civil Jurisdiction and Judgments Act 1982
which permits actions for damages for trespass to foreign land, unless the proceedings are
'principally concerned with' a question of title to, or right to possession of, that property.
[95] [1989] 2 Lloyd's Rep 479, CA.
[96] This then became Ord 11, r 1(1)(d) RSC.

claimed that, by a security agreement between him and the consortium, he had agreed to lend the consortium money and as security the consortium pledged and transferred to him the shares. The plaintiff claimed a declaration that it was, as against the defendant, solely beneficially entitled to the shares. Walton J, at first instance, held that the plaintiff was not seeking to do anything which affected the contract, ie the security agreement, in any way. The plaintiff was in fact bypassing the contract and saying that it is just not there for their purposes at all. Accordingly, the claim fell outside the scope of r 1(1)(f).[97] The contract head no longer requires that a claim must 'affect' a contract, instead it must be made in respect of a contract. However, it is unlikely that this drafting change was intended to have any substantive effect on the court's powers.[98] Moreover, even if the court's powers have been widened by this change of wording, it is submitted that such a claim, which bypasses a contract in this way, cannot be said to be made in respect of a contract.

7.57 These principles will now be applied to two examples of situations where the issue of the passing of property is raised in the context of a sales contract.

Insolvency and administration

7.58 This first example is the situation that occurred in the *Armour* case.[99] Is a claim by the receiver of the buyers for a declaration as against the sellers, that ownership of the steel had passed to the buyers on delivery, one made in respect of a contract? The contract for the purposes of this ground does not have to be between the claimant and the defendant.[100] Moreover, it can encompass a positive declaration.[101] Even so, it is doubtful whether such a claim can really be regarded as one made in respect of a contract. Such a claim would not appear to have fallen within the predecessor to this provision.[102] A claim that a reservation of title clause in a consignment note had been incorporated in the contract would be a contract claim; a claim that the clause worked effectively so as to prevent the passing of property to the buyer would not be. Furthermore, if one looks at the more

---

[97] The plaintiff appealed to the Court of Appeal but not on this point, which was accepted.
[98] See above, para 4.29, where the question of the extent to which cases decided under differently worded predecessors to r 6.20(5) are still relevant is also examined.
[99] n 27 above.
[100] 'Contract' covers contractual rights and liabilities which have become vested in one of the parties by assignment or transfer, see *DR Insurance Co v Central National Insurance Co* [1996] 1 Lloyd's Rep 74, 78; approved in *DVA v Voest Alpine* [1997] 2 Lloyd's Rep 279, CA.
[101] *BP Exploration Ltd v Hunt* [1976] 1 WLR 788; *Gulf Bank KSC v Mitsubishi Heavy Industries Ltd* [1994] 1 Lloyd's Rep 323, 328.
[102] Ord 11, r 1(1)(d) RSC; formerly r 1(1)(f).

detailed wording of that earlier provision, it cannot be said that such a claim is brought to 'enforce' a contract. Nor does it appear to 'otherwise affect' (i.e. produce a material effect on)[103] a contract. The claim affects property rights, rather than the sales contract itself.[104] We are, of course, concerned with the new wording contained in r 6.20(5). However, it is not intended that the drafting change should have any substantive effect on the court's powers.[105] It is submitted therefore that such a claim is not brought in respect of a contract. It is brought in respect of property and should be brought within the property ground in r 6.20(10).

A claim for the payment of the price

The second example of a situation which raises the question of the passing **7.59** of the property in the context of a sales contract is that where a claim is brought by the seller against the non-paying buyer for the price of goods, rather than for damages for non-acceptance. Under English law at least, the seller is almost always going to have to show that the property has passed to the buyer. This may be disputed by the buyer. The claim for the payment of the price would appear to be made in respect of a contract for the purposes of r 6.20(5) of the Civil Procedure Rules. But what of the dispute as to the issue of the passing of property? Does an English court have jurisdiction over the defendant by virtue of r 6.20(5) in relation to this dispute? In answering this question it is important to separate out the different contexts in which this issue can arise.

A claim for a declaration as to ownership If this is the only relief sought **7.60** by the claimant it is submitted that r 6.20(5) cannot apply. This is not a claim made in respect of a contract, even if the action is brought as a precursor to a subsequent action for payment of the price of the goods.

As part of the claim for payment During the course of the claim for **7.61** payment of the price, the question of the ownership of the goods will inevitably arise, at least if English law is applicable. This is something that the seller is going to have to establish in order to justify his claim for payment of the purchase price. It is part and parcel of his claim. It follows that, if service out of the jurisdiction can be effected under r 6.20(5) over the claim for payment of the price, the English court necessarily has jurisdiction in relation to any dispute over this aspect of the claim.[106]

---

[103] The *BP Exploration* case, n 101 above; the *Gulf Bank* case, n 101 above. In the latter case, at 328, Hobhouse J said that Ord 11, r 1(1)(d) would encompass 'claims for a declaration . . . in relation to the validity, status, or enforceability of a contract'.

[104] It is submitted that this is so even though the obligation to transfer property stems from the sales contract.

[105] See above, para 4.29.   [106] The position would be the same as under the EC rules.

7.62   The claimant seeks a declaration as to ownership and payment of the price   This is a more difficult situation, which raises starkly the question of whether there is just one 'claim' for the purposes of r 6.20, albeit what is sought are two different forms of relief, or two claims, i.e. one for a declaration and one for the price? In answering this question it is important to distinguish between, on the one hand, cases where the declaration is concerned with establishing one of the requirements for relief by way of the price of the goods, and, on the other hand, cases where the declaration is concerned with some other matter.

The declaration is concerned with establishing the case for the price

7.63   *One claim*   It is arguable that, where the declaration is concerned with establishing the case for the price, although two forms of relief are sought, there is only one claim, the one for the price. This claim is one made in respect of a contract. If service out of the jurisdiction can be effected in relation to the claim for the price under r 6.20(5), the English court would also necessarily have jurisdiction in relation to the declaration as to ownership which is just part of that claim.

7.64   *Two claims*   There is an alternative way of analyzing this scenario. This is that there are two claims[107] but that, if the claim for a declaration is concerned with establishing one of the requirements for the price, if service out of the jurisdiction can be effected in relation to the claim for the price under r 6.20(5) the English court should also have jurisdiction in relation to the claim for a declaration. The arguments and authority[108] in favour of giving this extended jurisdiction have already been given earlier in this chapter in the context of conversion and need not be repeated.[109]

7.65   The declaration is concerned with some other matter   A declaration of ownership may be concerned with some matter other than establishing one of the requirements for the price. Such a declaration should be regarded as being a separate claim from that for the price. The claim for a declaration looked at in isolation in this way is not one made in respect of a contract and accordingly falls outside the scope of r 6.20(5). However, it may be possible to use the property ground under r 6.20(10) as the basis for service out of the jurisdiction in relation to this claim.

7.66   The declaration is concerned with more than one matter   We now have to look at the situation where the declaration is concerned with more than one matter: first, establishing the case for the price; and second, some

---

[107] See *International Credit and Investment Co (Overseas) Ltd v Adham* [1994] 1 BCLC 66; discussed above, para 7.52.
[108] ibid.   [109] See above, paras 7.51–52.

other matter. It is submitted that in this situation, it is necessary to ask what the declaration is principally concerned with.[110] As regards the first situation, if service out of the jurisdiction can be effected in relation to the claim for the price under r 6.20(5) the English court should also have jurisdiction to grant the declaration. In contrast, when it comes to the second situation, an independent basis of jurisdiction should be needed in order to grant the declaration.

A Claim Against the Defendant as Constructive Trustee

A claim for a declaration as to the ownership of property may arise along- **7.67** side a claim in respect of a constructive trust. An example is *International Credit and Investment Co (Overseas) Ltd v Adham*.[111] The claimant sought a declaration that it was the owner of shares and that three of the defendants held these on constructive trust. Harman J held that the claims fell within the constructive trust ground for service out of the jurisdiction under the traditional English rules.[112] The constructive trust claim clearly fell within this ground and there was no suggestion that the claim for a declaration would not also do so.

2. FORUM CONVENIENS / FORUM NON CONVENIENS

Even though the terms of one of the grounds for service out of the juris- **7.68** diction have been met, the courts may refuse to permit service out of the jurisdiction. This is what happened in the *Banca Carige* case.[113] Lightman J refused to exercise the discretion in favour of permitting service out of the jurisdiction. One important factor in reaching this conclusion was that one of the defendants enjoyed immunity from enforcement of the judgment in this country. Trial in England would involve invasion into a sensitive area, i.e. whether the central bank of Cuba had dishonestly entered into an agreement, which the court should not undertake lightly. The character and relationship of the claim to property situated in England was not such as to give rise to a compelling reason why the court should assume jurisdiction. The connections of the parties and their dealings with England and the evidence relied on by the claimant and the value to the claimant of any judgment obtained were all too insubstantial to justify allowing service out of the jurisdiction.

---

[110] For the justification for this approach see above, para 7.55.

[111] [1994] 1 BCLC 66.

[112] ibid, at 70. The constructive trust ground, r 6.20(14) CPR, is discussed below, para 8.133. The restitution ground, r 6.20(15) CPR, discussed below, para 8.127, may also come into play.

[113] n 54 above, at 159–160.

7.69   What should be the attitude towards service out of the jurisdiction under this ground? The rationale of this ground is that where a question of the right to own or possess property physically within the jurisdiction is to be determined, the court of the place where the property is situated is the most appropriate one for trial because it is best placed to enforce any orders with regard to the property.[114] This suggests that the courts should not be reluctant to permit service out of the jurisdiction under this ground, at least in cases where the ownership or possession of the property is what is at issue.

3. No Subject-Matter Limitation on Jurisdiction

7.70   Under the English traditional rules, there are well established subject-matter limitations on jurisdiction in respect of foreign immovable property and foreign intellectual property rights. However, there is no such limitation in respect of other types of foreign property. Thus an English court can try an action in respect of movable property situated abroad, provided that there is personal jurisdiction against the defendant.[115]

---

[114]   See the *Saltram* case, n 63 above, at 160.
[115]   See *Hesperides Hotels Ltd v Aegean Turkish Holidays Ltd* [1979] AC 508.

8

Restitution and the International
Sale of Goods: Jurisdiction

I. INTRODUCTION

1. Restitutionary Claims and Jurisdiction

8.01 We are concerned in this chapter with restitutionary claims, i.e. claims that seek a restitutionary remedy, such as the return of money paid in advance. By and large there are no particular jurisdictional problems in respect of restitutionary claims in so far as jurisdiction is based on non-specific grounds, i.e. grounds, such as the domicile or presence of the defendant in England, which are not concerned with what the matter relates to or the nature of the claim. However, problems can arise in the situation where jurisdiction is based on a specific ground which requires that 'a claim is made in restitution'. It is easy enough to say when a claim is for a restitutionary remedy. But it is by no means always clear whether a claim for a restitutionary remedy is based on unjust enrichment or on contract or, indeed, tort or property or equity. The ground of jurisdiction relied upon may be that the matter relates to a contract or to tort, or that the claim is made in respect of a contract or is made in tort. The question then arises: can a restitutionary claim come within such a ground? Again this raises the question of what the claim is based on. The laws of different countries can disagree on the answer. Even if you look simply at the English substantive law of restitution, this is less well developed than say contract or tort. There is much theoretical discussion of what the different categories of restitution are and a shortage of case law that would provide firm conclusions to be drawn.

2. Restitutionary Claims in International Sale of Goods Cases

8.02 We are, of course, concerned, in particular, with restitutionary claims that arise in the context of a contract for the international sale of goods. The following are examples of common scenarios that can arise in this context. First, the buyer seeks recovery of money he paid under a contract for the international sale of goods which is void *ab initio*. Second, the buyer seeks recovery of money that he overpaid, for example after being overcharged for the goods. Third, the seller seeks to recover payment for goods which the seller had in error oversupplied to the buyer. Fourth, the seller delivers the goods to the wrong person and seeks restitutionary damages equivalent to the value of the goods received. Fifth, the buyer seeks recovery of money he paid on the basis that there has been a total failure of consideration, having treated the contract as having been discharged by breach. Sixth, the international sales contract is frustrated and the buyer seeks to recover payments made in advance. Seventh, the claimant seeks to rescind the international sales contract for misrepresentation.

Eighth, the claimant seeks to rescind a contract, consent to which was obtained by duress, undue influence or induced by mistake.

3. RESTITUTION FOR WRONGDOING

Under the English law of restitution, as well as unjust enrichment by sub- **8.03** traction there is the concept of restitution for wrongdoing. The wrong-doing could be contractual, tortious or equitable. Examples of restitution for wrongdoing could arise in the context of a contract for the inter-national sale of goods. However, such cases will be rare and raise particu-larly difficult problems of classification of the cause of action. Restitution for wrongdoing will therefore be considered separately[1] after examining the more usual restitution by way of unjust enrichment by subtraction.

4. *NEGOTIORUM GESTIO*

Civilian systems recognize the concept of *negotiorum gestio*, which is **8.04** concerned with the voluntary bestowal of a benefit entitling the inter-venor (gestor) to a measure of recovery. Continental writers regard it as coming within the broad ambit of restitution or quasi-contract, albeit distinct from unjustifiable enrichment. There is no such concept in com-mon law systems. The English courts could be faced with a claim based on the concept of *negotiorum gestio*. The question could then arise: is this a claim made in restitution? It should be classified as such. However, trans-border cases involving *negotiorum gestio* have been rare in the past.[2] The classic case where this has arisen has been that of salvage, i.e. one ship rendering help to another ship. A case of *negotiorum gestio* is very unlikely to arise in the context of a contract for the international sale of goods and, accordingly, no more need be said on this matter.

II. UNJUST ENRICHMENT

1. THE EC RULES

There are, with one very limited exception that does not concern us,[3] no **8.05** rules in the Brussels I Regulation dealing specifically with restitutionary

---

[1] See below, paras 8.89–105.

[2] See the Hamburg Group for Private International Law's Comments on the European Commission's Draft Proposal for a Council Regulation on the Law Applicable to Non-Contractual Obligations, 34.

[3] Art 5(4) of the Brussels I Regulation provides that a person domiciled in a Member State may, in another Member State, be sued 'as regards a civil claim for damages or restitution

claims.[4] Jurisdiction in relation to such claims must therefore be based on the provisions previously examined in this book.

Article 23

8.06   The contract for the international sale of goods in relation to which the restitutionary claim arises may contain an agreement by the parties providing that a court or the courts of a Member State are to have jurisdiction to settle any disputes which have arisen or which may arise between them within the meaning of Article 23 of the Brussels I Regulation.[5] Three major questions arise in relation to the application of this provision to restitutionary claims based on unjust enrichment. The first is whether Article 23 is wide enough in its wording to encompass such claims. The second is whether there is any particular difficulty in establishing that there is an agreement as to jurisdiction in unjust enrichment cases. The third is whether the agreement as to jurisdiction is wide enough to encompass claims based on unjust enrichment.

8.07   As regards the first question,[6] it is important to note that Article 23(1) is very widely worded in relation to its scope. It applies where the parties have agreed that a court or courts of a Member State are to have jurisdiction to settle 'any disputes' which have arisen or which may arise 'in connection with a particular legal relationship'. It does not state that the disputes must be contractual or that the particular legal relationship in connection with which the dispute has arisen or may arise is a contractual relationship. Indeed, Article 23(4) makes it clear that Article 23(1) encompasses the situation where a trust instrument confers jurisdiction and proceedings are brought against a settlor, trustee or beneficiary. Moreover, the Court of Appeal has applied Article 17 of the Brussels Convention, the predecessor of Article 23 of the Regulation, in a case involving claims in tort.[7] Even more to the point, a Scots court clearly assumed that a Scots traditional basis of jurisdiction modelled on Article 17 of the Brussels Convention could apply, in principle, to a claim

which is based on an act giving rise to criminal proceedings, in the court seised of those proceedings, to the extent that that court has jurisdiction under its own law to entertain civil proceedings'. We are not concerned in this book with the jurisdiction of criminal courts to entertain civil proceedings.

---

[4] See generally on jurisdiction under the Brussels Convention in restitution cases, G Panagopoulos, *Restitution in Private International Law* (Oxford: Hart, 2000) Ch 9; Peel, E, 'Jurisdiction under the Brussels Convention', Ch 1 in Rose (ed), *Restitution and the Conflict of Laws* (Oxford: Mansfield, 1995).

[5] See generally Panagopoulos, n 4 above, 219–221. Art 23 is discussed above, paras 3.22–27.

[6] See Panagopoulos, n 4 above, 219–221.

[7] *Kitechnology BV v Unicor GmbH Rahn Plastmaschinen* [1994] IL Pr 560, Ch D 568, CA; discussed above, para 6.03.

for restitution based on unjust enrichment.[8] It can be stated with confidence therefore that the wording of Article 23 is wide enough to encompass a restitutionary claim based on unjust enrichment.

Moving on to the second question, restitutionary claims often follow on **8.08** from contracts that are void *ab initio* or have been avoided. In such cases, is it possible to rely on a jurisdiction agreement contained in that void or avoided contract? The better view is that the answer should be in the negative.[9] Of course, there may be a dispute as to whether the contract is void *ab initio* or has been avoided. The courts of the Member State with exclusive jurisdiction under Article 23 also have jurisdiction in relation to such a dispute.[10]

When it comes to the third question, it will be recalled[11] that this involves **8.09** a question of construction of the clause. This question of the scope of the agreement is for the national court to determine, applying the law governing the jurisdiction agreement. If the applicable law is English then recourse must be had to the test laid down by the Court of Appeal in *Kitechnology BV v Unicor GmbH Rahn Plastmaschinen*.[12] The Court held that a jurisdiction clause providing that 'the parties hereto thereby submit to the exclusive jurisdiction of the English courts' included 'not only claims for breach of the relevant contract, but also other claims which are so closely connected with them that the parties can properly be taken to have intended that they should be decided by the same tribunal . . . But all such claims must be connected with the contract, rather than with any "legal relationship" between the parties other than the relationship established by the contract itself.'[13]

Commonly, claims for a restitutionary remedy arising from a contract for **8.10** the international sale of goods are based on unjust enrichment and not on a contractual obligation. Examples include a claim for repayment of money paid under a contract void *ab initio* or paid by the buyer in error after being overcharged, a claim for payment for goods oversupplied by the seller and retained by the buyer, a claim for restitutionary damages

---

[8] *Compagnie Commercial André SA v Artibell Shipping Co Ltd* 1999 SLT 1051, Lord Macfadyen in the Outer House. The problem arose as to whether the wording of the jurisdiction agreement would encompass such a claim, see below, para 8.10.

[9] See, e.g., *Egon Oldendorff v Libera Corp* [1995] 2 Lloyd's Rep 64, discussed above, para 3.31. But compare AG Colomer in Case C-269/95 *Benincasa v Dentalkit Srl* [1997] ECR I-3767 at 3785, para 75: 'any grounds of nullity which might affect the substantive elements of a contract should not have any impact on jurisdiction clauses'.

[10] The *Benincasa* case, ibid, at 3798–3799. The dispute is governed by the applicable law determined by the private international law of the Member State of the court having jurisdiction, ibid, at 3797.

[11] See above, paras 6.02–03.   [12] [1994] IL Pr 560, Ch D 568, CA.   [13] ibid, at 576.

after delivery to the wrong person, probably a claim for restitution follow-ing frustration[14] and arguably a claim for restitution consequent upon rescission for duress or undue influence. Is such a claim within the wide interpretation of the scope of a jurisdiction clause adopted by the Court of Appeal in the *Kitechnology* case? Such claims appear not to be con-nected with the contract but with a legal relationship other than the rela-tionship established by the contract itself. There does not appear to be any English authority on the scope of jurisdiction clauses and claims based on unjust enrichment. There is, though, the Scottish case of *Compagnie Commercial André SA v Artibell Shipping Co Ltd*.[15] Lord Macfadyen in the Outer House held that a jurisdiction clause that was worded to cover 'All disputes arising out of this contract' was not apt to cover a claim for restitution based on unjust enrichment nor a constructive trust claim.[16] The wording was only apt to cover contractual claims. Claims for restitu-tionary remedies that are based on contract, rather than unjust enrich-ment, are not common. One such example is arguably where money has been paid and there is a total failure of consideration.[17] Another example is possibly where rescission is sought for misrepresentation[18] or for mistake inducing the contract.[19]

General Jurisdiction: Article 2

8.11   The absence of a provision in Article 5 dealing specifically with the juris-diction of civil courts in restitution cases, combined with the unavail-ability of Article 5(1) (jurisdiction in matters relating to a contract) in most of the situations where a restitutionary claim is brought in the context of a contract for the international sale of goods, means that, where there is such a claim, the plaintiff normally will have to have recourse to Article 2 and pursue the defendant in the state where he is domiciled.

Special Jurisdiction: Article 5(1)

8.12   Whilst Article 5 of the Brussels I Regulation has special jurisdiction rules dealing with contracts and torts, it has no such rule dealing specifically with the jurisdiction of civil courts in unjust enrichment cases. The question therefore arises of whether claims for unjust enrichment can be

---

[14] If there is a dispute over whether the contract is frustrated it is arguable that both the claim relating to this and the claim dealing with the consequences of frustration should be treated as contractual, see below, para 8.23.

[15] 1999 SLT 1051.   [16] ibid, at 1063.   [17] See below, paras 8.20–21.

[18] See below, paras 8.24–25.   [19] See below, para 8.26.

brought within any of the existing provisions under this article. The most obvious of these provisions is Article 5(1),[20] which will now be discussed.

The scope of Article 5(1)

A contractual obligation In *Kleinwort Benson Ltd v Glasgow City* **8.13** *Council*,[21] a majority of the House of Lords[22] adopted the principle that a claim can only come within Article 5(1) if it is based on a particular contractual obligation, i.e. the obligation whose performance is sought in the judicial proceedings.[23] Applying this principle, it was held that a claim based on the concept of unjust enrichment, rather than on a part-icular contractual obligation, fell outside the scope of Article 5(1) of the Modified Convention (now Modified Regulation). On the other hand, a restitutionary claim that is based on a contractual obligation will fall within the scope of this provision. In the absence of a decision of the European Court of Justice on this matter, the English courts will have to follow the view of the majority in the *Kleinwort Benson* case in relation to restitutionary claims.

The key distinction that must be drawn between, on the one hand, claims **8.14** based on unjust enrichment (these fall outside Article 5(1)) and those based on a contractual obligation (these fall within Article 5(1)) will now be applied to the sort of restitutionary claims that can arise in the context of contracts for the international sale of goods. This analysis is rather tentative because of the shortage of authorities. Moreover, it must be remembered that we are having to decide whether a restitutionary claim falls within the community definition of a matter relating to a contract, a definition that is based on the common core of the legal systems of the Member States.[24] It is sometimes hard enough to say whether, under English law, a claim is based on unjust enrichment or contract; it is even harder to ascertain what a claim is based on according to the law of other Member States. There is always the possibility of a different classification being adopted under the law of other Member States from that adopted under English law.

A contract void ab initio This was the situation that arose in the *Kleinwort* **8.15** *Benson* case. A claim was brought for restitution of money paid under a

---

[20] See Panagopoulos, n 4 above, 194–196, 206–218.
[21] [1999] 1 AC 153; analysed by Panagopoulos, n 4 above, 206–215.
[22] Lord Nicholls, with whom Lord Mustill concurred, vigorously dissented.
[23] At 167–171 (*per* Lord Goff); 181 (*per* Lord Clyde); 189 (*per* Lord Hutton). A differently constituted House of Lords has endorsed the need for a contractual obligation, *Agnew v Lansforsakringsbolagens AB* [2001] 1 AC 223, 241 (*per* Lord Woolf), 250 (*per* Lord Hope), 233–234 (*per* Lord Nicholls), HL.
[24] See above, para 3.62.

purported contract subsequently accepted by both parties as being void *ab initio*. It was held that this claim was based on the concept of unjust enrichment, not on a particular contractual obligation, and, accordingly, fell outside the scope of Article 5(1). Moreover, this provision could not apply because there was no obligation, it having been accepted that the contract was void *ab initio*. The *Kleinwort Benson* case concerned interest rate swap transactions, which were subsequently held by the courts to be void *ab initio* as being *ultra vires* the local authority. However, the same situation of a claim brought for the restitution of money paid under a contract subsequently found to be void *ab initio* could arise in the context of the international sale of goods. For example,[25] a plaintiff agrees to buy goods from the defendant and the plaintiff pays in advance for these. After the delivery of one consignment, the defendant refuses to deliver any more, and alleges want of contractual capacity. If the plaintiff accepts this, or this is established, the plaintiff is entitled under English law to recovery of the payment in advance less the value of the consignment delivered. As a result of *Kleinwort Benson*, such a claim cannot be regarded as a matter relating to a contract. The Italian case of *Colorificio Paulin SpA v Soc Sogeref Artlin*,[26] which was decided before the *Kleinwort Benson* case, reached the same conclusion in relation to such a claim. An Italian company, after entering into a contract of sale with a French company, took delivery of a consignment of insecticide paint which subsequently proved to be unsaleable on the ground that it contained substances prohibited by the Italian Ministry of Health. The Italian company brought an action in Italy for a declaration that the contract was void and for reimbursement of the purchase price plus interest. The Corte di cassazione ruled that it lacked jurisdiction under Article 5(1) of the Brussels Convention. The Court went on to explain that Article 5(1) only concerned claims based on a specific contractual obligation. An obligation to reimburse the price paid pursuant to a contract of sale, which had been declared null and void and thus inoperative ex tunc, could not be regarded as a contractual obligation. Likewise, German case law and literature holds that Article 5(1) will not apply in relation to a claim for the restitution of money paid under a purported contract which was found to be void *ab initio*.[27]

8.16 *Overpayments of Money*   In *Eddie v Alpa Srl*,[28] the pursuer sought restitution of money paid in error after being overcharged for goods. Counsel for

[25] This example is given by Millett LJ in the Court of Appeal in the *Kleinwort Benson* case [1996] QB 678 at 701.

[26] Judgment of 29 November 1989, No 5224 Mass foro it 1989, 731; Nuovo giur civ comm 1990, I, 391, Note: Campeis/De Pauli; Riv dir int priv proc 1991, 1052; D Series I-5.1.1—B 31.

[27] See the written observations of Germany in Case C-346/93 *Kleinwort Benson Ltd v Glasgow City Council* [1995] ECR I-615. See also Panagopoulos, n 4 above, 206, n 100.

[28] 2000 SLT 1062.

the pursuer conceded that this was a claim for restitution based on unjust enrichment and was not a contractual obligation as such. This was a fatal admission in the light of the decision of the House of Lords in the *Kleinwort Benson* case. Counsel for the pursuer also conceded that it was difficult to distinguish the claim in that case from the one in the present case. Lord Eassie in the Outer House concluded that no relevant ground of jurisdiction under Article 5(1) of the Brussels Convention had been made out. This follows the earlier Scots case of *Strathaird Farms Ltd v GA Chattaway & Co,*[29] where it was held that a claim for the amount of an overpayment made through a mistake of fact was not based on contract and, accordingly, fell outside the scope of Article 5(1) of the Modified Convention.

In contrast, the Oberlandesgericht, Frankfurt am Main, appears to have **8.17** accepted that a claim for repayment of part of the purchase price of goods, in circumstances where it was alleged that part of the goods delivered had not been ordered and that the price of other goods had not been calculated according to the method stipulated in the contract, was a matter relating to a contract, even though it was based on unjust enrichment.[30]

Oversupply by the seller The seller may in error oversupply goods to the **8.18** buyer, who then accepts the goods. The seller may seek to recover payment for such excess goods retained by the buyer. The position is the same as that for overpayments of money. The claim should be regarded as being based on unjust enrichment and, therefore, there is not a matter relating to a contract.

Delivery or payment to the wrong person We are concerned here with the **8.19** situation where, for example, the seller delivers the goods to the wrong person, i.e. a person with whom he has no contractual relationship. The seller claims restitutionary damages equivalent to the value of the goods received by the defendant, the goods having been dissipated. The claim should be regarded as being based on unjust enrichment and, therefore, there is not a matter relating to a contract. There is another reason why there is not a matter relating to a contract, namely that there is

---

[29] 1993 SLT 36, Sh Ct.

[30] Judgment of 9 January 1979-5U109/78, DB 1979, 693; MDR 1979, 503; RIW 1979, 204; Note: Mauro, Gaz Pal 1979, Jur., 285; D Series I-5.1.2—B 19. At that time, when determining the place of performance of the obligation it was necessary to look at the applicable law. In this case, it was held that this meant the law applicable to the restitutionary obligation, rather than the law applicable to the contract of sale as such. There may in fact not be any difference between the two because under German private international law the law governing unjust enrichment is the law governing the contractual relationship giving rise to the unjust enrichment. See on the position in England, below, paras 19.07–09.

no contractual relationship between the parties.[31] Finally, Article 5(1) requires that there is a contractual obligation[32] and there is no such obligation in this situation.

8.20 *Discharge of a contract where there has been a total failure of consideration*   We are concerned here with the situation where, for example, the plaintiff agrees to buy goods from the defendant, the goods to be delivered in England. The plaintiff pays for the goods in advance but they are not delivered. Under English law the plaintiff has a choice of two different remedies. He can sue the defendant for damages for breach of contract, bringing the action in England. This would be a matter relating to a contract and the English courts would have jurisdiction under Article 5(1) of the Brussels I Regulation. Alternatively, the plaintiff can treat the contract as discharged by breach and sue to recover the payment on the basis of a total failure of consideration. Under English law this is a claim in restitution based on unjust enrichment.[33] However, it would be very odd to deny jurisdiction to the English courts simply because of the remedy sought by the claimant. It is also a very different situation from that arising in the *Kleinwort Benson* case. It is this very example that led Millett LJ in the Court of Appeal in the *Kleinwort Benson* case[34] to go on to argue that the restitutionary claim on the different facts in that case should be treated as a matter relating to a contract. Lord Goff in the *Kleinwort Benson* case, whilst disagreeing with Millett LJ on the treatment of a restitutionary claim where money has been paid under a supposed contract which it turns out was void ab initio, did take on board Millett LJ's breach of contract example. Lord Goff accepted, without deciding the point, that it was possible that a claim to recover, on the ground of failure of consideration following a breach of contract by the defendant, money paid under a valid contract, might be regarded as a matter relating to a contract. This is, he reasoned, because the claim is capable of being classified under some systems as contractual and the concept of contractual obligation may be broad enough to encompass this.[35] This acknowledges that the classification of whether a claim is based on contract or unjust enrichment should not be a matter for the national law of any one Member State, such as the forum, but is rather a matter to be determined by looking at the classification adopted by the different legal

---

[31] See Case C-26/91 *Jakob Handte & Co GmbH v Traitements Mécano-Chimiques des Surfaces SA (TMCS)* [1992] ECR I-3967.

[32] See the *Kleinwort Benson* case, n 27 above; the *Agnew* case, n 23 above.

[33] See AS Burrows, *The Law of Restitution* (2nd edn, Croydon: Butterworths, 2002) 480. This also seems to be the position in Scotland see the *Compagnie Commercial André SA* case, n 8 above, at 1054, 1059–1060.

[34] [1996] QB 678 at 701.   [35] [1999] 1 AC 153 at 167, 171.

systems in the EC. This is obviously correct, given that a community definition has been given to the concept of a matter relating to a contract.

It is important, therefore, to note that there is German support for regard- **8.21** ing the present situation as coming within the scope of Article 5(1). Under the Vienna Convention a buyer is entitled to avoid the contract on the basis of a defect in the goods and seek restitution of the purchase price.[36] There is German academic support for the view that such a claim is a matter relating to a contract; for the purposes of Article 5(1) what matters is the contractual obligation that a party has failed to perform, rather than the remedy being sought.[37] The place of performance of this obligation is considered later in this chapter.[38] Moreover, prior to the introduction of the Vienna Convention, the Oberlandesgericht, Oldenburg, in a case where the buyer alleged that the goods had not been delivered and claimed repayment of an amount paid in advance, held that this was a claim relating to a contract for the purpose of Article 5(1) of the Brussels Convention.[39]

Frustration We are concerned here with the situation where the buyer **8.22** makes payments in advance. The contract is then frustrated and the buyer seeks to recover these payments. It is by no means easy to say whether such a claim should be regarded as being based, on the one hand, on a contractual obligation or, on the other hand, on unjust enrichment. In favour of the former view, it can be pointed out that the situation is very different from that in the *Kleinwort Benson* case of a contract void *ab initio*. Moreover, frustration can be regarded as being a form of partial failure of consideration.[40] It has already been seen that there is an argument for a contractual classification in the situation where there has been a total failure of consideration, which might suggest the same classification in the situation where there has been a partial failure of consideration. But, in the former situation, the argument for a contractual classification is based in part on the fact that the plaintiff has a choice of remedies, which is not so with frustration. Under English substantive law the claim is probably best regarded as being one in unjust enrichment.[41] The argument for this is that the claim only arises after the extinction of the contract and therefore logically cannot be regarded as being based on a contractual obligation. What we do not know is how other Member States would

---

[36] Art 81.   [37] Schlechtriem, 373.   [38] See below, para 8.31.
[39] Judgment of 14 November 1975–6 U 74/75 of the Oberlandesgericht, Oldenburg, NJW 1976, 1043, D Series I-5.1.2—B 3.
[40] See G Virgo, *The Principles of the Law of Restitution* (Oxford: OUP, 1999), 373.
[41] See Virgo, ibid, 373–390. But compare Panagopoulos, n 4 above, 251 who describes a claim under s 1(3) of the Law Reform (Frustrated Contracts) Act 1943 as one arising under a statute, rather than in unjust enrichment.

regard such a claim. Nonetheless, it is submitted that the claim is probably best regarded as being based on unjust enrichment and, therefore, outside the scope of Article 5(1).

8.23 So far what we have been concerned with is the aftermath of frustration. The position is more complex where there is a dispute over whether the contract is frustrated. A declaration may be sought that the contract is frustrated coupled with a claim that is concerned with the consequences of frustration, such as for the recovery of payments made in advance.[42] The former claim is contractual. It could then be argued that the claim for the recovery of payments in advance consequent to the finding of frustration should also be treated as being contractual. The argument in favour of this rests on two grounds. First, the claim for a declaration that the contract is frustrated can be regarded as the primary claim with the claim for the return of payments in advance merely being ancillary to this. The classification of the primary claim should also dictate the classification of the ancillary claim. Second, for policy reasons it is undesirable to split the two claims for jurisdictional purposes.[43] This could lead to the undesirable situation of the primary claim being tried in one state and the ancillary claim in another.

8.24 *Rescission for misrepresentation*   In *Agnew v Lansforsakringsbolagens AB*,[44] the plaintiffs sought a declaration that they were entitled to avoid (i.e. rescind) insurance contracts on the basis of misrepresentations and non-disclosure. The House of Lords[45] held that the Court had jurisdiction under Article 5(1) of the Lugano Convention to entertain the claim. A claim to set aside a contract was a matter relating to a contract.[46] There was an obligation, which could variously be described as being to make a fair presentation of the risk, not to misrepresent the risk, or to disclose facts material to the risk,[47] and it was accepted by the parties that this was to be performed in London.[48] There must be a contractual obligation

---

[42] See *BP Exploration Co (Libya) Ltd v Hunt* [1976] 1 WLR 788, 797—a case decided under the traditional English rules on jurisdiction; discussed below, para 8.77.

[43] ibid. But the ECJ has been prepared to split claims, see Case 189/87 *Kalfelis v Schroder* [1988] ECR 5565.

[44] [2001] 1 AC 223, HL.

[45] Lords Hope and Millett dissenting.

[46] *per* Lord Woolf at 239, *per* Lord Nicholls at 233–234, *per* Lord Cooke at 246, *per* Lord Hope at 250. Lord Millett, at 262–266, dissented.

[47] *per* Lord Cooke at 246. According to Lord Woolf, at 239, the obligation was to disclose. Lord Nicholls, at 233–234, concurred with both Lords Cooke and Woolf, which leaves the precise nature of the obligation uncertain.

[48] *per* Lord Woolf at 239, *per* Lord Nicholls at 233–234, *per* Lord Cooke at 246–247. Compare the dissents of Lord Hope, at 257, contractual obligation means one arising when the contract was made and Lord Millett, at 266, an obligation does not extend to what is merely a condition precedent to the formation of a fully binding contract.

and this can include a pre-contractual obligation, which if not fulfilled provides a right to set aside a contract.[49]

In the *Agnew* case, the remedy of rescission was regarded as being a con- **8.25** tractual remedy.[50] This must be right since all the plaintiffs sought was a declaration that they were entitled to avoid the contracts. No money had been paid out by the plaintiffs so there was no question of a claim for recovery back of the money paid. But what if the plaintiff seeks to rescind the contract and to recover the property with which he has parted? For example the reinsurer in the *Agnew* case paid the claim and then sought to avoid the contract and recover the money paid. The rescission then has restitutionary consequences. In this situation, it is argued by restitution lawyers that rescission is a restitutionary remedy.[51] On the other hand, Lord Cooke in the *Agnew* case said that 'the remedy of repudiating the contract is essentially part of the law of contract. This is not only because of the subject-matter but also because the remedy is available to the reinsurer in his capacity as one of the parties to the contract.'[52] It is submitted that this goes too far and that rescission operates as a restitutionary remedy in cases where it has restitutionary consequences. If this is accepted then the question is: what is rescission which has restitutionary consequences based on?[53] Is it based on contract or on unjust enrichment? As far as English law is concerned, Millett LJ has said of rescission that the obligation to make restitution must flow from the ineffectiveness of the transaction under which the money was paid and not from a mistake or misrepresentation which induced it.[54] This means that all the plaintiff has to show is that the contract is voidable and not that the defendant was unjustly enriched.[55] This would suggest that the obligation is contractual.[56] Moreover, whatever the classification under the English substantive law, there is an argument for regarding a restitutionary claim

[49] Compare the situation where under Italian law there is pre-contractual liability that follows from the failure to conclude a contract. The ECJ in Case C-334/00 *Fonderie Officine Meccaniche Tacconi SpA v Heinrich Wagner Sinto Maschinenfabrik GmbH (HWS)* [2002] ECR I-7357, para 22 held that there was no obligation for the purposes of Art 5(1); see the discussion above, para 6.11. Moreover, for Art 5(1) to apply there must also be an obligation freely assumed by one party towards the other, see the discussion below, paras 8.28–30.

[50] *per* Lord Cooke at 246, *per* Lord Hope at 253.

[51] See Virgo, n 40 above, 28.

[52] n 44 above at 246.

[53] See Burrows, n 33 above, 610 who argues that the difficulty in distinguishing between contract and restitution in rescission cases means that it is strongly arguable that Art 5(1) should apply.

[54] *Portman BS v Hamlyn Taylor and Neck* [1998] 4 All ER 202, 208.

[55] Despite this Virgo, n 40 above, 29–30, still analyses rescission in terms of unjust enrichment, albeit as having a negative function.

[56] But compare the position in Germany. Where a contract is rescinded the consequential restitutionary claim lies in unjust enrichment, see Panagopoulos, n 4 above, 206, n 100.

consequent upon rescission for misrepresentation as being a matter relating to a contract. The case of rescission is analogous to that of where money has been paid where there has been a total failure of consideration. As in the latter case, with misrepresentation a plaintiff will have a choice of remedies, either rescission or damages. If the plaintiff seeks damages this will be a matter relating to tort (if there is a fraudulent or negligent misrepresentation) or a matter relating to contract (if there is an innocent misrepresentation). It would be very odd to deny jurisdiction to the English courts simply because a restitutionary remedy is sought by the plaintiff, rather than damages. In conclusion, it is submitted that a restitutionary claim consequent upon rescission following misrepresentation should be regarded as falling within Article 5(1) of the Brussels I Regulation.[57]

8.26 *Rescission for duress, undue influence, mistake inducing a contract*   We are concerned here with the situation where consent to a contract has been obtained by duress or undue influence or induced by a mistake. Under English law this gives a right to rescission. Lords Woolf (with whom Lord Nicholls concurred), in obiter dicta in the House of Lords in the *Agnew* case,[58] had doubts whether Article 5(1) could be relied upon in this situation. Under Article 5(1)[59] there must be a contractual obligation and one that is capable of being performed. Lord Woolf questioned whether it was appropriate to refer to an obligation not to be guilty of duress or undue influence or inducing a contract by mistake as relating to a contract.[60] Lord Millett thought that there was no 'obligation' in such cases.[61] Both went on to say that there could be no place of performance for such a negative obligation.[62] It follows that a restitutionary claim that is brought consequent to the rescission would also fall outside Article 5(1). However, there is an argument that mistake inducing a contract should be treated differently from duress and undue influence. With the latter, it is hard to see why a claim for restitution should be regarded as being contractual when someone has been 'forced' to enter into the contract. This argument does not apply to mistakes inducing a contract. Be that as it may, no such distinction was drawn in the *Agnew* case and mistake inducing a contract was treated the same as duress and undue influence.

---

[57] The same conclusion is reached by Burrows, n 33 above, 610.   [58] n 44 above.
[59] The case concerned Art 5(1) of the Lugano Convention.   [60] n 44 above, at 241.
[61] ibid, at 265. Lord Millett thought that there could be no obligation in misrepresentation cases either.
[62] ibid, at 241 (*per* Lord Woolf), 266 (*per* Lord Millett). The ECJ in Case C-256/00 *Besix SA v Wasserreinigungsbau Alfred Kretzschmar GmbH & Co KG (WABAG)* [2002] ECR I-1699 held that Art 5(1) is not applicable where the place of performance of the obligation in question cannot be determined because it consists in an undertaking not to do something which is not subject to any geographical limit and is therefore characterized by a multiplicity of places for its performance.

Alternative claims in contract/restitution We are concerned here with the **8.27**
situation where, for example, a buyer of goods makes a part payment in
advance of delivery. The seller subsequently denies the existence of the
contract and refuses to deliver the goods or to return the payment in
advance. The buyer brings an action for breach of contract but adds on an
alternative claim for return of the payment in advance should the court
hold the contract to be null and void. Alternatively, the claim may be
pleaded the other way round with the claim for return of the payment
pleaded first, and the claim in contract pleaded second. The court with
jurisdiction under Article 5(1) over the contractual claim probably will not
have jurisdiction by virtue of that Article over the alternative claim for
return of the payment.[63]

An obligation that is freely assumed Article 5(1) is restricted to **8.28**
'matters relating to a contract' and, according to the European Court of
Justice, this requirement is not met in 'a situation in which there is no
obligation freely assumed by one party towards another'.[64] The European
Court of Justice has said that there is no such obligation in the situation
where the obligation is imposed by a rule of law.[65] However, it has been
suggested earlier that even obligations that arise by virtue of the general
law can be regarded as being freely assumed where the parties have voluntarily entered into a contract.[66] This is on the basis that by voluntarily
entering into a contract the parties freely assume the legal incidents of the
contract.[67]

An obligation based on unjust enrichment arises by virtue of the general **8.29**
law, not because of any term of the contract.[68] Nonetheless, restitutionary
relief which is based on unjust enrichment may well be sought in circumstances where the parties have voluntarily entered into a contract. For
example, restitution of money paid in error may be sought by a buyer of
goods who has been overcharged. Restitution may be sought after an
oversupply of goods by the seller or there has been delivery or payment
to the wrong person. Restitution following the frustration of a contract
is also probably best regarded as being based on unjust enrichment. In

---

[63] The position is discussed further above, para 3.78.
[64] Case C-26/91 *Jakob Handte & Co GmbH v Traitements Mécano-chimiques des Surfaces SA*
[1992] ECR I-3967, 3394, para 15. See also Case C-51/97 *Réunion Européenne SA v Spliethoff's
Bevrachtingskantoor BV* [1998] ECR I-6511, [2000] QB 690; Case C-334/00 *Fonderie Officine
Meccaniche Tacconi SpA v Heinrich Wagner Sinto Maschinenfabrik GmbH (HWS)* [2002] ECR
I-7357; Case C-265/02 *Frahuil SA v Assitalia SPA* [2004] IL Pr 11.
[65] See the *Fonderie* case, n 64 above.
[66] See the discussion above, paras 3.64–66.
[67] *Agnew v Lansforsakringsbolagens AB* [2001] 1 AC 223, 264 (*per* Lord Millett), HL.
[68] See Panagopoulos, n 4 above, 196, who concludes from this that the obligation is not
freely assumed and therefore Art 5(1) cannot apply.

these cases where the parties have voluntarily entered into a contact, the restitutionary relief based on unjust enrichment can be regarded as being one of the legal incidents of the contract. In such cases, the obligation should be regarded as being freely assumed.[69] However, a restitutionary claim based on unjust enrichment may equally well arise in cases where the parties cannot be said to have voluntarily entered into a contract. For example, restitution may be sought where a contract is void *ab initio* or has been induced by duress or undue influence. In such cases, the obligation based on unjust enrichment cannot be regarded as being freely assumed by the parties. Accordingly, it falls outside Article 5(1).

8.30 What of the situation where there is a restitutionary claim based on a contractual obligation? Examples of this situation, it has been suggested above, are where money has been paid in advance for goods that are not subsequently delivered and the buyer seeks to recover the payment on the basis of a total failure of consideration, and where the restitutionary claim is consequent upon rescission following misrepresentation. This situation does not involve an obligation imposed by the general law. It is an obligation imposed by the contract and, accordingly, will not fall foul of the requirement that there is an obligation freely assumed by one party towards another.

The place of performance of the obligation in question

8.31 In the relatively uncommon situation where there is a restitutionary claim which falls within the scope of Article 5(1), it is necessary to identify the place of performance of the obligation in question under this provision. The process of identifying this place is the same as for contractual claims in relation to a contract for the international sale of goods, a process which has been discussed fully in Chapter 3. Let us take an example the situation set out above,[70] namely where money has been paid in advance for goods that are not subsequently delivered and the buyer seeks to recover the payment on the basis of a total failure of consideration. It is arguable that such a claim is a matter relating to a contract, being based on a contractual obligation, namely the obligation to deliver goods in conformity with the contract.[71] This is the obligation in question for the purpose of Article 5(1). According to Article 5(1)(b), unless otherwise agreed, the place of performance of the obligation in question is the place

---

[69] See Briggs and Rees, 2.119, who give the example of restitution following the discharge of a contract by frustration. There is however an argument that the principle that voluntarily entering into a contract is enough to constitute freely assuming an obligation should not apply to restitutionary claims based on unjust enrichment. This is not a situation, as it was in the *Agnew* case, n 67 above, where obligations could arise under the terms of the contract as well as under the general law. See also the discussion of *Agnew* above, paras 3.80–82.

[70] See above, paras 8.20–21.   [71] See above, paras 8.20–21.

in a Member State where, under the contract, the goods should have been delivered. The parties will normally have specified in the contract where this place is.[72]

Special Jurisdiction: Article 5(3)

Matters relating to tort, delict or quasi-delict

Can a claim for restitution come within the scope of Article 5(3)?[73] This **8.32** depends on whether it is a matter relating to 'tort, delict or quasi-delict' within the meaning of this concept, which must be given a community meaning.[74] The European Court of Justice has given a wide interpretation to the scope of Article 5(3), encompassing all actions which seek to establish the liability of a defendant which are not related to a 'contract' within the meaning of Article 5(1).[75] This would cover a claim for unjust enrichment,[76] although the European Court of Justice has not been faced with such a claim.[77] However, the House of Lords has. In *Kleinwort Benson Ltd v Glasgow City Council*,[78] the House of Lords has given a narrow interpretation to Article 5(3), holding unanimously that a claim for restitution based on unjust enrichment did not fall within this provision.[79] English judges when faced with such a claim will doubtless feel obliged to follow this decision, even though it is based on an interpretation of the scope of Article 5(3) which cannot be reconciled with more recent decisions of the European Court of Justice.[80] On the other hand, if a claim for restitution can be regarded as being based on tort, delict or quasi-delict, and provided there is a harmful event, it does fall within this provision.[81] Applying these English principles to the situations where restitutionary claims are made in the context of the international sale of goods gives the following results.

---

[72] The operation of Art 5(1)(b) in the case of contracts for the international sale of goods is discussed above, paras 3.143 and 3.178.

[73] See Panagopoulos, n 4 above, 197–205.

[74] Case 189/87 *Kalfelis v Schroder* [1988] ECR 5565.

[75] See above, paras 6.11–12.

[76] See the opinion of AG Darmon in Case C-89/91 *Shearson Lehman Hutton Inc v TVB* [1993] ECR I-139, para 102. See also *Re Concurrent Claims (Royalties)* (Case 4 Ob 66/01) [2003] IL Pr 30, Austrian Supreme Court.

[77] In the *Kalfelis* case, n 74 above, the ECJ was concerned with a concurrent action in contract and tort as well as unjust enrichment

[78] [1999] 1 AC 153.

[79] ibid, at 1722 (*per* Lord Goff), 185 (*per* Lord Clyde), 196 (*per* Lord Hutton), 172 (*per* Lord Mustill, 177 (*per* Lord Nicholls). If unjust enrichment came within Art 5(3) there would be considerable problems in identifying the place where the harmful event occurred, see Panagopoulos, n 4 above, 200–203, Peel, n 4 above, 23–31.

[80] See above, para 6.12.

[81] See the discussion of restitution for tortious wrongdoing below, para 8.91.

Application to restitutionary claims in international sale of goods cases

8.33   Claims flowing from the following are all based on unjust enrichment and therefore fall outside the scope of Article 5(3): money paid under a contract void *ab initio* (the situation in the *Kleinwort Benson* case); money mistakenly paid; oversupply by the seller; delivery or payment to the wrong person. Money paid where there has been a total failure of consideration and a restitutionary claim consequent on the rescission of a contract for misrepresentation should be regarded as matters relating to a contract.[82] If a matter falls within the scope of Article 5(1) it cannot fall within the scope of Article 5(3) since these two articles are mutually exclusive.[83] The alternative is that they are based on unjust enrichment and fall outside Article 5(3) for that reason. A claim for restitution following frustration is probably best regarded as one based on unjust enrichment. The alternative, which is arguable in the situation where there is a dispute over whether the contract is frustrated, is that the claim for restitution is a matter relating to a contract. In either event, Article 5(3) will not apply. A restitutionary claim consequent on the rescission of a contract for a mistake inducing the contract is as a matter of substantive law arguably based on contract,[84] rather than unjust enrichment. In either event, Article 5(3) will not apply. Whereas it is arguable that a restitutionary claim consequent on the rescission of a contract for duress or undue influence should be regarded as being based on unjust enrichment, rather than contract. Again, in either event Article 5(3) will not apply.

2. The Traditional English Rules

8.34   There are no particular problems in serving a claim form within the jurisdiction in the case of restitutionary claims. What must be discussed though is service out of the jurisdiction in such cases.[85]

Service out of the Jurisdiction

8.35   Rule 6.20 of the Civil Procedure Rules contains a special provision dealing with the situation where a claim is made for restitution. After examining this ground for service out of the jurisdiction, the contract and tort

---

[82] In the situation where rescission is sought as a contractual remedy the position is clear and Art 5(1) applies, see the *Agnew* case, n 67 above and text accompanying.

[83] The *Kalfelis* case, n 74 above; the *Agnew* case, n 67 above, at 244–245 (*per* Lord Woolf), at 233 (*per* Lord Nicholls), at 267 (*per* Lord Millett).

[84] Nevertheless, it falls outside the scope of Art 5(1), see above, para 8.26.

[85] See generally on service out of the jurisdiction under the traditional rules in restitution cases, Panagopoulos, n 4 above, Ch 10; Briggs, Ch 2 in Rose (ed), n 4 above.

grounds will examined to see whether claims for restitution can be brought within them.

Claims for restitution

Rule 6.20(15)[86] provides that a claim form may be served out of the juris- **8.36** diction with the permission of the court if:

a claim is made for restitution where the defendant's alleged liability arises out of acts committed within the jurisdiction.

This is a new ground for service out of the jurisdiction introduced by r 6.20 of the Civil Procedure Rules.

A claim is made for restitution It is unclear how widely or narrowly **8.37** this concept should be interpreted. A wide view, and this is probably the better view, would be that it covers all cases where a restitutionary remedy is sought, regardless of whether the claim is in fact based on unjust enrichment or contract. The arguments for adopting this wide view are as follows. This ground is grouped with four other grounds,[87] all of which are concerned with the remedy sought and come under the sub-heading entitled 'claims about trusts etc'.[88] The wording of the provision is also significant. It refers to a claim[89] that is made 'for' restitution, which also suggests that the provision is concerned with the remedy sought rather than the underlying basis. This wording is noticeably different from the tort ground which refers to where a claim is made 'in' tort, which is referring to it being founded on a tort.[90] If the concern had been with the underlying obligation then restitution would have appeared on its own after claims in relation to contracts and claims in tort.

A narrow view would be that this ground should be confined to cases **8.38** where the claim is based on restitution. This narrow view is analogous to the position under the EC rules. It will be recalled[91] that the House of Lords in the *Kleinwort Benson* case, when determining whether there was a matter relating to a contract or a matter relating to tort, delict or quasi-delict, was concerned with what a claim was based on and held that a claim based on unjust enrichment was neither one relating to a contract nor one relating to tort. In determining what a claim for restitution is based on, there can be acute problems of classification. However, we

---

[86] See generally Panagopoulos, n 4 above, 235–239; Briggs and Rees, 4.48.
[87] r 6.20(11), (12), (13), and (14).
[88] The word 'etc' is significant, making it clear that the four grounds are not just concerned with trusts. Indeed, grounds (12) and (13) are not so concerned. It follows that (15) cannot be confined to restitution claims in trust cases.
[89] This doubtless covers proprietary claims as well as personal, see below, para 8.124.
[90] See below, para 8.87.   [91] Above, para 8.32.

are not concerned here with a Community definition of the concept of 'a claim is made for restitution' or with how other legal systems classify the claim but rather with how English substantive law classifies the claim and, if it is based on what is classified under English law as unjust enrichment, then it should be classified as such for the purposes of r 6.20.

8.39   Whichever view of the width of r 6.20(15) is adopted, it must be the case that a claim for a restitutionary remedy that is based on unjust enrichment is undeniably a claim made for restitution. Normally a claim for a restitutionary remedy will be based on unjust enrichment. In such cases, it does not matter whether the wide definition or the narrow definition is adopted. The difficulty comes in the more unusual situation where there is a claim for a restitutionary remedy which is not based on unjust enrichment. This is arguably what happens where there is a claim that a contract is frustrated coupled with a claim for the return of money consequent on the frustration, a claim for restitution consequent upon rescission of a contract for misrepresentation or mistake inducing the contract, and in cases of restitution for wrongdoing.[92] The scope of the concept of a claim made for restitution then becomes crucial.

8.40   We can now examine the situations where claims for restitution commonly arise in the context of a contract for the international sale of goods and determine in which of these situations it can be said that a claim is made for restitution.

8.41   *A contract void ab initio*   The claim is undeniably one made for restitution. It clearly comes within the wide definition of that concept. Such a claim is based on unjust enrichment[93] and, therefore, also comes within the narrow definition.

8.42   *Overpayments of money*   This is also a claim that is undeniably one made for restitution. It clearly comes within the wide definition of that concept. Moreover, since such a claim is based on unjust enrichment,[94] it also comes within the narrow definition.

8.43   *Oversupply by the seller*   The position is the same as that where there is an overpayment of money. This is also a claim that is undeniably one made for restitution. It clearly comes within the wide definition of that concept. Moreover, since such a claim is based on unjust enrichment,[95] it also comes within the narrow definition.

---

[92] Discussed below, paras 8.94–97.
[93] See the *Kleinwort Benson* case, n 78 above, and para 8.15.
[94] See above, para 8.16.   [95] See above, para 8.18.

Delivery or payment to the wrong person This is also a claim that is **8.44**
undoubtedly one made for restitution. It clearly comes within the wide
definition of that concept. Moreover, since such a claim is based on unjust
enrichment,[96] it also comes within the narrow definition.

Discharge of a contract where there has been a total failure of considera- **8.45**
tion This is a more difficult case where the scope of the concept of a claim
made for restitution becomes important. A claim for a restitutionary
remedy following the discharge of a contract where there has been a total
failure of consideration clearly comes within the wide definition of that
concept. Under the narrow definition it is necessary to ask what the
claim is based on. According to English law, this is a claim in restitution
based on unjust enrichment.[97] It follows that the claim would also come
within the narrow definition as well. This gives rise to the curious
result that under the EC rules on jurisdiction this should be regarded as a
matter relating to a contract whereas under the traditional rules it comes
within the restitutionary ground for service out of the jurisdiction. The
explanation for this is that, as far as the EC rules are concerned, such a
claim is capable of being classified under some systems as contractual. In
contrast, under the traditional rules it is the classification adopted under
English law that matters.

Frustration A claim for the return of money following the frustration of **8.46**
a contract is one made for restitution. It clearly comes within the wide
definition of that concept. Moreover, since such a claim is probably best
regarded as being based on unjust enrichment,[98] it also comes within the
narrow definition. However, if, contrary to what is suggested, the claim is
regarded as being based on contract, and there is authority for this under
the traditional rules,[99] then it would fall outside the narrow definition.

The position is less clear where there is a dispute over whether the **8.47**
contract is frustrated coupled with a claim for the return of money consequent upon a finding of frustration. It is arguable that both claims
should be treated as contractual.[100] This would mean that even the second
claim dealing with the consequences of frustration would fall outside the
restitution ground if the narrow definition of a claim made for restitution
were to be adopted. It would though fall within the contract ground. On
the other hand, if the wide definition of the latter concept were to be
adopted, the second claim would fall within the restitution ground as well
as the contract ground.

---

[96] See above, para 8.19.   [97] See above, paras 8.20–21.   [98] See above, para 8.22.
[99] See *BP Exploration Co (Libya) Ltd v Hunt* [1976] 1 WLR 788; discussed and criticized
below, paras 8.77–79.
[100] See above, para 8.23.

8.48   *Rescission for misrepresentation*   This is the most difficult case of all, where the scope of the concept of a claim made for restitution becomes important. A claim for rescission for misrepresentation in circumstances where rescission operates as a contractual remedy, as in the *Agnew* case,[101] will fall outside even the wide definition of a 'claim made for restitution'. On the other hand, a claim for restitution consequent upon rescission for misrepresentation clearly comes within the wide definition of that concept. However, it is arguable that it does not come within the narrow definition. Under this narrow definition it is necessary to explore the basis of the claim. Under English substantive law, it is arguable that the claim is based on contract[102] and would, therefore, fall outside the scope of r 6.20(15).

8.49   *Rescission for duress, undue influence or a mistake inducing the contract*   A claim for rescission for duress, undue influence or a mistake inducing the contract in circumstances where rescission operates as a contractual remedy will fall outside even the wide definition of a 'claim made for restitution'. On the other hand, a claim for restitution consequent upon rescission for duress, undue influence or a mistake inducing the contract clearly comes within the wide definition of this concept. It is more difficult to say whether it comes within the narrow definition of a 'claim made for restitution'. The arguments are different for cases of duress or undue influence than for cases of a mistake inducing the contract. Accordingly, the two types of case will be examined separately. It is arguable in principle that restitution consequent upon rescission for duress or undue influence should be regarded as being based on the law of restitution. If a person has been forced to enter into a contract and the contract is set aside it is hard to see why the claim for restitution should be regarded as being contractual. Moreover, it has been doubted whether it is a matter relating to contract under Article 5(1) of the Brussels I Regulation.[103]

8.50   This argument of principle does not apply where the contract has been induced by a mistake. In this situation, it is arguable that the claim should be regarded as being based on contract. This may be the position under English substantive law.[104] This would be to treat rescission for mistake in the same way as rescission for misrepresentation. However, this view can only be put forward tentatively. It has been doubted whether restitution consequent upon rescission for mistake inducing the contract is a matter relating to contract under Article 5(1) of the Brussels I Regulation.[105] In

---

[101] n 67 above and text accompanying.   [102] See above, paras 8.24–25.
[103] See above, para 8.26.
[104] See the *Portman* case, n 54 above, where Millett LJ treated mistake in the same way as misrepresentation.
[105] See above, para 8.26.

this respect at least, it has not been treated differently from duress or undue influence.

The defendant's alleged liability arises out of acts committed within **8.51** **the jurisdiction**   A claimant who has established that a claim is made for restitution, then has to establish that the defendant's alleged liability arises out of acts committed within the jurisdiction. Acts may have been committed partly within the jurisdiction and partly outside the jurisdiction. The same problem has arisen with both the tort ground and the constructive trust ground. The position adopted in relation to those grounds should also be adopted in relation to this ground. Thus it is not necessary that all the acts have been committed within the jurisdiction.[106] It is enough that 'substantial and efficacious acts' have been committed within the jurisdiction, even if substantial and efficacious acts have also been committed outside the jurisdiction.[107]

It is not easy to say what the act is out of which the defendant's alleged **8.52** liability arises. Take the example of a claim by the buyer of goods for the return of money overpaid by him to the seller. Is the act out of which the liability of the defendant arises the act of the buyer (the claimant) in overpaying or is this referring to the act of the seller (the defendant) in refusing to return the overpayment? This raises a question of principle of whether the act is referring to an act by the defendant. Rule 6.20(15) does not say that it has to be such an act.[108] Moreover, the liability in question must be the liability of the defendant to make restitution. In the above example, the liability of the defendant is to repay the money overpaid. This liability arises out of the overpayment by the buyer (the claimant). The act in question therefore is the overpayment by the buyer (the claimant).

Turning now to examples of claims for restitution that arise in the context **8.53** of a contract for the international sale of goods, we can identify what the act out of which the alleged liability arises. We also need to identify where it is committed.

---

[106] See in relation to constructive trusts *ISC v Guerin* [1992] 2 Lloyd's Rep 430, 433, Hoffmann J; *Polly Peck International v Nadir* Independent, 2 September 1992, reversed by the Court of Appeal, The Times, 22 March 1993, but Hoffmann LJ said obiter that he adhered to his view in the *ISC* case. Compare *ISC v Guerin* (7 December 1990, Millett J).

[107] *Metall und Rohstoff AG v Donaldson Lufkin and Jenrette Inc* [1990] 1 QB 391, CA (a case decided under Ord 11, r 1(1)(f) RSC); overruled on a different point in *Lonrho plc v Fayed* [1992] 1 AC 448; *Nycal (UK) Ltd v Lacey* [1994] CLC 12—a case decided under Ord 11, r 1(1)(t) RSC, the successor to which, r 6.20(14), is discussed below, para 8.133.

[108] See Dicey and Morris, *Third Supplement to the Thirteenth Edition* (2003) 71. But compare the Art 5(3) constructive trust case of *Dexter Limited (In Administrative Receivership) v Harley* The Times, 2 April 2001.

8.54   *A contract void ab initio*   This is the situation where it is most difficult of all to identify an act. It is the fact that the contract is void ab initio that gives rise to the liability of the defendant to make restitution, rather than any act by a person. It is necessary therefore to create a fictional act for the purposes of r 6.20(15). One possibility would be the act of the parties of entering into the contract. This act would be committed in the state in which the contract was made.

8.55   *Overpayments of Money*   The act in question is that of overpayment by the buyer. It is submitted that this would be so even if the overpayment results from the buyer being overcharged by the seller. The act would be committed in the state where the buyer makes the overpayment.

8.56   *Oversupply by the seller*   The act in question is that of oversupply of goods by the seller. This act would be committed in the state where the goods are delivered.

8.57   *Delivery or payment to the wrong person*   The act in question is that of the delivery by the seller of the goods to the wrong person or the payment by the buyer to the wrong person. In the former case, the act is committed in the state where the goods are delivered and, in the latter case, where the payment is made.

8.58   *Discharge following a total failure of consideration*   The act in question is the breach of contract which constitutes the total failure of consideration. This will be an act committed by the defendant. If, for example, the breach consists of a failure to deliver the goods then the act in question is that failure to deliver. This act is committed in the state where the goods should have been delivered under the contract.

8.59   *Frustration*   The act in question is the frustrating event. This may be, for example, the destruction of the goods by an accidental fire. In such a case, the place where the act was committed is easy to ascertain. It is where the goods were situated at the time they were destroyed.

8.60   *Rescission for misrepresentation*   The act in question is the act of misrepresentation. This will be an act committed by the defendant. The question of where an act of misrepresentation has been committed is one of considerable complexity. In the *Agnew* case, it was, initially at least, common ground that it was committed in England during the course of the brokers' presentation of the risk to the reinsurers in their office or underwriting boxes in London.[109] In other cases, the answer may be less obvious. The question of where an act of misrepresentation is committed

---

[109] The *Agnew* case at first instance [1996] 4 All ER 978, 981, Mance J; in the Court of Appeal [1997] 4 All ER 937, 940; in the House of Lords, where the point was no longer common ground, n 67 above, at 247 (*per* Lord Cooke).

has already been examined in Chapter 6 in the context of the discussion of the torts of negligent misstatement and negligent and fraudulent misrepresentation and reference should be made to what was said there.[110]

Rescission for duress, undue influence or a mistake inducing the contract With **8.61** duress the act in question is an unlawful threat or the exertion of pressure.[111] With undue influence the act in question is the one by which the defendant exercises his undue influence.[112] This may be an act of coercion, although undue influence can be more subtle than this. The act of duress or undue influence is committed in the state where the threat is made or act of coercion is carried out. In a case of a contract induced by a mistake, it is not obvious what the act, out of which the defendant's liability arises, is. The act could be regarded as being that of entering into the contract under a mistake. This act would be committed in the state in which the contract was made.

The exercise of the discretion to permit service out of the jurisdic- **8.62** **tion** The normal principles on which the discretion to permit service out of the jurisdiction is exercised, set out by the House of Lords in *Spiliada Maritime Corp v Cansulex Ltd*,[113] apply to claims made for restitution under r 6.20(15). There is a lack of authority on the application of this ground and so any discussion of the typical factors of appropriateness that will arise in respect of such claims must be rather speculative. What we have been discussing are restitutionary claims arising out of a contract for the international sale of goods. This contract should be taken into account. It follows that typical factors of appropriateness will include those factors previously examined[114] that arise in cases where the buyer sues the seller, or vice versa, in contract. Perhaps more importantly, there are additional factors which take into account the fact that this is a claim made in restitution. That the acts out of which the defendant's alleged liability arises were committed in England is an important factor in pointing towards England as the clearly appropriate forum for trial. An analogous principle could be adopted to that in tort cases,[115] so that the fact that these acts were committed in England would make England prima facie the natural forum for trial.

Claims in relation to contracts
Rule 6.20(5), (6) and (7) are, according to the sub-heading encompassing **8.63** these three grounds, all concerned with claims in relation to contracts.[116]

---

[110] See above, paras 6.97–102.   [111] See Virgo, n 40 above, 192 et seq.
[112] ibid, at 251 et seq.   [113] [1987] AC 460.   [114] See above, paras 4.119–150.
[115] See above, paras 6.30–31. But see para 6.32 for criticism of this principle.
[116] See generally on the application of these grounds in restitution cases, Panagopoulos, n 4 above, 241–254.

Rule 6.20(5)

8.64   *A claim is made in respect of a contract*   Rule 6.20(5) requires that 'a claim is made in respect of a contract'. This ground does not say that the 'claim' must be for a contractual remedy. What is meant by 'made in respect of a contract'? It is noticeable that r 6.20(5) does not refer to a claim 'made in contract'. This contrasts with r 6.20(8), which refers to a claim 'made in tort', which means founded (i.e. based) on tort. This suggests that r 6.20(5) is intended to be wider than this and to cover cases which are not based on a contract.

8.65   It has previously been pointed out that the predecessors to r 6.20(5) were worded differently. There is a question over the extent to which cases on the scope of the former are still relevant when considering the scope of the latter. It has been argued above[117] that the new wording was probably not concerned to alter the substance of the court's powers and therefore, in principle, these old cases are a guide to what falls within the scope of the new rule.[118] But the important change that has taken place is the introduction of a restitution ground for service out of the jurisdiction. This raises the possibility of channelling some of the cases that used to fall within the contract ground, under what is now r 6.20(5), away from this ground and into the restitution ground. We can now turn to look at cases dealing with restitutionary claims decided under the predecessors of r 6.20(5).

8.66   *Restitutionary claims arising out of an implied contract*   The predecessors to this rule,[119] were not interpreted as being confined to contractual remedies and included restitutionary remedies arising out of an implied contract. In *Bowling v Cox*,[120] the Privy Council held that a claim for money had and received to the use of the plaintiff trustee in bankruptcy, where the cause of action arose out of a contract which the law implied, satisfied the requirement that a contract was made within the jurisdiction.[121] This was followed by Danckwerts J in *Rousou's Trustee v Rousou*,[122] where it was held that the claim of a trustee in bankruptcy to recover from defendants

---

[117] At para 4.29.
[118] Morever, the cases which will be examined in relation to restitution were concerned essentially with what is meant by a 'contract', rather than with the meaning of the words which have been changed. The change in wording does not therefore affect their relevance.
[119] Ord 11, r 1(1)(d) RSC (formerly Ord 11, r 1(1)(f) RSC) and Ord 11, r 2 (formerly Ord 11, r 1(e) RSC).
[120] [1926] AC 751, PC.
[121] ibid, at 754. The contract was made within the jurisdiction because the plaintiff's right to the money arose when the defendant executor got in the money under an implied contract and this took place in the forum.
[122] [1955] 1 WLR 545.

moneys formerly the property of the bankrupt was based prima facie on a right of a quasi-contractual nature[123] and, accordingly, fell within a predecessor to r 6.20(5).[124] Likewise, the Court of Appeal in *Re Jogia (A Bankrupt)*,[125] accepted in obiter dicta that an action to recover money had and received in breach of an English statute was quasi-contractual[126] and again fell within a predecessor to r 6.20(5).[127] More recently, Clarke J in *The Kurnia Dewi*,[128] said that not every claim which can be described as quasi-contractual was necessarily within a predecessor to r 6.20(5).[129] However, the quasi-contractual claim[130] in front of him, which was for *quantum meruit*, did so because it was the kind of quasi-contractual claim which arose out of an implied contract.[131] This implied contract arose in the situation where salvors were asked to mobilize after a ship was wrecked.

What is interesting about these cases is the use of the term quasi-contract. **8.67** At one time the law of restitution was based on a theory of implied contract, which is reflected in the use of this term. As a matter of the substantive law of restitution, it is clear that the law of restitution can no longer be regarded as being based on this theory. Moreover, as far as the private international law of jurisdiction is concerned, according to the House of Lords in *Kleinwort Benson*, restitution is different from contract. The cases considered above would now be regarded as being based on unjust enrichment not on implied contract. Furthermore, there was no express contract lurking in the background. In the days when claims were regarded as being based on quasi-contract, it is understandable that they should be regarded as coming within a contract head for service out of the jurisdiction, particularly when there was no restitution head for them to

---

[123] The same judge explained subsequently that he was basing his decision on this right that arose at common law and in no way on the statutory position, see *Trustee of Rousou v Rousou* [1955] 3 All ER 486.

[124] Ord 11, r 1(e) RSC.

[125] [1988] 1 WLR 484, CA. See also *Newtherapeutics Ltd v Katz* [1991] Ch 226, 255–256.

[126] Compare *BP Exploration Co (Libya) Ltd v Hunt* [1976] 1 WLR 788, discussed below, where a claim for relief under the Law Reform (Frustrated Contracts) Act 1943 was regarded as being based on rights of a contractual, not quasi-contractual, nature.

[127] Ord 11, r 1(f) RSC. The quasi-contract was said to be made or arise for the purpose of this provision where the money is received. Doubts were cast on the *Rousou* case on this point as to where the contractual obligation arose.

[128] *Smit International Singapore Pte Ltd v Kurnia Dewi Shipping SA Ocean Marine Mutual Protection and Indemnity Association and Ocean P & I Services Ltd (The Kurnia Dewi)* [1997] 1 Lloyd's Rep 552. The position is the same in New South Wales, see *McFee Engineering Pty Ltd (In Liqidation) v CBS Constructions Pty Ltd* (1980) 44 FLR 340.

[129] Ord 11, r 1(1)(d) RSC.

[130] Clarke J thought that the plaintiff had a claim in contract but discussed the alternative way in which it was pleaded as one in quasi-contract.

[131] n 128 above, at 561.

come within. It is much harder to justify claims based on unjust enrichment coming within r 6.20(5), particularly now that there is a restitution ground which encompasses such claims. It is submitted therefore that the above cases should not come within r 6.20(5).[132] They would, however, come within the restitution ground in r 6.20(15).

8.68 *Restitutionary claims arising in the context of a contract for the international sale of goods*   These cases are much more difficult than the ones just considered since there is now a contract lurking in the background. This starkly raises the question of what is meant by a claim 'made in respect of a contract'. Is the fact that the restitutionary claim arises in the context of a contract enough to satisfy this requirement (the wide interpretation)? Or must it be shown that the claim is actually based on contract (the narrow interpretation)? Most claims arising in the context of international sales are based on unjust enrichment and this narrow interpretation would put them outside r 6.20(5). It is certainly arguable that a restitutionary claim based on unjust enrichment where there is a sales contract in the background is 'made in respect of a contract'.[133]

In favour of this wide interpretation, is the wording of r 6.20(5). As has been seen, it is arguable that the choice of the words 'made in respect of a contract' is intended to cover claims which are not based on a contract. Some support for this wide interpretation can also be found in *BP Exploration Co (Libya) Ltd v Hunt*,[134] where Kerr J held that a claim for relief under the Law Reform (Frustrated Contracts) Act 1943 for such sums as the court considers just in respect of valuable benefits obtained by the defendant fell within a predecessor to r 6.20(5). There is however a question, which will be addressed below,[135] over whether this decision should be followed now.

8.69 In favour of a narrow interpretation of the scope of r 6.20(5), are two policy considerations. The first is that restitutionary claims based on unjust enrichment should not be placed within a contract ground when there is a restitution ground which is designed for such claims. The second is that it is not sensible to interpret r 6.20(5) in a way that opens up such a wide gap between Article 5(1) of the Brussels I Regulation, which requires the claim to be based on contract, and the traditional English rules.

8.70 Both of these policy considerations militate strongly in favour of the narrow interpretation of r 6.20(5). Moreover, at present there is no authority

---

[132] Briggs and Rees, 4.48; Burrows, n 33 above, 614. See also Panagopoulos, n 4 above, 241–242.

[133] Panagopoulos, n 4 above, 249–254.   [134] [1976] 1 WLR 788.   [135] At para 8.79.

on the meaning of a claim 'made in respect of a contract' that dictates that this should include claims based on unjust enrichment. In conclusion, it is tentatively suggested that a restitutionary claim based on unjust enrichment should fall outside r 6.20(5), even though there is a sales contract lurking in the background.[136] The position would be different though where the claim for restitution is based on contract; this should fall within r 6.20(5).

We can now examine the situations where restitutionary claims commonly arise in the context of a contract for the international sale of goods and see in which of these situations there can be said to be a claim made in respect of a contract. **8.71**

A CONTRACT VOID AB INITIO   The claim is based on unjust enrichment[137] and therefore should not be regarded as being a claim made in respect of a contract. In this particular situation, a further argument to those made above can be made for not bringing the claim within r 6.20(5). This is that it is uncertain whether a claim for a declaration that no contract exists (which could include a declaration that the contract is void *ab initio*) can come within this ground.[138] It was this very uncertainty that led to the introduction of r 6.20(7).[139] If such a declaration does indeed fall outside r 6.20(5) it would very odd to bring within this ground a restitutionary claim that only arises because no contract exists. However, as has been seen, this restitutionary claim will fall within the restitution ground. **8.72**

OVERPAYMENTS OF MONEY   This is also a claim for restitution based on unjust enrichment[140] and therefore it too should not be regarded as being a claim made in respect of a contract. However, as has been seen it will fall within the restitution ground. **8.73**

OVERSUPPLY BY THE SELLER   The position is the same as that where there is an overpayment of money. **8.74**

DELIVERY OR PAYMENT TO THE WRONG PERSON   This is also a claim for restitution based on unjust enrichment[141] and therefore it too should not be regarded as being a claim made in respect of a contract. Moreover, no contract exists and therefore the same problem in using r 6.20(5) arises as **8.75**

---

[136] See Panagopoulos, n 4 above, 249–254; Burrows, n 33 above, 615.
[137] See the *Kleinwort Benson* case, n 78 above, and para 8.15.
[138] Compare *Finnish Marine Insurance Co Ltd v Protective National Insurance Co* [1990] 1 QB 1078—not within the contract head, with *DR Insurance Co v Central National Insurance Co* [1996] 1 Lloyd's Rep 74—within the contract head if the agreement was entered into with intent to create legal relations. The latter view accords with the purpose behind the rule: *The Ines* [1993] 2 Lloyd's Rep 492; *Gulf Bank KSC v Mitsubishi Heavy Industries Ltd* [1994] 1 Lloyd's Rep 323. See also *The Olib* [1991] 2 Lloyd's Rep 108.
[139] See below, para 8.84.   [140] See above, para 8.16.   [141] See above, para 8.19.

with where a contract is void *ab initio*. However, as has been seen it will fall within the restitution ground.

8.76   DISCHARGE FOLLOWING A TOTAL FAILURE OF CONSIDERATION   Under the English substantive law the claim is based on unjust enrichment and therefore should not be regarded as being made in respect of a contract. However, as has been seen it will fall within the restitution ground. This gives rise to the curious result that under the EC rules such a claim should be regarded as a matter relating to a contract whereas under the traditional rules it is not a claim made in respect of a contract. The explanation for this is that, as far as the EC rules are concerned, such a claim is capable of being classified under some systems as contractual; whereas under the traditional rules it is the classification adopted under the English substantive law that matters.

8.77   FRUSTRATION   This is one of the rare instances where there is an authority dealing with the point. In *BP Exploration Co (Libya) Ltd v Hunt*,[142] Kerr J held that a claim for a declaration that a contract had become frustrated 'affected' a contract and, accordingly, was within a predecessor of r 6.20(5),[143] even though, in effect, there was no longer any contract. A further claim for relief under the Law Reform (Frustrated Contracts) Act 1943 for such sums as the court considers just in respect of valuable bene-fits obtained by the defendant was also held to be one which 'affected' the contract. Accordingly, this too fell within the same contract head. Kerr J pointed out the undesirable consequences of holding otherwise, namely that, the English court, whilst able to deal with the question of whether the contract was frustrated, would be unable to deal with the con-sequences between the parties which flow from that frustration according to the 1943 Act. It was argued by the plaintiff, as an alternative to this analysis, that this second claim was based on a statutory quasi-contractual obligation that arose once the contract had been frustrated and there-fore reliance could be placed on the *Bowling* and *Rousou* cases[144] as the authority for bringing this second claim within the contract head in question. Kerr J rejected this argument saying that: 'The reality is that there is only one contract, the original contract which has become frustrated, but that the statute engrafts upon this contract certain post-frustration rights and obligations which in the view of the legislature the justice between the parties requires. I therefore consider that from start to

---

[142] [1976] 1 WLR 788.
[143] Ord 11, r 1(f) RSC. This required an 'action begun . . . to enforce, rescind, dissolve, annul or otherwise affect a contract'. The newly worded contract ground in r 6.20(5) CPR does not require this, merely that a claim is made in respect of a contract.
[144] n 120 above and n 122 above respectively.

finish one is only dealing with one contract, but one which is 'affected' by the provisions of the Act. . . .'[145]

If this analysis is followed, the second claim dealing with the con- **8.78** sequences of frustration should be regarded as being made in respect of a contract.[146] It would then fall within this contract ground but outside the restitution ground if the narrow definition of a claim made for restitution were to be adopted. On the other hand, if the wide definition of the latter concept were to be adopted, it would fall within the restitution ground as well as the contract ground.

The *BP* case was decided in 1975 before recent developments in the law **8.79** of restitution and in private international law; so there is a question of whether this decision should still be followed. A claim for the return of money following the frustration of a contract is, under English substantive law, probably best regarded as one based on unjust enrichment[147] and therefore should not be regarded as being a claim made in respect of a contract. However, it would fall within the restitution ground. In a case where the claim is solely for the return of money, with the question of whether the contract is frustrated not being in issue, this is the analysis that should be applied. However, in a case, such as that facing the court in *BP*, where there are two claims, one for a declaration that the contract is frustrated and another dealing with consequences of frustration, there is much to be said for following the approach of Kerr J in the BP case in that it allows both claims to come within the one ground, the contract ground. The alternative is to classify the two claims differently, the first claim as being contractual and the second claim as being restitutionary. This prevents the two claims from being dealt with under the same ground. The former claim would not fall within the restitution ground and the latter would not fall within the contract ground under r 6.20(5). However, this does not mean that the English courts would lack jurisdiction in relation to both claims, which was what concerned Kerr J in the days before the introduction of the restitution ground. The claim for the return of money following the frustration of the contract would fall within the restitution ground. The claim for a declaration that the contract is frustrated is made in respect of a contract and therefore would fall within the scope of r 6.20(5). It would then need the contract to have been made in England or English law to govern the contract etc for this ground to be satisfied.[148]

---

[145] The *BP Exploration* case, n 126 above, at 797.   [146] Panagopoulos, n 4 above, 251, 254.

[147] See Virgo, n 40 above, 373–390. But compare Panagopoulos, n 4 above, 251 who describes a claim under s 1(3) of the Law Reform (Frustrated Contracts) Act 1943 as one arising under a statute, rather than in unjust enrichment.

[148] If this requirement is not satisfied then the claimant would be in no better position if the Kerr J contractual approach were to be adopted.

8.80   RESCISSION FOR MISREPRESENTATION   This is the most difficult case of all. A claim for rescission for misrepresentation in circumstances where rescission operates as a contractual remedy, as in the *Agnew* case,[149] should be regarded as being made in respect of a contract. But what of a claim for restitution consequent upon the rescission? Under English substantive law the restitutionary claim is arguably based on contract. If so, this would be a claim made in respect of a contract. Would it also come within the restitution ground? It has already been seen that this depends on the width of the definition adopted for the concept of a claim made for restitution. A restitutionary claim for rescission for misrepresentation clearly comes within the wide definition of that concept but arguably outside the narrow definition.

8.81   RESCISSION FOR DURESS, UNDUE INFLUENCE OR A MISTAKE INDUCING THE CONTRACT   A claim for rescission for duress, undue influence or a mistake inducing a contract in circumstances where rescission operates as a contractual remedy should be regarded as being made in respect of a contract. But what of a claim for restitution consequent upon the rescission? Where the claim for restitution is consequent upon rescission for duress or undue influence it is arguable that this is based on the law of restitution[150] and therefore should not be regarded as being a claim made in respect of a contract. However, the restitution ground will apply. Where the claim for restitution is consequent upon rescission for mistake inducing the contract it has been argued tentatively that this should be regarded as being based on contract.[151] The position would then the same as for restitution consequent upon rescission for misrepresentation. It would be a claim made in respect of a contract. The claim would also fall within the restitution ground if the wide definition of 'a claim made for restitution' were to be adopted but not if the narrow definition were to be adopted.

8.82   *Additional requirements*   Rule 6.20(5) requires not just a claim made in respect of a contract but also that one of four alternatives is satisfied, namely that the contract was made within the jurisdiction etc.[152] In those few situations where there is a restitutionary claim made in respect of a contract, i.e. arguably a claim for restitution consequent upon rescission for misrepresentation or mistake inducing the contract[153] and, if the *BP Exploration* case is followed, a claim dealing with the consequences of frustration of a contract in the situation where the frustration is in dispute,

---

[149]   n 67 above and text accompanying.
[150]   See above, para 8.26.   [151]   See above, para 8.26 .   [152]   See above, para 4.28.
[153]   A claim to rescind where this is sought as a contractual remedy is definitely made in respect of a contract.

there are no special difficulties in establishing one of these four alternatives.

Rule 6.20(6)   Rule 6.20 (6) requires that 'a claim is made in respect of **8.83** a breach of contract'.[154] In so far as this requires that a claim is made in respect of a contract, everything said about this concept when discussing r 6.20(5) is equally applicable to r 6.20(6). This would exclude most restitutionary claims that arise in the context of a contract for the international sale of goods. In those few situations where there is a claim made in respect of a contract, ie arguably a claim for rescission for misrepresentation or mistake inducing the contract[155] and, if the *BP Exploration* case is followed, a claim dealing with the consequences of frustration of a contract in the situation where the frustration is in dispute, it has to be further asked whether the claim is made in respect of a 'breach' of contract. A claim dealing with the consequences of frustration cannot be so regarded and would therefore fall outside the scope of r 6.20(6). The same is true of a claim for rescission.

Rule 6.20(7)   This requires that 'a claim is made for a declaration that no **8.84** contract exists'. If a buyer has paid money in advance for goods he may seek to combine such a declaration with a claim for reimbursement of this money.[156] A claim for a declaration that a contract has been frustrated or has been vitiated because of mistake or misrepresentation should be regarded as falling within this provision, even though it is alleged that the contract no longer exists, rather than that it has never existed.[157]

The exercise of the discretion to permit service out of the jurisdic- 8.85 tion   The typical factors of appropriateness in cases coming within the contract heads have previously been examined in Chapter 4[158] and reference should be made to what is said there.

Claims in tort

It will be recalled that r 6.20(8) provides that a claim form may be served **8.86** out of the jurisdiction with the permission of the court if:

a claim is made in tort where—
  (a) damage was sustained within the jurisdiction; or
  (b) the damage sustained resulted from an act committed within the jurisdiction.

---

[154] See Panagopoulos, n 4 above, 245 for Australian cases where restitutionary claims have been brought within their equivalent of this ground on the basis of an implied contract.

[155] This is definitely so if rescission is sought as a contractual remedy and arguably so where it is sought as a restitutionary remedy, see above, paras 8.80–81.

[156] See, e.g. the Italian *Colorificio* case, n 26 above, discussed above, para 8.15.

[157] See above, paras 4.90–93. It might be argued that misrepresentation or mistake go to validity of the contract, rather than its existence. However, the courts may well take a wide view of this provision and interpret it as covering validity, see above, para 4.93.

[158] At paras 4.103–109 and 4.119–150.

8.87 A claim is made in tort   This ground requires that 'a claim is made in tort'. A claim is 'made' in tort when it is founded on a tort, i.e. based on a tort.[159] It is worth recalling[160] that we are not concerned here with a community definition of a tort but rather with whether English substantive law classifies the claim as being one made in tort for the present purposes. We can now examine the situations where claims for restitution can arise in the context of a contract for the international sale of goods and see in which of these situations there can be said to be a claim made in tort.[161]

8.88 Application to claims for restitution in international sale of goods cases   The following claims are all based on unjust enrichment, rather than on a tort, and will therefore fall outside the scope of r 6.20(8): money paid under a contract void *ab initio* (the situation in the *Kleinwort Benson* case); money mistakenly paid; oversupply by the seller; delivery or payment to the wrong person; discharge following a total failure of consideration. A claim for restitution following frustration is probably best regarded as one based on unjust enrichment. The alternative, which is arguable in the situation where there is a dispute over whether the contract is frustrated, is that the claim for restitution is contractual. In either event, the claim is not based on a tort. A restitutionary claim consequent on the rescission of a contract for a mistake inducing the contract is as a matter of substantive law arguably based on contract,[162] rather than unjust enrichment. In either event r 6.20(8) will not apply. In contrast, it is arguable that a restitutionary claim consequent on the rescission of a contract for duress or undue influence should be regarded as being based on unjust enrichment, rather than contract. But again, in either event, r 6.20(8) will not apply.

III. RESTITUTION FOR WRONGDOING

1. THE SUBSTANTIVE LAW BACKGROUND

8.89   Commentators on the English law of restitution regard restitution for wrongdoing as part of the law of restitution. However, they are not agreed on how restitution for wrongdoing should be characterized. Four

---

[159] See above, para 6.23   [160] See above, para 6.24.

[161] See generally on the application of the tort ground in restitution cases: Panagopoulos, n 4 above, 254–259; Briggs, n 85 above, 57–60.

[162] A claim to rescind where this is sought as a contractual remedy is definitely based on contract.

different views have emerged.[163] First, restitution for wrongdoing is not founded on reversal of unjust enrichment.[164] The cause of action is in contract, tort or equity, and this triggers a restitutionary remedy.[165] Second, the cause of action is in restitution but the elements of this cause of action are the same as those for the wrong.[166] Third, restitution for wrongdoing is based on unjust enrichment but that this type of unjust enrichment is different from the more usual unjust enrichment by subtraction (or autonomous unjust enrichment).[167] With the former the cause of action to which restitution responds is the wrongdoing; with the latter the cause of action to which restitution responds is unjust enrichment. Less helpful to the private international lawyer, who has to classify the matter for the purposes of jurisdiction and choice of law, it has also been said that, 'restitution for a wrong can be equally well classified as part of the law concerning the wrong or as part of the law of restitution'.[168] Fourth, the cause of action is in unjust enrichment by subtraction.[169]

2. CONTRACTS FOR THE INTERNATIONAL SALE OF GOODS

The most likely form of wrongdoing to arise in the context of a contract **8.90** for the international sale of goods is tortious wrongdoing, rather than contractual or equitable wrongdoing. For example, the defendant may have sold the claimant's goods and this gives rise to the tort of conversion. The claimant may then seek the value of the proceeds of sale.[170] The remedy in such a case is restitutionary because it is assessed by reference to the defendant's gain rather than the claimant's loss.[171] Restitution for contractual wrongdoing is unlikely to arise in the context of a contract for the international sale of goods. Under English law it is only in the most exceptional circumstances that restitutionary remedies are available in the

---

[163] See generally Bird in Rose (ed), n 4 above, 72–76, who discusses three of these.

[164] Virgo, n 40 above, 445–448.

[165] Virgo, ibid, 445–448; Panagopoulos, n 4 above, 16–17, 81–84, 228; Friedmann in W Cornish, R Nolan, J O'Sullivan and G Virgo (eds), *Restitution: Past, Present and Future* (Oxford: Hart, 1998) 13; Bird, n 163 above, 74; P Birks, *Restitution-The Future* (Amandale, NSW: Federation, 1992) 1; *An Introduction to the Law of Restitution* (Oxford: Clarendon, 1985) 316.

[166] Bird, n 163 above, 72–73, who says that this theory seems to be confined to torts.

[167] Burrows, n 33 above, 5–6 and Ch 14. See also Birks, *An Introduction to the Law of Restitution*, n 165 above, Chs I and X but compare this with the more recent *Restitution: Past, Present and Future*, n 165 above Ch 1.

[168] Burrows, n 33 above, 459.

[169] J Beatson, *The Use and Abuse of Unjust Enrichment*, (Oxford: Clarendon, 1991) 25–28, 206–243.

[170] The claimant will do this if this figure is higher than the market value of the goods, i.e. the claimant's loss.

[171] Virgo, n 40 above, 490.

situation where the defendant has breached a contract,[172] circumstances which are very different from those arising where there is a contract for the international sale of goods. However, this still leaves the possibility, in theory at least, that a claim could be brought before the English courts for restitution for contractual wrongdoing based on a broader foreign law which allows such a claim even in cases of the international sale of goods. A claim for equitable wrongdoing[173] is most unlikely to arise in the context of a contract for the international sale of goods and so no more will be said on this type of wrongdoing.

3. Restitution for Tortious Wrongdoing

The EC Rules

Article 5(3)

8.91 There is some uncertainty over whether Article 5(3) will apply in the case of a claim for restitution for tortious wrongdoing. If the claim is regarded as being based on tort it will do so. On the other hand, if the claim is regarded as being based on unjust enrichment it will not do so.[174] So far so good. It is when one moves onto the next stage and asks how legal systems in the EC would classify restitution for tortious wrongdoing that the problems start. If one starts off by looking at the English substantive law of restitution, it has already been seen that commentators disagree on the classification to be adopted. If the first theory is adopted, namely that the cause of action is in tort, the answer is clear; the claim is based on tort. If the second theory is adopted, namely that the cause of action is in restitution but the elements of this cause of action are the same as those in tort, the answer is less clear, but, even so, the claim probably should be regarded as being based on tort. If the third theory is applied, the claim should be treated as one based on tort.[175] It is only if the fourth theory is applied, namely that the cause of action is in unjust enrichment by subtraction, that one gets the result that the claim cannot be regarded as one based on tort. It is submitted that, as a matter of substantive law, this is the least convincing of the four theories. The better view, which enjoys the greatest academic support,[176] is that as far as English substantive law is

---

[172] *Attorney-General v Blake* [2001] 1 AC 268, HL; *Satnam Investments Ltd v Dunlop Heywood & Co Ltd* [1999] 3 All ER 652, CA; *Experience Hendrix v PPX Enterprises Inc* [2003] EWCA Civ 323, [2003] 1 All ER (Comm) 830. See generally Virgo, n 40 above, Ch 17.

[173] The categories for such wrongdoing are: breach of fiduciary duty; abuse of relationships of confidence; unconscionability and dishonestly assisting in a breach of trust. See Virgo, n 40 above, 520–555.

[174] See the *Kleinwort Benson* case, n 78 above and text accompanying.

[175] Burrows, n 33 above, who puts forward the third theory says at 613 that Art 5(3) will encompass restitution for wrongs.

[176] See above, para 8.89.

concerned, restitution for tortious wrongdoing should be regarded as being based on tort. This would doubtless be enough to persuade an English court that Article 5(3) should apply. But the real question is how Member States, not just England, classify restitution for wrongdoing, assuming that they have this concept. Germany and Greece classify such cases under unjust enrichment by subtraction.[177] If most other Member States classify restitution for wrongdoing in this way then Article 5(3) should not apply.[178]

Article 5(1)

A claim for restitution for tortious wrongdoing, regardless of whether it is **8.92** based on tort or unjust enrichment, is certainly not based on contract and therefore cannot be regarded as being a matter relating to a contract within the meaning of Article 5(1).

The Traditional English Rules

Rule 6.20(8)

It is submitted that a claim for restitution for tortious wrongdoing should **8.93** be regarded as being a claim made in tort.[179] This is because such a claim is best regarded under the English substantive law of restitution, and this is what we are concerned with under the traditional rules, as being based on tort.[180] Once the claimant has established that a claim is made in tort, he must further establish that damage was sustained within the jurisdiction or the damage sustained resulted from an act committed within the jurisdiction. The meaning of these concepts has previously been examined in Chapter 6[181] and the reader is referred to what is said there.

Rule 6.20(15)

A claimant who can have recourse to the tort ground will have nothing to **8.94** gain from having recourse to the restitution ground. The latter is unlikely to allocate jurisdiction to England in circumstances where the tort ground would not do so. Both grounds allocate jurisdiction to England if the relevant act is committed in England. In a case of restitution for tortious wrongdoing, this act will presumably be the same for both grounds. Nonetheless, it is worth asking whether a claim for tortious wrongdoing

---

[177] See Panagopoulos, n 4 above, 228; for Germany see B Markesinis, W Lorenz and G Danneman, *The German Law of Obligations, Volume 1, The Law of Contracts and Restitution: A Comparative Introduction* (Oxford: Clarendon 1997), 741, 743–747.

[178] Not unless, contrary to the *Kleinwort Benson* case, a wide interpretation is given to the scope of that provision, see above paras 6.11–12.

[179] See Panagopoulos, n 4 above, 254.

[180] See above, para 8.89. [181] See above, paras 6.14–16.

would come within the restitution ground, given that counsel for the claimant routinely seek service out of the jurisdiction on the basis of a number of alternative grounds.

8.95 It is unclear whether a claim is made for restitution within r 6.20(15) in the situation where the claim is for restitution for tortious wrongdoing.[182] This depends on how widely or narrowly the concept of 'a claim . . . made for restitution' is defined.[183] If, as is suggested above, this concept is widely defined to encompass all cases where a restitutionary remedy is sought, regardless of what the claim is based on, then clearly a claim for tortious wrongdoing is made for restitution. The claim for tortious wrongdoing would fall within the restitution ground (as well as the tort ground).

8.96 In contrast, if this concept is narrowly defined so as to be confined to claims based on the law of restitution, then the position is much less clear. Restitution for tortious wrongdoing is part of the English law of restitution and to that extent the claim can be said to be based on the law of restitution. On this view, the claim would fall within the restitution ground (as well as the tort ground). However, when applying the narrow definition it is probably necessary to dig deeper and ask what restitution for tortious wrongdoing is based on. The answer is that it is best regarded under the English substantive law of restitution as being based on tort.[184] The claim would therefore fall outside r 6.20(15) (but still within the tort ground).

8.97 If, contrary to what is argued above, a claim for restitution for tortious wrongdoing is regarded as being based on unjust enrichment by subtraction[185] it will fall outside the tort ground but clearly within the restitution ground.

Rule 6.20(5), (6), (7)

8.98 A claim for restitution for tortious wrongdoing cannot be regarded as being a claim in relation to a contract.

4. Restitution for Contractual Wrongdoing

The EC Rules

Article 5(1)

8.99 There is the same uncertainty over whether Article 5(1) will apply in the case of a claim for restitution for contractual wrongdoing as there is over whether Article 5(3) will apply in a case of restitution for tortious wrong-

---

[182] But compare Panagopoulos who regards it as so falling, n 4 above, 235.
[183] See the discussion above, paras 8.37–39.
[184] See above, para 8.89.   [185] See theory four above, para 8.89.

doing. If the claim is regarded as being based on contract, it will come within Article 5(1). On the other hand, if the claim is regarded as being based on unjust enrichment by subtraction it will not do so. It is necessary to ask how legal systems in the EC would classify restitution for contractual wrongdoing. It is submitted that, as far as the English substantive law is concerned, although there is a lack of agreement amongst commentators as to the underlying cause of action, the claim should be regarded as being based on contract.[186] This would doubtless be enough to persuade an English court that Article 5(1) should apply. But the real question is how Member States, not just England, classify restitution for contractual wrongdoing, assuming that they have this concept. Germany and Greece classify such cases under unjust enrichment by subtraction.[187] If most other Member States classify restitution for wrongdoing in this way, then Article 5(1) should not apply.[188]

Article 5(3)

A claim for restitution for contractual wrongdoing, regardless of whether **8.100** it is based on contract or unjust enrichment by subtraction, is certainly not based on tort and therefore cannot be regarded as being a matter relating to tort, delict or quasi-delict within the meaning of Article 5(3).

The Traditional English Rules

Rule 6.20(5), (6), (7)

It is submitted that a claim for restitution for contractual wrongdoing **8.101** should be regarded as being a claim made in relation to a contract. This is because such a claim is best regarded under the English substantive law of restitution, and this is what we are concerned with under the traditional rules, as being based on contract.[189]

Rule 6.20(15)

It is conceivable that the restitution ground would operate in circum- **8.102** stances where the contract ground would not. It is important therefore to decide whether a claim for restitution for contractual wrongdoing would fall within this ground. Unfortunately, it is unclear whether such a claim is made for restitution within the meaning of r 6.20(15). The position is

---

[186] The argument for this is precisely the same as that above, para 8.89 in relation to tortious wrongdoing.

[187] See Panagopoulos, n 4 above, 228; for Germany see Markesinis, Lorenz and Danneman, n 177 above, 741, 743–747.

[188] For the autonomous definition to be given to 'Matters relating to a contract' see above, para 3.62.

[189] See above, para 8.89.

essentially the same as that where there is tortious wrongdoing.[190] It depends on how widely or narrowly the concept of 'a claim . . . made for restitution' is defined. If, as is suggested above, this concept is widely defined to encompass all cases where a restitutionary remedy is sought, regardless of what the claim is based on, then clearly a claim is made for restitution. The claim for contractual wrongdoing would fall within the restitution ground (as well as the contract ground).

8.103 In contrast, if this concept is narrowly defined so as to be confined to claims based on the law of restitution then the position is much less clear. Restitution for wrongdoing is part of the English law of restitution and to that extent the claim can be said to be based on the law of restitution. On this view, the claim would fall within the restitution ground (as well as the contract ground). However, when applying the narrow definition it is probably necessary to dig deeper and ask what restitution for contractual wrongdoing is based on. The answer is that it is best regarded under the English substantive law of restitution as being based on contract.[191] The claim would therefore fall outside r 6.20(15). It would though, of course, come within the contract ground.

8.104 If, contrary to what is argued above, a claim for restitution for contractual wrongdoing is regarded as being based on unjust enrichment by subtraction it will fall outside the contract ground but clearly within the restitution ground.

Rule 6.20(8)

8.105 The question of whether a claim for restitution for contractual wrong-doing is made in relation to a contract or is made for restitution is not easily answered[192] but whatever the answer the claim cannot be regarded as being made in tort. This is supported by the decision in *ISC v Guerin*,[193] where Hoffmann J held that equitable restitutionary remedies for breach of trust or fiduciary duty (i.e. restitution for equitable wrongdoing) were not founded on a tort.[194] The same must be true for restitution for contractual wrongdoing.

IV. PROPRIETARY RESTITUTION

8.106 Claims for proprietary restitution are particularly complex, raising as they do the relationship between the law of property and the law of restitution. There is then a further complication in that the defendant may hold

---

[190] Discussed above, paras 8.95–97.   [191] See above, para 8.89.
[192] See above, paras 8.101–102.   [193] [1992] 2 Lloyd's Rep 430.   [194] ibid, at 432.

property for the claimant by virtue of a trust. It is necessary therefore to distinguish between, on the one hand, proprietary claims which involve trusts and, on the other hand, proprietary claims which do not. Something also needs to be said briefly about tracing.

1. Proprietary Restitution (Without a Trust)

Introduction

How claims for proprietary restitution (without a trust) arise in the sales context

A claim for proprietary restitution (without a trust) could arise in the **8.107** context of a contract for the international sale of goods. For example, a seller delivers goods to the buyer and the latter fails to pay. Suppose that the seller wants the goods themselves back, rather than damages. If, and this will be unusual, title to the goods has already passed to the buyer, the seller would ask that the goods revest in him (the seller).[195] A claim for proprietary restitution (without a trust) can also arise in the case of rescission of the international sales contract. It is important to distinguish between cases where the claimant seeks damages to put him back in the position he was in before from cases where he seeks rescission of the transfer itself, i.e. he wants those exact goods back and to re-establish ownership. This may be important where the defendant is insolvent because proprietary claims have in English law priority over claims by unsecured creditors.

Classification of claims for proprietary restitution

Under English law there is considerable academic controversy over the **8.108** nature of a claim for proprietary restitution. Virgo regards such a claim as being proprietary (i.e. vindicating property rights).[196] Burrows,[197] though, distinguishes between two situations. The first is where the claimant is asserting that the property in the defendant's hands is and was the claimant's property. This claim is not based on unjust enrichment of the defendant. The return of the property simply rests on pre-existing ownership. It involves the vindication of a continuing property right. This first situation is sometimes referred to as 'a pure proprietary claim', rather than proprietary restitution,[198] and clearly involves a claim based on the law of property. The second situation is where a proprietary remedy is given because the law is creating new proprietary rights in response to the

---

[195] If title has not passed to the buyer the claim by the seller would be for vindication of his property rights.

[196] See Virgo, n 40 above, Ch 20.

[197] See Burrows, n 33 above, 60–75. This view has also been taken by Birks, n 167 above, at 70.

[198] Panagopoulos, n 4 above, 13–14.

defendant's unjust enrichment at the claimant's expense. Burrows has described the relationship between the law of restitution and the law of property in the following way. 'The law of restitution, being concerned with the principle of unjust enrichment, includes that part of the law of property in which proprietary remedies respond to (or, as one might otherwise express it, proprietary rights are created in response to) unjust enrichment.'[199] Under this second category, but not the first, the claim is based on unjust enrichment.[200]

8.109   Returning to the first example of where a claim for proprietary restitution (without a trust) may arise, it will be recalled that this was where a seller delivers goods to the buyer and the latter fails to pay. The seller wants the return of the goods, title to which has unusually already passed to the buyer, rather than damages. Virgo would regard the claim as being proprietary. In contrast, this revesting of property would appear to fall within the second of Burrow's categories[201] and should therefore, according to Burrows, be regarded as being based on unjust enrichment. The second example given above, namely where the claimant seeks rescission of the transfer of the goods, would also be regarded by Virgo as being proprietary. In contrast, it would again appear to fall within the second of Burrow's categories and should therefore, according to Burrows, be regarded as being based on unjust enrichment.

8.110   When it comes to the EC rules on jurisdiction it is important not just to look at the classification adopted under English law but also at that adopted in other Member States. However, most other Member States do not recognize proprietary restitution[202] and so it is not possible to have recourse to the classification adopted elsewhere.

8.111   This uncertainty over the classification to be adopted makes it very difficult for the private international lawyer when applying at least certain bases of jurisdiction. One way round this is for the private international lawyer to take a bold line and, rather than choosing between these competing theories under English domestic law, simply say that, for jurisdictional purposes, claims for proprietary restitution should be regarded as being based on property since property rights are ultimately at stake.[203] Where property rights are in issue, the jurisdictional provisions

---

[199]   Burrows, n 33 above, 62.

[200]   Panagopoulos, n 4 above, 226–227 adopts this classification for jurisdictional purposes.

[201]   If the title in the goods never passed to the buyer this would come within the first of Burrows' categories. A claim for return of the goods would be a claim to vindicate property rights.

[202]   See Panagopoulos, n 4 above, 11–12, 226–227. An exception is Ireland.

[203]   The same argument is made below, paras 19.69–73, in relation to choice of law and the application of the law of the situs.

tend to point to the place where the property is located, since it is that state which exercises control over the property and a judgment may need to be enforced there. These jurisdictional justifications exist regardless of the technical nature of the cause of action. In other words, they are result orientated jurisdiction rules and, as such, should apply wherever property rights are ultimately at stake. It is tentatively suggested that this bold approach be adopted and that, for jurisdictional purposes, claims for proprietary restitution should be regarded as being based on property. The application of the EC and the traditional rules of jurisdiction in proprietary restitution (without a trust) cases will now be examined.

The EC Rules

There is no special provision in the Brussels I Regulation dealing with **8.112** claims for proprietary restitution. It is therefore a question of fitting such claims within the normal rules contained in the Regulation. There are no particular difficulties in using Articles 23 (choice of jurisdiction agreement), 2 (defendant's domicile), and 5(5) (branch etc). What does need to be considered is whether it is possible to bring a claim for proprietary restitution within the special jurisdiction rules in Article 5(3) or 5(1).

Article 5(3)

This is where the difficulties over the classification of proprietary restitu- **8.113** tion really bite. The view has tentatively been put forward that, for jurisdictional purposes, a claim for proprietary restitution should be regarded as one based on property. We will therefore start by examining what happens if the claim is so regarded. However, given the uncertainty over the classification of claims for proprietary restitution, we need also to examine briefly what would happen if the claim is regarded, for jurisdictional purposes, as being based on unjust enrichment. It will be seen that in the former case it is doubtful whether it is possible to use Article 5(3), whereas in the latter case one can state with confidence that it is not possible to use this provision.

The claim is based on the law of property If a claim for proprietary **8.114** restitution is regarded for jurisdictional purposes as being based on the law of property, the first question that arises is: does such a claim fall within the scope of Article 5(3)? If it does, the next question is: where is the place where the harmful event occurred?

Does a claim for proprietary restitution fall within the scope of Article **8.115** *5(3)?* Applying the wide definition of the scope of Article 5(3) adopted by the European Court of Justice,[204] a claim for proprietary restitution will fall within this provision if it is one which seeks to establish the liability of a defendant and which is not related to a 'contract' within the meaning of Article 5(1). A claim for proprietary restitution is not a matter relating to a contract within the meaning of Article 5(1). It is a matter of property (or of unjust enrichment). Is it an action which seeks to establish the liability of a defendant?[205] Advocate General Jacobs has said that 'liability' comfortably encompasses types of legal liability other than the obligation to make financial reparation.[206] The remedy sought does not appear to matter. Nonetheless, it is arguable that a claim for proprietary restitution does not seek to establish the liability of a defendant. In *Reichert v Dresdner Bank (No 2)*,[207] the European Court of Justice held that an action whereby a creditor sought to set aside a gift of property made by a debtor, which allegedly defrauded him of his rights (an action paulienne under French law), did not seek to establish the liability of a defendant in the sense understood in Article 5(3). The Court explained that:

> The object of such an action is not to compel the debtor to make good the damage he has caused the creditor by his fraudulent act, but to set aside, as against the creditor, the effects of the disposition by the debtor.[208]

There are parallels between an action paulienne and an action for proprietary restitution. The object of an action for proprietary restitution is not to compel the defendant to make good the damage he has caused the plaintiff by his unlawful act. There does not appear to be an unlawful act.[209] And the action is not designed to compensate[210] but to get back those precise goods and to re-establish ownership.[211] A claim for proprietary restitution can also affect a third party in that in the case of a defendant who is insolvent, it gives the plaintiff priority over the claims by unsecured creditors. This too would indicate that the claim does

---

[204] See above, para 6.11.

[205] See generally Briggs and Rees, 2.138.

[206] Case C-167/00 *Verein Fur Konsumenteninformation v KH Henkel* [2002] ECR I-8111. See also the opinion of AG Jacobs in Case C-18/02 *DFDS v SEKO* [2004] IL Pr 10 at [37].

[207] Case C-261/90 [1992] ECR I-2149.

[208] ibid, para 19.

[209] But see Briggs and Rees, 2.138 who ask whether there would be an unlawful act if the plaintiff demanded return of the property and the defendant refused.

[210] Briggs and Rees, 2.138.

[211] We are concerned in this chapter with proprietary restitution based on the law of property or unjust enrichment. Proprietary restitution may be sought in a case of conversion. This situation is distinguishable on the basis that the claim is based on a wrongful act, i.e. the denial of title, and damages are payable for this (see Briggs and Rees, 2.138). It has been held in this situation that the claim is one to establish the liability of the defendant, see *Cronos Containers NV v Palatin* [2002] EWHC 2819 (Comm), [2003] 2 Lloyd's Rep 489; discussed above, para 6.46.

not seek to establish the liability of a defendant for the purposes of Article 5(3).[212]

Moreover, there is the further difficulty that, for the application of Article **8.116** 5(3), there must be a harmful event.[213] Considerable ingenuity is required to identify this in the case of such a claim, which raises serious doubts over whether proprietary restitution should really come within Article 5(3).

The upshot is that a claim for proprietary restitution probably should not **8.117** be regarded as falling within the scope of Article 5(3).[214]

Where is the place where the harmful event occurred?   If, contrary to what is **8.118** argued above, it were to be held that a claim for proprietary restitution does fall within the scope of Article 5(3), it would be necessary to identify the place where the harmful event occurred.

THE PLACE OF THE EVENT GIVING RISE TO THE DAMAGE   Let us turn to the **8.119** first example, given above, of where a claim for proprietary restitution (without a trust) may arise, namely where a seller delivers goods to the buyer and the latter fails to pay. The seller wants the return of the goods, the title to which has unusually already passed to the buyer, rather than damages. It is far from clear what the *event* giving rise to any damage is. Is it the buyer's promise to pay, his failure to pay, his taking delivery of the goods, his assuming ownership of the goods, his retaining the benefit he has received? This event must *give rise* to the damage. So it is helpful to identify the *damage* at this stage. It could be argued that the damage is the seller's loss of ownership in the goods. It follows that the event giving rise to the damage is the act of the buyer which gives rise to the loss of ownership by the seller. Under English law, with a CIF contract it is the act of the buyer of paying against shipping documents which gives rise to the property passing to the buyer.[215] If, for example, payment is made by a cheque but this is not subsequently honoured, it is this earlier act of 'payment' which has led to the property passing to the buyer. Again under English law, with an FOB contract property will presumptively pass when

---

[212] The ECJ in the *Reichert* case, n 207 above, para 19, also justified their decision on the basis that an action paulienne 'is directed not only against the debtor but also against the beneficiary of the disposition, viz a third party in relation to the debtor's obligation to the creditor, even if, where the disposition is by way of gift, the debtor does not commit a wrongful act'.

[213] As required by *Kleinwort Benson Ltd v Glasgow City Council* [1999] 1 AC 153 at 172 (*per* Lord Goff), 185 (*per* Lord Clyde), 196 (*per* Lord Hutton), 172 (*per* Lord Mustill), 177 (*per* Lord Nicholls).

[214] See generally Briggs and Rees, 2.138.

[215] Bridge, *The International Sale of Goods*, 10.08.

the goods are put on board a ship by the seller (i.e. the seller delivers the goods to the carrier).[216] This is, of course, not an act committed by the buyer. There are, however, acts committed by the buyer. The buyer takes delivery, and also assents to the seller's unconditional appropriation, through the person of the carrier (who is the buyer's agent). There are also acts committed by the buyer's agent, the carrier, without whose co-operation delivery cannot take place. But it cannot be said that these acts lead the seller to deliver the goods to the carrier. It would have to be argued that it is the buyer's act of promising to take delivery or the agent's promise to co-operate that leads the seller to deliver. Similarly, it might be argued that there is another act committed by the buyer that leads the seller to deliver the goods to the carrier, namely the promise to pay the seller. The conclusion from this analysis is that, whilst it is possible to fix upon a place which can be referred to as the place of the event giving rise to the damage, this looks increasingly like a fiction.

8.120   THE PLACE WHERE THE DAMAGE OCCURRED   As previously mentioned, it could be argued that the damage is the seller's loss of ownership in the goods. The place where this damage occurs must be the place where the goods are situated at the time that ownership passes to the buyer. With an FOB contract this will be the place where the ship is when the goods are put on board by the seller.[217] With a CIF contract it will be where the goods are when the 'payment' against shipping documents is made by the buyer.

8.121   **The claim is based on unjust enrichment**   If a claim for proprietary restitution is regarded as being based on unjust enrichment then the position should be the same as for any other case of a claim based on unjust enrichment.[218] The fact that a proprietary remedy is sought should not alter this. The use of Article 5(3) in the case of claims based on unjust enrichment has already been examined.[219] It will be recalled that the House of Lords in *Kleinwort Benson* held that Article 5(3) cannot be used where the claim is based on unjust enrichment.

Article 5(1)

8.122   A claim for proprietary restitution is not based on a particular contractual obligation, it is based on the law of property or on unjust enrichment, and, accordingly, it falls outside the scope of Article 5(1)

---

[216] ibid, 10.06. It is, however, very common for the FOB seller to reserve the right of disposal under s 19 of the Sale of Goods Act by retaining the bill of lading until payment is made.

[217] Again this is subject to the seller reserving the right to disposal.

[218] See Panagopoulos, n 4 above, 226–227.   [219] At para 8.32.

The Traditional English Rules

There are no special difficulties in serving a claim form within the juris- **8.123** diction in cases where the claim is for proprietary restitution. Nor are there any problems in service out of the jurisdiction using general grounds under r 6.20 of the Civil Procedure Rules. Moreover, the claimant may be able to rely on r 6.20(10), which is a special ground dealing with claims about property within the jurisdiction. This ground will now be examined, after which the question will be considered of whether a claim for proprietary restitution can be brought within the tort, contract or restitution grounds of r 6.20.

Rule 6.20(10)

Rule 6.20(10) of the Civil Procedure Rules[220] provides that a claim form **8.124** may be served out of the jurisdiction with the permission of the court if:

(10) the whole subject-matter of a claim relates to property located within the jurisdiction.

It can be said with some confidence that a claim for proprietary restitution 'relates to property', regardless of the classification adopted for such a claim. Even if you follow the Burrows approach and regard this claim as coming within his second category (ie where a proprietary remedy is given because the law is creating new proprietary rights in response to the defendant's unjust enrichment at the claimant's expense), the fact that proprietary rights are created means that the claim can be regarded as relating to property. Provided that the property in respect of which proprietary restitution is sought is located in England, service out of the jurisdiction will be permissible under r 6.20(10).

Rule 6.20(8)

There is uncertainty over the classification under English law of a claim **8.125** for proprietary restitution (ie whether it should be regarded as being based on the law of property or unjust enrichment). But whatever the answer to this, it cannot be regarded as being made in tort in the English sense, and this is the sense with which we are concerned in the present context, and therefore r 6.20(8) will not operate.

Rule 6.20(5) and (6)

Neither can a claim for proprietary restitution be regarded as being made **8.126** in respect of a contract for the purposes of r 6.20(5) or in respect of a breach of contract for the purposes of r 6.20(6). This will be so, regardless

---

[220] Discussed above, paras 7.27–38.

of whether the claim is regarded as being based on property or unjust enrichment, and even though there is a sales contract lurking in the background.[221] Therefore these grounds for service out of the jurisdiction cannot operate.

Rule 6.20(15)

8.127   It will be recalled[222] that this, the restitution ground, requires that 'a claim is made for restitution'. A 'claim' doubtless covers proprietary claims as well as personal ones.[223] If a claim for proprietary restitution is regarded as being based on unjust enrichment the requirement that the claim is 'made for restitution' is clearly met. What if the claim is regarded as being based on the law of property (ie it is a vindication of pre-existing property rights)? A wide view of this requirement would be that it covers all cases where a restitutionary remedy is sought, regardless of whether the claim is in fact based on contract, tort or property.[224] However, if a narrow view of this requirement is taken, so that what is required is that the claim is based on the law of restitution, this requirement would not be met. It is also required that the defendant's alleged activity arises out of acts committed within the jurisdiction.

2. PROPRIETARY RESTITUTION (WITH A TRUST)

Introduction

How claims for proprietary restitution (with a trust) arise

8.128   We are concerned here with the situation where the basis of the claim for proprietary restitution is that the defendant holds for the claimant by virtue of an express, resulting or constructive trust. As far as the English law on the international sale of goods is concerned, a constructive trust will arise in the situation where the contract is specifically enforceable. A buyer may argue that in such a case the seller, from the moment of the conclusion of the contract, holds the goods on constructive trust for him.[225] Few contracts of sale will be specifically enforceable. This is because what is required is that there are unique goods for which there would be no replacement on the open market. Again, if the buyer is the owner of goods, by virtue of an ownership clause in the sales contract, as

---

[221] See above, paras 8.108–109.   [222] Above at paras 8.37–50.
[223] See Panagopoulos, n 4 above, 235–236.
[224] It has been submitted earlier that this is the better view. The arguments in favour of this wide view are set out above, para 8.37.
[225] Or subject to an equitable lien. The language of constructive trusts is not normally used in sale of goods cases and that of the equitable lien is preferred: see, e.g., *Re Wait* [1927] 1 Ch 606.

soon as they are produced and the seller sells them to a third party, the proceeds are held on constructive trust.[226] Moreover, there may be a question of whether a constructive trust has arisen in the situation where the contract contains a retention of title clause in favour of the unpaid seller. But the buyer has permission to enter into a sub-sale and is able to pass good title on to a third party. Under English law, the *Romalpa* case held that the proceeds of sale were held by the buyer on constructive trust for the seller.[227] However, this conclusion was reached because of the buyer's concession that the bailment under which the goods were supplied gave rise to a fiduciary relationship. Subsequent cases have denied this.[228] It follows that, under English law, there may only be a personal action for money had and received. But a foreign law may govern the question of whether a constructive trust arises and hold that it does so.

Classification of claims for proprietary restitution (with a trust)

Constructive trusts themselves are not a cause of action. They are a **8.129** response to various different events in the law. For example, where a contract is specifically enforceable, a constructive trust arises. Classification of the claim is therefore the same as for a claim for proprietary restitution without a trust. The claim should be regarded as being based on either the law of property or on unjust enrichment, the better view being that it should be regarded as the former rather than the latter. Again, ultimately what is at stake is the assertion of property rights (this time the beneficial ownership). It has already been seen[229] that, where what is at stake is the assertion of property rights, there are good policy reasons (to do with the nature of the jurisdiction rules that apply in such cases) for regarding claims for proprietary restitution as being based on property for jurisdictional purposes. It might be argued that the nature of the property right being asserted by the claimant is slightly weaker in trusts cases than in cases where there is no trust, as the claimant only asserts equitable ownership. Whereas legal rights usually bind the world, the bona fide purchaser of the legal estate for value without notice can defeat equitable interests. Nonetheless, the good policy reasons for regarding the claim as being based on the law of property are just as strong for equitable interests as they are where absolute ownership is asserted. Moreover, the claimant

---

[226] See *Tate & Lyle Industries Ltd v Cia Usina Bulhoes and Cargill Inc* [1997] 1 Lloyd's Rep 355; discussed above, para 7.05.

[227] *Aluminium Industrie Vaassen BV v Romalpa Aluminium Ltd* [1976] 1 WLR 676.

[228] See, eg, *Clough Mill v Martin* [1985] 1 WLR 111; *Hendy Lennox (Industrial Engines) v Graham Puttick* [1984] 1 WLR 485.

[229] See the discussion of the classification of claims for proprietary restitution in cases where there is no trust, above, paras 8.108–111.

will usually assert in the sales context absolute beneficial entitlement. That being so, at least in English law, he can terminate the trust and claim absolute ownership of the property.[230]

The EC Rules

8.130   When it comes to the application of the EC rules on jurisdiction to claims for proprietary restitution (with a trust) the position is the same as that set out above for claims for proprietary restitution without a trust. In both cases, the claim is for proprietary restitution and, in both cases, should be classified for the purposes of jurisdiction in the same way. The fact that there is a trust should not affect the classification of the claim. It follows that everything said in the previous section (when dealing with the application of the EC rules of jurisdiction to proprietary jurisdiction (without a trust)) is equally applicable to those cases where there is a trust.[231] At the same time, the presence of a trust does have some jurisdictional significance. It raises the question of whether the plaintiff is able to found jurisdiction on Article 5(6) of the Brussels I Regulation, a provision dealing specifically with trusts. If the plaintiff is able to use this Article, it would provide an additional basis of jurisdiction to which the plaintiff can have recourse.[232] But is the plaintiff able to use this Article? Article 5(6) states that a person domiciled in a Member State may, in another Member State, be sued:

as settlor, trustee or beneficiary of a trust created by the operation of a statute, or by a written instrument, or created orally and evidenced in writing, in the courts of the Member State in which the trust is domiciled.

This provision is only concerned with trusts 'created by the operation of a statute, or by a written instrument, or created orally and evidenced in writing'. It applies to the internal relationship between the parties to a trust: 'as between the trustees themselves, between persons claiming the status of trustees and, above all, between trustees on the one hand and the beneficiaries of a trust on the other'.[233] It does not extend to claims by

---

[230]   Under the rule in *Saunders v Vautier* (1841) 4 Beav 115.

[231]   An interesting question arises as to whether, when there is a trust, it could sometimes be argued that the claim for proprietary restitution is based on a contractual obligation. An example would be where there is a contract of sale which has a retention of title clause in it. With the consent of the original seller, the buyer sells the goods on. It might be argued that the original seller's claim that the proceeds are held on constructive trust for him (according to the applicable law) is based on the original retention of title clause contained in the contract of sale and is, accordingly, based on a contractual obligation. The better view is that this is still a claim for proprietary restitution and that such a claim is based on the law of property or on unjust enrichment.

[232]   See Panagopoulos, n 4 above, 227.   [233]   Schlosser Report, para 111.

or against a third party, for which 'no adjustments to the 1968 Convention are necessary'.[234]

More importantly in the sales context, in *Chellaram v Chellaram (No 2)*, **8.131** Lawrence Collins J observed[235] that:

Both CPR 6.20(11) and Article 5(6) are in terms concerned with express trusts . . . Accordingly, neither CPR 6.20(11) nor Article 5(6) applies to constructive trusts. CPR 6.20(14) makes special provision for constructive trusts, and it is clear both from the text of Article 5(6) and from the Schlosser Report on the 1978 Accession Convention (by which the United Kingdom acceded to the 1968 Convention, and which introduced Article 5(6)), para 117, that Article 5(6) does not apply to constructive trusts.

It follows that Article 5(6) will not avail a plaintiff who seeks to assert that a constructive trust arises.[236]

Article 5(6) allocates jurisdiction to the courts of the Member State in **8.132** which the trust is domiciled.[237] In order to determine whether a trust is domiciled in the Member State whose courts are seised of the matter, the court applies its rules of private international law.[238] A trust is domiciled in the United Kingdom if and only if it is domiciled in a part of the United Kingdom.[239] A trust is domiciled in a part of the United Kingdom if and only if the system of law of that part is the system of law with which the trust has its closest and most real connection.[240]

The Traditional English Rules

The position under the traditional English rules is parallel to that under **8.133** the EC rules. In other words, when it comes to the application of the traditional English rules on jurisdiction to claims for proprietary restitution (with a trust) the position is the same as that set out above for the

---

[234] ibid, para 110. [235] [2002] EWHC 632 (Ch) at [137], [138], [2002] 3 All ER 17.

[236] Contrast Art 3 of the Hague Trusts Convention, which applies to 'trusts created voluntarily and evidenced in writing' and its statutory extension in the UK by s 1(2) of the Recognition of Trusts Act 1987 to '. . . any other trusts of property arising under the law of any part of the United Kingdom or by virtue of a judicial decision whether in the United Kingdom or elsewhere'. On the scope of these provisions, see Harris, *The Hague Trusts Convention* (Oxford: Hart, 2002) 122–150; Hayton (1987) 36 ICLQ 260.

[237] As at the date of the proceedings rather than the date when the cause of action arose: *Chellaram v Chellaram (No 2)* [2002] EWHC 632 (Ch) at [151], [2002] 3 All ER 17.

[238] Art 60(3) of the Brussels I Regulation.

[239] Civil Jurisdiction and Judgments Order 2001, SI 2001/3929, Sch 1, para 12(2).

[240] ibid, para 12(3). On the law applicable to a trust in the absence of choice, see Art 7 of the Hague Trusts Convention; Harris, n 236 above, 215–232 esp 232. See also *Chellaram v Chellaram (No 2)* [2002] EWHC 632 (Ch), [2002] 3 All ER 17.

application of the traditional English rules of jurisdiction to claims for proprietary restitution without a trust. Everything said in the previous section (when dealing with the application of the traditional English rules of jurisdiction to claims for proprietary restitution (without a trust)) is equally applicable to those cases where there is a trust. At the same time, the presence of a trust does have some jurisdictional significance, in that it provides an additional possible basis of jurisdiction. The plaintiff may be able to found jurisdiction on r 6.20(14) of the Civil Procedure Rules,[241] a ground for service out of the jurisdiction dealing specifically with the situation where a claim is made for a remedy against the defendant as constructive trustee. This provides that a claim form may be served out of the jurisdiction with the permission of the court if a claim is made for a remedy against the defendant as constructive trustee where the defendant's alleged liability arises out of acts committed within the jurisdiction. This replaces an earlier provision, Order 11, r 1(1)(t) of the Rules of the Supreme Court. This was explicit in specifying the remedy sought in such cases and also answered the question of who can commit the act in question. It allowed for service out of the jurisdiction where 'the claim is brought for money had and received or for an account or other remedy against the defendant as constructive trustee, and the defendant's alleged liability arises out of acts committed, whether by him or otherwise, within the jurisdiction'. It was doubtless not intended that these changes should have any substantive effect on the court's powers.[242] It follows that recourse probably can be had to the old wording and to the authorities under that provision.

8.134   A claim for proprietary restitution where a constructive trust has arisen can be regarded as one where a claim is made for a remedy against the defendant as constructive trustee. Provided that the defendant's alleged liability arises out of acts committed within the jurisdiction, service out of the jurisdiction will be permissible under r 6.20(14). It is not necessary that all the acts have been committed within the jurisdiction.[243] It is enough that 'substantial and efficacious acts' have been committed within the

---

[241] See generally Dicey and Morris, *Third Supplement to the Thirteenth Edition* (2003) 70–71; Briggs and Rees, 4.47.

[242] The introduction of r 6.20 was preceded by the Lord Chancellor's Department Consultation Paper on the CPR, *Service of Court Process Abroad*, para 22, which notes that a number of minor drafting changes were proposed which did not affect the substance. This appears to be another of these changes.

[243] See in relation to constructive trusts *ISC v Guerin* [1992] 2 Lloyd's Rep 430, 433, Hoffmann J; *Polly Peck International v Nadir* Independent, 2 September 1992, reversed by the Court of Appeal, The Times, 22 March 1993, but Hoffmann LJ said obiter that he adhered to his view in the *ISC* case. Compare *ISC v Guerin* (7 December 1990, Millett J).

jurisdiction, even if substantial and efficacious acts have also been committed outside the jurisdiction.[244]

Finally, a brief mention must be made of r 6.20(11) of the Civil Procedure **8.135** Rules. This ground for service out of the jurisdiction applies where:

a claim is made for any remedy which might be obtained in proceedings to execute the trusts of a written instrument where—
  (a) the trusts ought to be executed according to English law; and
  (b) the person on whom the claim form is to be served is a trustee of the trusts.

Lawrence Collins J in *Chellaram v Chellaram (No 2)* observed[245] that r 6.20(11) is in terms concerned with express trusts. Accordingly, it does not apply to constructive trusts. He went on to observe that r 6.20(14) makes special provision for constructive trusts. It follows that r 6.20(11) will not avail a claimant who seeks to assert that a constructive trust arises.

3. Tracing

Tracing is the process of identifying property where it has changed its **8.136** form through mixture or substitution or both. Tracing rules 'enable the plaintiff to identify property in the defendant's hands which the plaintiff has not previously owned but which can be considered to represent the plaintiff's original property'.[246] Tracing could easily arise in the international sale of goods context. For example, the buyer pays the seller and seeks recovery of the payment itself, not damages equivalent to its value. Let us assume that the payment was paid into the seller's bank account, where it was mixed with his own funds, or was used to purchase goods. There is then a problem in identifying the payment. Another example would be where the seller delivers oil to the buyer and the buyer mixes it with his own oil. The seller then seeks to establish a proprietary interest by claiming a share of the new blended product.[247]

Traditional thinking says that tracing is not a cause of action at all; it is an **8.137** evidential step in bringing a claim, i.e. it is simply the stage of determining

---

[244] *Metall und Rohstoff AG v Donaldson Lufkin and Jenrette Inc* [1990] 1 QB 391, CA (a case decided under Ord 11, r 1(1)(f) RSC); overruled on a different point in *Lonrho plc v Fayed* [1992] 1 AC 448; *Nycal (UK) Ltd v Lacey* [1994] CLC 12—a case decided under Ord 11, r 1(1)(t) RSC, the predecessor of r 6.20(14).

[245] [2002] EWHC 632 (Ch) at [137], [138], [2002] 3 All ER 17.

[246] Virgo, n 40 above, 642. See generally on tracing: Virgo at 642–655; Burrows, n 33 above, 78–104.

[247] This is similar to what happened in *Glencore International AG v Metro Trading International Inc (No 2)* [1999] 1 Lloyd's Rep 284. This case is discussed at length below in paras 17.60, 13.221–222, 18.37–38.

if property is still identifiable.[248] So, if A wishes to bring a claim for proprietary restitution he must show the following: first, that he had title in
the first place; second, that the defendant has the traceable proceeds of the
property; third, an unjust factor; fourth, a pre-existing fiduciary relationship. The question then arises of whether the defendant has any defence
to the proprietary claim, for example that he is the bona fide purchaser of
the legal estate for value without notice. If this analysis is correct, there
is no need to bring tracing within any basis of jurisdiction. It simply has
to be asked what the cause of action is. This may be in contract, tort,
property or unjust enrichment. The court with jurisdiction over the cause
of action also has jurisdiction to determine if the claimant's property is
still identifiable.[249]

---

[248]   Virgo, n 40 above, 643; Burrows, n 33 above, 78–79. But see J Harris, 'Tracing and the
Conflict of Laws' (2002) 73 British Ybk of Intl Law 65.
[249]   Tracing is more problematic when it comes to the applicable law, see below, paras
19.88–96.

9

Multiple-Party Claims Arising out of the International Sale of Goods: Jurisdiction

I. MULTI-DEFENDANT CLAIMS

1. MULTI-DEFENDANT INTERNATIONAL SALE OF GOODS CASES

9.01   A wide variety of different multi-defendant claims can arise in the context
of the international sale of goods. There can be multi-defendant claims
in contract, claims in tort and claims against one defendant in contract
and against the other defendant in tort. These multi-defendant claims
can arise out of the contract for the international sale of goods or out of
associated contracts, in particular out of the contract for the carriage of the
goods.

Multi-Defendant Claims in Contract

9.02   The simplest example of this would be where a buyer brings a claim for
breach of the sales contract against two sellers. This is essentially what
was alleged in *Tesam Distribution Ltd v Schuh Mode Team GmbH and
Commerzbank AG*.[1] The English plaintiff buyer brought an action for
breach of contract against two German defendants, the supplier and a
bank, which it alleged was a party to the sales contract. The action for
breach of contract was based on a failure to deliver shoes, which it was
argued were owned by the bank or the bank had a charge over. Moreover,
an officer of the bank attended a meeting along with the first defendant at
which there was an offer to sell the shoes to the plaintiff. Another example
would be where a French company brought an action in France for
rescission of a contract of sale against a German company and its French
subsidiary, which was a party to the contract of sale.[2] A final example
would be where a Spanish seller sued for payment a German company
and its sole director and shareholder.[3]

Multi-Defendant Claims in Tort

9.03   An example of how this can arise can be seen from the facts of *Re a
Consignment of Italian Wine*,[4] a decision of the German Bundesgerichtshof.
The German plaintiff buyer, a wholesale wine merchant, claimed damages

---

[1] [1990] IL Pr 149, CA.
[2] For the position where the subsidiary is not a party to the contract of sale see below,
para 9.23.
[3] Case 28 AR 8/01 (Kammergericht (Berlin Court of Appeal) April 9, 2001): [2002] Iprax
515; [2003] IL Pr 465. The second defendant was also German and so the question arose of
where in Germany the two defendants could be sued. Art 6(1) of the Brussels Convention
applied to determine this rather than German domestic law.
[4] [1988] ECC 159.

from the Italian defendant seller, a wine-trading company, and its director, alleging that they had negligently infringed wine regulations on the minimum alcohol content, in specifying the alcohol content in accompanying documents and in the illegal addition of sugar. It was also alleged that the defendants were in breach of their contractual obligations.[5] Equally the multi-defendant case could involve a claim in conversion brought by a company, which alleges that it has title to the property, against two buyers.[6]

Multi-Defendant Claims: Against One Defendant in Contract and The Other Defendant in Tort

This can arise where, for example, a buyer of goods brings an action **9.04** against the first defendant, the seller, for breach of contract, claiming that the goods do not conform with the contract in terms of quantity and quality, and against the second defendant in tort for negligently issuing the certificate stating that the goods did conform with the contract.[7] A buyer who is injured by defective goods may sue the retailer in contract and the manufacturer in tort.[8] Similarly, a purchaser who buys direct from the manufacturer a plane, which crashes, may be able to sue the manufacturer in contract and the supplier of a defective component in tort.[9]

The tort action brought against one of the defendants may be that of **9.05** inducement of breach of contract. This is illustrated by the *Tesam* case,[10] where the buyer argued in the alternative that if the second defendant, the bank, was not a party to the sales contract it was liable in tort for inducing a breach of contract by the first defendant, the supplier. This meant that there was a claim against the first defendant in contract and against the second defendant in tort.

Equally the tort action could be that of negligent misstatement. *Alfred* **9.06** *Dunhill Ltd v Diffusion Internationale de Maroquinerie de Prestige*[11] is an example. The claimant entered into contracts for the first two defendants (French companies) to manufacture and supply travel goods to be distributed under the claimant's brand name. These defendants subcontracted part of the work to the third defendant, an Italian company,

---

[5] The fact that there are parallel claims in contract and tort raises a serious problem when it comes to using Arts 5(1) and 5(3) of the Brussels I Regulation, see above, paras 3.71–73.

[6] See, e.g. *Glencore International v Metro (No 1)* [1999] 2 All ER (Comm) 899, the facts of which are set out below, para 9.50.

[7] *Goldenglow v Commodin* [1987] 2 Lloyd's Rep 569, CA.

[8] See the example given in *Watson v First Choice Holidays* [2001] EWCA Civ 972 at [33], [2002] IL Pr 1.

[9] See *Messier-Dowty Ltd v Sabena SA (No 2)* [2000] 1 WLR 2040 at 2043, CA.

[10] n 1 above. [11] [2002] IL Pr 13; discussed above, para 6.91.

which supplied defective fabric. The claim against the first two defendants was a straighforward sale of goods case. The claimant sued the third defendant, *inter alia*, for negligent misstatement, alleging that, acting in reliance on the alleged misstatements, the claimant instructed the first and second defendants to contract with the third defendant, which they did.[12]

Multi-Defendant Claims in Relation to Associated Contracts

9.07 The position as regards multi-defendant claims in relation to associated contracts is essentially the same as that in relation to the contract for the international sale of goods. If you take the example of carriage of goods by sea, which can often lead to multi-defendant claims, there may be claims against two or more defendants in contract, in tort or against one defendant in contract and against the other defendant in tort. An example of the latter is provided by *Réunion Européenne SA v Spliethoff's Bevrachtingskantoor BV*,[13] a decision of the European Court of Justice. The consignee of goods brought an action in contract against the first defendant, an Australian company, which issued the bill of lading (an action based on the contract of carriage), and actions in tort against two further defendants. The second defendant, a Dutch company, was the company which actually carried the goods, although it was not mentioned in the bill of lading, and the third defendant, who resided in Amsterdam, was the master of the ship which carried the goods.

9.08 Similarly, when it comes to payment for goods this can spawn multi-defendant claims in contract or tort or against one defendant in contract and against the other defendant in tort. *Bastone & Firminger Ltd v Nasima Enterprises (Nigeria) Ltd*[14] serves as an illustration. The unpaid seller brought proceedings in contract against the first and second defendants, the buyers, and the third defendant, Mr Saidi, the individual behind the buyer companies, after he had given two personal cheques which were not honoured. Leave was obtained for service out of the jurisdiction against the first two defendants but they were never served. Mr Saidi was served within the jurisdiction, but subsequently disappeared. The fourth defendant was the Nigerian bank which had been appointed by the plaintiff's English bank to collect payment by way of bills of exchange. It was alleged that the fourth defendant was liable in contract (on the basis of agency or assignment) and in tort for conversion of or wrongful interference with the consignments or documents sent to Nigeria.

---

[12] There were also claims against the third defendant based on negligent misrepresentation under the Misrepresentation Act 1967 and on negligent misstatement resulting in a contract between the claimant and the third defendant.

[13] Case C-51/97 [1998] ECR I-6511.   [14] [1996] CLC 1902.

2. THE EC RULES

It may be possible to bring actions against defendants in a multi- **9.09**
defendant action within one of the bases of jurisdiction examined in
previous chapters.[15] What has not been discussed so far is Article 6(1) of
the Brussels I Regulation, which is specifically designed to provide a basis
of jurisdiction in multi-defendant cases, thereby consolidating litigation
in one Member State.[16]

Article 6(1)

Article 6(1) of the Brussels I Regulation provides that a person domiciled **9.10**
in a Member State may also be sued:

where he is one of a number of defendants, in the courts for the place where any
one of them is domiciled,[17] provided the claims are so closely connected that it is
expedient to hear and determine them together to avoid the risk of irreconcilable
judgments resulting from separate proceedings;

The European Court of Justice had held in relation to Article 6(1) of the
Brussels Convention that there must exist between the various actions
brought by the same plaintiff against the various defendants a connection of such a kind that it is expedient to hear them together to avoid
irreconcilable judgments.[18] This requirement has been incorporated into
the wording of the Brussels I Regulation. Judgments may be irreconcilable
because they involve contradictory findings of fact, or contradictory legal
conclusions drawn from those facts,[19] or contradictory remedies.[20] There is
an obvious risk of irreconcilable judgments in cases where the claims
against the various defendants are substantially the same in law and fact,
such as where the defendants are joint debtors or joint tortfeasors.[21] But

---

[15] These are discussed above, paras 3.60 (Art 2), 3.61–301 (Art 5(1)), 6.08–16 (Art 5(3)), 3.302–312 (Art 5(5)), 3.22–59 (Art 23), 3.17 (Art 24).

[16] The place of Art 6 in the hierarchy of bases of jurisdiction is explained above, para 3.15.

[17] The time for determining the domicile of the defendant in the forum state is that of the initiation of the proceedings which in the case of England is the time when the claim form is issued, *Canada Trust Company v Stolzenberg (No 2)* [2002] 1 AC 1, HL.

[18] Case 189/87 *Kalfelis v Schroder* [1988] ECR 5565. The actions must be related at the time of the commencement of the proceedings, ibid, at 5584, on which see *Messier Dowty v Sabena SA* [2000] 1 WLR 2040, CA.

[19] *Gascoigne v Pyrah* [1994] IL Pr 82, CA. But see *Watson v First Choice Holidays* [2001] EWCA Civ 972, [2002] IL Pr 1 where the Court of Appeal referred to the ECJ the question, *inter alia*, of whether irreconcilable judgments can only arise from incompatible holdings of law. The case was settled before reaching the ECJ.

[20] *Société Commerciale de Réassurance v Eras* [1995] 1 Lloyd's Rep 64 at 78–79.

[21] See *Pearce v Ove Arup Partnership Ltd* [2000] Ch 403, CA.

even where the claims are largely based on different facts, there can be a risk of an inconsistent finding of fact in relation to a particular central matter.[22]

9.11 In order to prevent abuse, there are further requirements that have to be satisfied before this provision can be used. First, there must be a valid claim against the defendant domiciled in the forum.[23] Second, the second defendant must be a necessary or proper party to the action against the defendant domiciled in the forum.[24]

9.12 Finally, it is worth pointing out what this provision does not require and the great advantage of using it. It does not require that the matter relates to tort or contract or any other type of action. This means that it can be used where the action against a particular defendant relates to a number of different matters.

Application to International Sale of Goods Cases
Are the defendants domiciled in different Member States?

9.13 If the defendants are all domiciled in the same Member State they can all be sued there by virtue of Article 2. Article 6(1) is concerned with the situation where the defendants are domiciled in different Member States.[25] Although multi-defendant cases not uncommonly arise in the context of the international sale of goods, it is less common to find such cases where the defendants are domiciled in different Member States. Article 6(1) was not discussed in either the *Tesam* case[26] or in *Re a Consignment of Italian Wine*. The most likely explanation for this was because, seemingly, both defendants were domiciled in the same EC State, Germany in the former case and Italy in the latter. If the second defendant, the director, had been domiciled in England in the former case and in Germany in the latter then the plaintiff could have invoked Article 6(1) (provided the other requirements for the operation of this provision had been met) to found jurisdiction against both defendants in England in the former case and Germany in the latter case. Nonetheless, cases involving defendants from different Member States are not unknown.[27]

---

[22] The *Gascoigne* case, n 19 above.

[23] *The Rewia* [1991] 2 Lloyd's Rep 325 at 335–336, CA; the *Gascoigne* case, n 19 above.

[24] *Molnlycke AB v Proctor & Gamble Ltd (No 4)* [1992] 1 WLR 1112, CA.

[25] But see Case 28 AR 8/01 (Kammergericht (Berlin Court of Appeal) April 9, 2001): [2002] Iprax 515; [2003] IL Pr 465; and n 3 above.

[26] n 1 above.

[27] See, e.g. *Le Assicurazioni d'Italia SpA v Mannesmann Nederland BV* Judgment of 1 February 1983, Riv dir int priv proc 1983, 385; D Series I-6—B 10.

Are the claims so closely connected that it is expedient to hear and determine them together etc?

In answering this question it is important to look separately at the dif- **9.14** ferent types of multi-defendant claim that can arise in the context of the international sale of goods.

Multi-defendant claims in contract In the situation in the *Tesam* case, **9.15** where claims are brought for breach of contract against two or more sellers, there can be no doubt that the claims are substantially the same in law and fact. Accordingly, there is an obvious risk of irreconcilable judgments if the claims are brought in different Member States. The position would be the same in the situation where claims are brought against two buyers. Normally the claim would be for non-payment of the price of the goods. The defendants would be joint debtors and there would be an obvious risk of irreconcilable judgments if the claims were tried in different Member States.

Multi-defendant claims in tort In the situation in *Re a Consignment of* **9.16** *Italian Wine,*[28] where the claims in tort were against a company and its director as joint tortfeasors, there is an obvious risk of irreconcilable judgments if the claims are tried in different Member States and Article 6(1) will apply. A more complicated situation arose in the English case of *Messier-Dowty Ltd v Sabena SA (No 2).*[29] The claimant, a company which supplied defective landing gear on an aircraft, causing it to crash, sought in England a declaration of non-liability against the first defendant, the Belgian purchaser of the aircraft, the second defendant, the French manufacturer, and the third defendant, an English partner in the con- struction of the aircraft. The claimant argued that the third defendant had been negligent in providing data for the design and manufacture of the landing gear which was not sufficiently demanding. The third defendant was domiciled in England: was it possible to use Article 6(1) of the Brussels Convention to provide a basis of jurisdiction against the first defendant? If the first defendant had made a claim in tort against the claimant for breach of duty in the design and manufacture of the landing gear this would have been possible. According to the Court of Appeal there would then be a risk of irreconcilable judgments.[30] On the facts, the first defendant had made no such claim and therefore this requirement had not been met.

Multi-defendant claims: against one defendant in contract and the other **9.17** **defendant in tort** In the situation where the claim against one defendant is in contract and the other defendant is in tort, the position is less

---

[28] n 4 above.   [29] [2000] 1 WLR 2040, CA.   [30] ibid, at 2054.

straightforward. In the *Réunion Européenne* case,[31] the European Court of Justice said that two claims in one action for compensation, directed against different defendants and based in one instance on contractual liability and in the other on liability in tort or delict, cannot be regarded as being connected for the purpose of Article 6(1) of the Brussels Convention.[32] They were influenced[33] in so deciding by an earlier decision of the European Court of Justice,[34] which held that a court, which has jurisdiction under Article 5(3) over an action in so far as it is based on tort or delict, does not have jurisdiction over that action in so far as it is not so based.

9.18   It is not clear how this statement in the *Réunion Européenne* case fits in with the requirement that the claims are so closely connected that it is expedient to hear and determine them together to avoid the risk of irreconcilable judgments.[35] Is it an application of the latter principle, it being assumed that there cannot be irreconcilable judgments when the claim against one defendant is in contract and the claim against the other defendant is in tort? If this is the basis of the statement, it is making a false assumption. For it is possible to have a claim against one defendant in contract that is so closely connected to a claim against another defendant in tort that, if tried separately, this could lead to the risk of irreconcilable judgments. The facts of the *Tesam* case[36] illustrate this.[37] The claim against the first defendant for breach of contract in failing to supply the shoes and the alternative claim against the second defendant in tort for inducing the breach of contract by the first defendant are obviously different in law and fact. Nonetheless, there would be a risk of an inconsistent finding of fact in relation to one particular central issue if the two claims were litigated in different Member States. At the heart of the claim for breach of contract against the first defendant was the issue of whether a contract had in fact been made. This was denied by both of the defendants. This issue was also at the heart of the alternative claim in tort against the second defendant for inducing the breach of contract by the first defendant. If the

---

[31]   Case C-51/97 [1998] ECR I-6511; the facts are set out at para 9.07 above.

[32]   ibid, para 50. But if the claims against both defendants are in both contract and tort it may be possible to show the requisite connection, see *Clodagh Daly v Irish Group Travel Limited Trading as 'Crystal Holidays'* [2003] IL Pr 38, Irish High Court.

[33]   *Réunion Européenne*, n 31 above, para 49.

[34]   Case 189/87 *Kalfelis v Bankhaus Schroder, Munchmeyer, Hengst & Co* [1988] ECR 5565.

[35]   This requirement was laid down in relation to Art 6(1) of the Brussels Convention by the *Kalfelis* case, n 34 above. It is now enshrined in the wording of Art 6(1) of the Brussels I Regulation.

[36]   n 1 above. For another example of factual irreconcilability see *Watson v First Choice Holidays* [2001] EWCA Civ 972 at [31], [2002] IL Pr 1.

[37]   Compare the *Messier-Dowty* case, n 29 above at 2054, where one claim in contract and another claim in tort would not have involved the risk of irreconcilable judgments.

explanation of the statement in the *Réunion Européenne* is that it is a mis-
guided application of the principle of irreconcilable judgements then it
should be possible to separate out cases, where the claim against one
defendant is in contract and the claim against the other defendant is in
tort, into those where this leads to the risk of irreconcilable judgments
(which would fall within Article 6(1)) and those which do not involve
this risk (which would fall outside Article 6(1)). The fact that one claim
is in contract and the other in tort would be a relevant factor when determining the risk of irreconcilable judgments.[38]

Or is the statement based on the idea that the connection required under **9.19**
Article 6(1) is not to be determined solely by looking at the question of
whether allowing the two claims to be tried separately would lead to the
risk of irreconcilable judgments? More specifically, is the Court saying
that, even though there is a risk of irreconcilable judgments, Article 6(1)
cannot be used where the claim against one defendant is based on
contract and the claim against the other defendant is based on tort? The
Court of Appeal in *Watson v First Choice Holidays*[39] recognized that the
present law on this matter is not clear and specifically referred this last
question, inter alia, to the European Court of Justice.[40] The Court
was concerned that, if the statement in *Réunion Européenne* was applied
inflexibly, this would produce undesirable consequences. For example,
if an English buyer is injured in France by defective goods and wishes
to sue the English retailer in contract and the Spanish manufacturer in
tort there is no Member State in which it is possible to proceed against
both defendants, despite the clear connection between the two
claims.[41] Unfortunately, the case has subsequently been removed from the
Register[42] so the present uncertainty will remain.

In the meantime, we are left with the statement from the European Court **9.20**
of Justice in the *Réunion Européenne* case, a statement which cannot be

---

[38] This is the approach favoured by the Court of Appeal in the *Watson* case, n 39 below at
[37]. However, the Court seemed to accept that this approach cannot be squared with the
statement in *Réunion Européenne*.
[39] [2001] EWCA Civ 972, [2002] IL Pr 1.
[40] The precise question asked was: 'If proceedings have been brought in the courts of a
Contracting State against a defendant domiciled in that State for a claim in a matter relating
to contract, does Article 6(1) permit the claimant to join as an additional defendant a
person domiciled in another Contracting State against whom his claim amounts to a matter
relating to a tort, delict or quasi-delict and not a matter relating to tort, where (unless such a
conclusion is precluded by the different legal nature of the two claims) the national court
is satisfied that the connection between the claims against the two defendants is of such a
kind that it is expedient to determine the claims together in order to avoid the risk of
irreconcilable judgments resulting from the separate proceedings?'
[41] n 39 above at [33]. See also at [34]–[35].   [42] [2003] OJ C19/26 (25, January 2003).

ignored.[43] It has been applied by the French Cour de cassation chambre civil which has held that Article 6(1) of the Brussels Convention could not be applied in the situation where there was a claim against the foreign bank of the purchaser of goods based on tort and a claim against the bank of the seller based on contract.[44]

9.21 Multi-defendant claims in relation to associated contracts   The position where there is an associated contract, such as an insurance contract or one for the carriage of the goods, is no different from that where a claim is brought in respect of the sales contract. It is important to look at the type of claim that is being brought against the defendants. However, it is not always clear what the claim is based on. This is illustrated by the Italian national decision in *Le Assicurazioni d'Italia SpA v Mannesmann Nedeland BV*.[45] The plaintiff, an Italian insurance company, brought an action for damages in the Tribunale di Genova against three defendants, claiming that they were 'individually, jointly and severally, or proportionately' liable after steel rods bought by an Italian buyer were found to have manufacturing defects and also to have been damaged during shipment and unloading. The three defendants were the Dutch seller, the German company which had been entrusted with shipment of the goods and the Italian company which had been directly involved with unloading operations at the port. It is unclear from the brief report whether the claim brought by the insurance company against the seller, the company entrusted with the shipment of the goods and the company involved in unloading was in contract or tort or against one or more defendants in contract and the other defendant(s) in tort. The *Assicurazioni* case was decided before the European Court of Justice had introduced the requirement that, for Article 6(1) of the Brussels Convention to apply, there must exist a connection of such a kind that it is expedient to hear the actions together to avoid the risk of irreconcilable judgments and so this point was not discussed. If the case arose now this requirement would have to be satisfied.

9.22   The claims against the different defendants would not appear to be the same in law and fact since the goods were said to have had both manufacturing defects and to have been damaged during shipment and unloading. The plaintiff claimed that the three defendants were jointly and severally liable, but this is by no means self-evident. In such a case,

---

[43] See *Watson*, n 39 above, at [39]. However, the Court of Appeal in that case, at [40], said that there was some doubt as to whether the statement in *Réunion Européenne* formed part of the principles laid down by the Court in that case and therefore was binding on the English courts by virtue of s 3(1) of the Civil Jurisdiction and Judgments Act 1982.

[44] *Société KBC Bank v SA Crédit Lyonnais* [2003] IL Pr 144.

[45] Judgment of 1 February 1983, Riv dir int priv proc 1983, 385; D Series I-6—B 10.

the liability of the defendants looks more likely to be an individual liability rather than joint and several liability. Of course, even if the claims were not the same in law or fact, that is not the end of the matter. It may be that there is one particular issue that was common to all three separate claims and, accordingly, there would be a risk of irreconcilable judgments if the claims were tried in different Member States. However, there is no evidence that this was so on the facts of the *Assicurazioni* case.

There must be a valid claim against the defendant domiciled in the forum

This requirement was not met in a case[46] where a French plaintiff brought **9.23** proceedings in France for rescission of a contract relating to industrial parts against a German company and its French subsidiary. The Cour d'appel, Paris, found that the French company had acted purely as agent of the German company and was therefore not a party to the contract concluded between the German company and the plaintiff, with the result that the action for rescission could not be brought against it. Since it was wrong to proceed against the French company, Article 6(1) of the Brussels Convention could not be used against the German company. On the other hand, in the *Assicurazioni* case[47] the court came to the conclusion that the claim against the Italian defendant, which was involved in the unloading operations, did not appear to have been brought solely with the aim of ousting the jurisdiction of the courts which would normally have jurisdiction in relation to the other two defendants.

The second defendant must be a necessary or proper party to the action against the first defendant

This requirement was introduced in a case[48] where a German domiciled **9.24** defendant was added merely in order to obtain discovery of documents. It was held that this defendant (the second defendant) was not a necessary or proper party to the action against the anchor defendant (the first defendant). This appears to be the only reported case where this requirement has been applied. It was not a case arising out of the international sale of goods but there would be no particular difficulty in applying this requirement in such cases.

3. THE TRADITIONAL ENGLISH RULES

It may be possible to bring a claim against defendants in a multi- **9.25** defendant action within one of the bases of jurisdiction examined in

---

[46] *Soc Leybold-Heraeus and Leybold-Heraeus Sogev SI v Seima*, Judgment of 19 January 1978, RIW 1978, 271; D Series I-6—B 3.

[47] n 45 above.   [48] The *Molnlycke* case, n 24 above.

previous chapters.[49] What has not been discussed so far is r 6.20(3) of the Civil Procedure Rules, which is specifically designed to provide a basis of jurisdiction in multi-defendant cases.

Rule 6.20(3)

9.26 Rule 6.20(3) of the Civil Procedure Rules provides that a claim form may be served (otherwise than in reliance on this paragraph) out of the jurisdiction with the permission of the court if:

a claim is made against someone on whom the claim form has been or will be served and—

(a) there is between the claimant and that person a real issue which it is reasonable for the court to try; and

(b) the claimant wishes to serve the claim form on another person who is a necessary or proper party to that claim.

In order to come within this provision two requirements must be satisfied. The first is that there is between the claimant and the person on whom the claim form has been or will be served (the first or anchor defendant) a real issue which it is reasonable for the court to try.[50] This merits threshold test[51] protects the first defendant, who can be served with a claim form, from spurious claims being brought against him solely in order to obtain jurisdiction over the second defendant who is outside the jurisdiction. It also, of course, protects the second defendant. There will not be 'a real issue which it is reasonable for the court to try' if the claimant has no real prospect of succeeding on that issue.[52] 'Real' is to be contrasted with 'fanciful'.[53] This requirement will not be met if the claim against the first defendant is bound to fail. It will also not be met if the claim against the first defendant is not a bona fide one, i.e. the first defendant is joined with the sole object of subjecting the second defendant to the jurisdiction of the English courts.[54]

9.27 The second requirement is that the other person on whom the claimant wishes to serve the claim form (the second defendant) is a necessary or proper party to the claim against the first defendant. This serves to protect

---

[49] These are discussed above, paras 4.02–25 (service within the jurisdiction), 4.26–153 (service out of the jurisdiction under r 6.20((5), (6) and (7)), 6.10–16 (r 6.20(8))).

[50] The written evidence in support of the application for permission to serve the claim form out of the jurisdiction must state the grounds on which the witness believes that this is so, r 6.21(2).

[51] *De Molestina v Ponton* [2002] 1 Lloyd's Rep 271 at [37].

[52] *Owusu v Jackson* [2002] EWCA Civ 877 at [32], [2002] IL Pr 45.

[53] ibid. The Court said that r 6.20(3) introduces the language of r 24.2(a)(i) CPR and in that context 'real' contrasts with 'fanciful', citing *Swain v Hillman* [2001] 1 All ER 91 at [10].

[54] *Konamaneni v Rolls-Royce Industrial Power (India) Limited* [2002] IL Pr 40 at [44].

the second defendant from being improperly joined. The Court of Appeal has held that the issue, whether a person out of the jurisdiction is a proper party to an action against a person who has been served within the jurisdiction, must depend on the answer to this question: 'supposing both parties had been within the jurisdiction would they both have been proper parties to the action? If they would, and only one of them is in this country, then the rule says that the other may be served, just as if he had been within the jurisdiction.'[55] Generally a person who may be joined in proceedings in accordance with the English rules as to joinder of parties is a 'proper party'.[56] This second requirement will not be satisfied if: the second defendant has a good defence in law and the claim is therefore bound to fail;[57] the claimant's rights are predominantly against the first defendant;[58] or if the claim should have been principally brought against the second defendant.[59]

Although r 6.20(3) is, like Article 6(1) of the Brussels I Regulation, concerned with concentrating litigation in one state[60] and thereby avoiding the situation where there are two inconsistent judgments,[61] it does not require, like that provision, that the claims are so closely connected that it is expedient to hear and determine them together to avoid the risk of irreconcilable judgments resulting from separate proceedings. **9.28**

Rule 6.20(3) does not require that the claim be made in respect of a contract or is made in tort or in any other type of action. It thus has the advantage of encompassing a claim against a particular defendant which is based on more than one cause of action.[62] Moreover, unlike Article 6(1) **9.29**

---

[55] *Massey v Heynes & Co* (1888) 21 QBD 330 at 338 (*per* Lord Esher MR); quoted by May LJ in *Multinational Gas and Petrochemical Co v Multinational Gas and Petrochemical Services Ltd* [1983] Ch 258 at 274, CA. See also *Analog Devices BV v Zurich Insurance Co* [2002] 2 ILRM 366, SC of Ireland.

[56] *Petroleo Brasiliero SA v Mellitus Shipping Inc (The Baltic Flame)* [2001] EWCA Civ 418 at [33], [2001] 2 Lloyd's Rep 203. See also the *Eras Eil Actions* [1992] 1 Lloyd's Rep 570, CA; the *Owusu* case, n 52 above, at [9]. The English rules on joinder are contained in r 19 CPR. Rule 7.3 CPR provides that a claimant may use a single claim form to start all claims which can be conveniently disposed of in the same proceedings.

[57] *Multinational Gas and Petrochemical Co v Multinational Gas and Petrochemical Services Ltd* [1983] Ch 258, CA; *Borealis AB v Stargas Ltd* [1999] QB 863, CA, aff'd by the House of Lords on different grounds [2002] 2 AC 205.

[58] *Re Schintz* [1926] Ch 710.

[59] *Rosler v Hilbery* [1925] Ch 250, CA

[60] *Golden Ocean Assurance Ltd and World Mariner Shipping SA v Martin, (The Goldean Mariner)* [1989] 2 Lloyd's Rep 390, 400; [1990] 2 Lloyd's Rep 215, CA.

[61] *Amanual v Alexandros Shipping Co* [1986] 1 QB 464, 478. For the other reasons given by the English courts for the desirability of concentrating litigation in one state, see J Fawcett, 'Multi-party Litigation in Private International Law' (1995) 44 ICLQ 744 at 746.

[62] See, e.g. *ISC Technologies Ltd v James Howard Guerin* [1992] 2 Lloyd's Rep 430; discussed below, para 9.35.

of the Brussels I Regulation,[63] it can be used where there are claims against different defendants based on different causes of action.[64]

9.30   When it comes to the exercise of the discretion to serve out of the jurisdiction, special care is needed with this ground, 'in the sense that the court will give careful examination to the cause of action relied on, both as to its substance and its prospects (is it bound or very likely to fail?), whether it is brought in good faith or with some improper motive or ulterior purpose, and whether or not full and fair disclosure has been made'.[65] Establishing that England is the clearly appropriate forum for trial will not be easy because the rule applies to cases where there is no territorial connection between the claim which is the subject of the relevant action and the jurisdiction of the English courts. Nevertheless, this is a good provision in terms of litigational convenience, allowing for the consolidation of litigation in one state. This is a factor which may properly encourage a judge to lean in favour of allowing service out of the jurisdiction in the absence of positive counter-indications.[66]

Application to International Sale of Goods Cases

9.31   The fact that r 6.20(3) is not concerned with the question of how closely connected the claims are means that there are not the particular problems with international sale of goods cases that arise with Article 6(1) of the Brussels I Regulation. Nonetheless, there can be problems with the requirements that do exist under r 6.20(3).

A real issue which it is reasonable for the court to try between the claimant and the person on whom the claim form has been served

9.32   In *Goldenglow v Commodin*,[67] the English buyer of groundnuts, which did not conform to the contract in terms of quality or quantity, brought an action against three defendants: the first defendant, the English seller, for breach of contract; the second defendant, a Swiss company, for negligently certifying that the goods conformed with the contract; and the third defendant, an English company which was the first defendant's insurers. The second defendant's argument, that the sole or predominant reason why the action had been brought against the first and third defendants was to bring the claim against the second defendant which was outside the jurisdiction, was rejected by Rougier J on the basis that a

---

[63] See above, paras 9.10–12.   [64] See, eg, the *Owusu* case, n 52 above.
[65] *Petroleo Brasiliero SA v Mellitus Shipping Inc (The Baltic Flame)* [2001] EWCA Civ 418 at [21], [2001] 2 Lloyd's Rep 203.
[66] ibid, at [22].   [67] [1987] 2 Lloyd's Rep 569, CA.

good arguable case existed against the first and third defendant.[68] This was upheld by the Court of Appeal.[69]

In contrast, this requirement was not met in *Thierry Morin v Bonhams & Brooks Limited and Bonhams & Brooks SAM*.[70] The claimant bought a classic car at an auction in Monaco held by the second defendant, the Monegasque subsidiary of the first defendant, an English auction house. The first defendant sent an auction catalogue, printed in England and prepared for the second defendant, to the claimant in London. The claimant alleged that the catalogue misrepresented the kilometerage of the car. He sought, inter alia, damages for negligent misstatement from both defendants. The claimant sought to use r 6.20(3) to serve the second defendant out of the jurisdiction. Jonathan Hirst QC, sitting as a deputy High Court Judge, held that the claimant did not have a reasonably arguable case against the first defendant that they owed him a duty of care in tort for the purposes of the claim for negligent misstatement[71] nor was it a joint tortfeasor with the second defendant. The result of these findings was that the claimant had failed to establish a good arguable case that there was a real issue between the first defendant and the claimant which it was reasonable for the court to try.[72] Neither was this requirement met in the *Bastone* case.[73] It will be recalled that the third defendant, Mr Saidi, was served within the jurisdiction. It was argued that the fourth defendant, Ecobank, was a necessary or proper party to this action. There was no intention of pursuing the claim against Mr Saidi, who had disappeared, and, accordingly, there was no longer any real issue for the court to try between the plaintiff and Mr Saidi.[74] As Rix J bluntly put it, Ecobank was a necessary or proper party to nothing.[75]

The other person whom the claimant wishes to serve is a necessary or proper party to that claim

In the *Goldenglow* case, Rougier J, applying the test laid down by the Court **9.34** of Appeal that, supposing both parties had been within the jurisdiction,

9.33

---

[68] Service out of the jurisdiction was sought on the basis of Ord 11, r 1(1)(j) RSC which was differently worded from the present multi-defendant ground under r 6.20(3) CPR. What has to be shown now is that there is between the claimant and the person on whom the claim form has been or will be served a real issue which it is reasonable for the court to try, r 6.20(3)(a) CPR, discussed above, para 9.26. See also *The Ines* [1993] 2 Lloyd's Rep 492 at 493.

[69] n 67 above, at 578.

[70] [2003] EWHC 467 (Comm), [2003] IL Pr 25. The Court of Appeal affirmed the decision at first instance that Monegasque law governed the tort claim [2003] EWCA Civ 1802, [2004] IL, Pr 24. For an example arising out of the carriage of goods by sea where this requirement was not met see *The Rewia* [1991] 2 Lloyd's Rep 325, CA.

[71] The *Thierry Morin* case, n 70 above, at [46].

[72] ibid, at [61]. The alternative argument that service could be effected abroad using the tort ground is discussed above, para 6.103.

[73] n 14 above and accompanying text.   [74] ibid, at 1917.   [75] ibid, at 1918.

would they both have been proper parties to the action, held that the second defendants were proper parties to the action brought against the first and third defendants. This was affirmed by the Court of Appeal.[76] A differently constituted Court of Appeal in *Borealis v Stargas Ltd*,[77] was faced with a much more difficult decision, involving the determination of an unclear point of substantive law. Saudi Arabian shippers of a contaminated cargo of propane argued that they were not a necessary or proper party to an action brought by Swedish buyers against Jersey sellers. The buyers sought an indemnity or contribution from the shippers for any liability they might have to the Norwegian shipowners under the bills of lading. The Court of Appeal held that the buyers, having endorsed the bills of lading to third party purchasers, were automatically divested of any liability under the contract of carriage. Consequently, the shipowners' claim against the buyers was bound to fail. It followed that the buyers ought not to be permitted to join the shippers as parties and the judge erred in concluding that the case was a proper one for service out of the jurisdiction.[78]

9.35 The necessary or proper party requirement was also met in *ISC Technologies Ltd v James Howard Guerin*.[79] It will be recalled that the plaintiffs wished to serve Mr Pindell out of the jurisdiction in Pennsylvania, it being alleged that in collaboration with others he had knowingly participated in a fraudulent misrepresentation that a contract had been concluded when there was in fact no such contract. It was also claimed that he participated in the pretence that goods and services were being ordered to enable the plaintiffs to perform the contract and gave auditors a false version of a genuine contract. Service out of the jurisdiction had previously been permitted against another defendant, Radcliffe. The latter was not alleged to have been a party to the pretence that a sale contract had been concluded. He was concerned with the technical implementation of the plaintiff's contracts and was alleged to have participated in the fraudulent misrepresentations that the fictitious contracts were actually being implemented. The activities of both were alleged to be part of a scheme of fraudulent conduct organized by Guerin. Hoffmann J held that Pindell was a proper party to the action against Radcliffe. This case illustrates very well the usefulness of r 6.20(3) in terms of its application, regardless

---

[76] n 67 above, at 574.

[77] [1999] QB 863, CA; aff'd by the House of Lords on different grounds [2002] 2 AC 205.

[78] Counsel for the shippers argued the appeal on the basis that the discretion should not be exercised to permit service out of the jurisdiction, rather than alleging that the terms of Ord 11, r 1(1)(c) RSC—the predecessor of 6.20(3) CPR—had not been met. Earlier Waller J, at first instance, had held that the terms of Ord 1, r 1(1)(c) had been met, [1997] 1 Lloyd's Rep 635 at 639.

[79] [1992] 2 Lloyd's Rep 430.

of the cause of action. The relief sought against Pindell was: first, an account and restitution of the money paid out by the plaintiffs; second, damages for fraud; third, an account of profits. The claim for fraudulent misrepresentation fell within the tort head of Order 11.[80] But this only enabled the plaintiffs to claim remedies founded on tort. Their claims for equitable restitutionary remedies for breach of trust or fiduciary duty had to be brought within some other head. However, all the plaintiffs' claims could be brought within the multi-defendant head of Order 11, thereby allowing the plaintiffs to litigate the whole of their case in England.

Again by way of contrast, this requirement was not met in the *Bastone* **9.36** case.[81] The only claim brought against Mr Saidi was in respect of two personal cheques which were not met. Ecobank, whose alleged contractual liability was based upon the instructions that it received as a collecting bank and who was also allegedly liable in tort for conversion of or wrongful interference with the consignments or documents sent to Nigeria,[82] was not a necessary or proper party to this claim.

4. CASES INVOLVING BOTH SETS OF RULES

It is not uncommon in multi-defendant cases to have the situation **9.37** where one defendant is domiciled in an EC Member State and the other defendant is domiciled in a non-Member State. *Réunion Européenne SA v Spliethoff's Bevrachtingskantoor*[83] is an illustration of this. It will be recalled that the plaintiff consignee of goods brought proceedings against three defendants: first, the Australian company which issued the bill of lading; second, the Dutch company which actually carried the goods, although it was not mentioned in the bill of lading; and third, the master of the ship which carried the goods, who resided in Amsterdam. In such a case, the forum will have to apply its traditional rules of jurisdiction in relation to the first defendant and the EC rules in relation to the second and third defendants.[84] The European Court of Justice in the *Réunion Européenne* case held that Article 6(1) of the Brussels Convention must be interpreted as meaning that a defendant domiciled in a Contracting State cannot be sued in another Contracting State before a court seised of an action against a co-defendant not domiciled in a Contracting State on the ground that the dispute is indivisible rather than merely displaying a connection. This means that the fact that the French forum had jurisdiction under its

---

[80] See above, para 6.96. [81] n 14 above.
[82] Jurisdiction in relation to the tort claim is considered above, para 6.101.
[83] Case C-51/97 [1998] ECR I-6511.
[84] See the *Owusu* case, n 52 above. See also the *Canada Trust Company* case, n 17 above.

traditional national rules of jurisdiction against the first defendant did not allow it to use Article 6(1) to found jurisdiction against the other two defendants.

II. THIRD PARTY CLAIMS

1. Third Party Claims in International Sale of Goods Cases

9.38 Numerous illustrations can be given of where a third party claim has been brought in an international sale of goods case. The first illustration is the Dutch case of *Technisch Handelsbureau PJ van Londen BV v NV Gieterijen Technomet*.[85] A buyer of cast iron rings claimed against the Netherlands seller in the Netherlands on the basis that the goods supplied were defective and the latter sought to bring third party proceedings in the Netherlands against the Belgian manufacturer of the goods. The second illustration, *Rutschi Pumpen AG v SA Pompes Rutschi Mulhouse*,[86] is similar to the first but this time the French supplier of defective goods, having been sued in France by the buyer, issued third party proceedings not only against the Swiss manufacturer but also against its (the supplier's) insurer, which was also the manufacturer's insurer. The third illustration is where a buyer of goods, which are defective, brings a claim against the seller for breach of contract. The goods were carried on a ship and the seller serves a third party notice on shipowners, alleging breach of the charter and seeking an indemnity against the seller's liability to the buyer.[87] The fourth illustration is where a bank, which has been financing a party to the international sales contract is joined as the third party to an action in relation to the sales contract.[88] The fifth illustration is where a sale of goods contract contains a set-off clause which permits set off claims by any affiliates of the buyer and seller respectively. The buyer who is sued for the price of goods issues a third party notice against an affiliated company of the seller, which allegedly owes money to an affiliated company of the buyer under a separate contract.[89] The sixth illustration is

---

[85] Arrondissementsrechtbank, Arnhem, Judgment of 23 December 1982, NIPR 1983, No 246; D Series I-17.1.2—B 24. See also *Islanders Canning Corp Ltd v Hoekstra; Hoekstra v Schmalbach-Lubecca-Werke AG*, Arrondissementsrechtbank, Leeuwarden, Judgment of 2 September 1976; D Series I-17.1.1—B 4.

[86] [2002] IL Pr 6, Grenoble Court of Appeal.

[87] See the *Borealis* case, n 77 above.

[88] *Glencore International AG v Metro Trading International Inc (No 1)* [1999] 2 All ER (Comm) 899. The facts are set out below, para 9.50.

[89] *Sinochem International Oil (London) Ltd v Mobil Sales and Supply Corp Ltd (Sinochem International Oil Co Ltd, third party) (No 2)* [2000] 1 All ER (Comm) 758; discussed below, para 9.43.

where a buyer of shares in an English company sues the seller, a Canadian company, W, for deceit and fraudulent misrepresentation and the latter brings third party claims against, inter alia, the Canadian auditors of W, alleging negligence.[90] These illustrations are in addition to the most conventional case of all: the defendant seller who serves a third party notice on its own supplier, claiming against the latter for breach of contract in terms similar to those forming the basis of the plaintiff buyer's claim. In this illustration, the claim over in contract against the seller's supplier is to be distinguished from a claim over in tort against a party who may or may not be privy to a contract with the defendant seller.

2. THE EC RULES

Article 6(2)

Article 6(2) of the Brussels I Regulation provides that a person domiciled **9.39** in a Member State may also be sued:

as a third party in an action on a warranty or guarantee or in any other third party proceedings, in the court seised of the original proceedings, unless these were instituted solely with the object of removing him from the jurisdiction of the court which would be competent in his case;

This provision does not require the national court to accede to the request for leave to bring third party proceedings and the forum may apply the procedural rules of its national law on third party proceedings to determine whether the action is admissible.[91] This means that, as far as England is concerned, there must be a proper connection between the original claim and third party claim such as would be recognized by England's own third party statute.[92]

Application to International Sale of Goods Cases

In the *Technisch* case,[93] the Arrondissementsrechtbank, Arnhem, held that, **9.40** in principle, the Dutch courts had jurisdiction to hear the third party claim against the Belgian manufacturer by virtue of Article 6(2) of the Brussels Convention since it was the court seised of the original proceedings.[94] There was no question in that case but that there was a proper connection

---

[90] *Man Nutzfahrzeuge Aktiengesellschaft v Freightliner Ltd* [2003] EWHC 2245 (Comm).
[91] Case C-365/88 *Kongress Agentur Hagen GmbH v Zeehage BV* [1990] ECR 1845.
[92] *Caltex v Metro* [1999] 2 Lloyd's Rep 724 at 735.
[93] n 85 above.
[94] The Dutch court's jurisdiction was overridden by a Belgian choice of jurisdiction clause.

between claim and third party claim. Similarly, in the *Rutschi Pumpen* case,[95] Article 6(2) applied to give the French courts jurisdiction against the third party Swiss manufacturer. The close connection between the original claim and the third party proceedings could be seen from the fact that the cause of action and subject-matter of the main action and third party proceedings were identical.[96] Moreover, the original proceedings related to the loss caused by the very product manufactured by the third party.[97]

9.41   In contrast, the connection between the original claim and the third party proceedings raised problems in *Caltex v Metro*,[98] one of the many cases that arose out of the collapse of Metro, a company engaged in storing and trading in fuel oil. In that case, the issue was which if any of the oil claimants or Metro itself had title to such oil as remained in storage or could be traced, or to the proceeds of the sale of such oil. Rix J held that a fourth party claim in tort for wrongful interference with the oil did not fall within the English statutory provision allowing third and fourth party notices[99] since it did not relate to the original subject-matter of the third party action (interpleader relief whereby the plaintiff sought to be freed from accountability) and, accordingly fell outside Article 6(2) of the Brussels Convention.[100] The Italian national decision in *SA Salpa v SpA Co-Ar and Fallimento SpA Tanit* is to the same effect.[101] The buyer of artificial leather strips, following the bankruptcy of the seller, filed an application before an Italian court for the determination of a claim in bankruptcy, and in the framework of those proceedings commenced an action in damages against the French supplier of the goods. The Corte di cassazione, Sezioni unite, held that it had no jurisdiction under Article 6(2) of the Brussels Convention in relation to the damages claim. This was because the claims were not sufficiently related. Under the Italian procedural rule which governed third party claims, it was necessary for the basis and objective of the claims to be related, which was not the case in the proceedings in question.

---

[95] n 86 above.   [96] ibid, at [4].

[97] The third party proceedings against the insurer came within the insurance provisions under the Lugano Convention.

[98] [1999] 2 Lloyd's Rep 724.

[99] Ord 16, r 1(1) RSC; see now on addition and substitution of parties r 19.2 et seq CPR. For special rules about parties in claims for wrongful interference with goods, see r 19.5A CPR.

[100] n 98 above, at 734–735.

[101] Judgment No 246 of 15 January 1987, Foro it 1987, I, 2816; Riv dir int priv proc 1988, 285; D Series I-6—B 12.

3. THE TRADITIONAL ENGLISH RULES

Rule 6.20(3)

To introduce a foreign defendant into the English proceedings by way of **9.42**
a third party notice under Part 20 of the Civil Procedure Rules requires the
permission of the court under r 6.20 of those rules. When it comes to
establishing one of the grounds of jurisdiction under r 6.20, it is important
to note that r 6.20(3) of the Civil Procedure Rules[102] applies not only to
multi-defendant cases but also to third party claims.[103]

Application to International Sale of Goods Cases

The leading case is *Sinochem International Oil (London) Ltd v Mobil Sales and* **9.43**
Supply Corp Ltd (Sinochem International Oil Co Ltd, third party) (No 2),[104]
which is illustration number five above.[105] An English company (SL) sold
oil to a US subsidiary of a US company, MD. The contract, which contained an English choice of law and exclusive jurisdiction clause, also
contained a set-off clause which permitted set-off claims by any affiliates
of the buyer and seller respectively. The buyer failed to pay the full price
of the oil. An affiliated company of the buyer, MHK, a Hong Kong company, had previously sold oil to an affiliated company of the seller, SB, a
Chinese company. This separate contract contained a Hong Kong choice
of law and exclusive jurisdiction clause. Most of the purchase price under
this contract was unpaid. SL brought an action against MD in England for
the balance of the price due under the English contract. MD issued a third
party notice against SB, based on the Hong Kong contract, and applied
for leave to serve out of the jurisdiction under the predecessor of r 6.20(3),
Order 11, r 1(1)(c) of the Rules of the Supreme Court. Permission was
granted ex parte on the basis that SB was a necessary or proper party to
the proceedings in relation to the English contract. SB challenged the
jurisdiction of the court and sought the discharge of the third party notice.
Should leave to serve out of the jurisdiction be permitted? Rix J held that it
should. The case was complicated in that it involved two different contracts, with different choice of law clauses. The essential dispute between
the parties arose under the Hong Kong contract because it was by no
means clear that there was an obligation to pay under this contract,
given that there were allegations of smuggling. However, the Court of
Appeal had previously decided that MD was entitled to resist the present

---

[102] Discussed above, paras 9.25–27.
[103] See, eg, *Petroleo Brasiliero SA v Mellitus Shipping Inc (The Baltic Flame)* [2001] EWCA Civ
418, [2001] 2 Lloyd's Rep 203.
[104] [2000] 1 All ER (Comm) 758.   [105] At para 9.38.

proceedings by invoking MHK's claim to the balance of the price under the Hong Kong contract.[106] Rix J had also just decided in the instant case that the potential issues which may arise under the Hong Kong contract, did not necessitate the staying of the English proceedings, pending the litigation in Hong Kong.[107] In the light of these two facts, Rix J concluded that the interests of justice required that all the parties involved in such issues should be present in the proceedings in England.[108] He came to this conclusion more readily bearing in mind that SB was only nominally a different company from SL.

III. COUNTER-CLAIMS

1. COUNTER-CLAIMS IN INTERNATIONAL SALE OF GOODS CASES

9.44 The facts of a Danish case, *Cha Cha Denmark A/S v Commercial Textiles LDA*,[109] provide a simple example of how a counter-claim can arise in the context of the international sale of goods. The foreign plaintiff manufacturer brought a claim in Denmark for payment for delivery of clothes. The defendant Danish wholesaler and retailer counter-claimed, arguing that the price sought was higher than that agreed and that it was entitled to compensation for the costs and damage to reputation that had arisen because of the problem deliveries.

2. THE EC RULES

Article 6(3)

9.45 Article 6(3) of the Brussels I Regulation provides that a person domiciled in a Member State may also be sued:

on a counter-claim[110] arising from the same contract or facts on which the original claim was based, in the court in which the original claim is pending;

Application to International Sale of Goods Cases

9.46 In the *Cha Cha Denmark* case, the Danish Supreme Court found that the counter-claim fell within the scope of Article 6(3) of the Brussels

---

[106] [2000] 1 Lloyd's Rep 339, CA. [107] n 104 above, at 769–773.
[108] ibid, at 773. [109] [2002] IL Pr 5.
[110] This does not cover set-off as a defence (Case C-341/93 *Danvaern Production A/S v Schuhfabriken Otterbeck GmbH & Co* [1995] ECR I-2053) or a cross-claim made by a party who was not a defendant to the original claim (*Dollfus Mieg et Cie v CWD International Ltd* [2004] IL Pr 12).

Convention.[111] The Court pointed out that the claim and counter-claim concerned deliveries of clothes by the plaintiff to the defendant which took place as part of a long standing pattern of trade between the parties. Moreover, part of the counter-claim related to the same deliveries which were the subject of the plaintiff's claim and the other part of the counter-claim related to corresponding objections to deliveries from the same period. In these circumstances, the Court found that the requirement for a connection between the contract or facts of the claim and the counter-claim was satisfied. However, the answer would have been different if the parties had entered into two or more contracts and the contract on which the defendant's counter-claim was based (the second contract, under which the Dutch defendant sold computers to the Italian plaintiff) was a different contract from the one on which the plaintiff's claim for payment was based (the first contract, under which the plaintiff sold computers to the defendant).[112] The requirement that the counter-claim arise from the same contract or facts on which the original claim was based would not be met and the Dutch courts would not have jurisdiction under Article 6(3) of the Regulation in relation to the counter-claim.

3. The Traditional English Rules

A simple example of where a counter-claim would arise in the context of **9.47** the traditional rules would be where a New York seller brings a claim in England against the English buyer for payment of the price of the goods delivered. The defendant counter-claims for damages based on breach of the seller's obligation to deliver goods in conformity with the contract.

Permission is not needed for service of the counter-claim, even though **9.48** this is against a person outside the jurisdiction.[113] Commencing an action as claimant gives the English court jurisdiction over this person in respect of the counter-claim.[114] The counter-claim comes within the broad category of a Part 20 claim under the Civil Procedure Rules.[115] This category also encompasses a claim by a defendant against any person (whether or not already a party) for contribution or indemnity or some other

---

[111] n 109 above, at [28]. The wording of Art 6(3) of the Brussels Convention is the same as that of Art 6(3) of the Brussels I Regulation.

[112] *Deutscher Ring Lebensversicherungs-AG v Computer Hardware Corp CV*, Gerechtshof, Amsterdam, Judgment of 24 December 1981, NJ 1983, No 547; D Series I-17.3—B 4. See also *Piccioli v V en N Impag BV*, Gerechtshof, Leeuwarden, Judgment of 23 June 1982; D Series I-6—B 9.

[113] *Derby & Co v Larsson* [1976] 1 WLR 202 at 205; *Civil Procedure (The White Book)* (2003) vol 1, para 6.21.11.

[114] *Balkanbank v Taher (No 2)* [1995] 1 WLR 1067, CA.   [115] r 20.2(1)(a) CPR.

remedy.[116] If the person against whom this claim is brought is outside the jurisdiction then permission of the court for service abroad will be required. However, a claim form may be served out of the jurisdiction with the permission of the court under r 6.20(3A) where 'a claim is a Part 20 claim and the person to be served is a necessary and proper party to the claim against the Part 20 claimant'.

IV. MULTI-PARTY CLAIMS AND DECLINING JURISDICTION

1. Declining Jurisdiction Under the Brussels I Regulation

9.49   The complex nature of multi-party claims inevitably raises questions over whether the requirements for the application of Article 27 (*lis pendens*) of the Brussels I Regulation have been satisfied.[117] Two questions in particular arise: is the cause of action the same; and are the parties the same?

Is the Cause of Action the Same?

9.50   The way in which this question can arise is illustrated by *Glencore International v Metro (No 1)*.[118] Metro (M) agreed to sell and deliver cargoes of bunker fuel to SPC and IPC. Bills of lading were issued by a bank that had been financing M. Both SPC and IPC gave undertakings that they would pay the price of the goods to the bank for the account of M. The goods were delivered. The English proceedings were as follows. G, which alleged that it had title to the oil, brought proceedings in England against IPC and SPC for conversion. Receivers of M brought proceedings in England against IPC for the contract price. IPC served third party proceedings on the bank in both actions to ensure that it would be bound by the court's decision. The proceedings in France were as follows. The bank brought proceedings in Paris against IPC and SPC for recovery of the amounts due under the contracts of sale. SPC made third party claims against G and M.

9.51   The bank sought to stay the third party proceedings brought in England by IPC, basing the stay on Article 21 of the Brussels Convention. Moore-Bick J held that there could be little dispute as far as the 'cause' was concerned, despite the fact that the relief sought in England against the bank was merely declaratory, since both sets of proceedings were based on the same facts and depended on the same rules of law. What was less

---

[116] r 20.2(1)(b) CPR. See also r 20.2(1)(c).
[117] Art 27 is discussed above, paras 3.13–15.   [118] [1999] 2 All ER (Comm) 899.

clear was whether the proceedings had the same 'objet' (end which the action has in view), given that the bank's action was one to recover the price under the sales contract whereas IPC's third party proceedings merely sought to ensure that the bank was bound by the decisions made in G's action. Nonetheless, a decision in the English proceedings that IPC was liable to G because M had no title to the oil would, if binding on the bank, necessarily mean that IPC was not liable to the bank or to M. Equally a decision in the French proceedings that IPC was liable to the bank would be inconsistent with any right of G to recover damages for conversion in the English proceedings, or for that matter, any right of G to recover the price, since it was not suggested that IPC could be liable to make payment both to the bank and to M. The central issues in both sets of proceedings were whether G or M had title to the cargo loaded on board a ship and which of them was entitled to recover from IPC. In each case, judgment in the action would determine the rights and obligations of IPC, G and M amongst themselves in a manner which would bind them all. Moore-Bick J concluded that both sets of third party proceedings between the bank and IPC involved both the same cause and the same 'objet' as the proceedings between them in France.[119]

SPC sought a stay of G's action against it: again the stay was based on **9.52** Article 21 of the Brussels Convention. Moore-Bick J held that the proceedings between GI and SPC in France were intended to lead to a final decision on GI's right to recover against SPC in respect of wrongful interference with the cargo. Accordingly, it involved the same cause of action as the English proceedings between those parties, and was therefore subject to Article 21. This was despite the fact that in England G was claiming damages for wrongful interference with its property, whereas in France SPC was making no claim at all. It was merely doing what was necessary to ensure that G was bound by the outcome of the bank's action without itself asserting any claim or seeking any other kind of relief.[120]

The position is different where one set of proceedings involves an action **9.53** by B against S in respect of the proceeds of sale of oil bought by S from M and the other set involves interpleader relief sought by S against B, asking to be absolved from playing any further part in the proceedings, where what is in issue is not the liability of S but, rather, which of the interpleader claimants has the better title to S's debt. In such a case, the two sets of proceedings do not involve the same set of proceedings or share the same 'objet'.[121]

---

[119] ibid, at 908. [120] ibid, at 920.
[121] *Glencore International v Shell* [1999] 2 All ER (Comm) 922.

Are the Parties the Same?

9.54 This question also arose in *Glencore International v Metro (No 1)*.[122] The European Court of Justice has adopted a party by party approach towards multi-party cases, holding that 'the second court seised is required to decline jurisdiction only to the extent to which the parties to the proceedings before it are also parties to the action previously commenced; it does not prevent the proceedings from continuing between the other parties'.[123] In other words, 'the requirement of identity of parties is satisfied to the extent that the same parties are joined in both actions, whether or not other parties have been joined in one or both of the actions'.[124] In *Glencore International v Metro (No 1)*,[125] it was clear that this requirement was satisfied as far as the bank and IPC were concerned since both of them were parties to each of the English actions as well as one of the bank's actions in France.[126]

2. DECLINING JURISDICTION UNDER THE TRADITIONAL ENGLISH RULES

9.55 When exercising the discretion to stay the English proceedings on the ground of *forum non conveniens*[127] in multi-party cases a number of questions arise.[128]

9.56 First, in cases where one defendant is served within the jurisdiction (the burden then being on the defendant to show that the clearly appropriate forum is abroad) and the other is served out of the jurisdiction (the burden then being on the claimant to show that England is the clearly appropriate forum for trial), are different burdens of proof to be applied to each defendant when it comes to the question of the appropriate forum for trial? The 'overriding requirement is that justice must be done to all parties'.[129] This means that different burdens of proof should not be adopted when this would result in jurisdiction being taken against one defendant but not another defendant.

9.57 Second, where there are several defendants or groups of defendants should the appropriate forum be ascertained separately for each group? The answer to this is clear. The case must be looked at in the round, not reviewing the position of English defendants independently.[130]

---

[122] [1999] 2 All ER (Comm) 899.
[123] Case C-406/92 *Owners of the Cargo Lately Laden on Board the Ship Tatry v Owners of the Ship Maciej Rataj* [1994] ECR I-5439 at 5474.
[124] *Glencore International v Metro (No 1)* [1999] 2 All ER (Comm) 899 at 905.
[125] ibid.   [126] Ibid.   [127] See above paras 4.156–160.
[128] See generally Fawcett, n 61 above, at 755–760.
[129] *Du Pont (EI) de Nemours & Co v Agnew and Kerr* [1987] 2 Lloyd's Rep 585 at 595, CA.
[130] ibid, at 593 (*per* Bingham LJ).

Third, what weight is to be attached to the concentration of litigation **9.58**
factor? In the situation where England is the only state in which several
defendants can be joined together in a single action, this is an important
factor in favour of trial taking place in England.[131] Equally, if a foreign
state is the only one in which litigation can be consolidated this is an
important factor in favour of trial taking place there. This is illustrated
by *Donohue v Armco Inc*,[132] where, it will be recalled,[133] proceedings
were brought in New York in breach of an English exclusive jurisdiction
clause. The claimant's prima facie entitlement to enforce the contractual
bargain[134] was displaced because there were other defendants in the
New York proceedings who were potential co-claimants in the English
proceedings. The interests of justice were best served by the submission of
the whole suit to a single tribunal which could adjudicate on all matters in
issue, namely the New York courts.[135]

---

[131] See *Meadows Indemnity Co Ltd v Insurance Corp of Ireland Ltd and International Commercial Bank Ltd* [1989] 1 Lloyd's Rep 181, 190, aff'd [1989] 2 Lloyd's Rep 298, CA.
[132] [2001] UKHL 64, [2002] 1 All ER 749.
[133] See above, para 4.173.
[134] By means of an injunction restraining the proceedings in New York.
[135] n 132 above, at [34].

10

Electronic Commerce: Jurisdiction

I. INTRODUCTION

Electronic commerce has been defined in the context of private inter- **10.01**
national law[1] as 'commercial activities which are carried on by means
of computers interconnected by telecommunications lines'[2] and, more
simply, as 'business transactions conducted over the Internet'.[3] This still
leaves a question as to how widely or narrowly this basic definition is
interpreted. A narrow interpretation would look simply at transactions
taking an electronic form, most obviously contracts concluded or performed online.[4] This would include the situation where the parties communicate and conclude their contract by email.[5] A wider view[6] would go
further and encompass all situations where a person or company uses the

---

[1] The substantive law of electronic commerce is not entirely helpful. Neither the EC
Directive on Electronic Commerce [2000] OJ L178/1 nor the UNCITRAL Model Law on
Electronic Commerce of 1996 defines 'electronic commerce'. The full title of the former is
Directive 2000/31/EC of the European Parliament and of the Council of 8 June 2000 on
certain legal aspects of information society services, in particular electronic commerce, in the
Internal Market (Directive on electronic commerce). See also Arts 1 and 2 for scope and
definitions. The Directive applies to 'any information in the form of a data message used in
the context of commercial activities', Art 1. The term 'commercial' is widely defined to cover
matters arising from all relationships of a commercial nature, whether contractual or not.

[2] Prel Doc No 7 of April 2000, *Electronic Data Interchange, Internet and Electronic Commerce*
by Kessedjian for the attention of the Special Commission of May 2000 on general affairs and
policy of the Hague Conference on Private International Law, 17 (www.hcch.e-vision.nl/
index_en.php?act=progress listing&cat=9)

[3] *Colt Studio Inc v Badpuppy Enterprise* 75 F Supp 2d 1104 (1999). Strictly speaking,
electronic commerce can be conducted over other networks than the internet, see Prel Doc
No 7, n 2 above, 17.

[4] This is the view adopted by Kessedjian at the Hague Conference on Private International
Law in Prel Doc No 7, n 2 above, 17.

[5] ibid, 16.

[6] This wider view is adopted by courts in the US, see below, paras 10.247–248.

internet[7] (including email) as a means of carrying on its commercial activities, regardless of whether a contract was made or performed online. To illustrate the difference, think of the situation where a company creates a passive website to advertise its goods. The contract is made in a traditional way not via the internet. This situation would fall outside the narrow interpretation but within the broader interpretation. This situation can raise issues that do not arise in non-internet cases[8] and it is for this reason that, for the purposes of this chapter, the wider view will be adopted.

10.02 Statistics on the extent of electronic commerce make staggering reading. It is estimated that in 2000 commerce over the internet world wide[9] reached 214 billion EUR and is expected to reach as much as 7.64 thousand billion EUR by 2004.[10] Business to business transactions account for more than four-fifths of all transactions conducted online.[11] There is no doubt that electronic commerce is transforming the way in which business is being conducted. Inevitably, business transactions conducted over the internet give rise to legal proceedings. Indeed, they give rise to the same variety of proceedings as business transactions conducted in a more traditional manner. These include not just actions in contract but also actions in tort, such as for infringement of intellectual property rights.[12] When it comes to the international sale of goods, a buyer may bring an action for breach of contract, or in tort for negligent misstatement,[13] against a seller who conducts business over the internet.[14] There are no territorial boundaries with the internet and so jurisdictional problems will frequently arise. When it comes to solving these problems, there is no special regime of jurisdictional rules on electronic commerce. It is a question of applying

---

[7] The internet is 'a giant network which interconnects innumerable smaller groups of linked computer networks. It is thus a network of networks', *American Civil Liberties Union v Reno* 929 F Supp 824, 830–845 (ED Pa 1996).

[8] See the discussion below, paras 10.173–187, of negligent misstatement and negligent and fraudulent misrepresentation over the internet.

[9] 80% of e-commerce is US generated, see the Opinion of the Economic and Social Committee of the European Parliament on the E-Commerce Directive [1999] OJ C169/14 of 15 April 1999.

[10] The statistics are taken from Hague Conference on Private International Law Prel Doc No 17 of February 2002, *The Impact of the Internet on the Judgments Project: Thoughts for the Future*, 4 (www.hcch.e-vision.nl/index_en.php?act=progress.listing&cat=4). See also the ABA Cyberspace Report, 1–4.

[11] Prel Doc No 17, n 10 above.

[12] A narrow definition in terms of contracts made or performed over the internet would exclude many torts that might arise from internet activity.

[13] This assumes that English law, or that of some other state that has this tort, governs the claim.

[14] See, e.g. *Armouth Intern Inc v Haband Co Inc* 715 NYS 2d 438 (NYAD 2000), discussed below, para 10.247; *Weinstein v Todd Marine Enterprises Inc* 115 F Supp 2d 668 (ED Va 2000), discussed below, para 10.247.

the familiar EC and traditional English rules on jurisdiction to cases of electronic commerce. This is not always easy because of certain important characteristics of electronic commerce. It is worth looking at these characteristics before examining the application of jurisdictional rules in cases of electronic commerce. Something also needs to be said about the substantive law background to electronic commerce.

II. CHARACTERISTICS OF ELECTRONIC COMMERCE

The characteristics of electronic commerce can be grouped together under **10.03** various headings: namely, territorial connections; carrying on business; the sales contract; and the underlying policy in this area.

1. TERRITORIAL CONNECTIONS

Territorial Boundaries and Connections

Both US courts[15] and commentators[16] refer to the lack of territorial bound- **10.04** aries with the internet. But how significant is this lack of physical boundaries? It can affect what the parties to the contract foresee.[17] 'Physical boundaries typically have framed legal boundaries, in effect creating signposts that warn that we will be required after crossing to abide by different rules.'[18] It can also make it difficult to localize the business transaction in any single state. As an American court has said: 'When business is transacted over a computer network via a website accessed by a computer in Massachusetts, it takes place as much in Massachusetts, literally or figuratively, as it does anywhere'.[19] However, the English jurisdictional rules are not concerned with foreseeability or with the location of the business transaction. Moreover, the internet is not the only method of communication that ignores boundaries; so does the telephone. Indeed, the internet utilizes telephone lines. The internet shares many characteristics with earlier technology such as satellite broadcasting.[20] Most

---

[15] *Digital Equipment Corp v Altavista Technology Inc* 960 F Supp 456 at 463 (US District Court, District of Massachusetts 1997).
[16] See, e.g. G Kalow, 'Note, From the Internet to Court: Exercising Jurisdiction over World Wide Web Communications' (1997) 65 Fordham L Rev 2241; W Brodsky, 'Surfin' the Stream of Commerce: *Compuserve v. Patterson*' (1997) 70 Temple L Rev 825; D Johnson and D Post, 'Law and Borders: The Rise of Law in Cyberspace' (1996) 48 Stanford L Rev 1367.
[17] See the ABA Cyberspace Report, 9–10.
[18] The *Digital Equipment* case, n 15 above, at 463.   [19] ibid, at 462.
[20] *Dow Jones & Company v Gutnick* (2002) 210 CLR 575, HC of Australia, para 125 (*per* Kirby J), HC of Australia. This case is discussed at length at paras 10.169 and 21.125–132.

importantly of all, although the internet, as a method of communication, ignores boundaries this does not mean that there are no territorial connections in internet transactions and disputes arising therefrom.[21]

10.05 With an internet transaction there will be a communication between a person resident in a state and another person resident in a state. In an international sale of goods case there will be a seller resident in one state and a buyer probably resident in another. The communication will involve the use of at least two computers. Normally, these will be located in states. The exception to this would be where there is a laptop being used on a plane in mid air or on a ship on the High Seas. A computer that is situated in a state will usually be located in the state where the user is resident, although it is always possible for a user to take a lap top abroad and communicate with this. In an international sale of goods contract, there will often be tangible goods which are located in one state and are delivered to another state.[22] There are no courts in cyberspace. In the event of a dispute arising and the plaintiff wishing to resolve this by litigation, rather than by some other method, he will seek trial before the courts of a particular state. The defendant may well prefer the trial to take place before the courts of some other state.

Problems of Identity and Location of the Parties

10.06 The buyer may not know the identity of the seller or where he is resident. There are electronic addresses but these do not necessarily signify a geographical connection.[23] For example, a person may have an electronic address with a service provider whose domain name comprises a national identifier, such as 'uk', without being a resident there.[24] A domain name may lack a national identifier.[25] However, there has been an attempt within the EC to address these problems. According to the EC Directive on electronic commerce, the seller is required to provide his name, geographic address, and details, including his email address which enable him to be to be contacted rapidly and communicated with in a direct and effective manner.[26] But if the buyer is contracting with, for example, a US company, the problem of identifying the seller and his location will remain.

---

[21] See generally, C Reed, *Internet Law: Text and Materials* (London: Butterworths, 2000), 7.1.1.

[22] For the position in relation to digitized products see below, paras 10.44–75.

[23] See the ABA Cyberspace Report, 31.

[24] See Prel Doc No 7, n 2 above 26.

[25] e.g. it may end with . com, . net or . org, see the Scots case of *Bonnier Media Ltd v Greg Lloyd Smith and Kestrel Trading Corp* 2003 SC 36, [2002] ETMR 86.

[26] Art 5(1) of the Directive on electronic commerce, discussed below, para 10.27.

Equally, the seller may not know the identity of the buyer or where he **10.07** is resident.[27] Visitors to a website reveal their internet provider address generally assigned to them by the Internet Service Provider (ISP). But some ISPs assign a new address every time a user logs on to the web.[28] This lack of identification of location can also happen where a software provider makes its products or services available to users through an Application Service Provider business model.[29] Under this model recipients could give one address as their billing address, but may access the software products or services from any location in the world in which they can get access to the internet. The EC Directive on electronic commerce does nothing to address this problem. A seller can always ask the buyer for information on its identity and location but there is nothing to stop the buyer lying about this.[30] Even having details of a recipient's credit card does not always determine where a person is located. For example, a US company may issue a credit card to an Australian.[31]

Problems of Identity and Location of Computers

The parties will not know the identity of all the computers used in a **10.08** communication over the internet. Communication over the internet at its simplest can involve two computers, albeit with mail servers forwarding the messages.[32] This is the scenario with electronic mail. Communication via the world wide web is more complex and can involve the parties sitting at their computers communicating via intermediate web-servers,[33] intermediate web-servers and networks, or a virtual market place server, which handle and process the messages.[34] In these scenarios, communication is indirect with servers relaying information in the same way as post offices relay mail.

More importantly, it is not uncommon for users of electronic commerce to **10.09** communicate from one state to another without knowing the location

[27] See the *Dow Jones* case, n 20 above, para 169 (*per* Callinan J). In this case, the internet company admitted that it could not identify the addresses of all its subscribers.

[28] See the *Dow Jones* case, n 20 above, para 84 (*per* Kirby J).

[29] See Prel Doc No 17, n 10 above 7, 17.

[30] See *CompuServe Inc v Cyber Promotions Inc* 962 F Supp 1015 (SD Ohio 1997)—defendant falsified the point of origin information on its email and configured its network servers to conceal its internet domain name.

[31] See the *Dow Jones* case, n 20 above, para 85 (*per* Kirby J).

[32] See L Davies, 'Contract Formation on the Internet: Shattering a few myths', Ch 6 in L Edwards and C Waelde (eds), *Law and the Internet: Regulating Cyberspace* (Oxford: Hart, 1997) 106.

[33] A server is a computer which runs programs to provide services or serve up data on request, ibid, at 101–102.

[34] ibid, at 110. The parties may use a common server, such as where they use a single onLine service provider's system, ibid, at 107.

of information systems through which communication is operated.[35] The location of certain information systems may change without either of the parties being aware of the change.[36] The person sending the message and the person receiving it are unlikely to know where any intermediate servers are located. Nor will the sender necessarily know the location of the computer where a message is ultimately received. If information is downloaded on to a lap top it will be impossible for the person sending the message to know whether this has happened, let alone where this has happened. A domain name is not a reliable indicator of where a computer is located because the computer may be physically moved without any change in domain name.[37] Nor will the receiver of the message necessarily know where the computer from which it originated is located. A provider of digitized products may set up a number of mirror sites to speed up the transfer of information. If the provider chooses the site from which the information is to be sent to this particular recipient, the latter is unlikely to know where this site is located.

Location of Computers and Location of the Parties

10.10 Computers are not necessarily located in the same state as that where parties are resident or the place where their business is located. Thus a company may be domiciled in State A, carry on its activities in relation to its internet business, such as writing and editing information and billing recipients, in State B, and place information which is to be available to recipients on a web-server in State C.[38] There may also be intermediate servers that relay the information to recipients. These are unlikely to be situated in the state where the parties are located. Even when it comes to the computer where the data message is received or from which it is retrieved, often this is located in a jurisdiction other than that in which the addressee itself is located.[39] For example, the message may be received on a lap top computer which is being used abroad on a business trip. The recipient may be a mobile internet user (m-commerce). Similarly, when it comes to the computer from which the data message originates, a seller may lease an internet website on a server in another state from that where he is resident or has established his business. If a company which

---

[35] UNCITRAL Model Law on Electronic Commerce 1996, Guide to Enactment, para 100.

[36] ibid.

[37] M Berliri, 'Jurisdiction and the Internet, and European Regulation 44 of 2001' in D Campbell and S Woodley (eds), *E-Commerce: Law and Jurisdiction: The Comparative Law Year-book of International Business—Special Issue 2002* (Aspen, 2002) 1, 2.

[38] See the facts of *Dow Jones & Company v Gutnick* (2002) 210 CLR 575, HC of Australia; discussed below, para 10.169.

[39] See the UNCITRAL Model Law on Electronic Commerce 1996, Guide to Enactment, para 100.

transacts business over the internet sets up mirror sites in order to speed up the transfer of information, then all but one of these, or indeed all of these, will be located in a state other than the one in which the company is located.

Problems in Locating the Place where Events Take Place

Bases of jurisdiction that are specific to certain matters or causes of action **10.11** typically require the court to identify the place where something has happened, for example the place where the contract was made, where it was to be performed, where it was breached, the place where the tortious act giving rise to the damage occurred, or the place where the damage occurred. Identification of this place can be problematic in non-internet cases but this is exacerbated with internet cases. Doing business and communicating over the internet involve a complicated sequence of events, which can be spread across numerous states. As a result, it can be difficult to pinpoint the precise place where something has happened.

2. CARRYING ON BUSINESS

We are concerned here with characteristics that relate to electronic com- **10.12** merce as a method of carrying on business.

A Wide Variety of Different Business Activities

Conducting business over the internet can take a wide variety of different **10.13** forms. A person or company may create its own website. This in turn can take more than one form. It may be an inter-active website, ie one where a user can exchange information with the host computer.[40] Any contract will be concluded via that website. The level of interactivity and the commercial nature of the exchange of information that occurs on an inter-active website can vary considerably. This is hardly surprising since a website is custom-made for a business. For example, shopping online may take the form not only of contracting via the internet but also of providing information about a product, including its price, and allowing an order form to be printed from the site, a facility for recipients to check the status of their purchases and a possibility of communicating directly with online sales staff to facilitate purchasing via email.[41] Alternatively, it

---

[40] *Zippo Manufacturing Company v Zippo Dot Com Inc* 952 F Supp 1119 at 1124 (US District Court, WD Pennsylvania 1997).
[41] *Mienczkowski v Masco Corp* 997 F Supp 782 (US District Court, ED Texas 1998).

may be a passive website, i.e. one where information is simply posted on a website which is accessible to users.[42] The contract is not made online. The website may be being used as a form of advertising and to that extent what is happening is essentially no different from a company placing an advert in a newspaper or magazine or on the television. However, a passive website may involve more than mere advertising. A home page may, for example, provide a free phone number for recipients to ring.[43] Business can also be regarded as being conducted over the internet if someone else's website is used, as where a person uses an internet auction site or an internet advertising service. That person can be said to conduct business over the internet. In so far as jurisdiction is based on the defendant's activities in a particular state, as happens under US law, but only to a very limited extent under EC law, it becomes relevant to look at the nature of the internet business activity.

Unlimited Access

10.14 The internet 'enables anyone with the right equipment and knowledge . . . to operate an international business cheaply, and from a desktop'.[44] This means that it is easy to operate as an internet company with the result that a lot of the businesses that transact business in this way are small and medium sized enterprises. The internet gives the internet company unlimited access to the entire planet. There is unlimited access too for recipients. 'Anyone with a personal computer, a telephone modem, and appropriate computer software may gain access to the Internet.'[45] This is what is peculiar about this method of carrying on business.[46] All of this explains the tremendous growth in electronic commerce but also leads to the problems, addressed above, of identity and location.

Targeting the World

10.15 Unlike other more traditional forms of advertising and solicitations, such as those in newspapers, mail shots, radio and television, advertisements and solicitations on the internet are not normally directed[47] to a

---

[42] The *Zippo* case, n 40 above, at 1124.

[43] See, e.g. *Heroes Inc v Heroes Foundation* 958 F Supp 1 (US District Court, District of Columbia 1996).

[44] *CompuServe v Patterson* 89 F 3d 1257 at 1262 (6th Cir 1996).

[45] The *Heroes* case, n 43 above, at 4.

[46] See the Opinion of the Economic and Social Committee on the proposed Brussels I Regulation [2000] OJ C117/6, 4.2.2.

[47] The concept of directing activities is important for the definition of consumer contracts for the purposes of Section 4 of the Brussels I Regulation, Art 15(1)(c).

specific geographical area.[48] Nor are they directed to specific people or groups of people. Everyone with internet access is targeted.[49] Anyone who operates a business over the internet can foresee that it can be accessed[50] by anyone with the right equipment without geographic restriction.[51]

It has to be stressed that 'normally' the world is targeted. There are excep- **10.16** tions. The owner of a website can include a disclaimer that it will not sell its products outside a certain geographic area or will not sell in a certain specified state or states.[52] However, problems of identity and location of the buyer mean that this is not a guaranteed method of ensuring no sales take place in such areas or states.[53] If you ask a buyer where he comes from there is nothing to stop him lying.[54] There are also anonymizing techniques that enable recipients to mask their identity and location.[55] A disclaimer is a negative technique, attempting to restrict sales geographically. More positively, it is possible to target certain areas or states. A website may say that sales will only be made to recipients in England. There can also be implicit targeting. Thus if a website is in German it is German speaking states that are targeted and, arguably, individuals in other states that can speak German.[56] However, if a website is in English, this is such a commonly spoken language around the world, particularly in the business context, that this should not be regarded as a form of implicit targeting.

---

[48] *Millennium Enterprises Inc v Millenium Music* 33 F Supp 2d 907 at 914 (D Or 1999). Moreover a website is a permanent form of advertisement whereas any advert in a newspaper, magazine or on the television is temporary. Newspapers and magazines are discarded and an advert on the television is by its nature transient, see *Inset Systems Inc v Instruction Set* 937 F Supp 161 (D Conn 1996).

[49] See generally on targeting, the ABA Cyberspace Report, 30–32.

[50] With a membership site full access is denied to those without a user name and password.

[51] See the *Dow Jones* case, n 38 above, para 39; *Re The Maritim Trademark* (Case 416 0294/00) [2003] IL Pr 17, Landgericht (District Court), Hamburg.

[52] In *Re The Maritim Trademark*, n 51 above, the use of a national top level domain, i.e. '.dk' was said to lead the consumer to presume information content was tailored in content and language to that particular country.

[53] See Prel Doc No 17, n 10 above, 9, n 22; the *Dow Jones* case, n 38 above, paras 84–87 (*per* Kirby J).

[54] See the ABA Cyberspace Report, 153.

[55] The *Dow Jones* case, n 38 above, para 86 (*per* Kirby J).

[56] See the ABA Cyberspace Report, 30. But see the joint declaration issued by the European Parliament and Commission in relation to the consumer provisions under the Brussels I Regulation that the language or currency which a website uses does not constitute a relevant factor when working out if an internet seller is soliciting custom abroad. See also *Re The Maritim Trademark*, n 51 above, where use of German language by a Danish company was not regarded as targeting Germany.

Two Active Parties

10.17 Other forms of communication typically involve an active party and a passive party, a sender and a receiver of information. With the internet it is different. It often involves two active parties, a poster of information and a retriever.[57] For example, there is a seller who creates an interactive website and a buyer who accesses that website and places an order over the internet. Of course, there may still be an active seller and a relatively passive buyer but equally there can be an active buyer and a relatively passive seller, for example one who creates a passive website.[58]

3. The Contract

10.18 We are concerned here with characteristics that relate to the contract that is made in cases of electronic commerce.

Contracts Made via the Internet

10.19 Sales contracts can be negotiated and concluded via an interactive website. However, it is many years since contracts were routinely made at face to face meetings. Nowadays a contract can equally be made over the telephone, although this does not provide a record in the way that a contract made over the internet does; or it can be made by fax, which does provide a written record.

Performance Over the Internet

10.20 It is possible to purchase digitized products such as software, music and even statistical information and books, over the internet, including by email. The 'delivery' of such products may also take place via the internet.[59] Information is transferred from one computer to another with the information being downloaded on to the recipient's computer.[60] In such cases, there are conceptual problems over whether the contract is for the sale of goods, the provision of services or neither[61] and in locating the place where electronic performance takes place.[62] There are also practical problems. If the provider of the information sets up mirror sites

---

[57] See the *Bonnier Media* case, n 25 above, at [18].
[58] See the ABA Cyberspace Report, 34.
[59] It is possible to buy software and other digitized products which are contained on a disk and are delivered by post.
[60] The information may be uploaded on a web-server by the service provider and accessed by the recipient or may be sent by the service provider to the recipient as an email attachment.
[61] See below, paras 10.42–50.
[62] See below, paras 10.54–75. See also Prel Doc No 17, n 10 above, 7, n 17.

and chooses which one to send the information from to this particular recipient, it is impossible for the recipient to influence the choice of site from which the information is sent. Moreover, the recipient will not know the location of this place. Equally, it is impossible for the provider of the information to restrict where the information ends up being downloaded by the recipient on to the hard disk of his computer. For example, he could download it on to a lap top in any state he chooses to take the lap top. The provider of the information will not know where this place is. This difficulty is unique to electronic commerce.

Digitized Products as Intangible Property

If a digitized product, such as software, takes the form of a disk packaged **10.21** in a box this is tangible goods,[63] which may be bought via the internet but would have to be delivered by traditional means, such as by post. However, when the digitized product takes the form of information which is transferred over the internet, it is difficult, if not impossible, to identify anything that is tangible and the product is best regarded as being intangible property.[64]

4. THE UNDERLYING POLICY

We are concerned here with the final characteristic (of those listed above) **10.22** of electronic commerce, namely that underlying the substantive law of electronic commerce there is a policy of promoting business over the internet.

The Policy of Promoting E-Commerce

There is within the EC a policy of promoting business over the internet.[65] **10.23** The development of electronic commerce 'offers significant employment

---

[63] Software on a disk is goods for the purposes of the Vienna Convention, see the discussion below para 10.47.

[64] See Prel Doc No 7, n 2 above, 19, n 51. This is the position under English law, see *St Alban's City and District Council v International Computers Ltd* [1997] FSR 251, 265 (*per* Sir Iain Glidewell), CA. See, in relation to the US, RT Nimmer, 'Through the looking glass: What courts and UCITA say about the scope of contract law in the information age' (2000) 38 Duquesne L Rev 255. A number of states in the US regard software as tangible personal property, see S Bagert, 'South Central Bell v. Barthelemy: The Louisiana Supreme Court determines that computer software is tangible personal property' (1995) 69 Tulane L Rev 1367. There is a separate question of whether software transferred over the internet is 'goods' for the purposes of the Vienna Convention. This raises the question of whether intangible property is goods for this purpose, see the discussion below, para 10.47. Often software will be transferred under a licensing agreement under which ownership will not pass to the customer, see below, para 10.45.

[65] See the discussion of the Directive on electronic commerce, below, paras 10.24–33.

opportunities in the Community, particularly in small and medium sized enterprises, and will stimulate economic growth and investment in innovation by European companies, and can also enhance the competitiveness of European industry, provided that everyone has access to the Internet'.[66] The same policy is evident in individual Member States and in States outside the EC, such as the United States, Australia and Japan.[67] Jurisdiction rules have their part to play in achieving this objective. On the one hand, a company which wishes to conduct business over the internet, particularly a small or medium sized business, may be discouraged if, by virtue of doing so, it now finds itself becoming subject to jurisdiction abroad.[68] An excessively wide jurisdiction 'raises the possibility of dramatically chilling what may well be the most participatory marketplace of mass speech that . . . the world . . . has yet seen'.[69] On the other hand, recipients may be deterred from purchasing goods over the internet if it means that they have to sue the defendant in its home state.

III. THE SUBSTANTIVE LAW BACKGROUND

10.24 Electronic commerce has its own well developed substantive law background. In the EC this is contained principally in the EC Directive on Electronic Commerce.[70] At the world wide level, there is the UNCITRAL Model Law on Electronic Commerce of 1996.

1. The EC Directive on Electronic Commerce and its Implementation in the United Kingdom

10.25 Recital (1) of the EC Directive on Electronic Commerce states that the development of information society services within the EC is 'vital to eliminating the barriers which divide the European peoples'. However, this is hampered by legal obstacles arising from divergences in legislation and from legal uncertainty as to which national rules apply to such services.[71] The objective of the Directive is to create a legal framework

---

[66] Recital (2).   [67] See Prel Doc No 17, n 10 above, 5, n 9.
[68] *Millennium Enterprises Inc v Millennium Music* 33 F Supp 2d 907 (D Or 1999).
[69] *Digital Equipment Corp v Altavista Technology Inc* 960 F Supp 456, 463 (US District Court, District of Massachusetts 1997).
[70] Directive 2000/31/EC, n 1 above. There is also Directive 1999/93/EC on a Community framework for electronic signatures [2000] OJ L13/12, discussed below, para 21.104, and Directive 2000/46/EC of the European Parliament and of the Council of 18 September 2000 on the taking up, pursuit of and prudential supervision of the business of electronic money institutions [Electronic Cash Directive] [2000] OJ L275/39. See on the E-Commerce Directive and choice of law, and on electronic signatures, below, paras 21.08–34 and 21.105–107.
[71] Recital (5).

to ensure the free movement of information society services between Member States,[72] and to ensure legal certainty and consumer confidence.[73] It aims also to foster economic growth by European companies.[74] This legal framework contains provisions dealing with: the internal market;[75] establishment and information requirements;[76] commercial communications;[77] contracts concluded by electronic means;[78] and the liability of intermediary service providers.[79] Most of these provisions have been implemented in the United Kingdom by the Electronic Commerce (EC Directive) Regulations 2002.[80] These Regulations will now be examined.

Internal Market

Regulation 4 provides that the requirements[81] under the Regulations **10.26** apply to the provision of an information society service by a service provider established in the United Kingdom, irrespective of whether that information society service is provided in the United Kingdom or another Member State.[82] This implements that part of the Directive which provides that each Member State shall ensure that a service provider established on its territory must comply with the national laws of that State.[83] Moreover, according to the Directive, Member States may not restrict the freedom to provide information society services from another Member State.[84] What all of this means is that a service provider must comply with the laws of the Member State in which it is established, not with the laws of the other Member States. The philosophy underlying this is that, in order to ensure an effective protection of public interest objectives, information society services should be supervised at the source of the activity. Therefore the responsibility for supervision is placed on the Member State where the services originate.[85]

General Information to be Provided

Regulation 6(1)[86] provides that a person providing an information society **10.27** service, and this includes selling goods online,[87] must make available to the recipient of the service in a form and manner which is easily, directly and permanently accessible, inter alia, the following information: the name of the service provider; the geographic address at which the service

---

[72] Art (8). [73] Recital (7). [74] Recital (2). [75] Art 3. [76] Section 1.
[77] Section 2. [78] Section 3. [79] Section 4. [80] SI 2002/2013.
[81] The requirements must fall within the co-ordinated field, as defined under reg 2(1).
[82] This implements Art 3 of the Directive. For derogations see Art 5.
[83] Art 3 of the Directive. [84] For implementation in the UK see reg 4(3).
[85] Recital (22) of the Directive.
[86] Implementing Art 5(1) of the Directive. [87] Recital (18).

provider is established; the details of the service provider, including his electronic mail address; and details in any trade register. Prices must be indicated clearly and unambiguously and, in particular, must indicate whether they are inclusive of tax and delivery costs.[88]

Commercial Communications

10.28 A service provider must ensure that any commercial communication provided by him and which constitutes or forms part of an information society service must: be clearly identifiable as a commercial communication; and clearly identify the person on whose behalf the commercial communication is made; and clearly identify as such any promotional offer and any promotional competition or game.[89] A service provider must also ensure that any unsolicited commercial communication sent by him by electronic mail is clearly and unambiguously identifiable as such as soon as it is received.[90]

Information to be Provided where Contracts are Concluded by Electronic Means

10.29 Unless parties who are not consumers have agreed otherwise, where a contract is to be concluded by electronic means a service provider shall, prior to an order being placed by the recipient of a service, provide to that recipient in a clear, comprehensible and unambiguous manner the following information: the different technical steps to follow to conclude the contract; whether or not the concluded contract will be filed by the service provider and whether it will be accessible; the technical means for identifying and correcting input errors prior to the placing of the order; and the languages offered for the conclusion of the contract.[91] These requirements do not apply to contracts concluded exclusively by exchange of electronic mail.[92]

Placing of the Order

10.30 Unless parties who are not consumers have agreed otherwise, where the recipient of the service places his order through technological means, a service provider must acknowledge receipt of the order to the recipient of

[88] reg 6(2), implementing Art 5(2) of the Directive.
[89] reg 7, implementing Art 6 of the Directive.
[90] reg 8, implementing Art 7 of the Directive.
[91] reg 9, implementing Art 10 of the Directive.
[92] reg 9(4), implementing Art 10(4) of the Directive.

the service without undue delay[93] and by electronic means;[94] and make available to the recipient of the service appropriate, effective and accessible technical means allowing him to identify and correct input errors prior to the placing of the order.[95] Where the service provider has not made available such means the recipient is entitled to rescind the contract unless any court having jurisdiction in relation to the contract in question orders otherwise on the application of the service provider.[96] These requirements do not apply to contracts concluded exclusively by exchange of electronic mail.[97]

Liability of the Service Provider

The duties imposed on the service provider[98] by the Regulations are **10.31** enforceable, at the suit of any recipient of a service, by an action against the service provider for damages for breach of statutory duty.[99]

Liability of Intermediary Service Providers

A defence is created for intermediary service providers from any liability **10.32** incurred from the activities of mere conduits, 'caching'[100] and 'hosting'[101] in the circumstances set out in the Regulations.[102]

No Rules on Private International Law

It is also important to look at what the Directive and the UK Regulations **10.33** do not deal with. Very importantly for the purpose of this chapter, the Directive expressly provides that it does not establish additional rules on private international law nor does it deal with the jurisdiction of courts.[103]

---

[93] This phrase will presumably have an autonomous meaning.

[94] The order and the acknowledgement of receipt will be deemed to be received when the parties to whom they are addressed are able to access them, reg 11(2)(a). For the meaning of 'order' see reg 12.

[95] reg 11, implementing Art 11 of the Directive.

[96] reg 15; This is discussed further below, paras 21.91–92.

[97] reg 11(3).   [98] By regs 6, 7, 8, 9(1) and 11(1)(a).   [99] reg 13.

[100] 'Caching', according to Art 13, is: 'Where an information society service is provided that consists of the transmission in a communication network of information provided by a recipient of the service . . .'.

[101] 'Hosting', according to Art 14, is: 'Where an information society service is provided that consists of the storage of information provided by a recipient of the service . . .'.

[102] regs 17–19, implementing Arts 12–14 of the Directive. These Regulations do not prevent someone from agreeing different contractual terms, Art 20.

[103] Art 1(4) and Recital 23.

The Regulations have no such provisions.[104] However, the Directive requests Member States to ensure that appropriate court actions are available and should examine the need to provide access to judicial procedures by appropriate electronic means.[105]

2. THE UNCITRAL MODEL LAW ON ELECTRONIC COMMERCE OF 1996

10.34 The Model Law applies to any kind of information in the form of a data message used in the context of commercial activities.[106] It sets out a framework law to be supplemented by technical regulations in the implementing state. A 'functional-equivalent' approach is adopted.[107] This is based on the analysis of the purposes and functions of traditional paper-based requirements with a view to seeing how those purposes and functions could be fulfilled through electronic-commerce techniques.[108] For example, Article 6 provides that where the law requires information to be in writing, that requirement is met by a data message if the information contained therein is accessible so as to be usable for subsequent reference.[109] Where the law requires a signature of a person, the Model Law explains how that requirement is met by a data message.[110] The same applies where the law requires information to be presented or retained in its original form[111] and where it requires that certain documents, records or information be retained.[112] The Model Law also sets out default rules which may be used by the parties as a basis for concluding agreements and to fill in gaps in agreements.[113] These default rules may also be regarded as setting a basic standard for situations where data messages are exchanged without a previous agreement being entered into by the communicating parties. These rules deal with such matters as: formation and validity of contracts;[114] recognition by parties of data messages;[115] attribution of data messages;[116] acknowledgement of receipt;[117] and time and place of dispatch and receipt of data messages.[118] A number of states have adopted legislation modelled on the Model Law[119] and many other

---

[104] This was deliberately omitted as being inconsistent with regulation by the country of origin, see the discussion below, para 21.17. But for the relationship between the internal market provisions in Art 4 of the Regs and choice of law rules see reg 4(4) and the Schedule to the Regulations. For discussion of the implications of the Directive and Regulations as regards the applicable law in e-commerce cases see below, para 21.34.

[105] Recital 52.   [106] Art 1.

[107] See the accompanying Guide to Enactment, paras 15–18.   [108] ibid, para 16.

[109] Formalities for the conclusion of a contract by electronic means and the E-Commerce Directive are discussed below, paras 21.105–107.

[110] Art 7. The EC Directive on a Community Framework for Electronic Signatures is discussed below, para 21.104.

[111] Art 8.   [112] Art 10.   [113] Guide to Enactment, para 19.
[114] Art 11.   [115] Art 12.   [116] Art 13.   [117] Art 14.   [118] Art 15.
[119] See the UNCITRAL website (www.uncitral.org).

states have made use of the Model Law in legislation that has already been adopted or is in drafts under preparation.[120]

IV. BUSINESS-TO-BUSINESS E-COMMERCE: CONTRACT CLAIMS

When examining bases of jurisdiction and how they operate in cases of **10.35** electronic commerce it is important to distinguish between business-to-consumer e-commerce and business-to-business e-commerce. Consumer contracts[121] fall outside the scope of this book and so we are concerned only with business-to-business e-commerce, that is with business contracts[122] arising from the transaction of business over the internet. Arising from this there can be an action in contract between the parties to this contract.

1. THE EC RULES

The Brussels I Regulation contains only one provision that explicitly **10.36** acknowledges the advent of electronic commerce. This is Article 23(2), which is concerned with the requirement as to form where there is a choice of jurisdiction agreement. The Regulation also contains one other provision whose wording has been influenced by electronic commerce concerns, namely Article 15(1)(c) which is concerned with the definition of a consumer contract.[123] However, there are problems that arise with

---

[120] ibid. These include Australia and Canada. See also the Uniform Electronic Transactions Act prepared in the US by the United States National Conference of Commissioners on Uniform State Law.

[121] For the definition of a consumer contract under the Brussels I Regulation, see above, para 3.19. For discussion generally of jurisdiction in relation to consumer contracts, see Briggs and Rees, 2.73–2.78; Dicey and Morris, 370–374. For discussion more specifically on jurisdiction, e-commerce and consumers see J Oren, 'International Jurisdiction over Consumer Contracts in E-Europe' (2003) 52 ICLQ 665.

[122] This can be defined as a contract concluded by persons for a purpose within their trade or profession. This definition is based on the definition of a consumer contract under the Brussels I Regulation. Art 15(1) defines this in terms of 'a contract concluded by a person, the consumer, for a purpose which can be regarded as being outside his trade or profession'.

[123] Art 15(1) (c) covers cases where 'the contract has been concluded with a person who pursues commercial or professional activities in the Member State of the consumer's domicile or, *by any means, directs such activities* to that Member State or to several States including that Member State, and the contract falls within the scope of such activities' (emphasis added). This new wording is designed to make clear that point (c) applies to consumer contracts concluded via an interactive website accessible in the state of the consumer's domicile, see the Explanatory Memorandum in the Proposal for a Council Regulation COM (1999) 348 final, 16. Where a consumer simply had knowledge of a service or possibility of buying goods via a passive website accessible in his country of domicile the intention is that this will not trigger the protective jurisdiction for consumers, ibid.

many of the bases of jurisdiction in the Regulation when these are applied in cases of electronic commerce.

Article 23

10.37 Article 23(2) provides that: 'Any communication by electronic means which provides a durable record of the agreement shall be equivalent to "writing" '.[124] Thus, if a contract is made by emails which are saved on a computer, this can be regarded as being a contract in writing for the purposes of Article 23. If a contract is made online there will be a durable record if a copy of the agreement is printed off. But what if it is not? If the agreement is saved on the seller's or buyer's computer, this should be regarded as being a durable record.

10.38 Article 23(2) means that it cannot be argued that, as a matter of principle, an agreement on jurisdiction contained in an online contract cannot satisfy Article 23. However, as with an agreement in a more conventional form, questions may be raised if the writing is so small or illegible that the agreement goes unnoticed. This is a perfectly legitimate argument to make and can mean that the writing requirement under Article 23 is not met.[125] What is not legitimate is to argue that notice of the clause was obscured by virtue of its electronic format, in that only one page of the contract can be seen on the screen at any one time and to read it all requires scrolling down the document.[126] After all, a conventional written contract may be several pages long and these pages will need turning. To accept this argument would effectively mean that agreements on jurisdiction contained in an online contract would always fall outside the requirement as to writing under Article 23, when Article 23(2) makes it clear that this should not happen. This argument was raised before an Ontario court[127] in the context of whether that court had jurisdiction in the face of an agreement in an online contract providing for jurisdiction in Washington. The argument was rejected because it would 'move this type of electronic transaction into the realm of commercial absurdity. It would lead to chaos in the marketplace, render ineffectual electronic commerce

---

[124] Compare the wording in Art 6 of the UNCITRAL Model Law on Electronic Commerce of 1996 which provides that: 'Where the law requires information to be in writing, that requirement is met by a data message if the information contained therein is accessible so as to be usable for subsequent reference'. This inspired Art 4(2)(b) of the Hague draft Judgments Convention of 30 October 1999.

[125] See generally on this requirement, Cheshire and North, 241–242. This requirement of form is discussed above, para 3.22.

[126] See also the discussion on consent to a choice of law clause below, paras 21.36–39.

[127] *Rudder v Microsoft Corp* 1999 Carswell Ont 3195, Ontario Superior Court of Justice.

and undermine the integrity of any agreement entered into through this medium.'[128]

Apart from this requirement as to form, there appear to be no special **10.39** difficulties in satisfying the requirements of a jurisdiction agreement under Article 23 in the case of contracts concluded over the internet.[129] The process of inserting a choice of jurisdiction agreement into such a contract is not hard. For example, an owner of a website can set up an interactive 'clickwrap agreement'.[130] This requires a recipient to assent to the terms of the contract by clicking on an acceptance button on the website. If the recipient does not do this, the website will not accept the recipient's order. Such agreements are common on websites that sell or distribute software programs that the recipient downloads from the web-site. One of the terms that the website owner can insert into the agreement is a choice of jurisdiction clause.

Article 2

With contracts made over the internet there are the twin practical prob- **10.40** lems of identification and location of the parties.[131] Even if the plaintiff can identify and locate the party that it wishes to sue, it may be impossible to work out where that party is domiciled. The plaintiff seller may have no address for the defendant buyer. With a corporate defendant, even if the plaintiff finds an address for an e-commerce company, corporate decisions may be made following discussion over the internet between senior officers who reside in different states, rather than by face to face meetings. It is therefore very difficult to ascertain where the central administration[132] of the company is located.[133] Likewise, the way in which an internet company can carry on its business by locating its domicile,

---

[128] ibid, para 16.

[129] This was the view of the experts on jurisdiction and e-commerce at the Hague Conference on private international law when discussing a similarly worded provision, see the expert meeting on Electronic Commerce and International Jurisdiction organized by the Hague Conference on Private International Law held in Ottawa from 28 February to 1 March 2000, Summary of Discussions at 4. This was also the conclusion reached by the experts at the earlier Geneva Round Table (see the Report of Commission III set out in Prel Doc No 7, n 2 above, 22–23).

[130] *Stomp Inc v NeatO* 61 F Supp 2d 1074 at 1080–1081 (CD Cal 1999).

[131] See the expert meeting at Ottawa, n 129 above, at 5–6. See also the Geneva Round Table, Commission I, Prel Doc No 7, n 2 above, 19. These problems are discussed above, paras 10.06–07.

[132] For the purpose of Art 60(1)(b) of the Brussels I Regulation.

[133] The Report of the Special Commission on the future Hague Judgments Convention drawn up by Nygh and Pocar, Prel Doc No 11.

office and web-server in different states makes it difficult to ascertain where the principal place of business of the company is located.[134]

Article 5(1)

10.41 There are two problems in applying Article 5(1) in cases of business-to-business e-commerce.[135] First, is there a contract for the sale of goods, the provision of services or neither? Second, where is the place of performance of the obligation in question? The answer to this second question depends on the answer to the first question. If it is a contract for the sale of goods or the provision of services, Article 5(1)(b) will apply.[136] If it is neither, Article 5(1)(a) will apply and it is necessary to determine the place of performance of the obligation in question.[137]

Is there a contract for the sale of goods, the provision of services or neither?

10.42 In answering this question, it is important to distinguish three different scenarios. The first is where there is physical delivery, such as by post or by carriage by sea and land, of tangible goods. The second is where there is performance over the internet, i.e. transfer of a digitized product (an intangible) over the internet. There is then a third scenario which must be examined, namely where software is purchased from, and installed by, the service provider.

10.43 **Physical delivery**   We are concerned here with tangible goods, such as a computer, a computer chip, or software on a disk, that have been purchased and are delivered in a conventional way. This is a contract for the sale of goods.[138]

10.44 **Performance over the internet**   We are concerned here with the situation where not only has the contract been made over the internet but also it is to be performed over the internet. For example, a recipient buys a digitized product, such as a software program, or takes out a subscription to an online journal. Information is then transferred over the internet. In such cases, the question of whether the contract is for the sale of goods, the provision of services or neither is particularly difficult to answer. It is important to look separately at contracts, on the one hand, for the

---

[134] For the purpose of Art 60(1)(c) of the Brussels I Regulation.

[135] See generally on this topic, C Gringras, *The Law of the Internet*, (2nd edn, London: Butterworths, 2003) 51–52.

[136] See generally above, para 3.143.   [137] See generally above, para 3.236.

[138] Appellate Court (Oberlandesgericht) Koblenz of 17 September 1993 (translated at http://cisg3.law.pace.edu/cases/930917gi.html)—sale of a computer chip goods under the Vienna Convention. Software on a disk is regarded as goods for the purposes of the UCC in the US, see *Advent Systems Ltd v Unisys Corp* 925 F 2d 670 (1991 Pa). For criticism of the latter see Nimmer, n 64 above.

purchase of digitized products, such as software, and, on the other hand, for the provision of online services. But before doing so, a few words must be said about licensing agreements.

Licensing agreements   Contracts for the supply of computer software at **10.45** the business to business level often take the form of a licensing agreement[139] with ownership remaining with the licensor, rather than a sale to the recipient.[140] What the recipient is paying for is the right to use the information that constitutes the software.[141] Unless a licensing agreement can be classified as a contract for the sale of goods or as one for the provision of services, Article 5(1)(a) of the Brussels I Regulation will apply and it is necessary to identify the place of performance of the obligation in question.[142] It has been argued in Chapter 3 that the Vienna Convention definition of sale of goods should be adopted for the purpose of interpretation of sale of goods under Article 5(1)(b) of the Brussels I Regulation. Although the position is not clear, it is arguable that a licensing agreement (whether or not a disk is transferred), under which, of course, ownership does not pass, falls outside the concept of sale of goods under the Vienna Convention.[143] This is because Article 30 of the Vienna Convention requires the seller to transfer its property in the goods 'as' (not 'if') required by the contract and the Convention. It has been suggested earlier that the concept of the provision of services should be widely defined.[144] However, it would be surprising if a licensing agreement fell within even a wide definition of this concept. The provision of services connotes some sort of continuing activity by the person providing the service. With a licensing agreement there is merely a one off act by the grantor of the licence of entering into the agreement. It is submitted therefore that a licensing agreement should not be regarded as the provision of services.

Contracts for the purchase of software and other digitized products   What we **10.46** are concerned with here are those perhaps less common cases where

---

[139] See generally Gringras, n 135 above, 45–47. The nature of a licensing agreement is discussed in Fawcett and Torremans, 74.

[140] The *St Alban's* case, n 64 above; *Unisys Canada Inc v Imperial Optical Co* 44 BLR (2d) 311, aff'd 2 BLR (3d) 172, Ont CA. See generally Nimmer, n 64 above.

[141] Fawcett and Torremans, 74, state that: 'A licence contract is essentially a contract that grants the licensee the right to do something that would normally amount to an infringement of the intellectual property right'.

[142] See generally on Art 5(1)(a), above, paras 3.236–246. See specifically on the identification of the place of performance of the obligation in question for licensing agreements, Fawcett and Torremans, 79–81.

[143] See below, para 16.86.

[144] See generally the discussion above, para 3.300. The draft Council Directive on the liability of suppliers of services COM (90) 482 final-SYN 308 excludes from its definition of services any transaction which has as its direct and exclusive object the transfer of intellectual property rights. This would clearly exclude an assignment of an intellectual property right.

computer software or some other intangible product is 'purchased', i.e. the ownership is intended to pass. For example, a bank wants the security of owning the software rather than having a licence for a fixed period.[145] This could involve the purchase of standard software or the purchase of individual software developed for that particular customer. Is this a contract for the sale of goods, the provision of services, or neither? Each of these possibilities will now be examined.

10.47 SALE OF GOODS? Although there appears to be a sale, is what is being sold 'goods'? The recipient is not buying tangible property. What he is buying is an intangible product, namely information.[146] Nonetheless, German and Swiss courts, without drawing a distinction between the direct downloading of software and its transfer in the medium of a disk, have treated the sale of software as a sale of goods for the purposes of the Vienna Convention.[147] Thus, a standard computer software programme that has been delivered and installed by the supplier has been held by the District Court of Munich to constitute goods under the Vienna Convention,[148] which would suggest that the same programme transferred over the internet would be regarded in the same way. This fits in with the view that the Vienna Convention extends to intangible property, provided that it is movable.[149] There is also academic authority it favour of the proposition that software transferred online is goods for the purposes of the Vienna Convention.[150] In contrast, the English Court of Appeal has held that a computer program, as opposed to a disk containing such a program, does not constitute goods for the purposes of the Sale of Goods Act 1979.[151] However, the definition adopted by the English courts cannot be regarded as being decisive on this matter. It has been argued in Chapter 3 that the Vienna Convention definition of sale of goods should be adopted for the purpose of interpretation of sale of goods under Article 5(1)(b) of the Brussels I Regulation. It follows that the purchase of software or other digitized products transferred over the internet should be

---

[145] An English bank may buy software developed for England. The service provider may sell a modified version of the same software to a French bank for use in France.

[146] See the expert meeting at Ottawa, n 129 above, at 5.

[147] Oberlandesgericht, Koblenz, of 17 September 1993 (translated at http://cisg3.law.-pace.edu/cases/930917gi.html); Landgericht Munich of 8 February 1995 (translated at http://cisg3.law.pace.edu/cases/950208g4.html); the Commercial Court (Handelsgericht) of the Canton of Zurich of 17 February 2000 (translated at http://cisg3.law.pace.edu/cases/000217sl.html). Software is goods for the purposes of the Uniform Commercial Code, see *Advent Systems Ltd v Unisys Corp* 925 F 2d 670 (3d Cir 1991).

[148] Landgericht Munich of 8 February 1995, n 147 above.

[149] Oberlandesgericht, Koblenz, of 17 September 1993, n 147 above. See also below, paras 16.86–87.

[150] Schlechtriem, 23.

[151] See the *St Alban's* case, n 64 above, at 265 (*per* Sir Iain Glidewell).

regarded as being sold under a contract for the sale of goods for the purposes of Article 5(1)(b).

SERVICES?   It has been suggested by an English court that the purchase of **10.48** software is more akin to the provision of services than the sale of goods.[152] More importantly, the Electronic Commerce Directive sees electronic commerce, including selling of goods online,[153] in terms of an information service provider and recipient. It has been assumed from this that a service provider provides services for jurisdictional purposes.[154] However, the terminology used in the E-Commerce Directive should not be regarded as being conclusive on the classification of the contract. For example, if a service provider sells tangible goods (delivered in a conventional way) over the internet, there is clearly a contract for the sale of goods, even though the seller is described as a service provider under the Directive. The real question is whether what is described as a service provider under the Directive enters into a contract for the provision of services for the purposes of Article 5(1)(b) of the Brussels I Regulation. It is submitted that a service provider does so where it provides online services, such as providing recipients with access to the internet.[155] But where there is a contract for the sale of a digitized product with transfer of the property over the internet, the sale element (ie the transfer of ownership in property) makes the transaction very different from this example of an internet service and, indeed, from typical examples of services coming within Article 5(1)(b), such as a contact for the carriage of goods by sea or for the provision of financial services. Moreover, the provision of services commonly connotes a continuing service[156] whereas with a sale the alleged service is instantaneous. Nonetheless, there is one particular instance of the sale of software with transfer over the internet where there may be a contract for the provision of services. This is where the supplier has developed individual software for a particular customer where the element of labour is so large that the contract is excluded from the scope of the Vienna Convention.[157] The Court of Appeal, Koln, has described the development of software for an individual client as a contract for services and, accordingly, as not constituting 'goods' under the Vienna Convention.[158]

---

[152] ibid.   [153] See Recital (18) of the Directive.

[154] LJ Forner Delaygua, 'International Jurisdiction in "Business to Business" Online Performed Contracts: Lessons From the Hague' in JJ Barcelo and KM Clermont (eds), *A Global Law of Jurisdiction and Judgments: Lessons from the Hague* (The Hague/London: Kluwer Law, 2002) 70.

[155] See below, para 10.50.

[156] See generally MBM Loos, 'Towards a European Law of Service Contracts' (2001) 9 European Rev of Private Law 565.

[157] See, in outline, above, para 1.06 and, in detail, below, para 16.93.

[158] Oberlandesgericht Cologne of 26 August 1994 (translated at http://cisg3.law.pace.edu/cases/940826gl.html).

10.49 NEITHER   It is sometimes assumed that the contract must be one for either the sale of goods or for the provision of services,[159] but logically there is a third possibility, namely that it is neither. It is *sui generis*. However, the authorities in relation to the Vienna Convention that have been mentioned above would strongly indicate that this is not the way to classify the contract.

10.50 *Online services*   If the contract is for the provision of an online service, for example providing internet access to recipients[160] or designing a website for a customer,[161] this should be regarded as a contract for the provision of services for the purposes of Article 5(1)(b). With these examples, the classification looks to be reasonably clear. The difficulty though is whether certain commonly found contracts that are performed over the internet should be regarded as ones for online services. Take the example of a recipient who takes out a subscription to an online journal. The recipient may be a business or a university library and so is not a consumer. This may involve a licensing arrangement. But in cases where it does not, it would look to be the provision of a service. There is a continuing relationship and so it is unlike the purchase of software. The oddity is that the same journal may be available as a hard copy and this would be a contract for the sale of goods. Indeed, what you get for your subscription may be a hard copy and also access to the online version.

10.51 **Purchase and installation of software**   In the situation where a recipient purchases software, this may be contained on a disc. This is tangible property which will be delivered in a conventional way. This situation has been discussed above. Alternatively the software purchased may be just information stored on a web-server, intangible property, and performance is over the internet. This situation has also been discussed above. There is though a third scenario. The software purchased is contained on a disk but this is not delivered to the recipient. Instead, the service provider sends round an employee to the recipient. The employee brings the disk with him, installs the information on the recipient's computer and leaves with the disk. It is unclear whether this is a contract for the sale of goods, the provision of services or neither. The contract is for the purchase of software, intangible property, and its installation. As has been seen, the purchase of the software is probably a sale of goods. However, the installation element raises the possibility that the contract falls within

---

[159] See the ABA Cyberspace Report, 151.

[160] See, e.g. *Rudder v Microsoft Corp* 1999 Carswell Ont 3195, Ontario Superior Court of Justice; discussed below, para 10.111.

[161] *1st Mover APS v Direct Hedge SA* [2003] IL Pr 31, Eastern Court of Appeal, Denmark, which regarded this as the provision of a service for the purposes of the Rome Convention.

the exclusion from the Vienna Convention of 'contracts in which the predominant part of the obligations of the party who furnishes the goods consists in the supply of labour or other services'.[162] The District Court of Munich, in holding that a contract for the sale of software was one for the sale of goods under the Vienna Convention, raised no objection to the fact that the goods were installed by the supplier.[163] Nonetheless, the performance of installation and other ancillary services, such as training of staff, could mean that the predominant part of the obligations of the supplier is the provision of services.[164] The adaptation of software to meet the customer's needs, which could also be regarded as a service,[165] would also be a relevant consideration. The upshot is that a contract for the purchase of software and its installation should be regarded as either one for the sale of goods or the provision of services, depending on whether the predominant part of the obligations of the supplier is perceived as being the supply of services.[166]

References to the European Court of Justice

Given the uncertainty on the classification of the contract in many **10.52** instances of performance over the internet and in cases of purchase of software and its installation, what is needed is a decision or decisions from the European Court of Justice on the application of Article 5(1) in such cases. Faced with this matter, there are two approaches that that Court could adopt. The first is to say that, in cases where it is unclear whether the contract is one for the sale of goods, the provision of services or neither, Article 5(1)(b) does not apply.[167] According to Article 5(1)(c), in this situation, one must return to Article 5(1)(a) and identify the place of performance of the obligation in question. If one concentrates on the obligation in question, there is no need to decide on what type of contract it is. This approach may appeal to the European Court of Justice which can then leave it to the national court to identify this place.[168] The second, and better, approach is for the European Court of Justice, in cases where there is uncertainty over the classification of the contract, to decide definitively whether it is a contract for the sale of goods,

---

[162] See Art 3(2) of the Vienna Convention, discussed below, para 16.93.
[163] Landgericht Munich of 8 February 1995 (translated at http://cisg3.law.pace.edu/cases/950208g4.html).
[164] See the Commercial Court (Handelsgericht) of the Canton of Zurich of 17 February 2000 (translated at http://cisg3.law.pace.edu/cases/000217sl.html).
[165] See the discussion above of where the supplier has developed individual software for a particular customer.
[166] The way this is done in Vienna Convention cases is discussed below, para 16.93.
[167] See the discussion in relation to distribution agreements above, para 3.158.
[168] Case C-440/97 *GIE Groupe Concorde v Master of the Vessel Suhadiwarno Panjan* [1999] ECR I-6307.

provision of services or neither. The purpose of Article 5(1)(b) is to give an autonomous definition to the place of performance of the obligation in question for certain commonly found contracts. It is not within the spirit of this if contracts that are capable of being given a precise classification, which includes the possibility of a classification falling within Article 5(1)(b), are taken outside this provision because the European Court of Justice is unwilling to grasp the nettle and classify the contract. The classification it should adopt is summed up in the conclusions below.

10.53 *Conclusions*

(1) In the case of the physical delivery of tangible goods, there is a contract for the sale of goods for the purposes of Article 5(1)(b).

(2) In the case of a licensing agreement, this should be regarded as neither a contract for the sale of goods nor for the provision of services. Article 5(1)(a) will therefore apply.

(3) In the case of the purchase (as opposed to a licence) of standard software and other digitized products with transfer over the internet, this should be regarded as a contract for the sale of goods.

(4) In the case of the purchase (as opposed to a licence) of bespoke software with transfer over the internet, this should be regarded as a contract for the provision of services where the element of labour is so large that the contract is excluded from the scope of the Vienna Convention.

(5) In the case of a contract for the provision of an online service, this should be regarded as a contract for the provision of services.

(6) A contract for the purchase of software and its installation should be regarded as either one for the sale of goods or the provision of services, depending on whether the predominant part of the obligations of the supplier is perceived as being the supply of services.

Identification of the place of performance of the obligation in question

10.54 If, as is argued above, there is a contract for the sale of goods or the provision of services in cases of electronic commerce, Article 5(1)(b) will apply. The application of this provision in cases of e-commerce will now be examined. After which consideration will be given to the position if the approach advocated by the authors is not adopted by the European Court of Justice. In other words, at least in some instances of e-commerce, the European Court of Justice says that the classification of the contract is unclear and simply turns to Article 5(1)(a), or does classify the contract but as neither one for the sale of goods nor for the provision of services.

A contract for the sale of goods or the provision of services: Article 5(1)(b)

Physical delivery In cases of physical delivery of tangible goods, the **10.55** place where, under the contract, the goods were delivered or should have been delivered for the purposes of Article 5(1)(b) is no more difficult to ascertain if the international sale of goods contract has been made online over the internet than if it has been made by some more traditional method, such as by telephone, letter or fax.[169] The sales documentation will normally specify a place of delivery and, if it does not, it can be ascertained in the same way as for any other instance where no place of delivery is specified.[170]

Performance over the internet It is submitted that, under Article 5(1)(b), **10.56** when it comes to contracts involving performance over the internet, the place where the goods were delivered (where the contract is regarded as one for the sale of goods) is going to be exactly the same as that where the services were provided (where the contract is regarded as one for the provision of services). Accordingly, for present purposes, as long as the contract is either for the sale of goods or the provision of services it does not matter which it is.

NO AGREEMENT BY THE PARTIES ON THE PLACE OF DELIVERY/PROVISION OF **10.57** SERVICES If the parties have agreed on the place of delivery of goods/ provision of services, then this is the place of performance of the obligation in question. However, the problem with performance over the internet is that the parties agree (at least impliedly) that information is to be transferred from one computer to another, but they may not have expressly (or even impliedly) agreed on the place where this was to happen. Whilst there are internationally agreed terms (INCOTERMS) that can be used to identify the place of delivery of tangible goods, there are no such terms for the transfer of digitized products over the internet. A lack of agreement by the parties on this place has serious consequences. This raises the same conceptual difficulty in applying Article 5(1)(b) as arises with the sale of goods in non-internet cases where there is no agreement on the place of delivery.[171] It is arguable in such cases that Article 5(1)(b) does not apply and recourse must therefore be made to Article 5(1)(a).[172] Whatever the merits, or otherwise, of this solution in non-internet cases, recourse to Article 5(1)(a) is singularly unhelpful in the case of the transfer of information over the internet. This is because in such cases

---

[169] See the expert meeting at Ottawa, n 129 above, 5; the Geneva Round Table, n 129 above, 19; Reed, n 21 above, 7.1.3.1.
[170] See above, paras 3.177–199.   [171] See above, paras 3.192–199.
[172] See above, para 3.169.

the substantive applicable law is unlikely to have rules on the place of performance of the obligation in question, in the absence of agreement.[173]

10.58 AN AUTONOMOUS COMMUNITY DEFINITION OF THE PLACE FOR THE PURPOSES OF ARTICLE 5(1)(b) The better way of solving this problem of lack of agreement on the place of delivery of goods/provision of the services (i.e. transfer of the information) in cases where performance takes place over the internet is to give an autonomous Community definition to the concept of the place of delivery of goods/provision of services for the purposes of Article 5(1)(b). There is though no common core of substantive law in the Member States on which this definition could be based and so deciding upon a definition will not be easy.

10.59 It would perhaps be easier to decide upon a definition if an analogy could be drawn with the situation where there is a delivery of tangible goods.[174] However, with performance over the internet it is not clear whether the transaction should be regarded as being one where the recipient visits the service provider's website or vice versa.[175] If one tries to analogize it with a delivery of tangible goods, is it as if the buyer has gone to the seller's warehouse to pick them up[176]or the seller has delivered them to the buyer?[177] The truth is that where the information is put on a website and accessed by the recipient, as is likely to be the case with a contract for an online service, this is a complicated arrangement involving two active parties. There is a service provider which creates a website, places information on it and creates a procedure which allows the information to be transferred to recipients. There is also a recipient which accesses the website and requests the transfer of the information.

10.60 THE FOUR POSSIBILITIES The definition of the place of delivery of goods/ provision of services for the purposes of Article 5(1)(b) for cases where performance takes place over the internet could be based on one of the following. First, the place where the information was dispatched. But which computer is this referring to? The technical means by which the transfer of the information is made will be relevant. If information is uploaded (making the information available over the internet by placing

---

[173] Compare the position in non-internet sale of goods cases, see above, paras 3.195–198.
[174] But see Reed, n 21 above, 7.1.3.1 who draws the analogy.
[175] See the ABA Cyberspace Report, 8.
[176] See the ABA Cyberspace Report, 33–34; Reed, n 21 above, 7.1.3.1. The counterargument is that cyberspace is a method of communication rather than a place and so a buyer cannot be regarded as visiting the seller.
[177] Another way of putting it is to ask whether the information was pushed by the seller or pulled by the recipient, see the discussion by Hedigan J at first instance in the *Dow Jones* case [2001] VSC 305.

it in a storage area managed by a web-server)[178] and is then accessed by the recipient, the place of dispatch would appear to be the place where the information is uploaded by the service provider (ie the place where that web-server which is accessed by the recipient is situated). The process of transfer of the information may be complicated by the fact that the information is originally contained on a computer in State A but is then transferred and uploaded on to the web-server in State B, which is accessed by customers. Is the place of dispatch in State A or State B? The place of dispatch should be regarded as being in State B. It is the web-server in State B that really matters. This is what the customer access, not the computer in State A. As between the contracting parties the process is one of transfer from the web-server to the recipient. Where the information is located prior to it being placed on the web-server is of no concern to the customer. So far we have been discussing transfer of information from a web-server to a customer's computer. But information may be transferred by means of an email attachment.[179] Is the place of dispatch referring to the computer from which the email was sent or the one where the information contained in the attachment was originally held, which may be in a different state?

Second, the place where the information was received by the recipient. **10.61** Again this raises the problem of which computer is being referred to. The most obvious place of receipt is the place where the information was downloaded (i.e. the process by which the web-server delivers a document in response to a request by the recipient)[180] on to the computer of the recipient (i.e. the place where the recipient's computer was situated). But the technical means by which the transfer of information is made may raise other possibilities. If the information is transferred by means of an email attachment, it would be possible to regard the place of receipt as the place where the recipient's mailbox is situated.[181] This would be located on a server to which emails to the recipient are routed. This may not be in the state where the recipient has its place of business or where the email is actually downloaded (collected from the mailbox).

Third, the place where the service provider has some specified personal **10.62**

---

[178] See the *Dow Jones* case, (2002) 210 CLR 575, HC of Australia, para 16. A computer that makes documents available runs software usually referred to as a web-server. A computer that requests and receives documents runs software that is referred to as a web browser, ibid, para 15.

[179] See Reed, n 21 above, 7.1.3.1.   [180] The *Dow Jones* case, n 177 above, para 15.

[181] See Reed, n 21 above, 7.1.3.1. Another possible solution is to look at the place where the message enters the recipient's systems, i.e. the physical location of the server to which the recipient's domain name (if a company) points. See below, para 21.157 and discussion of the Australian Electronic Communications Act 1999.

connection, such as where it has its place of business, is established or domiciled.[182]

10.63　Fourth, the place where the recipient has some specified personal connection, such as where it has its place of business, is established or domiciled.

10.64　To complicate matters, it would be possible to have different solutions depending on which technical method of transfer of information was used. Thus transfer by email attachment would point to a place of receipt solution rather than a place of dispatch solution. This is where the customer acquires practical access to the information. A place of receipt solution reflects the fact that, as far as the transfer is concerned, the service provider is playing the active role by sending the email attachment, whereas the recipient is playing a passive role. However, in the situation where transfer is by means of the recipient accessing the website of the service provider, there is a case for a solution in terms of the place of dispatch. If one asks where the buyer acquires practical access to the information, the answer is in the place of dispatch.

10.65　The arguments for and against each of these four possible solutions will now be examined.

10.66　THE PLACE OF DISPATCH　The arguments in favour of this solution are as follows. First, given that what is being transferred is information from one computer to another, this more obviously refers to the place of dispatch or of receipt than to the place where one of the parties has a personal connecting factor.[183] Second, the process of the transfer of the information starts from the place of dispatch.

10.67　However, there are powerful arguments against this solution. First, there is the difficulty in identifying which particular computer constitutes the place of dispatch. With a subscription to an online journal, it is going to be the place of uploading (ie the place where the web-server, on which the information is made available to be accessed by customers, is located). If information is transferred by means of an email attachment it is more difficult to identify the place of dispatch.[184] It is then necessary to identify where this web-server/computer is situated. There are well known

---

[182] The problem of deciding which connecting factor to use is discussed below, para 10.71.

[183] Contrast this with the position where a definition is being sought of the place of performance of the obligation to transfer information for the purposes of developing a substantive law provision. There are precedents for the use of a personal connecting factor, see Art 15(4) of the UNCITRAL Model Law on Electronic Commerce of 1996, discussed below, para 10.70.

[184] Digitized products such as software may well be transferred in this way.

difficulties in ascertaining this place.[185] Second, in the typical scenario where the recipient is suing the service provider, this solution does not fit in well with the scheme of jurisdiction under the Brussels I Regulation. The plaintiff (recipient) can always sue the defendant (service provider) in the Member State in which the latter is domiciled. This place will often coincide with the place where the defendant has its web-server and, therefore, if the place of dispatch (where, as is likely to be the case, this means the place of uploading) is adopted, Article 5(1) will not, in practice, provide the plaintiff with an alternative forum in which to bring his action.[186] Third, the place of uploading can lead to manipulation by the service provider.[187] Fourth, it may be unknown to the recipient and it may even be unknown to the service provider.[188] Fifth, it may have no connection with the place where the service provider carries on its internet business activities, or with the place where the service provider is domiciled.[189] Sixth, a place of dispatch theory favours the service provider which can ensure that this place is its home state.

THE PLACE OF RECEIPT The arguments in favour of this solution are **10.68** these. First, at the time the information is transferred the recipient is perhaps more likely to be physically located where his computer is than the service provider. Second, there is some support for the autonomous definition under Article 5(1)(b) in cases of tangible goods being that of where the goods are ultimately supplied to the buyer;[190] and the analogy to this in cases of electronic commerce is the place of downloading of the information on to the computer of the recipient. Third, the place of receipt (where, as is likely to be the case, this refers to the place of downloading) looks to fit in reasonably well with the scheme of the Brussels I Regulation. It is likely to provide the plaintiff recipient with a choice of fora in which to sue since downloading will often take place in the plaintiff's home state. Fourth, given that what is being transferred is information from one computer to another, this more obviously refers to the place of dispatch or of receipt than to the place where one of the parties has a personal connecting factor.

---

[185] See above, paras 10.08–09.
[186] The two places will not always coincide. The defendant's web-server may be placed in a Member State other than the one in which the defendant is domiciled. The plaintiff will have a choice of fora in which to sue. But there may be little connection with the State in which the web-server is placed. The defendant is not domiciled there and may not carry out its internet activities there either. It is questionable whether, in such circumstances, the plaintiff should be allowed to sue in that Member State.
[187] See the *Dow Jones* case, n 177 above, para 130.   [188] Ibid, para 132.
[189] See, eg, in the non EC context, the facts of the *Dow Jones* case, n 177 above; discussed below, para 10.169.
[190] See above, para 3.197.

10.69 However, there are arguments against a place of receipt approach. First, there is the problem of identifying which computer constitutes the one of receipt. With a subscription to an online journal it is going to be the one where downloading on to the customer's computer takes place (i.e. the place where the customer's computer was situated). There may be a problem of identifying the location of this computer at the time of downloading. If information is transferred by means of an email attachment it is more difficult to identify the place of receipt.[191] Second, the recipient can manipulate the jurisdiction rules by deliberately choosing to download the information in a Member State in which he wishes to bring his action. Third, the service provider would not even know where the recipient downloads the information. Fourth, the place of downloading will be difficult to identify in the situation where this takes place in a number of different Member States. For example, the recipient agrees to purchase statistical information over the internet. This is something which the recipient pays for by a yearly subscription and can use as much as he wants over the year. The recipient may download the information at various times in various Member States as he moves around Europe downloading it on to a laptop computer. Fifth, the place of downloading favours the recipient because this place will tend to be the recipient's home state.

10.70 THE PLACE WHERE THE SERVICE PROVIDER HAS A SPECIFIED PERSONAL CONNECTING FACTOR In favour of this solution, the following points can be made. First, support for it can be found in the substantive law of electronic commerce contained in the UNCITRAL Model Law on Electronic Commerce of 1996, which introduces the concept of a deemed place of dispatch of a data message.[192] Article 15(4) provides that: 'Unless otherwise agreed between the originator and the addressee, a data message is deemed to be dispatched at the place where the originator has its place of business, and is deemed to be received at the place where the addressee has its place of business'.[193] This was introduced in the context of the substantive law on the formation of contracts set out in the Model Law but it can equally be used for the purposes of private international law.[194] Second, support for it can be found in the substantive law of

---

[191] Digitized products such as software may well be transferred in this way.

[192] See the expert meeting at Ottawa, n 129 above, at 5.

[193] If the originator or the addressee has more than one place of business, the place of business is that which has the closest relationship to the underlying business transaction or, where there is no underlying transaction, the principal place of business, Art 15(4)(a). If the originator or the addressee does not have a place of business, reference is to be made to its habitual residence, Art 15(4)(b). See also the Australian Electronic Communications Act 1999 which in s 4(5)(b) adopts a deemed place of receipt rule.

[194] See the attached Guide to the Model Law, para 105.

electronic commerce contained in the E-Commerce Directive. This adopts a country of origin principle that points to the place where the service provider is established. Third, because of the E-Commerce Directive, there should not be the problems of identity and location of the service provider.[195] Fourth, it is questionable whether a solution which allocates jurisdiction to the place of uploading or downloading provides an appropriate basis of jurisdiction. Both of these solutions can lead to: the allocation of jurisdiction to a place with which there is no meaningful connection which would justify it having jurisdiction; manipulation by one or other of the parties; and the place being unidentifiable by one or other of the parties.

The arguments against this solution are as follows. First, a decision has to **10.71** be made as to which personal connecting factor to adopt. The place of business is a connecting factor used in the Vienna Convention in the context of delivery[196] and is also used in the UNCITRAL Model Law on Electronic Commerce.[197] The E-Commerce Directive refers to the place of establishment.[198] The Brussels I Regulation uses the concept of domicile.[199] Second, it is too pro-defendant. This point needs some explanation. In some cases, the service provider will be the plaintiff suing the recipient of goods or services for non-payment. In other cases, the service provider will be the defendant being sued by the recipient, who complains that the goods have not been delivered (or services performed) or that the goods are defective (or the services have not been properly performed). However, the typical complaint in cases of e-commerce is by the recipient who says that he has paid for goods (or services) and these have not been delivered (performed) or that the goods are defective (services have not been properly performed). Whichever connecting factor is used, in the typical case of a recipient suing the service provider, the plaintiff recipient will normally not be provided with a place of trial that is different from that of the defendant service provider's domicile. If domicile is used as the connecting factor the plaintiff recipient will be given no choice at all. If the place of business (or place of establishment) is used this will normally coincide with the place of the defendant service provider's domicile and the plaintiff recipient therefore will rarely be given a choice. Under this solution, Article 5(1) would be much less plaintiff friendly in internet cases than it is in non-internet cases.

---

[195] See the discussion above, para 10.27, on the information to be provided by an information society service provider.   [196] Art 31.

[197] See Art 15(4)(a) and 4(b), quoted above, para 10.70, which deal with definitional problems in relation to this concept.

[198] For the meaning of this term see Recital (19) and Art 2 of the Directive, discussed below, paras 10.155–156. Case C-68/93 *Shevill v Presse Alliance SA* [1995] 2 AC 18 also uses this concept.   [199] See above, paras 3.12–14.

10.72 The place where the recipient has a specified personal connecting factor   In favour of this solution is, first, the fact that, it is supported by the UNCITRAL Model Law on Electronic Commerce of 1996. Second, it avoids the drawback of a place of receipt and dispatch rule in that they lead to jurisdiction being allocated to an inappropriate forum.

10.73   Against this solution, the following points can be made. First, there are the well-known problems of identity and location of the recipient, which the E-Commerce Directive does not address. Second, a rule based on a link with the recipient is too pro-plaintiff in the typical case of the plaintiff recipient suing the defendant service provider. If domicile is used as the connecting factor, the plaintiff recipient would be able to sue in his domicile. If the place of business (or establishment) is used as the connecting factor, this will normally coincide with the plaintiff recipient's domicile. However, the alternative solution of looking to the place where the service provider has its place of business etc is arguably even worse in that it rarely provides the plaintiff recipient with a choice of forum. Moreover, the pro-plaintiff nature of the rule would be mitigated by the fact that the parties can agree that the place of performance of the obligation in question is some place other than the place where the recipient has its place of business.[200]

10.74 The preferred solution   It is submitted that, on the basis of the above analysis, a solution based on a personal connecting factor is to be preferred to one based on the place of dispatch or receipt. The personal connecting factor should be that of the recipient rather than that of the service provider. This would fit in better with the scheme of the Brussels I Regulation than a solution based on a personal connecting factor relating to the service provider. When it comes to the choice of connecting factor, it is submitted that the place of business is to be preferred. It avoids the plaintiff being able automatically to sue in his own domicile and is likely to be easier to ascertain than the place of establishment. It is submitted therefore that, for the purposes of Article 5(1)(b), in the absence of agreement by the parties, the place where the goods are delivered/services provided should be regarded as being that where the recipient has its place of business.

10.75   *Purchase and installation of software*   It has been argued that a contract for the purchase of software and its installation should be regarded as either one for the sale of goods or one for the provision of services, depending on whether the predominant part of the obligations of the supplier is perceived as being the supply of services. In the case of a contract for the

---

[200] The parties cannot, though, agree on a fictitious place of performance, see above, para 3.214.

sale of goods, the place where the goods were delivered or should have been delivered is easy to identify. It is the place where the installation has taken place or should have taken place, i.e. where the computer on which the software was or should have been installed is located. In the case of a contract for the provision of services, the place where the services were provided or should have been provided is also easy to identify. It is the place where the installation has taken place or should have taken place, i.e. where the computer on which the software was or should have been installed is located.

A contract that is neither for the sale of goods nor for the provision of 10.76 services: Article 5(1)(a) We are not concerned here with the physical delivery of tangible goods (this is clearly a contract for the sale of goods) but with performance over the internet and the installation of software (where the position is less certain). What happens in these scenarios if, contrary to what is argued above, the European Court of Justice says that the classification of the contract is unclear and simply turns to Article 5(1)(a), or does classify the contract but as neither one for the sale of goods nor for the provision of services? If the contract is so classified, Article 5(1)(b) will not apply. In this situation, according to Article 5(1)(c), one must return to Article 5(1)(a) and identify the place of performance of the obligation in question.

The obligation in question At the outset it is necessary to identify the **10.77** obligation in question. Let us assume that the plaintiff is a recipient who is suing the service provider for breach of the obligation to provide the software or other digitized product (i.e. the information has not been provided at all) or for breach of the obligation to provide the software of the requisite quality. These are the most likely obligations to have been breached in cases of performance over the internet. Normally the product will not be transferred until payment has been made and so there is unlikely to be an action brought by the service provider for non-payment.

The place of performance of the obligation in question

NO RULE OF SUBSTANTIVE LAW The national court will have to apply **10.78** national choice of law rules, in order to identify the applicable substantive law and hence the place of performance of the obligation in question under that law. For the United Kingdom this will be the rules on the applicable law in the Rome Convention. In the case of performance over the internet, although there may be agreed terms and conditions, the parties may not have actually agreed on the place of performance of the obligation to provide the software/provide the software of the requisite quality. This is something they would have been likely to have specified in the case of delivery of tangible goods but the method of transfer over the internet makes this much less likely. A lack of agreement on this has serious consequences. The applicable national substantive law is unlikely to have an existing rule determining where this place is in the absence of agreement. The Vienna Convention has no provisions on performance over the internet. Neither does the substantive English law on the international sale of goods. The E-Commerce Directive and the Electronic Commerce (EC Directive) Regulations 2002 are silent on this.[201] In the absence of any domestic substantive law rule identifying the place of performance of the obligation in question, Article 5(1)(a) is unworkable.

10.79 INVENTING A RULE OF SUBSTANTIVE LAW   The European Court of Justice cannot fill in a gap in a Member State's national domestic substantive law. But if the national judge trying the case is applying local law, it may be possible for him to invent a rule of domestic substantive law.[202] This could be based on the location of computers or on the location of the parties to the contract. It is submitted that the choice would be between the following. First, the place where the information was dispatched.[203] Second, the place where the information was received by the recipient. Third, the place where the service provider has some specified personal connection, such as where it has its place of business, is established or domiciled. Fourth, the place where the recipient has some specified personal connection, such as where it has its place of business, is established or domiciled. These possibilities are familiar to us from the discussion of an autonomous Community definition of the place where goods are delivered/services provided for the purposes of Article 5(1)(b) of the Brussels I Regulation. However, it must be stressed that what we are now concerned with is a judge of a national court fixing upon the right definition under substantive domestic law of the place of performance of the obligation to provide the software/provide the software of the requisite quality. The definition adopted is not concerned with the allocation of jurisdiction to the courts of a particular Member State. Neither is it required that the definition adopted fits in with the scheme of jurisdiction rules under the Brussels I Regulation.

10.80 What we really need is European or international agreement on a definition for the place of transfer of information over the internet.[204] This agreement could take the form of an EC Directive or a Model Law prepared by UNCITRAL.

---

[201] But see Reed, n 21 above, 7.1.3.1, who uses EC tax law to assert that services are normally performed 'in the supplier's own jurisdiction'.

[202] But what if the judge is applying foreign law? If foreign law is inadequately proved, English law will apply by default, see R Fentiman, *Foreign Law in English Courts* (Oxford: OUP, 1998) 182–183.

[203] i.e. where the web-server accessed by the recipient is situated.

[204] See generally Forner Delaygua, n 154 above, 69–70.

Article 5(5)

Is there a branch, agency or other establishment?

When considering the application of Article 5(5) in cases of electronic **10.81** commerce, the obvious question arises: can a defendant, domiciled in one Member State and which conducts business over the internet, be regarded as having a branch, agency or other establishment in another Member State by virtue of the fact that it conducts business there in that way? It will be recalled that a branch etc. has been defined by the European Court of Justice in terms of a number of characteristics.[205] The branch etc. must: (i) have a fixed permanent place of business; (ii) be subject to the direction and control of the parent; (iii) have a certain autonomy; and (iv) act on behalf of and bind the parent. The various ways in which business is conducted over the internet will now be examined to see whether these characteristics can be met.

Activity involving the defendant's own website Let us assume that a **10.82** French domiciled company creates a website with a server located in France. This website can be accessed in every EC Member State and indeed outside the EC as well. Can a plaintiff bring an action in, for example, England on the basis that the website can be accessed there? Clearly the defendant has no fixed permanent place of business in England.[206] A defendant that sends a sales representative to England but has no office there will not satisfy this requirement[207] and neither will a company that has even less of a presence in England. As far as this requirement is concerned, the nature of the website, ie whether it is passive or interactive, is irrelevant. The view put forward here, that the mere fact that a website can be accessed in England is not enough to mean that there is a branch etc in England for the purposes of Article 5(5), ties in with the substantive law of e-commerce, which does not attach importance to the place where a website can be accessed. The E-Commerce Directive provides that the place of establishment of a company providing services via an internet website is not the place at which its website is accessible.[208]

Would it be any different if the French defendant set up its website in **10.83** Germany, with its server in that Member State? Does the defendant have a fixed permanent place of business in Germany? A website cannot constitute a branch office or establishment.[209] But what about the server on

---

[205] See above, para 3.303. [206] See Reed, n 21 above, 7.2.1.1.

[207] See Case 33/78 *Somafer v Saar-Ferngas* [1978] ECR 2183.

[208] Recital (19). According to this Recital, the Directive contemplates that there can more than one place of establishment so it is not using this term as the equivalent of, say, the seat of a company.

[209] See the expert meeting at Ottawa, n 129 above, at 9.

which the website is stored?[210] This will no doubt be located in a place that is fixed and permanent and so it could be argued that this requirement is met.[211] But would this 'branch' have a certain autonomy and act on behalf of and bind the parent? If a passive website is set up, these two requirements will not be met. What if an interactive website is set up which allows a recipient to contract online? This is very different from a conventional branch office. First, there is no person who acts on behalf of the parent and decides whether to contract.[212] Instead, a system is set up, admittedly by a person, that automatically provides for entering into the contract. Second, the interactive website can be accessed by someone from outside the Member State where the website and server are situated. The website is the means by which the defendant directs its commercial activities to other Member States and beyond. It is reaching out to recipients abroad and could be said to be as much in those countries as it is in the country where the website and server are situated.[213] If one were to analogize this situation with the one where there is a branch office and a person, it is as if the branch manager of a German branch regularly goes from Germany to England to contract with English recipients. It is very questionable whether Article 5(5) would operate to allow the parent to be sued in Germany in such a case. This is because the link with Germany is much reduced in such circumstances. It must always be remembered what the justification for this provision is.[214] Special jurisdiction is based on a close link between the court and the action or the facilitation of the sound administration of justice. Neither can be shown in such circumstances. The view expressed here, that the mere fact that a company has its server in Germany is not enough to mean that there is a branch etc in Germany[215] for the purposes of Article 5(5), ties in with the substantive law of e-commerce, which does not attach importance to the place where a server is situated. The E-Commerce Directive provides that the place of establishment of a company providing services via an internet website is not the place at which the technology supporting its website is located.[216]

---

[210] See generally L Gillies, 'A Review of the New Jurisdiction Rules for Electronic Consumer Contracts within the European Union' [2001] J of Information, Law & Technology 1 at 10; R Schu, 'Consumer Protection and Private International Law in Internet Contracts' (1997) 5 Intl J of Law & Information Technology 192 at 221–222.

[211] See generally Forner Delaygua, n 154 above, 58–59.

[212] See Reed, n 21 above, 7.2.1.1.

[213] This argument would, however, not apply where there is an attempt to restrict the website to customers in Germany. But there is still no person who acts on behalf of the parent and decides whether to contract.

[214] Recital (12) to the Brussels I Regulation.

[215] See also Gillies, n 210 above; Schu, n 210 above.   [216] Recital (19) and Art 2(c).

In conclusion, Article 5(5) cannot operate simply on the basis that the **10.84**
defendant has set up its own website, whether interactive or passive. This
view is supported by the experts at a meeting concerned with electronic
commerce and the Hague Judgments Convention.[217] The 1999 and 2001
versions of the draft Convention contained a provision that is virtually
identical in wording to Article 5(5) of the Brussels I Regulation.[218] There
was though a proposal at the Hague Conference that this provision
should be extended beyond branches, agencies and other establishments
to allocate jurisdiction to the courts of a state 'where the defendant has
carried on regular commercial activity by other means'.[219] It is clear from
the accompanying Nygh and Pocar Report[220] that this extension would
encompass electronic commerce where there is something more than
a mere passive website, but not just a passive website. Implicit in this
is the view that the original wording, that is virtually identical to that
in Article 5(5) of the Brussels I Regulation, was not adequate to cover a
website, even one where there is something more than a mere passive
website.

Activity involving someone else's website   We are concerned now with **10.85**
the situation where, for example, the defendant, domiciled in France, uses
an internet auction site or an internet advertising service which is owned
by an English company, which has set up its website and its server in
England. Is the English company a branch etc. of the French defendant?
The English company appears to have a fixed permanent place of
business in England.[221] However, there are difficulties in satisfying two
of the other characteristics of a branch etc. First, is the alleged English
branch under the direction and control of the French defendant, which
uses its website? The situation is similar to that where an independent
commercial agent is used to carry on business abroad. If a commercial
agent is free to arrange its own work, is not prevented from representing
other firms competing in the same sector, and transmits orders to the
parent without being involved in their terms or execution, then such an

---

[217] See the experts meeting at Ottawa, n 129 above, at 9.

[218] See the First Part of the Diplomatic Conference 6–20 June 2001, Interim Text, Art 9.
This replaced the version of the draft Convention adopted by the Special Commission on
30 October 1999.

[219] This proposal was not discussed in 2001 pending discussion of the 'activity jurisdiction' elsewhere in the draft.

[220] Nygh and Pocar Report, 57. The report discusses the version of the draft Convention
adopted by the Special Commission on 30 October 1999. The wording of the branch etc
provision was the same in this earlier version as that in the more recent 2001 version.

[221] It will not have a fixed permanent place of business in other Member States merely by
virtue of the fact that the website can be accessed in those other Member States, see above,
para 10.82.

agent does not have the character of a branch, agency or other establish-ment.[222] It is not under the direction and control of the parent. Second, there is difficulty in showing that the English company whose website is used acts on behalf of and can bind the French domiciled parent. If the website is merely used to advertise the goods, then this cannot be shown. Even if the website is used, for example, to auction the defendant's goods and is an interactive one so that a contract can be made online, it is doubt-ful whether the requirement that the branch acts on behalf of and can bind the parent can be regarded as being met. There is no person from the company whose website it is who acts in this way. Instead a system is set up, admittedly by a person, that automatically provides for entering into the contract. Moreover, even if one accepts that a person is not needed and setting up a website is enough, the website is reaching out to recipients abroad and could be said to be as much in these countries as it is in the country where the website and server are situated. It is very questionable whether Article 5(5) would operate in such a case for the reason outlined above.[223]

10.86 **Exchange of emails**   A French defendant may exchange emails by means of a server set up in Germany. The server cannot be regarded as a branch etc of the defendant. Although it is no doubt located in a place that is fixed and permanent, the server does not have a certain autonomy and it cannot act on behalf and bind the parent. This ties in with the substantive law of e-commerce, which does not attach significance to the place where a server is located.[224]

Is there a dispute arising out of the operations of the branch etc?

10.87 If, contrary to what has been argued above, it were to be held that the setting up of an interactive website in a Member State other than the one where the defendant was domiciled constituted a branch, there would probably be no difficulty in showing that the dispute arose out of the operations of the branch. If there is online contracting through an inter-active website, it could be said that the branch (i.e. the interactive website), acting on behalf of the seller, entered into a sale of goods contract with the buyer, thereby satisfying the requirement that the dispute arose out of the operations of the branch.[225] It should also be satisfied by showing that the branch is concerned with the performance of the undertakings out of which the dispute arises.[226]

---

[222] Case 139/80 *Blanckaert and Willems v Trost* [1981] ECR 819.   [223] At para 10.83.
[224] See Recital (19) of the E-Commerce Directive.   [225] See above, para 3.304.
[226] ibid.

2. THE TRADITIONAL ENGLISH RULES

Service Within the Jurisdiction

With a business-to-business contract it is possible that the defendant is an **10.88**
individual. If so, there is no more difficulty in serving such a defendant
within the jurisdiction in a case where the contract was made over the
internet than there is in the case of a contract made in a traditional way. It
is more likely though that the defendant will be a corporate one. In cases
of e-commerce, there are problems in serving such a defendant within the
jurisdiction.

Service under the Companies Act 1985

Is there a branch in Great Britain or the establishment of a place of 10.89
business (which is not a branch)? It will be recalled[227] that, in determining whether a place of business has been established, it is relevant
to see whether the business is carried on from a fixed and definite place
and whether the company uses an agent that can bind it contractually. If a
place of business has been established, it is then necessary to determine
whether this is a branch or not.[228] When considering the application of
these criteria in cases of electronic commerce, the question arises: can a
foreign corporate defendant, which conducts business over the internet,
be regarded as having a branch in Great Britain or as having established a
place of business, which is not a branch, in Great Britain by virtue of the
fact that it conducts business in that way? The various ways in which
business is conducted over the internet will now be examined to see
whether they can constitute a branch or the establishment of a place of
business, which is not a branch.

Activity involving the defendant's own website Let us assume that a New **10.90**
York incorporated company creates a website with a server in New York.
The website can be accessed in England. In such circumstances, business
is not carried out from a fixed and definite place of business in England
and the New York company therefore cannot be said to have established
a place of business in England.[229] The result is that the company neither
has a branch nor has established a place of business, which is not a branch,
in England and cannot be served within the jurisdiction. This view
ties in with the substantive law of e-commerce, which does not attach

---

[227] See above, para 4.12.
[228] A branch is a more permanent establishment than a mere place of business.
[229] Statements on the foreign company's website concerning its activities have not been
given much weight when determining whether it has an office in England, see *Matchnet v
Blair* [2002] EWHC 2128 (Ch), [2003] 2 BCLC 195.

importance to the place where a website can be accessed.[230] The E-Commerce Directive provides that the place of establishment of a company providing services via an internet website is not the place at which its website is accessible.[231]

10.91 Let us now assume that the New York company set up its server and website in England. The server will no doubt be located in a place which is fixed and definite. But does the company have an agent in England that can bind it contractually? If a passive website is set up then clearly not. But what if an interactive website is set up which allows a recipient to contract online? It is doubtful if the company can be said to have an agent in England. An agent is a person who acts on behalf of and can bind the principal. With electronic commerce there is no such person. Instead a system is set up, admittedly by a person, that automatically provides for entering into the contract. Even if it is accepted that a system like this could constitute an agency, what the rules contemplate is that the agent who binds the company is in England. What is required is that the company is there in England by virtue of its agent. But if the website is being accessed by people from outside England, it is reaching out to them abroad and is as much in those countries as it is in England.[232] It is analogous to the situation where a person who is the agent in England leaves the place of business and goes abroad to contract with people from abroad. The upshot is that it is doubtful, even where an interactive website is set up with its server in England, whether a foreign company can be said to have established a place of business in England. The result is that the foreign company neither has a branch nor has established a place of business, which is not a branch, in Great Britain and cannot be served within the jurisdiction. This conclusion ties in with the substantive law of e-commerce which does not attach importance to the place where a server is situated. The E-Commerce Directive provides that the place of establishment of a company providing services via an internet website is not the place at which the technology supporting its website is located.[233]

10.92 *Activity involving someone else's website* Let us assume that a New York company, instead of creating its own website, uses the auction or advertising website of an English company in order to conduct its business

---

[230] But compare the position in France, where, in the *Yahoo! Inc* case, Number RG: 0/005308 (2000), the Paris Tribunale de Grande Instance held that a Californian company was subject to French jurisdiction because its online auction website (on which people could sell Nazi memorabilia) could be accessed in France.

[231] Recital (19).

[232] This argument would however not apply where there is an attempt to restrict the website to customers in England. If, contrary to what is argued in this book, you accept that there is an agent, this agent should be regarded as being in England.

[233] Recital (19).

internationally. Is the English company whose website is used by the foreign company an established place of business of the company in England? The business may well be carried on from a fixed and definite place in England but there remain two difficulties. First, is the English company an agent that can bind the foreign company contractually? If the website is merely used to advertise the goods then it cannot be shown that the company whose website is used acts on behalf of and can bind the foreign company. Even if the website is used, for example, to auction the defendant's goods and is an interactive one so that a contract can be made online, it is doubtful whether the English company can be regarded as being an agent. There is no person who acts on behalf of and can bind the principal. Instead a system is set up, admittedly by a person, that automatically provides for entering into the contract. Moreover, even if you accept that a system could constitute an agent it is arguable that the agent who binds the company is not in England, but rather is abroad reaching out to foreigners who access the website. Second, does the English company act on behalf of the New York company or on its own behalf? This is always a problem where business is carried on through an independent commercial agent.[234] In the present situation, where the English company is acting in the same way for numerous companies, and the New York company has no control over which companies the English company acts for, it looks more realistic to regard the English company as acting on its own behalf rather than on behalf of the New York company. In conclusion, in the situation where a New York company uses the auction or advertising website of an English company in order to conduct its business internationally, the New York company cannot be regarded as having established a place of business in England.

Exchange of emails   We are concerned here with the situation where the **10.93** New York company exchanges emails using a server located in England. Has a place of business been established in England? The server is doubtless located in a place which is fixed and definite. But there is no agent in England which can bind the New York company in England. The server is a mere conduit of information. The conclusion therefore is that no place of business has been established in England. This ties in with the substantive law of e-commerce, which does not attach significance to the place where a server is located.[235]

Is service in respect of the carrying on of the business of the branch?   It **10.94** will be recalled[236] that, if the claimant seeks to serve the foreign company on the basis that it has a branch in England and uses the method of service

---

[234] See Cheshire and North, 294.
[235] See Recital (19) of the E-Commerce Directive.   [236] See above, paras 4.08–10.

set out in the Companies Act 1985, the claimant must establish a good arguable case that the process that is served on the foreign company is in respect of the carrying on of the business of the branch. If, contrary to what has been argued above, it were to be held that the setting up of an interactive website on a server in an office in England by the foreign company constituted a branch, there would probably be no difficulty in showing that the process that is served on the company is in respect of the carrying on of the business of the branch. If there is online contracting through the interactive website, it could be said that the branch, acting on behalf of the foreign company, enters into the contract with the customer, thereby satisfying this requirement. It is submitted that this requirement would, as an alternative, be satisfied by showing that the branch is concerned with the performance of the undertakings out of which the dispute arises. In many cases, the branch will be involved in the performance of this undertaking.

10.95 It is worth remembering that, if the defendant has established a place of business which is not a branch in England, there is no requirement that the document served on the company must be in respect of the carrying on of the business. It could be argued that setting up an interactive website on a server in an office in England, whilst not a branch, is an established place of business, which is not a branch. It does look very different from a typical branch office.[237] Moreover, any difficulty over the requirement that the document served on the foreign company must be in respect of the carrying on of the business of the branch can arguably be avoided if service is effected by one of the methods set out in Part 6 of the Civil Procedure Rules.

Service under Part 6 of the Civil Procedure Rules

10.96 It will be recalled that where there is service under Part 6 arguably it does not have to be shown that a foreign company 'establishes' a place of business in Great Britain.[238] The latter connotes a degree of formality and permanence of location which is not required by Part 6. However, Part 6 still requires there to be a 'place of business' of the company within the jurisdiction. Service on an address with which the company has no more than a transient or irregular connection will not be valid.

10.97 The fact that it is easier to show that the defendant has 'a place of business' than that it 'establishes a place of business' is not going to help in the

---

[237] See, e.g. *South India Shipping Corp Ltd v Export-Import Bank of Korea* [1985] 1 WLR 585—a case involving a foreign bank with a branch office in England.

[238] See above, para 4.22. But see at para 4.16 the narrow view of the relationship between Part 6 and the Companies Act 1985 to the effect that it still has to be shown that a foreign company establishes a place of business in Great Britain.

situations with which we are concerned here. If the defendant's website is situated on a server in New York, the mere fact that this can be accessed in England is not enough to show that the defendant has a place of business in England. If the defendant has a web-server and website in England, it is doubtful that this constitutes a place of business for these purposes, even where it is an interactive website. There is no agent in England and, even if there was, it cannot be shown that the foreign defendant is there in England by virtue of its agent.[239] If the foreign defendant uses the website and server in England of an English company (a separate entity), then it is likely that any place of business in England is that of the English company and not that of the defendant. It would be otherwise if the English company is acting as agent for the foreign company. The question of whose business is being carried on in England, that of the defendant or that of a third party, is crucial when it comes to showing 'a place of business' for the purposes of service under Part 6.[240]

Service Out of the Jurisdiction

The problem that can arise in cases of electronic commerce is in satisfying **10.98** those grounds for service out of the jurisdiction that require it to be established that something has happened in England. When it comes to claims in contract, the grounds in question are ones specifying that the contract was made there and that a breach of contract was committed there.[241] The problem in satisfying these grounds stems from the fact that the internet is a method of communication that is not concerned with the place where things happen. The difficulty in satisfying each of these grounds in cases of electronic commerce will now be examined.

The contract was made within the jurisdiction

Rule 6.20(5) of the Civil Procedure Rules provides that a claim form may **10.99** be served out of the jurisdiction with the permission of the court if a claim is made in respect of a contract where the contract was made within the jurisdiction.[242] The English rules on formation of a contract must be applied in order to determine whether the contract was made in England.

---

[239] See above, para 4.12 when discussing service under the Companies Act 1985. The great importance attached to there being an agent also applies in relation to service under Part 6, at least where a separate entity is acting on behalf of the defendant, see *Lakah Group v Al Jazeera Satellite Channel* [2003] EWHC 1231 (QB); aff'd [2003] EWCA (Civ) 1781.

[240] The *Lakah Group* case, n 239 above.

[241] In tort claims, there is the ground that the damage sustained resulted from an act committed within the jurisdiction. This ground is considered below, para 10.164.

[242] Spain also has a traditional basis of jurisdiction founded on the contract being made in the forum. For problems of using this where the contract is made online see Forner Delaygua, n 154 above, 59–60.

It has already been seen[243] that, even where traditional methods of communication, such as telex and telephone, are used by the parties, there can be real difficulty in identifying the place where a contract was made. Moreover, there can be a lack of connection with that place. These problems arise equally in cases of contracts concluded by exchange of emails. Each email will have to be analyzed to see when first there occurs an offer, and then standard offer-and-acceptance terminology will be applied to see if there has been an acceptance of it, or a counter-offer. The place of acceptance will be the place of receipt under the instantaneous communication rule.[244] Where the contract is concluded online by the customer clicking boxes there will be problems not only of working out which party made the offer and which party accepted but also of working out where these were made. An online auction should be treated just the same as a physical auction. Unusual cases apart (for example, auction sales advertised as being 'without reserve'), each bidder makes an offer and the auctioneer accepts when bringing down the hammer or signifying acceptance in some other way.[245] By and large this is unaffected by the Electronic Commerce (EC Directive) Regulations 2002. The only proviso to this is that it is arguable that any offer made to the service provider would lapse if the receipt of the order were not acknowledged as required by Article 11 of the Regulations since the parties' expectations as to a reasonable time for the currency of the offer might be conditioned by compliance with Article 11.

10.100 It has been accepted that it is not always possible to analyze a contract in terms of offer and acceptance, and that, as a matter of principle, a contract can be made in more than one jurisdiction.[246] This was so decided in the context of where neither party wished to give the other an advantage in terms of where the agreement was finalized. Accordingly, copies were signed by each party in England and California and completion was arranged by telephone. It was held that there was a good arguable case that the terms of r 6.20(5)(a) had been met. This approach would provide a solution to the problem of identifying the place of offer and acceptance in cases of e-commerce. But it would mean applying this approach in a very different context. It is one thing to decide that a contract can be made in two countries when the parties intend that this should be the case and adopt a procedure for finalizing the contract that reflects this. It is a very different thing to so decide when the parties have no such intention.

---

[243] See above, paras 4.32–36.
[244] But compare J Hogan-Doran, 'Jurisdiction in cyberspace: The when and where of online contracts' (2003) 77 Australian LJ 377.
[245] See *Payne v Cave* (1789) 3 TR 148; Sale of Goods Act 1979, s 57(2).
[246] *Apple Corps Ltd v Apple Computer Inc* [2004] EWHC 768 (Ch).

Rather than extending the use of r 6.20(5)(a), e-commerce should be the catalyst for its abolition.[247]

A breach of contract was committed within the jurisdiction

Rule 6.20(6) provides that a claim form may be served out of the juris- **10.101** diction with the permission of the court if a claim is made in respect of a breach of contract committed within the jurisdiction. In a case of non-performance, it is necessary to identify, applying English law, the place of performance of the obligation that has been breached.

The seller's obligation to deliver the goods The most commonly **10.102** breached obligations of the seller in an international sale of goods contract are those of delivering the goods or of delivering goods in conformity with the contract (which is treated as the same obligation for the purposes of the operation of this ground for service out of the jurisdiction). The breach of the seller's obligation to deliver the goods is committed in the state where the goods should have been delivered.

Delivery by traditional means When it comes to the sale over the internet **10.103** of non-digitized products, delivery will be made by traditional means, such as by carriage of goods by sea and road. The fact that the contract has been made online over the internet or by exchange of emails will make no difference. The position is exactly the same as for cases where the contract has been made by traditional means. The sales documentation will normally specify the place of delivery and, if it does not, it can be ascertained in the same way as in any other case where the place of delivery is not specified.[248]

Performance over the internet We are concerned here with the situation **10.104** where a contract has been made for the purchase of a digitized product, such as software, or for the provision of an online service, with transfer of the information over the internet. When the recipient tries to download the information, he is unable to do so. The service provider is in breach of its obligation to provide the information it contracted to provide. In particular, it could be described as being in breach of a sub-obligation to make the information available for downloading by the recipient. Alternatively, the recipient manages to download the software but finds that it is defective. Again the service provider is in breach of its obligation to provide the information it contracted to provide. However, it is not possible to particularize this obligation in the way that it is in the situation where the recipient tries to download the information, but finds that he is unable to do so. For the purposes of r 6.20(6), and, indeed, for service out

---

[247] See below, para 10.239.   [248] See above, paras 4.71–76.

of the jurisdiction generally, the nature of the contract is irrelevant. It does not matter whether the contract is regarded as one for the provision of services, the sale of goods (a view that has been rejected in the context of English sale of goods law),[249] or neither.[250]

10.105 It is for English law, as the law of the forum, to determine where the obligation to provide the information should have been performed. There is as yet no English domestic substantive law on the place of provision of information over the internet. However, it is submitted that the choice is between the place of dispatch of the information, the place of receipt, the place where the service provider has a specified personal connection and the place where the recipient has a specified personal connection.[251] In the situation where the recipient tries to download the information, but finds that he is unable to do so, and, accordingly, the service provider is in breach of its sub-obligation to make the information available for downloading by the recipient, the place where this sub-obligation should have been performed is obvious. It is the place where the web-server which the customer accesses to obtain the information is located, ie the place of dispatch. In contrast, in the situation where the recipient manages to download the software but finds that it is defective, and, accordingly, the service provider is simply in breach of its obligation to provide the information it contracted to provide, there is no obvious place where this obligation should have been performed. It is arguable that this place should be regarded as being the place of dispatch. This would provide consistency for all cases of breach of the obligation to provide information, regardless of the form which this breach takes.

10.106 **The buyer's obligation to pay for the goods** The most commonly breached obligation of the buyer is that of payment for the goods.

10.107 *Payment by traditional means* With business-to-business contracts, if delivery is made by conventional means, payment may also be made in a conventional way, such as by letter of credit. Moreover, even where a contract is made online over the internet or by the exchange of emails, payment may be made by traditional means. In such cases, the fact that the contract was made in this modern technological way will make no

---

[249] See *St Alban's City and District Council v International Computers Ltd* [1997] FSR 251. If it were necessary to classify the nature of the contract for the purposes of service out of the jurisdiction, the classification under the substantive English law would be adopted, which would rule out a sale of goods classification. Compare the discussion of the Unfair Contract Terms Act 1977 below, paras 21.113–118.

[250] Compare the position under Art 5(1) of the Brussels I Regulation, above, para 3.143.

[251] These solutions were discussed, above, paras 10.60–74, in the context of Art 5(1)(b) of the Brussels I Regulation, where some of the difficulties in ascertaining the location of these places are examined.

difference. In the case of non-payment, the place where payment should have been made will be the same, regardless of the way in which the contract was made. The sales documentation will normally specify the place of payment and, if it does not, or there is no sales documentation, it can be ascertained in the same way as in any other case where the place of payment is not specified.[252]

Payment over the internet   This is a common feature of business-to-con- **10.108** sumer contracts and will also arise with a business to business contract for the purchase of digitized products, such as software, or for the provision of online services. Payment may be made in this way for tangible goods as well. Payment is made online by direct use of a credit card or by means of electronic money (this can involve software based virtual cash)[253] and the order will not be accepted until payment has been made. This means that normally there will be no problem of non-payment. However, if such a case does arise, because, for example, the credit card is not honoured by the bank, ascertaining the place where payment should have been made is not easy. The internet contract will not expressly provide for a place of payment. The process of payment by credit card over the internet can involve credit card details being sent from the recipient's computer in State A to the service provider's web-server in State B which is automatically programmed to receive payment and then release the digitized goods or services from a web-server in State C. Is the place where payment should have been made in State A, B or C? The realistic choice has to be between State A and State B and it is submitted that payment should have been made in State B, the place where payment should have been received.[254] Under English law payment by credit card constitutes not conditional but absolute payment.[255] What the merchant must be given[256] is the information necessary to draw down payment from the card issuer. If the card issuer then defaults, there is no recourse of the merchant against the buyer. Payment should therefore be regarded as being made in State B. The place of supply of the information, State A, is an unattractive solution. It is the equivalent to saying with non-internet transactions that a buyer pays in State A when he puts a cheque in the post in State A.

---

[252] See above paras 4.83–86.

[253] The user downloads software from the website of an online issuer and opens an online wallet which has value added to it by a credit card. Online purchases involve deducting the amount from the wallet. See generally Simmons and Simmons, *E-Commerce Law* (2001) 54–55 and Ch 5 generally.

[254] See also the discussion below, para 21.239, of the situation where credit card details are provided to the wrong person.

[255] *Re Charge Card Services* [1989] Ch 497, CA.

[256] The decision in *Re Charge Card*, ibid, was based heavily upon an earlier agreement between the merchant and the card issuer.

Forum Conveniens/Forum non Conveniens

Internet cases in general

10.109   No special principles of *forum non conveniens* have been developed for internet cases. Instead, the normal principles will apply. There are as yet no English cases making this point but there are *forum non conveniens* internet cases in Canada[257] and Australia, including a decision of the High Court of Australia,[258] where the courts have simply applied the normal Canadian and Australian principles of forum non conveniens.

10.110   However, when it comes to the application of these principles and, in particular, to the identification of the appropriate forum for trial, it is possible to identify various internet connections, which are obviously unique to internet cases. At the same time, traditional connections will have to be examined in internet cases.

10.111   **Internet connections**   When it comes to ascertaining the appropriate forum, internet connections to be taken into account are as follows. First, where the computers (including web-servers) used by each party are located. In the Canadian case of *Rudder v Microsoft Corp*,[259] a class action by members of an online service[260] was brought against the service provider. Winkler J in the Ontario Superior Court of Justice, when considering whether to exercise the discretion to stay the Ontario proceedings,[261] took into account the fact that all the computers in which members' content and information were contained were located in the State of Washington. There was no problem in ascertaining this. Neither was there any problem in *Dow Jones & Company Inc v Gutnick*[262] in ascertaining that the defendant online journal provider made information available by transmitting it from a computer in New York either directly to computers at the defendant's premises in New Jersey or via an intermediate site operated by the defendant elsewhere in New Jersey. It was then loaded on to six servers in New Jersey. However, in some cases there may be difficulties in locating computers.[263] For example, information may be regularly downloaded on to a lap top by a person moving around Europe.

10.112   Second, it is relevant to consider where the internet service provider carried out the activities associated with the provision of its services. In the *Rudder* case, Winkler J took into account the fact that Microsoft (the defendant) carried out in Washington the following activities associated

---

[257]   *Alteen v Informix Corp* (1998) 164 Nfld & PEIR 301; *Kitakufe v Oloya* 1998 Ont Ct of Justice Carswell Ont 2494.

[258]   *Dow Jones & Company v Gutnick* (2002) 210 CLR 575.

[259]   1999 Carswell Ont 3195, Ontario Superior Court of Justice.

[260]   The service was providing internet access.

[261]   The case concerned the discretion to stay where there is a foreign jurisdiction clause.

[262]   n 258 above.   [263]   See above, paras 10.08–09.

with the provision of its services: the business management of accounts of recipients; recipient authentication; policy-making regarding member accounts; and billing and recipient services.

Third, the location of the party providing access to the internet is arguably **10.113** a relevant connection, at least where both parties use the same party to provide internet access or different providers are established in the same state. However, this connection should not be regarded as being of much weight.

Fourth, in the situation where there is a sale through another party's **10.114** website, such as an auction site, the location of the website and website owner's place of business should be relevant factors. However, if the service provider is clearly selling in its own right and merely makes use of a website hosted by someone else, the location of this website and the host's place of business should be given little weight.

Traditional considerations   Traditional considerations used in non- **10.115** internet cases will also be relevant. Thus in the *Rudder* case, Winkler J looked at where the evidence as to billing was located and where the Microsoft witnesses were located. There was no difficulty in ascertaining that the relevant evidence and witnesses were located in Washington where Microsoft carried out its activities associated with the provision of services. In the internet defamation case of *Dow Jones & Company Inc v Gutnick*, the High Court of Australia was much concerned with the applicable law.[264] There was a conceptual difficulty in defining the place where the tort was committed for defamation over the internet but once it was held that this was the place where the information was downloaded there was no difficulty in applying this rule and concluding that this took place in Victoria. However, as will be seen below, when it comes to the provision of digitized products which are transferred and paid for over the internet, there can be considerable difficulties in applying some of the traditional considerations.[265]

Internet sales/provision of information

We are concerned here with an action in contract between the recipient **10.116** and service provider arising out of the sale of goods or the provision of information.

---

[264] See below, paras 21.125–132.

[265] In Canada, it has been acknowledged that there are difficulties in establishing a real and substantial connection between the action and the forum, which is required for jurisdiction, in internet cases: *Craig Broadcast Systems Inc v Frank N Magid Associates Inc* 2000 Carswell Man 131, para 23, Manitoba Court of Appeal. However, this did not cause any problems in a case where goods were merely marketed on the internet: *Old North State Brewing Company Inc v Newlands Services Inc* [1999] 4 WWR 573, British Columbia Court of Appeal.

10.117 **Ascertaining the appropriate forum** This involves looking at internet connections, as identified above, and at the typical traditional connections that apply in sales cases.[266]

10.118 *The place where the computers used by each party are located* This internet connection will operate in the same way in internet sales as it does in any other type of internet case.

10.119 *The place where the service provider carried out the activities associated with sales/the provision of information* There are no obvious difficulties in ascertaining the location of this place. Thus in the *Rudder* case,[267] there was no problem in identifying where Microsoft carried out the activities associated with the provision of its services. The business management of accounts of recipients, recipient authentication, policy-making regarding member accounts, and billing and recipient service were all carried out in Washington. There would be no difficulty either if it had provided sales rather than services.

10.120 *The location of the party providing access to the internet* This internet connection will operate in the same way in internet sales as it does in any other type of internet case.

10.121 *Sale through another party's website: the location of the website and website owner's place of business* This internet connection will also operate in the same way in internet sales as it does in any other type of internet case.

10.122 *The place of delivery of the goods/provision of the information* In the situation where there is an internet contract for the sale of tangible goods which are delivered in a conventional way, for example by carriage by sea and land, the problem of ascertaining the place of delivery is precisely the same as in cases where the sales contract has been made in a conventional way, not over the internet.[268]

10.123 The position is very different in cases involving performance over the internet. In such cases, the difficulty involved in identifying the place where, in a case of non-performance, the information should have been provided is familiar to us from the discussion of the service provider's obligations for the purposes of r 6.20(6) of the Civil Procedure Rules.[269] This problem of identification will arise not only in cases of non-performance, i.e. a failure to provide the information, but also in cases where there has been performance. For example, the recipient has received the information and the service provider is suing for payment. In ascertaining the appropriate forum, one relevant connection is the place

---

[266] See above, paras 4.120–151.   [267] n 259 above.
[268] See above, para 4.125.   [269] See above, paras 10.102–105.

where the information was provided. Is this the place where the information was dispatched, the place where it was received, the place where the service provider has a personal connecting factor, or the place where the recipient has a personal connecting factor?[270] There is no clear answer to this question. In such circumstances, there may be a temptation to ignore the place of delivery/provision of services factor altogether.[271] But this would be to ignore a connection that will become increasingly important as e-commerce increases. A better approach would be to accept that it is not essential to define the place where the information is provided. It is possible for the purposes of *forum conveniens/forum non conveniens* to treat these four possible solutions to the definitional problem as separate connecting factors with each one to be weighed in the balance. It is, though, necessary to reach some conclusion on the relative weight to be attached to each of these four connecting factors. This will depend very much on the facts of the case. Thus in a case where the defendant has failed to upload software on to the web-server which the recipient was to access, the place of dispatch (i.e. the place where the web-server containing the software to be accessed by the recipient is located) should be regarded as being particularly important. In contrast, in a case where the customer has downloaded software but it is defective, the place of receipt (i.e. the place where the recipient's computer, on to which he downloaded the software, is located) becomes particularly important.

The place of payment for the goods/information   There is no special problem **10.124** in ascertaining the place of payment in an internet sales case if payment is made in a conventional way, for example by commercial letters of credit. The position is the same as with a sales contract not made over the internet.[272]

But what if payment is made over the internet? The difficulty involved in **10.125** identifying the place where, in a case of non-payment, the payment over the internet should have been made is familiar to us from the discussion of the recipient's obligations for the purposes of r 6.20(6).[273] This problem of identification will arise not only in cases of a failure to pay but also in cases where payment has been made. For example, the recipient has paid for the information but has not received it or it is defective. The recipient is suing the service provider for failure to provide the information which

---

[270] See generally the discussion, in the context of Art 5(1) of the Brussels I Regulation, of the merits of each of these rules, above, paras 10.60–74.

[271] This is by analogy with the position where it is difficult to work out where the contract was made, see above, para 4.136.

[272] See above, paras 4.128–132.   [273] See above, para 10.108.

he contracted to provide. In ascertaining the appropriate forum, one relevant connection is the place where the payment over the internet was made. Whilst it may be clear that payment has been made, it may be by no means easy to say where this occurred. Payment could be regarded as being made as soon as credit card details are provided by the recipient. But these details are sent from the recipient's computer in State A to the service provider's computer in State B which is automatically programmed to receive payment and then release the digitized product or online service from State C. Has the payment been made in State A, B or C? It has been argued above that it should be regarded as having been made in State B on the basis that what the merchant must be given is the information necessary to draw down payment from the card issuer.[274] However, this definitional difficulty need not detain us. It is possible for the purposes of *forum conveniens/forum non conveniens* to look at the whole of the payment process and weigh in the balance the fact that there is a connection with State A, B and C. In a case where there has been payment, the payment factor (i.e. the payment process connections) whilst arguably relevant should not be given much weight and should be regarded as being less important than the delivery factor.[275] In a case of non-payment over the internet, the payment factor should be given more weight. Where the customer has failed to provide credit card details, it is submitted that the most significant connection is with State A in the above example, ie where the customer's computer is located. This is on the basis that what the customer has failed to do is to upload the credit card details on to his computer.

10.126 *The place of performance of an obligation under the e-commerce contract (other than to deliver or pay for the goods/information)* Typical breaches of obligations under an international sale of goods contract (other than delivery or payment), such as the breach of a seller's obligation to hand over documents or breach of the buyer's obligation to take delivery, are only likely to arise with tangible goods delivered by conventional means. In such circumstances, the place where these obligations are to be performed is no more difficult to ascertain in a case where a contract is made over the internet than it is in a case where it is not made in this way.[276] However, one example of where there could be a problem is where the seller[277] of a digitized product that has been transferred over the internet has failed to transfer property in the product. It is not clear where the property in digitized goods is to pass. Arguably the analogy should be drawn with

---

[274] See *Re Charge Card Services* [1989] Ch 497; see above, para 10.108.
[275] See the discussion in relation to non-internet sales above, paras 4.128–131.
[276] For the latter see above, paras 4.133–134.
[277] This is assuming that there is a sale. Often there will not be, see above, para 10.45.

the identification of the place of delivery of the goods/provision of the information, which has been discussed above. This would mean looking at the place where the information was dispatched, the place where it was received, the place where the service provider has a personal connecting factor, and the place where the recipient has a personal connecting factor. Each would be treated as a separate connecting factor to be weighed in the balance.

The place where the e-commerce contract was made The difficulty in ascer- **10.127** taining the place where a contract is made online (rather than by exchange of emails) is familiar to us.[278] Even splitting it up into the component elements of an offer and acceptance and regarding each of these as a connection with a state, thereby avoiding the technical question of where the contract was made, does not help a lot because of the difficulty of ascertaining both where the offer and the acceptance were made in the situation where these took place over the internet. In cases where it is by no means easy to work out where the contract was made, this factor has not been regarded as being particularly significant.[279] However, if this attitude were to be taken in relation to contracts made online, it would mean ignoring this connection in all cases of contracts made in this way. In general, this would not matter because the mere fact that a contract was made in a particular state does not in itself constitute much of a connection with that state.

The law applicable to the e-commerce contract As will be seen,[280] ascertain- **10.128** ing the law applicable to an internet sales contract can be more difficult than a sales contract not made in this way. The real problem arises in cases where there is no choice of the applicable law by the parties.[281] The applicable law factor has been regarded as a significant one in non-internet sale of goods cases where the applicable laws are significantly different.[282] In internet cases where the applicable laws are significantly different, the applicable law should be ascertained despite the problems that are sometimes involved.

A jurisdiction agreement There are no particular problems in identifying **10.129** a choice of jurisdiction clause in internet cases. As noted earlier,[283] a click wrap agreement can contain terms and conditions on which the service provider contracts and these can include a choice of jurisdiction agreement.

---

[278] See above, paras 10.99–100.
[280] See below, paras 21.35–119.
[281] Nonetheless, the conclusion in Ch 21 is that the Rome Convention does work reasonably well for internet contracts.
[282] See above, paras 4.139–140.

[279] See above, para 4.136.

[283] See above, para 10.39.

10.130 *The availability of witnesses*   Many sales disputes concern the quality of the goods sold. If these are tangible goods delivered in a conventional way the question of where the witnesses as to the quality of the goods are located is no more difficult to answer in a case where the contract was made over the internet than it is in a case where it was made in a conventional way.[284] However, if there is a digitized product, such as software, that has been provided over the internet, and it is alleged that what has been provided is defective, it is less easy to say where witnesses as to their quality are located. The recipient may turn to an expert in his (the recipient's) home state to examine the software but could presumably send it for examination to an expert in a foreign state. By the time that the parties come to litigate over where to litigate, it may be clear which expert witness each party is going to use and where each is located.

10.131 *The residence of the parties*   Problems of location of the parties are a prominent feature of e-commerce sales and make it difficult to identify the residence of the parties, which is normally the easiest connecting factor to identify when ascertaining the appropriate forum. Nonetheless, in e-commerce cases, the personal connecting factor does provide a meaningful connection with a state which is not always the case with the place of receipt or place of dispatch. It is arguable therefore that in such cases the personal connecting factor should be given greater weight than either the place of receipt or the place of dispatch.

10.132 *A multiplicity of proceedings*   This factor will operate in exactly the same way in internet sales cases as it operates in more usual non-internet sales cases. The wide range of contacts with numerous other states that can arise with e-commerce means that the risk of a multiplicity of proceedings is certainly there with certain instances of e-commerce. An obvious example of which is the situation where subscribers to an online journal from around the world all sue the publisher in contract.

10.133 *Other considerations*   It is relevant to look at contracts related to the sales contract.[285] Thus the courts should look at the law governing the contract for the carriage of the goods,[286] its insurance and the contracts for payment by commercial letters of credit. With an internet contract which involves delivery of tangible goods by conventional means, there will be these related contracts and this factor will operate in the normal way. With a contract involving performance over the internet there will be no such related contracts.

---

[284] For the latter see above, para 4.142.
[285] See above, para 4.149.   [286] See below, paras 14.09–37.

Injustice abroad Any examination of whether there would be injustice **10.134**
in trial abroad will operate in exactly the same way in internet sales cases
as in non-internet sales cases.

A Foreign Jurisdiction Agreement

The normal principle that, prima facie, an English court will stay an action **10.135**
brought in England in defiance of an agreement providing for trial
abroad, will apply, even though the agreement is contained in an online
agreement. The claimant may raise the argument put forward in *Rudder v
Microsoft Corp*,[287] that an agreement in this form does not represent the
true agreement of the parties. The form in which the agreement is provided to recipients obscures the forum selection clause in that only a
portion of the agreement is presented on the screen at one time. This led
on to the argument that the rest of the agreement was essentially 'fine
print', which under Canadian law had to be brought specifically to the
attention of the party accepting the terms. English private international
law has not under the traditional rules on jurisdiction concerned itself
with the form which the agreement takes.[288] But even if it were so to
concern itself, the same answer should be given as was given by Winkler J
in the Ontario Superior Court of Justice, who rejected this argument on
the basis that, if accepted, this would undermine any online jurisdiction
agreement.

V. INTERNET TORTS

1. INTERNET TORTS GENERALLY

The most common internet torts are infringement of intellectual property **10.136**
rights (for example the defendant creates a website which infringes
another's trade mark) and defamation (for example the defendant's
journal is published online and a defamatory article appears on its website). Nonetheless, it is easy to envisage other internet torts, including
ones that arise out of the international sale of goods. In this section we will
look at internet torts generally and then in the following sections look at
the specific internet torts of negligent misstatement, and negligent and
fraudulent misrepresentation, conversion, a failure to sell, inducement of
breach of contract and negligence.

---

[287] n 259 above.
[288] Compare the position under Art 23 of the Brussels I Regulation, discussed above, paras
10.37–39. See also the discussion in relation to choice of law clauses below, paras 21.36–39.

The EC Rules

10.137 In internet tort cases, it may be possible to use as the basis of jurisdiction Article 23, Article 2, or Article 5(5) of the Brussels I Regulation,[289] none of which are concerned with whether the matter relates to tort or not. The application of these non-specific bases of jurisdiction in internet cases has already been examined and what has been said above[290] does not need to be repeated. When it comes to the application of Article 5(3) of the Brussels I Regulation to internet torts, the familiar questions arise: first, where is the place of the event giving rise to the damage; and second, where is the place where the damage occurred?

Article 5(3): the place of the event giving rise to the damage

10.138 **The difficulty involved** Experts at the Hague Conference on private international law, after much consideration of the problems of jurisdiction in cases of electronic commerce, have expressed the view that in cases of torts committed over the internet it is very difficult, if not impossible, to identify the place of the event giving rise to the damage.[291] The difficulty can be illustrated by looking at a typical case of an internet tort, namely where an online journal contains allegedly defamatory material. A contributor to the journal may send copy from his home state, State A. This is sent over the internet to a computer in State B, where the material for the journal is assembled. The process of transfer of the information over the internet to subscribers involves a sequence of events, starting with the original uploading (i.e. making the information available over the internet by placing it in a storage area managed by a web-server) by the publisher (i.e. the service provider) in State C and ending with its eventual downloading on to the computer of the subscriber (ie the recipient) in State D.[292] In between, the information may have passed through an intermediate web-server in State E. The European Court of Justice has held that, where it is difficult or impossible to determine the place of the event giving rise to the damage, the plaintiff will have to rely on bringing the action in the place where the damage occurred.[293] This was said in the context of a case where the Court was faced with having to determine the place where the cooling system in refrigerated containers broke down during a voyage

---

[289] In a multi-defendant case, or where there are third party proceedings, or where there is a counter-claim it may be possible to use Art 6, discussed above, paras 9.09–24, 9.39–41, 9.45–46.

[290] See above, paras 3.22–60, 3.302–312.

[291] See the conclusions of Commission II at the Geneva Round Table, Prel Doc No 7, n 2 above, 21–22; the expert meeting at Ottawa, n 129 above, at 5.

[292] These are essentially the facts of the *Dow Jones* case, n 258 above.

[293] Case C-51/97 *Réunion Européenne v Spliethoff's Bevrachtingskantoor BV* [1998] ECR I-6511.

from Australia to the Netherlands. It is one thing to say that the facts of a particular case pose a problem in identifying the place of the event giving rise to the damage and therefore this rule should not operate, but it is an entirely different thing to exclude the place of the event giving rise to the damage rule for all torts committed over the internet. This would exclude potentially large numbers of cases. There are already many instances of infringement of intellectual property rights[294] and of defamation over the internet.[295] The numbers of internet tort cases will only increase over the coming years. The European Court of Justice should define the place of the event giving rise to the damage in internet tort cases.

A definition for a particular tort The courts will be faced with, for **10.139** example, an internet defamation case or an internet negligent misstatement case, rather than an abstract internet tort case. In the multi-state defamation case of *Shevill v Presse Alliance SA*,[296] the European Court of Justice was at pains to identify the place of the event for the tort of multi-state defamation, taking into account the particular situation that arises in such cases. There are also national decisions defining the place of the event for particular torts. When it comes to internet torts, it seems likely that the European Court of Justice, if faced with such cases, would emphasize the tort in question and define the place of the event giving rise to the damage for that particular internet tort, rather than emphasize the fact that it is an internet tort and adopt one definition which would apply to all such torts. It is even more predictable that national courts would do likewise. The starting point is therefore going to be the definition adopted for the place of the event giving rise to the damage for this particular tort in non-internet cases. For example, with a case of defamation over the internet, the starting point will be the multi-state defamation case of *Shevill*.[297]

The alternative solutions In the absence of decisions from the European **10.140** Court of Justice and from national courts, it is unclear how the place of the event giving rise to the damage will be defined in relation to particular internet torts. Nonetheless, it is submitted that, for most internet torts,[298]

---

[294] See, e.g. *Re The Maritim Trademark* (Case 416 0294/00)) [2003] IL Pr 297, Landgericht (District Court), Hamburg. There are many cases in the US, see, eg, *Zippo Manufacturing Company v Zippo Dot Com Inc* 952 F Supp 1119 (US District Court WD Pennsylvania 1997); *Mattel Inc v Adventure Apparel* (SDNY 2001).

[295] See, e.g. *Braintech Inc v Kostiuk* [1999] BCCA 0169; *Blakey v Continental Airlines Inc* 751 A 2d 538 (2000); *Dow Jones v Gutnick*, n 258 above.

[296] Case C-68/93 [1995] ECR I-415.

[297] See PJ Borchers, 'Tort and Contract Jurisdiction via the Internet: The "Minimum Contacts" Test and the Brussels Regulation Compared' [2003] Netherlands Intl L Rev 401.

[298] An exception would be the tort of a refusal to sell. This takes place where the decision to refuse to sell was made, see below, para 10.200.

the alternatives that could be adopted for defining the place of the event giving rise to the damage are the same. First, there is a conventional definition in terms of the place of uploading of the information or downloading it on to the computer of the recipient. Second, there is a bolder definition in terms of the place where the defendant is established. The arguments in favour of and against these two alternative solutions will now be considered.

The place of uploading or downloading

10.141 THE ARGUMENTS IN FAVOUR   First, the uploading and downloading of information on the internet are both undeniably events. Although there is a whole sequence of events involved in communicating over the internet, it is submitted that the only two really significant events are the uploading and the downloading of the information. If the information is uploaded in Member State A and downloaded in Member State B, it would be absurd to allocate jurisdiction to Member State C where there is an intermediate web-server that relays the information. Neither is there a strong connection with the State where the service provider starts the process of uploading the information (in Member State X) that is eventually placed on a web-server (in Member State A) that can be accessed by customers (i.e. the place of uploading).[299] In contrast to the place of uploading or downloading, a definition in terms of the place where the defendant is established does not appear to be referring to an event at all.

10.142 Second, the definition of both the place of uploading and of downloading is a clear one. According to the *Dow Jones* case,[300] the place of uploading is the place where the web-server (on which the information that is being made available is stored) is situated. This is important in tort cases. It means that there is no definitional problem in the situation where a report is compiled by a number of contributors sending in information by email from different Member States. The report appears on the internet by being placed on a web-server in France and is defamatory or perhaps it contains misstatements that induced a contract. To complicate things the contributors may input information bit by bit on to their lap top computers as they move around the EC and only at some later point file their whole contribution to form part of the eventual report. Nevertheless, the place of uploading in relation to the report is undeniable, it is France. Similarly, in the *Dow Jones* case,[301] Dow Jones had its editorial offices for the online

---

[299] For an illustration of this scenario see the facts of the *Dow Jones* case, para 10.169 below. In many cases though the process will start in the same state as that where the web-server accessed by customers is located (ie the place of uploading).

[300] n 258 above.   [301] ibid.

journal in New York. Material for publication once prepared by its author was transferred to a computer in the editorial offices in New York. From there it was transferred either directly to computers at Dow Jones's premises in New Jersey or via an intermediate server operated by Dow Jones elsewhere in New Jersey. It was then loaded on to six servers in New Jersey. The information was uploaded in New Jersey.[302] According to the same case, information is downloaded (i.e. the process by which the web-server delivers a document in response to a request by the recipient)[303] on to the computer of the recipient. The place of downloading is therefore the place where the recipient's computer was situated. This too is a clear definition.

Third, both the place of uploading and that of downloading constitute **10.143** significant connecting factors which, depending on the circumstances, can be helpful as places of trial from the point of view of the evidence and of the conduct of the proceedings.[304]

THE ARGUMENTS AGAINST There are various disadvantages that are **10.144** common to both a place of uploading rule and a place of downloading rule. These were identified earlier in the context of the discussion of Article 5(1)(b).[305] These common disadvantages apply equally to tort cases. For example, the place of uploading and downloading can be manipulated by one or other of the parties. This danger is there as much in tort cases as in contract cases. A defendant service provider may deliberately upload the information on to a web-server in a particular Member State which is a favourable forum for him in the event of the trial of a tort action, whilst the recipient may deliberately download the information in a particular Member State for the same reason.

WHICH ONE TO APPLY: THE PLACE OF UPLOADING OR THE PLACE OF DOWN- **10.145** LOADING? If a conventional definition in terms of the place of uploading or downloading were to be adopted, then a decision has to be made as to which one it should be for internet tort cases. The respective merits of each of these two solutions were considered earlier when discussing contracts[306] and apply equally to torts. There are some additional arguments that arise with torts that do not arise with contracts because of the scenarios that can face the courts in the former but not in the latter.

---

[302] ibid, para 16.   [303] ibid, para 15.
[304] For interpretation of Art 5(3) in the light of this criterion see the opinion of Leger AG in Case C-168/02 *Kronhofer v Maier*.
[305] Above, paras 10.67, 10.69. The discussion there was of the merits of a place of dispatch and a place of receipt rule. In a typical tort case, where information is transferred by being placed on a website and accessed by the recipient, the place of dispatch is the place of uploading and the place of receipt is the place of downloading.
[306] Above, paras 10.66–69.

10.146 First, with certain torts the substantive law for that tort appears to favour one solution rather than the other. This is arguably the case with infringement of copyright, where the substantive law supports the place of downloading solution in that it is arguable that the downloading constitutes the copying in a case of copyright infringement.

10.147 Second, it could be argued that a tort that is essentially concerned with the conduct of the defendant, such as trespass, negligent misstatement or negligence, points to a place of uploading solution whereas the tort of defamation, which is concerned with publication, points to the place of downloading solution.[307]

10.148 Third, information will normally just be input by the defendant in one place. This favours a place of uploading rule. In contrast, information can be downloaded by numerous persons in numerous places. If a place of downloading rule were to be adopted, the defendant would then be subject to action in any EC Member State in which the information has been downloaded, giving the plaintiff opportunities for forum shopping. This would be a particular problem with defamation and infringement of intellectual property rights over the internet.[308] A plaintiff can have a reputation in lots of different states which is damaged in all of those states and an intellectual property right can be infringed in lots of different states. However, this is not a problem with all internet torts. For example, with negligent misstatement the individual plaintiff may simply be relying on the downloading of a web page containing the misstatement in a single specified Member State.

10.149 Fourth, the place of uploading fits in better with the concept of the place of the event giving rise to the damage than the place of downloading. With many torts, the common scenario will be the downloader suing the uploader. In this scenario, the place of uploading rule focuses on the act of the defendant, which is as it should be, given that what is sought to be established is jurisdiction against the defendant. In contrast, the place of downloading focuses on the act of the plaintiff.

---

[307] This is a distinction referred to by the Australian High Court in the *Dow Jones* case, n 258 above, paras 43–44, when searching for the place where a tort is committed.

[308] The High Court of Australia still favoured a place of downloading rule, see below, para 10.169. And see the Scots case of *Bonnier Media Ltd v Greg Lloyd Smith and Kestrel Trading Corp* 2003 SC 36, [2002] ETMR 86, a case of threatened passing off and trade mark infringement where the threatened delict involved setting up a website outside Scotland which could be accessed in Scotland. It was held that Scotland had jurisdiction under Art 5(3) of the Brussels Convention. The delict was potentially committed in every state in which the website could be seen but this was limited by saying that there would be no jurisdiction in a state where the impact of the website would be insignificant. The Landgericht, Hamburg, has also applied a place of downloading rule to trademark infringement over the internet in *Re The Maritim Trademark*, n 294 above.

The conclusion from this analysis is that, if a conventional definition in **10.150** terms of the place of uploading or downloading is adopted, in general the former is probably to be preferred to the latter. However, it is dangerous to generalize and considerations may arise with a particular tort which may point to the place of downloading. A tort by tort analysis is needed.

The place where the defendant is established   Under this solution jurisdiction **10.151** is allocated to the place in a Member State where the defendant is established. The defendant will typically be the service provider[309] whose online journal defames, whose website infringes a trade mark or contains a negligent misstatement.

THE ARGUMENTS IN FAVOUR   This solution can be supported, both in **10.152** terms of principle and in terms of precedent. In terms of principle, the following points can be made. First, there may be less difficulty in ascertaining where a defendant is established than there is in ascertaining where a computer is situated. Second, this solution fits in best with the substantive law of electronic commerce. It will be recalled that the E-Commerce Directive sees the origin of the information in terms of where the internet service provider is established.[310] Third, this solution is less likely to lead to one or other of the parties manipulating the place with jurisdiction than if a definition is adopted in terms of the place of uploading or place of downloading. Admittedly, a definition in terms of the defendant's place of establishment still involves the risk of manipulation: a company may establish itself in a Member State because it is favourable to it in the event of trial. But this would require much more effort than is required for manipulating the place of uploading or downloading.

There is a precedent for defining the place of the event giving rise to the **10.153** damage in terms of the place where the defendant is established. This is the definition adopted by the European Court of Justice in *Shevill v Presse Alliance SA*,[311] a case of multi-state defamation. It was held that, in the case of a libel by a newspaper article distributed in several Contracting States, the place of the event giving rise to the damage 'can only be the place where the publisher of the newspaper in question is established, since that is the place where the harmful event originated and from which the libel was issued and put into circulation'.[312] The case concerned the multi-state

---

[309]   In the sense in which this term is used in the E Commerce Directive, discussed above, para 10.26, i.e. a person providing an information society service.

[310]   See above, para 10.26.

[311]   Case C-68/93 [1995] ECR I-415.

[312]   The idea in *Shevill*, ibid, para 24, of looking at where the harmful event originated has been followed by AG Jacobs in Case C-18/02 *DFDS Torline v SEKO* [2004] IL Pr 10 at paras 70–71 of his opinion. The tort originated in Sweden where notifications of industrial action were issued and sent.

distribution of libel through the press but the principles laid down would doubtless also be applied to multi-state distribution of libel over the internet. It is then arguable that the rule for multi-state distribution of libel over the internet should apply equally to other torts involving multi-state distribution over the internet. The internet by its very nature involves multi-state distribution of information and so it is arguable that the rule for multi-state distribution of libel over the internet should apply to all other internet torts.

10.154 Finally, in support of this solution it can be mentioned that experts on electronic commerce and private international law, at meetings organized by the Hague Conference on private international in the context of the proposed Hague Judgments Convention, favoured something similar to this for internet torts in that they preferred to refer to a personal connect-ing factor related to the parties, rather than literally trying to find the place of the act.[313] Some experts favoured the use of a presumption that the place of the act causative of the injury would be situated in the place of habitual residence of the defendant or author of the act.[314] The Brussels I Regulation by and large does not use habitual residence as the relevant personal connecting factor and so it would not be appropriate to use this particular connecting factor. Other experts preferred a simpler solution making available a forum at the place of habitual residence of the plaintiff.[315] However, this pro-plaintiff stance would not be appropriate for Article 5(3) of the Brussels I Regulation. Its predecessor, Article 5(3) of the Brussels Convention, has been interpreted by the European Court of Justice in such a way as to avoid the situation where the plaintiff was able to sue in the Member State where he was domiciled.[316]

10.155 THE ARGUMENTS AGAINST   There is a number of arguments that can be made against adopting this solution. First, it would be necessary to define the place where a defendant is established. It would be possible to define this in terms of the place where the defendant internet company pursues its economic activity. This is the definition adopted in the E-Commerce Directive. Recital (19) states that 'the place of establishment of a company providing services via an Internet website is not the place at which the technology supporting its website is located or the place at which its website is accessible but the place where it pursues its economic activity'. Article 2(c) of the Directive goes on to define an 'established service

---

[313] Geneva Round Table, Prel Doc No 7, n 2 above, 21–22.   [314] ibid, at 22.
[315] ibid, at 21. It seems that, under this proposal there would not be a place of acting or a place of damage rule.
[316] Case C-364/93 *Marinari v Lloyd's Bank plc (Zubaidi Trading Co Intervener)* [1996] QB 217. See also the opinion of AG Leger in Case C-168/02 *Kronhofer v Maier*, para 26.

provider' as a 'service provider who effectively pursues an economic activity using a fixed establishment for an indefinite period. The presence and use of the technical means and technologies required to provide the service do not, in themselves, constitute an establishment of the provider.'[317] Where the company has only one place of establishment,[318] this will probably be in the same Member State as where it is domiciled (a company is domiciled, *inter alia*, where it has its principal place of business[319]).

What if the service provider has several places of establishment? Recital **10.156** (19) goes on to state that 'in cases where it is difficult to determine from which of several places of establishment a given service is provided, this is the place where the provider has the centre of his activities relating to this particular service'.[320] The alternative would be to define the place where the defendant is established as that where it has its place of business. In the situation where the defendant has more than one place of business, this is that which has the closest relationship to the underlying business transaction.[321] If a company has several places of establishment the place where it is established may not be in the same Member State as where it is domiciled.

Second, the place of establishment is not an event and is therefore **10.157** inappropriate for use in the context of Article 5(3). With some torts it is possible to get round this objection. It should be recalled that in *Shevill* the place of establishment was justified on the basis that this was where the harmful event originated. The latter is undeniably an event. But other torts may not originate where the defendant is established. For example, a negligent misstatement may be placed on a website on a web-server in State A by a company established in State B.

Third, a place of establishment rule ignores the features of particular torts. **10.158** It points to the same place, regardless of the tort in question. In other words, it emphasizes the fact that it is an internet case, rather than that it is a tort case. But the starting point for ascertaining the place of the event for any internet tort should be the identification of this place for this particular tort in non-internet cases. In the light of this, it looks to be inappropriate to adopt a solution that operates, regardless of the tort in question.

---

[317] Implemented in the UK by Art 2(1) of the Electronic Commerce (EC Directive) Regulations 2002.

[318] i.e. the place where it pursues its economic activity or, depending on the definition adopted, has its place of business.

[319] Art 60(1)(c) of the Brussels I Regulation.   [320] ibid.

[321] See Art 15(4)(a) of the UNCITRAL Model Law on Electronic Commerce of 1996.

10.159 Fourth, the place where the defendant is established does not form as strong a connection in internet cases, in terms of being helpful as a place of trial from the point of view of the evidence and of the conduct of the proceedings, as the place of uploading or downloading.

Article 5(3): the place where the damage occurred

10.160 Expert meetings organized by the Hague Conference on private international law appear to have disagreed on whether there are any particular problems in identifying the place of damage arising from the fact that the tort is committed over the internet.[322] However, as the examination of specific internet torts will show,[323] such problems can arise. The discussion of the possible places of damage in internet torts is best dealt with in the context of specific internet torts. Some of the experts at the meetings organized by the Hague Conference on private international law, aware of the problems that can arise with internet torts, favoured a presumption that the place where the injury arose would be at the place of habitual residence of the plaintiff.[324] But such a presumption could not be applied in the context of Article 5(3) of the Brussels I Regulation because this would be too pro-plaintiff.[325]

10.161 **Multiple damage**   With some internet torts there will be multiple damage occurring in a number of Member States. The best example is internet defamation.[326] Information placed on the internet can be read in every Member State in which the information can be accessed. The damage to the plaintiff's reputation will occur in each Member State where the information is read. The plaintiff will have the option of suing in any one of these Member States. However, forum shopping is discouraged by the limitation in the *Shevill* case[327] that the courts of the place of injury would only have jurisdiction to rule on the injury caused there to the victim's reputation, not in relation to injury caused in other Member States. The same problem of multiple damage arises with infringement of intellectual property rights[328] and with certain complementary torts such as passing off.[329] However, when it comes to the internet torts that arise out of the international sale of goods and with which we are concerned in this chapter, multiple damage is unlikely to arise, except perhaps in cases of a failure to sell. It does not appear to be a problem with negligent misstatement and negligent and fraudulent misrepresentation over the internet, or

---

[322] Compare the conclusions of the Geneva Round Table, Prel Doc No 7, n 2 above, 21–22, which envisages problems in relation to the place of damage, with those of the expert meeting at Ottawa, n 129 above, 8, which does not mention any such problems.
[323] See below, paras 10.173–220.
[324] See the Geneva Round Table, Prel Doc No 7, n 2 above, 22.
[325] See above, para 10.154.   [326] See Fawcett and Torremans, 400.   [327] n 311 above.
[328] See Fawcett and Torremans, 167–168.   [329] ibid, at 378.

with conversion, or inducement of breach of contract over the internet, or negligence.[330] The problem of multiple damage need not therefore detain us any further.

The Traditional English Rules

Service within the jurisdiction

The position as regards service within the jurisdiction is the same in inter- **10.162** net tort cases as for internet business to business contract cases.[331]

Service out of the jurisdiction: r 6.20(8) of the Civil Procedure Rules

In the situation where the claimant wishes to use the tort ground, r 6.20(8) **10.163** of the Civil Procedure Rules, for service out of the jurisdiction, the familiar questions must be asked: did the damage sustained result from an act committed within the jurisdiction or was the damage sustained within the jurisdiction?

Did the damage sustained result from an act committed within the juris- 10.164 diction? It has been submitted above,[332] when discussing the definition of the place of the event giving rise to the damage under Article 5(3) of the Brussels I Regulation, that the starting point must be the definition adopted for that particular tort in non-internet cases. The same is true when it comes to determining whether an act was committed within the jurisdiction. It has also been submitted that for torts in general there are only two really significant events involved in communicating over the internet, the uploading and the downloading of information and that, in general, the place of uploading is to be preferred to the place of down-loading (although this is subject to considerations that may arise with a particular tort). Many of the arguments employed above are equally applicable in the present context. In favour of the place of uploading is the fact that: it focuses on the act of the defendant; and information is normally just uploaded in one place.[333] However, there is one very important argument against the place of uploading that applies in the context of the traditional English rules of jurisdiction, but not in the EC context. A vast and disproportionate number of internet service providers are domiciled in the United States and their web-servers are located in the United States.[334] The English courts would normally not be able to serve a

---

[330] It could be a problem with a failure to sell. See below, para 10.201.
[331] See above, paras 10.88–97. [332] At para 10.139.
[333] However, all we are concerned with in the present context is whether the English courts have jurisdiction. The fact that the information is downloaded in many states would not lead to opportunities for forum shopping unless other countries took jurisdiction on the same basis.
[334] See the *Dow Jones* case, n 258 above, para 133 (*per* Kirby J).

claim form out of the jurisdiction against an American defendant on the basis of an act committed within the jurisdiction if the act is defined in terms of uploading. Moreover, with some torts the substantive law may point to the place of downloading.

10.165 What the English courts cannot do is adopt a bold definition that looks to the place where the defendant is established. This is permissible and, indeed, has the support of the European Court of Justice[335] in the context of Article 5(3) of the Brussels I Regulation, but this provision is differently worded from r 6.20(8) of the Civil Procedure Rules, referring to the place of the event giving rise to the damage rather than to an *act* committed within the jurisdiction. An act cannot be defined in terms of the place where the defendant is established.

10.166 **Was the damage sustained within the jurisdiction?** There are no particular problems in identifying the place of the damage arising from the fact that it is an internet tort.[336]

Forum conveniens/Forum non conveniens

10.167 When it comes to ascertaining the appropriate forum for trial regard should be had both to traditional considerations that apply in non-internet tort cases and to internet connections.

10.168 **Traditional considerations** It will be recalled[337] that, when it comes to determining whether England is clearly the appropriate forum for the purposes of service out of the jurisdiction, regard is to be had to the principle that the jurisdiction in which a tort was committed is, *prima facie*, the natural forum for trial. The use of this principle, which requires the identification of a single place where the tort was committed,[338] has been criticized in this book, apart from in cases of defamation.[339] One point of criticism is that it is by no means easy to ascertain the place where many torts are committed. This place will be even harder to ascertain if the tort is committed over the internet. There are two reasons for this. First, the precedents that could be used for determining the place where the tort was committed may be of limited value when it comes to internet torts.[340]

---

[335] The *Shevill* case, n 311 above.

[336] The position is the same as under Art 5(3) of the Brussels I Regulation, on which see above, para 10.160.

[337] See above, paras 6.30–32.

[338] This is not required under the traditional jurisdictional rules for service out of the jurisdiction in tort cases.

[339] See above, paras 6.31–32. For the difficulties in identifying the country in which the most significant elements of the events constituting the tort occurred for choice of law purposes see below, paras 17.27–30.

[340] See the discussion below, paras 10.184–187, of misstatements/misrepresentations communicated over the internet.

Second, it then becomes necessary to choose between a place of uploading rule and a place of downloading rule when the process of transfer of information involves both places and the policy arguments in favour of each are fairly evenly balanced. This raises the question of whether it is sensible to use a rule that necessitates the identification of a single place of an internet tort.

The one tort where the use of this principle can be justified is that of **10.169** defamation.[341] In *Dow Jones & Company Inc v Gutnick*,[342] the High Court of Australia had to determine the place where the tort of defamation was committed in the situation where the alleged defamatory material was contained in an online journal. The plaintiff lived in the State of Victoria and had his business headquarters there. The defendant was a Delaware corporation. Material for the journal was composed and finally edited in New York and then transmitted from a computer in New York either directly to computers at the defendant's premises in New Jersey or via an intermediate site operated by the defendant elsewhere in New Jersey. It was then loaded on to six servers in New Jersey. There were many subscribers from different countries, including some living in the State of Victoria. Where was the tort committed? Was this in New Jersey, where the material was uploaded, or in the State of Victoria, where it was downloaded? It was held that:

... ordinarily, defamation is to be located at the place where the damage to reputation occurs. Ordinarily that will be where the material which is alleged to be defamatory is available in comprehensible form assuming, of course, that the person defamed has in that place a reputation which is thereby damaged. ... In the case of material on the World Wide Web, it is not available in comprehensible form until downloaded on to the computer of a person who has used a web browser to pull the material from the web-server. It is where the person downloads the material that the damage to reputation may be done. Ordinarily then, that will be the place where the tort of defamation is committed.[343]

---

[341] See above, para 6.31.

[342] n 258 above; followed without discussion by Eady J in *Harrods Limited v Dow Jones & Company Inc* [2003] EWHC 1162 (QB) and in *Don King v Lennox Lewis* [2004] EWHC 168 (QB).

[343] *Dow Jones & Company Inc v Gutnick* (2002) 210 CLR 575, para 44. If the defamation was contained in a hard copy, not online, the tort would also be committed in Victoria if there were subscribers there. A place of downloading rule is more questionable if there are no subscribers, on which see the note by U Kohl, 'Defamation on the Internet—Nice Decision, Shame About the Reasoning: *Dow Jones v Gutnick*' (2003) 52 ICLQ 1049. But it could be argued that if a service provider is prepared to release the defamatory information world wide it must be prepared to be sued abroad. This argument was adopted by the Landgericht, Hamburg, in the trademark infringement over the internet case of *Re The Maritim Trademark*, n 294 above. The most difficult case is if the service provider has tried to prevent persons in a particular state from reading the material.

See below, para 10.251. See also in favour of an internet tort (of passing off and trade mark infringement) being committed in the place of downloading, the Scots *Bonnier Media* case, n 308 above and text in footnote.

The tort of defamation was committed in Victoria and, accordingly, the High Court refused to stay the proceedings in that State on the ground of *forum non conveniens*.[344] In England, Eady J has followed the *Dow Jones* case and held that the tort of defamation takes place where an internet posting is downloaded.[345]

10.170 It has been argued earlier on in this book[346] that we would be better off without presumptions. Instead, what we should look at in tort cases is the law applicable to the tort, which is, after all, the idea underlying the presumption, and that, if the law applicable to the tort is English law, this should be regarded as strong evidence in favour of England being clearly the appropriate forum for trial.[347] The particular difficulties in determining the law applicable to internet torts are examined below.[348]

10.171 **Internet connections**   It will be recalled,[349] that there are four connections that are unique to internet cases. The first is where the computers used by each party are located. In the internet defamation case of *Dow Jones & Company Inc v Gutnick*, there was no difficulty in identifying where these were situated, even though the defendant publisher used a fairly complex system of computers and web-servers located in several states. The second internet connection is where the internet service provider carried on the activities associated with the provision of its services. There should be no more difficulty in working this out in tort cases than there is in contract cases.[350] The third internet connection, admittedly one that should not be regarded as being of much weight, is the location of the party providing access to the internet. There should be no more difficulty in working this out in tort cases than there is in contract cases. The fourth is concerned with the situation where there is a sale through another party's website, such as an auction site, and involves taking into account

---

[344] The Australian doctrine of *forum non conveniens* requires a showing that Victoria is a clearly inappropriate forum for trial, which is a different and stricter test from that used in England, see *Voth v Manildra Flour Mills Pty Ltd* (1990) 171 CLR 538, HC of Australia. If the tort was committed in the forum this is likely to be decisive. See Gaudron J in *Oceanic Sun Line Special Shipping Company Inc v Fay* (1988) 165 CLR 197 at 266 (*per* Gaudron J—the selected forum should not be seen as an inappropriate forum if it is fairly arguable that the substantive law of the forum is applicable); the *Voth* case, ibid, at 566 (the fact that forum law was applicable was regarded as being very significant); *Régie National des Usines Renault SA v Zhang* (2002) 210 CLR 491 at 521 (an Australian court cannot be a clearly inappropriate forum merely by virtue of the fact that foreign law is applicable). See also the *Dow Jones* case, n 343 above, para 162 (*per* Kirby J). The Victoria courts had a basis of jurisdiction because the plaintiff suffered damage in Victoria.
[345] *Don King v Lennox Lewis* [2004] EWHC 168 (QB) at [15], [39] (Eady J). See also *Harrods Limited v Dow Jones & Company Inc* [2003] EWHC 1162 (QB) (Eady J); *Godfrey v Demon Internet Ltd* [2001] QB 201, 208–209; *Loutchansky v Times Newspapers Ltd* [2002] QB 783 at [58].
[346] See above, para 6.32.   [347] See the *Voth* case, n 344 above, at 566.
[348] At paras 21.120–174.   [349] See above, paras 10.111–114.
[350] For a contract case see above, para 10.112.

the location of the website and website owner's place of business. This internet connection could come into play with the internet torts of negligent misstatement or negligent or fraudulent misrepresentation.[351]

The importance attached to the place where the tort was committed **10.172** means that these internet connections are necessarily reduced in importance in tort cases. The High Court of Australia did not in fact attach any *forum non conveniens* significance to the place where computers were located or even mention where, on the facts of that case, accounts of recipients were managed and billing arrangements were carried out. This was because the High Court was solely concerned with the place of the tort.[352] If it was committed in Victoria, it could not be shown that Victoria was a clearly inappropriate forum for trial. Such territorial connections are not relevant to this.[353] Nonetheless, internet connections are still relevant under English law. The English principle that looks to the place where the tort was committed is phrased in terms that this is 'prima facie' the natural forum for trial. Other connections, including internet connections, can be used to rebut this inference, although this will not be easy to do.[354]

2. NEGLIGENT MISSTATEMENT, NEGLIGENT AND FRAUDULENT MISREPRESENTATION OVER THE INTERNET

An example of misstatement or misrepresentation over the internet **10.173** would be where this is set out on the defendant's website or is contained in an email from the defendant to the plaintiff in response to an email enquiry from the plaintiff about the quality of the goods.

The EC Rules: Article 5(3)

The place of the event giving rise to the damage

When it comes to negligent misstatements that are communicated by **10.174** traditional means, there is English authority to the effect that the place of the event giving rise to the damage is that where the misstatement originates, rather than where it is received and relied upon.[355] This is based on an analogy with defamation.[356] This authority is the starting

---

[351] Discussed below, para 10.184.
[352] The *Dow Jones* case, n 343 above, para 4.   [353] ibid, para 42.
[354] See also the discussion below, paras 17.35–39, in relation to the displacement rule under s 12 of the Private International Law (Miscellaneous Provisions) Act 1995.
[355] *Domicrest Ltd v Swiss Bank Corp* [1999] QB 548; discussed above, para 6.88.
[356] ibid, at 563, where Rix J quotes from the decision of the ECJ in Case C-68/93 *Shevill v Presse Alliance SA* [1995] 2 AC 18 at 62 where the event giving rise to the damage was seen in terms of the origin of the damage.

point when defining the place of the event giving rise to the damage when the misstatement or misrepresentation is communicated over the internet.

10.175 Misstatements or misrepresentations contained in an email   If the misstatement or misrepresentation is contained in an email sent by the defendant to the plaintiff, it is no more difficult to ascertain the place of the event giving rise to the damage than with any other form of instantaneous communication, such as by telephone. Applying the rule that this place is where the misstatement or misrepresentation originates, rather than where it is received and relied upon,[357] the place of the event giving rise to the damage is where the message is typed out and transmitted. This could be on a lap top being used on a plane flying across Europe or in a hotel room abroad, but this is no different from the situation where a misstatement or misrepresentation is made during the course of a phone conversation made from a mobile phone. In these cases where it is difficult or impossible to determine the place where the event giving rise to the damage occurred, the solution adopted by the European Court of Justice has been to deny the plaintiff the use of this limb of Article 5(3).[358] Instead, the plaintiff will have to rely on jurisdiction in the place where the damage occurred under Article 5(3) or on suing in the state where the defendant is domiciled under Article 2.

10.176 A misstatement or misrepresentation contained on the defendant's website   Identification of the place of the event giving rise to the damage is more difficult if the misstatement or misrepresentation is contained on the defendant's website, which is then accessed by the plaintiff. Where does the misstatement or misrepresentation originate? This must be in either the place where the web-server on which is stored the defendant's website (containing the misstatement or misrepresentation) is situated (i.e. the place of uploading the misstatement/misrepresentation) or, following the analysis adopted in the multi-state defamation *Shevill* case,[359] the place where the defendant is established. Given that the place of origin rule adopted for misstatements is based on the analogy with defamation, it is likely that an English court would opt for the latter solution. The European Court of Justice could well adopt the same solution.[360] However, if the decision on the best solution was based on policy, rather than precedent, it would be necessary to weigh up the more general advantages and disadvantages of adopting, on the one hand, a conventional

---

[357] See above, para 6.88.   [358] See the *Réunion Européenne* case, n 293 above.
[359] n 356 above and text accompanying.   [360] See above, para 10.153.

definition in terms of the place of uploading or downloading (with misstatement or misrepresentation it would be uploading) and, on the other
hand, a bolder definition in terms of the place where the defendant is
established.[361]

The place where the damage occurred

The starting point for the discussion of the specific internet torts of neg- **10.177**
ligent misstatement and negligent and fraudulent misrepresentation
should be the existing definition of the damage adopted in non-internet
cases. In a misstatement case, where, for example, the seller brings an
action against a bank, the damage can be the release of the goods by the
seller, acting in reliance on misstatements from the bank, without payment.[362] In internet cases, this place may be by no means easy to ascertain.
With physical goods it is easy enough to identify the place where the
goods are released; it is the place where they are held in storage.[363] But if
digital products are released the place where this happens is not so obvious. In a simple case, the release of the information involves information
that is contained on the service provider's computer being transferred to
the recipient's computer. Let us assume that the process of transfer is that
information is uploaded by the service provider on to a web-server and
downloaded by the recipient who accesses this web-server. The place
where the release takes place is presumably the place where the service
provider's web-server containing the information to be released is situated.[364] The information could be held on a server which is in a Member
State other than the one where the service provider is domiciled. Not only
may there be a lack of connection with the place where the server is
situated, but there is also a risk of manipulation by the service provider
who places the server in a Member State in which he least objects to being
sued as an alternative to being sued in his domicile.

In a more complex case, the information will be held on a number of **10.178**
mirror sites and will be released from these to customers. However, as far
as an individual recipient is concerned, the information released to him
will be released from just one site, which, if it has been selected by the
recipient, will allow the recipient to manipulate the place of damage, or, if
it has been selected by the service provider, will allow the service provider
to manipulate the place of damage.

---

[361] See above, paras 10.140–159. [362] See above, paras 6.93–95.
[363] See above, para 6.94.
[364] If information is transferred by means of an email attachment, the place of release is
referring either to the computer from which the email was sent or to the one where the
information contained in the attachment was originally held, which may be in a different
state.

The Traditional English Rules

10.179   The position as regards service within the jurisdiction is the same for the internet torts of negligent misstatement and negligent and fraudulent misrepresentation as for any other internet tort.[365] Service out of the jurisdiction requires a more detailed treatment.

Service out of the jurisdiction: r 6.20(8) of the Civil Procedure Rules

10.180   **Did the damage sustained result from an act committed within the jurisdiction?**   The starting point for answering this question should be the existing definition of the act for the specific torts of negligent misstatement and negligent and fraudulent misrepresentation that has been adopted in non-internet cases. It will be recalled that an act of misrepresentation is committed within the jurisdiction if the misrepresentation is made in England,[366] and that, if the misrepresentation is communicated by an instantaneous form of communication, such as a telex message, a telephone message or a fax, the misrepresentation is made where it is communicated, i.e. where it is received. It is submitted that an email message should be regarded as being an instantaneous form of communication and that these principles should equally apply to this form of communication. It follows that a misstatement or misrepresentation contained in an email message should be regarded as having been made in the country where the message is received.

10.181   The setting out of information on a website should also be regarded as being an instantaneous form of communication. It follows that the misstatement or misrepresentation which is set out on the defendant's website should be regarded as having been made in the country where the message is received. There is then the problem of identifying this place. It might be argued that the customer receives the information containing the misstatement or misrepresentation when he accesses the web-server containing the website. The place of receipt would therefore be the state of uploading, ie where the web-server is situated. However, it is difficult to say that the information is communicated to the recipient at that point. It is more realistic to argue that the place of receipt of the information is where it is downloaded on to the computer of the recipient, ie the place where the recipient's computer is situated at the time of downloading. Unless and until the information is downloaded by the recipient, there is no information which he can read and nothing upon which he might detrimentally rely. Moreover, before the recipient downloads the information, the other party may, of course, remove the information from the server, or issue a correction.

---

[365] See above, paras 10.162 and 6.17–20.   [366] See above, para 6.97.

Was the damage sustained within the jurisdiction? In many cases, the **10.182**
place where damage was sustained is no more difficult to ascertain in an
internet misstatement or misrepresentation case than in any other case
of misstatement or misrepresentation. Thus if the damage is that the
claimant as a consequence of the misrepresentations paid out money[367] it
matters not whether the misrepresentation was made over the internet or
not. This is illustrated by *Alteen v Informix Corp*,[368] a decision of Woolridge
J in the Newfoundland Supreme Court, Trial Division. The plaintiffs,
shareholders in Newfoundland, brought an action in tort against the
defendant US corporation for allegedly issuing false and misleading
statements regarding its current and future operations which artificially
inflated the price of its shares prior to the date of purchase. The shares
subsequently declined in value due to the misdeeds of the defendant.
Woolridge J held that the Newfoundland Court had jurisdiction on
the basis that the damage occurred there, this being the place where the
shares were purchased. The false information about the company's
operations was in fact disseminated, *inter alia*, over the internet but this
appears to have had no relevance when it came to ascertaining the place
of damage.

But what about the example given earlier[369] of where the claimant service **10.183**
provider, acting in reliance on a misstatement from the defendant bank
releases digitized products to the recipient without prior payment? With
digitized products, that are 'delivered' over the internet, information is
transferred from the service provider's computer to the recipient's computer. Let us assume that the process of transfer of information is that it
is uploaded by the service provider on to a web-server and downloaded
by the recipient who accesses the web-server on which the information is
stored. If you accept that the damage is the release of the information
without payment,[370] it would appear that this occurs at the place where
the service provider's web-server containing the information that is
released is situated.[371] It has been suggested above that this is the position
in cases under Article 5(3) of the Brussels I Regulation. This analysis is
supported by a non-internet case defining damage for the purposes of
r 6.20(8) of the Civil Procedure Rules. In a case involving the loss of consignments shipped to the buyer following misrepresentations made by a

---

[367] See above, para 6.104.   [368] (1998) 164 Nfld & PEIR 301, 507 APR 301.
[369] Above, para 10.177.
[370] This is so in Brussels I Regulation cases, see above, para 10.177.
[371] If information is transferred by means of an email attachment, the place of release is
referring either to the computer from which the email was sent or to the one where the
information contained in the attachment was originally held, which may be in a different
state.

bank, it appears that damage was sustained in England because this was
the place from which the goods were shipped.[372] Applying this analogy to
digitized goods, it would appear that the damage was sustained at the
place from which the information was transferred, ie the place where the
service provider's web-server containing the information was situated. It
has to be pointed out though that there may be lack of connection with
this place and also a risk of manipulation of jurisdictional rules by the
service provider.[373]

Forum conveniens/forum non conveniens

10.184 When it comes to ascertaining the appropriate forum for trial, regard
should be had both to internet connections and to traditional considerations that apply in non-internet cases of negligent misstatement and
negligent and fraudulent misrepresentation.[374] As regards internet connections, what has been said earlier when discussing internet torts in
general is equally applicable to the specific internet torts of negligent
misstatement and negligent and fraudulent misrepresentation.

10.185 When it comes to traditional considerations, it has already been seen that,
the principle of England being prima facie the natural forum for
determination of the dispute if the tort was committed England, has been
applied to the torts of negligent misstatement and negligent and fraudulent misrepresentation.[375] These cases enable us to determine where
this tort was committed, at least in non-internet cases. Identification
of this place depends on whether there was, on the one hand, a non-
instantaneous communication and, on the other hand, some instantaneous form of communication. In the latter case, the tort is committed
where the misstatement/misrepresentation is received and acted upon. In
the past, a distinction has been made between these two different
methods of communication. If the parties communicate by email, it is
possible to apply this distinction. An email should be regarded as being
an instantaneous form of communication. It follows that where the misstatement or misrepresentation is contained in an email the tort should be
regarded as having been committed in the place where it is received and
acted upon. The setting out of information on a website should also be
regarded as being an instantaneous form of communication. It follows
that, where the misstatement or misrepresentation is set out on the
defendant's website, the tort should also be regarded as having been
committed in the place where it is received and acted upon.

---

[372] See *Bastone & Firminger Ltd v Nasima Enterprises (Nigeria) Ltd* [1996] CLC 1902,
discussed above, para 6.106.
[373] See above, para 10.177.   [374] See above, paras 6.110–114.
[375] See above, para 6.110.

Normally, the place of receipt of information will be the same as the place **10.186** where it is acted on. In cases where the two take place in different states, it is submitted that the place of receipt should be treated as the more significant element and that the tort should be treated as being committed in that place.[376]

This still leaves the difficulty in cases where the misstatement or mis- **10.187** representation is set out on the defendant's website of ascertaining the place of receipt. Is this the place of uploading, ie where the web-server containing the website is situated or the place of downloading on to the computer of the recipient, ie the place where the recipient's computer is situated at the time of downloading? For the reasons already given, the place of receipt should be regarded as being the place of downloading on to the recipient's computer. In conclusion, where the misstatement or misrepresentation is set out on the defendant's website the tort should be regarded as having been committed in the place where the information is downloaded by the recipient on to his computer.

3. CONVERSION OVER THE INTERNET

An example of conversion over the internet would be where a buyer **10.188** enters into a sales contract via the seller's interactive website and subsequently takes delivery of tangible goods. If the act of receiving the goods amounts to an assertion of dominion over the goods which is inconsistent with owner's rights, this act will amount to conversion under English law. Equally the unauthorized disposal of the goods by selling them over the internet could amount to a conversion. Another example of conversion over the internet would be where the defendant gives an order which results in tangible goods being transferred,[377] the order being sent by email.

In the situation where the recipient receives a digitized product via the **10.189** internet, this raises the thorny question of whether a digitized product can be the subject of conversion. The law of conversion is concerned with protecting an owner's property rights in chattels and documentary intangibles, such as cheques. It protects any corporeal moveable property.[378] There is Canadian authority to the effect that computer software can be the subject of conversion.[379] Hoilett J at first instance accepted the view that 'knowledge in some permanent form, for example, on . . . a

---

[376] See also the discussion in relation to choice of law below, para 21.176.

[377] See, eg, *Van Oppen v Tredegars* (1921) 37 TLR 504.

[378] WVH Rogers (ed), *Winfield and Jolowicz on Tort* (16th edn, London: Sweet & Maxwell, 2002) 596, para 17.7.

[379] *Unisys Canada Inc v Imperial Optical Co* 44 BLR (2d) 311, aff'd 2 BLR (3d) 172, Ont CA.

disc used for computers, would seem to have the character of a chattel, and should be capable of being converted'.[380] The software was described as being physically in the possession of the first defendant,[381] although it is not clear whether this was because it was on a floppy disk or because it was on the hard disk in the first defendant's computer. The decision of the New Zealand Court of Appeal in *Pacific Software Technology Ltd v Perry Group Ltd*[382] is to the same effect. The case concerned a dispute over the ownership of software and the intellectual property incorporated in it. The Court said that: 'Copyright is a *sui generis* form of "personal property". It is a bundle of rights conferred by law. . . . Denial of those rights can, on the facts of a given case, amount to conversion.' It is submitted therefore that a digitized product transferred over the internet can be the subject of conversion, even though it constitutes intangible property. This is consistent with the view put forward above[383] that such property can constitute 'goods' under the Vienna Convention.

10.190   An example of the conversion of a digitized product transferred over the internet would be as follows. The service provider agrees to sell a bespoke[384] computer program to a customer. The service provider then arranges to sell the same program to another person, X, and makes the software available to X to download, which X duly does. Suppose that the product is uploaded by the service provider on to a server located in State A. X downloads the product in State B. The original customer is resident in State C, where one might have expected him to download the product. The original customer claims that by a particular law he has the right to possession of the digitized product and that X and the service provider have wrongfully interfered with this right.

The EC Rules: Article 5(3)

10.191   It has previously been argued that a claim for damages for conversion should be regarded as being a matter relating to tort, delict or quasi-delict.[385] It is now necessary to identify the place of the event giving rise to the damage and the place where the damage occurred in cases of electronic commerce.

---

[380] He was quoting from G Fridman, *The Law of Torts in Canada* (Toronto: Carswell, 1989) Vol 1, 98. See also S Todd, *The Law of Torts in New Zealand* (3rd edn, Wellington: Brookers, 2001) 565.

[381] For conversion there is no need to show that the defendant had actual possession of the goods.

[382] [2004] 1 NZLR 164.   [383] At para 10.47.

[384] Conversion must be to the exclusion of others. In most cases, the converter will only obtain a copy of the product and so this requirement will not be satisfied.

[385] See above, para 6.46.

The place of the event giving rise to the damage

It is argued above that with the tort of conversion the event giving rise to **10.192** the damage is the act, such as the disposing or receiving of goods, which this tort requires. With tangible goods there is no problem in identifying the place where this act occurred. The fact that the contract was made online does not affect this. This place will be the same, regardless of whether the contract was made via the internet or by more traditional means. With digitized products transferred via the internet, there is more of a problem in identifying the relevant place. Reverting to the example above of such a case, the act of conversion by the defendant service provider is that of disposal to X. This involves a transfer of the product over the internet from the service provider to X. In our example, what happened was that the service provider uploaded the product on to a server in State A, from where it was accessed by X. The place of the act of disposal by the defendant service provider should therefore be regarded as being in State A. It is true that the product eventually ends up in State B after being downloaded by X, but this does not involve an act by the defendant service provider. The downloading is an act committed by X. As regards a claim against defendant X, the act of conversion by X is receiving the product. It is submitted that X receives the product in State B where he downloads it.

The place where the damage occurred

It is argued above[386] that, if conversion by the defendant takes the form of **10.193** receiving goods where this amounts to an assertion of dominion over the goods which is inconsistent with the owner's rights, the *direct* damage to the plaintiff is the loss of the goods. It is not enough to show merely that financial consequences of the conversion are felt in England. With tangible goods, there is no problem in identifying the place where the loss of the goods occurred.[387] The fact that the contract was made online does not affect this. This place will be the same, regardless of whether the contract was made via the internet or by more traditional means. With digitized products 'delivered' via the internet, there is more of a problem in identifying the place where the loss of the product occurred. Is this the place where the product was unavailable for the customer to access (State A) or where the customer expected to download it (State C)? On balance, the former is probably better regarded as being the place where the loss occurred.

---

[386] See above, para 6.54.   [387] See above, para 6.54.

The Traditional English Rules

10.194   The position as regards service within the jurisdiction is the same for the internet tort of conversion as for any other internet tort. Service out of the jurisdiction needs more discussion.

Service out of the jurisdiction: r 6.20(8) of the Civil Procedure Rules

10.195   A claim for conversion has been accepted as falling within this provision.[388] The fact that it is an example of conversion over the internet should not make any difference and this too should fall within this provision.

10.196   **Did the damage sustained result from an act committed within the jurisdiction?**   The act in question is the act of dealing with a chattel in a manner inconsistent with another's rights, such as the act of receiving goods where this amounts to an assertion of dominion over the goods which is inconsistent with the owner's rights. This is the same act, which, it has been suggested above, should constitute the event giving rise to the damage for the purposes of Article 5(3) of the Brussels I Regulation. As noted in that context, with tangible goods there is no problem in identifying the place where this act occurred and thus whether it was committed within the jurisdiction. When it comes to the above example of a digitized product transferred via the internet, again the same rule should be adopted as that adopted for the purposes of Article 5(3) of the Brussels I Regulation. The place of the act of disposal of the product by the service provider should be regarded as being in State A where he uploaded the product on to a server from which it could be accessed by X. The place of the act of receiving the product by X should be regarded as being in State B where he downloaded the product.

10.197   **Was the damage sustained within the jurisdiction?**   It has been seen that damage is sustained where the goods are lost to the claimant.[389] It is not enough to show merely that financial consequences of the conversion are felt in England. With tangible goods, there is no problem in identifying the place where the loss of the goods occurred. The fact that the contract was made online does not affect this. This place will be the same, regardless of whether the contract was made via the internet or by more traditional means. With digitized products transferred via the internet, there is more of a problem in identifying this place. The same rule should be adopted as that adopted for the purposes of Article 5(3) of the Brussels I Regulation. In the above example, the place where the loss of the product occurred should be regarded as being the place where the product was

---

[388] See above, para 6.58.   [389] See above, para 6.62.

unavailable for the customer to access (State A), rather than the place where the customer expected to download it (State C).

Forum conveniens/forum non conveniens

When it comes to ascertaining the appropriate forum for trial, regard **10.198** should be had both to internet connections[390] and to traditional considerations that apply in non-internet cases of conversion.[391] As far as traditional considerations are concerned, it has been argued above[392] that the tort of conversion should be regarded as having in substance been committed in the state where the act of conversion took place. As has been seen,[393] ascertaining this place raises no particular difficulty where tangible goods have been sold via the internet. Even in cases where a digitized product has been transferred over the internet, it is possible to identify this place.[394] Reverting to the example above of such a case, the act of conversion by the defendant service provider was that of disposal to X by uploading the product on to a server in State A, from where it was accessed by X. The place of the act of disposal by the defendant service provider should therefore be regarded as being in State A. As regards a claim against defendant X, the act of conversion by X is receiving the product by downloading it in State B. The place of the act of receiving should therefore be regarded as being in State B.

4. A Failure to Sell

It is easy to envisage cases of a refusal to sell arising in the context of **10.199** e-commerce. The contract between the buyer and the seller, who now refuses to supply a particular range of goods to the buyer, may have been made by an exchange of emails. The seller may have an interactive website and the contract may have been made via the internet. The contract may be for the purchase of digitized products and the service provider may have refused to provide a certain range of these products.

The EC Rules: Article 5(3)

The place of the event giving rise to the damage

There is French authority holding that a refusal to sell takes place at the **10.200** actual moment, and therefore at the place, at which the decision to refuse the offer was made. In the case in question, this was at the seat of the defendant seller.[395] In a non-internet case, this will often be the place where this decision is made. However, if the defendant is an internet company, it may be very difficult to ascertain where decisions were

[390] See above, paras 10.171–172. [391] See above, para 6.65. [392] At para 6.65.
[393] Above, para 10.196. [394] See above, para 10.196. [395] See above, para 6.119.

made. The decision may be made following discussions over the internet between senior officers who reside in different states. The alternative solution for defining the place of the event giving rise to the damage is to do so in terms of the place where the refusal to sell was communicated to the 'buyer'. This solution was rejected earlier in this book when discussing non-internet torts.[396] However, it is worth asking now, whether, despite its weaknesses, it would be a better solution for internet cases. The answer must be in the negative. A refusal to sell is communicated to the buyer in the place where the message is received. This could be in a Member State where the recipient happens to be using a lap top computer, a Member State that has no connection with the parties or the transaction.

The place where the damage occurred

10.201 Again there is French authority in a non-internet case that this is the place or places where resale of the items in question was anticipated.[397] If there is a refusal to sell tangible goods, there is no more difficulty in identifying this place in cases of electronic commerce, where the contract was made over the internet or by exchange of emails, than there is in cases where the contract was made by traditional means. However, if there is a refusal to sell digitized products there can be considerable difficulty in identifying this place. The purchaser of the digitized product may be an internet company which is going to advertise the product on its website with a view to selling it on throughout the world, including throughout the EC. The place of resale for the purposes of Article 5(3) would literally be every Member State of the EC. The European Court of Justice would not adopt an interpretation of Article 5(3) that would lead to the plaintiff being given such a wide choice of fora.[398] In such a case, it would be better to define the place where the damage occurred in terms of the place of transfer for resale. Assuming that the intended process of transfer for resale is that information is uploaded by the plaintiff internet company on to a web-server and downloaded by the recipient who accesses this web-server, this would be the place where the web-server containing the information which is accessed by its customers is located.

The Traditional English Rules

10.202 The position as regards service within the jurisdiction is the same for the internet tort of a failure to sell as for any other internet tort. Service out of the jurisdiction cannot be dealt with so easily.

---

[396] See above, para 6.120.   [397] See above, para 6.121.
[398] See Case C-256/00 *Besix SA v Wasserreinigungsbau Alfred Kretzschmar GmbH & Co KG (WABAG)* [2002] ECR I-1699, discussed above, para 3.206.

Service out of the jurisdiction: r 6.20(8) of the Civil Procedure Rules

Did the damage sustained result from an act committed within the **10.203**
jurisdiction? It is submitted that there would be an act committed
within the jurisdiction if the decision to refuse to sell was made in
England.[399] This is the same rule as that applied for identifying the place
of the event giving rise to the damage under Article 5(3) of the Brussels I
Regulation. The problems in applying this rule in cases of electronic
commerce have already been examined in that context and the reader is
referred to what is said there.[400]

Was the damage sustained within the jurisdiction? It is submitted that **10.204**
damage is sustained within the jurisdiction if resale of goods is anticipated in England.[401] This is the same rule as that adopted when identifying the place where the damage occurred for the purposes of Article 5(3)
of the Brussels I Regulation. The problems of applying this rule in cases of
electronic commerce have already been examined in that context and the
reader is referred to what is said there.[402] In the situation where the purchaser of a digitized product is an internet company which advertises the
product on its website with a view to reselling it world wide, it would be
better to define the place where the damage occurred in terms of the place
of transfer for resale, i.e. the place where the web-server containing the
information which is accessed by the customers of the plaintiff internet
company is located.[403] In such a case, defining damage in terms of the
place where resale was anticipated would automatically give the English
courts jurisdiction, despite the fact that there is no greater connection with
England than with anywhere else in the world.

Forum conveniens/forum non conveniens

When it comes to ascertaining the appropriate forum for trial, regard **10.205**
should be had both to internet connections and to traditional considerations that apply in non-internet cases of a failure to sell.[404] As regards
traditional considerations, this involves ascertaining where the tort was
committed. This is hard enough in a non-internet case of a refusal to sell.
It is even harder in an internet case. It has been submitted earlier that in
non-internet cases the tort of a failure to sell should be regarded as having
been committed in the state where the decision not to sell was made,
rather than where it was communicated to the 'buyer'.[405] As has been
seen,[406] if the defendant is an internet company, it may be very difficult to

---

[399] See above, para 6.124.   [400] See above, para 10.200.
[401] See above, para 6.126.   [402] See above, para 10.201.
[403] For identification of this place for this internet tort see the above discussion of the place
where damage occurred under Art 5(3) of the Brussels I Regulation.
[404] See above, para 6.128.   [405] See above, para 6.128.   [406] See above, para 10.40.

ascertain where decisions were made by senior officers residing in different states.

5. Inducement of Breach of Contract

10.206 A number of examples can be given of inducement of breach of contract in
the context of electronic commerce. The first is where the defendant A
induces the service provider B to transfer digitized products (with an
exclusive right to sell on) to it in breach of the contract B has with the
plaintiff, C. The act of inducement is communicated via an email. The
second example would be where the defendant A concludes a contract
with the service provider B by electronic means which is inconsistent with
the service provider's contractual obligation to the plaintiff C, as where he
agrees to buy a product already the subject of a contract of sale between
C and B. The third example is where the contract between the service
provider B and the customer C states that the digitized products should
be available for downloading from a website by the customer. The
defendant A hosts a server used by the service provider. The defendant A
makes this unavailable for a prolonged period of time in order to upgrade
it. This may have the effect of making it impossible for the service provider B to transfer the digitized product to the plaintiff C. The fourth
example involves an act of inducement being communicated by being set
out on a website. A possible instance of this would be where the defendant A's website contains a general offer to purchase particular digitized
products (with an exclusive right to sell on) at an inflated price, knowing
that B has these products but has contracted with the plaintiff C at a lower
price. This would raise the substantive law question of whether there is a
sufficient act of inducement by merely making a general offer on a website. Moreover, this situation is unlikely to arise. It is much more likely
that A, knowing that B has these products, would communicate directly
with B, rather than communicate to the world in general via its website.

The EC Rules: Article 5(3)

The place of the event giving rise to the damage

10.207 It is submitted that the place of the event giving rise to the damage is the
place where the act of inducement of breach of contract was committed.[407]
This act usually involves communication by the defendant (A) to the person (B) who then breaks his contract with the plaintiff (C). It has been
argued that the act of inducement is committed where the communication
is received.[408] If the communication takes the form of an email, as in the

---

[407] See above, para 6.139.   [408] ibid.

first example, the place of the event is that where B's computer is situated. The position would appear to be the same under the second example. The relevant place is that where the defendant A communicates his willingness to buy the product, ie where B's computer is situated. There may then be a problem of locating where this computer is situated. It may be a lap top which is taken from one Member State to another. It may be that the email is received by a computer in one Member State (X) but an employee of internet company B accesses this computer from another computer in another Member State (Y). In which Member State is the communication received? It would be best to ignore intermediate computers and therefore the email should be regarded as being received in Member State Y. The third example does not involve communication. The act of inducement by the defendant A is the failure to provide a properly functioning server. This act is located in the state where A's server is situated. When it comes to the fourth example, in the unlikely event of the act of inducement being communicated by being set out on the defendant A's website, again one is concerned with where the communication is received,[409] i.e. where B's computer is situated.

The place where the damage occurred

It is suggested that the direct damage in a sale of goods case is the failure **10.208** to receive the goods and that the place where the damage occurred is therefore the place where the goods should have been delivered to the plaintiff.[410] Ascertaining this place usually presents no particular problem in the case of tangible goods: this place will normally have been agreed. However, if what is being provided is a digitized product there is the problem of identifying the place where it should have been provided. It is suggested[411] that this place is where the information, if it had been provided, would have been downloaded on to the plaintiff's computer (i.e. where the plaintiff's computer is located).

The Traditional English Rules

The position as regards service within the jurisdiction is the same for **10.209** the internet tort of inducement of breach of contract as for any other internet tort. However, service out of the jurisdiction needs some discussion.

---

[409] If one were concerned with where the communication originated the same problems would arise as with misstatements and misrepresentations, see above, paras 10.175–176.

[410] See above, para 6.140.

[411] See also in relation to choice of law, below, para 21.197.

Service out of the jurisdiction: r 6.20(8) of the Civil Procedure Rules

**10.210 Did the damage sustained result from an act committed within the juris-
diction?**   The act in question is the act of inducement by the defendant
and, seemingly, in the case of the first, second and fourth examples, this
is committed within the jurisdiction if the communication containing the
inducement is received in England,[412] i.e. if B's computer is located there.
As regards the third example, the act of inducement by the defendant is
committed within the jurisdiction if the non-functioning server is located
in England. This is the same position as under the EC rules and what is
said above about identifying the place where the act of inducement
occurred in cases of electronic commerce is equally applicable here.

10.211 Was the damage sustained within the jurisdiction?   It is suggested that
the damage in a sale of goods case is the failure to receive the goods and
that this damage is sustained within the jurisdiction if England is the
place where the goods should have been delivered to the claimant.[413] This
is the same position as under the EC rules and what is said above about
identifying the place where the damage occurred in cases of electronic
commerce also applies here.

Forum conveniens/forum non conveniens

10.212 When it comes to ascertaining the appropriate forum for trial, regard
should be had both to internet connections and to traditional considerations that apply in non-internet cases of inducement of breach of
contract.[414] As regards the traditional considerations, it will be recalled
that, in determining where in substance the tort of inducement of breach
of contract was committed, it is necessary to take into account not only
where the act of inducement was located but also, looking at the matter
more broadly, where the breaches (particularly the effective breaches)
induced and the effective damage were located. If the two latter connections were in England, this will mean that the tort was committed
in England, even if the act of inducement was committed abroad. The
problem of ascertaining where the damage occurred in cases of electronic
commerce has already been examined. Where is the effective breach of
contract committed in a case of electronic commerce? In the first, second
and fourth examples, the effective breach is that of the service provider
failing to deliver the tangible goods, or, in the case of a digitized product
transferred over the internet, the failure of the service provider to transfer
the product. In the third example, the breach is the failure of the service
provider, B, rather than the defendant server host, A, to transfer the
product to the customer. The problem of identifying the place where

---

[412] See above, para 6.144.   [413] See above, para 6.145.   [414] See above, para 6.146.

digitized products should have been provided over the internet has previously been examined in this chapter[415] and the reader is referred to what is said there.

6. NEGLIGENCE

Although an action in negligence brought by a buyer of tangible goods **10.213** against the seller or a third party is not common, it is possible to think of examples of where this could arise where there is a sale of digitized products transferred over the internet. First, the service provider fails to warn the recipient of a problem with the digitized product which comes to light after transfer of the product, such as a virus, a security problem or incompatibility with other software. The recipient's computer is damaged and he wishes to sue in respect of this damage and also possibly for consequent economic loss caused by the digitized product. Second, a service provider uses a server hosted by a third party, X, who is the defendant. The recipient downloads the digitized product from the server, which contains a virus that damages the recipient's computer.[416] The recipient wishes to sue in respect of this damage and also possibly for consequent economic loss caused by the digitized product. Third, the server hosted by X is unavailable for a prolonged period, preventing the customer from downloading the product which he has purchased. The customer seeks to sue X for economic loss arising from the delay in being able to access and use the digitized product.

The EC Rules: Article 5(3)

Is there a matter relating to tort, delict or quasi-delict?

In the first of the above examples, the plaintiff has a contractual relation- **10.214** ship with the defendant. In the situation where they have such a relationship and a claim is brought in negligence, the question has to be asked whether there is concurrent liability in tort and contract. If parallel claims, that is claims based on the same facts, are brought in contract and tort, there is authority to the effect that the claim in tort is excluded from the scope of Article 5(3).[417] The same authority says that, where there is concurrent liability in contract and tort, the result would be the same even if the only claim is in tort.[418] In the first example, the claim in negligence is based on a failure to warn customers of the problem with the digitized product. In contrast, a claim in contract would be based on the defect in the product itself. It is submitted therefore that the claim in negligence

---

[415] See above, para 10.105.
[416] The recipient may prefer to sue the service provider in contract.
[417] See above, para 3.72.   [418] See above, para 3.72.

cannot be regarded as a parallel one to the claim in contract. Accordingly, it is not excluded from the scope of Article 5(3). In the other two examples, there is no contractual relationship between the plaintiff and defendant and so there is no doubt that there is a matter relating to tort etc.

The place of the event giving rise to the damage

10.215 In the first example, the event giving rise to the damage is a failure by the service provider to warn the recipient. This takes place where the warning should have been given.[419] When the product was placed on the web-server by the service provider so that customers could access this, there should have been an accompanying warning.[420] The place where the warning should have been given is therefore the place where the web-server on which the product is uploaded is located. In the second example, the event giving rise to the damage is the failure by X to protect the host server from becoming infected by a virus which then infected information stored on the host server. Alternatively, the event is a failure to destroy the virus once it had infected the host server. This event would take place in the state where the host server was situated. In the third example, it is submitted that the event giving rise to the damage is the failure to make the digitized product available for downloading by the customer. This takes place in the state where the host web-server which is unavailable for a prolonged period is located.

The place where the damage occurred

10.216 In the first two examples, the customer is suing for damage to his computer, which is damaged by becoming infected by the digitized product. It could be argued that the direct damage to the customer consists of the damage to the software, and that the consequent damage to the customer's computer is a form of indirect damage. This analysis appears to be supported by the decision of the European Court of Justice in the *Marinari* case.[421] It is by no means easy to locate the place where the digitized product itself is damaged.[422] It could be argued that the digitized product is made to be transferred to customers and should be free of defects at the time when it is made available to customers to access, i.e. it is put on the web-server which customers access. The place where this occurs is the place where this web-server is located. The alternative to

---

[419] See in relation to tangible goods, J Fawcett, 'Jurisdiction', Ch 6 in A Grubb and G Howells (eds), *The Law of Product Liability* (London: Butterworths, 2000) 6.19.

[420] This is the equivalent to putting the product on the market without warning for tangible goods, ibid.

[421] Case C-364/93 *Marinari v Lloyd's Bank plc (Zubaidi Trading Co Intervener)* [1996] QB 217.

[422] See the discussion below, para 21.199.

this is to argue that the damage we are concerned with is the damage to the computer itself. It is much easier to identify the place where this damage occurs. This occurs in the state where the customer's computer is situated at the time of downloading by the customer. The position should be the same if the plaintiff also claims for consequent economic loss. The claim is for damage to the customer's computer and the economic loss is contingent upon that claim. In the third example, the customer is suing for economic loss arising from the delay in being able to access and use the digitized product. The immediate harm to the customer will occur in the state in which the computer is located on to which the product would have been downloaded by the customer had it been available.

The Traditional English Rules

The position as regards service within the jurisdiction is the same for **10.217** internet negligence as for any other internet tort. Service out of the jurisdiction needs a bit more analysis.

Service out of the jurisdiction: r 6.20(8) of the Civil Procedure Rules

Did the damage sustained result from an act committed within the 10.218 jurisdiction? The question of what the negligent act is and where it takes place in cases of internet negligence has been examined when discussing the EC rules. What was said there is equally applicable here.

Was the damage sustained within the jurisdiction? The question of **10.219** what the damage is and where it occurs in cases of internet negligence has been examined when discussing the EC rules. What was said there is equally applicable here.

Forum conveniens/forum non conveniens When it comes to ascertain- **10.220** ing the appropriate forum for trial, regard should be had both to internet connections and to traditional considerations that apply in non-internet cases of negligence.[423] As regards the traditional considerations, it will be recalled that, in cases where the essential ingredients of the wrongful act and the ensuing damage occur in different states, the tort of negligence has been regarded as having been committed in the state where the wrongful act was committed, rather than the state where the damage occurred. In the three examples given above, the wrongful act was committed respectively in the state where: the web-server on which the digitized product was uploaded was located; the host web-server was

---

[423] See above, para 6.172.

located; and the host web-server which was unavailable for a protracted period was located. If this place was in England, then England is, prima facie, the natural forum for trial. This analysis is supported by obiter dicta of the High Court of Australia in the *Dow Jones* case. It will be recalled that the High Court adopted a place of downloading rule when determining the place where the internet tort of defamation was committed. However, the High Court was at pains to point out that defamation was not, like trespass or negligence, concerned with the conduct of the defendant,[424] which is what a place of uploading rule reflects.

VI. PROPERTY CLAIMS

10.221 We are concerned here with jurisdiction in relation to property matters arising out of business conducted over the internet. For example, a customer commissions bespoke software (a new database program) from a software development company. The defendant refuses to deliver up the source code giving access to the software, claiming that it had already developed independently most of the software in the program. The customer seeks an order for delivery up of the source code. This raises an issue as to the ownership of the source code.[425] Of course, if the customer has simply entered into a licensing agreement there is no issue as to the ownership of the software.[426]

1. The EC Rules

10.222 As has been seen, there are no special rules in the Brussels I Regulation dealing with movable property.[427] It may be possible to bring property matters within Article 5(3) or Article 5(1) of the Regulation.[428] The difficulties in using these provisions in internet cases has already been considered in this chapter[429] and what is said there need not be repeated.

---

[424] *Dow Jones & Company Inc v Gutnick* (2002) 210 CLR 575 para 43.
[425] These are the facts of *Pacific Software Technology Ltd v Perry Group Ltd* [2004] 1 NZLR 164, discussed above, para 10.189.
[426] The question, nevertheless, still arises of whether the property ground for service out of the jurisdiction under the traditional rules (r 6.20(10) CPR) can be used, see below para 10.227.
[427] See above, para 7.11   [428] See above, paras 7.12–25.
[429] See above, paras 10.41–87, 10.138–161.

2. The Traditional English Rules

It will be recalled that, under r 6.20(10) of the Civil Procedure Rules, a **10.223**
claim form may be served out of the jurisdiction with the permission of
the court if the whole subject-matter of a claim relates to property located
within the jurisdiction.[430] There are a number of difficulties in applying
this ground in cases of property claims arising out of business conducted
over the internet.

Is a Digitized Product Property?

A digitized product, such as software, which is transferred over the inter- **10.224**
net should be regarded as being intangible property.[431] The concept of
property under r 6.20(10) is wide enough to encompass such property.

Where is Digitized Property Located?

It is suggested below that a digitized product should be regarded as being **10.225**
located in the place where the web-server on which the product is stored
is located.[432] In the situation where the service provider uses a number of
mirror sites, located in different states, the property should be regarded as
being located in the place where the web-server, from which the recipient
was to download or did actually download the information which is
the subject of the litigation, is located. This avoids the spectre of having
property located in more than one state with the attendant problems that
this raises.[433] This still leaves a problem where the gist of the complaint by
the claimant is that the service provider has failed to put the information
on its web-server.

When is it Located in England?

If the service provider's web-server on which the information is stored **10.226**
is located in England, then it can be said that property is located within
the jurisdiction. However, given the realities of electronic commerce,
the likelihood is that the internet company providing the information

---

[430] For discussion see above, paras 7.27–38.
[431] See above, para 10.21   [432] See below, paras 21.224–226.
[433] Property can probably be located in England for the purposes of r 6.20(10) when at
the same time it is also located abroad. This would be consistent with the tort ground
under which it is enough if substantial and efficacious acts have been committed within
the jurisdiction even if substantial and efficacious acts have also been committed outside the
jurisdiction, see above, para 6.26. However, there may be problems in establishing that the
whole subject-matter of the claim relates to this property, see above, para 7.30.

will be based in the United States. If the internet company has just one web-server, this is likely to be also situated in the United States. In the more complicated situation where the information is contained on a number of web-servers located in different countries, then there is property situated in England if the web-server that the recipient accesses is situated there.

Does the Whole Subject-Matter of the Claim Relate to Property?

10.227 The subject-matter of the dispute is the intangible property (i.e. the software or other digitized product) transferred over the internet. As regards the question of whether the subject-matter of the dispute 'relates to' property, a dispute as to whether the ownership of the digitized product has passed to the customer will clearly do so. But, as has been seen,[434] the concept of 'relates to' has been widely construed and can extend to a claim for damages arising from a breach of contract relating to property located within the jurisdiction. This means that a claim for damages for breach of contract alleging that software transferred[435] over the internet and now located in England is defective would fall within r 6.20(10). The whole subject-matter of the claim 'relates to' property because compensation is sought for damage to that property. In contrast, a claim for compensation based on the breach of the exclusive right to use the software under a licensing agreement would not 'relate to' the property.

Is the Property Located within the Jurisdiction?

10.228 It is important to identify specifically which property is the subject of the claim. Thus, in the situation where the provider of information uses mirror sites, if the subject of the claim is the property downloaded by the claimant from a web-server in England, it can said that the whole subject-matter of the claim relates to property located within the jurisdiction.

VII. RESTITUTION AND E-COMMERCE

10.229 Examples of how a personal restitutionary claim could arise in the context of electronic commerce would be where the service provider erroneously delivers tangible goods or erroneously transfers a digitized product to the wrong person. The service provider then seeks restitutionary damages equivalent to the value of the goods/digitized product, the latter

---

[434] See above, para 7.31.
[435] The software could be transferred under a licensing agreement (ie with no transfer of ownership) and then there could be a complaint that it is defective.

having been dissipated. Another example would be where the recipient erroneously pays the wrong person for the goods/digitized product and then seeks restitution of the money.

1. THE EC RULES

Normally, restitutionary claims fall outside the scope of Article 5(1) of the **10.230** Brussels I Regulation.[436] As a result the law on jurisdiction becomes much simpler. There is no need in cases of the sale of a digitized product with transfer over the internet to agonize over the application of Article 5(1). The plaintiff is instead normally going to have to sue the defendant in the Member State in which he is domiciled. However, in certain circumstances, Article 23 can apply to restitutionary claims.[437]

2. THE TRADITIONAL ENGLISH RULES

Service Within the Jurisdiction

There are no particular problems of service within the jurisdiction where **10.231** there is a restitutionary claim arising out of electronic commerce. Service out of the jurisdiction needs more discussion.

Service Out of the Jurisdiction

It will be recalled[438] that r 6.20(15) of the Civil Procedure Rules provides **10.232** that a claim form may be served out of the jurisdiction with the permission of the court if a claim is made for restitution where the defendant's alleged liability arises out of acts committed within the jurisdiction. In internet cases, there is the familiar problem of identifying where the acts were committed. It has been argued that, in a case where the seller has delivered goods to the wrong person, the act in question is that of delivery and that this act is committed in the state where the goods are delivered to the wrong person.[439] If it is an online contract and tangible goods are delivered in a conventional way, there is no more difficulty in identifying where this act was committed than in a case where the contract was not made online. But what if the online contract involved transfer of a digitized product over the internet to the wrong person? It is submitted that the act is providing the information to the wrong person and this act is committed in the state where the information was downloaded on

---

[436] See above, paras 8.13–27.
[437] For problems in using this provision in relation to restitutionary claims see above, paras 8.06–10.
[438] See above, para 8.36.   [439] See above, para 8.57.

to the computer of the recipient, i.e. where the recipient's computer was located.[440] It has also been argued that, in a case where the buyer has paid money to the wrong person, the act in question is the payment by the buyer to the wrong person and that this is committed where the payment is made.[441] Where is payment over the internet made? The process of payment over the internet to the wrong person can involve credit card details being sent from the recipient's computer in State A to the defendant wrong person's computer in State B. Is the place where payment was made in State A, or B? It is submitted that it should be regarded as being made in State B, where it is received by the wrong person.[442]

10.233 The claimant, instead of seeking personal restitutionary damages, may seek to assert or obtain a proprietary interest in the digitized product made available to the defendant.[443] In this situation, recourse can be had to the restitution ground under r 6.20(15), since this doubtless covers proprietary claims as well as personal.[444] Recourse can also be had to the property ground under r 6.20(10), since it can be said with some confidence that a claim for proprietary restitution 'relates to property'. The use of r 6.20(10) in the context of e-commerce has been described above when discussing property claims. Moreover, a constructive trust may arise where, for example, bespoke software is transferred over the internet to the wrong person, and this will bring into play the constructive trust ground under r 6.20(14).[445]

VIII. EVALUATION OF THE EXISTING LAW

1. THE EC RULES

10.234 The emphasis in the EC has been upon the substantive law of electronic commerce rather than on the private international law aspects. In so far as the latter have been addressed, the concentration has been almost entirely on consumer contracts, rather than business to business transactions. There has not been the systematic examination of bases of jurisdiction of the sort that has been undertaken at the Hague Conference on private international law.[446] We are left with jurisdiction rules that, when applied to certain cases of electronic commerce, are both uncertain and unpredictable.

---

[440] For the definition of downloading see above, para 10.61.
[441] See above, para 8.57.
[442] Compare the position in relation to choice of law, see below, paras 21.241–245.
[443] See in relation to non-internet cases, the discussion above, paras 8.107–127.
[444] See above, para 8.127.   [445] Discussed above, para 8.133.
[446] See below, para 10.251.

Uncertainty and Unpredictability

As has been seen, electronic commerce causes problems when applying **10.235**
a number of jurisdictional rules. There is the problem of identifying
and locating the defendant when using Article 2. There are several
unanswered questions when Article 5(1) is applied to cases where not
only is the contract made via the internet but is also performed via the
internet. Is a contract for the purchase of a digitized product transferred
over the internet one for the sale of goods, provision of services or
neither? Regardless of how the contract is characterized, there is
uncertainty over the identification of the place where the services were
provided/goods delivered. Article 5(1)(a) is unworkable because of gaps
in the substantive law which make it impossible to identify the place of
performance of the obligation in question. It is unclear whether the place
of the event giving rise to the damage under Article 5(3) will be defined
for a particular tort in terms of the place of uploading/downloading or in
terms of the place where the defendant is established. Nor is it always
possible to identify the place where damage occurred when digitized
products have been transferred over the internet. Whilst Article 5(5)
normally is easy to apply in cases of electronic commerce, the position is
not entirely certain where a defendant sets up its server containing its
website in another Member State. This uncertainty and unpredictability
is not only bad for the parties because it can lead to litigation but will
also discourage both recipients and service providers from conducting
business over the internet, thwarting the policy objective of developing
electronic commerce within the EC.

**Bases of Jurisdiction and Situations where there are no
E-Commerce Concerns**

The problems raised by electronic commerce should not be exaggerated. **10.236**
Not all bases of jurisdiction are problematic. It is worth remembering that
there is no difficulty in using Article 23. If the parties insert a choice of
jurisdiction agreement in their contract then there is no uncertainty or
unpredictability. Even where a provision can potentially cause problems,
it may not do so in all cases of electronic commerce. For example, in some
cases where Article 2 is used the seller will know the identity of the buyer.
There is no difficulty in using Article 5(1)(b) in cases where, although the
contract is made online, delivery is effected by traditional methods. It is
digitized products transferred over the internet and online services that
cause the biggest headache.

2. THE TRADITIONAL ENGLISH RULES

10.237 No thought has officially been given to any problems that may arise when the traditional English rules on jurisdiction are applied in cases of electronic commerce. The same criticism of uncertainty and unpredictability can be made as was made in relation to the EC rules. Moreover, there is at least one basis of jurisdiction that looks to be inappropriate in cases of electronic commerce.

Uncertainty and Unpredictability

10.238 It is uncertain whether a foreign defendant can be served within the jurisdiction in the situation where it sets up its own website and server in England. It is not easy to say whether it has established a branch or a place of business, other than a branch, in England. The same uncertainty exists in the situation where a defendant uses someone else's website in England. It is also very difficult to say where a contract negotiated and concluded via the internet was made. Nor is it easy to ascertain whether a breach of contract was committed within the jurisdiction in the situation where digitized products or services have been provided over the internet. With a tort claim for negligent misstatement, negligent or fraudulent misrepresentation there is uncertainty over where the act of misstatement or misrepresentation from which the damage resulted was committed in the situation where the misstatement or misrepresentation was contained on the defendant's website. There is also uncertainty over the place of damage when this consists of digitized goods being released by the claimant prior to payment being made.

Inappropriate Bases of Jurisdiction

10.239 To allow service out of the jurisdiction on the mere basis that a contract was made in England has for many years been a dubious basis for asserting jurisdiction. The advent of electronic commerce should be regarded as being the final nail in the coffin of this basis of jurisdiction. The inappropriateness of the concept of the place where a contract was made in the light of electronic commerce has been accepted as far as the EC rules are concerned. The drafters of the Brussels I Regulation recognized the difficulty or impossibility of identifying the place where a consumer took the necessary steps for the conclusion of the contract, as required under the Brussels Convention,[447] in the situation where the contract has been concluded via an interactive website, and actually got rid of this con-

---

[447] Art 13(3)(b) of the Brussels Convention.

cept.[448] Moreover, the drafters could see that the necessary steps for the conclusion of the contract may be irrelevant to creating a link between the contract and the consumer's state. Yet English traditional rules still allow jurisdiction on the basis that a contract was made in England, which inevitably involves an enquiry into the steps leading up to the conclusion of the contract.

Of course, the requirement under the doctrine of forum conveniens that **10.240** England is the clearly appropriate forum for trial filters out cases where it is inappropriate to have trial in England but, as has been seen, there are difficulties in using this doctrine in cases of e-commerce.

Bases of Jurisdiction and Situations where there are no E-Commerce Concerns

As with the EC rules, the problems raised by electronic commerce should **10.241** not be exaggerated. There are no serious problems in relation to service out of the jurisdiction where the ground used is that there is an English choice of jurisdiction clause or that the contract is governed by English law.[449] Even where a provision can potentially cause problems, it will not do so in all cases of electronic commerce. Thus there is no difficulty in using the breach ground if goods are delivered by traditional means. It is performance via the internet that causes the problems.

IX. REFORM

There are three models that could be applied for the reform and develop- **10.242** ment of the law of jurisdiction in cases of electronic commerce. These are as follows: first, apply the normal rules on jurisdiction, leaving it to the courts to develop the law; second, reform the law by modifying the normal rules on jurisdiction; third, reform the law by introducing a special regime of rules of jurisdiction for cases of electronic commerce.

1. LEAVING IT TO THE COURTS

This is the fall back position that applies in default of adopting either of **10.243** the other two models. This is what has happened in the EC with regard to

---

[448] See Art 15(1)(c) of the Brussels I Regulation.
[449] There can, of course, be a problem in ascertaining whether English law governs a contract made over the internet, see below, paras 21.35–119. There can also be difficulty in ascertaining whether England is the clearly appropriate forum for trial.

the Brussels I Regulation, in England with regard to the traditional rules of jurisdiction, and in other states outside the EC.

The EC

10.244 When the Brussels Convention became the Brussels I Regulation, the experts involved in drafting the changes recognized that there would be problems in applying the new Article 5(1) to cases of digitized products but, in the absence of an obvious solution, at least in the time available to them, left this to be resolved by the courts. The absence of any special provision in Article 5(1) for electronic commerce also can be seen as reflecting a philosophy that electronic commerce contracts should be treated the same as other contracts.

10.245 The way in which the European Court of Justice should solve the problems created by electronic commerce has already been discussed in this chapter. Thus the European Court of Justice should solve the problem of the application of Article 5(1)(b) to cases of digitized products transferred over the internet, by providing that, in the absence of agreement by the parties, the place where the goods are delivered/services provided should be regarded as being that where the recipient has its place of business. Internet torts should be dealt with by the European Court of Justice defining the place of the event giving rise to the damage for each particular internet tort, as suggested above.

England

10.246 As far as the traditional English rules are concerned, there appear to be no plans for reform and so it will be left to the courts to grapple with problems of applying the existing jurisdictional rules to cases of electronic commerce. The way in which the English courts should solve these problems has already been set out in this chapter. Thus when it comes to the application of r 6.20(6) (the breach of contract ground) to the situation where the recipient tries to download the information, but finds that he is unable to do so, and, accordingly, the service provider is in breach of its sub-obligation to make the information available for downloading by the recipient, the place where this sub-obligation should have been performed is where the web-server which the customer accesses to obtain the information is located, ie the place of dispatch. The application of r 6.20(8) to internet torts should be dealt with by looking separately at each particular internet tort, as suggested above.

States Outside the EC

The United States

In the United States, the courts continue to apply traditional jurisdictional **10.247** requirements[450] in internet cases.[451] The courts have had to address the question of whether jurisdiction can be founded on internet connections and have developed certain principles to assist them in answering this question.[452] A sliding scale approach has been adopted, at one end of which are situations where a defendant clearly does business over the internet. For example, the defendant enters into contracts with residents of a foreign jurisdiction that involve the knowing and repeated transmission of computer files over the internet.[453] This is grounds for the exercise of personal jurisdiction. At the opposite end of the scale are situations where a defendant has simply posted information on a passive internet website which is accessible to users in foreign jurisdictions. This is not grounds for the exercise of personal jurisdiction.[454] The middle ground is occupied by interactive websites where a user can exchange information with the host computer. In these cases, the exercise of jurisdiction is determined by examining the level of interactivity and commercial nature of the exchange of information that occurs on the website.[455] The majority of cases using these principles are based upon a defendant's conduct over its own website and they have not been regarded as being particularly useful in cases of activity involving someone else's website,[456] such as an online auction site.[457] Emails have been treated as being no different from more traditional methods of communication, such as letters and phone calls.[458] These principles, developed in cases of the infringement of intellectual property rights, have been applied in cases involving breach of a sale of goods contract.[459]

---

[450] See ABA Cyberspace Report, 32–92. Leading Supreme Court cases are *International Shoe Co v Washington* 326 US 310, 316 (1946); *Helicópteros Nacionales de Colombia SA v Hall* 466 US 408, 416 (1984); *Keeton v Hustler Magazine Inc* 465 US 770, 774 (1984); *Burger King Corp v Rudzewicz* 471 US 462, 475–476 (1985).

[451] *Dagesse v Plant Hotel NV* 113 F Supp 2d 211 at 220–221 (District Court New Hampshire 2000).

[452] See the ABA Cyberspace Report, 57–65, 69. The leading case is *Zippo Manufacturing Company v Zippo Dot Com Inc* 952 F Supp 1119 (US District Court WD Pennsylvania 1997).

[453] eg, *CompuServe Inc v Patterson* 89 F 3d 1257 (6th Cir 1996).

[454] eg, *Bensusan Restaurant Corp v King* 937 F Supp 295 (SDNY 1996).

[455] eg, *Maritz Inc v Cybergold Inc* 947 F Supp 1328 (ED Mo 1996).

[456] *Metcalf v Lawson* 148 A 2d 1221 (NH 2002).

[457] ibid. See also *Winfield Collection Ltd v McCauley* 105 F Supp 2d 746 (ED Mich 2000).

[458] *Internet Doorway Inc v Parks* 138 F Supp 2d 773 (SD Miss 2001).

[459] *Armouth Intern Inc v Haband Co Inc* 715 NYS 2d 438 (NYAD 2000) (defendant uses its own website); *Weinstein v Todd Marine Enterprises Inc* 115 F Supp 2d 668 (ED Va 2000) (using an online classified advertisements service); *Metcalf v Lawson*, n 456 above (using an online auction site).

10.248 These US principles of internet jurisdiction could not be adopted in Europe. It must be repeated that they involve the application of traditional jurisdictional requirements in internet cases. In many states in the United States, jurisdiction is exercised to the fullest extent allowed under the Constitution.[460] There are constitutional limitations on the exercise of personal jurisdiction, namely that the defendant has engaged in systematic and continuous activities in the forum[461] or, for forum related activities, that the relationship between the defendant and the forum falls within a framework of minimum contacts,[462] the touchstone of which is whether the defendant purposefully established contacts with the forum state.[463] Provided that these flexible criteria are satisfied, there is jurisdiction. These criteria are very different from the EC rules on jurisdiction. The flexible nature of the US criteria and its emphasis on activity based jurisdiction allows for easy judicial development of the law of jurisdiction in response to the challenge of the internet, by looking at internet activities in a way that is unthinkable to judges in Europe who have to act within the structure and provisions of the Brussels I Regulation.

Australia and Canada

10.249 The same pattern of leaving it to the courts can be found in Australia and Canada where courts have applied traditional jurisdictional concepts to internet cases. The High Court of Australia in *Dow Jones & Company Inc v Gutnick*[464] was invited to adopt a bold solution and re-express the principles of the common law in the light of this new technology but refused to do so.[465]

2. MODIFICATION OF THE NORMAL RULES

10.250 Under this approach, the starting point is the normal rules on jurisdiction, whether derived from national law, EU law or a multilateral Convention, but these are modified and where appropriate supplemented by additional rules to take account of electronic commerce concerns.

THE HAGUE JUDGMENTS CONVENTION

10.251 This approach was the model proposed at the Hague Conference on Private International Law for the first two drafts of the Hague Judgments

---

[460] This is the position in Pennsylvania, see the *Zippo* case, n 452 above.
[461] See the *Helicópteros* case, n 450 above.
[462] The *International Shoe* case, n 450 above.
[463] The *Burger King* case, n 450 above.   [464] n 424 above.
[465] ibid, paras 88–90. What it was being asked to re-express was the law of defamation, para 111 (*per* Kirby J).

Convention.[466] The problems posed by electronic data interchange is a topic on the agenda of the Hague Conference, separate from the Judgments Convention, although obviously of relevance to that project. The examination of these problems has been very thorough, with a number of expert meetings and reports on this topic.[467] At the time when what was contemplated was a Judgments Convention that was very wide in its scope and to some extent, at least as regards jurisdiction, resembled the Brussels Convention, it was never suggested at the Hague Conference that electronic commerce should be excluded from such a Convention.[468] What was proposed was that the normal rules in the Convention should apply, supplemented by some additional rules to take account not only of the recording of a jurisdiction agreement[469] but also for contracts performed online and, in the situation where jurisdiction was based explicitly on the defendant conducting activity in a state, to deal with defendants who took steps to avoid entering into obligations in a particular state.[470] The proposal that contracts performed online should be dealt with by a special rule is of particular interest because it was made in relation to a provision with almost identical wording to Article 5(1) of the Brussels I Regulation.[471] Other electronic commerce concerns were identified but no

[466] There were two preliminary drafts of a wide Convention on jurisdiction and foreign judgments in civil and commercial matters (the Hague Judgments Convention). First, there was the draft Convention adopted by the Special Commission on 30 October 1999. Second, the First Part of the Diplomatic Conference 6–20 June 2001 Interim Text. Difficulties in reaching agreement on these drafts by the Member States of the Hague Conference has meant that a third draft has been prepared which is much narrower in scope than the two earlier drafts. This is the Draft on Exclusive Choice of Court Agreements prepared by the Special Commission on Jurisdiction, Recognition and Enforcement of Foreign Judgments in Civil and Commercial Matters (1 to 9 December 2003) Working Document No 49 E Revised. See http://hcch.e-vision.nl/index_en.php?act=progress.listing&cat=4

[467] See the Geneva Round Table on Electronic Commerce and Private International Law held jointly by the Hague Conference on Private International Law and the University of Geneva 2, 3 and 4 of September 1999 (seven commissions met simultaneously); the expert meeting on Electronic Commerce and International Jurisdiction organized by the Hague Conference on Private International Law held in Ottawa from 28 February to 1 March 2000. The conclusions of both of these meetings are set out by Kessedjian in Prel Doc No 7, n 2 above. For the work that needs to be done in the future in relation to the internet within the context of the Judgments Convention see Prel Doc No 17, n 10 above. See generally Forner Delaygua, n 154 above, 47 et seq.

[468] The expert meeting at Ottawa, ibid, at 11.

[469] Art 4(2)(b) of the 30 October 1999 version of the draft Convention. This was repeated in the 2001 Interim Text.

[470] See the 2001 Interim Text: Art 6, Alternative A[3] (contractual matters), Art 7[3] (consumer contracts)—there was no consensus on this proposal; Art 10[3] (torts)—there was no consensus on this proposal. See also Art 7(1) (consumer contracts). These proposals were not contained in the earlier 30 October 1999 version of the draft Convention.

[471] The expert meeting at Ottowa, n 467 above, at 5. They were concerned in particular about whether this was a contract for sale or the provision of services. See also Prel Doc No 7, n 2 above, 19.

suggestion was made for special rules to deal with these particular concerns.[472]

The EC Rules

10.252 The Brussels I Regulation does involve a modification of existing rules in so far as it contains the two provisions reflecting electronic commerce concerns. However, there is no special rule under Article 5(1) for contracts performed online. It is possible in the future to introduce such an amendment.[473] A new rule could be introduced into Article 5(1)(b) of the Brussels I Regulation by means of a third category to follow the current two categories, i.e. the special rules for identifying the place of performance of the obligation in question in the case of the sale of goods and in the case of the provision of services. This third category could apply 'in the case of performance over the Internet'.[474] But this would be to treat electronic commerce contracts differently from other contracts, which goes against the current philosophy towards Article 5(1). As regards internet torts, any special rule[475] would doubtless crudely apply the same rule to every internet tort and would not focus, as it should, on the intricacies of particular internet torts. The European Court of Justice is capable of resolving the problems of the application of Article 5(1) in cases of performance online and the application of Article 5(3) to internet torts and should be left to do so. If the Regulation were to be constantly modified in the light of changes in technology this would destroy the very flexibility of the Regulation which is one of its strengths.

---

[472] Art 10 of the 30 October 1999 draft Convention; the expert meeting at Ottawa, n 467 above, at 8 (the place where a tortious act occurs), ibid (application of a foreseeability test in tort cases); Art 9 of the 30 October 1999 draft Convention; the expert meeting at Ottawa, n 467 above, at 9 (what constitutes carrying on regular commercial activity). These Articles are also to be found in the 2001 Interim Text. There was a proposal that the tort provision in the Hague Judgments Convention should contain a proviso that there would be no jurisdiction in a state in situations where the defendant has taken reasonable steps to avoid acting in or directing activity into that state: Art 10(3). There was no consensus on this proposal.

[473] Art 73 of the Brussels I Regulation provides that the Commission must report on the application of the Regulation within five years of its entry into force. The report shall be accompanied, if need be, by proposals for adaptations to the Regulation.

[474] It could provide that, 'in the case of performance over the Internet, the place in a Member State where, under the contract, information was transferred or should have been transferred. In the absence of agreement by the parties on this place, it shall be deemed to be the place where the recipient of the information has its place of business'. This would be to adopt the same rule as has been put forward in this chapter for application by the ECJ.

[475] This could, for example, allocate jurisdiction to the place in a Member State where the defendant was established or the damage occurred.

The Traditional Rules

It would be possible to introduce new grounds for service out of the **10.253**
jurisdiction for cases of e-commerce. Rule 6.20(6) of the Civil Procedure
Rules could be amended to deal with contracts performed online.[476] Rule
6.20(8) could also be amended to deal with internet torts.[477] But this would
go against the current practice which is have grounds for service out of
the jurisdiction which are based on claims. This refers to causes of action
and types of proceeding, rather than to problems posed by technology. It
is also likely to lead in the case of internet torts to a special rule that would
crudely apply the same rule to every internet tort, rather than focusing, as
it should, on the intricacies of particular internet torts. The English courts
are capable of solving such contractual and tortious problems and should
be left to do so. If the Civil Procedure Rules were to be constantly modified in the light of changes in technology this would destroy the very
flexibility of the Rules which is one of their strengths.

The one exception where modification of the rules is necessary is in rela- **10.254**
tion to r 6.20(5)(a). It should no longer be possible for service out of the
jurisdiction to be permitted on the mere basis that a contract was made in
England and this ground should be deleted from r 6.20. This is not a
matter that can be left to the courts, as that would be to usurp the judicial
function. But this suggestion is not just a response to electronic commerce.
This would affect all cases where a claim is made in respect of a contract,
not just those involving electronic commerce.[478] But then this ground is a
dubious one not just in cases of electronic commerce.[479]

3. INTRODUCTION OF A SPECIAL REGIME OF JURISDICTIONAL RULES FOR E-COMMERCE

There has to be good reason for taking an increasingly important area **10.255**
outside the scope of the normal rules on jurisdiction. There are those that
favour a special regime of jurisdictional rules for electronic commerce
on the ground that territorially based concepts of jurisdiction are not

---

[476] This could provide, for example, that service out of the jurisdiction would be permissible if England is the place of the online performance of that obligation. In the absence of
agreement by the parties, online performance should be regarded as taking place in England
if the recipient has its place of business there.

[477] This could, for example, provide that service out of the jurisdiction would be
permissible if the defendant was established or the damage occurred in England.

[478] For criticism of the use of the place where the contract is made as a basis of jurisdiction,
at least for online contracts where delivery is online, see Prel Doc No 7, n 2 above, 19.

[479] See also Hogan-Doran n 244 above.

appropriate in cyberspace.[480] This treats cyberspace as if it were a place rather than what it is, a means of communication,[481] and ignores the territorial connections that undoubtedly exist in cases of electronic commerce. There is no compelling underlying conceptual reason for radical reform[482] that sweeps away the existing law and replaces it by a special regime of jurisdictional rules. There would, though, be a practical reason for doing so if it could be shown that the majority of the existing rules on jurisdiction are inappropriate in cases of electronic commerce. But this is not the case. It is hard to see the European Commission wanting to become involved in a special regime of jurisdictional rules for electronic commerce. Electronic commerce has been considered recently when the Brussels Convention became the Brussels I Regulation and the concentration has been upon the substantive law of electronic commerce. Moreover, although questions of private international law raised by the information society have been included in the agenda for the future work of the Hague Conference,[483] one of the conclusions reached so far is that, as far as possible, existing rules of private international law should be applied in cases of electronic commerce.[484] There is no suggestion of a special regime of jurisdiction rules for e-commerce cases.[485]

10.256 If a special regime of rules were to be introduced, there would be the problem of defining when the rule would apply, ie what is meant by electronic commerce,[486] and determining what these rules should be. Fundamental questions would have to be answered, such as: when should a company which conducts its business over the internet be subject to jurisdiction in states abroad? A principle could be adopted that the company is subject to jurisdiction abroad in circumstances where it is deliberately seeking to expand beyond its traditional marketing area to

---

[480] M Burnstein 'Conflicts on the Net: Choice of Law in Transnational Cyberspace' (1996) 29 Vanderbilt J of Transnational Law 75, 82; Johnson and Post, n 16 above.

[481] See the discussion in the ABA Cyberspace Report, 7–10; Lord Drummond Young in *Bonnier Media Ltd v Greg Lloyd Smith and Kestrel Trading Corp* 2003 SC 36, [2002] ETMR 86 at [18]. But see the comments of Kirby J in the *Dow Jones* case, n 424 above, para 164 whose intuition suggested to him that it is more than another method of communication. This matter is discussed further below, paras 21.265–267.

[482] See the *Dow Jones* case, n 424 above, at 125 (*per* Kirby J).

[483] See Minutes, No 1, Commission I, Nineteenth Session (21 June 2001). See also Gen Affairs Prel Doc No 10 of June 2000, 13–15. It is not part of the current work programme, see Conclusions of Commission I (22–24 April 2002). E-Commerce is a global problem and so there is a case for a global solution: see the ABA Cyberspace Report, 24–26; Prel Doc No 7 of April 2000, 18.

[484] See p 2 of the Press Release for the Geneva Round Table, n 467 above.

[485] But see J Castel, 'The Internet in Light of Traditional Public and Private International Law Principles and Rules Applied in Canada' [2001] Canadian Ybk of Intl Law 3.

[486] For the difficulty in defining this concept see above, para 10.01.

that foreign country.[487] This would mean that a company which is only concerned with the local market would not be subject to jurisdiction abroad.

There are various national and international initiatives that could be con- **10.257** sulted. However, their usefulness is distinctly limited. There are the ICC Electronic Commerce Project and the Canadian Consultation Document on the Determination of Jurisdiction in Cross-border Business-to-Consumer Transactions, but both of these initiatives are only concerned with business to consumer electronic commerce.[488] For consideration of business to business as well as business to consumer electronic commerce there is the ABA Cyberspace Report and various reports prepared for the Hague Judgments Convention. However, neither of these sets out a complete regime of jurisdictional rules for electronic commerce. What the Hague reports tell us is which bases of jurisdiction do and do not work in cases of electronic commerce, but there is no Hague Convention on electronic commerce and jurisdiction. The ABA Cyberspace Report sets out principles and strategies that are designed to guide any body that is drafting a set of rules.[489] However, these principles bear a distinct resemblance to the internet principles developed by the US courts which are concerned with activity based jurisdiction. It follows that such an approach could not be adopted in Europe.

4. Conclusion

The conclusion from this analysis is that reform and development of the **10.258** law of jurisdiction in cases of electronic commerce should be left to the courts, which are certainly capable of solving the problems raised by this new method of communication.

---

[487] See the Opinion of the Economic and Social Committee on the proposed Brussels I Regulation [2000] OJ C117/6, 4.2.2.

[488] Moreover, the former only sets out principles, rather than a set of rules.

[489] The ABA Cyberspace Report, 20–23. It is contemplated that these could be applied by the courts as well as by a legislature or organization.

PART II
RECOGNITION AND ENFORCEMENT OF FOREIGN JUDGMENTS

11

The Recognition and Enforcement of Foreign Judgments

I. INTRODUCTION

11.01 The recognition and enforcement of judgments obtained overseas in England is, of course, a subject of fundamental importance in the conflict of laws. In the international sales context, it will be very common for a foreign judgment to require recognition and enforcement in England, if the defendant's assets are located in a state other than that in which the judgment was obtained. However, it is equally clear that most of the law in this area is not specific to sale of goods contracts. Accordingly, the general rules of recognition and enforcement are set out rather briefly.[1]

---

[1] For more detail, see Dicey and Morris, Ch 14; Cheshire and North, Chs 15 and 16; Briggs and Rees, Ch 7.

The chapter then seeks to highlight certain issues which might prove particularly problematic in relation to the enforcement of judgments relating to sale of goods contracts. These issues are primarily concerned with the fact that many judgments in this area may not order the payment of a fixed sum of money. These might include an order for the delivery of goods to the buyer, or a declaration that title has passed to the buyer. There is surprisingly little learning on the enforcement of such non-monetary judgments in England. If such judgments may not be enforced in England, there is a further question as to the circumstances in which the claimant might sue afresh on the cause of action in England. Moreover, if the judgment is enforced, there is a question as to the effect that it would have on any related litigation in England. This might include a claim by one of the parties for damages. Where a foreign judgment affecting delivery or possession has been issued, the question arises as to which third parties, if any, might be affected by such an order.

II. THE RULES OF RECOGNITION AND ENFORCEMENT: GENERAL REMARKS

1. RECOGNITION OR ENFORCEMENT?

Where an English court *recognizes* a foreign judgment, it recognizes it as **11.02** conclusive as to the *liability* of the parties to the litigation. Where an English court *enforces* a foreign judgment, it also gives effect to a *remedy* granted in the foreign court. For a foreign judgment to be enforced by a claimant, it must also be entitled to recognition. Enforcement will be required by a judgment creditor who has been awarded a remedy overseas and now wishes to secure access to the defendant's assets in England. Recognition alone will suffice where the foreign court's decision is merely declaratory. It will also suffice where a defendant who has been sued overseas wishes to use the foreign judgment as a defence to further litigation against him in England.

2. THE SCHEMES OF RECOGNITION AND ENFORCEMENT OF FOREIGN JUDGMENTS APPLICABLE IN THE UNITED KINGDOM

Four major schemes of recognition and enforcement of foreign[2] judgments **11.03** are applicable in England: the Brussels I Regulation,[3] the Administration

---

[2] i.e. judgments from outside the UK.

[3] Regulation on Jurisdiction and the Recognition and Enforcement of Judgments in Civil and Commercial Matters (the 'Brussels I Regulation'): Council Regulation (EC) No 44/2001 of 22 December 2000 [2001] OJ L12/1.

of Justice Act 1920, the Foreign Judgments (Reciprocal Enforcement) Act 1933 and the common law. The appropriate scheme depends upon the court which delivered judgment and/or the basis of its jurisdiction. There are also rules contained in the Civil Jurisdiction and Judgments Act 1982 on the recognition and enforcement of a judgment from a court of one part of the United Kingdom in another part.

III. THE EUROPEAN REGIME OF RECOGNITION AND ENFORCEMENT

1. Scope of Application

11.04   The rules in the Brussels I Regulation apply to a judgment delivered in the courts of a Member State in a civil and commercial matter[4] regardless of the basis on which the court of origin took jurisdiction. This means that if an English court has taken jurisdiction pursuant to its traditional national rules in a matter falling with the scope of Article 1 of the Brussels I Regulation,[5] the rules of the Brussels I Regulation regime apply to determine whether the judgment qualifies for recognition and enforcement in other Member States.[6] This is the case even if jurisdiction was taken under the court of origin's national jurisdictional rules pursuant to Article 4. It follows that only where a matter is excluded altogether from the Regulation by Article 1 will one of the other schemes of recognition and enforcement apply to a Member State's judgment. However, the English court will be entitled to check for itself that the judgment is indeed within the scope of the Regulation when recognition is sought.[7]

11.05   If the judgment was delivered in Denmark, the Brussels Convention will apply to its recognition and enforcement. The Brussels Convention will also apply to foreign judgments delivered before 1 March 2002. The Lugano Convention will apply to a judgment delivered in Iceland, Norway, or Switzerland.[8] However, we shall concentrate upon the Brussels I Regulation rules in the following discussion.

2. Meaning of 'Judgment'

11.06   The word 'judgment' is defined in Article 32 to mean 'any judgment given

---

[4]   Within the meaning of Art 1 of the Regulation.
[5]   Pursuant to Art 4.
[6]   Or, in the case of Denmark, the Brussels Convention.
[7]   See Briggs and Rees, 432–433.
[8]   Poland became a Contracting State to the Lugano Convention on 1 August 2000: see SI 2000/1824. However, it joined the EU on 1 May 2004.

by a court or tribunal of a Member State, whatever the judgment may be called, including a decree, order, decision or writ of execution, as well as the determination of costs or expenses by an officer of the court'. This broad definition none the less excludes purely procedural rulings[9] and without notice applications[10] (including an asset freezing order).[11]

3. Automatic Recognition

Article 33(1) of the Regulation provides that 'a judgment given in a **11.07** Member State shall be recognized in the other Member States without any special procedure being required'. There is no requirement that the judgment be a final one.[12] Moreover, unlike the common law position, the judgment need not be a monetary award. An order of specific performance would be entitled to enforcement under the Regulation.[13]

4. Defences—Lack of Jurisdictional Competence

A party cannot generally resist enforcement by arguing that the overseas **11.08** court lacked jurisdiction. Nevertheless, under Article 35 the debtor may in very limited circumstances object to the Member State's jurisdiction. A judgment will not be recognized if it conflicts with the exclusive jurisdiction provisions of Article 22 or the insurance[14] or consumer contract[15] provisions, i.e. if those provisions gave jurisdiction to the courts of another Member State and not to those of the state where the judgment was delivered.[16] It should be noted that violation of a choice of court agreement[17] is not given as a reason to refuse enforcement.[18] In all cases, the court seised shall be bound by the findings of fact on which the court of the state of origin based its jurisdiction.[19] Hence, only legal errors in application of the Regulation will fall within these limited provisions.

[9] Schlosser Report [1979] OJ C59/127, para 187.
[10] *Denilauler v SNC Couchet Frères* [1980] ECR 1553. The problem is that such decisions are likely to fall foul of the natural justice defence in Art 34(2) (on which, see below, paras 11.11–12). See also Case C-39/02 *Maersk Olie & Gas A/S v Firma M de Haan*, judgment of 14 October 2004.
[11] See Briggs and Rees, 431–436.
[12] Schlosser Report, 126; Case 143/78 *De Cavel v De Cavel* [1979] ECR 1055.
[13] See further the Schlosser Report, 132.
[14] Contained in Arts 8–14.
[15] Contained in Arts 15–17.
[16] Although in the cases of the last insurance and consumer contracts, enforcement will still be possible if the defendant had submitted to the overseas jurisdiction.
[17] The choice of court provisions are contained in Art 23.
[18] Compare Case C-116/02 *Erich Gasser GmbH v Misat Srl* [2004] IL Pr 7.
[19] Art 35(2).

5. Substantive Defences

11.09   Article 34 provides four substantive defences to recognition.

Recognition would be Manifestly Contrary to English Public Policy

11.10   This provision should be construed narrowly, a fact emphasized by the word 'manifestly'.[20] Recognition of the judgment itself, not the underlying subject-matter of the dispute in which judgment was given, must be contrary to public policy. The fact that the judgment of the state of origin is allegedly illegal is not in itself enough to justify use of the public policy defence. In *Krombach v Bamberski*[21] the European Court of Justice held that:

> In order for the prohibition of any review of the foreign judgment as to its substance to be observed, the infringement would have to constitute a manifest breach of a rule of law regarded as essential in the legal order of the State in which enforcement is sought or of a right recognized as being fundamental within that legal order.[22]

The European Court of Justice ruled in *Régie Nationale des Usines Renault SA v Maxicar SPA*[23] that even an alleged breach of EC law, such as the rules on free movement of goods, is not in itself enough to justify invoking the defence.

The Judgment was given in Default of Appearance and the Defendant was not Duly Served with the Document which Instituted the Proceedings or with an Equivalent Document in Sufficient Time and in such a way as to Enable him to Arrange for his Defence, Unless the Defendant failed to Commence Proceedings to Challenge the Judgment when it was possible for him to do so

11.11   Only default judgments are covered by this defence. It appears that the phrase 'default judgment' has a European autonomous meaning. In *Hendrikman v Magenta Druck & Verlag GmbH*,[24] the European Court of Justice held that a judgment given against a person who had no knowledge that proceedings had been initiated against him was not entitled to recognition in other Member States, even where a lawyer had appeared on behalf of that person. As to what constitutes due service, it must be shown that the defendant was 'duly served' in a way which would reasonably have allowed him to ensure that a default judgment was

---

[20]   Which was added in the Regulation and which was not previously found in the Brussels Convention.
[21]   Case C-7/98 [2000] ECR I-1935.
[22]   ibid, at 1968–1969, para 37.   [23]   Case C-38/98 [2000] ECR I-2973.
[24]   Case C-78/95 [1996] ECR I-4943. See also Case C-39/02 *Maersk Olie & Gas A/S v Firma M de Haan*, judgement of 14 October 2004.

not entered against him.[25] In this regard, the fact that he was properly served according to the national procedural rules of the state of origin is a necessary, but not sufficient, condition.[26] The state where recognition is sought may re-examine for itself whether the time was sufficient.[27]

The Regulation makes clear that if the defendant failed to commence **11.12** proceedings overseas to challenge the judgment when it was possible for him to do so, he will be precluded from raising the defence at the recognition stage.

The Judgment is Irreconcilable with a Judgment between the same Parties in the Court in which Recognition is Sought

In *Hoffman v Krieg*,[28] the European Court of Justice held that judgments are **11.13** 'irreconcilable' if they lead to consequences which are mutually exclusive. In civil and commercial matters, the court first seised mechanism in Article 27 of the Regulation[29] should prevent irreconcilable judgments between the same parties being delivered in different Member States. Where this does occur, however, the English court's judgment prevails in England, even if it is delivered subsequent to the foreign judgment. This provision might also apply where there are two causes of actions which are not identical, so that Article 27 is not invoked, and no stay is granted by the court under Article 28. Article 34(3) will also be relevant if the foreign court took jurisdiction within the Regulation and there is a related action in England which falls outside the scope of the Regulation. In such a case, the court first seised mechanism of the Regulation would not be triggered.

The Judgment is Irreconcilable with an Earlier Judgment given in another Member State or in a Third State involving the same cause of Action and between the same Parties, provided that the Earlier Judgment fulfils the Conditions necessary for Recognition in the Member State Addressed

If a judgment was given in a non-Member State, such as the United States, **11.14** and is entitled to recognition by our common law rules, it would prevail if delivered prior to a German judgment.

---

[25] Case 166–80 *Klomps v Michel* [1981] ECR 1593.
[26] Case 49/84 *Debaecker v Bouwman* [1985] ECR 1739.
[27] Case 228/81 *Pendy Plastic Products BV v Pluspunkt Handels GmbH* [1982] ECR 2723.
[28] Case 145/86 [1988] ECR 645. See also Case C-80/00 *Leather SpA v WECO Polstermobel GmbH & Co* [2002] ECR I-4995.
[29] Discussed above, paras 3.313–329. See also Art 28, which deals with related actions between the same parties.

11.15 There had been a lacuna in the Brussels Convention as to what should happen where two judgments delivered in overseas Member States, such as, for example, France and Germany, were irreconcilable with one another. The Regulation clarifies matters by providing that a Regulation judgment shall be refused recognition if irreconcilable with an earlier judgment given in another Member State qualifying for recognition. In other words, the first judgment to be handed down will prevail.

6. A Treaty Based Exception

11.16 Article 59 of the Brussels Convention allowed a Contracting State to enter into a treaty with a non-Contracting State which exempted certain persons from the Convention recognition regime where the courts of a Member State had taken jurisdiction under their national rules pursuant to Article 4. Article 72 of the Brussels I Regulation provides that such treaties as were entered into when the Convention was in force will still be effective. The United Kingdom has two such treaties, which apply respectively to defendants domiciled or habitually resident in Australia[30] and Canada.[31] However, it should be noted that Article 72 of the Brussels I Regulation does not confer on Member States the power to enter into new treaties of this nature.

7. No Review on the Substance

11.17 Aside from the grounds mentioned above, Article 36 states that 'under no circumstances may a foreign judgment be reviewed as to its substance'. This means that an English court cannot refuse recognition to a judgment of another Member State on the basis that the court of origin applied different substantive sale of goods provisions to those applicable in English law and thereby reached a decision on the merits which differs to that which the English court would have reached had it heard the case.

8. The Enforcement Procedure

11.18 The enforcement procedure is set out in detail in Articles 38–52. The provisions are not complex and it is not necessary to examine them at any length. A judgment shall be enforced in England when, on the application

---

[30] Reciprocal Enforcement of Foreign Judgments (Australia) Order 1994, SI 1994/1901, Sch 3, Art 3.
[31] Reciprocal Enforcement of Foreign Judgments (Canada) Order, SI 1987/468.

of any interested party, it has been registered for enforcement in England.[32] The claimant seeking enforcement[33] should apply without notice for an order for registration before the High Court[34] and produce a copy of the judgment.[35] When a judgment is entitled to recognition under the Regulation, the applicant may seek such interim relief as is available in the state of recognition prior to obtaining a declaration of enforceability.[36]

Article 41 provides that 'the judgment shall be declared enforceable **11.19** immediately on completion of the [requisite] formalities ... without any review under Articles 34 and 35'. In other words, the defendant to the enforcement proceedings will at this stage get no opportunity to argue that one of the defences to recognition is applicable. Instead, that person must launch an appeal on this basis pursuant to Article 43(1). This streamlines the enforcement procedure, but has the result of putting the judgment debtor firmly on the back foot.

However, if an appeal is pending overseas, the court may stay its pro- **11.20** ceedings on the question of enforcement.[37] Once registration is granted, the defendant may then appeal to the High Court against the registration.[38] If registration was refused, the claimant may appeal.[39] When the judgment is conclusively registered in whole or in part,[40] it is treated for the purposes of English law as equivalent to a High Court judgment.[41]

IV. THE COMMON LAW RECOGNITION AND ENFORCEMENT RULES

1. General Remarks

Where the Regulation rules are inapplicable, the common law will govern **11.21** enforcement, or one of the statutory schemes which modifies the rules in relation to judgments of certain states. The common law applies unless

---

[32] Art 38(2).   [33] Pursuant to s 4 of the Civil Jurisdiction and Judgments Act 1982.
[34] Annex II to the Regulation.   [35] Art 53.   [36] Art 47(1).   [37] Art 37.
[38] Art 43. The court may also stay the appeal against registration if an appeal is pending overseas: Art 46 (cf the Brussels Convention position: Case C-432/93 *SISRO v Ampersand* [1995] ECR I-2269).
[39] Art 43(5) states that: 'An appeal against the declaration of enforceability is to be lodged within one month of service thereof. If the party against whom enforcement is sought is domiciled in a Member State other than that in which the declaration of enforceability was given, the time for appealing shall be two months and shall run from the date of service, either on him in person or at his residence.'
[40] Partial enforcement is permitted by Art 48(1).
[41] Civil Jurisdiction and Judgments Order 2001, SI 2001/3929, Sch 1, para 1(3).

the United Kingdom has entered into a bilateral treaty with another state pursuant to the 1920 or the 1933 Act. This means that, for example, a judgment from any state in the United States of America will be subject to the common law regime of recognition and enforcement in England. Since the Acts are largely a codification of the common law, attention will focus primarily on the common law. Discussion of the statutes will consider any material differences from the common law.

11.22 In order to enforce at common law, a party cannot rely on a registration procedure. Instead, an action must be brought on the judgment itself seeking summary judgment.

2. RECOGNITION RULES: THE JURISDICTIONAL COMPETENCE OF A FOREIGN COURT

11.23 A judgment will not be recognized if the foreign court was not jurisdictionally competent in the eyes of English law. The English court will assess this question for itself. It will regard a foreign court as jurisdictionally competent on two grounds. First, if the defendant had the necessary territorial connection with the state of origin. Second, if the defendant submitted to the jurisdiction of the court of origin. We shall now look at these two grounds a little further.

The Defendant was Present and/or Resident in the Overseas Jurisdiction

Individuals

11.24 It is somewhat uncertain whether the defendant must be resident in the state of origin, or whether his presence at the time of instigation of proceedings will suffice. The classic judgment of Buckley LJ in *Emanuel v Symon*,[42] suggests that residence is required. However, the Court of Appeal in *Adams v Cape Industries*[43] reviewed the law and suggested that presence was sufficient.[44] It left open the situation where the defendant was resident, but not present, in the jurisdiction at the time of commencement. However, it would be surprising[45] if this were not sufficient.

Companies

11.25 Where the defendant is a company, it was decided in *Adams* that there must be a fixed place of business maintained at the company's own

---

[42] [1908] 1 KB 302.   [43] [1990] Ch 433.
[44] It relied in part on *Carrick v Hancock* (1895) 12 TLR 59.
[45] Although not inconceivable, since presence alone is sufficient in an English court to give it jurisdiction as of right. However, the enforcement rules are not intended exactly to mirror the jurisdiction rules.

expense from which it has carried out its own business in the overseas jurisdiction whose courts gave judgment.[46] It will suffice that its business is transacted at that place through representatives of the company carrying out the corporation's business.[47] Particularly relevant in this respect will be whether it may enter into contracts on the corporation's behalf.[48]

Submission

A court to which a defendant has submitted will also be seen as juris- **11.26** dictionally competent in the eyes of English law. The most obvious means of submitting is by voluntarily pleading to the merits. However, s 33 of the Civil Jurisdiction and Judgments Act 1982 states that an appearance solely to contest the jurisdiction of the court, or to ask it to dismiss or stay proceedings for another country's courts, or for arbitration, or to protect or obtain the release of property seized or threatened with seizure, shall not constitute submission.[49]

A defendant may also have contractually agreed[50] to submit litigation to **11.27** the courts of a particular state. It is uncertain whether the contractual term must be express or can also be implied into a contract.[51] It is difficult to see any reason why the agreement should not be implied, provided that there is clear evidence that this reflects the parties' intentions.

Finally, it is important, if not self-evident, to note that a claimant, by **11.28** instigating proceedings, will be deemed to have submitted to the court.

3. Judgment Final and Conclusive on the Merits

A judgment will not be recognized unless it is also final and conclusive on **11.29** the merits. The word 'final' means that the judgment is binding in the court which gave judgment and cannot be reopened therein, even if

---

[46] Where a defendant (be it an individual or a company) is sued in a federal jurisdiction, it was suggested in *Adams* that it must be present in the particular state which gave judgment (eg, Texas, not simply anywhere in the US), unless the judgment is from a federal, rather than a state, court.

[47] See also *Littauer Glove Corp v FW Millington* (1928) 44 TLR 746.

[48] *Vogel v R & A Kohnstamm Ltd* [1973] QB 133.

[49] Compare the pre-Act position in *Henry v Geoprosco International Ltd* [1976] QB 726.

[50] In a suitable case, submission might even occur by estoppel. This might be the case where a party issues an assurance that he will agree to litigation in a particular jurisdiction and the other party has acted reasonably in detrimental reliance upon that assurance.

[51] In favour of the view that it may be implied, see *Blohn v Desser* [1962] 2 QB 116; against, see *Vogel v R & A Kohnstamm* [1973] QB 133.

the same matter can be appealed to a higher court.[52] A default judgment may thus not be final until the time for setting aside has expired.[53] The judgment will not be conclusive if further defences to its recognition are available in the overseas court.

11.30 The requirement that the judgment be on the merits of a point means that it '. . . establishes certain facts proved or not in dispute, states what are the relevant principles of law applicable to such facts and expresses a conclusion with regard to the effect of applying those principles to the factual situation concerned'.[54]

4. FURTHER CONDITIONS FOR ENFORCEMENT[55]

11.31 A judgment which satisfies the above conditions is entitled to recognition in England. However, if it is sought also to enforce the judgment, the claimant must satisfy further conditions.

The Judgment must be for a Fixed Sum of Money

11.32 The judgment must be for a fixed sum; accordingly a judgment for specific performance or injunctive relief will not be enforced. Nor can a damages claim be enforced if the total sum to be awarded has not been finally quantified. This area of law can raise real difficulties in relation to the sale of goods, which will be examined below.[56] An order that X has title to, or possession of goods, or an order that the seller deliver the goods to the buyer do not qualify for enforcement. They are, however, entitled to recognition.

The English Court will not Enforce a Foreign Penal, Revenue or Public Law Judgment

11.33 A tax liability[57] or an order for confiscation of property[58] in the name of the state would not be enforceable. An order to pay penal damages will certainly not be enforceable if payable to a state authority.[59] How-

---

[52] *Nouvion v Freeman* (1889) 15 App Cas 1.   [53] Briggs and Rees, 483.

[54] *The Sennar (No 2)* [1985] 1 WLR 490, *per* Lord Brandon. A decision that an action was time-barred would be on the merits: s 3 of the Foreign Limitation (Periods) Act 1984.

[55] These further conditions do not need to be satisfied if only recognition is sought. For a foreign judgment to be recognized at common law, the foreign court need only be jurisdictionally competent in the eyes of English law.

[56] At paras 11.70–81.

[57] *United States v Inkley* [1989] QB 225.

[58] *Attorney-General for New Zealand v Ortiz* [1984] AC 1.

[59] *Huntington v Attrill* [1893] AC 150.

ever, exemplary or punitive damages which are awarded to a private individual should not be caught by this exclusion.[60] In any event, if it is possible to sever the compensatory part of a judgment, that alone may be enforced.[61]

The Judgment Must not Order the Payment of Multiple Damages

Where 'a judgment is for an amount arrived at by . . . multiplying a sum **11.34** assessed as compensation',[62] it shall not be enforced.[63] This provision seeks largely to counteract the antitrust legislation of the United States. If the defendant has already paid multiple damages to the defendant, he may reclaim in an English court that part of the damages which was not paid as compensation.[64]

5. Inoperative Defences to Recognition and Enforcement

A judgment debtor will not be able to resist recognition or enforcement on **11.35** either of the following grounds.

Error of Law

The fact that a foreign court has allegedly misapplied the law, or applied **11.36** a law which seems inappropriate, cannot be pleaded in defence.[65] The English court will also not review an alleged error of fact in the court of origin, as it should not go into the merits of the foreign decision.

The Foreign Court Lacked Jurisdiction by the Procedural Law of the State of Origin

Even if it is alleged that the particular court, which heard the case in the **11.37** state of origin lacked jurisdiction, this will be irrelevant, unless the error made the judgment null and void in that state.[66]

In the case of both error of law and error of jurisdiction, it is inherently **11.38**

---

[60] *SA Consortium General Textiles v Sun & Sand Agencies Ltd* [1978] QB 279.
[61] *Raulin v Fischer* [1911] KB 93.
[62] Protection of Trading Interests Act 1980, s 5(3).
[63] ibid, s 5(1).   [64] ibid, s 6(2).   [65] *Godard v Gray* (1870) LR 6 QB 288.
[66] *Vanqueilin v Brouard* (1863) 15 CBNS 341; *Pemberton v Hughes* [1899] 1 Ch 781.

more likely that the court of origin will apply its law and rules of jurisdiction correctly than that an English court will.

6. Operative Defences to Recognition and Enforcement

11.39 If properly made out, the following will provide valid defences to recognition[67] of a foreign judgment at common law.

The Judgment was Procured by the Claimant's Fraud

11.40 English courts are prepared effectively to retry the case on its merits where fraud is alleged. It matters not that the foreign court rejected this allegation on the basis of the same evidence,[68] nor that the defendant had the opportunity to raise the defence overseas but did not do so.[69] However, the Privy Council in *Owens Bank Ltd v Etoile Commerciale SA*,[70] suggested that the defence should be struck out '. . . in the absence of plausible evidence disclosing at least a prima facie case of fraud'.[71]

11.41 There is one exception to the availability of the defence. Where a separate judgment has been delivered on the fraud issue, the defendant will be estopped from raising it in England.[72]

The Judgment was in Breach of Natural Justice

11.42 It is apparently open to a party resisting recognition to allege that standards of natural justice have been violated in the state of origin, even if such an allegation had been made overseas,[73] or the defendant failed to take advantage of any procedures existing in the state of origin to make his complaint.[74]

11.43 The English courts have traditionally been reluctant to condemn foreign procedures and to find that a foreign judgment was in breach of natural justice.[75] However, in *Adams v Cape Industries*,[76] it was suggested obiter

---

[67] And therefore also to enforcement of a foreign judgment.
[68] *Abouloff v Oppenheimer & Co* (1882) 10 QBD 295.
[69] *Syal v Hayward* [1948] 2 KB 443.   [70] [1995] 1 WLR 44.
[71] ibid, at 51, *per* Lord Templeman. He went on to state that no precise test could be laid down and that the court must '. . . decide whether justice requires the further investigation of alleged fraud or requires that the plaintiff, having obtained a foreign judgment, shall no longer be frustrated in enforcing that judgment'.
[72] *House of Spring Garden v Waite (No 2)* [1991] 1 QB 241.
[73] An unlikely event if the alleged breach is a lack of opportunity to be heard.
[74] *Adams v Cape Industries* [1990] Ch 433.
[75] Whether the Human Rights Act 1998 will increase the scope of the natural justice defence remains to be seen.
[76] [1990] Ch 433.

that the court could refuse to enforce the judgment if the foreign proceedings amounted to 'a breach of an English court's views of substantial justice'.[77] In that case, the judge, with the assistance of counsel, awarded compensation to the plaintiffs on a basis which did not obviously reflect the extent of the injuries each had suffered and it was said obiter that this amounted to a breach of natural justice.

Recognition would be Contrary to Public Policy

This defence is rarely pleaded successfully.[78] In *Israel Discount Bank of New* **11.44** *York v Hadjipateras*,[79] the defendant alleged that a New York judgment for the plaintiff was obtained because his father had exercised undue influence over him to make him enter into a contract of guarantee. The public policy defence to enforcement was rejected by the Court of Appeal, on the grounds that the defendant failed to raise the issue overseas. It is doubtful if this is a fair view, however, given that the defence is that *English* public policy, not that of the state of origin, has been infringed.

In *Soleimany v Soleimany*,[80] the Court of Appeal suggested obiter that it **11.45** would be contrary to public policy to recognize a foreign judgment which upheld a contract, even though the foreign court had found that the common intention of the parties was to perpetrate an act which was illegal in what an English court would regard as a friendly foreign state.[81]

The Judgment was in Breach of a Choice of Court or Arbitration Agreement

If the judgment was in breach of a valid[82] exclusive jurisdiction clause, **11.46** s 32(1) of the Civil Jurisdiction and Judgments Act 1982 states that the judgment shall not be enforced.[83] The only exception is where the defendant submitted to the court delivering judgment or counterclaimed therein.

---

[77] ibid, at 564.   [78] But see *Re Macartney* [1921] 1 Ch 522.
[79] [1983] 3 All ER 129.   [80] [1999] QB 785.
[81] See also the discussion of public policy in relation to Art 16 of the Rome Convention, below, paras 13.282–294.
[82] That is to say it is not illegal, void, unenforceable or incapable of performance: s 32(2) of the Civil Jurisdiction and Judgments Act 1982.
[83] It should be noted that an English court is not bound by the foreign court's finding that the jurisdiction clause was invalid or did not apply to the facts and may decide this issue itself: ibid, s 32(3).

The Judgment is Inconsistent with Another Judgment

11.47 It is a valid defence to the recognition of a foreign judgment that there is an irreconcilable[84] English judgment.[85] Where there are two irreconcilable foreign judgments, the Privy Council has held that the first judgment to be delivered will prevail.[86]

V. THE STATUTORY SCHEMES

11.48 Judgments of some states falling outside the Brussels regime are enforced under one of two statutory schemes of registration, rather than by an action on the judgment at common law. The criteria for recognition and enforcement and the available defences are similar to those of the common law.

1. THE ADMINISTRATION OF JUSTICE ACT 1920

11.49 The Administration of Justice Act 1920 allows for the reciprocal enforcement of money judgments between the United Kingdom and certain Commonwealth and colonial countries.[87] Its provisions are not mandatory and the claimant may choose instead to rely on the common law rules.[88] The Act applies to judgments of superior courts,[89] which may be registered if 'just and convenient'[90] within 12 months. The court of origin must have been jurisdictionally competent in the eyes of English law. In this regard, the rules are similar to the common law, save that an individual defendant must have resided or carried on business in the state of origin (or submitted to the jurisdiction of the courts of that state).[91] The available defences are much the same:[92] fraud, lack of due service, affront to public policy, or that an appeal is pending in the court of origin.[93]

11.50 Registration is made without notice and notice of the registration is then served on the defendant. No permission is required to do so, even if he is

---

[84] On the question of whether the English judgment must have been delivered prior to the foreign judgment, see Cheshire and North, 454.

[85] *Vervaeke v Smith* [1983] 1 AC 145. [86] *Showlag v Mansour* [1995] 1 AC 431.

[87] The list is lengthy, but includes the Bahamas, Belize, Bermuda, Botswana, British Virgin Islands, Cayman Islands, Cyprus, Falkland Islands, Fiji, Ghana, Gibraltar, Jamaica, Kenya, Malaysia, Malta, Mauritius, New Zealand, Nigeria, Papua New Guinea, Singapore, Solomon Islands, Sri Lanka, Uganda, Zambia and Zimbabwe. For a full list, see Briggs and Rees, 498, n 469.

[88] Although he will generally not recover costs if he chooses not to use the Act's provisions.

[89] s 9(1). [90] ibid.

[91] s 9(2). [92] ibid.

[93] Although not expressly so stated, s 32 of the Civil Jurisdiction and Judgments Act 1982 will also apply to preclude recognition of a judgment in breach of a jurisdiction clause.

outside the jurisdiction.[94] The defendant may apply to have service set aside if he shows due cause.[95]

2. The Foreign Judgments (Reciprocal Enforcement) Act 1933

The Foreign Judgments (Reciprocal Enforcement) Act 1933 applies to **11.51** enforcement and recognition of money judgments of superior courts in countries to which an Order in Council has been made extending its provisions. Like the Administration of Justice Act 1920, the enforcement regime is reciprocal between the two countries. It applies to judgments from a broad range of countries.[96] Unlike the Administration of Justice Act 1920, registration is mandatory by the court where the requisite provisions are satisfied. Nor can the claimant choose to rely on the common law rules in lieu.[97]

The circumstances in which a foreign court is considered to have juris- **11.52** dictional competence in the eyes of English law are much the same as at common law,[98] except that presence of the defendant will not suffice; rather, an individual must be resident, or a company have its principal place of business,[99] in the state of origin. The judgment must be final, conclusive and for a fixed sum.[100]

The substantive defences are: fraud, failure to receive notice of pro- **11.53** ceedings in time to defend oneself and affront to public policy.[101] The court may set aside or stay registration pending an appeal in the state of origin.[102] Registration may also be set aside if the foreign judgment was given after a judgment of another jurisdictionally competent[103] foreign court.[104]

Registration should be sought without notice within six years of judg- **11.54** ment or any appeals against the judgment.[105] A notice of registration

---

[94] s 9(4).   [95] ibid.

[96] The list includes Austria, Australia, Belgium, Canadian provinces (excluding Quebec), France, some Indian provinces, the Isle of Man, Israel, Italy, Jersey, Netherlands and Norway. However, in the case of states which are now within the Brussels I Regulation, Brussels Convention or Lugano Convention schemes, it is those rules, not the 1933 Act, which will govern recognition and enforcement. For a full list of the states to which the 1933 applies, see Briggs and Rees, 500, nn 494–496.

[97] s 6.   [98] s 4(2).

[99] It will also suffice if the company had an office in the state, through whose transactions the claim arose.

[100] s 1(2).

[101] s 4(1)(a). Presumably, breach of a jurisdiction clause would also be a defence pursuant to s 32 of the Civil Jurisdiction and Judgments Act 1982.

[102] s 5. It is not obliged to do so.

[103] ie jurisdictionally competent in the eyes of English law.   [104] s 4(1)(b).

[105] s 2(1).

should be served on the defendant,[106] who may apply to have the registration set aside.

VI. INTRA-UNITED KINGDOM JUDGMENTS

11.55   The Civil Jurisdiction and Judgments Act 1982 provides for the automatic recognition and enforcement of a judgment of the courts of one part of the United Kingdom in any other part.[107] Enforcement may only be achieved by registration.[108] There are no requirements of jurisdictional competence. The provisions are not limited to monetary awards; hence, an order for specific performance, or injunctive relief, will fall within these provisions.

11.56   The 'standard' common law defences do not apply; nor, it seems, does s 32 of the Civil Jurisdiction and Judgments Act 1982 dealing with judgments in breach of a jurisdiction clause. Hence, a jurisdictional objection must be made in the court of origin and not at the enforcement stage. However, enforcement may be refused where the judgment conflicts with one previously given by another court of competent jurisdiction.[109]

VII. JUDGMENTS *IN REM*

11.57   A judgment *in rem* is one which determines the status of a person or thing that is conclusive in respect of all persons, regardless of whether they were parties to the litigation. It must be distinguished from an *in personam* judgment which determines the particular interest of a party to the litigation.[110] 'The former looks beyond the individual rights of the parties, the latter is directed solely to those rights.'[111] In the present context, it may be that a foreign judgment *in rem* will determine title to goods.

11.58   Where a judgment orders the sale of a chattel, it will be treated as an *in rem* judgment if the object of the sale is to appropriate the chattel in order to satisfy the claimant's action. However, if the order is made solely so as to satisfy a claim against the general estate of the defendant, the action will be in personam.[112] An *in rem* judgment ordering the sale of chattels will be entitled to recognition and enforcement[113] in England if the

---

[106] s 2(2).   [107] ss 18 and 19; Schs 6 and 7.   [108] s 18(8).

[109] Sch 6, para 10(b); Sch 7, para 9(b).

[110] See *Lazarus-Brown v Regent Estates Co Ltd* [1949] 2 KB 465, 475. See also Cheshire and North, 423–426; Dicey and Morris, 508–512.

[111] Cheshire and North, 424. See *Dolfus Mieg et Compagnie SA v Bank of England* [1949] Ch 369.

[112] *Castrique v Imrie* (1860) 8 CBNS 405; rev'd, 405; reversal aff'd (1869-70) LR 4 HL 414.

[113] On the enforcement of judgments in rem, see Cheshire and North, 426; *The City of Mecca* (1879) 5 PD 28; *The Despina GK* [1983] 1 QB 214.

property was located in the state of origin at the time of the action.[114] If a foreign court orders the sale of chattels in the course of administering an estate in bankruptcy or upon death, the sale will be treated as conferring a valid title upon the purchaser in England.

VIII. THE EFFECT OF FOREIGN JUDGMENTS UPON LITIGATION IN ENGLAND

It is not only the overseas claimant that might seek to obtain recognition **11.59** of a foreign judgment in England. The overseas defendant might seek recognition of that foreign judgment in order to prevent the same matter being considered afresh in an English court. He might claim that the overseas claimant is estopped from raising the matter in England.

1. CAUSE OF ACTION ESTOPPEL

A successful claimant overseas may none the less feel that he could have **11.60** obtained higher damages in England. Rather than seeking recognition of the foreign judgment, he might attempt to sue afresh in the courts of England. He will be estopped from doing so by s 34 of the Civil Jurisdiction and Judgments Act 1982, which provides that:

no proceedings may be brought by a person in England and Wales or Northern Ireland on a cause of action in respect of which a judgment has been given in his favour in proceedings between the same parties, or their privies, in a court in another part of the United Kingdom or in a court in an overseas country, unless that judgment is not enforceable or entitled to recognition in England and Wales or, as the case may be, Northern Ireland.

The phrase 'cause of action' is broadly construed. In *The Indian Grace*,[115] a cargo of munitions was damaged in transit. A small amount of the cargo was discharged in France. The remainder was found to be useless when it was unloaded in India. The consignees sued the shipowner in the Indian courts in respect of the short delivery of the cargo discharged in France. They then brought an action in rem in England in respect of the remainder of the cargo. The Indian court ruled in the plaintiff's favour. The House of Lords held that s 34 provided the defendant with a defence to the English

---

[114] Dicey and Morris, 508, Rule 40(1). This accords with the provision in s 4(2)(b) of the Foreign Judgments (Reciprocal Enforcement) Act 1933. See also *Minna Craig Steamship Co v Chartered Bank of India* [1897] 1 QB 55; aff'd, 460; *Air Foyle Ltd v Centre Capital Ltd* [2002] EWHC 2535; [2003] 2 Lloyd's Rep 753, considered further below, para 18.62.

[115] *India v India Steamship Co Ltd* [1993] AC 410, HL.

action. Their Lordships held that the causes of action were the same. True, one claim was in respect of defective delivery in India and the other in England in respect of damage to the cargo. However, they were both brought in relation to a breach of contract arising from the alleged inadequate carriage of the goods.[116] Upon a further petition to the House of Lords, their Lordships ruled that s 34 applied even though the foreign action was brought in personam and the English action *in rem*.[117]

11.61   In determining whether the causes of action are the same, it may be relevant to have regard to the cases concerning Article 27 of the Brussels I Regulation.[118] This requires that:

> where proceedings involving the same cause of action and between the same parties are brought in the courts of different Member States, any court other than the court first seised shall of its own motion stay its proceedings until such time as the jurisdiction of the court first seised is established.[119]

An obvious example of the application of this Article would be if a buyer brought proceedings in a Member State for damages for breach of contract and the seller subsequently sought to bring proceedings in another Member State for a declaration that he was not liable to the buyer.[120] Another example arose in *Gubisch Maschinefabrik KG v Palumbo*.[121] A German seller sued the buyer in Germany for the unpaid purchase price of a woodworking machine. Subsequently the Italian buyer sought rescission of the contract in Italy. The European Court of Justice ruled that Article 27 prevented the purchaser from so doing. Although the claims were not identical, the risk of irreconcilable judgments was clear. In each case, the key question arising was whether the contract was binding upon the parties. This demonstrates that it is the substance of the claim which is crucial, not the form in which the cause of action is brought.[122]

---

[116] Contrast *Kloeckner & Co AG v Gatoil Overseas Inc* [1990] 1 Lloyd's Rep 177. In that case, a basic agreement provided the framework for a large number of oil sale contracts, purchase contracts and book-out contracts. Hirst J ruled that each separate contract gave rise to a its own cause of action.

[117] *India v India Steamship Co Ltd (The Indian Grace) (No 2)* [1998] AC 878, HL. Briggs and Rees, 492 note that: 'The striking result was that a judgment in the Indian courts for a measly £9,000 precluded an action in the English courts in respect of a multi-million pound claim'.

[118] See Chapter 3 on jurisdiction under the Brussels I Regulation, above, paras 3.313–329.

[119] See Case C-406/92 *The Tatry* [1994] ECR I-5439. The ECJ ruled that in order for the cause of actions to be the same for the purposes of what was Art 21 of the Brussels Convention (what is now Art 27 of the Brussels I Regulation), they must be based upon the same rule of law and facts and they must have the same end in view.

[120] ibid; and see the decision of the Munich Court of Appeal in *Re a Clothing Sale Contract* [1995] IL Pr 172.

[121] Case 144/86 [1987] ECR 4861. See also the German Federal Supreme Court decision in *Re a Sale of Shares* [1996] IL Pr 292.

[122] See also *SpA Silpol Pears Plastics Belgium NV*, judgment of 26 September 1978, Foro pad

If the claimant was unsuccessful overseas, the defendant may argue that **11.62** the matter is now *res judicata*, if the same cause of action between the same parties[123] is in issue. Furthermore, if the dispute in question in England is not identical, but could have been raised in the foreign court, estoppel will not operate, but it may be deemed an abuse of process to allow the claimant now to litigate in England.[124]

2. Issue Estoppel

It may be that, whilst overseas litigation does not prevent a related action **11.63** from being brought in England, an issue decided by the foreign court in the process of reaching its judgment will bind an English court in resolving its dispute. This may effectively make litigation in England futile.

It is clearly desirable that an issue effectively determined between two **11.64** parties in a jurisdictionally competent foreign court should not generally be considered anew in England. However, English courts have urged caution in the application of the issue estoppel doctrine,[125] stressing that it may be very hard to determine whether a foreign court has decided a particular issue in reaching its judgment. A court must satisfy itself that the issue in question in the foreign and English courts is identical, that the parties are identical and that the foreign ruling was final and conclusive.[126] This last requirement can be especially difficult to demonstrate when the court expresses a view on a matter which is none the less not a critical part of its reasoning process.

3. Issue Estoppel and the International Sale of Goods

In *Air Foyle Ltd v Center Capital Ltd*[127] the first claimant claimed ownership **11.65** of an aircraft purchased at an auction in the Netherlands in December 2000, pursuant to an order of the Dutch court directing the holding of the

---

1978, I, 394, D Series I-21-B4. In Case C-11/01 *Gantner Electronic GmbH v Basch Exploitatie Maatschappij BV*, [2003] IL Pr 37, the ECJ ruled that in applying the *lis alibi pendens* provisions of the Brussels Convention, account should be taken only of the claims of the applicants and not of any defences raised by the defendant.

[123] See *Wiltshire v Powell* [2004] EWCA Civ 534.
[124] *Henderson v Henderson* (1843) 3 Hare 100.
[125] *Carl Zeiss Stiftung v Rayner & Keeler* [1967] 1 AC 753, HL.
[126] Logic would suggest that estoppel should only operate once a foreign court has been shown to be jurisdictionally competent in the eyes of English law. But see *Desert Sun Loan Corp v Hill* [1996] 2 All ER 487, CA.
[127] [2002] EWHC 2535, [2003] 2 Lloyd's Rep 753.

auction. The defendants asserted ownership of the same aircraft pursuant to a purchase in Russia in October 2000 and relied upon a Russian judgment to this effect.[128] They went on to claim that the Russian judgment was entitled to recognition in England and so estopped the claimant from relying upon the Dutch judgment to assert ownership. Gross J ruled that neither cause of action estoppel nor issue estoppel operated on the facts. The Russian court had refused to recognize the effect of the Dutch order. However, Gross J found that the Russian court had not addressed the issue of the ownership allegedly acquired by the claimant in the Netherlands. The claimant's Dutch title prevailed over the defendant's Russian title.[129]

11.66 There are, however, a number of examples of where issue estoppel might operate with respect to the international sale of goods. Suppose, for example, that a foreign court gave a judgment as to the passing of title to goods and ruled that title to the goods remained presently with the seller. If the buyer were to sue the seller for damages for breach of contract in England, on the basis that the seller did not transfer a good title to the buyer, then he should not be required to prove afresh that title remained with the seller. Provided that the foreign judgment is entitled to recognition in England, the matter is *res judicata*. It should be likewise if the buyer seeks specific performance of the obligation to pass title. But if the foreign court had ruled that the seller did transfer a good title to the buyer at the designated time, then the action in England must fail.

11.67 Again, suppose that a foreign court, in litigation between a buyer and a seller, rules that the buyer does not have possession of goods, or the right to possession of goods. The buyer then brings an action in an English court against the seller for the tort of conversion. If the foreign judgment is entitled to recognition in England, then the question of possession of the goods is *res judicata*. Since the claim must demonstrate the existence of such a right in order to sue in conversion, it follows that the buyer's action in conversion will fail.[130]

11.68 It must be stressed that a foreign judgment in personam can only create an estoppel if both the issue and the parties to subsequent litigation in England are the same. For example, suppose that the claimant buyer brings a successful action in conversion overseas on the basis that his right to possession has been infringed by the defendant seller. If a third

---

[128] As a matter of Russian law, the aircraft was deemed to be located in Russia, where it was registered, even though the aircraft itself was not physically in Russia at the time.

[129] One reason for this was that Gross J refused to accept that Russia was ever the *situs* of the aircraft: see further below, paras 18.62 and 18.67.

[130] Assuming that the tort claim is allegedly governed by English law.

party asserts the right to possession of the goods in litigation against the buyer in England, then the foreign judgment will not render the question of possession *res judicata*, since it did not involve the same parties.[131] Conversely, suppose that a third party successfully obtained an overseas order in personam to recover his goods from the buyer. If the buyer sues the seller in England for failure to pass good title to him, the foreign judgment will not make the matter res judicata. Rather, the buyer will have to establish afresh that the seller did not pass a good title to him.

However, if the foreign judgment is delivered *in rem*, then it conclusively **11.69** determines the status of the goods themselves and the property rights of the parties in those goods. Such a judgment is capable of binding third parties to the litigation, so that the status of the goods will be *res judicata*.

IX. THE SALE OF GOODS AND FOREIGN JUDGMENTS CONFERRING NON-MONETARY REMEDIES: SPECIFIC PERFORMANCE, ORDERS FOR THE DELIVERY OF GOODS, ETC

1. Enforcement at Common Law and Under the Administration of Justice Act 1920 and the Foreign Judgments (Reciprocal Enforcement) Act 1933 Prohibited

An action to enforce a foreign judgment is essentially an action in debt. **11.70** Briggs and Rees state that:

As the common law generally awarded monetary remedies and as the action for enforcement is an action in debt, only judgments for sums of money can be enforced by the judgment creditor. As the effect of a judgment entitled to recognition is to oblige the defendant to pay the debt adjudicated, and as an action for debt could not be brought in respect of an unliquidated sum, a judgment can only be enforced if it has been finally quantified.[132]

We have seen above that a foreign judgment which does not order the payment of a fixed sum is entitled to recognition, but not enforcement, at common law.[133] Such a judgment is also not entitled to enforcement under either the 1920[134] or the 1933[135] scheme. 'It follows that there can be no

---

[131] And it was not a judgment *in rem* as to the status of the goods.
[132] Briggs and Rees, 488.
[133] It may be recognized and enforced under the Brussels I Regulation, Brussels Convention or Lugano Convention.
[134] s 12(1) of the 1920 Act defines a 'judgment' as one where 'any sum of money is made payable'.
[135] s 1(2)(b) of the UK 1933 Act states that a judgment must order the payment of a sum of money, not being a sum payable in respect of taxes or other charges of a like nature or in respect of a fine or other penalty.

question of enforcing a foreign decree for specific performance or for the specific delivery or restitution of chattels.'[136] The close interface between contract and property in the contract of sale means that such remedies might frequently be conferred by foreign courts. This raises a very important, yet little considered, question as to what effect foreign orders conferring non-monetary remedies have in English courts.

2. Cause of Action Estoppel and Non-Monetary Foreign Judgments: the Common Law and the Administration of Justice Act 1920

11.71 Suppose that a foreign court has ordered specific performance of a contract or required the seller to deliver goods to the buyer. Although an English court would not *enforce* a judgment which does not order the payment of a fixed sum either under the 1920 or 1933 statutes or at common law, it is much less certain whether it would *recognize* the foreign judgment as conclusive of liability as between claimant and defendant. If it did, the effect of this would arguably be to make the matter *res judicata* as to liability between the parties to the litigation.

11.72 It is unclear whether s 34 of the Civil Jurisdiction and Judgments Act 1982 applies to a judgment which is not for a fixed sum. It will be recalled that this section prevents a party who has obtained a judgment in his favour overseas from litigating the same matter against the same party in England, 'unless that judgment is not enforceable or entitled to recognition in England . . .'. The trouble is that if a judgment which orders the seller to deliver to the buyer *is* entitled to recognition in England, this may prevent the claimant from suing afresh in England. Could it be said as a result of this statutory provision that a successful claimant overseas who finds his judgment to be unenforceable in England (because it is not for a fixed sum) cannot sue afresh in England, on the basis that there is no reason why the judgment cannot be *recognized* in so far as it imposes a *liability* on the defendant? If so, it would follow that the parties would be estopped from litigating the issue of the liability of the defendant in an English court. In other words, the right of the claimant, but not his remedy, would be given legal effect in England. But that could be a catastrophic result for the claimant, since it might mean that a judgment which could not be enforced in England would nevertheless prevent the claimant from suing afresh in England to establish liability *and obtain a suitable remedy.*

---

[136] Cheshire and North, 429.

Briggs and Rees[137] state that: 'An argument that [the judgment] is entitled **11.73** to recognition (so that s.34 bars an action to establish liability), but cannot be enforced (so the claimant can do neither one thing nor the other) cannot be correct'. Hence they convincingly argue that no estoppel should operate *at all*, so that the claimant who finds his foreign judgment unenforceable in England, because not for a fixed sum, should be entitled to relitigate the entire matter in England. They go on to contend that:

a judgment to the effect that there is liability, but of a size, or for a remedy, that English law cannot give effect to is a very strange thing; as the remedy is so closely part of the right, it is thought that if the judgment cannot be enforced as to its remedy, it cannot be enforced at all.[138]

Accordingly, it is suggested that where a foreign judgment falls within **11.74** the scheme of the common law or 1920 Act and is not for a fixed sum, the claimant should not be estopped from relitigating the matter in England by s 34 of the Civil Jurisdiction and Judgments Act 1982. Instead, he may treat the foreign judgment as having no legal effect in England.

3. Cause of Action Estoppel and Non-Monetary Foreign Judgments: the Problems Created by the Foreign Judgments (Reciprocal Enforcement) Act 1933

However, it is suggested that this common sense approach is not avail- **11.75** able where the foreign judgment falls under the scheme of the Foreign Judgments (Reciprocal Enforcement) Act 1933. Section 8(1) of the 1933 Act contains a provision, described by Dicey and Morris as 'obscure',[139] which effectively provides that where a judgment falls within Part I of the Act, and *would have been enforceable under the Act had a sum of money been payable*, then that foreign judgment '*shall be recognized in any court in the United Kingdom as conclusive between the parties thereto in all proceedings founded on the same cause of action* and may be relied on by way of defence or counter-claim in any such proceedings'.[140] This suggests that a judgment other than for a fixed sum would be entitled to recognition in England; and, if so, it would appear that s 34 of the 1982 Act would estop the claimant from litigating afresh on the same cause of action in England. But what then is the claimant to do if he cannot enforce the judgment in England? On one view, he would be *unable* to obtain a remedy in the English courts.

---

[137] A Briggs and P Rees, (2nd edn, London: LLP, 1997) 355, n 315. The matter is not discussed in the third edition.
[138] ibid, 355.MMM   [139] Dicey and Morris, 541.   [140] Emphasis added.

11.76   In order to prevent this catastrophic consequence, it is to be hoped that an English court would interpret s 8(1) of the 1933 Act as meaning that although the *liability* of the defendant in English proceedings following a foreign order cannot be denied, the claimant is at liberty to seek a new *remedy* on that cause of action in England. Otherwise, the claimant would be a victim of his own success in a foreign court.

11.77   It is suggested that an English court should grant *its own remedy* in support of the liability created by the foreign order. This could, of course, mean that the English court might grant an order differing from that granted in the foreign court. It might, for example, be unwilling to allow specific performance of the contract, but be prepared to award damages to the claimant instead. However, in order to reduce the artificiality of splitting the right and the remedy, the case for the English court granting a remedy which is *identical* to the (unenforceable) remedy awarded overseas in support of a right created overseas (and recognized in England) would be strong, at least where there is no public policy objection to the foreign remedy.[141] The result would be, in substance, *indirectly* to adopt the same remedy as was awarded in the court of origin in aid of a right generated in that foreign court.

4. Could Foreign Judgments which Award Equitable Remedies, such as Specific Performance, ever be Enforceable in England at Common Law?

11.78   White argues that the orthodox view that a foreign judgment may only be enforced at common law if for a fixed sum of money is historically inaccurate.[142] He notes that, prior to the Judicature Act 1873, foreign judgments were enforced by the Court of Chancery as well as in Superior Courts of Law. The former courts would not insist upon the judgment being for a fixed sum.[143] An example is *Houlditch v Marquis of Donegal.*[144] The Court of Chancery in England granted the plaintiff an order for the appointment of a receiver of the defendant's Irish estate. The plaintiff sought enforcement of that order in Ireland and injunctive relief to prevent the defendant from interfering with the receiver's receipt of income from the estate. The House of Lords, on appeal from the Irish Chancery

---

[141]   Such as, in the case of an order for specific performance, if this would impose excessive burdens on the defendant or the court.

[142]   R White, 'Enforcement of Foreign Judgments in Equity' (1982) 11 Sydney L Rev 631.

[143]   *Morgan's Case* (1737) 1 Atk 408; *Houlditch v Marquis of Donegal* (1834) 8 Bligh NS 301.

[144]   ibid.

Court, held that the order could be enforced in an Irish court.[145] The case was cited with approval in *Henderson v Henderson*. Lord Denman CJ noted that some foreign judgments might be enforceable *only* in equity 'because they may invoke collateral and provisional matters to which a Court of Law can give no effect'.[146]

White argues that with the emergence of the obligation theory[147] of foreign **11.79** judgments 'there is no suggestion during this period that equity would not follow the law in the principles upon which foreign judgments should be enforced'.[148] He contends that: 'If equitable remedies are available to enforce a foreign judgment on the basis that the defendant has an obligation to obey it, the foreign judgment must be conclusive on the merits. If the defendant's conscience is bound by the judgment, it is irrelevant to consider the original cause of action.'[149]

Moreover, if a judgment other than one which orders payment of a sum of **11.80** money may be sufficient to found recognition and give rise to a cause of action estoppel,[150] it follows that the underlying cause of action is acknowledged in English law. It is not immediately apparent why equitable remedies should not be granted to support that right. 'There is no basis for treating a foreign judgment as less conclusive on a suit by a plaintiff to enforce it than on a defence to the plaintiff's claim'.[151]

It is suggested that White's conclusions should be accepted only in **11.81** part. The need for a foreign judgment to be for a fixed sum is now well established, both at common law and by statute. It was argued above that cause of action estoppel should not operate at common law or under the 1920 Act where the foreign judgment is not for a fixed sum. Accordingly, the claimant should simply be permitted to litigate afresh in England. Where the 1933 Act applies, however, it is suggested that cause of action estoppel does operate in relation to the liability of the parties. Accordingly, whilst the English court should not directly enforce a foreign equitable remedy, such as a decree of specific performance, it may do so indirectly by awarding a suitable *English* remedy, which may very well coincide with that awarded by the foreign court of origin. However,

---

[145] See also *Paul v Roy* (1832) 15 Beav 433; *Reimers v Druce* (1857) 26 LJ Ch 196; both discussed by White, n 142 above, at 633.

[146] (1844) 6 QB 288, 297. But cf *Bonn v National Trust Co Ltd* [1930] DLR 820; discussed by White, n 142 above, at 636.

[147] This doctrine states that the judgment itself imposes an obligation upon the defendant to comply with it, which obligation can be enforced in a court of enforcement. See further *Godard v Gray* (1870) LR 6 QB 139.

[148] White, n 142 above, at 637.   [149] ibid, at 638.

[150] A matter of some dispute; see the discussion in the previous section.

[151] White, n 142 above, at 638.

since equitable relief is in its nature discretionary, an English court might refuse to grant specific performance in circumstances where it would be available in the courts of origin. White suggests that the relief might be refused if 'the plaintiff is guilty of laches and presumably such defences as hardship, or the necessity for the continual supervision by the court of its order, will be available'.[152]

X. CONCLUSION

11.82 The interaction between contract and property law in the sale of goods contract means that it is by no means inevitable that a foreign judgment will order the payment of a fixed sum of money. This can create real difficulties as to the effect of such orders in England. A claimant who will need to enforce such an order in England should think long and hard as to the consequences of litigating overseas. If, for example, the claimant seeks the delivery of goods to him in England, it is likely to be much more straightforward for him to litigate the claim in England, where possible, rather than suing overseas[153] and then seeking to enforce the foreign judgment in England.

---

[152] ibid, at 647.
[153] At least where the foreign judgment would not be subject to the Brussels I Regulation, Brussels Convention or Lugano Convention schemes.

PART III
CHOICE OF LAW

12

Introduction to Choice of Law: Nature of Problems

I. THE NATURE OF SALE OF GOODS CONTRACTS: A HYBRID OF CONTRACT AND PROPERTY

The sale of goods contract is characterized by the interaction of contract **12.01** and property law. It has been remarked that: 'The sale of goods is a hybrid of contract and conveyance in which the contractual and proprietary aspects are virtually inseparable . . .'.[1] This may appear to be the case where, for example, the contract contains a retention of title clause, or the buyer seeks specific performance of the contract. Of course, the difficulty confronting the choice of law process is that it is necessary to determine which matters ought properly to be characterized as contractual, and

---

[1] Bridge, *The Sale of Goods*, 35.

subject to the applicable law of the sales contract, and which should be characterized as proprietary, and subject to the law of the *situs* of the goods at the time of a purported transfer of them. One must distinguish between those rules which relate to the agreement to transfer goods and those which relate to the transfer itself. As Dicey and Morris note:

> The fact that the English Sale of Goods Act deals with both [contractual and proprietary] problems should not be allowed to obscure this basic difference. The principle of English domestic law that, within certain limits, the time and mode of the transfer of property in movables are determined by the intention of the parties is a rule which belongs to the law of property, not to the law of contract, and applies only to goods situate in England, irrespective of the governing law.[2]

12.02 To a large extent, the law which regulates contractual obligations is contained in the Rome Convention on the Law Applicable to Contractual Obligations.[3] This is an EC Convention which harmonizes choice of law in contract in Contracting States for matters within its scope. The Convention is given the force of law in the United Kingdom by the Contracts (Applicable Law) Act 1990.[4] However, it is clear that the Convention does not apply to property rights.[5] In contrast, the law which regulates proprietary matters is still essentially determined by common law choice of law rules.

II. SALES SPECIFIC CHOICE OF LAW QUESTIONS

1. CONTRACT[6]

12.03 There are many sales specific issues which may arise in applying the choice of law rules in contract. For example, there are questions as to the relationship of the Rome Convention with the Vienna Convention, and with the Hague Conventions on choice of law in sales contracts of 1955 and 1986. There are questions about whether the parties chose a law to govern the contract and the relevance of trade practice in relation to the sale of particular types of goods. There are questions about the applicable law in the absence of choice and the relevance of various factors in typical sales contracts, such as the FOB and CIF contracts. There are questions as to the relevance of the law of the place of performance. There are questions about allocation of risk, for example, if the goods cannot be

---

[2] Dicey and Morris, 1334.

[3] [1980] OJ L 266/1. The Convention was concluded on 19 June 1980.

[4] Which entered into force on 1 April 1991. See generally Ch 13 on choice of law in contract and the international sale of goods, esp paras 13.02–10.

[5] See the Guiliano and Lagarde Report [1980] OJ C282/1, 10.   [6] See Ch 13.

delivered owing to a failure to obtain an export or import licence. There are questions about the role and overriding effect of legislation, such as the Unfair Contract Terms Act 1977, and as to the extent to which the implied obligations contained in the Sale of Goods Act 1979 may be excluded or limited. There are also questions about the limits of the applicable law of the contract, for example, where it contains rules on the passing of property between the parties, or where the buyer seeks the remedy of specific performance of the contract.

However, cases on the application of the Rome Convention to sales con- **12.04** tracts are relatively rare. This may be explained, in part, by the high degree of harmonization of substantive law achieved in the field. More-over, as Benjamin notes, the relatively modest number of cases may be partially explained by the need for a party relying on foreign law to plead its contents[7] and the fact that in many cases where conflicts points might have been made, neither party attempted to plead them.[8]

2. Transfer of Contractual Rights and Obligations

Of course, international sale of goods contracts do not exist in a vacuum. **12.05** The CIF seller will be contractually required to transfer the bill of lading and the benefit of the insurance contract to the buyer.[9] This gives rise to difficulties as to the nature of the relationship between the buyer and the carrier or insurer, upon which authority is sparse. In particular, the question arises as to whether the buyer, as transferee of a bill of lading, is bound by a choice of law clause contained in the bill.

3. Property[10]

The application of property choice of law rules also poses a number of **12.06** specific challenges in the sales context. The proper limits of the law of the situs must be ascertained. Should it, for example, apply to determine the passing of property where goods are in transit? What is its role in relation to documentary transfers, the right to retain documents and the effect of a document such as a bill of lading on the relationship between the

---

[7] See generally R Fentiman, *Foreign Law in English Courts* (Oxford: OUP, 1998)

[8] C Morse, 'Conflict of Laws' in Benjamin, 25–003. A prime example, which Benjamin gives, is *Aluminium Industrie Vaassen BV v Romalpa Aluminium Ltd* [1976] 1 WLR 676.

[9] See Ch 5, above, on jurisdiction and the transfer of contractual rights and obligations and Ch 14, below, on choice of law and the transfer of contractual rights and obligations, below. Under English law, the transfer of rights and obligations is by virtue of the Carriage of Goods by Sea Act 1992. See also Ch 9, above, on jurisdiction disputes involving multiple parties.

[10] See Ch 18, below.

contracting parties to the sales contract and the carrier? To what extent should the law of the *situs* be applied to determine the effects of a retention of title clause? How does it apply to other claims over property, such as liens, charges, pledges and chattel mortgages? The question also arises as to whether a different choice of law rule might apply to proprietary disputes that involve only the contracting parties to that which applies where third parties to the contract are affected.

4. Other Claims: Tort[11] and Restitution[12]

12.07 Although the great majority of claims arising from a sale of goods contract will be contractual or proprietary, other types of claim are also of considerable importance. A seller may owe the buyer obligations in the law of tort, if, for example, he is alleged to have induced the buyer to contract by a misrepresentation, or to have committed the tort of conversion, or to have wrongfully refused to sell the goods to the buyer. There might also be claims which involve third parties. These might include an action against a carrier for negligence,[13] or a claim in respect of an alleged inducement to a party to the sales agreement to breach the contract.

12.08 Where the contract is void or rescinded, it is possible that one of the parties will seek the return of money or benefits already rendered. There may also be questions which arise in the aftermath of frustration. These raise questions relating to the law of restitution. This is a subject on which authority is sparse and where it is uncertain to what extent the law applicable to the 'contract' may be applied to its restitutionary aftermath.

5. Concurrent Claims[14]

12.09 There may be situations in the sale of goods context where there is a possibility of concurrent actions. These might be, for example, in contract and in tort. This might arise if, for example, an action for breach of contract is combined with an action against the seller for negligent performance of a collateral obligation to install or assemble the goods. Again, there may be concurrent claims in contract and restitution, as where a party sues for damages for breach of contract, or in the alternative for restitutionary damages upon the rescission of a contract. These claims raise issues as to whether the claimant is entitled to choose how to frame his cause of action or whether he may sue in the alternative. The concurrent claims might involve the same alleged breach arising from

---

[11] See Ch 17, below.   [12] See Ch 19, below.
[13] Where this falls to be classified as tortious.   [14] See Ch 20, below.

the same facts, as where a claimant sues for damages for the misrepresentation which induced him to contract, and in the alternative for damages for breach of contract, on the basis that the misrepresentation was incorporated as a term of the contract. In such a case, the question arises whether he is forced to bring his action in contract where such a claim is available to him on the facts.

Sometimes, a buyer or seller might bring proceedings against the other **12.10** contracting party, but also against one or more third parties.[15] This might arise if, for example, a party allegedly induced the buyer or seller to breach the sales contract. The claimant might sue the third party in tort, and bring proceedings against the other contracting party for breach of contract.

6. THE IMPACT OF ELECTRONIC COMMERCE[16]

The ever increasing number of sales transactions which are concluded **12.11** by email or via a website has posed a formidable number of challenges for legislators. There are difficulties in devising suitable substantive law rules which respond to the global nature of the e-commerce market and its tendency to delocalize transactions. In private international law, this poses questions at the choice of law level. It is not immediately clear to what extent personal connecting factors upon which the choice of law process has hitherto placed reliance, such as the domicile, habitual residence or place of business of the parties, are of relevance in such transactions. The place of conclusion of a contract can be arbitrary, as can the place where a buyer or seller places an order or receives acceptance of an offer sent by email. A website used by a seller may have its server located in a state which is otherwise wholly unconnected with a contract. It may also be difficult to determine whether the parties have genuinely consented to a choice of a particular law which appears as a standard term on the seller's website and which might not be immediately visible to the buyer. Where claims in tort arise, the place of the tort in question may be very difficult to determine and may not necessarily have a close connection with the cause of action. It is not immediately clear whether existing choice of law rules can adequately deal with the demands of e-commerce, or whether specific choice of law rules are needed in this area.

---

[15] See Ch 9 on jurisdiction in multi-party litigation.
[16] See Ch 21, below; and see Ch 10 on jurisdiction and e-commerce.

III. SALES SPECIFIC CONVENTIONS

1. THE HAGUE SALES CONVENTIONS OF 1955 AND 1986[17]

12.12 Important sales specific initiatives have been effected on the global stage. However, these have not been adopted in England. Nonetheless, they are still of interest to the English lawyer. They raise the question of whether English law would benefit from more sale of goods specific choice of law rules and whether either of these Conventions should be ratified in England.

12.13 The Hague Convention of 1955[18] deals with choice of law in contract and is in force in a number of states. There is also a more detailed Hague Convention of 1986,[19] although this has failed to find favour and is not presently in force. These Conventions raise the question of how far party autonomy can be pushed, and in particular whether it may extend to certain matters which would ordinarily be regarded as proprietary.

2. THE VIENNA CONVENTION[20]

12.14 The Vienna Convention is, of course, the most important source of harmonized substantive law rules. Although not in force in England, it has had an enormous impact elsewhere across the globe. Closer examination of the Convention reveals that it also contains certain provisions of a private international law nature. The impact of these is not always clear. It is, for example, not immediately clear how the Vienna Convention interacts with the Rome Convention and with the Hague Sales Convention 1955. In the English courts, difficult questions may arise where, for example, the governing law of a contract is that of a state that is Party to the Vienna Convention, or where the parties seek directly to choose the law of the Vienna Convention to govern their contract.

IV. CLASSIFICATION

12.15 Complex questions of characterization may arise in respect of international sales litigation. There are some claims, such as those based upon

---

[17] See Ch 15, below.

[18] The Hague Convention of 15 June 1955 on the Law Applicable to International Sales of Goods.

[19] The Hague Convention of 22 December 1986 on the Law Applicable to Contracts for the International Sale of Goods.

[20] See Ch 16.

misrepresentations alleged to have induced a contract, which might be classified as contract, or tort, or even both. There are cases whose classification is unclear because they partake of elements of different areas of law: for example where a contract is allegedly breached and a party seeks rescission on the basis of the breach. Although the claim is based upon the non-fulfilment of a contractual obligation, the remedy might be seen as either a proprietary or restitutionary one, if the party seeks the vesting or revesting of property in himself. Indeed, the question of remedies may pose a number of difficulties. It will first be necessary to determine whether the remedy is to be treated as procedural (and so subject to the law of the forum) or substantive (and so subject to the law applicable to the cause of action). If the latter, the question arises whether there are any limits upon the forum's willingness to grant a remedy which does not exist in its domestic law, or which would not be granted on the facts. There is a further question whether the fact that the claimant seeks a proprietary, rather than a personal remedy might itself affect the law which is applied to the whole claim.

There are areas where it may be necessary to separate carefully the dif- **12.16** ferent elements of the claim, for example where a seller seeks to recover property from the buyer or a third party on the basis of a retention of title clause in the contract of sale. Again, there are claims in tort which have as a prerequisite that the claimant should have a sufficient proprietary or possessory right, as in the case of the tort of conversion.

V. THE POTENTIAL FOR A CONFLICT OF LAWS IN INTERNATIONAL SALES TRANSACTIONS

In determining the extent to which a conflict of laws[21] might arise in **12.17** international sales law, it is obviously important to assess to what extent the rules of different legal systems might differ. A brief assessment of some of the issues on which conflict might arise is given below.

1. 'Goods' in Private International Law[22]

The definition of goods may vary as between legal systems. In English **12.18** law, the term is defined in s 61 of the Sale of Goods Act 1979 as including 'all personal chattels other than things in action and money', in particular 'emblements, industrial growing crops, and things attached to or forming

---

[21] i.e. a choice of law problem where the laws of various states differ as to substance.
[22] See Ch 1, above, for more detailed discussion of the meaning of 'goods'.

part of the land which are agreed to be severed before sale of under the contract of sale'.[23] The Vienna Convention[24] offers no definition of 'goods'.[25] It does lay down some specific exclusions, such as money, securities and negotiable instruments.[26] These would not be goods in English law either. However, it also excludes the sale of ships and aircraft,[27] which are goods in English law, and the sale of electricity, which is arguably within the meaning of 'goods' in English law.[28] More generally: 'There is much to be said for giving "goods" a broad meaning, so that it embraces all tangible, corporeal things . . .'.[29] This might extend to minerals and crops.[30]

2. Goods and Tangible Movable Property[31]

12.19   It is important to appreciate that the word 'goods' is not a term of art in the conflict of laws. Certainly, the category is very similar to the recognized, and much more important category of 'tangible movable property'.[32] However, Benjamin notes the overlap between this category and 'goods' may not be complete. The authors give the example of crops growing in a field which might be classified as immovables, even though they are regarded as goods in domestic law.[33] Again, gas and electricity may be regarded as intangibles, even though they may also be considered to be goods.[34] The law of the *situs* of the property will determine whether the property is classified for conflicts purposes as tangible movables, intangible movables or immovables.[35]

---

[23] See Bridge, *The Sale of Goods*, Ch 2.
[24] Compare also Art 1 of the Hague Sales Convention 1955 and Arts 2 and 3 of the Hague Sales Convention 1986.
[25] See further Bridge, *The International Sale of Goods*, 45.   [26] Art 2(d).
[27] See also the discussion of the Cape Town Convention on International Interests in Mobile Equipment 2001, below, paras 18.126–131.
[28] *County of Durham Electrical Power Distribution Co v IRC* [1909] 2 KB 604; Bridge, *The International Sale of Goods*, 45.
[29] Bridge, ibid, 47. The statement is made specifically in connection with the meaning of 'goods' under the Vienna Convention. The suggested interpretation is consistent with the wording of the Convention, which contains certain exclusions but not a positive definition of 'goods'.
[30] Since, according to Art 3(1), the Convention applies to goods which are 'produced': Bridge, ibid, 47–48.
[31] See Ch 1, above.
[32] On the choice of law rules applicable to *inter vivos* transfers of tangible movable property, see *Dicey and Morris*, 963–977; *Cheshire and North*, Ch 30.
[33] Benjamin, 25–004. These are goods for the purposes of the Sale of Goods Act 1979, s 61(1).
[34] ibid.
[35] *Freke v Carbery* (1873) LR 16 Eq 461; *Re Hoyles* [1911] 1 Ch 179; *Re Berchtold* [1923] 1 Ch 192.

3. A 'Sale' of Goods[36]

The Sale of Goods Act 1979 defines a contract of sale as comprising 'an **12.20** agreement to sell' and 'a sale'.[37] The sale of goods contract is one where the buyer pays a money consideration called the price. This excludes contracts of exchange of goods or consideration through the provision of services.[38] The Vienna Convention does not define 'sale'. It does not specifically exclude exchange and barter agreements. It has been argued that 'there seems no reason . . . to exclude the CISG if the two supplies of goods can sensibly be rationalized as back-to-back sales with a set-off of the two prices due to each supplier'.[39] The Vienna Convention, though, does specifically exclude certain types of sale,[40] such as judicial sales and sales by auction[41] and goods which are purchased for personal, family or household use.[42] Article 3(2) of the Convention also excludes contracts where the 'preponderant' part of the supplier's obligation is the provision of labour or services.[43] It is unclear how this compares to the distinction in English law between work and materials contracts and sale of goods contracts.[44] That latter distinction is of little importance in English law. However, the distinction drawn in Article 3(2) will be crucial,[45] since contracts which are predominantly concerned with the provision of labour or other services will be excluded from the Convention and not subject to its uniform law.[46]

4. English Sales Law and the Vienna Convention[47]

It is undoubtedly true that the potential for a conflict of laws has been **12.21** much reduced by the advent of the Vienna Convention. However, there are still many areas in which conflict could arise. One obvious point is that not all states are party to the Vienna Convention. Major commercial centres, such as, for example, England and Japan, are not.

English substantive sales law differs in many key respects from the **12.22** Vienna Convention. This is not the place for detailed discussion of those

---

[36] See Ch 1, above.
[37] ss 2(1),(4) and (5). Discussed in Bridge, *The Sale of Goods*, 36–38.
[38] See ibid, 46–49 for a discussion of works and materials contracts.
[39] Bridge, *The International Sale of Goods*, 48.   [40] See below, paras 16.83–88.
[41] Art 2(b) and (c).   [42] Art 2(a).   [43] Art 3(2).
[44] Bridge, *The Sale of Goods*, 46–49.
[45] See also Art 1(3) of the Hague Sales Convention 1955 and Art 4 of the Hague Sales Convention 1986.
[46] Bridge, *The International Sale of Goods*, 46–47.   [47] See Ch 16.

differences.[48] Bridge identifies three categories of differences.[49] First, there are rules in the Vienna Convention which have no counterpart in English law,[50] such as those on the remedy of price reduction,[51] on cure,[52] on giving notice to the seller of the lack of conformity of the goods[53] and on the preservation of rejected goods.[54] Second, there are rules of the Convention which appear at face value to differ from the provisions of English law and which might or might not lead to the same outcome on the facts. Bridge gives the example of Article 79 on exemptions, which 'is structured very differently from its English counterpart dealing with frustration and impossibility of performance'.[55] Third, there are Convention rules which appear at first sight to be similar to those of English law but which in fact differ significantly. An example is the duty to supply goods in conformity with the contractual description under Article 35 of the Convention.[56]

12.23 Even within Contracting States to the Vienna Convention, a conflict of laws may arise. The Vienna Convention does not cover all contractual matters that may arise in an international sales contract. Moreover, the scope of the Convention is not uniform. All states must apply the Convention where the conditions of Article 1(1)(a) are met, that is where the parties have their places of business in different Contracting State. Moreover, Article 1(1)(b) states that the Convention should also be applied where application of the forum's private international law rules point to the law of a Contracting State. However, states are free to enter a reservation[57] in respect of Article 1(1)(b). A state which does so will not apply the Vienna Convention where the conditions of Article 1(1)(a) are not met, even if its rules of private international law point to the law of a Contracting State.[58] Again, the parties are free to contract out of the Convention, in whole or in part.[59]

5. Non-Contractual Claims

12.24 The Vienna Convention is limited in its scope.[60] It applies only to the 'rights and obligations of the seller and buyer arising from' a contract of sale.[61] It does not apply to 'matters of validity[62] of the contract, of any of its

---

[48] For a comparison of English law and the Vienna Convention, see generally Ch 3, esp paras 3.34–35, 3.87–108, 3.118–124, 3.130–136, 3.257–297. See also Bridge, *The International Sale of Goods*, Ch 3.
[49] ibid, 71–72.   [50] ibid, 71.   [51] Art 50.   [52] Arts 37 and 48.
[53] Arts 39, 40 and 44.   [54] Arts 85–88.   [55] Bridge, *The International Sale of Goods*, 71.
[56] ibid, 72.   [57] Pursuant to Art 95.
[58] The US is one of the states which has entered this reservation. See Ch 16, below.
[59] Art 6.   [60] See Bridge, *The International Sale of Goods*, 50–54.   [61] Art 4.
[62] Although the Convention shall determine what are matters of validity or property. See further Bridge, *The International Sale of Goods*, 50–51.

provisions or of any usage',[63] nor to 'the effect the contract may have on the property[64] in the goods sold'.[65] A number of causes of action might arise in connection with a sales contract upon which there is only limited, or no substantive harmonization. So, there will be claims which arise in tort,[66] such as those relating to misstatements or misrepresentations, conversion or interference with contractual relations. There will also, of course, be proprietary issues relating to the goods, which will have to be determined by applying national rules of property law. Again, there may be claims in unjust enrichment, as where a contract is declared void, rescinded or frustrated and the buyer seeks the return of payments made to the seller. In all these areas, the substantive law of different states may vary considerably. It then becomes essential to ascertain which state's law governs the matter, since this may be determinative of the outcome of the case.

VI. LIMITED HARMONIZATION OF CHOICE OF LAW RULES

There is also, to date, limited harmonization of choice of law rules. There **12.25** is, of course, the Rome Convention on choice of law in contract. However, this only applies in the courts of European Contracting States. Moreover, it contains a number of exclusions.[67] There are also the Hague Sales Conventions of 1955 and 1986.[68] However, the latter is not in force and the former has had only a relatively modest global impact. In other areas of law related to the contract for the sale of goods, there is still no significant harmonization of private international law. This includes areas such as torts, property and restitution.

VII. CONCLUSION

Together, all these factors indicate a substantial potential for choice of law **12.26** problems arising in the context of the international sale of goods. They give rise to important questions of classification and determination of the applicable law. These will be examined in detail in the following chapters.

---

[63] Art 4(a).
[64] But the Convention states that the seller is obliged to transfer property in accordance with the terms of the contract and the Convention: Arts 30, 41 and 42.
[65] Art 4(b).
[66] The Convention also excludes claims for death or personal injury caused by the goods: Art 5.
[67] Arts 1(2) and (3) of the Rome Convention, discussed in Ch 13 on choice of law in contract and the international sale of goods, below, paras 13.22–42.
[68] See the discussion in Ch 15.

13

Choice of Law in Contract and the International Sale of Goods

I. SYNOPSIS

The application of the choice of law rules in contract to the international **13.01** sale of goods cannot be understood without some discussion of the general framework rules on choice of law in contract applicable in England. These rules apply to contracts of sale as to many other types of contracts. Accordingly, relatively concise discussion of the framework principles will be given in this chapter.[1] However, attention will naturally be focused on the application of those rules to the international sale of goods.[2]

II. PRELIMINARY ISSUES

1. The Legislation

Choice of law in contract is now governed by the Contracts (Applicable **13.02** Law) Act 1990, which enacts the provisions of the Rome Convention on

---

[1] For fuller discussion of the general principles of choice of law in contract, see Dicey and Morris, Ch 32; Cheshire and North, Ch 18; R Plender and M Wilderspin, *The European Contracts Convention*, (2nd edn, London: Sweet and Maxwell, 2001). On the application of these principles to the sale of goods, see Dicey and Morris, 1323–1337; C Morse, 'Conflict of Laws' Ch 25 in Benjamin.

[2] Since this book is not concerned with consumer contracts, they will not be examined in detail in this chapter. See, however, the brief discussion below, paras 13.265–268, and the examination of the Unfair Contract Terms Act 1977, below, para 13.320.

the Law Applicable to Contractual Obligations 1980.[3] For matters within its scope, the Convention harmonizes the choice of law rules in contract for Contracting States.[4] Section 2(1) of the Rome Convention states that the Convention 'shall have the force of law in the United Kingdom'. The Convention appears as Sch 1 to the Contracts (Applicable Law) Act 1990.

2. Time Frame

13.03 The Rome Convention applies to contracts made on or after 1 April 1991. Earlier contracts are governed by the common law choice of law rules. For contracts made after that date, matters will continue to be governed by the common law only if they fall outside the scope of the Convention.[5]

3. Why Common Rules?

13.04 The harmonization of private international law rules in contract has several advantages. The fact that parties will find their relationship subject to the same legal system, no matter in which Contracting State they might be, clearly promotes predictability in commerce. It also furthers the free movement principles of European law. A seller exporting his goods across Europe would face a serious competitive disadvantage if he had to satisfy the requirements of the contract laws of several legal systems. Moreover, the fact that different states' courts will apply the same law on the merits should facilitate the liberalization of rules on free movement of judgments, since the fear that a state might have reached a judgment on the merits by application of an 'unsuitable' law is very much reduced. Again, common choice of law rules complement the rules of jurisdiction in Europe. A claimant who would face the same state's law on the merits, no matter which Contracting State he sued in, has a substantially reduced incentive to engage in forum shopping.

---

[3] [1980] OJ L 266/1. The Convention was concluded on 19 June 1980.

[4] These are the current EU Member States. Initially, the Convention applied to what were then the ten Member States: Belgium, Denmark, France, Germany, Greece, Ireland, Italy, Luxembourg, Netherlands and the United Kingdom. (The Convention on the Accession of the Hellenic Republic 1984 ('the Luxembourg Convention') was concluded before the Rome Convention entered into force: see [1984] OJ L 146/1.) There have since been a Convention on the Accession of the Kingdom of Spain and the Republic of Portugal 1992 ('the Funchal Convention' [1992] OJ L333/1) and a Convention on the Accession of Austria, Finland and Sweden 1996 ('Austrian, Finnish and Swedish Accession Convention' [1997] OJ C15/ 10; implemented in the UK by the Contracts (Applicable Law) 1990 (Amendment) Order 2000, SI 2000/1825). The latest version of the Convention can be found at [1998] OJ C27/ 34. The Joint Declaration attached to the Convention envisages that each state which joins the European Union will become party to the Convention.

[5] See the discussion of the exclusions from the Convention below, paras 13.22–42.

4. TERRITORIAL APPLICATION OF THE CONVENTION

Application Irrespective of the Parties' Domicile and Residence

Although a European Convention, the Rome Convention applies in English **13.05**
courts *irrespective of the domicile or residence of the parties*. So, for example,
the Rome Convention would still be applied in English courts in litigation
between a claimant domiciled in Texas and a defendant domiciled in
Brazil in relation to a contract of sale governed by Argentinean law.

Application Irrespective of the Applicable[6] Law

Moreover, Article 2 states that: 'Any law specified by this Convention **13.06**
shall be applied whether or not it is the law of a Contracting State'. So, if a
buyer domiciled in England and a seller domiciled in France choose the
law of Japan to govern a contract, an English court should apply the rules
of the Rome Convention.[7]

Intra-UK Contracts

Article 19(2) states that a state consisting of more than one territorial unit, **13.07**
each having its own system of law, is not bound to apply the Convention
between such states. Of course, states which wish to apply the Convention to such a scenario are free to do so. To this end, the United Kingdom
has extended the application of the Convention to cross-border contracts
with connections only to England and Scotland and Northern Ireland.[8]

5. OFFICIAL REPORT

In English courts, the Official Report by Giuliano and Lagarde[9] 'may be **13.08**
considered in ascertaining the meaning or effect of any provision of . . .
[the] Convention'.[10] The Report has no binding effect but may be highly

---

[6] The phrases 'applicable law' and 'governing law' are used interchangeably in this
chapter to denote the law designated by the Convention's rules to apply to the contract. The
phrase 'proper law' is used in relation to the common law approach to determining which
law governs a contract.

[7] Indeed, it would do so even if the parties were both domiciled and resident in non-
Contracting States.

[8] s 2(3) of the Contracts (Applicable Law) Act 1990.

[9] M Giuliano and P Lagarde, *Report on the Law Applicable to Contractual Obligations* [1980]
OJ C282/1.

[10] s 3(3)(a) of the Contracts (Applicable Law) Act 1990. The court may also make reference
to the Explanatory Report by Tizzano in determining the meaning of terms of the First
Protocol on the Interpretation by the Court of Justice of the European Communities of
the Convention on the Law Applicable to Contractual Obligations: hereafter 'the Brussels
Protocol' [1990] OJ C129/1.

persuasive in determining the meaning or scope of a provision in the Convention.

6. References to the European Court of Justice

13.09 Two Protocols to the Convention allow the European Court of Justice to give preliminary rulings on the interpretation of the Convention. The first of these, contained in Sch 3 to the Contracts (Applicable Law) 1990 Act,[11] confers jurisdiction on the ECJ. It is commonly known as the 'Brussels Protocol'.[12] An appellate court of a Contracting State may request a ruling at its discretion. Even the House of Lords is not obliged to make a reference.[13] However, as the Protocols are yet to be ratified, they are not yet in force. There is a fear in some quarters[14] that the Protocol will make England a less attractive place to sue. A New York claimant suing a Japanese defendant would not obviously want an action in England delayed pending an ECJ ruling. If, in due course, the Convention is replaced by a Regulation,[15] then it will be possible to request a ruling from the European Court of Justice.[16] The House of Lords would be bound to refer questions of interpretation of the Convention to the European Court.[17]

---

[11] The Brussels Protocol [1989] OJ L48/1.

[12] The Second Protocol on the Interpretation by the Court of Justice of the European Communities of the Convention on the Law Applicable to Contractual Obligations states that the ECJ has jurisdiction even if the Convention is not yet in force in all Contracting States. This was not scheduled to the Contracts (Applicable Law) Act 1990. It can be found in [1989] OJ L48/17.

[13] Art 2 of the First Protocol. If an English court does not make a reference, it will still be bound by any relevant decision of the ECJ: s 3(1) of the Contracts (Applicable Law) Act 1990. Judicial notice shall be taken of decisions or opinions of the ECJ in such matters: ibid, s 3(2). Benjamin (para 25–018) points out that it is not wholly clear whether 'relevant decisions' are only ones on the Rome Convention itself, or whether they also include other matters of EC law, or interpretation of terms appearing in other instruments which also appear in the Rome Convention. The authors convincingly argue that only decisions on the Convention itself are binding, although, of course, other decisions may be highly persuasive.

[14] Belgium and Ireland have yet to ratify the Protocol. See further http://ue.eu.int/Accords/default.asp?lang=en.

[15] See below, paras 13.11–12.

[16] Art 234 of the EC Treaty.

[17] The prevailing interpretation of Art 234(3) EC is that all national courts against whose decision in the case under review there is no judicial remedy are under a duty to make a reference to the ECJ. However, even such courts may lawfully decide not to make a reference when (i) the ECJ has already delivered a judgment on the point in question pursuant to any procedure laid down in the EC Treaty (Joined Cases 28–30/62 *Da Costa en Schaake NV, Jacob Meijer NV and Hoechst-Holland NV v Nederlandse Belastingadministratie* [1963] ECR 31; Case 182/81 *Sri CILFIT and Lanificio di Gavardo SpA v Ministry of Health* [1982] ECR 3415) or (ii) the provision in question is sufficiently clear so as to make a reference unnecessary (the 'acte claire' doctrine, introduced in *CILFIT*).

7. Subordination to Community Law

In application of the Convention, a court is required to give precedence to **13.10**
any rules of Community law.[18] One such example is the Unfair Terms in
Consumer Contract Regulations.[19]

8. The Future: A Rome Regulation?

The Treaty of Amsterdam has brought measures relating to judicial **13.11**
co-operation in civil matters having cross-border implications that are
necessary for the completion of the internal market within the First Pillar
of European Community Law.[20] This means that, whereas the Community
had previously to proceed with private international law initiatives by
Convention, they may now do so by Regulation.[21] The most prominent
example of such an initiative is, of course, the transformation of the
Brussels Convention into a Regulation.[22] Although the United Kingdom
and Ireland have an opt-out from initiatives made pursuant to Article 65
EC, contained in Articles 1 and 2 of the Protocol on the position of

---

[18] Art 20 of the Rome Convention.
[19] SI 1999/2083 (replacing the 1994 Regulations, SI 1994/3159, implementing Directive
93/13/EEC [1993] OJ L95/29). The Directive contains an anti-avoidance provision in Art
6(2). See also the Sale and Supply of Goods to Consumers Regulations 2002, SI 2002/3045,
implementing Directive (EC) 99/44 on Certain Aspects of the Sale of Consumer Goods and
Associated Guarantees (especially the anti-avoidance provision in Art 7(2) of the Directive).
See further joined Cases C-240/98, C-241/98, C-242–98, C-243/98 and C-244/98 *Océano
Grupo Editorial SA v Rocio Murciano Quintero* [2000] ECR I-4941; C Withers, 'Jurisdiction
Clauses and the Unfair Terms in Consumer Contracts Regulations' [2002] LMCLQ 56.
[20] [1997] OJ C340/1. See Art 65 of the EC Treaty.
[21] Or by Directive; but the Regulation is the preferred route in this area. The legal basis for
the Regulations adopted so far in private international law has been Art 61(c) of the Treaty. It
is likely that the same basis would be used for transforming the Rome Convention into a
Regulation.
[22] Regulation on Jurisdiction and the Recognition and Enforcement of Judgments in Civil
and Commercial Matters ('Brussels I Regulation'): Council Regulation (EC) No 44/2001 of
22 December 2000 [2001] OJ L12/1. Many other substantial advances have already been
made in this respect, such as: Council Regulation (EC) No 1348/ 2000 of 29 May 2000 on the
Service in the Member States of Judicial and Extra-judicial Documents in Civil or Commercial Matters [2000] OJ L160/ 37; Council Regulation (EC) No 1346/ 2000 of 29 May 2000
on Insolvency Proceedings [2000] OJ L 160/1 (on which, see below, paras 18.122–125); and
Council Regulation (EC) No 2201/2003 of 27 November 2003 Concerning Jurisdiction and
the Recognition and Enforcement of Judgments in Matrimonial Matters and the Matters of
Parental Responsibility [2003] OJ L 338/1 (repealing Council Regulation (EC) No 1347/ 2000
of 29 May 2000 on Jurisdiction and Recognition and Enforcement of Judgments in
Matrimonial Matters and in Matters of Parental Responsibility for Children of Both Spouses
[2000] OJ L160/ 19). See also the Commission's Proposal for a Regulation of the European
Parliament and the Council on the Law Applicable to Non-Contractual Obligations
('Rome II'), COM/2003/0427 Final, available at http://europa.eu.int/eur-lex/pri/en/lip/
latest/doc/2003/com2003_0427en01.doc. This Proposal is considered further below, paras
17.165–182, 19.98–100, 21.203–210.

the United Kingdom and Ireland,[23] it is willing to opt back into private international law initiatives.[24]

13.12 It is envisaged that the Rome Convention will be transformed into a Regulation pursuant to Article 65 EC. So much was said in the Community Action Plan of December 1998.[25] The European Commission launched a consultation on the matter in January 2003.[26] At this stage, one can speculate that there are likely to be some significant substantive changes, as there were with the advent of the Brussels I Regulation, and that these will focus on the problems of e-commerce and consumer protection. However, it is also unlikely that there will be anything approaching root and branch changes to the existing choice of law rules.[27]

III. ARTICLE 1(1): 'CONTRACTUAL OBLIGATIONS INVOLVING A CHOICE BETWEEN THE LAWS OF DIFFERENT COUNTRIES'

13.13 Article 1(1) of the Rome Convention states that 'the rules of the Convention shall apply to contractual obligations involving a choice between the laws of different countries'. At first sight, this does not seem particularly controversial or difficult to apply. However, the closer one looks at this provision, the more apparent its complexity is.

1. 'CONTRACTUAL OBLIGATIONS'

13.14 In order to ensure the uniform application of the Convention throughout the Contracting States, the term 'contractual obligations' must have an

---

[23] Art 69 EC preserves the Protocol on the position of the UK and Ireland (for the text of which, see [1997] OJ C340/99).

[24] And has opted back into initiatives such as the Brussels I Regulation and Regulations on: Service in the Member States of Judicial and Extra-Judicial Documents in Civil or Commercial Matters; the Jurisdiction and Recognition and Enforcement of Judgments in Matrimonial Matters and in Matters of Parental Responsibility; and Insolvency Proceedings.

[25] Action Plan of the Council and Commission on How Best to Implement the Provisions of the Treaty of Amsterdam Establishing an Area of Freedom, Security and Justice, adopted on 7 December 1998 [1999] OJ C19/1 (esp point 40(c)). Initially, it was hoped that the amendments would be drawn up within two years of the entry into force of the Treaty.

[26] See the Commission's 'Green Paper on the Conversion of the Rome Convention of 1980 on the Law Applicable to Contractual Obligations into a Community Instrument and its Modernisation' COM/2002/0654 Final. See further the Press Release of the European Commission: IP/03/45 of 14 January 2003. See also the proposals of the European Group for Private International Law (GEDIP), available at www.drt.ucl.ac.be/gedip.

[27] One significant change will be the immediate conferring of competence on the ECJ once the Regulation enters into force, with the result that one can expect a series of cases finally to reach the ECJ on the interpretation of a number of key provisions.

autonomous meaning. Indeed, Article 18 states that in the '. . . interpretation and application of the preceding uniform rules, regard shall be had to their international character and to the desirability of achieving uniformity in their interpretation and application'. Any other approach would undermine the uniformity and predictability for which the Rome Convention strives. 'It would be deplorable if the nations should . . . reach agreement. . . . And . . . their several courts should then disagree as to the meaning of what they appeared to agree upon.'[28]

In the absence of any further elucidation in the Convention, it will be tempting to look for other sources of guidance as to what a European meaning of 'contractual obligations' might be.

The most natural comparator is the provision in Article 5(1) of the **13.15** Brussels I Regulation, which allocates jurisdiction in 'matters relating to contract'.[29] In *Jakob Handte GmbH v Traitements Mécano-Chimiques des Surfaces*,[30] the ECJ said that there was not a 'matter relating to contract' where a buyer had sold goods on to a sub-purchaser who sought to sue the original seller. This was the case notwithstanding that under French law it appeared that all the contractual rights of the purchaser against the seller were assigned to the sub-purchaser on sale. The Court said that Article 5(1) could not apply, as the proceedings did not seek to enforce as 'an undertaking freely entered into by one party in relation to another'.[31] This tends to suggest that if the obligation in question is freely undertaken, and is undertaken by one party towards another specific, identified person or company, the matter relates to contract. If the same approach were taken under the Rome Convention, then it would certainly be the case that a voluntary agreement with an identified party unsupported by consideration would fall within the Convention.[32] It might also be the case that, for example, litigation concerning freely offered, but negligent advice given by an accountant to a client (or friend) would fall within the Convention.[33]

However, it is important to note that it is not essential for the definition of **13.16** 'contractual obligations' in Article 1(1) of the Rome Convention exactly to reflect the definition of 'matters relating to contract' in Article 5(1) of the Brussels I Regulation. In *Handte*, Advocate General Jacobs observed that:

---

[28] *per* Viscount Simonds in *Scruttons v Midland Silicones Ltd* [1962] AC 446, 471.
[29] See the discussion above, paras 3.62–82.
[30] Case C-26/91 [1992] ECR I-3967.   [31] ibid, para 15.
[32] Compare the common law position in *Re Bonacina* [1912] 2 Ch 394.
[33] Compare, in the context of non-disclosure in the negotiation of a contract of reinsurance, the decision of the House of Lords in *Agnew v Länsfösäkringsbolagens AB* [2001] 1 AC 223. But see the discussion of negligent misstatement and fraudulent and negligent misrepresentation, below, paras 17.90–100.

It is above all important to stress that the jurisdiction rules of the [Brussels] Convention deal solely with the issue of jurisdiction. They do not affect the classification of the action for such purposes as determining the applicable principles of liability or deciding what limitation period applies. A court that acquires jurisdiction under Article 5(1) is not prevented by the Convention from proceeding with the action on the basis that it is delictual and a court that acquires jurisdiction under Article 5(3) is not prevented by the [Brussels] Convention from proceeding with the action on the basis that it is contractual.[34]

It should be noted the wording of Article 1(1) of the Rome Convention refers to 'contractual obligations', whereas the wording of Article 5(1) of the Brussels I Regulation uses the words 'matters relating to contract'. A matter could 'relate' to contract without being itself a contractual obligation. This might suggest that a narrower construction should be taken of the scope of Article 1(1) of the Rome Convention than Article 5(1) of the Brussels I Regulation.

13.17 Against this, Article 5(1) of the Brussels Convention was interpreted in *Handte* so that even a claim involving a contractual obligation would fall outside the scope of that provision, if the defendant did not freely assume the obligation to a foreseeable, other party. It is not necessary to adopt the same approach to Article 1(1) of the Rome Convention and impose this further requirement. The Rome Convention should simply apply to any claim involving a contractual obligation.[35] This may be particularly important in the context of the carriage of goods by sea, and in particular in relation to the transfer of rights and duties to a third party holder of a bill of lading. In English law, the transferee obtains contractual rights and duties against the carrier by the operation of statute.[36] There is no doubt that these are contractual obligations, albeit that they are not freely assumed by the parties to the bill of lading, and that the carrier may not be able to foresee to whom he will owe these contractual obligations. They should accordingly fall within the scope of the Rome Convention,[37] even if there is doubt as to whether they fall within the scope of Article 5(1) of the Brussels I Regulation.[38]

2. 'Involving a Choice'

13.18 The Convention will clearly apply where there are objective elements of the contract located in more than one state, for example if the parties

---

[34] Case C-26/91 [1992] ECR I-3967, para 24 of the Opinion.
[35] Not otherwise falling outside the scope of the Convention by Art 1(2).
[36] s 2 of the Carriage of Goods by Sea Act 1992; see above, paras 5.08, 5.22 and below, paras 14.03–05, 14.52.
[37] See below, paras 14.03–05.   [38] See above, paras 5.22–27.

reside in different states, or performance is to be made in a state other that where the parties are resident.[39] It appears that the Convention also applies even when the only international aspect of the contract is the choice of law clause. In this respect, it contrasts notably with the Hague Sales Convention 1986,[40] which applies only where the parties have their places of business in different states or where there is a choice between the laws of different states. Article 1(b) thereof expressly states that a choice of law clause or a choice of court or arbitration clause by itself is insufficient to create a choice between the laws of different states. In other words, it requires there to be *objective* connections to more than one state. This is not required under the Rome Convention. It would thus appear that a contract between a buyer resident in Germany and a seller also resident in Germany would fall within the Rome Convention's ambit, if the parties stated that the contract was to be governed by English law, or subject to the jurisdiction of the English courts.[41] As we shall see below, the possibility that parties might thus 'evade' certain laws which they would otherwise be subject to in what is, in all respects save the choice of law or jurisdiction clause, a purely domestic contract, is specifically regulated elsewhere in the Convention.[42] This largely eliminates the need to insist upon a contract being *objectively* transnational in nature before the Rome Convention applies.

3. THE CONVENTION 'SHALL APPLY'

The Convention states that its specified rules 'shall apply'.[43] In English **13.19** private international law, there is a general principle that if foreign law is not pleaded here, the court will apply the law of the forum.[44] It is unclear whether this position can be maintained under the Rome Convention. One argument for saying that it can is that this could be said to be a rule of procedure or evidence. Such matters are excluded from the Convention by Article 1(2)(h).[45] This view attracts the support of Benjamin.[46]

---

[39] Giuliano and Lagarde Report, 10.   [40] See below, paras 15.65–129.

[41] An English jurisdiction clause may be sufficient to infer an implied choice of English law, pursuant to Art 3(1) of the Rome Convention (on which, see below, paras 13.44–55, esp paras 13.50, 13.52.

[42] Art 3(3) of the Rome Convention; see below, paras 13.99–102.   [43] Art 1(1).

[44] See generally R Fentiman, *Foreign Law in English Courts* (Oxford: OUP, 1998).

[45] See also *Thierry Morin v Bonhams* [2003] EWCA Civ 1802, [2004] IL Pr 24, where the Court of Appeal applied the choice of law rules in tort to claims for misrepresentation and negligent misstatement and held that they were governed by the law of Monaco. It did so even though there was evidence that the latter claim would be treated as contractual by the law of Monaco. The parties did not dispute the classification of the claims. The court showed no inclination to consider of its own motion whether one or both claims fell within the scope of the Rome Convention. See further below, paras 17.90–97.

[46] Benjamin, 25–029.

Alternatively, it might be argued that by proceeding as though the law of the forum were the applicable law, the parties have tacitly and consensually changed the applicable law pursuant to Article 3(2) of the Convention.[47]

13.20 The counter-arguments are two-fold. First, that the wording of Article 1(1) is in mandatory terms. Second, any other view would frustrate the uniform application of the Convention,[48] potentially leading to it failing to be applied in English courts in circumstances where it would be applied in the courts of other Contracting States. On balance, it is suggested that Article 1 should be construed as requiring an English judge of his own motion to apply the rules of the Convention, even if the parties do not plead its application.[49] Moreover, it seems clear that the parties cannot take contractual freedom to its ultimate limits and contract out of the application of the Rome Convention's choice of law rules altogether.[50]

4. 'DIFFERENT COUNTRIES'

13.21 Finally, it should be noted that Article 1(1) refers to the laws of 'different countries'. As the authors of Benjamin note,[51] the Giuliano and Lagarde Report refers instead to choices between 'different legal systems'.[52] Moreover, Article 19(1) provides that where a state has several territorial units each of which has its own contract rules, each unit is to be treated as a country when identifying the applicable law under the Convention. It must accordingly be the case that application of the Convention would be triggered in respect of a contract having connections with, for example, New South Wales and Queensland, even if it has no connections to any other legal system outside Australia.

IV. SPECIFIC EXCLUSIONS[53]

13.22 Certain matters are excluded from the Convention altogether by Articles 1(2) and 1(3). The provisions of Article 1(2) are considered briefly below, with particular emphasis on those most likely to arise in the sales context.

---

[47] On which, see below, paras 13.107–111.   [48] On which, see Art 18.

[49] A view shared by Cheshire and North, 545.

[50] But see F Mann, 'The Proper Law of the Contract- an Obituary' (1991) 107 LQR 353; G Hogan, 'Contracting Out of the Rome Convention' (1992) 108 LQR 12. See also Benjamin, 25–027.

[51] Benjamin, 25–021.   [52] Giuliano and Lagarde Report, 10.

[53] For a useful, concise summary of these exclusions, see Peel, E, 'Conflict of laws', Ch 15 in E McKendrick (ed), *Sale of Goods* (London: LLP, 2000) 15–019.

1. Status and Capacity

A person's capacity to contract may be limited for a number of reasons, **13.23** including age and mental incapacity.

Individuals

The status or legal capacity of natural persons is excluded from the scope **13.24** of the Rome Convention by Article 1(2)(a). It is thought that individuals should not be able to choose the law applicable to this question. Rules which restrict the ability of a certain group of persons to enter into a contract have an intrinsically mandatory characteristic and it would be inappropriate if such rules could be avoided by the simple expedient of choosing a particular law to govern the matter. However, the common law rule as to the capacity of individuals to contract is itself highly unclear.[54] The rule in Dicey and Morris[55] reads thus:

The capacity of an individual to enter into a contract is governed by the law of the country with which the contract is most closely connected or by the law of his domicile or residence:

(a) If he has capacity to contract by the law with which the contract is most closely connected, the contract will (*semble*) be valid so far as capacity is concerned.

(b) If he has capacity to contract by the law of his domicile and residence, the contract will (*semble*) be valid so far as capacity is concerned.

Given that questions of status are intrinsically personal, it seems sensible for issues of capacity to be determined by the law of the domicile of the individual alleged to lack capacity. However, in the modern commercial world it would be impractical for all questions of capacity to be governed solely by the law of the domicile. If X, domiciled in Japan, enters into a contract with Y, an English domiciliary, which is governed by English law, it would be very inconvenient if X could escape liability for an alleged breach of contract on the grounds that he lacked capacity by the law of his domicile, Japanese law. Y may have no knowledge of X's domicile, especially if the contract is concluded at a distance by electronic means.[56]

The law of closest connection approach attempts to reconcile the un- **13.25** desirability of a potential lifelong burden being imposed on a person by

---

[54] Some cases favour the domicile of the parties, such as *Sottomayor v de Barros (No 1)* (1877) 3 PD 1, 5 and *Cooper v Cooper* (1888) 13 App Cas 88; others favour the law of the place of contracting, such as *Sottomayor v de Barros (No 2)* (1879) 5 PD 94 and *Male v Roberts* (1800) 3 Esp 163; others still favour the objective proper law of the contract, such as *Bodley Head v Flegon* [1972] 1 WLR 680 and *Charron v Montreal Trust Co* (1958) 15 DLR (2d) 240.

[55] Rule 179(1), 1271–1272.   [56] See generally Ch 21 on e-commerce and choice of law.

the law of his domicile with the need to prevent evasion of capacity rules by choosing a particular law to govern the contract. It ensures a strong connection between capacity and the contract itself. However, it may be very difficult to determine the law of closest connection and may lead to excessive uncertainty, not least because the common law rules on the objective proper law will have to be used, rather than those found under Article 4 of the Rome Convention,[57] for determining the applicable law in the absence of choice.

13.26 Dicey and Morris's rule attempts to take the best features of the law of the domicile and the law of closest connection. The rule tends to uphold contracts, in that a person need only have capacity by one of two laws. However, given that both connecting factors are inherently uncertain, it is difficult to see how commercial certainty can be fostered by a choice of law rule which may require the court to consider not one but two connecting factors.

13.27 In any event, Article 11 of the Rome Convention limits the application of the common law rule on capacity. It provides that:

> in a contract concluded between persons who are in the same country, a natural person who would have capacity under the law of that country may invoke his own incapacity resulting from another law only if the other party to the contract was aware of this incapacity at the time of the conclusion of the contract or was not aware thereof as a result of negligence.

It is important to appreciate the effect of this provision. It limits the circumstances in which an individual *can invoke his own incapacity* under the common law rules. It does not apply where a person seeks to invoke the common law rules to demonstrate his capacity. Nor does it apply where, for example, a buyer alleges that the contract is invalid because the seller lacked capacity.

13.28 An example of the operation of this Article is as follows. Suppose that an 18-year-old buyer domiciled in Utopia concludes a contract with a seller domiciled in Ruritania for the purchase of whisky. The contract is concluded face to face between the parties in Ruritania. It states that the seller shall deliver the goods to Utopia and the buyer shall pay in Utopian currency. Suppose that by Utopian law, but not Ruritanian law, a buyer aged under 21 lacks capacity to enter into a contract for the purchase of alcohol. Let us also suppose that an English court concludes that the law of closest connection to the contract is Utopian law. If one applies the rule in Dicey and Morris, the buyer would have capacity if he possessed it by

---

[57] On which, see below, paras 13.112–139.

either the law of his domicile or the law of closest connection to the contract. Since, in both cases, this is Utopian law, it follows that the common law rules indicate that the buyer lacks capacity. Now suppose that the seller sues the buyer to obtain the purchase price of the goods. The buyer states by way of defence that he never had capacity to conclude the contract in the first place according to the common law rules on capacity. However, by the law of the place where both parties were at the time of conclusion of the contract, Ruritania, the buyer had capacity and the contract is valid. Article 11 has the effect that the buyer would only be able to invoke his common law incapacity, and so successfully defend the action, if he could prove that the seller either knew that the buyer lacked capacity by the common law rules, or, if the seller did not actually know, he had knowledge of sufficient facts that he should have been aware of this fact. Article 11 will not apply often in the international sales context, since it will be relatively rare for the parties to be in the same country at the time of conclusion of the contract.

Companies

The capacity of companies to contract is excluded from the Rome Convention. The relevant provision is Article 1(2)(e), but it makes sense to consider the issue at this point. The incapacity of a company may stem from one of two sources: the constitution itself, which may render certain activity ultra vires, or a general provision of the law of the place of incorporation.[58] In England, it seems that the 'general' capacity of companies is governed by the law of closest connection to the contract. However, that law cannot confer capacity on a company beyond that which it has under its constitution. The law of the place of incorporation of the company will decide what limits the constitution places on the company's capacity.[59] Since a company is itself set up by law, it makes sense for the law of the place where it is incorporated to apply. The question whether an organ of the company is authorized to conclude a certain contract is excluded by virtue of Article 1(2)(f).[60] **13.29**

---

[58] Giuliano and Lagarde (at 13) state that the exclusion in Art 1(2)(e) is concerned with restrictions imposed upon the company's capacity by law. However, as Benjamin notes (para 25–085), the combined effect of Arts 1(2)(e) and (f) seems to be to exclude all issues of capacity of a corporation from the Convention.

[59] Dicey and Morris, Rule 154, 1109–16; *Risdon Iron and Locomotive Works Ltd v Furness* [1906] 1 KB 49; *Carl Zeiss Stiftung v Rayner and Keeler Ltd (No 2)* [1967] 1 AC 853; *Janred Properties Ltd v ENIT* [1989] 2 All ER 444.

[60] Considered below, para 13.38.

2. Wills, Succession, Matrimonial Property, etc.

13.30 Article 1(2)(b) deals with wills, succession, matrimonial property and rights and duties arising out of family relationships. This is not significant in the present context.

3. Obligations under Bills of Exchange, Cheques, Promissory Notes and other Negotiable Instruments

13.31 This has the effect that many typical payment arrangements arising pursuant to a contract of sale fall outside the scope of the Convention.[61] The Giuliano and Lagarde Report states that it is for the conflicts rules of the forum to decide if the instrument is negotiable.[62]

This has the effect that such documents as bills of lading, similar documents issued in connection with transport contracts, and bonds, debentures, guarantees, letters of indemnity, certificates of deposit, warrants and warehouse receipts are only excluded . . . if they can be regarded as negotiable instruments.[63]

Even then, the exclusion only applies in so far as the obligation arises out of the negotiable character of the instrument.[64]

4. Choice of Court and Arbitration Agreements

The Brussels I Regulation; Formal and Essential Validity; Incorporation

13.32 International sales contracts will frequently contain a clause referring any disputes between the parties to arbitration in,[65] or to the courts of,[66] a particular state. The existence, consent to and validity[67] of such clauses are largely treated as jurisdictional issues and fall outside the ambit of the Rome Convention. Where the clause stipulates for the jurisdiction of the courts of a Member State of the European Community,[68] the effectiveness of the clause is largely governed by Article 23 of the Brussels I Regulation.[69]

---

[61] See, in the UK, s 72 of the Bills of Exchange Act 1882 (discussed by Plender and Wilderspin, n 1 above, 65–7). See also Benjamin, 25–077; Dicey and Morris, 1431–54.

[62] Giuliano and Lagarde Report, 11.

[63] It may be argued that Giuliano and Lagarde somewhat confuse the words 'negotiable' and 'transferable'.

[64] Giuliano and Lagarde Report, 11.

[65] See, eg, *XL Insurance v Owens Corning* [2000] 2 Lloyd's Rep 500.

[66] See above, paras 3.28 and 4.47, for examples of standard form contracts which contain a jurisdiction clause.

[67] See *Akai Pty Ltd v People's Insurance Co Ltd* [1998] 1 Lloyd's Rep 90, 98.

[68] Or a Contracting State to the Brussels or Lugano Conventions.

[69] Or Art 17 of the Brussels or Lugano Convention.

However, Article 23 of the Brussels I Regulation is largely[70] concerned **13.33**
with the formalities for a choice of court clause. What if, for instance, the
clause meets the requirements of Article 23, but is alleged nonetheless
not to have been incorporated in the contract, or to have been included as
a result of a mistake, or duress or undue influence? This matter is considered in the discussion of Article 23 of the Brussels I Regulation and
readers should refer to that discussion for a full consideration.[71] Suffice
it to say here that whilst a jurisdiction clause for a Member State of the
European Community must, of course, comply with the requirements of
Article 23, it is nor clear whether that Article exclusively regulates the
validity of jurisdiction clauses. The view preferred by the authors is that it
does not, so that the clause may be struck down if it is essentially invalid
according to the governing law of the contract. However, it should be
noted that the law which putatively[72] governs the contract according to
common law principles should determine the material validity of the
jurisdiction clause, since the matter lies outside the scope of the Rome
Convention.[73]

Common Law

If the jurisdiction clause does not designate the courts of a Member State **13.34**
of the European Community,[74] the English court will have to determine
its existence, formal and essential validity by its own conflicts rules. At
least where the contract is governed by English law, it appears that the
jurisdiction clause need not satisfy any general formality requirements.
However, English law insists that a jurisdiction clause be express and that
it may not be implied into a contract.[75]

---

[70] Although it does seek also to ensure that there is consent between the parties. However,
it is nothing like a failsafe in this respect. A clause might be in writing or evidenced in
writing, yet not incorporated into the contract, or incorporated by mistake or the duress of
one of the parties.

[71] See above, paras 3.29–39.

[72] In making this assessment of the putative proper law, the court is likely to ask what the
proper law would be, assuming that the jurisdiction clause were valid.

[73] However, in *Egon Oldendorff v Libera Corp (No 1)* [1995] 2 Lloyd's Rep 64, Mance J
regarded the issue of the incorporation of an arbitration clause as an issue of material
validity of the contract and applied the rules of the Rome Convention, not the common law
choice of law rules. This may be justified on the basis that the issue of incorporation of a
clause often raises questions of offer and acceptance, and of which party's terms are being
used. These matters are concerned with the formation of the contract. There is nothing
intrinsically wrong with the clause itself.

[74] Or Contracting State to the Brussels or Lugano Convention.

[75] *Sridhar Gordian Singh v Rajah of Faridkote* [1894] AC 670; *Schibsby v Westenholz* (1870) LR
6 QB 161; *New Hampshire Insurance Co v Strabag Bau AG* [1992] 1 Lloyd's Rep 361 (affirming
the first instance decision of Potter J; [1990] 2 Lloyd's Rep 61).

13.35 In the event of a dispute between the parties as to whether they agreed to the jurisdiction clause, or whether it was the product of duress or mistake, the proper law of the contract,[76] as determined by common law choice of law rules, should resolve the matter.[77]

Relevance of Jurisdiction Clause to the Applicable Law of the Contract

13.36 Once the validity of the jurisdiction clause is established by application of rules outside the scope of the Rome Convention, the jurisdiction clause may itself become a relevant term of the contract when determining the applicable law of the contract under the Convention. It may, for example, be evidence from which a court may determine that the parties impliedly chose the law of the state whose courts are identified.[78]

5. Questions Governed by the Law of Companies and other Bodies Corporate or Unincorporate

13.37 This exclusion covers the creation[79] and internal organization of the company. It would exclude from the Rome Convention a contract contained in the articles of association of a company, or a shareholder's agreement to wind up a company. It also excludes the legal capacity of companies.[80] However, contractual questions which are not peculiar to the law of companies are not excluded.

6. The Ability of an Agent to Bind a Principal

13.38 Only the question of the agent's ability to bind the principal is excluded (for example, whether an organ of a company can bind the company).

---

[76] But see the comment on the *Egon Oldendorff* decision in n 73 above. It may be that if the jurisdiction clause is itself valid, the question of whether it is incorporated into the contract will be determined by the rules of the Rome Convention.

[77] Where the clause is not subject to the Brussels regime, the court will determine, according to the law of the forum whether, and when, the parties are *permitted* to confer jurisdiction on the court by such a clause, or to derogate from its jurisdiction by a foreign jurisdiction clause. In *Re Claim by a Polish Producer of Zinc and Copper Products* [1998] IL Pr 727, the Oberlandesgericht Cologne was faced with a Polish jurisdiction clause in a contract between a Polish company and a German company. The court remarked that 'an agreement upon the jurisdiction of a court is a contract on relations under procedural law. The validity and effect of an agreement on international jurisdiction made before the proceedings start are determined, if application is made to a German court, in accordance with German procedural law . . .' (at 730). However, for choice of law purposes, the key question is not whether a valid jurisdiction clause would actually be *effective* in the courts of a particular state. Rather, the key question is whether that clause *was validly agreed upon* by the parties, so that it became a term of the contract. As the German court went on to recognize, that is a matter for the proper law of the contract.

[78] Pursuant to Art 3(1), considered below, paras 13.50–52.

[79] By registration or otherwise.   [80] Which is considered above.

Other contractual disputes between the principal and agent arising from the agency contract itself are not excluded. In England, the common law rules dictate that the proper law of the contract between an agent and a third party determines whether the principal is bound to the third party by virtue of the agent's acts.[81]

7. THE CONSTITUTION OF TRUSTS

The constitution of trusts and the relationship between settlor, trustees **13.39** and beneficiaries falls outside the Convention. This provision is apparently concerned with express trusts only.[82] If a seller, S, were to contract to transfer goods to T to hold on trust for the buyer, B, the question whether and when the trust was constituted would be a matter outside the Convention's scope.[83]

8. EVIDENCE AND PROCEDURE

This preserves the familiar rule in the English conflict of laws that matters **13.40** of evidence and procedure are not proper subjects for the choice of law process.[84] These matters will governed by the law of the forum. An example of a procedural matter would be the question of whether a party may sue or be sued in an English court at all.[85] Questions of evidence, such as whether a party may give evidence on their own behalf and whether they may cross-examine witnesses, will be also be governed by the law of the forum.[86]

However, the traditional understanding in English law of what are **13.41** matters of evidence and procedure may necessitate some reconsideration for the purposes of the application of the Rome Convention. For example,

---

[81] See further Benjamin, 25–073, 25–081 and 25–082; Dicey and Morris, 1464–1481. See also below, paras 14.08, 14.105–108.

[82] *Chellaram v Chellaram (No 2)* [2002] 3 All ER 17. This suggests that it would not apply, for example, to determine whether a constructive trust arises pursuant to a specifically enforceable contract of sale.

[83] It would probably be a matter for the law of the situs: see J Harris, 'Launching the Rocket: Capacity and the Creation of *Intern Vivos* Trusts', Ch C2 in J Glasson (ed), *International Trust Laws* (Bristol: Jordans, looseleaf).

[84] See Dicey and Morris, Ch 7; Cheshire and North, Ch 6.

[85] *Banque Internationale de Commerce de Petrograd v Goukassow* [1923] 2 KB 682. But the question of whether a party who is, in principle, capable of suing or being sued in England is a proper party to the instant case should be regarded as a substantive question, at least in so far as it affects that party's substantive rights under the contract. See *General Stores Navigation Co v Guillou* (1843) 11 M & W 877; *Re Doetsch* [1896] 2 Ch 836.

[86] *Appleton v Braybook* (1817) 6 M & S 34; *Brown v Thornton* (1837) 6 Ad & E 185.

although there is common law authority in the shape of *Leroux v Brown*[87]
for the proposition that a requirement under English law that a contract
be evidenced in writing may be regarded as a procedural matter,[88] formality rules are treated as substantive and within the scope of the Rome
Convention.[89] Moreover, Article 14(1) makes clear that presumptions[90]
and burdens of proof[91] contained in the law of contract[92] come within the
Convention and are determined by the governing law of the contract.
Furthermore, the remedies available for a breach of contract are subjected
to the applicable law of the contract, in accordance with Article 10(1)(c).[93]
Finally, it should be noted that, partly in anticipation of Article 10(1)(d)
of the Rome Convention, the question of limitation of actions, having
previously been regarded as procedural,[94] was designated a substantive
matter by s 1(1) of the Foreign Limitation Periods Act 1984. The combination of these two provisions ensures that the limitation period of the
applicable law of the contract shall be applied.[95]

9. ARTICLE 1(3)—EXCLUSION OF CERTAIN INSURANCE RISKS

13.42 This exclusion covers risks situated in the territories of the Member States
of the European Community.[96] Article 1(4) states that this exclusion does
not apply to contracts of reinsurance.

---

[87] (1852) 12 CB 801; and see *Maddison v Alderson* (1883) 8 App Cas 467, 474. But contrast
Monterosso Shipping Co Ltd v International Transport Workers' Federation [1982] 3 All ER 841.
[88] *Leroux* concerned the requirements of s 4 of the Statute of Frauds, which prevented a
party from bringing an action on certain contracts unless they satisfied certain formality
requirements. The court applied these requirements to a contract governed by French law.
The case is heavily criticized by Cheshire and North, 69.
[89] Art 9. See also Art 14(2), which states that 'a contract or an act intended to have legal
effect may be proved by any mode of proof recognized by the law of the forum or by any of
the laws referred to in Art 9 under which that contract or act is formally valid, provided that
such mode of proof can be administered by the forum'. See below, paras 13.256–264.
[90] At common law, irrebuttable presumptions of law were regarded as substantive (*Re
Cohn* [1945] Ch 5). The position with regard to rebuttable presumptions of law was much less
clear. On one view, they were to be regarded as procedural: see Dicey and Morris, 165–166.
[91] This is a change to the common law approach, which treated burdens of proof as
procedural: *The Roberta* (1937) 58 Ll LR 159; *In the Estate of Fuld (No 3)* [1968] P 675, 696–697.
[92] In practice, it seems that any substantive rules on burden of proof of the governing law
should be applied, even if they are not specific to the law of contract: Giuliano and Lagarde
Report, 36. See also Benjamin, 25–198.
[93] As long as it is within the procedural competence of the court to grant such a remedy at
all. See the discussion of this provision below, paras 13.205–239. On the question of who may
properly be made parties to litigation, see Dicey and Morris, 160–162.
[94] See ibid, 173–174.
[95] Subject to a public policy exception in s 2(1) of the Foreign Limitation Periods Act 1984.
[96] See further Dicey and Morris, 1337–1383; *Third Supplement to the Thirteenth Edition*, 352–
390; R Merkin and A Rodger, *EC Insurance Law* (London: Longman, 1997), Ch 6; F Seatzu,
Insurance in Private International Law: a European Perspective (Oxford: Hart Publishing, 2003).

V. THE PRIMARY CHOICE OF LAW RULE: FREEDOM OF CHOICE

1. EXPRESS CHOICE OF LAW

Article 3(1) states that 'a contract shall be governed by law chosen by the **13.43** parties'.[97] Normally, the choice will be expressly contained in a choice of law clause in the contract. Choice of law clauses are very common in international sale of goods contracts.[98] Such clauses may be found in many standard form contracts.[99]

2. IMPLIED CHOICE OF LAW

Relevant Factors

A choice can also be 'demonstrated with reasonable certainty by the terms **13.44** of the contract or the circumstances of the case'. This is a stringent test. The court is looking for a choice that the parties actually did make, albeit not expressly. It does not allow the court to infer a choice of law which the parties might have made if they had thought about the matter, if they had not actually made a choice.[100] The Giuliano and Lagarde Report states that, in the absence of a choice of law clause, the following factors might be sufficient to infer a choice of law with reasonable certainty:[101]

use of terminology related to a particular law, or use of a standard form;[102]

---

[97] The parties themselves must have agreed to the clause. See *Insurance Company of North America v Société Intramar* [1999] IL Pr 315, French Court de Cassation; compare the decision of the English High Court in *Youell v Kara Mara Shipping Co Ltd* [2000] 2 Lloyd's Rep 102. See also *Baytur SA v Dinagro Holdings SA* [1992] QB 610.

[98] See A Briggs, 'On Drafting Agreements on Choice of Law' [2003] LMCLQ 389.

[99] See above, paras 4.41–42, for examples of contracts that typically contain choice of law clauses. See also below, paras 14.11–14.

[100] See J Hill, 'Choice of Law in Contract under the Rome Convention: the Approach of the UK Courts' (2004) 53 ICLQ 325, 328.

[101] [1980] OJ C282/1, at 17.

[102] Such as a Lloyd's policy of marine insurance, which is known to be governed by English law. See *Amin Rasheed Shipping Corp v Kuwait Insurance Co* [1984] AC 50. In *Tiernan v Magen Insurance* [2000] IL Pr 517, Longmore J was faced with a reinsurance contract on a Lloyd's standard form. He found that the parties had impliedly chosen English law to govern the contract. He remarked (at 522–3) that he was 'particularly influenced by the Giuliano and Lagarde Report, where it is stated in terms that a contract may be in a standard form known to be governed by a particular legal system of law even though there is no express statement to that effect and a Lloyd's policy of marine insurance is instanced'. See also *King v Brandywise Reinsurance Co Ltd* [2004] EWHC 1033 (Comm); *RYG Baltica International (UK) Ltd v Boston Compañía de Seguros SA* [2004] EWHC 1186 (Comm).

a choice of law clause in a previous course of dealing[103] or in a related transaction between the parties;

an arbitration[104] or choice of court clause for a particular country.

Terminology; Standard Forms

13.45 The importance of the first factor may be illustrated by the common law decision in *Gill and Duffus Landauer Ltd v London Export Corp GmbH*.[105] In that case, English sellers sold shelled almonds to German buyers FAS California. Payment was due against the presentation of the documents. The contract was evidenced by written confirmation, signed by an English company which acted as brokers. This confirmation was made subject to the terms and conditions of the Dried Fruit Association of California (DFA). The DFA's terms included an arbitration clause for California. The goods were shipped in California and consigned for Hamburg. A dispute arose as to whether the goods were of the appropriate quality specified in the contract and the buyer rejected the documents. The sellers sought leave to serve proceedings outside the jurisdiction. One of the bases on which they did so was that the contract was governed by English law. Robert Goff J emphatically disagreed. The 'only' factors which pointed to England were the fact that the claimants were an English company, the brokers were in England and the defendant's holding company was an English company. In contrast, the shipment was to be made in California and the standard terms referred to in the contract were Californian. He ruled that Californian law was 'plainly'[106] the governing law.[107]

Previous Course of Dealing

13.46 The role of the second factor is illustrated by the common law case of *Kloeckner & Co AG v Gatoil Overseas Inc*.[108] The parties had concluded a large number of contracts for the purchase of cargoes of North Sea crude oil on 15 day terms. These contracts were subject to a basic agreement of

---

[103] It appears that one previous transaction between the parties containing a choice of law clause is not enough to constitute a 'course of dealing': see the first instance decision in *Iran Continental Shelf Oil Co v IRI International Corp* [2002] CLC 372.

[104] Such clauses are relatively common in the standard terms of various commodities contracts. See the examples given above, paras 3.04–06.

[105] [1982] 2 Lloyd's Rep 627. See also *Gan Insurance Co Ltd v Tai Ping Insurance Co Ltd* [1999] IL Pr 729, CA; Hill, n 100 above, at 331.

[106] [1982] 2 Lloyd's Rep 627, 629.

[107] Of course, standard form terms can only be an indicator of an implied choice of law where it is clear that both parties agreed to those terms: see the first instance decision in *Iran Continental Shelf Oil Co v IRI International Corp* [2002] CLC 372.

[108] [1982] 2 Lloyd's Rep 627–629.

terms made in June 1986. The practice of the parties was to enter into 'book out' contracts under which before the time when performance of the sales contract was due, they would agree to annul the sales contract in consideration of payment of a certain sum by one party to the other. Subsequently, from July to October 1988, the parties entered into over 150 contracts of sale under the basic agreement. This incorporated the general conditions of Shell UK for the sale of crude oil. However, these contracts were not booked out. The price of oil fell substantially and the defendants failed to pay the sum due. In November 1988, the claimants sent a telex in which they terminated all the contracts under the Shell conditions. The defendants then filed a claim for a declaration of liability in the German courts on 23 November 1988. On 25 November 1988, the claimants issued a claim form against the defendants, seeking to recover the sums due, which amounted to some $200 million, in the English courts. They obtained leave to serve out of the jurisdiction. When this leave was challenged, a number of questions of jurisdiction and *lis alibi pendens* were raised. Hirst J rejected the *lis alibi pendens* objection, finding that the courts of England were first seised of the matter. He then observed that all of the contracts of purchase and sale and the book-out agreements provided for the application of English law and the jurisdiction of the English courts.[109] However, the basic agreement itself did not contain a jurisdiction clause. Nevertheless, Hirst J found that it was governed by English law and subject to the jurisdiction of the English courts. He stated that:

I have already held that the basic agreement contemplated and provided the framework for, *inter alia*, the making of contracts between Kloeckner and Gatoil for the sale and purchase of 15 day North Sea cargoes. Such cargoes are inevitably traded on terms containing English law and jurisdiction clauses . . . and this must have been well known to Gatoil, who have actively traded in Brent crude-oil since at least 1985. It follows in my judgment that there is an overwhelmingly strong inference that the parties must have intended the basic agreement to be governed by the same law as the multifarious agreements for which it provided the framework. Moreover it seems to me wholly artificial to divorce the basic agreement from the remainder . . .[110]

The case demonstrates that the court will strive wherever reasonably possible to find that a network of mutually dependent contracts are subject to the same law. It also indicates that the existence of a trade practice will be of considerable importance to determining whether the parties impliedly chose a certain law. However, it also suggests that their

---

[109] With the consequence that (what was then) Ord 11, r 1(d)(iii) and (iv) RSC (now 6.20(5) (c) and (d) CPR) were satisfied.
[110] [1990] 1 Lloyd's Rep 177, 206.

familiarity with the industry in question is a material factor. If they are new to the industry and unaware of trade practices, it is less likely that an implied choice will be found. It would seem that the same approach should be adopted under the Rome Convention. Where the parties have experience of operating in a field where contracts of sale are habitually subject to a particular law,[111] their own silence as to the governing law may be seen as a strong inference that they are content for the law which 'normally' governs such a contract to apply.

13.47 In *Banque Paribas v Cargill International SA*,[112] the question arose as to whether a previous course of dealings between parties was relevant when the parties entered a different market for the first time. The claimant, Banque Paribas, was incorporated in France and had a London branch. It alleged that it was the valid assignee under two contracts, a sale and a 'washout' agreement.[113] The original contracting parties were Blue Energy Ltd, a company incorporated in the British Virgin Islands and operating through agents in Monaco (the assignor), and Cargill, a company incorporated in Antigua with its main oil trading branch in Geneva. The washout agreement was accepted by both parties to be governed by English law. When the buyers failed to pay, the sellers sued. This raised issues as to whether the assignment to the claimant was valid and as to whether the defendant had a right of set-off. In turn, it was argued that the resolution of these issues depended upon which was the applicable law of the contract. On this point, the claimants argued that English law governed the contract of sale, since all previous transactions between the contracting parties, Cargill and Blue, had contained an English choice of law and jurisdiction clause. The defendants, Cargill, pointed out that the previous contracts had been on CIF terms, whereas this contract was on FOB barge terms and that in that market it would be understood that Dutch law was the proper law. Parker LJ did not rule conclusively on the matter. He stated that it was 'arguable'[114] that the contract was governed by English law. However, he also stated that if the jurisdiction of the English court hinged upon this question (which, in the event, he found that it did not), it was not sufficiently arguable to make it proper to grant leave to serve the claim form out of the jurisdiction. Hence, although nothing conclusive can be gleaned from the decision, it can be said that the previous dealings of the parties will certainly not give rise to an inference to the requisite level of reasonable certainty that the same law should

---

[111] See also *Gan Insurance Co Ltd v Tai Ping Insurance Co Ltd* [1999] IL Pr 729, CA.

[112] [1992] 2 Lloyd's Rep 19.

[113] The latter agreement provided for the payment by Cargill to Blue of $30,000 in consideration of the cancellation of two contracts between the parties.

[114] [1992] 2 Lloyd's Rep 19, 25.

govern a contract between them in a new market.[115] At best, it is merely an indicator which might tilt the balance in favour of an implied choice of that law only if there are other relevant factors also pointing to that law.

It is not clear how these principles should be applied to 'string' sales con- **13.48** tracts involving successive sales of the same goods. Invariably, these contracts contain choice of law clauses. However, if, for example, the first contract in the 'string' contains a choice of law clause, but subsequent contracts are silent as to the applicable law, is there an inference that the parties to those contracts intended the same law to govern them as that which governed the first contract? One might argue that the answer should be 'no'. The contracts, although on a 'string', are separate contracts between different parties and there should be no inference that the law which happened to govern an earlier contract should bind those later parties.

However, the essence of string contracts is that they are absolutely identi- **13.49** cal save as to price.[116] The idea is that the parties are in effect dealing with *the same abstract commodity*. So, if they are in a market which entertains those expectations, then it is arguable that the parties to later contracts intend to abide by the applicable law clause in the head contract in so far as there may be a highly foreseeable likelihood that a given seller may not be the shipper.

Arbitration and Choice of Court Clauses

The third factor, an arbitration or choice of court clause, is likely to be an **13.50** especially strong,[117] although not conclusive,[118] indicator of a choice of law, at least where neither of the first two factors exists and points to a different law. In *Egon Oldendorff v Libera Corp (No 1)*,[119] there was a

---

[115] A view also supported by the decision of McCombe J at first instance in *Iran Continental Shelf Oil Co v IRI International Corp* [2002] CLC 372. Compare *SIPAL Rexons Società Italiana Prodotti Auto E Locomozione SpA v Sprl Gold's Products* [1990] IL Pr 386, 391, Court of Appeal, Mons.

[116] Possibly too the quantity, in that a contract for 30,000mt might be broken up into parcels of, for example, 10,000mt with three sub-strings developing.

[117] As in *Egon Oldendorff v Libera Corp (No 1)* [1995] 2 Lloyd's Rep 64 and *Egon Oldendorff v Libera Corp (No 2)* [1996] 1 Lloyd's Rep 380. See also the common law decision in *Compagnie Tunisienne de Navigation SA v Compagnie d'Armement Maritime SA* [1971] AC 572. This last case also suggested that, at common law, English courts would tend to infer that the applicable law of the contract was one by which the contract was valid. It is not stated that this is a relevant factor under the Rome Convention. However, it may be thought inherently unlikely that the parties would have chosen a law by which the contract was invalid. As such, one could not be 'reasonably certain' that the parties had chosen that law, as Art 3(1) requires.

[118] The Giuliano and Lagarde Report indicates that the jurisdiction clause must still be considered subject to the other terms of the contract and the circumstances of the case.

[119] [1995] 2 Lloyd's Rep 64.

claimant resident in Germany, a defendant resident in Japan, a Japanese shipbroker who acted as an intermediary and the chartered ships were to be delivered to Japan. There was also an English arbitration clause. This factor pointing to England was found to be enough to demonstrate a good arguable case[120] that the parties impliedly chose English law to govern the contract.[121]

13.51 This accords with the common law approach. For example, in *SAIL v Hind Metals Inc*[122] Hobhouse J was faced with a contract having no real objective connection to England. The seller was from Calcutta and the buyer was from New York. There were numerous objective connections to India, which was the place of conclusion, manufacture and shipment. The documents would also be presented by the sellers in Calcutta. New York was the destination of the goods. However, the parties provided that the contract should be subject to arbitration in London. Hobhouse J found this to be a conclusive indicator that English law was intended by the parties to govern the contract. His reasoning appears equally forceful today:

> The arbitration clause . . . does give rise to an inference of an intention to choose English law as the proper law and this inference is not rebutted. . . . Here the parties were choosing a neutral forum to decide their disputes and, by implication, a neutral legal system to govern their contractual relations and liabilities.[123]

> In the face of an English arbitration clause, it would take an overwhelming implication from the other terms all pointing to one single other system of law as the proper law of the contract,[124] to displace the inference that the parties intended English law to govern the contract. Indeed, it is the very fact that the contract does *not* have any objective connection to England which leads to such a strong inference that, if the parties opted for arbitration in England, they intended a wholly neutral forum, and *a wholly neutral law* to govern the contract.

---

[120] Which was all that was required for the purpose of service out of the jurisdiction. See also the decision of Clarke J on the applicable law of the contract in *Egon Oldendorff v Libera Corp (No 2)* [1996] 1 Lloyd's Rep 380.

[121] In *Marubeni Hong Kong & South China Ltd v Mongolian Govt* [2002] 2 All ER (Comm) 873, Aitken J went further still. In the face of a non-exclusive English jurisdiction clause contained in a contract, and an English choice of law clause which had been deleted during negotiations, Aitken J found that it was reasonably certain that the parties had impliedly chosen English law to govern the contract. As A Briggs, 'Decisions of British Courts During 2000: Private International Law' (2002) 73 British Ybk of Intl Law 453, 473–475 points out, the decision seems difficult to justify. Since the question of the applicable law arose in the context of service out of the jurisdiction, Briggs argues that the most one can say is that there was a good arguable case that there was an implied choice of English law. Even this, however, seems a dubious conclusion on the facts of the case. See also Hill, n 100 above, at 328, 329–330.

[122] [1984] 1 Lloyd's Rep 405.   [123] ibid, at 409.   [124] ibid.

That said, it is clear that a choice of court or arbitration clause is not in and **13.52** of itself tantamount to an implied choice of law. Imagine that the parties to a sales contract opt for arbitration in London. However, they have a previous course of dealings, which have been expressly subject to Japanese law. They have also used terminology in their contract which particularly identifies it with Japanese law. In such a circumstance, it could not be said to be demonstrated with 'reasonable certainty' that English law (or, perhaps, any law) was intended to govern the contract. In a case such as *Egon Oldendorff*, had one or more of the other, subjective factors mentioned by Giuliano and Lagarde been present and pointed to a different law to that indicated by the arbitration clause, it is unlikely that the courts would have found an implied choice of English law.

Other Factors

It is not stated by Giuliano and Lagarde that objective factors such as **13.53** currency, place of conclusion of the contract and place of performance can be considered when determining whether the parties impliedly chose a governing law of the contract. It would appear that they are only relevant in determining the applicable law in the absence of choice and in considering the application of Article 4(5).[125] It is also appears that objective factors cannot be relied upon to rebut an implied choice which otherwise appears to exist. So, if there is an English jurisdiction clause in an English standard form contract, the fact that the parties are both resident in Texas, that the contract was concluded in Ontario and was to be performed in Ontario would not dissuade the court that the parties impliedly chose English law to govern the contract.[126]

Surrounding Circumstances

It should be noted that the court is not confined to the terms of the **13.54** contract itself.[127] If it is unsure whether the parties have made a choice of law, it may look at the surrounding circumstances, such as a previous course of dealings, to satisfy itself conclusively on the matter.[128] Although the surrounding circumstances will normally operate positively to show

---

[125] Discussed below, paras 13.127–139.
[126] *Egon Oldendorff v Libera Corp (No 2)* [1996] 1 Lloyd's Rep 380.
[127] See *Gan Insurance Co Ltd v Tai Ping Insurance Co Ltd* [1999] IL Pr 729, CA; *American Motorists Insurance Co v Cellstar Corp* [2003] EWCA Civ 206, [2003] IL Pr 22, CA.
[128] Indeed, Potter LJ observed in *Aeolian Shipping SA v ISS Machinery Services Ltd* [2001] 2 Lloyd's Rep 641 that the factors to which the court may have regard in looking for an implied choice were in some respects wider than those to which it might ordinarily have regard in implying a term into a written agreement.

an implied choice of law, they need not do so. In *Land Rover Exports Ltd v Samcrete Egypt Engineers and Contractors SAE*,[129] Potter LJ indicated that, taken alone, the contract of guarantee with which it was faced may have been intended by the parties to be governed by English law, especially as the underlying contract of distribution was subject to English law. However, the circumstances of the case indicated that Land Rover had purported expressly to subject the contract to English law and that the guarantor had deleted this clause during negotiations. On this basis, the court could not hold that it was the implied intention of both parties for the contract to be governed by English law.

Implied Choice and Subsequent Conduct

13.55 In determining whether the parties made an implied choice of law, it is not certain whether the court may have regard to the conduct of the parties after conclusion of the contract. Despite common law reluctance to permit this,[130] it is suggested that any factor which sheds light on the intentions of the parties *at the time of conclusion of the contract* is one of the 'circumstances of the case'. Provided that such evidence is not used to attribute an intention to the parties that they did not have at the time of contracting, such evidence should be permitted in principle.[131]

3. WHAT LAW DECIDES IF THE PARTIES HAVE AGREED ON A CHOICE OF LAW AT ALL?

13.56 Article 3(4) states that in determining whether the parties agreed to a choice of law clause and whether that clause is valid, the rules in Articles 8, 9 and 11 should be applied. Of particular relevance is Article 8(1), which makes clear that the existence and essential validity[132] of any term of the contract is a matter for the law which would govern the contract if it were valid.[133] This means that the choice of law is pulled up by its own bootstraps. If there is a dispute between buyer and seller as to whether they agreed upon a choice of German law to govern the contract, an English court should apply German law to determine whether the parties did

---

[129] [2001] EWCA Civ 2019, [2002] CLC 533.

[130] *James Miller and Partners Ltd v Whitworth Street Estates (Manchester) Ltd* [1970] AC 583, 603; *Amin Rasheed Shipping Corp v Kuwait Insurance Co* [1984] AC 50, 69.

[131] This is also the view of Benjamin, 25–032; and of Dicey and Morris, 1216. See also Plender and Wilderspin n 1 above, 98–8; P Lagarde (1991) 80 Revue Critique de Droit International Privé 287.

[132] The formal validity of the clause will be determined by Art 9, considered below, paras 13.256–260.

[133] Subject to the limited exception in Art 8(2), which will be considered below in discussing the formation of the contract, paras 13.150–153.

indeed agree to the choice of that law.[134] If it finds that they did, then German law governs the contract; if it finds that they did not, then the applicable law of the contract must be determined[135] in the absence of choice[136] under Article 4.[137]

4. A 'BATTLE OF THE FORMS' AS TO THE GOVERNING LAW[138]

The problem of the 'battle of the forms' arises where a buyer and seller **13.57** each put forward their own differing terms during negotiations and never conclusively decide upon which set of terms applies, yet purport to perform their obligations nonetheless. In the event of a dispute arising between the parties, an obvious question arises as to which set of terms governs the contract. Although this may be a messy problem in domestic law, for choice of law purposes, the general principle is relatively clear: namely that the law putatively applicable to the contract will determine whether there is a contract, which law governs it and what the terms of the contract are.

Where one party has purported to introduce a choice of law clause in his **13.58** set of terms, say for Utopian law, and the other party has not, it may be said that Utopian law *putatively* governs the contract and that it should

---

[134] A choice might be struck down if, for example, the clause was the product of mistake, duress or undue influence. In the consumer contract context, it might also be struck down if it infringes the Unfair Terms in Consumer Contracts Regulations 1999 n 19 above. See the joined Cases C-240/98, C-241/98, C-242-98, C-243/98 and C-244/98 *Océano Grupo Editorial SA v Rocio Murciano Quintero* [2002] 1 CMLR 43, ECJ. The ECJ ruled that the Regulations allow national courts to determine whether any contractual term, including a jurisdiction clause, is unfair. See also the decision of Steel J in *Standard Bank London Ltd v Apostolakis* [2001] Lloyd's Rep Bank 240. See Withers, n 19 above; D Staudenmayer, 'The Directive on the Sale of Consumer Goods and Associated Guarantees—A Milestone in European Consumer and Private Law' (2000) 8 ERPL 547; see also the case comments on how a case such as *Océano Grupo* would have been decided by the national courts of a number of jurisdictions in (2002) 10 ERPL 157–173.

[135] Unless it is then alleged that another law was impliedly chosen. If so, the law which is alleged to have been impliedly chosen should determine whether an implied choice of law was indeed made.

[136] See the first instance decision by McCombe J in *Iran Continental Shelf Oil Co v IRI International Corp* [2002] CLC 372. Each party alleged that a different law had been chosen by the parties to govern the contract. However, McCombe J made no reference to either putative applicable law and appeared simply to apply English law rules to determine whether the parties had consented to either law applying. In the event, the conclusion reached was that neither law was chosen and the applicable law was ascertained in the absence of choice under Art 4. See further Hill, n 100 above, at 326–327.

[137] Unless it is a consumer or employment contract; in which case Arts 5 and 6 respectively apply.

[138] See G Dannemann, 'The "Battle of the Forms" and the Conflict of Laws', Ch 11 in F Rose (ed), *Lex Mercatoria—Essays on International Commercial Law in Honour of Francis Reynolds* (London: LLP, 2000) 199.

be used to decide these questions.[139] Where neither party purports to choose a governing law, it may be said that, pursuant to the presumption of characteristic performance considered below, the law of the seller's habitual residence is putatively applicable and should resolve these matters and decide which set of terms applies.

13.59 The most complex question is what should happen if the buyer includes in his terms a clause stating that the contract shall be governed by the law of Utopia, whereas the buyer includes in his terms a clause stating that the contract shall be governed by the law of Ruritania. Article 8(1) states that the law putatively applicable to the contract shall determine whether the contract is valid and what its terms are. But here, which law, Utopian or Ruritanian, is putatively applicable?

13.60 A similar problem arose in *OTM v Hydranautics*.[140] The seller's standard terms included a Californian choice of law and arbitration clause; the buyer's standard terms included a clause for arbitration 'in the UK and conducted in accordance with UK law'. Moreover, it appeared that English and Californian law would resolve the battle of the forms in different ways: English law would tend to favour the last set of terms;[141] Californian law would not.[142] In the event Parker J did not find it necessary on the facts to formulate a conflicts rule to deal with this scenario. In an unconvincing turn of reasoning, he found that at the stage where the buyer sent its purchase order containing a reference to an English arbitration clause and the application of 'UK law', the parties reached an agreement. This was notwithstanding that these terms were not expressly agreed by the parties, and notwithstanding that the seller subsequently issued a conditional acceptance, setting out its standard terms, including a Californian arbitration and choice of law clause, which the buyer signed and returned to the seller. Parker J held that all this came too late, as the parties had already concluded a contract on the buyer's terms.

13.61 There clearly was a much more complex question on the facts as to whether and when the contract was concluded and on what terms. Parker

---

[139] In accordance with Arts 3(4) and 8(1). See also *Land Rover Exports Ltd v Samcrete Egypt Engineers and Contractors SAE* [2001] EWCA Civ 2019, [2002] CLC 533.

[140] [1981] 2 Lloyd's Rep 211. See the discussion by Dannemann, n 138 above, esp 207–210. He refers also to an Austrian decision (OGH 7.6.90, Iprax 1991, 419) and a German decision (AG Kehl 6.10.95, NJW-RR 1996, 565) where similar problems arose. See also *Iran Continental Shelf Oil Co v IRI International Corp* [2002] EWCA Civ 1024. At first instance, each party had claimed that the parties had agreed upon a different law to govern the contract. McCombe J effectively simply applied English law to determine what the parties had agreed upon. In the event, the conclusion was that they had chosen neither law: see [2002] CLC 372.

[141] See *Butler Machine Tool Ltd v Ex-Cell-O Corp (England) Ltd* [1979] 1 WLR 401.

[142] Its exact approach to the resolution of the problem was not clear, save that it did *not* simply invoke the last set of terms: see the discussion by Dannemann, n 138 above, 208

J did not consider which of the two putative applicable laws, English and Californian law, determined these issues. A plausible approach to the resolution of such questions is offered by Dannemann.[143] He points out that whether the parties agreed to the choice of Californian law should today be determined by the law of California, in accordance with Articles 3(4) and 8(1) of the Rome Convention. English law should likewise decide whether the parties agreed upon a choice of English law. In other words, at this stage, both laws are putatively applicable. If one law finds that its own law was agreed upon and the other does not, there is no true conflict and the law agreed upon should govern the contract and determine its validity and its terms. If neither law considers that the parties agreed to a choice of its law, then the parties did not choose any law and the applicable law should be determined as in the absence of choice under Article 4. But if both laws consider the choice of the choice of law clauses for their respective laws as agreed upon by the parties, the stalemate remains. In that scenario, Dannemann contends that Article 3(1) has the effect that neither choice should be accepted, since 'two different choices of law within the same contract cannot be considered "express" or "certain" '.[144] However, the present authors would disagree. Both choices are apparently 'express' and both laws are sufficiently 'certain' that the parties designated their legal system to apply to the contract. Moreover, it is clear that if one party designates the law of Utopia to govern the contract and the other the law of Ruritania, rejecting both choices may defeat the expectation of both parties, and any third parties relying upon the contract. In other words, the fact that both parties cannot have their preferences respected is not obviously a sound reason for saying that we should respect neither. Accordingly, it is suggested that in this circumstance, the law of the forum should determine which of the two laws was agreed upon, applying its own rules of the battle of the forms. True, this is an imperfect solution. The Rome Convention very much suppresses the role of the forum in determining the consent to a choice of law; and reliance on the law of the forum raises an obvious forum shopping objection. However, the law of the forum steps in to deal with the fact that there are two laws apparently 'agreed' upon by the parties, according to the choice of law rules of the Convention. The law of the forum is simply playing a residual and mediating role of trying to make sense of the Rome

---

[143] ibid, 209 10. See also Peel, n 53 above, 15 047.

[144] ibid, 210. One might also support Dannemann's position by reference to the decision of the ECJ in Case 12/76 *Industrie Tessili Italiana Como v Dunlop AG* [1976] ECR 1473. In that case, the order form contained standard terms which included the designation of a particular forum. The acceptance (the invoice) contained standard terms which included the designation of a different forum. The ECJ ruled that there was, accordingly, no written agreement upon the courts of a particular forum for the purposes of (what was then) Art 17 of the Brussels Convention.

Convention's choice of law rules. In England, this is likely to favour the application of the law contained in the last set of terms laid down.

5. STRIKING DOWN THE CHOICE OF LAW CLAUSE

13.62 The choice of law clause, like any other term of the contract, or the contract itself, is subject to the rules which safeguard the consent of the parties in Article 8[145] and to the provisions concerning mandatory rules and public policy in the Convention.[146] However, it is less certain when, if ever, a court would be justified in striking down a choice of law, simply because they regard the choice made as unacceptable. One might expect this only to be permitted in the most exceptional of circumstances, since it is a framework rule of the Convention that the parties may choose the law that they desire, even if it has no objective connection to the contract.

13.63 Despite this, the appellate court of Düsseldorf has, more than once, invoked mandatory rule provisions in order to justify striking down what appeared to be a freely agreed[147] choice of English law to govern a consumer contract.[148] Instead, it imposed German law as the governing law of the contract. A German individual was approached by a German company which advertised the services of a British broker. The broker employed the German company to promote the broker on the German futures market. The German individual concluded a contract with the broker which contained an English choice of law clause. The court held that the choice of law clause was invalid for a number of reasons. First, Article 31(2), EGBGB provides, in similar terms to Article 8(2) of the Rome Convention,[149] that a party may rely upon the law of his habitual residence to demonstrate that no contract was concluded. Second, Article 29(1), EGBGB, in similar terms to Article 5 of the Rome Convention, provides that a consumer contract containing a choice of law clause shall not deprive the consumer of the mandatory rules of his habitual residence.[150]

---

[145] Considered below, paras 13.143–155.   [146] Below, paras 13.271–300.

[147] This is not wholly clear. On one view, the court regarded the clause as not agreed by the parties at all. However, the case is objectionable in that it goes beyond this and strikes down the clause, even if it was agreed upon, as 'unusual' and therefore not part of the contract, in accordance with s 3 of the AGBG, which deals with standard form contracts.

[148] Case 17 U 129/93, decision of 14 January 1994; ZIP 4/1994, 288. J Schmidt, 'The Invalidity of Certain Choices of Law Clauses under German Law' [1995] JBL 308. The court reaffirmed its stance in *Re Futures Transactions* [1998] IL Pr 327, where it also struck down an English arbitration clause for similar reasons.

[149] Which is discussed when considering the formation of contracts below, paras 13.150–153.

[150] Provided also that pre-conditions such as are found in Art 5 of the Rome Convention are also met.

Third, the German Law on General Terms and Conditions, AGBG, was held to be a set of mandatory rules which could not be derogated from by choosing a different law to govern the contract. In particular, s 3 states that conditions which are so abnormal that a person entering into a contract would not typically expect to find them are not regarded as constituting part of the contract. The English choice of law clause, contained in a contract precipitated by a German company approaching a German individual and concluded in Germany, was such an unusual clause that it should be struck down.

Although the decision was confined to consumer contracts[151] involving **13.64** the provision of a service, it is a troubling one. If the court had found only that, in the circumstances, it was unreasonable to determine the purchaser's consent by English law alone, and that by the law of his habitual residence, Germany, he did not consent to the clause *at all*, that would be quite unobjectionable.[152] But the court also held that, regardless of the Convention's rules on *consent*, such a clause was sufficiently 'unusual' that it should be struck down. Moreover, whilst the Rome Convention preserves the application of mandatory rules, including those of consumer protection,[153] these are to be *superimposed* onto the governing law. There is no provision which states that they can override the framework rules of the Convention itself. This is what the court effectively did, since it did not preserve the application of English law but also require compliance with certain German consumer protection rules; rather, it ruled that it was a mandatory rule of German law that the choice of law would be rejected in such circumstances. This is effectively to allow the AGBG to trump the framework rules of the Rome Convention, which clearly respects any choice of law between the parties to which they consented and requires Contracting States to give effect to the choice. Accordingly, it is suggested that the correct interpretation of the Rome Convention is that the choice of law by the parties may be fettered by the need to comply with certain mandatory rules of another law specified by the Convention; but no court should use its mandatory rules to strike down the choice of law altogether, if the evidence is that the parties did indeed consent to that clause.[154]

---

[151] And only then when they met the conditions of Art 5 of the Rome Convention.
[152] Art 8(2) of the Rome Convention sanctions this.
[153] Under the provisions of Art 5.
[154] In *Re Futures Transactions* [1998] IL Pr 327, the court also struck down the 'unusual' English arbitration clause. To the present authors, the decision on this point is equally objectionable. Moreover a consumer who does consent to a contract containing an English arbitration and choice of law clause might legitimately be said to have made a rod for their own back and be expected to abide, at least to some degree, by these decisions.

6. The Need to Choose the Law of a Recognized Legal System; Freezing a Choice of Law in Time; Meaningless Choice of Law

Recognized Legal System

13.65 It seems that the parties must choose the law of a recognized legal system in force at the time of contracting.[155] This means that a choice of the *lex mercatoria* to govern a contract would be ineffective in an English court.[156] This would result in the applicable law being determined in the absence of choice.[157]

13.66 In the case of arbitration agreements, which fall outside the scope of the Rome Convention,[158] there is a long tradition of arbitrators being empowered to dispose of disputes according to principles and provisions that do not represent state law, for example, general principles of law, the *lex mercatoria* and so on. In such cases, English law, for example, recognizes the binding character of such an arbitral reference.[159] This is reinforced by the express language of the Arbitration Act 1996.[160]

---

[155] See *Shamil Bank of Bahrain EC v Beximco Pharmaceuticals Ltd* [2004] EWCA Civ 19, where the application of Sharian law was rejected. See, in particular, at [48], per Potter LJ. See also Dicey and Morris, 1223. Compare the position at common law in *Amin Rasheed Corp v Kuwait Insurance Co* [1984] AC 50, 60, 65. Lord Diplock was clear that the proper law of a contract had to be a system of law, when he said that 'contracts are incapable of existing in a legal vacuum' and 'are mere pieces of paper devoid of all legal effect unless they are made by reference to some system of private law . . .'. See also *EI Du Pont de Nemours v Agnew* [1982] 2 Lloyd's Rep 592, 595, CA.

[156] But it would be effective in arbitration, by virtue of s 46(1)(b) of the Arbitration Act 1996. Compare the Inter-American Convention on the Law Applicable to International Contracts 1994. As Cheshire and North, 560, note, this seems implicitly to sanction a choice of the lex mercatoria in Arts 3, 9 and 10.

[157] Benjamin, 25–029, argues that once the law applicable in the absence of choice has been determined, that law should then determine if a choice of the *lex mercatoria* is effective. However, this is by no means clearly correct. The argument in its favour would be that if that law sanctions the choice of the *lex mercatoria*, it does so because this *is* part of that legal system. Against this, however, it does seem to undermine the principle in Art 3(1) that the law which governs the contract must be a recognized body of legal rules which apply in a particular state. On balance, it is suggested that a choice of the *lex mercatoria* is ineffective for all purposes under the Rome Convention.

[158] Art 1(2)(d).

[159] *Deutsche Schachtbau- und Tiefbohrgesellscaft mbH v Ras Al Khaimah National Oil Co* [1987] 2 All ER 769, 778–79 (*per* Donaldson MR—'internationally accepted principles of law governing contractual relations'). The arbitration had been conducted under ICC Rules enabling the parties to 'determine the law to be applied by the arbitrator' (Art 13(3)). See also *Home and Overseas Insurance Co Ltd v Mentor Insurance Co (UK) Ltd* [1989] 3 All ER 74, 84–85, CA.

[160] An arbitrator may decide a dispute either 'in accordance with the law chosen by the parties as applicable to the dispute' or 'in accordance with such other considerations as are agreed by them or determined by the tribunal' (s 46(1)(b)). This latter formula is very wide.

Freezing the Law in Time

It seems equally clear that the parties cannot provide that the law of state **13.67**
X applies 'as it stood on 1 January 2004', ignoring any changes to the
content of that legal system after that date.[161] The argument against
freezing the applicable law in time is akin to that which prevents choice
of anational law. The connecting factor employed under the Rome Convention allows the parties to choose to subject the contract to a particular
legal system but they must choose a system which exists in a particular
state and must also apply that state's domestic law as it would be applied
from time to time in the selected legal system.[162]

It might be argued that such a choice is shorthand for the parties **13.68**
excluding, *inter se*, any new provisions of the chosen law. This might suggest that it is the chosen law, the law of State X, which should determine
whether a clause which 'freezes' the law in time is valid and effective.
However, it appears that the Rome Convention autonomously determines
that a choice of law clause which freezes the law in time is invalid.[163]

Meaningless Choice of Law

It should be noted that even where the parties have clearly intended to **13.69**
choose a governing law, such a choice will be ineffective if the choice is
essentially meaningless. In *Compagnie D'Armement Maritime SA v Cie
Tunisienne de Navigation SA*,[164] the parties chose the law of the flag to
govern a contract for the carriage of oil, even though the goods in question were to be shipped by a number of ships carrying different flags. The
Court of Appeal[165] felt unable to determine to which law the clause
referred. The House of Lords accepted the principle that a meaningless
clause cannot be given effect. However, it demonstrated that it would
strive to determine what the parties meant, if at all possible. On the facts,

---

[161] Dicey and Morris, 1223–4; *Rossano v Manufacturers' Life Ins Co* [1963] 2 QB 352, 362.

[162] 'The prevailing view is that the selection of the law by the parties supplies the connecting factor under the law of the forum, which thereupon will apply the law, as it stands at the
relevant time, to determine the rights and liability of the contract': P Nygh, *Autonomy in
International Contracts* (Oxford Monographs in Private International Law: Clarendon Press,
1999) 63. See also F Mann, 'The Time Element in the Conflict of Laws' (1954) 32 British Ybk of
Intl Law 217; J Morris, 'The Time Factor in the Conflict of Laws' (1966) 15 ICLQ 422; J
Grodecki, 'Conflict of Laws in Time' (1959) 35 British Ybk of Intl Law 58; E Spiro, 'The
Incidence of Time in the Conflict of Laws' (1969) 19 ICLQ 357.

[163] This should be contrasted with the incorporation of *terms* found in a particular legal
system, which may, it seems, be incorporated as they stood at a particular time. This is
because incorporation is a means of stipulating those rights and obligations intended by the
parties to govern the contract.

[164] [1971] AC 572. The case is fully considered by Cheshire and North, 559.

[165] [1969] 1 WLR 1338.

it found that the parties had chosen French law, as the law of the flag of the ships primarily responsible for carriage of the oil.

7. APPLICATION OF THE VIENNA CONVENTION

Choice of the Law of a State which is Party to the Vienna Convention[166]

Effect in a forum which is a Contracting State to the Vienna Convention[167]

13.70 One question that has emerged in the case law concerns the significance of a choice of law clause in the contract selecting as the applicable law the law of a state that happens to be a Contracting State to the Vienna Convention. The parties might choose the law of a Contracting State where otherwise the Vienna Convention is applicable because the parties are resident in different Contracting States to the Vienna Convention. If their choice, as interpreted by the forum of a Contracting State to the Vienna Convention, were to lead to the Vienna Convention by way of Article 1(1)(b), then the result would be the same as if the applicable law clause had been disregarded and the Vienna Convention applied by way of Article 1(1)(a).

13.71 Where they are resident in different states, where neither or only one of these is a Contracting State to the Vienna Convention, the effect of that choice[168] in a forum that accepts the autonomy of the parties to select their own applicable law is that where the forum is a Contracting State to the Vienna Convention, it will be bound to apply that Convention on the basis of Article 1(1)(b).[169]

Effect in a forum which is a non-Contracting State to the Vienna Convention

13.72 If the forum is not a Contracting State to the Vienna Convention, such as England, the position is more difficult. This forum is under no obligation to apply the Vienna Convention directly. The Vienna Convention could only be reached by way of the forum's private international law rules (an approach similar to the Article 1(1)(b) route taken by Contracting States to the Vienna Convention). This would mean giving effect to the clause as

---

[166] See paras 16.28–31 and 16.128–136 on the Vienna Convention for further discussion.

[167] If the law chosen is the law of a non-Contracting State to the Vienna Convention, there should be no real difficulty: Art 6 of the Vienna Convention permits its own ouster, thus avoiding any inconsistency with any rule of national or treaty origin compelling recognition of the parties' choice of an applicable law. A clearer implied exclusion of the Vienna Convention could hardly be imagined. It should be respected, even if only to avoid an unnecessary conflict between the Vienna Convention and the Rome Convention.

[168] Subject to what precisely they mean by the selection clause: see the discussion of the construction of a clause for a Contracting State to the Vienna Convention, below, paras 13.77–82.

[169] On the inter-relationship of the Vienna Convention and the Rome Convention and which prevails in the case of conflict, see below, paras 16.96–113.

leading into the Vienna Convention in so far as the forum respects the parties' freedom to choose their own applicable law.

Effect in a forum which is a non-Contracting State to the Vienna Convention: is the forum ever bound to apply the Vienna Convention?[170]

It might appear that where the English court's choice of law rules point **13.73** to the application of a state which applies the Vienna Convention, all is relatively straightforward. Indeed, sometimes, there will be no meaningful 'conflict' of laws, because, the parties have their places of business in different Contracting States to the Vienna Convention, States X and Y and, on any view, one of these two states' law is applicable.

However, Benjamin casts doubt upon whether an English court is ever **13.74** obliged to apply the Vienna Convention, even if the law of the state identified by the Rome Convention would do so on the facts. The authors point out that Article 21 of the Rome Convention[171] only preserves the application of Conventions to which Contracting States are, or become, parties. Given that the United Kingdom is *not* a party to the Vienna Convention, it could be argued that its application is not required in the United Kingdom.[172]

Cogent though this argumentation is, it is suggested that the conclusions **13.75** to which it leads should be rejected for several reasons. First, Article 21 is primarily concerned with preserving the application of other instruments governing choice of law. Whilst the Vienna Convention does contain private international law aspects, it is essentially a substantive law Convention. Second, an English court which applies the Vienna Convention in the circumstances described is not doing so directly, but because this *is* the content of the law of the state whose law the Rome Convention designates. Third, if an English court were to refuse to apply the Vienna Convention in such circumstances, then it would have to apply the national law of the state identified. However, states which are party to the Vienna Convention would apply the Vienna Convention on the facts. This would undermine the uniform application of the Rome Convention, to which Article 18 expressly refers. It would also introduce forum shopping opportunities for the parties. Finally, it would mean that an exporter would potentially have to satisfy both the requirements of the Vienna Convention and of national law, so creating a disincentive to free

---

[170] See also below, paras 16.98–113.   [171] On which, see below, paras 16.98–113.
[172] Benjamin, 25–026. The same argument is made by Dicey and Morris, 1331, who comment that: 'It is possible to construe Art 21 of the Rome Convention as rendering international conventions applicable, even in this circumstance, only as between Contracting States which are parties thereto. If the latter view is correct, then since the United Kingdom is not a party to the United Nations Convention, the law applicable to a contract of sale, if that of a foreign country which is a party to the United Nations Convention, will be the contract law of that country, excluding the rules of the latter Convention'.

movement. For all of these reasons, the present authors contend that if the rules of the state identified by the Rome Convention's choice of law rules lead to the application of the Vienna Convention, then an English court must apply the Vienna Convention to resolve the dispute.[173]

13.76 This then raises the question of how the English court should construe, for example, the parties' choice of 'French law' to govern their contract. This arguably gives rise to problems of renvoi, in so far as, if a French forum were to apply the Vienna Convention in a case falling outside Article 1(1)(a),[174] it would perforce be applying the Vienna Convention directly pursuant to its private international law rules, as directed by Article 1(1)(b), since that is the only other way that it could end up applying the Convention. It is argued elsewhere[175] that a Contracting State, applying the Convention because its private international law rules lead to the law of another Contracting State, is not as such infringing any prohibition on renvoi. The same argument does not apply in quite the same terms in the present case, where the forum is in a non-Contracting State to the Vienna Convention. Nevertheless, if an English court is bound to apply French law pursuant to the Rome Convention (and therefore bound also to respect the prohibition on renvoi),[176] it could fairly be said that the French *internal* law for sales of an international character is the Vienna Convention. As such, the English court should apply the Vienna Convention. This is the domestic law of the state to which the Rome Convention's choice of law rules point.

Construction of a choice of law clause for a Contracting State to the
Vienna Convention

13.77 The remaining question is what do the parties mean when they stipulate that the *law* of a country, which happens to be a Contracting State to the Vienna Convention, shall apply to their contract? Clauses of this sort are highly ambiguous.[177] Do they signify an intention to select the domestic law of that state minus the Vienna Convention?

---

[173] No such difficulties would arise if the applicable law is that of a state which is party to the Uniform Law on the International Sale of Goods 1964 (ULIS). This contains rules of substantive law which an English court may apply, if the requirements for application of ULIS are met: see below, paras 13.95–98 and 16.12–15. See also Peel, n 53 above, 15–017.

[174] Which applies where the parties are resident in different Contracting States to the Vienna Convention.

[175] See below, paras 16.28–31, on the Vienna Convention.

[176] Art 15 of the Rome Convention: see below, para 13.141.

[177] See the following recommended clause, for parties seeking the application of domestic law, in Art 14(a) of the UN Model Contract . . .: 'This law is governed by the domestic law of _____ (country)'. See the criticism of Klotz, 'Critical Review of The ICC Model International Sale Contract' (www.cisg.law.pace.edu/cisg/biblio/klotz.html), who suggests adding: 'The application of the CISG is expressly excluded'.

This question has been treated by the Austrian Oberster Gerichtshof[178] as **13.78** one of the hierarchy of norms within the designated state with the Vienna Convention ranking above the rules of domestic sale law. With respect, this is a fundamentally misconceived approach to the matter. In view of the freedom given to the parties to oust the application of the Vienna Convention, the matters to be considered are, first, whether the Convention may be excluded by implication or must be excluded expressly, and second, whether the parties by designating a national law have thereby indicated an intention to exclude the Convention in favour of the rules applicable to non-international sale transactions.[179]

The provision in the Uniform Law on International Sale of Goods 1964[180] **13.79** equivalent to Article 6 of the Vienna Convention referred to above is Article 3, which makes it clear that exclusion need not be express. It states that: 'The parties to a contract of sale shall be free to exclude the application thereto of the present Law either entirely or partially. Such exclusion may be express or implied.'

However, in the Vienna Convention context, a number of tribunals have **13.80** rejected in principle the possibility of implied exclusion.[181] However, they are to be faulted for their failure to look at the history of the Convention. The better view, in a Convention that eschews formal requirements for a contract of sale, is that the parties may achieve by implied means an exclusion or derogation from the provisions of the Vienna Convention.[182] The clarity of an implied exclusion is of course a different matter.

---

[178] Judgment of 22 October 2001. The court declined to regard the selection of a national law as tantamount to the exclusion of the UN Sale Convention under Art 6: 'The choice of law without an explicit declaration that the Convention be excluded does not constitute an implicit exclusion, and because the CISG is a part of the chosen law, it is therefore included in the referral, and takes precedence over the non-unified law which would otherwise be applicable...'.

[179] The choice of a Contracting State's law might in certain cases indicate an intention to opt into only a part of the Convention, for example, where that state has made a declaration under Art 92 that it will not be bound by Part II of the Convention (formation). Again, the choice of a state's law may be significant where the states of the seller's and buyer's residence have made a declaration under Art 94 that the Convention (or Part II or Part III of it) shall not apply as between them. If the Contracting Parties then choose as the applicable law the law of a third state which has not made such a declaration, then the clause should be interpreted in the courts of any Contracting State making an Art 94 declaration as providing for the application of the UN Sale Convention to the contract. See the discussion of declarations and reservations below, paras 16.121–145.

[180] See also below, paras 13.95–98 and 16.12–15.

[181] See Landgericht Landshut of 5 April 1995 (translated at http://cisgw3.law.pace.edu/cases/950495g1.html); International Court of Commercial Arbitration (Chamber of Commerce & Industry of the Russian Federation) of 24 January 2000 (Case No 054/1999) (translated at http://cisgw3.law.pace.edu/cases/000124r1.html).

[182] For those states making a declaration under Art 96, implied derogation might give rise to difficulties in some cases (for example, informal modification). See the discussion of Art 96 of the Vienna Convention, below, paras 16.137–141.

13.81 So the question that has to be faced is what the parties mean when they select the law of a Contracting State to the Vienna Convention to govern the contract. The question is not easy and depends upon varied circumstances. Nevertheless, the case law heavily favours the view that they do not intend thereby to opt out of the Vienna Convention under Article 6. First of all, if they are not resident in different Contracting States to the Vienna Convention, the selection of the law of a Contracting State is the most effective way of reaching the Vienna Convention since it brings them in under Article 1(1)(b). It would take quite compelling additional evidence to show that their intention was to oust the Vienna Convention in this instance. In the case of a contract entered into on a standard form predating the entry into force of the Vienna Convention in 1988, the use of such a form should not of itself indicate a contrary intention under Article 6. The use of a standard form postdating the entry into force of the Vienna Convention advances the cause of implied exclusion a little further. The same arguments apply, *mutatis mutandis*, to the use of forms selecting as the applicable law one that is not the law of a Contracting State to the Vienna Convention at the time the form is published but which has become so by the time the parties use the form for their particular contractual adventure.[183] If the applicable law clause is bespoke for the present contractual adventure, then the argument that this amounts to implied exclusion acquires yet more substance, at least if the parties are resident in different Contracting States to the Vienna Convention.[184]

13.82 The position is very difficult to unravel and the only practical advice to give is that parties, if seeking to avoid the application of the Vienna Convention, should do as is done by the various commodities trading forms and exclude the Convention in express terms. However inadvisable it might be to seek such a result impliedly by reference to a stated national law, sound contractual practice should not be necessary as a matter of law for the Vienna Convention to be excluded between the parties.

The impact of the reservation permitted by Article 95 of the Vienna Convention

13.83 If the parties do not have their places of business in different Contracting States to the Vienna Convention, difficulty may arise, since the application of the Vienna Convention then hinges upon Article 1(1)(b) thereof and whether the conflicts rules point to the law of a Contracting State to the Vienna Convention. However, not all Contracting States to the Vienna Convention are bound by Article 1(1)(b). Contracting States to the Vienna

---

[183] Subject to the point made about Art 1(1)(b) below, paras 16.28–31 and 16.39–41.
[184] The temptation to confuse applicable law and jurisdiction clauses should be resisted. Hence, it is no argument to say that the parties chose Dutch law not on its own merits but because they wished any disputes to go before the Dutch courts.

Convention have the right to opt out of the application of Article 1(1)(b), pursuant to Article 95.[185] China, Singapore, St Vincent and Grenadines and the United States have done this.[186] In such states, the scope of the Vienna Convention is determined by Article 1(1)(a).

Suppose now that a dispute arises in an English court between an English **13.84** buyer and a New York seller. The English court finds that New York law governs the contract by applying the rules of the Rome Convention. However, the United States has entered the reservation in Article 95. It is suggested that an English court should apply the national law of New York, rather than the rules of the Vienna Convention. The Rome Convention tells the English court to apply the internal law of New York. On the facts, New York law decrees that the Vienna Convention does not apply.[187] Any other approach would distort the application of New York law and potentially create opportunities for forum shopping.

However, this may not be the position in a forum which is party to the **13.85** Vienna Convention and which has not itself entered the reservation in Article 1(1)(b). Bridge takes the example of a contract between a New York buyer and an English seller, where proceedings take place in the Netherlands. Suppose that the Dutch Court finds that New York law governs the contract according to its rules of private international law.[188] The United States has made the Article 1(1)(b) reservation, but the Netherlands has not (and has not pledged to respect the US reservation). One could argue that the forum should apply the internal law of the state whose law is identified; and if the state identified would not itself apply the Vienna Convention on the facts, because it has opted out of Article 1(1)(b), then neither should the forum. However, Bridge argues that the Dutch court *should* apply the rules of the Vienna Convention on the facts, and not the domestic law of New York. True, a New York court would not apply the Convention on the facts. However, the Netherlands has not made the reservation, and so has pledged to apply the Vienna Convention where its rules of private international law point to *the law of a Contracting State* (not to the law of a Contracting State which would, on the facts, itself apply the Vienna Convention). This has the consequence that an English

---

[185] For discussion of other reservations and declarations under the Vienna Convention, see below, paras 16.121–127 and 16.137–145.

[186] There is some doubt as to whether the reservation initially entered by Czechoslovakia now applies in the Czech Republic and in Slovakia. It appears that it does apply to these states. For more details on the reservations made by Contracting States to the Vienna Convention, see www.cisg.law.pace.edu/cisg/countries/cntries.html.

[187] This is *not* tantamount to application of the doctrine of renvoi, which is prohibited by Art 15 of the Rome Convention. It is a question of determining what the *internal* law of New York is on the facts. It does not involve a reference to the choice of law rules of New York.

[188] Bridge, *The International Sale of Goods*, 2.44.

court would apply the national law of New York on the facts, whilst a Dutch court would apply the Vienna Convention.[189] This, in turn, does tend to undermine Article 18 of the Rome Convention, which urges states to have regard to the international character of the Convention and the desirability of achieving uniformity in its interpretation and application.[190]

Direct Choice of the Vienna Convention

Nature of difficulty

13.86 A related question is what should happen if the parties to a contract of sale do not make a choice of legal system to apply to the contract, but seek directly to apply the Vienna Convention, as where they state that 'this contract shall be governed by the rules of law contained in the Vienna Convention'. Such an express selection may cause difficulties whether or not the forum state is a party to the Vienna Convention.

13.87 The parties might directly choose the Vienna Convention because, for example: the contract is for a type of sale excluded from the scope of the Vienna Convention, such as the sale of a ship; or it might be between parties who are resident in the same state so that the contract fails to pass the international test laid down in Article 1(1)(a) of the Vienna Convention; or the parties might use this expedient instead of expressly choosing the law of a state that has adopted the Vienna Convention; or the contract might be not a contract of sale at all as defined by the Convention. The last case occurred indirectly in a Dutch case where the contract of engagement was between the owner of a painting attributed to a named artist and an auctioneer. The agreement was that the rules applicable to contracts of sale were also applicable to the agreement between the parties as far as 'material and juridical defects' of the painting destined to be auctioned were concerned. Although the Convention was not specifically named as the applicable law, the parties were resident in different Convention States so the Dutch court at first instance applied the Convention to the owner's liability in respect of non-conforming goods.[191] This was reversed by an appellate court, on the ground that the parties had incorporated a set of standard terms invoking German law in terms that excluded the application of the Convention.[192] Consequently, the question whether parties

---

[189] See further below, paras 16.128–136.

[190] See also P Winship, 'Private International Law and the U.N. Sales Convention' [1988] Cornell Intl LJ 487; cf J Honnold, *Uniform Law for International Sales under the 1980 United Nations Convention* (2nd edn, Deventer: Kluwer, 1990) 84–94.

[191] Arnhem District Court of 17 July 1997 (www.unilex.info via http://cisgw3.law. pace.edu/ cases/970717n1.html).

[192] Arnhem Appellate Court of 9 February 1999 (www.unilex.info via http://cisgw3.law. pace.edu/cases/990209n1.html).

might select the Convention for a non-sale contract was not tested in the higher court.

The role of the Rome Convention

However the issue might arise, its resolution is not to be determined **13.88** within the Vienna Convention itself. Rather, the question is whether the forum's rules of private international law recognize such a choice. We have seen that Article 1(1) of the Rome Convention is clear in stating that the Convention applies 'in any situation involving a choice between the laws of different countries'.[193] The Vienna Convention is not a system of law and is part of a system of law only to the extent that it is incorporated in the domestic law of a system of law selected by a choice of law rule. It could accordingly be argued that the parties cannot under the Rome Convention opt into the Vienna Convention.

Incorporation by reference?

Nonetheless, where the forum is England, it is suggested that a direct **13.89** choice of the Vienna Convention should be accepted. The Vienna Convention contains a detailed set of rules which command very wide acceptance around the world as a body of substantive contract rules. It is of central importance to the sales law of many states. Moreover, failure to respect the choice will defeat the expectations of the parties. The problem can be largely side-stepped if it can be argued that the clause contained in the parties' contract involves the incorporation by reference of the set of terms contained in the Vienna Convention, i.e. that it is simply a shorthand for a series of contractual terms which the parties could individually have included in their contract.[194] The provisions of the law which would apply but for the choice of the Vienna Convention are ousted, at least in so far as that 'default' law permits its own provisions to be displaced by terms agreed by the parties.[195]

Of course, the Vienna Convention does not exhaustively determine all **13.90** issues of contract law which might arise between the parties. The question arises as to which law should 'plug the gaps' in the above example. It is suggested that the choice of 'the Vienna Convention' should be regarded as introducing a potential 'splitting' of the contract. With regard to the remaining issues, it should be asked whether the parties have made an

---

[193] See also Giuliano and Lagarde Report, 10: 'It must be stressed that the uniform rules apply . . . only "in situations involving a choice between the law of different countries" '.

[194] In support of the view that the parties may choose the law of the Vienna Convention where that Convention does not apply directly under its Art 1(1), see the Dutch Supreme Courts' decisions: Hoge Raad 26.5.1989, NJ 1992.105 and 5.1.2001, NJ 2001.391.

[195] Compare *Shamil Bank of Bahrain EC v Beximco Pharmaceuticals Ltd* [2004] EWCA Civ 19, esp at [50]–[52], *per* Potter LJ.

express or an implied choice of law;[196] if they have not, then the applicable law for those residuary issues should be determined in the absence of choice.

Other possible approaches

13.91 There is a less advanced position which pays some heed to the parties' choice of a non-systemic body of law. Suppose that a contract is before the courts of New York in circumstances where, if the parties' choice of the Vienna Convention is not recognized, the contract will be held subject to English law. The express choice clause could be regarded as a shorthand way of excluding all provisions of the English law of sale that are capable of being excluded and that are inconsistent with their counterpart rules in the Vienna Convention. This would create space for the insertion in the contract of terms based upon those rules in the Convention. The same approach would be appropriate too where contracting parties opt into the Vienna Convention in a case where the Convention on its own terms does not apply, for example, where a ship or electricity is being sold. In the former case, it would be more straightforward for the parties to select as the applicable law the law of a Contracting State.

13.92 There is also another means by which parties, arguably, might seek to contract into the Vienna Convention in circumstances where it would not otherwise apply. Article 6 of the Vienna Convention permits the contracting parties to 'vary the effect of any of [the] provisions' of the Convention. Could they, for example, vary Article 2 of the Vienna Convention in the case of the sale of a ship so as to render the Convention applicable to their sale contract? Or could they transform their work and materials contract into a contract of sale by altering the test for excluded contracts in Article 3 of the Vienna Convention? It has been argued that the latter expedient is possible.[197] If this correct, then there is every reason why parties should be free to alter Article 2 of the Vienna Convention so as to bring ship sales within the Vienna Convention. And if this also is possible, why should they not be free to depart from Article 5 so as to extend the Vienna Convention to personal injuries, or even modify Article 1 so that the Convention applies on the basis of their different nationalities? It is submitted that Article 6 cannot be read literally and that it should be confined in its

---

[196] In this regard, the choice of the Vienna Convention might itself be evidence as to the system of national law impliedly chosen to govern the residue of the contract. This would only be the case where the contract has connections only to one State Party to the Vienna Convention, or to one State which is party to the Vienna Convention and another that is not. It would not assist where there are connections to two or more States Party to the Vienna Convention, since it would not reveal which of the States' national laws is to apply.

[197] P Schlechtriem, *Uniform Sale Law—The UN Convention on the International Sale of Goods* (Vienna: 1986) 31 (available in full text form at www.cisg.law.pace.edu).

effect to Parts II and III of the Vienna Convention and not extend to Part I ('Sphere of Application and General Provisions') and Part IV ('Final Provisions'). Article 6 presupposes that the parties are contracting parties under the Vienna Convention: if they are not under the Convention, then they cannot avail themselves of the freedom given by Article 6.[198] In the work and materials case, however, the parties could go part way towards Vienna Convention coverage by splitting one contract into two so as to create separate contracts of sale and for services.

Choice of the Law of a State Minus the Rules of the Vienna Convention

What if the parties choose the law of a state which *is* party to the Vienna **13.93** Convention[199] to govern a contract, but specifically stipulate that they want the domestic law of that state to govern the contract and *not* the rules of the Vienna Convention? This may be the case in certain standard form contracts. For example, clause 28 of the Federation of Oils, Seeds and Fats Associations Ltd standard FOB terms (FOFSA)[200] and clause 33 of the Grain and Feed Trade Association (GAFTA) contract no 100 on Shipment of Feedingstuffs in Bulk Tale Quale on CIF terms[201] specifically state that the Vienna Convention does not apply to the contract.

It is suggested that such a choice must be upheld. The Vienna Convention **13.94** is not of mandatory application in Contracting States. Article 6 of the Vienna Convention permits the parties to disapply the Convention in whole or in part.[202] If they do so, then the domestic law of the state identified will apply.[203]

Choice of Law and the Uniform Law on International Sale of Goods 1964 (ULIS) and Uniform Law on the Formation of Contracts for the International Sale of Goods 1964 (ULFIS)

ULIS and ULFIS were enacted into English law by the Uniform Laws **13.95** on International Sales Act 1967. Their practical impact today is very marginal. ULIS would apply if the parties to the sales contract stipulated that it should apply[204] and, as Benjamin notes, '. . . in practice such a choice is rarely, if ever, made'.[205] Indeed, standard form contracts may, for

---

[198] This argument does not go so far as to prevent the parties to a Convention contract from modifying Art 5.
[199] And which has not entered a reservation as to the application of Art 1(1)(b).
[200] These can be found in Bridge, *The International Sale of Goods*, appendix 1, 448, 455.
[201] These can be found in ibid, appendix 2, 456, 466.
[202] Subject to Art 12. [203] A view endorsed by Schlechtriem, 55.
[204] s 1(3) of the Uniform Laws on International Sales Act 1967.
[205] Benjamin, 25–003, n 14.

the avoidance of doubt, specifically exclude ULIS. For example, clause 28 of the FOFSA standard FOB terms[206] and clause 33 of GAFTA contract no 100[207] specifically state that ULIS does not apply to the contract.

13.96 Moreover, even if a choice of ULIS is made, Article 1 of that Convention[208] states that it only applies if the parties have their places of business in different Contracting States to the Convention and: (a) the contract involves the sale of goods which are at the time of conclusion of the contract in the course of carriage or will be carried from the territory of one state to the territory of another; or (b) the acts constituting the offer and the acceptance have been effected in the territories of different states; or (c) delivery of the goods is to be made in the territory of a state other than that within whose territory the acts constituting the offer and the acceptance have been effected.

13.97 If these conditions are not satisfied, the parties may still choose to apply ULIS. They may do this even if the parties do not have their places of business in different states, and even if their state(s) of residence are not parties to ULIS. However, such a choice would then not be permitted to prevent the application of those mandatory rules which would have applied save for the choice of ULIS.[209] Section 1(4) of the Uniform Laws on International Sale Act 1967 indicates that, for these purposes, the undertakings in ss 12 to 15 of the Sale of Goods Act 1979 are mandatory rules. So, a choice of ULIS by the parties will not prevent the application of those sections of the 1979 Act, where, but for the choice, the contract would have been governed by English law.

13.98 ULFIS also has a very marginal practical impact.[210] It applies to contracts which, if concluded, would be governed by ULIS.

8. Limits on the Freedom of Choice

13.99 An express choice of law clause will be valid, even if the contract is otherwise wholly unconnected with the law chosen.[211] However, Article 3(3) states that such a choice:

shall not, where all the other elements relevant to the situation at the time of the choice are connected with one country only, prejudice the application of the rules of laws of that country which cannot be derogated from by contract, hereinafter 'mandatory rules'.

---

[206] These can be found in Bridge, *The International Sale of Goods*, appendix 1, 448, 455.
[207] This can be found in ibid, appendix 2, 456, 466.
[208] Sch 1 to the 1967 Act.   [209] Art 4 of ULIS.   [210] See also Peel, n 53 above, 15–015.
[211] Compare the common law position in *Vita Food Products v Unus Shipping Co Ltd* [1939] AC 277, 290 where Lord Wright stated that a choice must be '*bona fide* and legal'. See also *United Services Fund v Richardson Greenshields of Canada Ltd* (1987) 40 DLR (4th) 94.

Article 3(3) does not invalidate the choice of law by the parties.[212] Rather, it preserves the application of the laws of the state with which a contract is, save for the choice of law clause, wholly connected, in so far as those rules cannot be derogated from by contract.[213] This is a reference to 'domestic' mandatory rules,[214] that is the rules of law of the state of objective connection from which the parties could not have derogated *if that law had been the governing law of the contract*.[215] So, for example, if an English buyer and an English seller conclude a contract to be performed in England and subject to an English jurisdiction clause, but they expressly state that the contract is to be governed by Japanese law, the parties would still be subject to those 'mandatory rules' which cannot be contracted out of in English contract law.[216] Such 'framework' rules of English contract law might include the requirements of valid consideration[217] and that the contract does not contain a penalty clause[218] which is not a genuine estimate of the parties' potential loss.[219]

---

[212] Compare the position in Australia: *Akai Pty Ltd v People's Insurance Co Ltd* [1997] 141 ALR 389, HC of Australia; [1998] 1 Lloyd's Rep 90, 98, QBD.

[213] Art 3(3) refers to the 'elements relevant to the situation'. It does not say what these elements are. See *Caterpillar Financial Services Corp v SNC Passion* [2004] EWHC 569 (Comm). In *Golden Acres Ltd v Queensland Estates Pty Ltd* [1969] Qd R 378, a choice of Hong Kong law by the parties was struck down as not being made in good faith. The contract was entirely connected to Queensland, save for the fact that the claimant company was incorporated in Hong Kong. If the same approach is taken under the Convention, it might suggest that the place of incorporation is not a relevant factor in determining the elements relevant to the situation.

[214] The idea is to prevent the parties from evading all those rules which they could not have derogated from by the law that would otherwise have applied if the parties had not chosen a different law. Moreover, where the Convention intends to refer to international mandatory rules, as in Art 7(2), it uses more forceful language. Art 7(2) refers to mandatory rules that apply *'irrespective of the law otherwise applicable to the contract'* (emphasis added). The nature and application of mandatory rules is discussed below, paras 13.271–281.

[215] In other words, it is not limited to those 'international' mandatory rules which the law of objective connection would insist on being applied regardless of the governing law of the contract.

[216] Of course, the very nature of international sales contracts means that there usually will be objective connections to more than one state, so that the role of Art 3(3) will be limited: Benjamin, 25–037; P North, 'Reform, but not Revolution', (1990-I) 220 Recueil des Cours 9, 184

[217] Although whether the English courts would insist upon the application of the rules of consideration, which are neither protectionist rules nor justified on strong policy grounds, is debatable. Compare *Re Bonacina* [1912] 2 Ch 394.

[218] The buyer or seller may have chosen a foreign law in order to be able to insert a penalty clause. Such clauses may be considered oppressive by English law where they are not a genuine estimate of loss. As such, English contract law has a strong reason to invalidate such a clause.

[219] It might also allow for the application of 'international' mandatory rules, such as where the conditions described in s 27(2) of the Unfair Contract Terms Act 1977 exist and the circumstances are those described in Art 3(3) of the Rome Convention. See the discussion of the Unfair Contract Terms Act 1977 below, paras 13.301–320.

13.100 However, this gives rise to something of a paradox. For, the law of England might state that such rules must be applied *where English law governs the contract*. But, it may allow the parties to derogate from those laws *by choosing a foreign law to govern the contract*. In that scenario, can it really be said that these are 'mandatory' rules? As Benjamin notes:

> If this is correct, a court applying Article 3(3) would be required to apply, as a mandatory rule, a rule of country which would not regard that rule as applicable in relation to a contract containing a choice of law clause ... It cannot be the purpose of the Convention to give greater effect to these rules than the legal system of which they form part would give them.[220]

As Benjamin convincingly concludes, Article 3(3) must be interpreted so as to *permit* the law of objective connection to apply such rules as it considers must be applied to the transaction; but it does not *require* that law to insist upon application of all such rules. It is likely that, where the law of objective connection is England, an English court will not insist upon application of rules to foreign law to a contract, where it accepts that they are rules which can be freely avoided by choice of a foreign law.[221]

13.101 It should be noted that Article 3(3) does not have to lead to the application of the domestic mandatory rules of the forum. If the parties choose the law of England to govern a contract of sale, but all the objective elements of the contract point to the law of Japan, the domestic mandatory rules of Japanese law will be applied.

13.102 Finally, it is important to appreciate the limited scope of Article 3(3). It is only triggered if *all* the objective elements of the situation,[222] save the choice of law clause, point to a single, other law.[223] Suppose that a contract is concluded between a French seller and an English buyer. The contract is concluded in France but provides for delivery in England. The parties choose Japanese law to govern the contract. Although this is a choice of a law unrelated to the contract, the objective elements of the contract do not point to a single, other law. Accordingly, Article 3(3) is inapplicable and the choice of Japanese law unrestricted.[224]

---

[220] Benjamin, 25–039.

[221] ibid. But where the rule *is* intended to apply to the facts even though the parties chose a foreign law, it must continue to be applied: see, eg, s 27(2)of the Unfair Contract Terms Act 1977, discussed below, paras 13.315–320.

[222] See *Caterpillar Financial Services Corp v SNC Passion* [2004] EWHC 569 (Comm). Cooke J noted (at [18]) that 'elements relevant to the situation' is a broader term than 'elements relevant to the contract'.

[223] On this point, see *NM Rothschild Ltd v Equitable Life Assurance Society* [2002] EWHC 1021, QB.

[224] Save by the provisions on special contracts and the general provisions on mandatory rules and public policy in the Convention.

9. 'Splitting' the Applicable Law

Article 3(1) states that the parties can select the law to apply to the whole **13.103** or *any part of the contract*. Hence it is possible for different parts of the contract to be governed by different laws.[225] If the parties choose a governing law for only part of the contract, then the law applicable to the remainder will be determined in the absence of choice.[226]

The Giuliano and Lagarde Report states that the choice of a law to govern **13.104** a particular part of the contract must be sufficiently independent that application of that law will not lead to logically inconsistent results under the contract.[227] If it does, it is very likely that both choices will fail and the applicable law will be determined in the absence of choice.[228] Giuliano and Lagarde suggest that the parties could validly stipulate that an 'index-linking clause' be subject to a separate law to the rest of the contract. However, the parties could not provide that the same issue, such as the right to get out of the contract, be governed by a different law depending upon whether the seller or the buyer is the person seeking to terminate the contract.[229]

Article 3(1) does not expressly say that the parties should be permitted **13.105** expressly to choose *different* laws to govern different parts of the contract. However, provided that the choices are logically consistent, there seems no compelling principled reason not to permit such express choices.[230]

10. Incorporation of a Foreign Law's Terms by Reference

Closely related to the choice of law under a contract is the concept of **13.106** incorporation by reference of the terms of a contract. Imagine a contract between an Irish seller and a Japanese buyer. Rather than stating that the contract shall be governed by the law of England, the parties might provide, for example, that all the implied[231] terms contained in the United

---

[225] See also the discussion of 'splitting' the contract in the absence of choice, below, para 13.140.

[226] See *Centrax Ltd v Citibank* [1999] 1 All ER (Comm) 557; *XL Insurance Ltd v Owens Corning* [2000] 2 Lloyd's Rep 500. See also Benjamin, 25–057.

[227] Giuliano and Lagarde Report, 17. [228] ibid.

[229] ibid. See also *Shamil Bank of Bahrain EC v Beximco Pharmaceuticals Ltd* [2004] EWCA Civ 19. But see below, paras 14.25–27.

[230] It could be objected that this lets the parties 'mix and match' between different laws and does not result in the application of the law of any one recognized legal system. However, once the principle of contract splitting is allowed at all by the Convention, it should be permitted however it comes about, provided of course, that this is the will of the parties and that the issues are sufficiently separable from each other.

[231] Although there is a certain paradox in expressly incorporating implied terms under the Sale of Goods Act 1979, the meaning of this phrase is tolerably clear.

Kingdom's Sale of Goods Act 1979, as amended, shall apply to their contract. This is clearly not a choice of law as such; 'the clause is merely a "shorthand device" for adding terms to the contract'.[232] Although the Rome Convention appears to require the parties to choose the law of a particular legal system to govern the contract, it seems that such incorporation by reference should be permitted.[233] It is, after all, simply a way of describing terms of the contract which the parties could have spelt out in full in the contract. Since this is essentially just a way of fleshing out their intended rights and obligations, these should continue to apply and not be affected by any subsequent change in the content of those terms according to the law of the state from which they originate.[234] It must, of course, be possible to determine conclusively which terms the parties intended to incorporate into their contract.[235]

11. Changing the Applicable Law

Bilateral Change, Unilateral Change and 'Floating' Choices of Law

13.107 Article 3(2) states that: 'The parties may agree at any time to subject the contract to a law other than that which previously governed it'. It should be noted that the right to change the governing law of the contract is not a choice of law rule as such.[236] Rather, it is an example of a uniform rule of substantive law.[237] If the parties seek to change the governing law from English to Japanese law, the fact that the change is not permitted by one or both of these laws is immaterial.[238] Whilst this might seem pragmatic,

---

[232] Benjamin, 25–028.

[233] Dicey and Morris say (at 1226) that there is 'no doubt' that such incorporation is permitted. See also the Giuliano and Lagarde Report, 17.

[234] A view shared by Benjamin, 25–028 and by Dicey and Morris, 1227. See also *Vita Food Products Inc v Unus Shipping Co Ltd* [1939] AC 277.

[235] *Shamil Bank of Bahrain EC v Beximco Pharmaceuticals Ltd* [2004] EWCA Civ 19. A choice of English law, but 'subject to the principles of the Glorious Sharia'a' was rejected, as it was impossible to tell what terms were being incorporated into the contract.

[236] The position at common law was much less certain. See A Briggs, 'The Validity of "Floating" Choice of Law and Jurisdiction Clauses' [1986] LMCLQ 508; A Beck, 'Floating Choice of Law Clauses' [1987] LMCLQ 523; D Pierce, 'Post-Formation Choice of Law in Contract' (1987) 50 MLR 176.

[237] Contrast Art 10 of the Hague Convention on the Law Applicable to Trusts and on their Recognition 1985, enacted in the UK by the Recognition of Trusts Act 1987. This states that: 'The law applicable to the validity of the trust shall determine whether that law or the law governing a severable aspect of the trust may be replaced by another'.

[238] One could argue that Japanese law must still approve the change to that law. This is because Arts 3(4) and 8(1) state that the existence and validity of a choice of Japanese law should be determined by that law. However, those provisions are concerned with whether the parties *agreed* to the choice of Japanese law. They are not concerned with the issue of whether a contract's governing law may be *changed* to Japanese law.

it does have the unfortunate consequence that an English court may consider the contract to be valid and governed by Japanese law, even if the courts of Japan would consider the change of law ineffective.

It is not wholly clear whether the parties to a contract may give either the **13.108** buyer or the seller the right to change the applicable law unilaterally. It is true that Article 3(2) refers to a change of law by the 'parties' in the plural. However, the *right* for one of the parties to change the governing law will have been agreed by both *parties*. Accordingly, it seems that such a choice should be effective.[239]

It may happen that the parties do not stipulate any law as applicable at **13.109** the time of conclusion of the contract and only later select the governing law.[240] If so, the correct approach would be to say that, prior to the choice of law, the applicable law of the contract is determined in the absence of choice, in accordance with Article 4.[241]

Implied Change of Law

Presumably, the change of law need not be expressly agreed and an **13.110** implied agreement would suffice. However, the court would need to be 'reasonably certain' that such a change was intended. In *Aeolian Shipping SA v ISS Machinery Services Ltd*,[242] ISS had installed a turbo charger into A's ship and subsequently concluded a contract with A to supply replacement parts for that charger. Japanese law was the applicable law of the contract.[243] ISS sued for the price of the parts and for damages based on A's refusal to take further parts. A brought a counter-claim alleging that the goods were of unsatisfactory quality. ISS had received an undertaking from A's Protection and Indemnity Club to pay the amount of any judgment awarded against A, in consideration for the claimants refraining from arresting the ship. That undertaking was expressly stated to be governed by English law. The defendants argued that this amounted also to a variation of the applicable law of the turbo-charger contract. The Court of Appeal rejected the argument. It stated that, had the parties intended to change the governing law of the turbo-charger contract, they would have done so expressly. As they did not, there was no basis on the facts to imply such a choice into the contract. Indeed, such a change

---

[239] See below, paras 14.25–27.
[240] See the discussion of floating choices of law below, paras 14.22–28.
[241] Unless the contract is a consumer of employment contract, in which case Arts 5 and 6 respectively apply.
[242] [2001] 2 Lloyd's Rep 641.   [243] As determined in the absence of choice by Art 4.

would have been most unfavourable to the claimants, as it would have deprived them of complete defences to the defendant's counter-claim and there would have been no reason for them to have agreed to the change. However, Mance LJ did state that, on suitable facts, a change of law could be implied, if it could be demonstrated with reasonable certainty.[244] It is submitted that this is correct. The conditions upon which the parties may agree to change the governing law should be exactly the same as those under which the governing law is determined in the first place.[245]

Formal and Essential Validity; Effect on Third Parties

13.111 Article 3(2) goes on to state that the formal validity of the contract will not be affected by the change of law. Nor should a change of law adversely affect the rights of third parties, who will, of course, not have been party to any agreement to vary the governing law and who may have relied upon a particular law governing the contract.[246] Whilst this is desirable in order not to invalidate the contract retrospectively, it does not state that the *essential validity* of the contract shall be unaffected. It might accordingly be possible that a contract is initially governed by English law, by which it is valid. The parties might then change the governing law to Japanese law, by which the contract is essentially invalid. In such a circumstance, Article 8(1) would appear to lead to the conclusion that the contract is invalidated. This would have a manifestly undesirable effect on the parties themselves,[247] and, especially, on any third parties relying on the existence of the contract.[248]

VI. THE APPLICABLE LAW IN THE ABSENCE OF CHOICE: CHARACTERISTIC PERFORMANCE

1. THE LAW OF CLOSEST CONNECTION

Nature of Test

13.112 Where there is no express choice of law and one cannot be inferred, Article 4 determines the applicable law of the contract. Article 4(1) states

---

[244] [2001] 2 Lloyd's Rep 641, 647.
[245] See also the Giuliano and Lagarde Report, 18.   [246] ibid.
[247] Although it could be said that they have only themselves to blame.
[248] Such as a person who has lent money to the seller on the expectation that the seller will shortly receive payment due under the contract of sale.

that, in the absence of choice, 'the contract shall be governed by the law of the country with which it is most closely connected'.[249] It is not clear whether the search is for the *legal system* with which the contract has its closest connection (in which case, such factors as the use of terms in the contract which are resonant of a certain legal system would be relevant) or for the *state* with which the contract has closest connection. The language of Article 4(1) suggest the latter and that the test is purely objective. The importance of this distinction can be illustrated by the common law case of *James Miller & Partners Ltd v Whitworth Street Estates (Manchester) Ltd.*[250] A Scottish company agreed to make alterations to an English company's premises in Scotland. The language of the contract and its form pointed to English law as the *legal system* of greatest connection. Geographically, however, the key factors pointed to Scotland, such as the fact that it was the place of performance of both obligations under the contract. As Cheshire and North point out,[251] the application of Article 4(1) to the facts of such a case would point to the application of Scottish law.

The Time Factor

The state of closest connection should be assessed at the time that the **13.113** contract is concluded. However, Giuliano and Lagarde, suggest that, exceptionally, the court may take account of factors supervening after the conclusion of the contract.[252] However, one would have thought that a court should be slow to do this and would only be justified in doing so for one of two reasons: first, if it is alleged that the supervening factors shed further light on the law of closest connection at the time of conclusion of the contract; or second, if it alleged that the law of closest connection has subsequently been changed by the express or implied intention of the parties.[253] However, notwithstanding the view of Giuliano and Lagarde,

---

[249] Compare the Danish position under the International Purchase of Chattels Act no 722, 24 October 1986, which applied the law of the seller's domicile in the absence of choice: *Scan-Expo Hans Worthmann GmbH v Ringkobing County* [1994] IL Pr 335, Western Court of Appeal, Denmark. Contrast the decision of the District Court of Monza in *SpA OMV Officine Meccaniche Ventura v Prometal SA* [1990] IL Pr 184. In that case, the court found that the pre-Rome Convention rule applicable in Italy in the absence of a choice of law by the parties was that the law of the place of the conclusion of the contract applied. See, especially, at 189–90 of the judgment.

[250] [1970] AC 583.

[251] Cheshire and North, 567–8.   [252] Giuliano and Lagarde Report, 20.

[253] It is not clear whether a new law of closest connection may replace the law of closest connection at the time of the conclusion of the contract. The language of Art 3(2) speaks of the parties *agreeing* to change the applicable law, suggesting that any change of governing law must be express or implied. However, it is difficult to see why this need be the case, if the contract is now clearly more closely connected to a different law. The only concern would be that a very clear case for replacing one law of closest connection with another should be

English courts are still likely to be very reluctant to look at such supervening factors. The antipathy shown at common law to reliance upon such factors is clear in the judgment of the House of Lords in *Whitworth Street Estates (Manchester) Ltd v James Miller & Partners Ltd.*[254] Lord Reid, for instance, observed that:

> ... it is not legitimate to use as an aid in the construction of the contract anything which the parties said or did after it was made. Otherwise one might have the result that a contract meant one thing the day it was signed, but by reason of subsequent events means something different a month or a year later.[255]

2. A Rebuttable Presumption of Closest Connection; Characteristic Performance; Article 4(2)

13.114 Article 4(1) on its own would have rendered the choice of law process very uncertain, and therefore impractical in an area such as international contract law, where a high premium is placed upon predictability. To ameliorate this problem, Articles 4(2), (3) and (4) introduce a series of rebuttable presumptions as to which law is the law of closest connection. That which is most important to the contract of sale is the presumption contained in Article 4(2)). This states that this law of closest connection will be presumed to be the law of the place:

> ... where the party who is to effect the performance which is characteristic of the contract has, at the time of conclusion of the contract, his habitual residence, or, in the case of a body corporate or unincorporate, its central administration.

If the contract is entered into by that party in the course of business, that relevant country is the one in which its principal place of business is situated or the place of business through which it is to effect performance.

13.115 'Characteristic performance' is explained by the Official Report to mean, in most cases, the main obligation for which money is due. In a contract of sale, the characteristic performance is ordinarily that of the seller.[256] In this

---

required, so as not to introduce intolerable legal uncertainty for all concerned. See further *Aeolian Shipping SA v ISS Machinery Services Ltd* [2001] 2 Lloyd's Rep 641. Compare the common law position in *Libyan Arab Foreign Bank v Bakers Trust* [1989] QB 728, where a single contract related to bank accounts in New York and London. New York applied only in part to the London account.

[254] [1970] AC 583. See also *Watcham v Attorney-General of East Africa Protectorate* [1919] AC 533; *Wickman Tools v Schuler AG* [1974] AC 235.

[255] ibid, at 603. Similar objections were voiced by Lord Hodson (at 606), Viscount Dilhorne (at 611) and Lord Wilberforce (at 614).

[256] Giuliano and Lagarde Report, 20. *Williams Grant & Sons International Ltd v Marie Brizard España SA* 1998 SC 536, Outer House. In a contract of service, the characteristic performance is that of the provider of the service.

respect, it matters not whether the contract is on FOB, CIF or other sale terms.[257] This would remain the case even if the buyer and seller had ancillary obligations under the contract.[258]

It should be noted that it is the habitual residence of the party rendering **13.116** that obligation which is crucial, irrespective of where that obligation is to be performed and of whether that is the obligation in dispute. So, if a contract of sale is concluded between a corporate seller with its principal place of business in France and an English purchaser for delivery of goods in London, the contract would be presumed to be governed by French law.

3. The Meaning of 'Habitual Residence', 'Central Administration' and 'Principal Place of Business'

Habitual Residence

There is no Convention definition of 'habitual residence'.[259] This is **13.117** unfortunate, since the concept is far from a clear cut one and it is likely that different states will determine habitual residence differently.[260] This undermines the intended uniform interpretation of the Convention.[261] What is clear is that the relevant time for ascertaining habitual residence is the conclusion of the contract.[262]

It is possible that a state will conclude that the seller has his habitual **13.118** residence in more than one state, or indeed, in no one state.[263] If that is the case, then, presumably, the correct approach is to hold that it is impossible to identify the relevant law under Article 4(2) and, instead, the law of the state of closest connection should be applied, pursuant to Article 4(5).[264]

---

[257] See the decision of the Dutch Supreme Court in *Société Nouvelle des Papéteries de l'Aa v BV Machinenfabriek BOA* [1992] NJ 750, RvdW [1992] No 207; T Struycken, 'Some Dutch Judicial Reflections on the Rome Convention Art.4(5)' [1996] LMCLQ 18.

[258] See also Dicey and Morris, 1326–1327.

[259] And no guidance in the Giuliano and Lagarde Report. Compare Case C-90/97 *Swadling v Administrative Officer* [1999] ECR I-1075.

[260] See further, Cheshire and North, 161–76; Dicey and Morris, 156–52; Plender and Wilderspin, n 1 above, 151–2; Benjamin, 25–056, points out that English courts have themselves not applied a consistent definition of habitual residence.

[261] Art 18.

[262] Giuliano and Lagarde Report, 12.

[263] Benjamin, 25–056, citing *Hack v Hack* (1976) Fam Law 177 and *Re J (A Minor)(Abduction)* [1990] 2 AC 562.

[264] Although as Benjamin, 25–062, suggests, where the seller has two places of habitual residence, an alternative approach would be to work out which is more closely connected with the performance of the characteristic obligation.

Central Administration

13.119 Equally, the Convention does not define phrases such as 'central administration' or 'principal place of business'. As to the former, it is possible that
some parallel will be drawn to the definition of domicile of a company
contained in the Civil Jurisdiction and Judgments Act 1982 and in the
Brussels I Regulation.

13.120 Under the Brussels Convention, there was no European definition of the
domicile of companies and each state was left to apply its own rules. The
United Kingdom enacted provisions to the effect that a corporation is
domiciled where it has its seat. It has its seat in the United Kingdom if
it was incorporated or formed under the law of a part of the United
Kingdom and has its registered office or central management and control
in the United Kingdom.[265] It is domiciled in England if these criteria apply
to that part of the United Kingdom.[266] It is domiciled overseas if the same
conditions apply to an overseas state, unless it is demonstrated that the
overseas state would not regard the company as having its seat there.[267]

13.121 However, the Brussels I Regulation introduced a European autonomous
definition of domicile for companies, which replaced the definition in
the Civil Jurisdiction and Judgments Act 1982. Article 60(1) provides that:
'a company or other legal person or association of natural or legal persons
is domiciled at the place where it has its: (a) statutory seat; or (b) central
administration; or (c) principal place of business'. The statutory seat
means, for the purposes of the United Kingdom and Ireland, 'the
registered office or, where there is no such office anywhere, the place of
incorporation, or where there is no such office anywhere, the place under
the law of which the formation took place'.[268] However, whilst this
definition replaces the United Kingdom's definition of corporate domicile
contained in the Civil Jurisdiction and Judgments Act 1982, it does not
appear significantly to affect the substantive criteria. But more importantly for present purposes, it does not really resolve the question of where
a company's central administration is located. Benjamin convincingly
suggests that the place of central management and control of a company
is likely to be the most important factor in determining where a company
has its central administration.[269] In the end, the test of what constitutes a
company's central administration does not appear to be a technical one,
but one which depends simply upon examining the centre of gravity of
where the company carries out its operations.[270]

---

[265] Civil Jurisdiction and Judgments Act 1982, s 42(3).   [266] ibid, s 42(4).
[267] ibid, s 42(6), (7).   [268] Art 60(2) of the Brussels I Regulation.
[269] Benjamin, 25–063.   [270] See further ibid.

Principal Place of Business

It will be recalled that where a contract of sale is entered into the course of **13.122**
a business by a seller, the law of its principal place of business applies.[271]
Benjamin notes that in determining what a 'place of business' is, the
courts may have regard to the cases on jurisdiction *in personam* at common law. These show that a place of business 'constitutes a places which
is fixed and definite and that the activity carried on at that place must
have been carried on for a sufficient period of time for it to be characterized as a business'.[272] If a company has more than one place of business,
the court should simply examine the amount of activity taking place at
each in order to determine which is the principal place of business.

Companies Incorporated in One State but with Branches Elsewhere

Difficulties may arise if a company has a branch in a state other than **13.123**
the place of incorporation. Article 4(2) states that the law of a place other
than the company's principal place of business shall apply '. . . where
under the terms of the contract the performance is to be effected through
a place of business other than the principal place of business'. In *Iran
Continental Shelf Oil Co v IRI International Corp*,[273] a Delaware company,
which operated though a UK branch office, had contracted to supply the
claimants, three Iranian corporations, with parts and other equipment for
repair of an Iranian oil rig. The defendants were alleged to have failed to
perform their obligations under the contract by reason of an order of the
President of the United States precluding such dealings with Iranian
companies. At this point, the question of whether English, Iranian or
Texan law governed the contract arose. At first instance, the claimants had
alleged that the parties had chosen Iranian law to govern the contract; the
defendants that Texan law was chosen. McCombe J held that neither had
been chosen and determined that, in the absence of choice, Texan law, the
law of the place of central administration of the defendant, the characteristic performer, applied under Article 4(2) of the Rome Convention. He
found that the UK branch was solely a channel of communication. On
appeal, the claimants argued that Article 4(2) in fact pointed to the law
of England. The Court of Appeal agreed and allowed the appeal. Their

---

[271] Unless performance is to be effected from a different place of business, in which case
that place's law applies.
[272] Benjamin, 25–064. The authors cite *Adams v Cape Industries plc* [1990] Ch 433, 512–50;
The Theodohos [1977] 2 Lloyd's Rep 428; and *Dunlop Pneumatic Tyres v AG Cudell & Co* [1902]
KB 342. See also see *The Rewia* [1991] 2 Lloyd's Rep 325; *Harrods v Dow Jones* [2003] EWHC
1162 (QB). The phrase 'place of business' is used under r 6.5(6) CPR; see the discussion
above, para 4.22.
[273] [2002] EWCA Civ 1024.

Lordships noted that the UK office was much more than just a channel of communication. The contract was in terms which suggested that the United Kingdom was the relevant place of business of the company for the purposes of shipment and supply. The parties had agreed that the characteristic performance was to be carried out through the UK office. 'The outward appearances were that an English entity was contracting with an Iranian one.'[274] Accordingly, Article 4(2) pointed to the law of England, not the law of Texas.[275]

4. CONTRACTS OF SUPPLY AND DISTRIBUTION[276]

13.124 The concept of characteristic performance is much more complex to apply where the contract involves not just the sale of goods, but also the distribution of goods. If X agrees to supply goods to Y, who will distribute them exclusively on X's behalf in State A, which is the characteristic performance?[277] It could be said that the ultimate aim of the contract is the distribution of goods and that this is the key obligation. Indeed, this is arguably the *characteristic* that is distinct about the contract, since the obligation to supply may exist in other contracts.[278] But the counter-

---

[274] Briggs, n 121 above, at 476.

[275] But see *Ennstone Building Products Ltd v Stanger Ltd* [2002] 1 WLR 3059, 3068, CA, where Keene LJ stated that the law of the principal place of business of the characteristic performer (in this case, England) would apply 'unless the contract terms specify that performance is to be effected through some other place of business' (at [31]). The Court of Appeal ruled that the fact that the parties *anticipated* that performance would be effected through another office in Scotland would not suffice; they must be shown to have intended, expressly or impliedly, that the contract should contain such a provision. This seems to contradict the decision in *Iran Continental Shelf Oil Co*, which '. . . applies a test of whether the performance agreed on *was understood and agreed to be* effected through the English office; *Ennstone* asks whether the performance *was contractually required to be* performed through the Scottish office': Briggs, n 121 above, at 479 (emphasis in original). Since both decisions were delivered by the Court of Appeal on the same day, it is not easy to say which will be followed. However, Briggs goes on convincingly to argue that the *Iran Continental Shelf Oil Co* approach is the preferable one. If it is anticipated that performance is to be performed through another place of business, there is likely to be a strong connection with that state and its law, even if the contract did not actually contractually required performance through that place of business. However, the opposite view is taken by Hill n 100 above, at 338–339: 'Not only does the English version of the Convention use the phrase "under the terms of the contract" . . . [but] . . . in policy terms . . . it should be possible to tell solely from a consideration of the terms of the contract whether or not the relevant connecting factor for the purposes of Art 4(2) is the characteristic performer's principal place of business or some other place of business. A more open-textured test would be likely to generate unnecessary and undesirable uncertainty.'

[276] See the discussion of distribution agreements above, paras 3.158–162; and in para 16.95, below, on the Vienna Convention.

[277] See *Dicey and Morris*, 1238.

[278] O Lando [1987] CML Rev 159, 204; Hill, n 100 above, at 335–336. See also the Dutch Supreme Court decision in *Elinga BV v British Wool International Ltd*, Nederlands International Privaatrecht 1998, No 288, where the court found that the performance by the distributor was characteristic of the contract.

argument would be that without the supply by X, there is nothing to distribute. The distribution agreement contains an implied promise by X to supply goods to Y as and when required by Y. The distribution is, in other words, contingent upon, and ancillary to, the supply. It is this latter argument which won the day in *Print Concept GmbH v GEW (EC) Ltd.*[279] Longmore LJ observed of the obligations of supply and of distribution that:

No doubt they . . . [are] both important; but the penetration of the . . . market could not even take place without the supply and purchase of the . . . [goods], and it was performance of that supply obligation . . . which was . . . characteristic of what was a distributorship agreement intended to be fulfilled by individual contracts of sale and purchase.[280]

Had the contract solely involved distribution of goods, without a sale element, the characteristic performance would have been that of the distributor.[281]

5. OTHER REBUTTABLE PRESUMPTIONS

Rights in Immovable Property; Article 4(3)

The characteristic performance test does not apply to contracts the subject **13.125** of which is rights in immovable property[282] which, in the absence of a choice of law, are presumed[283] to be governed by the law of the place where the property is situated (Article 4(3)). These contracts are, of course, unlikely to come within the definition of 'goods'. However, it is possible that difficulties of classification will arise as to whether certain property should be classified as immovable or movable. A good example of this would be crops growing in a field. Although the distinction between

---

[279] [2001] EWCA Civ 352, [2001] ECC 36, CA. See also C Forsyth and P Moser, 'The Impact of the Applicable Law of Contract on the Law of Jurisdiction under the European Conventions' (1996) 45 ICLQ 190.

[280] ibid, at [34].

[281] Although the question of whether, and when, the agent, as distributor, could bind the principal falls outside the scope of the Rome Convention, pursuant to Art 1(2)(f). Compare the decision of the Paris Court of Appeal in *Printed Forms Equipments Ltd v Société Matériel Auxiliary d'Informatique* [2000] IL Pr 597, where the court applied the law of the place where the agent operated to an exclusive distribution contract concluded before the entry into force of the Rome Convention.

[282] Compare Art 22(1) of the Brussels I Regulation on the meaning of this term, which deals with proceedings *'which have as their object* rights *in rem* in immovable property or tenancies of immovable property . . .' (emphasis added).

[283] Giuliano and Lagarde Report, 21, make clear that this presumption could be rebutted under Art 4(5) on appropriate facts. They give the example of two Belgian residents making a contract for the rental of a holiday home in Italy. Such a contract may be considered more closely connected to Belgium and Belgian law may be applicable by virtue of Art 4(5).

movable and immovable property is made here for the purposes of determining the law applicable to the contract, it clearly relates to the type of property in question. Accordingly, in the absence of an autonomous definition of 'immovable property' in the Rome Convention, one would expect that an English court would apply the law of the situs of the property to determine whether it is immovable or movable. This is consistent with general choice of law in property principles.[284]

Contracts for the Carriage of Goods; Article 4(4)

13.126 Article 4(4) states that contracts for the carriage of goods shall be presumed to be governed by the law of the place where the carrier has his principal place of business at the time when the contract is concluded, provided that that country is also either: (a) the principal place of business of the consignor; or (b) the place of loading; or (c) the place of discharge. This provision is examined further in Chapter 14.[285]

6. EXCEPTION TO THE PRESUMPTIONS IN ARTICLE 4(2), (3) AND (4): ARTICLE 4(5)

Nature and Application of the Exception

13.127 Article 4(5) states that the presumptions in Article 4(2), (3) and (4) shall not apply if the characteristic performance cannot be determined,[286] or if, notwithstanding the above presumptions 'it appears from the circumstances as a whole that the contract is more closely connected with another country'. Naturally, we will focus on the possible displacement of Article 4(2), which is the key presumption applicable in the sales context.[287]

---

[284] See *Freke v Carbery* (1873) LR 16 Eq 461; *Re Hoyles* [1911] 1 Ch 179; *Re Berchtold* [1923] 1 Ch 192.

[285] At paras 14.33–37.

[286] This is, of course, very unlikely to present a problem in a straightforward contract of sale. However, it may be more complex where the seller has further obligations under the contract, such as to manufacture the goods, or to arrange contracts of carriage and insurance. Nevertheless, on any view, it is still the seller who is rendering the characteristic performance and the law of his habitual residence or place of business should be applied. A much more difficult case is a contract of exchange or barter. Here, it is impossible to tell which party is rendering the characteristic performance. Accordingly, the law of the state of closest connection will need to be applied, pursuant to Art 4(5). A further situation where Art 4(2) will not apply is where both parties undertake obligations *not* to pursue a particular activity, as where two parties agree not to infringe each other's trademarks: see *Apple Corps Ltd v Apple Computer* [2004] EWHC 768 (Ch).

[287] See Hill, n 100 above; S Atrill, 'Choice of Law in Contract: the Missing Pieces of the Art 4 Jigsaw?' (2004) 53 ICLQ 549.

At this stage, the test is wholly objective.[288] As Hobhouse LJ remarked in **13.128** *Crédit Lyonnais v New Hampshire Insurance Co:*[289]

... the question of choice and absence of choice becomes irrelevant to the question of ascertaining with what State the contract is most closely connected. Similarly, to refer to contemplation by one party or another that certain local laws may or may not be relevant is to be influenced by considerations of inferred choice and connection with a legal system and not with questions of performance and the location of the performing parties.[290]

The court may have regard to a wide range of objective factors.[291] **13.129** These include such factors[292] as the places of business of the parties,[293] the place of performance of the obligations of the parties,[294] the place of conclusion of the contract,[295] and the currency of account and of

---

[288] See also the discussion above, paras 4.103–109, 4.111–151, 4.156–159 and 4.161–163, of the natural forum in contract cases involving the international sale of goods and the significance to be attached to different factors.

[289] [1997] 2 Lloyd's Rep 1. In *Land Rover Exports Ltd v Samcrete Egypt Engineers and Contractors SAE* [2001] EWCA Civ 2019, [2002] CLC 533, Potter LJ agreed obiter with this view and regarded it as largely irrelevant, when determining the law applicable to a contract of guarantee in the absence of choice, that the underlying contract of loan contained a choice law clause for English law.

[290] *Crédit Lyonnais* [1997] 2 Lloyd's Rep 1, 7.

[291] Common law case law indicated that any relevant factors could be used to help determine the law of closest connection. Dicey and Morris, 1328, suggest that any circumstances considered relevant at common law may now be considered under Art 4(5). However, common law authority must be treated with caution, since an English court should not be too ready to displace the presumption in Art 4(2).

[292] See also the discussion of how Art 4(5) should operate in the case of sales by electronic means, below, paras 21.58–90.

[293] Benjamin notes (25–009) that, at common law, English courts would be particularly influenced in sales contracts if the parties had their place of business in the same state. However, today, if the buyer has his place of business in the same state as the seller, the presumption in Art 4(2) is very unlikely to be rebutted. If the buyer has his place of business in a different state, the buyer and seller's places of business will cancel each other out as connecting factors and provide no basis to rebut the presumption in Art 4(2).

[294] Benjamin, ibid, notes that this factor was of importance at common law where the parties did not have their place of business in the same state. Where the obligations of the parties were to be performed in different states, the place of delivery of the goods by the seller to the buyer (or, as the contract might require, the place where the seller made the goods available to the buyer, or to a carrier to transport to the buyer) would be the most important factor in determining the proper law (*Benaim & Co v Debono* [1924] AC 514; *NV Handel Maatschappij J Smits v English Exporters (London) Ltd* [1955] 2 Lloyd's Rep 317). The place of payment is, on its own, unlikely to be given much weight. The buyer's obligation is not the characteristic obligation under the contract and, as such, it is unlikely to be significant where this obligation is to be performed. On the relevance of the place where property in the goods is to pass under the contract, see the discussion of Art 4(5), below, paras 21.77–79.

[295] However, it is difficult to see that this provides any enduring connection to the contract, especially where the parties contract at arm's length. It is suggested that this factor will be given little weight in the application of Art 4(5).

payment.[296] It is suggested that the law of the forum should be used to identify these connecting factors. Accordingly, reference should not be made to a foreign law at this stage, if, for example, the place of perform-ance or conclusion of the contract is itself a matter of dispute.[297]

13.130 Lagarde gives the example of a sub-contract as one to which Article 4(5) might be applied.[298] In the sales context, this might allow the law applic-able to the principal contract between the original seller and purchaser[299] to apply to the contract between a purchaser and a sub-purchaser.[300] However, it is not inevitable that this will be the case. The sub-purchase is a separate agreement between different parties and it is not imperative for it to be subject to the same law as the main sales contract.

13.131 An example of the operation of Article 4(5) can be found in *Bank of Baroda v Vysya Bank*.[301] An Indian bank had issued a letter of credit. The con-firming bank, which was also based in India, was to effect its performance through its London office. Article 4(2) pointed to the application of English law to the contract between the issuing and the confirming bank and to the contract between the confirming bank and the beneficiary. However, Article 4(2) pointed to Indian law as the governing law for the contract between the issuing bank and the beneficiary. Mance J took the view that it would be undesirable for these contracts to be governed by different laws, since letters of credit give rise to a network of separate,

---

[296] *The Assunzione* [1954] P 150; *Rossano v Manufacturers Life Insurance Co* [1963] 2 QB 352. However, Benjamin, 25–010, n 59, notes that this factor would be less significant where an international currency such as sterling was used, citing *Sayers v International Drilling Co NV* [1971] 1 WLR 1176, 1183 and 1186 in support. Certainly, if currency is stipulated in Euros, this will provide no enduring connection to a particular state (save, perhaps, where the only two countries with which the contract is connected are one state which does and one state which does not use the Euro). More generally, there seems little reason to accord weight to the currency used. English courts are able to give judgment in a foreign currency (see the discussion of Art 10(1)(c), below, paras 13.211–214), even where the contract is governed by English law and there is no particular difficulty in a contract being governed by a law other than that whose currency is stipulated in the contract.

[297] This issued is considered further in relation to the particularly difficult case of e-commerce in paras 21.65–68, 21.71 and 21.75, to which the reader is referred.

[298] Lagarde, P, 'The European Convention on the Law Applicable to Contractual Obliga-tions: An Apologia' (1981) 22 Virginia J of Intl Law 91, 97–98—though the example that he gives concerns a contract of employment and the use of a sub-contractor.

[299] In relation to the main contract of sale, Art 4(2) leads to a presumption that the law of the place of business of the seller applies. However, in relation to a sub-sale, the original buyer will now be the sub-seller and characteristic performer and Art 4(2) will point to the law of his place of business. Hence, there is a strong possibility that Art 4(2) will lead to a presumption that a different law governs the main sales contract and the sub-sale, if the original buyer and seller have their respective places of business in different states.

[300] This would be desirable where the rights of the purchaser against the original seller are assigned to the sub-purchaser. See the discussion of string contract, and of claims involving third parties to a contract of sale, below, paras 13.137 and 13.249–255.

[301] [1994] 2 Lloyd's Rep 87, esp 93.

but clearly inter-related contracts between the parties and the banks involved. Mance J invoked Article 4(5) in relation to the contract between the issuing bank and the beneficiary and held that it, too, was governed by English law.[302]

Recent English[303] case law demonstrates that the most common circum- **13.132** stance in which the presumption may be rebutted is where the characteristic obligation is to be performed in a state other than that of the characteristic performer's habitual residence.[304] This is well illustrated, in the context of a contract of service, by *Definitely Maybe (Touring) Ltd v Karek Lieberberg Konzertagentur GmbH (No 2)*.[305] The claimants were based in England and provided the services of the pop group Oasis to concert organizers. They arranged with the defendants, a German company, for Oasis to play two concerts in Germany. In the event, an internal rift in the band meant that the lead guitarist did not play in the concert. The defendants then refused to pay the full price. The claimants sued them in England for the balance.[306] The contract contained no express or implied choice of law. Clearly, Article 4(2) would have pointed to England, as the place of business of the service provider. However, this was a contract with a German company for the performance of a service exclusively in Germany. Save for the location of the claimants and Oasis in England, there was no connection between England and the contract. Morison J described the position in Article 4(2) as the ' "normal" rule'[307] and stated that a wide interpretation of Article 4(5) 'will render the presumption of no value and represent a return to the English common law test of ascertaining the proper law . . .'.[308] He pointed out that there are 'two schools of thought'[309] as to how readily Article 4(5) should be invoked.

---

[302] For criticism of the decision, see Hill, n 100 above, at 339–341.

[303] In Scotland, see *Ferguson Shipbuilders v Voith Hydro GmbH* [2000] SLT 229; *Caledonia Subsea Ltd v Microperi Srl* 2001 SC 716.

[304] Or, in the case of corporate sellers, central administration or principal place of business. This was also a factor in *Bank of Baroda v Vysya* [1994] 2 Lloyd's Rep 87, as the place of performance of the issuing bank was not its place of business. Contrast, in the context of Art 5(1) of the Brussels I Regulation, the decision of the Court of Appeal in *Crédit Agricole Indosuez v Chailease Finance Corp* [2001] 1 Lloyd's Rep 348.

[305] [2001] 2 Lloyd's Rep 455; noted by R Fentiman, 'Commercial Expectations and the Rome Convention' (2002) 61 CLJ 50. See also Atrill, n 287 above, at 553–555.

[306] In fact, the central issue in the case was whether the English court had jurisdiction under Art 5(1) of the Brussels Convention, on the basis that the place of performance of the obligation to pay was in England. English law stated that payment should be made at the place of the creditor, ie England; however, German law provided that payment should be made at the residence of the debtor, ie Germany. The court needed to work out the governing law of the contract, so that it could use it to determine where the place of performance of the payment obligation was.

[307] [2001] 2 Lloyd's Rep 455, 456.

[308] ibid. See also *Caledonia Subsea Ltd v Microperi Srl* 2001 SC 716.

[309] ibid, at 457.

One view, namely that of Dicey and Morris[310] and the court in *Crédit Lyonnais v New Hampshire Insurance Co*,[311] is that the presumption is relatively weak and might easily be rebutted if the place of performance of the characteristic obligation is not the place of the characteristic performer's residence. The other view is exemplified by the Dutch Supreme Court decision in *Société Nouvelle des Papéteries de L'AA SA v BV Machinefabriek*.[312] It stated that the presumption should only give way if the law specified by it had no significant connection to the contract.[313] In the event, Morison J did not clearly decide between these viewpoints in *Definitely Maybe*. He commented that:

I accept that it is for the defendant to show that the presumption should be disregarded, by establishing factors which point to Germany. I accept that this will be more readily achievable where the place of performance is different from the place of the performer's business. But in carrying out what must be regarded as a comparative exercise, due weight must be given to the factor identified in Article 4(2).[314]

On the facts, the centre of gravity of the contract was so clearly Germany that this turned out not to be a 'hard case'. On any reasonable view, the presumption should be disapplied and German law was treated as the governing law under Article 4(5).[315]

13.133   In *Land Rover Exports Ltd v Samcrete Egypt Engineers and Contractors SAE*,[316] a contract of guarantee had been concluded between an Egyptian surety

---

[310] Dicey and Morris, 1240–1

[311] [1997] 2 Lloyd's Rep 1, 5. In this case, the Court of Appeal saw Art 4(2) as little more than a tie breaker where it could not be determined what the law of the country of closest connection was. It stated (at 5) that Art 4(5) had the effect of making 'the presumption [in Art 4(2)] very weak'.

[312] [1992] NJ 750, RvdW [1992] No 207; Struycken, n 257 above; Atrill, n 287 above, at 550–552.

[313] The Scottish Court of Session, Inner House stated in *Caledonia Subsea Ltd v Microperi Srl* 2001 SC 716 that Art 4(5) should only be invoked if, on a comparison of the factors which point to the law specified in Art 4(2) with those which point to another law, there is a clear preponderance of factors which point to another law. Lords Cameron and Marnoch expressly applied the test used by the Dutch Supreme Court in *Société Nouvelle des Papéteries de L'AA SA v BV Machinefabriek*. Indeed, Hill demonstrates that the Scottish courts have consistently applied the presumption in Art 4(2) in a more robust manner than the English courts: n 100 above, at 345–346.

[314] [2001] 2 Lloyd's Rep 455, 458.

[315] Contrast *Ennstone Building Products Ltd v Stanger Ltd* [2002] 1 WLR 3059, CA. In that case, the claimants alleged that the defendant, a company with its principal place of business in England, had breached its duty in failing adequately to investigate the staining of stonework on a building situated in Scotland. The claimant sued in contract and in tort. As to the contract claim, the Court of Appeal found that Art 4(2) pointed to the law of England and that clear evidence would be needed to rebut that presumption. Although the investigation was to be performed in Scotland, the claim arose from the advice given by one English company to another and communicated in England. See Hill, n 100 above, at 344.

[316] [2001] EWCA Civ 2019, [2002] CLC 533. See also *Bergmann v Kenburn Waste Management Ltd* [2002] IL Pr 33.

and an English creditor. The Court of Appeal ruled that the obligation of the guarantor to provide payment under the guarantee was the characteristic obligation under the contract.[317] This pointed to the law of Egypt. However, the court looked to the underlying contract between creditor and debtor and found that the payment was to be made in England. It ruled that this[318] provided sufficient grounds to rebut the presumption in Article 4(2) and instead to apply the law of England to the contract. In doing so, it cited with approval a passage from Dicey and Morris, where the authors state that:

... the presumption may most easily be rebutted in those cases where the place of performance differs from the place of business of the party whose performance is characteristic of the contract ... The situations in which they are performed elsewhere may (but by no means inevitably) provide material to rebut the presumption.[319]

It has been suggested that the court placed undue weight upon the place of performance.[320] Indeed, Hill argues that although recent English decisions have paid lip service to the strength of the presumption in Art 4(2), they have in fact been ready to rebut the presumption when the characteristic obligation is to be performed overseas. There is nothing in the Rome Convention of the Giuliano and Lagarde Report to justify this approach, which comes close to the substitution of one connecting factor for another.[321]

The Importance of the Place of Performance[322] to the Law Applicable to FOB,[323] CIF[324] and Other Contracts

Benjamin points out that where FOB contracts are concerned, the common law cases show that: **13.134**

---

[317] As Giuliano and Lagarde, 21, state. See also *Bloch v Soc Lima*, Court of Appeal of Versailles 14e ch, 6 February 1991 [1992] JCP 21972.

[318] Although it also referred to the continuing obligation of Land Rover to supply goods to Samcrete 'delivery ex UK works' and the fact that payment was due in sterling.

[319] Dicey and Morris, 1240–1; cited in *Land Rover* at [43]. To similar effect, see the Court of Appeal's decision in *Ennstone Building Products Ltd v Stanger Ltd* [2002] 1 WLR 3059, CA. See also the decision of the Scottish Court of Session, Inner House in *Caledonia Subsea Ltd v Microperi Srl* 2001 SC 716.

[320] Compare the discussion of its importance to the *forum conveniens* test in relation to jurisdiction at common law above, paras 4.120–127.

[321] Hill, n 100 above, at 341–342.

[322] See further above, paras 3.179–226 and 3.257–297, for discussion of the place of delivery in typical international sales contracts. See also Atrill, n 287 above, at 557–559.

[323] On the law applicable to FOB contracts, see also D Sassoon, *C.i.f. and F.o.b. Contracts* (4th edn, London: Sweet and Maxwell, 1995) paras 732–739.

[324] On the law applicable to CIF contracts, see ibid, paras 393–404.

there was an observable tendency in the relatively few authorities to treat the country of shipment as the place of performance by delivery on board the ship and to regard the contract as governed by the law of that place in the absence of any countervailing considerations. Implicit in the view was the idea that shipment at the stipulated port was the most important act of performance of an FOB contract.[325]

It is likely that the place of shipment will also be the most important factor to which the court has regard when applying Article 4(5) of the Rome Convention to FOB contracts, if this is other than the place of business or habitual residence of the seller.[326] It is also likely to be significant for other contracts where the obligation to ship is of primary importance, such as FAS contracts.[327] Of course, the place of shipment will commonly coincide with the place of the seller's residence or business in any event, so that there will be no question of displacing the presumption in Article 4(5). However, given the significance of the presumption in Article 4(2), the mere fact that delivery is to be effected in a state where the seller has no place of business should not in and of itself be sufficient to invoke Article 4(5).[328] However, Dicey and Morris note that Article 4(5) may be triggered if the delivery is to take place in the state where the *buyer* has his place of business, since it is likely in such a case that there will be other objective connections to that state.[329]

13.135 For other contracts, such as ex works contracts, the place where the buyer collects the goods is likely, though will not inevitably, coincide with the seller's place of business under Article 4(2). To the extent that it does not, the place of collection may be a relevant factor under Article 4(5). For ex ship contracts, the place where the goods are to be brought to the buyer under the contract is unlikely to coincide with the law designated by Article 4(2) and may be a significant factor in determining whether to invoke the exception under Article 4(5).[330]

13.136 In relation to CIF contracts, Benjamin observes that '. . . there was slender judicial authority, and some academic authority, to the effect that where

---

[325] Benjamin, 25–011. The authors cite *Benaim & Co v Debono* [1924] AC 514; *Re Viscount Supply Co Ltd* (1963) 40 DLR (2d) 501 and *Restatement 2nd, Conflict of Laws*, § 191d in support.

[326] It is very unlikely that Art 4(5) will be invoked if the seller's place of business and the place of shipment are in the same state: Dicey and Morris, 1328–1329.

[327] And also FOR and FOT contracts: see Benjamin, 25–013, since this would remove the legal certainty for which Art 4(2) strives.

[328] Dicey and Morris comment (at 1329) that: 'It is most unlikely, however, that a case for displacement of the presumption will be found to exist if the seller is merely obliged to deliver goods from his place of business to that of the buyer in a different country unless further connections with the latter country are established'.

[329] Dicey and Morris, ibid; this is also the view of Benjamin, 25–066.

[330] See Benjamin, 25–013.

the parties carried on business in different countries, the law of the country of shipment of goods should, *prima facie*, be the proper law'.[331] However, the authors rightly observe that less weight might be attached to this factor than is the case in relation to an FOB contract, since the CIF seller's duties are not as concentrated upon the place of shipment. This is because the tender of documents by the seller is the key feature of the CIF contract and the duty to tender appropriate documents may very well arise in a state other than that of shipment, such as the buyer's home state. The seller may also be permitted to tender the documents with respect to goods sold afloat. Benjamin convincingly concludes that: 'The most that might be said is that in a situation where the seller has no right to tender goods afloat (e.g. where he is bound to manufacture and ship the goods CIF in a specified country) there could be a strong pointer towards . . . [the country of shipment's] law . . .'.[332] The same is likely to be true for variant contracts, such as the C&F contract.

'String' Contracts

It is not clear how Article 4(5) might operate in relation to 'string' sales **13.137** contracts involving successive sales of the same goods.[333] If each seller in the 'string' has its place of business or habitual residence in a different state to the others, Article 4(2) will subject each contract to a different law in the absence of choice. Could it be said, under Article 4(5), that the same law should be applied to all contracts in the 'string'? The nature of string contracts is that they are absolutely identical save as to price. The parties are effectively dealing with the same abstract commodity. As such, one might argue that string contracts should be subject to the same law. However, the fact remains that the contracts are legally independent agreements between different parties and there seems no compelling reason for subjecting them all to the same law.[334]

The Need for Caution in Applying Article 4(5)

It must be reasserted that the basic presumption is contained in Article **13.138** 4(2). Certainly, there is nothing like a rule of law that Article 4(5) should be invoked where the characteristic obligation is to be performed in a

---

[331] Benjamin, 25–012, citing *Lewis Construction Co Ltd v Tichauer SA* [1966] VR 341; *Johnson v Taylor Bros & Co Ltd* [1920] AC 144.

[332] Benjamin, ibid. Dicey and Morris, 1329, also state that the presumption should not give way if the seller has the right to tender documents relating to goods afloat.

[333] The problem is unlikely in view of the almost invariably present applicable law clause in such contracts.

[334] See also Benjamin, 25–068.

state other than the performer's habitual residence or principal place of business, since this would remove the legal certainty for which Article 4(2) strives. All other relevant factors need to be considered, including the place of performance of other obligations such as payment, and the place of business of the buyer. Only if, having weighed all the objective factors, a state other than that of the seller's habitual residence or principal place of business is clearly more closely connected to the contract should the presumption in Article 4(2) give way.[335]

13.139 In *Iran Continental Shelf Oil Co v IRI International Corp*,[336] the Court of Appeal ruled that where a Delaware company had a UK branch, from which it undertook to perform its obligations to supply and ship equipment for the repair of an oil rig in Iran for three Iranian companies, Article 4(2) indicated that the law of England was presumed to apply. The claimants argued that if this were so, the state of closest connection was nonetheless Iran,[337] and that this law should be applied pursuant to Article 4(5). This was, of course, the place of performance of the characteristic obligation. However, the Court of Appeal noted that the UK branch had other functions to perform in the United Kingdom in giving technical advice, and that the parties had connections with a number of jurisdictions. In the circumstances, the presumption in Article 4(2) prevailed.[338]

7. 'SPLITTING' THE CONTRACT IN THE ABSENCE OF CHOICE

13.140 Article 4(1), second sentence indicates that a contract may be 'split' in the absence of choice, if a certain part of it is more closely connected with a state other than that whose law governs the rest of the contract. It follows that Article 4(5) could be used to displace the presumption in Article 4(5) only in part. Of course, the part in question must be logically severable from the rest of the contract. However, there is little to be said in favour of partial displacement of the presumption in Article 4(2). This will complicate matters, may defeat the expectations of the parties and will lead to the combined application of a set of laws such as would be applied domestically in no country in the world. Contract splitting may be justi-

---

[335] An example of where Art 4(5) might be invoked is given by Dicey and Morris (at 1329). They suggest that it might apply if an agent for the seller stores the seller's goods in the buyer's home state and is bound to deliver those goods to the buyer in that same state.

[336] [2002] EWCA Civ 1024.

[337] The defendants argued that it was Texas.

[338] Compare the Versailles Court of Appeal's decision in *Bloch v Lima*, 6 February 1991, 14e ch, referred to by Potter LJ in *Land Rover Exports Ltd v Samcrete Egypt Engineers and Contractors SAE* [2001] EWCA Civ 2019, [2002] CLC 533, at [42].

fied where it represents the express will of the parties. Where it is not, however, it is best kept to an absolute minimum.[339]

VII. RENVOI

1. Exclusion

Article 15 states that the law which is applicable under the Convention is **13.141** the *domestic* law of the state identified by the Convention's rules, ignoring any choice of law rules of that state. So, if X and Y choose Japanese law to govern a contract, it is irrelevant that a Japanese court might, on the facts, apply English law to resolve the dispute.[340] The English court would apply the law of Japan to the contract. Likewise, if application of the Rome Convention leads to the application of the law of a state which has enacted the Hague Sales Convention 1955, an English court will not itself apply the rules of that Convention, which contain a set of choice of law rules. Instead, it will apply the domestic law of the state identified. If the purpose of letting the parties choose the law applicable to a contract is to give effect to their expectations, then it can be said that, almost invariably, where the parties have chosen a law, they would have meant that country's domestic law only and did not mean to include also its conflict of laws rules. Even where the applicable law is determined in the absence of choice, the purpose of Article 4(2) is to make it relatively clear to the parties which law will be presumed to apply. Again, some of that predictability and simplicity would be sacrificed by application of the doctrine of renvoi.

2. The Scope of a State's Domestic Law

It must be stressed that Article 15 only prevents the application of the **13.142** private international law of the state whose law is identified by the Convention's rules. In other words, the fact that the designated law itself has choice of law provisions which would lead to the application of a different law is irrelevant. But where the law identified has provisions which simply define what the content and scope of application of *its own* law is on the facts, these are not choice of law rules and an English court must give effect to them. In particular, if the state whose law is applicable

---

[339] Giuliano and Lagarde urge states 'to have regard to severance as seldom as possible': 23.

[340] In principle, renvoi could be applied to matters falling outside the scope of the Convention. However, it is most unlikely that an English court would do this in relation to contractual matters.

is party to an international Convention, such as the Vienna Convention, and, on the facts, that state would hold that the Vienna Convention is applicable,[341] it would seem that an English court must apply the Vienna Convention to determine the merits of the dispute.[342]

VIII. FORMATION OF THE SALES CONTRACT; THE ESSENTIAL VALIDITY OF THE CONTRACT AND ITS TERMS

1. GENERAL RULE: FORMATION AND ESSENTIAL VALIDITY DETERMINED BY THE PUTATIVE APPLICABLE LAW

Essential Validity of the Contract and its Terms

13.143   It may be that a party to a sales 'contract' contests the validity of the contract or its terms. It might do so on the basis, for example, they did not agree to be bound by the contract itself, or by some of its terms, or that the contract or some of its terms were induced by undue influence or mistake. In such a case, which law determines whether the contract or its terms are valid?

13.144   Article 8(1) provides that: 'The existence and validity of a contract, or of any term of a contract, shall be determined by the law which would govern it under this Convention if the contract or term were valid'. Suppose that X and Y purport to enter into a contract of sale containing a Texan choice of law clause. X argues that the entire contract is void because induced by mistake. Texan law decides if the contract was formed and is essentially valid.

13.145   Article 8(1) also subjects the essential validity of each term of the contract[343] to the putative applicable law.[344] This includes the question of whether the parties have agreed to a choice of law clause. In the event of a

---

[341] This will be determined by Art 1 of the Vienna Convention. However, if the circumstances described in Art 1(1)(a) are not met and the state whose law is applicable has entered a reservation that it will not apply the Convention if only the conditions of Art 1(1)(b) are met, then the Convention is *not* applicable according to the law of that state. Accordingly, an English court should apply the national rules of the state identified.

[342] See further the discussion of the Vienna Convention in relation to Art 3(1), above, paras 13.70–94.

[343] Other than those excluded from the scope of the Convention, such as jurisdiction and arbitration clauses.

[344] Benjamin points out (at 25–089) that the law applicable to the contract will accordingly determine whether a clause which seeks to vary standard FOB terms is valid and also whether (subject to any relevant mandatory rule provisions), an exclusion or limitation clause will be valid.

dispute between the parties as to whether a Texan choice of law clause was included in the contract, Texan law shall determine this matter.[345]

It follows that the Convention pulls itself up by its own bootstraps.[346] It assumes what it sets out to prove by using the law of State X to determine whether a contract exists and, if so, whether it is governed by the law of State X. This may be pragmatic, but it is certainly not logical.   **13.146**

Essential Validity and Implied Choice of Law

Where the formation of the contract is in issue, and it contains no choice of law clause, matters are more complex, since it is less clear what law would govern the contract if it were valid. If it is alleged that the parties made an implied choice of law, because, for example, they concluded a valid jurisdiction or arbitration clause for a certain state,[347] then it appears that this is the law which *putatively* governs the contract and that it should be used to determine the validity of the contract itself and its terms. In *Egon Oldendorff v Libera Corp (No 1)*,[348] Mance J applied English law to determine whether an English arbitration clause was incorporated into a contract. He reasoned that if the clause did form part of the contract, it would give rise to a strong inference that the parties had impliedly chosen English law to govern the contract.   **13.147**

Essential Validity and the Applicable Law in the Absence of Choice

Where there is no law putatively chosen by the parties, either expressly or impliedly, the applicable law has to be determined in the absence of choice. This creates a further paradox. For until one knows all of the terms of the contract, it is not possible to say what the law of the state of closest connection to the contract is. Perhaps even more than where there is an alleged express or implied choice, there appears to be a problem of   **13.148**

---

[345] See also Art 3(4), considered above, para 13.56.

[346] Although it appears that the common law did much the same thing: see, eg, *Re Bonacina* [1912] 2 Ch 394; *Albeko Schuhmaschinen AG v Kamborian Shoe Machine Co Ltd* (1961) 11 LJ 519. *Chevron International Oil Co Ltd v A/S Sae Team (The TS Havprins)* [1983] 2 Lloyd's Rep 356; *Dubai Electricity Co v Islamic Republic of Iran Shipping Lines (The Iran Vojdan)* [1984] 2 Lloyd's Rep 380; *Union Transport plc v Continental Lines SA* [1992] 1 WLR 15. Discussion in English periodicals includes: A Jaffey, 'Essential Validity of Contracts in the English Conflict of Laws' (1974) 23 ICLQ 1; A Jaffey, 'Offer and Acceptance and Related Questions in the English Conflict of Laws' (1975) 24 ICLQ 603; D Libling, 'Formation of International Contracts' (1979) 42 MLR 169; A Thomson, 'A Different Approach to Choice of Law in Contract' (1980) 43 MLR 650; A Briggs, 'The Formation of International Contracts' [1990] LMCLQ 192.

[347] By Art 1(2)(d), the validity of these clauses would not be determined by the Convention's rules.

[348] [1995] 2 Lloyd's Rep 64. See also *Welex AG v Rosa Maritime Ltd (The Epsilon Rosa) (No 2)* [2002] EWHC 2033 (Comm), [2002] 2 Lloyd's Rep 701, QBD (Comm).

circular reasoning. Until the court knows what the terms of the contract are, how can it decide what law it should be applying to determine the validity of the whole contract?

13.149 In fact, it is suggested that the Rome Convention allows this problem to be sidestepped. It may be said that, in accordance with Article 4(2), the law of the seller's habitual residence or principal place of business is that which is presumed to govern a contract in the absence of choice. Unless and until the validity of each of the terms of the contract is conclusively established, there can be no clear case for rebutting this presumption pursuant to Article 4(5). That being the case, the law of the seller's habitual residence or principal place of business *putatively* applies to the contract and it is this law which, in accordance with Article 8(1), should determine both the existence and essential validity of the contract itself and the terms thereof.[349] This solution has more logical backbone than that employed where there is an express or implied choice, since it is not wholly dependent upon pulling itself up by its own bootstraps.

2. Exception: Use of the Law of a Party's Habitual Residence to show Lack of Consent to the Contract or a Term of the Contract

13.150 There is one exception to the general rule in Article 8(1), which is contained in Article 8(2). This provides that a party[350] may rely on the law of his habitual residence[351] to show lack of consent if it is not reasonable to rely solely on the putative applicable law to determine this matter.

13.151 The application of this provision can be illustrated by the following example. Suppose that X sends Y an offer through the post to purchase office equipment from X, which Y simply ignores. X's offer stated that 'if I do not hear from you within one month, you will be deemed to have accepted the offer and to have agreed that the contract between us shall be governed by Utopian law'. By Utopian law, silence constitutes acceptance of an offer. Article 8(1) suggests that Utopian law should be used to determine whether the contract was agreed upon and that the answer will

---

[349] Of course, once the terms have been conclusively established by this process, it may then transpire that the law of the state of closest connection is a different law under Art 4(5). However, that does not render the approach taken to determining the existence and essential validity of the contract invalid. Art 8(1) tells the court to apply the law which is *putatively* applicable to the contract and, at that stage, the law of the seller's habitual residence or principal place of business was putatively applicable.

[350] This may be either the offeror or the offeree: Giuliano and Lagarde Report, 28.

[351] But not his nationality: see the German Federal Supreme Court decision, Case XI ZR 42/92, 2 September 1992, discussed by Schmidt, n 148 above.

be in the affirmative. In that situation, Y may, by exception, rely upon the law of his habitual residence to show that he did not agree to the contract.[352]

In *Egon Oldendorff v Libera Corp (No 1),*[353] Mance J applied English law to **13.152** determine whether an English arbitration clause was incorporated into a contract and, if so, whether the parties had impliedly chosen English law to govern the contract. However, the contract had very little objective connection to England. The defendants sought to rely on the law of their place of business, Japan, to demonstrate their lack of consent to the term. They alleged that Japanese law required them to confirm their assent to contractual terms and that they had not done so. Mance J ruled that the party seeking to rely on Article 8(2) must prove that it is unreasonable to determine consent solely by reference to the general rule stated in Article 8(1). On the facts, in the face of an English arbitration clause, Mance J held that it would defeat commercial expectations to subject the incorporation of the clause to anything other than English law. Moreover, this was not a case where the defendants had not given their consent *at all* and they patently had their work cut out to show that the Japanese law went to the question of whether they consented to the term's incorporation at all, as opposed to whether the consent that they had given was valid.[354]

It should be noted that a party may not rely upon Article 8(2) to show that **13.153** they *did* consent to a contract which is *not* valid according to Article 8(1). Moreover, a party cannot rely on the lack of consent of *the other party* by invoking Article 8(2).

3. VITIATING FACTORS

If a party alleges that the contract, or a term thereof, was induced by **13.154** duress,[355] undue influence, mistake or misrepresentation, the law putatively applicable to the contract under Article 8(1) will determine the substance of the claim.[356] However, the rule in Article 8(2) may not be invoked in such circumstances. It appears that Article 8(2) is concerned

---

[352] Although Giuliano and Lagarde (at 28) make clear that Art 8(2) can be used to determine the effects of positive conduct by a party, as well as the omission of silence.

[353] [1995] 2 Lloyd's Rep 64. See also *Welex AG v Rosa Maritime Ltd (The Epsilon Rosa) (No 2)* [2002] EWHC 2033 (Comm), [2002] 2 Lloyd's Rep 701, QBD (Comm), considered below, para 14.76.

[354] A point made by Cheshire and North, 589.

[355] See *Dimskal Shipping Co SA v International Transport Workers Federation (The Evia Luck)* [1992] 2 AC 152.

[356] Compare, at common law, *British Controlled Oilfields Ltd v Stagg* [1921] WN 31; *Mackender v Feldia AG* [1967] 2 QB 590; *Dimskal Shipping SA v International Transport Workers Federation* [1992] 2 AC 152; *The Evia Luck* [1992] AC 152, 168.

only with the *existence* of consent. It does not help if a party alleges that the consent which he gave was vitiated.

13.155 It might be thought that if the contract is voidable, this gives rise to a logical paradox. For, if the contract is voidable by its governing law, it could be argued that the choice of law clause is also invalidated. However, it appears that this is not the case. An arbitration agreement is capable of surviving notwithstanding that a contract is voidable.[357] The same is arguably true also of a jurisdiction clause.[358] It is likely that the same approach will be taken under the Rome Convention to choice of law clauses.[359] However, it should ultimately be for the law applicable to the contract to determine what effect the voidability of the contract has on the choice of law clause.

IX. SCOPE OF THE APPLICABLE LAW

13.156 Once the applicable law of the contract has been identified, it will determine most questions arising in relation to the contract. In particular,[360] Article 10(1) provides that it will apply to the matters discussed below.

1. INTERPRETATION[361]

13.157 The applicable law will determine the construction of ambiguous terms in the contract. It will also determine whether those terms might properly be construed in the light of subsequent conduct of the parties.[362] The governing law will also determine the relevance of trade custom in a particular field, or in a particular state.

13.158 Of course, in determining the meaning of a term of the contract, a party may seek to adduce evidence of a kind which is not permitted in

---

[357] *Heyman v Darwins Ltd* [1942] AC 356; *Ashville Investments Ltd v Elmer Contractors Ltd* [1989] 1 QB 488; *Harbour Assurance Co (UK) Ltd v Kanza General International Insurance Co Ltd* [1993] QB 701. For a recent affirmation of these principles, see *IFR Ltd v Federal Trade SpA* (19 September 2001, QBD (Comm Ct), 2001 WL 1677001). See also s 7 of the Arbitration Act 1996.

[358] *Mackender v Feldia* [1967] 2 QB 590; *The Parouth* [1982] 2 Lloyd's Rep 351. But see Case 269/95 *Benincasa v Dentalkit Srl* [1997] ECR I-3767; Case C-159/97 *Transporti Castelletti Spedizioni Internazionali SpA v Hugo Trumpy SpA* [1999] ECR I-1597.

[359] See Nygh, n 162 above, 84. See also J Harris, 'Contractual Freedom in the Conflict of Laws' (2000) 20 OJLS 247, 252–255.

[360] The list is illustrative and not exhaustive.

[361] Art 10(1)(a). See also the discussion above, paras 13.77–82, on the meaning of a choice of law clause for a Contracting State to the Vienna Convention.

[362] But subject to the comments made above about ascertaining the applicable law of the contract in the light of the parties' subsequent conduct.

English domestic law. Since matters of evidence are excluded from the Convention,[363] it is for English law to determine what evidence may be adduced.[364] However, the applicable law will determine, in the light of that evidence, how the contract or term is to be interpreted.

2. PERFORMANCE[365]

The Applicable Law

This key provision subjects the obligations of the parties and their per- **13.159** formance to the applicable law of the contract. The Giuliano and Lagarde Report gives the following examples of matters covered by this provision:

the diligence with which the obligation must be performed; conditions relating to the place and time of performance; the extent to which the obligation can be performed by a person other than the person liable; the conditions as to performance of the obligation both in general and in relation to certain categories of obligation (joint and several obligations, alternative obligations, divisible and indivisible obligations, pecuniary obligations); where performance consists of the payment of a sum of money, the conditions relating to the discharge of the debtor who has made the payment, the appropriation of the payment, the receipt, etc.[366]

The Role of the Law of the Place of Performance; Article 10(2)

However, Article 10(2) muddies the water significantly.[367] This states that **13.160** in respect of the *manner* of performance and the steps to be taken in the event of defective performance, *regard is to be had* to the law of the place of performance.[368] This only raises a further set of questions.

It should be stressed that Article 10(2) *requires* states to examine the law of **13.161** the place of performance on issues concerning the manner of performance. However, having done so, it is at the court's *discretion* what effect, if

---

[363] Art 1(2)(h).

[364] But in respect of the proof of acts intended to have legal effect, see Art 14(2).

[365] Art 10(1)(b)

[366] Giuliano and Lagarde Report, 32. The capacity of the performing party and any conditions relating to the form of the act which is to be done in performance of the obligation are not covered by this provision (ibid).

[367] For an example of its application in the context of carriage of goods, see the decision of Thomas J at first instance in *East West Corp v DKBS AF 1912 A/S* [2002] EWHC 83 (Comm), [2002] 2 Lloyd's Rep 182, 194 considered below, paras 14.94–96 (the point was not argued in the Court of Appeal [2003] EWCA Civ 83, [2003] QB 1509).

[368] Contrast the position at common law, where the governing law determined these matters: *Compagnie Tunisienne de Navigation SA v Compagnie d'Armement Maritime SA* [1971] AC 572; *Amin Rasheed Shipping Corp v Kuwait Insurance Co* [1984] AC 50, 60.

any, to give to that law.[369] It may apply the law of the place of performance in whole, in part, or not at all.[370] Moreover, Article 10(2) does not state that, where applicable, the law of the place of performance *replaces* the governing law of the contract on issues relating to manner of performance. At face value, it suggests that the governing law and the law of the place of performance will work in tandem. However, it is difficult to see how a court can apply both laws if, for example, they differ as to what constitutes an acceptable time for delivery.[371] In practice, a court which decides to apply the law of the place of performance on a particular matter will, in case of conflict, apply the rules of that state *rather than the rules of the governing law of the contract.*[372]

13.162 A central question is when an issue of performance can be said to relate to *manner* of performance. Benjamin explains that:

> The broad distinction (which is to drawn according to the *lex fori*),[373] under each régime is that between the substance of the obligation, governed by the applicable law, and matters of detail which affect the mode or manner of performance but which do not impinge on the substance of what must be done under the contract. . . . Thus if waiver of any particular obligation is alleged, its validity and effect is a matter for the applicable law, whereas if a contract governed by, say, English law, provides for delivery in Paris during 'usual business hours', French law will determine what hours those are.[374]

Giuliano and Lagarde state that whilst no definition of 'manner of performance' was formulated in drafting this provision, it might cover such matters as 'the rules governing public holidays, the manner in which goods are to be examined, and the steps to be taken if they are refused'.[375]

13.163 As Benjamin points out, matters affecting the manner of delivery, such as usages governing delivery at a particular port, should be determined by

---

[369] It is therefore not correct to say, as Thomas J did in *East West Corp v DKBS AF 1912 A/S* [2002] EWHC 83 (Comm), [2002] 2 Lloyd's Rep 182, 194 that: 'The effect of art. 10 of the Rome Convention is to maintain a distinction between the substance of the obligation which is governed by the proper law . . . and the mode (or manner and method) of performance which is governed by the law of the place of performance . . .'.

[370] Giuliano and Lagarde Report, 33.

[371] Thomas J in *East West Corp v DKBS AF 1912 A/S* [2002] EWHC 83 (Comm), [2002] 2 Lloyd's Rep 182, 194 seemed to envisage that the law of the place of performance would apply in lieu of the governing law of the contract.

[372] This seems to be the view of Giuliano and Lagarde, 32.   [373] ibid, 33.

[374] Benjamin, 25–149 and n 96.

[375] Giuliano and Lagarde Report, 33. Compare Art 4 of the Hague Sales Convention 1955, which states that unless the parties expressly provide to the contrary, the domestic law of the place where inspection of goods delivered pursuant to a contract of sale is to take place shall apply to the form in which, and period within which, the inspection must take place, the notification concerning the inspection and the measures to be taken in case of refusal of the goods: see below, paras 15.49–58.

the law of the place of performance by invoking Article 10(2).[376] The question of time of delivery is more controversial. Although listed as a matter to be referred to the applicable law by Giuliano and Lagarde, it does also appear to relate to the way in which performance is to be effected. Indeed, it would seem unacceptable for the applicable law of the contract to lay down a time of delivery which is prohibited in the place of performance. For this reason, the following approach is tentatively suggested. In the first place, the governing law of the contract should, in principle, determine the times of delivery. However, the English court should then have regard to the rules of the place of performance. If, by that law, some or all of the times of delivery stipulated by the governing law are *prohibited*, an English court should not sanction delivery during those times. So, if, for example, the applicable law states that delivery may be made at any time between 9am and 6pm, but the law of the place of performance states that delivery must take place between 8am and 5pm, the applicable law should in principle be applied. However, since the law of the place of delivery would prohibit delivery after 5pm, delivery should not be permitted after this time. On these facts, this would lead an English court to conclude that delivery should take place between 9am and 5pm.[377]

It is particularly likely that an English court will invoke Article 10(2) **13.164** and give effect to the rules of the place of performance in the situation where the contract violates a mandatory rule of the law of the place of performance. The paradigm case would be where one or both parties have acted, or contracted to act, in a manner which is illegal by the law of the place of performance. Certainly, if the goods are to be delivered to a certain state, and that state prohibits the import of the goods, it would seem positively desirable to give effect to its laws. So, if state X, the place of delivery, prevents the import of goods, its law should be given effect to and performance should not be required in that state. The governing law of the contract, not the law of state X, should then determine whether, and in what circumstances, performance should be effected in another state.

However, the law of the place of performance will not always be applied **13.165** simply because the contract is illegal by that law. This is illustrated,[378] in the context of a contract of insurance, by the decision in *Euro-Diam Ltd v Bathurst*.[379] Staughton J was faced with an action by a plaintiff company

---

[376] Benjamin, 25–150.

[377] Benjamin, ibid, also suggests that if the applicable law states that delivery must be made at a 'reasonable' hour, the law of the place of performance should decide what hours it considers reasonable and its rules applied.

[378] Albeit not in the context of a case concerning manner of performance.

[379] [1990] 1 QB 1.

incorporated in the United Kingdom which supplied diamonds to whole-salers. Some of its diamonds were exported to West Germany, where they were stolen from a German company's warehouse. The plaintiffs sued the defendant, an insurer, for the loss under its contract of insurance. However, the diamonds in question formed part of two consignments negotiated by an Israeli citizen acting in breach of West German immigration laws. Moreover, the defendants alleged that the plaintiffs had mis-represented the value of one of the consignments so as to evade import taxes. In view of this illegality, they argued that the plaintiffs should not be able to enforce the insurance contract. The Court of Appeal disagreed. Although the understating of the value of the diamonds was a criminal offence in Germany, the plaintiffs had recorded the true value properly on their own record and had paid the due premiums and not deceived the defendants. The invoice was not relied upon in the action against the defendants. The illegality did not contribute to the loss of the goods and the court refused to imply a warranty in the contract that the parties would comply with the laws of the place where the dealings with the goods were to be effected.

13.166 Of course, the performance of the parties may also be affected by any relevant mandatory rules of another state. In particular, where exclusions or limitations of liability in relation to the performance of certain obliga-tions are contained in a contract, those provisions must satisfy the requirements of the Unfair Contract Terms Act 1977 in an English court, in those circumstances where the Act is intended to apply irrespective of the law governing the contract.[380]

Performance of the Key Obligations of the Buyer and the Seller[381]

Duty to deliver

13.167 The applicable law will regulate the delivery obligations of the seller.[382] Hence, the place or places of delivery, the acceptable delivery times, the persons to whom the seller might deliver, the nature and quantity of goods to deliver, the packaging of the goods and the documents which the seller must tender to the buyer are all a matter for the applicable law. The seller's obligations related to the contract of sale will also be covered, including obligations that he might have to procure a contract of carriage and to insure the goods.

---

[380] Pursuant to Art 7(2) of the Rome Convention. The operation of the Unfair Contract Terms Act 1977 is considered in detail below, paras 13.301–320.

[381] See generally the account in Benjamin of these issues: 25–150 to 25–165.

[382] Subject to Art 10(2) and the discretionary application of the law of the place of performance with respect to manner of performance.

Duty to take delivery

In principle, the applicable law should determine if, and in which circum- **13.168** stances, the buyer is entitled to refuse to take delivery of the goods. This will extend, as appropriate, to accepting goods tendered by the seller. The applicable law will determine the buyer's obligations to inform the seller of the time and place of delivery. It will also cover obligations which the buyer might have related to the sales contract, such as arranging for the carriage of the goods and informing the seller of the carriage arrangements. Giuliano and Lagarde indicate that if the buyer is justified in refusing delivery by the governing law, the question of what consequences should follow from this may be determined by the law of the place of performance, pursuant to Article 10(2). This might include the question of whether the seller is entitled to deliver further goods of a suitable quality, or fitting the description, within the time available for delivery.

Duty to pass property

This fundamental obligation of the seller is a matter for the law applicable **13.169** to the contract. This will determine the existence of the duty to pass property and the nature of the property which the seller is obliged to pass to the buyer.[383]

Matters are relatively straightforward if the applicable law contains an **13.170** implied duty to pass property similar to that contained in s 12 of the Sale of Goods Act 1979,[384] and if the circumstances in which that duty may be excluded or restricted are identical to, or more limited than, those of the Unfair Contract Terms Act 1977. Difficulties will arise, however, if the governing law contains less extensive implied terms as to the passing of property, or if it would permit those terms to be excluded or restricted in circumstances where this would not be possible according to the Unfair Contract Terms Act 1977. It is to this question that we now turn.

The application of the Unfair Contract Terms Act 1977 to international **13.171** sale of goods contracts is considered extensively below.[385] However, in summary, the rules on exclusion and limitation contained in the 1977 Act do not apply if the contract is an 'international supply contract' within the meaning of s 26. In such a case, the applicable law of the contract will

---

[383] Although, of course, the question of whether property has passed to the buyer is a proprietary one and for the law of the situs to determine.

[384] Oddly, s 12 speaks to the *quality* of the title passed by the seller; it does not as such require the seller to pass the property in the goods. In fact, no provision in the Sale of Goods Act 1979 does. Such a duty seems to be implied from the terms of the parties' contract when they use words such as 'sell' and 'buy'.

[385] At 13.301–320.

alone determine the nature and extent of the seller's duty to pass title and whether that duty may be excluded or restricted.

13.172 If s 26 is inapplicable, then the provisions of the 1977 Act will normally be applicable in full force if the law of a part of the United Kingdom *is* the governing law of the contract. Even here, however, the rules of the 1977 Act will not apply if the parties choose the law of a part of the United Kingdom to govern the contract but, save for that choice, the law of a foreign state would have governed the contract.[386]

13.173 Conversely, the rules of the 1977 Act *do* apply if the parties choose[387] a foreign law to govern the contract and that term was imposed by a party wholly or principally to evade the restrictions in the Act.[388] These rules include, in s 6, a provision prohibiting the exclusion or restriction of liability for breach of the seller's undertakings as to title. This may be seen as a mandatory rule of the forum, which may be applied pursuant to Article 7(2) of the Rome Convention.

13.174 Despite this, the Sale of Goods Act 1979 does not itself explicitly state that the implied terms contained therein shall be applied even where a contract is governed by foreign law. Accordingly, s 27(2) of the Unfair Contract Terms Act 1977 appears not only to limit the circumstances in which the obligations contained in the Sale of Goods Act 1979 Act may be restricted or excluded, but it also seems explicitly to apply them in circumstances where the 1979 Act itself does not expressly insist upon their application.[389] Although this might seem somewhat curious, this clearly appears to be the outcome intended by s 27(2) of the 1977 Act and the result is that, where applicable, the undertakings as to title must be complied with even if the governing law of the contract would permit the seller to exclude or restrict them.

13.175 The remedies available to the buyer in the event of a breach of the duty to pass property will be determined by the applicable law of the contract.[390]

Duty to pay the purchase price; interest upon failure to pay the purchase price

13.176 There is no doubt that the duty to pay the purchase price is, in principle, a matter for the governing law of the contract. If the parties' stipulation as to the purchase price is unclear or ambiguous, the applicable law[391] will

---

[386] s 27(1).   [387] Or purport to choose.

[388] s 27(2)(a), UCTA 1977. See also the provision on consumer contracts, contained in s 27(2)(b) and discussed below, para 13.320.

[389] See also Benjamin, 25–152; Peel, n 53 above, 15–058.

[390] Art 10(1)(c), discussed below, paras 13.205–239.

[391] Unless the parties have chosen a different law to govern the interpretation of the contract (see the discussion of contract splitting in relation to Art 3(1), above, paras 13.103–105).

determine the construction of their words.[392] The applicable law will determine the time and place of payment[393] and the credit period available to the buyer.

If the buyer defaults in paying, the issue of whether the seller might **13.177** have the right to resell the goods is a question for the governing law of the contract.[394] However, the question whether a seller with power to resell actually *has* passed a good title to a third party is a property law matter and subject to property choice of law rules.[395]

The governing law should also determine, in default of payment, **13.178** whether, and if so, at what rate, interest might be charged on the purchase price.[396] However, this is qualified by s 12 of the Late Payment of Commercial Debts (Interest) Act 1998.[397] In contracts for the supply of goods and services between parties, both of whom are acting in the course of business, the Act provides, subject to certain exceptions,[398] that simple interest shall be payable upon a debt which is not paid on time.

The Act has a qualified, mandatory application. Section 12(1) states that **13.179** the Act does *not* apply to a contract governed by the law of a part of the United Kingdom which has no significant connection with *that part*[399] of the United Kingdom, if that law only applies by virtue of the choice of the parties and, but for that choice, the law of a state outside the United Kingdom[400] would have been applicable. This means that the Act will be applicable if English law is chosen by the parties and there is *a* significant

---

[392] Art 10(1)(a). As Benjamin notes (25–154), if the parties do not name a price at all, or if it is required to resolve the meaning of an ambiguous phrase, the court should examine any relevant trade usage. The authors cite the Supreme Court of Manitoba's decision in *Sanitary Packing Co Ltd v Nicholson and Bain* (1916) 33 WLR 594 where a court referred to Ontarian trade usage where that law governed the contract and the meaning of the words 'opening price' were in issue.

[393] Although subject to the possible application of Art 10(2), considered above, paras 13.160–166.

[394] Art 10(1)(c).   [395] See Benjamin, 25–182.

[396] *Mount Albert Borough Council v Australasian Temperance and General Mutual Life Assurance Society Ltd* [1938] AC 224. But see Benjamin, 25–184 on the payment of interest on an award of damages, where the authors argue that the law of the forum should apply.

[397] See also the discussion of the Directive on Combating Late Payment in Commercial Transactions (EC) 2000/35, below, paras 18.104–107.

[398] s 1(1).

[399] Emphasis added. So, the Act would not affect a contract stipulated to be governed by English law, which had no significant objective connection to England, but did have a significant connection to Scotland (at least if, but for the choice of law, the contract would have been governed by the law of a state outside the UK).

[400] This has the curious effect that if the parties chose English law to govern the contract, which had no significant connection to the contract, but, in the absence of choice, Scottish law would have applied, the Act will still apply. This is because, in the absence of choice, the applicable law would not have been that of a state outside the UK. See s 12(1)(b) and Benjamin, 25–155.

connection to England,[401] even though, in the absence of choice, a different law would have governed the contract. Of course, if the law of a state of the United Kingdom governs the contract, and the exclusionary conditions of s 12(1) of the 1998 Act are not met, the simple interest provision in the Act will be given effect as part of the governing law.

13.180 Conversely, the Act *will* apply in relation to a contract governed by the law of a state outside the United Kingdom if, save for that choice, the governing law would have been that of a part of the United Kingdom and there is no significant connection between the contract and any country other than that part of the United Kingdom. If the parties chose Japanese law to govern their contract, but, save for this choice, English law would have been the governing law, the Act will apply *unless* the contract has a significant connection to some state other than England. If the contract *does* have a significant connection to some other state, such as Germany, the Act will not apply, *even though the contract has no objective connection with the state whose law was chosen*, in this case Japan.

Duties to supply goods fit for purpose, complying with description, sample and in the correct quantity

13.181 These key duties of the seller are relatively uncontroversial in the conflict of laws. In principle, all are subject to the governing law of the contract.[402] That law will be used to interpret any provisions in the contract relating to these matters. But more significantly, that law will also determine what implied undertakings are included in the contract and the extent to which those undertakings may be excluded, or liability for their breach restricted.[403]

13.182 Of course, it is very likely that most states will imply obligations of this nature into a contract. The Vienna Convention contains a set of rules on the obligations and liabilities of the seller in Articles 30 to 52.[404] In Italy, even before the entry into force of the Vienna Convention,[405] the importance of the seller's obligation to provide goods of a satisfactory

---

[401] Benjamin, ibid, suggests that a significant connection would exist if England is the place of business of the buyer or the place of payment or the place of delivery. Despite the existence of one or more of these connections, English law would not necessarily have applied in the absence of choice. This is because Art 4(2) would lead to a presumption that the law of the habitual residence or principal place of business of the seller would apply.

[402] As are the remedies available for breach of these obligations. Thus, the applicable law would determine such questions as whether the buyer is entitled to reject the goods or the documents: Art 10(1)(c), discussed below, paras 13.205–239.

[403] Compare *Henry Kendall & Sons v William Lillico & Sons Ltd* [1969] 2 AC 31. See also the discussion of s 2 of the Fertilizers and Feeding Stuffs Act 1926 in this case (discussed further by Benjamin, 25–164).

[404] Although the Vienna Convention is not mandatory, in the sense that the parties may exclude its application, or vary its provisions, pursuant to Art 6.

[405] The Convention entered into force in Italy on 1 January 1988.

quality arose before the District Court of Monza in *SpA OMV Officine Meccaniche Ventura v Prometal SA*.[406] The court had to determine the seller's obligations for the purposes of allocating jurisdiction under Article 5(1) of the Brussels Convention. It ruled that the duty of the seller to provide a guarantee as to defects was inextricably bound up with the obligation to deliver goods[407] to the buyer free from defects.[408] This was described as one of the principal obligations of the seller and it seems very likely that an Italian court would insist upon it being satisfied, even if the applicable law imposed no such requirement.[409]

Where the governing law imposes as rigorous, or more rigorous, implied **13.183** terms than the Sale of Goods Act 1979, and where its rules on exclusion or limitation of liability are at least as robust as those under the Unfair Contract Terms Act 1977, little difficulty will arise.[410] However, if the implied terms are less rigorous than the Sale of Goods Act 1979, or the rules on exclusion and limitation of liability are wider than those under the Unfair Contract Terms Act 1977, problems may ensue.

As will be seen below,[411] the 1977 Act provides in s 6(2)(a) that the obliga- **13.184** tions in ss 13 to 15 of the Sale of Goods Act 1979 may not be excluded or restricted at all as against a person dealing as a consumer. In the case of business contracts, s 6(2)(b) states that ss 13[412] to 15 may be excluded or restricted, but only if the clause complies with the requirement of 'reasonableness'.[413] In circumstances where the Act is applicable, any exclusion or limitation clause must be reasonable in the eyes of English law. To the extent that it is not, the clause will be invalid.[414]

---

[406] [1990] IL Pr 184.

[407] As to the source of the obligation, and whether it is derived from the obligation to deliver, see the discussion, above, paras 3.110–111 and 3.261–271.

[408] Pursuant to s 1492 of the Civil Code. See also Cassazione no 5774, judgment of 3 November 1982.

[409] [1990] IL Pr 184, 188–189.

[410] Save in the unlikely event that the implied terms are so rigorous, and the rules on exclusion and limitation so restrictive, that application of the governing law is manifestly contrary to English public policy under Art 16 of the Rome Convention.

[411] At 13.186, 13.320.

[412] The undertakings as to title in s 12 may not be excluded in a consumer or a business contract.

[413] This is defined in s 11 UCTA. The test of reasonableness requires that 'the term shall have been a fair and reasonable one to be included having regard to the circumstances which were, or ought reasonably to have been, known to or in the contemplation of the parties when the contract was made'.

[414] Because the provisions of UCTA 1977 will be treated as international mandatory rules and may be applied pursuant to Art 7(2) of the Rome Convention. It is possible, in the case of consumer contracts, that the state of the consumer's habitual residence may also contain mandatory rules on the exclusion and limitation of liability for these various obligations of the seller. If that is the case, then the buyer should get the benefit of them, if they are more protective of him than the rules of the governing law.

13.185 That said, the Court of Appeal in *Aeolian Shipping SA v ISS Machinery Services Ltd*[415] was faced with a contract for the supply of parts for a turbo-charger on a ship. The purchaser argued that the charger was of unsatisfactory quality and durability. The contract was found to be governed by Japanese law. It was accepted by the parties in the Court of Appeal that Japanese law did not imply into a supply contract an implied term of satisfactory quality or durability. The purchasers did not seek to argue that this infringed a mandatory rule of English law, or a rule of public policy, and the court gave no indication that it found the Japanese law objectionable. The defendant failed in his claim for damages based upon the condition and durability of the goods.

Exclusion of the Implied Undertakings in the Sale of Goods Act 1979

13.186 It should be clear from the above discussions that the parties to a contract could not provide that 'this contract shall be governed by the law of England, but shall exclude all undertakings and liabilities contained in the Sale of Goods Act 1979'. There are two serious objections to such a clause. First, that if the parties chose a law to govern a contract, they must take it as they find it.[416] Second, that it is clear from the terms of the Unfair Contract Terms Act 1977 that its rules on exclusion and limitation of liability are capable of application even to contracts governed by a foreign law. This has the result that the Sale of Goods Act 1979 is itself rendered a mandatory rule, in the sense that the key obligations of the parties under that Act may not be excluded or restricted, or may only be excluded or restricted when it is reasonable to do so.[417]

Currency of Account

13.187 Article 10(1)(b) would presumably also cover questions relating to the currency of account and the currency of payment. These are matters properly submitted to the law applicable to the contract. If the currency of account stipulated by the parties is itself not wholly clear, this raises an issue of interpretation of the contract.[418] If the law applicable to the contract has been split, and a separate law governs the question of interpretation of the contract, then it is that law which would resolve any ambiguity as to meaning. Otherwise, matters of interpretation are determined by the governing law of the contract.

---

[415] [2001] 2 Lloyd's Rep 641.

[416] They may 'split' the contract under Art 3(1), but they must still apply *all* of the domestic law of the state whose law applies to a particular issue.

[417] See the discussion of the UCTA 1977 below, paras 13.301–320.

[418] Art 10(1)(a). Compare *Bonython v Commonwealth of Australia* [1951] AC 201.

In *W J Alan & Co v El Nasr Export*,[419] two contracts for the sale of coffee had **13.188** been concluded between Kenyan sellers and an Egyptian state trading corporation with an office in Tanzania, FOB Mombasa. The contract incorporated the terms of the London Coffee Trade Association, which stipulated English law as the proper law of the contract. However, the contract also stated a price of 'shs. 262 . . . per cwt'. Payment was to be by irrevocable letter of credit. The buyer sold the coffee on to sub-buyers who opened an irrevocable letter of credit in Madrid in sterling. The buyers obtained the transfer to a bank in Tanzania of the letter of credit for an amount not exceeding £131,000 in favour of the sellers. The sellers accepted the terms of the letter of credit and operated the credit. Subsequently, the sellers prepared an invoice expressed in sterling in respect of coffee supplied under the second contract. Before they presented the documents, sterling was devalued. The sellers then claimed that since Kenyan shillings was the currency of account in the sales contracts, the buyers, having paid in sterling, were liable for an additional amount which would bring the price up to 262 Kenyan shillings at the present rate. The Court of Appeal agreed that the currency of account had to be construed according to the proper law of the contract, English law. As a matter of construction of the contract, this was Kenyan shillings, as demonstrated by the abbreviation 'shs', which was not used in respect of shillings in sterling. However, the Court of Appeal then went on to find that because the sellers had accepted the sterling letter of credit, it had, according to the proper law of the contract, conditionally discharged the buyer of liability; a liability which was absolutely discharged when the payment was made.

This case illustrates what must still be the position today under the Rome **13.189** Convention, namely that: (1) the law applicable to the contract determines the currency of account;[420] (2) where the parties have made a stipulation as to the currency of account, the construction of that term of the contract is governed by the applicable law of the contract. However, if the contract has been split in accordance with Article 3(1) and a separate law chosen to govern the construction of the contract, that law shall determine the meaning of a stipulation as to currency in the contract; (3) where a seller accepts payment by a letter of credit in a different currency, and where full payment is made under the letter of credit, this will be construed as a variation of the agreement as to the currency of account, at least where the contract of sale is governed by English law.

---

[419] [1972] 2 QB 189.
[420] And will determine what is legal tender in that state: *Pyrmont Ltd v Schott* [1939] AC 145.

13.190   Otherwise, where a contract is governed by English law, Benjamin points out that the parties will be presumed to have intended that the currency of the state of closest connection to the contract should be used.[421] If they have selected a place of payment and made no provision as to currency, it will be presumed that the currency of that place is the currency of account,[422] unless there is more than one potential place of payment.[423]

13.191   The applicable law of the contract will determine the effect of any fluctuations of exchange rate on the price payable.[424] However, as Benjamin points out, almost every state accepts the principle of nominalism, namely that the price stated in the contract shall not be affected by such fluctuations.[425]

Currency of Payment

13.192   The currency of payment[426] clearly relates to the buyer's performance under the contract. However, it is at first sight not wholly clear whether the applicable law alone should determine this matter, or whether the issue should be treated as relating to the 'manner of performance', so that the law of the place of payment may also be invoked.[427] The matter is far from clear. Giuliano and Lagarde suggest that the applicable law should apply to determine the conditions of discharge of the buyer's payment

---

[421]   Benjamin, 25–158, citing *Bonython v Commonwealth of Australia* [1951] AC 201; *National Bank of Australasia v Scottish Union and National Insurance Co Ltd* [1952] AC 493; and *WJ Alan & Co Ltd v El Nasr Export and Import Co* [1972] 2 QB 189.

[422]   *Mount Albert Borough Council v Australasian Temperance and General Mutual Life Assurance Society Ltd* [1938] AC 224; *National Mutual Association of Australasia Ltd v AG for New Zealand* [1956] AC 369, 387; *WJ Alan & Co Ltd v El Nasr Export and Import Co* [1972] 2 QB 189.

[423]   Or, of course, if the terms of the contract point to a different law.

[424]   Where the money of account and the money of payment are not the same, the governing law of the contract should determine the exchange rate between them: Dicey and Morris, 1600–4; Benjamin, 25–160.

[425]   Benjamin, 25–159. However, the authors point out that if the currency is devalued after the conclusion of the contract and before payment becomes due, the applicable law should determine whether the buyer should be required to pay a higher sum. In such a case, this might more accurately reflect the intended 'value' placed on the goods by the parties. See *Re Schnapper* [1936] 1 All ER 322.

[426]   English law is prepared to award damages in a foreign currency (*Miliangos v George Frank (Textiles) Ltd (No 1)* [1976] AC 443). The governing law should determine in which currency damages are awarded: Art 10(1)(c); compare *Services Europe Atlantique Sud v Stockholms Rederiaktebolag SVEA (The Folias)* [1979] AC 685, 700. It is a matter of construction of the contract (under Art 10(1)(a)) whether the parties intended that the currency of account and/or payment should also be the currency in which damages are awarded. Where a contract is governed by English law and it does not appear that the parties intended the currency of account and/or payment also to be the currency in which damages are award, the court will award damages in the currency which best reflects the party's loss: *The Folias*, ibid, 700; see further, Benjamin, 25–186 and 25–193. See further the discussion of Art 10(1)(c), below, 13.211–214.

[427]   Pursuant to Art 10(2).

obligation.[428] However, whilst it seems sensible for the applicable law to determine when the payment obligation has been met, the currency in which that obligation *may* be met does naturally seem to be a question of *how* the payment obligation can be discharged. Accordingly, it is likely that the law of the place of payment will be applied to this matter under Article 10(2).[429]

As Benjamin notes, where England is the country of payment, English law **13.193** adopts a presumption that the currency of payment will be the same as the currency of account.[430]

Inspection

It is not wholly clear which law should determine the right of the buyer to **13.194** inspect the goods, the place of inspection and the time and form of inspection. It would seem that the *right* to inspect the goods is a matter for the governing law of the contract. Matters relating to time, place and form of inspection appear to relate to the *manner* in which the inspection is carried out.[431] They may accordingly be subject to the law of the place where performance is to be carried out.[432]

The right of the buyer to reject the goods must be a matter for the govern- **13.195** ing law of the contract, as will be the question of whether the contract may be repudiated by the breach.[433] The applicable law will also determine whether the buyer must inform the seller of the rejection of the goods and whether the seller has the right to provide substitute goods in the event of rejection.[434]

---

[428] Giuliano and Lagarde Report, 42–43.

[429] This view is shared by the authors of Benjamin, 25–160, who in turn draw support from Plender and Wilderspin, n 1 above, 11–07. However, it appears that Plender is dealing with a different point, namely that the *construction* of a term stipulating a currency of payment 'will only be readily ascertainable by reference to the law of the country whose currency it is'. He is not dealing with the situation where there is no stipulation at all as to the currency of payment.

[430] Benjamin, 25–160, citing *Auckland Corp v Alliance Assurance Co Ltd* [1937] AC 587.

[431] Benjamin, 25–189, suggests that issues concerning the 'general custody' of the rejected goods should also be determined by the law of the place of performance, in accordance with Art 10(2). However, it is questionable whether this can be said to concern the manner of performance of the obligations arising under the contract. It may be that the law applicable to the contract will alone be applied to this issue.

[432] Art 10(2). Of course, until the place of inspection is determined, it may not be possible to ascertain which law this is, if the parties have not stipulated where inspection is to occur. The English court will have to apply the law of the place where, putatively, the inspection is to be carried out at this stage. See below, paras 15.53–55, on the Hague Sales Conventions, for discussion as to the place of inspection in English domestic law.

[433] Art 10(1)(c).

[434] See the discussion of rejection of goods in relation to Art 10(1)(c), below, paras 13.234–235.

Risk

13.196 The question of which party, if either, has taken the risk of certain events happening must be a matter for the law applicable to the contract. This issue does not naturally fit within any one provision of Article 10. However, this is certainly not fatal to the application of the governing law, since Article 10 only provides a non-exhaustive list of matters subjected to that law. Risk may relate, for example, to the performance of the contract, if goods cannot be delivered owing to a failure to obtain an export or import licence. It may relate to the condition of the goods, if, for example, they are lost or damaged before reaching the buyer. It may relate to the extinguishing of obligations under the contract, if, for example, after the contract is concluded performance of the contract becomes illegal by the law of the place of performance. In that case, the question may arise as to whether the contract is frustrated, or whether one party bore the risk of such an occurrence.[435] It is suggested that the question whether the non-delivering seller has a defence that the contract was frustrated to an action for damages for non-delivery is a matter for the applicable law of the contract. The same law should be applied to the question of whether the buyer still has to pay despite what has happened to the goods.

13.197 Of course, the question of risk is closely connected to the passing of property.[436] In English law, s 20 of the Sale of Goods Act 1979 provides that risk is presumed to pass with the property, unless the parties agree to the contrary. However, the fact that risk may pass with property in the domestic law of a particular state does not mean that risk itself is a proprietary matter. It is clearly concerned with the question of the personal liability of the parties under the contract. As such, a contractual classification is clearly appropriate and the governing law of the contract should be applied.[437] This is the same approach as is adopted expressly by Article 12(d) of the Hague Sales Convention 1986.[438]

13.198 To this general principle, *Benjamin* suggests a somewhat controversial exception. The authors point out that where parties enter into a contract governed by English law, they may assume, in the absence of a provision to the contrary, that property will pass under ss 16 to 19 of the Sale of Goods Act 1979 and that, according to s 20 of the Act, risk will pass at the

---

[435] This would also be subject to the applicable law, though presumably by virtue of Art 10(1)(d).

[436] See the discussion of risk below, paras 18.132–134.

[437] A view shared by Benjamin, 25–147; Dicey and Morris, 1333, n 92. See also G Zaphiriou, *The Transfer of Chattels in Private International Law: a Comparative Study* (London: Athlone Press/University of London, 1956) Ch 10.

[438] See the discussion on the Hague Sales Conventions, below, para 15.111.

same time. If the goods are situated overseas and the law of the situs provides that property passes at a different time to that which ss 16 to 19 lay down, Benjamin argues that application of s 20 will lead to risk passing at a time other than that which the parties might have expected. The authors suggest that:

It is therefore possible that in such a case the court would hold that the parties may properly be taken to have displaced section 20 by an implicit contrary agreement, this being in effect that risk should pass at the time when the property *would* have passed if its passing had been regulated by sections 16 to 19, instead of by the foreign *lex situs*.[439]

With due respect, in the present authors' view, such a statement should be **13.199** treated with considerable caution. Contracting parties must take choice of law rules as they find them. If those rules lead to a result which they might not have expected, then there is a strong argument to say that they only have themselves to blame. Moreover, if the application of choice of law rules were based upon the expectations of the parties, then there would be a strong general argument for rejecting the law of the situs and applying the applicable law of the contract to questions of the passing of property; yet it is clear that the law of the situs holds sway on such matters.[440] In any event, s 20(1) of the Sale of Goods Act 1979 is a statutory default rule that owes nothing to actual party intention.

That said, ultimately, the question of when the parties intended risk to **13.200** pass is essentially one of *construction* of the contract. It should accordingly be for the law which governs this issue (which, in the absence of contract splitting, will be the governing law of the contract) to determine when the parties intended risk to pass.[441] However, it is suggested that, where that governing law is the law of England, it is stretching matters too far to construe the parties' silence as to when property and risk would pass as indicating a *positive intention* that risk should pass at the point when property would have passed in English law. Not the least problem with this argument is that if the parties really did intend from their silence that property and risk should pass *together*, the suggested approach of Benjamin would lead precisely to the result that they would *not*, since the passing of the property would clearly be a matter for the law of the situs. On balance then, it is suggested that a court should be slow to adopt the suggestion made by Benjamin.

---

[439] Benjamin, 25–148. Emphasis in original. The authors also cite *Kursell v Timber Operators and Contractors Ltd* [1927] 1 KB 299, 312 as a case consistent with their suggestion (though it is not a suggestion which was actually adopted by the court in that case).

[440] *Glencore International AG v Metro Trading International Inc (No 2)* [2001] 1 Lloyd's Rep 284, QBD (Comm).

[441] Art 10(1)(a).

Licences

13.201 The question of whether an import and/or export licence is needed for goods can only sensibly be answered by reference to the law of the place of import or export.[442] Since these matters relate to the manner of performance of the seller, an English court may apply the law of the state of export or import, as appropriate, by reference to Article 10(2). In so far as one or more licences is required, the applicable law of the contract will determine which of the parties is responsible for obtaining them.[443] That law will also determine the liability of the parties in the event of a failure to obtain a relevant licence[444] and whether this has the effect of discharging the parties from their obligations.[445]

At least where a contract is governed by English law, the fact that it expressly requires the buyer to obtain an import licence will be almost conclusive evidence that the contract will not be frustrated if, for any reason, the import of goods into the buyer's home state become unlawful.[446] He will be viewed as having taken the risk of obtaining a licence. The same principles will apply if a party expressly agrees to obtain an export licence.

13.202 If the contract is governed by English law and is silent on the question of who should obtain an import licence, it may be that the contract will be viewed as frustrated[447] if the performance of the contract becomes illegal by the law of the place of import.[448]

Exchange Control[449]

13.203 The applicable law of the contract should be applied, in so far as it contains exchange control restrictions. This may lead to the contract being declared invalid.[450] At least where a contract is governed by English law, it may also be invalidated if it infringes exchange control legislation of

---

[442] Compare the House of Lords decision in *AV Pound & Co Ltd v MW Hardy & Co Inc* [1956] AC 588, 601.

[443] Art 10(1)(b). See also *AV Pound & Co Ltd v MW Hardy & Co Inc*, ibid; *Partabmull Rameshar v KC Sethia (1944) Ltd* [1951] 2 Lloyd's Rep 89; *Peter Cassidy Seed Co Ltd v Osuustukkukappa IL* [1957] 1 WLR 273.

[444] Art 10(1)(c).

[445] Art 10(1)(d). Of course, the governing law of the contract is likely to make reference to the law of the place of import or export, in order to determine whether a party's failure to obtain a licence was: (i) reasonable; (ii) foreseeable; and (iii) a circumstance which that party took the risk of occurring.

[446] *Bangladesh Export Import Co Ltd v Sucden Kerry SA* [1995] 2 Lloyd's Rep 1, 6–7.

[447] See *Partabmull Rameshar v KC Sethia (1944) Ltd* [1951] 2 Lloyd's Rep 89; *Walton (Grain and Shipping) Ltd v British Italian Trading Co SA* (1949) 80 LL R 530.

[448] Or, in the case of an export licence, the state of export.

[449] See Dicey and Morris, Rule 212, 1612–22.   [450] Pursuant to Art 8(1).

the law of the place of performance.[451] The United Kingdom also has international obligations under the Bretton Woods Agreement. In relation to exchange contracts involving the currency of a Member State of the International Monetary Fund, any exchange controls of a Member State which are permitted by the Bretton Woods Agreement must be respected and a contract failing to comply with those controls will not be enforceable in England.[452]

Any other exchange control regulations which might enter in force in the **13.204** forum and which are intended to apply irrespective of the governing law may be applied as mandatory rules pursuant to Article 7(2) of the Rome Convention.[453]

3. Within the Limits of the Powers Conferred on the Court by its Procedural Law, the Consequences of Breach, Including the Assessment of Damages in so far as it is Governed by Rules of Law

General Principle

In principle, the contractual remedies available to a party are to be deter- **13.205** mined by the governing law of the contract. However, Article 10(1)(c) makes it clear that the courts of the forum do not have to grant a remedy given by the applicable law of the contract if they are not procedurally competent to do so. Accordingly, it does not seem that an English court would be expected to grant a remedy which is unknown in English domestic law.[454]

Specific Performance

It is less clear whether an English court would be required to grant a **13.206** remedy available by the governing law, if that remedy is known to English law, but would be granted only exceptionally and would not be

---

[451] *Ralli Bros v Compañía Naviera Sota y Aznar* [1920] 2 KB 287. This is on the basis that the contract is frustrated on the grounds of supervening illegality.

[452] See Art 3 of the Bretton Woods Agreements Order in Council 1946, SR & O 1946, pursuant to the Bretton Woods Agreements Act 1945 (the Act was later repealed but the Order in Council is still in force). See Benjamin, 25–113.

[453] See, e.g. *Boissevain v Weil* [1949] 1 KB 482.

[454] Compare the position at common law: *Phrantzes v Argenti* [1960] 2 QB 19; *Monterosso Shipping Co Ltd v International Transport Workers Federation* [1982] 3 All ER 841, 6. See also *John Pfeiffer Pty Ltd v Rogerson* (2000) 172 ALR 625. Benjamin, 25–183, concludes that this position is not significantly different to that at common law: 'At common law, the correct rule was . . . that whilst the law applicable to the contract determined the available remedy, it would not be granted unless such remedy, or a reasonably close equivalent, is to be found within the procedural law of the forum and was accordingly one which the forum has adequate machinery to grant and to enforce'.

available in English domestic law on the facts. The paradigm example would be specific performance, which is much more readily available in some states than in England.[455] Dicey and Morris suggest 'with some hesitation that . . . [specific performance] is . . . a matter for the *lex contractus*'.[456] The present authors would concur.[457] It is suggested that such a remedy should be granted, since it is clearly within the procedural competence of an English court to grant specific performance. Wherever possible, it is desirable that the law which confers contractual rights upon a party should also determine the remedial consequences of a failure by the other party to respect those rights. This avoids artificiality, reduces incentives for forum shopping and is more likely to give effect to the expectations of the parties.[458]

13.207 However, there may still be procedural limitations of the forum which might justify the court in not granting the remedy, as where, for example, specific performance would impose a constant supervision burden on the court. In such a circumstance, the English court would be justified in not awarding specific performance, even if it is available by the applicable law.[459] Subject to this caveat, however, the governing law should be applied to determine if specific performance is available.

Damages Claims by the Seller or Buyer; Heads of Damages, Quantification, etc.

13.208 Obviously, the right of either party to obtain damages for breach of contract will be determined by the governing law of the contract. The seller might sue the buyer for failure to pay the purchase price or to accept the goods.

13.209 Where damages are sought by the buyer, a question may arise as to whether his acceptance of the goods, or late notification to the seller of rejection, prevents him from recovering damages.[460] This is a matter for the applicable law of the contract.

13.210 The availability of heads of damages is a matter for the applicable law of the contract.[461] So too is the quantification of damages, in so far as this is

---

[455] See, in particular, Arts 46 and 62 of the Vienna Convention, which give the buyer and seller respectively the right to require performance of the other party's key obligations under the contract.

[456] Dicey and Morris, 1265. Contrast *Baschet v London Illustrated Standard Co* [1900] 1 Ch 73.

[457] As does Benjamin, 25–194.

[458] *Amin Rasheed Shipping Corp v Kuwait Insurance Co* [1984] AC 50, 60.

[459] See Dicey and Morris, 1265 and Benjamin, 25–194.   [460] Benjamin, 25–192.

[461] *Boys v Chaplin* [1971] AC 356; *Edmunds v Simmonds* [2001] WLR 1003; *Hulse v Chambers* [2001] 1 WLR 2386. See J Carruthers,' Substance and Procedure in the Conflict of Laws: a Continuing Debate in Relation to Damages (2004) 53 ICLQ 691.

determined by rules of law. This also means that rules on remoteness of damages of the governing law will be applied in an English court.[462] However, quantification of damages, in so far as it is not governed by rules of law, will be determined by the law of the forum as a procedural matter.[463] So too, the availability of a counter-claim is likely to be treated as a procedural matter.[464]

Currency of Judgment

Can the English courts award a judgment in a foreign currency?

Benjamin notes that the question of whether the English court *can* **13.211** award damages in a foreign currency is procedural in nature. As such, Article 10(1)(c) of the Rome Convention and the question of whether the governing law of the contract takes the same view, will not be relevant at this stage.[465] That said, English courts may order the payment of a liquidated debt[466] or damages,[467] either in pounds sterling or a foreign currency.

Should the court award a judgment in a foreign currency on the facts?

However, given that English law decrees that damages *can* be awarded **13.212** in a foreign currency, the next question is to determine whether such a judgment *should* be given in a foreign currency in the instant case. This, it is contended, is a question of substance. The English court has determined that it is procedurally competent to grant the award in a foreign currency and it should then be for the law governing the contract to determine in which currency judgment should be given.[468] It follows that the governing law will determine the currency in which a debt is enforced, or damages

---

[462] *J D'Almeida Araujo Lda v Sir Frederick Becker & Co Ltd* [1953] 2 QB 329. The duty to mitigate would also be governed by the applicable law: ibid.

[463] ibid; *Boys v Chaplin* [1971] AC 356; *Edmunds v Simmonds* [2001] WLR 1003; *Hulse v Chambers* [2001] 1 WLR 2386. The question of whether interest may be awarded by way of damages is substantive but, the rate of that interest is procedural. See Benjamin, 25–184; *Miliangos v George Frank (Textiles) Ltd (No 2)* [1977] QB 489.

[464] Benjamin, 25–184, citing *South African Republic v Compagnie Franco-Belge du Chemin de Fer du Nord* [1897] Ch 487. However, the authors point out that a *right* of set off against the claimant's action substantively alters the nature and extent of the claimant's remedy and should be determined by the applicable law: ibid, citing *Macfarlane v Norris* (1862) 2 B & S 783; *Meridien BIAO Bank GmbH v Bank of New York* [1997] 1 Lloyd's Rep 437.

[465] Benjamin, 25–187; *Miliangos v George Frank (Textiles) Ltd (No 1)* [1976] AC 443, 465. Matters of procedure are excluded from the scope of the Rome Convention by Art 1(2)(h).

[466] *Miliangos (No 1)*, ibid; *Schorsch Meier GmbH v Hennin* [1975] QB 516.

[467] *Kraut AG v Albany Fabrics Ltd* [1977] QB 182; *The Folias* [1979] AC 685. See Dicey and Morris, 1609–1611; Cheshire and North, 90–98.

[468] Cheshire and North, 94–95.

are awarded for a breach of contract, such as the buyer's refusal to accept the goods.[469]

13.213 If English law governs the contract, the court's approach was laid down in *The Folias*.[470] If the parties have expressly stated a single currency of account and payment, it is likely that this will also be the appropriate currency in which an English court will award damages.[471] Where the purchase price alone is expressed in a foreign currency, an English court may also award damages in that foreign currency, even if the contract is governed by English law, or some other foreign law.[472] It has been noted that in cases where the contract does not clearly reveal the parties' intentions as to which currency judgment should be given in, English courts tend to award damages in the currency which best expresses the claimant's loss.[473] Where the claim is brought by the buyer, 'this is likely to be the currency in which he is compelled to buy goods in substitution for those promised in the contract or to arrange for defects to be put right in the goods which the seller has delivered'.[474]

Execution of a judgment given in a foreign currency

13.214 Where payment is ordered in a foreign currency and the debtor fails to pay, the claimant will need to enforce the judgment. Dicey and Morris, rule 211(2)[475] states that: 'For procedural reasons the amount of the judgment must be converted into sterling before execution can be levied'. Conversion should be made as from the date of payment,[476] which will normally be the date when the court authorizes enforcement of the judgment, unless there is a statutory provision to the contrary.[477]

Interest Upon the Judgment

13.215 Benjamin suggests that once the English court has invoked the applicable law and ordered the payment of damages, English law should determine at what rate interest on those damages is awarded,[478] irrespective of the currency in which judgment was given. It should do so by applying s 35A

---

[469] *Services Europe Atlantique Sud (SEAS) v Stockholms Rederiaktebolag SVEA ('The Folias')* [1979] AC 685; Benjamin, 25–186.

[470] [1979] AC 685.   [471] *Bain v Field & Co Fruit Merchants Ltd* (1920) 5 ILR 16.

[472] Benjamin, 25–187.   [473] ibid, 25–186.   [474] ibid, 25–193.

[475] Dicey and Morris, 1605. Rule 211 is explained at 1604–9.

[476] *Miliangos v George Frank (Textiles) Ltd (No 1)* [1976] AC 443; Benjamin, 25–187.

[477] *Miliangos (No 1)*, ibid, at 468–9.

[478] Benjamin, 25–184, citing, inter alia, *Miliangos v George Frank (Textiles) Ltd (No 2)* [1977] QB 489; *Shell Tankers (UK) Ltd v Astro Comino Armadora SA (The Pacific Colocotronis)* [1981] 2 Lloyd's Rep; but contrast *Helmsing Schiffarts GmbH v Malta Drydocks Corp* [1977] 2 Lloyd's Rep 444, 449–50.

of the Supreme Court Act 1981, by which it has a discretion to determine the rate of simple interest.[479]

In the event of the buyer making a late payment,[480] and the currency of payment having depreciated in the meantime, the governing law should determine if the buyer is liable to compensate the seller for the ensuing loss.[481] **13.216**

Contractual or Proprietary Remedy?

The Rome Convention applies only to 'contractual obligations'.[482] However, whilst the *obligation* must be contractual, the Rome Convention does not expressly stipulate that the *remedy* awarded must also be contractual in nature.[483] This gives rise to difficulties if the remedy awarded for the breach of a contractual obligation is proprietary in nature. **13.217**

However, it is suggested that the Rome Convention should be construed as applying only to *contractual* remedies for breaches of *contractual* obligations. The application of the law of the *situs* rule in relation to property is largely result orientated and based upon the need to ensure that, where property rights are at stake, an English court reaches a decision in conformity with that which a judge in the situs would reach. Whatever the source of the obligation, it is desirable that the law of the *situs* apply to proprietary remedies, since, ultimately, rights in property are in issue. **13.218**

This, in turn, raises a difficult problem of classification, where it is unclear if the remedy in question is essentially contractual or proprietary in nature. Benjamin suggests that this classification should be conducted by the law of the forum. The authors of that work reject the application of the law of the *situs*, on the basis that this 'is likely to present problems as to time, and possibly even circularity, if the goods change *situs*'.[484] It is **13.219**

---

[479] The authors of Benjamin, ibid, suggest that in exercising this discretion, the court will normally award the rate of interest applicable to the currency of payment, at least where that currency was stated in the contract (citing *Miliangos (No 2)* in support). The authors go on to suggest that if the creditor is reasonably required to borrow in his own currency rather than the currency of account, the rate should be that at which a loan will ordinarily be repayable in the state where he borrowed (citing *Hemsing*, ibid, and *The Pacific Colocotronis*, ibid, in support).

[480] See also the discussion of the Directive on Combating Late Payment in Commercial Transactions (EC) 2000/35 below, paras 18.104–107.

[481] Benjamin, 25–185.

[482] Art 1(1); Giuliano and Lagarde Report, 10.

[483] Indeed, the Rome Convention allows the applicable law to deal with the consequences of breach, without restriction. Not all legal systems are like English law in treating remedies, like damages, as derived from secondary obligations of the contract.

[484] Benjamin, 25–171.

suggested that this is correct in principle, there being no reason to classify a dispute as to whether a remedy is contractual or proprietary by either the law applicable to the contract or the law of the *situs.*

13.220   That said, there is no clear guidance in the Rome Convention as to what constitutes a contractual remedy. Benjamin suggests that where the only parties to the litigation are the seller and the buyer, the remedy awarded should be classified as contractual.[485] Where the competing interests of a third party, such as the carrier or a sub-buyer are involved, Benjamin argues that this is essentially a proprietary matter.

13.221   However, it is suggested that this distinction can not be accepted, at least on the present state of the authorities.[486] The question of who the parties to the litigation are cannot be determinative of the nature of the right in question. It was stressed in *Glencore International AG v Metro Trading International Inc (No 2)*[487] that a property claim remains a property claim, and the law of the *situs* must be applied to it, notwithstanding that the only parties to the litigation are the buyer and seller under a contract. Even in litigation between the buyer and the seller, the question may arise as to the respective interests of the parties in the goods or purchase monies. Any finding of the court on this matter may bind third parties. The distinguishing characteristic of a property right is that it is *capable* of binding third parties. Furthermore, one might argue that the justifications for applying the law of the *situs* remain, in that the *situs* will effectively have control over the property in question[488] and will provide a choice of law rule that is predictable for the contracting parties and third parties alike.[489]

13.222   Moore-Bick J remarked in *Glencore* as follows:[490]

I do not think that questions of title to movables can properly be considered simply by reference to the positions of the parties to the transaction under which they are intended to be transferred. Consistency of principle requires that the same rule should apply whether or not third party interests are involved . . . [I]t would be highly anomalous if questions of title to the goods were to be governed by . . . the proper law of the contract if the seller had not purported to re-sell the

---

[485]   ibid.
[486]   Although it does have something to commend it in principle: see below, paras 18.37–54. See also the discussion of the Hague Convention on the Transfer of Property 1958, below, paras 18.71–73.
[487]   [2001] 1 Lloyd's Rep 284, QBD (Comm).
[488]   Of course, this argument is less strong in relation to movable property than immovable property, in that the situs of movable property may change.
[489]   Compare Cheshire and North, 940–1; P Lalive, *The Transfer of Chattels in the Conflict of Laws* (Oxford: Clarendon, 1955) 115.
[490]   [2001] 1 Lloyd's Rep 284, 294–6, QBD (Comm).

goods to a third party, but by . . . the *lex situs* if he had.[491] Questions of title are most likely to be of importance when one party to the transaction is insolvent. The interests of third parties in the form of a general body of creditors may clearly be affected in such a case,[492] but it would be equally anomalous if the law governing the passing of property depended on considerations of this kind. . . . Practical control over movables can ultimately only be regulated and protected by the state in which they are situated and the adoption of the *lex situs* rule in relation to the passing of property is in part a recognition of that fact. That is just as much true in relation to the passing of property between the parties to the transaction as it is in relation to the passing of property between one or other of them and a third party.

The decision in *Glencore* suggests that the key distinction to be drawn is between personal remedies binding only two parties, such as a claim by the buyer against the seller for damages, and rights in the goods or purchase monies themselves, which can endure against third parties. The former should be regarded as contractual; the latter as proprietary.[493] We shall now look at certain remedies whose classification is less than straightforward, or where it may be necessary to separate the contractual elements from the proprietary elements of the remedy and to apply a separate choice of law rule to each.

Lien[494]

The right of the seller to retain possession of goods where he has not **13.223** received payment from the buyer[495] is regarded by Benjamin as a contractual remedy to be determined by the governing law of the contract.[496] However, the authors suggest that where third parties claim rights in the goods unencumbered by the seller's lien, as where the buyer has transferred documents to a sub-buyer, the property choice of law rules should apply.

---

[491] However, one might retort that in English domestic law, we separate the two questions of when property passes to the buyer under the contract of sale and whether the buyer has the power to transfer title to third parties. And we underline that separation by using different words, 'property' and 'title', for the two cases. It would be possible for the law of State A to deal with passing of property and the law of State B to deal with transfer of title. English domestic law builds the passing of property upon the intention of the parties.

[492] English law does not treat creditors as third parties, in the sense that there is no disposing transaction in their favour. The liquidator stands in the shoes of the company in winding-up (also the trustee qua bankrupt) and represents the unsecured general creditors.

[493] But see below, paras 18.37–54, on the question of whether property law questions arising solely between the buyer and the seller might be governed by the applicable law of the contract.

[494] See also below, paras 18.42-44; M Chesterman, 'Choice of Law Aspects of Liens and Similar Claims in International Sale of Goods' (1973) 22 ICLQ 213.

[495] On maritime liens, see A Mandaraka-Sheppard, *Modern Admiralty Law* (London: Cavendish, 2001) 154–9.

[496] Benjamin, 25–173, citing *Livesley v Clemens Horst Co* [1925] 1 DLR 159, 160–161.

13.224 In the light of the *Glencore* case,[497] one might question the validity of this distinction. Even where the issue of the lien is raised in litigation solely between the buyer and the seller, the question may arise as to the *nature of the seller's interest in the goods*.[498] The lien may be capable of binding third parties, albeit that it might, in some circumstances, be defeated by a third party. It might seem undesirable for the law governing the contract, law X, to determine that the seller has a lien over the buyer's property, only for the law of the situs, law Y, to determine that this lien cannot be enforced against a third party, on the basis that, by the law of State Y, that lien never arose in the first place. One might respond that the appropriate question to ask of the law of State Y is rather 'assuming that the seller has a lien over the buyer's property, does this lien bind a third party?'. However, this is an artificial question which involves distortion of the law of State Y.

13.225 Nevertheless, the unpaid seller's lien can be seen in parallel, contractual terms as the right not to deliver except in accordance with the terms of the contract. For example a seller might in certain circumstances decline to deliver to a buyer not ready and willing to pay.[499] A seller who stands on his contractual entitlement is exercising a contractual right. And, if no third party interest has supervened, it ought not to matter whether the property has already passed to the buyer. Accordingly, this question can properly be determined by the applicable law of the contract.

13.226 It is suggested that one must distinguish between the exercise of a *contractual* right of the seller to refuse to deliver to the buyer and the *proprietary* effects of the lien. The former should be governed by the applicable law of the contract. The latter should determine whether the right in question is one which may endure against third parties.

Stoppage in Transit[500]

13.227 Benjamin notes that there is no clear authority as to whether the right of stoppage in transit should be treated as a contractual or a proprietary remedy.[501] The authors go on to suggest that the existence of a right of stoppage between the buyer and the seller alone, and the means by which it may be exercised, are to be determined by the applicable law of the contract. They point out that application of the law of the *situs* makes it

---

[497] Discussed above, paras 13.221–222.
[498] See *Willis v Glenwood Cotton Mills* 200 F 301, 305 (1912).
[499] See Art 30 of the Vienna Convention.   [500] See below, paras 18.43–45.
[501] Benjamin, 25–176. The authors note that the decision in *Inglis v Usherwood* (1801) East 515 is of limited assistance, since the law applied was both the law of the *situs* and the proper law of the contract.

harder for the parties to vary the right of stoppage by agreement and may also lead to problems where goods are in transit.[502] However, the authors suggest that where the seller seeks to invoke the right of stoppage against a third party, such as a sub-buyer, proprietary choice of law rules should apply.[503]

In the light of *Glencore*,[504] one might question whether this approach **13.228** should be followed. The right of stoppage in transit, although derived from the contract of sale, itself creates a form of proprietary interest which entitles the claimant to demand stoppage. That right, once in being, may be *capable* of enduring against third parties. As such, it could be seen as a proprietary right.

However, Article 71(2) of the Vienna Convention treats stoppage in transit **13.229** in effect as a contractual matter where it concerns only the seller and the buyer. It provides that:

If the seller has already dispatched the goods before . . . [an anticipatory breach by the buyer] becomes evident, he may prevent the handing over of the goods to the buyer even though the buyer holds a document which entitles him to obtain them. *The present paragraph relates only to the rights in the goods themselves as between the buyer and the seller.*[505]

Stoppage in transit is in contractual terms a reversal of delivery with the enforced assistance of a third party carrier. Stoppage says nothing about the location of property. It sets up the possibility of resale[506] Accordingly, it is suggested that the distinction in Benjamin should be adopted in this area and that the seller's right of stoppage in transit should be governed by the applicable law of the contract when invoked against the buyer, and by the law of the *situs* when invoked against a third party.

Rescission[507]

Benjamin suggests that the law applicable to the contract should apply **13.230** where the right of rescission involves only the seller and the buyer.[508] Where it involves a third party, the authors suggest that property choice

---

[502] Benjamin, 25–177.
[503] ibid, 25–178. See also the discussion of the position of the carrier at 25–180 and 25–181.
[504] See above, 13.221–222.
[505] Emphasis added. Note also Art 4(b) of the Vienna Convention.
[506] Which may be regarded as a contractual remedy: see below, para 13.233.
[507] This is discussed in more detail elsewhere. See below, paras 18.46 and 19.57–61.
[508] Rescission *ab initio* does not necessarily entail proprietary consequences, as in the case of a purely executory contract.

of law rules should determine the right to rescission.[509] It is suggested that this distinction should not be applied. Rather, one should, in the first instance, distinguish between the right to rescind a contract and the aftermath of rescission. The former issue should be treated as a contractual matter, as it is a remedy which determines whether the parties can avoid the contract itself.

13.231 The aftermath of the rescission claim is more naturally to be viewed as a claim in unjust enrichment.[510] As such, restitutionary choice of law rules should apply. In Chapter 19 on restitution and choice of law, it is suggested that one must distinguish personal claims where the claimant seeks damages to restore him to his pre-contractual position from cases where the claimant seeks rescission of the transfer itself and the revesting of property in himself.[511] It is argued that personal restitutionary claims should be determined by the law which governed the 'contract'. However, since a claim to rescind the transfer itself will ultimately result in a ruling as to ownership of property, it is suggested that the law of the situs should determine its availability in a claim between the buyer and the seller, and also whether that right may be invoked against a third party.[512]

13.232 Hence, the following choice of law rules are suggested:

(1) The right of a party to a contract to obtain rescission of that contract shall be determined by the applicable law of the contract.
(2) If rescission is available by that law:
    (a) the right of the claimant to obtain damages to restore him to his pre-contractual position shall also be determined by the applicable law of the contract;
    (b) the right of the claimant to rescind the transfer itself shall be determined by the law of the *situs*.[513]

---

[509] Benjamin, 25–177 and 25–178. See also the Canadian cases cited in Benjamin, 25–176, n 54. See, in particular *Rhode Island Locomotive Works v South Eastern Ry Co* (1886) 31 LCJ 86; *Re Hudson Fashion Shoppe Ltd* [1926] 1 DLR 199; *Re Viscount Supply Co Ltd* (1963) 40 DLR (2d) 501; *Re Modern Fashions Ltd* (1969) 8 DLR (3d) 590; *Re Satisfaction Stores* [1929] 2 DLR 435; *Re Farley and Grant* [1936] 1 DLR 57.

[510] Arts 81(2) and 84(2) of the Vienna Convention lend support to this approach.

[511] See below, paras 19.57–61.

[512] It is true that this matter is addressed by the Vienna Convention, even though the Convention excludes property matters (Art 4(b)). Moreover, revesting upon contractual termination is in English law seen as a matter of implied contractual terms—*Ward v Bignall* [1967] 1 QB 534. However, the application of the law of the *situs* is justified by the fact that property rights are ultimately at stake and may need to be enforced in the courts of the *situs*. As such, it is suggested that the law of the *situs* should be applied to the question of the proprietary effects of rescission. This is consistent with the decision in *Glencore International AG v Metro Trading International Inc (No 2)* [2001] 1 Lloyd's Rep 284, QBD (Comm).

[513] i.e. the *situs* of the property in question at the time of the last actual or purported dealing in it.

Right of Resale

It is important to distinguish the right of an unpaid seller to resell goods[514] **13.233** from his ability to confer a good title on a third party to whom he purports to resell. The former is a right arising from the contract itself and should be determined by the applicable law of the contract.[515] The latter is a question concerning the ability to confer property rights on a third party and ought clearly to be governed by property choice of law rules.[516]

Rejection of the Goods[517] or Documents

The buyer's right to reject the goods owing to the seller's breach is a **13.234** matter for the governing law of the contract.[518] The question of whether, and if so, when rejected goods should be returned to the seller will also be determined by this law, as will the consequences of failure to return the goods.[519] Benjamin rightly notes that the proprietary effect of an act of rejection upon the goods is a matter falling outside the scope of the Rome Convention and for the law of the *situs* to determine.[520]

The right to reject documents tendered to the buyer by the seller is also a **13.235** matter for the governing law of the contract. This law will determine the extent to which this right is dependent upon an ongoing right to reject the goods themselves.[521]

Termination for Breach

It is important to note that the phrase 'consequences of breach' in Article **13.236** 10(1)(c) means that the governing law will determine whether a party might be justified in terminating the contract following the other party's breach.[522] As Peel points out,[523] the applicable law might hold that the

---

[514] English law, in the form of s 48 of the Sale of Goods Act 1979, does not attach the right of resale to the revesting of property—it is perfectly possible to see the seller acting as agent for the buyer to effect a resale. But see *Ward v Bignall* [1967] 1 QB 534.

[515] The same is true of the right to sue for a deficiency on resale: Benjamin, 25–182.

[516] This is also the view of Benjamin, ibid. See also *Livesley v Clemens Horst Co* [1925] 159, 160–161.

[517] See also the above discussion of the inspection of goods and their subsequent rejection in relation to questions of performance, paras 13.194–195; and see Arts 10(1)(b) and 10(2). The effect of Art 10(2) is that the law of the place of performance may be applied to questions concerning the manner of performance under the contract.

[518] Giuliano and Lagarde Report, 33. At common law, see *Benaim & Co v Debono* [1924] AC 514; *Glynn (Covent Garden) Ltd v Wittleder* [1959] 2 Lloyd's Rep 409; Benjamin, 25–189.

[519] Benjamin, ibid. [520] ibid, 25–190. [521] ibid, 25–191.

[522] This result could conceivably also be reached by applying Art 10(1)(d), which states that the applicable law shall determine the ways in which the obligations of the parties are extinguished.

[523] Peel, n 53 above, 15–075.

existence of this right depends, as it does in English domestic law, upon whether the term is a condition (in which case the innocent party may terminate the contract) or an innominate term (in which case, he may only terminate in respect of a breach which strikes at the heart of the contract). He goes on to note that this issue may be better seen as a point of interpretation. However, Article 10(1)(a) would lead back to the governing law to determine this point of interpretation.

Fundamental Breach of Contract and its Effect on the Operation of a Choice of Law Clause

13.237   An important question that might arise is the effect of a finding of fundamental breach by the governing law of the contract on the validity and effect of a choice of law clause. The Federal Court of Canada was faced in *ZI Pompey Industrie v ECU-Line NV*[524] with a contract of carriage containing a jurisdiction clause for the courts of Antwerp. The carrier was required to carry the goods, photo-processing equipment, port-to-port by sea. Instead, he shipped the goods part of the way and then sent them by rail to their ultimate destination. The court found this to be a fundamental breach, since it was particularly important that such sensitive equipment be carried entirely by sea. It then ruled that when the goods were discharged from the ship, this fundamental breach brought the contract to an end. This had the effect of also rendering all of the terms of the contract, including the jurisdiction clause, inapplicable.

13.238   Presumably, the court would have reached the same conclusion if the contract had contained a choice of law clause.[525] But if this is the case, then should the law which initially governed the contract pursuant to the choice of law clause be used to determine the remedies available upon such a fundamental breach? After all, if there is no longer a choice of law clause, why should it determine the remedies available to a party?[526]

13.239   Although a claim to recover payments made pursuant to a contract discharged by fundamental breach may best be regarded as restitutionary,[527]

---

[524] [2000] IL Pr 600.

[525] Although this is something of a paradox, as one would expect the law applicable to the contract at its inception to determine whether a breach occurred and the effect of that breach on the contract and its terms.

[526] Compare the comments of Lord Simon LC in *Heyman v Darwins Ltd* [1942] AC 356, 366: 'if one party to the alleged contract is contending that it is void *ab initio* . . . the arbitration clause cannot operate . . .'. See also the decision of the Court of Appeal in *Trendtex Trading Corp v Crédit Suisse* [1980] QB 629.

[527] See Art 81 of the Vienna Convention; Schlechtriem, 373; *Kleinwort Benson Ltd v Glasgow City Council* [1999] 1 AC 153.

it is clearly *based* upon a contractual obligation which a party has failed to perform. If, in a sale contract, the seller fails to provide goods conforming to description, the *obligation* which has been breached is contractual and the law applicable to the contract would decide whether this gives the buyer the right to treat the contract as discharged.[528] It would seem artificial not to let that law also decide the *consequences* of that discharge, including whether the buyer can recover any sums already paid. Indeed, Article 10(1)(c) envisages that the law applicable to the contract will also determine the consequences of breach. Moreover, the applicable law of the contract may give the buyer the choice of affirming the contract and suing for damages for breach of contract, or treating it as discharged and seeking repayment. It would seem unsatisfactory for the ability of the claimant to recover in each case to be determined by different laws, since both rest upon the breach of a single contractual obligation.[529]

4. The Various Ways of Extinguishing Obligations and Prescription and Limitation of Actions

Extinguishing Obligations by Performance[530]

Article 10(1)(d) has the effect that the question of whether, and when, the **13.240** parties have discharged their individual obligations will be determined by the law applicable to the contract. That law will also determine when the whole contract has been discharged by performance.[531]

Discharge by Frustration

The applicable law of the contract will determine whether a contract is **13.241** frustrated.[532] It is, of course, entirely sensible that the same law which determines the question of risk[533] should also determine whether a contract is frustrated. After all, that law might find that neither party took the

---

[528] Art 10(1)(d).   [529] See further below, para 19.48.
[530] Termination of a contract on the basis of a breach by the other contracting party is considered in relation to Art 10(1)(c), above.
[531] Or, at least, a combination of this provision and Art 10(1)(b) will have this effect. Compare the common law approach: *Mount Albert Borough Council v Australasian Temperance and General Mutual Life Assurance Society Ltd* [1938] AC 224; *Bonython v Commonwealth of Australia* [1951] AC 201; *WJ Alan & Co Ltd v El Nasr Export and Import Co* [1972] 2 QB 189. On novation, see *Re United Railways of the Havana and Regla Warehouses Ltd* [1960] Ch 52, *Wight v Eckhardt Marine GmbH* [2003] UKPC 37, [2004] 1 AC 147; and see below, paras 14.49–51 and 14.56. On accord and satisfaction, see *Ralli v Denistoun* (1851) 6 Exch 483.
[532] Compare *Jacobs v Crédit Lyonnais* (1884) 12 QBD 589.
[533] Considered in relation to Art 10(1)(b), above, paras 13.196–200.

risk of it being impossible for certain obligations under the contract to be carried out owing to an unforeseen event.

13.242 However, it must be stressed that the applicable law under the Rome Convention will only apply to determine *if* a contract is frustrated. The consequences of that frustration, and claims which might arise for restitution of money or benefits conferred, will not be subject to the Convention's rules, at least in the United Kingdom.[534] This is because the United Kingdom has not enacted Article 10(1)(e) of the Rome Convention, which would have submitted these consequences to the law which (previously) governed the contract.[535]

Discharge by Illegality, Impossibility, etc.

13.243 Article 10(1)(d) would also cover the questions of whether the contractual obligations of the parties have been extinguished by legislation,[536] by illegality[537] or by impossibility of performance.[538]

Discharge by Bankruptcy

13.244 However, it seems that Article 10(1)(d) will not apply to discharge by bankruptcy.[539] The law of bankruptcy has its own set of conflicts rules and these cannot lightly be subordinated to the law chosen by the parties to govern a contract.

Prescription and Limitation

13.245 Article 10(1)(d) also covers the time within which a claim may be brought. This matter, previously regarded as procedural in English law,[540] is now

---

[534] This claim is considered further below, paras 19.42–47, where the question is considered whether English law ought nonetheless to apply the proper law of the 'contract' to the aftermath of frustration. See also Benjamin, 25–169.

[535] s 2(2) of the Contracts Applicable Law (Act) 1990.

[536] Compare *Re Anglo-Austrian Bank* [1920] 1 Ch 69. See also Peel, n 53 above, 15–079, who points out that if the effect of the legislation is to transfer contractual rights to a third person, this may be treated as a property matter and subject to property choice of law rules.

[537] Subject to the application of any relevant mandatory rules and provisions of public policy. The effect of illegality upon a contract is discussed in the section on mandatory rules and public policy, below, paras 13.295–300.

[538] See Plender and Wilderspin, n 1 above, 221.

[539] This is the view of Benjamin, 25–170, n 36; Dicey and Morris, 1137–1141.

[540] *Black-Clawson International Ltd v Papierwerke Waldhof-Aschaffenburg AG* [1975] AC 591, 630.

generally treated in the English conflict of laws process as a substantive matter, to be determined by the law governing the cause of action.[541] However, this is not entirely uncontroversial. A comparison with the Hague Sales Convention 1986 is instructive. Although Article 12(g) of the 1986 Convention subjects the prescription and limitation of causes of action to the applicable law of the contract, Article 21(1)(d) of that Convention allows Contracting States to enter a reservation to the effect that they will not apply the governing law to these issues.[542] The Rome Convention contains no such reservation and the governing law of the contract must be applied.

Boele-Woelki considers what would happen if the applicable law of the **13.246** contract of sale were that of a state that was party to the Vienna Convention.[543] She refers to a judgment of the German Oberlandesgericht Hamm.[544] The court accepted that as the parties chose German law, and as the parties were based in different Contracting States to the Vienna Convention, it had to apply the Vienna Convention. However, the Convention is silent on the issue of prescription.[545] That being so, the court applied the relevant German national provisions on prescription. As Boele-Woelki rightly points out, this is not to say that two different laws applied to the contract—the Vienna Convention and German national law. It is simply that application of German law leads to the rules of the Vienna Convention where they have something to say on a matter, and German national law fills the gaps where they do not.[546]

---

[541] s 1(1) of the Foreign Limitation Periods Act 1984. This is subject to a public policy exception in s 2(1). As Plender and Wilderspin, n 1 above, 221, point out, there is no express provision in this Act stating that English statutes of limitation are substantive and not procedural. Such a statement might have helped some courts in non-Contracting States to determine whether they should be applied where English law is the governing law (although, of course, such states are free in any event to depart from the classification of limitation periods used in English law). However, in Contracting States, the effect of Art 10(1)(d) is that English statutes of limitation should be applied if English law is applicable to the contract.

[542] See further para 15.119 on these provisions of the Hague Sales Convention 1986.

[543] See also the discussion above, paras 13.70–85.

[544] K Boele-Woelki, 'The Limitation of Rights and Actions in the International Sale of Goods' (1999) IV(3) Uniform L Rev 621, 629, discussing the decision of 9 June 1995, Rechtsprechung des OLG Hamm 1995, 169–70; UNILEX D 1995–17.

[545] But see the UN Convention on the Limitation Period in International Sale of Goods 1974; below, paras 16.146–148.

[546] Boele-Woelki, n 544 above, 630. See also the discussion of a decision of the International Chamber of Commerce of 23 August 1994, discussed, ibid, 630–1.

5. The Consequences of Nullity of a Contract

13.247 The United Kingdom has reserved the right not to apply Article 10(1)(e) of the Rome Convention in its courts;[547] a reservation which is permitted by the terms of the Rome Convention.[548] This provision would have used the (putative) applicable law of the contract to determine the consequences of nullity of a contract. This may be seen in English law as essentially a matter of restitution, not contract law.[549] As such, it is not clear that it should be subordinated to contractual choice of law rules.[550] The law applicable to such claims is considered in Chapter 19, which deals with restitution and choice of law.[551]

13.248 However, parties to a contract must be aware that, if litigation were to take place in the courts of another Contracting State which has not entered this reservation, Article 10(1)(e) may be applied. This has the unfortunate effect that the consequences of nullity may be determined by different laws in different Contracting States. This, in turn, may create incentives for a party to forum shop in the state whose law is more favourable to it.

X. CLAIMS INVOLVING THIRD PARTIES TO A CONTRACT OF SALE

1. Extended Warranties

13.249 Suppose that a contract is concluded between a producer and a wholesaler which is governed by the law of State A. That contact contains a warranty by the producer in favour of the wholesaler. The wholesaler then sells the goods on to the buyer pursuant to a contract governed by the law of State B. The buyer then claims the benefit of the producer's warranty.[552] How should an English court determine the matter?

---

[547] By s 2(2) of the Contracts (Applicable Law) Act 1990.

[548] Art 22(1)(b) of the Rome Convention.

[549] See the decision of the Scottish Court of Session in *Barings Bros & Co Ltd v Cunninghame District Council* [1997] CLC 108. See also *Arab Monetary Fund v Hashim* [1993] 1 Lloyd's Rep 543, aff'd [1996] 1 Lloyd's Rep 589.

[550] But compare Art 12(h) of the Hague Sales Convention 1986, which states that the governing law of the contract shall apply to 'the consequences of nullity or invalidity of the contract'. There is no opt-out provision from Art 12(h) in the 1986 Convention. See further below, para 15.120.

[551] See also Dicey and Morris, Ch 34; Cheshire and North, Ch 20.

[552] See Bridge, *The Sale of Goods*, 376–380, who explains that such extended warranties have their origins in the US.

It is suggested that the claim should be classified as contractual. It is in **13.250** substance a claim that the *benefit of a contractual warranty* has passed to the claimant by virtue of the *contract* of sale. The question then arises as to which law or laws should apply. It appears that the solution is to be found in Article 12 of the Rome Convention. Article 12(2) states that:

The law governing the right to which the assignment relates shall determines its assignability, the relationship between the assignee and the debtor, the conditions under which the assignment can be invoked against the debtor and any question whether the debtor's obligations have been discharged.

In other words, in order for the buyer to claim the benefit of the producer's warranty, the law applicable to the contract between the producer and wholesaler, that of State A, must state that the right is capable of being assigned to a third party buyer. If, by that law, the right is incapable of being assigned, then there is no question of the buyer claiming the benefit of the extended warranty. However, if the right is capable of being assigned by that law, a second question arises as to whether the benefit of the warranty has indeed passed to the buyer. Article 12(1) of the Rome Convention states that:

The mutual obligations of assignor and assignee under a voluntary assignment of a right against another person ('the debtor') shall be governed by the law which under the Convention applies to the contract between the assignor and assignee.

This suggests that the law of State B should determine whether the benefit of the warranty has passed from the wholesaler to the buyer. Only if the answer to this second question is also in the affirmative can the buyer claim the benefit of the producer's warranty.[553]

2. CLAIM BY ORIGINAL SELLER AGAINST SUB-PURCHASER

If a contract of sale contains a retention of title clause, it may also stipulate **13.251** that if the purchaser sells the goods on to a sub-purchaser before payment is received by the seller in full, the purchaser's claim for the purchase price of the goods against the sub-purchaser should vest in the seller.[554] It seems that the rules of Article 12 of the Rome Convention should again apply to determine whether the seller can claim the purchase price from the sub-purchaser. The assignability of the purchaser's right against the sub-purchaser should accordingly be determined by the law governing

---

[553] See also *Raiffeisen Zentralbank Osterreich AG v Five Star General Trading LLC* [2001] 2 WLR 1344. In that case, the Court of Appeal rejected the argument that the law of the *situs* could be applied to the assignment of the benefit of a marine insurance policy.

[554] Benjamin, 25–142.

that contract of sub-sale, pursuant to Article 12(2). If, by that law, the right is assignable, Article 12(1) states that the law applicable to the original contract of sale will determine whether the right to sue the sub-purchaser has been assigned to the seller. The law applicable to the contract of sub-sale will determine what defences, if any, the sub-purchaser might have to a claim by the seller.[555]

3. Rights of Third Parties Under a Contract

13.252 The Contracts (Rights of Third Parties) Act 1999[556] has the effect that in English domestic law a third party might in certain circumstances have the right to enforce a benefit conferred upon him under a contract to which he was not party.[557] Suppose that A agrees with B that he will transfer goods to X in return for B paying a sum of £10,000 to A. If A then fails to transfer the goods to X, can X sue A for damages for breach of contract?

13.253 It could be argued that the matter in question falls outside the scope of the Rome Convention, which applies only to 'contractual obligations'.[558] In *Jakob Handte GmbH v Traitements Mécano-Chimiques des Surfaces*,[559] a manufacturer sold a suction system to a purchaser, who sold the system on to a sub-purchaser. The sub-purchaser alleged that the system was unfit for purpose. The ECJ ruled that the claim did not 'relate to contract'[560] for the purposes of Article 5(1) of the Brussels Convention. However, one relevant consideration in that case was that the manufacturer had not voluntarily undertaken obligations to that particular sub-purchaser. In the instant case, the seller will clearly undertake obligations to a specific, foreseeable party and the matter should fall within the scope of the Rome Convention.[561] The question of whether the third party acquires the right to sue under the contract should simply be determined

---

[555] Art 12(2).

[556] The Act is also considered below, paras 14.116–120. See also R Stevens, 'The Contracts (Rights of Third Parties) Act 1999' (2004) 120 LQR 292.

[557] The French *stipulation pour autrui* is also contractual in nature: see Art 1121 of the French Code Civil.

[558] Art 1(1), discussed above, paras 13.14–17.

[559] Case C-26/91 [1992] ECR I-3967; see above, paras 3.63–66 and 5.22–27.

[560] Note that this wording is somewhat broader than the phrase 'contractual obligations' in Art 1(1) of the Rome Convention: see above, paras 13.14–17, and below, paras 14.02–06.

[561] Compare *Atlas Shipping Agency (UK) Ltd v Suisse Atlantique Société d'Armament Maritime SA* [1995] IL Pr 600, HC. Briggs and Rees, 125, comment that it is 'clear beyond doubt' that a claim by an intended beneficiary under the 1999 Act will be regarded as contractual for the purposes of the Brussels I Regulation.

by the law applicable to the contract.[562] True, the third party might be bound by a choice of law clause between the contracting parties to which he did not himself consent. However, he is claiming the benefit of rights existing under that contract and must take the terms of the contract as he finds them. Moreover, there is no reason from the seller's point of view why his position should be determined by any law other than that to which he agreed to subject himself in the original contract.[563]

It seems clear that the Contracts (Rights of Third Parties) Act 1999 will not **13.254** be regarded as a mandatory rule of English law. Section 1(2) states that even where a contract purports to confer a benefit on a third party, the third party does not obtain the right to enforce a term of the contract 'if on a proper construction of the contract it appears that the parties did not intend the term to be enforceable by the third party'.[564] Clearly, the parties may derogate from the Act's provisions even where the contract is governed by English law. *A fortiori*, the Act should not apply where the contract is governed by a foreign law.

4. AGENT'S LIABILITY UNDER THE CONTRACT OF SALE

Where an agent signs the contract on behalf of the seller, a question could **13.255** arise as to whether that agent might render himself liable under the terms of the contract to the other contracting party. This appears to be a question for the governing law of the contract of sale. *Dicey and Morris* suggest that that law will determine whether the agent has created privity of contract between himself and the other party to the sales contract and the liability of the agent for the acts of the principal.[565]

---

[562] Where a party succeeds by law to the rights of party to a contract which contained a choice of court clause, the ECJ has ruled that he may be bound by that clause: Case 201/82 *Gerling v Italian Treasury* [1983] ECR 2503; Case 71/83 *The Tilly Russ* [1984] ECR 2417; Case C-159/97 *Transporti Castelletti Spedizioni Internazionali SpA v Hugo Trumpy SpA* [1999] ECR I-1597; Case C-387/98 *Coreck Maritime GmbH v Handelsveem BV* [2000] ECR I-9337. See above, paras 5.06–10. See also Briggs and Rees, 98–99. The authors comment that although a jurisdiction clause may be seen as a burden affecting the third party, it is 'an integral part of the benefit which the contract confers'.

[563] Similarly, the law applicable to the contract should determine what defences A might have to the claim by X. See also s 3 of the 1999 Act.

[564] s 1(4) states that the third party does not have the right to enforce a term of the contract 'otherwise than subject to and in accordance with any other relevant term of the contract'.

[565] Dicey and Morris, 1479–1480. For discussion of the rights and liabilities of the principal and agent to one another, see ibid, Rule 197, 1464–1473. For discussion of the liability of the principal, see ibid, Rule 198, 1473–1479. See also *Benjamin*, 25–082.

XI. THE FORMAL VALIDITY OF THE CONTRACT

1. GENERAL RULE[566]

13.256 It may not always be clear whether the issue confronting the court is one of formal or essential validity. Giuliano and Lagarde describe formality rules as 'every external manifestation required on the part of a person expressing the will to be legally bound and in the absence of which such expression would not be regarded as fully effective'.[567] They give the examples of a requirement that a contract be witnessed by two signatures, or be duplicated, or that the contract be concluded in writing. However, they state that a requisite for an act to bind third parties, such as notice of statutory assignment which is needed in England for a chose in action, is not a formality requirement. Ultimately, it is left to national courts to decide if the issue is one of formal validity.

13.257 Article 9 adopts a policy of ensuring that the contract is not rendered formally invalid. A contract of sale will be formally valid if it satisfies either the requirements of the law which governs the contract[568] or the law of the country where it was concluded, if both parties were in the same country at the time of conclusion.[569] If they were in different countries at the time of conclusion, the contract need only satisfy one of three laws: the applicable law of the contract, or the law of the place where either party was at the time of its conclusion.[570]

13.258 Of course, the application of Article 9 is subject to the provisions on mandatory rules and public policy in the Convention.[571] In particular, the liberal nature of Article 9 could lead to the conclusion that a contract is valid in circumstances which are manifestly incompatible with English public policy.[572] Moreover, 'Article 7 of the Convention, which contains a reservation in favour of the application of mandatory rules, may lead to the rejection of the liberal system based on the application in the alterna-

---

[566] See also the discussion of formal validity and Art 96 of the Vienna Convention below, paras 16.137–141.

[567] Giuliano and Lagarde Report, 29.

[568] More accurately, the law which would govern the contract if it were formally valid. In the event that the contract is 'split' so that different laws govern different parts of it, Giuliano and Lagarde suggest that the applicable law is that which governs the part of the contract most closely connected with the disputed condition upon which the formal validity of the contract hinges.

[569] Art 9(1).

[570] Art 9(2). Art 9(3) states that if the contract is concluded by an agent, the country in which the agent acts is the relevant country for the purposes of Arts 9(1) and (2).

[571] See below, paras 13.271–300.   [572] Art 16.

tive of either the law governing the substance of the contract or the law of the place where it was entered into'.[573] This may be the case where the forum imposes formality requirements to provide protection to one or both parties to the contract and such protection would be denied to those parties if Article 9 were given its full force.

2. CONSUMER CONTRACTS[574]

The provisions on formal validity considered in the previous paragraph **13.259** are not used where the consumer contract provisions of Article 5 apply. In that case, formal validity is in all cases governed solely by the law of the state where the consumer has habitual residence.[575]

3. CONTRACTS FOR THE SALE OF RIGHTS IN IMMOVABLE PROPERTY[576]

When it comes to contracts for the sale of rights in immovable property, **13.260** the general rules of Article 9 are applied. However, if the law of the *situs* has any formality rules of a mandatory nature which are intended to apply regardless of the governing law of the contract, those rules must also be satisfied.[577]

4. BURDEN OF PROOF; PRESUMPTIONS; ACTS INTENDED TO HAVE LEGAL EFFECT

Burdens of Proof

Although some formal requirements could be regarded as procedural, **13.261** and thus as falling outside the Rome Convention, the tenor of the Convention is to treat them as substantive where possible. Article 14(1), for example, states that the governing law 'applies to the extent that it contains, in the law of contract, rules which raise presumptions of law

---

[573] Giuliano and Lagarde Report, 32; in the UK, only Art 7(2), which preserves the application of the international mandatory rules of the forum, is in force.

[574] Although this book is concerned with commercial contracts, it is important to establish that the contract in issue is not caught by the definition of a consumer contract: see the brief discussion of consumer contracts below, paras 13.265–268.

[575] Art 9(5).

[576] These contracts are not our concern in this book. However, it may not always be immediately clear whether a contract relates to the sale of 'goods' or of 'immovable property', for example where crops are growing in a field. See also the discussion of Art 4(3), above, para 13.125.

[577] Art 9(6).

or determine the burden of proof'.[578] This provision applies both to rebuttable and irrebuttable presumptions of law.

13.262 The qualification that the presumption or burden of proof be contained in the governing law's 'law of contract' is less than clear. In particular, if the governing law has a general principle that the burden of proof in civil litigation rests upon a particular party, should an English court apply this? Giuliano and Lagarde suggest that a provision concerning the burden of proof must effectively be a substantive rule of contract in order for Article 14(1) to apply.[579] On this view, it is suggested that an English court should not apply the governing law's general principles of civil litigation as to the burden of proof. Rather, Article 14(1) would apply only to what is in effect a rule of law. Giuliano and Lagarde give the example of Article 1147 of the French Code Civil, which states that a defendant who is in breach of contract will be liable in damages *unless he demonstrates that the breach results from circumstances outside his control.* In effect, this rule relates to the question of when the defendant will be liable for breach of contract. As such, it should be applied by an English court if French law governs the contract.[580]

Presumptions

13.263 In relation to rebuttable[581] presumptions, Benjamin takes the example of the presumption of undue influence as a 'genuine' substantive presumption of English domestic law.[582] However, the authors note that this presumption is not specific to the law of contract, and also exists, for example, in equity. Nevertheless, the authors conclude that the presumption can be said to be 'contained in the law of contract'.[583] It is suggested that this is correct. Article 14(1) does not say that the rule must be contained *exclusively* in the law of contract. True, 'there must be a point at which a presumption is of such general scope that it ceases to be "contained in the law of contract" because of its generality'.[584] However, there is no reason for an English court officiously to find that a presumption of the governing law is not 'contained in the law of contract' and refuse to apply it. Where the presumption has a substantive character, this would simply result in a distortion of the foreign law and may create the potential for forum shopping in England.

---

[578] Discussed in Benjamin, 25–198. Contrast the common law position, which treated these matters as procedural: *The Roberta* (1937) Ll L R 159.

[579] Giuliano and Lagarde Report, 36.   [580] Benjamin, 25–198.

[581] Irrebutable presumptions are effectively rules of law and so should be treated as substantive in character. See the discussion of s 184 of the Law of Property Act 1925 in *Re Cohn* [1945] Ch 5.

[582] Benjamin, 25–198.   [583] ibid.   [584] ibid. See further Dicey and Morris, 167–8.

Acts Intended to have Legal Effect

Article 14(2) states that a contract or act intended to have legal effect[585] in **13.264** relation to a contract[586] may be proved by any mode of proof recognized by the law of the forum or by any of the laws specified in Article 9 under which the contract or act is formally valid.[587] This is a very liberal provision. The only qualification is that, where a more liberal mode of proof exists by one of the laws specified in Article 9 than would be used in the domestic law of the forum, that mode of proof must be one which the forum is *capable* of administering. As Giuliano and Lagarde observe:

... the liberalism should not lead to imposing on the trial court modes of proof which its procedural law does not enable it to administer ... This is the explanation of the provision which in substance enables a court, without reference to public policy, to disregard modes of proof which the law of procedure cannot generally allow, such as an affidavit, the testimony of a party or common knowledge.[588]

XII. PARTICULAR CONTRACTS

1. Consumer Contracts[589]

The Rome Convention contains special choice of law rules to deal with **13.265** consumer contracts and with employment contracts. Consumer contracts may, of course, be contracts of sale. However, our concern in this book is with commercial contracts of sale. Accordingly, it is inappropriate to discuss consumer contracts in detail. Nevertheless, the consumer contract provisions do have a limited potential to interact with the rules for commercial sales contracts. As such, the basic provisions will be briefly stated. It will not always be easy to tell whether the contract in issue is a

---

[585] These may include 'notice of termination, remission of a debt, declaration of rescission or repudiation, etc.': Giuliano and Lagarde Report, 29.

[586] An act must be connected with the contract to fall within the scope of the Convention: Giuliano and Lagarde Report, 29.

[587] See also Art 9(4), which states that: 'An act intended to have legal effect relating to an existing or contemplated contract is formally valid if it satisfies the formal requirements of the law which under this Convention governs or would govern the contract or of the law of the country where the act was done'.

[588] Giuliano and Lagarde Report, 36–7

[589] See Dicey and Morris, 1284–1303; Benjamin, 25–044 to 25–054; Plender and Wilderspin, n 1 above, Ch 7. The scope of the consumer provisions is likely to be one of the most closely considered issues if and when the Rome Convention is transformed into a Regulation. Substantive changes in the law in this area are likely. For some of the options being considered, see the Commission's 'Green Paper on the Conversion of the Rome Convention of 1980 on the Law Applicable to Contractual Obligations into a Community Instrument and its Modernisation' COM/2002/0654 Final, para 3.2.7.

commercial sales contract, or whether it falls within the Rome Convention's definition of a consumer contract.[590] Accordingly, parties to a sales contract should satisfy themselves as to whether the consumer provisions might be applicable to their contract.

13.266 Article 5 describes a consumer contract as one whose object 'is the supply of goods or services to a person for a purpose which can be regarded as outside his trade or profession'. It is thus the *purpose* of the transaction which is paramount. A buyer not currently in business who enters into a contract of sale with a view to setting up a business is thus not a consumer.[591] Although Article 5 does not say so, it is also necessary that the other party *is* contracting for a purpose *within* his trade or profession.[592]

13.267 In addition, a contract will not fall within the consumer contract provisions unless at least one of three alternative pre-conditions laid down in Article 5(2) is satisfied. They are that in the country of the consumer's habitual residence:

the conclusion of the contract was preceded by a specific invitation addressed to him or by advertising, and he had taken in that country all the steps necessary on his part for the conclusion of the contract; or

the other party or his agent received the consumer's order in that country; or

the contract is for the sale of goods and the consumer travelled from his habitual residence to another country and there gave his order, provided that the consumer's journey was arranged by the seller for the purpose of inducing the consumer to buy.

If these conditions are satisfied,[593] the position is as follows. The parties may still choose the applicable law under Article 3(1), but the contract must also satisfy the mandatory rules of the state of the consumer's habitual residence.[594] However, if the parties do not make an express or implied choice of law, the applicable law is determined not by Article 4, but by Article 5(3). This lays down an irrebuttable rule that the law of the

---

[590] See further J Harris, 'Consumer Protection in Private International Law', Ch 11 in F Meisel and P Cook (eds), *Property and Protection: Essays in Honour of Brian Harvey* (Oxford: Hart Publishing, 2000).

[591] See, in the context of Art 13 of the Brussels Convention, Case C-88/91 *Shearson Lehman Hutton v TVB* [1993] ECR I-139; Case C-269/95 *Francesco Benincasa v Dentalkit Srl* [1997] ECR I-3767; Case C- 167/00 *Verein fur Konsumenteninformation v Henkel* [2002] ECR I-8111; Case C-96/00 *Gabriel v Schlank & Schick GmbH* [2002] ECR I-6367.

[592] Giuliano and Lagarde Report, 23.

[593] Subject to the exceptions in Art 5(4). For present purposes, it is worth noting that Art 5(4)(a) excludes contracts of carriage (unless the contract provides for a combination of carriage and accommodation, as in the case of a package holiday; in such a case, Art 5(5) states that the consumer contract provisions apply if the other conditions in Art 5 are met).

[594] Art 5(2). There are numerous mandatory rules of English law which apply to consumer contracts. See, in particular, ss 26 and 27 of the UCTA 1977, discussed below, paras

consumer's habitual residence shall be the applicable law of the contract.

The formal validity of a consumer contract is determined by the law of the **13.268** place of the consumer's habitual residence.[595]

2. CONTRACTS OF SALE AND MANUFACTURE, CONSTRUCTION OR SERVICE[596]

A contract for the sale of goods might also require the seller to perform **13.269** a service for the buyer. For example, the seller might be required to manufacture and sell the goods in question; or, he might contract to sell machinery parts to a buyer and then assemble the machinery. This does not give rise to any particular choice of law problem if the obligations are contained in a single contract. If the contracts of service and sales are separate, then the applicable law should be determined separately for each contract.[597]

It should be noted that a contract for the provision of services is not a **13.270** contract of employment. Accordingly, the special rules for employment contracts in the Rome Convention[598] will not apply. In *Shenavai v*

13.301–320. See also the anti-avoidance provisions of the Unfair Terms in Consumer Contracts Regulations 1999, SI 1999/ 2083, reg 9, the Consumer Protection (Distance Selling) Regulations 2000, SI 2000/2334, implementing Directive 97/7/ EC of the European Parliament and Council, 20 May 1997, on the Protection of Consumers in Respect of Distance Contracts [1997] OJ L144/19 and the Sale and Supply of Goods to Consumers Regulations 2002, SI 2002/3045, implementing Directive (EC) 99/44 on Certain Aspects of the Sale of Consumer Goods and Associated Guarantees [1999] OJ L171/12. For detailed discussion of the application of these provisions to international consumer contracts, see Morse, C, in Benjamin, 25–090 to 25–111 and in Benjamin (Special Supplement) (2003) 1–035 to 1–049.

[595] Art 9(5).

[596] See also paras 16.91–94 on the Vienna Convention.

[597] Although both contracts will normally point to the same law. The parties may have chosen the law applicable to the two contracts. Usually, they will choose the same law, though they need not, of course, do so. In the absence of choice, Art 4(2) will point to the law of the principal place of business of the seller, or service provider.

[598] Employment contracts are dealt with in Art 6. See Dicey and Morris, 1303–23; Plender and Wilderspin, n 1 above, Ch 8. The basic rule for contracts of employment is that the parties may still choose the applicable law pursuant to Art 3(1). However, the employee will obtain the protection of the mandatory rules of the state in which he habitually works in performance of the contract, or, if he does not habitually work in one country, of the place of business through which he is engaged. In either case, he may obtain the protection of the mandatory rules of a different law instead, if it appears from the circumstances as a whole that the contract is more closely connected with another country.

If the parties have not chosen a governing law, then the applicable law in the absence of choice is determined by Art 6. That law will be the law of the state in which the employee habitually works in performance of the contract, or, if he does not habitually work in one country, of the place of business through which he is engaged. Once again, either of these laws can be displaced, if it appears from the circumstances as a whole that the contract is more closely connected with another country.

Kreischer,[599] the European Court Justice had to determine the scope of the provision in Article 5(1) of the Brussels Convention on individual contracts of employment.[600] It will be recalled that it ruled that a claim by an architect for payment for plans drawn up for the building of houses was not a contract of employment.[601] An employment contract creates an enduring connection between the employee and the employer, and to the place where the employee works. Moreover, Giuliano and Lagarde comment that Article 6 seeks to provide 'more adequate protection for the party who from the socio-economic point of view is regarded as the weaker in the contractual relationship'.[602] A commercial contract of sale which also involves the provision of services does not have these characteristics.[603]

XIII. MANDATORY RULES AND PUBLIC POLICY

1. NATURE

13.271 The Convention contains a number of provisions limiting the impact of the applicable law. These provisions may deal with mandatory rules or with public policy. The nature of these rules is outlined briefly below.[604]

13.272 The essential difference between mandatory rules and public policy is that the former is a positive concept and the latter a negative one. Where a state applies a mandatory rule, it *superimposes* that rule on to the applicable law, so that the parties must satisfy the requirements of both laws. Mandatory rules are triggered not because the state in question objects to the content or application of the governing law of the contract. It is simply that the relevant state itself has a rule of law, whose intended scope of application is such that it may not be derogated from by the parties.

13.273 Public policy, on the other hand, involves the *disapplication* of a provision of the governing law, in whole or in part. Public policy does not operate because of any particular rule of the forum which must be applied and which cannot be derogated from by the parties. Rather, it operates because application of the foreign law on the facts would lead to a result which

---

[599] Case 266/85 [1987] ECR 239. See above, para 3.21.
[600] There are now separate Articles in the Brussels I Regulation to deal with individual employment contracts: Arts 18–21.
[601] The case is considered more fully above, paras 3.21, 3.85.
[602] Giuliano and Lagarde Report, 25.
[603] See further Cheshire and North, 208–209; Plender and Wilderspin, n 1 above, 159–164.
[604] See further Cheshire and North, Ch 8 and pp 575–586; Dicey and Morris, Ch 5 and pp 1242–1250, 1276–1283; Plender and Wilderspin, n 1 above, Ch 9.

would be unacceptable to the law of the forum. To the extent that this is the case, the relevant provisions of the governing law of the contract will not be applied.

2. MANDATORY RULES

Mandatory rules are laws from which the parties may not derogate by contractual stipulation. There are two types of such rules.[605] **13.274**

Domestic Mandatory Rules

Domestic mandatory rules are rules of law which cannot be derogated from by agreement where a given law is applicable. In English law, a domestic mandatory rule is one from which the parties cannot derogate where English law governs the contract, regardless of whether they may derogate from it if a foreign law governs the contract.[606] Plender gives the example of the rule in English law against the enforceability of wagering contracts as a domestic mandatory rule.[607] **13.275**

International Mandatory Rules

International mandatory rules are rules which cannot be derogated from by the parties' agreement and which are intended to apply regardless of the law applicable to the contract. They have been described by the European Court of Justice as: **13.276**

national provisions compliance with which has been deemed to be so crucial for the protection of the political, social or economic order in the Member State concerned as to require compliance therewith by all persons present on the national territory of that Member State and all legal relationships within that State.[608]

A clear example of an international mandatory rule, which we will examine in detail below,[609] is s 27(2) of the Unfair Contract Terms Act 1977. This has the effect that many terms of a contract, including implied

---

[605] Cheshire and North, 578.

[606] This category is broad enough to cover *any* rule from which the parties cannot derogate where English law governs the contract. This will also include those rules which apply regardless of the governing law, such as s 27 UCTA 1977. However, unlike Art 7(2) of the Rome Convention, it will not be limited to such rules.

[607] Plender, and Wilderspin, n 1 above, 106–107, though he notes that there is some uncertainty as to whether an English court would apply this rule to a contract governed by a foreign law.

[608] Cases C-369/96 and C-376/96 *Criminal Proceedings against Jean-Claude Arblade and Arblade & Fils SARL and Bernard Leloup, Serge Leloup and Sofrage SARL* [1999] ECR I-8453, para 30.

[609] At paras 13.315–320.

undertakings contained in the Sale of Goods Act 1979, cannot be excluded in certain circumstances, even if the contract is not governed by English law.

Domestic Mandatory Rules and the Rome Convention

13.277 The references to mandatory rules in Article 3(3) and the consumer and employment contract provisions in Articles 5 and 6 respectively are to the broader category of domestic mandatory rules. In each case, they are confronting the 'problem' of the parties having chosen a law, for example, the law of State A, where, but for the choice, the contract would have been governed by another law, that of State B. They have the effect that the parties still must satisfy all those rules of State B from which they could not have derogated by contractual stipulation *if the law of State B had governed the contract*.[610]

13.278 It is generally considered[611] that mandatory rules must be protectionist in nature, such as rules of consumer and employee protection. Cheshire and North describe mandatory rules as '. . . rules which are concerned with protecting some group of persons or the national economic system—rules that arise as the result of state interference with contracts'.[612] Accordingly, framework rules of the English law of contract, such as the need for valid consideration, would not be mandatory rules. This makes eminent sense in relation to the consumer and employment contract provisions of the Rome Convention.[613] However, it could be argued that Article 3(3) of the Convention is concerned with identifying those rules of English law which the parties would have been bound by had it not been for the choice of a foreign law to govern the contract. In other words, it is anti-evasionary, rather than protectionist in nature. If this is correct, then it could be argued that framework rules of English contract law, such as the requirement for consideration, are domestic mandatory rules for the purposes of Article 3(3). This is on the basis that, in a purely domestic contract, the parties cannot bypass the requirement for consideration. At the same time, the need for consideration is not intended to apply to a

---

[610] In other words, if English law's mandatory rules are applicable by virtue of one of these Articles, all those rules which could not be derogated from in English contract law will be applied. This will include *both* rules intended to apply *only* where English law is the governing law and rules which would be equally applicable to a contract governed by a foreign law, such as s 27 UCTA.

[611] Cheshire and North, 575; A Jaffey, 'The English Proper Law Doctrine and the EEC Convention' (1984) 33 ICLQ 531, 538. See also C Morse, 'Consumer Contracts, Employment Contracts and the Rome Convention' (1992) 41 ICLQ 1.

[612] Cheshire and North, 575.

[613] Arts 5 and 6.

contract which is governed by foreign law,[614] and so is not an international mandatory rule.[615]

International Mandatory Rules and the Rome Convention

International mandatory rules of the forum

Article 7 deals with the application of international mandatory rules. **13.279** The key provision applicable in an English court is Article 7(2). This provides a general exception that, in relation to all contracts covered by the Convention:

> nothing . . . shall restrict the application of the rules of the law of the forum in a situation where they are mandatory irrespective of the law otherwise applicable to the contract.

The phrase 'mandatory *irrespective of the law otherwise applicable to the contract*',[616] uses stronger, more forceful language than the references in Article 3(3) and the consumer and employment contract provisions. This emphasizes that Article 7(2) is concerned with the stronger, narrower category of international mandatory rules.

This provision is a general exception to any provision of the Convention. **13.280** Any relevant international mandatory rules of English law will be applied in an English court irrespective of the applicable law. Giuliano and Lagarde note that the provision has in mind, in particular, '. . . rules on cartels, competition and restrictive practices, consumer protection and certain rules concerning carriage'.[617] As Benjamin notes,[618] many such rules in the sales arena are related to consumer contracts, including provisions of the Unfair Contract Terms Act 1977,[619] the Unfair Terms in Consumer Contracts Regulations 1999,[620] the Consumer Protection (Distance Selling) Regulations 2000[621] and the Sale and Supply of Goods to Consumers Regulations 2002.[622] The discussion below[623] will focus on the

---

[614] Hence, an agreement governed by Italian law unsupported by consideration can nonetheless be recognized as a valid contract in England: *Re Bonacina* [1912] 2 Ch 394.

[615] So that it certainly cannot be invoked pursuant to Art 7(2).

[616] Emphasis added. [617] Giuliano and Lagarde Report, 28.

[618] See Benjamin, 25–090 to 25–111. [619] s 27(2). [620] SI 1999/2083, reg 9.

[621] SI 2000/2334, implementing Directive 97/7/EC of the European Parliament and Council, 20 May 1997, on the Protection of Consumers in Respect of Distance Contracts [1997] OJ L144/19.

[622] SI 3045/2002, implementing Directive (EC) 99/44 on Certain Aspects of the Sale of Consumer Goods and Associated Guarantees (especially the anti-avoidance provision in Art 7(2) of the Directive). Note that the anti-avoidance provision contained in the Directive is not expressly implemented in the Regulations: see Benjamin (Special Supplement) (2003), 1–035.

[623] At paras 13.310–320.

Unfair Contract Terms Act 1977, since its provisions may also affect the application of the governing law of commercial contracts of sale.

International mandatory rules of a state of close connection

13.281 It is important to note that the United Kingdom opted out of applying Article 7(1), which would have allowed for the discretionary application of the international mandatory rules of 'the law of another country with which the situation has a close connection'.[624] This was felt to lead to excessive uncertainty and restriction on the autonomy of the parties.[625] However, one must be aware that, if litigation were to take place in the courts of another Contracting State, Article 7(1) may be applied.[626] Accordingly, one cannot simply assume at the drafting stage of a contract that the mandatory rules of a country of close connection can be ignored.

3. PUBLIC POLICY

The Public Policy of the Forum

13.282 Article 16 states that: 'The application of a rule of the law of any country specified by this Convention may be refused only if such application is manifestly incompatible with the public policy of the forum'. This provision is an exception to all of the rules of the Convention. It allows an English court to disapply the law designated by the Convention, in so far as to apply it would be manifestly contrary to English[627] public policy. The word 'manifestly' indicates a strong threshold and that public policy should be invoked only in clear cut cases, so as not to undermine the uniform application of the Convention.[628]

---

[624] By s 2(2) of the Contracts (Applicable Law) 1990. See Art 22 of the Rome Convention.

[625] But compare the rule of English common law that an English court would not enforce a contract which would harm relations between the British Government and a friendly foreign state: *Foster v Driscoll* [1929] 1 KB 470; *Regazzoni v KC Sethia* [1958] AC 301. There is some uncertainty as to whether this can be described as a rule of *English* public policy (which may continue to be applied under Art 16) or the application of an overriding rule of a foreign state (in which case, it may not be applied, since the UK has not enacted Art 7(1)). See the discussion of 'Whose Public Policy?', below, paras 13.292–294, where the latter interpretation is preferred by the authors.

[626] See *Caterpillar Financial Services Corp v SNC Passion* [2004] EWHC 569 (Comm).

[627] This must include any rules of Community law public policy: Giuliano and Lagarde Report, 38. Compare, in the context of the Brussels Convention and Brussels I Regulation, Case C-7/98 *Krombach v Bamberski* [2000] ECR I-1935; Case C-38/98 *Régie National des Usines Renault SA v Maxicar SA* [2000] ECR I-2973. These cases suggest that it would offend public policy if the governing law were inconsistent with fundamental human rights. However, the ECJ also indicated that it would be willing to review the proper limits to the scope of public policy in Contracting States, to ensure that a court did not overstep the mark in its purported application of public policy. See also Benjamin, 25–043.

[628] Giuliano and Lagarde Report, 38. See also *City of Gotha (A Body Corporate) v Sotheby's (No 2)* The Times, 8 October 1998.

It should be stressed that Article 16 is not concerned with domestic rules **13.283** of public policy which are not intended to have any effect in relation to international contracts.[629] Rather, Article 16 is concerned with the application of English law's body of 'international' public policy, that is, public policy which is sufficiently powerful that it must be upheld even in respect of a contract governed by a foreign law.[630] An English court will normally only invoke its international public policy where the case has some connection with England, as, for example, where a contract governed by a foreign law restrains a party from trading in England.[631]

An example of the possible application of a public policy provision would **13.284** be if the limitation period of the governing law of the contract was oppressively short or long. Section 2(1) of the Foreign Limitation Periods Act 1984 states that the limitation period of the applicable law shall not be applied 'to the extent that its application would [conflict with English public policy]'. This is an English rule of international public policy, in the sense that it may lead to the disapplication of a foreign governing law of the contract.

Of course, some rules of a given law may be so offensive that most states **13.285** of the world, including England, would agree that public policy is violated by them. If, for example, a provision of the governing law is racially or sexually discriminatory or infringes human rights, it will be disapplied. In other cases, the interests of maintaining harmonious relations with a particular foreign state may weigh so heavily that English public policy dictates that the contract should not be enforced on its terms, because a foreign state considers the contract, or one or more of its terms, to be offensive or illegal.

However, it should be noted that it is only the public policy of the *forum* **13.286** that may be invoked under the Convention. There is no provision anywhere in the Convention which permits an English court to apply the public policy of a foreign state. Accordingly, an English court should be slow to invoke public policy on the grounds that it is seeking to maintain good relations with another state, where it is in substance giving effect to the law of a foreign state.[632] Certainly, it should not do so simply because the contract has strong, or very strong, objective connections to that state.[633]

---

[629] Cheshire and North, 584–585.   [630] *Vervaeke v Smith* [1981] Fam 77.
[631] The example given by Cheshire and North, 585; and see ibid, 123–128.
[632] See the discussion of 'whose public policy?', below, paras 13.292–294.
[633] *Akai Pty Ltd v People's Insurance Co Ltd* [1998] 1 Lloyd's Rep 90, 98.

Nature of Public Policy[634]

13.287 The nature and operation of public policy is a subject of considerable complexity and cannot be examined in detail here. Nevertheless, it may briefly be mentioned that a number of different circumstances exist in which an English court might invoke English public policy. Cheshire and North suggest four main categories of cases:[635]

13.288 **Where fundamental conceptions of English justice are disregarded** For example, if a party is subject to extreme duress to enter into a contract, the contract will not be enforced, even if it is valid and enforceable by its governing law.[636]

13.289 **Where the contract infringes English concepts of morality** This category would cover, for example, payment for the use of personal influence to secure a contract, if the place of performance also regards the activity as immoral.[637]

13.290 **Where application of the governing law would prejudice interests of the United Kingdom or good relations with a friendly foreign state** There are numerous examples of cases under this category. For example, an agreement to import liquor contrary to a prohibition law was not enforced in *Foster v Driscoll*.[638] Perhaps the best known example is *Regazzoni v KC Sethia (1944) Ltd*.[639] The case involved a contract governed by English law for the sale of jute bags. The buyer was English, the seller was Swiss. The contract was governed by English law. Both parties were aware that the sole source of supply was India and that the goods would be resold in South Africa. Indian law provided that it was illegal to export jute bags to South Africa. The House of Lords refused to enforce the contract, on the basis that it required the performance of an act which was illegal in India.

---

[634] For recent detailed discussion of public policy in the conflict of laws, see M Rubino-Sammartano and C Morse, *Public Policy in Transnational Relationships* (The Hague: Kluwer, 1992). See also, P Carter, 'Rejection of Foreign Law: Some Private International Law Inhibitions' (1984) 55 British Ybk of Intl Law 111; P Carter, 'The Role of Public Policy in English Private International Law' (1993) 42 ICLQ 1; N Enonchong, 'Public Policy in the Conflict of Laws: a Chinese Wall around Little England?' (1996) 45 ICLQ 633; J Harris and F Meisel, 'Public Policy and the Enforcement of International Arbitration Awards: Controlling the Unruly Horse' [1998] LMCLQ 568; R Leslie, 'The Relevance of Public Policy in Legal issues Involving Other Countries and their Laws' (1995) 6 Juridical Rev 477; A Briggs, 'Public Policy in the Conflict of Laws: a Sword and a Shield?' (2002) 6 Singapore J of Intl and Comparative Law 953.

[635] Cheshire and North, 126–128.

[636] *Royal Boskalis Westminster NV v Mountain* [1999] QB 674.

[637] *Lemenda Trading Co Ltd v African Middle East Petroleum Co* [1988] QB 448; *Westacre v Jugoimport* [1999] 2 Lloyd's Rep 65.

[638] [1929] 1 KB 470.   [639] [1958] AC 301.

Application of the governing law offends English conceptions of **13.291**
human liberty and freedom of action This body of public policy is
likely to be shared throughout the civilized world. In England, it would
include refusing to enforce a contract which defeated a right protected
by the European Convention on Human Rights,[640] or an act in violation of
rules of public international law.[641]

Whose Public Policy?

Sometimes, it was difficult to tell at common law whether the English **13.292**
court was applying *English* principles of public policy or was giving effect
to foreign mandatory rules or public policy. Of the above categories, the
'friendly foreign state' category is the most controversial,[642] since it is not
wholly clear whether the reasons for upholding the rules of that state are
because *English* public policy so requires, or because the foreign law's
rules are themselves being directly applied in an English court.[643] Today, it
is crucial to determine which interpretation is correct. If it is the former,
then this category is preserved under the Convention and is simply
a manifestation of English public policy, which may be applied under
Article 16. However, if the latter view is correct, then this appears to be
the application of the mandatory rules of a third state. Since the United
Kingdom has not enacted Article 7(1) of the Convention, which would
have allowed it to give effect to the mandatory rules of a state of close
connection to the contract, it would appear that there is no room for
application of such rules in an English court.[644]

One might argue that if the maintenance of international relations with a **13.293**
particular state is critical to England, then the English court's primary
motivation is not to *apply* a mandatory rule of a law of a friendly foreign
state, but to *disapply* the governing law because it undermines the *English*
policy of maintaining good relations with that state. If, on the contrary,
English law feels relatively neutral, but a friendly foreign state has especially strong views on a particular matter, then if the English court gives
effect to those views, it appears to be invoking a *foreign* rule or policy.[645]

---

[640] Enforced in the UK by the Human Rights Act 1998.
[641] *Kuwait Airways Corp v Iraqi Airways Co (Nos 4 and 5)* [2002] 2 AC 883; Briggs, n 634
above.
[642] Cheshire and North, 585, comment that, at common law, this was '. . . a very different
category of public policy . . . based on the comity of nations'.
[643] See Harris and Meisel, n 634 above.
[644] And if these were regarded as rules of foreign public policy, there is no provision in the
Convention permitting application of the public policy of a third state.
[645] A case such as *Lemenda Trading Co Ltd v African Middle East Petroleum Co* [1988] QB 448
may be a hybrid, involving as it does the combination of the morality of two different states.

13.294 However, it is suggested, on balance, that the entire 'friendly foreign state' category should today be viewed as an example of the application of the international mandatory rules of a third state.[646] In *Regazzoni*, important though relations with India were, what the court actually did was to give effect to *a rule of Indian law* which was designed to apply regardless of the law governing the contract. Had the United Kingdom wished to continue to give effect to the mandatory rules of a third state, it should have enacted Article 7(1) of the Convention. Since it has not done so, it would be undesirable to seek to find ways indirectly to give effect to the mandatory rules of a third state by reinterpreting them as provisions of English public policy. This much restricts the importance of the 'friendly foreign state' category in an English court under the Rome Convention.[647]

4. The Effect of Illegality upon a Contract

13.295 It is self-evident that a contract which requires the performance of an act, illegal by its governing law,[648] will not be enforced in England.[649] It is also scarcely surprising that a contract which involves the commission in England of an act which is illegal by English law will not be enforced in England.[650] The English court may invoke Article 7(2), on the basis that an international mandatory rule of the forum has been infringed. Benjamin gives two cogent examples of this which relate to sale of goods. The first is where a statutory provision concerning the minimum deposit in a credit sale is violated. The second is where a foreign seller packs goods destined for England in such a way as will help the buyer to smuggle them into the country.[651] A contract governed by a foreign law will also be unenforceable if it is illegal by English law, even if the relevant

---

[646] See Harris, n 359 above, at 260–264; Cheshire and North, 585–6.

[647] But see Peel, n 53 above, 15–059, who comments that 'this would be an unintended consequence of the Convention and it is highly unlikely that it is an interpretation which would be applied by the English courts. For the purposes of the Convention, the rule should be characterized as a rule of public policy falling within Art 16.' See also Plender and Wilderspin, n 1 above, 185.

[648] Or the law which would have governed the contract had it been valid: Art 8(1).

[649] Unless, of course, the foreign illegality is itself repugnant to English law and offends its public policy under Art 16: *Royal Boskalis Westminster NV v Mountain* [1999] QB 674; *Kuwait Airways Corp v Iraqi Airways Co (Nos 4 and 5)* [2002] 2 AC 883.

[650] Although, as Benjamin 25–112, notes, this will not be the case if the rule of English law is not intended to affect the validity of the contract.

[651] ibid; citing *Clugas v Penaluna* (1791) 4 TR 466; *Waymell v Reed* (1794) 5 TR 599; *Vandyke v Hewitt* (1800) 1 East 96; and *Pellecat v Angell* (1835) 2 CR M & R 311.

acts are committed overseas, if, on a true construction of the legislation,[652] it is intended to apply extra-territorially to the facts of the case.[653]

If the contract does not infringe any specific legislation of English law, **13.296** but application of the governing law on the facts would be repugnant to English public policy, the foreign law may be refused application, pursuant to Article 16. Benjamin gives a number of examples of the operation of public policy in English law which relate to the sale of goods.[654] These include: contracts which involve trading with an alien enemy;[655] contracts in unreasonable restraint of trade;[656] where the parties conclude a contract intending to perform an act which is illegal in a friendly foreign state;[657] and where the contract is immoral according to English law and is also considered immoral and unenforceable in the place of performance of the contract.[658]

However, the most well known case of illegality concerns the situation **13.297** where a contract requires the performance of an act which, after conclusion of the contract, become illegal in the place of performance. In *Ralli Bros v Compañía Naviera Sota y Aznar*,[659] a contract was concluded between Spanish shippers and English charterers to carry goods from India to Spain. The contract was governed by English law. The cost of the carriage was to be £50 per ton of freight. Whilst the ship was en route, a law was enacted in Spain to the effect that the price of the freight should not exceed £10 per ton. An action brought by the carrier for the additional £40 per ton failed.

A number of interpretations of the case are possible. One is to say that the **13.298** contract was governed by English law and the Spanish rule was simply one which frustrated the contract according to English law.[660] On this

---

[652] On the construction of statutes and their application in private international law, see also F Mann, 'Statutes and the Conflict of Laws' (1972–3) 46 British Ybk of Intl Law 117; S Dutson, 'The Conflict of Laws and Statutes: the International Operation of Legislation Dealing with Matters of Civil Law in the United Kingdom and Australia' (1997) 60 MLR 668.

[653] *Boissevain v Weil* [1950] AC 327. A statute that is silent as to its overriding effect, but contains a provision as to its territorial scope is likely to be treated as having an overriding effect within that territorial scope. Compare *The Hollandia* [1983] 1 AC 565.

[654] Benjamin, 25–112 (citing, inter alia, the authorities in the ensuing footnotes).

[655] *Dynamit AG v Rio Tinto Co Ltd* [1918] AC 260.

[656] *Rousillon v Rousillon* (1880) 14 Ch D 351. See also *Apple Corps Ltd v Apple Computer Inc* [1992] FSR 431.

[657] *Regazzoni v KC Sethia* [1958] AC 301; *Foster v Driscoll* [1929] 1 KB 470. But see the discussion of 'whose public policy?' above, paras 13.292–294, on the question of whether this involves the application of *English* public policy. The present authors conclude that it does not.

[658] *Lemenda Trading Co Ltd v African Middle East Petroleum Co Ltd* [1988] QB 448.

[659] [1920] 2 KB 287.

[660] See, eg, *Kahler v Midland Bank* [1950] AC 24, 48; *Walton (Grain and Shipping) Ltd v British Italian Trading Co SA* (1949) 80 LL R 530, 543–4; *Royal Boskalis Westminster NV v Mountain* [1999] QB 674, 733–4.

view, the only relevance of *Ralli* today is that where English law governs the contract, it will regard subsequent illegality by the law of the place of performance as extinguishing the relevant obligations under Article 10(1)(d). Again, it could be argued that the court was applying a mandatory rule *of the place of performance*. If that is the case, then, given that the United Kingdom has not enacted Article 7(1) of the Rome Convention, it cannot give effect to the mandatory rules of a third state.[661] An alternative view is that the action would have failed even if the contract had not been governed by English law, because it is a rule of *English* public policy[662] that a contract which requires the performance of an act which becomes illegal in the place of performance is unenforceable, regardless of what the governing law of the contract says on the matter.[663] However, this stretches the notion of English public policy beyond its natural limits[664] and might allow the provisions of the applicable law to be undermined too readily. Another approach is to say that the *Ralli* principle may relate to manner of performance and that the law of the place of performance can be applied under Article 10(2). However, it is doubtful whether this can be said to relate to the 'manner' of performance. On balance, it is suggested that the *Ralli* case should not be viewed as giving rise to a rule of public policy or requiring the application of a mandatory rule under the Rome Convention.

13.299 Whatever the scope of the common law rule, it was clearly the case that where a contract was governed by English law, the English courts would not compel performance in a state where that performance had become illegal.[665] This rule may continue to be applied under the Rome

---

[661] Save if the conditions of Art 3(3), or the consumer or employment contract provisions, lead to the application of that state's mandatory rules.

[662] But the *Ralli* case did not use the terminology of public policy. Cases that have purported to follow the *Ralli* decision tend to use the language of comity: Cheshire and North, 602, citing, *inter alia*, *Toprak v Finagrain* [1979] 2 Lloyd's Rep 98, 107 (aff'd by the Court of Appeal at 112, but not addressing this point); *Euro-Diam Ltd v Bathurst* [1987] 1 Lloyd's Rep 178, 187; *Lemenda Trading Co Ltd v African Middle East Petroleum Co Ltd* [1988] QB 448.

[663] See, e.g. *Zivnostenska Bana v Frankman* [1950] AC 57, 78; *Mackender v Feldia AG* [1967] 2 QB 590

[664] Public policy is an inherently negative process; whereas, in so far as English courts refused at common law to enforce a contract that was illegal by the law of the place of performance, this may be more naturally seen as involving the positive application of a rule of the law of the place of performance. See Cheshire and North, 602.

[665] Whether it also covered initial illegality is unclear (see, in favour of the view that it did, *Cunningham v Dunn* (1873) 3 CPD 443 and *Walton (Grain and Shipping) Ltd v British Italian Trading Co SA* (1949) 80 LL R 530; contra, see *Partabmull Rameshar v KC Sethia (1944) Ltd* [1951] 2 Lloyd's Rep 89, 96). It is hard to see why the *Ralli* principle should not apply to initial illegality, at least if, according to the governing law of the contract, neither party has taken the risk of that illegality. If one party has taken the risk of illegality, the court would not order performance of the contract, but might require him to pay damages to the other party for failure to perform.

Convention, on the basis that the contract is frustrated.[666] However, there must be two qualifications to this statement. First, the court needs to satisfy itself that the contracts *requires* performance in a certain country. As Millett LJ remarked in *Bangladesh Export Import Co Ltd v Sucden Kerry SA*:[667]

> Where a contract is governed by English law, the mere fact that its performance has become illegal under the law of a foreign country does not of itself amount to a frustration of the contract unless the contract requires performance in that country . . . The fact that performance in that country was within the contemplation of both parties is not enough; such performance must be required by a term of the contract express or implied.

In particular, if A agrees to sell goods cigarettes on CIF terms to B, the goods to be loaded on a ship in State X bound for State Y, it cannot be said that A's performance *requires* that the goods successfully arrive in State Y. The seller is bound only to ship the goods, take out a contract of insurance and deliver the documents to the buyer.[668] If, after the contract was concluded, State Y passed a rule prohibiting the import of tobacco products, an English court would not regard such a rule as having any effect on the contract between the parties.[669] Only if it was stated to be a condition of the contract that it would become frustrated if the seller could not import the goods into State Y would the legislation be relevant.

Second, the consequence of subsequent illegality by the law of the place of performance will normally be that the contract is frustrated. However, if, according to the law governing the contract, it appears that one party took the risk of an unforeseen event rendering performance overseas illegal, that party will be liable in damages for failure to perform.[670]   **13.300**

---

[666] Pursuant to Art 10(1)(d), considered above, paras 13.240–246, esp paras 13.241–242. See also *Luiz Barros Mattos Jnr v MacDaniels Ltd* [2004] EWHC 1188 (Ch) (a case which makes no reference to the Rome Convention).

[667] [1995] 2 Lloyd's Rep 1, 5–6. See also *Kleinwort Son & Co v Ungarische Baumwolle Industrie Aktiengesellschaft* [1939] 2 KB 678; *Toprak Mahsulleri Ofisi v Finagrain Compagnie Commerciale Agricole et Financière* [1979] 2 Lloyd's Rep 98; *The Playa Larga* [1983] 2 Lloyd's Rep 171.

[668] See Bridge, *The International Sale of Goods*, 157–158, who comments that: 'Shipment under a carriage contract and the taking out of insurance, coupled with the delivery of the documents that record their accomplishment, may be seen as a substitute for the physical delivery of the goods to the buyer under a conventional contract of sale . . . [T]he seller is not positively bound to deliver the goods at the port of discharge, and is not answerable for a failure by the carrier to do likewise . . .'

[669] This applies a fortiori to an FOB contract, since the seller's obligations are discharged when he loads the goods free on board ship.

[670] Benjamin, 25–112, gives the example of a collateral warranty that a contract is legal under the foreign law; *Peter Cassidy Seed Co Ltd v Osuustukkukappa IL* [1957] 1 WLR 273; *The Playa Larga* [1983] 2 Lloyd's Rep 171.

XIV. THE APPLICATION OF THE UNFAIR CONTRACT TERMS ACT 1977 TO INTERNATIONAL COMMERCIAL CONTRACTS OF SALE

1. INTRODUCTION

13.301 The provisions of the Unfair Contract Terms Act 1977[671] may restrict the effectiveness of an exclusion or limitation clause contained in a contract of sale.[672] They may do so even if the contract is governed by a foreign law. In this sense, the Act is clearly an example of a mandatory rule of international application. Nevertheless, the ambit of the Act, and its application to international commercial[673] contracts of sale is not straightforward and demands closer examination.

2. INTERNATIONAL SUPPLY CONTRACTS TO WHICH THE PROVISIONS OF THE UNFAIR CONTRACT TERMS ACT 1977 ARE INAPPLICABLE, REGARDLESS OF THE GOVERNING LAW OF THE CONTRACT

13.302 A look at s 26 of the Act suggests that the role of the Unfair Contract Terms Act 1977 will be limited in relation to sale of goods contracts. It states that:

(1) The limits imposed by this Act on the extent to which a person may exclude or restrict liability by reference to a contract term do not apply to liability arising under such a contract as is described in subsection (3) below.

(2) The terms of such a contract are not subject to any requirement of reasonableness under section 3 or 4: and nothing in Part II of this Act shall require the incorporation of the terms of such a contract to be fair and reasonable for them to have effect.

(3) Subject to subsection (4), that description of contract is one whose characteristics are the following—

(a) either it is a contract of sale of goods[674] or it is one under or in pursuance of which the possession or ownership of goods passes; and

(b) it is made by parties whose places of business (or, if they have none, habitual residences) are in the territories of different States (the Channel Islands and the Isle of Man being treated for this purpose as different States from the United Kingdom).

---

[671] Which applies to contracts made on or after 1 February 1978.

[672] See also paras 16.61–70 on the Vienna Convention.

[673] Its significance to consumer contracts is considered briefly below, para 13.320. However, it will not be examined in any detail, as this book is concerned with commercial contracts of sale. For detailed discussion of this matter, see Benjamin, 25–098 and 25–099.

[674] This will have the same meaning as under the Sale of Goods Act 1979. The word 'goods' is defined in s 61 of the 1979 Act.

(4) A contract falls within subsection (3) above only if either—

   (a) the goods in question are, at the time of the conclusion of the contract, in the course of carriage, or will be carried, from the territory of one State to the territory of another; or

   (b) the acts constituting the offer and acceptance have been done in the territories of different States; or

   (c) the contract provides for the goods to be delivered to[675] the territory of a State other than that within whose territory those acts were done.

Hence, the provisions of the 1977 Act do not apply to 'international supply contracts', within the meaning of ss 26(3) and (4). Of course, this very much limits the scope for reliance upon the Act. However, it is clear that there will be a limited category of international sales contracts which are not caught by the exclusion in s 26. For those contracts, the provisions of the Act may still be applied, whether as rules of English law (if that is the governing law of the contract) or as mandatory rules of the forum of international application.[676]

13.303 Section 26 (3) indicates that it only applies to a contract of sale where the parties[677] have their places of business in different states. A contract of sale between a buyer based in England and a seller also based in England, but involving delivery of goods in Portugal would not be caught by s 26. So too, a contract between a buyer based in England and a seller also based in England, but containing a Portuguese choice of law clause, would fall outside s 26. The effect of this provision is to discriminate against English sellers selling to English buyers, as the contract will be subject to the provisions of the 1977 Act. Had the seller had its place of business in Portugal, s 26(3) would have been triggered and the Act would not have applied.[678]

13.304 In addition, even if the parties *do* have their places of business in different states, the contract will still not be an 'international supply contract' within the meaning of s 26, unless at least one of the conditions of s 26(4) is met. Imagine a contract between a seller based in France and a buyer based in England. If, for example, the contract involves the carriage of the goods from England to France, it will fall within the s 26 exclusion, by

---

[675] It will not suffice that the contract provides for delivery *within* the territory of a state other than that within which those acts were done. The goods must pass from one state to another. See *Amiri Flight Authority v BAE Systems plc* [2003] EWCA Civ 1447, [2003] 2 Lloyd's Rep 767, CA, reversing [2002] EWHC 2481, [2003] 1 Lloyd's Rep 50, discussed below, paras 13.305–307.

[676] Most naturally, under Art 7(2) of the Rome Convention; but also, potentially, under Art 3(3), or in the case of consumer and employment contracts, Arts 5 and 6.

[677] This is a reference to the places of business of the principals to the contract and not any agents that they might employ: *Ocean Chemical Transport Inc v Exnor Cragg Ltd* [2000] 1 Lloyd's Rep 446.

[678] Provided that one of the conditions in s 26(4) was also met.

virtue of s 26(4)(a). But if the contract contains no carriage obligation,[679] it will not fall within s 26 unless one or both of the conditions in s 26(4)(b) or (c) are satisfied. The former requires that the acts of offer and acceptance have been done in the territories of different states;[680] the latter that the contract requires the goods to be delivered to the territory of a state other than that where the acts of offer and acceptance were done. So, in our example, if the buyer and seller concluded the contract by exchange of letters from their respective home states, s 26 would be satisfied. But if they concluded the contract by face-to-face negotiations in France,[681] and the goods were to be collected by the buyer from the seller's factory in France,[682] the contract does not satisfy s 26, notwithstanding that it is a contract of sale and that the parties have their places of business in different territories. That being so, the provision of s 27 as to the scope of application of the Act to international contracts becomes relevant.

13.305 Another example of where s 26 does not apply arose in *Amiri Flight Authority v BAE Systems plc*.[683] Amiri brought a claim as successor to the Private Department (PD) of the ruler of the United Arab Emirates. In 1987, PD had concluded a contract in Abu Dhabi for the purchase of an aircraft from the first defendant, BAE. The aircraft was to be delivered in England. It contained an English choice of law and choice of court clause. It stated that BAE would provide a maintenance programme for the aircraft after delivery. In 1999, the fuel tanks were found to be badly corroded owing to fungal contamination, which was a known risk and could have been prevented using biocidal agents. Amiri sued BAE, claiming that it was in breach of an implied term of the contract, and also liable in negligence, for

---

[679] So that the condition in s 26(4)(a) is not met.

[680] This being a UK statute designed to determine the ambit of its own application, it must be for English law to determine what these acts of offer and acceptance are and where they take place.

[681] The condition in s 26(4)(b) would not be met here, as the acts of offer and acceptance must occur in different states. Nor would s 26(4)(b) apply if the acts of offer and acceptance both took place in England. It would also not apply if the acts of offer and acceptance occurred in a third state, such as Germany. Although the acts of offer and acceptance occur in a state other than that where the parties have their places of business, they nonetheless occur in a *single* state. S 26(4)(b) applies only where these acts occur in *different* states.

[682] s 26(4)(c) applies where the goods are to be delivered to a state *other than that where the acts of offer and acceptance occurred*. In the given example, the acts of offer and acceptance took place in France, the same state where the goods were to be collected. As such, s 26(4)(c) does not apply. Nor would this case be caught by s 26(4)(a), as it does not involve carriage of the goods. The same would be true if the acts of offer and acceptance had taken place in a third state, such as Germany, and the buyer was required to collect them from a warehouse in Germany in which they were stored. Even though Germany was not the place of business of either party, the condition of s 26(4)(c) would not be met and, since there was no carriage obligation, the condition of s 26(4)(a) would not be met either.

[683] [2003] EWCA Civ 1447, [2003] 2 Lloyd's Rep 767, CA, reversing [2002] EWHC 2481, [2003] 1 Lloyd's Rep 50.

failure to prevent this corrosion as part of their maintenance obligation. The contract contained a clause excluding the seller's liability in contract and in tort. Amiri pleaded that this clause was not fair or reasonable and was invalid under the Unfair Contract Terms Act 1977.

The question then arose as to whether the contract was caught by the **13.306** exclusion in s 26, as an 'international supply contract'. This, in turn, raised the issue of whether one of the pre-conditions in s 26(4) was satisfied. The goods themselves were to be transported from one part of the United Kingdom to another part, rather than from one state to another. It was accepted that neither s 26(4)(a) nor s 27(4)(b) applied, because the goods were not to be transported from one state to another and the acts of offer and acceptance all occurred in Abu Dhabi. The central question was whether s 26(4)(c) applied. This applies if the contract 'provides for the goods to be delivered to the territory of a State other than that within whose territory those acts [of offer and acceptance] were done'. Delivery was to take place in England, whereas the contract was concluded in Abu Dhabi. However, Mance LJ[684] held that it could not be said that the goods were to be delivered *to* a state other than that where the contract was concluded. Rather, they were to be delivered *within* a state other than that where the contract was concluded. Mance LJ stated that: 'The words "delivered to the territory of a state" import movement from elsewhere into that state'.[685] He rejected the view of Tomlinson J at first instance that there was no rational basis for such a technical distinction, which would frustrate the aim of s 26 of providing parties to international supply contracts with freedom of contract.

The Law Commission[686] had modelled the pre-conditions in s 26(4) of the **13.307** 1977 Act on the Uniform Law on the International Sale of Goods,[687] Article 1(1)(c) of which refers to 'where delivery of the goods is to be made *in* the territory of a State other than that within whose territory the acts constituting the offer and the acceptance have been effected'.[688] Accordingly, it does not require movement of the goods from one state to another. However, Mance LJ noted that s 26(4)(c) of the 1977 Act had received careful attention in its drafting and ruled that he could not dismiss the use of the word 'to' in s 26(4)(c) as a technical oversight. He conceded that: 'The scheme of s. 26 leads on any view to what may be regarded as narrow or

[684] With whom Potter LJ and Rix LJ concurred.
[685] [2003] 2 Lloyd's Rep 767, 775, at [32].
[686] Law Commission First Report on Exemption Clauses in Contracts (Law Com No 24), para 120; Second Report on Exemption Clauses (Law Com No 69), paras 213 and 214; but see cl 14(3)(c) of the draft bill annexed to the Second Report, which speaks of the goods being delivered 'to' a state other than that where the acts of offer and acceptance were effected.
[687] Scheduled to the Uniform Law on International Sales Act 1967.
[688] Emphasis added.

even arbitrary distinctions'.[689] However, he noted that there was some evidence in the drafting of s 26(4)(a) and (c) that they were focused on the international movement of goods and found no justification for giving s 26(4)(c) anything other than its natural meaning. The result was that s 26 was inapplicable. Mance LJ remitted to the trial judge the question of whether the clause was invalid under the provisions of the 1977 Act.

13.308   In consequence, s 26 involves a rather technical test, which appears somewhat removed from the key policy question of which international sales contracts have a sufficient connection with England to merit the application of the Unfair Contract Terms Act 1977. Arguably, s 26 is in need of reform.[690] One might argue that where the buyer and seller have their places of business in different states, as where the buyer is based in England and the seller is based in Portugal, English law only has a legitimate territorial interest in the application of the Act where delivery of the goods is to take place in England. If the buyer is based in England and the seller is based in Portugal and delivery occurs in Portugal, arguably the Act should not apply, it being the legitimate concern of Portuguese law, not English law, to regulate unfair contractual terms in such circumstances.[691]

3. International Contracts of Supply Falling Outside the Scope of the s 26 Exclusion: The Ambit of the Unfair Contract Terms Act 1977

Contracts Governed by the Law of The United Kingdom Only by Virtue of a Choice of Law by the Parties

The provision

13.309   Section 27(1) states that:

(1) Where the [law applicable to][692] a contract is the law of any part of the United Kingdom only by choice of the parties (and apart from that choice would be the

---

[689] [2003] 2 Lloyd's Rep 767, 779, at [44].

[690] The Law Commission is currently considering reforms to UCTA: see the Joint Consultation Paper on *Unfair Terms in Contracts* (Law Commission Consultation Paper No 166; Scottish Law Commission Discussion Paper No 119).

[691] However, if both buyer and seller are based in England, but delivery is to take place in Portugal, s 26 would not presently apply, as the parties have to have their places of business in different states (s 26(3)). Accordingly, UCTA is applicable. It is suggested that this is desirable. There is an argument that English law does have a legitimate interest here in regulating unfair contract terms in contracts where both parties have their places of business in England, even if delivery occurs overseas. This is likely to reflect the parties' expectations of protection under the Act. Moreover, if the parties chose English law to govern the contract, this is not a case where UCTA would be disapplied pursuant to s 27(1) of the Act.

[692] Words substituted by Contracts (Applicable Law) Act 1990, s 5, Sch 4, para 4, to reflect change in terminology from 'proper' law to 'applicable' law under the Rome Convention.

law of some country outside the United Kingdom) sections 2 to 7 and 16 to 21 of this Act do not operate as part [of the law applicable to the contract].[693]

The law of a part of the United Kingdom applies only by choice of the parties

Section 27(1) requires the court to work out which would be the applic- **13.310** able law in the absence of choice, but for the choice of English law. Presumably, it should do this today[694] by applying Article 4 of the Rome Convention.[695] If the applicable law in the absence of choice is that of a part of the United Kingdom, the rules of the 1977 Act will still prevail, at least in respect of those international supply contracts not caught by s 26. However, if the applicable law in the absence of choice is not that of a part of the United Kingdom, ss 2 to 7 and 16 to 21 of the 1977 Act will not apply, notwithstanding that the parties chose English law[696] to govern the contract. This means that if, for example, a Japanese buyer and a Japanese seller conclude a contract containing a choice of law clause for English law, and the contract has no significant objective connection to England, the contract will not be subject to the provisions of ss 2 to 7 and 16 to 21. It is clear that, but for the choice of law, the contract would not have been governed by English law.[697]

The key question in s 27(1) is whether the applicable law in the absence of **13.311** choice would have been that of a part of the United Kingdom, rather than English law specifically. Hence, if the parties choose English law to govern a contract, but the contract would, in the absence of choice, be governed by Scottish law, then the exclusion is not triggered. The same would be true in the converse scenario.

Implied choice of the law of a part of the United Kingdom

It is not wholly clear whether s 27(1) is only triggered where the parties **13.312** have *expressly* chosen the law of a part of the United Kingdom and the contract has no connection with any part of the United Kingdom. Section 27(1) refers only to a 'choice' of the parties. What if the parties have *impliedly* chosen such a law, for example by including an English juris- diction or arbitration clause? It is suggested that s 27(1) is equally applic- able in this scenario. The purpose of the section is to deal with cases where a contract is governed by the law of a part of the United Kingdom,

---

[693] ibid.
[694] At the time when the Sale of Goods Act 1979 was concluded, the common law choice of law rules in contract would have applied.
[695] Discussed above, paras 13.112–140; or, for consumer or employment contracts, Arts 5 and 6 respectively.
[696] Or, as the case may be, Scottish law.
[697] Art 4(2) would lead to a presumption in favour of the law of the place of business of the seller, Japanese law.

notwithstanding that it would not have been the applicable law in the absence of choice. Whether it is the governing law by virtue of an express or implied choice of the parties does not seem material.[698]

The effect of s 27(1)

13.313 Where s 27(1) is applicable, this means that *inter alia*, the following provisions of the Act will not apply to commercial contracts of sale: the exclusion or restriction of negligence liability;[699] the exclusion or restriction of the liability of the seller for breach of his implied undertakings as to title;[700] and the reasonableness requirement for the exclusion or restriction of the seller's liability for conformity of the goods with description and quality or fitness for purpose.[701] For consumer contracts, the following, additional provisions of the Act will not apply: the requirement that where a contract contains a clause excluding or restricting the liability of the other party for breach of contract, or entitling that other party to render a substantially different performance from that which was reasonably expected of him, or to render no performance at all, that clause be reasonable;[702] the reasonableness requirement for the imposition of an indemnity obligation upon a consumer;[703] the exclusion or restriction of liability in a manufacturer's guarantee for goods proving defective in consumer use and resulting from negligence in manufacture or distribution;[704] and the exclusion or restriction of the seller's liability for conformity of the goods with description and quality or fitness for purpose.[705]

The parties expressly stipulate that the Act should apply

13.314 A particular problem might arise if the parties to a contract to which s 27(1) applies *want* the rules of the Unfair Contract Terms Act 1977 to apply to their contract. Imagine that a contract is concluded between a Japanese buyer and a Japanese seller.[706] They provide that English law shall govern the contract, *including all the substantive rules on the exclusion and limitation of liability clauses contained in the Unfair Contract Terms Act 1977*. It could be argued that such a choice is ineffective. If the parties

---

[698] This is also the view of Benjamin, 25–092. The authors cite the case of *Surzur Overseas Ltd v Ocean Reliance Shipping Co Ltd* [1997] CLY 906. See also the Giuliano and Lagarde Report, 17.

[699] s 2 UCTA. This is a blanket restriction in the case of death and personal injury; in other cases, it is subject to a reasonableness test.

[700] ibid, s 6. This is a blanket restriction.   [701] ibid.

[702] ibid, s 3. This section also applies to a commercial contract where one party deals on the other's written standard terms of business.

[703] ibid, s 4.   [704] ibid, s 5. This is a blanket restriction.

[705] ibid. This is a blanket restriction in the case of consumer contracts, whereas it is subject to a reasonableness test in the case of commercial contracts.

[706] This will not be caught by s 26, since the parties do not have their places of business in different states.

choose English law to govern a contract, then they must take it as they find it. We saw in the discussion of Article 3(1) that the parties are required to choose the provisions in force of a recognized legal system.[707] English law stipulates in s 27(1) that, on facts such as these, ss 2 to 7 and 16 to 21 of the 1977 Act are inapplicable. It might be said that this is, in effect, a mandatory rule of English law and that, as English law governs the contract, it must be complied with by the parties. Against this, one might argue that the purpose of s 27(1) is not to *force* the parties to comply with the restrictions in the Act, where the law of the part of the United Kingdom is not the law of the state of closest connection. But if they *want* to comply with those restrictions, it is not clear why they should not be permitted to do so. Alternatively, it could be argued that the express choice by the parties of the rules of the 1977 Act is not a distortion of English law as such, but involves the incorporation by reference of a set of terms into the contract.[708] It is suggested that there is no cause to object to such incorporation by reference on facts such as these and that, accordingly, all of the rules of the Act should apply in this scenario.

Application of the Unfair Contract Terms Act 1977 Notwithstanding a Choice of the Law of a Foreign State

The provision

Section 27(2)(a) then provides that the Act shall apply: **13.315**

. . . notwithstanding any contract term which applies or purports to apply the law of some country outside the United Kingdom where . . .:
 (a) the term appears to the court, or arbitrator . . . to have been imposed wholly or mainly for the purpose of enabling the party imposing it to evade the operation of this Act. . . .

Evasion of the operation of the Act

The effect of this provision is that if the parties choose a foreign[709] law **13.316** to govern their contract, and if that choice appears to the court to be motivated entirely, or primarily, by the desire[710] to evade the Unfair Contract Terms Act 1977, the Act will still be applied to the contract.[711]

---

[707] Above, paras 13.65–66.   [708] This argument is presented by Benjamin, 25–093.
[709] As Benjamin, 25–100, points out, the parties may be able to evade certain provisions of UCTA by invoking the terms of the Uniform Law on International Sales 1964, as this is a part of the law of the UK by virtue of the Uniform Law on International Sales Act 1967.
[710] Specifically, s 27(2)(a) refers to the desire of 'the party imposing [the term] . . .'.
[711] The relevant provisions of UCTA might be applied either pursuant to Art 7(2) of the Rome Convention, as international mandatory rules of the forum, or pursuant to Art 3(3). However, the latter may only be applied if, but for the choice of law, the contract is entirely objectively connected to England. As such, it will be easier to rely upon Art 7(2).

This only raises another question as to when a court might reasonably conclude that this was the purpose behind the choice of a foreign[712] law. There are parallels to the common law requirement that a choice of law had to be *'bona fide* and legal'.[713] One would have thought that the prime concern of s 27(2)(a) would be the converse of s 27(1): namely to ensure that the 1977 Act applies where a foreign law is chosen, but the applicable law in the absence of choice would have been the law of a part of the United Kingdom. Unfortunately, s 27(2)(a) differs materially from s 27(1) in making its application hinge on the subjective intentions of the parties. In particular, the word 'evade'[714] suggests that the key question is whether the parties have intended to act with an element of bad faith, by manipulating the choice of law process so as to escape the clutches of the 1977 Act. This has two consequences. First, in the case of a contract of sale which, save for a choice of law clause for Japanese law, is wholly domestic to England,[715] the Act will not apply if it does not appear to the court that the intention of the parties to the contract was wholly, or principally, to evade the application of the Act. Second, if English law is not the law which would have applied to the contract in the absence of choice, but the parties, fearing that it might be, deliberately chose the law of a state outside the United Kingdom to govern the contract,[716] it would appear that the rules of the 1977 Act must be applied, since the *purpose* of the choice of law clause was to evade application of the Act. This might be the case if, for example, a Japanese buyer and a Japanese seller conclude a contract for the delivery of machine parts to England, where the buyer intends to use them to manufacture machinery. The parties choose Japanese law to govern the contract, to make absolutely sure that the Act does not apply. In this scenario, Japanese law would in all probability have applied anyway in the absence of choice.[717] Yet, it seems that s 27(2)(a) requires the English court to apply the 1977 Act to the contract. Whatever the state of

---

[712] s 27(2)(a) is not triggered by a choice of the law of another part of the UK. However, it is, of course, extremely unlikely in any event that such a choice would be motivated by the desire to evade the provisions of UCTA.

[713] per Lord Wright in *Vita Food Products v Unus Shipping Co Ltd* [1939] AC 277, 290.

[714] Which is used rather than the word 'avoid'. The word 'avoid' does not suggest an element of *mala fides*.

[715] Such a contract will not be caught by s 26, as the parties do not have their places of business in different states.

[716] This scenario is comparatively unlikely, since if there is a realistic prospect of English law applying in the absence of choice, but it is not, in fact, the law of the state of closest connection, the contract will usually fall within s 26. However, the example given in this paragraph illustrates that this will not always be the case.

[717] It is the habitual residence or principal place of business of the characteristic performer, the seller. Nor does there seem much prospect of that law being rebutted under Art 4(5), since England is certainly not clearly more closely connected to the contract.

mind of the parties, it is difficult to see that it provides a sufficient principled justification for the application of the Act in this scenario.

The clause was 'imposed'

In fact, s 27(2)(a) speaks of a term being 'imposed'. This might suggest **13.317** that its principal concern is with standard form contracts, rather than choice of law clauses which are individually negotiated by the parties. However, it seems that a clause may be 'imposed' even if it is not a standard term. As Benjamin convincingly argues:

If a party having a dominant bargaining position expressly insists or insidiously ensures that the other party agree to the selection of a foreign law and he does so 'wholly or mainly' with a view to ensuring that one or more exemption clauses operating in his favour should not be struck down by the Unfair Contract Terms Act, there is, it is submitted, an 'imposition' of the foreign law with the 'purpose' of 'evading' the Act. . . . [T]he interest sought to be protected is not so much United Kingdom law (in the abstract) as that of the weaker party or parties.[718]

Implied choice of a foreign law

As with s 26, it is not immediately clear whether s 27(2)(a) applies where **13.318** the choice of a foreign law is implied by the parties, rather than being stated expressly. Two principal arguments against the application of the provision in the case of an implied choice can be made. First, that s 27(2) refers to a contract 'term' which applies or purports to apply the law of a country outside the United Kingdom.[719] Frequently, an implied choice of law will not be determined by any one term of the contract, as, for example, where the whole contract is on standard terms usually indicative of a particular governing law, or where the parties have subjected their previous course of dealings to a certain law. Moreover, if the contract contains an exclusive jurisdiction or arbitration clause, although this may be a very strong indicator of an implied choice of law, it is not a choice of law by itself and must always be considered in the light of other relevant factors. However, it is suggested that this point is not fatal to implied choices being relevant under this sub-section. One might argue that from whatever sources the English court draws to conclude that an implied choice of law has been made, that choice, once determined, is itself a term of the contract.[720] Second, it is arguably inherently much more likely that parties who wish to evade the 1977 Act will expressly choose a foreign

---

[718] Benjamin, 25–097.   [719] A point made by Benjamin, 25–095.

[720] And one whose essential validity hinges, principally, upon Arts 3(4) and Art 8(1) of the Rome Convention.

law to govern the contract.[721] Those who do not do so are much less likely, in the course of their implied choice, to have been motivated by evasionary tactics. However, this is a point which should go only to the question of whether the court rules that the parties had sought to evade the Act; it should not itself be a reason to reject the role of implied choice under this sub-section. Ultimately, if it can be established that a foreign law was impliedly chosen so as to evade the application of the Act, there seems absolutely no principled reason not to apply s 27(2)(a) with the equal force that would have applied if the choice of foreign law had been express.

The term 'purports' to apply a foreign law

13.319 It should be noted that s 27(2)(a) applies not only where the parties do apply a foreign law, but when they 'purport' to do so. This suggests that even an ineffective choice of foreign law in these circumstances described by s 27(2)(a) will trigger the application of the Act.[722] Such choice might be ineffective because the term which one party sought to impose was not incorporated into the contract, or was not freely agreed upon by the other party. However, in the great majority of cases where a purported evasionary choice fails, the law applicable in the absence of choice will in any case be the law of England,[723] so that the 1977 Act will apply as part of the governing law in any event. There would, after all, have been little motivation for the purported evasion were this not the case. However, there is one situation where a failed choice of a foreign law for evasionary reasons might trigger the application of s 27(2)(a), even though the applicable law in the absence of choice is not English law. To return to an earlier example, imagine that a Japanese buyer and a Japanese seller conclude a contract for the supply of machine parts.[724] These are to be delivered to the buyer in England, where he intends to use them to manufacture machinery. After the contract has been concluded, the seller, anxious to avoid any prospect of the application of the 1977 Act, sends a confirmation letter in which, for the first time, he states that the contract 'shall be governed by the law of Japan and that, in particular, the provisions of the United Kingdom's Unfair Contract Terms Act 1977 shall not apply between the parties'. The buyer does not respond to this term. In subsequent litigation in England, the buyer satisfies the court that the

---

[721] Although the truly sophisticated choice of law shopper might select the governing law impliedly, rather than expressly, so as to deflect suspicion that he is purporting to evade UCTA.

[722] See Benjamin, 25–096; though the authors appear to provide only a limited answer to the problem.

[723] Or Scotland.

[724] Since the parties do not have their places of business in different states, the matter is not caught by s 26.

term was not incorporated into the contract. The applicable law in the absence of choice will almost certainly be Japanese law, since it is the law of the habitual residence of the characteristic performer, the seller, and since there does not appear to be a sufficiently strong case for disapplying that law[725] and applying English law instead, given that all factors, save the place of performance, are connected to Japan.[726] Nevertheless, it can be said that one party[727] purported to apply the law of a country outside the United Kingdom and that it was imposed 'wholly or mainly for the purpose of enabling the party imposing it to evade the operation of . . . [the] Act'. As such, the 1977 Act will apply to the contract. The seller is, in this scenario, the victim of trying too hard to evade the Act. Ironically, by unsuccessfully seeking to do so, he triggers its application in circumstances where the Act would otherwise not be applicable.

Consumer Contracts

This book is essentially concerned with commercial contracts of sale. **13.320** Nevertheless, there may be difficult cases where it is unclear whether the contract is a commercial or a consumer contract. The parties should accordingly satisfy themselves whether their agreement is a consumer contract within the meaning of the 1977 Act, or other applicable legislation.[728] It should be noted briefly[729] that s 27(2)(b) provides, as an alternative to s 27(2)(a), that the 1977 Act will still be applied notwithstanding a term which applies or purports to apply the law of a country outside the United Kingdom if:

in the making of the contract one of the parties dealt as consumer, and he was then habitually resident in the United Kingdom, and the essential steps necessary for the making of the contract were taken there, whether by him or by others on his behalf.[730]

---

[725] Pursuant to Art 4(5) of the Rome Convention.

[726] Although it was shown above that the most common case for rebutting the presumption in Art 4(2) is where the characteristic obligation is to be performed in a state other than that of the seller's habitual residence, this is most unlikely to happen if the parties are *both* habitually resident in the same state and the contract was concluded in that state.

[727] s 27(2)(a) refers in the singular to 'the party' imposing, or purporting to impose, a term stipulating that the law of a state outside the UK is to govern the contract.

[728] See above, paras 13.265–268. See also, in relation to consumer contracts, the anti-avoidance provisions of SI 1999/2083, SI 2000/2334 and SI 2002/3045, n 594 above. For detailed discussion of the application of these provisions to international consumer contracts, see Morse in Benjamin, 25–090 to 25–111 and Benjamin (Special Supplement) (2003), 1–035 to 1–049.

[729] See further Benjamin, 25–098.

[730] Compare the Joint Consultation Paper on *Unfair Terms in Contracts* (Law Commission Consultation Paper No 166; Scottish Law Commission Discussion Paper No 119). It comments (at 250) that: 'In consumer contracts, it should be made clear that, if the contract has a close connection with the UK, the new legislation will apply irrespective of a choice of another system of law'.

The word 'consumer' is defined in s 12 thus:

(1) A party to a contract 'deals as consumer' in relation to another party if—
   (a) he neither makes the contract in the course of a business nor holds himself out as doing so; and
   (b) the other party does make the contract in the course of a business; and
   (c) in the case of a contract governed by the law of sale of goods or hire-purchase, or by section 7 of this Act, the goods passing under or in pursuance of the contract are of a type ordinarily supplied for private use or consumption.[731]

It is not immediately clear in which circumstances the 'essential steps' for the making of the contract will have been made in the United Kingdom, within the meaning of s 27(2)(b) of the 1977 Act. It may be that the meaning of this term is modelled on the pre-conditions in Article 5 of the Rome Convention.[732] If so, s 27(2)(b) would apply[733] where the conclusion of the contract was preceded in the state of the consumer's habitual residence, England, by a specific invitation addressed to him or by advertising and the consumer took there all steps necessary by him for the conclusion of the contract; or if the seller or his agent received the buyer's order in that country; or if the consumer travelled abroad because the seller arranged the journey with the aim of selling goods to him.[734]

XV. CONCLUDING REMARK

13.321 The rules of the Rome Convention are an exercise in qualified pragmatism. They uphold the parties' freedom to choose the governing law. However, they maintain a fair element of control of party autonomy, in the shape of provisions on mandatory rules and public policy. Indeed, the Convention is, in one sense, conservative. The defining feature of a contract of sale of goods is its mixture of issues relating to contractual rights and duties on the one hand, and the passing of property on the other. The Convention does not deal with this latter aspect. Instead, the forum's property choice of law rules are left intact.[735] Unlike the Hague

---

[731] Although s 12(2) states that where the buyer participates in an auction or competitive tender, he will never be treated as a consumer. In all other cases, where s 12(1) is satisfied, a party alleging that the other person is not a consumer has the burden of proving that the other party is not: s 12(3).

[732] Compare Benjamin, 25–098.

[733] But note that in many cases, the provisions of UCTA will in any event be excluded by s 26 of UCTA.

[734] Although note that these conditions do not apply under Art 5 of the Rome Convention to a contract of carriage: Art 5(4)(a), unless the contract is to provide, for an inclusive price, travel and accommodation (Art 5(5)).

[735] Subject to the limited provisions on assignment (Art 12) and subrogation (Art 13).

Sales Convention 1986, there is no attempt, for example, to extend the role of the applicable law of the contract to such matters as the time when the buyer becomes entitled to the products, fruits and income deriving from the goods[736] or to the effect as between the parties of a retention of title clause.[737] It may be precisely because the Rome Convention does not extend party autonomy beyond its acceptable limits, or purport to stray from its natural terrain of contractual obligations, that the Convention has provided a set of solutions which, in general, work effectively in respect of international sale of goods contracts.[738]

---

[736] Art 12(c) of the Hague Sales Convention 1986. See chapter 15 on the 1955 and 1986 Hague Sales Conventions below, para 15.110.

[737] ibid, Art 12(e).

[738] And which have marginalized the role of the Hague Sales Convention 1986, in particular.

Sales Convention 1980, there is no attempt, for example, to extend the role of the applicable law of the contract to such matters as the time when the buyer becomes entitled to the products, fruits and income deriving from the goods, or to the extent as between the parties of a retention of title clause. It may be precisely because the Rome Convention does not extend party autonomy beyond its acceptable limits of purport to stray from the natural extent of contractual obligations, that the Convention has provided a set of solutions which in general work effectively in respect of international sales of goods contracts.

All three of the Hague Sales Convention 1986. See chapters 15 and 17 on the 1955 and 1986 Hague Sales Convention above: paras 15.1.1.

Ibid, Art 11(2).

and which have marginalized the role of the Hague Sales Convention 1986 in particular.

14

Transfer of Contractual Rights and Obligations: Choice of Law

I. SCOPE OF DISCUSSION

We are concerned in this chapter with choice of law problems arising out **14.01** of the transfer of rights and obligations between the seller and buyer. Our primary concern is with the performance of CIF contracts and the process by which the buyer acquires rights and incurs duties under the bill of lading contract. The question arises as to the relationship between the buyer, who is a transferee of the bill of lading, and the carrier. This may create choice of law problems, owing to the fact that the transferee is not a party to the original contract of carriage made between the shipper and the carrier, but may nevertheless seek to invoke contractual rights against the carrier.[1] Different legal systems may differ as to the nature and extent of the rights which the transferee of the bill of lading[2] has against

---

[1] Or the carrier may seek to invoke contractual rights against the transferee of the bill of lading.

[2] On bills of lading, see below, paras 18.78–92.

the carrier. In particular, the question arises as to the effect of a choice of law clause in the bill of lading upon claims between the carrier and the transferee of the bill.[3]

II. DOES THE ROME CONVENTION APPLY? ARTICLE 1(1) AND 'CONTRACTUAL OBLIGATIONS'

1. Obligations between the Shipper and Carrier

14.02   By definition, the contract of carriage, as evidenced by the bill of lading, concerns 'contractual obligations' entered into between the original parties to that bill. It accordingly falls within the scope of the Rome Convention. There is no difficulty in establishing this where the action in contract is between the shipper and the carrier.[4] Moreover, it is in the nature of the contract that there will almost always be a 'choice between the laws of different countries' in a carriage of goods by sea case. Indeed, there may be a wide range of connecting factors, such as personal connecting factors relating to the carrier, shipper and consignee, the places of loading and discharge of the goods and the flag of the vessel.[5]

2. Obligations between the Transferee of the Bill of Lading and the Carrier; s 2 of the Carriage of Goods by Sea Act 1992

14.03   It is less clear what the position is where the bill of lading lawfully changes hands and the holder brings a claim against the carrier, or vice versa. If the claimant argues that a foreign law applies,[6] by which there are no contractual obligations between the holder and the carrier, then the claim cannot fall within the scope of the Rome Convention.[7] However, suppose that the claimant brings a claim under English law,[8] on the basis

---

[3] See further above, paras 5.01–05, for discussion of the duties of a CIF seller in relation to the contract of carriage and contract of insurance and the types of legal problem to which these may give rise.

[4] Compare *Gracechurch Container Line Ltd v SpA Assicurazioni Generali* [1994] IL Pr 206, Italian Supreme Court.

[5] See Gaskell, 19.5. The authors further point out that some bills of lading provide for the application of the law of a non-Contracting State to the Rome Convention, such as the provision in the Mitsui OSK Lines Combined Transport Bill 1993 for the application of Japanese law (ibid, 19.16). The Rome Convention applies even if the governing law is that of a non-Contracting State: Art 2.

[6] See *DVA v Voest Alpine* [1997] 2 Lloyd's Rep 279 at 287 (*per* Hobhouse LJ), 291 (*per* Morritt LJ), CA.

[7] Compare, in relation to jurisdiction at common law, *Enichem Anic SpA v Ampelos Shipping Co Ltd (The Delfini)* [1990] 1 Lloyd's Rep 252, CA.

[8] Or another applicable national law by which the third party holder of the bill of lading is alleged to succeed to the rights and obligations of the shipper.

of the machinery of the Carriage of Goods by Sea Act 1992.[9] The nature of the claim, and whether it can be regarded as a 'matter relating to contract' for the purposes of Article 5(1) of the Brussels I Regulation, was considered at length in Chapter 5, to which the reader is referred.[10] Many of the arguments made there are equally applicable here. It was argued in chapter 13[11] that the definition of 'contractual obligations' in Article 1(1) of the Rome Convention is a European autonomous one and that, in the absence of further guidance, the European Court of Justice case law on the autonomous meaning of 'matters relating to contract' in Article 5(1) of the Brussels I Regulation is the best available source of guidance.

It will be recalled that there is considerable doubt as to whether the claim **14.04** by the transferee of the bill against the carrier pursuant to s 2 of the Carriage of Goods by Sea Act 1992 is a 'matter relating to contract'. Since the phrase 'contractual obligations' in Article 1(1) of the Rome Convention appears at first sight to be narrower, if anything, than the phrase 'matters relating to contract', one might think that similar doubts exist as to whether the choice of law rules in contract apply to this claim. However, the meaning of 'matters relating to contract' under the Brussels I Regulation has been complicated by the decision in *Jakob Handte et Cie GmbH v SA Traitements Mécano-Chimiques des Surfaces*[12] and the need for the obligation to be *both contractual and freely assumed*. The latter requirement casts doubt upon the application of Article 5(1) of the Brussels I Regulation, given that the contract between the transferee of the bill and the carrier arises by operation of statute, and given that the carrier will usually be unable to foresee the party to whom he owes contractual obligations by virtue of the machinery of s 2 of the Carriage of Goods by Sea Act 1992.[13]

When it comes to Article 1(1) of the Rome Convention, there seems no **14.05** reason to impose the further requirement that an obligation be freely assumed to an identifiable person. Article 1(1) quite clearly *only* requires that there be a contractual obligation. If, for whatever reason, the obligation between the parties is contractual, be that by express agreement or by the operation of a statute, then the Rome Convention applies. The obligations under s 2 of the Carriage of Goods by Sea Act 1992 are

---

[9] On which, see R Bradgate and F White, 'The Carriage of Goods by Sea Act 1992' (1993) 56 MLR 188; M Bridge, 'The Carriage of Goods by Sea Act 1992' [1993] JBL 379; F Reynolds, 'The Carriage of Goods by Sea Act 1992' [1993] LMCLQ 436; J Wilson, *Carriage of Goods by Sea*, (4th edn, Harlow; Longman, 2001).

[10] See above, paras 5.19–28.   [11] See above, paras 13.14–17.

[12] Case C-26/91 [1992] ECR I-3967, paras 16 and 20. See also the opinion of AG Jacobs at para 39.

[13] See above, paras 5.19–28. Nonetheless, there is an argument for regarding a carrier as having freely assumed an obligation towards the third party: above, para 5.25.

contractual.[14] It follows that claims made pursuant to s 2 of the Carriage of Goods by Sea Act 1992 by the transferee of a bill of lading against the carrier, or vice versa, are subject to the choice of law rules in contract.[15]

3. An Action between a Consignee and a Sub-Carrier

14.06 In this situation, there is an action involving a third party but, unlike under the Carriage of Goods by Sea Act 1992, there is in this case no transfer of rights and duties. In its discussion of Article 5(1) of the Brussels Convention, the European Court of Justice in *Réunion Européenne SA v Spliethoff's Bevrachtingskantoor BV*[16] held that in this situation the bill of lading discloses no contractual relationship[17] between the consignee and the sub-carrier. The same approach should be taken for choice of law purposes, so that the Rome Convention is inapplicable.

III. SPECIFIC EXCLUSIONS FROM THE ROME CONVENTION

1. Obligations Arising under Bills of Exchange, Cheques and Promissory Notes and other Negotiable Instruments

14.07 The main exclusions from the Rome Convention are listed in Article 1(2) and (3). These were discussed in Chapter 13, to which the reader is referred.[18] However, of particular relevance to bills of lading is the exclusion in Article 1(2)(c) of 'obligations arising under bills of exchange, cheques and promissory notes and other negotiable instruments to the extent that the obligations under such other negotiable instruments arise out of their negotiable character'. Giuliano and Lagarde make it clear that bills of lading are only excluded if they are negotiable and that even then

---

[14] See above, paras 5.22–23 and 5.27.

[15] Compare, in relation to jurisdiction at common law, *Compañía Continental del Perú SA v Evelpis Shipping Corp (The Agia Skepi)* [1992] 2 Lloyd's Rep 467; and *Ilyssia Compañía Naviera SA v Ahmed Abdul-Qawi Bamaodah (The Elli 2)* [1985] 1 Lloyd's Rep 107, where a claim based on the contract of carriage brought by the carrier against a third party, who, according to the applicable law, had assumed liability under the contract of carriage, was treated as a claim made in respect of a contract for the purposes of service out of the jurisdiction by the Court of Appeal. See above, paras 5.32–43, esp 5.38–39, 5.42–43.

[16] Case C-51/97 [1998] ECR I-6511.

[17] Although there was a further problem in relation to Art 5(1) of the Brussels Convention that any relationship between the parties was not freely entered into. It has been suggested in the above section that this further requirement does not exist under the Rome Convention. Nevertheless, there must be a contractual obligation under the Rome Convention and none existed on the facts of the case.

[18] See above, paras 13.22–42.

only obligations arising from their negotiable character are excluded.[19] However, whether the document is regarded as a bill of lading is a matter for the law of the forum and its rules of private international law.[20] One might question whether some bills of lading are caught by this exclusion, on the basis that they are order or bearer bills of a negotiable character. However, it is suggested that the Rome Convention still applies to such bills, on the basis that: 'Under English law the characteristic feature of a negotiable instrument is that the *bona fide* transferee for value of the instrument obtains a better title than the transferor or a previous holder. It is probable that the negotiability of the bill of lading does not affect substantive proprietary rights.'[21]

2. AGENT'S ABILITY TO BIND PRINCIPAL

The question of whether an agent may bind a principal is excluded by **14.08** Article 1(2)(f). This issue may also arise in the bill of lading context. It may be disputed whether a party signed the bill of lading as an agent and whether that person had authority to bind a carrier by signing the bill.[22]

IV. THE LAW APPLICABLE TO THE BILL OF LADING

Our primary concern is not with the law applicable to the bill of lading **14.09** itself,[23] but with the exercise of determining the choice of law problems that may arise from the seller's obligation under a CIF contract to transfer the bill of lading to the buyer. Nevertheless, we cannot properly look at the choice of law issues raised by the transfer of the bill of lading without first considering the law applicable to the bill of lading.[24]

In principle, most of the choice of law rules on the law applicable to the **14.10** bill of lading will be determined by the rules examined in Chapter 13 on the Rome Convention. We shall concentrate here solely upon choice of law issues which are specific to the bill of lading.

---

[19] However, one might question whether this view confuses true negotiability and transferability.

[20] Giuliano and Lagarde Report, 11.

[21] Gaskell, 19.8, citing dicta of Lloyd LJ in *The Future Express* [1993] 2 Lloyd's Rep 542, 547 in support.

[22] See above, para 13.38, see also the discussion of agency and Himalaya clauses below, paras 14.105–108. See further Benjamin, 25–073, 25–081 and 25–082; Dicey and Morris, 1464–1481; Gaskell, 19.10.

[23] On which, see further Gaskell, Ch 19. See also Wilson, n 9 above, 310–316.

[24] Strictly speaking, the bill of lading is evidence of the contract of carriage and not the contract of carriage itself. However, we need to examine the law applicable to the bill, since it is the transfer of rights and duties contained in the bill which concerns the subsequent holder of the bill of lading.

V. EXPRESS CHOICE OF LAW

14.11 It is very common for a bill of lading expressly to provide which law applies to it. That choice will commonly be for the law of England.[25] This may be the case even though neither party is English and neither the port of loading nor the port of destination is England.[26]

14.12 The choice of law may be made by naming a particular system of law, or by reference to a connecting factor, such as the law of the carrier's principal place of business.[27] The latter choice should be equally acceptable, since it will normally be clear who the carrier is[28] and it will be possible to ascertain their principal place of business.[29] Where the bill of lading is issued by the carrier[30] and signed by the ship's master or agent, it will contain the standard terms and conditions laid down by the carrier. The choice of law clause will often therefore provide for the application of the law of the carrier's home state. Alternatively, it might refer to a choice of law clause contained in a charterparty.[31]

14.13 Any choice of law clause will very commonly sit alongside a jurisdiction[32] or arbitration clause for the state whose law is applicable. Once again, this may be contained in the bill itself, or the bill may refer to a jurisdiction clause contained in a charterparty.[33] However, there are certain standard form bills of lading which contain an English choice of law clause but no jurisdiction clause.[34]

---

[25] Gaskell, 19.13–19.19, gives examples such as: the Shell Bill of Lading (which provides for the application of English law); the ANL/ Australia/ South East Asia Service Bill (the law of Victoria, Australia); the Mitsui OSK Lines Combined Transport Bill 1993 (Japanese law); and the Conlinebill (the law of the place where the carrier has his principal place of business). The authors of Gaskell also note that the contract may be 'split', as in the case of the Shell and Mitsui OSK Lines Combined Transport Bill 1993: see ibid, 562, n 48.

[26] See, e.g. *Compañía Continental del Perú SA v Evelpis Shipping Corp (The Agia Skepi)* [1992] 2 Lloyd's Rep 467; *Ilyssia Compañía Naviera SA v Ahmed Abdul-Qawi Bamaodah (The Elli 2)* [1985] 1 Lloyd's Rep 107; and *Enichem Anic SpA v Ampelos Shipping Co Ltd (The Delfini)* [1990] 1 Lloyd's Rep 252, CA.

[27] As in the case of the Conlinebill.

[28] But see the discussion of the identity of the carrier, below, paras 14.38–45.

[29] Albeit that the principal place of business may not be immediately evident: see *Owners of Cargo Lately Laden on Board the Rewia v Caribbean Liners (Caribtainer) Ltd (The Rewia)* [1991] 2 Lloyd's Rep 325; *Harrods v Dow Jones* [2003] EWHC 1162 (QB).

[30] Some bills of lading will be carriers' bills—see the discussion of *Homburg Houtimport BV v Agrosin Private Ltd (The Starsin)* [2003] UKHL 12, [2004] AC 715, below, para 14.38.

[31] See below, para 14.14.

[32] See above, paras 5.04–05, for examples of such clauses.

[33] If there is an arbitration or choice of court clause but no choice of law clause, there may nevertheless be an implied choice of the law of that state whose jurisdiction is specified: see below, paras 14.15–21.

[34] See, e.g. Shell Bill of Lading, cl 10(A); Ellerman East Africa/Mauritius Service Bill, cl 24.

VI. INCORPORATION OF A CHOICE OF LAW CONTAINED IN A CHARTERPARTY

The bill of lading may expressly incorporate the terms of a charterparty,[35] **14.14** including a choice of law clause contained in the charterparty.[36] It is likely that this will be regarded as an express choice of law in the bill of lading. This is because the bill of lading expressly stipulates which law will govern it, albeit by incorporating a clause from the charterparty by reference. This will be the case even where the charterparty to which the bill of lading refers expressly provides only that 'the charterparty shall be governed by the law of state X'.[37] However, it is suggested that the question of whether the clause is incorporated is itself a choice of law question. Accordingly, if the question is whether the choice of law clause for the law of State X was incorporated into the bill of lading, the law of State X should itself determine this question.[38]

VII. IMPLIED CHOICE OF LAW; INCORPORATION OF A CHOICE OF COURT OR ARBITRATION CLAUSE CONTAINED IN THE CHARTERPARTY

1. The Inference to be Drawn from an Exclusive Jurisdiction or Arbitration Clause

Alternatively, the bill of lading may refer only to a choice of court[39] or **14.15** arbitration clause[40] in the charterparty.[41] If so, and if the charterparty

---

[35] See J Cooke, T Young, A Taylor, J Kimball, D Martowski and L Lambert, *Voyage Charters*, (2nd edn, London: LLP, 2001) 1.27–1.66; S Boyd, A Burrows and D Foxton, *Scrutton on Charterparties and Bills of Lading*, (20th edn, London, Sweet and Maxwell, 1996) 13–16, 79–80.

[36] As is the case with, for example, the Congenbill 1994, the Heavyconbill, the HIBL Bill and the Orevoybill, all of which are considered by Gaskell, 19.41, 19.42, 19.44–19.46.

[37] A point made by Gaskell, ibid, 19.20, citing *The Nerano* [1996] 1 Lloyd's Rep, in support. On the scope of an arbitration clause in a charterparty, see the decision of the Federal Court of Australia (Full Court) in *Hi-Fert Pty Ltd v Kiukang Maritime Carriers Inc* [1999] 2 Lloyd's Rep 782.

[38] Pursuant to Arts 3(4) and 8(1) of the Rome Convention. In addition, the interpretation of terms of the 'contract' is a matter for the governing law of the contract: Art 10(1)(a). See *Egon Oldendorff v Libera Corp* [1995] 2 Lloyd's Rep 64.

[39] Compare *Hellenic Steel Co v Svolamar Shipping Co Ltd (The Komninos S)* [1991] 1 Lloyd's Rep 370; noted F Reynolds, '*Vita Food* Resurgent' (1992) 108 LQR 395; R Asariotis, 'Implications of a "British" Jurisdiction Clause' [1992] JBL 321. See also *Vita Food Products v Unus Shipping Co Ltd* [1939] AC 277.

[40] On arbitration and bills of lading, see Gaskell, 20.243–20.279. See also M Wilford, T Coghlin and J Kimball, *Time Charters*, (5th edn, London: LLP, 2003) Ch 29.

[41] As is the case with, for example, Cementvoybill, which refers to the arbitration clause in the charterparty. See Gaskell, 19.43.

contains an exclusive jurisdiction or arbitration clause,[42] this should be regarded as strong evidence of an implied choice of the law of the specified forum to govern the bill of lading.[43]

14.16 However, in *Hapag Lloyd Container Line GmbH v La Réunion Européenne*[44] the French Cour de cassation was faced with a contract of carriage which contained a German jurisdiction clause. The court nonetheless went on to determine the applicable law of the contract in the absence of choice and found it to be French law. Little explanation is offered in the judgment as to why this was the case. The ruling is not altogether convincing. Certainly, it does not appear to be consistent with the very strong inference of a choice of law which is drawn by the English courts from an exclusive jurisdiction clause.[45]

2. Non-Exclusive Jurisdiction or Arbitration Clauses

14.17 It may be that the bill of lading will contain a non-exclusive jurisdiction or arbitration clause. In that event, it will not be possible to determine to the requisite standard of reasonable certainty[46] which law the parties intended to govern the contract.[47]

3. Incorporation and Choice of Law

14.18 In all cases, the question of whether a term is incorporated into the bill of lading is ultimately a matter for the governing law of the contract. It will

---

[42] But see the decision of the Federal Court of Australia in *Hi-Fert Pty Ltd v United Shipping Adriatic Inc* 165 ALR 265, noted J Goldring, 'Jurisdiction and Applicable Law in the Carriage of Goods by Sea' (2000) 5 Uniform L Rev 348. In that case, an arbitration clause for London contained in the voyage charter was incorporated into the bill of lading. The Federal Court held that this had, in principle, the effect of incorporating the clause in the bill. However, it proceeded to strike the clause down as infringing the Australian Carriage of Goods by Sea Act 1991, which gives effect to the Hague-Visby Rules in Australia. Section 11 of that Act invalidates a provision in a contract for the carriage of goods by sea to an Australian port which purports to restrict the jurisdiction of an Australian court in disputes arising from the contract.

[43] *Egon Oldendorff v Libera Corp (No 1)* [1995] 2 Lloyd's Rep 64; *Egon Oldendorff v Libera Corp (No 2)* [1996] 1 Lloyd's Rep 380. See also Dicey and Morris, 33–260. Compare the position at common law: *Tsortzis v Monark Line A/B* [1968] 1 Lloyd's Rep 337; *Compagnie Tunisienne de Navigation SA v Compagnie d'Armement Maritime SA* [1971] AC 572.

[44] [2003] IL Pr 51 at 779, Cour de cassation.

[45] *Egon Oldendorff v Libera Corp (No 1)* [1995] 2 Lloyd's Rep 64; *Egon Oldendorff v Libera Corp (No 2)* [1996] 1 Lloyd's Rep 380. See above, paras 13.50–52.

[46] Laid down in Art 3(1) of the Rome Convention.

[47] *The Star Texas* [1993] 2 Lloyd's Rep 445.

be recalled that in *Egon Oldendorff v Libera Corp (No 1)*,[48] Mance J was faced with a charterparty between German charterers and Japanese owners. One question was whether the charterparty incorporated an English arbitration clause contained in previously agreed terms. If the term were incorporated, it would be very strong evidence of an implied choice of English *law* to govern the contract. Accordingly, English law was putatively applicable to the contract. In accordance with Articles 3(4) and 8(1) of the Rome Convention, English law was accordingly used to determine if the arbitration clause was incorporated into the contract. The answer was in the affirmative.[49]

4. INCORPORATION OF THE TERMS OF THE CHARTERPARTY WITH NO EXPRESS REFERENCE TO A CHOICE OF LAW, JURISDICTION OR ARBITRATION CLAUSE

The most difficult case is where the bill of lading expressly states that it **14.19** incorporates the terms and conditions of the charterparty, but does not expressly state that this includes a choice of law clause and/or a jurisdiction or arbitration clause in the charterparty.[50] One might simply argue that these are terms of the charterparty and so incorporated expressly into the bill of lading. Alternatively, it may be held that a choice of law clause, arbitration or choice of court clause is not itself a term or condition of the charterparty, on the basis that it does not confer rights and obligations, but simply determines the law by reference to which those rights and obligations are interpreted. If so, the clause is not itself expressly incorporated in the bill of lading.[51] However, one might rebut this argument by contending that if the parties have expressly included the terms and conditions in the charterparty, there is a natural inference that they did not wish to divorce those terms from their original context. As such, one might conclude that the parties intended that arbitration clause also to apply to the bill of lading.[52] In turn, that arbitration clause may give rise

---

[48] [1995] 2 Lloyd's Rep 64. See also *Welex AG v Rosa Maritime Ltd (The Epsilon Rosa) (No 2)* [2002] EWHC 2033 (Comm), [2002] 2 Lloyd's Rep 701, QBD (Comm).

[49] Mance J went on to say that the Japanese owners could not rely upon Art 8(2) of the Rome Convention to establish that they had not consented to the choice of law clause according to the law of their state of habitual residence, Japan; see above, paras 13.150–153.

[50] See Congenbill 1978; Caokell, 19.43.

[51] See *Siboti K/S v BP France SA* [2003] EWHC 1278 (Comm), [2003] 2 Lloyd's Rep 364; *Prifti v Musini Sociedad Anónima de Seguros y Reaseguros* [2003] EWHC 2796 (Comm). These cases suggest a reluctance to find that general words of incorporation in a bill of lading, such as a reference to 'any terms whatsoever' in the charterparty, suffice to incorporate an English jurisdiction or choice of law clause.

[52] See Gaskell, 19.49 (and see 19.47–19.54). See further *The Njegos* [1936] P 90; *Wahda Bank v Arab Bank* [1996] 1 Lloyd's Rep 470.

to an inference that the parties intended the *law* of the state of arbitration to govern the bill of lading.[53]

Ultimately, this is a question of the construction of a term in the bill of lading. It is suggested that if the question is whether the parties intended to incorporate a choice of law clause in a charterparty for State X, the law of State X should itself determine whether the parties so intended and whether the clause is validly incorporated.[54]

5. No Incorporation of the Terms of the Charterparty

14.20 If the bill of lading contains no express choice of law and no clause incorporating any of the terms of the charterparty, then the law applicable to the bill of lading will normally be determined in the absence of choice. However, even here, it might just be possible to infer that the law chosen to govern the charterparty is also intended to apply to the bill of lading.[55] Giuliano and Lagarde state that a choice of law clause[56] in a related transaction between the *same* parties may give rise to an inference that the same law[57] was intended by the parties to govern the instant contract.[58] However, it seems very unlikely that such an inference will be drawn here, as the parties to the charterparty and the contract of carriage are not the same. Ultimately, though, it is suggested that if the question arises as to whether the parties to the contract of carriage intended to incorporate a choice of law clause for the law of State X contained in the charterparty, even though they did not say so, this is a matter for the law of State X to determine.[59]

6. A Previous Course of Dealings

14.21 If the carrier and the shipper have previously contracted with one another on terms which included a choice of law clause, it may be possible to infer that they intended the same law to govern the present contract of carriage, albeit that it contains a choice of law clause. Against this, the very fact that they excluded the choice of law clause in the instant agree-

---

[53] But contrast Gaskell, 19.65. The authors of Gaskell argue that if the facts of *The Njegos* arose today, there would not be an implied choice of law, since the bill of lading did not incorporate the arbitration clause in the charterparty. If so, the relevance of the law applicable to the charterparty will be in relation to the law applicable to the bill of lading in the absence of choice, pursuant to Art 4(5) of the Rome Convention.

[54] Arts 3(4), 8(1) and 10(1)(a) of the Rome Convention. See also the discussion in the section above, para 14.18.

[55] See Dicey and Morris, 33–260.   [56] Or an arbitration clause.

[57] Or the law of the place of arbitration, where the charterparty contains no choice of law clause.

[58] Giuliano and Lagarde Report, 17.   [59] Arts 3(4) and 10(1)(a) of the Rome Convention.

ment may suggest that they intended the omission to be deliberate and that they did not want the same law to govern the instant contract. The question of the relevance of a previous course of dealings is examined further in Chapter 13, to which the reader is referred.[60]

VIII. A 'FLOATING' CHOICE OF LAW

1. NATURE OF PROBLEM

It is common practice for a bill of lading to contain a floating choice of law **14.22** clause.[61] These clauses tend to give one party the right unilaterally to choose the governing law, usually from a limited range of alternatives.[62] Some clauses go further and give the *plaintiff* the right to choose the governing law. For example, clause 24 of the P & O Containers Bill stated[63] that: 'Unless clause 25 applied, any claim or dispute arising under this Bill of lading shall be determined, at the option of the plaintiff, either by the courts of the country where the Carrier, or the defendant if not the Carrier, has his principal place of business according to the laws of that country'. This is a particularly difficult clause for three reasons: first, it is a 'floating' clause, which appears to lay down no applicable law unless and until one is chosen; second, the choice may be made unilaterally by one of the parties, without securing the agreement of the other party; and third, and most surprisingly, the applicable law is not determined by one or other party to the contract, but by the *plaintiff*[64] *in the instant litigation*. This suggests that unless and until litigation is commenced, no choice of law *can* be chosen.[65] It also has the effect of creating a potential rush for litigation, in that the plaintiff in the proceedings is the party that can choose the governing law.[66]

At common law, there was considerable doubt as to the validity of **14.23** floating choice of law clauses.[67] The effect of the case law appeared to be

---

[60] See above, paras 13.46–49. [61] Gaskell, 19.23–40.

[62] See the P & O Nedlloyd Bill, the Hapag-Lloyd Bill of Lading 1996 and the ANL Trantzas Bill of Lading; these are all to be found in Gaskell, 19.25, 19.28 and 19.29 respectively.

[63] Gaskell notes that the clause has been superseded.

[64] As the example given, cl 24 of the P & O Containers Bill, refers to the 'plaintiff', this term is used in the present section rather than the term 'claimant'.

[65] Although the authors of Gaskell note that if the carrier is the defendant, the other party is given no choice as to the governing law; only if the carrier is the plaintiff may he have a choice of law. However, the effect is still to render it all important which party is the plaintiff in the instant proceedings.

[66] See also Combidoc, cl 5b, considered by Gaskell, 19.23.

[67] A Briggs, 'The Validity of "Floating" Choice of Law and Jurisdiction Clauses' [1986] LMCLQ 508; A Beck, 'Floating Choice of Law Clauses' [1987] LMCLQ 523; D Pierce, 'Post-Formation Choice of Law in Contract' (1987) 50 MLR 176.

that there had to be a governing law at the inception of the contract[68] and that law could not be chosen unilaterally at a later stage.[69] However, it was permissible if a contract stipulated that the law of State X should govern a contract, unless the clause was unenforceable, in which case the law of State Y applied.[70] This was on the basis that there was a governing law at the time of conclusion of the contract.[71]

2. The Effect of Article 3(2)

14.24 Article 3(2) of the Rome Convention appears to authorize all floating choice of law clauses. It states that: 'The parties may agree at any time to subject the contract to a law other than that which previously governed it'.[72] This means that the parties may bilaterally vary any choice of law made at the time of the conclusion of the contract. Giuliano and Lagarde also sanction choices of law made only *after* the contract is concluded.[73] It would appear that where no choice is made at the time of conclusion of the contract, the contract is initially governed by the law applicable in the absence of choice, as determined by Article 4 of the Convention. If the parties later choose a governing law, that is in effect a change of law.

3. Unilateral Choice

14.25 If this is correct, it still does not expressly address the fact that many bills of lading confer the right to choose the governing law *on one party only*. Article 3(2) refers to the 'parties' in the plural agreeing to change the governing law, and does not expressly authorize one party alone to do so. Nor do Giuliano and Lagarde refer to the permissibility of unilateral change. However, they do speak of Article 3(2) conferring 'maximum freedom as to the time at which the choice of applicable law can be made'.[74] Moreover, one might say that the *parties* bilaterally agree that *one* of them may stipulate which law applies at a later date. In that sense, the decision is still the product of an agreement between the parties. For this

---

[68] *Armar Shipping Co Ltd v Caisse Algérienne d'Assurance et de Réassurance (The Armar)* [1981] 1 WLR 207.

[69] *Dubai Electricity Company v Islamic Republic of Iran Shipping Lines (The Iran Vojdan)* [1984] 2 Lloyd's Rep 380.

[70] *Astro Venturoso Compañía Naviera v Hellenic Shipyards SA (The Mariannina)* [1983] 1 Lloyd's Rep 12.

[71] Compare the Hapag-Lloyd Bill of lading 1996, considered by Gaskell, 19.28, which provides for the application of German law, unless the clause is inapplicable by that law. If that is the case, the carrier may choose either the law of the place of loading or the law of the place of discharge.

[72] The consent of the parties to the choice of the new law will be determined in accordance with Arts 3(4) and 8 of the Convention.

[73] Giuliano and Lagarde Report, 17.   [74] ibid.

reason, it is likely that clauses which give one party the right to stipulate, or change, the governing law, will be effective under Article 3(2).[75]

There is then a further complication. We have seen that a bill of lading **14.26** may confer a right on the *plaintiff* to choose the governing law, so that which party commences litigation is all important. In a different context, when discussing the 'splitting' of a contract, Giuliano and Lagarde expressly state that a choice must be logically consistent. They suggest the same legal issue cannot be determined under more than one law, so that '. . . it is unlikely that repudiation of the contract for non-performance would be subjected to two different laws, one for the vendor and one for the purchaser'.[76] However, the problem in that case is of two laws potentially governing one issue *simultaneously*. One might distinguish our present difficulty by arguing that before litigation is commenced, the contract of carriage is governed by the applicable law determined in the absence of choice. When the plaintiff commences proceedings, he may change that law to another law. At any time, the contract is subjected to a single law and, accordingly, such clauses should be permitted.

Even if this is correct, the question arises as to whether the plaintiff's **14.27** choice must be made at the time of commencement of the proceedings, or may be made during the proceedings themselves. Giuliano and Lagarde argue that: 'If the choice of law is made or changed in the course of proceedings, the question arises as to the limits within which the choice or change can be effective. However, the question falls within the ambit of the national law of procedure, and can be settled only in accordance with that law.'[77] The common law did not permit a party unilaterally to choose the law after the commencement of proceedings.[78] It appears that the same result would be reached in an English court today.[79]

4. CONCLUSION

In conclusion, it is suggested that the parties may validly agree in the bill **14.28** of lading to confer the right on the parties, or one of the parties, to choose the governing law after the conclusion of the contract. Before this choice is made, the contract is governed by the applicable law in the absence of choice. Even a clause which confers the right to choose the law on a

---

[75] Although Art 3(2) states that the change must not affect the rights of third parties and does not prejudice the formal validity of the contract. See above, para 13.111.

[76] Giuliano and Lagarde Report, 17.

[77] ibid, 18. See Art 1(2)(h) of the Rome Convention, which excludes matters of procedure and evidence from its scope.

[78] See *Dubai Electricity Company v Islamic Republic of Iran Shipping Lines (The Iran Vojdan)* [1984] 2 Lloyd's Rep 380.

[79] This is also the view of Gaskell, 19.39.

plaintiff[80] should be accepted, though it is likely that any choice which the plaintiff makes must be made at the commencement of proceedings[81] and not subsequently.

IX. CONSTRUCTION OF A CHOICE OF LAW CLAUSE IN THE BILL OF LADING

1. MUST THE APPLICABLE LAW BE EVIDENT ON THE FACE OF THE BILL?

14.29 Must a choice of law clause contained in a bill of lading be formulated in such a way that it is possible to identify the governing law from the wording of the clause alone? A similar problem has arisen with respect to jurisdiction clauses under the Brussels Convention. In *Coreck Maritime GmbH v Handelsveem BV*,[82] the European Court of Justice was faced with a jurisdiction clause in the bill of lading which provided for trial in the country 'where the carrier has his principal place of business'. It held that it was not necessary for the jurisdiction clause to be formulated so that it was possible to identify the court having jurisdiction on its wording alone, provided that it laid down objective factors which were sufficiently precise to enable a court to determine which state's jurisdiction was referred to in the clause. In principle, a similar approach should be taken for choice of law purposes. As long as the law in question can be identified by a court, there is no reason to insist upon a particular form of wording.

2. CONSTRUCTION OF A CHOICE OF LAW CLAUSE; A BOOTSTRAPS PROBLEM

14.30 Suppose that a bill of lading states that the law of the state where the carrier has his principal place of business applies. Although it may not be certain who the carrier is,[83] or where its principal place of business, these are questions that can be resolved by application of the putative governing law. Moreover, Article 10(1)(a) states that the construction of a contract is a matter for the applicable law of the contract. But how can we determine which law this is, when the law specified in the clause is the very question in issue? This creates something of a logical paradox.

14.31 It is suggested that English law as the law of the forum must first determine which law is *putatively* applicable. It must determine who *it*

---

[80] Such as cl 24 of the P & O Containers Bill.
[81] At least if the proceedings are in an English court.
[82] Case C-387/98 [2000] ECR I-9337. See further above, para 5.11.
[83] See below, paras 14.38–45.

considers to be the carrier and where it considers that carrier to have its principal place of business. If the clause is so ambiguous that an English court is *unable* to determine a law to which the contract putatively refers, then the case must proceed on the basis that there is no valid choice of law.

However, suppose that the English court is able to find a law which is **14.32** *putatively* specified in the choice of law clause and *putatively* applicable to the contract. Suppose that this is the law of State X. It is suggested that Article 10(1)(a) of the Rome Convention has the effect that the construction of that choice of law clause should then be determined, finally, by the law of State X. We can then arrive at a law which is putatively applicable to the contract. That law can then determine, finally, whether the choice of law clause is valid, pursuant to Articles 3(4) and 8(1) of the Rome Convention.[84]

X. APPLICABLE LAW IN THE ABSENCE OF CHOICE

1. CONTRACTS FOR THE CARRIAGE OF GOODS; ARTICLE 4(4)[85]

The law applicable to a contract of carriage will normally be determined **14.33** in the same manner as for a contract of sale. If there is an express or implied choice of law, such choice will be effective,[86] subject to the application of any relevant mandatory rules or public policy provisions of the Rome Convention.[87] The major departure comes where there is no express or implied choice of law and the applicable law must be determined in the absence of choice. In such a case, there is a special provision for the carriage of goods.[88] Article 4(4) provides[89] that contracts for the carriage of goods[90] shall be presumed to be governed by the law of the place where

---

[84] It could theoretically be that the law of State X will adopt different canons of construction and find that the choice of law clause is one for the law of State Y. If so, then the law of State Y should determine the validity of the clause, pursuant to Arts 3(4) and 8(1).

[85] See Dicey and Morris, Rules 189 and 190, 1395–1418.   [86] Art 3(1).

[87] See above, paras 13.271–294.

[88] So that the presumption in Art 4(2) discussed in Ch 13 does not apply.

[89] Although it should be recalled that Art 21 of the Rome Convention has the effect that other international conventions dealing with choice of law in relation to carriage contracts shall take precedence over the Rome Convention. See Dicey and Morris, 1395–1418, for detailed discussion of the impact of other Conventions.

[90] But not passengers. Contracts for the carriage of passengers are subject to the presumption in Art 4(2). A contract for the carriage of goods and passengers will, in the absence of a choice of law, require the separate application of Arts 4(4) and 4(2) respectively to the different parts of the contract.

the carrier[91] has his principal place of business[92] at the time when the contract is concluded,[93] provided that that country is also either: (a) the principal place of business[94] of the consignor;[95] or (b) the place of loading; or (c) the place of discharge.[96]

14.34 It may not always be apparent whether the contract in question is one for the 'carriage of goods', within the meaning of Article 4(4).[97] Article 4(4) goes on to state that: 'In applying this paragraph single voyage charter-parties and other contracts the main purpose of which is the carriage of goods shall be treated as contracts for the carriage of goods'.[98] More generally, in order to ensure a uniform application of the Convention, it seems that 'carriage of goods' must bear an autonomous meaning.[99] It is the primary purpose of the contract that is paramount. It matters not whether the carriage is by sea, air, rail or other means.[100]

2. Where the Conditions in Article 4(4) are not Met

14.35 If the contract is for the carriage of goods, but the conditions in Article 4(4) are not met,[101] that provision is inapplicable. In such a case, the presumption in Article 4(2) does not apply in lieu. Rather, no presumption is used

---

[91] See R Plender and M Wilderspin, *The European Contracts Convention* (2nd edn, London: Sweet & Maxwell, 2001) 132 for discussion of the meaning of this term. Giuliano and Lagarde, 22, state that this refers to '. . . any person who undertakes to carry the goods, whether or not he performs the carriage himself'. See also Dicey and Morris, 33–263.

[92] Plender and Wilderspin, ibid, 132–133, argue that this refers 'to the "real seat" rather than to "the place of incorporation" of the company'. See also Dicey and Morris, 1406–1407. However, compare Art 60 of the Brussels I Regulation, which draws a distinction between the seat and principal place of business of a company for the purposes of determining where it is domiciled.

[93] Giuliano and Lagarde Report, 22.

[94] Dicey and Morris, 1407–1408.

[95] On the meaning of this term, see Plender and Wilderspin, n 91 above, 132–133; Dicey and Morris, 1408. Giuliano and Lagarde, 22, comment, not terribly helpfully, that this refers to 'any person who consigns goods to the carrier'.

[96] The places of loading and discharge are those agreed at the time of conclusion of the contract. Even if the parties subsequently change one or more of these places, this will not lead to a change in the governing law.

[97] See Dicey and Morris, Rule 190, 1401 and 1403–1404.

[98] Plender and Wilderspin, n 91 above, 133 suggest that consecutive voyage charters and freight contracts would also be caught by Art 4(4), but that time charters and demise charters would not be. See also Benjamin, 25–071.

[99] See Plender and Wilderspin, n 91 above, 131–132; but see the decision of the Arrondissementrectsbank of Roermond, 27 November 1986 [1988] Schip en Schade No 97, 278, discussed ibid, 131–132.

[100] Contrast the definitions of 'contract of carriage' and 'goods' in Art 1(b) and (c) respectively of Sch 1 to the Carriage of Goods by Sea Act 1971. The effect of this Act is discussed by Dicey and Morris, 1412–1414.

[101] Gaskell, 19.65, notes that the common law case of *The Njegos* [1936] P 90 is one where the conditions in Art 4(4) would not have been met if the facts had arisen today.

and the applicable law will simply be the law of the country of closest connection to the contract. For example, in *Hapag Lloyd Container Line GmbH v La Réunion Européenne*,[102] the carrier, Hapag Lloyd had its principal place of business in Germany. The shipper had its place of business in Mexico. The goods were dispatched under a combined transport bill of lading from Houston, USA, via Antwerp to Rungis in France. It followed that the place of business of the carrier, Germany, did not coincide with the place of loading or discharge or the place of business of the consignor. The French Cour de cassation determined the applicable law under Article 4(5)[103] and found French law to be the governing law of the contract of carriage. The judgment gives little explanation as to why this was the case. France was the place where the goods were physically[104] to be delivered, and the place of business of the consignee. This suggests that where the conditions in Article 4(4) are not met, and the place of actual delivery of the goods[105] and the place of business of the consignee coincide, this law will be the law of the state of closest connection.[106]

3. DISPLACEMENT OF THE PRESUMPTION; ARTICLE 4(5)

Relevance of the Law Applicable to the Contract of Sale

Of course, a carriage of goods contract will normally be closely related to **14.36** a contract of sale. However, there is no necessary reason why the contract of carriage need be governed by the law applicable to the contract of sale, not least because the parties to them will not be identical. Indeed, the requirement that the carrier's principal place of the business also has a further connection with the contract should ensure that Article 4(4) points to the application of a law with a substantial connection to the contract. As

---

[102] [2003] IL Pr 51 at 779, Cour de cassation.

[103] Arguably, it should have applied Art 4(1) instead. Art 4(5) applies to rebut a presumption in Arts 4(2)–(4) (of which none was applicable on the facts) or where the presumption in Art 4(2) cannot be determined. It does not apply where Art 4(4) is simply inapplicable. However, this is very unlikely to make a difference in practice. See further Dicey and Morris, 1405.

[104] Even though, of course, the bill of lading may be handed over elsewhere.

[105] Compare *The Assunzione* [1954] P 150, CA; Dicey and Morris, 1408–1409.

[106] By analogy to the case law on the rebuttal of Art 4(2) under Art 4(5), one might say that the carrier performs the 'characteristic' obligation for which money is due and that the place of performance of that obligation is the state of delivery. see above, paras 13.127–136. (Although it must be reiterated that Art 4(2) itself is inapplicable to contracts of carriage, even where the conditions in Art 4(4) are not met). However, this analogy works less well in the case of carriage, if the bill of lading is transferred in another state. Compare the position at common law in respect to contracts of carriage: *Moore v Harris* (1876) 9 App Cas 318; *The Industrie* [1894] P 58; *The Assunzione* [1954] P 150; *Coast Lines Ltd v Hudig* [1972] 2 QB 34, 47; *Partenreederei M/S Heidberg v Grosvenor Grain & Feed Co Ltd (The Heidberg) (No 2)* [1994] 2 Lloyd's Rep 287. See also Dicey and Morris, 1401–1402.

such, a court should not be too ready to rebut the presumption under either Article 4(2) of 4(4), so as to ensure that the same law governs the sale and carriage contracts pursuant to Article 4(5).

Relevance of the Law Applicable to The Charterparty

14.37 More difficult is the question of the relevance of the law applicable to a charterparty.[107] If the bill of lading does not expressly incorporate the terms[108] of the charterparty, might one nevertheless argue, pursuant to Article 4(5), that the bill of lading is more closely connected with the law applicable to the charterparty than to the law to which Article 4(4) points? Gaskell suggests that the answer to this question may be 'yes' and draws support from the decision in *Bank of Baroda v Vysya Bank*.[109] However, Mance J was dealing in that case with the network of contracts created from a confirmed letter of credit. The contracts were clearly legally connected. By contrast, a charterparty and a bill of lading may be factually connected, but they are clearly independent of one another.[110] It is suggested that if the law applicable to the charterparty is determined in the absence of choice, and the bill of lading does not expressly incorporate those terms,[111] there is no clear reason for the two agreements to be governed by the same law.[112]

XI. IDENTITY OF THE CARRIER

1. GENERAL PRINCIPLES OF ENGLISH LAW; *THE STARSIN*

14.38 In *Homburg Houtimport BV v Agrosin Private Ltd (The Starsin)*,[113] the House of Lords had to deal with the construction of a bill of lading, in circumstances where it was unclear whether the shipowner or time charterer was party to the bill of lading. Page 1 of a bill of lading (which contains the

---

[107] Gaskell, 19.65.

[108] i.e. a choice of law clause, or, failing that, an exclusive jurisdiction or exclusive arbitration clause from which a choice of law can be inferred. See above, paras 14.14–21.

[109] [1994] 2 Lloyd's Rep 87, esp 93. See above, para 13.131.

[110] Although the bill of lading may expressly incorporate the terms of the charterparty. However, in such a case, it is likely that there will be an express or implied choice of the law applicable to the bill of lading. Our present concern is with the situation where the law applicable to the bill of lading is determined in the absence of choice.

[111] See further Gaskell, 19.65; *The Njegos* [1936] P 90.

[112] Of course, the terms of the charterparty and the bill of lading may be sufficiently similar that they lead to the application of the same law in the absence of choice. However, the key point is that Art 4(5) is applied to the instant bill of lading contract, and not by 'infection' from the law applicable to the charterparty.

[113] [2003] UKHL 12, [2004] AC 715; noted by E Peel, 'Actual Carriers and the Hague Rules' (2004) 120 LQR 11.

small print) will very frequently contain both a demise and an identity of carrier (IOC) clause, the terms of which will provide that the shipowner is the carrier. However, the House of Lords gave a 'commercial' construction to the bill of lading.[114] This meant looking only at page 2 (having the appearance of the front page and containing the various boxes of information and the signature), disregarding page 1 with its clauses contradicting the appearance of page 2.[115] In consequence, the House of Lords found that the charterer was the carrier and party to the bill of lading.[116]

2. IDENTITY OF THE CARRIER AND CHOICE OF LAW

Different laws may take differing views as to who is a party to a bill of lading.[117] For example, in the case of *The Rewia*,[118] under English law the shipowners were the carriers; however, under German law the sub-charterers were the carriers. In so far as an issue of construction of the bill is raised, this is a question to be determined by the law applicable to the contract of carriage between the parties to the original contract. This is consistent with Article 10(1)(a) of the Rome Convention, which refers questions of interpretation of a contract to the applicable law of that contract.[119] Furthermore, in the context of the application of the Brussels Convention, Advocate General Alber said in *Coreck Maritime GmbH v Handelsveem BV*,[120] that 'it is for the national court to establish whether it is clear from the bill of lading who, for the purposes of the bill of lading . . . is to be deemed the carrier'.[121] **14.39**

In *The Forum Craftsman*,[122] the plaintiff cargo owners entered into a contract with charterers who had chartered a ship belonging to the defendant shipowners. The Court of Appeal applied Japanese law, the **14.40**

---

[114] Praying in aid Art 23 of UCP500, which deals with the type of documents against which banks will pay out under documentary letters of credit.

[115] As a decision on the construction of the particular bill of lading, of course it does not bind where the details of the bill are subtly different, but it does indicate that a robust view will be taken as a general matter.

[116] As a consequence of *The Starsin*, there may be more claims over by charterers against shipowners, claiming an indemnity for the liability of the charterers under the bill of lading contract where there has been poor stowage, unseaworthiness etc.

[117] On the question of who is the carrier and the choice of law problems that this raises, see Dicey and Morris, 1405–1406.

[118] *Owners of Cargo Lately Laden on Board the Rewia v Caribbean Liners (Caribtainer) Ltd (The Rewia)* [1991] 2 Lloyd's Rep 325, CA.

[119] It could theoretically be argued that this is a matter of procedure: T Sing, 'Conflict of Laws Implications of the Carriage of Goods by Sea Act 1992' [1994] LMCLQ 280, 283. However, what are in issue are substantive rights and duties under a contract and it is suggested that the issue must be treated as substantive.

[120] Case C-387/98 [2000] ECR I-9337. See further above, para 5.11.

[121] ibid, para 35 of the Opinion. [122] [1985] 1 Lloyd's Rep 291, CA.

law applicable to the bills of lading, to determine whether the shipowner was a party to this contract. It was accepted that under Japanese law these were charterers' bills and not owners' bills and that they evidenced a contract solely between the cargo-owners and the charterers.[123]

3. A BOOTSTRAPS PROBLEM

14.41 The hard case is one where the contract of carriage contains no express or implied choice of law clause, so that the applicable law has to be determined in the absence of choice. Suppose that the shipowner has its place of business in State X (which is also the place of loading of the goods) and the charterer has its place of business in State Y (which is also the place of discharge of the goods). Suppose also that the laws of State X and State Y differ as to whether the shipowner or the charterer is party to the bill of lading. If the shipowner is the carrier, then the law of State X will apply by virtue of Article 4(4) of the Rome Convention. However, if the charterer is the carrier, then the law of State Y will apply by virtue of the same provision.

14.42 At this point, it is suggested that the English court can only apply the law which it considers to be *putatively* applicable to the contract to determine the construction of the clause. The English court should apply the law of the forum and English canons of construction to determine who it considers to be the carrier of the goods. Having done this, it can determine which law is putatively applicable to the contract and use that law to determine, finally, who is the carrier of the goods.

4. CAN THERE BE MORE THAN ONE CARRIER?

14.43 The House of Lords in *The Starsin*[124] rejected the possibility of there being more than one carrier under the bill of lading. Lord Hoffmann referred to the observation of Rix LJ in the Court of Appeal[125] that such an approach would be 'novel and inconsistent with the settled expectation of the shipping trade'.[126] It is possible that a foreign legal system might disagree on

---

[123] ibid, at 295.

[124] *Homburg Houtimport BV v Agrosin Private Ltd* (The Starsin) [2003] UKHL 12, [2004] AC 715.

[125] [2001] EWCA Civ 56 at [73], [2001] 1 Lloyd's Rep 437, 452.

[126] [2003] UKHL 12 at [85], [2004] AC 715, 757. In fact, this quotation is taken slightly out of context. Rix LJ was considering the arguments of counsel as to whether there could be more than one carrier and went on ([2001] EWCA Civ 56 at [74], [2001] 1 Lloyd's Rep 437, 452), to say that 'I can visualize the argument that when CPS (in fact their agents) signed the bills for their own account as carriers . . . they created a contract in respect of which both they and their principal, the owner, had rights and liabilities . . . The fact that a contract contemplates only one buyer does not mean that both the signatory to the contract and his principal may not have rights and liabilities under it.'

this point and hold that there can be more than one carrier. Indeed, in *Coreck Maritime GmbH v Handelsveem BV*,[127] the Rechtbank Rotterdam took the view that there was a possibility of there being two carriers.

We have seen that the construction of a contract is a matter for the **14.44** applicable law of that contract by virtue of Article 10(1)(a) of the Rome Convention. If that law holds that there is more than one carrier, then this should be accepted.[128] The liabilities of each of the parties will be determined by the applicable law of the contract.[129] However, the liabilities of a shipowner and charterer *inter se* would still be governed by the law applicable to the charterparty.

5. LIABILITY OF THE SELLER TO ENTER INTO A REASONABLE CONTRACT OF CARRIAGE

A CIF seller has a contractual duty to enter into a reasonable contract of **14.45** carriage and it may be questioned whether compliance with this duty has occurred where the identity of the carrier is hard to determine. Since this is a question as to a possible breach of the seller's obligations under the contract of sale, it is the law governing the CIF contract which should determine this question.[130]

XII. THE OPERATION OF S 2 OF THE CARRIAGE OF GOODS BY SEA ACT 1992: SUBSTANCE OR PROCEDURE?

Section 2 of the Carriage of Goods by Sea Act 1992 transfers the rights and **14.46** duties of the shipper to the transferee of the bill of lading. A question arises as to the nature of this process of transfer, which may in turn

---

[127] Case C-387/98 [2000] ECR I-9337. See further above, para 5.11.

[128] Although AG Alber, ibid, para 35 of the Opinion said that where there was more than one carrier, a jurisdiction clause in a bill of lading must fail.

[129] If there is no express or implied choice of law in the bill of lading, it is theoretically possible that different laws will govern the two contracts between the shipper and shipowner on the one hand, and the shipper and charterer on the other. This could arise in the above example where the shipowner has its place of business in State X (which is also the place of loading of the goods) and the charterer has its place of business in State Y (which is also the place of discharge of the goods). However, it seems likely that an English court would strive to avoid such a conclusion, if necessary by invoking Art 4(5), so that the two contracts were governed by the same law. If the place of business of either the charterer or the shipowner coincides with the place of business of the shipper, the court may conclude that both contracts should be governed by the law of this place.

[130] On which, see Ch 13.

determine whether the transferee is subject to a choice of law clause contained in the bill of lading.

14.47   It could be argued that the effect of s 2 of the Carriage of Goods by Sea Act 1992 is to determine which party may invoke contractual rights against the carrier. As such, it could be treated as a rule of procedure, rather than a rule of substance which affects the nature of the contractual rights themselves.[131] If so, the Act would be applied in an English court regardless of the law applicable to the contract of carriage.

14.48   However, it is suggested that this approach must be firmly rejected. The Act clearly confers contractual rights on the transferee. It is not simply a question of which party can enforce existing contractual rights under the contract of carriage. The terms of the bill of lading determine the contractual rights and duties of the transferee of the bill of lading; whereas the shipper's contractual rights and duties are determined by the contract of carriage, of which the bill is only evidence. Moreover, the shipper retains liability when the bill of lading is transferred. The effect of a procedural classification could be the 'creation of contractual rights between parties where none exist under the relevant foreign laws' and encourage the shipper or transferee 'to forum shop in England for an action in contract'.[132] Accordingly, a substantive classification of the 1992 Act is strongly preferable,[133] with the effect that the Act should only apply where English law governs the contract.[134]

XIII. THE POSITION OF THE TRANSFEREE OF A BILL OF LADING; ASSIGNMENT, NOVATION AND *SUI GENERIS* OBLIGATIONS

1. NATURE OF TRANSFER OF CONTRACTUAL RIGHTS AND DUTIES

14.49   It is important to determine the process by which the transferee of a bill of lading acquires contract rights and duties with respect to the carrier. If the process is regarded as being one of assignment, then the transferee clearly acquires rights under the original contract. It is very likely that any con-

---

[131]   Sing, n 119 above, at 283. See *Jeffrey v M'Taggert* (1817) 6 M & S 126; cf *O'Callaghan v Thomond* (1810) 3 Taunt 82. See also *Re Doetsch* [1896] 2 Ch 836.

[132]   Sing n 119 above, at 283.

[133]   Although Sing, ibid, at 285, notes that in practice the parties might fail to plead the application of a foreign law, so that the Carriage of Goods by Sea Act 1992 is applied by default: *The Blue Wave* [1982] 1 Lloyd's Rep 151; *Mendala III Transport v Total Transport Corp (The Wilomi Tanana)* [1993] 2 Lloyd's Rep 41.

[134]   But see the discussion of the mandatory effect of the Act below, paras 14.97–101.

tractual claim between the carrier and the transferee will be determined by the same law which governed the original contract of carriage. Otherwise, the nature and extent of those rights might be determined by reference to a law other than under which they arose and those rights might be distorted in the process of assignment.

If the process is treated as one of novation, then it involves a new contract **14.50** arising between the carrier and transferee and it will not necessarily be the case that this contract will be subject to the same law as that which governed the contract of carriage. This is illustrated in a different context by the decision in *Wight v Eckhardt Marine GmbH*.[135] A German company agreed to sell a vessel to a buyer in Bangladesh. Pursuant to this agreement, a letter of guarantee had been issued by the Chittagong branch of a bank incorporated in the Cayman Islands. All branches of the bank were closed and no payment was made under the guarantee. A winding-up order against the bank was made in the Cayman Islands in January 1992. In August of that year, a scheme was established in Bangladesh vesting the assets and liabilities of the bank in a newly formed bank. In 1995, the liquidators in the Cayman Islands rejected the seller's claim to a proof, on the basis that all claims against the old bank were now assumed by the new bank. The Privy Council applied the law of Bangladesh to determine whether the claim against the original bank was discharged. This was the law which had passed the decree establishing the scheme, and it was this law which should determine the effect of the scheme on the liability of the original bank. However, Lord Hoffmann[136] considered the judgment of Jenkins LJ in *Re United Railways of the Havana and Regal Warehouses Ltd*,[137] who suggested that a transfer of liability for a debt constituted a statutory novation, involving the extinction of the original debtor's liability and its replacement by the liability of a new debtor. Jenkins LJ accepted that '. . . these two aspects of the transaction were not necessarily governed by the same law . . .'.[138] If this analysis were also to be applied in the context of the rights acquired by the consignee pursuant to a bill of lading, it would be theoretically possible for different laws to determine the law applicable to the original contract of carriage and the law applicable to the contract between the holder of the bill of lading and the carrier.

Again, the transfer may be treated as *sui generis*, in that it involves a **14.51** hybrid of assignment and novation. If so, it is less than clear what choice of law rules are applicable. In particular, it may be unclear whether the

---

[135] [2003] UKPC 37, [2004] 1 AC 147.   [136] At [13]–[15], pp. 153–154.
[137] [1960] Ch 52, 84–88.
[138] [2003] UKPC 37, [2004] 1 AC 147, 153 (*per* Lord Hoffman, explaining the views of Jenkins J). See also *Borealis AB v Stargas Ltd (The Berge Sisar)* [2001] UKHL 17, [2002] 2 AC 205, HL.

law applicable to the original contract of carriage is equally applicable to the contract between the carrier and the transferee.

2. THE POSITION IN ENGLISH LAW: A *SUI GENERIS* SOLUTION

14.52 It was suggested in Chapter 5 that the position in English law under the Carriage of Goods by Sea Act 1992 is *sui generis*.[139] It cannot amount to assignment in that it involves the transfer of burdens as well as benefits. Furthermore, the terms of the bill of lading become the contract between any subsequent holder of the bill and the carrier;[140] whereas as between shipper and carrier, the bill of lading is only evidence of the terms of the contract of carriage.[141] However, it is unlikely to be seen as novation either, since the liabilities of the shipper are not wholly extinguished.[142] Moreover, the transfer of rights and duties take place at different times.

3. CHOICE OF LAW: ASSIGNMENT AND *SUI GENERIS* TRANSFERS

14.53 It is suggested that the law applicable to the original contract of carriage should determine whether the contractual rights and duties under a bill of lading may be transferred. This is consistent with Article 12(2) of the Rome Convention. That law should also determine the nature of the process by which the transfer operates.

14.54 Suppose that the law governing the contract of carriage determines that the process of transfer is one of assignment or *sui generis*.[143] It is suggested that the law applicable to the contract of carriage should also go on to determine whether, and, if so, when a contract arises between the carrier and the current holder of the bill of lading. It is true that Article 12(1) of the Rome Convention hints that the question of whether the contractual right *has* been assigned (as opposed to whether it can be assigned) might be a matter for the law governing the contract of assignment between assignor and assignee. Here, this might be taken to refer to the contract of sale between seller and buyer. However, although the seller under a CIF contract may have a duty to pass the bill of lading to the buyer, the contract of sale cannot itself be described as a contract of assignment of contractual rights. Nor does Article 12(1) clearly apply to

---

[139] At paras 5.22–23. [140] *Leduc v Ward* (1888) 20 QBD 475.
[141] *The Ardennes* [1951] 1 KB 55.
[142] s 3(3) of the Carriage of Goods by Sea Act 1992 provides that the liabilities imposed under s 3 on the person in whom rights are vested under s 2(1) (the holder of the bill of lading) 'shall be without prejudice to the liabilities under the contract of any person as an original party to the contract'.
[143] If it regards it as one of novation, the comments in the following section should be consulted.

this issue. It states only that the mutual obligations of assignor and assignee are governed by the law governing the contract of assignment. It does not say that the question of whether the right has been assigned must be determined by that same law. These arguments apply *a fortiori* in the case of English law, which we have seen is not strictly speaking an 'assignment' of the contract of carriage, but a sui generis transfer.[144]

It is suggested that it is rather more sensible for the law applicable to the **14.55** contract of carriage to determine both whether contractual rights and duties can be transferred to the transferee and whether they have been transferred. Article 12(2) of the Rome Convention states that the relationship between the debtor and assignee is a matter for the law applicable to the contract to which the assignment relates. 'There is a certain conceptual neatness in having rights created under the contract governed by its proper law throughout their existence, including the issue of against whom they are subsequently exercisable.'[145]. This also has the effect that, from the carrier's point of view, his rights and obligations are not altered by a contract to which he was not party. That same law should also determine what obligations the shipper retains by virtue of the contract and when those obligations are extinguished.

4. Choice of Law: Novation

If the law applicable to the original contract of carriage regards the **14.56** process of transfer as one of novation, it should determine the point at which the contractual obligations between the shipper and carrier are extinguished.[146] The law applicable to the 'new' contract between the transferee of the bill and the carrier should then be determined. Theoretically, this might be a different law to that which applied to the first contract. For example, suppose that the bill of lading contains no express or implied choice of law. Suppose also that the carrier has its place of business in State X. The shipper under the contract has its place of business in State Y. The place of loading of the goods is State X, with the effect that that law governed the original contract under Article 4(4) of the Rome Convention. However, the transferee of the bill has its place of business in State Y, which is also the state where the bill is transferred and where the goods are to be delivered. It is just arguable that the law of State Y has a closer connection to the contract than the law of State X, and so should apply pursuant to Article 4(5). This, however, could create serious difficulties. The law of State Y might consider that novation does not take

---

[144] Since Art 12 of the Rome Convention refers only to assignment.
[145] Sing, n 119 above, at 285.   [146] Art 10(1)(d) of the Rome Convention.

place, or that there is no valid contract between the carrier and the current holder of the bill. Accordingly, it is suggested that even if the law of State X were to regard the process as one of novation, an English court would strive to ensure that the law which governed the 'new' contract would be the same one which governed the original contract. The two contracts are intimately connected, both in fact and in law and it would be highly undesirable for them to be subject to different laws.

5. FOB Contracts—Carrier Contracts as Principal and 'Assigns' to the Buyer

14.57 In a minority of cases, the FOB seller may conclude a contract of carriage as principal and then transfer that contract to the buyer via the machinery of the Carriage of Goods by Sea Act 1992 in performance of his duty to place goods free on board. In accordance with the arguments advanced in the preceding sections, is suggested that the law applicable to the contract of carriage should determine whether that contract may be, and has been, transferred to the buyer.[147]

6. The Shipper's Obligations

14.58 In all cases, it is for the law applicable to the original contract of carriage to determine whether, and at what point, the shipper's obligations are extinguished. This is consistent with Article 10(1)(d) of the Rome Convention.[148]

7. Insurance

14.59 Under a CIF contract, the seller also transfers the insurance policy[149] to the buyer.[150] Under English law the transfer is effected under the Marine

---

[147] Art 12(2) of the Rome Convention. The law applicable to the contract of sale should not apply to this matter, as it is one which relates to the transfer of the contract of carriage and is enforceable against the carrier. However, if the seller fails to fulfil his duties, the law applicable to the contract of sale will, of course, determine his liability to the buyer.

[148] On which, see above, paras 13.240–246.

[149] On the law applicable to contracts of insurance, see *Dicey and Morris*, 1337–1383; *Third Supplement to the Thirteenth Edition*, 352–390; R Merkin and A Rodger, *EC Insurance Law* (London: Longman, 1997), Ch 6; F Seatzu, *Insurance in Private International Law: a European Perspective* (Oxford: Hart Publishing, 2003).

[150] On the law of marine insurance, see H Bennett, *The Law of Marine Insurance* (Oxford: Clarendon, 1996); D Rhidian Thomas (ed), *The Modern Law of Marine Insurance* (London: LLP, 1996).

Insurance Act 1906 and operates as a type of statutory assignment.[151] It is suggested that the choice of law rules applicable to assignment and *sui generis* transfers considered above in relation to the bill of lading are equally applicable here.[152] This means that the law applicable to the insurance policy determines its assignability, pursuant to Article 12(2) of the Rome Convention. As to the assignment of the policy itself, one might argue that Article 12(1) suggests that the law applicable to the contract of assignment applies. However, it is difficult to describe the CIF contract itself as a contract of assignment, albeit that it imposes a contractual duty *to assign* on the seller. In any event, Article 12(1) only deals with 'the mutual obligations of the assignor and assignee' and not expressly with the question whether the benefit has been assigned. In contrast, Article 12(2) applies the law governing the right to which the assignment relates to questions of the relationship between the assignee and the debtor. In the absence of a contract of assignment between the seller and the buyer, it is suggested that the law applicable to the contract of insurance should also determine whether, and when, the buyer becomes the assignee of the insurance policy.

XIV. THE EFFECT OF A CHOICE OF LAW CLAUSE ON A TRANSFEREE OF THE BILL OF LADING

1. General Principles

If, by the law applicable to the contract of carriage, the transferee of a bill **14.60** of lading acquires contractual rights and duties with respect to the carrier, then he will be subject to a choice of law found in the bill of lading.[153] The same will be true in relation to the contract of insurance.[154]

---

[151] On the effect of an arbitration clause on a transferee of rights under the Third Parties (Rights against Insurers) Act 1930, see *Socony Mobil Oil Co Inc v West of England Ship Owners Mutual Insurance Association (London) Ltd (The Padre Island) (No 1)* [1984] 2 Lloyd's Rep 408.

[152] See Y Baatz, 'The Impact of the EC Conventions and Directives on Governing Law and Jurisdiction in Marine Insurance and Reinsurance Contracts', Ch 10 in Rhidian Thomas (ed), n 150 above, 334–346. See also G Bowtle and K McGuiness, *The Law of Ship Mortgages* (London: LLP, 2001) 237–273.

[153] Sing, n 119 above, at 283. See, in the context of the Brussels Convention, Case 71/83 *Partenreederei ms Tilly Russ v Haven & Vervoerbedrijf Nova* [1984] ECR 2417; Case C-387/98 *Coreck Maritime GmbH v Handelsveem BV* [2000] ECR I-9337. See further above, paras 5.06–09. See also, in relation to arbitration clauses and the Contracts (Rights of Third Parties) Act 1999, *Nisshin Shipping Co Ltd v Cleaves & Co Ltd* [2003] EWHC 2602 (Comm), [2004] 1 Lloyd's Rep 38, QBD (Comm).

[154] Under English law insurers may also succeed to the rights and liabilities of the shippers and they too will then take the benefit and burden of all the contract terms including the choice of law clause. See also *Socony Mobil Oil Co Inc v West of England Ship Owners Mutual Insurance Association (London) Ltd (The Padre Island) (No 1)* [1984] 2 Lloyd's Rep 408.

14.61 The position is illustrated by the decision of the Court of Appeal in *Welex AG v Rosa Maritime Ltd (The Epsilon Rosa)*.[155] Welex was a Swiss company that purchased steel plates from a German company on CFR terms, free out Szczecin in Poland. By the terms of the contract, the seller was permitted to tender bills of lading incorporating the terms of a charterparty, without needing to provide a copy of the charter. A shipowner, Rosa, had its vessel chartered to carry the steel plates from Ukraine to Szczecin. The voyage charter contained an English choice of law clause, as well as a London arbitration clause. The bill of lading was issued on the Congenbill 1994 form on behalf of the ship's master. The bill contained the words 'freight payable as per charterparty' on its face, although the date of the charterparty to which this referred was not completed.[156] Only after the bill of lading was issued was a formal charterparty executed. The goods were found to be damaged when discharged. Welex claimed in respect of the price reduction it had been obliged to offer its buyer as a result of the damage. Welex arrested the ship in Portugal but then commenced proceedings against Rosa and Alexia, the new owner of the ship, in Poland. Rosa argued that this was in breach of the arbitration clause for London and sought an anti-suit injunction from the English courts to restrain Welex from continuing with the Polish proceedings. Welex claimed that the arbitration clause was not incorporated in the bill of lading. Steel J granted the anti-suit injunction, on the basis that the arbitration clause was incorporated into the bill of lading.[157] Even though no final charterparty had been drawn up when the bill of lading was issued, a telex sent to Rosa by the chartering brokers and the standard form charterparty referred to in that telex sufficed as a matter of English law to incorporate the arbitration and choice of law clause into the bill of lading.[158] This decision was upheld by the Court of Appeal.

14.62 However, if, by the law applicable to the contract of carriage, there is no equivalent to s 2 of the Carriage of Goods by Sea Act 1992,[159] so that the transferee of the bill of lading does not succeed to the rights and obligations of the shipper, there can be no question of that transferee being

---

[155] [2003] EWCA Civ 938, [2003] 2 Lloyd's Rep 509.

[156] Compare *Orinoco Navigation Ltd of Cyprus v Ecotrade SpA (The Ikariada)* [1999] 2 Lloyd's Rep 365, QBD (Comm)

[157] [2002] 2 Lloyd's Rep 81, [2002] 1 All ER (Comm) 939.

[158] See also *Partenreederei M/S Heidberg v Grosvenor Grain & Feed Co Ltd (The Heidberg) (No 2)* [1994] 2 Lloyd's Rep 287.

[159] See *Insurance Company of North America v Société Intramar* [1999] IL Pr 315, French Cour de cassation.

bound by a choice of law clause in the contract of carriage.[160] This is consistent with the European Court of Justice's case law on the effect of jurisdiction clauses on third party holders of a bill of lading.[161]

The situation where a foreign law contains no equivalent to s 2 of the **14.63** Carriage of Goods by Sea Act 1992 is illustrated by the decision in *Hapag Lloyd Container Line GmbH v La Réunion Européenne*.[162] It will be recalled that the French Cour de cassation found that a contract of carriage was governed by French law, notwithstanding the existence of a German jurisdiction clause. The question then arose as to whether the German jurisdiction clause bound the consignee and the company which was subrogated to the rights of the consignee. Consistently with European Court of Justice case law on the matter,[163] the Cour de cassation held that this depended upon whether the consignee succeeded to the rights and obligations of the shipper by the governing law of the contract, French law. It held that there is no rule of French law to this effect. It followed that the consignee could only be bound by the jurisdiction clause if it had agreed to that clause at, or before, the time of delivery.[164] As this had not happened, the jurisdiction clause did not bind the consignee, and the insurer which was subrogated to the consignee's rights.[165] One would expect the same approach to be taken with respect to a choice of law clause.

2. A Bootstraps Problem; does the Transferee have a Claim in Contract?

Suppose that there is a contract of carriage governed by the law of **14.64** England. The bill of lading is transferred to the transferee, who now wishes to sue the carrier. By English law, the transferee has a claim in contract by virtue of the Carriage of Goods by Sea Act 1992. However, a question arises as to whether the transferee has an action in contract or might instead sue in tort. If the claim is one in tort, it would be governed

---

[160] Compare *The Blue Wave* [1982] 1 Lloyd's Rep 151 at 154. In this case, no evidence was adduced as to the content of the foreign applicable law and the case proceeded on the basis that it was the same as English law. See also *Standard Chartered Bank v Pakistan National Shipping Corp* [1995] 2 Lloyd's Rep 365, 371–372.

[161] Case 71/83 *Partenreederei ms Tilly Russ v Haven & Vervoerbedrijf Nova* [1984] ECR 2417; Case C-387/98 *Coreck Maritime GmbH v Handelsveem BV* [2000] ECR I-9337. See also Case 201/82 *Gerling v Italian Treasury* [1983] ECR 2503; Case C-159/97 *Trasporti Castelletti Spedizioni Internazionali SpA v Hugo Trumpy SpA* [1999] ECR I-1597. See above, paras 5.06–09.

[162] [2003] IL Pr 51 at 779, Cour de cassation.

[163] See above, paras 5.06–09.

[164] In circumstances which complied with Art 23 of the Brussels I Regulation.

[165] See also *Insurance Company of North America v Société Intramar* [1999] IL Pr 315, discussed above, para 5.61.

by the law of State X, by which law the transferee obtains no right of action in contract and can only sue in tort. Which law should determine whether the claimant has an action in contract? 'To use the proper law [of the contract] concept would presuppose a contract already existent between the two parties of carrier and transferee when the whole enquiry is precisely to determine if that is so by asking whether there has been a statutory assignment of rights.'[166]

14.65 However, it is suggested that use of the putative applicable law of the contract to resolve this issue is the correct approach under the Rome Convention. There is a contract of carriage governed by English law between the carrier and the shipper. The transferee holds the bill of lading. On any view, there is *putatively* a contract between the carrier and the transferee. Article 8(1) of the Rome Convention states that whether a valid contract between the parties does exist is a matter for the law which would govern that contract if it indeed does exist. English law would govern such a contract and should accordingly be used to decide the matter. If it concludes that there is a contract between the carrier and the transferee of the bill, so be it. This is admittedly a bootstraps approach; but it is consistent with legislative provision. Moreover, since Article 1(1) of the Rome Convention states that it 'shall apply to contractual obligations', the effect of the finding that there is a claim in contract may be to extinguish a claim in tort.[167]

3. Benefit and Burden

14.66 The bill of lading will normally be on the carrier's terms and contain a choice of law clause providing for the application of the law of the carrier's home state. As such, it may well be to the disadvantage of the transferee of the bill to be bound by the choice of law clause.

14.67 In the context of jurisdiction clauses, the issue was discussed as to whether it makes any difference whether the jurisdiction clause in the bill of lading benefits the transferee, or imposes a burden upon him.[168] It was

---

[166] Sing, n 119 above, at 283.

[167] This issue is discussed below, paras 17.20–22 and 20.12–13.

[168] In relation to the question whether a 'beneficiary' under the Contracts (Rights of Third Parties) Act 1999 was subject to an arbitration clause in the original contract, Colman J remarked in *Nisshin Shipping Co Ltd v Cleaves & Co Ltd* [2003] EWHC 2602 (Comm) at [42], [2004] 1 Lloyd's Rep 38, 45, QBD (Comm) that: 'The third party never was expressed to be a party to the arbitration agreement but, in view of the fact that he has in effect become a statutory assignee of the promisee's right of action against the promisor and by reason of the underlying policy of the 1999 Act expressed in s. 1(4) he is confined to the means of enforcement provided by the contract to the promisee, namely arbitration, he is to be treated as standing in the shoes of that promisee for the purpose only of the enforcement of the substantive term'.

suggested in Chapter 5 that no distinction should be drawn between a third party taking the benefit of a jurisdiction clause and having the burden of that imposed on him.[169] The same should be true for choice of law purposes. Ultimately, however, this is simply a matter for the (putative) governing law of the contract between the transferee and the carrier. If the contract of carriage contains a choice of law clause for State X, and the issue is whether that choice of law clause is applicable to the contract between the transferee and the carrier, the law of State X should determine this matter. If that law does not draw a distinction between benefits and burdens of a choice of law rule, as is likely to be the case,[170] there is no reason for the English courts to treat the distinction between the 'benefit' and 'burden'[171] of a choice of law clause as significant.[172]

XV. CONSENT OF THE TRANSFEREE TO THE CHOICE OF LAW CLAUSE

1. The Validity of the Choice of Law Clause

In *Coreck Maritime GmbH v Handelsveem BV*[173] the European Court of **14.68** Justice held that the validity of a jurisdiction clause under the Brussels Convention should be determined by reference to the relationship between the parties to the original contract. This makes eminent sense for choice of law purposes too. If the question is whether the transferee of a bill of lading is subject to a choice of law clause in the bill of lading, it must first be asked whether that choice of law clause in the bill was formally and essentially valid. This must be determined by the law which would govern that clause if it were valid.[174]

However, in *Coreck*, the European Court of Justice held that if the third **14.69** party bearer of the bill of lading has succeeded by virtue of the applicable law to the shipper's rights and obligations when he acquired the bill

---

[169] At para 5.49. See also C-387/98 *Coreck Maritime GmbH v Handelsveem BV* [2000] ECR I-9337.

[170] And as is the case under English law in the Carriage of Goods by Sea Act 1992.

[171] If the choice of law clause can be described as imposing either. It is not a substantive term of the contract imposing rights and duties; it is simply the law by which the rights and duties of the parties are determined. See the discussion of Himalaya clauses below, paras 14.110–111. See also *The Mahkutai* [1996] AC 650, 666, PC.

[172] See more generally Briggs and Rees, 2.89. If the applicable substantive law of carriage only transfers rights to the third party, there would be no objection to this including the right to rely on a choice of law clause.

[173] Case C-387/98 [2000] ECR I-9337. See further above, para 5.10.

[174] Arts 3(4) and 8(1) of the Rome Convention.

of lading, it is not necessary to determine whether he accepted the jurisdiction clause in the original contract.[175] If the same approach is adopted for choice of law clauses, no separate enquiry would take place as to whether the transferee consented to the choice of law clause. The clause would be valid if expressly agreed to by the parties to the contract of carriage. Equally, if the parties to the contract of carriage impliedly chose a law to govern the contract, as where the clause is in a form which accords with practices which the parties have established between themselves, it might suggest that the transferee is bound by the implied choice even if no such practice existed between the transferee and the carrier.[176]

14.70   However, case law and principle suggest that for choice of law purposes, the question of whether a choice of law made between the parties to the contract of carriage binds the transferee must be determined separately. In English law, it has been seen that s 2 of the Carriage of Goods by Sea Act 1992 is not, strictly speaking, an assignment of contractual rights and duties, but a sui generis transfer. Moreover, this is one area of law where the analogy to jurisdiction clauses breaks down. Under the Brussels regime, the European Court of Justice has studiously refused to allow any reference to the governing law of the contract to determine whether the parties consented to a jurisdiction clause.[177] Rather, it has held that the requirements for the validity of the clause are autonomously determined by the provisions of (what is now) Article 23 of the Brussels I Regulation. In contrast, the consent of the parties to a choice of law clause is expressly referred to the (putative) governing law of the contract by Articles 3(4) and 8(1) of the Rome Convention. It is the applicable *national* law which determines the consent of the parties to a term of the contract, and the validity of that term.

14.71   Nevertheless, the practical importance of this position should not be overstated. It will be the law applicable to the bill of lading which normally[178] determines if the transferee is bound by an express or implied choice of

---

[175] The same approach has been taken in the context of jurisdiction clauses in insurance contracts by the ECJ in Case 201/82 *Gerling Konzern Speziale Kreditversicherung AG v Amministrazione del Tesoro dello Stato* [1983] ECR 2503. A third party beneficiary may rely upon a choice of jurisdiction clause inserted for his benefit in a contract if that clause satisfies the requirement as to form between an insurer and a policyholder, even though the third party has not satisfied the requirement as to form.

[176] See above, paras 5.10 and 512–13.

[177] Case C-269/95 *Benincasa v Dentalkit Srl* [1997] ECR I-3767 para 25; Case C-159/97 *Transporti Castelletti Spedizioni Internazionali SpA v Hugo Trumpy SpA* [1999] ECR I-1597, paras 49 and 51.

[178] Subject to the possible application of the exception in Art 8(2) of the Rome Convention, considered below, para 14.76.

law in the original contract.[179] If, by that law, the transferee is subject to the contractual rights and duties specified in the bill of lading, that law is equally likely to say that the transferee is bound by the choice of law made in, or appertaining to, the bill of lading.

2. THE CONSENT OF THE TRANSFEREE OF THE BILL OF LADING TO A CHOICE OF LAW CLAUSE OR ARBITRATION CLAUSE: ARTICLE 8(1)

In *Michael S Evryalos Maritime Ltd v China Pacific Insurance Co Ltd (The MV* **14.72** *Michael S)*,[180] a trip time charter contained a London arbitration clause and an English choice of law clause. The questions arose as to whether these clauses were incorporated into the bill of lading and whether they bound the indorsees of the bill of lading and their insurers. The upper left hand corner of the bill of lading contained the words 'Code Name "CONGEN-BILL" Edition 1994'. Congenbill 1994 states that 'all terms and conditions, liberties and exceptions of the Charter Party, dated as overleaf, including the Law and Arbitration Clause, are herewith incorporated'. However, the face of the bill merely stated that: 'All terms, conditions and exceptions of governing charter party are deemed incorporated therein'. The reverse of the bill was to similar effect, with no mention of an arbitration or choice of law clause.

Colman J applied English law to determine whether the arbitration and **14.73** choice of law clause were incorporated in the bill of lading and bound the transferee who succeeded to the rights and duties of the shipper.[181] Neither party argued that any other law governed the bill of lading. In any event, the approach taken is consistent with the approach taken in Articles 3(4) and 8(1) of the Rome Convention, which subject the question of whether a choice of law clause is agreed upon and valid to the law which would govern it if it were indeed valid. English law was putatively applicable to the bill of lading.

Colman J went on to say that the question of whether a choice of law **14.74** or arbitration clause bound the consignee could not be determined by asking whether the initial parties to the contract of carriage had them-selves agreed to, and incorporated, that clause. Rather, '. . . it must be remembered that the court has to put itself in the position of a third party transferee of the bill of lading reading it for the first time and wholly unaware of any discussion or understanding between the shippers and

---

[179] Since this is the law putatively applicable to claims between the carrier and transferee.
[180] Judgment of 20 December 2001, QBD (Comm Ct).
[181] Contrast the decision of the French Cour de cassation in *Insurance Company of North America v Société Intramar* [1999] IL Pr 315. On the position in American Law, see Wilford, Coghlin and Kimball, n 40 above, 58–9.

carrier that underlay the issue of the bill in question'. He held that, as a matter of English law, general words of incorporation such as contained on the front and reverse of the bill were not effective to incorporate the choice of law and arbitration clause.[182] There was nothing on the face of the bill which indicated an intention to incorporate the terms of the 1994 edition of the Congenbill.

14.75   Colman J emphasized that the Carriage of Goods by Sea Act 1992 does not create a contract on the terms of the contract of carriage, but that: 'What is transferred to the holder of the bills is.. all rights of suit and by virtue of section 3 [of the Carriage of Goods by Sea Act 1992], all continuing obligations under the contract "contained in or evidenced by" the bill of lading'. This demonstrates that one cannot simply say that, if a choice of law or arbitration clause is effective as between the original parties to the contract of carriage, it binds the holder of the bill of lading. It must separately be determined whether, according to the law putatively incorporated into the bill of lading, the clause binds the holder of the bill. This should be determined from the terms of the bill, and not by any private understanding between the original parties to the contract of carriage which is not evidenced by the bill of lading.[183]

3. Article 8(2) and the Effect of the Choice of Law or Arbitration Clause on the Transferee

14.76   The facts of *Welex AG v Rosa Maritime Ltd (The Epsilon Rosa)*[184] were given above.[185] In *Welex AG v Rosa Maritime Ltd (The Epsilon Rosa) (No 2)*,[186] Steel J had to decide whether it was reasonable for the question of whether the arbitration clause was incorporated into the bill of lading to be determined solely by English law.[187] Welex argued that by virtue of Article 8(2), they should be able to rely upon the law of their 'home' state, Switzerland,[188] to establish that they did not consent to the clause. The judge rejected this argument. Welex had the burden of proof as to why it was unreasonable for English law alone to determine whether the arbitration

---

[182] See *W Thomas Co Ltd v Portsea Steamship Co Ltd* [1912] AC 1.

[183] See *Leduc v Ward* (1888) 20 QBD 475; *SS Ardennes (Cargo Owners) v SS Ardennes (Owners)* [1951] KB 55; *Partenreederei M/S Heidberg v Grosvenor Grain & Feed Co Ltd (The Heidberg) (No 2)* [1994] 2 Lloyd's Rep 287.

[184] [2003] EWCA Civ 938, [2003] 2 Lloyd's Rep 509.   [185] At para 14.61.

[186] [2002] EWHC 2033 (Comm), [2002] 2 Lloyd's Rep 701. This point did not arise in the Court of Appeal.

[187] Pursuant to Art 8(1) of the Rome Convention.

[188] The case proceeded on the basis that Swiss law would only hold the consignee to such terms as the original shipper had agreed to; and that by Ukrainian law, the original shipper had not agreed to the arbitration clause.

clause was incorporated in the bill of lading. Welex had succeeded to the shipper's rights and duties under the contract of carriage. It had accepted that it was reasonable for it to be bound by the contract of carriage as a whole; and arbitration clauses were commonplace in such contracts. Steel J concluded that: 'There is nothing "eccentric" let alone unjust in the English law in those circumstances holding that both the shipper and the consignee are bound by the terms of the dispute resolution clause'.[189]

XVI. THE EFFECT OF A CHOICE OF LAW CLAUSE ON OTHER PARTIES

1. CAN A SHIPOWNER WHO IS NOT PARTY TO THE BILL OF LADING RELY UPON AND BE BOUND BY A CHOICE OF LAW CLAUSE IN THE BILL OF LADING?

A question may arise as to whether a shipowner whose ship has been **14.77** chartered can rely on, and is bound by, a choice of law clause in the bill of lading. In the first place, it must be established whether the shipowner is a party to the bill of lading. We have seen that the law applicable to the contract determines if the shipowner is the contracting carrier.[190]

Where the shipowner is not a party to the bill of lading, any relationship **14.78** between the cargo owner and the shipowner is likely to be based on tort.[191] However, it might be argued that the contract of carriage imposes burdens upon the shipowner, which is somewhat unlikely, or that it confers benefits upon the shipowner, for example, immunity from suit under the terms of an exclusion clause. If so, the question may arise as to whether the shipowner is subject to a choice of law clause in the bill of lading. This raises an issue of privity of contract. Accordingly, it must be determined by the law applicable to the contract of carriage whether shipowners who are not a party to that contract have an enforceable

---

[189] [2002] EWHC 2033 (Comm) at [11], [2002] 2 Lloyd's Rep 701, 704.

[190] Above, paras 14.39–42.

[191] In English law, since the shipper's/consignee's/indorsee's claim lies against the charterer under the bill of lading contract, that party might not be too concerned about going after the shipowner, especially in view of the steer given by the House of Lords in the direction of charterers' bills in *The Starsin* [2003] UKHL 12, [2004] AC 715. But of course charterers may be insolvent (as in *The Starsin*) and there may be no ship to arrest. So that leaves the action in negligence against the shipowner, which will usually fail because the damage has been done before the holder of a bill of lading acquires rights in the underlying cargo. Unusually, one of the holders of a set of bills in *The Starsin* had a bill of lading transferred before the damage caused by defective loading/stowage.

right[192] to invoke that clause. In *The Forum Craftsman*,[193] Japanese law held that the terms of a bill of lading cannot be invoked to protect shipowners, who by Japanese law are not parties to the bill, in a claim in tort brought against them by the buyers.

2. CAN A SHIPOWNER WHO IS A SUB-CONTRACTOR RELY UPON A CHOICE OF LAW CLAUSE IN ITS CONTRACT WITH THE CARRIER AGAINST A CARGO OWNER?

14.79 A related problem arises in the case where a carrier, having issued bills of lading to a cargo owner, then sub-contracts a part of the voyage to a shipowner which, for that part, issues a separate bill of lading to the carrier. Under English law there is no contractual relationship[194] between the shipowner and the cargo owner.[195] The question then arises as to whether, despite the absence of a contract between that shipowner and the cargo owner, the shipowner can still rely on the choice of law clause in the contract with the carrier to rule upon the effectiveness of a clause in that contract granting the shipowner immunity from an action brought by the cargo owner. It is suggested that the shipowner must first establish that under the law governing the contract between the shipowner and carrier, it has an enforceable right to invoke the choice of law clause against the cargo owner.

14.80 However, one might argue that there is no reason for the cargo owner to be adversely affected by a choice of law clause in a sub-contract to which it was not party.[196] Accordingly, it is suggested that it must also be shown that, by the law applicable to the contract of carriage between the carrier and the cargo owner, the cargo owner may be bound by a choice of law clause in the sub-contract between the carrier and shipowner.[197]

---

[192] That law should also determine whether the shipowner can be bound by the clause.

[193] [1985] 1 Lloyd's Rep 291, CA.

[194] Though a relationship of sub-bailment on terms comes into existence.

[195] *Owners of Cargo Lately Laden on Board the KH Enterprise v Owners of the Pioneer Container (The Pioneer Container)* [1994] 2 AC 324, PC. However, the case shows that, if English law governs the bill of lading contract, the shipowners may have an enforceable right to invoke a jurisdiction clause against the cargo-owner by virtue of the law of bailment: See *The Starsin* [2003] UKHL 12, [2004] AC 715, HL; *East West Corp v DKBS AF 1912 A/S* [2003] EWCA Civ 83, [2003] QB 1509, CA.

[196] Compare Art 12(2) of the Rome Convention. The situation is different to that of the transferee of a bill of lading, who may be subject to contractual rights and obligations in respect of the carrier.

[197] See the discussion of *The Pioneer Container* [1994] 2 AC 324, PC, below, paras 14.121–123.

3. Effect of a Choice of Law Clause where Neither Party is Privy to the Original Contract of Carriage

Suppose that there is a dispute between the third party holder of the bill of **14.81** lading and the agent of the ship and of the carrier.[198] Suppose that there is a choice of law clause which, according to its putative governing law,[199] is valid between the shipper and the carrier. The law specified by that clause, let us say the law of State X, determines whether the transferee of the bill of lading succeeds to the rights and obligations of the shipper, and is subject to the choice of law clause in the bill of lading. Similarly, the law of State X determines whether the agent succeeds to the rights and obligations of the carrier and is subject to the same choice of law clause. Only if the answer to both questions is 'yes' will the choice of law clause be effective as between the third party holder of the bill of lading and the agent of the ship and of the carrier.

4. Direct Claims Against a Cargo Owner's Insurers

In determining whether a choice of law or arbitration clause binds a third **14.82** party, it is essential for the court to ascertain the precise basis upon which the claimant's action rests. This is well illustrated by the decision in *Through Transport Mutual Insurance Association (Eurasia) Ltd v New India Assurance Co Ltd*.[200] A claimant, N, who was the insurer of a cargo owner whose cargo was lost in transit, brought a claim against T, who was the insurer of the shipper, B. The insurance contract between B and T contained an English choice of law clause and a London arbitration clause, both of which purported to extend to disputes involving third parties, including assignees. N's right to sue T arose by virtue of s 67 of the Finnish Insurance Contracts Act 1994, which allowed a claimant to sue a defendant's insurer directly where the defendant was insolvent. The question arose as to whether N was bound by the London arbitration clause. This depended upon whether N asserted an independent right of action arising by virtue of its right of action against an insolvent insured (so that it could not be bound by the arbitration clause and Finnish law governed the claim), or a derivative claim, in effect as assignee of the insurance policy between T and B (so that, as assignee, N was subject to the London arbitration clause in the insurance policy). Moore-Bick J ruled

---

[198] It was suggested above in the context of a discussion of jurisdiction clauses that the fact that neither party was privy to the original contract does not change the basic position: para 5.18.

[199] Arts 3(4) and 8(1) of the Rome Convention.

[200] [2003] EWHC 3158 (Comm), [2004] 1 Lloyd's Rep 206, QBD (Comm).

that this raised a matter of classification and that this must be conducted by English law, even though the case concerned the construction of a Finnish statute. He further held that he must classify the issue before him, which was whether N was bound by the London arbitration clause. This, in turn, depended upon the nature of the rights asserted by N. Moore-Bick J ruled that N did not seek to enforce an independent right of action. Rather, the Finnish legislation allowed a party with a claim against an insolvent insured party to bring proceedings directly against the insurer *to obtain the benefit that the insured would have been entitled to receive under the contract of insurance*. In effect, the claimant, N, was bringing a claim parasitic upon the contract of insurance between T and B by virtue of a statutory assignment. Accordingly, the claimant was bound by the arbitration clause.

14.83 The same approach should be adopted in relation to choice of law clauses. If the issue is whether a claimant is bound by a choice of law clause for State X, then the law of State X determines the process by which the claimant acquires rights against the defendant, and whether he is bound by the choice of law clause.[201]

XVII. CHOICE OF A LAW WITH NO CONNECTION TO THE CONTRACT BETWEEN THE CARRIER AND THE TRANSFEREE OF THE BILL OF LADING: APPLICATION OF ARTICLE 3(3)

14.84 A question may arise as to the application of Article 3(3) of the Rome Convention between the transferee of the bill of lading and the carrier. In particular, should this be determined by looking at the parties to, and terms of, the contract of carriage, or by looking at the parties to, and terms of, the contract between the transferee of the bill and the carrier?

14.85 It will be recalled that Article 3(3) preserves the application of the mandatory rules of a country with which a contract is entirely connected objectively, where another law is chosen by the parties to govern the contract.[202] Imagine that a contract is concluded between a shipper and a carrier, who have their places of business in France, for the carriage of goods from one port in France to another. The contract is stated to be governed by English law. In this situation, Article 3(3) would apply, as the contract is entirely objectively connected to France and the mandatory

---

[201] Arts 3(4) and 8(1) of the Rome Convention.
[202] See above, paras 13.99–102.

rules of France would be applied notwithstanding the choice of English law.

Suppose now that the bill of lading is transferred to a holder of the bill **14.86** with its place of business in England. English law, as the governing law of the contract, holds that a contract arises between the transferee of the bill and the carrier. It can no longer be said that all objective elements of the contract are connected to England. But is the contract between the transferee and the carrier subject to Article 3(3) and the domestic mandatory rules of France?

It is suggested that the answer to this question is 'no'. In other words, **14.87** Article 3(3) should be applied to the contract between the transferee and the carrier. It is true that s 2(1) of the Carriage of Goods by Sea Act 1992 provides that a person who is the lawful holder of a bill of lading, the identified consignee in a sea waybill, or the person entitled to delivery of goods to which a delivery order relates, has the right to sue the carrier under the contract of carriage *'as if he had been a party to that contract'*.[203] However, we have already seen that the machinery of the Carriage of Goods by Sea Act 1992 is not strictly speaking an assignment of the same contractual rights which the shipper had to the carrier. The carrier is subject to burdens as well as benefits, and the shipper's liability remains. The *sui generis* transfer of contractual rights and obligations means that the choice of law rules in contract must be applied specifically to the contract between the carrier and the transferee. Accordingly, in the example given, the choice of English law to govern the contract would be unrestricted by Article 3(3).

XVIII. FORMAL VALIDITY OF THE CONTRACT BETWEEN THE CARRIER AND THE TRANSFEREE OF THE BILL OF LADING

1. Nature of Problem

A related question concerns the formal validity of the contract between **14.88** the transferee and the carrier. Suppose that a contract of carriage is concluded between a shipper and a carrier and is subject to the law of State W. The carrier has its place of business in State X and the shipper has its place of business in State Y.[204] The contract is formally invalid by the laws

---

[203] Emphasis added.
[204] And these parties are in these respective states at the time of conclusion of the contract.

of State W and State X. However, it is valid by the law of State Y. The effect of Article 9(2) of the Rome Convention[205] is to render the contract formally valid, since the contract must satisfy the formality rules of at least one of the following: (i) the governing law; and/ or (ii) the law of the place where one party was at the time of conclusion of the contract; and/ or (iii) the law of the place where the other party was at the time of conclusion of the contract. The contract satisfies the law of the place where the shipper was at the time of conclusion of the contract.

14.89   Suppose now that the bill of lading is transferred to the present holder, who brings an action against the carrier. The governing law of the contract, State W, is in similar terms to s 2 of the Carriage of Goods by Sea Act 1992 and the transferee brings an action in contract. The transferee has its place of business in State W. If the formal validity of the 'contract' between the transferee and the carrier is determined afresh, then the contract will fail, since it satisfies neither the formality rules of the governing law (State W), nor the law of the place of business of the carrier (State Y), nor the law of the place of business of the transferee (again, State W).

2. The Need to Determine Separately the Formal Validity of the Contract between Carrier and Transferee

14.90   There is a hint in the Rome Convention that the formal validity of the contract should not be adversely affected by the transfer of the bill of lading. Article 3(2) states that where parties change the law applicable to the contract, this shall not prejudice the contract's 'formal validity or adversely affect the rights of third parties'.[206] However, this provision is concerned with a single contract, whose law changes. We are concerned here with a different problem of the sui generis transfer of contractual rights and duties, in circumstances where the liability of the shipper remains. There is no change of law.[207] We are concerned with whether the transferee acquires substantive contractual rights which he did not have at the time of conclusion of the contract of carriage. As such, it is difficult to say that the transferee's position is *prejudiced* by applying the rules of formal validity to the 'contract' which later arises between the transferee and the carrier. Moreover, it is difficult to say that the carrier's position

---

[205] On which, see above, paras 13.256–258.

[206] See also Art 9(4) which provides that an act intended to have legal effect relating to an existing contract is formally validity if it satisfies the formality rules of the law which governs the contract or the law of the country where the act was done. See further Art 14(2).

[207] Although see the remarks about novation, above, paras 14.50, 14.56.

is prejudiced, at least in English domestic law, since the liability of the shipper remains.

A further argument is that in the context of jurisdiction clauses and Article **14.91** 17 of the Brussels Convention, the European Court of Justice held in *Coreck Maritime GmbH v Handelsveem BV*[208] that the validity of a jurisdiction clause under the Brussels Convention should be determined by reference to the relationship between the parties to the original contract. The earlier decision of the European Court of Justice in *Gerling Konzern Speziale Kreditversicherung AG v Amministrazione del Tesoro dello Stato*[209] as to the impact of a jurisdiction clause upon a third party beneficiary is to the same effect.

If the same approach is adopted for choice of law purposes, it might **14.92** suggest that provided that the contract of carriage is formally valid as between the carrier and the shipper, its formal validity should not be revisited when the bill is transferred to the third party holder. Certainly, there can be no question of a transferee being bound by a bill of lading, if the original contract between the carrier and the shipper was not formally valid. The third party holder of the bill can hardly be bound as *transferee* of the bill of lading, if the original contract of carriage, of which the bill is evidence, was not binding as between the carrier and the shipper. However, it is suggested that the fact that the contract of carriage is formally valid as between carrier and shipper is a necessary, but not sufficient condition for the bill of lading to bind the transferee of the bill of lading. Since the Carriage of Goods by Sea Act 1992 is not strictly speaking an assignment of contractual rights to the transferee, but is *sui generis* in nature, there is no reason why the formal validity of the bill of lading should be determined once and for all by the choice of law rules applicable as between the carrier and the shipper.[210] Accordingly, it is suggested that the formal validity of the bill of lading as between the carrier and the transferee of the bill must be determined separately.

For all these reasons, it is suggested that Article 9 of the Rome Convention **14.93** should be applied to the specific contract between the transferee and the carrier. In our above example, this leads to the conclusion that the contract between the parties is formally invalid.

---

[208] Case C-387/98 [2000] ECR I-9337. See further above, paras 5.10, 5.12–13.
[209] Case 201/82 [1983] ECR 2503.
[210] Especially since, as between shipper and carrier, the bill of lading is only evidence of the terms of the contract of carriage. The bill of lading itself supplies the terms of the contract between the carrier and the transferee.

XIX. PERFORMANCE OF THE CARRIER'S OBLIGATIONS: ARTICLE 10(1)(b) AND 10(2) OF THE ROME CONVENTION

14.94 It will be recalled[211] that Article 10(1)(b) of the Rome Convention states that questions relating to the performance of a contract are a matter for the governing law of the contract. However, Article 10(2) states that in relation to the manner of performance of the contract, the court must have regard to the law of the place of performance.[212] In *East West Corp v DKBS AF 1912 A/S*,[213] the defendant shipping lines carried goods owned by the claimants to Chile. The contracts of carriage contained an English choice of law clause. The bills of lading issued by the defendants identified the claimants as shippers and consigned the goods to the order of certain Chilean banks. The claimants indorsed the bills and delivered them to the banks, who were to collect the purchase price due from the various buyers. When the goods arrived in Chile, the defendants[214] cleared them through customs and delivered them to one of the buyers without presentation of the original bills of lading. The buyer in question did not pay for the goods and the claimants sued the defendants.

14.95 One question which arose at first instance[215] was as to the nature and extent of the shipping line's obligations under the contract of carriage. Thomas J stated that: 'The effect of art. 10 of the Rome Convention is to maintain a distinction between the substance of the obligation which is governed by the proper law (in this case English law) and the mode (or manner and method) of performance which is governed by the law of the place of performance—Chile'.[216]

---

[211] See above, paras 13.159–204.

[212] See also Dicey and Morris, 1409–1410. As the authors note, a similar approach to that specified in Art 10(2) of the Rome Convention was previously adopted at common law: see *Norden SS Co v Dempsey* (1876) 1 CPD 654; *The Stettin* (1889) 14 PD 142; *Aktieselskab August Freuchen v Steen Hansen* [1919] 1 Ll LR 393.

[213] [2002] EWHC 83 (Comm), [2002] 2 Lloyd's Rep 182, 194 (the point was not argued in the Court of Appeal [2003] EWCA Civ 83, [2003] QB 1509). See also *Orinoco Navigation Ltd of Cyprus v Ecotrade SpA (The Ikariada)* [1999] 2 Lloyd's Rep 365, QBD (Comm); *Import Export Ltd v Compañía Sud Americana de Vapores SA* [2003] EWHC 11 (Comm), [2003] 1 Lloyd's Rep 405, QBD (Comm Ct).

[214] With the assistance of warehouse operators and port agents.

[215] But not on appeal. The appeal was primarily concerned with the liability of the shipping lines to the claimants, and in particular whether they could be liable as bailees (there being no contractual claim, available to the claimants, who were not the holders of the bills of lading).

[216] *per* Thomas J at first instance in *East West Corp v DKBS AF 1912 A/S* [2002] EWHC 83 (Comm) at [64], [2002] 2 Lloyd's Rep 182, 194. In the Court of Appeal, Mance LJ summarized the findings of Thomas J on this point [2003] EWCA Civ 83, at [8]–[11], [2003] QB 1509, 1523–1524. However, his Lordship was not required to comment on the correctness of these findings.

This is not self-evidently correct. Article 10(2) of the Rome Convention **14.96** gives the English court the discretion whether to invoke the law of the place of performance in relation to the manner of performance. It imposes no obligation to do so. Nor does Article 10(2) expressly oust the application of the governing law of the contract to such issues.[217] Nevertheless, Thomas J continued:

> . . . as a matter of English law, I am satisfied that the obligation in bailment and contract upon [the shipping lines] . . . was only to deliver against presentation of an original bill of lading. However, these carriers relied on the distinction under art. 10 of the Rome Convention between the substance of that obligation and the manner and mode of its performance. . . . To the extent that the law of Chile contained provisions specifying the manner in which cargo in Chile had to be delivered, then in my view it must be correct to have regard to the law of Chile under art. 10. Thus, for example, under the law of Chile . . . the original bills of lading had to be retained by the customs agent. They could only therefore be presented to the carrier and had to be returned (marked if necessary to show delivery had been made); to that extent the obligations under the bill of lading are modified by the law of Chile.[218]

This suggests that an English court is unlikely to require a carrier to perform in a manner which is incompatible with the law of the place of performance.[219] In effect, it involves the application of the law of the place of performance to questions as to the manner of performance, to the exclusion of the applicable law of the contract.

XX. MANDATORY RULES

1. Is the Carriage of Goods By Sea Act 1992 An International Mandatory Rule of the Forum?

An important question is whether the Carriage of Goods by Sea Act 1992 **14.97** is an international mandatory rule of the forum, so that its provisions must be applied in an English court, notwithstanding that English law does not govern the bill of lading.[220] The Law Commission considered this question but did not decide upon it;[221] and the Act is silent on the matter.

---

[217] On one view, the two laws can operate simultaneously: see above, paras 13.160–161.

[218] *per* Thomas J, [2002] EWHC 83 (Comm) at [130]–[131], [2002] 2 Lloyd's Rep 182, 205–206.

[219] See further Cooke et al, n 35 above, 1.54–1.66 on the effect of illegality upon the contract of affreightment.

[220] Dicey and Morris, 1414; *Scrutton on Charterparties and Bills of Lading*, n 35 above, 35–43; see also *Sewell v Burdick* (1884) 10 App Cas 74.

[221] 'Rights of Suit in Respect of Carriage of Goods by Sea', Law Com No 196, Scot Law Comm No 130 (1991); J Beatson and J Cooper, 'Rights of Suit in Respect of Carriage of Goods by Sea' [1991] LMCLQ 196, 199.

14.98   In the absence of any express statement on the issue, there is a presumption that the Act is not an international mandatory rule.[222] As Sing points
out:[223] 'Perhaps, the only plausible claim to mandatory character which
[this statute has] . . . is . . . its facilitation of a contractual relationship so
that carriers and transferees of bills of lading are more certain of their
respective positions and recourse to actions in tort and bailment
often ingeniously conceived, need not be had'. However, these are not
sufficiently pressing reason for the Act to apply in an English court if a
foreign law governs the contract.[224]

14.99   English law itself had, until fairly recently, relatively few exceptions to the
doctrine of privity of contract.[225] It would hardly seem reasonable for it to
have refused to accept the application of a foreign governing law which
did not create a contractual relationship between the carrier and the transferee of the bill of lading.[226] Moreover, the argument as to the commercial
convenience of a contractual relationship cannot be decisive. Commercial
convenience demands that the autonomy of the parties to a contract of
carriage be respected. If they happen to choose a law by which no contractual rights arise between the carrier and transferee, so be it. It could be
said to be inherent in Article 12(2) of the Rome Convention that the
assignability[227] of a right is a matter for the law governing the original
contract of carriage.

14.100   One complication is that there are some cases which support the mandatory application of the predecessor to the 1992 Act, namely the Bills of
Lading Act 1855.[228] However, it has been pointed out that many of these
decisions are opaque or not precisely on the point and that: 'It was not
even remotely suggested in these cases that a forum mandatory statute
was involved'.[229] In the era of the Rome Convention, where a concept of

---

[222] See F Mann, 'Statutes and the Conflict of Laws' (1972–3) 46 British Ybk of Intl Law 117;
S Dutson, 'The Conflict of Laws and Statues: the International Operation of Legislation
Dealing with Matters of Civil Law in the United Kingdom and Australia' (1997) 60 MLR 668.
[223] Sing, n 119 above, at 281.
[224] Dicey and Morris, 1414.
[225] See the discussion below, paras 14.104–125. But see now the Contracts (Rights of Third
Parties) Act 1999, considered below, paras 14.116–120.
[226] See *Scott v Pilkington* (1862) 2 B & S 11. Conversely, the English courts have accepted
the validity of a foreign contract unsupported by consideration: *Re Bonacina* [1912] 2 Ch 394;
Sing, n 119 above, at 281.
[227] We saw above that it may not be correct to describe the process of s 2 of the Carriage of
Goods by Sea Act 1992 as assignment. However, the analogy to Art 12(2) of the Rome
Convention still remains. See above, paras 14.49–55.
[228] See the cases considered by Sing, n 119 above, at 281–283. See in particular: *Sewell v
Burdick* (1884) 10 App Cas 74, 85; *The St Joseph* [1933] P 119, 129; *Pacific Molasses Co and United
Molasses Trading Co v Entre Ríos Compañía Naviera SA (The San Nicholas)* [1976] 1 Lloyd's
Rep 8.
[229] Sing, n 119 above, at 282–283.

international mandatory rules has evolved, there seems no reason to be fettered by these authorities relating to an earlier statute. Moreover, when applying the rules of the Rome Convention, Contracting States are urged to have regard to 'the desirability of achieving uniformity in their interpretation and application'.[230] It is accordingly suggested that the Carriage of Goods by Sea Act 1992 should not be treated as an international mandatory rule of the forum for the purposes of Article 7(2) of the Rome Convention.

2. THE CARRIAGE OF GOODS BY SEA ACT 1992 AS A DOMESTIC MANDATORY RULE

However, the Carriage of Goods by Sea Act 1992 should be regarded as a **14.101** *domestic* mandatory rule of the forum.[231] It is a rule which is intended to apply *whenever English law is applicable to the contract*. At several points in the Rome Convention, reference is made to domestic mandatory rules and their application preserved.[232] Article 3(3), for example, preserves the application of the domestic mandatory rules of the state with which the contract is entirely objectively connected, if the parties choose the law of another state to govern the contract.[233] This could be triggered in the case of carriage from one port in the England to another, in circumstances where the parties involved all have their places of business in England. If the bill of lading contains a choice of law clause for a foreign law, and by that foreign law no contractual liability arises between the carrier and the transferee, Article 3(3) has the effect that the provisions of the Carriage of Goods by Sea Act 1992 are nevertheless applicable. This is because but for the choice of law clause, the contract would have been governed by English law; and if English law had applied, the Carriage of Goods by Sea Act 1992 would have been triggered.

3. OTHER MANDATORY RULES; THE HAGUE AND HAGUE-VISBY RULES

There are English authorities pre-dating the Rome Convention which **14.102** struck down the parties' choice of law if the choice had the effect of reducing the carrier's liability beyond the levels specified in the Hague-Visby Rules.[234] If the conditions for the application of the Rules in England

---

[230] Art 18.   [231] See above, paras 13.275, 13.277–278.   [232] Notably, Arts 3(3), 5 and 6.

[233] Art 3(3) will rarely apply in the carriage of goods context, since it requires all the relevant objective elements to be connected to a single state other than that whose law is chosen to govern the contract.

[234] Gaskell, 19.55–19.62; see also Wilson, n 9 above, 186–9. See, in particular, *Vita Food Products v Unus Shipping Co Ltd* [1939] AC 277, 290 (a case involving the Hague Rules); *Owners of Cargo on Board the Morviken v Owners of the Hollandia (The Hollandia)* [1983] 1 AC 565; *Hellenic Steel Co v Svolamar Shipping Co Ltd (The Komninos S)* [1991] 1 Lloyd's Rep 370; *The European Enterprise* [1989] 2 Lloyd's Rep 185.

are satisfied,[235] they apply notwithstanding a choice of law clause for the law of a state which imposes a lesser liability. If one 'translates' this into the terminology of the Rome Convention, the Hague-Visby Rules were regarded as mandatory rules of the forum within their intended scope of application.[236] Such mandatory rules may today be invoked pursuant to Article 3(3), where the parties choose a foreign law to govern a bill of lading which is otherwise entirely connected with England.[237] Clearly, such cases will be very rare. More importantly, the Hague-Visby Rules have been applied in England where a foreign law was chosen to govern the bill of lading. As such, within their intended scope they have effectively been treated as international mandatory rules[238] of the forum.[239] The application of the international mandatory rules of the forum is preserved by Article 7(2) of the Rome Convention.[240]

14.103 It appears, however, that it is unnecessary[241] for an English court to rely upon the provisions of the Rome Convention in order to invoke the Hague-Visby Rules. Article 21 of the Rome Convention[242] states that: 'This Convention shall not prejudice the application of international conventions to which a Contracting State is, or becomes, a party'. This means that the Hague-Visby Rules prevail over the rules of the Rome Convention.

---

[235] In particular, if the bill is issued in a contracting state and concerns a contract for carriage from a port in a contracting state. See Art X of the Rules, set out in the Schedule to the Carriage of Goods by Sea Act 1971. See *Parson Corp v CV Scheepvaartonderneming (The Happy Ranger)* [2002] EWCA Civ 694, [2002] 2 Lloyd's Rep 357, CA, noted D Martin-Clark, 'Where are you leading us, Ranger?' (2002) 2 Shipping and Trade Law 1; and see the earlier decision of Tomlinson J [2001] 2 Lloyd's Rep 530, QBD (Comm). See also *The Starsin* [2003] UKHL 12, [2004] AC 715.

[236] See *Benjamin*, 25–071; P Todd, *Bills of Lading and Bankers' Documentary Credits*, (3rd edn, London: LLP, 1998), 291–2. See further *Owners of Cargo on Board the Morviken v Owners of the Hollandia (The Hollandia)* [1983] 1 AC 565; *The Happy Ranger* [2002] EWCA Civ 694, [2002] 2 Lloyd's Rep 357, CA.

[237] See further above, paras 13.99–102.

[238] On which, see above, paras 13.276, 13.279–281.

[239] They are part of the law of the forum, as they were enacted by the Carriage of Goods by Sea Act 1971. See also the decision of the Federal Court of Australia in *Hi-Fert Pty Ltd v United Shipping Adriatic Inc* 165 ALR 265, noted Goldring, n 42 above, in which an arbitration clause for proceedings in London was struck down as infringing the Australian Carriage of Goods by Sea Act 1991, which gives effect to the Hague-Visby Rules in Australia. Contrast the decision of the District Court of Maryland, USA in *Van Ommeren Bulk Shipping v Cooper/T Smith Stevedoring Co*, summarized in (1999) Uniform L Rev 1024, where the court upheld a US jurisdiction and choice of law clause in circumstances where proceedings were threatened in Belgium and it was accepted that the Belgium court would not have enforced the choice of court clause and could have applied the Visby SDR Protocol. The Maryland court suggested that an injunction could have been issued to restrain proceedings in Belgium.

[240] See Dicey and Morris, 1412–1414.

[241] Not to mention strictly speaking incorrect.

[242] Art 21 is considered further below, paras 15.05–08 and 16.98–113.

XXI. THE EFFECT OF A HIMALAYA CLAUSE IN A BILL OF LADING

1. Nature of a Himalaya Clause

In English law, the insertion of a Himalaya clause[243] into the bill of lading **14.104** will give servants, agents and independent contractors of the carrier the benefit of exceptions and limitations in the bill of lading contract. According to classic Himalaya language, of the type set out in *The Starsin*,[244] the Himalaya beneficiary is deemed to be a party to the contract contained in or evidenced by the bill of lading (the purpose of this language being to protect the beneficiary as against subsequent holders of the bill of lading).[245]

2. The Law of Agency

In order for a party to claim the protection of a Himalaya clause, it will be **14.105** necessary to show that the clause extends to him. If the clause applied to agents of the carrier, a question may arise as to the whether a party is indeed an agent of the carrier.

A bill of lading may be signed by someone other than the shipowner, such **14.106** as the master (acting as his agent). The question may arise as to whether the shipowner is a party to the bill of lading.[246] Furthermore, the House of Lords in *The Starsin* accepted that the shipowner could be the charterer's independent contractor or agent for the purpose of carrying the goods and so could shelter behind the protective language of a Himalaya clause.[247] The validity and effect of a Himalaya clause will determine in what circumstances an action in negligence might fail against a shipowner who is not the carrier, on the ground that the shipowner can claim the protection of the clause as the agent of the charterer.

The choice of law rules applicable to agency must determine whether **14.107** the master or other person signs the bill of lading as agent of the shipowner. The same rules will determine whether the charterer acts as the

---

[243] See *Adler v Dickson* [1955] 1 QB 158, CA; *New Zealand Shipping Co Ltd v AM Satterthwaite & Co Ltd (The Eurymedon)* [1975] AC 154, PC.

[244] [2003] UKHL 12, [2004] AC 715.

[245] Lord Bingham was of the view that this produced a contract of carriage in the Hague-Visby sense but only to a limited extent, that extent being Art III, r 8, which prevents the exclusion of liability for negligence.

[246] See the discussion of the identity of the carrier, above, paras 14.38–44.

[247] This is curious in that, under standard time charterparties, the charterer under an agency and employment clause can act as agent of the shipowner.

shipowner's agent, or vice versa.[248] It will be recalled that the question of the agent's ability to bind the principal to a third party is excluded from the scope of the Rome Convention.[249] The English common law rules provide that the proper law of the contract between an agent and a third party determines whether the principal is bound to the third party by virtue of the agent's acts.[250]

14.108 Other contractual disputes between the principal and agent arising from the agency contract itself are not excluded from the Rome Convention.[251] The rights and liabilities of the principal and agent in relation to one another will be governed by the law applicable to the contract between them, as determined by the rules of the Convention.[252]

3. THE EXTENT OF THE PROTECTION AFFORDED BY THE TERMS OF THE HIMALAYA CLAUSE TO SERVANTS, AGENTS AND INDEPENDENT CONTRACTORS

14.109 The law applicable to the contract of carriage which contains the Himalaya clause determines the intended scope of that clause. It will also determine the extent of the protection that it affords to servants, agents and independent contractors. This is consistent with Article 10(1)(a) of the Rome Convention. This view is also supported by the decision in *The Forum Craftsman*.[253] In that case, the court applied Japanese law, which was the law governing the bill of lading. By Japanese law, the terms of a bill of lading cannot be invoked to protect shipowners, who under Japanese law are not parties to the bill, where a claim is brought against them in tort by the buyers.

4. DOES A HIMALAYA CLAUSE EXTEND TO A CHOICE OF LAW CLAUSE?

14.110 The usual language in the Himalaya clause refers to exceptions and limitations, which connotes clauses with a one-way protecting effect and

---

[248] It is possible that, while a charterer may not be the carrier, yet in signing the bill of lading as agent of the shipowner or carrier it has incurred personal liability on the contract. This is not the general position in the English law of agency but may be so by a relevant other law. As the question relates to liability on the contract, it should be determined by the law which governs the contract of carriage.

[249] Art 1(2)(f); see above, paras 13.38 and 14.08.

[250] Dicey and Morris, Rule 198, 1473. But see also *ibid*, at 1475–1479.

[251] See further Benjamin, 25–073, 25–081 and 25–082; Dicey and Morris, 1464–1481.

[252] Dicey and Morris, Rule 197, 1464. See also *W & R Fletcher (New Zealand) Ltd v Sigurd Haavik Aksjeselskap (The Vikfrost)* [1980] 1 Lloyd's Rep 560, CA, discussed above, para 5.50.

[253] [1985] 1 Lloyd's Rep 291, CA, considered above, paras 14.40, 14.78 and 5.63–65 Although the case pre-dates the Rome Convention, it is suggested that it should be followed under the Convention.

that do not impose obligations on the shipper. Hence the language will not be apt to cover choice of court or arbitration clauses.[254] Hobhouse LJ in the Court of Appeal in *Bouygues Offshore SA v Caspian Shipping Company*[255] ruled that this was not merely a matter of construction of the Himalaya clause. Rather, a jurisdiction clause could simply not be described as an exception or limitation and was, accordingly, not the proper subject of a Himalaya clause. The same is presumably true of a choice of law clause. As with a jurisdiction clause: 'Such a clause can be distinguished from terms such as exceptions and limitations in that it does not benefit only one party, but embodies a mutual agreement . . . which creates mutual rights and obligations'.[256]

Nevertheless, Hobhouse LJ in *Bouygues Offshore SA* did acknowledge[257] **14.111** that it would be possible to draft a Himalaya clause which might have the effect of enabling a third party to rely on a jurisdiction clause. Moreover, for reasons which are not clear, *The Mahkutai*[258] was decided on the basis of English law, even though the bill of lading was governed by Indonesian law. It is suggested that the question of whether an appropriately drafted Himalaya clause is intended to confer the benefit of a choice of law clause on servants, agents and independent contractors is a question of the construction of the Himalaya clause. Article 10(1)(a) of the Rome Convention subjects the construction of a term of the contract to the applicable law of the contract.[259] The law specified in the bill of lading is that which is *putatively* applicable to the servant, agent or independent contractor. It is that law which should determine whether the Himalaya clause is intended also to cover the choice of law clause contained in the bill of lading. If, by that law, the Himalaya clause is not intended to extend to the choice of law clause in the bill of lading, it is suggested that the choice of law clause does not apply to servants, agents and independent contractors of the carrier.

5. THE EFFECT OF A CHOICE OF LAW CLAUSE ON SERVANTS, AGENTS AND INDEPENDENT CONTRACTORS

If the Himalaya clause *is* intended as a matter of construction to extend to **14.112** a choice of law clause contained in the contract between the shipper and the carrier, it is suggested that a second question arises as to the *validity*

---

[254] *The Mahkutai* [1996] AC 650.   [255] [1997] IL Pr 472, CA.
[256] Lord Goff in *The Mahkutai* [1996] AC 650, 666.
[257] [1997] IL Pr 472, 476.   [258] [1996] AC 650, PC.
[259] On the applicability of Roman-Dutch law to a bill of lading clause, see H Staniland, 'The Himalaya Clause in South Africa' [1992] LMCLQ 317.

of that clause. The question of the validity of the clause in respect of servants, agents and independent contractors ought properly to be subject to the law applicable to that contract. This is consistent with Articles 3(4) and 8(1) of the Rome Convention, which subject the existence and validity of a term of the contract, and a choice of law clause in particular, to the law which would govern it if the term were valid. If[260] by that law, the clause is also valid, then it will be applicable to servants, agents and independent contractors of the carrier.

6. Contractual Defences to Tort Claims

14.113 However, it may be incorrect in principle to subject all questions relating to a Himalaya clause to the applicable law of the contract. A claim may be brought against an servant, agent and independent contractors in respect of that party's liability in tort.[261] In substance, the Himalaya clause may be used as a contractual defence to a tort action.[262] Arguably, it is to the choice of law rules in *tort* that we should first look.

14.114 The proper approach to the problem of contractual defences to tort actions is considered in Chapter 20 on concurrent claims and choice of law.[263] There, it is suggested that the law applicable to the tort claim should determine whether a party may avoid liability by a valid contractual provision. If the answer is 'no', then the claim in tort will be determined exclusively by the law applicable to the tort. If the answer is 'yes', however, a second question arises as to whether the clause is valid. This should be determined by the law applicable to the contract.[264]

14.115 However, at least on the present state of authorities, it seems more likely that an English court will directly apply the law applicable to the contract and simply ask whether, according to that law, the Himalaya clause is valid and effective to protect servants, agents and independent contractors.

---

[260] But only if.

[261] Advocate General Colomer in Case C-440/97 *GIE Groupe Concorde v Master of the Vessel Suhadiwarno Panjan* [1999] ECR I-6307, para 34 of the Opinion, stated that a claim by the consignee of the goods against the ship's master lay in tort. See further *Scrutton on Charterparties*, n 35 above, 44–58.

[262] *Adler v Dickson* [1955] 1 QB 158. Although there is some doubt on this point, as *The Starsin* [2003] UKHL 12, [2004] AC 715, suggests that the Himalaya beneficiary is deemed to be a party to the contract contained in or evidenced by the bill of lading.

[263] At paras 20.53–58.

[264] See P North, 'Contract as a Tort Defence in the Conflict of Laws' (1977) 26 ICLQ 914. See also *Sayers v International Drilling Co NV* [1971] 1 WLR 1176.

XXII. OTHER MEANS OF GETTING AROUND PRIVITY OF CONTRACT

1. DOES THE GOVERNING LAW OF THE CONTRACT CONFER AN ENFORCEABLE BENEFIT UPON A THIRD PARTY? THE IMPACT OF THE CONTRACTS (RIGHTS OF THIRD PARTIES) ACT 1999

General Principles

The Himalaya clause, with its complexities, may arguably be dispensed **14.116** with in English domestic law as a result of the Contracts (Rights of Third Parties) Act 1999.[265] However, s 6(5)(a) of the Act states that the Act confers no rights on a third party in the case of 'a contract for the carriage of goods by sea'. Section 6(6)(a) states that this includes a contract 'contained in or evidenced by a bill of lading,[266] sea waybill or a corresponding electronic transaction'. It is unclear whether the special 'contract' between the non-carrying shipowner and the shipper is a contract of carriage as set out in the exclusionary language of the Act. It may, however, be evidenced by a bill of lading.[267]

However, it is ultimately a matter for the governing law of the contract to **14.117** determine whether a party might obtain an enforceable benefit under that contract.[268] That law should also determine whether a choice of law clause in a contract is capable of benefiting, or binding, a third party.[269]

The Position of Subsequent Holders of the Bill of Lading

There may be difficulties with subsequent holders of the bill of lading, **14.118** not parties to the original contract of carriage that created a benefit for the shipowner. In English law, it is unclear how these holders are to be bound by the 1999 Act's conferral of an enforceable benefit[270] against the original contracting parties.

More generally, the Carriage of Goods by Sea Act 1992 only imposes upon **14.119** transferees of the bill of lading the burdens of the contract of carriage.

---

[265] See further above, paras 13.252–254. See also R Stevens, 'The Contracts (Rights of Third Parties) Act 1999' (2004) 120 LQR 292.
[266] Which is in turn defined by s 6(7)(a).   [267] Though not contained therein.
[268] See further *Nisshin Shipping Co Ltd v Cleaves & Co Ltd* [2003] EWHC 2602 (Comm), [2004] 1 Lloyd's Rep 38, QBD (Comm).
[269] Arts 3(4), 8(1) and 10(1)(a) of the Rome Convention.
[270] In so far as the 1999 Act does confer enforceable benefits in the carriage context: see above, paras 14.116–117.

Section 5(1) appears to assume only one contract contained in or evidenced by the bill of lading.[271]

14.120 Once again, it must be for the law applicable to the bill of lading to determine the question of the effect of a clause protecting third parties upon the transferee of the bill of lading. If, according to that law, the transferee is subject to all obligations by which the original contracting parties were bound, then the third party may invoke the benefit against the transferee.

2. *The Pioneer Container*

14.121 Where a carrier entrusts the cargo to a sub-carrier, a case of sub-bailment may arise. The Privy Council in *The Pioneer Container*,[272] used the English[273] law of bailment to get around the privity of contract problem between the shipper and the sub-bailee. It held that where goods had been sub-bailed with the authority of the shipper, the obligation of the sub-bailee towards the shipper was that of a bailee for reward and the shipper could proceed directly against the sub-bailee under the law of bailment. The shipper is not normally bound by the terms of the contract between the bailee and sub-bailee, including a choice of law clause in that contract, as he is not privy to that contract. However, if the shipper consents to the carriage of the goods on terms agreed between the carrier and sub-carrier, he will be bound by a choice of law clause in the contract between carrier and sub-carrier. It is suggested that the law applicable to the contract of carriage should determine whether the shipper has agreed to be bound by any choice of law clause in the contract between the bailee and sub-bailee.[274]

14.122 It is suggested that the sub-bailee must also show that it has an enforceable right to invoke the choice of law clause in the contract between the bailee and sub-bailee against the shipper. The law applicable to the

---

[271] This same difficulty might arise with the continuing use of the Himalaya clause, as the special contract of exemption or limitation of liability was explained in *New Zealand Shipping Co Ltd v AM Satterthwaite & Co Ltd (The Eurymedon)* [1975] AC 154. In that case, Lord Wilberforce indicated that consignees (and one may add subsequent indorsees) might not be bound under the machinery of the old Bills of Lading Act 1855. He nevertheless was of the view that consignees would be bound by the Himalaya clause by virtue of the *Brandt v Liverpool* machinery (though this was said before the scope of such contracts was restricted).

[272] *Owners of Cargo Lately Laden on Board the KH Enterprise v Owners of the Pioneer Container (The Pioneer Container)* [1994] 2 AC 324, PC.

[273] This was regarded as identical to Hong Kong law. However, the bill of lading containing the foreign jurisdiction clause was governed by Chinese law and it is not altogether clear why the court did not have regard to this law.

[274] The shipper's position should not be adversely affected by a contract to which it was not party, so that the question of the shipper's consent cannot simply be determined by the law applicable to the contract between the bailee and sub-bailee. Compare Art 12(2) of the Rome Convention.

contract between the bailee and sub-bailee should determine this matter. This is consistent with Articles 3(4) and 8(1) of the Rome Convention, which subject the existence and validity of a choice of law clause to the law which would govern it if the choice were valid.

By contrast, the shipper will not normally be able to rely upon a choice of **14.123** law clause in its contract with the carrier against a bailee or sub-bailee who has not consented to that clause. Only if it could be shown that, according to the law specified in the contract of carriage, the bailee or sub-bailee had consented to the choice of law clause in the contract of carriage, could that bailee or sub-bailee be bound by the choice of law clause.[275] Even then, it is doubtful whether a bailee should be adversely affected by a choice of law clause in a contract of carriage to which it was not party. Accordingly, it must also be shown that, according to the law applicable to the contract of bailment, the bailee may be bound by a choice of law clause in the contract of carriage.

3. *BRANDT V LIVERPOOL CONTRACTS*

In *Brandt v Liverpool*:[276] 'Essentially, the courts invented a theory whereby **14.124** they implied a contract between the presenter of a bill (who fell within one of the gaps in s1 of the Bills of Lading Act 1855) and the carrier, under which a contract on the terms of the bill of lading came into existence when the carrier delivered the cargo in exchange for the holder presenting the bill and paying any freight'.[277] Our present concern is with the choice of law issues which such a contract might generate.

In *The Elli 2*,[278] the court assumed that a *Brandt v Liverpool* contract could **14.125** be subject to a foreign governing law.[279] Yet the courts have studiously refused to apply the putative applicable law of the contract to determine if such a contract arises by a foreign law.[280] Instead, they have applied English contractual doctrines to determine the existence of the contract. It has been suggested that a two stage test may be in operation.[281] First, the English court applies English law to determine if the contract arises. Second, if it does, it then determines its governing law by the choice of law rules in contract. However, there is no reason to do this. The Rome

---

[275] *The Forum Craftsman* [1985] 1 Lloyd's Rep 291, CA.
[276] *Brandt v Liverpool Brazil and River Plate Steam Navigation Co Ltd* [1924] 1 KB 175.
[277] Gaskell, 4.13.
[278] *Ilyssia Compañía Naviera SA v Ahmed Abdul-Qawi Bamaodah (The Elli 2)* [1985] 1 Lloyd's Rep 107.
[279] Sing, n 119 above, at 285–286.
[280] *The Aramis* [1989] 1 Lloyd's Rep 213 and *Mitsui & Co Ltd v Novorossiysk Shipping Co (The Gudermes)* [1993] 1 Lloyd's Rep 311.
[281] Sing, n 119 above, at 285–286.

Convention dictates that the *existence* and validity of a contract should be determined by the law which would govern it if it existed and were valid. Although the *Brandt v Liverpool* contract is separate from the contract of carriage and could be governed by a different law to that which governs the contract of carriage:[282] 'Delivery under a *Brandt v Liverpool* contract being almost by definition delivery on bill of lading terms ... there [is] a strong case for arguing that the *Brandt v Liverpool* contract ... [is] governed by the law governing the bill of lading'.[283] One might say that the law applicable to the contract of carriage is *putatively* applicable to a *Brandt v Liverpool* contract. It should accordingly simply be that law which determines whether the contract arises on the facts.[284]

XXIII. CONCLUSION

14.126   We have seen that the seller's duties under a CIF contract to transfer rights and duties to the buyer create particular choice of law problems, upon which authority is sparse. These problems are particularly acute in relation the transfer of the bill of lading. However, it has been suggested that if, by the putative governing law, the claim by the transferee of the bill of lading against the carrier is regarded as contractual, then the choice of law rules in contract should apply and determine whether the parties are bound by a choice of law clause in the bill of lading. It has also been suggested that the choice of law rules in contract should be applied specifically to the 'contract' between the transferee and the carrier and that it should not suffice to apply the choice of law rules to the original contract of carriage, in order to determine such questions as the transferee's consent to a choice of law clause, the formal validity of the 'contract' and the operation of mandatory rules pursuant to Article 3(3) of the Rome Convention.

---

[282] See *The St Joseph* [1933] P 119.

[283] F Reynolds, 'Proper Law of a Brandt *v* Liverpool Contract' [1985] LMCLQ 188, 189.

[284] Contrast ibid, 189. Reynolds goes on to suggest that the *Brandt v Liverpool* contract is a remedial device of English law and that: 'Since it corrects defects in the transmission of contracts governed by English law, there are "strong grounds" for applying it whatever the governing law of the contract of carriage'. It is suggested that this argument cannot be accepted. It is tantamount to treating the *Brandt v Liverpool* contract as an international mandatory rule of the forum simply because a foreign law would not recognize it. Neither commercial convenience, nor the need to escape the rigidity of privity of contract rules of a foreign law are sufficient to justify such an approach (see the discussion of mandatory rules, above, paras 14.97–103). Moreover, the argument that the *Brandt v Liverpool* contract is a remedial device of the forum lacks conviction. It clearly results in the existence of a (substantive) contractual relationship between the parties. It would be contrary to conflict of laws doctrine, as well as a recipe for forum shopping, for that contract to be governed by English law in an English court even where the contract of carriage was not governed by English law (and may have had no significant connection with England).

15

The Hague Sales Conventions of 1955 and 1986

I. INTRODUCTION

15.01 The Hague Conference on Private International Law has concluded a number of Conventions specific to the international sale of goods.[1] Of these, two lay down contractual choice of law rules for the international sale of goods. These Conventions seek to harmonize choice of law rules in the area, so as to bring predictability to international trading as to which

---

[1] The Hague Convention of 15 April 1958 on the Jurisdiction of the Selected Forum in the Case of International Sales of Goods was signed by Austria, Belgium, Germany and Greece but was not ratified by a single state. There is no prospect of this Convention ever entering into force. The Convention was drawn up in French and is available at http://hcch.e-vision.nl/index_en.php?act=conventions.text&cid=34. The Hague Convention of 15 April 1958 on the Law Governing Transfer of Title in International Sales of Goods was ratified only by Italy (and was signed, but not ratified, by Greece). It never entered into force. It was drawn up in French and is available at http://hcch.e-vision.nl/index_en.php?act =conventions.text&cid=32. There is an Explanatory Report by L Julliot de la Morandière on these Conventions: *Actes de la Septième session*, t I, 1951, 360. Given the age of these Conventions and their failure to enter into force, they are not discussed in this chapter. The latter Convention, is, however, considered below, paras 18.71–73.

state's law will be applied and so as to reduce incentives to forum shopping. It is upon these two Conventions that this chapter will focus.

The first Convention, concluded in 1955,[2] has proved reasonably success- **15.02** ful. It has entered into force and has been ratified in a number of states.[3] The later Convention of 1986[4] contains choice of law rules that are substantially more detailed than those of the 1955 Convention. However, the 1986 Convention has proved much less successful. It has never entered into force and has had very little impact. This may be explained by three factors: first, reservations as to the choice of law rules contained in the Convention itself; second, the advent of the Rome Convention and general satisfaction with the rules contained therein and their application to international sales; and third, the level of harmonization of substantive law brought about by the Vienna Convention, which reduces the importance for many states of adopting a sales specific choice of law Convention and which in any event itself contains some provisions on choice of law.[5]

It seems unlikely that either the 1955 or 1986 Hague Sales Convention will **15.03** be ratified by, or will enter into force in, the United Kingdom.[6] However, the 1955 Convention is important in international sales transactions where trial takes place in another state which applies that Convention.[7] The 1986 Convention can usefully be compared with the solutions reached under the Rome Convention in international sales cases to see

---

[2] The Hague Convention of 15 June 1955 on the Law Applicable to International Sales of Goods was drawn up in French, and is available at http://hcch.e-vision.nl/index_en.php?act=conventions.text&cid=31. The Explanatory Report is by L Julliot de la Morandière, ibid. There is an English translation of the Convention: see (1965) 74 Yale LJ 463.

[3] For a list of the states which have ratified the Convention, see below, para 15.10. The idea of a Convention in this area had been on the agenda for some considerable time. The possibility of a Convention on choice of law for sales of tangible goods was discussed at the Sixth Hague Conference in 1928. See M Pelichet, *Report on the Law Applicable to International Sales of Goods* (Preliminary Document No 1 of the Hague Conference, 1982).

[4] The Hague Convention of 22 December 1986 on the Law Applicable to Contracts for the International Sale of Goods, available at http://hcch.e-vision.nl/index_en.php?act=conventions.text&cid=61. There is an Explanatory Report by von Mehren: *Proceedings of the Extraordinary Session of October 1985*.

[5] See Ch 16.

[6] Accordingly, discussion of both Conventions in this chapter is limited to consideration of the key provisions. More detail should be sought by referring to the works mentioned in the course of discussion below. In particular, no attempt is made to consider in any detail the extensive case law of the Contracting States to the 1955 Convention on the application of that Convention.

[7] It may also be important in the law of jurisdiction. It may be necessary to apply the choice of law rules of the 1955 Convention in an EU Member State when applying Art 5(1) of the Brussels I Regulation and determining the place of performance of a contractual obligation (although, in the case of sale of goods, there is a provision autonomously laying down the place of performance). See above, paras 3.242–247 and 3.254.

whether the United Kingdom and other Member States might benefit from ratification of the former Convention.

II. THE INTER-RELATIONSHIP OF THE 1955 AND 1986 HAGUE SALES CONVENTIONS

15.04 Article 28 of the Hague Sales Convention 1986 states that where a state is party to the Hague Sales Convention 1955 and then consents to be bound by the 1986 Convention, the 1986 Convention shall replace the application of the 1955 Convention.[8] The Netherlands signed the 1955 Convention on 15 June 1955. It signed the 1986 Convention on 2 February 1990. However, since it never ratified the 1955 Convention, and since the 1986 Convention has not entered into force, no conflict has arisen.

III. THE INTER-RELATIONSHIP OF THE HAGUE SALES CONVENTIONS WITH THE ROME CONVENTION[9]

1. The Hague Sales Convention 1955 and the Rome Convention

15.05 As to the inter-relationship of the Rome and Hague Sales Conventions, Article 21 of the Rome Convention makes clear that it does not purport to prejudice the application of international conventions to which a Contracting State is, or becomes a party.[10] This means that where a state has enacted the Hague Sales Convention 1955 and also the Rome Convention,

---

[8] Assuming, of course, that it has brought the 1955 Convention into force in that state and that the 1986 Convention eventually comes into force.

[9] The inter-relationship of the Vienna and Hague Conventions is considered in below, paras 16.114–120. See also Ch 13 for discussion of the application under the Rome Convention of the law of a Contracting State to the Vienna Convention, the impact of the reservation permitted in Art 95 of the Vienna Convention and a direct choice of the Vienna Convention by the parties: paras 13.70–94.

[10] There is a consultation procedure for states which wish to become party to a multinational convention which is primarily concerned with providing choice of law rules in respect of any matter falling within the scope of the Rome Convention. This is laid down in Arts 23 and 24 of the Rome Convention. However: 'The [1986] Hague Sales Convention is excluded from this provision because its object is to revise a convention to which many European states are already a party . . .': C McLachlan, 'The New Hague Sales Convention and the Limits of the Choice of Law Process' (1986) 102 LQR 591, 612. Additionally, a Contracting State to the Rome Convention need not go through the consultation procedure if it wishes to ratify a Convention already in force in other Contracting States. R Plender and M Wilderspin, *The European Contracts Convention* (2nd edn, London: Sweet & Maxwell, 2001), 15 comment that '. . . the consultation procedure would not be obligatory if the United Kingdom wished to accede to the Hague Convention on the Law Applicable to International Sales of Goods of June 15, 1955'.

the former will apply to determine the choice of law rules applicable to a contract of sale falling within the scope of that Convention.[11] So, the 1955 Convention will continue to apply between Denmark, Finland, France, Italy and Sweden. Although both the 1955 and Rome Conventions are aimed at the harmonization of choice of law, paradoxically, the existence of both is 'capable of impeding to some degree the harmonisation of laws within the European Community'.[12]

2. THE HAGUE SALES CONVENTION 1986 AND THE ROME CONVENTION

However, matters are less clear with regard to the inter-relationship of the **15.06** Rome Convention and the Hague Sales Convention 1986, since the latter Convention also contains a give way provision. Article 22 states that:

(1) This Convention does not prevail over any convention or other international agreement which has been or may be entered into and which contains provisions determining the law applicable to contracts of sale, provided that such instrument applies only if the seller and buyer have their places of business in States Parties to that instrument.

(2) This Convention does not prevail over any international convention to which a Contracting State is, or becomes, a Party, regulating the choice of law in regard to any particular category of contracts of sale within the scope of this Convention.

Article 22(1) of the 1986 Convention is not triggered by the Rome Convention. This is because the Rome Convention is applicable even where the buyer and seller do not have their places of business in States Parties to that Convention. As to Article 22(2), it cannot be denied that the Rome Convention, although not sales specific, does contain choice of law provisions which cover, *inter alia*, contracts for the sale of goods. However, Article 22(2) refers to choice of law conventions regulating a *particular* category of sales contract. It does not refer to a convention which applies to *all* sales contracts; and still less to one which applies generally

---

[11] Of course, as C Saf, 'A Study of the Interplay between the Conventions Governing International Contracts of Sale' (www.cisg.law.pace.edu/cisg/text/saf90.html) points out, it would be possible for states to denounce the Hague Sales Convention 1955, as Belgium did. It might also be possible for Contracting States to both the 1955 Hague Convention and the Rome Convention to agree to apply the Rome Convention to disputes involving a choice solely between the application of the law of one of those states. Alternatively, it has been suggested by Plender and Wilderspin, n 10 above, 14 that under Art 30(3) and (4)(a) of the Vienna Convention on the Law of Treaties 1969, an earlier treaty should only be applied in so far as it is compatible with a later treaty. This would argue for the application of the Rome Convention to the exclusion of the Hague Sales Convention 1955. Nor would this conflict with Art 21 of the Rome Convention, which *permits* earlier legislation to be applied, but does not *require* it. However, the *intention* of the Rome Convention to give way to earlier or later Conventions dealing with choice of law rules for specific contracts is clear and it is suggested that the 1955 Convention should accordingly prevail.

[12] ibid, 13.

to international contracts. It is accordingly dubious whether Article 22 applies and purports to give way to the Rome Convention.

15.07 Even if Article 22 of the 1986 Convention did purport to give way to the Rome Convention, we have seen that Article 21 of the Rome Convention itself contains a give way provision. It is suggested that the general convention should yield to the more specific one. In other words, the Rome Convention lays down choice of law rules intended to apply to international contracts, save where there is an international instrument or convention which lays down specific rules for a particular type of contract. This seems correct in principle and accords with the fact that the Hague Sales Convention 1986 in turn yields to any more specific provisions relating to a particular type of contract of sale.[13]

15.08 However, it should be noted that Article 21(1)(a) of the 1986 Convention allows states to enter a reservation which will have the effect that they will only apply the Convention in the circumstances described in Article 1(a).[14] Article 1(a) applies the 1986 Convention 'between parties having their places of business in different States'. Suppose that a state had entered this reservation and was also party to the Rome Convention.[15] If the parties had their places of business in States A and B, there would be a possible conflict between the 1986 Convention and the Rome Convention and, for the reasons given above, the 1986 Convention should prevail. However, if the parties both had their places of business in State A, Article 1(a) of the 1986 Convention would not triggered. In such a circumstance, there would be no conflict with the Rome Convention. The Rome Convention would, accordingly, be applied.

3. Conclusion on the Inter-relationship of the Hague Sales Conventions and the Rome and Vienna Conventions

15.09 One might be forgiven for doubting whether the network of private international law and substantive law Conventions aimed at clarifying the law and rendering it more predictable to apply has entirely done its job.[16]

---

[13] As Art 22(2) of the Hague Sales Convention 1986 expressly states.

[14] See the discussion of the scope of the 1986 Convention, below, paras 15.68–75, esp paras 15.68–70.

[15] Until recently, there was no such state. The position has changed upon the accession of the Czech and Slovak Republics to the European Union in May 2004. Both states have made the reservation in Art 21(1)(a) of the 1986 Hague Convention. In the First Joint Declaration made on Signature of the Rome Convention, 19 June 1980, para II, the Signatory States '. . . express[ed] the view that any State which becomes a Member of the European Communities should accede to . . . [the Rome] Convention'. See also Art 28 of the Rome Convention; Plender, and Wilderspin, n 10 above, 18.

[16] See also McLachlan, n 10 above, at 610–615.

Certainly, their inter-relationship is a matter of complexity. Nevertheless, it may be helpful to draw together here the conclusions reached in this book on the inter-relationship of the Hague Conventions with each other, with the Rome Convention and with the Vienna Convention.[17]

(1) Where the Hague Sales Convention 1955 is in force in a particular state and it enacts the Hague Sales Convention 1986, the latter will prevail (if and when it enters into force) and the 1955 Convention will cease to be applicable in that state.

(2) Where a state is party to the Rome Convention and to the Hague Sales Convention 1955, the latter should prevail. Where a state is party to the Rome Convention and to the Hague Sales Convention 1986, the latter should prevail where there is a conflict between the two.[18]

(3) We shall see in Chapter 16 that the Vienna Convention and Hague Sales Convention 1986 appear to suggest that they operate without prejudice to each other.[19] The Hague Sales Convention 1986 says so expressly. This must be taken to mean that in so far as the Vienna Convention contains private international law provisions which conflict with the 1986 Convention, the latter should give way. However, even if the Vienna Convention can be said to contain conflicts rules, most notably in Article 1(1)(a), the Vienna Convention certainly does not contain detailed private international law rules. It is suggested that where the conditions of that Article are satisfied, but the parties choose the law of a non-Contracting State to the Convention, their choice of law should be upheld and that this is sanctioned by Article 6 of the Vienna Convention. However, where they make no choice of law, the rules of the Vienna Convention should be applied in Contracting States to that Convention, even if the rules of the Hague Sales Convention 1986 point to the application of a different law. It is suggested[20] that the same approach should be adopted with regard to the Hague Sales Convention 1955 and that where the conditions of Article 1(1)(a) of the Vienna Convention are met, an express choice of the law of a non-Contracting State to the Vienna Convention should be respected. However, where there is no such choice, the position is less clear. It is tentatively suggested that the Vienna Convention's substantive rules should be applied, even if the private international

---

[17] The last of which is discussed below, paras 16.114–120.

[18] There would be no conflict between the two if a state had entered the reservation in Art 21(1)(a) of the 1986 Convention and the parties both had their places of business in the same state. The Rome Convention would be applicable and the 1986 Convention would not be. See above, para 15.08.

[19] At paras 16.118–120.

[20] Albeit more tentatively.

law rules of the Hague Sales Convention 1955 suggest that the law of a non-Contracting State to the Vienna Convention is applicable.[21]

(4) The Vienna Convention periodically refers to the need to apply rules of private international law, most notably in determining the sphere of application of the Convention under Article 1(1)(b). The Hague Sales Convention 1955 should determine those rules of private international law in states where it is in force.[22] The Hague Sales Convention 1986 should be applied, if and when it enters into force, in states where it is enacted.[23]

IV. THE HAGUE SALES CONVENTION 1955[24]

1. CONTRACTING STATES

15.10 To date, the 1955 Convention has undoubtedly achieved much more success than its 1986 counterpart. That said, its impact is still relatively modest. It first came into force on 1 September 1964. It is presently in

---

[21] The give way provision of Art 90 of the Vienna Convention does not apply; the Hague Convention 1955 is simply silent on the matter. The Vienna Convention's position might be considered to be a more reflective attempt to consider its inter-relationship with other Conventions and it might be inferred that, where its give way provision is not triggered, the Vienna Convention should indeed prevail. But the position with respect to the 1955 Convention cannot be stated with confidence because neither the 1955 Convention nor the Vienna Convention gives way to the other: see below, paras 16.114–117.

[22] An example of where the rules of the Hague Sales Convention 1955 were invoked to determine whether the Vienna Convention applied by virtue of Art 1(1)(b) of the latter Convention can be found in the decision of the French Cour d'appel de Colmar in *Pelliculest v Morton International*, decision of 24 October 2000 (www.cisg.law.pace.edu/cases/001024f1.html).

[23] In England, where neither of the Hague Sales Conventions has been signed, still less brought into force, the Rome Convention should be applied to determine the matters of private international law referred to in the Vienna Convention.

[24] For discussion of the Convention, see K Boele-Woelki, 'Convention sur la Loi Applicable aux Ventes à Caractère International d'Objets Mobiliers Corporels, du 15 Juin 1955' in M Sumampouw (ed), *Les Nouvelles Conventions de la Haye* (Dordrecht: Martinus Nijhoff, 1984) 15; M Chesterman, 'Choice of Law Aspects of Liens and Similar Claims in International Sale of Goods' (1973) 22 ICLQ 213; G Droz, 'Entrée en Vigueur de la Convention sur la Loi Applicable aux Ventes à Caractère International d'Objets Mobiliers Corporels' [1964] Revue Critique de Droit International Privé 663; J Foyer, 'La Convention de La Haye du 15 Juin 1955' [1990] Revue Critique de Droit International Privé 712; L Frédéricq, 'La Vente en Droit International Privé (Quelques Conventions Récentes)' (1958) 93-I Recueil des Cours de l'Académie de Droit International de La Haye 1; D Jacobson, 'The International Sale of Goods' (1954) 3 ICLQ 659; P Kahn, 'La Convention de La Haye sur la Loi Applicable aux Ventes à Caractère International d'Objets Mobiliers Corporels'' [1966] Journal du Droit International 301; O Lando, 'The 1955 and 1985 Hague Conventions on the Law Applicable to the International Sale of Goods' [1993] 1/2 Rabels Zeitschrift für Ausländisches und Internationales Privatrecht 155. A detailed and regularly updated bibliography to the 1955 Convention can be found at http://hcch.e-vision.nl/index_en.php?act=conventions.publications&dtid=1&cid=31. See also the Official Report by Julliot de la Morandière, *Actes de la Septième session*, t I, 1951, 360.

force[25] in Denmark,[26] Finland,[27] France,[28] Italy,[29] Niger,[30] Norway,[31] Sweden[32] and Switzerland.[33] It has also been signed, but not ratified, in Luxembourg,[34] the Netherlands[35] and Spain.[36] It was brought into force but later denounced in Belgium.[37]

2. SCOPE

Article 1 states that the Convention applies to 'international sales of **15.11** goods'.[38] No definition as such is provided of this term, although the Article does go on to mention certain types of contract which fall inside and outside the scope of the Convention.

'Goods'

Sales of securities, as well as sales of ships, of registered boats and aircraft **15.12** are excluded from the scope of the Convention.[39] Also excluded are 'sales upon judicial order or by way of execution'.[40] Beyond that, it is

---

[25] Art 10 provides that the Convention shall apply in the metropolitan territories of a ratifying state, but that it shall only apply to its other territories if it expressly declares this to be the case and gives due notification in accordance with the requirements of that Art.

[26] Signed on 23 October 1956; ratified on 3 July 1964; brought into force on 1 September 1964.

[27] Signed on 12 April 1957; ratified on 3 July 1964; brought into force on 1 September 1964.

[28] Signed on 25 July 1955; ratified on 30 July 1963; brought into force on 1 September 1964.

[29] Signed on 13 April 1956; ratified on 17 March 1958; brought into force on 1 September 1964.

[30] Accession on 11 October 1971; brought into force on 10 December 1971. Niger is the only non-Member State of the Hague Conference on Private International Law to have signed the Convention and to have brought it into force.

[31] Signed on 24 October 1956; ratified on 3 July 1964; brought into force on 1 September 1964.

[32] Signed on 23 October 1956; ratified on 8 July 1964; brought into force on 6 September 1964.

[33] Signed on 20 September 1971; ratified on 29 August 1972; brought into force on 27 October 1972.

[34] Signed on 15 June 1955.

[35] Signed on 15 June 1955. However, it should be noted that Dutch courts have, on occasions pre-dating the entry into force of the Rome Convention, referred to provisions of the 1955 Convention and treated them as accurately representing the law in the Netherlands. They have even extended the 1955 Convention's rules to other types of contract. See the decisions of the court in Arnhem of 10 January 1980; Asser 12.198 and of 14 August 1980; Asser 12.343, both summarized by Boele-Woelki, n 24 above, at 18–19.

[36] Signed on 12 April 1957.

[37] Signed on 1 August 1955; ratified on 29 October 1962; brought into force on 1 September 1964; denounced pursuant to Art 12 on 19 February 1999, with effect from 1 September 1999.

[38] See also the discussion above, paras 1.04–15 and 12.18–20.

[39] Art 1(2).   [40] ibid.

unclear what 'goods' are.[41] There is, for example, no express exclusion of certain types of contract expressly excluded in the Vienna Convention. That Convention excludes, *inter alia*, the sale of stocks, shares, negotiable instruments and money.[42] Section 61(1) of the Sale of Goods Act 1979 defines goods as including all personal chattels save choses in action and money.[43]

15.13 In the absence of further elucidation, three approaches are possible: (i) that the Convention applies to all sales save those items specifically excluded by Article 1; (ii) that an autonomous meaning of the word 'goods' is to be given; (iii) that each state should apply its own understanding of what a sale of 'goods' is.[44]

15.14 Option (i) must be rejected. The Convention must clearly exclude sales of, for example, land, even though this is not expressly excluded. It also almost certainly excludes sales of choses in action and money, which are very unlikely to be understood in any legal system as goods. Option (ii) is the most attractive, since it ensures the uniform application of the Convention. If one is to harmonize choice of law rules in a given area, it makes sense that one should also harmonize the scope of application of those rules, not least to control forum shopping. The difficulty, of course, is the absence of established criteria for defining 'goods'. Option (iii) is accordingly the most realistic. In principle, it appears objectionable, in that it may lead to a different scope of application of the Convention between Contracting States. In practice, those states which have adopted the Vienna Convention are likely to adopt a very similar understanding of what 'goods' are; those which have not should be encouraged to adopt an understanding of 'goods' for the purposes of private international law, rather than that used in purely domestic scenarios in that state, both because this is likely to lead to greater uniformity of application and because it seems inappropriate to adopt too inward looking an approach to classification of a contract which may very well turn out not to be governed by the law of the forum. In practice, this is today likely to mean

---

[41] In *SA Compagnie Française BK v Hatzatz Haedumin* [1996] IL Pr 569, the Paris Court of Appeal applied the 1955 Convention to a sale of a crushing and sifting installation for the production of sand. It did so simply 'in the absence of evidence as to whether the installation supplied was an immovable by nature' (at 571). In other words, the court assumed that, in case of doubt, it would apply the 1955 Convention and that the contract should be treated as one for the sale of goods.

[42] Art 2 of the Vienna Convention. Contracts for the sale of electricity are also excluded.

[43] See further Bridge, *The Sale of Goods*, 21–31. Note that the UK Sale of Goods Act 1979 does cover the sale of ships and aircraft: ibid, 22.

[44] That understanding might itself differ depending upon whether the state uses its purely domestic understanding of 'goods' or whether it adopts a special private international law definition.

the application of the Convention to those contracts of the type falling within the scope of the Vienna Convention.

'Sale'

The Convention also fails to explain what the word 'sale' means.[45] Section **15.15** 2(1) of the UK Sale of Goods Act 1979 describes this as the process by which 'the seller transfers or agrees to transfer the property in the goods for money consideration called the price'. Since it is the very essence of a sale contract that property passes from the buyer to the seller, the transfer of property element is likely to be the defining factor under any Convention, including the Hague Sales Convention 1955, in determining what constitutes a sale.

Matters are a shade more complex where the contract is for the delivery of **15.16** goods which first have to be manufactured or produced.[46] The question is whether the sale itself can any longer be considered the essence of the contract. This time, however, the 1955 Convention provides an answer: namely that the contract still falls within the scope of the Convention as long as the party who is to deliver the goods is to provide the raw materials for the manufacture or production.[47] If so, it can be said that he is passing property in those materials to the buyer, albeit in a new form. Hence, if a party agrees to manufacture machinery using its own raw materials, and undertakes to deliver the machinery to the buyer, the contract is one for the 'sale' of goods, within the meaning of the 1955 Convention.

'Contract'

It is also unclear what the meaning of the word 'contract' is for Conven- **15.17** tion purposes. Different states will obviously have different views as to what constitutes a contract and a private international law meaning of 'contract' needs to be given, in order to ensure the uniform application of the Convention. At common law,[48] English private international law recognized as a contract a voluntary agreement governed by Italian law that was unsupported by consideration.[49] Under the Brussels I Regulation, a matter relating to contract has been defined[50] as 'an undertaking freely

---

[45] Compare the position under the Vienna Convention, below, paras 16.84–90.
[46] Compare the position under the Vienna Convention, below, paras 16.91–94.
[47] Art 1(3).
[48] See also the discussion of the words 'contractual obligation' in Art 1 of the Rome Convention, considered above, paras 13.14–17.
[49] The agreement was valid by Italian law: *Re Bonacina* [1912] 2 Ch 394.
[50] For the purposes of Art 5(1) of the Regulation.

entered into by one party in relation to another'.[51] It is likely under the 1955 Convention also that the key elements of a contract are (i) the voluntary agreement to undertake an obligation; and (ii) to a specific, foreseeable person.[52] This is supported by the fact that the Convention expressly excludes 'involuntary' sales upon judicial order of by way of execution.

15.18 It should be noted that there is no provision equivalent to that in the Vienna Convention that the private international law rules must lead to the application of the law of a Contracting State to the Convention.[53] Rather, as with the Rome Convention,[54] the 1955 Convention applies regardless of the law governing the contract.

3. 'INTERNATIONAL' SALES

15.19 The Convention applies only to 'international' sales contracts. This is not defined in a positive way, but the Convention does state[55] what would be insufficient to render a contract 'international' for these purposes. If A, a seller resident in France, contracts to sell goods to B, a buyer resident in France, and the goods are to be delivered from Paris to Marseilles, the contract is clearly a domestic one. But what if the contract contains a clause stating that it shall be subject to the law of England? It appears that under the Rome Convention, this is enough to bring the matter within its scope as creating a choice between the laws of different countries within the meaning of Article 1(1).[56] However, under the Hague Sales Convention 1955 it is expressly provided that the mere choice of a foreign law by the parties does not render the contract 'international'. Moreover, if the facts had been as described above but the contract had instead contained an exclusive jurisdiction clause for a country other than France, this is again insufficient to bring the matter within the scope of the 1955 Convention. Presumably, the same would be true if the contract contained both a choice of law and a jurisdiction clause. This is because the Convention essentially adopts the philosophy that the parties cannot themselves create a conflict of laws in respect of what is otherwise a domestic contract. The 'international' element must come from the objective elements

---

[51] Case C-26/91 *Jacob Handte GmbH v Traitements Mécano-Chimiques des Surfaces* [1992] ECR I-3967, para 15. See the discussion above, paras 3.63–82.

[52] Although it is not certain that this second requirement will be imposed. It may suffice that the obligation is undertaken voluntarily. See the discussion of Art 1(1) of the Rome Convention above, paras 13.17 and 14.04–05.

[53] Art 1(b) of the Vienna Convention; although, of course, the matter might otherwise fall within the scope of the Vienna Convention under Art 1(a).

[54] Art 2 of the Rome Convention, discussed above, para 13.06.

[55] Art 1(4) of the 1955 Convention.   [56] Discussed above, para 13.18.

of the contract. So, if the purchase price were to be payable in pounds sterling, or the goods to be delivered from Milan to Marseilles, the contract would fall within the scope of the Convention.

It is not clear whether there need to be *substantial* objective connections to more than one state before the Convention applies, or whether *any* degree of objective connections to more than one state will suffice. In principle, it seems that some substantial connection should be required; otherwise, the restriction of the Convention to genuinely international sales means little. In the above example, the mere fact that the parties happened to conclude the contract in London does not obviously make a contract between two French residents for sale and delivery within France an international one. However, the fact that the goods are to be delivered, say, from Paris to London almost certainly means that another state, England, has a significant, enduring connection to the contract. Accordingly, it is suggested that the Convention requires there to be a significant objective connection of the contract to more than one state. Perhaps the most obvious way for this to be supplied would be where the contracting parties are habitually resident in different states. **15.20**

4. EXCLUSIONS

The Convention at no point positively states its scope of application. It does, however, define its limits in Article 5. None of these exclusions would appear to be particularly controversial or surprising, **15.21**

The first exclusion is the capacity of the parties.[57] In other words, rules which restrict the ability of a particular group of persons, such as children or the mentally handicapped, to enter into a contract which persons at large may validly conclude are outside the Convention's scope. There is an understandable reluctance to allow questions of capacity to be determined by the law chosen by the parties to govern a contract.[58] Capacity is not something which parties should be able to confer upon themselves by selection of an appropriate law. The whole point about restrictions on age, **15.22**

---

[57] This includes both natural persons (individuals) and legal persons (corporate entities).

[58] The capacity of natural persons is excluded from the scope of the Rome Convention by Art 1(2)(a) (subject to a limited provision in Art 11; discussed above, paras 13.27–28). English common law authority shows considerable reluctance to allow the law chosen by the parties to govern this question. See, e.g. *Sottomayor v De Barros (No 1)* (1877) 3 PD 1, 5; *Male v Roberto* (1800) 3 Esp 163; *Bodley Head Ltd v Flegon* [1972] 1 WLR 680. Rule 181(1) in Dicey and Morris, 1271–1272 reads thus: 'The capacity of an individual to enter into a contract is governed by the law of the country with which the contract is most closely connected or by the law of his domicile or residence: (a) If he has capacity to contract by the law with which the contract is most closely connected, the contract will (*semble*) be valid so far as capacity is concerned. (b) If he has capacity to contract by the law of his domicile and residence, the contract will (*semble*) be valid so far as capacity is concerned.' See the discussion above, paras 13.24–28.

mental capacity etc is that they have a mandatory characteristic bound up with the parties' status, or at least with the law with which the contract has, objectively, its closest connection.

15.23 The second exclusion concerns the formal validity of the contract. On one view, formal validity is more naturally to be seen as a procedural matter.[59] In any event, formality rules, which may be designed to protect one or both parties by ensuring their genuine consent, are not obviously ones which the parties should be able to avoid by choosing a particular law to govern the contract.

15.24 The third exclusion concerns the transfer of ownership.[60] There is then a rider that the obligations of the parties, especially those concerning the passing of risk, are subject to the applicable law under the Convention.[61] However, the passing of risk is essentially a personal matter;[62] the passing of ownership is an altogether different matter. Although it is, of course, possible that risk will pass when ownership passes, the latter is clearly not an issue which concerns contractual obligations. It accords to the claimant a right which may endure against third parties and should normally be determined by the law of the situs.

15.25 It is less clear what should happen where a contract of sale contains a retention of title clause. Since this is a clause which affects ownership, and the transfer of ownership is outside the scope of the Convention, it is tempting to think that the Convention has nothing to say about the validity or effect of such clauses. However, it is suggested that this is true only in part. The *effect* of the retention of title clause must be a matter for the law of the situs, since it is in any view a property question.[63] However, no state is going to consider the clause to be effective to prevent property from passing unless the clause is a valid term of the contract. Since this is solely a question about the validity of a contractual term, it is suggested that the 1955 Convention should apply to determine this matter. In other

---

[59] *Leroux v Brown* (1852) 12 CB 801; but not under Art 9 of the Rome Convention, where the issue is treated as a substantive one: above, paras 13.256–263.

[60] The Hague Convention of 15 April 1958 on the Law Governing Transfer of Title in International Sales of Goods was ratified only by Italy (and was signed, but not ratified, by Greece). It never entered into force. See below, paras 18.71–73.

[61] Nothing is said of property rights short of ownership, such as a charge or the right to possession. As these are essentially proprietary, and not contractual, matters, it is suggested that the 1955 Convention does not apply to them. See also the discussion of Art 5(c) of the 1986 Sales Convention, below, paras 15.78–80.

[62] See above, paras 13.196–200.

[63] Compare *Goetschius v Brightman* 245 NY 186 (1927); *Century Credit Corp v Richard* (1962) 34 DLR (2d) 291; *Zahnrad Fabrik Passau GmbH v Terex Ltd* 1986 SLT 84; see also Cheshire and North, 945–947. But contrast Art 12(e) of the 1986 Sales Convention, discussed below, paras 15.112–115.

words, a two stage test should operated: first, is the clause valid according to the applicable law of the contract, as determined by the 1955 Convention; second, if so, is the clause effective to prevent property from passing to the buyer, according to the law of the situs?

The final matter excluded from the Convention is the effect of the sale on **15.26** third parties. One would clearly not expect a Convention that regulates the contractual relationship between buyer and seller to be capable of affecting the position of third parties. Certainly, it cannot affect issues of title to property, which are not contractual matters at all. However, it should also not affect typical related parties in the sale transaction. Hence, the Convention has nothing to say on the contract of carriage, or the payment obligations which might arise and the relationship of the parties to issuing or confirming banks. Perhaps the only reservation is where, according to the law governing the contract of sale, the contractual rights of the seller against the carrier are assigned to the buyer. However, the rights which parties have against the carrier are matters which relate to the contract of carriage and not to the contract of sale. Accordingly, it must be the law governing the contract of carriage, not the law governing the contract of sale, which determines whether the buyer can sue the carrier in contract.[64]

It should be noted that the list of exclusions is nowhere near as broad as **15.27** that contained in Article 1 of the Rome Convention. There is, for instance, no express exclusion of matters of evidence or procedure; nor is the validity of a jurisdiction clause expressly excluded. It is difficult to believe that either is intended to be regulated entirely by the 1955 Convention. General conflicts principles would dictate that matters of procedure would not be subject to choice of law principles. If necessary, a court might be willing to find that the application of procedural rules of a foreign state offends its public policy.[65] As to jurisdiction clauses, it may be said that most issues concerning their validity are questions of form[66] and matters of form are expressly excluded from the 1955 Convention. But as to questions of *material* validity, such as whether the clause really was agreed upon and incorporated into the contract by the parties, or whether it is the result of a mistake, duress or undue influence, it would appear that the Convention applies. This means that the law putatively

---

[64] Of course, the law governing the contract of carriage will insist that the contract of sale is valid according to its governing law. If it is, the law governing the contract of carriage should decide what rights the buyer has against the carrier. See generally Ch 14, esp paras 14.49–56, 14.64–65.

[65] Pursuant to Art 6.

[66] At least in the Brussels regime under Art 23 of the Brussels I Regulation; see above, paras 3.22–40, 3.44–59.

applicable to the contract will determine the substantive validity of the jurisdiction or arbitration clause.

5. THE CHOICE OF LAW RULES

Express or Implied Choice

General rule; exclusion of renvoi

15.28 Article 2 states that the domestic law of the country designated by the parties shall apply.[67] The reference to 'domestic' law excludes application of the doctrine of renvoi. So, if X and Y agree that the law of Utopia should govern a contract of sale, the fact that a Utopian judge would refuse to accept the choice of law and would instead apply Ruritanian law, as the law of the place of contracting, is ignored and Utopian law should be applied under the Convention.

Choice of the Vienna Convention

15.29 It is not clear what should happen if the parties have their habitual residences in different states, neither of which is party to the Vienna Convention, but choose simply 'the rules of the Vienna Convention' to govern the contract. The Vienna Convention is clearly part of the substantive sales law of very many Contracting State and it might seem churlish to refuse to give effect to such a choice.[68] However, the choice might be viewed as objectionable, since it is not the choice of the law of a given state as such. It is a body of rules which is incorporated as part of the legal system of a Contracting State. The issue is discussed further elsewhere,[69] where it is suggested that a choice of the Vienna Convention should be regarded as the incorporation by reference of the terms of the Convention into the contract, at least where the law which would otherwise have governed the contract permits the parties to exclude its provisions.

Choice of the law of a state which is party to the Vienna Convention

15.30 Suppose that the buyer and seller have their places of business in states which are party to the Hague Sales Convention 1955, but not to the

---

[67] Art 2(2) refers to a choice 'contained in an express clause'. This might suggest that the clause needs to be contained in writing. However, the matter is not certain from the wording of the provision. Moreover, Art 5(2) states that the Convention does not apply to 'the form of the contract'. It may accordingly be that the choice can be made orally, provided that it was the product of consent between the parties.

[68] But the choice of the *lex mercatoria* is much more controversial, since this is not the law of any legal system. It is very doubtful whether such a choice may be made under the Hague Sales Convention 1955. Art 2 refers to 'the domestic law *of the country* designated by the Contracting Parties' (emphasis added); see also the references to the domestic law of a country in Arts 3 and 4. See further the discussion of Art 3(1) of the Rome Convention, above, paras 13.65–66.

[69] See the discussion of Art 3(1) of the Rome Convention, above, paras 13.86–92.

Vienna Convention. They choose the law of a state that is party to the Vienna Convention to govern their contract. Which rules should the forum apply: those of the Vienna Convention or the domestic rules of the state identified?[70] The Vienna Convention indicates that it should apply in such circumstances, pursuant to Article 1(1)(b), because the rules of private international law lead to the law of a State Party to the Vienna Convention.[71] The forum should apply the Vienna Convention, as it is simply giving effect to the law of the state whose law is applicable by virtue of the choice of law rules in the Hague Sales Convention 1955.[72]

Implied choice of law

The choice must be 'contained in an express clause, or unambiguously **15.31** result from the provisions of the contract'.[73] This is very close to the requirements in the Rome Convention that the choice be either express or implied to the standard of reasonable certainty.[74] However, the 1955 Convention seems to be even stricter in its requirements for an implied choice. The standard of 'unambiguous' choice may be stronger than that of 'reasonable certainty'.[75] The 1955 Convention requires that an implied choice result from the contract itself.[76] In contrast, Article 3(1) of the Rome Convention also lets the choice be determined by 'the circumstances of

---

[70] See McLachlan, n 10 above, at 614, who discusses the matter with regard to the Hague Sales Convention 1986.

[71] If the state whose law is identified has entered a reservation under Art 95 (as the US, amongst others, has done) and does not apply Art 1(1)(b) of the Vienna Convention, it could be argued that the domestic law of the state identified should be applied. However, Bridge, *The International Sale of Goods*, 66–67, argues that the question turns upon whether the forum is itself party to the Vienna Convention and whether *it* has made the reservation in Art 95 of the Vienna Convention. If it not a party to the Vienna Convention, or if it is a party thereto but has made the reservation in Art 95, then it should apply the domestic law of the state identified. If it is a party to the Vienna Convention and has not made the reservation, then it is bound to apply the Vienna Convention whenever its own private international law rules point to *the law of a Contracting State* (regardless of whether that Contracting State would itself apply the Vienna Convention on the facts). Accordingly, it should apply the rules of the Vienna Convention. See also P Winship, 'Private International Law and the U.N. Sales Convention' (1988) Cornell Intl LJ 487; cf J Honnold, *Uniform Law for International Sales under the 1980 United Nations Convention* (2nd edn, Deventer: Kluwer, 1990), 84–94. See further above, paras 13.83–85.

[72] It is true that the 1955 Convention refers to the domestic law of the state identified (Art 2(1)). However, this is principally to exclude the doctrine of renvoi, rather than to insist on the application of the law identified as it would be applied if the facts were entirely domestic to the state in question.

[73] Art 2(2) of the 1955 Convention.

[74] Art 3(1) of the Rome Convention. See above, paras 13.44–55.

[75] This is certainly the view of Plender and Wilderspin, n 10 above, 93.

[76] But for an example of an implied choice of law under the Convention, see the Belgian decision, Justice de Paix de Zaventem, 21 May 1982; RW 1982–83, 662, summarized by Boele-Woelki, n 24 above, at 17.

the case'. This would appear to suggest that the 1955 Convention allows reliance to be placed upon the existence of a jurisdiction or arbitration clause, or upon the use of a standard form contract. However, it would also suggest that a previous course of dealing between the same parties in which a choice of law clause had been contained in the contract would not be relevant.[77]

15.32 It would appear that objective factors would be irrelevant to determining an implied choice. So, the place of conclusion, the place of performance, the currency and such matters cannot be said unambiguously to determine that the parties designated a particular law to govern the contract.

No objective connection to the chosen law required

15.33 There is no requirement that the chosen law have a substantial connection to the contract. This might appear surprising, as it seems to extend party autonomy very far and to permit a choice of law motivated by nothing more than evasion. The response would be that the requirement that the contract should be 'international' in the first place[78] militates against the worst excesses of choice of law shopping. That said, there is nothing to prevent, for example, a Danish seller who enters into a contract with a Norwegian buyer from choosing the law of a third state, such as Sweden, to govern the contract.

Consent to the Choice of Law Clause

15.34 Article 2(3) states that: 'Conditions affecting the consent of the parties to the law declared applicable shall be determined by such law'. In other words, if it is alleged that the parties chose Utopian law to govern the contract, but one party claims that he did not agree to that term of the contract, or, indeed, that he did not agree to the whole contract, of which the choice of law clause is but one term, Utopian law shall determine whether the choice of law was made.

15.35 This raises the familiar 'bootstraps' objection that until one knows whether a valid contract exists and what law governs it, there can be no logical reason to invoke the law which *might* apply if there is indeed a contract governed by that law. However, application of Utopian law can be justified as the *putative* applicable law of the contract and pragmatism, if nothing else, strongly favours this approach.[79]

---

[77] A view shared by Plender and Wilderspin, n 10 above, at 14.
[78] Art 1(4), discussed above, paras 15.19–20.
[79] See the discussion of Arts 8(1) and (2) of the Rome Convention above, paras 13.143–155.

Article 2 speaks only of the *consent* of the parties. Presumably, this covers **15.36** both allegations that one party did not agree to that term of the contract *at all* and also allegations that the consent was in some way deficient, because, for example, one or both parties had made a mistake, or the contract was induced by duress or undue influence.

It is less clear immediately what should happen if the alleged defect in **15.37** consent is a formality requirement of a given law. The Convention does not lay down rules of formalities, save in the limited respect that it appears to suggest that an express choice of law clause should be in writing[80] and an implied choice is to be determined from the provisions of the contract itself.[81] However, Article 5(2) states that the Convention does not apply to 'the form of the contract'. Accordingly, it can be determined that Article 2 refers only to questions concerning the essential validity of the consent.

Applicable Law in the Absence of Choice; General Rule

Article 3(1) provides that, in the absence of choice, the governing law shall **15.38** be the domestic law of the state in which the vendor has his habitual residence[82] at the time when he receives the order.[83] If the order is received by an establishment of the vendor, the governing law is the domestic law of the state where the establishment is situated.

The reference to the habitual residence of the vendor is a forerunner of **15.39** Article 4(2) of the Rome Convention and the doctrine of characteristic performance. It has the important effect that a vendor selling his goods across the globe is not required to satisfy the standards laid down in the contract law of each state in which the goods are to be sold. As long as he complies with the domestic law of his 'home' state, that will suffice. Today, within the European Union, any other approach would be a potentially serious impediment to the free movement of goods.[84]

---

[80] Although the phrasing is not entirely clear. Art 2(2) of the 1955 Convention states that the '. . . designation must be contained in an express clause . . .'.

[81] Although, presumably, this contract may be an oral one, if its provisions can be clearly ascertained.

[82] The term 'habitual residence' is not defined.

[83] See the summaries by Boele-Woelki, n 24 above, at 15–17, of the Finnish decision of Court of Appeal of Helsinki, 3 February 1982/997 and the Dutch decisions of the courts of Arnhem of 7 February 1980; Asser 12.1.96 and Breda, 14 September 1982; NIPR 1983 nr 208.

[84] In some cases, Dutch courts have used the law specified by Art 3 of the Convention to determine where the place of performance of a contractual obligation is for the purposes of Art 5(1) of the Brussels Convention: the Hof's-Hertogenbosch, decision of 27 March 1979; NJ 1980, 512 and court of Arnhem, 21 February 1980; Asser 12.225, both considered by

The Role of the Law of the Buyer's Habitual Residence

15.40 Article 3(2) contains a sting in the tail. If the order of the buyer was received by the vendor in the state where the buyer is habitually resident, or where the buyer has an establishment that gave the order, that state's law shall instead apply.[85] This will also be the case if the order was received there by the vendor's representative, agent or commercial traveller.[86] In *SA Compagnie Française BK v Hatzatz Haedumin*,[87] the Paris Court of Appeal was faced with a contract of sale between a French seller and an Israeli buyer. In determining whether to enforce an Israeli judgment in France, the court ruled that it would not do so unless the Israeli court had reached its decision by applying the same law on the merits that a French court would have applied had the case been heard in France. That meant that it had to have regard to the Hague Sales Convention 1955. The contract contained no choice of law clause. It had been concluded in Israel between the buyer, an engineer of the French company and a company representing the French company in Israel. The court ruled that, pursuant to Article 3(2), Israeli law governed the contract.

15.41 In one sense, Article 3(2) might be seen as an early form of consumer protection. It gives the buyer the benefit of his 'home' law in circumstances where the goods are ordered in his own state. However, the rule is indiscriminate, in the sense that it will apply to commercial sales as much as it does to consumer sales. Furthermore, the rules stated in Article 3 are not subject to a flexible exception on the basis that the contract clearly has an objectively closer connection to another state.

15.42 The result is that the place of receipt is given very great and, arguably, disproportionate importance. This might be thought regrettable, but at

Boele-Woelki, ibid, at 19–20. In *San Carlo Gruppo Alimentaire SpA v SNC Vico* [1996] IL Pr 493, the French Cour de cassation had to determine the place of performance of the payment obligation under a sales contract for the purposes of Art 5(1) of the Brussels Convention. In order to do so, it first had to work out the applicable law, in the absence of choice, of a contract between a seller resident in France and a purchaser resident in Italy. In accordance with Art 3(1) of the Hague Sales Convention 1955, it found that French law governed the contract. According to French law, payment was due at the domicile of the debtor. See also *Anton Huber GmbH v Polyspace SA* [2003] IL Pr 10 at 203, Cour de Cassation. See further above, paras 3.175–297, esp paras 3.242–247 and 3.254, on the identification of the place of performance for the purposes of Art 5(1) of the Brussels I Regulation.

[85] This provision was the inspiration for the second of the alternative pre-conditions for the application of the consumer contracts provisions contained in Art 5 of the Rome Convention.

[86] See *Anton Huber GmbH v Polyspace SA* [2003] IL Pr 10 at 203, Cour de cassation.

[87] [1996] IL Pr 569.

least clear cut. The fact that Articles 3(1) and (2) are stated as rules of law, rather than rebuttable presumptions, suggests that there is a greater level of certainty in these rules than in their Rome Convention counterparts.[88] However, this assumes that the place of 'receipt' of the 'order' will be easy to determine. That would not necessarily have been the case in 1955, since different laws might take differing views as to whether what the buyer has sent constitutes an 'order', as opposed to what English law would call a mere invitation to treat. That would appear to introduce a choice of law question as to which law should determine whether, and at what point, the buyer made an 'order'. That question is itself beset with difficulty, since at this stage we do not yet know the governing law of the contract. Presumably, the law putatively applicable to the contract should apply, But even that will be hard to determine if, for example, the 'buyer' has first handed a letter alleged to constitute an order to the seller in the buyer's home state and has then posted a letter of confirmation to the seller in the seller's home state. It may be unclear which is putatively the order and, accordingly, which is the putative applicable law.

A further difficulty is that today, determining the place where an order **15.43** is received can be a complex question. An order might be placed by telephone, fax, by email or via a website. As to the first of these, it is unclear whether the order itself needs to be in writing or evidenced in writing. Since the Convention is silent on the matter, one might assume that an oral order would suffice.[89] Presumably, the place of receipt would be the place in which the seller takes the telephone call. It is less clear what should happen if a buyer habitually resident in State A telephones the seller whilst the latter is on a business trip to State A and places an order, which is subsequently confirmed in writing by the buyer sending a letter to the seller at the latter's permanent place of business in State B. The wording of Article 3 suggests that 'the order' refers to the telephone conversation itself in which the order was placed, rather than the act of confirmation; in which case, the law of State A would be applied.

As to communications by fax, irrespective of the rules which different **15.44** states may have as to the place of *conclusion* of a contract, it is clear that Article 3 refers to the place of receipt of the fax. So, if X faxed an order to Y from State A to State B, the place of receipt is State B. However,

---

[88] Arts 4(2), (3) and (4) of the Rome Convention.
[89] But this is not certain, as the Convention does not apply to formality requirements: Art 5(2).

suppose that X faxed an order from the state of his habitual residence, State A, to State B, the place of business of the seller, Y, but that Y was away on business in State A at the time. What if the fax was forwarded to Y's hotel in State A? Which is the state of receipt of the order? Presumably, if the buyer has sent the order to the proper, permanent place of business or to a representative or agent of the seller, the place of receipt should be State B. The buyer scarcely 'deserves' or would obviously expect that his 'home' law should apply simply because the order was first brought to the attention of the seller in State A. However, if the order was sent to a party in State B not authorized to act on behalf of the seller and that party simply forwarded the fax to the seller's proper place of business in State A, it must be the case that the applicable law in the absence of choice would be that of State A, since neither the seller nor an authorized representative of the seller had received the order in State B.

15.45 Where orders by email and through a website are concerned, it becomes substantially more difficult to determine a place of receipt.[90] Should this be the place from which: (1) the buyer sends the order; or (2) the place where the website has its domain; or (3) the place of business of the seller (if different)?[91] The first option does not seem appropriate, since the buyer's 'home' state cannot be said to be the place of receipt[92] by the seller. However, if the buyer is approached by the seller to contract by the sending of an email which the buyer will, in all probability, read in his home state, it could be said that any order made should be deemed to be received in the buyer's home state. But even here, it is difficult to see how a place which is neither the place of business of the seller nor the location of his email account or website could sensibly be said to be the place where he 'receives' an order. As to the third option, it is true that this will, in all probability, be the place where the seller will read the email in which an order is placed, or become aware of an order placed on the website. But equally, the seller could happen to read his email whilst away on business (or even on holiday whilst simply periodically checking his email) in a different state. In such circumstances, it would surely be most unfortunate

---

[90] See below, paras 21.64–90 for more detailed discussion; see also paras 21.150–174 on the position in the law of tort.

[91] See also Directive (EC) 2000/31 of the European Parliament and Council, 8 June 2000, on Certain Legal Aspects of Information Society Services, in particular Electronic Commerce [2000] OJ L178/1. This is implemented in the UK by the Electronic Commerce (EC Directive) Regulations 2002, SI 2002/2013 (most of the provisions of which entered into force in the UK on 21 August 2002). This is discussed above; paras 10.25–33, and below, paras 21.08–33.

[92] Unless of course, it happens to coincide with the location of the website or place of business of the seller.

if the place of 'receipt' should vary with where he happened to check his email and it is not at all clear why the law of the buyer's habitual residence should apply simply because the seller happened to be in that state at the time that he read his email. Accordingly, it is suggested that the second option should be accepted and that the place of receipt should be either the place where the website upon which the order is placed has its registered domain, or the place where the email address of the seller is located. Of course, this might allow a seller to manipulate the place of registration to avoid the application of an otherwise unfavourable law; but there might be much more potent and obvious reasons for doing this anyway than avoidance of Article 3 of the Hague Sales Convention 1955 and it is difficult to believe that a seller who wanted to go to so much trouble would not simply insert a choice of law clause as a standard term into its contracts of sale.

Where an order is received by an agent or representative of the seller, it **15.46** should suffice that this person has authority to receive orders on behalf of the vendor. It should not matter if he does not have authority to bind the vendor contractually. This is because the focus is on the act of *receipt* in the state of the buyer's habitual residence and not upon the conclusion of the contract itself.

6. AUCTION SALES

The final paragraph of Article 3 contains a special rule for contracts con- **15.47** cluded at an exchange or public auction.[93] In such a case, the domestic law of the state in which the exchange is situated or the auction took place shall apply in the absence of choice. This seems eminently sensible. If the vendor should put his goods up for sale at auction in an overseas state, or the buyer should attend an auction in an overseas state, neither can reasonably expect that the law of his own habitual residence will apply to the contract. The territorial connection of an exchange or auction with the place where it occurs makes it very likely that that law will have the closest connection with the contract. Once again, however, problems may arise if the auction is held online. In that case, it may be difficult to determine the location of the auction. It may be deemed to be the place where the auctioneer has its principal place of business, at least where this place is clearly identified on the website. This is the state whose law both parties might reasonably expect to govern a contract between them and,

---

[93] Such contracts are excluded altogether from the Vienna Convention by Art 2(b). See also the Finnish decision of the Court of Appeal of Rovaniemi, 9 November 1983/326 and the Tribunal of Suomussalmi of 15 September 1982/147. Both are discussed by Boele-Woelki, n 24 above, at 17.

wherever the location of the auctioneer's website, it will be the auctioneer itself that will regulate the proceedings.[94]

15.48 One problem with Article 3(3) is that rather than adopting a rebuttable presumption, it lays down an irrebuttable rule that the specified law will apply. So, even if a vendor habitually resident in State A puts goods up for auction which are purchased by a buyer also habitually resident in State A, the law of State B will apply in the absence of choice, if that is the place of the auction.

7. THE ROLE OF THE LAW OF THE PLACE WHERE THE GOODS ARE TO BE INSPECTED[95]

The Provision

15.49 Article 4 states that unless the parties expressly provide to the contrary:

> . . . the domestic law of the country in which inspection of goods delivered pursuant to a sale is to take place shall apply in respect of the form in which and periods within which the inspection must take place, the notifications concerning the inspection and the measures to be taken in case of refusal of the goods.

Choice of Law Clauses

15.50 It would appear that a choice of law clause contained in the contract would be sufficient to oust the application of this Article.[96]

Nature of the Rule in Article 4

15.51 There is a similarity here to Article 10(2) of the Rome Convention. That provision states that although matters of performance are to be governed by the applicable law of the contract, where issues relating to manner of performance are concerned, 'regard shall be had' to the law of the place of performance.[97] However, Article 10(2) of the Rome Convention allows a court to superimpose rules of the law of the place of performance onto the governing law. Article 4 of the Hague Convention is at first sight more ambiguous. It is not clear whether it lays down a choice of law rule, or simply provides for the application of what today would be

---

[94] See further the discussion of Art 4(5) of the Rome Convention and the applicable law in the absence of choice for contracts concluded by electronic means, below, paras 21.64–90, esp paras 21.86–89.

[95] See also below, para 16.116, for discussion of the interaction of this Article with the Vienna Convention.

[96] Von Mehren, n 4 above, says that this would be the case in respect of the equivalent Article (Art 13) of the Hague Sales Convention 1986: paras 140–141.

[97] See above, paras 13.160–166.

called mandatory rules. Imagine that a contract contains no choice of law clause, that the seller is habitually resident in State A and that the buyer, habitually resident in State B, places an order which is received by the seller in State A. Article 3(1) of the 1955 Convention states that the law of State A shall apply. But imagine now that the parties have arranged for the delivery, and inspection, of the goods in State B. Does Article 4 have the effect that those matters mentioned in Article 4 relating to inspection are governed entirely by the law of State B, or is it that the law of State A still applies to issues relating to inspection, but that in so far as there are provisions of the law of State B which conflict with those of State A, or which are additional to those of the law of State A, State B's law must also be applied? It would appear that the former is the correct answer. Article 4 says that the law of the place of inspection 'shall apply'. This appears to mean exactly what it says: that it will apply to the exclusion of any other law for matters within its scope. But if this is correct, it is a rare example of a Convention expressly incorporating *dépeçage*. In other words, in the absence of choice, the governing law of the contract determines most issues falling within the scope of the Convention, but not those specified in Article 4.

Delimiting the Scope of Article 4

This might, of course, create certain difficulties. First, the place where the **15.52** seller is obliged to 'deliver' the goods might not be the place where the goods are to be inspected. If, for example, the seller's obligation is to deliver FOB a ship in State A, the goods may be then be shipped to State B, where they are inspected by the buyer.[98] It seems clear that the law of State B nonetheless applies to questions of inspection.[99] Second, whilst the inspection itself and the form which it takes are matters for the law of the place of inspection, what if there is a dispute between the parties as to *who* should inspect the goods and, in particular, whether an inspection agency should be used?[100] In the absence of a clause in the contract so stipulating, the law of the place where inspection is to take place should decide whether this should be carried out by an agency. But what if the seller alleges that the parties *have* expressly agreed to an agency inspection clause and the buyer contests the essential validity of that clause? Which law should determine the validity of that clause: the law applicable to the

[98] Although this may be comparatively rare: inspection by an agency will normally take place on shipment: see Bridge, *The International Sale of Goods*, 15.

[99] Normally, the inspection will be as to the quality of the goods. However, Art 4 is not expressly limited to this and would appear to extend to inspection as to whether the goods are as described, and/or are fit for purpose.

[100] On inspection agencies, see Bridge, *The International Sale of Goods*, 15–16.

contract or the law of the place of inspection? The argument in favour of the former would be that this relates to the essential validity of a clause of the contract; the argument in favour of the latter would be that the validity of the clause will affect the form in which inspection will take place. It is suggested that the former approach must be correct. Article 4 clearly states that it applies in the absence of an express stipulation to the contrary. If there is an express stipulation as to the form of inspection, that must be respected. Hence the law applicable to the contract should determine whether the parties have validly agreed upon inspection by an agency.

The Place of Inspection

15.53 Of course, the place where inspection is to take place will normally be clear cut. But this is not inevitably so. There could, for example, be a dispute as to whether goods are to be inspected upon shipment or upon arrival at their destination. In that case, a choice of law question might arise as to which law determines where inspection is to take place. However, we cannot, of course, use the law which governs the inspection to determine this question, for that puts the cart before the horse. It must, accordingly, be the law which *putatively* governs the inspection which falls to be applied. That is, in itself, a complex question. On the one hand, it could be argued that the seller provides goods which, at the point of shipment, either are or are not of the requisite quality and fitness for purpose. Moreover, he is unlikely to warrant that the ship upon which the goods are placed will reach its destination. Accordingly, it could be said that the place of inspection is most naturally the place of shipment. But on the other hand, where goods are to be sold and delivered to a buyer, it might be said that the natural place for him to inspect those goods as to quality, description and fitness is in the place of delivery.[101] In so far as the goods need to be inspected to determine their condition,[102] this has to be done at the place where the buyer was to receive them.

15.54 Ultimately, an English court will have to apply its own principles of international sales to determine the putative place of inspection. English law is

---

[101] Compare *Viskase Ltd v Paul Kiefel GmbH* [1999] 1 WLR 1305, discussed above, paras 3.111, 3.181, 3.211, 3.265–269, where the Court of Appeal held that the obligation to supply goods fit for the purpose was to be effected at the place to which the goods were to be delivered. It rejected the argument that, upon dispatch, the goods either were or were not fit for purpose and that the obligation had been discharged at that point. See also *Boss Group Ltd v Boss France SA* [1996] 4 All ER 970.

[102] On the possible distinction between quality and condition, see Bridge, *The International Sale of Goods*, 18–19 and *Cremer v General Carriers SA* [1974] 1 WLR 341.

thin as regards any presumption about where inspection should take place but the starting point is the place of delivery. This comes from the typical case of a face-to-face transaction in the market place. In the case of FOB contracts, it was recognized that the place of shipment might not be always a practical place, so case law extended it to discharge ports and the buyer's establishment.[103] In the case of CIF contracts, it was certainly recognized that a buyer could not examine the goods at discharge prior to paying[104] but of course the buyer would have the right to examine the *documents* at the point of tender and a CIF contract is a documentary sale. In CIF commodity sales (and FOB sales for that matter) the contractual practice grew up of stipulating for inspection by a disinterested agency at the load port. This (i) clarified the application of risk in transit being on the buyer (leaving no room for arguments that damage did not incur in transit but was present on shipment); and (ii) it prevented the buyer from exploiting the seller by claiming defects and the right to reject in a distant place far removed from the seller's establishment. This all suggests that there is a clear expectation in commercial transactions involving *commodities* that inspection should take place on shipment. As for manufactured goods, the position is not so clear-cut and protection for the buyer might be sought by other means: in some cases of obvious damage, a master would not sign a clean bill of lading, and the buyer would have a right to complain if the goods had not been properly packed. There cannot be a systematic third party inspection service in the case of manufactured goods, so the likely expectation is that the buyer would inspect at discharge or when the goods arrived at his establishment.

Once the *putative* place of inspection has been determined, that law **15.55** should determine, finally, where the place of inspection actually is; and once that place has been found, its law applied to the matters designated in Article 4.

Application of Article 4

As to those matters expressly covered by Article 4, the law of the place of **15.56** inspection decides the form of the inspection and the time within which this must take place. In this respect, the time limit is regarded as a substantive matter.[105] The law of the place of inspection also determines the notifications concerning the inspection. Again, one might have

---

[103] *Scaliaris v E Ofverberg & Co* (1912) 37 TLR 307; *JW Schofield & Sons v Rownson, Drew and Clydesdale Ltd* (1922) 10 Ll L R 480.
[104] *E Clemens Horst Co v Biddell Bros* [1912] AC 18.
[105] Compare the Foreign Limitation Periods Act 1984.

been tempted to think of this as an essentially procedural step; but the Convention makes clear that it is to be regarded as substantive.

15.57 The final matter specified in Article 4 is also the most complex. The measures to be taken in the event of refusal of the goods are also for the law of the place of inspection to determine. This is a curious provision, given that the acceptance or refusal of the documents associated with the transaction is unlikely to occur in the place where the goods are to be inspected. Nor is it at all clear what these 'measures' might be. It would appear that the law of the place of inspection should determine if the refusal was justified. This in turn raises the issues of: (i) whether the goods were in some way unsatisfactory; and (ii), if so, whether the defect was sufficient to justify a refusal to accept the goods. Whether the refusal is or is not justified, however, inevitably raises the subsequent question of remedies. If the buyer unlawfully refused to accept the goods, the seller might wish to sue him to obtain specific performance of the contract or the agreed purchase price. If the buyer lawfully refused to accept the goods, he might wish to terminate the contract and/or sue for damages for breach of contract based upon his expected profit had the goods been satisfactory. Alternatively, the issue might arise whether the seller may provide alternative goods in a satisfactory condition, rather than paying damages to the buyer. It is not obviously to be expected that the law of the place of inspection has any great connection to the remedies for breach of contract, just because the inspection in that state revealed the defect. One might expect remedies either to be treated as procedural and hence determined by the law of the forum;[106] or, alternatively, if they are treated as substantive,[107] one might expect the law which determines the essential validity of the contract and the rights and duties of the parties under that contract also to determine what remedies are available in the event of those duties being violated. Nevertheless, in the absence of any provision in the Convention spelling out the scope of the governing law, and given the specific reference in Article 4 to the law of the place of inspection applying to the 'measures' to be taken in case of refusal, it would appear that it is the law of the place of inspection which should, in the absence of an express clause to the contrary, apply to the question of remedies. After all, if a court compels one of the parties to pay damages, or orders the specific performance of the contract, both can be described as 'measures' flowing from the refusal to accept the goods. Where there is a refusal of goods, so there is also inevitably a question of whether that refusal was justified and how to redress the consequences of that refusal.

---

[106] *Phrantzes v Argenti* [1960] 2 QB 19.
[107] Compare Art 10(1)(c) of the Rome Convention; discussed above, paras 13.205–239.

Finally, it should be noted that Article 4 does *not* govern the right to **15.58** inspection. That is a matter which should be determined by applying the governing law of the contract.

8. Consumer Contracts

It should be noted that consumer contracts fall within the scope of the **15.59** Convention. No special rules are applicable to them. This means that, in most cases, a seller acting in the course of business will be able to insist upon the application of a particular law to a contract with a consumer. Even where no such clause is included in the contract, the law applicable in the absence of choice will normally be that of the seller's habitual residence. This adverse position for consumers was one reason for dissatisfaction with the 1955 Convention and a catalyst for the drawing up of the 1986 Convention. It also led to a declaration being issued by the states present at the fourteenth session of the Hague Conference on Private International Law[108] to the effect that Parties to the 1955 Convention were not prevented from applying their own special rules to consumer sales contracts.[109]

9. Public Policy

No choice of law Convention is complete without a public policy **15.60** derogation. Article 6 duly obliges. However, there is no indication of how strictly the threshold is to be applied. It is not, for instance, stated that application of the governing law must be 'manifestly' contrary to public policy.[110] Nor is it expressly stated that the public policy to be applied must be that of the forum. It might, for instance, be possible to give effect to the public policy of a state of close connection, such as the place of performance.[111]

It is notable that no other derogation from the governing law appears in **15.61** the Convention. The phrase 'mandatory rules' does not appear in the Convention. However, in so far as the forum has a rule of law which is

---

[108] *Acts and Documents of the Fourteenth Session (1980)*, tome I, *Miscellaneous Matters*, 62.
[109] A step taken by Denmark, Finland and Sweden. It is recommended that states that do apply special rules for consumers should notify the Permanent Bureau at the Hague of this fact. See further C Saf, 'A Study of the Interplay between the Conventions Governing International Contracts of Sale' (www.cisg.law.pace.edu/cisg/text/saf90.html).
[110] Compare Art 16 of the Rome Convention; discussed above, paras 13.282–294.
[111] Compare *Ralli Bros v Compañía Naviera Sota y Aznar* [1920] 2 KB 287, which, on one view, suggests that an English court was willing at common law to give effect to a provision of the law of the place of performance rendering a contract illegal after it was concluded (see the discussion of the effect of illegality, above, paras 13.295–300).

intended to be applied to a contract of sale regardless of its governing law, it is inconceivable that effect would not be given to this rule. Rather, a court would hold that it is contrary to its public policy to apply rules of a foreign law to the extent that they conflict with such a provision. Similarly, although there are no consumer protection provisions in the Convention, in so far as a consumer contract infringes statutory consumer protection provisions of the forum which are designed to apply irrespective of the applicable law, application of that foreign law will be deemed to infringe the forum's public policy.

10. Concluding Remarks on the 1955 Convention

15.62 Overall, one is left with the impression of a Convention which has become overtaken by events. It is not terribly ambitious, in the sense that it contains relatively few provisions and a number of exclusions. Then again, the great majority of contracts for the sale of goods fall within its scope; and the list of exclusions is scarcely unreasonable.

15.63 The choice of law rules of the Convention are in one sense more pragmatic and commercially appealing than those of the Rome Convention. The freedom of choice of the parties is upheld and subject to no specific imposition of the mandatory rules of another law. The only requirement is that the sale be genuinely international. The applicable law in the absence of choice is, in most cases, the same as that applicable under Article 4(2) of the Rome Convention (i.e. that of the seller's habitual residence). However, the provision which instead allows for the law of the buyer's habitual residence to apply has a dated feel, in that it places considerable and inflexible reliance upon the place of receipt, a concept which may be difficult to determine and somewhat arbitrary in an era of instantaneous communication. Moreover, the provision relating to the law of the place of inspection creates considerable difficulty in determining its meaning, scope and application and can lead to an artificial separation of the law governing the parties' rights and their remedies.

15.64 Taken as a whole, one is bound to question whether the Convention provides any better choice of law rules for sale of goods contracts than the 'general' contract choice of law rules of the Rome Convention. In many respects, they are similar. And in so far as the 1955 Convention differs by, for example, applying a limited buyer's residence rule and a limited law of the place of inspection rule, or by not laying down a solution to the formal validity of a contract, it is arguable that the Rome Convention provides a preferable solution. There is not, accordingly, a convincing case for the United Kingdom to ratify the 1955 Convention.

V. THE HAGUE SALES CONVENTION 1986[112]

1. INTRODUCTION

The 1986 Convention was fuelled[113] largely by reservations in many **15.65** quarters[114] about the relatively undetailed nature of the 1955 Convention and its sweeping, inflexible rules[115] which seemed inappropriate to consumer sales[116] and yet also excluded much from their scope. It was also fuelled by the advent of the Vienna Convention.[117] The references in that Convention to rules of private international law re-emphasizes the close relationship between choice of law and substantive law in providing suitable working rules for international contracts of sale.[118]

---

[112] For discussion, see D Cohen and B Ughetto, 'La Nouvelle Convention de La Haye Relative à la Loi Applicable aux Ventes Internationales de Marchandises' (1986) 20 Recueil Dalloz 149 (continued in (1987) 21 Recueil Dalloz 157); M Gilmore, 'Hague Conference on the Law Applicable to Contracts for the International Sale of Goods' (1987) 28 Harvard Int LJ 526; P Lagarde, 'La Nouvelle Convention de La Haye sur la Loi Applicable aux Contrats de Vente Internationale de Marchandises' in Journées de la Société de Législation Comparée (1985) 7 Revue Internationale de Droit Comparé 327; O Lando, 'The 1985 Hague Convention on the Law Applicable to Sales' [1987] Rabels Zeitschrift für Ausländisches und Internationales Privatrecht 60; Lando, n 24 above; Y Loussouarn, 'La Convention de La Haye d'Octobre 1985 sur la Loi Applicable aux Contrats de Vente Internationale de Marchandises' [1986] Revue Critique de Droit International Privé 271; Z Matic, 'The Hague Convention on the Law Applicable to Contracts for the International Sale of Goods—Rules on the Applicable Law', Ch 4 in P Sarcevic (ed), *International Contracts and Conflicts of Laws: a Collection of Essays* (London, Graham & Trotman, 1990) 51; McLachlan, n 10 above; M Pelichet, 'La Vente Internationale de Marchandises et le Conflit de Lois' (1987) 201-I Recueil des Cours de l'Académie de droit international de La Haye 9. The Official Report to the Convention by Arthur Taylor von Mehren can be found in *Actes et Documents de la Session Extraordinaire d'Octobre 1985* (also available at http://hcch.e-vision.nl/index_en.php?act= publications.details&pid=2950&dtid=3). For a detailed and regularly updated bibliography to the Convention, see http://hcch.e-vision.nl/index_en.php?act= conventions.publications &dtid=1&cid=61.

[113] For discussion of the genesis of the Hague Sales Convention 1986, see the von Mehren Report, paras 1–14.

[114] But not the Nordic countries of Denmark, Finland, Norway and Sweden. McLachlan, n 10 above, at 601, points out that these countries were all parties to the 1955 Convention and generally happy with its operation. None has signed the 1986 Convention.

[115] As one might have expected, the common law countries were keen for Contracting States to retain a substantial element of discretion under the 1986 Convention.

[116] The Hague Conference had also been considering a possible Convention on the Law Applicable to Certain Consumer Sales, although this never reached a successful conclusion.

[117] And, prior to that, the earlier uniform law conventions: Uniform Law on the International Sale of Goods and Uniform Law on the Formation of Contracts for the International Sale of Goods. It could be argued that, in an ideal world, the parties to the Vienna Convention would also successfully conclude and ratify a choice of law convention. However, prospects for this seem extremely remote. See further N Vilkova, 'The Unification of Conflict of Laws Rules in the CIS Countries' (2000) 26 Rev of Eastern European Law 75.

[118] Most notably under Art 1 when determining the scope of application of the Vienna Convention: see below, paras 16.16–31.

At the same time, the European Community sought a set of rules that would complement the approach taken by the Rome Convention.

15.66 Faced with these various considerations, the task for the drafters of the 1986 Convention was never going to be easy. In the event, the Convention has proved to be unsuccessful. It has been ratified only by Argentina.[119] It was signed, but not ratified by the Czech Republic,[120] the Netherlands[121] and Slovakia.[122] Only one non-Member State of the Hague Conference has acceded to the Convention, namely Moldova.[123] The Convention has never entered into force.[124] Most European states are satisfied with the solutions offered by the Rome Convention. Those which apply the 1955 Convention show little interest in ratifying the 1986 Convention. Accordingly, it appears that the prospects for entry into force of the Hague Sales Convention 1986 are bleak.

15.67 Unlike the 1955 Convention, the 1986 Convention's focus is on contracts which do not require special protection for either party.[125] Otherwise, the 1986 Convention shares much in common with the Rome Convention and contains a similar hierarchy of choice of law rules. The 1986 Convention is set against the background of the Vienna Convention[126] and, if and when the 1986 Convention enters into force, would be used by Contracting States to each Convention to determine those matters to which the Vienna Convention defers to the forum's rules of private international law.[127]

---

[119] It was signed and ratified on 4 October 1991.

[120] Signed by Czechoslovakia on 22 December 1986. The Czech Republic declared on 28 January 1993 that it would be bound by the Convention (including such reservations and declarations made by Czechoslovakia) as from 1 January 1993 (the date of the division of Czechoslovakia).

[121] Signed on 2 February 1990.

[122] Signed by Czechoslovakia on 22 December 1986. Slovakia declared on 15 March 1993 that it would be bound by the Convention (including such reservations and declarations made by Czechoslovakia) as from 1 January 1993 (the date of the division of Czechoslovakia).

[123] Accession on 24 December 1997.

[124] It would require five ratifications for the Convention to enter into force.

[125] Art 2(c). However, the Convention does apply if, at the time of conclusion of the contract, the seller neither knew nor ought to have known that the goods were bought for personal, family or household use. See also the von Mehren Report, para 14.

[126] As the Preamble expressly states.

[127] Such as Art 1(1)(b) on the scope of the Vienna Convention and Art 7(2) which provides that matters left unresolved under the Vienna Convention should be determined by rules of the law designated by the forum's rules of private international law. See below, paras 16.26–31, 16.42–74.

2. Scope of the 1986 Convention; the Meaning of 'Sale of Goods'

The Requisite Cross-Border Element

The Convention applies to determine the law applicable to 'contracts of **15.68** sale of goods'.[128] However, it will only apply to such contracts where (i) the parties have their places of business in different states; or (ii) in any other case involving a choice between the laws of different states, unless that choice arises solely by virtue of a choice of law clause and/or a jurisdiction or arbitration clause.[129] There are obvious, and deliberate[130] parallels to the scope of the Vienna Convention. However, it would be inappropriate for the scope of the two Conventions to be identical, both because they are largely concerned with quite different things and because the Hague Sales Convention 1986 might lead to the application of the law of a state which has not ratified the Vienna Convention.

In the event, Article 1 simply seems concerned to ensure that the contract **15.69** of sale truly is international.[131] Almost certainly, a contract falling under Article 1(a) involving parties which have their places of business in different states would meet that definition. However, in contrast to Article 1(1)(a) of the Vienna Convention, there is no requirement that the states in question be Contracting States to the 1986 Convention. As to Article 1(b), the concern is to ensure that, where the parties have their places of business in the same state, there is some genuine, objective connection to another state.[132] Hence, two parties with businesses in the same state cannot trigger the application of the Convention simply by their subjective choice of the law of another state to govern the contract, or by a foreign choice of court or arbitration clause. Nor will a jurisdiction clause *and* a choice of law clause be sufficient. But, of course, if the contract

---

[128] Art 1. Unlike Art 1 of the 1955 Convention, the phrase 'international sale of goods' is not used (though it is, of course, used in the title to the Convention and in the Preamble). In effect, the following provisions of Art 1 make clear that the sales contract must be objectively transnational.

[129] Art 1 of the 1986 Convention.

[130] Von Mehren Report, para 23. Earlier, he comments that '. . . the view was widely and consistently held that Vienna's language should, to the extent possible, be adapted for use in the draft . . . because the choice-of-law convention would thereby be rendered more comprehensible and easier to administer for those States that might put both instruments into force': para 11.

[131] Art 20 provides that a state which consists of different territorial units each having their own systems of law is not bound to apply the Convention to conflicts which are substantially between the laws of those units. Art 26 provides that if a state has two or more territorial units in which different systems of law are applicable, it may declare that the Convention shall extend to all, one or some units only (and may, of course, subsequently modify this declaration).

[132] 'The proviso eliminates the major situation in which states could object to the operation of party autonomy': McLachlan, n 10 above, at 603.

provides for the delivery of goods to a state other than where the parties have their places of business[133] that would suffice to bring the contract of sale within the scope of the Convention. It is less clear whether, for example, the mere fact of conclusion of the contract in a foreign state, or the fact that payment is to be made in a foreign currency, would suffice to bring the matter within the scope of the Convention.[134] However, the wording of Article 1(b) does suggest that the Convention applies where there is any kind of choice between the laws of different states, save where that choice arises only *subjectively* from a choice of law clause and/or a jurisdiction or arbitration clause. Moreover, since the Convention does not generally apply to consumer contracts,[135] a broad approach to the Convention, and to the autonomy of the parties to select the governing law, might properly be taken. Accordingly, it is suggested that the examples of conclusion of the contract overseas or payment in a foreign currency should suffice to bring the matter within the Convention.

15.70 Just as it is possible to restrict the application of the Vienna Convention to cases where the parties both have their place of business in different Contracting States,[136] so too it is possible to do so under the Hague Sales Convention 1986. Article 21(1)(a) of the 1986 Convention allows a state to enter a reservation to the effect that it will not apply the Convention in the circumstances described in Article 1(b).[137] This reservation was entered into by Czechoslovakia. Both the Czech Republic and Slovakia have both since affirmed that they wish the reservation to apply in their states.

Meaning of 'Sale of Goods'

15.71 The Convention does not specifically define what 'sale of goods' means. It does, however, contain a list of specific types of sales contracts excluded from the Convention.[138] The list draws upon the exclusions in the 1955 Convention and the Vienna Convention,[139] but is not identical to either. Involuntary sales by way of execution or by authority of law are

---

[133] And if that choice is not a sham: compare Case C-106/95 *Mainschiffahrts-Genossenschaft eG v Les Gravières Rhénanes Sarl* [1997] ECR I-911; discussed above, para 3.214.

[134] Under the Rome Convention, a liberal view of the scope of the application of the Convention can be taken, because the worst excesses of choice of law shopping can be controlled by the application of the mandatory rules of a state with which the contract is otherwise wholly objectively connected, under Art 3(3). No such provision exists in the Hague Sales Convention 1986.

[135] Art 2(c).   [136] Art 95 of the Vienna Convention.

[137] See the von Mehren Report, paras 176–178.

[138] Von Mehren also indicates that sales of intellectual property rights fall outside the Convention: ibid, para 34.

[139] See paras 15.21–27 and 16.84–88.

excluded,[140] as under the 1955 Convention.[141] The 1986 Convention also excludes sales of 'stocks, shares, investment securities, negotiable instruments or money . . .'.[142] This wording is identical to that contained in Article 2(d) of the Vienna Convention.

The final exclusion is also the most significant: namely sale of goods **15.72** bought 'for personal, family or household use'. This definition of consumer contracts, introduced so that the Convention would be uniformly applied in Contracting States, is identical to that in Article 2(a) of the Vienna Convention. It focuses attention not on the *status* of the parties, but on the *purpose* for which the buyer entered into the transaction.[143] Of course, the essence of the consumer contract is the unequal bargaining position of the parties. If the party acting in the course of business did not know that he was dealing with someone acting outside the course of business, nor ought to have known this, the potential for that party to exploit his bargaining position is extremely limited. For this reason, contracts of sale which are formed in such circumstances will fall within the Hague Sales Convention 1986.[144]

More positively, although the Convention contains no definition of 'sale **15.73** of goods', it does expressly state certain matters which do fall within the definition.[145] So, a sale of goods based on documents will fall within the Convention.[146] Of course, if that were not the case, the practical scope of the Convention in international sales transactions would be vastly restricted. Also covered by the Convention are sales of 'ships, vessels, boats, hovercraft and aircraft'.[147] Sales of such items are expressly excluded from the scope of the Vienna Convention[148] and also from the Hague Sales Convention 1955.[149] However, the Diplomatic Conference at the Hague felt that, whilst special substantive rules would apply to such contracts of sale, they did not raise unique choice of law questions and so

---

[140] Art 2(a) of the 1986 Convention.   [141] Art 1(2) of the 1955 Convention.
[142] Art 2(b) of the 1986 Convention. It goes on to state that the Convention does apply to 'the sale of goods based on documents'.
[143] Compare C-269/95 *Benincasa v Dentalkit Srl* [1997] ECR I-3767.
[144] There is no such express provision determining the scope of the consumer protection provisions in either the Brussels I Regulation or the Rome Convention.
[145] It is uncertain to what extent digital products fall within the Convention. H Kronke, 'Applicable Law in Torts and Contracts in Cyberspace' in K Boele-Woelki and C Kessedjian (eds), *Internet: Which Court Decides? Which Law Applies?* (The Hague: Kluwer, 1998) 65, argues at 75–76 that data and images should fall within the scope of the Convention '. . . if a parallel with the Vienna Convention is to be maintained, as the von Mehren Report recommends'. However, he goes on to doubt whether information falls within the scope of the Convention, on the basis that 'rights were deliberately excluded from the scope of application [of the Convention]' (citing *Explanatory Report No 34* at 721).
[146] Art 2(b).   [147] Art 3(a).   [148] Art 2(e) of the Vienna Convention,
[149] Art 1(2) of the Hague Sales Convention 1955.

could comfortably be included within the Hague Sales Convention 1986.[150] For similar reasons, the 1986 Convention extends to the sale of electricity,[151] which is excluded from the Vienna Convention.[152]

15.74 The 1986 Convention deals with contracts for the supply of goods to be manufactured or produced[153] and contracts involving the supply of labour or other services. As to the former, Article 4(1) states that contracts involving manufacture or production shall still be treated as contracts of sale unless the *buyer* undertakes to supply a substantial part of the materials for manufacture or production. As von Mehren points out, this provision, directly taken from Article 3(1) of the Vienna Convention,[154] is slightly curious in that it focuses not upon whether the *seller* provides a substantial amount of the materials for manufacture or production, but upon the role of the buyer. Hence, he suggests that a contract to tailor a suit should still come within the Convention, even if the buyer supplied the lining for the suit.[155]

15.75 Contracts involving the supply of labour or other services will not be treated as contracts of sale if the provision of labour or other services is the preponderant part of the obligations of the party who furnishes the goods.[156] Once again, the wording of the Vienna Convention has been directly reproduced.[157]

3. Specific Exclusions

15.76 Having determined what a contract of sale is (or, perhaps more clearly, what it is not), the Convention goes on to provide a list of specific issues which are not to be determined by the Convention. These are contained in Article 5. The first of these relates to the capacity of the parties.[158] This issue is frequently excluded from private international law conventions, and most notably, for present purposes, from the 1955 Sales Convention[159] and the Rome Convention.[160] Contractual rules of a legal system restricting a party's capacity are intended to have a mandatory effect on that party which would be undermined if that state's law could be bypassed by the simple expedient of choosing a different law to govern

---

[150] Von Mehren Report, para 33.   [151] Art 3(b) of the 1986 Convention.
[152] Art 2(f) of the Vienna Convention.
[153] Compare Art 1(3) of the Hague Sales Convention 1955, above, paras 15.15–16.
[154] On which, see below, paras 16.91–94.   [155] Von Mehren Report, para 12.
[156] Art 4(2) of the 1986 Convention.   [157] Art 3(2) of the Vienna Convention.
[158] Art 5(a) of the 1986 Convention. The exclusion relates to the capacity of legal and natural persons.
[159] Art 5(1) of the 1955 Convention.
[160] Art 1(2)(a) of the Rome Convention. Capacity is also excluded by Art 1(2) of the Brussels I Regulation.

the contract.[161] Also excluded are the consequences of nullity or invalidity of the contract resulting from incapacity. Hence, it would appear that restitutionary claims arising from the nullity of the contract on the grounds of one party's incapacity fall outside the Convention.[162]

The questions of whether an agent can bind a principal, or whether an **15.77** organ can bind a company or unincorporated association, are also excluded.[163] However, it should be noted that the consequences of an agent lacking authority will be regulated by the 1986 Convention.[164]

Article 5(c) excludes issues relating to the transfer of ownership. That is **15.78** not in the least bit surprising. Questions of ownership will normally be governed by the law of the situs. The question whether ownership is with the seller or the buyer, although ostensibly a matter which affects only the contracting parties, will inevitably confer a right on one of those parties which is capable of binding third parties. It is, accordingly, not properly to be subjected to the law which the parties select to govern the contract.

However, Article 5(c) is expressly subject to the matters specifically men- **15.79** tioned in Article 12, which remain governed by the law designated by the Convention. In particular, the time at which the buyer becomes entitled to the products, fruits and income deriving from the goods is governed by the Convention;[165] so too is the passing of risk to the buyer[166] and the validity and effect as between the parties of a retention of title clause.[167] These provisions are considered further below.

Curiously, Article 5 does not deal with property rights short of ownership **15.80** between the parties. The question whether, for example, a contracting party[168] has a charge over goods, or the right to possession of goods, or the question of priority to goods, are not expressly mentioned and excluded from the Convention. However, since none of these are, properly speaking, contractual questions, they should not be determined under the Convention. Notwithstanding that the contract itself may contain express provisions on these matters, the effect of such provisions should be a

---

[161] On the common law rules on capacity, see *Dicey and Morris*, Rule 181(1), 1271–1272, and above, paras 13.23–29.

[162] Although the consequences of nullity or invalidity arising from the formal or essential invalidity of the contract will be covered by Art 12(h) of the 1986 Convention.

[163] Art 5(b) of the 1986 Convention.

[164] Art 12(h); a fact confirmed by von Mehren, para 40.   [165] Art 12(c).

[166] Art 12(d): although it is suggested that risk is an allocation of personal liability and is not proprietary in nature.

[167] Art 12(e).

[168] The question whether a third party has such an interest is excluded by Art 5(d).

matter to determined by the law designated by the forum's property choice of law rules.

15.81 Article 5(d) also makes clear that the effect of the sale in respect of third parties is outside the scope of the Convention. If not already covered by Article 5(c), the rights of third parties in the goods themselves, including whether they have title, possession or a charge over the goods,[169] are not regulated by the Convention. So too, the effect of the sale on third parties who may contract with the parties to the sale, such as a carrier, or a bank, are not matters which are regulated by the sales contract itself.

15.82 Finally, Article 5(e) excludes choice of court and arbitration agreements, even when contained within the text of the contract of sale. This accords with the approach of the Rome Convention.[170] Where a choice of the courts of a Member State of the European Community is made, the formal requirements for the validity of the clause will be determined by the Brussels I Regulation.[171] In so far as the substantive validity of the clause may be questioned because, for example, it was allegedly entered into by duress or mistake, the forum must apply its own national choice of law rules to determine the clause's validity.[172] Once the clause has been declared valid, however, the arbitration or choice of court clause may be a material factor in determining whether the parties impliedly chose a governing law.[173]

4. DETERMINING THE GOVERNING LAW

Express or Implied Choice

Express choice

15.83 In Article 7(1), the Convention enshrines the basic principle of party autonomy. The law[174] chosen by the parties will be applied, even if it

---

[169] There is no such express exclusion of these issues between the contracting parties themselves. Art 5(c) excludes only the transfer of ownership. See, however, the remarks in the preceding paragraph.

[170] Art 1(2)(d) of the Rome Convention.   [171] Art 23 of the Brussels I Regulation.

[172] But on the question whether a party may contest the material validity of a jurisdiction clause for a Member State, see the discussion of Art 23 of the Brussels I Regulation above, paras 3.25–27 and 3.29–40.

[173] Pursuant to Art 7(1) of the 1986 Convention, discussed in the subsequent section.

[174] The Convention does not expressly address the issue of whether the parties might choose a law other than that currently in force in a particular state, such as the *lex mercatoria*, or the rules of the Vienna Convention (especially in states which are not party to the Vienna Convention, or in circumstances where the conditions for the application of the Vienna Convention in Art 1 are not satisfied). The provision in Art 7 dealing with express choice of law simply refers to the choice of a 'law' but Art 8, which applies in default of choice, refers several times to 'the law of the State'. There is some suggestion in Art 15 that

has no objective connection to the contract and even if it is the law of a non-Contracting State.[175]

It is not immediately clear what should happen if the parties have their **15.84** places of business in different states which are *not* parties to the Vienna Convention and choose the law of a state which *is* party to the Vienna Convention to govern their contract. Under the 1986 Sales Convention, should a court apply the rules of the Vienna Convention, or the domestic law of the state identified? Article 1(1)(a) of the Vienna Convention is not satisfied, as the parties do not have their places of business in different Contracting States to that Convention. However, Article 1(1)(b) of the Vienna Convention prescribes its application where the rules of private international law point to the law of a state which has ratified the Vienna Convention. The rules of private international law are those of the 1986 Convention. It follows that if they point to the law of a state which has ratified the Vienna Convention, then the rules of the Vienna Convention should be applied.[176]

the parties must choose the law in force in a particular state. This provides that the word ' "law" means the law *in force in a State* other than its choice of law rules' (emphasis added). However, Art 15 was primarily dealing with the exclusion of renvoi and von Mehren indicates that the dominant view was that it did not intend to deal one way or another with the question whether the *lex mercatoria* might be chosen: para 156. See also McLachlan, n 10 above, at 603–604, 615–620. As to the choice of 'the Vienna Convention', since this effectively is the law (or a large part of the law) of many recognized legal systems, it is suggested that such choice should be upheld. If necessary, one might argue that the choice of the Vienna Convention is simply a shorthand method of incorporating by reference the provisions of that Convention into the contract. See further the arguments in relation to the 1955 Convention above, paras 15.29 and 13.65–69, 13.86–94.

[175] Art 6.

[176] If, however, the state whose law is chosen has entered a reservation pursuant to Art 95 of the Vienna Convention to the effect that Art 1(1)(b) of the Vienna Convention does not apply (as the US, amongst others, has done), matters are more complex. It could be argued that the domestic law of the state identified should apply, on the basis that a court in that state would not itself apply the Vienna Convention on the facts. However, Bridge, *The International Sale of Goods*, 66–67, suggests that the key question is rather whether the forum is itself a party to the Vienna Convention and, if so, whether it has itself entered the reservation in Art 95. If it is not a party to the Vienna Convention, or if it has entered the reservation in Art 95, it should apply the domestic provisions of the governing law. If it is a party to the Vienna Convention and it has not entered the reservation, it is *bound* to apply the Vienna Convention wherever its rules of private international law lead to the application of the law of a Contracting State to the Vienna Convention *regardless of whether that Contracting State itself would apply the Vienna Convention on the facts*. This means that it should apply the Vienna Convention. This, in turn, has the unfortunate effect that different Contracting States to the 1986 Convention might apply different laws on the facts, even though Art 16 of the Convention urges that: 'In the interpretation of the Convention, regard is to be had to its international character and to the need to promote uniformity in its application'. See also Winship, n 71 above; McLachlan, n 10 above, at 613–615; cf Honnold, n 71 above, 84–94. See also the arguments made in relation to the 1955 Convention, above, para 15.30, see also above, paras 13.83–85, and below, paras 16.128–136.

Implied choice

15.85 If no express choice has been made, a choice may be 'clearly demonstrated
by the terms of the contract and the conduct of the parties, viewed in their
entirety'.[177] The language used is a touch more liberal than the Rome
Convention equivalent, which requires a choice to be 'demonstrated with
reasonable certainty . . .'.[178] The choice under the 1986 Convention may be
demonstrated by looking both at the contract's terms and the parties'
conduct and a court may apparently look at conduct both before and after
conclusion of the contract.[179] It appears that the approach is broader than
that in the Rome Convention, where the search for an implied choice
hinges on subjective factors such as an arbitration clause, a previous
course of dealings between the parties governed by a particular law, or a
standard form contract.[180] Under the 1986 Convention, no factor is apparently excluded from the search for an implied choice. However, von
Mehren suggests that a single element pointing to a particular law, such
as the place of performance[181] or conclusion of the contract, would not
suffice in itself to demonstrate an implied choice. Presumably, even an
arbitration or choice of court clause alone would not suffice in and of
itself.[182]

Splitting the Contract

15.86 The parties may also choose a law to govern only a part of the contract.[183]
If so, the law governing the remainder of the contract will be determined
in the absence of choice under Article 8. Although the Convention does
not say so expressly, it appears that the parties could expressly choose
different laws to govern different parts of the contract.[184]

---

[177] Art 7(1) of the 1986 Convention.   [178] Art 3(1) of the Rome Convention.
[179] Von Mehren Report, para 48.
[180] Giuliano and Lagarde Report [1980] OJ C282/1, at 17; see above, paras 13.44–55.
[181] Indeed, it is envisaged in Art 8(2)(b) that a designation of the buyer's place of business
as the place of performance will make that law applicable *in the absence of choice*. This
suggests that the mere choice of a place of performance is not enough to constitute an
implied choice of the governing law.
[182] Ironically, although the wording of Art 7 of the 1986 Convention suggests a more
liberal implied choice test than Art 3(1) of the Rome Convention, an English arbitration
clause has been treated as nearly conclusive evidence that the parties intended English law
to govern a contract with little objective connection to England: *Egon Oldendorff v Libera Corp
(No 2)* [1996] 1 Lloyd's Rep 380 (and see the earlier decision at [1995] 2 Lloyd's Rep 64).
[183] Art 7(1), final sentence. Logically, the choice must relate to a separable issue under the
contract, such as its construction. However, the Hague Conference decided not to address
the matter in any further detail.
[184] Von Mehren Report, paras 51–54. The Rome Convention also omits to say whether the
parties may expressly choose different laws to govern different parts of the contract. See
further A Diamond, 'Harmonisation of Private International Law Relating to Contractual
Obligations' (1986-IV) 199 Hague Recueil 233, 259.

Changing the Governing Law

The parties may agree to change the law applicable to all or part of the **15.87** contract.[185] They may do this regardless of whether the law previously governing the contract was chosen by them. The only rider is that the change cannot prejudice the formal validity[186] of the contract nor affect the rights of third parties.[187] In effect, the 1986 Convention lays down a rule of uniform law:[188] the validity of a change of law is determined not by the law initially governing the contract, nor by the law which the parties intend to govern it subsequently, but is autonomously sanctioned by the Convention.

The Applicable Law in the Absence of Choice

General presumption in favour of the law of the seller's place of business: Article 8(1)

In the absence of an express or implied choice of law, the applicable **15.88** law shall be determined by Article 8. The rules contained in this Article were the subject of much debate at the Hague Conference and are more complex than those found in either the Rome Convention or the 1955 Sales Convention.

The general presumption, contained in Article 8(1), is very similar to that **15.89** in Article 4(2) of the Rome Convention: namely that the law of the state where the seller[189] has its place of business at the time of conclusion of the contract applies.[190] Article 14(1) states what happens if the seller has more than one place of business. The relevant place of business is that '. . . which has the closest relationship to the contract and its performance, having regard to the circumstances known to or contemplated by the parties at any time before or at the conclusion of the contract'. Although this provision is taken from Article 10 of the Vienna Convention, and reference to its case law could presumably be made in cases of difficulty, the provision is not as clear as it might be. For one thing, the court may only consider factors 'known to or contemplated by the parties' before or

---

[185] Art 7(2).

[186] This suggests that the *substantive* validity of the contract may be prejudiced.

[187] So, for example, an assignee under the original contract should not have his rights adversely affected: von Mehren Report, para 55.

[188] In similar terms to Art 3(2) of the Rome Convention.

[189] Art 4(2) of the Rome Convention refers more generally to the performance which is characteristic of the contract. However, it is clear that this performance is that of the seller in a contract of sale. See above, paras 13.114–116.

[190] For criticism, see McLachlan, n 10 above, at 605–606 and the passage that he cites from J D'Oliveira, 'Characteristic Obligation in the draft EEC Obligation Convention' (1977) 25 AJCL 303, 328.

at the time of conclusion. It is obvious that this could create difficult questions of proof. Furthermore, Article 14(1) refers to the place of business of closest connection to the contract *and* its performance. Yet the place of business which has the greatest factual connection with the contract as a whole may not be the same place of business as that where performance should take place. In such a scenario, is the place of closest connection or the place of performance to be given greater weight? It is suggested that a similar approach to that taken under the Rome Convention should be adopted. Essentially, this gives greater weight to the place of business through which performance is to be carried out.[191] Article 4(2) of the Rome Convention states that the law of the principal place of business is to be used, unless performance is to be effected through a place of business other than the principal place of business; in which case, the place where the party[192] will effect performance applies. In the converse scenario where a seller has no place of business, Article 14(2) of the 1986 Convention states that reference is to be made to his habitual residence.[193]

Circumstances where a presumption in favour of the law of the buyer's place of business applies: Article 8(2)

15.90   However, Article 8(2) departs significantly from the approach of the Rome Convention by providing that in certain circumstances the law of the *buyer's* place of business at the time of conclusion of the contract applies in the absence of choice. There are three such circumstances. The first[194] is where the negotiations[195] were conducted and the contract concluded by and in the presence of the parties in the state of the buyer's place of business. Von Mehren states that it would suffice that a substantial amount of the negotiations took place in that state, even if not all of them took place there.[196] However, it would appear that these negotiations *and* the conclusion[197] of the contract must occur in this state and that it must

---

[191] A view shared by Schlechtriem, 83.

[192] i.e. the characteristic performer under the Rome Convention. In a contract of sale, this will be the seller.

[193] This is also taken from Art 10 of the Vienna Convention.   [194] Art 8(2)(a).

[195] McLachlan, n 10 above, at 606 comments that: 'It is unclear what is required for "negotiations". This will remain a question of fact for the judge, but may, for instance, the mere proffering of a standard form contract amount to negotiations?' In fact, one could argue that what constitute 'negotiations' is a matter of law, on which different legal systems might disagree. Strictly speaking, it could be argued that a judge should apply the law putatively applicable to the contract to determine this matter, namely that of the buyer's place of business.

[196] Von Mehren Report, para 65.

[197] Of course, different states might take differing views as to what suffices for the conclusion of the contract. Presumably, the law which is putatively applicable (i.e. that of the buyer's place of business) should decide if the contract was indeed 'concluded' in that state.

be a face-to-face transaction. In such circumstances, it could scarcely be doubted that the law of the buyer's place of business has the closest connection to the contract.

The second scenario[198] where the law of the buyer's place of business **15.91** applies in the absence of choice is where the contract expressly states that the seller must perform his obligation to deliver goods in that state. Whilst this might accord with the expectations of the parties, it can, of course, create difficulties as to where the place of delivery is.[199] This is particularly so where the seller passes goods to a carrier for delivery to the buyer's state. Von Mehren states that:

In international transactions, INCOTERMS such as 'CIF' or 'FOB' coupled with a specific designation of the destination of the goods are frequently encountered. Such 'transport' clauses do not in themselves establish the obligation to deliver the goods at the specified destination.[200]

Accordingly, it seems that unless the seller expressly undertakes not merely to arrange for a contract of carriage to a certain destination, but also undertakes to deliver the goods to that destination and that the goods will arrive there, this provision will not be triggered.[201]

The final circumstance which triggers the buyer's place of business rule **15.92** relates to calls to tender by the buyer, where the contract was concluded 'on terms mainly determined by the buyer'.[202] This proposal makes sense, since '. . . a buyer (the caller) can hardly compare the proposals received unless they are subject to a single law known to him'.[203] Moreover, both parties are likely to focus attention on the terms of the tender drawn up by the caller and it is unlikely that they would anticipate any other law being applied. Of course, some uncertainty exists as to when the terms are

---

[198] Art 8(2)(b).

[199] Compare the discussion of this problem above, paras 3.175–297, in respect of Art 5(1) of the Brussels I Regulation. The place of delivery will be especially difficult to determine in the case of transfer of digitized products: see the discussion of Art 5(1) of the Brussels I Regulation, above, paras 10.54–74, 10.78–80. See also the criticisms of the application of Art 8(2)(b) of the 1986 Convention in Kronke, n 145 above, at 76–77.

[200] Von Mehren Report, para 76. See also *SIPAL Rexons Società Italiana Prodotti Auto E Locomozione SpA v Sprl Gold's Products* [1990] IL Pr 386, Cour d'appel, Mons.

[201] See also McLachlan, n 10 above, at 607, who comments that ' "Delivery" itself is another legal concept which varies in meaning from legal system to legal system. The paragraph does not settle the issue of whether the *lex fori* or the *lex causae* is to be applied to answer this question.' Although this author would agree, it is suggested that the latter approach should be preferred. It would reduce forum shopping opportunities and promote uniform application of the Convention if the law *putatively* applicable under this Article, ie that of the place of the buyer's place of business, determined this question.

[202] Art 8(2)(c).   [203] Von Mehren Report, para 79.

'mainly' determined by the buyer.[204] However, such difficulties should not be exaggerated, as it is likely that most contracts of tender will clearly satisfy this condition on any reasonable view.

A general exception: Article 8(3)

15.93 Both Articles 8(1) and 8(2) are only rebuttable presumptions as to the applicable law in the absence of choice. Article 8(3) states that they may be rebutted under where 'in the light of the circumstances as a whole, for instance any business relations between the parties, the contract is manifestly more closely connected with a[nother] law . . .'. This provision has similarities to Article 4(5) of the Rome Convention.[205] However, it makes clear what the Rome Convention does not,[206] namely that the general presumptions are to be rebutted by the exception only there is a 'manifestly' closer connection with another law.[207] Commercial certainty demands that presumptions as to the governing law are rebutted only in cases where it is abundantly clear that another law is more closely connected.

15.94 All factors may be considered in determining whether Article 8(3) should be invoked, although the 'business relations between the parties' are singled out. What this means is less than clear. It appears to suggest that where the contract in issue forms part of a course of dealings between the parties typically governed by a particular law, the same law might properly govern this contract. Of course, that network of relations could be enough to infer a choice of law under Article 7 in any case.

Reservation on the application of the exception in Article 8(3)

15.95 Article 8(3) introduces an element of flexibility which seeks to strike a balance between clear rules of law and a restricted exception which allows another law to apply where it is manifestly more closely connected to the contract. Nevertheless, some states preferred to keep the rules absolutely rigid, and therefore wholly predictable, as the Hague Sales Convention 1955 had done. The eventual compromise was that states which did not want to apply Article 8(3) could make a reservation pursuant to Article 21(1)(b). This reservation was entered into by Czechoslovakia. Both the Czech Republic and Slovakia have both since affirmed their wish to be bound by the same reservation.

---

[204] Any uncertainty as to what the terms are, and whether they were determined 'mainly' by the buyer, should arguably be resolved by the law putatively applicable to the contract, namely that of the buyer's place of business.

[205] And nothing in common with the Hague Sales Convention 1955, which contains no exception to its choice of law rules in the absence of choice.

[206] See the discussion of Art 4(5) of the Rome Convention, above, paras 13.127–139.

[207] Note also that Art 4(5) of the Rome Convention refers to a closer connection to another country, rather than another law.

However, it is important to appreciate that the reservation would not in **15.96**
itself prevent the application of Article 8(3). It is not a blanket reservation,
and is phrased in curious terms. It allows a state which enters the reservation not to apply Article 8(3) '. . . except where neither party to the contract has his place of business in a State which has made a reservation
provided for under this sub-paragraph'. In other words, a state which has
made the reservation would only be able to invoke it where at least one
of the parties had their place of business in a state which had made the
reservation. Suppose that the 1986 Convention were to be ratified in all
the states which have presently only signed it[208] and were to enter into
force. To date, only the Czech Republic and Slovakia have made the
reservation in Article 21(1)(b). If a court in the Czech Republic were asked
to determine the applicable law in the absence of choice of a contract
between a buyer with its place of business in Argentina and a seller with
its place of business in Slovakia, the reservation would be triggered
and it would not apply Article 8(3). However, if the seller had its place of
business in the Netherlands,[209] the reservation would not be triggered
and the Czech court would have at least to consider whether to invoke the
exception in Article 8(3).

Conversely, Article 8(4) states that even a forum which has *not* made **15.97**
the reservation in Article 21(1)(b) shall not apply Article 8(3), if *both*
parties have their places of business in states which *have* made that
reservation. So, if a court in the Netherlands were asked to determine
the applicable law in the absence of choice of a contract between a
buyer with its place of business in the Czech Republic and a seller with
its place of business in Argentina, it would have to consider whether to
invoke the exception in Article 8(3). However, if the seller had its place
of business in Slovakia, it could not apply Article 8(3), since both the
Czech Republic and Slovakia have entered the reservation in Article
21(1)(b). In such circumstances, the Dutch court would simply apply the
rules of Articles 8(1) and (2) as inflexible rules of law in the absence of a
choice of law by the parties.[210] It is hard to see these provisions as
anything other than convoluted and it is unfortunate[211] that the law
which the forum will apply may depend upon whether some foreign
states in which the parties have their places of business have entered a
reservation.

---

[208] Or, in the case of Moldova, acceded to it.
[209] Or in a non-Contracting State to the 1986 Convention.   [210] Art 8(4).
[211] Not to say close to application of the doctrine of renvoi, which is otherwise excluded
from the Convention by Art 15. See para 15.99 below.

Non-application of Article 8(3) where parties have their places of business in different States Parties to the Vienna Convention

15.98 Even in respect of states which were willing to adopt the exception in Article 8(3), there was some disquiet about whether it was appropriate in respect of matters regulated by the Vienna Convention. Where, on any view, Article 8(1) or (2) would lead to the application of the rules of the law of a state which applies the Vienna Convention, it was felt that the Vienna Convention should apply and the possibility of the law of another state being applied instead as the law of closest connection should be removed.[212] So, Article 8(5) states that where, at the time of conclusion of the contract, the buyer and seller have their places of business in different states which are both parties to the Vienna Convention,[213] the exception in Article 8(3) does not apply in respect of issues which are regulated by the Vienna Convention. 'The theory underlying this proposal was that simple and rigid rules of the kind enunciated in Article [8(1) and (2)] . . . are acceptable when they lead to the application of an international and widely accepted body of substantive law rules.'[214] In such a scenario, the applicable law in the absence of choice shall be determined by Articles 8(1) and (2), which must be applied as inflexible rules of law and not subject to any exception. However, such a rule can readily be criticized. Choice of law rules are essentially supposed to be neutral as to the content of the various substantive choice of law rules that are to be applied. Yet this provision essentially involves saying that once the Vienna Convention's rules have been designated by Article 8(1) or (2), a 'suitable' law has been identified; where, however, those Articles do not lead to the application of the Vienna Convention, the possibility that another law could be applied as the law of closest connection is left open.[215]

5. EXCLUSION OF RENVOI

15.99 Once the applicable law has been identified, the domestic law of that state shall be applied. Article 15 provides that the word 'law' in the Convention excludes reference to the choice of law rules of the state identified.[216] This is consistent with other conventions on choice of law in contractual

---

[212] Even if it is hard to imagine that such a law would be 'manifestly more closely connected to the contract', as Art 8(3) requires.

[213] The condition in Art 1(a) of the Vienna Convention.

[214] Von Mehren Report, para 91.

[215] In particular, the law of a non-Contracting State to the Vienna Convention might be displaced by the law of a Contracting State to the Vienna Convention.

[216] Although, as we shall see in the following section, the Convention does in fact sanction a limited application of renvoi in the case of auction sales.

matters.[217] Where the parties have selected a law to govern the contract, they will clearly envisage that the domestic law of that state will be applied. Where the applicable law has to be determined in the absence of choice, the rules of Article 8 are designed to select the most suitable law to govern the contract. The domestic law of the state identified arguably remains the most suitable law[218] notwithstanding any choice of law rules of that state which would lead to the application of a different law in the courts of that state. For these reasons, the doctrine of renvoi is sensibly excluded.[219]

6. Auction Sales

As with the Hague Sales Convention 1955,[220] the 1986 Convention **15.100** contains a special choice of law rule for auctions.[221] This is contained in Article 9 of the 1986 Convention. This time, however, the provision is distinctly curious. It states that the parties may still choose the governing law of the contract under Article 7 '. . . to the extent to which the law of the State where the auction[222] takes place. . . does not prohibit such a choice'. The guiding principle is that party autonomy should, in principle, still be respected. However, given the strong territorial connection of an auction to the state where it takes place,[223] the law of that state has a power of veto in so far as it objects to the application of the law chosen by the parties. Yet this is tantamount to an express application of the doctrine of renvoi. Article 9 makes express reference *to the choice of law rule* of the place where

[217] Most notably, Art 2 of the 1955 Convention, above, para 15.28, and Art 15 of the Rome Convention, above, para 13.141. It is also consistent, as von Mehren points out, with the traditional approach of the Hague Conventions: para 148.

[218] Although a possible counter-argument is that the exception in Art 8(3) may be invoked where there is another *law* which is manifestly more closely connected to the contract (whereas Art 4(5) of the Rome Convention refers to another *country* of closer connection). It could be argued that where Art 8(1) or (2) of the 1986 Convention points to the law of State X, and a judge in State X would himself not apply that law, but would instead apply *the law of State Y*, there is a closer connection with the latter law.

[219] There was some discussion during the drafting of the Convention as to whether Art 15 had a function beyond excluding renvoi and whether the reference to 'the law in force in a State' was intended to preclude the parties from selecting the *lex mercatoria* to govern a contract. Von Mehren concludes that there was '. . . a very general—but not complete— agreement that Art 15 was intended to regulate only the issue of *renvoi*': para 156.

[220] Art 3(3) of the 1955 Convention, discussed above, paras 15.47–48.

[221] Which are not covered by the Vienna Convention. Art 2(b).

[222] Or commodity or other exchange. Note that in contrast to the 1955 Convention, no reference is made to the auction being 'public'.

[223] At least an auction which is not conducted by electronic means. Where the auction takes place using the internet, it is very difficult to determine its location and there is a case for saying that such auctions should be regarded as outside the scope of the Convention altogether: Kronke, n 145 above, at 77. See also the discussion of Art 3(3) of the 1955 Convention, above, paras 15.47–48.

the auction occurs. Such reference is extremely unusual in the private international law of contract. This is especially curious since Article 15 excludes the doctrine of renvoi by stating that the word 'law' in the Convention refers to 'the law in force in a State other than its choice of law rules'. It is difficult to see Article 9 as anything other than an unnecessary convolution of the law.[224]

15.101 Where no choice of law is made, or where the choice of law is prohibited according to the law of the place where the auction occurs, the law of the place of the auction applies. This is consistent with the approach taken in Article 3 of the 1955 Convention. It does, however, pose the same problem of identifying where an auction taking place over the internet takes place.[225]

7. The Essential Validity of the Contract and its Terms

15.102 Article 10 deals with the consent of the parties to the terms of the contract, including a choice of law clause, and with the essential[226] validity of the contract as a whole. It contains rules which are almost identical to those found in the Rome Convention.[227] Those rules represent a clear triumph of pragmatism over principle and allow the contract and its terms to be pulled up by their own bootstraps.

15.103 If it is disputed by the parties whether a choice of law clause for Utopian law exists at all, or whether the parties had consented to that clause, the law of Utopia will be applied to determine these matters.[228] If the answer is 'yes', then Utopian law will govern the contract. If the answer is 'no', then the applicable law will be determined in the absence of choice under Article 8. Article 10(1) is poorly worded. It states that questions of the existence and consent of the parties to the choice of law clause shall be determined by the law chosen (ie the law putatively chosen) 'where the choice satisfies the requirements of Article 7'. This does not make a great deal of logical sense, since until it is known whether a choice of law was indeed made, it cannot be said whether Article 7 is satisfied. Article 10(1) presumably means that there must, at least, be a *prima facie* case as to the existence of a choice of law and the consent of the parties to it before that law can be applied.

---

[224] Although von Mehren dismisses the renvoi point as a 'somewhat conceptual objection': para 99.

[225] See above, paras 15.47–48. See also below, paras 21.86–89.

[226] But not formal validity, which is dealt with in Art 11.

[227] Principally in Art 8 of the Rome Convention (but also in Art 3(4) thereof); discussed above, paras 13.56, 13.143–155.

[228] Art 10(1). Utopian law should be consulted only on these issues. It is irrelevant that Utopian law does not permit parties to choose the governing law of a contract.

The existence and essential validity of the contract itself, or of any terms of **15.104** the contract are governed by the law which would govern the contract if it were valid.[229] So, if the buyer and seller dispute whether a draft contract of sale was agreed upon, which contains a clause subjecting it to the law of Ruritania, Ruritanian law shall be used to determine whether the contract exists and is valid and whether it is indeed subject to Ruritanian law. If the parties accept that there is a contract governed by Ruritanian law, but dispute the validity of a term of it, for example stipulating that delivery should occur in the buyer's home state, Ruritanian law should similarly be applied to determine the validity of that term. Where the 'alleged' contract contains no choice of law clause, the law which would apply in the absence of choice were all the terms valid (which will be either the law of the seller's place of business, or, in certain circumstances, that of the buyer's place of business, in accordance with Article 8(1) and (2))[230] applies.

As with the Rome Convention,[231] the 1986 Convention contains an excep- **15.105** tion for the circumstance where using the putative applicable law to determine the existence and validity of the contract would work serious injustice on one party. Suppose that a seller were to send an email or letter to a party with a place of business in Arcadia, offering to sell it goods on particular terms, one of which is a choice of law clause providing that the law of Suburbia applies. Suppose that the buyer ignores the offer, but that, by Suburbian law, silence is deemed after the elapse of a certain period to constitute acceptance of an offer and agreement with its terms. Strictly speaking, Article 10(2) states that the court must apply Suburbian law to determine whether a contract exists and is valid. According to Suburbian law, the answer to both questions is 'yes'. Such manifest injustice is corrected in Article 10(3) by permitting the offeree to rely on the law of his place of business, Arcadia, to show that he did not consent to the contract,[232] if he can show that it would be unreasonable to determine this matter solely by the law putatively applicable to the contract.[233]

8. FORMAL VALIDITY[234]

The rules on formal validity are contained in Article 11. They are very **15.106** similar to those found in Article 9 of the Rome Convention.[235] Like the

---

[229] Art 10(2). [230] Considered above, paras 15.88–92.
[231] Art 8(2) of the Rome Convention; discussed above, paras 13.150–153.
[232] Or to any term of the contract, including a choice of law clause.
[233] Compare, under the Rome Convention, *Egon Oldendorff v Libera (No 1)* [1995] 2 Lloyd's Rep 64 (and see *Egon Oldendorff (No 2)* [1996] 1 Lloyd's Rep 380). These cases are discussed above, para 13.152.
[234] See also the discussion of the relationship of Art 11 to Art 96 of the Vienna Convention; below, paras 16.137–141.
[235] On which, see above, paras 13.256–263.

Rome Convention's rules, they are very liberal. Where the parties are in the same state at the time of conclusion, a contract[236] will be formally valid if it satisfies the formality rules of the law of the state of conclusion *or* the governing law of the contract, as determined under Articles 7 and 8.[237] Where the parties were in different states at the time of conclusion, a contract will be formally valid if it satisfies the formality rules of the law of the place where the buyer was at that time, *or* the law of the place where the seller was at that time *or* the governing law of the contract.[238]

15.107 Article 21(1)(c) deals with the problem of states which have legislation which *requires* that a contract of sale be concluded, or evidenced, in writing.[239] Rather than risk such states routinely refusing to apply the formality rules of Article 11 by treating their own rules as international mandatory rules of the forum,[240] the Convention allows them to enter a reservation[241] to the effect that they will not apply the Convention's rules on formal validity if, but only if, one or more of the parties has his place of business in the territory of that state at the time of conclusion of the contract. To date, only Argentina has entered such a reservation.

15.108 More curiously, Article 11(5) states that the formality rules of the Convention applicable to contracts of sale[242] do not apply 'where one of the parties to the contract has, at the time of its conclusion, his place of business in a State which has made the reservation provided for in Article 21, paragraph 1, sub-paragraph c)'. This appears to be the case *regardless of whether the forum has itself entered the reservation*. So, if the Convention were to enter into force and be applied in the Netherlands, which has not entered the reservation, it should not apply the formality rules of Article 11 to a contract of sale[243] governed by Dutch law between a seller with its place of business in Argentina and a buyer with its place of business in

---

[236] But Art 11 must not be applied so as to impose formal requirements on the validity of a choice of law clause. The requirements for a valid choice of law clause are solely those specified in Art 7: von Mehren Report, para 111.

[237] Art 11(1).

[238] Art 11(2). Where a contract is concluded by an agent, the place where the agent acts is the relevant state for the purposes of these rules: Art 11(3). Art 11(4) states that an act intended to have legal effect in relation to an existing or contemplated sales contract is formally valid if it satisfies the formality requirements *either* of the governing law of the contract *or* of the law of the state where the act was done.

[239] But is silent on any other kind of formality rule.   [240] Pursuant to Art 17.

[241] Modelled on Art 96 of the Vienna Convention.

[242] The reservation applies only to the contract of sale itself and not to a choice of law clause. Art 7 of the Convention decrees that a state may not impose a formality requirement for a choice of law clause: von Mehren Report, para 114.

[243] Von Mehren Report, para 117, notes that the exclusion does not apply to the consequences of formal invalidity.

the Netherlands.[244] It seems distinctly curious that the application of the Convention's formality rules should hinge upon a reservation made in a foreign state and not in the forum. The justification for this can scarcely be to give effect to the mandatory formality rules of a third state, in this case Argentina, since the Convention contains no other provision for applying the mandatory rules of a third state.[245]

9. SCOPE OF THE APPLICABLE LAW

Interpretation and Performance

The matters which are subjected to the applicable law of the contract **15.109** are set out in Article 12. The list is 'illustrative but not exhaustive'.[246] Many of them are quite uncontroversial. So, the applicable law will determine issues relating to the interpretation of the contract[247] and the rights and obligations of the parties and performance of the contract.[248] However, other provisions are substantially more controversial.

Entitlement to Products, Fruits and Income

Article 12(c) refers to 'the time at which the buyer becomes entitled to **15.110** the products, fruits and income deriving from the goods'. Whilst this might not seem controversial, the word 'entitled'[249] suggests a passing of property in those products; and, of course, one would normally expect such questions to be treated as matters for the law of the situs, not the governing law of a contract. It is notable that the Hague Convention on the Law Governing Transfer of Title in International Sales of Goods 1958, which also applies a contractual approach to the passing of fruits between the parties, has also failed ever to enter into force.[250]

Risk

Article 12(d) refers to the time from which the buyer bears the risk **15.111** with respect to the goods. This is a contractual, rather than a proprietary,

---

[244] Although, of course, there is nothing to stop it from adopting identical formality rules to those contained in Art 11: ibid, para 114, n 101.

[245] Art 17 only deals with the international mandatory rules of the forum.

[246] Von Mehren Report, para 118.

[247] Art 12(a). See also the discussion of Art 10(1)(a) of the Rome Convention, above, paras 13.157–158.

[248] Art 12(b). See also the discussion of Art 10(1)(b) of the Rome Convention, above, paras 13.159–13.204.

[249] Compare the French version: 'droits aux produits et aux fruits des marchandises'.

[250] See Art 2(1) of the 1958 Convention. See further below, paras 18.71–73.

issue. The passing of risk and the passing of title may, but certainly need not necessarily, be simultaneous.[251] However, they are clearly subject to different classifications for choice of law purposes.[252] The passing of risk does not confer a property right on the buyer; it is a question relating to the respective liabilities of the parties for loss and appropriately subject to the applicable law of the contract.[253]

Retention of Title

15.112   Article 12(e) is more complex. It applies to 'the validity and effect as between the parties of clauses reserving title to the goods'.[254] So, if A contracts to sell goods located in Arcadia to B and the contract of sale is governed by Baratarian law, the latter applies to the retention of title clause and determines whether it is valid and effective to prevent title from passing to B. That might seem sensible and commercially sound.[255] After all, the retention of title clause is a term of the contract and it is logical that the applicable law of the contract should determine its validity. However, the key point is that whilst it is indeed logically correct for the essential *validity* of a term in the contract to be subjected to the governing law of the contract, it is a quite different question whether a retention of title clause validly concluded in a contract has the *effect* of preventing property from passing to B. That is a matter relating to the passing of property and one might expect it to be governed by the law of the *situs*, Arcadian law.

15.113   It could be countered that, as between the parties, it would defeat their expectations if Arcadian law were applied. Moreover, since Article 12(e) only applies *between the parties*, no harm can obviously be done by letting them make their own arrangements as to the passing of property. The effect of the clause on third parties can be treated as a property matter and subjected to the law of the situs.[256] However, the obvious objection to this argument is that property rights which are determined in litigation between the contracting parties are nonetheless capable of binding third

---

[251] See, e.g. s 20 of the Sale of Goods Act 1979.

[252] See paras 12.03–04 and 12.06 on introduction to choice of law, paras 13.196–200 on choice of law in contract and the international sale of goods, and paras 18.132–134 on choice of law in property.

[253] But not all agree: see McLachlan, n 10 above, at 609. See also *Jacobs v Crédit Lyonnais* (1884) 12 QBD 589.

[254] See also above, para 13.251, and below, paras 18.93–111 and 19.81–87.

[255] For arguments in support, see below, paras 18.39–54, 18.100–111.

[256] A similar distinction between inter partes and third party scenarios can be found in the (unsuccessful) Hague Convention on the Law Governing Transfer of Title in International Sales of Goods 1958, ratified only by Italy (though signed, but not ratified, by Greece). The Convention is extremely unlikely ever to enter into force.

parties. That is, after all, the essence of a property right.[257] The question whether A or B owns the goods in question may affect third parties who purport to acquire title from one of those parties, or who claim that they were the pre-existing owner of the goods, or that they have a charge over the assets of one of the parties. It is this argument that won the day in *Glencore International AG v Metro Trading International Inc (No 2)*. Moore-Bick J remarked that:[258]

... I do not think that questions of title to movables can properly be considered simply by reference to the positions of the parties to the transaction under which they are intended to be transferred. Consistency of principle requires that the same rule should apply whether or not third party interests are involved ... [I]t would be highly anomalous if questions of title to the goods were to be governed by ... the proper law of the contract if the seller had not purported to re-sell the goods to a third party, but by ... the *lex situs* if he had.[259]

In our above example, suppose that Baratarian law, the law applicable to **15.114** the contract, regards the retention of title clause as valid, and effective to prevent title from passing to B. Arcadian law, the law of the *situs*, considers the clause ineffective to prevent title from passing to B. Article 12(e) of the 1986 Convention suggests that Baratarian law applies, and that title is retained by A. What, though, if B then purports to sell the goods in question to C in Arcadia? The law of Arcadia will presumably state that B can pass good title, on the basis that by that law, he has a good title himself. Yet the situs of the goods has remained unchanged throughout.

In short, it must be questioned whether it is possible wholly to separate **15.115** the effect of the retention of title clause between the contracting parties from the effect of that clause on third parties. A more conservative approach would have been for the law governing the contract to determine the essential validity *only* of the retention of title clause. If the clause is essentially valid by that law, it should then be asked whether, according to the law of the situs, that valid[260] clause has the *effect* of reserving title in the seller. This approach, which recognizes the legitimate concerns of both property and contractual choice of law rules in retention of title clauses,

---

[257] *Glencore International AG v Metro Trading International Inc (No 2)* [2001] 1 Lloyd's Rep 284; but contra, see M Bridge, 'English Conflicts Rules for Transfers of Movables: A Contract-based Approach?', Ch 7 in M Bridge and R Stevens (eds), *Cross Border Security and Insolvency* (Oxford, OUP, 2001) 123, esp 130–134. See also *Zahnrad Fabrik Passau GmbH v Terex Ltd* 1986 SLT 84.

[258] *Glencore*, ibid, at 294–295. See also the discussion of Art 10(1)(c) of the Rome Convention, above, paras 13.217–222.

[259] But for criticism of *Glencore*, see below, paras 18.38–54.

[260] The law of the *situs* must take for granted that the clause is essentially valid if the law designated by the forum's choice of law in contract rules so decrees.

would have the further advantage that it would not treat the retention of title clause differently for choice of law purposes, depending upon whether the dispute concerned only the buyer and seller, or also involved third parties.

Consequences of Non-Performance

15.116 Article 12(f) deals with the consequences of non-performance, including the categories of loss for which compensation may be recovered.[261] These 'consequences' of non-performance include the remedies available to the other party, such as rescission, damages, specific performance, the right of stoppage in transit and the right of resale. However, whilst it is unquestionably desirable that the law which confers contractual rights on the parties should also determine the remedies available to them, Article 12(f) applies 'without prejudice to the procedural law of the forum'. Whilst one would not normally ever expect rules of procedure to be determined other than by the law of the forum, it is notable that the Convention contains no general exclusion of matters of procedure. However, the concern in this area is that the applicable law of the contract might confer a remedy which is simply unknown in the courts of the forum and which they do not consider themselves competent to grant. In such circumstances, the remedy need not be granted.

15.117 More difficult are cases where the remedy does exist under the law of the forum, but would not be available on the facts. Discussions during the drafting of this Article focused on the remedy of specific performance, which is much more widely available in some legal systems than in others. Many wanted to make it express in the Convention that they would not be compelled to order such a remedy if it would not be available on the facts by the law of the forum.[262] Such an approach would reflect the approach taken in Article 28 of the Vienna Convention. Certainly, the 1986 Convention appears to permit states to refuse specific performance on these grounds as being contrary to the procedural law of the forum.[263] That said, it is suggested that it would be preferable for the courts of a Contracting State only to refuse to give effect to the governing law's remedy where that remedy is wholly unknown to the courts of the

---

[261] Many of the issues raised are similar to those under Art 10(1)(c) of the Rome Convention. The reader is referred to the discussion of that Article, above, paras 13.205–239.

[262] Von Mehren Report, paras 126–132.

[263] One effect of this provision is to provide an incentive to forum shop according to the remedy sought: see F Ferrari, ' "Forum Shopping" Despite International Uniform Contract Law Conventions' (2002) 51 ICLQ 689, 701.

forum. If the remedy is known in the courts of the forum, but would not be granted by it had the facts arisen in a purely domestic contract governed by the law of the forum (as might, for example, be the case with the granting of specific performance), then it is within the *competence* of the court to grant that remedy and it is not obvious there are sufficiently compelling reasons to refuse to give effect to the remedy stipulated by the applicable law of the contract. It is undesirable to separate the law governing a right from the remedy which it awards, and is likely to lead to a distortion of the foreign law.

Where the remedy in issue is damages, many states may wish to dis- **15.118** tinguish between issues relating to the types of loss for which recovery is possible and the quantification of damages under each head of damages. Article 12(f) refers expressly only to the former. This would be consistent with the approach taken in English law, where the availability of heads of damages is treated as a substantive matter for the governing law, but the quantification of damages is procedural and for the law of the forum to determine.[264]

The Ways of Extinguishing Obligations

Article 12(g) applies to the ways of extinguishing obligations, as well as **15.119** to prescription and limitation of actions.[265] It is entirely sensible that the law under which the parties' obligations arise should determine in which ways those obligations can be extinguished. More controversial is the provision on limitation and prescription. In some states, this may be regarded as a matter of procedure and properly governed by the law of the forum.[266] Accordingly, Article 21(1)(d) allows Contracting States to enter a reservation to the effect that they will not apply Article 12(g) in so far as it relates to prescription and limitation periods.[267]

---

[264] *Boys v Chaplin* [1971] AC 356; *Edmunds v Simmonds* [2001] WLR 1003; *Hulse v Chambers* [2001] 1 WLR 2386. Von Mehren, paras 133–135, suggests that the courts of the forum might refuse to allow penal damages to be awarded on the facts, even where they are available according to the governing law of the contract. Some states might see the availability of penal damages as procedural. However, even where the availability of penal damages is viewed by states as substantive, they might refuse to permit them on public policy grounds under Art 18 (but see ibid, paras 167–168 for rather inconclusive discussion about whether, and if so when, Art 18 might be invoked). See further J Carruthers, 'Substance and Procedure in the Conflict of Laws: a Continuing Debate in Relation to Damages' (2004) 53 ICLQ 691.

[265] See also the discussion of Art 10(1)(d) of the Rome Convention, above, paras 13.240–246.

[266] But not in England, where the Foreign Limitation Periods Act 1984 makes limitation periods a substantive matter (as does Art 10(1)(d) of the Rome Convention).

[267] Although no state has yet entered such a reservation. Note that Art 23(b) states that the 1986 Convention does not prejudice the application of the Convention on the Limitation

The Consequences of Nullity or Invalidity of the Contract

15.120 The final provision on the scope of the applicable law, Article 12(h), relates to the consequences of nullity or invalidity of a contract.[268] A similar provision in Article 10(1)(e) of the Rome Convention causes considerable controversy.[269] Some states were unwilling to apply the law governing a contract which had been shown to be null or invalid to determine the consequences of nullity. It may be seen as logically difficult to defend the application of the law of a 'contract' which is void.[270] Moreover, the restitutionary claims which might arise are on one view wholly independent legal causes of action and should be subject to their own choice of law rule.[271] However, whereas states were permitted to enter a reservation that they would not apply Article 10(1)(e) of the Rome Convention,[272] no such option has been left open in the 1986 Convention. That is likely to prove an ongoing disincentive to states of the same mind as the United Kingdom to ratifying the 1986 Convention.

Conclusion

15.121 Overall, it can be seen that the desire to push pragmatism to its limits has led to the formulation of a list extending beyond those matters which one might traditionally expect to be governed by the applicable law of the contract. This progressive approach is evidently one which has failed to convince a sufficient number of states to sign up to and ratify the Convention.

10. THE ROLE OF THE LAW OF THE PLACE OF INSPECTION

15.122 As with the 1955 Convention,[273] so the 1986 Convention contains a provision giving the law of the place of inspection a role with respect to the inspection process. Article 13 states that, in the absence of an express

---

Period in the International Sale of Goods (New York, 14 June 1974) or the Protocol amending that Convention (Vienna, 11 April 1980). See K Boele-Woelki, 'The Limitation of Rights and Actions in the International Sale of Goods' (1999) IV(3) Uniform L Rev 621, esp 628–631.

[268] However, the consequences of nullity or invalidity of a contract on the grounds of incapacity fall outside the Convention under Art 5(a).

[269] See the discussion above, paras 13.247–248, and below, paras 19.15 and 19.36.

[270] But see below, paras 19.20–31.

[271] Compare the decision of the Outer House of the Court of Session in *Barings Bros & Co Ltd v Cunninghame District Council* [1997] CLC 108, considered below, paras 19.11–12.

[272] Art 22(1)(b) of the Rome Convention. The UK has entered this reservation: see s 2(2) of the Contracts (Applicable Law) Act 1990.

[273] Art 4 of the 1955 Convention, considered above, paras 15.49–58.

clause to the contrary, this law will apply to 'the modalities and procedural requirements for such inspection'. As with the 1955 Convention, this does not appear to superimpose these rules onto the otherwise applicable law; rather, the law of the place of inspection is *the applicable law* for such matters. However, a choice of law clause complying with Article 7 will be sufficient to oust the application of this Article.[274]

Article 13 applies only to the form in which inspection shall take place **15.123** and the procedure for inspection. It must not be applied to the right to inspect the goods, which is a matter for the governing law of the contract to determine; nor can it be applied to the time period for inspection.[275] This is a departure from the 1955 Convention's position. Moreover, Article 4 of the 1955 Convention deals also with 'the measures to be taken in case of refusal of goods'. We saw above that this is an uncertain and unsatisfactory provision. It is not included in Article 13 of the 1986 Convention and it appears that such matters must be determined by the governing law of the contract.[276]

11. Mandatory Rules and Public Policy

Mandatory Rules

Even a modern choice of law Convention as embracing of party **15.124** autonomy as the 1986 Convention must contain some restrictions on the scope of that autonomy. That said, the 1986 Convention contains just one Article each on mandatory rules[277] and public policy.[278] It is notable that the scope of application of these provisions is subtly different to those found in the Rome Convention.

Article 17 preserves the application of the international mandatory rules **15.125** of the forum. In other words, the forum is not prevented from applying its rules of law from which the parties may not derogate, where those rules must be applied irrespective of the law applicable to the contract. However, after prolonged discussion, the Hague Conference decided to have no equivalent provision to Article 7(1) of the Rome Convention, which permits a court to apply the mandatory rules of a state of close connection to the contract.[279] Although states were free to opt out of the

---

[274] Von Mehren Report, para 140.   [275] ibid, paras 140–141.
[276] Art 4 of the 1955 Convention also mentions the notification concerning the inspection. This is not mentioned in Art 13 of the 1986 Convention but is presumably governed by it, since it could be said to relate to the procedural requirement for the inspection.
[277] Art 17 of the 1986 Convention.   [278] Art 18 of the 1986 Convention.
[279] For discussions on a proposal to introduce an Article in the same terms as Art 7(1) of the Rome Convention, or a modified version of it, see the von Mehren Report, paras 158–165.

application of that Article,[280] and the United Kingdom has done so,[281] it is notable that the 1986 Convention does not even tolerate the possibility of the application of such rules. In that respect, as in many others,[282] the 1986 Convention is extremely embracing of party autonomy.[283]

Public Policy

15.126 Article 18 permits the forum to refuse to apply the law identified by the Convention if, but only if, such application would be manifestly contrary to public policy. As with Article 16 of the Rome Convention, so too here the word 'manifestly' is intended to emphasize that use of public policy is a route of last resort and that, wherever possible, the law specified by the Convention should be applied. However, Article 18 curiously does not expressly limit itself to the public policy of the *forum*. This is a curious situation and a departure from Article 16 of the Rome Convention, which allows only the forum's public policy to be applied. In theory, a court could apply the public policy of a state of close connection, such as the place of performance, under the 1986 Convention. It is very hard to understand why the forum may only apply its own international mandatory rules, but might be permitted to invoke the public policy of a third state. It is suggested that it is important for states to construe Article 18 narrowly, in order not to undermine the promotion of party autonomy elsewhere in the Convention.[284] That suggests that states should be very slow to invoke the public policy of a third state. This would make the application of the Convention unpredictable and would result in differential application between Contracting States.

12. Concluding Remarks on the 1986 Convention

15.127 There is much to admire in the Hague Sales Convention 1986. It is ambitious, detailed and progressive. It seeks to marry itself with the Vienna

---

[280] Art 22(1)(a) of the Rome Convention so provides.

[281] s 2(2) of the Contracts (Applicable Law) Act 1990.

[282] Most notably with regard to the matters listed in Art 12 to which the applicable law of the contract applies, which include the effect of a reservation of title clause, the time at which the buyer becomes entitled to the products and fruits deriving from the goods and the consequences of nullity or invalidity of the contract (there being no opt out from any of these provisions). See above, paras 15.109–121.

[283] See further McLachlan, n 10 above, at 623 (esp n 133).

[284] Art 16 also states that when interpreting the Convention, regard should be had 'to its international character and to the need to promote uniformity in its application'. This might add further support to the proposition that the public policy restriction should be narrowly construed, since it is in the nature of an international Convention that Contracting States will have to apply rules substantially different to those found in their, or another state's, domestic law.

Convention, whilst recognizing the differing functions of a private international law Convention and the fact that, since the 1986 Convention might lead to the application of the law of a state not party to the Vienna Convention, exact uniformity in the scope of its various Articles is inappropriate. Yet, the 1986 Convention has proved unsuccessful.

The Convention is more progressive than the 1955 Convention or the **15.128** Rome Convention in protecting party autonomy. The list of matters subjected to the governing law of the contract covers matters not usually associated with that law, such as the effect of a retention of title clause, the entitlement of the buyer to the products fruits and income derived from goods, and the consequences of nullity or invalidity of a contract.[285] Although the Convention contains a number of opt-outs, they do not relate to these matters. There is a danger that party autonomy has been extended too far. The fact that the Convention includes matters which might traditionally be regarded in common law states as properly subjected to property or restitution choice of law rules might lead to some hesitation in those states in embracing the Convention. Moreover, alongside these progressive rules are certain Articles which appear unnecessarily complex and somewhat convoluted, such as the rule on auction sales, the rules on exactly when the law of closest connection may or may not be considered under Article 8(3), and the effect of the reservation on formal validity.

For Contracting States to the Rome Convention, there is a serious doubt **15.129** about whether ratification of the 1986 Convention would be an improvement upon the rules of the Rome Convention. Many of the key choice of law rules are very similar to those in the Rome Convention. Since the contract of sale is perhaps the archetypal contract, the Rome Convention was obviously drafted with the need to provide workable solutions to sales contracts in mind. Like the 1986 Sales Convention, it allows the parties expressly or impliedly to choose the governing law of the contract and normally[286] applies the law of the seller's place of business in the absence of choice. Where the rules of the 1986 Convention differ from those of the Rome Convention, it is a moot point whether they improve the law. As stated above, the 1986 Convention's rules could rather be seen as too embracing of party autonomy. For example, Article 1(1) of the Rome Convention limits the scope of that Convention to 'contractual obligations'.[287] Article 12 of the 1986 Convention extends the scope of the

---

[285] Other than for reasons of incapacity.

[286] Art 4(2) of the Rome Convention. This is subject to Art 4(5). See above, paras 13.112–140.

[287] See above, paras 13.14–17.

law applicable to the contract to certain matters which may appropriately be classified as proprietary.[288] Moreover, whilst both Conventions subject the consequences of nullity to the applicable law of the contract,[289] only the Rome Convention permits Contracting States to enter a reservation, as the United Kingdom has done, to the effect that they will not apply this provision. At the same time, the 1986 Convention's rules are too complex in certain areas in comparison with the Rome Convention. For example, the additional rules on determining the applicable law in the absence of choice,[290] the auction provisions[291] and the reservation on formal validity[292] have no counterpart in the Rome Convention. Any conceivable benefits that these provisions might have in laying down more specific, and more appropriate, choice of law rules for the international sale of goods, are easily outweighed by the complexity and uncertainty to which they give rise.[293] Today, there would need to be compelling arguments for a Contracting State to the Rome Convention to sign and ratify the 1986 Convention and it appears that such arguments do not exist. It is suggested that the United Kingdom should not adopt the 1986 Convention. More generally, prospects do not augur well for the 1986 Convention ever to enter into force.

VI. CONCLUSION

15.130 That the Hague Conference should twice[294] have concluded Conventions on the law applicable to contracts for the international sale of goods only serves to illustrate the fundamental importance of having appropriate choice of law rules in this area. A uniform approach to choice of law means that the parties can be sure that they will meet the same law in whichever Contracting State they might sue or be sued. The Hague Sales Convention 1955 has been modestly successful, but has failed to attract significant interest, not least because it also applies to consumer contracts,

---

[288] Notably Art 12(c) on the time at which the buyer becomes entitled to the products and fruits derived from the goods and Art 12(e) on the effect as between the parties of a retention of title clause; see above, paras 15.110 and 15.112–115.

[289] Art 10(1)(e) of the Rome Convention, above, paras 13.247–248, and below, paras 19.15 and 19.36; Art 12(h) of the 1986 Convention.

[290] Art 8(2), (3), (4) and (5) and the reservation in Art 21(1)(b), discussed above, paras 15.90–98.

[291] Art 9 of the 1986 Convention, discussed above, paras 15.100–101.

[292] Arts 11(5) and 21(1)(c) of the 1986 Convention, discussed above, para 15.108.

[293] This also helps to explain why even states which are party to the 1955 Convention have largely shunned the 1986 Convention.

[294] As well as the two unsuccessful Conventions of 1958 on the Jurisdiction of the Selected Forum in the Case of International Sales of Goods and on the Law Governing Transfer of Title in International Sales.

without offering consumers any special protection. The 1986 Convention, triggered by concern about the appropriateness of the rules of the 1955 Convention and the advent of the Vienna Convention, is a sophisticated attempt at a set of choice of law rules for commercial contracts, but has failed to strike a chord with the Conference's Member States. It must now be doubtful whether the Hague Conference will ever have a major global impact on the international sale of goods.

16

Uniform and Harmonized Sales Law: Choice of Law Issues

I. INTRODUCTION

16.01 The purpose of this chapter is mainly two-fold: first, to determine the respective spheres of, on the one hand, harmonized and uniform law and, on the other hand, the choice of law process; and second, to track the role of choice of law rules within harmonized and uniform law. To determine the roles of uniform law and of choice of law rules is as necessary in a book dealing with private international law as it is to select between competing laws in the choice of law process. Nevertheless, though competing choices of national law may each repel the other, it is a fallacy to believe that uniform substantive law and choice of law are mutually exclusive processes, which is why a careful account has to be taken of their interaction. This account will be based preponderantly upon the United Nations Convention on International Sale of Goods 1980.[1]

1. CHOICE OF LAW AND UNIFORM LAW DISTINGUISHED

16.02 Choice of law is a process that, amongst competing laws, permits the selection of an applicable law to one or more issues arising under a legal relationship. The rules applied in the choice of law process are the rules of the legal system whose courts are seised of the matter. In that sense, choice of law rules are part of the domestic law of the forum state whose courts apply those rules. In consequence, choice of law rules may vary from state to state unless and to the extent that different states by convention have adopted uniform choice of law rules. The Hague Conference on Private

---

[1] Hereinafter, Vienna Convention. It is common to abbreviate this Convention as the CISG (Convention on International Sale of Goods) but the Convention exists in the six official languages of the UN and an abbreviation that is true to only one of those languages (English) may be thought to be lacking in the spirit of internationalism.

International Law has been the source of numerous multilateral conventions adopted more or less by individual states.[2] Outside the Hague Conference, the various European Community countries have bound themselves by multilateral treaty, the Rome Convention on the Law Applicable to Contractual Obligations 1980, to legislate for uniform choice of law contract rules.

The adoption of uniform choice of law rules brings about the convergence **16.03** of different states' laws, but only up to a point. In so far as a contractual matter, for example, might be litigated in different Member States of the European Community, then in principle it ought not to matter whether the matter is brought before the courts of England, Belgium, Germany or any other Contracting State. The applicable law should be the same. If the parties expressly choose Belgian law to be the applicable law, then the courts of any Contracting State will apply Article 3 of the Rome Convention to uphold the parties' choice. Alternatively, if the parties have not selected an applicable law, all national courts, pursuant to Article 4, will turn to the law of closest connection,[3] which is presumed to be the law of the place where the characteristic performer is resident.[4]

2. FEATURES OF UNIFORM LAW

The relatively modest aims of uniform choice of law rules should be **16.04** noted. They discourage forum shopping but they do nothing to diminish the plethora of substantive laws that might be applied to a contractual matter, except in this respect. So far as uniformity in the choice of law process promotes party autonomy—which is not a necessary component of this process—it encourages the development of substantive laws so that they accommodate the commercial aspirations of contracting parties, even as it reduces in practice the number of laws applied in the various courts of the Contracting States, as parties tend to select the more commercially friendly and predictable laws. Even so, the burden of handling or mastering a multiplicity of laws imposes costs on business. Individual contracting parties cannot be sure of imposing their own preferred law on each other. Moreover, as far as sale goes, party autonomy applies only to the contractual aspects of sale and not to its proprietary aspects.[5]

---

[2] Apart from conventions attracting different numbers of Contracting States, the number of such states required before the convention enters into force will vary from convention to convention. The Unidroit Convention on International Financial Leasing (Ottawa 1988), for example, came into force upon its adoption by only three states (Art 16(1)). On the other hand, the number required for the Vienna Convention was ten states (Art 99(1)).

[3] Art 4(1). See Ch 13 above.   [4] Art 4(2).   [5] See Ch 18 below.

16.05   Uniform choice of law also has two significant shortcomings that it shares, though not necessarily to the same degree, with uniform substantive law. To the extent that interpretation of the terms of a choice of law convention rests ultimately with the highest courts of Contracting States, as opposed to an international commercial court of one sort or other, there is no binding means, apart from exhortative or mandatory provisions in the Convention, to be guided by international considerations in interpreting the Convention, to maintain uniformity.[6] The protocol to the Rome Convention, if ever it comes into effect,[7] will resolve this problem by vesting ultimately in the European Court of Justice the task of interpreting the Convention. The other significant shortcoming concerns the distinction between substantive and procedural law. Procedure is a matter for the law of the forum, which also defines what constitutes procedure.[8] The extent of uniformity in the choice of law process depends greatly upon how extensive and how uniform are the definitions of procedure in the laws of the various Contracting States. The prevailing trend, however, seen more clearly in the case of uniform choice of law, is to diminish the grip of the

---

[6] For an unfortunate recourse to national considerations in interpreting the Vienna Convention, see Cour d'appel de Chambéry of 25 May 1993, *R. J. com.* 1995, 242, note C Witz, where in applying Art 3(1) the court was clearly influenced by the French national distinction between contracts of sale and 'contrats d'entreprise'. A correct interpretation of the Convention, guided by international considerations, would have led to the opposite conclusion. For an illustration of the latter approach, see Oberlandesgericht Frankfurt of 17 September 1991 (translated at www.cisg.law.pace.edu/cisg/wais/db/cases2/910971g1.html).

[7] See the Green Paper on the Conversion of the Rome Convention of 1980 on the Law Applicable to Contractual Obligations into a Community Instrument and Its Modernisation (COM(2002) 654, Brussels 14 January 2003) (known and referred to hereinafter as Rome I Green Paper 2003). If the Rome Convention is superseded by a choice of law regulation, as is likely, then the ECJ will in any event be the ultimate arbiter of its meaning.

[8] Subject to any convention that defines as a matter of substantive law something that under the law of the forum would be perceived as procedure. See, e.g. Art 14 of the Rome Convention (burden of proof). As far as the Vienna Convention goes, there is authority for the view that it deals with issues of the burden of proof: see Bundesgerichtshof of 9 January 2002 (translated at http://cisgw3.law.pace.edu/cases/020109g1.html). So far as the parol evidence rule operates as a rule of evidence in the US, American decisions to the effect that it has no part to play in the application of the Vienna Convention support the view that the Convention supersedes rules of domestic procedural law arrived at by way of the law of the forum: see *Mitchell Aircraft Spares v European Aircraft Service* (Federal District Court (Illinois) of 27 October 1998 at http://cisgw3.law.pace.edu/cases/981027u1.html); *MCC Marble Ceramic Center Inc v Ceramica Nuova D'Agostino* (Federal Court of Appeals 11th Circuit of 29 June 1998 at http://cisgw3.law.pace.edu/cases/980629u1.html); *Filanti v Chilewich International Corp* (Federal District Court (New York) of 14 April 1992 at http://cisgw3.law.pace.edu/cases/920414u1.html); *Calzaturinifico Claudia v Olivieri Footwear* (Federal District Court (New York) of 6 April 1998 at http://cisgw3.law.pace.edu/cases/980406u1.html). For the view that the parol evidence rule still applies, see *Beijing Metals & Minerals Import/Export Corp v American Business Center* (Federal Court of Appeals 5th Circuit of 15 June 1993 at http://cisgw3.law.pace.edu/cases/930615u1.html). Limitation periods will be discussed below.

law of the forum by subjecting procedural issues to the law applicable to the contract. If anything, the above drawbacks to uniformity in the choice of law process are even more pronounced for uniform substantive law given the greater ambition and expanse of uniform law.

3. HARMONIZATION OF LAW

Whereas uniformity of law strives for identicality among the laws of the **16.06** various states, the goals of harmonization are not so fine-tuned. Within the European Community, the difference between the two processes can be observed in the distinction between regulations, directly applicable in identical terms in all Member States,[9] and directives, which are binding as to 'the result to be achieved'[10] but leave it to the national law how the directive itself should be transposed into domestic legislation and are thus to that extent tolerant of diversity. In so far as directives permit national difference, then the selection of the applicable law by way of the choice of law process to define the content of the law within that margin of tolerance remains significant.

Taking the Directive on Unfair Terms in Consumer Contracts as an **16.07** example,[11] the applicable law would determine the extent to which terms on the indicative 'grey list' of unfair terms gave rise to a significant imbalance in the contract in breach of good faith[12] and indeed would determine the type of conduct that accorded with good faith.[13] A reference instead to the law of the forum would be inconsistent with the Rome Convention 1980.[14] This is preferable to leaving the issue to the law of the forum. Similarly, to take as an example the Directive on Guarantees in Consumer Sales,[15] it should be the applicable law that determines whether a consumer buyer has elected to take the remedies transposed from the Directive or the remedies laid down instead by national sale of goods law. In determining the line between national and community law, it is submitted, a distinction should be drawn between, on the one hand, the meaning of undefined concepts that determine the application of the

---

[9] Art 249 of the EC Treaty.   [10] Art 249 of the EC Treaty.
[11] Council Directive (EEC) 93/13 of 5 April 1993, transposed as the Unfair Terms in Consumer Contracts Regulations 1999, SI 1999/2083.
[12] reg 5(1).
[13] Case C-478/99 *Commission of the European Communities v Kingdom of Sweden* [2002] ECR I-4147, para 11: since the grey list is non-exhaustive, it may pursuant to Art 8 of the Directive be amplified or restricted in the national laws of Member States.
[14] See Ch 13. It need hardly be said that the significance of the contents on the grey list, itself operating from within a directive, cannot be given an autonomous European interpretation.
[15] (EC) 1999/44 of the Parliament and the Council of 25 May 1999 (transposed into English law by SI 2002/3045, amending the Sale of Goods Act 1979).

Directive (or rather its transposed equivalent) and the application of discretionary standards contained within the Directive together with its detailed implementation. For example, expressions such as 'supply of goods' and 'supply of services' in the Distance Selling Directive[16] should be given an autonomous community meaning because, if they received divergent national interpretations, the harmonization process itself would be undermined.

16.08 The transposition of directives can be seen as producing sectoral harmonization of law within the European Community. The aspirations of the process of harmonization relate not to the outcomes of individual cases but rather to the attainment of certain systemic goals, such as the production of level competitive conditions and the evolution of a generation of consumers with the confidence to shop across national frontiers in the European Community.[17] The attainment of identical outcomes in individual cases, sought by uniform law in both its choice of law and substantive law manifestations (though the outcomes are differently defined), is not one of the goals of this harmonization process.

4. Harmonized Law and Choice of Law

16.09 Since harmonization does not bring about identical outcomes, it follows that the choice of law process remains an active one amongst the states subject to that harmonized law.[18] Furthermore, to the extent that harmonization sets minimum standards, as it does in the consumer arena in the European Community, the choice of law process is further boosted so far as consumers might be able to rely upon higher standards of protection in certain states. The choice of law issues presented by uniform law are just conventional issues of choice of law in contract.[19] To the extent that the laws of England and of Germany, for example, are similar but not identical in the case of the Directive on Consumer Sales Guarantees 1999,[20] then it will remain important to select the applicable law. It might happen that the transposition of the Directive in England, in a way that leaves open the remedial structure of the Sale of Goods Act 1979 alongside the new provisions, will raise questions of election by the consumer buyer

---

[16]   (EC) 1997/7 of the Parliament and the Council of 20 May 1997 (transposed into English law by SI 2000/2334).

[17]   See S Weatherill, 'Consumer Guarantees' (1994) 110 LQR 545.

[18]   Nevertheless, insurance contracts relating to risks within the EU Member States are excluded from the choice of law rules in the Rome Convention: Art 1(3). On one view, this is because the various directives had achieved substantive harmonization, but a more realistic view is that it was expected that specific rules for insurance contracts would later be devised (which in fact never happened).

[19]   See Ch 13 for choice of law in contract.   [20]   1999/44.

between these two remedial regimes of a kind not to be found as a result of changes to the German Civil Code, as part of the process of adapting German law to the sum of community law in the area of consumer protection.[21] Determining whether the applicable law is German or English law might therefore be significant for the purpose of determining the remedies left open to a consumer buyer. This question goes beyond the rules in the Rome Convention designed to ensure that the consumer is not prejudiced by the selection of the applicable law in the choice of law process.[22]

II. THE UNITED NATIONS CONVENTION ON THE INTERNATIONAL SALE OF GOODS 1980[23]

1. The History of the Vienna Convention

The uniform law movement in sale has a documentary history going back **16.10** three-quarters of a century. The detailed history is recorded elsewhere[24] but its principal milestones are as follows. Upon the foundation of the International Institute for the Unification of Private Law in 1926,[25] the great German jurist Ernst Rabel was successful in placing the subject of a uniform law of international law on its agenda. A first draft was prepared in 1935 but the Second World War halted further progress. After the war, the matter was carried forward with a series of drafts between 1958 and 1963, the process culminating in two Hague conventions of 1964 containing uniform laws on the international sale of goods (ULIS) and on the formation of contracts for the international sale of goods (ULF). These attracted very little support, most of it from western Europe, largely because of the effective absence of the United States and the developing and socialist nations from the legislative process. The process of achieving real uniformity was given a major boost with the establishment in

---

[21] See P Schlechtriem, 'The German Act to Modernize the Law of Obligations' (*Oxford Comparative Law Forum*: http://ouclf.iuscomp.org); R Zimmermann, 'Breach of Contract and Remedies under the New German Law of Obligations', in *Centro di studi e ricerche di diritto comparato et stranieri: Saggi, Conferenzi e Seminari* (No 48, Rome 2002).

[22] See Art 5.

[23] This will be referred to in this text as the Vienna Convention, though it is more common to use the acronym, CISG (Convention on International Sale of Goods), the drawback to which is that it is unique to English, which is only one of the six official languages of the UN though it was the language of the proceedings.

[24] K Sono, 'The Vienna Sale Convention: History and Perspective' in P Volken and P Sarcevic (eds), *International Sale of Goods: Dubrovnik Lectures* (New York: Oceana, 1986); Schlechtriem, 1–3.

[25] Based in Rome, this is an inter-governmental organization originally set up as a League of Nations agency.

1966 of the United Nations Commission on International Trade Law (UNCITRAL), an act largely inspired by the desire to give birth to a new economic order. Work on (initially) two new instruments was launched in 1968, taking as its basis the uniform laws of 1964. A draft convention was prepared in 1978 uniting contractual formation and the substantive law of sale of goods and the final version was adopted at a diplomatic conference in 1980, coming into force in 1988 when the requisite number of signatures had been obtained. The Vienna Convention 1980 has now been adopted by many nations, including the greater part of the world's major trading nations.[26]

16.11   In view of the importance of following the legislative history of the Vienna Convention[27] when interpreting its provisions, the process of enactment set in train by the UNCITRAL should be understood. It consisted first of the efforts of a Working Group meeting on nine occasions from 1970 to 1977, which worked on the texts of ULIS and ULF to produce drafts of 1976 and 1977.[28] These were reviewed by the full Commission from 1977 to 1978, unanimously approved and combined into a single 1978 draft. The third stage was the 1980 diplomatic conference in Vienna. Its work was entrusted to two committees[29] meeting simultaneously, in each of which all states attending the Conference were represented.[30] This final phase culminated in a plenary meeting which adopted the present text of the Vienna Convention.

2. THE USE OF CHOICE OF LAW IN DETERMINING THE SCOPE OF THE VIENNA CONVENTION

The Uniform Law on the International Sale of Goods

16.12   The part played by choice of law in determining the scope of the Vienna Convention[31] can be seen in its clearest light by means of a preliminary examination of its predecessor, ULIS. ULIS has attracted strong criticism

---

[26] The major exceptions are the UK, Japan, India and Brazil.

[27] See the invaluable compilation by J Honnold, *Documentary History of the Uniform Law for International Sales* (Deventer: Kluwer, 1989), taken from the relevant volumes of the UNCITRAL Yearbooks and the Official Records of the 1980 Diplomatic Conference in Vienna. The proceedings are also available online (www.cisg/law/pace.edu/cisg/proceedings.html).

[28] The first was on the substantive law of sale and the second on formation of the contract.

[29] The first Committee dealt with Parts I–III (Arts 1–88), while the second dealt with Part IV (Final Provisions).

[30] See Honnold, n 27 above, at 1–4.

[31] See generally P Winship, 'Private International Law and the U.N. Sales Convention' (1988) 21 Cornell Intl LJ 487; I Dore, 'Choice of Law under the International Sales Convention: a US Perspective' [1983] American J of Intl Law 521; J Kimball and S Harter, 'Choice of Law Issues in Contracts for the International Sale of Goods: Getting What You Bargained for in the United States' (1997) 1 Intl Trade LQ 28.

for its so-called universalism.[32] It is universal in the sense that the forum state, if a Contracting State, is bound to apply ULIS, provided that the contract complies with the factual requirements of an international sale as defined in ULIS, regardless of whether the parties themselves, or even one of them, resides in a Contracting State. In consequence, a jurisdiction agreement in a contract of sale might have the inadvertent consequence, for parties to a contract not containing an applicable law clause, that their relations are governed by ULIS, an instrument to which they might not have intended to commit themselves and of whose existence they might have been quite unaware. The parties, indeed, might reside in non-Contracting States and have, apart from the jurisdiction agreement or the accident of litigation in a Contracting State, no connection at all with any Contracting State.[33] This state of affairs will arise if the forum state is a Contracting State and the parties have not in their contract, by means for example of an express applicable law clause, availed themselves of the facility granted by ULIS to exclude some or indeed all of its provisions.[34] The universalist approach of ULIS was seen by some critics as amounting to the forcing of a foreign convention upon a non-acceding country and the conferment of benefits upon a non-signatory. One response to this latter criticism, however, is to treat ULIS as part of the domestic law of the incorporating state so that the incorporating state is applying the Convention to itself and not to other states.[35]

The purity of ULIS's universalism comes at a price. The Convention **16.13** introducing ULIS[36] permits Contracting States to make one or more declarations that will in varying degrees circumscribe the universalist character of ULIS. First, they may declare that they will apply ULIS only in those cases where the parties reside in different Contracting States.[37]

---

[32] For practical purposes, ULIS has very little scope for application but it would be premature to treat it as a dead letter. The UK is still a party to it (though with reservations), likewise San Marino and Gambia. Israel denounced it with effect from 1 February 2003 consequent upon its accession to the Vienna Convention. The instrument concerning the latter was deposited with the UN on 22 January 2002, so that Israel became a Contracting State 12 months later (see Art 99(2) of the Vienna Convention). For jurisdiction cases where ULIS was the applicable law, see Ch 3 above.

[33] See *Report of the Secretary-General, Pending questions with respect to the revised text of a uniform law on the international sale of goods* (UN Documents A/CN.9/100, annex III), para 10 [1975] 6 UNCITRAL Yearbook 88, 89.

[34] Art 3 of ULIS permits contracting parties to exclude ULIS either entirely or partially.

[35] See L Réczei, 'The Area of Operation of the International Sale Conventions' (1981) 29 American J of Comparative Law 513, 515–516.

[36] Convention Relating to a Uniform Law on the International Sale of Goods (1964).

[37] Art III: '... [A]ny State may ... declare ... that it will apply the Uniform Law only if each of the parties to the contract of sale has his place of business or, if he has no place of business, his habitual residence in the territory of a different Contracting State ...'. Declarations under Art III were made by West Germany, the UK, San Marino and the Netherlands. See the Uniform Law on International Sales Act 1967.

16.14 Second, they may declare that they will apply ULIS only where, pursuant to a conflicts convention dealing with the international sale of goods and to which they have acceded or which they have ratified, they are bound to apply ULIS.[38] This is primarily a reference to the 1955 Hague Sales Convention; it confines the application of ULIS to those cases where the forum's rules of private international law lead to the law of a (ULIS) Contracting State. Third, they may declare that ULIS will apply only if the parties choose ULIS as the applicable law.[39] Of the small number of states adopting ULIS, only Israel did so without making one or more of these three declarations.

16.15 This universalist stance of ULIS reflects (subject to permitted declarations) its repudiation of private international law as an engine for determining the application of the uniform law. ULIS applies to those contracts of sale where the parties' places of business are in different states and one of the following three requirements is satisfied: first, the goods are to be carried from one state to another, or, at the time of conclusion of the contract, are in the course of so being carried; second, the acts constituting offer and acceptance are effected in different states; and third, delivery of the goods takes effect in a state other than the one where the acts constituting the offer and acceptance are effected.[40]

Application of the Vienna Convention

16.16 The scope of application of the Vienna Convention was a matter for intensive debate throughout the process leading to its conclusion. The basic

---

[38] Art IV: 'Any State which has previously ratified or acceded to one or more Conventions on conflict of laws in respect of the international sale of goods may . . . declare . . . that it will apply the Uniform Law in cases governed by one of those previous Conventions only if that Convention itself requires the application of the Uniform Law'. Italy and Belgium made declarations under Art IV.

[39] Art V: 'Any State may . . . declare . . . that it will apply the Uniform Law only to contracts in which the parties thereto have . . . chosen that Law as the law of the contract'. The UK and Gambia made declarations under Art V. See the Uniform Law on International Sales Act 1967.

[40] These tests of internationality correspond almost exactly (and depart only accidentally?) from the test of an international supply contract which is exempted from the controls on exclusion and limitation clauses in the Unfair Contract Terms Act 1977 by virtue of s 26 thereof. See *Amiri Flight Authority v BAE Systems plc* [2003] EWCA Civ 1447, [2003] 2 Lloyd's Rep 767, CA, where the court, reversing Tomlinson J below ([2002] EWHC 2481 at [28], [2003] 1 Lloyd's Rep 50), ruled that a minor difference in the wording of the test in the Unfair Contract Terms Act 1977 (s 26(4)(c): 'goods to be delivered to the territory of a State other than that within whose territory [acts amounting to offer and acceptance] were done') and ULIS ('delivered in etc') had the practical effect that a contract where formation occurred in one state and delivery occurred in another, but without crossing national borders, was not an exempt international sale of goods contract. See further the discussion above, paras 13.305–306. The test for the exclusion of unfair contract terms legislation from international contracts is currently under active consideration by the Law Commission.

elements of the scope provision, Article 1, were the subject of debate and proposed amendment as late as the 1980 Diplomatic Conference. The main features of Article 1 that differentiate it from its ULIS predecessor are first that it eschews any factual test of internationality. Hence it contains no requirements concerning the transport of goods across national frontiers or the formation of contracts in states other than those where delivery takes place. Furthermore, the Vienna Convention differs from ULIS in allotting a role to the place of business of the parties in different states and to private international law.[41]

According to Article 1(1) of the Vienna Convention: **16.17**

This Convention applies to contracts of sale of goods between parties whose places of business are in different States:
  (a) when the States are Contracting States; or
  (b) when the rules of private international law lead to the application of the law of a Contracting State.

A few preliminary points should be taken. First, the nationality of the **16.18** parties is explicitly disregarded for the purpose of determining the application of the Vienna Convention.[42]

Second, while the Convention will not as such be applied retrospectively **16.19** to the contracting parties,[43] a forum may well find itself enforcing the Convention in the case of a contract that was entered into before the forum state itself adopted the Convention. If, for example, the United Kingdom were to adopt the Convention in the case of a French buyer and a German seller, its courts would apply the Convention by virtue of Article 1(1)(a) to a contract concluded after the adoption of the Convention by Germany and France but before adoption by the United Kingdom.

Third, the test in Article 1(1) is a disjunctive one. There will be cases where **16.20** the application of either head could lead to the Vienna Convention. One example of this is that of a German seller and a Belgian buyer where, under the Rome Convention (the forum state being a Contracting State), the applicable law is German law as the law of the place of business of the characteristic performer.[44] Article 1(1)(b) directs the application of the Vienna Convention. In addition, both Germany and Belgium are Contracting States under the Vienna Convention, which is stated to be applicable under Article 1(1)(a). Of the two grounds for the application of the

---

[41] The role and scope of the place of business being in different states and of private international law depend upon whether the Vienna Convention applies by virtue of Art 1(1)(a) or Art 1(1)(b).
[42] Art 1(3).   [43] See the discussion below, paras 16.39–41, of commencement dates.
[44] Art 4(2), since the parties have not selected their own applicable law under Art 3.

Convention, however, the one in Article 1(1)(a), as a matter of common understanding, is the dominant one. A measure of controversy is still attached to the role of private international law in Article 1(1)(b), as witnessed by the debate surrounding its very existence and the Article 95 declaration permitting states to opt out of Article 1(1)(b).[45]

16.21 Fourth, Article 1(1), it should be noted, applies to states and not to legal systems. The contract of a New York seller and a California buyer will not fall under Article 1(1)(a). In the event that the United Kingdom becomes a Contracting State, the same will be true for a Scots seller and an English buyer. Suppose that a French court were to be led, by its rules of private international law, to apply Scots law pursuant to Article 1(1)(b) in a dispute between a Scots whisky seller and a Japanese buyer (Japan being a non-Contracting State). It is submitted that no distinction should be drawn between the law *in* and the law *of* a Contracting State. The Vienna Convention permits partial territorial application of the Convention in the case of states with different laws applying in two or more territorial units.[46] Consequently, if the United Kingdom were not to elect in favour of severance,[47] by for example adopting the Convention with regard to Scotland but not to England and Wales, it should be treated as a unified territory for the purpose of Article 1(1)(b). Hence, in the above example, the French court should apply the Vienna Convention in the event of the United Kingdom becoming a Contracting State and should not declare that Scotland is excluded from the operation of the Convention.

16.22 A final preliminary point to consider before Article 1 is examined in detail is this. In the conventional choice of law process, it is for the parties themselves to plead and prove foreign law. They may, quite often to diminish legal costs and expedite proceedings, elect to have the forum treat their case as though it were subject to the domestic law of the forum. In this chapter, it will be argued that the Vienna Convention is in Contracting States a part of the domestic law of the Contracting State. In that state's courts, the Convention is not foreign law but rather local, specialized law that applies in the same way as is applied any separate

---

[45] Discussed below, paras 16.128–136.   [46] Art 93.
[47] By making a declaration under Art 93 (discussed below, para 16.125). Upon accession on 23 April 1991, Canada made such a declaration so that the Convention applied only to Alberta, British Columbia, Manitoba, New Brunswick, Newfoundland, Nova Scotia, Ontario, Prince Edward Island and the Northwest Territories. At later dates, Canada had the Convention extended to Quebec, Saskatchewan and the Yukon Territory, as well as later to the Territory of Nunavut, carved out of the Northwest Territories. An Art 93 reservation was initially combined by Canada with an Art 96 reservation, so that British Columbia was excluded from the application of Art 1(1)(b), but the declaration respecting British Columbia was later withdrawn.

laws for commercial and consumer contracts of sale. If the Convention is part of the forum state's domestic law in this way, and if that state subscribes to the principle of *jura novit curia*,[48] then its courts will be bound to apply the Convention even if the parties themselves do not invoke it.[49] It is also arguable that the forum state as a Contracting State is bound to ensure that its courts apply the Convention as required by Article 1. Nevertheless, it is submitted, and in view of the long-standing freedom of litigants to ignore applicable foreign law, Article 1 does not with sufficient clarity abridge this freedom if it is to be applicable on its own terms. A further point is that, as the parties are free to vary or detract from the Convention,[50] their conduct in litigation might be seen as consensually varying their contract so as to subject it to the national law that the forum would apply in default of the Convention.[51] This point appears decisive: the forum state itself has no interest in the choice of applicable law made by private contracting parties in those cases where that state subscribes to the principle of freedom of choice and there are no issues of public policy or mandatory principles to restrict that choice.[52]

Article 1(1)(a) and Dual Contracting State Residence

Because of its disjunctive relationship to Article 1(1)(b), the dual place of **16.23** business in Contracting States provision in Article 1(1)(a) has on the face of it no connection with rules of private international law. The Vienna Convention therefore seems to apply as the law of the forum, but this of course can only occur where the forum state is a Contracting State. Contracting States are treaty-bound to see to it that their courts apply the Vienna Convention, an obligation clearly absent where the forum state is a non-Contracting State. Because this latter state's courts will be indifferent to the dual place of business test in Article 1(1)(a), it follows that contracts which might have been dealt with by the courts of a Contracting State under Article 1(1)(a), or either under sub-paragraph (a) or (b), will often be dealt with instead by the courts of a non-Contracting State, further to its choice of law rules, in a way that is consistent with the application

---

[48] The court knows the law: the court seeks out the law captures the idea better, since the court should not wait to be instructed by the parties.

[49] See, e.g. the decision of the Tribunale Civile di Vigevano of 12 July 2000 translated at http://cisgw3.law.pace.edu/cisg/wais/db/cases2/00712i3/html.

[50] Art 6.

[51] A post-contractual change in the applicable law is permitted by Art 3(2) of the Rome Convention.

[52] In the case of those states that have made a declaration (see Art 96 of the Convention) departing from the rule that contracts may be informally modified (see Art 29(1)), this argument could not readily be run unless the modification were regarded as implicit in written pleadings.

of the rule in Article 1(1)(a) by Contracting States. This is because an application of the non-Contracting State's choice of law rules will often lead it to the law of either the seller's or the buyer's country of business residence. For example, the application of the characteristic performance rule in Article 4 of the Rome Convention will lead to the application of the seller's law.[53] Precisely how such a reference to the seller's law then leads into the Vienna Convention raises very similar issues to those arising when a Contracting State applies the Vienna Convention pursuant to Article 1(1)(b) and will be dealt with when that provision is discussed.

An Incomplete Rule of Private International Law?

16.24 It may be orthodoxy to state that the dual business rule is not a rule of private international law, yet the proposition has been advanced that Article 1(1)(a) may be an incompletely formed rule of private international law binding on Contracting States. In his explanatory report on the Hague Sales Convention 1986, Professor von Mehren writes that Article 1(1)(a) 'can be seen as including a kind of choice-of-law rule, one which makes the Vienna Convention as adopted and interpreted by *either* the buyer's State *or* the seller's State applicable where both States are Parties to the Vienna Convention'.[54] This notion emerged in the course of the conference proceedings without being fully developed, so on that account it should not be accorded a great deal of importance. Subject to that, if Article 1(1)(a) is a choice of law rule, then it is an incomplete one because it gives the forum no direction as to whether the applicable law should be the seller's or the buyer's law.[55] As a choice of law rule,

---

[53] See Art 4(2). See the decision of the Cour d'appel de Grenoble of 26 April 1995 (translated at www.cig.law.pace.edu/cisg/wais/db/cases2/950426f1.html; CLOUT Case 152), applying the Vienna Convention pursuant to Art 1(1)(b), since the seller's place of business was in France (a Contracting State) and the buyer resided in Portugal (a non-Contracting State). But the court applied, not the Rome Convention, but Art 3 of the Hague Sales Convention 1955 (as the French courts do) (which in most cases applies the seller's law directly and not as the law of the characteristic performer). Cf Schiedsgericht der Handelskammer Hamburg of 21 March 1996 (translated at www.cig.law.pace.edu/cisg/wais/db/cases2/960321g1.html; CLOUT Case 166).

[54] Report on the Hague Sales Convention 1986, Proceedings of the Extraordinary Session of October 1985, para 192. He does however go on to say that, given the part played by Art 1(1)(a) in defining the application of the Vienna Convention, it 'seems both unnecessary and undesirable' also to interpret it as a choice of law rule, especially when its value as such is 'limited and problematical': ibid, at 57–59. On Art 1(1)(a) as a choice of law rule, see also Dore, n 31 above; C Saf, 'A Study of the Interplay between the Conventions Governing the International Sale of Goods' (www.cisg/law/pace.edu/cisg/text/saf90.html).

[55] If both rules of application of the Vienna Convention in Art 1 together are taken to be choice of law provisions, then Art 1 itself is an incomplete choice of law provision in the further sense that it gives no direction at all as to the governing law for those international contracts of sale that fall outside Art 1. On statutes and private international law, see *Dicey and Morris*, 16–26.

Article 1(1)(a) would therefore play a different role than that played by an internal rule of demarcation of the forum state, determining which of two sales laws existing side-by-side in the law of the forum, the domestic sales law or the Vienna Convention, should apply to the case in hand.

If Article 1(1)(a) does amount to an incomplete choice of law rule, this **16.25** clearly has implications for the resolution of any conflicts between a choice of law convention and the Vienna Convention in the case of a state which is party to both.[56] To the extent that the forum state resolves any conflict by applying the Vienna Convention, it ought not in principle to matter whether the Vienna Convention is applied as domestic law of the forum state or by virtue of the forum's choice of law rules. This is because the Vienna Convention is supposed to be uniform law whether the law of the forum is the seller's law, the buyer's law or some third system of law. To the extent, supposing this happens, that the Vienna Convention acquires different settled meanings and scope in different legal systems,[57] the question raised by Professor von Mehren will take on greater significance. It may then be important to determine whether it is the Vienna Convention of the seller's or the buyer's state that disposes of the matter. Having raised the issue, it is perhaps unfortunate that Professor von Mehren does not give a clear direction as to how it ought to be resolved. It is submitted that Article 1(1)(a) should be taken at face value as directing the application of the Vienna Convention as part of the law of the forum. This avoids both needless complexity and any criticism of Article 1(1)(a) as an incomplete rule, and it builds upon the express reference to private international law in Article 1(1)(b) and the absence of any such reference in Article 1(1)(a).

Article 1(1)(b) and Private International Law

In applying the Vienna Convention under Article 1(1)(b), the conventional **16.26** view is that the courts of the forum state are not applying their own substantive law, at least in those cases where their choice of law rules lead them to a substantive law other than their own. Rather, they are applying the substantive law of the state identified by the forum's choice of law rules. The text of Article 1(1)(b) does not say whose rules of private international law are being applied, but practical sense and the absence of

---

[56] e.g. the prohibition on renvoi in Art 15 of the Rome Convention.

[57] One area where there is a real risk of this happening is where states give varying degrees of scope to rules of private international law (discussed below) in filling gaps in the Vienna Convention, pursuant to Art 7(2).

any intelligible alternative mean that only the forum's own rules could be applied.[58]

16.27 Some of the accidental character of the application of ULIS is evident also in Article 1(1)(b). Even if neither seller nor buyer is resident in a Contracting State, the conduct of litigation in the courts of one Contracting State may lead to the application of the Vienna Convention when the different choice of law rules of another Contracting State would not have had this consequence.[59] Suppose, for example, that an Australian court is seised of a dispute between an English seller and an Indian buyer[60] under a contract lacking an applicable law clause and calling for performance in Australia.[61] Under Article 1(1)(b), an Australian court concluding that the applicable law is the law of the place of performance[62] should have to apply the Vienna Convention.[63] This is because the court's choice of law rules lead to the law of a Contracting State (Australia). If the dispute were litigated instead in a Belgian court, that court applying the characteristic performance rule in Article 4 of the Rome Convention,[64] then the applicable law would be English law as the law of the seller's residence (or place of business).

---

[58] The application of the Vienna Convention under Art 1(1)(b) is a more complex matter in the case of arbitration, in that the origin of the private international rules applied by the arbitrator is no straightforward matter. The Rome Convention, for example, does not apply to arbitration agreements (including arbitration clauses in agreements otherwise covered by the Rome Convention) (see Art 1(2)(d)). But that does not preclude an arbitrator from applying choice of law rules as laid down in the Rome Convention. In the case of an arbitration with an English seat, the arbitrator is required under English law to act in accordance with s 46 of the Arbitration Act (since the notion of a delocalised arbitration is not accepted by English law: see Dicey and Morris, para 16–030, n 1). Section 46(1) requires the arbitrator to respect the parties' choice of applicable law. If there is no choice, the arbitrator applies 'the law determined by the conflict of laws rules that [he] considers applicable' (s 46(3)—a formula identical to Art 28(2) of the UNCITRAL Model Law on Arbitration and Art 33(2) of the UNCITRAL Arbitration Rules). The arbitrator is therefore not bound by Rome but, though at liberty to select his own choice of law rules, should be open to the argument that the Rome Convention is a respected and widely accepted statement of applicable conflict rules. The arbitrator is therefore given a significant degree of freedom in practice in moving to the application of the Vienna Convention.

[59] Conventions on uniform choice of law will obviously diminish the likelihood of this.

[60] Like the UK, India is not yet a party to the Vienna Convention.

[61] Since Australia did not make a severance declaration under Art 93, the state in which the Australian court is located and the state of performance need not be identified.

[62] In accordance with the pre-Rome English position: see *Bonython v Commonwealth of Australia* [1951] AC 201, PC.

[63] If the forum, as is the case with Rome Convention Contracting States (Art 4 and characteristic performance), applies a choice of law rule based upon the residence or place of business of one of the contracting parties, then the same degree of accidental contact with the Vienna Convention is absent.

[64] On which, see Ch 13 above.

How the Forum Applies the Convention under Article 1(1)(b)

An interesting question now presents itself as to how the forum arrives at **16.28** the Vienna Convention once it is directed by its choice of law rules to apply the law of a foreign, Contracting State. Before that question is resolved, it should be asked how the forum arrives at the Vienna Convention when its choice of law rules direct it to apply its own substantive law. Suppose, for example, that a Belgian court, seised of a dispute between a Belgian seller and an English buyer, applies Belgian law pursuant to Article 4(2) of the Rome Convention and the characteristic performance rule.[65] Belgian law consists of the domestic rules of sale to be found in the Code civil and of the international rules of sale as expressed in the Vienna Convention. It seems clear that the forum must consider internal Belgian rules of legal demarcation to determine which of these two sales laws it applies to the case in hand. This choice is no different in kind from the type of choice a court might have to make in a purely domestic case where it has to determine whether its consumer sales law or a commercial sales law is applicable.

Now, suppose that the Belgian court is handling a dispute between a **16.29** German seller and an English buyer and is led, again by Article 4(2) of the Rome Convention, to the law of the seller's residence, in this case German law. On one view, it considers the mass of German sales law and sees that there is a sales law for domestic cases and a sales law for international cases. It therefore does not consider German choice of law rules and so exercises an internal choice no different from the choice that the Belgian forum made in the earlier example when it applied the Belgian international sales law. The forum is therefore not infringing provisions of conflict of laws conventions that proscribe the use of renvoi.[66] But this view, if it is correct, comes at a price. In treating the Vienna Convention as part of the domestic law of the state whose law is the applicable law, it domesticates the Vienna Convention as Belgian law, German law, New York law and so on, which has substantial implications for the uniform future of uniform law.

There is a way of invoking the machinery that avoids altogether the risk **16.30** that a forum, in applying the law of another state, is reaching the Vienna Convention by way of that state's private international law rules. A different approach to the conventional reading of Article 1(1)(b) would

---

[65] Belgium is chosen instead of France in this example because a French court would apply the Hague Sales Convention 1955 rather than the Rome Convention, whereas Belgium has denounced the Hague Sales Convention.

[66] e.g. Rome Convention Art 15 (the applicable law is the law in force in the country in question, minus its rules of private international law).

build upon the literal wording that the 'Convention applies' when the rules of private international law 'lead to the law of a Contracting State'. The text does not say that the Vienna Convention is applied as the law of that selected Contracting State. On the other hand, it does not say that the rules of private international law would 'otherwise' lead to the law of a Contracting State. Putting aside this last linguistic point, the forum might be seen, pursuant to the treaty commitments of the forum state, to be applying the law of the forum which has supplanted the law that would otherwise have been applicable by virtue of the private international law rules of the forum, these rules having been displaced to the extent of the Vienna Convention's coverage. This approach too would treat the Vienna Convention as part of a domestic law, this time the domestic law of the forum. In the above example, the Belgian court whose private international law rules led to the application of German law would desist from applying German law at all and would instead look to its own law as requiring the application of the Vienna Convention. As with the above approach interpreted as avoiding the use of renvoi, this approach also leads to the 'nationalisation' of the Vienna Convention. This alternative approach cannot be adopted for a forum in a non-Contracting State. To the extent that that forum's choice of law rules lead to a foreign law, it will apply the Vienna Convention if so directed by the foreign law's rules of internal demarcation or by its rules of private international law.

16.31 In sum, it may not matter whether, under Article 1(1)(b), the Vienna Convention is applied as part of the law of the forum or pursuant to a rule of internal demarcation of the state whose substantive law is called into play by the forum's private international law rules. The former approach is simpler—which is a good reason for promoting it—though the latter approach is somewhat more consonant with the forces of internationalism that have arrested the homeward trend towards the law of the forum and is more attuned to the spirit that lies behind the Vienna Convention. Yet, on balance, the former approach—based on the notion that the forum state is not truly engaged with the choice of law process—is preferable for the added reason that describing the application of the forum's own law as the application of the law of the forum is subtly misleading. Different states incorporate the provisions of multilateral conventions into their own laws by different means. The United Kingdom makes use of implementing legislation to which the terms of a treaty or at least some of them are scheduled.[67] Most other states[68] may simply declare adherence to the

---

[67] See, e.g. the Contracts (Applicable Law) Act 1990 to which the Rome Convention on the Law Applicable to Contractual Obligations 1980 (discussed in Ch 13 above) is scheduled.

[68] Adopting a monist view of public international law, as opposed to the dualist view of the UK.

treaty by a declaration of the executive, whereupon the treaty has direct effect. This latter style brings out vividly the point that the content of the law of the forum is not of domestic provenance but consists of norms of public international law, albeit norms that are superimposed upon norms, dealing for example with civil procedure, of the law of the forum. To treat the application of the Vienna Convention, wherever possible, as the application of the law of the forum in this special sense does not diminish its standing as international uniform law but rather enhances it. In the case of the Vienna Convention, this point is further emphasized by Article 7(1), which requires the interpretation of the Convention in an internationalist spirit. This approach, which looks directly to the text of the multilateral convention, has the merit of countering any 'nationalization' of the Vienna Convention. It preserves the uniform character of the Convention even as it is being absorbed within the legal systems of the different Contracting States.

The Place of Business

A number of other issues arise out of the place of business test in Article 1. **16.32** First of all, the place of business of the parties in different states is to be 'disregarded' if 'this fact does not appear either from the contract or from any dealings between, or from information disclosed, by the parties at any time before or at the conclusion of the contract'.[69] The first point to note is that this provision applies equally to both sub-paragraphs (a) and (b) of Article 1(1). The second point is that the Vienna Convention does not define 'place of business' at all. A joint Argentinian and Belgian proposal to amend what became Article 10, which deals with the absence of a place of business and choice between two or more places of business, was submitted to the Plenary Conference.[70] It sought to define 'place of business' as 'a place where the party maintains a business organization having power to negotiate or conclude contracts of sale or purchase in the name of the party'.[71] As such, this amendment would have ruled out places where a party's interests were looked after by an agent having only powers of representation. The proposed amendment was voted down at the Plenary Conference, partly because of perceived difficulties presented by multinational corporations, partly because of a general resistance to providing definitions in the Vienna Convention and partly because the

---

[69] Art 1(2).

[70] On 7 April 1980. See Honnold, n 27 above, at 727. It was one of the few proposed amendments submitted to the Plenary Conference.

[71] This came after the Belgian delegate had during the First Committee Deliberations (para 66) unavailingly sought an explanation for the lack of any definition: Honnold, n 27 above, at 490.

amendment came very late in the day.[72] It was not just that any definition of 'place of business' was rejected. In addition, any attempt to narrow the meaning of place of business to a fixed establishment which had contract-making power was also rejected. The definition of 'place of business' is therefore at large and capable of giving rise to disagreement. A French court has held that a seller's liaison office through which the buyer placed its order was not a place of business under the Vienna Convention since it lacked legal personality.[73] Unless the office is just a letter box and is not involved in the performance of the contract, this seems unduly restrictive. The Vienna Convention does not require a place of business to have a legal personality.

16.33   The third point arises out of the somewhat loose wording of Article 1(2), the mischief of which seems reasonably clear: the parties should not become bound by the Vienna Convention when they are ignorant of a basic jurisdictional requirement upon which the application of the Convention depends, namely that their places of business are in different states. Nevertheless, the wording of Article 1(2) raises some difficulties. First of all, both parties, dealing with each other for the first time, may be well aware that their places of business are in different states even if this (perhaps unusually) is not stated in the contract and is not communicated around the time of conclusion of the contract. Article 1(2) should not, it is submitted, be read too literally in such a case. For example, a tribunal should be prepared to accept knowledge of different national places of business in those cases where this is implicit in the corporate titles of the parties.[74]

Only one party aware of foreign place of business

16.34   A more troublesome difficulty presents itself where only one party is aware that the other's place of business is in a different country. For example, a pre-contract communication from the seller may alert the buyer to the fact that buyer and seller have their places of business in different countries without the seller itself ever becoming aware of this fact. This difficulty requires a close examination of the mischief behind Article 1(2), which above all seems to be to prevent surprise. For the purposes of a forum's choice of law rules, knowledge of different places of business is unlikely to play a role.[75] A party is not protected from the

---

[72] Decisions of the Plenary Conference, 6 April 1980, paras 65–90 (Honnold, n 27 above, at 738–740).

[73] Cour d'appel de Paris (15th Division) of 22 April 1992 (*Société Fauba v Société Fujitsu*: CLOUT Case 159; UNILEX 1996). (The UNILEX reports of international arbitral awards (albeit few in number) are most helpful and are now available without subscription on the internet (www.unilex.info)). See C Witz, *Recueil Dalloz Sirey* 1995, Chronique 143.

[74] e.g. SpA and GmbH.   [75] e.g. it does not appear in the Rome Convention.

application of foreign law by ignorance, however justifiable, of the other's place of business. In the absence of an express choice of the applicable law, however, a forum's choice of law rules will lead to the application of foreign law only if performance of the contract or part of it takes place outside the forum state. And a contracting party's knowledge of the cross-border character of the contract will itself put that party on notice of its exposure to a foreign law. Now, it is because the application of the Vienna Convention does not depend at all upon cross-border performance, because for example it can apply to a contract concluded in state X where performance takes place wholly within state X, as where goods are sold ex warehouse with payment in the seller's currency, that the issue of ignorance of exposure is presented and resolved in the way that it is in Article 1(2).

What then is the effect of excluding the application of the Vienna Conven- **16.35** tion? The forum will instead apply its choice of law rules to determine the applicable law. Take a case where the seller's place of business is in the forum state. It may be that the conclusion and performance of the contract took place wholly within the forum state, in which case there will be no choice of law process at work in any event. But if a substantial element of performance takes place outside the forum state, the effect of excluding the Vienna Convention may only be to apply a law other than the law of the state where the seller's place of business is located. Where the parties are unaware that their places of business are in different states, this precludes the application of the whole of Article 1(1) and so blocks the application of the Vienna Convention. This means that a court applying its choice of law rules in search of the applicable law may not apply the Vienna Convention even in those cases where its rules lead to the law of a Convention state. Regardless of the way in which the Vienna Convention might otherwise be applied by the law of the forum, the Convention, in its own terms, denies its applicability.

In the light of the position set out above, it is not at all obvious that a **16.36** broad reading should be given to Article 1(2) so as to require both parties to be aware of their places of business being in different states. It is therefore submitted that, for the aware buyer and ignorant seller in the earlier example, more particularly where a substantial element of performance takes place outside the unaware seller's state, Article 1(2) should not be applied so as to remove the contract from the reach of the Vienna Convention. The problem, nevertheless, is not an easy one. Another possibility, which may be criticized for undue complexity, is to apply the Convention when it is in the interests of the unaware party to do so. Although it might have been difficult to draft an appropriate provision, it would have been better explicitly to limit Article 1(2) to cases where formation and performance of the contract took place exclusively within one state.

Locating the place of business

16.37 The next issue is to determine the location of the parties' places of business. This is dealt with, but only partly, in Article 10. Where a party does not have a place of business as such, reference is made instead to his habitual residence.[76] In the case of a party with more than one place of business, the relevant place of business will be the one that has 'the closest relation to the contract and its performance' in the light of the circumstances known to or contemplated by the parties before or at the time of conclusion of the contract.[77] This provision departed from an earlier draft which presumptively favoured the principal place of business,[78] which was replaced by the present text drawn from the Limitations Convention.[79] The issue of choosing the particular place of business of a party with more than one place of business is of importance in two cases: first, where one of these places of business is the same as the other contracting party's place of business; and second, where one of these places of business is located in a non-Contracting State.[80] In the first of these two cases, the conclusion may be that the Vienna Convention is not to be applied at all. In the second, the Vienna Convention may not be applicable under Article 1(1)(a), though the possibility will remain of its applicability under Article 1(1)(b).

16.38 It may not be straightforward to apply the closest connection test in Article 10(1). If, for example, the head office of a company deals with the conclusion of a contract but performance is rendered through a branch office in another country, then a hard choice will have to be made as to which of the two offices is the more closely involved. Since the Vienna Convention is a unified text of substantive sales law and formation provisions, there does not appear to be any possibility of splitting it so as to assign Part II (Formation of the Contract) and Part III (Sale of Goods) to different offices, which might have the result that only one of these two parts applies to the contract in hand. Modern choice of law rules dealing with the essential validity and performance of contracts place more emphasis upon performance than upon formation. It may be that the same trend will lead to the place of business for the purpose of Article 10

---

[76] Art 10(2).

[77] The existence of more than one place of business was not dealt with in ULIS.

[78] See the 1976 Working Group Draft, Art 4(a) (Honnold, n 27 above, at, 243).

[79] Vienna Convention on the Limitation Period in the International Sale of Goods 1974, Art 2(c).

[80] See UN Secretariat Commentary on the 1978 Draft, para 3 of Commentary to Art 9 (Honnold, n 27 above, at 409).

being regarded as the branch office through which performance takes place. This weighting in favour of the branch office will nevertheless be diminished in so far as the extent of the branch office's involvement in performance is not known or contemplated by both parties at the contract date.

Place of business and commencement

The place of business is also important in connection with the com- **16.39** mencement provisions in Article 100. For the purpose of whether a state is or is not a Contracting State under Article 1, a distinction has to be drawn between Parts II and III of the Convention. In the case of Part II, the critical date, according to Article 100(1), is the date when 'the proposal for concluding the contract' is made. The Vienna Convention draws a distinction between proposals for concluding contracts and offers. It defines the latter as a subset of the former consisting of those proposals that are 'sufficiently definite and [indicate] the intention of the offeror to be bound in case of acceptance'. Proposals for concluding contracts, however, are not defined, which gives rise to problems under Article 1. As tempting as the interpretation may be, it would be a cavalier reading of Article 100(1) to conclude that it simply means offers when it refers to proposals: it would have been easy enough to say so explicitly if that had been the intention.[81] Moreover, if the Vienna Convention is to apply intelligibly to a stream of communications in order to pinpoint offer and acceptance, and if it is not to collide with some other law applicable to the issue of formation,[82] it seems sensible to apply it only if all the relevant communications between the parties occur after the commencement date or dates in Article 1.

If this approach is defensible, the unanswered question is, 'What is a **16.40** relevant communication for the purpose of amounting to an undefined proposal in Article 100(1)?' Does any communication taking place between the contracting parties, and made before the relevant commencement date, have the effect of removing the ensuing contract from the reach of the Vienna Convention? If the answer were yes, then the sending of a manufacturer's catalogue, *a fortiori* if this is accompanied by a price list, perhaps months before the purchaser places an order, will take formation issues outside the Vienna Convention. Yet it is hard to know where the line is to be drawn at some point in the spectrum between proposals like the sending of the catalogue and offers unless an impressionistic approach is taken that looks only to proposals with some

---

[81] Yet Art 100, like the other provisions of Part IV of the Vienna Convention, was drafted by the Second Committee in Vienna, a body consisting of diplomats rather than lawyers.
[82] It is not inconceivable that the two laws might both conclude that a contract has been validly formed but disagree about time and place, which could have various implications.

plausible claim to being treated as offers or proposals that are made in the immediate run-up to, or are an integral part of, the conclusion of a contract (as the putative application of Part II might show). Alternatively, one can oppose the view expressed above, that Article 100 is not confined to offers, and say that it is indeed confined to proposals that become offers for the purpose of Part II, which can only be adjudicated upon as and when the conclusion is reached that Part II is applicable. On this view, Article 100 does not explicitly mention offers because offers are defined in Part II and defined terms in Part II cannot be putatively mentioned to determine the commencement date of Part II. Nothing in the documentary history of the Vienna Convention gives any guidance on this issue. It is submitted that the best solution to what is a problem of limited duration, given the large number of states that have already implemented the Vienna Convention and the disappearance of ageing contracts from the system, is to apply Part II as from the date of commencement of negotiations in the immediate lead-in to the contract. This may not be the easiest of tests to apply but it minimizes the risk of a dépeçage with Part III of the Convention applying to the rights and duties of buyer and seller and some other system of law dealing with formation. This type of dépeçage is, admittedly, as undisruptive as any dépeçage can be.[83]

16.41 In the case of Part III, the critical date for the purpose of Article 100 is the date of conclusion of the contract. It is therefore perfectly possible to have a contract governed by Part III of the Vienna Convention but not by Part II, even though no state with an Article 1 connection to the contract has entered under Article 92 a declaration that it will not be bound by Part II. In some cases, the effect of Article 100 will merely be to shift the basis on which Part II of the Convention is applied. If a proposal for concluding a contract is made at a time when the law of the buyer's place of business has not yet acceded to the Vienna Convention, but the forum state and the seller's state have already acceded, then Part II, inapplicable under Article 1(1)(a), will be applicable under Article 1(1)(b), by virtue of

---

[83] Even here, the discord between Arts 14 (Part II) and 55 (Part III), on whether the price needs to be fixed, may give rise to trouble. It is notorious that Art 14 requires at least the existence of price-fixing machinery for there to be a contractual offer, whereas Art 55 assumes that a reasonable price can be implied if the contract is silent on the price. In the UN Secretariat's Commentary on the 1978 draft (see Honnold, n 27 above, at 435), the discrepancy is explained away on the ground that Art 55 (Art 52 in the draft) applies in this respect only as to states that have not adopted Part II of the Vienna Convention (Formation), but note that the debates and the views of various commentators (see, eg, Schlechtriem, 108–110) suggest that the discrepancy cannot so easily be resolved. Unlike a Hague Conference Report, a Secretariat Commentary is adopted along with the draft as amended. Nevertheless, whilst that Commentary is of persuasive power under Art 7(1) of the Vienna Convention, it is submitted that, especially given its brevity, it cannot be treated as the last word on any subject.

the forum's private international law rules, if these point to the law of the seller's place of business as dealing with formation issues.

3. THE USE OF PRIVATE INTERNATIONAL LAW IN FILLING GAPS IN THE VIENNA CONVENTION

General

The enactment of the UK Sale of Goods Act in 1893[84] had the effect of **16.42** creating boundaries between the law of sale, on the one hand, and the law dealing with other special contracts and the general law of contract, on the other. Various devices, nevertheless, served to efface any sharp separation between sale and cognate areas of law. One way was to apply the Sale of Goods Act by analogy to other types of contract.[85] Another was to invoke that provision of the Sale of Goods Act that rendered the general law applicable to contracts of sale to the extent that it was not inconsistent with the provisions of the Act.[86] A third way was to monitor the application of the Sale of Goods Act and modify the interpretation of its provisions so as to keep the law of sale on track with a developing general law of contract.[87] The overall effect was that the law of sale was anchored in the general law so that it was not a matter of great moment to know whether a particular issue in a sale of goods contract fell to be disposed of under the Act or by reference to the general law. For that reason, too, the inclusion to only a limited extent in the Act of doctrines such as mistake and frustration did not cause undue tension in the law. In sum, this interplay between sale of goods law and the general law of contract has deprived of significance the definition of the outer limits of the law of sale and any need to distinguish a matter that falls beyond these outer limits and one that falls within these limits but is not explicitly dealt with in the Sale of Goods Act.

As uniform law, the Vienna Convention is not integrated into any com- **16.43** plementary body of law. This means that the outer limits of its application

---

[84] Consolidated with various amendments as the Sale of Goods Act 1979, itself the subject of later amending legislation.

[85] *Young & Marten Ltd v McManus Childs Ltd* [1969] 1 AC 454.

[86] This appears as s 62(1) of Sale of Goods Act 1979: 'The rules of the common law, including the law merchant, except in so far as they are inconsistent with the provisions of this Act, and in particular the rules relating to the law of principal and agent and the effect of fraud, misrepresentation, duress or coercion, mistake, or other invalidating cause, apply to contracts for the sale of goods'.

[87] e.g. *Cehave NV v Bremer Handelsgesellschaft mbH* [1976] QB 44 (the introduction of intermediate stipulation analysis to express terms in a contract of sale); *Harlingdon and Leinster Enterprises Ltd v Christopher Hull (Fine Art) Ltd* [1991] 1 QB 654 (the introduction of reliance into the description condition in s 13 of the Sale of Goods Act).

have to be defined. It also means that provision has to be made for filling gaps in the coverage of sale by the Convention. Of prime importance is Article 7 of the Convention. Paragraph (1) states:

In the interpretation of this Convention, regard is to be had to its interpretation and to the need to promote uniformity in its application and the observance of good faith in international trade.

The aim of this provision is to maintain the Vienna Convention as international uniform law and to prevent its absorption by the various domestic laws of the Contracting States. Apart from resolving a disagreement concerning the role of good faith in defining the rights and duties of the contracting parties, the reference to good faith creates a uniform standard for carrying on the Convention through the case law of courts and arbitral tribunals worldwide. This, together with the explicit reference to uniformity, is designed to prevent the Convention from being overborne by domestic bias and therefore to deprive of as much significance as possible the growth of a choice of law process in the application of the Convention. Further mention is made of Article 7(1) below.[88]

16.44   According to Article 7(2):

Questions concerning matters governed by this Convention which are not expressly settled in it are to be settled in conformity with the general principles on which it is based or, in the absence of such principles, in conformity with the law applicable by virtue of the rules of private international law.

As with Article 1(1)(b), the rules of private international law are those of the forum state. The role allocated to private international law is thus a secondary one, designed to be filled only in default of discovering general principles within or about the body of the Vienna Convention itself. The reason for subordination is obvious. Just as the defined approach to interpretation in Article 7(1) is to frustrate the development of an active choice of law process in determining which Contracting State's Convention is to be applied, so too private international law is forced into the background in Article 7(2) in aid of the same purpose.

Private International Law and Interpretation

16.45   Article 17 of ULIS, the equivalent of Article 7(2), made no reference at all to private international law rules and quickly attracted criticism on the ground that it was difficult or even impossible to discern general principles in a uniform law when that law had no domestic legal background.[89]

---

[88] See below, paras 16.52, 16.56–57, 16.61.
[89] First Session of the Working Group, para 57 (Honnold, n 27 above, at 20).

In the meetings of the Working Group, there was extensive discussion on the controversial topic of whether there should be a reference to private international law, alongside the question whether there should be a formal separation of interpretation and the filling of gaps in the Convention.[90] Neither approach, however, had been adopted by the time of the 1977 draft.[91] When the 1977 draft was considered in 1978 by the full Commission, a proposal was introduced that matters arising between the contracting parties and not covered by the Convention ought to be determined by the law of the state of the seller's place of business. This was rejected on the ground that a private international law rule had no part to play in the Convention.[92] The 1978 draft (Article 6) contained no reference to private international law; indeed, it did not deal with gaps in the Convention at all. At the fifth meeting of the First Committee's deliberations at the 1980 Diplomatic Conference, the Bulgarian delegation introduced a proposal to deal with gaps with the aid of the law of the seller's place of business, on the ground that it was a 'costly illusion to imagine that all gaps in a legal instrument could be filled solely by means of the interpretation of its own provisions'.[93] A Czechoslovakian proposal substituted for the seller's law the rules of private international law.[94] Meanwhile, the Italian delegation preferred to fill gaps by means of the general principles contained in the Convention.[95] The solution adopted was to combine the Czechoslovakian and Italian proposals, which was accepted by a majority. A provision identical to the present Article 7(2) was subsequently presented to the Plenary Conference by the First Committee[96] and adopted unanimously.[97] The reference to private international law in Article 7(2) was therefore the price to be paid for invoking general principles underpinning the Vienna Convention in order to fill gaps.

Defining the Scope of the Convention

The reference to general principles in Article 7(2) brings out a point made **16.46** earlier which concerns the relationship between the UK Sale of Goods Act

---

[90] Ultimately settled in favour of separation, in the form of the current Art 7(1), (2).

[91] See the Sixth Session of the Working Group, para 54 (Honnold, n 27 above, at 245).

[92] See the Report of the Committee of the Whole, paras 141–43 (Honnold, n 27 above, at 327–328).

[93] ibid, para 7 (Honnold, n 27 above, at 476).

[94] ibid, para 11 (J Honnold, n 27 above, at 476).

[95] ibid, para 16 (Honnold, n 27 above, at 476). For the text of these three proposals, see Honnold, ibid, at 659. Though not present in the 1978 draft, this proposal can be traced back to Rabel's 1935 draft (Art 11) which in turn was inspired by the famous Art 38 of the Statute of the International Court of Justice at the Hague ('the general principles of law recognized by civilised nations'), though Art 38 opens the door much wider to comparative legal analysis than does the text of Art 7(2).

[96] Art 6(2) (Honnold, n 27 above, at 714).   [97] Honnold, n 27 above, at 737.

1979 and the general law. Simply put, there is no developed body of positive, international uniform contract law to turn to, whether to fill gaps in the Vienna Convention or to run on from it at the margins of its application. Defining the scope of the Convention is therefore much more important than defining the scope of the Sale of Goods Act in English sales law. In particular, it cannot necessarily be inferred from coverage of topics in the Convention where the outer limits of the Convention lie; the existence of gaps within the Convention in central areas of the sales law deprives of any great significance the silence of the Convention on a matter that might be seen as lying either at the outer limits of sale or beyond and within general contract law. In addition, the explicit exclusion in Article 4 of certain matters from the Convention, notably 'validity', invites an expansive interpretation of the scope of the Convention, on the ground that matters for which a strong case can be made for exclusion could have been dealt with explicitly in the same way as validity. Furthermore, taking English law as a comparator and looking at the coverage of contractual material in a sale of goods book and a general contract book, it might fairly be said that most of what is covered in a general contract text is repeated, often in lesser detail, in a sale of goods text, which then places the material in the sale of goods context. This is an argument for taking a very broad view of what constitutes a sales matter for the purpose of the Vienna Convention,[98] which is likely to exercise some considerable appeal for international arbitrators in particular. It would clearly diminish the scope of private international law for dealing with general contractual matters arising in the context of sale.

The Unidroit Principles of International Commercial Contracts

16.47 The extent to which material located in the general law of contract can be seen as replicated in the special law of sale is evident on a comparison between the Vienna Convention and the Unidroit Principles of International Commercial Contracts 1994,[98.1] once the exclusion of validity from the Vienna Convention is taken into account. The Unidroit Principles can be seen in a number of cases as adding detail to the coverage of matters in the Vienna Convention.[99] They are also a complementary instrument given the similarity of philosophy that unites them with the Vienna Convention. This is hardly surprising in view of the influence that

---

[98] This is discussed further below, paras 16.83–95.

[98.1] The 2004 edition of the Principles contains only minor amendments to the 1994 Principles.

[99] See, e.g. the provisions dealing with interest (Art 7.4.10), interpretation (Arts 4.6–7), payment (Arts 6.1.7–10), fundamental breach (or non-performance) (Art 7.3.1) and cure (Art 7.1.4).

the Vienna Convention has exercised in the uniform law movement[100] and the overlap of personalities engaged in the development of the two instruments. Yet, it should not be forgotten that the Unidroit Principles are not the work of UNCITRAL but rather the work of the International Institute for the Unification of Private Law, a quite separate body and not a United Nations agency. In consequence, they cannot represent a formal source of law for the purpose of supplementing the Vienna Convention. Furthermore, the Principles were not published in the aftermath of a diplomatic conference and have no pretensions to being the type of law laid down in the Vienna Convention. The role of the Principles is laid down in their Preamble. This states that they shall apply when the parties agree that their contract will be governed by them, or by the *lex mercatoria* or similar expression. The Preamble goes on to proffer the Principles as a source of inspiration for dealing with problems in those cases where it is impossible to discover the relevant rule of the applicable law, as a model law for legislators and as a means of interpreting or supplementing international uniform law instruments.

This last function contains a veiled reference to the Vienna Convention. **16.48** Nevertheless, just because it is legitimate under the Principles to supplement the Vienna Convention does not mean that it is legitimate under the Vienna Convention for it to be supplemented in this way. If the principles are to be invoked, a route to them has to be found in the text of the Vienna Convention. One way might be for the parties themselves to call the Unidroit Principles into play, either expressly or under the cover of a general formula, such as 'general principles of law' or 'the *lex mercatoria*'. The selection of the Unidroit Principles by the contracting parties will be dealt with below. The following discussion centres on the invocation of the Principles through the text of the Vienna Convention without reference to party choice.

In dealing with matters governed by the Convention but not expressly **16.49** settled in it, Article 7(2) directs a reference to 'the general principles on which [the Convention] is based'. It is uncontroversial that this permits an inductive exercise which, taking the provisions of the Convention in gross, generalizes from them by drawing out broad principles. A more difficult question is whether, more accurately to what extent, an outside enquiry is permitted to seek the sources of the Vienna Convention with a view to determining whether these sources may provide further inspiration not so far expressed in the written text of the Convention.

---

[100] For its influence in recent drafts of a revised Art 2 of the Uniform Commercial Code, see A Rosett, 'UNIDROIT Principles and Harmonization of International Commercial Law: Focus on Chapter 7' (1997) 2 Uniform L Rev (NS) 441.

16.50   If a causal relationship of influence could be demonstrated between the Unidroit Principles and the Vienna Convention, it would be uncontroversial to look at the Principles when settling the content of the Vienna Convention. But the unyielding difficulty remains that the Vienna Convention dates from 1980 and the Unidroit Principles from 1994. The special Working Group that settled down in earnest to produce the Principles was not constituted until 1980. While this abridges the temporal gap, it does not eliminate it. This temporal objection to calling in the Principles under Article 7(2) of the Vienna Convention has been dismissed as a 'rather formalistic argument',[101] but respect for the wording of Article 7(2) requires it to be taken seriously. Now, if the Unidroit Principles merely expressed existing international practice as gleaned from a comparative survey spanning many legal systems, it would be appropriate to backdate them to see whether, in their 'uncodified' form, they might have influenced the Vienna Convention. In conducting such an enquiry, the similarity of philosophy and language as between the two instruments would surely be significant.

16.51   Nevertheless, like other bodies of a similar character,[102] whether or not explicitly engaged upon a restatement exercise (which the Unidroit Working Group was not), the temptation to opt for the better rule, rather than merely to record an existing rule of positive law, is overpowering. Indeed, the Introduction to the Unidroit Principles that accompanied their publication in 1994 stated that: 'Since the Principles are intended to provide a system of rules especially tailored to the needs of international commercial transactions, they also embody what are perceived to be the best solutions, even if still not generally adopted'.[103] This point is not however fatal to the utility of the Principles when dealing with the Vienna Convention. The same appeal that a rule might have had for the Unidroit Working Group may well have been experienced by national delegates responsible for the text of the Vienna Convention. The reality, however, is that the Unidroit Principles form a useful expedient for courts, and more particularly for arbitrators. In the case of the latter, it is tempting to see their unreasoned calling in of the Unidroit Principles[104] as the easy expedient of tribunals who know that their awards will not be challenged for error of law, which is not a ground for non-recognition of awards under the New York Convention 1958.[105] One ought not perhaps be too

---

[101] MJ Bonell, 'The UNIDROIT Principles as a Means of Interpreting and Supplementing International Law' (2002) 13 ICC Intl Court of Arbitration Bulletin (Special Supplement) 29, 33.
[102] e.g. the American Law Institute and the Lando Commission on European Contract Law.
[103] p viii (Rome: Unidroit, 1994).   [104] See the examples given below.
[105] The limited grounds for refusing to recognize and enforce a foreign arbitral award are set out in Art V.

critical if this is the case: arbitrators do not have the resources to engage upon a full comparative survey regardless of cost to the disputants. As the Principles are more and more called upon by tribunals, then any controversy about their legitimacy will fade away. The passage of time will confuse cause and effect. One commentator has remarked: 'in my view the UNIDROIT Principles may be regarded as drawing upon, explaining and being explained by the CISG . . .'.[106] This tendency will increase to the extent that the Vienna Convention is treated as a living and evolving instrument. In that event, questions of temporal precedence between the Vienna Convention and the Unidroit Principles will clearly diminish. The influence of the Principles is likely to increase over time if only because, unlike the Convention, there is no need to convene a diplomatic conference in order to revise them.

In addition, the Principles might well be invoked under Article 7(1) by a **16.52** tribunal engaged in the task of providing an international interpretation of the Vienna Convention. It would be systemically difficult to usher in the Principles under Article 7(1) whilst expelling them under Article 7(2), given that the dividing line between interpretation and the filling of gaps is not clear-cut. Not all laws draw the same clear line as English law does between interpretation and implied terms. The distinction between the two emerged only with painful and protracted difficulty in the proceedings leading to the Vienna Convention. Even in English law, looser modern standards in the interpretation of contracts erase the clarity of that line.[107]

Unidroit Principles and usage

Another way of introducing the Unidroit Principles into international **16.53** sales as governed by the Vienna Convention might be to treat them as international trade usages. According to Article 9(2):

The parties are considered, unless otherwise agreed, to have impliedly made applicable to their contract or its formation a usage of which the parties knew or ought to have known and which in international trade is widely known to, and regularly observed by, parties to contracts of the type involved in the particular trade concerned.

A number of points may be noted here. First, the Principles would be **16.54** dealt with severally under this provision and not as a package. For each Article of the Principles, a case would have to be made that it represents

---

[106] Rosett, n 100 above.
[107] See, e.g. *Investors Compensation Scheme Ltd v West Bromwich Building Society Ltd* [1998] 1 WLR 896 and *C Itoh & Co Ltd v Cia de Navegaçao Lloyd Brasilieiro* (17 July 1998), aff'd [1999] 1 Lloyd's Rep 115, CA.

binding usage.[108] Usage, of course, as incorporated pursuant to Article 9(2) would be evolving usage. The dating of the Unidroit Principles 14 years after the Vienna Convention would therefore be no objection to their incorporation in an international sale contract. Over time, particular provisions might acquire increasing (or diminishing) binding force in particular contracts. Nevertheless, even though 'usage' is not defined in the Vienna Convention, and so is not subject to the confinement of a definition, it is a very loose treatment of the word that equates it to the rules of law laid down in the Unidroit Principles or similar instruments. An arbitrator's familiarity with individual rules in the Principles is not at all the same thing as contracting parties' familiarity with trade practices. Nevertheless, there may well be certain Articles in the Principles that might be regarded as eligible for treatment as usages. This is particularly likely in the various provisions dealing with payment, notably the place, method and currency of payment.[109] The same however could not be said, for example, in the case of Article 7.3.1, no matter how useful the additional guidance it might provide on the meaning of a fundamental breach of contract.[110]

Tribunal references to Unidroit Principles

16.55 From time to time, arbitral tribunals have referred to the Unidroit Principles when dealing with international sales[111] but the cases in which this has been justified under Article 7(2) of the Vienna Convention are few in number. They have been used to supplement the content of Article 78, which directs the award of interest in appropriate cases without specifying the rate or method of calculation, whether it is simple or compound or even when it begins to run.[112] The tribunals were in no doubt that the applicable interest rate was a gap in the Vienna Convention, and not something falling outside it. In eliciting a general principle of full compensation from the Convention, a comparative reference was made to the Unidroit Principles[113] without reasons being given for their citation. The same lack of explanation emerges from other awards where recourse

---

[108] In ICC Award No 8873, the tribunal concluded that the Unidroit rules on hardship did not correspond to prevailing practice in international trade.

[109] See Arts 6.1.6–10.

[110] A Russian arbitral tribunal, however, applied Art 7.4.13(2) of the Unidroit Principles, in order to reduce a penalty clause, on the ground that it was binding usage under Art 9(2) of the Vienna Convention: award 229/1996 of 5 June 1997 (cited in Bonell, n 101 above, at 36).

[111] See the discussion in Bonell ibid, at 29.

[112] International Court of Arbitration of the Federal Chamber of Commerce of Vienna: Award Nos SCH 4318 and SCH 4366 of 15 June 1994 (cited in UNILEX as UNILEX/CISG E.1994–13 and E.1994–14).

[113] Art 7.4.9 (average bank short-term lending rate to prime borrowers for the currency of payment at the place of payment).

was made to the Unidroit Principles to settle the interest rate.[114] One tribunal did however go so far as to say of the Unidroit Principles that 'they are said to reflect a world-wide consensus in most of the basic matters of contract law'.[115]

General Principles on which the Convention is Based

In order to determine the potential of private international law under **16.56** Article 7(2), it is first necessary to consider the potential of general principles on which the Vienna Convention is 'based', which is a rather ambiguous word.[116] These principles may be either immanent and unstated, to be drawn out of the express provisions of the Vienna Convention itself, or else they may be external to the Convention and influential in its drafting. They may not simply be discovered outside the Convention itself pursuant to a comparative legal analysis: they have to be principles upon which the Convention is 'based' and not merely float in some kind of international ether alongside the Convention. In a real sense, general principles in the Vienna Convention constitute the spirit of the law emerging from the text of the Convention as a whole. To the extent that they may properly be called in under Article 7(2), the Unidroit Principles or the source of them will be the basis of the Vienna Convention in the latter sense. Whether it is a case of invoking the Unidroit Principles, or divining the presence of uncodified principles in the text of the Convention, the exercise is an important one which is determinative of the role that private international law is going to play. If the Convention is to be an effective uniform law, then its application must be as wide as possible. This means that the line between general contract and sale should be drawn as much in favour of sale as is practicable and the application of private international law must be kept to a minimum. This last function depends, therefore, on an imaginative use of Article 7(2), in harmony with the internationalist spirit of interpretation laid down in Article 7(1).

---

[114] ICC Award Nos 8128 (1995) and 8769 (1996) (see (1999) 10:2 Intl Court of Arbitration Bulletin 75). In the former case, the tribunal simply states that the Unidroit Principles (as well as the Lando Principles of European Contract Law) are general principles for the purpose of Art 7(2). See also ICC Award No 8817 (1997) (see (1999) 10:2 Intl Court of Arbitration Bulletin 75). The Unidroit Principles have even been used to fill gaps in ULIS and ULF: see ICC Award No 8547 (see (2001) 12:2 Intl Court of Arbitration Bulletin 57, 58–59).

[115] ICC Award No 9117 (1999) 10:2 Intl Court of Arbitration Bulletin 96, 100). The same tribunal also applied rules of private international law to invoke the law of the RSFSR (the Russian Federation) to fill gaps in the Vienna Convention.

[116] The French version refers to general principles from which the Convention draws its inspiration ('dont elle s'inspire'), which is a looser formula than its English equivalent.

16.57   Extracting uncodified principles from within the body of the Vienna Convention[117] is a highly subjective exercise and the following should therefore be seen only as possible examples. The Convention is underpinned by the notion of freedom of contract (or party autonomy), as evidenced by the lack of controls on unfair contract terms and the freedom given in Article 6 to exclude the Convention or any of its provisions. The reference to good faith in Article 7(1) is confined to the interpretation of the Convention and does not extend to the rights and duties of the parties under the contract.[118] Given the extensive range of Article 6 and the way it can literally be applied on its own terms, there is no need to use it as a general principle in the way that the next example is used. This principle concerns the avoidance of loss or economic waste, evidenced by the provisions on cure,[119] the duty to preserve undelivered or rejected goods[120] and the rule of mitigation of damages.[121] The Convention does not state that a buyer preserving rejected goods is bound to return them to the seller, but circumstances may well arise where this is the most efficient way to avoid deterioration or to assist the seller to avoid market loss from rapidly depreciating goods. An extension of the rules on the basis of the general principle might then be justified in some instances.

16.58   It might be also permissible to invoke the principle of waste avoidance in a bolder way to permit set-off between seller and buyer, at least where both claims arise under the contract of sale.[122] Set-off is not the subject of explicit treatment in the Vienna Convention. The standard example concerns the seller bringing an action for the price and the buyer who claims damages. In some cases, the buyer's claim will go beyond the limits of his price revision remedy.[123] There might be a claim for consequential damages caused by the seller's delay in delivering the goods or by damage to the buyer's property caused by defective goods. The price

---

[117] See G Eörsi, 'General Provisions' in NM Galston and H Smit, *International Sales: The United Nations Convention on Contracts for the International Sale of Goods* (Parker School of Comparative Law, 1984); U Magnus, 'General Principles of UN-Sales Law' (1997) 3 Intl Trade and Business L Annual 33.

[118] The clarity of this division is however a matter of controversy, given the statement of the contractual rights and duties of buyer and seller in the body of the Convention. If the court is required under Art 7(2) to interpret provisions of the Convention conferring rights and imposing duties on the contracting parties, this is not so different from imposing good faith directly on the parties themselves. Indeed, some delegates took comfort from the greater status conferred upon the good faith principle when it was translated from the parties to the interpretation of the Convention.

[119] Arts 37, 48.   [120] Arts 85 et seq.   [121] Art 77.

[122] For support, see Magnus n 117 above, at 47.

[123] In Art 50. The buyer may have suffered consequential losses or may, even if the damage is direct in that the value of the goods is affected, prefer to sue for damages, which are more favourable to him on a rising market.

revision remedy in Article 50, as limited as it is, might be seen as the germ of a principle of self-help and expeditious procedures.[124] Added expense would be generated if the buyer had to bring separate proceedings for damages. Set-off has been dealt with under private international law rules in a number of German cases, but at least in some of them the cross-claim has arisen under a contract that itself is not one of sale and in some the court has dealt with an express clause precluding set-off.[125] In further support of set-off is Article 81 which, on the avoidance of a contract, requires seller and buyer to effect restitution concurrently.

Another example of an immanent general principle may be reliance pro-   **16.59**
tection. Reliance is to be seen explicitly in the Convention in a number of provisions. Article 16(2)(b) states that an offer may not be revoked after the offeree has relied upon it. There is also Article 29(2), under which the conduct of a party in relation to an informal modification of contract may prevent him from asserting a contractual clause that the modification ought to have been in writing. In addition, Article 35(2)(b) enacts the principle of the buyer's reliance on the seller's skill and judgment. Lastly, Article 80 prevents a party, whose act or omission was responsible for the other's failure to perform, from relying upon that failure. Taken together, these examples may be said to ground support for a general principle of estoppel (*venire contra factum proprium*).[126] This type of approach—inferring general principles from isolated examples—requires an intellectual approach rather different to that of a common lawyer, who might consider that the limited appearance of reliance in the Convention shows only that it was designed to have a limited role to play. The scope for estoppel under the Convention is not as great as it is in the common law of

---

[124] Another instance of self-help is to be found in Art 65 which permits the seller to specify the form, measure or other features of the goods in those cases where the buyer fails to do so after a reasonable request from the seller.

[125] e.g. a framework distribution contract. On set-off, see the following: Oberlandesgericht Hamm 9 June 1995 (translated at www.cig.law.pace.edu/cisg/wais/db/cases2/950609g1.html; CLOUT Case 125); Hamburg Arbitral Tribunal 21 March 1996 (translated at www.cig.law.pace.edu/cisg/wais/db/cases2/960321g1.html; CLOUT Case 166); Oberlandesgericht München 11 March 1998 (translated at www.cig.law.pace.edu/cisg/wais/db/cases2/980311g1.html; CLOUT Case 232); Kantonsgericht Freiburg 23 January 1998 (CLOUT Case 259); Oberlandesgericht Koblenz 17 September 1993 (translated at www.cig.law.pace.edu/cisg/wais/db/cases2/930917g1.html; CLOUT Case 281); Oberlandesgericht München 28 January 1998 (translated at www.cig.law.pace.edu/cisg/wais/db/cases2/980128g1.html; CLOUT Case 288); Oberlandesgericht Stuttgart 21 August 1995 (translated at www.cig.law.pace.edu/cisg/wais/db/cases2/950821g1.html; CLOUT Case 289); Oberlandesgericht Celle 2 September 1998 (translated at www.cig.law.pace.edu/cisg/wais/db/cases2/980902g1.html; CLOUT Case 318).

[126] More extensively, *venire contra factum proprium non valet* or *venire contra factum proprium nemini licet* (going against one's own act), which means that a person may not invoke a right in a way that is contrary to a position previously assumed by that person.

contract: there is no requirement of consideration to create a binding contract of sale and therefore no need to circumvent an obstacle to informal variations and changes in the modalities of performance. Nevertheless, a seller who stands by while a buyer makes an overt mistake, concerning the attributes of goods for which the seller has not accepted responsibility, may well find himself liable under Article 35, which deals with quality and fitness.[127]

16.60 The above technique may also be applied to problems where the Convention makes some provision but it is incomplete. The principle of full compensation for loss (subject to remoteness of damage) can be drawn out of the Convention by way of Article 74 on the recoverability of damages. In the same way, the principle of restitution of benefits arising under a contract that is avoided is to be found in the provisions requiring the seller and buyer to restore to each other the fruits of performance when the goods and the price are returned on the avoidance of the contract.[128] In the circumstances, a party who is bound to pay the other a sum of money and who incurs an obligation under the Convention to pay interest could be required, according to the circumstances, to pay a sum representing the rate that it would have cost the obligee to borrow the money (compensation) or the rate representing the use value of the money in the obligor's hand (restitution) from the time the sum becomes payable. In such a case, there is no need to turn to a national law chosen under the forum's rules of private international law to decide when interest begins to run and the principles determining selection of the interest rate.[129]

Exclusion Clauses and Penalty Clauses

16.61 Having sought to draw general principles from the Vienna Convention, let us now turn to problem areas to determine the extent to which they are or are not subject to the Vienna Convention. The first example concerns exclusion clauses and the second penalty clauses (which also brings in acceleration clauses). The second example, which alone of the two also brings in the Unidroit Principles,[130] bears some relation to the

---

[127] In such a case, the tribunal would have to be satisfied also that the estoppel prevents the matter from being treated as a pure question of validity, taken out of the Convention by Art 4(a).

[128] Arts 81(2), 82(2)(a), 84.

[129] It is nevertheless common for tribunals to refer to private international law in matters of interest: see, e.g. ICC International Court of Arbitration Award Nos 7565 of 1994 and 7585 of 1992.

[130] The Unidroit Principles deal only with penalty clauses.

first.[131] Legal systems in varying degrees apply legislative controls to exclusion clauses in commercial cases.[132] There is similar variety in their approach to the more complex case of penalty clauses. Penalty clauses may be permissible within limits[133] or even without them. They may be unlawful,[134] in which case they might be seen as unenforceable or as void. In view of the express exclusion of validity from the Vienna Convention, the first question is whether this exclusion embraces the subjects of exclusion and penalty clauses. If it does not, the second question is whether express provision is made for them in the Convention. If the answer to this is no, the third question is whether the Convention treats them as part of the law of sale and subjects them to implicit coverage in the Convention. If they are covered, the fourth question is to determine, with the aid of internal and external guides to the filling of gaps, how exclusion and penalty clauses are disposed of under the Convention. The fifth question, if an answer cannot be found by means of such guides, is to determine the applicable law under the rules of private international law of the forum.

Taking first the example of exclusion clauses, we start with the observa- **16.62** tion that the Vienna Convention does not define validity. This lack of definition is itself a gap in the Convention if one accepts, as one must, that the meaning of its own concepts is the property of the Vienna Convention. The clearest alternative to this position would be to look to the putative applicable law to determine the meaning of validity, which of course would lead in different cases to national definitions of varying width. This would be a blow to uniformity and, in particular, would transgress the requirement in Article 7(1) that the Convention be interpreted in an internationalist manner. The best way to ensure a uniform, and therefore an internationalist, interpretation of validity would be to seek its unstated

---

[131] The EU Directive on Unfair Terms in Consumer Contracts is certainly capable of embracing penalty clauses as defined in English law. See Law Commission, *Unfair Terms in Contracts* (Consultation Paper No 166, 2002), para 4.141.

[132] The Unfair Contract Terms Act 1977 regulates exclusion and similar clauses in commercial contracts. (See further above, paras 13.301–319.) The German Civil Code (BGB) (as revised with effect from 1 January 2002 by the Act on the Reform of the Law of Obligations (Schuldsrechtsreformgesetz)) in §§307–10 invalidates standard business terms if in contravention of good faith they place a contracting party at an unreasonable disadvantage (see www.iuscomp.org/gla/statutes).

[133] As in modern French law, where a second paragraph was added to Code civil, Art 1152 in 1985 (loi no 85–1097 of 11 October 1985) so that the court might reduce or increase the penalty where this was manifestly excessive or derisory. In French law, penalty is defined in very broad terms to embrace all agreed payments to be made or things to be transferred in the event of non-performance of the contract: Code civil, Art 1226.

[134] As they are in English law. In German law, penalty clauses in standard business terms are invalid: BGB (as revised) §309(6).

meaning under Article 7(2). In so doing, it is submitted that a tribunal should not give validity an expansive meaning, for otherwise it would defeat the underlying purpose of the Vienna Convention as an instrument of uniform law.

16.63 What then does Article 7(2) tell us about validity? Given the exclusion of matters of validity from the Vienna Convention, this is a question of some difficulty since it results in the absence of contextual assistance within the Convention. There are no examples of validity from which one might infer a broader definition. One cannot infer, from the absence of familiar contract material from the Convention, such as contractual capacity, that this material must pertain to validity. There are gaps in the Convention, both in respect of matters covered in insufficient detail, such as interest, and matters not covered at all. There are also matters that appear to be covered but perhaps are not. Taking first this last possibility, controls on the validity of exclusion clauses might intuitively seem to be a matter of validity, but for Article 6 which gives the parties full freedom to modify or exclude the text of the Convention itself. On one view, this incorporates the subject of exclusion clauses within the Convention and permits the parties full freedom to exclude. But there is another view, which prompts the question of what it means to exclude validity. Different national laws more or less connected to the contract of sale will have different rules concerning the control of exclusion clauses. In so far as the subject-matter of these rules pertains to validity, the Vienna Convention in effect is doing two things. First, it is stipulating that it chooses not to deal with exclusion as a matter of validity; and second, it is adopting a neutral posture with regard to the applicable law, leaving this to the choice of law rules of the forum.

16.64 If this second view is correct, suppose that the United Kingdom has adopted the Vienna Convention and consider the following example. A contract of sale between an English seller and a Belgian buyer is concluded, in the course of negotiations conducted in England, for delivery at the seller's premises. The parties have not chosen an applicable law and proceedings subsequently take place in a Belgian forum. The contract contains a provision excluding the seller's liability for goods that are not reasonably fit for the buyer's purpose. The Belgian court concludes that the contract is governed by the terms of the Vienna Convention but the buyer contends that the seller, notwithstanding Article 6, is not at liberty to exclude liability for fitness under Article 35. According to the buyer, this raises a matter of validity and the issue is governed by English law pursuant to the characteristic performance rule in Article 4 of the Rome Convention. Turning to the Unfair Contract Terms Act 1977, the buyer contends (correctly) that the case does not come within the disapplication provisions in section 26[135] since these require, *inter alia*, either cross-border contract formation or delivery by means of cross-border carriage.[136] At this point, the buyer runs into some difficulty. The text of the Unfair Contract Terms Act imposes a requirement of reasonableness on the exclusion of liability for fitness, but it refers to fitness under s 14 of the Sale of Goods Act 1979. The seller contends that s 14 is inapplicable; its fitness responsibilities lie in Article 35 of the Vienna Convention, which of course is not dealt with at all under the Unfair Contract Terms Act 1977.

The seller's argument would appear to be fatal for the buyer's case. Might **16.65** the buyer argue, however, that s 14 of the Sale of Goods Act 1979 has a shadow existence for the purpose only of the relevant provisions of the Unfair Contract Terms Act? Or that this Act recharacterizes the seller's obligations under Article 35 as obligations under s 14? The answer must clearly be no. First, since the seller's obligation under s 14 does not match its obligation under Article 35, there must be at least the possibility that its s 14 exposure is more extensive than its Article 35 exposure. To apply the Sale of Goods Act along with the Vienna Convention would give rise to a type of dépeçage for which there is no warrant under the Convention. In other words, the extent of the seller's responsibility for fitness is a matter dealt with fully by the Vienna Convention and the parties have not sought to modify it by reference to s 14. Second, as for going directly to the Unfair Contract Terms Act itself, there is the insurmountable obstacle that the Act says nothing about exclusion under the Vienna Convention.

Suppose now that the Unfair Contract Terms Act were modified so that it **16.66** explicitly extended to the seller's fitness duty, whether arising under the Sale of Goods Act or under the Vienna Convention. Should the Belgian court in the above example apply the Act? The question whether controls on exclusion clauses go to validity is squarely presented. Given the very clear language of Article 6, which states that '[t]he parties may . . . derogate from or vary any of [the Convention's] provisions', one has to conclude that the Convention means what it says. The parties have derogated from Article 35 and their decision may not be undermined through the validity exception in Article 4(a). The buyer is then left to fall back on a further argument, that the principle of good faith is employed in the

---

[135] s 27 is not relevant because it applies only where there is an express choice of law clause.

[136] s 26 of the Unfair Contract Terms Act 1977 complements the test for an international sale in ULIS (see *Amiri Flight Authority v BAE Systems plc* [2003] EWCA Civ 1447, [2003] 2 Lloyd's Rep 767) (broadly—but see note 40 above) and therefore does not fit the radically different test in the Vienna Convention.

interpretation of the Convention, so as to temper the free language of Article 6. The existence and extent of this argument is further support for the view that exclusion clauses are dealt with in full within the body of the Convention. In consequence, under the five question analysis set out above, we stop at the second question, having concluded that exclusion clauses are dealt with expressly under the Convention.

16.67 The text of Article 6 is important too in the matter of penalty clauses. Suppose, in our above example, that the contract had provided for payments in the event of delay by the seller, in a way that offended the rule against penalties in English law. The seller pleads that the clause is a penalty and the buyer states that the clause pursuant to Article 6 derogates from Article 74 to the extent that the latter lays down the rule that damages are recoverable in so far as they represent loss caused by the seller's breach. Article 74 states:

> Damages for breach of contract by one party consist of a sum equal to the loss . . . suffered by the other party as a consequence of breach. Such damages may not exceed the loss which the party in breach foresaw or ought to have foreseen at the time of the conclusion of the contract . . . as a possible consequence of the breach of contract.

This provision, on its terms, does not apply to acceleration clauses in that these do not deal with damages at all but, in the case of sale, only with the collapse into one present lump sum of the buyer's price instalments, a matter of primary performance and not secondary, or damages, performance. As for true penalty clauses, the first question is whether in the words of Article 4 they pertain to 'the rights and obligations of the seller and the buyer' and so fall within the scope of the Vienna Convention.[137] This is not the same thing as determining whether any extant rule dealing with penalties or liquidated damages is part of the law of sale. Since legal systems will not draw the line between general contract law and the special contract law of sale in identical ways, it was obviously wise to avoid any ideal definition of the law of sale which the Vienna Convention itself could neither confirm nor deny. The formula adopted in Article 4 is wider than any such ideal definition; indeed, it altogether eliminates any division between general and special contract law. In consequence, it tends to diminish the significance of asking whether the Unidroit Principles could be invoked in support of the Vienna Convention. An entitlement to receive and a liability to pay a penalty clearly pertain to 'the rights and obligations of the seller and the buyer' in that it is in their capacities as seller and buyer that the penalty is agreed.

---

[137] The opening flush.

The next question is whether penalty clauses go to the matter of validity **16.68** so that they are taken out of the Vienna Convention by Article 4(a). Once again, there arises the intractable difficulty of defining validity under the Convention without any real assistance from the remaining provisions of the Convention itself. One argument against treating penalties as pertaining to validity is that penalty clauses are by no means universally condemned across all legal systems. Some measure of universality, it is submitted, should be required of a provision to pass the test of validity since any unduly liberal definition of validity will impair the uniform purpose of the Vienna Convention. In addition, to overcome the difficulty of defining validity within the Convention, recourse to the Unidroit Principles is useful for the very reason that they do cover issues of contractual validity. First, in Chapter 3 on Validity, there is no mention of penalty clauses, which suggests that the subject of penalties is not taken out of the Vienna Convention. Second, there is in the section on damages, contained in the chapter on Non-Performance, a provision to the effect that an agreed sum can be recovered in the event of non-performance but that it may be reduced to a reasonable amount where it is 'grossly excessive in relation to the harm resulting from the non-performance'.[138] This now leads on to how the Vienna Convention should deal with penalty clauses in a contract of sale, in the course of which a reference to the Unidroit Principles, if legitimate, might be useful.

Turning to Article 7(2), the general principles on which the Vienna **16.69** Convention is based must first be examined for a solution before any recourse to the private international law rules of the forum takes place. Although Article 74, which deals generally with damages, expresses a compensation principle and links damages to loss caused by contractual non-performance, from which it might therefore be inferred that a penalty sum should not be recoverable, there are indications pointing the other way. First, the general support for self-help in the Convention[139] supports the autonomy of the parties in pre-empting a judicial resolution of the recoverable damages by setting their own figure. Second, as Article 6 in particular affirms, the Convention supports the freedom of the parties to depart from any rule of the Convention establishing their rights and obligations. This would appear to tilt the balance in favour of penalty clauses since Article 6 should not be confined to express derogations from the provisions of the Convention.[140] One possible though somewhat weak counter-argument, nevertheless, might be that the parties should consciously depart from the Convention to exercise their Article 6

---

[138] Art 7.4.13.
[139] See discussion above, para 16.58.   [140] Discussed below, para 16.110.

entitlement, such intention being absent in many penalty clause cases. In sum, it does not seem that there is any scope in Article 7(2) for turning to the private international law rules of the forum to assess the lawfulness or enforceability of a penalty clause.

16.70 With respect to case law and arbitral awards,[141] the response, as might fairly be predicted for any difficult issue in a legally varied world, is mixed and unhelpful, partly because the separation in English law of penalties, liquidated damages clauses and limitation clauses is not universally familiar. In a number of cases, resort has been had to the rules of private international law pursuant to Article 7(2), which supposes that the matter is in principle subject to the Vienna Convention but that no solution can therein be found.[142] In other cases, the Convention is said not to apply[143] or there is simply a reference to a national law.[144] Penalties have also been upheld on the simple ground that they are not inconsistent with the Convention[145] or are supported by 'the international practice stated in the Unidroit Principles of International Commercial Contracts'.[146] Provisions of the Convention have also been invoked, though not always in a convincing way.[147] A clause containing a 'compensation fee' expressed as a percentage of the price has also been considered with a view to determining whether it excludes a claim for damages under the Convention.[148] What is entirely lacking is any systematic and convincing attempt to work through the principles of the Convention and stake out its role relative to the rules of private international law of the forum.

---

[141] P Koneru, 'The International Interpretation of the UN Convention on Contracts for the International Sale of Goods: An Approach Based on General Principles' (1997) 6 Minnesota J of World Trade 105.

[142] ICC Court of Arbitration (No 7197 of 1992) (http://cisgw3.law.pace.edu/cases/927197i1.html); Appellate Court Arnhem (Holland) of 22 May 1995 (http://cisgw3.law.pace.edu/cases/931230nl.html), where the court found that references to Convention provisions (Arts 7 (good faith), 8(3) (interpretation) and 77 (mitigation)) provided no assistance.

[143] Oberlandesgericht Munich of 8 February 1995 (http://cisgw3.law.pace.edu/cases/920414gl.html).

[144] Rechtbank van Koophandel Hasselt (Belgium) of 21 January 1997 (http://cisgw3.law.pace.edu/cases/970121b1.html).

[145] Tribunal of International Commercial Arbitration at the Russian Federation Chamber of Commerce (No 3 of 1996) (http://cisgw3.law.pace.edu/cases/970513rl.html).

[146] Tribunal of International Commercial Arbitration at the Russian Federation Chamber of Commerce (No 229 of 1996) (http://cisgw3.law.pace.edu/cases/970605rl.html).

[147] ICC Court of Arbitration (No 8247 of June 1996) (http://cisgw3.law.pace.edu/cases/968247i1.html), where the penalty was recoverable as a claim for the price under Art 53.

[148] ICC Court of Arbitration (No 7585 of 1992) (http://cisgw3.law.pace.edu/cases/927585i1.html) (no: cf ICC Court of Arbitration (No 251 of 1993) (http://cisgw3.law.pace.edu/cases/941123i1.html)).

Validity and Misrepresentation

A more difficult validity question concerns common law rules of innocent **16.71** misrepresentation which have no equivalent in the Vienna Convention. Briefly, the problem is this. If the area of misrepresentation is taken out of the Vienna Convention by Article 4(a), so as to permit national mis-representation rules to apply to sale contracts, then there is the threat of such rules undermining the rule of fundamental breach in Article 25, which serves the purpose of rendering difficult the avoidance of the con-tract for breach. This is because misrepresentation and breach are capable of overlapping and it is relatively easy to rescind a contract for mis-representation,[149] which, though different from avoidance as a means of escaping the contract, remains nevertheless a means of escape. The same problem of accommodating misrepresentation and sale of goods rules is present in common law systems,[150] though it is not so pressing because the doctrine of promissory conditions and the use of such conditions to define implied terms in sale of goods legislation[151] makes it significantly easier to terminate a contract for breach under such legislation than it is to avoid a contract for non-performance under the Vienna Convention.

In so far as any misrepresentation induces entry into a contract of sale, **16.72** then the question is whether it pertains to 'the rights and obligations of the seller and buyer arising from such a contract'.[152] It is clear that any rights and obligations engendered by an inducing misrepresentation do not arise from the contract as such but from the circumstances pre-ceding that contract. Any attempt, therefore, to spell out a position in the Vienna Convention on misrepresentation by reference to the principles on which the Convention is based[153] should fail *in limine*. Furthermore, a seller's duty in Article 35(1) to deliver the goods in conformity with their 'description'[154] is not, even when broadly understood, capable of embracing misrepresentation since the governing description is the one 'required by the contract' and misrepresentation exists dehors the con-tract. The best means for controlling the destructive threat of innocent misrepresentation, so as to preserve the integrity of Convention rules on avoidance for breach and non-performance, would be for states adopting the Convention to restrict by legislation any liberal rules of rescission already in existence under their domestic laws. The case of the

---

[149] Notwithstanding (in England) the discretion given to a court or arbitrator under s 2(2) of the Misrepresentation Act 1967 to declare a contract subsisting.
[150] See, e.g. *Leaf v International Galleries* [1950] 2 QB 86; *Riddiford v Warren* (1901) 20 NZLR 572; *Watt v Westhoven* [1933] VLR 458.
[151] Sale of Goods Act 1979, ss 11–15.   [152] Art 4.   [153] Art 7(2).
[154] A word that should not be given the narrow artificial meaning that it has acquired under the English law of sale.

misrepresentation that is incorporated in the contract as, to use the language of the Convention, a requirement of it,[155] raises a different matter which will be dealt with in the next section. The question here is whether a claimant should have freedom to elect between a claim under the Convention and a claim under the applicable law dealing with an inducing misrepresentation.

Validity and Property

16.73 Article 4(b) excludes from the scope of the Vienna Convention 'the effect which the contract may have on the property in the goods sold'. The Convention does not define 'the property' but it would seem that the expression signifies ownership. The law applicable to property matters[156] would come into play to determine whether and when the property would pass. It should however be recognized that the Convention is not silent on property matters. First of all, it recognizes that the seller does have a duty as a matter of contract to transfer the property in the goods to the buyer.[157] It further recognizes that that property must not be impaired by third party rights. Hence the seller is required in stated conditions to deliver goods 'free from any right or claim of a third party based on industrial property or any other intellectual property'. In thus speaking to the *quality* of the property transferred, the Convention is again dealing with property as a matter of contractual obligation. Furthermore, it seems plain that the transfer of the property does not extend to possession of the goods, notwithstanding that possession may in some systems of law amount to a proprietary interest in goods capable of protection.[158] The Convention does indeed deal with possession in a way that compromises the existence of any clear distinction between property and contract law.[159]

16.74 The first way in which it does this is to recognize that the seller may make it a condition of handing over the goods, or of their surrender by the carrier, that the buyer first pay for them.[160] This right, which operates in a way that is equivalent to the unpaid seller's lien in English law,[161] is not expressed to be subject to any rights that the buyer might have acquired as owner under the relevant applicable law. Furthermore, even a seller who makes no provision for it is recognized as having a right of stoppage

---

[155] Art 35(1).   [156] Ch 18 below.   [157] Art 30.
[158] As is the case in English law: *On Demand Information plc v Michael Gerson* [2002] UKHL 13, [2003] 1 AC 368.
[159] See Ch 18 generally on whether the law of the situs should apply to the passing of property as between buyer and seller. See also above, paras 13.221–222.
[160] Art 58   [161] Sale of Goods Act 1979, s 41.

in transit[162] where it becomes apparent that the buyer will not perform a substantial part of its obligations under the contract.[163] Again, this is stated without regard to the passing of property to the buyer, to the corresponding stoppage provisions in national law[164] or to national insolvency law. Indeed, the Convention does not refer to the right as one of stoppage at all, but rather treats it as a matter of suspension of the contract.[165] There seems no good reason to subject the plain language of the Convention to any unstated qualification in the cause of preserving the integrity of property as a category distinct from contract. To this extent, the adoption by states of the Vienna Convention modifies their private international rules in matters relating to possessory rights over movables.

4. THE BOUNDARIES OF SALE IN THE VIENNA CONVENTION

The previous section was devoted to identifying gaps in the Vienna Convention and exploring ways of filling them, one such way being resort to the private international law rules of the forum. In this section, the focus is on two issues. The first concerns overlap between the Convention and certain national law subjects such as tort law and consumer protection law. In case of conflict between the Convention and national tort law, for example, does the Convention simply apply on its own terms or may the relevant body of national law be applied by the forum? In answering this question, a further question arises: are the rules of national law dealing with overlapping or cumulative liability in tort and contract invoked to deal with conflict between the Convention and national law? The second issue concerns the outer boundary of sale and raises two matters, namely, the very definition of a sale contract and the scope of certain express exclusions from the Convention. All of these issues and questions go to the heart of any role played by the forum's private international law rules alongside the Convention.   **16.75**

The Convention and National Law

More difficult issues concerning the scope of the Vienna Convention lie in **16.76** respect of the relationship between the law of sale and the law of tortious

---

[162] It is broader than the common law right in that it is not confined to the insolvency of the buyer. Cf Sale of Goods Act 1979, s 44.

[163] Art 71(1), (2).

[164] Which might be confined to insolvency or might define transit in a narrower way than the Convention.

[165] Note that national legislation on stoppage constitutes an interference with the carrier's rights and duties, whereas Art 71(2) is clearly limited to rights in the goods as between buyer and seller. Whether the carrier would be bound by the stop notice would therefore be a matter for the law governing the contract of carriage.

(or delictual) liability as well as, for common law systems, equity (mis-representation).[166] This is not so much a case of examining exclusions of sale material from the Vienna Convention but rather of determining the boundary between the Convention and a body of domestic law that has the potentiality of undermining the uniform implementation of the Convention. To the extent that the Convention permits the buyer of goods to recover damages, whether direct or consequential, arising from the supply of defective goods, in circumstances where the applicable law of tort would likewise order an award of damages, whether on the basis of fault-based or strict liability, then there is on the face of it no evident collision between that applicable law and the Convention. Moreover, domestic laws that take a stricter line than English law does on the choice between causes of action in contract and tort see contract as the dominant category, which points to the supremacy of the Convention over national tort law, so that in the event there is no retrenchment in the application of the Convention on its own terms.

Tort Law

16.77 One possible point of collision between the Vienna Convention and national tort law comes with respect to Article 39 which requires the buyer to give a notice specifying any nonconformity in the goods within a reasonable period after discovering it or after the time when it should have been discovered.[167] A buyer who fails to comply with Article 39 is deprived of the right to rely upon the nonconformity of the goods, with the exception of a limited damages claim or a reduction of the price in those cases where there was a reasonable excuse for the failure to give the required notice.[168] Suppose that the buyer fails to give the necessary notice but is able to present a claim under the applicable tort law which is not dependent upon the giving of any notice and which indemnifies the buyer against types of loss that are generally recoverable under the terms of the Vienna Convention. In view of Article 5, which excludes liability for personal injury and death from the Convention, the types of loss in question will be property damage and financial loss, the latter of which may not readily be recoverable in some tort law systems.

16.78 The critical issue here is whether the Vienna Convention is being undermined by a tort claim that outflanks the notice requirement in Article 39.

---

[166] An American view that in surveying a broad field seems to support the coexistence of tort and misrepresentation with the Vienna Convention is *Geneva Pharmaceuticals Technology Corp v Barr Laboratories Inc*, 201 F Supp 2d 236 (2002) (USDC, NY).

[167] This latter period is defined by reference to Art 38, which calls on the buyer to examine the goods within as short a time as is practicable in the circumstances.

[168] Art 44.

Since all legal systems, more or less, have to cope with the problem of overlapping liability in contract and tort, this must have been firmly in the minds of the architects of the Convention. Indeed, Article 5 may be seen as an attempt, however limited, to minimize the potential of such a conflict involving the Convention as part of the relevant contract law. It does this by shrinking the scope of contract law. It is submitted that it would read too much into the Convention to go further than this and ascribe to the Convention an intention to reach into national law and dispose of the internal problem of contract and tort overlap, so that a buyer who is able to assert a claim in tort ought to be allowed to do so. Still less does the Convention suppress contract law in favour of tort. The tort claimant, indeed, may have to prove fault and so be deprived of the benefit of strict contractual liability.

Article 5 has an important conflict of laws dimension in that it determines **16.79** in some cases whether there is a selection to be made between a choice of law rule in tort and the terms of the Vienna Convention. It provides that the 'Convention does not apply to the liability of the seller for death or personal injury caused by the goods to any person'. This provision came in at a late stage in the drafting process, its declared purpose being to minimize conflict between the Convention and domestic tort laws. The provision is unfortunately worded, which can be seen from the following example. Suppose that A sells goods to B under a transaction governed by the Convention and B in turn onsells the goods, or new manufactured or processed goods embodying the original goods, to C under a transaction governed by national law. C suffers personal injuries or death as a result of a defect in the original goods and is able to recover either damages, in tort or for breach of contract, under national law, or the benefit of a settlement. B now seeks to recover from A the sums it has had to pay to A.

Now, if the language of Article 5 is read literally, then the Convention **16.80** cannot apply, so far as A's liability in respect of C's injury is concerned, since C is 'any person'. Nevertheless, a literal interpretation of Article 5 hardly seems to satisfy any duty resting on the tribunal under Article 7(1) to have 'regard . . . to . . . the international character' of the Convention; the broad drafting style of the Convention encourages a purposive approach to its interpretation, in contrast with common law drafting styles and techniques of interpretation.[169] Moreover, a literal interpretation would lead to an untidy dépeçage in respect of A's claim against B, in that a claim for the recovery of or reduction of the price would fall under the Convention, while a claim to be indemnified in respect of B's liability to C would have to be dealt with under a national system of tort or contract

---

[169] See *Fothergill v Monarch Airlines Ltd* [1981] AC 251.

law. The principle of dépeçage is widely recognized[170] but is awkward enough in its practical application to be avoided wherever reasonably possible since it complicates suits and inhibits settlements. In addition, to place too much emphasis upon the words 'any person' reduces the significance of the words 'liability of the seller for death or personal injury'. In the above example, B is not seeking to hold A liable for death or personal injury. Rather, B is seeking recovery for its financial loss in having to compensate C. That is a matter which the Convention is well able to handle,[171] there being no difference between the way it would handle this type of consequential loss claim and the way it would handle a claim following on from damage to C's property.

16.81   There is little case law on Article 5 but a German court, in a case where an American seller had sold a cutting machine to a German buyer, which in turn had sold it on to a Russian sub-buyer, in whose factory the machine caused a death and a number of personal injuries, has ruled that B's claim is governed by the Convention.[172] The court did so, however, without referring to the text of Article 5.

Misrepresentation

16.82   It was stated above that circumstances might arise in which a statement could function under national law as a misrepresentation inducing the making of a contract of sale and at the same time as an express term, or requirement of the contract, under Article 35 of the Vienna Convention. Just as Article 39 could prove a problem in handling the overlap of tort and contract, so it has some potentiality for causing a problem at the point of overlap between contract and inducing misrepresentation. In one respect, the prospect of collision is greater here—misrepresentation does not suffer the limits of tort law in dealing with financial loss—but in a more important respect the prospect is less. This is because the abbreviated nature of the right to rescind under national law[173] reduces the risk of a buyer falling foul of Article 39 whilst retaining an active right to rescind. To the extent that the national law confers a right to damages for misrepresentation, then there is a very real point of collision with the Convention. A national court may be less willing to assert the supremacy of the contract (and the Convention with it) over a statutory action for damages for misrepresentation than over an action in tort. Nevertheless,

---

[170] Rome Convention, Art 3(1).   [171] See Art 74.
[172] Oberlandesgericht Düsseldorf of 2 July 1993 (translated at http://cisgw3.law.pace.edu/cisg/wais/db/cases2/930702g1.html).
[173] Because of the lapse of time, for example.

for the same reason as stated above in the case of tort, it is submitted that there is no good reason for courts to shrink the application of any domestic law of misrepresentation. There is a strong case to be made for states acceding to the Convention to anticipate problems of this nature and prepare their domestic laws to receive the Convention so that there is a minimum of friction between the two.

The Outer Boundary of Sale

Not all sale contracts come under the Vienna Convention. Furthermore, **16.83** not all contracts that contain certain essential features of the contract of sale, involving the transfer of the property in goods in return for payment, are regarded as sale of goods contracts under the Convention. In addition, there are issues concerning whether the relations between the parties are governed by one master sale of goods contract or consist of a master contract that itself is not one of sale coupled with individual contracts of sale executed thereunder from time to time.

Sale Contracts Excluded from the Convention

Besides not defining sale,[174] the Convention excludes certain types of sale **16.84** from its scope. In the case of excluded sales, recourse will have to be had to the private international law rules of the forum to select the applicable law. For reasons stated earlier, the scope of the exclusions has to be determined under the Convention itself. The list is to be found in Article 2:

This Convention does not apply to sales:
   (a) of goods bought for personal, family or household use, unless the seller, at any time before or at the conclusion of the contract, neither knew nor ought to have known that the goods were bought for any such use;
   (b) by auction;
   (c) on execution or otherwise by authority of law;
   (d) of stocks, shares, investment securities, negotiable instruments or money;
   (e) of ships, vessels, hovercraft or aircraft;
   (f) of electricity.

Apart from cases where the use of the goods for personal, family or **16.85** household purposes has been obvious, the Vienna Convention was applied in one case where at first glance the goods were sold for such a use.[175] The contract was for the sale of a generator by a German seller to the Danish owner of a yacht, who needed it to operate a cooling system so

---

[174] Discussed below, paras 16.89–90.
[175] Landgericht Düsseldorf of 11 October 1995 (translated at http://cisgw3. law.pace.edu/cases/951011g1.html).

that he could sail his yacht in the Caribbean. No indication was given as to why the Convention applied in such a case. It is possible that the buyer might have had a mixed recreational/domestic use in mind. The Convention is not clear on whether the personal, family or household use has to be the exclusive, or even the primary, use that the buyer has in mind. Furthermore, this exception to the application of the Convention arises only if the seller either was aware or should have been aware that the goods were being bought for such a use.[176] Both cases open up the possibility of a contract of sale being governed both by the Convention and also by a national system of consumer protection law that defines 'consumer' or related concepts in such a way that the seller's knowledge is not relevant.[177] In such a case, it would seem that the national consumer protection law should apply as an overlay on the Convention, even though there is no saving clause in the Convention for mandatory rules of the forum state or of any other state.[178] If national law can apply so as to support a buyer's tort claim when its Convention claim would fail for want of timely notice of defect, then there is no reason why national law should not exclude a seller's claim under the Convention.

16.86 The exclusion of auction sales, likewise sales by authority of law, has not given rise to difficult problems in the case law.[179] The same can be said for the various exclusions of documentary intangibles in Article 2(d).[180] These exclusions are so specific that they prompt the question whether the Convention should otherwise be given an expansive interpretation so as to cover intangible property,[181] or at least documentary intangible property, not specifically listed. The exceptions also prompt the question

---

[176] According to the Austrian Oberstergerichthof, in a decision of 11 February 1997, the seller seeking the application of the Convention in a case concerning the sale of a sports car has the burden of showing that he did not know that the goods were being acquired for personal use and could not have been expected to know this (*Recueil de jurisprudence concernant les textes de la CNUDCI*, no 90).

[177] See Bundesgerichtshof of 31 October 2001 (translated at http://cisgw3.law.pace.edu/cases/011031g1.html).

[178] For the application of mandatory rules, pursuant to the Rome Convention, to a Vienna Convention case, see discussion below, paras 16.111–112. See further the discussion of mandatory rules above, paras 13.274–281.

[179] For an attempt by owner and auctioneer to extend the Vienna Convention to their agency agreement, see the discussion below.

[180] For a decision that the Convention does not apply to the sale of shares in an Ivory Coast company, see Bezirksgericht der Saane (Zivilgericht) of 20 February 1997 (translated at http://cisgw3.law.pace.edu/cases/981009s1.html).

[181] It is noteworthy that, in one case, the refusal to apply the Convention to a contract for the preparation of a market study was reached, not on the ground that the contract was not one of sale, but because (for the purpose of Art 3(2)) the preponderant part of the analyst's obligations consisted of labour or other services (Oberlandesgericht Cologne of 26 August 1994, translated at http://cisgw3.law.pace.edu/cases/940826g1.html).

whether the Vienna Convention applies to software contracts, since any disk incorporating the software is just the physical means of embodying intangible matter.[182] In a similar vein, a law firm's opinion letter will take a paper form, but the sending of that letter can hardly be called a supply of goods. In considering the position of software, the preliminary question, which seems not to have been addressed in the reported cases, is whether a licensing agreement can be said to be one of sale at all.[183] So dominant is licensing as a means of conferring rights in respect of software that the failure of the case law to mention it gives rise to an inference that licensing has been tacitly regarded as sale for the purpose of the Convention. This tacit conclusion is to say the least contentious. Licensing is chosen as the preferred medium for dissemination precisely because the licensor wishes to retain control of the material and not to surrender its rights in the same way as a seller of goods. Since Article 30 of the Vienna Convention requires the seller to transfer its property in the goods 'as' (not 'if') required by the contract and the Convention, it seems to follow ineluctably that a licensing of software, whether or not a disk is transferred,[184] is not a sale of goods under the Convention. This point, nevertheless, has not been taken in the case law that holds software supplies to be sales of goods covered by the Convention.[185]

Moreover, on the question whether software is capable of being treated as **16.87** goods under the Convention, the courts, without drawing a distinction between the direct downloading of software and its transfer in the medium of a disk, have treated the sale of software as a sale of goods,[186] subject to an exception for the case of non-standard software bespoke for the buyer's needs where the element of labour on the part of the supplier is so large that the contract is excluded from the Convention.[187] This division in the cases tracks the distinction in Article 3 between sale of goods contracts and labour and materials contracts[188] and supports the expansive approach, referred to above, that embraces intangible property in the definition of goods. Given the various national backgrounds to the

---

[182] Obviously, software can be transferred without the use of any disk at all.

[183] See further above, para 10.45, and below, paras 21.113–118.

[184] But see above, para 10.45.   [185] See the cases referred to below, para 16.87.

[186] Oberlandesgericht Koblenz of 17 September 1993 (translated at http://cisgw3.law.-pace.edu/cases/930917gi.html); Landgericht München of 8 February 1995 (translated at http://cisgw3.law.pace.edu/cases/950208g4.html); Handelsgericht Zürich of 17 February 2000 (translated at http://cisgw3.law.pace.edu/cases/000217s1.html).

[187] Handelsgericht Zürich of 17 February 2000. See also Oberlandesgericht Cologne of 26 August 1994 (translated at http://cisgw3.law.pace.edu/cases/940826g1.html).

[188] The associated services that accompany the supply of hardware and software can tip the balance so that the contract is not overall one of sale of goods at all: see Handelsgericht Zürich of 17 February 2000 (translated at www.cisg.wais.db.cases2/0217s1.html).

Vienna Convention and its character as a unifying device, it seems on balance correct to extend the concept of goods to intangible property that is not expressly excluded from the Convention. The difficulty presented by the licensing issue, however, is by no means so easily overcome.

16.88   Article 2 also excludes the sale of 'ships,[189] vessels, hovercraft, or aircraft'. ULIS contained an exception for 'any ship, vessel or aircraft, which is or will be subject to registration'.[190] The reference to registration has been dropped, which among other things means there is doubt about the application of the Vienna Convention to small and inland boats,[191] though the word 'vessels' suggests an expansive interpretation of the exclusion. The more expansive the interpretation, however, the less rational seems the exception. Moreover, the existence of a title register of ships hardly amounts to any justification for excluding ships from a Convention that does not deal with the transfer of the property in the goods. It is clearly established, however, that spare parts for ships and aircraft, even aircraft engines, come within the Convention.[192]

The Definition of Sale under the Convention

16.89   Although the Vienna Convention does not define sale, there is guidance to be obtained from Article 30, the general provision that lays down the basic duties of the seller. This calls on the seller to 'transfer the property in the goods as required by the contract and this convention'. The definition of 'the property' can only have the same meaning as under Article 4(b), which excludes from the Convention the effect of the contract on the property in the goods sold. When Article 4(b) was examined, it was seen that 'the property' did not mean all property interests; the Convention did deal with possession in a number of instances. In English law, 'the property' means the general property in (or ownership of) goods. As undesirable as it might be to give expressions used in the Convention the same meaning as they might have in one or more system of national law, in this case it does seem that 'the property' means ownership or what passes for it in national law. In consequence, it would seem that financial and equipment leases should not be regarded as contracts of sale of goods under the Convention. This view depends upon legal expressions being interpreted in a legal, as opposed to a functional or economic, sense. Even

---

[189] Russian Federation arbitration proceeding (No 236/1996) of 6 April 1998 (translated at http://cisgw3.law.pace.edu/cases/980406r1.html).
[190] Art 5(1)(b).   [191] Schlechtriem, 35–37.
[192] *Mitchell Aircraft Spares v European Aircraft Service* (Federal District Court (Illinois) of 27 October 1998, http://cisgw3.law.pace.edu/cases/981027u1.html); Budapest Metropolitan Court of 10 January 1992 (translated at http://cisgw3.law.pace.edu/cases/920110h1.html).

though a line denoting lengthy possession and enjoyment will over the useful life of goods eventually converge with a line denoting the same thing with the addition of ownership, this does not sanction an interpretation of 'the property' in Article 30 that catches transactions where ownership never passes.[193]

A more difficult question concerns hire purchase contracts where the **16.90** transfer of the property in the goods turns upon the exercise of an option by the hirer, the hirer never coming under a contractual duty in the course of the hire to exercise that option. In English law terms, the exercise of the option amounts to the acceptance by the buyer of a standing and irrevocable offer made by the seller, conditional upon payment by the buyer of the antecedent instalments of hire. Now, expressed in these terms, the contract of hire purchase is capable of falling under Article 30 because the 'seller's' obligation to transfer the property 'as required by the contract' is to do so in the event of the buyer duly exercising the option. An alternative would be that there is a contract of hire (of a particular type) succeeded by a contract of sale sprung by the exercise of the option, with the latter contract only governed by the Convention. This is a less elegant solution and creates a dépeçage that is best avoided. The outcome of this analysis is that financial leases stand outside the Convention but that hire purchase comes within, which is pragmatically awkward but unavoidable so long as the Convention hinges on legal rather than economic definition.[194] The exclusion of financial leases does have the merit of avoiding any need to draw the line between those leases that are economically the equivalent of sale and those that are not.[195]

Contracts Akin to Sale

A perennial issue in the sale of goods concerns the boundary separating **16.91** sale from similar types of contract involving work and materials. In English law, the importance in current law is not great[196] since by a variety of means, case law and statutory, the law governing sale and work and

---

[193] In support, see Resolution No. 1/03 of the Presidium of the Supreme Arbitration Court of the Russian Federation of 28 January 2003 (translated at http://cisgw3.law.pace.edu/cases/030128r1.html).

[194] Note however that the existence in a financial lease of an option to purchase still keeps the lease within the scope of the Unidroit Convention on International Financial Leasing (Ottawa, 1988): see Art 1(3).

[195] An issue that has bedevilled the scope of modern statutes dealing with personal property security, notably Art 9 of the Uniform Commercial Code and its Canadian descendants.

[196] But see the discussion of the Hague Sales Conventions in Ch 15.

materials has become more or less identical.[197] The Vienna Convention seeks also to draw the line between the two types of contract, though the importance of drawing the line is greater, since there is no uniform law, or any assurance of a domestic law similar to the Vienna Convention, available for work and materials contracts. In the case of such contract, the forum's rules of private international law come into play in the usual way.

16.92　According to Article 3(1), with one exception, contracts for the sale of goods to be produced or manufactured are to be considered as contracts of sale under the Convention. This provision has been referred to in a number of cases in an unhelpful and unanalytical way as tribunals simply note their entry into the provisions of the Convention. The exception concerns contracts where the buyer supplies 'a substantial part' of the materials needed for such production or manufacture. The exception appears regrettably large—the English language exception being wider than its French counterpart which refers to 'une part essentielle'.[198] The latter formula would permit a qualitative, rather than a mere quantitative, assessment to be made. There is little sign, however, of this provision causing difficulties in practice.

16.93　Article 3(1) is not connected to Article 3(2), which provides that the Convention does not apply to contracts where 'the preponderant part' of the obligations of the supplier of goods consists of the provision of labour or services. The first point to note is that this services exception is more narrowly phrased than its Article 3(1) equivalent. Second, it is not clear what is meant by 'preponderant'. A UK proposal to limit the Article 3(2) exception to 'the major part of value' won no support at the diplomatic conference.[199] Yet, the case law on balance favours a quantitative monetary evaluation of goods against services, so that if the goods are worth more than the services then the contract comes under the Convention.[200] Some cases take an impressionistic view of the importance to the contract of the goods versus the services,[201] which is also a default position if there

---

[197]　See Bridge, *The Sale of Goods*, 46–49.

[198]　All six language versions of the Convention possess equal validity.

[199]　OR, 84.

[200]　See, eg, Oberlandesgericht Munich of 3 December 1999 (translated at www.cisg.wais.db.cases2/991203g1.html); Cour d'appel de Grenoble of 26 April 1995 (translated at www.cisg.wais.db.cases2/950426f2.html); Russian Federation Arbitration Proceeding 356/1999 of 30 May 2000 (translated at www.cisg.wais.db.cases2/000530r1. html).

[201]　Landgericht München of 16 November 2000 (translated at www.cisg.wais.db.cases2/ 001116g1.html); Handelsgericht Zürich of 9 July 2002 (translated at www.cisg. wais.db.cases2/020709s.1.html) (the Convention does not apply to turnkey contracts with all of their various obligations); Richteramt Lanfern des Kantons Berne (translated at www.cisg.wais.db.cases2/930507s1.html).

is no invoice evidence of the monetary value of the two parts of the seller's performance.[202] The language of the Convention, however, seems more aptly to embrace the quantitative approach, however mechanical this may seem. Going beyond the question of preponderance is the case of a pure service which is rendered in a recorded form so that it is inapt to speak even of goods being supplied under the contract.[203]

Finally, there is a division between paragraphs (1) and (2) that deserves **16.94** further consideration and prompts an exploration of any link between the two. Paragraph (1) contemplates a case where work and materials are blended to produce something new. Apart from the exception relating to the buyer's intervention, it does not appear to matter whether, in terms of quality or quantity, the services element dominates the goods (materials) element. On this analysis, a contract to paint the portrait of the president of the buyer company would be a contract of sale of goods, no matter how much time and artistry it takes. Paragraph (2), on the other hand, contemplates a case where services are not blended with goods, as where machinery is supplied and then installed in the buyer's factory and maintained over a period. Unless the preponderance test or something like it is imported into paragraph (1), the question of inclusion in the Convention will produce anomalous comparisons of cases decided under the separate paragraphs, but there is no textual justification for repairing the connection between them.

Framework Contracts

Another problem arising under the Convention relates to what may be **16.95** termed framework contracts. Individual contracts of sale are often concluding between contracting parties on a recurrent and unconnected basis. Sometimes, however, they take place within the frame of a master contract which itself may lack terms that are typical of sale contracts, such as those relating to delivery and payment. The buyer, for example, may be an authorized distributor in a named territory. Are framework contracts, like distributorship agreements, contracts of sale for the purpose of the Vienna Convention? This will depend in part upon whether individual purchases are to be treated as instalments delivered under such contracts, as opposed to individual contracts of sale in their own right. The better view is that the framework contract itself is not a contract of sale under

---

[202] Landgericht Mainz of 26 November 1998 (translated at www.cisg.wais.db.cases2/981126g1.html).

[203] Oberlandesgericht Köln of 26 August 1994 (translated at www.cisg.law.pace.edu/wais/db/cases2/940826g1.html) (delivery of scientific study).

the Convention[204] but that individual sales concluded thereunder are.[205] This gives rise to a type of dépeçage in that different laws apply to closely connected contracts that are designed to work hand in glove. As awkward as this may be, it is hardly an unprecedented legal phenomenon. To avoid such dépeçage, a different approach would treat the framework contract and the individual sales as one whole contract, weighing the distributorship obligations against the sale obligations further to the preponderance test in Article 3(2)[206] in order to determine whether the contract is on the whole one of sale or some other contract instead. This approach, it is submitted, is unsound in the case of distributorship. Some of the obligations of the contract, respecting for example confidentiality or the promotion of products in a defined territory, are not germane to contracts of sale so that it is impossible to conduct a balancing exercise of different and discrepant elements to produce a complex contract that can be styled a contract of sale. In the case of other framework contracts, of the type that arises where the seller binds itself to sell its entire output at intervals to the buyer, or the buyer pledges itself to purchase all of its requirements of a particular type from a named seller, the problem of discrepant obligations does not arise. The one-contract solution appears quite feasible in such a case. Moreover, there does not seem to be a need to resort to the test in Article 3(2) in the case of such contracts.

5. Conflicts and Overlaps Between the Vienna Convention and the Rome and Hague Conventions

16.96 Many states are parties to both the Vienna Convention and to either or both of the Rome Convention on the Law Applicable to Contractual Obligations[207] and the Hague Convention on the Law Applicable to International Sales of Goods 1955.[208] The last of these Conventions was designed to be superseded by a later Hague Convention that was signed in 1986, but this 1986 Convention has not received the number of

---

[204] See *Helen Kaminski v Marketing Australian Products* (21 July 1997, Fed Dist NY) (very unclear but semble no) (available at http://cisgw3/law.pace.edu/cases/970721u1.html); Handelsgericht Zürich of 8 April 1999 (translated at www.cisg.wais.db.cases2/990408s1. html).

[205] See Oberlandesgericht Koblenz of 17 September 1993 (translated at http://cisgw3. law.pace.edu/cisg/wais/db/cases2/930917g1.html), Oberlandesgericht Düsseldorf of 11 July 1996, *Recht der Internationales Wirtschaft* 1996, 958, Gerechtshof Amsterdam of 16 July 1992, *Nederlands International Privaat-recht* 1992, no 420, Obergericht des Kantons Luzern of 8 January 1997 (see D 1998 Somm 325, observations C Witz).

[206] See ICC Arbitration Case No 8817 of December 1997 (translated at www.cisg.wais.db.cases2/978817i1.html), at [5].

[207] On which, see Ch 13 above.

[208] For the relationship between the Rome Convention and the two Hague Conventions, see Ch 15 above.

adoptions required for entry into force. Given the adoption of the Vienna Convention by more than 60 countries with further adherents likely in the future, the 1986 Convention is unlikely ever to come into force, if only because the scope that remains after uniformity for the choice of law process is so severely reduced as a result of the large number of states adopting the Vienna Convention.[209] The Hague Convention 1986, however, may be looked at to throw some light on the question of how a state's adoption of what, on the face of it, appear to be conflicting Conventions can be reconciled. The first point to note in the treatment of this subject is that these Conventions do not call upon Contracting States to denounce their obligations under one or more of the others.[210] Indeed, to contrary effect, each appears to defer to the others so as to give the initial impression of désistement, with treaty commitments in aggregate withdrawing to leave a space vacated of obligations.

First of all, the language of the provisions in these various Conventions **16.97** will be analyzed to determine how far they overlap each other. The next question will be to see how far if at all the Conventions would lead to different choice of law outcomes.

The Rome Convention

Article 21 of the Rome Convention provides that it 'shall not prejudice the **16.98** application of international conventions to which a Contracting State is, or becomes, a party'.[211] In other words, Article 21 announces the retirement of Rome, not just as to the Contracting State's previous commitments, but also as to any future commitments. It is hard to imagine a formula broader than that set out in Article 21, which amply embraces the Vienna Convention. Article 90 of the latter Convention states:

This Convention does not prevail over any international agreement which already has been or may be entered into and which contains provisions concerning the matters governed by this Convention, provided that the parties have their places of business in States parties to such agreement.[212]

The appearance of a circle is thus created, as each Convention defers to the other.

---

[209] Furthermore, in the vanguard of these adopting states will be states that might, because of their commitment to international conventions, might otherwise have been expected to adopt the 1986 Hague Convention.

[210] With the exception of the Hague Convention 1986 respecting its 1955 predecessor.

[211] Of the states that are parties to the Rome Convention, all of them with the exception of Portugal, Ireland and the UK are also parties to the Vienna Convention.

[212] The equivalent of Art 90 in the UN Convention on the Limitation Period in the International Sale of Goods 1974 is Art 37.

16.99   Article 90 of the Vienna Convention raises a number of points. First, so far as the United Kingdom remains outside the Vienna Convention, it is unlikely to experience significant difficulties with this Article[213] in relation to contracts of sale.[214]

16.100   Second, if the Rome Convention is ever replaced by an EC Regulation directly applicable in the Member States of the European Community, Article 90 would seem to have no application since an EC regulation is not as such a matter of international agreement. It would strain matters somewhat to say that the 'agreement' referred to is the EC Treaty itself under which the Community might adopt regulations within the sphere of its competence, especially since Article 90 requires that 'agreement' to contain 'provisions concerning the matters' in the Vienna Convention, which the EC Treaty itself does not.

16.101   Third, the Rome Convention is of universal application for its Contracting States in that it applies to all choice of law matters within its scope and is not confined to intra-European Union conflicts. That is to say, the whole of a Contracting State's pre-existing choice of law rules in contract, to the extent of the coverage of the Rome Convention, are superseded by its terms; they are not superseded merely to the extent that they might otherwise apply to contractual relations involving parties domiciled or resident within the European Community. Now, Article 90 defers to the Rome Convention only so far as the parties have their places of business in one or more States Parties to the Rome Convention, and would seem moreover to require this of both parties to a contract of sale. This formula falls considerably short of the full scope of the Rome Convention, which is capable of applying where neither party has a place of business in a Contracting State.[215]

16.102   Fourth, certain types of *sale* are excluded by the Vienna Convention,[216] whereas certain types of *contract* are excluded by the Rome Convention, and these contracts happen not to be types of sale contracts. What this in effect means is that a wider variety of sale contracts can

---

[213] Although the UK did enact ULIS by the Uniform Law on International Sales Act 1967, it is unlikely to create practical problems. ULIS will apply if, but only if, the parties choose its provisions as the applicable law of the contract (s 1(3)). Such a choice should anyway be sanctioned by Art 3(1) of the Rome Convention.

[214] In relation to carriage of goods, the application of the Hague-Visby Rules, which were enacted in the UK by the Carriage of Goods by Sea Act 1971, will be preserved.

[215] e.g. where non-residents of an EC State select the law of an EC State as the applicable law. (Note that the applicable law under the Rome Convention need not be the law of a Contracting State: Art 2.)

[216] See in particular Art 2.

fall under the Rome Convention than can fall under the Vienna Convention. To the extent that the former overlaps the latter, contracts in the overlap area cannot be subject to any conflicting demands of the two Conventions.

Fifth, the Vienna Convention defers to the Rome Convention only in **16.103** respect of 'matters governed by' the Vienna Convention.[217] The Rome Convention is a uniform choice of law Convention and applies to all contracts unless otherwise excluded, including sale of goods contracts. The Vienna Convention is overwhelmingly a uniform substantive law Convention which, as we have seen, incorporates a significant measure of choice of law. Besides Article 1(1)(b), choice of law is also capable of intruding under Article 7(2) of the Vienna Convention. It would only be in respect of the choice of law aspects of the Vienna Convention that it would be necessary to determine the question of primacy between the Rome and Vienna Conventions. Apart from that, it is necessary to revisit the basis upon which the Vienna Convention is rendered applicable in the first instance under Article 1.

The view advanced above was that, despite Professor von Mehren's **16.104** hypothesis that the dual residence test in Article 1(1)(a) of the Vienna Convention could be seen as an imperfectly stated choice of law rule, it is nothing of the sort. Rather, it is a domestic rule of the adopting state that, in stated circumstances, a sale of goods law other than any law that would be selected by the choice of law process will be applied to the contract at hand. The view was also advanced above that the private international law basis for the application of the Vienna Convention, in Article 1(1)(b), could and should also be seen as a domestic rule of the adopting state. By this domestic rule, a sales law, other than the law that would be selected by the choice of law process, would be substituted for the combination of that state's former choice of law rule and the national law to which that rule pointed. The virtue of domesticating the Vienna Convention in the above way is that it removes conflict between the Rome Convention and the Vienna Convention. The argument, nevertheless, that the two Conventions thus deal with different 'matters' is nevertheless somewhat formalistic.

An argument against a formal interpretation of this sort comes in **16.105** Article 99. The conventions that are most likely to cover the 'same matters' as the Vienna Convention are the two 1964 Hague Conventions laying

---

[217] One explanation for this formula is that it makes it clear that the Vienna Convention can be amended by the flexible procedures laid down in the Vienna Convention on the Law of Treaties 1969 (see Art 40(2), (3)) rather than by denunciation and readoption: see J Honnold, *Uniform Law for International Sale of Goods* (3rd edn, Deventer: Kluwer, 1999) 531.

down a Uniform Law on the Formation of Contracts for the International Sale of Goods (ULF) and a Uniform Law on the International Sale of Goods (ULIS). Article 90 does not defer to these two uniform laws. On the contrary, Contracting States are bound to denounce either or both of the two 1964 Hague Conventions depending upon whether they have made an Article 92 declaration, which permits states to opt out of the formation provisions (Part II) or the substantive sale of goods provisions (Part III) of the Vienna Convention. Article 99 largely eliminates the ground for deference if Article 90 is supposed to be given the formalistic interpretation stated above.

16.106 The removal of conflict, however, is not the entire key to rendering the Rome and Vienna Conventions formally compatible in the courts of a Contracting State since, if there is no operative language of deference and if both Conventions on their terms are applicable at the same time, then the court applying them is in an impossible position. There seem to be two possible escape routes from this predicament. The first is to compare the language of deference. It is, as we have seen, expressed in narrower terms in the Vienna Convention than it is in the case of the Rome Convention. It might therefore be concluded that the Rome Convention retreats whilst the Vienna Convention stands its ground.

16.107 The second approach is to consider a range of cases where it might be thought that an application of the two Conventions would lead to different results and then to ask whether this is in fact the case.[218] First, where the Vienna Convention applies because the choice of law rules of the forum state, a party to that Convention, lead to the law of another Contracting State,[219] the outcome is exactly the same as would be arrived at under the Rome Convention. This is regardless of how the choice of law rules of the Rome Convention would arrive at that same outcome, whether pursuant to an express or implied choice of law, the law of the residence of the characteristic performer, or the law of closest connection. If there is an express choice of the law of a Contracting State, then the forum state will, pursuant to its Vienna Convention obligations, apply that Convention. Pursuant to its Rome Convention obligations, the forum state will apply the appropriate sales statute of the applicable

---

[218] Where the buyer, asserting an inconsistency between the Rome and Vienna Conventions, sought the Tribunal de Commerce Bruxelles to refer the matter to the ECJ, the court, for unclear reasons, seeing no conflict, declined to make the reference: Tribunal de Commerce Bruxelles of 5 October 1994, available in the original French at www.law.leuven.ac.be/int/tradelaw and translated at http://cisgw3.law.pace.edu/cisg/wase/db/cases2/941005b1.html.

[219] Art 1(1)(b).

law, designated by that law as apt for international sales of this character,[220] which will be the domesticated Vienna Convention.[221]

Exceptionally, a conflict between the Rome and Vienna Conventions **16.108** might arise on special facts. Suppose that a German court is seised of a dispute between a French seller and a German buyer in respect of a contract for the sale of machinery concluded at a trade fair in England. The German buyer needs the machinery for its English factory and the goods are to be delivered there by the French seller. It is just arguable that, under the Rome Convention, the presumption in the absence of choice in favour of the law of the characteristic performer's place of business is ousted in favour of the law of the country of closest connection in Article 4(5). If this were so, then English law would apply under the Rome Convention even though, under Article 1(1)(a) of the Vienna Convention, the latter would be applicable. This is an unlikely type of case, for the further reason that it comes close to an English place of business having a closer connection to the contract than the German buyer's main place of business in Germany. In such an event, the German buyer would be deemed to be resident in England under Article 10 of the Vienna Convention, with the result that Article 1(1)(a) would have no application. Apart from that, and accepting this mere possibility of conflict between the two Conventions, it is submitted that the Vienna Convention should prevail since, despite its choice of law rules, it is overwhelmingly a substantive law instrument.

A less straightforward reconciliation of the two Conventions than **16.109** tracking their application to the same result comes in cases where the Vienna Convention applies by virtue of the dual residence test in Article 1(1)(a). Suppose that an Italian forum is adjudicating on a contract concluded between a German seller and a Belgian buyer, all three states being parties to both the Rome and the Vienna Conventions. The greater part of the contract is to be performed in Belgium. Suppose further that, under the Rome Convention, German law would apply by virtue of

---

[220] See further above, paras 13.74–75.

[221] No Rome States have made an Art 95 declaration under the Vienna Convention, excluding Art 1(1)(b) and the private international law route unto the latter Convention. If such a state existed (as might be the case if the UK adopted the Vienna Convention), the Rome route into the Vienna Convention (as embedded in the substantive applicable law) would remain available. So far as the UK remains outside the Vienna Convention, the Art 95 declaration poses problems for the maintenance of uniformity within the *Rome* Convention. If an English court were led by its private international law rules to New York law, it would apply New York substantive law. A Dutch court, on the other hand, if not recognizing the US declaration under Art 95 (see discussion below, paras 16.128–136), would apply Art 1(1)(b) and treat the US as a Contracting State, with the result that it would apply the Vienna Convention. Art 18 of the Rome Convention, it should be noted, requires states to have regard to the international character of the Convention and the desirability of achieving uniformity in its interpretation and application.

the presumption in the absence of choice in favour of the law of the characteristic performer's place of business,[222] but that Belgian law would apply if the law of the country of closest connection were held applicable,[223] while Italian law would apply if the court were convinced that the choice of an Italian forum amounted to an implied choice of Italian law as the applicable law.[224] Whilst, without the Vienna Convention, it would be critical for the purposes of the Rome Convention to determine which of the above three approaches was correct, the Vienna Convention robs the selection of any practical importance since the same Vienna Convention is found in the domestic sale laws of all three states and is applicable to the contract of sale in these circumstances. In such a case, the Vienna Convention simplifies the application of the Rome Convention and is not in conflict with it at all.

16.110 It is quite difficult to manufacture an example involving the dual residence test that displays conflict between the two Conventions. Suppose, however, that the seller is Belgian and the buyer German but the parties expressly select English law as the applicable law. The dispute is taken to the courts of a state that is party to both Conventions. On the face of it, there is a conflict if it is thought that the Rome Convention requires the application of English law but the Vienna Convention is on its own terms applicable. The possibility of such a conflict is raised because the United Kingdom has not adopted the Vienna Convention, which prompts the observation that, the more universal the Vienna Convention becomes in the European Union, the less likelihood there is of any conflict between the two Conventions. On closer analysis, however, the Vienna Convention excludes itself and leaves the field to the Rome Convention. This is because Article 6 of the Vienna Convention permits the parties to derogate from it in whole or in part. In choosing English law as the applicable law, it would seem that the parties have clearly demonstrated that they do not intend their agreement to be governed by the Vienna Convention.[225] A narrow view that Article 6 should be read as permitting only an express exclusion of the Vienna Convention would have the unacceptable consequence of placing a Rome Contracting State in an

---

[222] Art 4(2).   [223] Art 4(1), (5).

[224] Art 3(1): see *Marubeni Hong Kong and South China Ltd v Ministry of Finance of Mongolia* [2002] 2 All ER (Comm) 873 (good arguable case for jurisdiction purposes). See also *Egon Oldendorff v Libera Corp (No 1)* [1995] 2 Lloyd's Rep 64 and *Egon Oldendorff v Libera Corp (No 2)* [1996] 1 Lloyd's Rep 380. See further above, paras 13.44–55.

[225] Obviously, the applicable law clause chosen here is not as clear as an express provision that the Vienna Convention does not apply.

intolerable dilemma.[226] However, if one party (at least) claims that it was unaware that the United Kingdom had not adopted the Vienna Convention, so that Article 6 had not been satisfied, then there might indeed be a conflict between the two Conventions.[227]

Article 6 of the Vienna Convention is relevant with regard to mandatory **16.111** rules, an expression that is used on six occasions in the Rome Convention.[228] The concept of mandatory rules is not expressly defined and, moreover, its meaning is evidently a variable one according to which of the several references to it in the Convention is applicable. Article 7(1) of the Rome Convention, for example, permits (not obliges) a court to give effect to the mandatory rules of a country with which the 'situation' is closely connected.[229] The difficulty of giving the expression as used in Article 7(1) an exact meaning, as well as the discretionary basis for its application, explains why the UK Government entered a permissible reservation to this provision.[230] One definition of mandatory rules as used in Article 7(1) would be based on the following:

... provisions to which a state attaches such importance that it requires them to be applied whenever there is a connection between the legal situation and its territory, whatever law is otherwise applicable to the contract. What is special about the mandatory rules within the meaning of Article 7(1) is that the court does not even apply its conflict rules to see what law would be applicable and assess whether its content might be repugnant to the values of the forum but automatically applies its own law.[231]

The problem that mandatory rules, as dealt with in Article 7(1), poses for **16.112** the compatibility of the two Conventions is this. In view of the extensive freedom that the Vienna Convention gives the parties to vary or derogate from its provisions—provisions that lay down rights and obligations—is this freedom taken away by a Convention (the Rome Convention) that permits deference to another country's mandatory rules? Suppose the parties agree on performance that departs from the substantive provisions

---

[226] See C McLachlan, 'The New Hague Sale Convention and the Limits of the Choice of Law Process' (1986) 102 LQR 591, 612, arguing cogently that the express choice of the law of a state that has not adopted the Vienna Convention should be recognized by the courts of Contracting States pursuant to Art 6.

[227] It would depend upon what the parties meant when they selected English law as the applicable law (were they evincing an intention to have the Sale of Goods Act 1979 applied?) if they believed that the UK had adopted the Vienna Convention. The intention of the ignorant party would be assessed according to the test laid down in Art 8 of the Vienna Convention, which starts from a subjective premise but is in substance an objective test that looks to the reasonable contracting counterparty.

[228] See above, paras 13.274–281. See further Rome I Green Paper 2003 (see part 3.2.8); Cheshire and North, 577–578.

[229] Whatever that might mean. For a criticism of Art 7(1), see Cheshire and North's 584.

[230] See above, para 13.281.   [231] Rome I Green Paper 2003, para 3.2.8.1.

of the Vienna Convention and also infringes the relevant mandatory rules of a closely connected state. The response is clear: Article 7(1) of the Rome Convention only permits a court to invoke foreign mandatory rules and does not compel it. There is no reason why a State Party to the Vienna Convention should not sign away the freedom given by the Rome Convention to invoke the mandatory rules of a connected state. In any case, attention should be given to the precise meaning of Article 6. It refers only to varying or derogating from Vienna Convention rules and does not state in unrestricted terms, not specific to that Convention, that the seller is free to exclude all liability for the quality and fitness of goods. Article 6 does not purport to grant freedom with respect to rules of a different, non-UN provenance, so there is no conflict between it and the mandatory rules of a connected state in the first place.

16.113   Another possible source of conflict between the Vienna Convention and the Rome Convention disappears on close analysis. Under Rome, the forum state is permitted to apply its own public policy notions.[232] This is not a matter of obligation—so there is no conflict with the Vienna Convention—and in any case matters of public policy would surely amount to matters of validity for the purpose of the Vienna Convention, such matters being excluded from that Convention by Article 4(a). With regard to formal validity, there is in principle no scope for conflict between the Rome Convention and the Vienna Convention, given that the latter does not impose any requirements of form. Nevertheless, certain difficulties might arise as a result of the latter Convention permitting certain states to opt out of the rule of informality: these will be discussed below[233] when the relevant provision, Article 96 of the Vienna Convention, is discussed.

Hague Sales Convention 1955

16.114   The terms of Article 90 of the Vienna Convention have already been noted. The Hague Convention on the International Sale of Goods 1955 contains no deference (or give way) clause akin to Article 90 of the Vienna Convention or Article 21 of the Rome Convention. This opens up, initially at least, the possibility that the Hague Sales Convention 1955 will apply in the case of a conflict with the Vienna Convention. The first question to address is whether the matters governed by the two Conventions are the same, an enquiry previously conducted in relation to the Rome Convention.[234] In just the same way, the response is that the Vienna Convention, whilst containing some private international law material, is

---

[232] Art 16. See above, paras 13.282–294.   [233] At paras 16.137–141.
[234] See above, para 16.103

nevertheless overwhelmingly a Convention that deals with substantive sales law. Apart from the importation of substantive law by way of Article 7(2), the private international law content of Article 1[235] might be seen as conditioning the application of the Vienna Convention, rather than as being something 'governed' by the Convention.

The second question is to consider whether, on the assumption that the two Conventions are both applicable, they are in conflict with each other. In just the same way as it was seen that the Rome Convention was not in conflict with the Vienna Convention, so all that the Hague Convention does is to furnish the rules of private international law that may or may not in a given case lead to the application of the Vienna Convention by way of Article 1(1)(b) of the latter. This will happen where the parties select a law that incorporates the Vienna Convention:[236] the Hague Convention 1955[237] recognizes the parties' choice of a governing law.[238] As for the dual residence test in Article 1(1)(a), this is compatible with the rule in the Hague Convention 1955 that, according to the circumstances, either the law of the seller's or of the buyer's habitual residence or place of business is the controlling law.[239] The scope for conflict between the two conventions is further reduced by the exclusion from the Hague Convention 1955 of matters of formal validity. **16.115**

In one respect, however, the Hague Convention could depart from the Vienna Convention, and that is where, under Article 4, it presumptively applies the law of the place where the buyer conducts his examination, as to the form of such examination and the time within which it must occur, as well as to any notice given in consequence of such examination. Under this same provision, the law of the place of examination will also deal with any measures that have to be taken in the case of goods rejected by the buyer.[240] The reasonable time within which an examination must be conducted may under Article 39 of the Vienna Convention be informed by the law of the place of examination, but the other issues covered by Article 4 could be subject to a law that does not incorporate the Vienna Convention, in circumstances where this Convention under its own terms **16.116**

---

[235] For the sake of completeness, one might mention again the hypothesis mentioned by Professor von Mehren, not adopted in this text, that Art 1(1)(a) is an imperfectly expressed choice of law rule: see above, para 16.24.

[236] Assuming they do not by this choice impliedly intend to exclude the Vienna Convention: see above discussion. See also para 15.30.

[237] Art 5(2). There are certain complexities arising under the Vienna Convention as a result of the permitted declaration in Art 96 that serves to exclude the Convention rule that contracts can be concluded and modified informally.

[238] Art 2. Note that the Hague Convention 1955 proscribes renvoi in the same way as does the Rome Convention: Arts 2–4.

[239] Art 3.   [240] On the meaning and scope of this provision, see above, paras 15.49–58.

would be applicable. In effect, this possibility will arise where goods are delivered in a non-Contracting State under the Vienna Convention. If the Vienna Convention is to prevail over the Hague Convention 1955 in this case, it must be because the Vienna Convention defers to other conventions only in respect of matters 'governed' by the Vienna Convention, an expression that does not extend to choice of law rules. This, however, is a strained expedient.[241] Furthermore, the recollection of one distinguished delegate, that he could not in the legislative process have imagined the assembled delegates accepting that the Hague Convention should prevail in these circumstances,[242] is no substitute for reading the text of Article 90 of the Vienna Convention and asking what else that provision could have meant. There has to be a limit on the extent to which the interpretative process can be stretched to avoid pitfalls arising out of the legislative process.

16.117 The final question, bound up with the previous one, is to determine the matter of primacy between the two conventions in that narrow range of cases where there is conflict between the two. This issue is more complex than the equivalent issue concerning the Rome and the Vienna Conventions, because there is no give way clause in the Hague Convention 1955. Consequently, an interpretation of the Vienna Convention along the lines that it does not truly defer to the Hague Convention, taking account of the matters 'governed' by the former Convention, is not conclusive when the Hague Convention on its own terms remains applicable. Reducing a problem to minor proportions by shrinking the area of conflict does not make it go away. In the absence of a doctrine of implied repeal, as might be applied in the case of two conflicting statutes so that the later prevails over the earlier, there is no machinery for reconciling a Contracting State's conflicting engagements. One response is to say that if the State of Plutonia engages with Urania to go to its assistance if it finds itself at war with Cobaltia, and engages similarly to go to the assistance of Cobaltia if it finds itself at war with Urania, then Plutonia's dilemma cannot be resolved by legal means. A more constructive response is to build upon the Vienna Convention as the more developed instrument. This would involve noting that the Hague Convention 1955 is silent on the matter and that Article 90 of the Vienna Convention on its terms does not apply since it comes into play only where any two conventions have provisions governing the same matter. This approach in favour of applying the Vienna Convention is to be preferred.[243]

---

[241] See the similar argument, based on Art 99 of the Vienna Convention, advanced above in respect of the Rome Convention.
[242] Honnold, n 217 above, at 535.
[243] See Ch 15, n 21 and accompanying text.

Hague Sales Convention 1986

Unlike the Hague Convention 1955, the Hague Convention 1986,[244] which **16.118** is not yet in force and which, because of the great success of the Vienna Convention, is unlikely ever to enter into force, does contain a give way clause and a very specific one at that. According to Article 23: 'This Convention does not prejudice the application: (a) of the United Nations Convention on Contracts for the International Sale of Goods ...'.[245] This leaves the give way clause in Article 90 of the Vienna Convention, but it is submitted that the latter provision has no application in any event, given that the word 'prevail' in Article 90 supposes a conflict between the two conventions that the language of the Hague Convention 1986 has sought studiously to avoid.[246] The latter Convention has retreated, leaving the Vienna Convention in sole occupation of any field that the two conventions might otherwise have contested.

Notwithstanding this interpretation of Article 90, so far as conflict might **16.119** arise between the UN and Hague Conventions, the arguments rehearsed above in relation to the Rome Convention once again come into play.[247] The Vienna Convention deals overwhelmingly with substantive sales law. Schlechtriem[248] indeed comments that the representatives of the Hague Conference on Private International Law, speaking at the diplomatic conference establishing the Vienna Convention, had argued that Article 90 of this Convention was unnecessary, since that Convention contained no private international law rules. The point may be made again that Article 1(1)(a), despite Professor von Mehren's hypothesis that it is an imperfect choice of law rule, should not be seen as such:[249] this diminishes any

---

[244] Convention on the Law Applicable to International Sale of Goods. See Ch 15; see also McLachlan n 226 above.

[245] See also Arts 8(5) and 22(1). The latter provision provides that the Convention 'does not prevail over any convention or international agreement which has been or may be entered into and which contains provisions determining the law applicable to contracts of sale, provided that such instrument applies only if the seller and the buyer have their places of business in States Parties to that instrument'. Art 22(2) goes on to say that the Convention does not prevent the application of international conventions to which a state is or becomes party and which regulate choice of law in regard to particular categories of contract of sale. See further above, paras 15.67–67.

[246] The Hague Convention was drafted in contemplation that its provisions would complement those of the Vienna Convention. One might have hoped that the details of the relationship between the two conventions would have been worked out in more detail and more clearly. For a view to this effect, see McLachlan, n 226 above, at 613.

[247] See above, paras 16.98–113.   [248] Schlechtriem, 688.

[249] Especially since he rejects as 'unnecessary and undesirable' the treatment of Art 1(1)(a) in this way: Report on the Hague Sales Convention 1986, Proceedings of the Extraordinary Session of October 1985, para 193.

possibility that both conventions retreat from a given case, thus creating a 'negative conflict'.[250]

16.120   Apart from that, the Hague Convention 1986, like its 1955 predecessor, supplies private international rules that can lead to the Vienna Convention by way of the latter's Article 1(1)(b). In particular, it recognizes the parties' choice of an applicable law.[251] In default of choice, it applies the law of the seller's residence[252] and, so far as it recognizes the Vienna Convention as part of the law of the seller's residence in cases where that Convention would apply on its own terms under the dual residence test of Article 1(1)(a), it steers clear of conflict. The Hague Convention 1986 reinforces this appearance of non-conflict in other ways too. The same definitions of goods and excluded types of sale contract are, for practical purposes, common to the Hague Convention 1986[253] and the Vienna Convention. Furthermore, an expansive number of sale issues are placed within the province of the applicable law in the Hague Convention 1986;[254] the test of an international sale in the two conventions is the same;[255] and the law of the place of inspection is restricted in scope to formal matters,[256] thus diminishing any real possibility of conflict with the Vienna Convention. In one respect, however, there is considerable scope for interplay between the provisions of the Hague Convention 1986 and the Vienna Convention. This occurs in respect of states that have departed from the latter Convention's eschewal of forms by making a declaration under Article 96. This will be considered below when the Article 96 declaration is discussed.

6. The Effect of Reservations and Declarations

General

16.121   The Vienna Convention in a number of places expressly allows states to make 'declarations' that affect the extent to which they are bound by specified parts of the Convention.[257] It also provides in Article 98 that: 'No reservations are permitted except those expressly authorized in this Convention'. Neither expression, 'declaration' or 'reservation', is defined in the Convention but it is noteworthy that the only place in which the Convention uses the word 'reservation' is in Article 98 itself, which plainly contemplates the existence of some reservations in the Conven-

---

[250] ibid.   [251] Art 7.   [252] Art 8(1).
[253] Arts 2–4, though the Hague Convention does apply to auction sales (Art 9).
[254] Art 12. See above, paras 15.09–12.
[255] See Art 1(a) of the Hague Convention 1986.
[256] Art 13.   [257] Namely Arts 92–96. Art 97 makes formal provision for declarations.

tion. The UN Convention on the Law of Treaties[258] defines a reservation as 'a unilateral statement, however phrased or named, made by a State, when signing, ratifying, accepting, approving or acceding to a treaty, whereby it purports to exclude or modify the legal effect of certain provisions of the treaty in their application to that State'.[259] From this it may be inferred that what the Vienna Convention calls a declaration is a reservation for the purpose of both the Convention itself and the UN Convention on the Law of Treaties. A declaration under the Vienna Convention is no less 'unilateral' for being a permitted option granted by the Convention itself.

The Convention on the Law of Treaties provides that a state may not, in a case where only specified reservations are permitted, make other reservations.[260] Article 98 of the Vienna Convention, as seen, expresses the same prohibition. The effect of a permissible reservation is to modify for a Reserving State, in its relations with other States Parties to the treaty, the provisions of the treaty to which the reservation relates.[261] It is not transparently clear how the effect of such reservations is translated into the private law relations of buyer and seller under the Vienna Convention, since reservations are defined in terms of the way that treaty provisions apply to the Reserving State.[262] It is nevertheless clear that such reservations must affect the way in which the courts[263] of the Reserving State enforce contracts governed by the Vienna Convention and coming before them. Whatever the impact of the reservations, they must first be interpreted to see how far they are intended to go. **16.122**

The Article 92 Declaration

The most radical declaration in the Vienna Convention is that contained in Article 92; it permits a Contracting State to declare that it is not bound by either Part II (formation of the contract) or Part III (the substantive sale of goods provisions) of the Convention. A number of states have made declarations in respect of Part II but no declarations have been made in respect of Part III. The effect of any such declaration will be to create a gap in the Convention, respecting the Declaring State, for the operation of rules of private international law. The rules in question will be those of the **16.123**

---

[258] Signed at Vienna on 23 May 1969 and entering into force on 27 January 1980. Although a large number of states have acceded to this Convention, their number represents less than half of all nation states members of the UN. The Convention, however, is widely accepted (in parts at least) as representing customary international law.

[259] Art 2(1)(d).   [260] Art 19(c).   [261] Art 21(1)(a).

[262] Art 2(1)(d) of the UN Convention on the Law of Treaties.

[263] *Quaere* arbitrators (as opposed to the enforcement of arbitral awards through the justice system of the reserving State) (see n 58 above)?

forum state. As a matter of treaty law, the forum state must respect the declaration in question if it too is a Contracting state.[264] If the forum state is a non-Contracting State, the effect of the declaration will be to redefine the area of operation of the Vienna Convention so that the forum state is deflected to another body of the Reservation State's law of sale when the substantive law of this latter state is selected by the forum's rules of private international law.

16.124   A further feature of the Article 92 declaration should be considered. According to paragraph (2), a Declaring State is regarded as not being a Contracting State for the purpose of Article 1(1) to the extent of its declaration. So, if a Contracting State enters a declaration in respect of Part II, then the courts of another Contracting State must respect the declaration in the following two examples based upon the Article 92 declaration made in fact by Sweden. A Russian seller and an English buyer conclude a contract subject to Swedish law as the applicable law.[265] Under Article 1(1)(b), Swedish law cannot be applied by the courts of a Contracting State to contractual formation because the applicable law under the forum's rules of private international law is not, so far as formation goes, the law of a Contracting State. Similarly, if the seller is Russian and the buyer is Swedish, Part II will not be applied by the courts of a Contracting State invoking the Vienna Convention under Article 1(1)(a) because Sweden, for the purpose of formation issues, is not a Contracting State under Article 1(1)(a).[266] To return to the first of these two examples, if the buyer had been German instead of English, then the Convention would have been applied by virtue of Article 1(1)(a)[267] without reference to Sweden.

The Article 93 Declaration

16.125   The declaration contained in Article 93 permits Contracting States with 'two or more territorial units' subject to 'different systems of law' to declare that the Convention will apply either to all[268] or some of those

---

[264]   Art 21(1) of the UN Convention on the Law of Treaties.

[265]   It is here assumed that this express choice of law is not regarded as displaying an intention to exclude the Vienna Convention under Art 2.

[266]   The same two outcomes will follow from the ordinary choice of law process where the forum is in a non-Contracting State.

[267]   Subject to the possible meaning of the applicable law clause as evincing an intention to subject formation issues to Swedish domestic law.

[268]   If the Contracting State makes no declaration, the Convention will apply to all of its territorial units: Art 93(4). The equivalent of Art 93 in the UN Convention on the Limitation Period in the International Sale of Goods 1974 is Art 31.

territorial units.[269] Those different laws must coexist as a matter of the state's constitutional law, an expression that requires some consideration in those cases where a state has no true written constitution.[270] Paragraph (3) states explicitly that a contracting party is not resident in a Convention State if he is resident in a territorial unit to which, under the state's declaration, the Convention does not apply. Although Article 93 does not say so in as many words, the rules of private international law of the forum should not lead to the law of a Contracting State under Article 1(1)(b) where they lead to the law of an excepted territorial unit. Article 93 appears to be most useful in the case of federal states that have to secure the assent of each state or province to the Convention, so as to allow adoption of the Convention in an incremental way as individual territorial units accede to the Convention at intervals.[271]

The Article 94 Declaration

Another permitted declaration is to be found in Article 94, which allows **16.126** two or more states with 'the same or closely related legal rules on matters governed by this Convention' to declare that the Convention shall not apply where the parties have their place of business 'in such States'.[272] The declarations 'may be made jointly or by reciprocal unilateral declarations',[273] so that one such state can declare and wait for as long as is required for one or more other eligible states to declare, which can take place after the latter state (or states) has acceded in an unreserved way to the Convention by one of the usual means.[274] If the declaring states are parties to a Convention laying down a uniform law, an alternative

---

[269] There is no reason why an Art 93 declaration might not be combined with other declarations. Canada initially entered before later withdrawing a declaration under Art 95 to the effect that British Columbia only of its provinces and territories would not be bound by Art 1(1)(a).

[270] e.g. the UK, where surely the Act of Union 1707 would qualify as constitutional law.

[271] See the experience of Canada as set out at www.uncitral.org (Status of Texts). This point emerges from the contribution of the Australian delegate at the first meeting of the Second Committee at the Vienna Conference, commenting on two earlier alternative drafts of what became the current Art 93. See the Official Records of the conference (OR, 434 et seq).

[272] Obviously, in any two of such states if they are more than two in number. The equivalent of Art 94 in the UN Convention on the Limitation Period in the International Sale of Goods 1974 is Art 34.

[273] p (1).

[274] Art 94(1) declarations have been made inter se by Norway, Sweden, Denmark and Finland.

route to the declaration process might have been found in the give way provision, Article 90,[275] but the process in Article 94 is clearer.

16.127 The process in Article 94 is available also in respect of relations between Contracting and non-Contracting States.[276] One or more Contracting States may make (unilateral)[277] declarations as regards one or more non-Contracting States. If, for example, Australia wished to make a declaration under Article 94(2) in respect of the United Kingdom, then the close relationship between the law of sale in both countries ought to allow it.[278] Article 94(3) makes provision for a declaration under Article 94(2) to be converted into a declaration under Article 94(1) in the event of the non-Contracting State becoming a Contracting State.[279]

The Article 95 Declaration

16.128 Perhaps the most challenging declaration to understand is the one in Article 95: 'Any State may declare . . . that it will not be bound by sub-paragraph (1)(b) of article 1 of this Convention'.[280] To date, declarations have been made by a number of states including China and the United States,[281] and there are indications that, if the United Kingdom were to accede to the Convention, then it too would make a declaration.[282] During the legislative process, invoking the new uniform law by means of rules of private international law was regarded as controversial.[283] As seen

---

[275] When Hungary acceded to the Convention it purportedly made a declaration under Art 90 to the effect that it considered the General Conditions of Delivery of Goods between Organizations of the Member Countries of the Council for Mutual Economic Assistance (COMECON) to be subject to Art 90 of the Convention (and thus to prevail over the Convention). No other COMECON country made a similar declaration.

[276] Declarations were made by Norway, Sweden, Denmark and Finland as regards Iceland, at a time when Iceland was a non-Contracting State.

[277] The non-Contracting State cannot of course make a declaration.

[278] In the case of Canada, the position is not so clear because the law of sale of the of the province of Quebec is based upon the civil law and does not derive from the imperial Sale of Goods Act 1893. It does not appear possible to combine a declaration under Art 94(2) with a declaration under Art 93 (so that the Art 94(2) declaration is made in respect only of the common law provinces and territories of Canada). The differences between English and Scots sale of goods law, as expressed in the Sale of Goods Act 1979, are in comparison quite minor.

[279] This occurred on 12 March 2003 in the case of Iceland (as regards Norway, Sweden, Denmark and Finland) after it had become a Contracting State.

[280] See also the discussion of the impact of this reservation on the Rome Convention above, paras 13.83–85. See further Ch 15, n 9.

[281] The other states are the Czech Republic, Slovakia, Singapore and St Vincent and the Grenadines.

[282] Law Com No 250 (1997), *Thirty-Second Annual Report*, para 2.17 (referring to a response sent to the Department of Trade and Industry and dated 28 November 1997). We are grateful to the Law Commission for letting Michael Bridge see this response.

[283] At the 1980 diplomatic conference, some delegates proposed the deletion of Art 1(1)(b): Honnold, n 27 above, at 457–459.

above, Article 1(1)(b) is best regarded as a secondary gateway into the application of the Vienna Convention if the Convention does not already apply, pursuant to Article 1(1)(a), by virtue of the buyer's and seller's places of business in different Contracting States. Obviously, the more states that accede to the Convention, the less likely it is that a forum will have to consider Article 1(1)(b) and its own rules of private international law. Given the success of the Convention, the Article 95 declaration represents a dying problem.

A number of objections have been expressed to the introduction of the **16.129** Vienna Convention by means of the choice of law process provided for in Article 1(1)(b). First, there is an element of distrust expressed of the choice of law process. It is a common observation that courts applying foreign law very frequently make mistakes in determining and applying it. In some cases too the choice of law rule, especially in less sophisticated legal systems, is difficult to discern. Against these criticisms, it may be said that much good work has been done in the cause of concluding conventions laying down clear and systematic choice of law rules.[284] Moreover, if the choice of law process leads to a Convention State's law, the law that is applied for the purpose of Article 1(1)(b) is the Vienna Convention and not some obscure or misunderstood body of domestic sales law. Uniform law is designed to deal with the problem of misapplication.

Other objections that have also been expressed to Article 1(1)(b) are that it **16.130** introduces an undesirable measure of complexity, and that it amounts to an excessive concession on the part of Contracting States towards non-Contracting States. Taking first the complexity argument, the rules of private international law of the forum may lead to different laws for different aspects of the contract that are subject to separate laws. The forum might select one law to deal with matters of formation and another law to deal with essential validity. The result might be that the Vienna Convention is selected for one of these matters with the law of a non-Contracting State for the other. A number of points can be made here. First, the Vienna Convention is not an integral whole—with rules on formation that are so closely interwoven with those on the substantive law of sale that neither works properly without the other—and so on that account ought not to be separated. In Article 92, declarations are permitted so that a Contracting State can opt out of either Part II or Part III of the Convention. Second, if a Contracting State has separate rules of private international law for formation and the substantive law of sale,

---

[284] e.g. the Rome Convention on the Law Applicable to Contractual Obligations 1980: the Inter-American Convention on the Law Applicable to International Contracts 1994 (Mexico City).

Article 1(1)(b) will not further complicate the matter. All that will happen will be that the Vienna Convention will be substituted for a national law further to one of these rules. Third, such a separation, or dépeçage, of different contractual aspects is permitted under the Rome Convention which, fourth, demonstrates a tendency to subject those different aspects to the same applicable law.

16.131   The other main argument behind the Article 95 declaration concerns the balance between Contracting and non-Contracting States and was expressed by the US President in his Message to the US Senate.[285] Reducing the argument to its bare essentials and assuming that an Article 1(1)(b) declaration were not made, if a US court were led by its rules of private international law to the law of one of its own states, then it would be bound to apply the Vienna Convention. If, however, those rules led to the law of a non-Contracting State (say, Dystopia), then Dystopian law and not the Convention would be applied. US law in the shape of Article 2 of the Uniform Commercial Code, in other words, would be sacrificed without a corresponding sacrifice on the part of Dystopian law.

16.132   This reasoning is, to say the least, odd in that it assumes that national sales law in the US is superior to the Convention so as to prompt the question why did the United States accede to the Convention in the first place. In addition, a US court might under Article 1(1)(a) apply the Convention in circumstances where a Dystopian court, despite the residence of buyer and seller in different Convention countries, would have applied the law of a non-Contracting State because, for example, it was the law of the place of performance of the contract (assuming that this is the applicable Dystopian choice of law rule). The sacrifice argument could thus also be made in respect of Article 1(1)(a). In addition, a US court might sometimes, where Article 1(1)(a) does not apply, be led by its rules of private international law to the law of another Contracting State whose domestic sales law it would have to apply because of the Article 95 declaration. There is no question of Article 2 of the Uniform Commercial Code being preserved in this case and no obvious reason why the Convention should not be applied if that Contracting State has not itself made an Article 95 declaration. The case for fracturing uniformity by means of this declaration is not a strong one.

16.133   In addition to the rational underpinning of Article 95, there is the difficulty of determining how far the declaration goes. The difficulty centres mainly on the position of foreign tribunals in the event that they deal with a case involving a US element. The following two examples can be

---

[285] US Senate Treaty Doc No 98–99, 98th Cong, 1st Sess 1–18 (1983), reprinted at (1984) 22 Intl Legal Materials 1368.

considered. First, a Belgian court is seised of a dispute between a New York seller and an Irish buyer where the contract contains a clause selecting Belgian law as the applicable law. The second example is a variation on the first, differing only to the extent that the contract contains a choice of law clause in favour of New York law.[286]

Taking the first example, if the dispute had been litigated in the New York **16.134** courts, the Vienna Convention could not have been applied under Article 1(1)(a), the reason being that the Irish buyer is not resident in a Contracting State. In consequence, the New York court would take notice of the Article 95 declaration of the United States and would, on the face of it at least, apply Belgian domestic law. At this point, the question should seriously be asked: what is the relevant Belgian domestic law for dealing with international sales of this type? The argument was advanced at the beginning of this chapter that, even under Article 1(1)(b), the Convention could be regarded as having been incorporated in the domestic law of the state whose law is applicable. If the New York court were prepared to take this point, then it could sensibly confine the Article 95 declaration to cases where its own law, namely, Article 2 of the Uniform Commercial Code, is being preserved. The extent to which it can take this point, however, might depend upon the view that a Belgian court might take when seised of this dispute.

The attitude of the Belgian court, it is submitted, turns upon how far **16.135** the US declaration is interpreted as going. Belgium has made no such declaration, and the declaration made under Article 95 merely recites that the United States shall not be bound by Article 1(1)(b). Nevertheless, there has to be considered the extent to which, as a matter of treaty law, non-Reserving States should respect the reservations (including the declarations) of Reserving States. The Article 95 declaration is one that is expressly provided for by the Vienna Convention, which means that it does not require any subsequent acceptance by other Contracting States.[287] The effect of that declaration is to 'modif[y] for the Reserving State in its relations with [other parties] the provisions of the treaty to which the reservation relates to the extent of the reservation . . .'[288] It should also be remembered that a reservation (including a declaration) 'purports to exclude or to modify the legal effect of certain provisions of the treaty *in their application to that [Reserving] State*'.[289] It is submitted that a Belgian court applying Belgian law in a case involving a US contracting

---

[286] In the reverse case of the Irish seller and the New York buyer, the Belgian court would by its own private international law rules be led to Irish domestic law since Ireland is not a Contracting State.

[287] Art 20(1) of the UN Convention on the Law of Treaties 1969.

[288] ibid, Art 21(1)(a).   [289] ibid, Art 2(1)(d). Emphasis added.

party is not concerned with the application of the provisions of the Vienna Convention to the United States or any of its states. The Convention is being applied to private contracting parties and the courts of New York are not being implicated in the application of the Convention to those parties.[290] Moreover, the fact that the dispute might have led to a different result had it been tried in the New York courts makes no difference at all to this analysis. It should however be noted that Germany, when it acceded to the Convention and although it did not itself make a declaration under Article 95, nevertheless declared that it would not apply Article 1(1)(b) in respect of any state that had made a declaration that that state would not apply Article 1(1)(b).[291] Apart from the fact that this appears to be itself an unauthorized declaration, its meaning is unfathomable. Would a German court placed in the position of the Belgian court refrain from applying the Convention, on the ground that it would be applying Article 1(1)(b) in respect of the United States because one of the parties had a place of business there?

16.136 This leaves the slightly more difficult case of the Belgian court, dealing with a dispute between a New York seller and an Irish buyer, whose rules of private international law lead it to New York law. What makes this case harder is first that the question is squarely posed whether the United States, having made an Article 95 Declaration, can be regarded as a Contracting State for the purpose of Article 1(1)(b) and Belgian private international law rules. On this point, it is submitted that the Belgian court has been led to the law of a Contracting State. Unlike Article 92 declarations, Article 95 does not state that the Declaring State shall not be regarded as a Contracting State under Article 1(1)(b): the absence of similar wording in Article 95 is telling. But the question must still be asked, for the purpose of treaty law, whether the action of the Belgian court, in applying the Convention under Article 1(1)(b), involves the application of the Convention to the United States or any of its states. For the reasons given above, it is submitted that the answer is no. This finally leaves the question whether the Belgian court in applying the Convention is purportedly applying New York law, further to its rules of private international law, or is instead applying the Convention as part of its own domestic law. Earlier in this chapter, the latter view was advanced in relation to the process involved in Article 1(1)(b).[292] Consequently, the Belgian court should simply apply the Vienna Convention: Belgium did

---

[290] Nor, it is submitted, would the New York or other US courts be subject to the Convention by way of Art 1(1(b) just because a foreign judgment based on the Convention was being enforced: the enforcing court would not go behind the judgment save in the most exceptional cases.

[291] See www.uncitral.org (Status of Texts).   [292] See above, paras 16.28–31.

not enter an Article 95 reservation and its courts should not behave as though it had done. If, however, the former view is correct, then it has an awkward consequence. The Belgian court, applying the provisions of the Vienna Convention, could not be said to be applying New York law if it applied a law (the one contained in the Convention) which is not the law designated by New York for international sales of this type. If this is the accurate way to depict the process, and if it does not transgress the prohibition on renvoi in the Rome Convention,[293] then the Belgian court should apply Article 2 of the Uniform Commercial Code as incorporated in New York law. Nevertheless, the better view is that the Belgian court is applying the Vienna Convention under Article 1(1)(b) as part of Belgian law and not as part of New York law. Consequently, the Belgian court has no cause to turn to Article 2 of the Uniform Commercial Code.

The Article 96 Declaration

This leaves Article 96 of the Vienna Convention, by which a Contracting **16.137** State, whose legislation requires contracts of sale to be concluded or evidenced in writing, may make a declaration that certain provisions of the Convention do not apply where any party has his place of business in that state.[294] The provisions in question are Article 11, the general rule dispensing with the need for writing or written evidence in the formation and enforcement of contracts, Article 29, which allows for contracts to be modified or terminated informally, and the whole of Part II, which deals with the process of contractual formation and contains rules that could conflict with any national writing requirement.[295]

There is first of all the relatively minor problem of determining which **16.138** states are entitled to make the declaration. On a literal reading, it would be only those states that required all contracts of sale to be concluded or evidenced in writing, which could hardly be correct in view of the common exception for small-scale transactions. At the other end of the scale, most if not all states have legislation requiring writing for some sale of goods transactions, even if they are only consumer transactions. The sensible *interpretation* in a Convention concerned with commercial sales is to read Article 96 as confined to states that require at least some commercial sales to conform to a writing requirement, but the sensible

---

[293] Art 15.
[294] Declarations have been made by Argentina, Belarus, Chile, China, Estonia, Hungary, Lithuania, Russia and Ukraine. This declaration, though made 'in accordance with Art 12', will be referred to hereinafter as the Art 96 declaration. A French court has stated that contracting parties are not free to exclude Art 12: Cour d'appel de Paris of 6 November 2001 (see witz.jura.uni-sb.de/CISG/decisions/061101v.htm).
[295] e.g. Art 18(1) in so far as it permits offers to be accepted by conduct.

conclusion is to recognize that there is no real issue here since only states with a serious writing requirement would ever wish to make an Article 96 declaration. A further, odd feature of Article 96 is that a state requiring writing in the formation of contracts, but not with regard to their modification or termination, could make a declaration in respect of Article 29, which deals only with modification and termination.

16.139   The Article 96 declaration is unclear in its effect for a number of reasons. The consequence of the declaration is that the relevant rule of informality 'does not apply where any [*sic*] party has his place of business' in the Declaring State. The purpose of Article 96 is obscure: is it designed to protect contracting parties steeped in a culture of written contracts and liable to be surprised by informal obligation, or does it exist for the sake of a judicial system that is ill equipped to handle the enforcement of unwritten contracts? Consider the following two examples. First, the contracting parties are before a forum in a state that has made an Article 96 declaration. Neither party, however, is resident in that state. The Declaring State is treaty-bound to enforce an informal contract of sale concluded between those parties, or an informal modification, and the unease of its courts in handling informal contracts is not a relevant consideration, since the Article 96 declaration does not apply in such a case. If one or other contracting party has its place of business in another state that has made an Article 96 declaration, the situation is no different from the case of a forum in a state that has not made an Article 96 declaration and will be considered below. The second example concerns a party that has a place of business in a Declaring State and contracts with another party, which does not have a place of business in a Contracting State, on terms providing that the applicable law is the law of a Contracting State that is not the Declaring State. Although the parties are commercial entities and may by their choice have clearly evinced an intention to avoid formal requirements imposed by the law of the Declaring State, that state as the forum state will not enforce the contract or the modification (as the case may be).

16.140   If a non-Declaring State is the forum state, this raises the question of how far states should go in recognising the Article 96 declaration of another state.[296] Article 96 is not confined expressly to those cases where proceedings under a contract of sale are brought in a state that has made an Article 96 declaration. If the declaration were seen as expressing the forensic and evidentiary policy of the Declaring State—which, as seen in

---

[296] The same issue, discussed in relation to Art 95 above, of the extent to which states are bound to recognize and give effect to the reservations of another state arises here too.

the example above, is not fully protected by the Article 96 declaration—then the non-Declaring State would be at liberty to disregard the declaration of another state. On the other hand, it is certainly not easy to see how the declaration pursues a policy of protecting the Declaring State's citizens from inadvertent contractual commitment. For one thing, the contracting party seeking to enforce the contract or its informal modification may be a citizen of the Declaring State. Article 96 amounts to a compromise that was necessary to prevent the Convention from running aground during the legislative process. It is anathematic to one of the key features of the Vienna Convention—informality—and so should not be expansively interpreted. It is therefore submitted that it should be confined in its scope to actions brought in the courts of a Declaring State. Nevertheless, as will now be seen, too much ought not to be made of the scope of the Article 96 declaration.

Article 96 merely disposes of a substantive rule (or rules) in the Vienna **16.141** Convention without supplying any others or the means of discovering others. In particular, if the forum state had to obey the Article 96 declaration of another state, it is under no obligation at all to apply any domestic writing requirement of the Declaring State to the contract.[297] The way is open for the application of a private international law rule of the forum to determine the requirements of form. As seen above, the Hague Convention 1955 contains no rule at all for formal validity. Its 1986 successor provides that a contract is formally valid if it either satisfies the formal requirements of the applicable law or of the law of the country where the contract was concluded, or of the law of the country where either party is located (in those cases where they are located in different states).[298] But it then goes on to provide that a state may make a reservation[299] in respect of this choice of law rule for formal validity, provided that either party has its place of business in that state. Not only is the Reserving State exempt from applying the Convention to the formal validity of the contract,[300] but the Convention itself is stated not to apply to formal validity questions.[301] This is tantamount to providing that,

---

[297] cf to the opposite effect, which must be wrong, the High Arbitration Court of the Russian Federation of 16 February 1998 (translated at www.cisg.law.pace.edu/cases/980216i1.html). A proposal to require the implementation of the Declaring State's formal requirements was rejected: Doc A/CN.9/SR 208 (referred to in Schlechtriem, 699).

[298] Art 11(1), (2).

[299] This word, rather than declaration, is used in the Hague Convention 1986 to deal with the same material as is dealt with by declarations in the Vienna Convention.

[300] Art 21(1)(c).

[301] Art 11(3). But the Convention does not in terms deal with modification and termination as regards forms.

where either contracting party is resident in a Reserving State, no state is a Contracting State for the purpose of formal validity. The Hague Convention 1986 is therefore significantly clearer than the Vienna Convention in showing the effect of a treaty reservation on states that have not made the reservation.[302] The Rome Convention displays the same catholic view towards the selection of the law governing the formal validity of contract, namely, either the applicable law of the contract or the law of the country where the contract was concluded or the law of the country where either party was resident if they were resident in different countries.[303] It differs however from the Hague Convention 1986 in that there is no permitted reservation for formal validity. Consequently, so far as the Rome Convention applies, the effect of an Article 96 declaration by a State Party to the Vienna Convention will be minimal.

Article 28 and Specific Performance

16.142   Although Article 28 of the Vienna Convention is not as such based on a declaration, it exhibits some of the characteristics of a declaration and so can conveniently be dealt with here. The starting point is that the primary remedy for non-performance in the Convention is not damages but the requiring (or enforcement) of performance obligations. This departs from the common law philosophy of damages as the primary remedy and specific performance as exceptional.[304] One means of protecting common law susceptibilities might have been to permit states to make a declaration to the effect that their courts should administer the remedies in the Convention in line with the prevailing national philosophy, but it would have been difficult to draft a declaration that would have sufficiently fed into the text of Part III of the Convention. There is instead Article 28 which does not depend upon a declaration to be made and gives national courts flexibility in administering the Convention in such a way as not to upset the settled domestic order. The outcome of this discretion given to certain national courts is not at all unlike the outcome of a declaration to similar effect.

16.143   Article 28 provides that a court is 'not bound' to enter a judgment for 'specific performance', in those cases where one contracting party has the right to require performance of the other, unless it 'would do so under its

---

[302] See above, paras 15.106–108, for discussion of the formality provisions of the 1986 Convention and of the formalities reservation.

[303] Art 9; on which, see above, paras 13.256–258.

[304] See also the discussion of Art 10(1)(c) of the Rome Convention, above, paras 13.205–206.

own law' in respect of 'similar contracts of sale' that are not governed by the Vienna Convention. In those cases where the court exercises the discretion,[305] it is not immediately clear whether the court in departing from uniform law simply applies the law of the forum, as proposed by an American court,[306] or engages in the choice of law process. The purpose of Article 28 being to protect the domestic curial process, it is submitted that the right approach is to apply the law of the forum ('its own law'). The next and related issue then is to identify 'similar contracts of sale'. It is submitted that the forum should simply 'domesticate' the contract for present purposes and treat it as though all parties and features were national, rather than look for the narrower case of an international sale of goods contract where the parties have opted out of the Convention or which predates the Convention.[307] In the case of English law, examples of specific performance of sale of goods contracts are few and far between, the most likely cases involving goods such as ships and aircraft whose sales stand outside the Vienna Convention in any event.

16.144 The final issue, and the most difficult, relates to which law—the uniform law contained in the Convention or the law of the forum—defines 'specific performance'. The drafting history of the Convention[308] reveals the common law impetus for Article 28. In addition, Article 28 itself is the only place where the expression 'specific performance' is used. Elsewhere, the Convention speaks of requiring performance, which brings out a point that in the past has so bedevilled attempts to compare the availability of specific performance in the civil law and common law. The more expansive availability of 'specific performance' in the civil law is to a large extent due to the more expansive definition of what constitutes specific performance (enforced performance or direct execution or similar expressions). For example, a buyer to whom goods are not delivered and whose damages are measured by the cost of acquiring replacements might be seen as enforcing the contract as in some way an 'agent' of the seller. Or an action by the seller to recover the price of goods might also be seen as specific performance.

16.145 The significance of defining the scope of specific performance is that, it is submitted, contrary to the normal rule that Convention terms are defined under the Convention in an internationalist way,[309] in this one case the requirements of internationalism and uniformity point in exactly

---

[305] There is only one reported case under Art 28. See CLOUT No 417 (US).
[306] ibid: 'Simply put, [Art 28] looks to the availability of such relief under the UCC'.
[307] A range of examples that would anyway lack critical mass.
[308] Honnold, n 27 above, at 525–526 (First Committee).   [309] Art 7(1).

the opposite direction. It is no accident that specific performance is mentioned only in this one place. A common law court, it is submitted, if uneasy about the Convention's rules on the (easier) recovery of the price[310] or the recovery of damages, not according to the market but instead according to the acquisition cost of replacement goods,[311] is not at liberty to revert to domestic law but must interpret 'specific performance' as it is more narrowly understood in domestic law. Any other approach would unduly exploit the 'quasi-declaration' in Article 28.

7. Limitation Periods and International Sale

16.146 It was stated earlier in this work that the matter of burden of proof was treated under the Rome Convention, and in case law under the Vienna Convention as a matter of substantive rather than procedural law.[312] Prior to the Foreign Limitation Periods Act 1984, limitation periods were regarded in English law as procedural matters for the law of the forum. However that may be, the UN Convention on the Limitation Period in International Sale of Goods 1974 (the Limitation Convention) imposes a uniform limitation period (four years from the date of breach)[313] and rules[314] operating in lieu of the choice of law process,[315] so that the limits of the Convention have to be determined. The Limitation Convention complements the Vienna Convention and indeed applies in the same circumstances as it, namely, when the contracting parties have their places of business in different Contracting States or in different states where the rules of private international law of the forum lead to the law of a Contracting State as applicable to the law of sale.[316] The Limitation Convention does not direct Contracting States to treat limitations as either a matter of substantive or procedural law, and so like the Vienna Convention displays no control over a Contracting State's choice of law process.[317] The range of excluded sale of goods contracts in the Limitation Convention is the same as in the Vienna Convention;[318] the treatment of contracts

---

[310] Compare s 49 of the Sale of Goods Act 1979 and Art 62.

[311] Compare s 51 of the Sale of Goods Act 1979 and Art 75.

[312] Art 14(1) of the Rome Convention; see above, para 13.41.

[313] Arts 8, 9(1) and 10(1).

[314] The content of these individual rules fall just as much outside the scope of this chapter as do the substantive rules in the Vienna Convention itself.

[315] To date, the Convention has been adopted by 24 states, of which 18 states have adopted both the 1974 Convention and its 1980 Protocol (see Arts 43 bis and 43 ter). References to provisions of the Convention are to the Convention as supplemented by the 1980 Protocol.

[316] Arts 1(1), 2(a) and 3. The second head was added by the 1980 Protocol to the Convention.

[317] But note that the Rome Convention, in Art 10(d), treats limitations as a matter for the applicable law (as opposed to the law of the forum); see above, para 13.240.

[318] Art 4 of the Limitation Convention; Art 2 of the Vienna Convention.

as other than sale of goods contracts because services or labour are supplied along with the goods is the same in both instruments.[319] Liability in respect of personal injuries and death is also excluded by both conventions.[320] The Limitation Convention also has to be interpreted in an internationalist spirit,[321] but there is no provision for dealing with gaps in this Convention corresponding to Article 7(2) of the Vienna Convention. Article 7(2) appeared late in the day and at a time when the Limitation Convention had been concluded several years earlier. In any case, there is a greater need for a provision like Article 7(2) in a convention that covers a much broader field than limitation of actions.

The Limitation Convention permits declarations of the type that are also **16.147** allowed under the Vienna Convention, notably those concerning states with more than one territorial law[322] and groups of states with closely related laws.[323] As in the Vienna Convention, the stated declarations are the only ones permitted, and reservations and declarations are assumed to be the same thing.[324] There are also declarations not to be found in the Vienna Convention. First, a state may declare that it will not apply the Limitation Convention to actions to annul the contract.[325] This appears to avoid any difficulties concerning the effect of a state's declaration on other Contracting States since it pertains only to the way that the forum of the Declaring State applies the uniform law. No definition is given of 'annulment'. This expression does not appear in the Vienna Convention, which uses 'avoidance' to signify termination for breach. One may infer that annulment refers to the process—however it might be described in domestic law terms—for setting aside contracts for reasons of invalidity. It would seem to follow that the forum state controls the characterisation of annulment. Similarly, a declaration that affects only the forum in the Declaring State is to be found in Article 36, by which courts may preserve their freedom to raise the issue of limitation even if the litigants themselves do not.[326]

The Limitation Convention contains a declaration provision identical to **16.148** that found in Article 95 of the Vienna Convention,[327] by which the private international law gateway into the application of the Convention is closed.[328] It contains a give way provision that is identical to the one found

---

[319] Art 3 of the Vienna Convention; Art 6 of the Limitation Convention.
[320] Art 5(a) of the Limitation Convention; Art 5 of the Vienna Convention. Art 5(b) of the Limitation Convention goes further than the Vienna Convention and excludes all nuclear damage caused by the goods.
[321] Art 7.   [322] Art 31.   [323] Art 34.   [324] Art 39.   [325] Art 35.
[326] The rule that it is for the litigants to raise the matter is to be found in Art 24.
[327] Art 36 bis.
[328] See the above discussion of Art 95 of the Vienna Convention.

in Article 90 of the Vienna Convention[329] and a declaration is permitted in order that the state can redefine a contract of international sale of goods so that it accords with the definition of international sale of goods in an existing convention to which the Declaring State is a party.[330]

---

[329] Art 37.

[330] The declaration provision appears to be for the benefit of States Parties to one or both of the Hague Conventions of 1964 (containing ULIS and ULF).

17

Torts Arising out of the International Sale of Goods: Choice of Law

1. INTRODUCTION

17.01 The essence of the sale of goods is the interaction between contract and property law. However, the parties to the sales contract may place themselves in a position where they are also potentially subject to liability in tort. The concern of this chapter is with torts which arise directly out of the relationship between the buyer and seller of goods. Accordingly, discussion will focus particularly upon the torts of conversion, negligent misstatement and negligent and fraudulent misrepresentation, failure to sell, inducement of breach of contract and negligence. Discussion of the substantive elements of these claims can be found in Chapter 6 on jurisdiction in tort claims, to which the reader is referred.[1]

The choice of law rules in tort applicable in England were radically changed when they were placed upon a statutory footing by the Private International Law (Miscellaneous Provisions) Act 1995, Part III.[2] This applies to torts committed after 1 May 1996. Discussion in this chapter

---

[1] Above, paras 6.33–41, 6.67–74, 6.116, 6.130–135, 6.147–159.
[2] Hereafter 'the 1995 Act', or 'the Act'.

will focus principally upon this statutory regime. However, there is, at present, a dearth of relevant authority as to the application of the provisions of the Act generally and, *a fortiori*, their application to the sale of goods context. By necessity, therefore, the opinions offered in this chapter are often largely speculative.

II. THE CHOICE OF LAW RULES OUTLINED

We need first to examine, relatively briefly, the choice of law rules in tort **17.02** which are applicable in England.[3] Having done so, we may then examine how these rules might be applied to specific sales related torts.

1. THE COMMON LAW

The Rule of Double Actionability

It is not proposed exhaustively to examine the common law rules, which **17.03** are discussed extensively elsewhere.[4] In essence, however, the plaintiff was required to show both that the alleged wrong would have constituted a tort according to English domestic law and that it would also give rise to some form of civil liability by the law of the place where the tort occurred (often referred to as the *'lex loci delicti'*).[5] This test, which had been developed in the nineteenth century[6] and recast as the rule of 'double actionability' in the twentieth century,[7] was a rather plaintiff unfriendly one,[8] since it required the availability of a particular cause of action under two different laws. Moreover, the plaintiff also had to show that each substantive head of damages was available by both laws.[9]

Exceptions

However, the perceived strictness of the double limbed general rule had **17.04** been significantly relaxed in recent years. In *Boys v Chaplin*,[10] the House of Lords ruled that in a suitable case, the law of the place of the tort could be disapplied, in whole or in part, so that some or all issues could be resolved exclusively by English law. The precise operation of the exception was not wholly clear. Lord Wilberforce appeared to suggest that it could be

---

[3] For greater detail, see Dicey and Morris, Ch 35; Cheshire and North, Ch 19.
[4] See Dicey and Morris, 1508–1514; Cheshire and North, 609–614.
[5] *Phillips v Eyre* (1870) LR 6 QB 1.   [6] ibid.   [7] *Boys v Chaplin* [1971] AC 356.
[8] See *M'Elroy v M'Allister* 1949 SC 110 for an example of the harshness of the rule.
[9] Compare the Scottish case of *M'Elroy v M'Allister*, ibid.
[10] [1971] AC 356.

applied where the law of the place of the tort had no interest in being applied to a particular issue,[11] although it also seemed that if the centre of gravity of the claim was England, that could suffice to invoke the exception.[12] Indeed, the exception[13] was invoked solely where both parties were domiciled in England.[14]

17.05 In *Red Sea Insurance Co Ltd v Bouygues SA*,[15] the Privy Council allowed the exception to work the other way around, by holding that in an appropriate case English law could be disapplied in whole or in part and the law of the place of the tort alone applied under the exception.[16] It appeared[17] that the exception would operate where the centre of gravity of the tort was overwhelmingly in the law of the place of the tort and had no significant connection to the forum. In any event, both the House of Lords in *Boys* and the Privy Council in *Red Sea* stressed that the exception should not be invoked lightly and that: 'The general rule must apply unless clear and satisfying grounds are shown why it should be departed from'.[18]

Evaluation

17.06 The development of the exception was to lead to a choice of law rule which, it could be argued, was appropriate to the area of torts. The importance of the law of the place of the tort to most disputes is self-evident. It is likely to be the law of closest connection to the dispute and it is also likely to be a law with a strong legitimate 'interest' in regulating activity within its territory. Furthermore, although parties may not anticipate a tort occurring, they may, in certain factual situations, anticipate that there is a real risk of liability arising in tort. Application of the law of the place of the torts is likely best to give effect to their intentions as to which law regulates their liability in tort.

---

[11] ibid, at 391.

[12] *Boys* itself was a case concerning a road accident in Malta involving two members of the armed forces resident in England. The exception was applied in relation to damages for pain and suffering, which were available by English law but not by Maltese law.

[13] At least prior to *Red Sea Insurance Co Ltd v Bouygues SA* [1995] 1 AC 190.

[14] *Johnson v Coventry Churchill International Ltd* [1992] 3 All ER 14, QBD; *Church of Scientology of California v Metropolitan Police Commissioner* (1976) 120 Sol Jo 690, CA.

[15] [1995] 1 AC 190. See also *Pearce v Ove Arup* [2000] Ch 403.

[16] On one view, the Privy Council sanctioned the application, by exception, of *any* law which was clearly the law of closest connection as the (only) governing law of the tort. This would create something like a proper law of the tort approach: *Red Sea*, n 13 above, at 206.

[17] Although the exception barely had time to take root, since it was quickly superseded by the statutory reform of choice of law in tort.

[18] Lord Wilberforce in *Boys v Chaplin* [1971] AC 356, 391; considered by Lord Slynn in *Red Sea Insurance Co Ltd v Bouygues SA* [1995] 1 AC 190, 201. See also the dissenting judgment of Lord Scott in *Kuwait Airways Corp v Iraqi Airways Co (Nos 4 and 5)* [2002] 2 AC 883, HL.

At the same time, the fact that a claim had ordinarily to succeed by **17.07** English domestic law as well meant that a plaintiff could not successfully sue a defendant in England for conduct which the latter was free to engage in by English domestic law. The role of English law, as the law of the forum, stemmed from the intimate connection of tortious liability with the law of civil liberties and fundamental values of the forum which are often embedded in its law of tort.

The exception in *Boys v Chaplin* dealt with cases where the connection **17.08** with England was especially strong and where the place of the tort might be arbitrary, or have no enduring connection with, or interest in, the claim in tort. However, for torts where infringement of English civil liberties was less of a concern, the *Red Sea* exception meant that the law of the place of the tort alone could be applied under the exception if the matter had little real connection with England.[19]

Against this, the two pronged general rule was still a plaintiff unfriendly **17.09** one and led to precious few cases being brought in English courts which were subject to the rule. Moreover, the two pronged test may once have served an important role in preventing forum shopping in English courts. However, since the development of the forum non conveniens doctrine,[20] forum shopping could be controlled directly through rules of jurisdiction and it was no longer necessary for choice of law rules to perform this role. Moreover, the general choice of law rule led to the routine application of the law of the forum in transnational cases. This could be criticized as being inward looking and out of line with other areas of choice of law. Even post-*Red Sea*, this placed the burden on the plaintiff to show why the law of the forum should be disapplied. Furthermore, the price to pay for the extension of the exception to double actionability was greater uncertainty as to which law or laws an English court would apply. All this created a momentum for statutory reform, which culminated in the reforms made by the 1995 Act.

Common Law Rules Applicable to Defamation Claims and Torts Pre-Dating the Act

The common law rules are still applied in relation to acts or omissions **17.10** giving rise to a claim which occurred before 1 May 1996.[21] It seems that the

---

[19] The fact that a tort has little connection with England does not necessarily mean that the English court will not take jurisdiction over it. If the common law rules of jurisdiction are applicable, the English court will only stay proceedings if the defendant seeks a stay; given the defendant-friendly common law choice of law rules in tort, the defendant would be unlikely to do so. See further above, paras 6.30–32.

[20] See above, paras 4.154–171.   [21] s 14(1) of the 1995 Act.

common law will apply if the act giving rise to the damage[22] occurred before this date, even if the resulting harm was manifested only after that date.

17.11 The common law rules are also applicable to the torts of libel, slander, slander of title, slander of goods, other malicious falsehood and other torts of a similar nature, to which the Act does not apply.[23] This is because most of these torts may raise profound questions of freedom of speech. Had the rules of the Act applied, then it might have been possible for a claimant to sue successfully in England in respect of statements made in England and published overseas. Although the defendant might have complied with English libel and slander rules, the claimant might successfully rely upon the libel or slander rules of the law of the place of publication,[24] which might not have defences available by English domestic law.[25] The preservation of double action-ability in this area means that such claims cannot succeed if the claim would not also give rise to tortious liability by English domestic law.

17.12 It is not obvious that malicious falsehood should have been excluded from the scope of the Act. As Cheshire and North point out,[26] this tort is not concerned principally with protecting the personal *reputation* of the claimant; rather, it is concerned with protecting goodwill and economic reputation.

17.13 It is not wholly clear which other torts are excluded from the ambit of the Act by s 13(2)(b). It would rather undermine the impact of the Act if the exception were widely construed. The exception should only be invoked in the limited circumstances which might justify it. Since the exclusion is clearly concerned principally with matters of personal repu-tation, it is likely that torts which protect related, but nonetheless differ-ent interests, will not be excluded. So, for example, a claim for invasion of privacy would be governed by the Act.[27] So too would a claim for passing off. Although related to the tort of malicious falsehood in the

---

[22] Where there is more than one such act, it will be necessary to identify the principal act.

[23] s 13 of the 1995 Act.

[24] Which is deemed to be the place where the tort occurs: see *Berezovsky v Michaels* [2000] 1 WLR 1004, HL.

[25] The foreign law might also be used to suppress criticism of the foreign government and its ministers.

[26] Cheshire and North, 655.

[27] A view supported by *Douglas v Hello! Ltd (No 2)* [2003] EWCA Civ 139, [2003] EMLR 28.

sense of protecting economic interests, it seems removed from the essence of s 13, which is concerned with torts affecting freedom of speech. The same is true of a claim under a foreign law[28] for unfair competition.

2. STATUTORY REFORM: THE PRIVATE INTERNATIONAL LAW (MISCELLANEOUS PROVISIONS) ACT 1995, PART III[29]

General Comment

The 1995 Act has purported to replace the double actionability rule and its **17.14** exception with a simple choice of law rule in favour of the law of the place of the tort.[30] It is no longer necessary that the alleged conduct be tortious by English domestic law, if it constitutes a tort by the law of the place of the tort.

The Act has prompted a degree of criticism.[31] Briggs has commented **17.15** that: 'It is the view of this writer that legislation was unnecessary . . . and that the actual form taken by the legislation is user-hostile and intellectually weak'.[32] This is largely on the basis that a number of uncertainties are generated by the Act, and a number of pre-existing uncertainties maintained by it. Against this,[33] the Act sweeps away the rather insular, and claimant unfriendly common law choice of law rules in favour of a single governing law approach, largely based upon where the most significant elements of the events constituting the tort occur.[34] The automatic, and arguably unwarranted, application of the law of the forum has ended.[35]

---

[28] Such as Swiss law: Cheshire and North, 655–656. For a claim in respect of unfair competition in German law under Art 3 of the Law on Unfair Competition (involving the use of a website), see *Estée Lauder Cosmetics Ltd v Fragrance Counter Inc and Excite Inc*, [2000] ETMR 843, Hamburg District Court. The court stated that the applicable law is the law of the place where the competitive act forming the subject of the complaint affects the competitors in the local market. The court held that German unfair competition legislation is applicable to internet advertising if it is aimed at least partially at the German market.

[29] See C Morse, 'Torts in Private International Law: A New Statutory Framework' (1996) 45 ICLQ 888; A Reed, 'The Private International Law (Miscellaneous Provisions) Act 1995 and the Need for Escape Devices', (1996) 15 CJQ 305.

[30] Or, more accurately in the case of s 11(2)(c) of the Act, the place where the most significant element or elements of the tort occurred.

[31] A Briggs, 'Choice of Law in Tort and Delict' [1995] LMCLQ 519; P Carter, 'The Private International Law (Miscellaneous Provisions) Act 1995', (1996) 112 LQR 190; J Harris, 'Choice of Law in Tort—Blending in with the Landscape of the Conflict of Laws?' (1998) 61 MLR 33.

[32] Briggs ibid, at 520.   [33] See Cheshire and North, Ch 19.

[34] See s 11 of the 1995 Act.   [35] Subject to ss 13 and 14 of the 1995 Act.

The Scope of the Act;[36] Classification; 'Issues Relating to Tort'

Issues relating to tort

17.16 The Act applies to 'issues relating to tort'.[37] Certainly, this will cover the key question of whether an actionable tort has occurred.[38] Beyond that, the term 'issues relating to tort' is itself not defined.[39] 'Issues relating to tort' would seem to include such matters as heads of damages,[40] substantive defences, vicarious liability[41] and capacity.[42] It is much less clear whether the Act applies to such matters as the transmission of claims upon death.[43] Claims for contribution between joint tortfeasors are better regarded as claims seeking restitution and, accordingly, outside the scope of the Act.[44]

Characterization

17.17 However, matters are further complicated by the fact that an English court may be faced with a claim which, although not classified in its domestic law as a tort, is so classified in a foreign state where the wrong allegedly occurred. Alternatively, the claimant may be suing in respect of a cause of action which simply does not exist in English domestic law. In both cases, an English court would have to decide whether, for the purposes of private international law and the application of the Act, the claim should be treated as tortious. Section 9(2) provides that:

> The characterisation for the purposes of private international law of issues arising in a claim as issues relating to tort or delict is a matter for the courts[45] of the forum.

---

[36] See also the discussion of the exclusion in s 13 of the 1995 Act of libel, slander and related claims above, paras 17.11–13.

[37] s 9(1). See also Briggs, n 31 above, at 523. Note that the Act also applies in an English court even if the only potentially applicable law is the law of another part of the UK, such as Scotland: s 9(7).

[38] s 9(4).

[39] The Law Commission considered the matter in its Report No 193 (1990).

[40] *Boys v Chaplin* [1971] AC 356; *Edmunds v Simmonds* [2001] WLR 1003, QBD; *Hulse v Chambers* [2001] 1 WLR 2386, QB. See J Carruthers, 'Substance and Procedure in the Conflict of Laws: a Continuing Debate in Relation to Damages' (2004) 53 ICLQ 691.

[41] Compare *Armagas Ltd v Mundogas SA* [1986] AC 717.

[42] Law Commission Report No 193 (1990), 3.34–3.39, 3.44.

[43] ibid, 3.41–3.43, 3.45–3.46, 3.51.

[44] But see *Arab Monetary Fund v Hashim (No 11)* The Times, 11 October 1994, QBD (Comm); A Briggs, 'The International Dimension to Claims for Contribution' [1995] LMCLQ 437, where the Civil Liability Contribution Act 1978 was effectively treated as a mandatory rule of the forum. See also *Petroleo Brasiliero SA v Mellitus Shipping Inc* [2001] 2 Lloyd's Rep 203.

[45] It is assumed that the Act meant to refer to the *law* of the forum. Self-evidently, an English *court* applying the Act has to classify the claim or issue in question. In *Thierry Morin v Bonhams & Brooks Ltd* [2003] EWCA Civ 1802 at [12], [2004] IL Pr 24 at 394, Mance LJ commented that: 'The law of England as the place of the forum determines the proper characterisation of the present claims as tort claims'.

This is highly problematic. As the rule in *Boys v Chaplin*[46] had generally required the claim to constitute a tort according to English domestic law, it followed that claims which would not be recognized as constituting tortious conduct by English domestic law were not brought in English courts.[47] Accordingly, no private international law definition of 'tort' had emerged and the Act offers no guidance on the matter.[48]

There are further difficulties created by s 9(2) of the 1995 Act. One might **17.18** think that, in the absence of a private international law understanding of a tort, an English court might refer to its domestic law definition of 'tort'. However, tempting though this is, it would rather undermine the search for a private international law definition. It would also almost certainly lead to the exclusion of certain non-contractual claims which are not regarded as tortious in English domestic law, such as breach of confidence, which share much in common with tortious claims.

It is suggested that the 1995 Act's rules should apply to those claims **17.19** which share the characteristics of tortious claims, however classified in English, or foreign, domestic law.[49] The essence of such tortious claims should be upon non-contractual claims *which seek compensation for the claimant's loss*.[50]

Relationship to the Rome Convention

A further complication is the scope of application of the Rome Convention **17.20** on choice of law in contract.[51] Where applicable, it is stated that its provisions 'shall apply'.[52] The Convention applies to 'contractual obligations

---

[46] [1971] AC 356, as interpreted in *Church of Scientology of California v Commissioner of the Metropolitan Police* (1976) 120 Sol Jo 690, CA and *Coupland v Arabian Gulf Oil Co* [1983] 1 WLR 1136, CA.

[47] Although the exception introduced in *Red Sea Insurance Co Ltd v Bouygues SA* [1995] 1 AC 190 would potentially have required an English court to deal with causes of action not known in England (or not regarded as claims in tort in English domestic law) where the matter was entirely connected with the place of the tort and the court was minded by exception to disapply English domestic law and apply solely the law of the place of the tort.

[48] For suggestions as to how the characterization exercise should be conducted, see *Cheshire and North*, 618–622.

[49] Save where the tort in question is specifically excluded from the scope of the Act by s 13.

[50] Compare *Briggs and Rees*, 149–157. This suggests that a claim for compensation for breach of confidence might fall within the Act (see *Douglas v Hello! Ltd (No 2)* [2003] EWCA Civ 139, [2003] EMLR 28); whereas a claim to recover the value of the enrichment received by the defendant from making use of that confidential information would not.

[51] Enacted by the Contracts (Applicable Law) Act 1990. See above, paras 13.13–21.

[52] Art 1(1) of the Rome Convention. But A Briggs, 'Choice of Choice of Law?' [2003] LMCLQ 12, 27 argues that this phrase is inconclusive because Art 2 of the Brussels I Regulation says that a defendant *shall* be sued in the state of his domicile; yet it has always been apparent that there are exceptions to this rule and alternative fora in which to sue the defendant. See also R Fentiman, *Foreign Law in English Courts* (Oxford: Clarendon Press, 1998) 80–97. Compare *Raiffeisen Zentralbank Osterreich AG v Five Star General Trading LLC* [2001] QB 825.

involving a choice between the laws of different countries'.[53] The phrase 'contractual obligations' has a European autonomous meaning, but not one that has been defined. In the Brussels I Regulation context, however, the term 'matters relating to contract' has been defined[54] negatively in *Jakob Handte GmbH v Traitements Mécano-Chimiques des Surfaces*[55] as excluding claims which do not seek to enforce 'an undertaking freely entered into by one party in relation to another'. A 'matter relating to contract' is one where (i) a contractual obligation is involved; and (ii) that obligation was entered into voluntarily, with a specific, or identifiable, person or company. If this European autonomous meaning is followed for Rome Convention purposes,[56] the impact might be that the contractual choice of law rules of the Rome Convention could be applied[57] to certain claims which would be regarded in English domestic law as tortious.[58]

17.21 If claims exhibiting these characteristics should be classified as contractual, the question arises as to whether the classifications of 'contract' in the Rome Convention and of 'tort' in the Act are mutually exclusive? Given that the definition of 'contract' is a European autonomous one, and the definition of 'tort' is the product of a UK statute, this cannot be assumed.[59] If not, this means that a single claim[60] arising under a domestic law might at once fall to be classified for choice of law purposes as both contractual and tortious.

17.22 However, it is possible to reason that the definition of 'tort' in the Act and of 'contract' in the Rome Convention are mutually exclusive, so that a

---

[53] Art 1(1), discussed above, paras 13.13–21.

[54] For the purposes of Art 5(1) of (what was then) the Brussels Convention.

[55] Case C-26/91 [1992] ECR I-3967, para 15.

[56] Some support for this view may be gleaned from the ECJ decision in Case 9/87 *Arcado Sprl v Haviland SA* [1988] ECR 1539 (though this is a jurisdiction case and pre-dates the entry into force of the Rome Convention). However, contrast the remarks of AG Jacobs in *Handte*, para 24 of the Opinion, who saw no reason for the classification for jurisdiction and choice of law purposes to be identical.

[57] It is suggested in Ch 13 that Art 1(1) of the Rome Convention requires *only* that there be a contractual obligation. The further limitation in *Handte* that it be freely entered into with regard to an identifiable party is not required. This is particularly significant in relation to the rights of a transferee of a bill of lading against the carrier: on which, see above, paras 14.03–05.

[58] The most significant example for present purposes might be claims involving negligent misstatement or misrepresentation. The classification of these claims is discussed below, paras 17.90–97.

[59] Contrast the approach to 'matters relating to tort' for the purposes of Art 5(3) of the Brussels I Regulation, above, paras 6.11–13.

[60] Note that we are *not* concerned here with the question of where a claimant has more than one cause of action by his domestic law and seeks to bring concurrent claims in respect of these. Our concern is whether a single cause of action in domestic law might be classified for private international law purposes both as contractual and tortious. See below, paras 20.12–13.

single claim must be classified as one or the other[61] for choice of law purposes. It could be argued that when the Rome Convention was enacted, matters falling within its scope ceased to be governed by double actionability and its flexible exception.[62] If so, the 1995 Act does not apply to them, as it does not purport to replace anything but the double action-ability rule and its flexible exception.[63] In effect, such claims would be treated as exclusively contractual. If this is correct, then the application of the 1995 Act is residual and a single claim cannot be classified for choice of law purposes as both contractual and tortious.[64]

What does the 1995 Act replace?

Technically, even if a matter is to be characterized for private international **17.23** law purposes as tortious, it does not follow that it will be governed by the Act. Section 14(2) states that 'nothing in this Part affects any rule of law (including rules of private international law) except those abolished by section 10 above'. Section 10 states the double actionability rule and its exceptions and then abolishes them.[65] If this is taken literally, it suggests that some claims,[66] although characterized for the purposes of private international law as tortious, will continue to be governed by the common law, since they were nonetheless not formerly subject to the double actionability rule.[67] There were at common law situations where it was clear that the double actionability rule and its exception did not apply, such as certain torts occurring on the high seas.[68] The Act preserves these common law situations.[69]

However, it was much less certain whether certain other claims were **17.24** subject to the rule of double actionability and its exception at common law.[70] There was, for example, no authority on the law applicable to claims

---

[61] Or, of course, neither, if the claim relates to some other branch of the law.

[62] On the basis that the Rome Convention has mandatory effect for matters within its scope, since Art 1(1) states that it 'shall apply'. But see R Plender and M Wilderspin, *The European Contracts Convention* (2nd edn, London: Sweet & Maxwell, 2001) 8–28 and 8–29. See also Briggs, n 52 above, at 20; *Base Metal Trading Ltd v Shamurin* [2004] EWCA (Civ) 1316.

[63] ss 10 and 14(2), considered below, paras 17.23–24.

[64] See A Briggs, 'Decisions of British Courts During 2000: Private International Law' (2002) 73 British York of Intl Law 453, 486–7. See further the discussion of negligent misstatement and misrepresentation below, paras 17.90–97. See also paras 20.12–13.

[65] Save in the case of defamation and related claims, where the common law rule is preserved by s 13.

[66] It may be especially difficult to determine whether claims arising by foreign law would formerly have been subject to the rule in *Boys v Chaplin*. The fact that the plaintiff had to succeed according to the English domestic law of torts meant that such claims were not brought in English courts, so authority on them is lacking. It is equally unclear whether, for example, a claim for breach of confidence was formerly governed by the rule of double actionability.

[67] See Briggs, n 31 above, at 521.   [68] These are discussed below, para 17.34.

[69] See Cheshire and North, 623–624, 628, 661–664.   [70] ibid, at 624.

for breach of confidence, or to invasion of privacy.[71] In such cases, it would create excessive uncertainty to speculate whether these claims were subject to the rule of double actionability and its exception. Section 14(2) is a saving provision and should be interpreted narrowly, so as not to create arbitrary exclusions from the Act. It is suggested that the Act should be construed as applying to those claims which are classified for the purposes of private international law as tortious[72] and for which there is no authority to suggest that a special choice of law rule was applied at common law.[73] There is no intrinsic merit in excluding such claims from the scope of the statutory choice of law rules in tort.

Torts occurring in England

17.25 A further complexity arises with torts which occur in England. Section 9(6) states that 'for the avoidance of doubt' the Act applies to events occurring in England as it applies to events occurring overseas, subject to the provisions of s 14. However, torts occurring in England were *not* subject to the double actionability rule and its flexible exception, but rather to a separate rule in *Szalatnay-Stacho v Fink*[74] that English domestic law alone would apply to them. Literally, if s 14(2) only replaces the rule of double actionability and its exceptions stated in s 10, and the *Szalatnay-Stacho* rule was not part of the rule of double actionability, then arguably it was not abolished by s 10 and replaced by the Act's provisions.[75] This would suggest that the Act does not apply to torts occurring in England. However, given the express wording of s 9(6), such an objection should be dismissed as a technical one. There seems no good reason in principle to exclude torts occurring in England from the scope of the 1995 Act. Accordingly, it is suggested that the Act will be applied to torts occurring in England. In *Roerig v Valiant*,[76] the Court of Appeal applied the Act where a tort was governed by English law.[77]

The Governing Law of the Tort

All elements occur in one state

17.26 Section 11(1) of the Act lays down the general choice of law rule, namely that 'the applicable law is the law of the country in which the events

---

[71] But see *Douglas v Hello! Ltd (No 2)* [2003] EWCA Civ 139, [2003] EMLR 28.
[72] And not otherwise specifically excluded from the scope of the Act by s 13.
[73] Cheshire and North, 624–625.   [74] [1947] KB 1.
[75] Morse n 29 above, at 890 argues that the *Szalatnay* rule could be said to have become subsumed within the double actionability rule post-*Red Sea*, as the double actionability rule had become sufficiently flexible to deal with torts occurring in England. This view is somewhat speculative, given that there is no authority to this effect.
[76] [2002] 1 Lloyd's Rep 681.   [77] For criticism, see Briggs, n 64 above, at 487–490.

constituting the tort or delict occur'.[78] This section applies if all the events 'constituting' the tort occur in a single country. The word 'constituting' is not a helpful one as it is not one formerly used at common law and is not elucidated in the Act. However, it is clear that the word 'events' refers to the constituent elements of the tort itself. The domicile or residence of the parties is not an 'event'. So, for example, in a negligent misstatement, negligent or fraudulent misrepresentation case, s 11(1) would apply and French law would govern the tort if the statement or representation was made in France, received in France and relied upon in France, even if one or both of the parties was resident in Germany. Conversely, it would not apply if the statement or representation was made in France and received and relied upon in Germany, even if both parties were resident in France.

Elements of the tort occur in more than one state

However, the more problematic situation is where elements of these events occur in different countries. In that case, s 11(2) states that the applicable rule shall be: **17.27**

   (a) for a cause of action in respect of personal injury caused to an individual or death resulting from personal injury,[79] the law of the country where the individual was when he sustained the injury;

   (b) for a cause of action in respect of damage to property, the law of the country where the property was when it was damaged; and

   (c) in any other case, the law of the country[80] in which the most significant element or elements of those events occurred.

This provides a choice of law rule which will usually be clear in respect of claims for personal injury or damage to property. However, in other cases, it may be far from obvious which law applies pursuant to s 11(2)(c) of the 1995 Act.

The most significant element or elements of the events

There is no real guidance in the Act as to how the most significant element or elements of the events should be ascertained for the purposes of applying s 11(2)(c). When applying the common law choice of law rules and identifying the place of the tort, it was held in *Metall und Rohstoff AG v Donaldson Lufkin & Jenrette Inc*[81] in the context of assessing where the   **17.28**

---

[78] That law determines whether the defendant is liable. It is irrelevant that the law identified does not *itself* consider that the liability is in tort.

[79] s 11(3) states that this definition includes 'disease or any impairment of physical or mental condition'.

[80] This is a geographical test of the country in which the most significant element or elements of the events occurred: *Thierry Morin v Bonhams & Brooks Ltd* [2003] EWCA Civ 1802 at [16], [2004] IL Pr 24 at 396.

[81] [1990] 1 QB 391, CA.

natural forum is for jurisdictional purposes, that one should ask where in substance the cause of action arose. It was also established in *Armagas Ltd v Mundogas SA*[82] that the place of the tort would be identical for jurisdictional and common law choice of law purposes. Given the lack of indication in the Act as to the presumed locus of a tort, one might assume that guidance should accordingly be drawn from the common law jurisdiction cases.[83] Accordingly, reference will be made to certain of these cases when we come to look at the application of the choice of law rules to particular torts which might affect the relationship between buyer and seller.

17.29   However, it is also important to recognize that s 11(2)(c) lays down a broader, more flexible test than the *Metall* approach, which is not strictly concerned with identifying the place of the tort. In *Protea Leasing Ltd v Royal Air Cambodge Ltd*,[84] Moore-Bick J remarked that:

> For my own part I would be cautious about turning too readily to the earlier authorities for assistance . . . [in ascertaining the governing law]. The 1995 Act establishes a new set of principles which makes it unnecessary for the court to identify a single country in which the tort was 'in substance' committed. Section 11(2)(c) only requires the court to identify the country in which the most significant element of the events constituting the tort occurred. That seems to me to be a much more flexible principle and one which might yield different answers in different cases even in relation to the same kind of tort'.

This passage was cited with approval by Mance LJ in *Thierry Morin v Bonhams & Brooks Ltd*.[85]

17.30   Whilst it is true that s 11(2)(c) does not necessitate a mechanical approach to ascertaining the place of the tort, the danger with Moore-Bick J's approach is that s 11(2)(c) might be treated as little more than a proper law of the tort approach. That being so, a very large element of uncertainty is introduced into the law. Moreover, the importance of the rule of displacement in s 12[86] would be very much reduced.[87] It is suggested that

---

[82] [1986] AC 717, HL.   [83] Briggs, n 31 above, at 524.

[84] [2002] EWHC 2731, The Times, 13 January 2003, QBD (Comm). This view was endorsed by Hirst QC (sitting as a Deputy Judge of the High Court) in *Thierry Morin v Bonhams & Brooks Ltd* [2003] IL Pr 25 at 431, QBD (Comm Ct) and affirmed in the Court of Appeal in *Morin* by Mance LJ, [2003] EWCA Civ 1802 at [18], [2004] IL Pr 24 at 396–397. Mance LJ commented that, 'I do not say that the two schemes may not amount to much the same . . . But it is inappropriate for disputes under a new statutory wording to become clogged with an overlay of arguments about whether and how far this was true, based on authorities on different and now irrelevant wording.'

[85] [2003] EWCA Civ 1802 at [18], [2004] IL Pr 24 at 396–397. The case is discussed below, paras 17.84, 17.91, 17.99, 17.03–104, 17.110–111, 17.113, 17.120.

[86] On which, see below, paras 17.35–39.

[87] But not removed altogether: s 11(2)(c) only looks at the *events* giving rise to the claim; s 12 is broader than this and allows consideration of such factors as the residence of the parties and the circumstances and consequences of the events.

matters would be clearer if, for any given tort, a particular element of the tort were habitually regarded as the most significant one for the purposes of s 11(2)(c). That law may then be displaced if, but only if, it is substantially more appropriate for another law to apply under the exception in s 12. Accordingly, whilst recognizing that s 11(2)(c) lays down a flexible test, continued reference to common law authorities on the place of the tort will be made in this chapter.

Claims involving more than one head of damages

Section 11(2), is phrased in terms of a particular 'cause of action' in respect **17.31** of personal injury, damage to property or any other case. However, these are not causes of action in the sense of being separate torts, such as negligence, nuisance, conversion and so forth. In effect, it is suggested that s 11(2) determines the choice of law rule by reference to *the head of damages* sought. In the case of a sale of goods, however, it is possible to suppose that a claim for damages might be brought both in respect of any damage to the goods *and* for consequential financial loss. For example, if goods are damaged in transit from state X to state Y, as a result of the alleged fault of the defendant (with whom the claimant does not have a contractual relationship),[88] the claimant might sue both for the damage to that property and for the economic loss of the opportunity which he had to sell those goods to a particular sub-buyer in another state, State Z.[89] It could be argued that s 11(2)(b) applies in respect of damage to the property; however, s 11(2)(c) applies in respect of damage other than personal injury or damage to property. Could it then be that claims in respect of different heads of damages resulting from a single alleged act of negligence, which would routinely be brought together, might be governed by different laws under s 11?[90]

There might be two ways out of this unattractive situation. First, it could **17.32** be said that s 11(2) invites the court to assess the *principal* nature of the remedy sought. However, in more complex factual scenarios, this would make the outcome of litigation very difficult to predict in advance. Second, it could be argued that the focus under s 11 should be on the

---

[88] See the discussion of negligence above, paras 6.152–153, for discussion of where a claim in negligence might be brought in the carriage context.

[89] See also s 3(2) of the Torts (Interference with Goods) Act 1977. This envisages (in subsection (a)) that the defendant might have both to deliver the goods and pay consequential damages.

[90] Another example might relate to the tort of passing off. This primarily protects the claimant's economic interest (and so, where the elements of the tort occur in different states, s 11(2)(c) should apply). However, it might be possible also to seek damages in respect of the damage to goodwill (which, as a claim in respect to damage to intangible property, may fall within s 11(2)(b). However, it is not certain whether the latter provision extends to intangible property: see Cheshire and North, 633–634).

immediate damage to the claimant.[91] In our example, the immediate damage was to the property itself; any further financial loss was consequential upon the damage to the property and indirect. Pursuant to s 11(2)(b), this is 'a cause of action in respect of damage to property'. Accordingly, s 11(2)(b) should apply to the whole claim. It is this second solution which is preferred by the present authors.[92]

Maritime torts[93]

17.33 It is less clear how these rules apply in respect of maritime torts.[94] Where the tort occurs in territorial waters, the common law treated that physical state where the alleged tort occurred as the relevant place for the purposes of the double actionability rule, and not the law of the ship's flag.[95] The same approach should be taken under the Act.[96]

17.34 Where a tort occurs on the high seas, the key question is whether the events in question took place upon on board a single vessel or involved an external act, such as a collision. As to the former, the law of the flag was regarded as the place of the tort at common law.[97] The court would then apply the rule of double actionability to such torts. It follows that the matter is now governed by the 1995 Act.[98] The relevant law should be regarded as the law of the flag,[99] and that law alone applied.[100] However, where an external act is alleged to give rise to a tort on the high seas, English common law did *not* apply the law of the flag, but rather applied the general maritime law as applied in England.[101] Since the 1995 Act only abolishes and replaces the rule of double actionability and its flexible exception, of which this was not part, it follows that this rule is preserved today.

---

[91] Compare, in the context of Art 5(3) of the Brussels I Regulation, Case C-220/88 *Dumez France v Hessische Landesbank (Heleba)* [1990] ECR I-49. See above, para 6.16.

[92] There is always the possibility that s 12 will displace the governing law in whole or in part. However, in the ordinary case, it is desirable for a single law to apply where the claimant seeks more than one head of damages.

[93] See Cheshire and North, 661–664.

[94] See *Roerig v Valiant* [2002] 1 Lloyd's Rep 681, CA, criticized by Briggs, n 64 above, at 488.

[95] See the decision of the Scottish Court of Session in *McKinnon v Iberia Shipping Co Ltd* [1954] 2 Lloyd's Rep 372.

[96] See Law Com No 193 (1990), para 3.26; but cf Law Commission Working Paper No 87 (1984), para 5.71–5.88. The general rule might be displaced by the law of the flag in a case where the tort appears to have little connection to the physical place of the tort.

[97] *R v Anderson* (1868) LR 1 CCR 161, 168; *R v Keyn* (1876) 2 Ex D 63, 94.

[98] ss 10 and 14(2), considered above, paras 17.23–24.

[99] This was accepted by both parties in *Roerig v Valiant* [2002] 1 Lloyd's Rep 681, CA.

[100] Unless displaced by the exception in s 12.

[101] See, e.g. *The Johann Friedrich* (1839) 1 Wm Rob 36; *The Wild Ranger* (1862) Lush 553; *Chartered Mercantile Bank of India, London and China v Netherlands Steam Navigation Co Ltd* (1883) 10 QBD 521; *The Esso Malaysia* [1975] QB 198;

Displacement of the General Rule

It should be noted that s 11 only lays down the general rule. It may be **17.35**
displaced under s 12, which provides as follows:

(1) If it appears, in all the circumstances, from a comparison of—

  (a) the significance of the factors which connect a tort or delict with the
  country whose law would be the applicable law under the general rule;
  and

  (b) the significance of any factors connecting the tort or delict with another
  country,

that it is substantially more appropriate for the applicable law for determining the
issues arising in the case, or any of those issues, to be the law of the other country,
the general rule is displaced and the applicable law for determining those issues
or that issue (as the case may be) is the law of that other country.

(2) The factors that may be taken into account as connecting a tort or delict
  with a country for the purposes of this section include, in particular, factors
  relating to the parties, to any of the events which constitute the tort or
  delict in question or to any of the circumstances or consequences of those
  events.

It would appear that s 12 is primarily concerned with an objective test
of closest connection.[102] It is not concerned with policy considerations
or interest analysis.[103] The Law Commission envisaged that the exception might be applied where the place of the tort is fortuitous (for
example, if it occurs upon a ship during transit) and both parties are
resident in the same state (which is other than the place of the tort), or
where there was a prior relationship between the parties (for example,
if a group of English people travel together overseas), or where all
other objective factors point to another law.[104] These are all clear cut
examples and suggest that the threshold for displacement of the general
rule is high.

It is clear from the wording of s 12 that the governing law need not be **17.36**
displaced in its entirety and may be disapplied in relation to a *particular
issue*. It may be that a particular matter, such as the question of vicarious
liability, is more closely connected with a law other than that to which
the general rule in s 11 points. This allows the principle of dépeçage to
operate in tort.

---

[102] i.e. of closest connection to another country; it is not concerned with whether there is
another *law* which it is substantially more appropriate to apply.
[103] Contrast *Johnson v Coventry Churchill International Ltd* [1992] 3 All ER 14.
[104] Law Com No 193 (1990), para 3.8. See also Cheshire and North, 643–644.

17.37 The exception was applied in *Edmunds v Simmonds*.[105] In that case, two English domiciliaries[106] on holiday together were involved in a road traffic accident in Spain. The claimant sought compensation for severe personal injuries suffered, which left her needing constant medical supervision. The claimant had been travelling in the same car as the defendant. The court stressed that the domicile of the parties is an important factor under s 12. The court noted that the factors pointing to Spain were that it was the place of collision and that the car was insured there (but largely discounted the second factor, on the basis that insurers of hire cars would contemplate that drivers might be foreign). In contrast, the claimant and defendant were English domiciliaries and the claimant's injuries had manifested themselves and would need treatment in England. This led Garland J to apply English law pursuant to s 12. It also suggests that the mere existence of some objective connection to the law of the place of the tort will not necessarily prevent the exception being invoked.[107]

17.38 However, it is likely that the court may be more willing to invoke the exception in a case concerned with physical injury, since the claimant would need ongoing treatment for that injury in his home state. The domicile of the parties may be less significant where the claim is solely in respect of economic loss.[108]

17.39 In *Roerig v Valiant*,[109] the Court of Appeal emphasized that s 12 presents a high threshold and that the general rule in s 11 should not lightly be disapplied. In this case, the claimant was a Dutch citizen suing for dependency damages following the death of Dutch fisherman on a trawler. The trawler was registered in England and owned by an English company. The tort took place in international waters off Mauritania. However, as it was internal to the English registered vessel, both parties agreed that the general rule in s 11 led to the application of English law. Under Dutch law, but not English law,[110] the claimant would have to give credit for damages already awarded for her loss when assessing her damages for loss of dependency. The Court of Appeal ruled that English law should apply, pursuant to s 11, and that there was no case pursuant to s 12 of the 1995 Act for applying Dutch law to the question of damages.[111] The court stressed that the mere fact that the deceased and the claimant were Dutch domiciliaries did not suffice to displace English law under s 12. The defendant was an English domiciliary and the tort occurred in England

---

[105] [2001] WLR 1003, QBD.   [106] Compare *Harding v Wealands* (27 May 2004, QBD).
[107] Although on the facts, there was the additional factor pointing to England that the parties knew each other beforehand.
[108] Cheshire and North, 639–641.   [109] [2002] 1 Lloyd's Rep 681, CA.
[110] s 4 of the Fatal Accidents Act 1976.
[111] Even if this could be classified as a substantive issue.

and it could not be said to be 'substantially more appropriate' to apply Dutch law.[112]

Exclusion of the Doctrine of Renvoi

Section 9(5) states that the applicable law 'shall exclude any choice of law **17.40** rules forming part of the law of the country or countries concerned'. In other words, the doctrine of renvoi is excluded.[113] This simplifies the law and conforms to the expectation of the parties that the domestic law of the place of the tort will apply. It is the decision of the English courts which state's domestic law to apply in its own courts. It can be argued that the choice of law rules of a foreign state should not determine which law is applied in an English court. Moreover, if one function of the doctrine of renvoi is to escape the application of inflexible choice of law rules, one might observe that there is already sufficient flexibility in the choice of law rules in Part III of the 1995 Act.[114]

That said, there are some arguments which support the application of the **17.41** doctrine of renvoi in tort. The general choice of law rules in s 11 point to the law which will typically have the closest connection with the dispute and the greatest 'interest' in having its law applied to the dispute. However, if English choice of law rules point to the application of the law of State A, it might be thought surprising that State A's domestic law will be applied, even if a court in State A would apply the law of State B. To an extent, application of the law of State A by an English court is a substitute for the case actually being heard in the courts of State A. If an English court is not prepared to apply the law that a court in State A would actually apply, that might somewhat undermine the purpose of referring to the law of State A in the first place, since the conditions in the foreign court will in no sense be reproduced. Moreover, if an English court would apply the law of State A on the merits, but the courts of State A would apply the law of State B on the merits, the possibility of forum shopping by the claimant to ensure litigation in the country which will apply the law most favourable to his case is a very real one.[115] The result is that the exporter of goods will find himself potentially exposed to tortious

---

[112] See also *Anton Durbeck GmbH v Den Norske Bank ASA* [2002] EWHC 1173 (Comm) 1173 (reversed on a different point, [2003] EWCA Civ 147, [2003] QB 1160).

[113] This was also the recommendation of the Law Commission: see Law Commission Working Paper No 87 (1984), para 4.23; Law Com No 193 (1990), para 3.56.

[114] Cheshire and North, 627.

[115] One possible solution would be to say that where a judge in the courts of State A would not himself apply the law of State A, but would rather apply the law of State B, it is 'substantially more appropriate' for the English court to apply the law of State B, pursuant to s 12. However, this approach amounts to renvoi by the back door and, in the light of s 9(5), is unlikely to be adopted.

liability unless he satisfies the standard of care required under the law of more than one country and hence faces a real disincentive to trade in comparison to the purely domestic seller. However, whatever one's views are on the merits or demerits of the argument for the application of renvoi in tort, s 9(5) of the Act makes it quite clear that the doctrine is inapplicable.

Limits on the Role of the Governing Law

17.42 Sometimes, an English court will wish to retain the right to apply the law of the forum, even if the most significant elements of the alleged tort occur overseas. This may be because the area is a particularly sensitive one, where civil liberties concerns weigh heavily. An English court might not wish a party to succeed in a claim by invoking a foreign law, where the defendant would be free to act in the manner that he has done in England. On other occasions, it will simply be that application of the foreign law on the facts is repugnant to English law. An English court can limit the operation of the governing law of the tort either by the application of a mandatory rule of English law, which is designed to apply regardless of the governing law of the tort,[116] or by holding that application of a foreign law is contrary to English public policy.[117] However, care should be taken in invoking either. Both undermine the purpose of the Act, which is to allow claims to succeed by a foreign law, even if they would not succeed on the facts by the law of the forum.

17.43 Section 14(3)(a) states that nothing in Part III of the Act:

authorizes the application of a law of a country outside the forum for determining issues arising in any claim in so far as to do so—

(i) would conflict with principles of public policy; or

(ii) would give effect to such a penal, revenue or other public law as would not otherwise be enforceable under the law of the forum.

Public policy

17.44 There is no statement as to the threshold before the public policy provision may be invoked. It is not stated that application of the governing law must be 'manifestly' incompatible with public policy, as Article 16 of the Rome Convention stipulates. The risk is that, the 1995 Act having displaced the rule of double actionability[118] and the requirement that the act complained of give rise to a tort by English domestic law, there may be a

---

[116] The application of mandatory rules of English law designed to apply whatever the applicable law is preserved by s 14(4).
[117] Invoking s 14(3)(a)(i).   [118] And its flexible exception.

significant expansion in the use of public policy by English courts to limit the application of foreign tort laws. However, this would drive a coach and horses through the new provisions. The choice of law rule in s 11 of the 1995 Act has as a consequence that claims governed by a foreign law can succeed in an English court where they would not have succeeded if they had been governed by English domestic law. Moreover, application of the public policy escape route by an English court might be said to be almost calculated to cause offence, since it emphasizes the unacceptable nature of a foreign law.[119]

A further difficulty is that because at common law an action had to suc- **17.45** ceed by English domestic law, there was very little case law on the use of public policy in tort.[120] That said, likely examples of public policy include where the foreign law gives rise to a claim which infringes the European Convention on Human Rights, or violates fundamental principles of public international law. The Law Commission suggested that the public policy exception may also the cover the award of multiple damages for infringement of American antitrust law.[121] They also suggested that it may cover cases where vicarious liability is, in the eyes of English law, unreasonably imposed by a foreign law.[122]

Curiously, it is not stated that only *English* public policy may be invoked **17.46** under the Act. However, there seems no case for applying the public policy of a third state. This was not done at common law. It is also not permitted under Article 16 of the Rome Convention. Accordingly, it is suggested that only English public policy may be invoked.

Giving effect[123] to a foreign penal, revenue and public laws

The concepts of foreign penal, revenue and public laws are well know in **17.47** private international law.[124] The Act does not explain how these concepts apply specifically in tort. The Law Commission has suggested that a civil claim under antitrust laws might be covered.[125] The provision might also

---

[119] Something which was unnecessary under the rule of double actionability. As the claim had also to succeed by English domestic law, it was rarely necessary to pass judgment on the content of a foreign law.

[120] But for an example of a refusal to apply the law of the place of the tort, Iraq, where it had seized property in breach of the rules of public international law, see *Kuwait Airways Corp v Iraqi Airways Co (Nos 4 and 5)* [2002] 2 AC 883, HI

[121] Law Commission Working Paper No 87 (1984), para 5.63.

[122] ibid, paras 6.11–6.13; Law Com 193 (1990) para 3.36.

[123] On the question of what constitutes giving effect to a foreign tort law, see the dissenting judgment of Lord Scott in *Kuwait Airways Corp v Iraqi Airways Co (Nos 4 and 5)* [2002] 2 AC 883, HL.

[124] See Cheshire and North, 107–116.

[125] Law Commission Working Paper No 87 (1984), para 5.62.

cover a foreign tort which is principally designed to protect the interests of the state or the government.[126]

Mandatory rules

17.48 Section 14(4) provides for the application of mandatory rules which have effect irrespective of the law applicable to the tort. This is a reference to international mandatory rules.[127] There is no learning on what constitutes an international mandatory rule of the forum at common law, since the rule of double actionability had meant that English domestic law would be applied, regardless of whether the rules of English law in question were of mandatory effect. However, one example of an international mandatory rule is the Civil Liability (Contribution) Act 1978. Its provisions on the right to seek a contribution from a joint tortfeasors have been applied irrespective of whether the claim was alleged to be governed by a foreign law.[128]

17.49 Curiously, the provision is not expressly limited to the mandatory rules of the forum. Could an English court give effect to the mandatory rules of a third state,[129] such as the law of the place where the act giving rise to damage occurs, or the law of the claimant or defendant's domicile? It is suggested that this provision should only be applied to the mandatory rules of the forum. Given the hostility shown by the United Kingdom to Article 7(1) of the Rome Convention,[130] which would have permitted the application of the international mandatory rules of a state of close connection, it is unlikely that Parliament would have wished to allow a third state's mandatory rules to apply in tort. Moreover, s 14 is about *preserving* the status quo in certain matters. Since there was no evidence that a third state's mandatory rules could be applied at common law, it would be very curious if s 14 had introduced such a rule.

Evidence and procedure

17.50 Section 14(3)(b) preserves the familiar rule that the law of the forum will still determine matters of procedure, evidence, pleading and practice. One consequence of this is that the rules on proof of foreign law are preserved. If the parties do not plead that a foreign law should apply, the law of the forum will determine the matter, even though the tort may have little to do with England.[131]

---

[126] Morse, n 29 above, at 892. See also Cheshire and North, 647.

[127] See the discussion on the nature of mandatory rules, above, paras 13.274–281.

[128] See above n 44. See further Cheshire and North, 650–652. However, one might argue that this is a rule of restitution, rather than a rule of tort.

[129] Assuming that this is not the law applicable to the tort.

[130] The UK opted out of this provision by s 2(2) of the Contracts (Applicable Law) Act 1990.

[131] See generally Fentiman, n 52 above.

The Law Commission has suggested that the question of quantification of **17.51** damages will be treated as procedural.[132] However, rules of remoteness and the question of heads of damages are a substantive matter. These statements have since been confirmed by the courts.[133] The Law Commission also suggested that methods of enforcement and the mode of trial were matters for the law of the forum.[134]

III. APPLICATION TO SPECIFIC TORTS RELATED TO THE SALE OF GOODS

We shall now consider the application of the choice of law rules in tort to a **17.52** number of torts which may arise in the sale of goods context. We shall examine the law as it applies to a tort occurring after the entry into force of the 1995 Act.

1. CONVERSION

Substantive Law Background

Section 1 of the Torts (Interference with Goods Act) 1977 introduces a **17.53** generic term, 'wrongful interference with goods', to cover the torts of conversion, trespass to goods, negligence resulting in damage to goods and any other tort which results in damage to goods or an interest in goods. Of these, perhaps the most important are conversion and trespass to goods. The former is concerned with intentional dealing with goods in a manner that is inconsistent with the possession, or right to immediate possession, of the claimant. The latter concerns direct and intentional or negligent interference with goods in the possession of the claimant. For choice of law purposes, they raise similar issues. The former is of greater

---

[132] Law Commission Working Paper 87 (1984), para 4.4. In *Kuwait Oil Tanker Co SAK v Al Bader (No 3) Independent*, 11 January 1999, QBD (Comm) the court treated the availability of interest by way of damages as a matter of procedure; the Court of Appeal did not express a view on this point: [2000] 2 All ER (Comm) 271. See further, Benjamin, 25–184. See also *Harding v Wealands* (27 May 2004, QBD), where Elias J held that the question of whether interest on a particular head of damages is available is a matter of procedure and to be determined by the law of the forum.

[133] The position was first stated by the House of Lords in *Boys v Chaplin* [1971] AC 356. It has been affirmed as representing the position under the 1995 Act in *Edmunds v Simmonds* [2001] WLR 1003, QBD; *Hulse v Chambers* [2001] 1 WLR 2386, QB and in *Roerig v Valiant* [2002] 1 Lloyd's Rep 681, CA. In the last case, the court held that the assessment of damages under s 4 of the Fatal Accidents Act 1976 was a procedural matter. See also *Harding v Wealands* (27 May 2004, QBD). See further Carruthers, n 40 above.

[134] Law Commission Working Paper 87 (1984), para 4.4.

relevance in the sale of goods context. It is not proposed here to outline the substantive requirements for the tort of conversion. The reader is referred to the discussion in Chapter 6 on torts and jurisdiction.[135]

Classification

17.54 Where a claim is based upon conversion, there can be no real doubt that the cause of action would be classified as tortious for the purposes of the 1995 Act.[136] It is a claim based upon non-contractual wrongdoing. The fact that an action by a buyer against a seller for the tort of conversion might be combined with an action for breach of contract does not mean that the action for conversion is itself anything other than tortious.[137] It has been accepted by the court without argument in *Glencore International AG v Metro Trading International Inc (No 2)*[138] that conversion falls within the scope of the 1995 Act. It has also been accepted in a number of common law jurisdiction cases that a conversion action falls within r 6.20(8) of the Civil Procedure Rules, which deals with service out of the jurisdiction where a claim is made in tort.[139]

Claims Founded Upon a Foreign Law

17.55 However, whilst English domestic law treats claims for interference with property rights as part of the law of tort, this is not the case in many other legal systems.[140] Civil law states often tend to treat the claim as part of the law of property. The claim is one for revendication, not damages. In French law, the fact that possession is tantamount to ownership[141] in any event prevents many potential claims arising against third parties where in English law there would be a claim for the tort. The result is that most claims are simply assertions of property rights. In German law, there may be a delictual claim for interference with the substance of a thing where

---

[135] Above, paras 6.33–41.

[136] Compare, in relation to Art 5(3) of the Brussels regime of jurisdiction, *Cronos Containers NV v Palatin* [2002] EWHC 2819, QBD (Comm), [2003] 2 Lloyd's Rep 489; *Bank of Tokyo-Mitsubishi Ltd v Baskan Gida Sanayi Ve Pazarlama AS* [2004] EWHC 945 (Ch). See above, paras 6.42–48 and 7.12.

[137] A buyer might also wish to bring an action for the tort against a third party and combine this with a claim for breach of contract against the seller.

[138] [2001] 1 Lloyd's Rep 284, QBD (Comm). The case is examined below, paras 17.76–81, 17.84.

[139] See *Bastone & Firminger Ltd v Nasima Enterprises (Nigeria) Ltd* [1996] CLC 190; *Beecham Group plc v Norton Healthcare Ltd* [1997] FSR 81. These cases were decided on the basis of the predecessor to r 6.20(8) CPR, namely Ord 11, r 1 (1)(f) RSC. See further above, paras 6.57–58.

[140] See the discussion on torts and jurisdiction, above paras 6.39–41.

[141] Code civil, Art 2279, al 1.

fault can be established;[142] but where it cannot, the rules on property are applicable.

This might lead us to question whether such civil law claims involving **17.56** interference with property rights should be classified for the purposes of *English* private international law as tort or property claims. Suppose that a claimant brings an action for revendication under the Code civil, and seeks to establish that his claim is governed by French law. Although the process of classification is one for *English* and not French law, it would be absurd to ignore the nature of the claim and its classification by its law of origin. Accordingly, this should lead to the action being classified as proprietary and subject to property choice of law rules.[143]

The 'hard' case would be where the claimant argues his claim in the **17.57** alternative on the basis of English and French law. He might allege that *if* the act of interference is found to occur in England, then he has a cause of action in tort; whereas if it is found to occur in France, the claim should be treated as proprietary. In such a case, an English court needs to ask itself where the most significant acts of interference with the property took place. It can only do this at this stage by applying the law of the forum to this question. For example, if the defendant has taken delivery in England from a person who does not himself have title to the goods, the most significant act of interference occurs in England. If the defendant uses the claimant's goods in France, the act of interference occurs in France. If the defendant disposes of the goods to a third party in England, the act of interference occurs in England. If, having conducted this exercise, the English court finds that the most significant act of interference by the defendant took place in England, then it should proceed on the basis that the claimant is suing for the tort of conversion and apply the tort choice of law rules; if, on the other hand, it finds that the most significant act of interference took place in France, it should consider the claimant's cause of action under the Code civil.

In short, the fact that different states of the world may take differing views **17.58** of whether claims based on interference with property rights are tortious or proprietary can be reflected in different classifications of such claims, depending upon how they are classified in the relevant state whose law

---

[142] BGB § 823 I. For more detailed explanation, see above, para 6.41; and see B Markesinis, *The German Law of Obligations, Volume II, The Law of Torts: A Comparative Introduction*, (3rd edn, Oxford: Clarendon, 1994).

[143] The position is less certain with a claim for fault based dispossession under German law: see above, paras 6.41, 6.47, 6.58. For the reasons given there, it is suggested that such a claim gives rise to delictual liability under BGB §823 I.

the claimant alleges is applicable. It is not necessary for an English court to form a unitary classification of all claims concerning acts of interference with goods which might arise under any legal system of the world.

A Preliminary Question of Property Law

17.59 However, the fact that a claim for conversion is likely to be classified as tortious does not mean that *all* issues arising in the case should be subject to the tort choice of law rules. In particular, the tort of conversion protects an owner's possessory rights. Unless and until he shows that he has such rights, he cannot found a claim for the tort. The existence of such rights is a matter of property law. As such, it should be determined by the law of the situs. Accordingly, there is a two-staged test: (i) does the claimant have possession, or the right to possession, according to the law of the situs of the property at the time of the last transaction said to have altered possession; and (ii) if so, can he bring a successful action for the tort of conversion according to the choice of law rules in tort? The importance of separating property issues from other issues arising in a case, and subjecting them to the *lex situs*, is evident in the decision of Moses J in *City of Gotha (A Body Corporate) v Sotheby's (No 2)*.[144] In that case, the claimants brought an action for the tort of conversion, seeking the return of a painting. However, the main issue arising in the claim was whether the Federal Republic of Germany could show a good title to the property in question. To that issue, Moses J applied the law of the situs.

17.60 This approach is also supported by the decisions in *Kuwait Airways Corp v Iraqi Airways Co (Nos 4 and 5)*[145] and in *Glencore International AG v Metro Trading International Inc (No 2)*.[146] In each case, the court first considered the property law issues arising by application of the property choice of law rules and *then* went on to consider whether, if the property was that of the claimant, he could found a claim in tort by the tortious choice of law rules.

---

[144] The Times, 8 October 1998, QBD. See also *Empresa Exportadora de Azúcar v Industria Azucarera Nacional SA (The Playa Larga and Marble Islands)* [1983] 2 Lloyd's Rep 171 where the property law point was 'barely argued' before the Court of Appeal (*per* Ackner LJ, at 180).

[145] [2002] 2 AC 883; noted E Peel, 'The Scope of Double Actionability and Public Policy' (2003) 119 LQR 1, esp 5–6; R O'Keefe, 'English Public Policy Internationalized—and Conversion Clarified Too' (2002) 61 CLJ 499; J Carruthers and E Crawford, 'Kuwait Airways Corporation v Iraqi Airways Company' (2003) 52 ICLQ 761; P Rogerson, '*Kuwait Airways Corp v Iraqi Airways Corp*: the Territoriality Principle in Private International Law—Vice or Virtue?' (2003) 56 CLP 265; A Briggs, 'Public Policy in the Conflict of Laws: a Sword and a Shield?' (2002) 6 Singapore J of Intl and Comparative Law 953; Briggs n 64 above, 487–490.

[146] [2001] 1 Lloyd's Rep 284, QBD (Comm). See also N Curwen, 'Title to Sue in Conversion' [2004] Conveyancer and Property Lawyer 308.

The law of the *situs* must also be referred to if the question arises as to **17.61** whether the parties are co-owners.[147] The same is true if the defendant alleges that a third party has a better right in the property than that of the claimant.[148]

The Significance of the Remedy Sought: A Subsequent Question of Property Law?

One difficulty with the tort of conversion is that although it is be **17.62** founded upon non-contractual wrongdoing, s 3(2) of the Torts (Interference with Goods) Act 1977 states that where the defendant is in possession or control of the goods, the *remedy* granted to the claimant may be either damages or the delivery of the property itself, or both. Indeed, the defendant might be given the alternative of whether to deliver the goods or to pay damages by reference to their value.[149] Furthermore, s 5(1) goes on to state that where damages are assessed on the basis that the claimant is being compensated for the whole of his interest in the goods,[150] the payment of these damages 'extinguishes the claimant's title to that interest'. In effect, the payment of the damages forces a sale to the defendant.

All this means that where the cause of action exists *in tort*, there will be **17.63** *proprietary* consequences which ensue.[151] For reasons of control and enforceability, it is usual to expect the law of the *situs* to determine such questions. Indeed, there is an obvious concern that if the law applicable to the tort and the law of the *situs* differ,[152] any award granted by the former law would be ineffective, if the courts of the *situs* did not concur as to the respective property rights of the parties. Furthermore, since the law of the *situs* determines the preliminary question of whether the claimant has the right to possession in the first place, it could be argued that it should also determine what property rights the parties have as a *consequence* of the act of conversion.

If this is correct, then a possible approach would be the following. First, **17.64** the law of the *situs* decides whether the claimant has possession, or the

---

[147] Although this will be no defence to a conversion action in many cases: see s 10 of the Torts (Interference with Goods) Act 1977
[148] ibid, s 8(1).   [149] In either case, he must also pay any consequential damages.
[150] Or for the whole of his interest subject to a reduction for contributory negligence.
[151] Compare *Cronos Containers NV v Palatin* [2002] EWHC 2819, QBD (Comm), [2003] 2 Lloyd's Rep 489; discussed above, para 6.46.
[152] This would not be very common, since the place of conversion is likely to be the law of the *situs* too. However, the general rule in tort may, of course, be displaced under s 12 by another law and could possibly be so displaced if, for example, both the parties were domiciled in a different state.

right to possession, of the goods. If so, then the law applicable to the tort should determine whether the defendant has committed the tort of conversion in respect of those goods. If the answer is 'yes', then it is suggested that the law applicable to the tort should also determine whether the claimant has the *right* to obtain an order for delivery of the goods and/or for damages. However, it could then be argued that, if an order for delivery *is* made, the question of whether it has the effect of restoring peaceful possession to the claimant is a matter for the law of the situs. More importantly, if an order is made for full compensatory damages in lieu, then the law of the *situs* should decide what *proprietary effect* such an order has and whether it is effective to extinguish the claimant's title to his interest in the goods.

17.65 An obvious objection to this approach is that it leads to a fragmentation of the claim. An obvious retort is that this simply reflects the fact that the claim is at the intersection of tort and property law. A more serious objection is that although the law of the tort might order the payment of full compensatory damages for the whole of the claimant's interest in the goods, the law of the *situs* might consider that this does *not* extinguish the claimant's title to that interest. If so, the defendant faces double jeopardy. However, there are three possible retorts to this. First, that it seems inherently unlikely that the law of the *situs* would so rule. Second, even if it does, it is important nonetheless to have regard to the law of the *situs*, because property rights are in issue and the question of enforceability of any order of an English court affecting title to an interest in the goods in the place where they are located is an important matter. Third, where the law of the *situs* appears to be wholly unacceptable, it is possible to disapply that law, on the basis that it offends English public policy.[153]

17.66 All that said, the present state of authorities does not support the application of this 'subsequent' property choice of law rule. It is likely that a court, having determined that the claimant has possession or the right to possession in the first place, will then apply tort choice of law rules to determine all subsequent questions as to whether the cause of action is made out and what remedies should be awarded. This does also have the advantage of ensuring the coherent application of the rules of a single legal system.[154]

---

[153] See *Kuwait Airways Corp v Iraqi Airways Co (Nos 4 and 5)* [2002] 2 AC 883, HL; *Winkworth v Christie* [1980] Ch 496.

[154] At least after the right to possession has been established by the law of the *situs*.

The Governing Law of a Claim for Conversion

Suppose that the claimant does bring an action based for conversion, rather **17.67** than a property claim for revendication by the law of a civil law state. It will be necessary to apply the tort choice of law rules of the 1995 Act.[155]

All elements occur in a single state

Of course, where all elements of the events constituting the tort occur in **17.68** one state, that law is applicable by virtue of s 11(1).

Elements occur in more than one state

Where the elements of the events constituting the tort do not occur in a **17.69** single state, s 11(2) must be applied. It is not immediately clear whether the general rule should be determined in accordance with s 11(2)(b) or (c). Clearly, the tort hinges upon the interference with possession, or right to possession, of property. However, it would be stretching the natural meaning of the term to say that interference with the right to possession is tantamount to causing 'damage' to goods. Rather, it is suggested that the general rule should be determined by s 11(2)(c).

If this is correct, then it is important to determine what the most signifi- **17.70** cant element or elements of the events in a conversion action are. In *Bastone & Firminger Ltd v Nasima Enterprises (Nigeria) Ltd*,[156] English sellers sold chemicals to a Nigerian company and shipped the goods to Nasima, a Nigerian company, in Nigeria. Ecobank, a Nigerian bank, was the collecting bank and was required to warehouse the goods upon arrival and release shipping documents upon acceptance by Nasima of the bills of exchange. The goods were released by Ecobank, but the plaintiffs were not paid. They brought an action alleging wrongful interference with the goods and documents. The court accepted that the tort took place in Nigeria. The key element of the tort was the release of the goods and documents and this took place in Nigeria. Although this decision arose in the context of determining whether an English court had jurisdiction at common law,[157] there seems little doubt that Nigeria would be the place where the most significant elements of the events occurred, if these facts arose today when determining the law applicable to the claim under s 11(2)(c) of the 1995 Act. The fact that the plaintiff might feel the financial consequences of the act of conversion in England is of little importance. The key question is where the events which gave rise to liability on the part of the defendant in tort took place and that was clearly Nigeria.[158]

---

[155] Assuming, of course, that the tort occurs on or after 1 May 1996.
[156] [1996] CLC 190. [157] See above, paras 6.59, 6.62.
[158] See also *The Eras Eil Actions* [1992] 1 Lloyd's Rep 570, 589–591; *Beecham Group plc v Norton Healthcare Ltd* [1997] FSR 81.

17.71   Sometimes, that law will be more difficult to ascertain, as in the case of a refusal to deliver goods to the true owner. Although the goods should have been transported to a particular state, there is no positive act in that state, only an omission to deliver in that state. Section 11(2)(c) refers to 'events' and this seems to suggest positive action. Do the most significant elements occur in the place where the refusing party is located, let us say State A, or the place where that refusal is communicated to the owner, State B, or the place to which the goods should have been transported, State C? It could be argued that the tortious *act* is the act of refusal itself, which points to the refusing party's home state, State A. True, the refusal will normally be communicated to the claimant in State B. However, a party who simply refuses to deliver goods need not necessarily communicate his refusal at all. He may simply decline to enter into correspondence. As such, communication is arguably not an essential element of the refusal. Indeed, the focus of the liability in the Torts (Interference with Goods) Act 1977 is on acts rather than words. Furthermore, if the goods are located in State A, that state exercises a degree of control over them.

17.72   Against this, although the tort of conversion is separate to any contractual claims, it is likely, where a contract of sale is concerned, that the claimant will also sue for breach of the contractual obligation to deliver goods at the place of delivery. It may be said that where the defendant refuses to deliver the goods, the most significant elements of the tort of conversion occur in the place of delivery under s 11(2)(c). Accordingly, the law of State C should be applied,[159] at least where the claim for conversion is accompanied by a claim for breach of contract.[160] Even where there is no accompanying claim for breach of contract, State C will normally be the place where the claimant suffers the immediate damage arising from the defendant's failure to deliver and there is a strong case for the application of the law of State C to the claim for conversion pursuant to s 11(2)(c).[161]

17.73   More generally, it is important to recall that the act of conversion can be committed in a variety of ways. It may include: buying and taking delivery from a person without title; use of goods; a disposition to a third party; or a refusal to deliver to the true owner.[162] Where more than one such act has apparently occurred, it would seem that the claimant can

---

[159]   Although the law applicable to the contract may be relevant only, if at all, in relation to the exception in s 12: see below, paras 17.84 and 17.120. In *Thierry Morin v Bonhams & Brooks Ltd* [2003] EWCA Civ 1802 at [16], [2004] IL Pr 24 at 396, Mance LJ remarked that 'S. 11 of the 1995 Act adopts a geographical test'.

[160]   Although, of course, the contract may be governed by another law.

[161]   Contrast the discussion of the tort of failure to sell, below, paras 17.132–134. In this case, there will be no contract and no place of delivery under the terms of the contract.

[162]   See above, paras 6.33–38.

select the particular act of conversion that he wishes[163] and that the law of the place where that act of conversion took place applies. Where the claimant sues on the basis of more than one act, each of which could independently give rise to a claim for the tort, it would appear that the applicable law for each should be determined separately under s 11(2)(c). However, pursuant to s 12 it is likely that a court will consider it 'substantially more appropriate' that all such claims be governed by the same law. As such, it is likely to look at the fact pattern of all the acts of conversion alleged, to determine which law should apply to them all.

Displacement of the General Rule Under s 12

Where all the elements of the tort occur in a single state and the applicable **17.74** law is determined in s 11(1), it might nevertheless be displaced under s 12. It is possible that although the 'events' all occurred in one state, the parties themselves are domiciled in the same, other state.

Where the elements of the events occur in different states, it is relatively **17.75** unlikely that it will be found to be substantially more appropriate for another law to apply under s 12. This is because the law which governs a claim for the tort is itself determined by the law with which the most significant elements of the events occurred under s 11(2)(c). Nonetheless, it is far from inconceivable that this section will be invoked in respect of conversion claims, since s 12 permits consideration of a broader range of factors than s 11(2)(c),[164] such as the domicile of the parties and any surrounding circumstances. The most important of these circumstances in the sales context is the sales contract itself and the question may arise as to whether the law applicable to the sales contract should influence the law applicable to a claim for conversion. It is to this question that we now turn.

The Influence of the Law Applicable to the Contract of Sale Under s 12

Where the contract does not contain a clause purporting to apply the applicable law of the contract to related tort claims

It appears that no relevance can be attached to the law applicable to the **17.76** contract of sale if the claim for the tort of conversion does not involve the two parties to the original sales contract. So, the law applicable to the contract of sale would not be relevant in a claim brought by a purchaser

---

[163] Just as he can in a domestic case.
[164] *Thierry Morin v Bonhams & Brooks Ltd* [2003] EWCA Civ 1802 at [21] [2004] IL Pr 24 at 397, *per* Mance LJ.

against a third party.[165] However, matters may be considerably different where the conversion action involves only the buyer and seller under the original contract. Although the conversion action is logically distinct from the contract, it might be 'substantially more appropriate' for the law which applies to a contract between the buyer and seller also to determine an action for conversion between the same parties. These propositions can be demonstrated by the decision in *Glencore International AG v Metro Trading International Inc (No 2)*.[166]

17.77 In that case, the defendant, MTI was involved in buying, blending and selling of fuel oil. MTI habitually commingled the oil which it received with oil that it already held in storage of the same grade. These activities were carried out in the waters of Fujairah aboard four vessels. Four parties delivered oil to MTI. Meanwhile, Texaco entered into an agreement with MOC, an associated company of MTI, to deliver crude oil to MOC and to receive refined oil. Texaco alleged that MOC habitually stored the oil and supplied Texaco with the refined product using MTI facilities. The five parties who dealt with MTI and MOC were collectively described as the 'oil claimants'.

17.78 When MTI became insolvent, it obtained finance from a number of banks who claimed first charge over the money due to MTI from the oil purchasers and over the products in storage. However, MTI sold various amounts of fuel oil to third parties ('the oil purchasers') and the oil claimants asserted proprietary rights over the proceeds.

17.79 The issues arising in the litigation focused primarily upon the property rights of the various parties. However, the claimants also brought actions in tort against MTI and against the oil purchasers for wrongful interference with goods.[167] It was clear that any acts of interference had taken place in Fujairah. Notwithstanding this, one relevant question was

---

[165] Where a contract of sale contains a retention of title clause in favour of the seller, the sub-buyer may not get good title from by the buyer by the law of the *situs*. That being so, the seller might have a cause of action for wrongful interference with his goods by the sub-buyer if he can show that he still has title by the law of the *situs*. If all acts of interference are in one state and so are the goods, the law of that country will apply. Benjamin, 25–141, points out that in such a case, it is unlikely that the applicable law will be displaced under s 12. The fact that the sub-sale contact is governed by a different law to that applicable under the tort choice of law rules is not a reason to invoke s 12, as the seller was not, of course, party to that sub-sale agreement.

[166] [2001] 1 Lloyd's Rep 284, QBD (Comm).

[167] This was how the action was described. The term 'conversion' was not used. However, there is no specific tort of wrongful interference with goods. The term 'wrongful interference with goods' in s 1 of the Torts (Interference with Goods Act) 1977 is a generic term to cover the torts of conversion, trespass to goods, negligence resulting in damage to goods and any other tort which results in damage to goods or an interest in goods.

whether it might be substantially more appropriate to apply a different law, on the basis that the contracts between the various parties and MTI were governed by English law.

In relation to the claim against the oil purchasers, Moore-Bick J emphatic- **17.80** ally and convincingly rejected the argument:

The only basis for that submission was the fact that in each case the purchaser agreed to buy the goods on English law terms. . . . [T]here was no direct relationship between the oil claimant and the purchaser in any of these cases and I am quite unable to accept that the mere fact that MTI agreed to sell bunkers on English law terms is sufficient to displace the general rule in s. 11. The fact that all the event in question occurred in Fujairah where the goods themselves were situated seems to me to provide the strongest possible connection with that country.[168]

However, in relation to the claim against MTI, the parties accepted that English law should apply to any claims in tort 'because they arise out of the relationship created by the contract and are closely related to the contract claim. . . . [T]his case falls within section 12 of the Private International Law (Miscellaneous) Provisions Act, 1995 so far as concerns claims in tort.'[169] The only exception was the claim brought by Texaco. Its contract with MOC was governed by New York law. Applying s 12, the parties agreed that the New York law should govern its claim in tort.[170]

Despite this, it is not clear precisely which factor under s 12 led to the **17.81** disapplication of the law identified in s 11. Section 12 refers to the 'circumstances or consequences' of the '*events*'[171] constituting the tort. It is not clear that a contractual relationship is an 'event'. Moreover, whilst it is true that, *factually*, the allegations of wrongful interference would not have arisen had the various parties not been in contractual relationships with MTI,[172] the claimants were *legally* entirely independent. A party can, of course, wrongfully interfere with another person's goods, even in the absence of any contractual relationships. The effect of the judgment is to subordinate the (free-standing) tort claim to the law applicable to the contract. This might be justified on the basis that it gives best effect to the intentions of the parties. In principle, however, it is not clear that this is a correct way to proceed or that it gives sufficient weight to the independence of an action in tort.

---

[168] [2001] 1 Lloyd's Rep 284, 298, QBD (Comm).   [169] ibid, at 296.
[170] Compare *Ennstone Building Products Ltd v Stanger* [2002] 1 WLR 3059, CA (decided on the basis of the common law choice of law rules); noted J Perkins, 'Identifying the Locus of the Tort' [2003] CLJ 274.
[171] Emphasis added.   [172] Or, in the case of Texaco, with MOC.

Where the contract contains a choice of law clause which is, on its natural construction, intended to extend to related claims in tort involving the same parties

17.82   In *Empresa Exportadora de Azúcar v Industria Azucarera Nacional SA, (The Playa Larga and Marble Islands)*,[173] the plaintiff brought an action in respect of a breach of a contractual warranty of quiet possession of goods alongside a claim in tort. The contract contained an arbitration clause in respect of 'all disputes arising out of the contract'. Ackner LJ ruled that it was simply a matter of construction whether this clause was intended also to cover a claim for the tort and that 'the claim for the tort has a sufficiently close connection with the claims in contract that it came within the arbitration clause ... [The] agreement to arbitrate on one can properly be construed as covering the other.'[174]

17.83   More generally, can it be argued that, if a contract contains a choice of law clause[175] purporting to apply to 'all disputes arising out of the contract', the chosen law should also govern a claim in tort, provided that it involves the same parties to the contract?[176] In favour of this suggestion is the fact that it may protect the expectations of the parties and that it will lead to the application of the same law where closely related claims for breach of a warranty and a claim in tort are combined. 'Consistency and harmony of result is likely to be brought about if the chosen law governs the totality of the obligations arising between parties in a contractual relationship; for, though some of the obligations may not be voluntary or self-defined, the relationship which caused them to impinge will have been.'[177] Against this, it might be argued that this approach tends to undermine the independent nature of the tort claim. Tortious liability is imposed as part of the framework law of non-contractual obligations and it is not obvious that it should be the proper subject of a choice by the parties. Furthermore, s 12 may be invoked where it is substantially more appropriate to apply the law of a *country* other than that where the tort occurred. As Briggs points out, this suggests, on a literal construction, that: 'It is not therefore the appropriateness of the other law, but the territorial connections with another state, which

---

[173] [1983] 2 Lloyd's Rep 171, CA. See also *The Pioneer Container* [1994] 2 AC 324, PC; *Donohue v Armco Inc* [2002] I Lloyd's Rep 425, HL. Compare also s 46 of the Arbitration Act 1996.

[174] *The Playa Larga*, ibid, at 183.

[175] Or a choice demonstrated with reasonable certainty under Art 3(1) of the Rome Convention. The arbitration clause may indicate an implied choice of law: see *Egon Oldendorff v Libera Corp (No 2)* [1996] 1 Lloyd's Rep 380.

[176] There should be no question of the contractual stipulation being relevant if the claim in tort does not involve the same parties.

[177] A Briggs, 'On Drafting Agreements on Choice of Law' [2003] LMCLQ 389, 392.

determine whether another law—the contractually and chosen law—will apply'.[178]

Nevertheless, in *Thierry Morin v Bonhams & Brooks Ltd*,[179] Mance LJ **17.84** remarked obiter[180] that: 'In general terms, it would seem odd, if an express choice of law were not at least relevant to the governing law of a tort . . . The law of a country is after all a feature of the country.' Commercial certainty demands some reference to the governing law of the contract. In the light of the approach taken in *Glencore*, it is suggested that the following principles should be applied. First, the claim in tort must still be classified as one in tort for choice of law purposes and the general rule determined by s 11 of the 1995 Act. However, when applying s 12, it is likely that very considerable weight will be attached to a choice of law clause which, on its natural construction,[181] is intended also to govern a related tort arising out of the contract and involving the same parties.[182] This is likely to lead to the law governing the contract displacing the general rule under s 12. However, all the other provisions of Part III of the 1995 Act will still apply to the claim in tort.

Public Policy

An exception to the application of the tort choice of law rules was **17.85** invoked in *Kuwait Airways Corp v Iraqi Airways Co (Nos 4 and 5)*.[183] The case was decided under the common law choice of law rules in tort. In 1990, the Iraqi state adopted resolutions proclaiming the sovereignty of Iraq over Kuwait. The Iraqis removed ten aircraft from Kuwait to Iraq. The Iraqi State then passed a resolution dissolving Kuwait Airways and vesting all its property worldwide in Iraqi Airways (the State owned airline). Later, Iraq accepted the illegality of its purported sovereignty over Kuwait. Kuwait Airways sued for conversion. The law of the place of the alleged conversion was Iraq. However, Iraqi law said that there was no claim, as title to the aircraft was acquired by the Iraqi State in

---

[178] ibid, at 394. He earlier suggests (at 393) that the applicable law of the contract may have been of greater relevance to the application of the exceptions to the common law choice of law rules in tort. This is on the basis that they were more flexible and able to take into account connections to another *law*, as well as to another *country*.

[179] [2003] EWCA Civ 1802 at [23], [2004] IL Pr 24 at 398.

[180] Whilst Mance LJ suggested that a choice of law clause would be a relevant factor under s 12, he expressly stated that he did not need to decide this point to reach his judgment and declined to do so.

[181] The construction of the clause is a matter for the applicable law of the contract: Art 10(1)(a) of the Rome Convention.

[182] Mance LJ in *Thierry Morin v Bonhams & Brooks Ltd* [2003] EWCA Civ 1802 at [23], [2004] IL Pr 24 at 398.

[183] [2002] 2 AC 883, HL; noted Peel, n 145 above; Briggs, 'Public Policy in the Conflict of Laws: a Sword and a Shield?', n 145 above.

Iraq. The House of Lords (Lord Scott dissenting) stated that there must be a public policy exception to the application of the law of the place of the tort. The circumstances in which this would be invoked would include breaches of human rights and fundamental breaches of public international law. The court ruled that the Iraqi Resolution vesting title in the Iraqi State would be disapplied on public policy grounds. Having done so, their Lordships then went on to apply Iraqi law *on the footing that title did not vest in the Iraqi State* and to ask whether, on this basis, Iraqi airways had committed the tort of conversion in respect of *the Kuwait Airways' property*. Unsurprisingly, the answer to this question was 'yes'.

17.86 However, there is clearly some force in the dissent of Lord Scott. Public policy is an essentially negative process involving the disapplication of the governing law in whole of in part.[184] Lord Scott noted that the majority of their Lordships had effectively *created* a cause of action where clearly none existed by Iraqi law. When an English court invokes public policy, we cannot simply edit out those bits of the governing law which lead to there being no recovery and leave those parts which would give rise to a claim.

17.87 That said, the conclusion reached on the facts of the case did appear satisfactory. In effect, it seems that the court simply did not consider the outcome of application of the law of the place of the tort as acceptable on the facts. That being so, it might be preferable simply to ignore the law of the place of the tort altogether on public policy grounds and to apply solely the law of the forum in such a case. The same result can be reached where the 1995 Act is applicable by invoking s 14(3)(i) of the Act.

2. Negligent Misstatement, Negligent and Fraudulent Misrepresentation

Nature of Claims in English Law

17.88 In English domestic law, a number of torts deal with misstatements and misrepresentations. These torts are considered in greater detail in Chapter 6 on tort claims and jurisdiction, to which the reader is referred.[185] In summary, these claims include: the tort of deceit;[186] the common law tort of negligent misstatement exemplified by *Hedley Byrne & Co v Heller and*

---

[184] See above, paras 13.282–294.   [185] Above, paras 6.67–71.

[186] Which deals with deliberate or reckless representations issued by the defendant with the intention that claimant should act in reliance on the representation, where this causes loss to the claimant.

Partners;[187] the statutory tort of negligent misrepresentation in s 2(1) of the Misrepresentation Act 1967;[188] and innocent misrepresentation.[189] Our present discussion will focus principally upon fraudulent and negligent misrepresentations which allegedly induce a buyer[190] to conclude a contract. We will also consider the common law tort of negligent misstatement, which may be relevant where an action is brought against a third party to the sales contract.

Civil Law Claims Relating to Pre-Contractual Conduct

In certain civil law systems, other forms of liability may arise from pre- **17.89** contractual conduct.[191] These are explained in Chapter 6 on tort and jurisdiction, to which the reader is referred.[192] Very briefly, it should be recalled that German law has the principle of *culpa in contrahendo*. Italian law provides in Article 1337 of the Codice civile that, in the negotiation and formation of a contract, the parties must act in good faith.[193] French law has a general principle of *non-cumul*, preventing a party from combining claims in contract and in tort to augment liability, or from proceeding in delict where the parties have a contractual relationship which covers the operative facts. However, French law has limited rules on delictual fault under Article 1382 of the Code civil which permit the delict claim to proceed where the obligation breached is pre-contractual and remains outside the contract.[194]

---

[187] [1964] AC 465, HL. This claim may give rise to liability in a pre-contractual context where there is a special relationship between the parties. *Hedley Byrne* liability will be important in the sales context where the statement was not made by one of the contracting parties, as where a company erroneously certifies that the goods conform with the contract.

[188] Where the misrepresentation is made by one of the parties to the sales contract, the statutory tort of negligent misrepresentation in s 2(1) of the Misrepresentation Act 1967 is much easier to establish than the tort of deceit and no less restricted in terms of what the claimant can recover.

[189] s 2(2) of the Misrepresentation Act 1967. There is the possibility, in respect of innocent misrepresentation, that the court will exercise its discretion not to grant rescission of the contract and to award damages in lieu. However, it is concluded above, para 6.67, that this last possibility should not be classified as a tortious claim for the purposes of private international law, as it is a remedial alternative to the contractual remedy of rescission.

[190] Or, less frequently, a seller.

[191] See further P Giliker, 'A Role for Tort in Pre-Contractual Negotiations? An Examination of English, French and Canadian Law' (2003) 52 ICLQ 969.

[192] Above, paras 6.72–74.

[193] See further, in the context of the Brussels Convention, C-334/00 *Fonderie Officine Meccaniche Tacconi SpA v Heinrich Wagner Sinto Maschinenfabrik GmbH (HWS)* [2002] ECR I-7357, discussed above, paras 6.11–12, 6.76.

[194] It also has rules of delict covering the negotiation process and liability for breaking off negotiations where the other party would expect a contract to be concluded; these are considered separately in the discussion of 'failure to sell', above, paras 6.73, 6.116, and below, paras 20.37, 20.41. See further paras 17.122–134 below.

Classification

English law claims

17.90 For the purposes of common law jurisdiction, negligent misstatement and fraudulent misrepresentation claims have been classified as tortious on many occasions.[195] Furthermore, fraudulent misrepresentation was classified by the House of Lords, in a case which pre-dated the 1995 Act, as a tort for choice of law purposes in *Armagas Ltd v Mundogas SA*.[196] However, these cases are of only limited guidance in the present day in the classification for choice of law purposes. This is because (i) there is now a European autonomous meaning of 'contract' for the purposes of the Rome Convention; and (ii) the 1995 Act requires an English private international law classification of issues arising in a claim as relating to tort. The common law decisions do not address these concerns.

17.91 In *Thierry Morin v Bonhams & Brooks Ltd*,[197] claims were brought for misrepresentation and negligent misstatement. The Court of Appeal had to decide whether these claims were governed by the law of England or the law of Monaco. Mance LJ ruled that the law of Monaco applied. In reaching this conclusion, he applied the 1995 Act and did so on the basis that it was 'common ground that under English law the proposed claims . . . are . . . tort claims. This is so, although, on the evidence of Monegasque law . . . any claim based on alleged negligent misstatement . . . would under that law probably be regarded as lying in contract, rather than delict.'[198] However, the case is far from conclusive as to the classification for private international law purposes of misrepresentation and negligent misstatement, since both parties accepted that the 1995 Act applied.

17.92 In our earlier discussion of the scope of the 1995 Act, we saw that it is far from clear which claims should be characterized as torts for choice of law purposes. Furthermore, some claims which might be classified as tortious in domestic law might conceivably be treated as 'contractual obligations' within the meaning of Article 1 of the Rome Convention on the Law Applicable to Contractual Obligations, which states that for matters

---

[195] On Ord 11, r 1(1)(f) RSC, the predecessor of the current r 6.20(8) CPR, see: *ISC Technologies Ltd v James Howard Guerin* [1992] 2 Lloyd's Rep 430; *ABCI v Banque Franco-Tunisienne* [2003] 2 Lloyd's Rep 146, CA (and see the earlier proceedings in *Arab Business Consortium International Finance and Investment Co v Banque Franco-Tunisienne* [1996] 1 Lloyd's Rep 485, [1997] 1 Lloyd's Rep 531). On the predecessor to this rule, Ord 11, r 1(1)(h) RSC, see *Cordova Land Co Ltd v Victor Bros Inc* [1966] 1 WLR 793; *Diamond v Bank of London and Montreal Ltd* [1979] QB 333, CA; *The Albaforth* [1984] 2 Lloyd's Rep 91. See further above, para 6.96.

[196] [1986] AC 717, 783, HL.

[197] [2003] EWCA Civ 1802, [2004] IL Pr 24, affirming [2003] IL Pr 25 at 431, QBD (Comm).

[198] [2003] EWCA Civ 1802, at [12] and [22], [2004] IL Pr 24 at 394, 398, *per* Mance LJ.

within its scope, the Convention 'shall apply'.[199] This immediately raises the question of whether a claim based for negligent misstatement, negligent or fraudulent misrepresentation is properly subject to tortious choice of law rules at all.[200]

It is possible that the claimant will allege that a misstatement or mis- **17.93** representation was incorporated as a term of the contract and that a concurrent action lies for breach of contract. This issue is considered in Chapter 20, which deals with concurrent claims.[201] Where, however, a claim is brought solely in respect of a misstatement or misrepresentation, classification is less clear cut. In the context of the Brussels I Regulation, Briggs and Rees suggest that a difference should be drawn between representations or statements made where the parties are 'in a relationship equivalent to privity, where advice was given directly be defendant to claimant . . .' and where 'the claimant is merely a foreseen and predictable non-party to the advice-giving relationship, though relying on the advice given'.[202] They suggest that the former would be treated as 'matter[s] relating to contract';[203] the latter as 'matter[s] relating to tort'.[204]

This distinction could also be applied when in comes to the choice of law **17.94** process. This may be justified on the basis that a European autonomous definition of 'contractual obligations' is needed for the application of the Rome Convention,[205] just as a European autonomous definition is given to 'matters relating to contract' in the Brussels I Regulation.[206] As to the latter category of Briggs and Rees, it is very likely that such claims will fall outside the ambit of the Rome Convention. They should certainly be classified as tortious for private international law purposes and the rules of the 1995 Act applied. This means that where the misstatement or

---

[199] Art 1(1) of the Rome Convention; above, paras 13.14–17 and 13.19–20. Compare the scope of Art 5(1) of the Brussels I Regulation. The House of Lords ruled in *Agnew v Länsfösäkringsbolagens AB* [2001] 1 AC 223 that the phrase 'matters relating to contract' in that Article included a claim to avoid a contract of reinsurance on the basis of a failure to make full and frank disclosure of relevant facts and risks. See above, paras 6.77–85 and 13.14–17. See further Briggs and Rees, 134–135.

[200] It also suggests that the court in *Morin* should arguably not have accepted the parties' view that the 1995 Act applied and should have considered of its own motion whether the Rome Convention applied.

[201] Below, paras 20.14, 20.28–52.   [202] Briggs and Rees, 127–128.
[203] For the purposes of Art 5(1) of the Brussels I Regulation.
[204] For the purposes of Art 5(3) of the Brussels I Regulation.
[205] Art 1(1) of the Rome Convention.
[206] Art 5(1) of the Brussels I Regulation; see above, paras 3.62–82. Of course, it is possible that the phrase 'matters relating to contract' is broader than 'contractual obligations'. A claim can *relate* to contract without actually being contractual. However, it is suggested in Chs 13 and 14 that in some respects the definition of 'contractual obligations' in the Rome Convention may actually be broader than the definition of 'matters relating to contract' in the Brussels I Regulation: see above, paras 13.17, 14.03–05.

misrepresentation was made by a third party to the sales contract, the choice of law rules in tort will apply.

17.95 It could be argued that the former category suggested by Briggs and Rees, where the parties are in a relationship equivalent to privity and the advice was given directly by defendant to claimant, would fall within the ambit of the Rome Convention. 'In the former case, it is only the absence of consideration which prevents the relationship being contractual as a matter of substantive law . . . It may be that . . . where the claim is brought by the person who sought and obtained the advice, the claim will be contractual; where it is instead brought by a third party, who has relied on it, such a conclusion will be more difficult to reach.'[207] If this is correct, then it may be that claims for negligent misstatement and fraudulent misrepresentation should be treated as 'contractual obligations' where the statement or representation is made by the seller to the buyer[208] within the European autonomous meaning of that term in Article 1(1) of the Rome Convention.

17.96 However, it is suggested that it is very doubtful that any claims for negligent misstatement and negligent and fraudulent misrepresentation would be regarded as falling within the scope of the Rome Convention and that they are much more likely to be governed by the 1995 Act. In our discussion of Article 5(1) of the Brussels I Regulation, which concerns 'matters relating to contract', we saw that this Article requires there to be a *contractual obligation* freely assumed by one party towards another.[209] In *Agnew v Länsfösäkringsbolagens AB*,[210] Lord Millett said there is no *contractual* obligation in English law not to misrepresent the facts during contractual negotiations. Article 1(1) of the Rome Convention expressly applies only to 'contractual obligations'. On balance, it is unlikely that such claims would be treated as falling within the ambit of the Rome Convention.

17.97 Furthermore, even if some misrepresentation or misstatement actions were to fall within the ambit of the Rome Convention, it does not necessarily follow that they could not fall within the scope of the 1995 Act as well. Under the Brussels I Regulation, the definitions of 'matters relating to contract' and 'matters relating to tort' are mutually exclusive.[211] That is not

---

[207] Briggs and Rees, 128, 153.   [208] Or, less commonly, by the buyer to the seller.

[209] See above, paras 3.67–69. See also Case C-26/91 *Societe Jakob Handte et Cie GmbH v Societe Traitements Mécano-Chimiques des Surfaces (TMCS)* [1992] ECR I-3967, 3994, para 15; Case C-51/97 *Réunion Européenne SA v Spliethoff's Bevrachtingskantoor BV* [1998] ECR I-6511, paras 17 and 19; Case C-334/00 *Fonderie Officine Meccaniche Tacconi SpA v Heinrich Wagner Sinto Maschinenfabrik GmbH (HWS)* [2002] ECR I-7357, para 23; Case C-265/02 *Frahuil SA v Assitalia SPA* [2004] IL Pr 11.

[210] [2001] 1 AC 223 at 265.

[211] Case 189/87 *Kalfelis v Bankhaus Schroder, Munchmeyer, Hengst & Co* [1988] ECR 5565.

necessarily the case for choice of law purposes when determining the ambit of the Rome Convention and the 1995 Act.[212] It may be that the claim may also be classified as a tort within *English* private international law's understanding of the term and the 1995 Act applied. If so, then the claimant may[213] be given a choice whether to frame his claim in contract of in tort.[214]

Civil law claims

The classification of a civil law claim concerning pre-contractual conduct **17.98** may be complex. The first question must be whether the claim falls within the European autonomous meaning of 'contractual obligations' in Article 1(1) of the Rome Convention. If it does, then the claimant may proceed in contract and the choice of law rules of that Convention shall apply.[215]

If not, the question arises as to whether the claim should be classified as **17.99** tortious and the 1995 Act applied.[216] In making this classification, the issue arises as to whether the English court should have regard to the classification of the cause of action or issue in the domestic law of the state whose law is putatively applicable, or whether the English court should apply its own classification, ignoring the classification of the foreign law. The fact that s 9(2) of the 1995 Act states that classification is to be done by the forum's private international law categories may suggest that the foreign classification is irrelevant. This view is arguably supported by the decision in *Thierry Morin v Bonhams & Brooks Ltd*,[217] where the Court of Appeal applied the 1995 Act and ruled that the law of Monaco applied to claims for misrepresentation and negligent misstatement, even though there was evidence that the latter claim would be treated as contractual by the law of Monaco.

---

[212] Although it may well be the case; see above, paras 17.20–22.

[213] The counter-argument would be that the Rome Convention states that it *shall* apply to claims involving 'contractual obligations', within the meaning of Art 1(1).

[214] In fact, it is suggested above, paras 17.20–22, that a single substantive claim in a domestic legal system may be classified as contractual or tortious, but not both. See further below, paras 20.12–13. See also Harris, n 31 above.

[215] It is unclear if the claim may also be classified as tortious for choice of law purposes, so that the claimant has a choice how to frame his action: see above, paras 17.20–22, and below, paras 20.12–13.

[216] Compare Case C-334/00 *Fonderie Officine Meccaniche Tacconi SpA v Heinrich Wagner Sinto Maschinenfabrik GmbH (HWS)* [2002] ECR I-7357. In this case, the ECJ ruled that where a third party sought to enforce the obligation imposed by Art 1337 of the Italian Codice civile on parties to negotiate in good faith, the matter related to tort and was covered by Art 5(3) of the Brussels Convention. However, the question did not arise as to whether the matter would have been regarded as relating to contract within Art 5(1) of the Brussels Convention had it been the other (putative) contracting party who had sought to enforce the obligation to act in good faith. Nonetheless, one might argue that such a claim should still be classified as a matter relating to tort if there is no *contractual* obligation to act in good faith. See further above, paras 6.11–12, 6.76.

[217] [2003] EWCA Civ 1802, [2004] IL Pr 24. However, on the facts, the classification of the claims was not in dispute by the parties.

17.100 However, it is suggested that a purely English classification should not be adopted for several reasons. First, there is absolutely no reason why, as a matter of *English* private international law, an English court should not be influenced in its characterization process by the classification made in a foreign law. Second, if an English court classifies the cause of action by a foreign law differently to the classification employed in that law, the result will be that foreign law may end up being applied in an English court in circumstances where the courts of the state whose law is applicable would not *themselves* apply that law on the facts (or vice versa).[218] Accordingly, it is suggested that the classification of civil law claims as tortious should be essentially determined by the law which English law considers is putatively applicable.

The Governing Law of a Claim for Negligent Misstatement, Fraudulent or Negligent Misrepresentation

All elements occur in a single state

17.101 Where a misrepresentation or misstatement is made in one state and relied upon to the claimant's detriment in that same state, then s 11(1) of the 1995 leads to the application of the law of that state.

Elements occur in more than one state

17.102 The difficulty arises where the relevant elements of the tort do not occur in a single state. It becomes important to determine, for the purposes of s 11(2)(c), where the most significant element or elements of the events occurred. A similar exercise was conducted in determining the place of the tort in a number of common law[219] jurisdiction cases[220] concerning fraudulent misrepresentation. It also seems that the principles in those cases applied with equal force to negligent misstatement and negligent misrepresentation claims.

17.103 Of course, the test in s 11(2)(c) is not strictly based upon the place of the tort. The common law jurisdiction cases can, accordingly, be of only limited relevance when considering the application of s 11(2)(c) authorities. Indeed, in *Thierry Morin v Bonhams & Brooks Ltd*, Mance LJ commented that: 'It is undesirable that submissions about the new wording of the 1995 Act should be complicated by increasingly outdated debate

---

[218] Compare *Ogden v Ogden* [1908] P 46.

[219] On the Brussels I Regulation and Art 5(3), see the discussion in Ch 6 dealing with tort and jurisdiction claims, paras 6.86–95.

[220] Although it is not necessarily the case that the place of the tort need be the same for jurisdiction and choice of law purposes: *David Syme & Co Ltd v Grey* (1992) 38 FCR 303 at 314; *Dow Jones v Gutnick* 210 CLR 575, HC of Australia; [2002] HCA 56, para 145, Kirby J.

about the precise nuances of old law'.[221] Nevertheless, in the absence of extensive case law under the Act at this stage, it is suggested the common law cases should remain of at least some persuasive effect as to which are likely to be the most significant elements of the events for the purposes of s 11(2)(c) of the 1995 Act.

More limited guidance might be gleaned from case law on Article 5(3) of **17.104** the Brussels I Regulation. That provision does not make it necessary to identify a single place where the tort occurs.[222] Moreover, Mance LJ in *Thierry Morin v Bonhams & Brooks Ltd* expressed particular reluctance to refer to Brussels Regulation cases in the application of the 1995 Act.[223]

With the caveats expressed by Mance LJ in *Thierry Morin v Bonhams &* **17.105** *Brooks Ltd* in mind, let us turn to look at the pre-1995 Act authorities. In the common law jurisdiction case of *Cordova Land Co v Victor Bros Inc*,[224] the court looked at the entirety of the events, in order to determine where the substance of the wrongful conduct alleged to give rise to the claim took place. It was not prepared to concentrate upon a single factor, such as the place where the representation was relied upon, or where it induced financial loss.[225] The case concerned the issuing of clean bills of lading. It was held that the place of making the misrepresentation was the key matter, and that this was made where clean bills of lading had been issued by the ships' masters and passed to the shippers.

However, in *Diamond v Bank of London and Montreal*,[226] the Court of Appeal **17.106** ruled that a misrepresentation by an instantaneous means of communication such as a telephone or telex occurs where it is received and acted on and not where it is made. The decision was followed by the Court of Appeal in *Cordoba Shipping Co v National State Bank, Elizabeth, New Jersey (The Albaforth)*.[227] Likewise, in *Armagas Ltd v Mundogas SA*,[228] a case concerned with choice of law, the court held that the alleged tort of fraudulent misrepresentation occurred where the representation was

---

[221] [2003] EWCA Civ 1802 at [18], [2004] IL Pr 24 at 396–397. The case is discussed below, paras 17.110–111, 17.113, 17.120.

[222] See above, paras 6.14–16 and 6.86–95.

[223] [2003] EWCA Civ 1802, [2004] IL Pr 24 at 396–397. He observed at [18] that: 'It seems to me even less fruitful to try to refer for inspiration . . . to other schemes, such as that under the Brussels Convention or Regulation 44/2001'.

[224] [1966] 1 WLR 793.

[225] See also *Base Metal Trading Ltd v Shamurin* [2002] CLC 322, [2003] EWHC 2419 (Comm), [2004] IL Pr 5, where Tomlinson J was not prepared to apply a mechanical test to identify the place where the tort occurred. See also the Court of Appeal's decision: [2004] EWCA (Civ) 1316.

[226] [1979] QB 333.

[227] [1984] 2 Lloyd's Rep 91, CA. Both *Diamond* and *The Albaforth* were cases concerned with jurisdiction at common law: see above, paras 6.101–102, 6.110.

[228] [1986] AC 717, HL.

communicated orally and relied upon. These cases were accepted as accurately representing the law in *Metall und Rohstoff AG v Donaldson Lufkin & Jenrette Inc.*[229]

17.107 In *Minster Investments Ltd v Hyundai Precision and Industry Ltd*[230] a case concerned with Article 5(3) of the Brussels Convention, Steyn J was faced with a claim by English buyers against South Korean sellers and against a French company with a Korean office which had certified that the goods complied with contractual specifications. The certification was performed in France and Korea, but the certificates were received in England, where the buyers detrimentally relied upon them by instructing the bank to pay the Korean sellers. Steyn J took the view that the essence of the tort was the communication of the advice and detrimental reliance upon it, and that this occurred in England.

17.108 The most difficult case is where advice is given in one state, received in another and causes harm to the claimant in another state. In *Domicrest Ltd v Swiss Bank Corp*,[231] a misstatement was made in Switzerland and communicated to England. The claimant relied upon this in England and ordered the release of goods located in Switzerland and Italy without prior payment. Rix J held that, for the purposes of Article 5(3) of the Brussels Convention, the act giving rise to the damage occurred in the place where the misstatement originated, Switzerland, not in the place of receipt of that misstatement, England. Moreover, it appeared that the harmful event itself was not the receipt of the misstatement in England, but the detrimental reliance upon it which inflicted direct damage upon the claimant. Rix J rejected the approach taken in *Minster Investments* by Steyn J of asking 'where in substance the cause of action arises?', which was incompatible with Article 5(3) of the Brussels Convention. The decision was followed, in the context of service out of the jurisdiction under RSC Order 11, r 1(1)(f),[232] by the Court of Appeal in *ABCI v Banque Franco-Tunisienne*,[233] where a fraudulent misrepresentation was allegedly sent from Tunisia to England and relied upon by the claimant making

---

[229] [1990] 1 QB 391, CA. In this case, the law applicable to the tort had to be determined in the context of the application of the rules of jurisdiction.

[230] [1988] 2 Lloyd's Rep 621, QBD (Comm). Contrast *Domicrest Ltd v Swiss Bank Corp* [1999] QB 548. See also *Raiffeisen Zentralbank Osterreich AG v National Bank of Greece SA* [1999] 1 Lloyd's Rep 408, QBD (Comm); *Raiffeisen Zentral Bank Osterreich AG v Alexander Tranos* [2001] IL Pr 9, QBD (Comm); *ABCI v Banque Franco-Tunisienne* [2003] 2 Lloyd's Rep 146, CA.

[231] [1999] QB 548; followed in *Alfred Dunhill Ltd v Diffusion Internationale de Maroquinerie de Prestige*, [2002] IL Pr 13.

[232] Which was the then applicable basis of service out of the jurisdiction for tort claims. It has since been replaced by r 6.20(8) CPR.

[233] [2003] EWCA Civ 205, [2003] 2 Lloyd's Rep 146, CA. See the earlier proceedings: *Arab Business Consortium International Finance and Investment Co v Banque Franco-Tunisienne* [1996] 1 Lloyd's Rep 485, [1997] 1 Lloyd's Rep 531.

payments out of an account in Switzerland. The act giving rise to the damage took place in Tunisia and the damage itself occurred in Switzerland, with the consequence that the English court, the place of receipt, lacked jurisdiction. Admittedly, in neither case was it necessary to determine a single place of the tort, whereas for choice of law purposes one governing law must, of course, be determined. At common law, the English court would have had jurisdiction if either the place of the act giving rise to the harmful event or the harm itself had occurred in England.[234] However, it is notable that neither of these places was the place of mere receipt of the advice.

The cases considered above suggest that no one factor can be determina- **17.109** tive of the governing law of the tort for choice of law purposes. However, it is suggested that matters will be fairly straightforward where the negligent misstatement or fraudulent or negligent representation is received and is relied upon in the same state. That state's law will be applicable by virtue of s 11(2)(c) of the 1995 Act, even if the misstatement or misrepresentation was sent from abroad.[235] This state should be preferred to the state where the misstatement or misrepresentation originated, regardless of the means of communication used.[236] A misstatement or misrepresentation which is made but never communicated to the defendant cannot give rise to a cause of action. As such, it is very hard to see how it can habitually be said to be the place where the most significant element of the tort occurs, at least where this is the only factor which points to that state.[237]

Where receipt and reliance take place in different states, matters are less **17.110** clear. In *Thierry Morin v Bonhams & Brooks Ltd*,[238] the claimant purchased a classic car at an auction in Monaco conducted by Bonhams and Brooks Monaco (B & B Monaco), the subsidiary of a London company, Bonhams and Brooks Ltd (B & B London). The contract of sale was governed by the law of Monaco. The contract stated that B & B Monaco acted as the seller's agent and was not itself party to the contract. The claimant later discovered that the odometer had been tampered with and the car was

---

[234] r 6.20(8) CPR (formerly Ord 11, r 1(1)(f) RSC); see above, paras 6.26–28, 6.92.

[235] It is difficult to deny that the sending of the misstatement or representation is an element of the events, so that s 11(2)(c) should apply rather than s 11(1).

[236] But see *Diamond v Bank of London and Montreal* [1979] QB 333, 346 *per* Lord Denning (discussed above, paras 6.101–102, 6.110), considering *Cordova Land Co Ltd v Victor Brothers Inc* [1966] 1 WLR 793.

[237] But see the comments of Mance LJ in *ABCI v Banque Franco-Tunisienne* [2003] EWCA Civ 205, [2003] 2 Lloyd's Rep 146, CA, at [41]. In that state, the representations were made in Tunisia. However, there was also a fraudulent conspiracy alleged to have been hatched there and the representations were made with a view to securing investment in a Tunisian company.

[238] [2003] EWCA Civ 1802, [2004] IL Pr 24, affirming [2003] IL Pr 25 at 431, QBD (Comm Ct).

'clocked'. He argued that B & B London and/or B & B Monaco had mis-represented to him the mileage of the car prior to the sale and that this was a key factor which had induced him to enter into the contract of sale. The misrepresentation was contained in a brochure sent to the claimant in London. The court, in determining the jurisdiction of the English court at common law, had to decide what law would govern the actions for mis-representation and negligent misstatement against B & B London and B & B Monaco respectively. The case was not an easy one: the misrepresenta-tion was received in England but, argued the defendants, was continuing up to the point of purchase in Monaco. Although the claimant incurred expenses in travelling to Monaco, the main act of reliance was the pur-chase itself, which occurred in Monaco, where the principal loss to the claimant also occurred.

17.111 At first instance, Hirst QC[239] expressly cautioned against reliance on pre-Act common law cases on identifying the place of the tort. He held that under s 11(2)(c) of the Act, one could not generalize as to where the most significant element of the events takes place and look at a single connect-ing factor. Rather, one must take a broader view of the chain of events in order to determine where the most significant elements occur. That might lead to a different answer even in relation to claims for the same kind of tort.[240] Mance LJ agreed with this statement in the Court of Appeal and affirmed the ruling of Hirst QC that the claim against B & B Monaco was governed by Monegasque law. The fact that the representation was ongoing until the moment of contracting in Monaco, that the main act of reliance occurred in Monaco and the vast majority of the claimant's dam-age was sustained there meant that 'by far the major elements of his reliance and of the loss caused and claimed in this case'[241] occurred in Monaco.[242] The place of initial receipt of the representations, London, paled into insignificance by comparison.[243]

---

[239] Sitting as a Deputy Judge of the High Court.

[240] [2003] IL Pr 25 at [34], endorsing *Protea Leasing Ltd v Royal Air Cambodge Ltd* [2002] EWHC 2731, The Times, 13 January 2003, QBD (Comm). The latter case was also cited with approval by Mance LJ in the Court of Appeal in the *Morin* case [2003] EWCA Civ 1802 at [18] [2004] IL Pr 24 at 396–397.

[241] But note that Mance LJ did not expressly consider the law applicable to the contract in reaching this conclusion.

[242] [2003] EWCA Civ 1802 at [19], [2004] IL Pr 24 at 397. However, Mance LJ commented that had Mr Morin bid by telephone from his office in England, rather than attending the auction in person, 'the balance of significant elements under s 11(2)(c) might, geographically, have shifted from Monaco to London': ibid, at [21] and 397.

[243] However, in relation to the claim against B & B London, Hirst QC at first instance ruled that all of the defendant's relevant acts had occurred in London and 'the essential communi-cation to [the claimant] . . . occurred in London' with the result that English law governed the claim: [2003] IL Pr 25 at [38]. Mance LJ was not required to rule on this point on appeal, but commented that he had 'considerable doubt about that proposition': [2003] EWCA Civ 1802 at [20], [2004] IL Pr 24 at 397.

Conclusions on Application of s 11(2)(c)

There is little doubt that an entirely flexible approach to s 11(2)(c) fits **17.112** within the wording of that provision.[244] It may, however, give rise to an excessive level of uncertainty. It would be somewhat clearer if courts were habitually to regard a particular element as the most significant one in a negligent misstatement, fraudulent or negligent misrepresentation case. This would provide a starting point for determining the applicable law, much as Article 4(2) of the Rome Convention does for contracts where there is no express or implied choice of law.[245] It would then be incumbent upon the party alleging that some other law applied to plead that it is substantially more appropriate to apply that other law pursuant to s 12. In that way, a set of rules which were reasonably clear, but not rigid, might emerge.

If such an approach were adopted, should the courts regard the most **17.113** significant element of the events in a negligent misstatement, fraudulent or negligent misrepresentation case as the receipt of the misstatement or misrepresentation, or detrimental reliance upon it? It could be argued, notwithstanding *Thierry Morin v Bonhams & Brooks Ltd*,[246] that the more important element under the 1995 Act should usually be the receipt of the representation. It is true that the recipient might detrimentally rely on the statement in another state, for example by investing money there, and that unless and until he does so and suffers loss, there is no claim. However, it is suggested that the focus under s 11(2)(c) of the 1995 Act should be upon the acts of the defendant[247] which are alleged to found a claim against him in tort. Once the defendant has issued a misstatement or misrepresentation and communicated it to the claimant, he has committed all relevant acts that might potentially render him liable in tort. So, the *communication* of the statement is the key, and final, act on the defendant's part which may give rise to liability. It is also a law whose application should be foreseeable to both parties.

It is argued that the place of receipt is especially important where the **17.114** communication is instantaneous.[248] However, even where a misstatement or misrepresentation is made by post, it is suggested that the applicable law under s 11(2)(c) should be that of the place of receipt, not the place of

---

[244] *Protea Leasing Ltd v Royal Air Cambodge Ltd* [2002] EWHC 2731, The Times, 13 January 2003, QBD (Comm); *Thierry Morin* case [2003] EWCA Civ 1802, [2004] IL Pr 24.

[245] See above, paras 13.114–116.   [246] [2003] EWCA Civ 1802, [2004] IL Pr 24.

[247] A counter-argument would be that ss 11(2)(a) and (b) look at the place of damage and not to the acts of the defendant.

[248] See also *Diamond v Bank of London and Montreal* [1979] 1 QB 333; *Bastone & Firminger Ltd v Nasima Enterprises (Nigeria) Ltd* [1996] CLC 190.

posting.[249] The tort of misrepresentation in domestic law is not complete until the communication is received and acted upon.[250] If the receipt is an essential ingredient of a misrepresentation claim,[251] then it should not matter what method of communication is used.[252]

17.115 One might also observe that recent jurisdiction cases such as *Domicrest Ltd v Swiss Bank Corp*[253] and *ABCI v Banque Franco-Tunisienne*[254] have emphasized that an English court has jurisdiction only if England is the place from which a misstatement or misrepresentation originates or the place where it causes immediate damage. The fact that the representation was received in England has not been treated as relevant. However, this is in the context of jurisdiction rules which look to the place where the act giving rise to damage occurs and the place where immediate damage is sustained. The place of receipt is neither of these. That, of course, does not mean that it is not the most significant element of the events for choice of law purposes under s 11(2)(c) of the Act. It is the communication of the misstatement or misrepresentation to the claimant that exposes the defendant to potential liability.

17.116 It is suggested that the law of the place of receipt is a more important factor than the place of detrimental reliance, or immediate financial loss to the claimant.[255] Whether and where[256] the claimant chooses to rely on that advice detrimentally is then outside the defendant's control. Moreover, the place where damage occurred can be a very difficult matter to determine,[257] and may have little concrete connection with the *events*[258] which

---

[249] But see *Diamond v Bank of London and Montreal* [1979] 1 QB 333, 346; *Cordova Land Co Ltd v Victor Brothers Inc* [1966] 1 WLR 793. See also *Domicrest Ltd v Swiss Bank Corp* [1999] QB 548, per Rix J; *The Albaforth* [1984] 2 Lloyd's Rep 91, CA; *National Bank of Canada v Clifford Chance* (1996) 30 OR (3d) 746.

[250] *Diamond v Bank of London and Montreal*, [1979] 1 QB 333, per Stephenson LJ, at 349; (but see ibid, at 346, per Lord Denning). See also *Original Blouse Co Ltd v Bruck Mills Ltd* (1963) 42 DLR (2d) 174, 182.

[251] Furthermore, the English courts are not, of course, fettered by common law authority on the application of s 11(2)(c), which adopts a different test to that used previously of identifying the most significant element or elements of the events.

[252] See *Arab Business Consortium International Finance and Investment Co v Banque Franco-Tunisienne* [1996] 1 Lloyd's Rep 485; *ABCI v Banque Franco-Tunisienne* [2003] EWCA Civ 205, [2003] 2 Lloyd's Rep 146, CA.

[253] [1999] QB 548, QBD.

[254] *ABCI v Banque Franco-Tunisienne* [2003] EWCA Civ 205, [2003] 2 Lloyd's Rep 146, CA

[255] But see *Domicrest Ltd v Swiss Bank Corp* [1999] QB 548, QBD; *ABCI v Banque Franco-Tunisienne* [2003] EWCA Civ 205, [2003] 2 Lloyd's Rep 146, CA.

[256] It may be impossible to foresee where the claimant is himself located at the time when he decides to rely upon the misstatement or misrepresentation, even if it is foreseeable where, for example, the claimant might choose to invest funds upon the basis of the defendant's misstatement or misrepresentation.

[257] An example, which is considered in para 6.95, above, is *Raiffeisen Zentral Bank Osterreich AG v Alexander Tranos* [2001] IL Pr 9, QBD (Comm).

[258] The word used in s 11(2)(c) of the 1995 Act.

gave rise to the claim. It may very well lead to the application of a law wholly unforeseeable to the party making the representations.

Admittedly, the approach advocated here does mean that the place of **17.117** receipt by the claimant becomes very important. However, there may be cases where this place is quite arbitrary,[259] or at least has no real connection with the tort. An example would be a misstatement or misrepresentation sent by fax, which the claimant happens to read whilst on a business trip abroad, rather than in his home state. In such a case, it is not likely that this state of receipt will be the place where the 'most significant elements of the events occur' for the purposes of s 11(2)(c). As such, the emphasis will shift to the other objective factors, especially the place where the representation was made, and the place where it was relied upon.[260]

On balance, there is a strong case for the courts to find in most cases **17.118** that the most significant element of the tort for the purposes of s 11(2)(c) is the communication of the misstatement or misrepresentation to the claimant.[261] This provides an important element of legal certainty. It may be better that this law be dislodged, if at all, pursuant to s 12 of the Act. However, it must be reiterated that, on the present state of authorities, the courts do not seem inclined to identify a single element as the most significant one under s 11(2)(c) and prefer to look at the facts as a whole.

Displacement of the General Rule Under s 12

When might s 12 be invoked?

Suppose that a court concludes that the applicable law by virtue of **17.119** s 11(2)(c) is the law of the place of the receipt of a misstatement or misrepresentation. It should go on to consider whether the exception in s 12 should be invoked. This might occur if, for example, the place of receipt is arbitrary, such as where it is in a state in which the claimant is temporarily located. It might also occur if, for example, the communication is made in State A, communicated to State B, but relied upon and causes direct damage to the claimant in State A. In that case, the act of communication and the place of detrimental reliance and damage all take place in a different

---

[259] See also the discussion below, paras 21.175–182.

[260] But, on the basis of the argument presented in this paragraph, it is suggested that the place of detrimental reliance should be less significant, since it is not an element of the defendant's tortious conduct (even if it is, of course, a sine qua non of the claim.)

[261] That is, the place of receipt of the misstatement or misrepresentation by the claimant.

state to the place of receipt.[262] Given that the cases show no overwhelming attachment to a single connecting factor, it is contended that the suggested general rule in favour of the law of the place of receipt of the communication, State B, would be dislodged in such a case under s 12 in favour of the law of State A.

Influence of the law applicable to the contract

17.120 We saw in the discussion of conversion above[263] that it is not clear what relevance should be attached to the law applicable to the contract in the application of s 12. In *Thierry Morin v Bonhams & Brooks Ltd*,[264] Mance LJ noted that s 12 does not obviously allow the court to consider this factor. However, he went on to suggest obiter that this may be considered as a relevant factor, on the basis that: 'The law of a country is after all a feature of the country'.[265] He also suggested that the existence of a jurisdiction clause for a particular state may be a relevant factor in the application of s 12. However, he expressly left open the issues of the relevance of the law applicable to the contract and of a jurisdiction clause in the contract, as they did not need to decided on the facts of the case.

17.121 It was suggested in the discussion of conversion above that very considerable weight should be attached to a choice of law clause which, on its true construction, is intended to govern a claim in tort arising out of the contract.[266] This would also apply to the torts of fraudulent or negligent misrepresentation. However, where a claim for negligent misstatement is brought against a third party to the contract of sale, the law applicable to the contract of sale should not be relevant to determining the law governing the claim in tort. Any choice of law clause contained in the contract of sale between buyer and seller should not affect the law that might be applied to a claim against a third party who in no way consented to the application of the law applicable to the contract of sale.[267]

---

[262] Compare *ABCI v Banque Franco-Tunisienne* [2003] EWCA Civ 205, [2003] 2 Lloyd's Rep 146, CA. In that case, Mance LJ commented at [41]: '... even assuming that the right question is where in substance did this cause of action arise or was this tort committed, we take the view that the answer would be Tunisia, where the fraudulent conspiracy . . . is said to have been hatched, the fraudulent accounts were prepared and from where they were sent with a view to inducing an investment in the Tunisian company to which they related'. See the earlier proceedings: *Arab Business Consortium International Finance and Investment Co v Banque Franco-Tunisienne* [1996] 1 Lloyd's Rep 485, [1997] 1 Lloyd's Rep 531.

[263] See above, paras 17.76–84, where the relevance of the applicable law of the contract is considered in detail.

[264] [2003] EWCA Civ 1802, [2004] IL Pr 24.   [265] ibid, at [23], p 398.

[266] At paras 17.82–84.

[267] Compare *Glencore International AG v Metro Trading International Inc (No 2)* [2001] 1 Lloyd's Rep 284, QBD (Comm). The case is examined above, paras 17.76–81.

3. FAILURE TO SELL

Classification

Clearly, it is endemic in the choice of law rules contained in the 1995 Act **17.122** that claims governed by a foreign law can now be classified[268] for the purposes of English private international law as tortious and successfully brought in English courts. One such claim, which is relevant in the sale of goods context, is the French tort of failure to sell.[269]

It was suggested above in relation to other civil law claims affecting pre- **17.123** contractual conduct that although classification is a matter for English private international law, it is important to have regard to the classification of such claims by their governing law.[270] Otherwise, that law may be applied in circumstances where it was not intended to be applied, or vice versa. This can lead to distortion of the foreign law and give rise to forum shopping opportunities.

In *Max Mara SA and Manifatture Del Nord SpA v Galerie Kleber SA*,[271] the **17.124** French Cour de cassation was faced with a jurisdiction dispute concerning a claim for compensation for failure to sell goods. The court held that the claim was a matter relating to tort for the purposes of Article 5(3) of the Brussels Convention. Although this was in the context of a European autonomous definition of 'matters relating to tort', it is suggested that the claim would also be classified by an English court as tortious for choice of law purposes. Given that the French Cour de cassation has classified the claim for failure to sell as tortious, there would be little obvious merit in an English court adopting a different classification, either for jurisdiction or choice of law purposes.

Is the Claim Excluded by s 13 of the 1995 Act?

A more important question is whether the French claim for failure to sell **17.125** is excluded from the Act by virtue of s 13. The claim for failure to sell is related to the protection of unfair competition. It is true that slander of goods and title, which are excluded from the 1995 Act, also have the effect of preventing anti-competitive behaviour. However, those torts are concerned with protection of economic *reputation* and it is for this reason, not the fact that they affect competition, that they are excluded from

---

[268] Pursuant to s 9(2) of the 1995 Act, above, paras 17.17–19.
[269] The substantive elements of this claim were discussed above, paras 6.115–116. See further Giliker, n 191 above.
[270] At paras 17.98–100.
[271] [1996] IL Pr 629, French Cour de cassation.

the Act. The claim for failure to sell is not based upon protection of reputation, and accordingly, it should fall within the scope of the 1995 Act.

The Governing Law of a Claim for Failure to Sell

All elements occur in a single state

17.126 If the refusal to sell is made and communicated to the claimant in a single state, where the claimant suffers financial loss, that state's law will apply pursuant to s 11(1).

Elements occur in more than one state

17.127 If elements of the tort occur in more than one state, it will be necessary to apply s 11(2)(c) of the 1995 Act and to determine where the most significant element or elements of the events occurred. However, there is no relevant authority on this matter. There are cases on the application of Article 5(3) of the Brussels Convention to a refusal to sell. In *Schimmel Pianofortefabrik GmbH v Hubert Bion*,[272] the court treated the act giving rise to the claim as being the place where the act of refusal was made,[273] not the place to which the refusal was communicated and received by the 'buyer'. In *Max Mara*, the court said that the *damage* occurred in the place where resale of the goods was contemplated, which was the place where the respondent had its place of business and intended to resell the designs.

17.128 However, when applying Article 5(3), there is no need to identify a single place of the tort. In contrast, this is necessary for choice of law purposes,[274] so as to determine the governing law. For choice of law purposes, it is suggested that the key focus should be on the elements of the defendant's conduct which potentially give rise to the claim. Once the defendant has refused to sell, he has committed all the acts[275] necessary to render him potentially liable. It is suggested that it is preferable to focus upon the acts of the defendant, rather than upon the place of intended resale of the goods by the claimant 'buyer'. The 'buyer' may not have intended to resell the goods at all. Even if he did, the place of intended resale may, from the defendant's point of view, be arbitrary and unpredictable.

17.129 This leaves the question of whether the relevant law for the purposes of s 11(2)(c) of the 1995 Act is the place where the defendant made his decision to refuse to sell, or the place of communication of that refusal to the

---

[272] [1992] IL Pr 199, French Cour de cassation.

[273] ie when, and at the place where, the decision not to sell was made.

[274] Or, rather, it is necessary to identify where the most significant element or elements of the events took place for the purposes of application of s 11(2)(c) of the 1995 Act.

[275] Or omissions.

'buyer'. A number of arguments point to the latter law. First, until the refusal is communicated, the 'seller' may change his mind. Second, the law of the place to which the refusal is communicated is the law which the 'buyer' might expect to be applied and it is a law whose application is reasonably foreseeable to the 'seller'. Indeed, otherwise the 'home' law of the alleged wrongdoing 'seller' would routinely be applied. Third, it was argued above in relation to the torts of negligent misstatement, fraudulent and negligent misrepresentation that the key element of the torts is the receipt of the misstatement or misrepresentation by the claimant.[276] One might argue that the same approach should be adopted with respect to a failure to sell.[277] For the same reasons as were given above in respect of negligent misstatement, fraudulent and negligent misrepresentation, this law would apply irrespective[278] of the means of communication involved.[279]

However, it is suggested that application of the law of the place of com- **17.130** munication to the 'buyer' should be rejected. That law may, on a given set of facts, have little connection to the events which give rise to the claim in tort. For example, if the refusal is communicated by email, and the 'buyer' happens to read that email whilst on a business trip overseas, it seems unsatisfactory for the law of the place where he read the message to be applied, if there is no other connection to the place of receipt.[280]

Rather, it is suggested that the law of the place where the 'seller' makes his **17.131** decision not to sell should apply under s 11(2)(c). It is true that this departs from the position advocated above in the case of negligent misstatement and fraudulent and negligent misrepresentation, where it is argued that the law of communication of the misstatement or misrepresentation should apply. However, the key difference with refusal to sell is that communication is not a necessary ingredient of the tort. A 'seller' who refuses to sell may be liable in tort, *whether or not he communicates that refusal to the 'buyer'*. It was argued in relation to negligent misstatement and fraudulent and negligent misrepresentation that the key

---

[276] At paras 17.102–118.

[277] See also the discussion of where the tort of conversion is committed by a refusal to deliver goods to their true owner, above, paras 17.71–72. However, the claim in conversion will often be brought alongside a claim for breach of contract, for failure to deliver to the specified state. In the case of a refusal to sell, there will be no contract and no place of delivery under the terms of the contract.

[278] In particular, and notwithstanding the decision in *Schimmel Pianofortefabrik GmbH v Hubert Bion* [1992] IL Pr 199, this law would also apply where the refusal was communicated by post.

[279] At paras 17.102–118; but subject to the comment below, para 21.175–182, about e-commerce and the possibility that on the facts of the case, the place of receipt may have no enduring connection to the case.

[280] See below, paras 21.191–192.

focus for the choice of law rules in tort should be upon the conduct of the defendant which is sufficient to render him liable in tort; and in the present case, this is simply the act of refusing to sell.

Pure omissions

17.132 It may be that the refusal to sell will never be communicated to the 'buyer'. The 'seller' might simply omit to conclude a sales contract with the 'buyer', without serving notice upon him that he is refusing to do so. In such a case, one could say that the tort takes place where the refusal should have been communicated to the buyer, which will normally be in the latter's place of business or residence. However, it is very difficult to say that a *refusal* to sell, itself an unlawful activity, *should* have been communicated anywhere.

17.133 An alternative argument is that where the 'seller' remains wholly silent, he has failed to conclude a contract *and to meet his obligation to deliver goods to the buyer*. Accordingly, one might argue that the law of the state to which the seller would have been contractually obliged to deliver the goods should instead apply pursuant to s 11(2)(c).[281] However, it is difficult to sustain this argument. In effect, a defendant could be lured into committing a tort abroad when quite possibly ignorant of that country's law, by virtue of being called upon to supply the buyer. Moreover, focusing upon the non-performance of a contract which by definition the wrongdoing seller did not enter into has a further awkward consequence. Suppose that there are two disappointed buyers, one proposing an FOB sale in the seller's country and the other an ex ship sale in the buyer's country. Do we apply different laws in the two cases? Can the buyer unilaterally fix the governing law in this way? To say that it is a wrong not to sell to the buyer is not the same as saying it is a wrong not to sell *on the buyer's particular terms*.

17.134 Rather, where there is no communication to the 'buyer', the failure to sell is made by pure omission. The 'seller' can be liable in tort for failure to sell, whether or not he positively indicates that intention by words, and whether or not he communicates those words to the 'buyer'. Accordingly, it is suggested that where the 'seller' remains wholly silent, the law of the place where the 'seller' has its place of business should apply by virtue of s 11(2)(c). This is consistent with the argument in the previous section that the law of the place of refusal, rather than the law of the place of communication, should apply.

---

[281] Compare the discussion of where the tort of conversion is committed by a refusal to deliver goods to their true owner: above, paras 17.71–72.

4. INDUCEMENT OF BREACH OF CONTRACT

Substantive Law Background

We saw in Chapter 6 that English law prevents anti-competitive conduct **17.135**
by imposing civil liability[282] through a series of contractual and tortious
claims.[283] Perhaps the most relevant of these in relation to the sale of goods
is the tort of inducing a breach of contract. A third party to a contract, C,
may commit this tort in a number of ways, if he employs unlawful[284]
means in interfering with the contractual relationship between A and B.
These would include: unjustifiable[285] persuasion, through advice[286] or
otherwise, or physical interference with performance by one of the contracting parties, A; and concluding a contract with A which is inconsistent
with A's contractual obligations to B.[287]

It will be recalled that French law imposes delictual liability for induce- **17.136**
ment of breach of contract under Article 1382 of the Code civil.[288] In
Germany, there are a number of principles of delictual liability. One of
these, in § 826 BGB covers liability for intentional injury *contra bonos
mores*.[289]

Classification

There seems little doubt that the tort of inducement of a breach of contract **17.137**
will be classified as tortious for the purposes of application of the 1995
Act. It matters not that the claimant also brings a separate claim for breach
of contract. The Court of Appeal in *Metall und Rohstoff AG v Donaldson
Lufkin & Jenrette Inc*,[290] when determining whether to permit service out of
the jurisdiction, held that a claim for inducement of a breach of contract
was founded upon tort and proceeded to work out the governing law of
that tort.[291] There seems no reason to believe that this is not also the case

---

[282] As well as possible criminal penalties.
[283] See the discussion above, paras 6.130–133.
[284] *DC Thomson & Co Ltd v Deakin* [1952] Ch 646; *Merkur Island Shipping Corp v Laughton*
[1983] 2 AC 581.
[285] *Brimelow v Casson* [1924] 1 Ch 302.
[286] *JT Stratford & Co Ltd v Lindley* [1965] AC 269, 333.
[287] *BMTA v Salvadori* [1949] Ch 556.
[288] J Bell, S Boyron and S Whittaker, *Principles of French Law* (Oxford: Clarendon, 1998)
370–371. See further the discussion above, para 6.134.
[289] K Zweigert and H Kötz, (trans A Weir), *An Introduction to Comparative Law, Vol. 2: The
Institutions of Private Law* (Oxford: Clarendon Press, 1987) 292–299. See the discussion above,
para 6.135.
[290] [1990] 1 QB 391, CA.
[291] It did this in order to establish whether there was a serious issue to be tried on the
merits. See above, paras 6.141–146.

for choice of law purposes. Likewise, inducement of breach of contract is regarded as a form of delictual liability in French and German law and should be subject to the choice of law rules in tort.

17.138 However, it does not follow that every issue arising in a claim for inducement of a breach of contract will be classified as tortious. Section 9(2) of the 1995 Act makes it clear that the English court should characterize each issue for the purposes of private international law to determine whether it is subject to the choice of law rules in the Act. In particular, it is not immediately apparent which law should determine whether: (i) there is a contract; and (ii) whether it has been breached. It could be argued that the cause of action for inducement of a breach of contract lies in tort, so that the law which governs the tort should determine all elements of the claim. In other words, the question of whether there is a contract and whether it is breached would be treated as incidental questions.[292] However, the whole basis to the tort action is the breach of contract and this can scarcely be treated as an 'incidental' matter. Accordingly, it is suggested that the preliminary questions of: (i) whether there is a contract; and (ii) whether it has been breached should be determined by the law applicable to the contract. If there is a breach of contract, then the law applicable to the tort will determine[293] whether: there was an actionable inducement; the defendant had the necessary state of mind; the defendant employed unlawful means; the inducement had a sufficient causal role in the breach; and there is a defence available, such as justification.[294]

The Governing Law of a Claim for Inducement of Breach of Contract

All elements occur in a single state

17.139 Where all elements of the tort occur in one state, that state's law is applicable by virtue of s 11(1). This will be so if the acts of inducement were made and communicated in State A and the breach of contract also occurred in State A, causing damage to the claimant in the same state.

Elements occur in more than one state

17.140 Matters become more complex where the elements of the events occur in more than one state and it is necessary to apply s 11(2)(c) of the Act to

---

[292] Compare, in the context of jurisdiction under the English traditional rules, *Atlantic Underwriting Agencies Ltd and David Gale (Underwriting) Ltd v Compagnia Di Assicurazione Di Milano SPA* [1979] 2 Lloyd's Rep 240

[293] The applicable law of the tort must take it as read that there has been a breach of contract and answer the question, 'given that there is a breach of contract, is there a cause of action for inducement of that breach by the defendant?'

[294] *South Wales Miners' Federation v Glamorgan Coal Co Ltd* [1905] AC 239; *Edwin Hill & Partners v First National Finance Corp* [1989] 1 WLR 225.

determine which law governs a claim for financial loss to the claimant. Some support can be drawn in this respect from the common law authorities. In *Metall und Rohstoff AG v Donaldson Lufkin & Jenrette Inc,*[295] the Court of Appeal was faced with a claim in tort for inducement of a breach of contract. It held that the tort took place not in New York, the place where the acts of inducement took place, but in London, where the breach of contract itself was committed and where the defendant suffered the resulting damage. Cheshire and North argue that if the facts arose today and the applicable law was in issue, English law should apply under s 11(2)(c) of the 1995 Act, as the most significant elements of the events occurred in London.[296]

It could be objected that the key element of the *defendant's* conduct is the **17.141** act of inducement itself, and that this clearly[297] took place in New York. Indeed, it has been argued above that the focus of s 11(2)(c) should normally be on the acts of the defendant which, once committed, may potentially render him liable in tort. In *Protea Leasing Ltd v Royal Air Cambodge Ltd,*[298] R was the national air carrier of Cambodia, whose business was managed by M using aircraft leased from M and from P. R's monopoly status was subsequently revoked. R failed to meet its repayments under the leases. P terminated the leases and sought repayment. It also sued M on the basis that it had put its own interests ahead of R's by using funds which should have been used for R to repay P instead of to repay R's debts to M. Moore-Bick J viewed the claim against M as analogous to an allegation that M had induced a breach of contract. He ruled that the law of Cambodia applied, as this was the place where M had allegedly improperly managed the business of R. This was so even though, under the leases, payment was to be made to a French bank account and thus the economic consequences of non-payment were felt in France. Moore-Bick J ruled that this was merely fortuitous and that the place where the economic consequences were felt was not the country in which the most significant element of the events constituting the tort occurred. He went on to say that s 11(2)(c) required a flexible approach to ascertaining the place of the tort and that no one factor could invariably be deemed conclusive, even in relation to claims concerning a single tort.[299]

---

[295] [1990] 1 QB 391, CA.

[296] Cheshire and North, 636. See also the first instance decision in *Dimskal Shipping Co SA v International Transport Workers' Federation (The Evia Luck) (No 2)* [1989] 1 Lloyd's Rep 166, 177.

[297] A more difficult case would arise if the inducement was sent by post, telephone, fax or email from one state to another. In such a case, the inducement may be deemed to be made in the place where it is received: *Metall und Rohstoff AG v Donaldson Lufkin & Jenrette Inc* [1990] 1 QB 391, 448, CA.

[298] [2002] EWHC 2731, The Times, 13 January 2003, QBD (Comm).

[299] In doing so, he cast doubt on the approach taken in *Metall und Rohstoff AG v Donaldson Lufkin & Jenrette Inc* [1990] 1 QB 391, CA.

17.142 However, if the courts adopt such a flexible approach to s 11(2)(c), a large measure of unpredictability will inevitably ensue. In turn, this is likely to lead to increased litigation to determine the governing law. Since s 12 itself contains a rule of displacement largely based on objective factors, it is suggested that it is better for s 11(2)(c) routinely to point to a particular law, based on a particular point of contact. That law may then be displaced if, but only if, it is substantially more appropriate to apply another law under s 12.

17.143 The question then arises as to which are the most significant element or elements of the events for the purposes of s 11(2)(c). The tort of inducement of a breach of contract necessarily revolves around a contractual relationship and the inducement to breach a contract. The places where the contract is breached and the consequences of that breach are felt are 'significant elements' of the tort. Accordingly, the view of Cheshire and North should be endorsed that English law would apply today to the facts of *Metall*, as the place of breach and immediate damage to the claimant.

17.144 It is suggested that where the place of breach and the place where the claimant suffers immediate financial loss are not one and the same state, the place of breach should be regarded as the most significant element of the events for the purposes of s 11(2)(c). It has been argued throughout this chapter that the damage to the claimant should not be the principal focus of s 11(2)(c). It is the breach of contract induced by the defendant which is at the root of his tortious liability. Moreover, a party who takes it upon himself to induce a breach of a contract can scarcely argue that his expectations are defeated if the court applies the law of the place of breach of the contract.

The role of the law applicable to the contract; s 12 of the 1995 Act

17.145 One final question is whether, pursuant to s 12 of the 1995 Act, it might be substantially more appropriate for the law which governs the contract itself also to determine whether the defendant is liable in tort. One might argue that given that the law applicable to the contract determines if there has been a breach of contract,[300] it should also determine whether the defendant induced that breach. Moreover, use of the law applicable to the contract is unlikely fundamentally to undermine the expectations of the defendant or the claimant. However, whilst it is suggested that some weight should be attached to the law applicable to the contract, this should not be enough in and of itself to displace the general rule in s 11. There are two main reasons for this. First, the test in s 12 looks to a *country* whose law it is substantially more appropriate to apply; in other words, it is, at face value, a geographical test. It does not look directly at whether it

---

[300] Art 10(1)(c) of the Rome Convention.

is substantially more appropriate to apply some other *law* on the basis that a claim related to the present action in tort might be governed by a different law.[301] Second, the claim against a party who induced a breach of contract is separate from a claim for breach of conduct. It looks to the wrongful act of inducement. An analogy might be drawn with the decision in *Glencore International AG v Metro Trading International Inc (No 2)*.[302] In that case, s 12 of the 1995 Act was applied to a claim for wrongful interference with goods, where the claim involved the parties to the sales contract. This was on the basis that the claim arose from the relationship created between the parties by the sales contract and was closely related to it.[303] However, in respect of claims by the buyers under the sales contracts against third parties who had bought goods from the same seller, the court held that there was no basis to invoke s 12. Likewise, where a claim for inducement of breach of contract is brought, the parties will not both be privy to the sales contract and there is no clear basis for invoking s 12 so as to apply to the tort claim the same law which governed the sales contract.

5. NEGLIGENCE

Substantive Law Background

Claims for negligence[304] between a buyer and seller of goods are compara- **17.146** tively rare. They might arise, for example, from a failure by the seller to warn of a problem with the goods which comes to light after delivery. Alternatively, the seller might have a collateral obligation to assemble the goods.

In English law, questions of negligence liability are much more common **17.147** in connection with the carriage of the goods. We saw above[305] that where an owner's or charterer's bill of lading has been issued, there is a preliminary question of who is the other party to the contract and whether the consignee may sue in contract. In English law, this depends upon s 2 of the Carriage of Goods by Sea Act 1992. A consignor might sue in tort where, for example, the bill of lading has been transferred to the consignee and the consignor has been divested of his contractual rights. He might wish to do so if he is still on risk and if the consignee does not wish to sue for damages for the account of the consignor.

---

[301] But see the obiter remarks of Mance LJ in *Thierry Morin v Bonhams & Brooks Ltd* [2003] EWCA Civ 1802 at [23], [2004] IL Pr 24 at 398.

[302] [2001] 1 Lloyd's Rep 284, QBD (Comm); discussed in connection with the tort of conversion, above, paras 17.76–81.

[303] See also *Ennstone Building Products Ltd v Stanger* [2002] 1 WLR 3059 (decided on the basis of the common law choice of law rules in tort); noted Perkins, n 170 above.

[304] For a claim in respect of deception (alleged watering down of wine), see *Re An Italian Cargo of Adulterated Wine* [1991] IL Pr 473, Oberlandesgericht, Koblenz.

[305] See above, paras 5.06–09, 5.15, 6.152–153, 14.03–05, 14.38–44.

Classification

17.148   There can be no real doubt that a claim for the tort of negligence, brought on its own, will be classified as tortious.[306] The fact that the action might be combined with a *separate* claim for breach of contract should not alter this fact.[307] However, where a claim is brought for breach of contract and for negligence, but the obligation breached arises from the same facts, it may prove more difficult to classify the negligence action.[308] In *Source Ltd v TUV Rheinland*,[309] the court was faced with concurrent claims by a buyer for breach of contract and negligence in respect of quality control inspection of goods by the defendant. It held that the claims must both be classified as matters relating to contract for the purposes of Article 5(1) of the Brussels Convention. However, it is questionable whether this decision is correct and it was doubted obiter by Toulson J in *Raiffeisen Zentralbank Osterreich AG v National Bank of Greece SA*.[310] The House of Lords in *Kleinwort Benson Ltd v Glasgow City Council*[311] stated that, for the purposes of Article 5(1) of the Brussels Convention, 'a matter relating to contract' had to concern the performance of a contractual obligation. A claim for the tort of negligence may be based upon the same *facts* as the claim for breach of contract, but it is clearly not based upon the performance of the contractual obligation itself. It is suggested that on facts such as those in the *Source* case, the claim for the tort should be classified for choice of law purposes as tortious.[312]

17.149   However, matters are less straightforward where the issue is whether a single[313] domestic law claim should be classified as contractual or tortious for choice of law purposes. This issue is most likely to arise in the context of carriage of goods. It is suggested that the following approach should be taken. First, the applicable law of the contract should determine who are the parties to the contract, what rights and obligations they have and

---

[306] *Edmunds v Simmonds* [2001] WLR 1003, QBD; *Hulse v Chambers* [2001] 1 WLR 2386, QB and *Roerig v Valiant* [2002] 1 Lloyd's Rep 681, CA. It has been so classified numerous times at common law, most notably, of course, in *Boys v Chaplin* [1971] AC 356 itself. The same classification has also been taken for the purposes of service out of the jurisdiction under the tort ground: *Monro (George) Ltd v American Cyanamid and Chemical Corp* [1944] KB 432, CA; *Distillers Co (Biochemicals) Ltd v Thompson* [1971] AC 458, PC (Australia); *Castree v ER Squibb & Sons Ltd* [1980] 1 WLR 1248, CA.
[307] Compare *Domicrest Ltd v Swiss Bank Corp* [1999] QB 548, QBD.
[308] Concurrent claims are considered separately in Ch 20.
[309] [1998] QB 54, CA.   [310] [1999] 1 Lloyd's Rep 408, 411.   [311] [1999] 1 AC 153.
[312] This situation must be distinguished from the discussion above, paras 17.20–22, as to whether a *single domestic law cause of action* may be classified as contractual for Rome Convention purposes and tortious for the purposes of the 1995 Act. In the present case, there are two different domestic law causes of action and each should be classified separately.
[313] In *Source* there was more than one claim.

at what point those rights and obligations are acquired and divested.[314] The justification for this is that where there is a contractual relationship, Article 1(1) of the Rome Convention states that it 'shall apply'.[315] If, by that law, there is a contractual relationship, then the claim should be classified as contractual and not tortious and the rules of the Rome Convention applied. If, however, there is no such relationship, then the claim should be classified as tortious and the rules of the 1995 Act applied.

The Governing Law of a Claim for Negligence

17.150 It is difficult to generalize as to the governing law for negligence claims, given the wide ranging contexts in which they might arise in the sales arena.[316] Nevertheless, some conclusions can be reached.

All elements occur in a single state

17.151 If the act of negligence and the damage which results both occur in a single state, that state's law shall apply pursuant to s 11(1) of the 1995 Act.

Elements occur in more than one state

17.152 However, matters are more complicated if the elements of the events occur in different states. A number of particular problems arise, as we shall see below.

17.153 **Damage to goods** In the first place, it is important to determine whether the claim is in respect of *damage* to the goods resulting from the negligent act or omission. If so, the law of the place where the property was at the time that it was damaged applies, pursuant to s 11(2)(b). So, if it is alleged that the seller has assembled the goods in such a way as to have permanently damaged them, the law of the place of assembly should apply. If he also claims for consequent economic loss from being unable to use the goods, it was suggested above that s 11(2)(b) should still be applied to the entire claim, since the direct cause of damage to the claimant arises from the damage to the goods themselves.[317]

17.154 However the claimant might bring an action on the basis that the goods were not properly assembled, but not claim that they were 'damaged' by their negligent assembly. He may simply *solely* seek compensation for the

---

[314] See above, paras 14.03–05, 14.38–44, 14.49–58, 14.94–96.
[315] See above, paras 13.19–20.
[316] Compare *Base Metal Trading Ltd v Ruslan Borisovich Shamurin* [2002] CLC 322, [2003] EWHC 2419 (Comm), [2004] IL Pr 5, where Tomlinson J was not prepared to apply a mechanical test to identify the place where the tort occurred when applying the common law choice of law rules. See also the Court of Appeal's decision: [2004] EWCA (Civ) 1316.
[317] See above, paras 17.31–32.

cost of hiring another person to reassemble the goods correctly. In such a case, it is still likely that the law of the place of assembly will apply but this time it will be pursuant to s 11(2)(c).

17.155   Where a claim is brought in respect of damage to the goods, it will not always be so easy to determine where the property was when it was damaged. For example, in the case of an omission, such as a failure to warn, it may be difficult to identify the place where the property was at the time of the ongoing failure, if the goods are, or have been, in transit during this time. Section 11(2)(b) is silent as to what should happen if it cannot be determined where the goods were when they were damaged. It is suggested that the best approach is to hold in such a case that the goods are damaged in the place to which they were to be transported and that the law of this place should be applied.[318] It is in this state that the goods will be located and can be inspected at the point of discharge and its law may be said to have the greatest connection with the claim.[319]

17.156   **The role of the law applicable to the contract; s 12 of the 1995 Act**   Where a claim for negligence arises between two parties to a contract, it might be argued that the general rule under s 11 should be disapplied pursuant to s 12, on the basis that it is substantially more appropriate for the law[320] governing the contract also to determine the claim for negligence between the same parties.[321] Indeed, this may well reflect the expectations of the parties. By analogy to the decision in *Glencore International AG v Metro Trading International Inc (No 2)*[322] in the context of wrongful interference with goods, it could be argued that the claim only arises factually because the parties entered into a contractual relationship and that it is appropriate for the law applicable to the contract also to determine the claim in tort. However, it is suggested that overwhelming weight should not be attached to the law applicable to the contract[323] in relation to the tort of negligence.[324] For one thing, the claim in tort may not be combined with a

---

[318]   Compare *Viskase Ltd v Paul Kiefel GmbH* [1999] 1 WLR 1305.

[319]   See also the discussion of 'carriage claims' below, paras 17.157–162.

[320]   Briggs, n 52 above, at 35 points out that s 12 actually refers to the connections between different *countries*, not different *laws*. In principle, this makes reference to the law governing the contract more difficult to defend.

[321]   Briggs, ibid, at 33 comments that '. . . where the claim is one . . . which as a matter of domestic law could be advanced in contract as well as in tort, the tort claim could, one hopes, be held to be governed by the *lex contractus*, by reason of s. 12 of the 1995 Act if not otherwise'.

[322]   [2001] 1 Lloyd's Rep 284, QBD (Comm); discussed above, paras 17.76–81.

[323]   A view supported by the judgment of Moore-Bick J in *Base Metal Trading Ltd v Ruslan Borisovich Shamurin* [2002] CLC 322, QBD (Comm Ct). See also the Court of Appeal's decision: [2004] EWCA (Civ) 1316.

[324]   Contrast the discussion of conversion, above, paras 17.76–84, and of negligent misstatement and fraudulent and negligent misrepresentation, above, paras 17.120–121.

claim in contract. Furthermore, although it might be true to say that *factually* the claim may not have arisen but for the existence of a contractual relationship between the parties, the claim is *legally* freestanding. As Panagopoulos argues in a different context: 'One has to be careful to distinguish those cases where the existence of a particular relationship is an essential component of the issue in dispute and those where the particular relationship is a mere circumstantial fact'.[325] For example, the buyer may have a claim in respect of the negligent assembly of the goods. Where the act of assembly is undertaken by a third party, it is clearly a distinct legal obligation. If the act of assembly is undertaken by the seller, the claim for negligence is still legally independent from the contract of sale. It is suggested that the applicable law of the contract should accordingly be *a* relevant factor under s 12 of the 1995 Act[326] but that, in and of itself, it does not provide sufficient grounds to displace the general rule in s 11.[327]

Carriage claims In the context of carriage claims, it may not be clear **17.157** where the relevant act of negligence on the part of the defendant took place. Moreover, this place may or may not coincide with the place where the damage to the claimant occurs. If the claim is in respect of negligent unloading of cargo, then the law of the place of unloading will almost certainly apply under s 11(1), since all the elements of the events occur in one state.

In cases where the wrongful act and the damage occur in different **17.158** states, claims in respect of damage to the goods should be determined by s 11(2)(b). This will point to the law of the place where the goods were at the time of damage.

This works well enough when it is clear where the property was at the **17.159** time when it was damaged. However, it works much less well when a single place where the property was located cannot be identified. In *Réunion Européenne SA v Spliethoffs Bevrachtingskantoor BV,*[328] a consignee of pears sued a Dutch sub-contractor and the master of a ship carrying the goods by sea from Australia to Rotterdam and then by road to France. The cooling system on the ship had failed and the pears were overripe on

---

[325] G Panagopoulos, *Restitution in Private International Law* (Oxford: Hart, 2000), 150.

[326] However, if the contract contains a choice of law clause which is clearly intended to govern any claims in negligence arising between the parties to the contract, a court is likely to accord this very considerable weight: compare *Glencore International AG v Metro Trading International Inc (No 2)* [2001] 1 Lloyd's Rep 284, QBD (Comm); discussed above, paras 17.76–81.

[327] There is a hint of this in the judgment of Hirst QC (sitting as a Deputy Judge of the High Court) in *Thierry Morin v Bonhams & Brooks Ltd* [2003] IL Pr 25, QBD (Comm Ct), esp at [33], although he does not offer a final view on the matter (see [37]). See also the comments of Mance LJ in the Court of Appeal in *Morin* [2003] EWCA Civ 1802 at [23], [2004] IL Pr 24 at 398, to similar effect.

[328] Case C-51/97 [1998] ECR I-6511.

arrival. In applying Article 5(3) of the Brussels Convention, the European Court of Justice did not find it easy to say where the act giving rise to the damage had occurred. However, the place where the damage occurred was found to be Rotterdam, where the maritime carrier was to surrender the goods. It is suggested that this place is also likely to be considered as the place where the property was at the time when it was damaged under s 11(2)(b) of the 1995 Act for choice of law purposes. This approach has a number of advantages. It leads to the application of the law of a place which: (i) is easier to determine than the place of the 'act' which gives rise to damage; (ii) is likely to have a closer connection to the tort than the place of the 'act'; and (iii) is reasonably foreseeable and certain. There should be no question of France being treated as the place where the property was when it was damaged on facts such as those in *Réunion*. The sea carrier might not know the ultimate destination of the goods, which may in any event change mid-voyage; and even if he did, it is hard to see that this has much connection with the tortious liability of the sea carrier.[329]

17.160 The general rule may be displaced under s 12 in relation to carriage claims. As we have seen, s 11(2)(b) attributes importance to the place where property was when it was damaged, even though this place may be very difficult to determine. In contrast, some common law jurisdiction cases have held that the natural forum in a negligence case is the place where the *wrongful act* took place and not the place of damage.[330] Although the test in s 11(2)(b) is different to the natural forum test, it is suggested that the common law approach should be of some persuasive value when it comes to applying the exception under s 12 of the 1995 Act. Moreover, if the court looks to the place where the defendant's act of negligence occurred, this is consistent with the argument made throughout the chapter that considerable importance should be attached in tort claims to the acts of the defendant which are sufficient to expose him to potential liability in tort.

17.161 However, it is suggested that the law of the place of the negligent act can be given substantial weight under s 12 if, *but only if*, it is clear where the act occurred. In a case such as *Réunion*, the European Court of Justice noted that it would be almost impossible to determine where the act giving rise to the damage occurred. It would follow that the act of negligence itself would be given no weight on such facts for the purposes of s 12 of the 1995 Act.

17.162 Beyond that, should any other factors be considered relevant under s 12 in respect of a negligence claim concerning the carriage of goods? It is

---

[329] See also the discussion of 'damage to goods', above, paras 17.153–155.

[330] *George Monro Ltd v American Cyanamid and Chemical Corp* [1944] KB 432; *Castree v ER Squibb & Sons Ltd* [1980] 1 WLR 1248, CA; *Distillers Co (Biochemicals) Ltd v Thompson* [1971] AC 458, PC (Australia).

suggested that neither the law applicable to the contract of sale nor the law applicable to the contract of carriage should be given great weight. This would be to undervalue the separate nature of the claim in tort. The fact that the claim takes place against the factual backdrop of such contracts does not of itself mean that it is necessary, or substantially more appropriate, for this law to apply to a claim in tort. The place where the claimant suffers immediate damage may be a relevant factor. So too, a relevant factor might be that the parties are both domiciled in the same state, which is different to that whose law is applicable under s 11. However, personal connecting factors may be of less weight in respect of claims which are not based upon personal injury.[331]

Economic loss   Of course, a claim for the tort of negligence might not be **17.163** based upon damage to the goods. A simple example would be where the buyer wishes to sue the carrier for late delivery of the goods. Suppose that by the putative applicable law, the buyer has no claim in contract against the carrier and can sue only for the tort of negligence. In such a case, if elements of the events occur in different states, then s 11(2)(c) must be applied. This is likely to be the case, at least if the lateness of delivery cannot be attributed to a single factor occurring in a single state. Under s 11(2)(c), the most significant element of the events is almost certainly the negligent failure *to deliver* to the buyer on time. The applicable law will, accordingly, be the law of the state to which the carrier was bound to deliver the goods.

Property Law Issues

One final important point is that the applicable law of the tort may **17.164** require, in the context of carriage claims, that the claimant has legal ownership of the goods, or a possessory right in them, before he can sue in tort.[332] In the decision of the New Zealand High Court Auckland Registry in *The Seven Pioneer*,[333] the court had to apply the rule of double actionability to a claim for the tort of negligence, where the alleged tort took place in Indonesia. In determining whether a claim existed in tort by the law of the forum, New Zealand law, counsel for both parties proceeded on the basis that the Indonesian law on whether property had passed to the plaintiff was irrelevant. However, it is suggested that this is not a correct approach. It is inconsistent with that taken by English courts in respect of claims for wrongful interference with goods.[334] It undermines the

---

[331] Cheshire and North, 639–641.

[332] See *Leigh & Sillivann Ltd v Aliakmon Shipping Co Ltd* [1986] 1 AC 785.

[333] [2001] 2 Lloyd's Rep 57.

[334] See the discussion of the preliminary issue of property law in respect of wrongful interference with goods, above, paras 17.59–61.

paramount importance usually attached to the law of the *situs* in respect of property law issues.[335] Rather, it is suggested that *if* the law applicable to the tort requires the claimant to have a particular proprietary interest before he might sue for the tort of negligence, the law of the situs at the time at which that interest was allegedly acquired should be applied to determine if he has that requisite interest. If he does not, then he may not sue successfully for the tort; but if he does, then the law governing the tort should then decide whether the other ingredients of the negligence claim are made out.

IV. REFORM ON THE HORIZON: A PROPOSED EUROPEAN REGULATION ON CHOICE OF LAW FOR NON-CONTRACTUAL OBLIGATIONS (THE 'ROME II' REGULATION)

1. Proposed Choice of Law Rule

17.165 Plans are presently afoot for a Regulation on the Law Applicable to Non-Contractual Obligations[336] (the 'Rome II' Regulation).[337] The European

---

[335] See below, paras 18.29–38.

[336] Negotiations had begun to draw up a European Convention on the Law Applicable to Non-Contractual Obligations ('Rome II') [1999] OJ C19/1, at 10. These were postponed when it was decided to focus attention instead in the first instance upon revision of the Rome Convention and upon turning it into a Regulation. However, the harmonization of choice of law rules for non-contractual obligations is now firmly back on the European agenda. On 3 May 2002, the European Commission issued a Consultation on a Preliminary Draft Proposal for a Council Regulation on the Law Applicable to Non-Contractual Obligations: see http://europa.eu.int/comm/dgs/justice_home/index_en.htm. See also the 'Follow-up of the Consultation on a the draft Rome II Regulation', available at http://europa.eu.int/comm/justice_home/unit/civil/consultation/contributions_en.htm. On the UK Government's position on the draft Rome II Regulation, see www.lcd.gov.uk/consult/general/eurocom.htm. On 22 July 2003, the Commission published a Proposal for a Regulation of the European Parliament and the Council on the Law Applicable to Non-Contractual Obligations ('Rome II'), COM/2003/0427 Final, available at http://europa.eu.int/eur-lex/pri/en/lip/latest/doc/2003/com2003_0427en01.doc. See also the Report of the UK House of Lords European Union Committee, available at www.publications.parliament.uk/pa/ld200304/ldselect/ldeucom/66/6602.htm; and the amendments proposed by the draft report of the European Parliament Committee on Legal Affairs and the Internal Market (Rapporteur Diana Wallis MEP), available at www.aig.org/r2g/downloads/dw_romeii_draftreport_090304.pdf

[337] The Regulation will be made pursuant to Title IV of the EC Treaty. The UK and Ireland have an opt-out from initiatives made pursuant to Title IV of the EC, contained in Arts 1 and 2 of the Protocol on the position of the UK and Ireland. They have the right to opt-into initiatives on a case-by-case basis. Both states indicated at the Council Meeting (Justice and Home Affairs) of 12 March 1999 that they intended to opt-into measures relating to judicial co-operation in civil matters. Title IV does not apply at all to Denmark. For concerns as to the legal basis of the proposed Rome II Regulation, see the Report of the UK House of Lords European Union Committee, n 336 above, para 72.

Commission's Proposal for a Regulation of the European Parliament and the Council on the Law Applicable to Non-Contractual Obligations lays down in Article 3(1) a general choice of law rule in tort in favour of the state in which the damage arises, or is likely to arise.[338] This applies regardless of where the event giving rise to the damage took place and of where the indirect consequences of the event are felt.[339] The general rule refers to the place of direct damage.[340] This would appear to be the law of the place where a claimant sustains personal injury, or where his property is when damaged. In that sense, the general rule accords with the approach taken in s 11(2)(a) and (b) of the 1995 Act.[341] However, in the case of financial loss, such as where a claimant detrimentally relies upon the defendant's misstatement or misrepresentation, the general rule would appear to point not to the place of communication of that misstatement or misrepresentation, but to the state where the recipient invests his money and suffers direct loss. So, if a misstatement or misrepresentation is sent by mail from France to England, and detrimentally relied upon by the recipient to invest in German companies, German law would be the law applicable to the tort.

The advantage of such an approach is that the place of immediate damage may sometimes be easier to foresee than the state where the recipient received the advice. If, for example, the defendant had placed a misstatement or misrepresentation in a newspaper article, it may be very difficult to determine who might read that misstatement or misrepresentation. However, if the misstatement or misrepresentation related to the financial affairs of one or more German companies, then it is reasonably foreseeable to both claimant and defendant that the claimant might detrimentally rely on the misstatement or misrepresentation to invest in Germany, and suffer direct damage in the form of financial loss in Germany. **17.166**

Against this, the actions of the defendant which potentially render him liable in tort are completed at the stage of communication of a misstatement or misrepresentation. Whether the claimant detrimentally relies upon that advice is a matter outside his control. **17.167**

---

[338] It is immaterial whether the governing law is that of a European Member State bound by the Regulation: Art 2; criticized by the Report of the UK House of Lords European Union Committee, ibid, para 93.

[339] The doctrine of renvoi is excluded: Art 20.

[340] See the UK Government's position, paras 5 and 6, on the earlier Preliminary Draft Regulation, which had referred to the place where loss is sustained. See also the Report of the UK House of Lords European Union Committee, n 336 above, para 100.

[341] UK Government's position, para 8.

17.168 A further controversial aspect of the proposal is that it effectively ends the 'single tort' approach of English law to most torts.[342] Instead, the commentary to the Draft Regulation comments that '. . . where damage is sustained in several countries, . . . the laws of all the countries concerned will have to be applied on a distributive basis . . .'.[343] So, if a defendant makes a misstatement or misrepresentation which the claimant detrimentally relies upon to invest in three different states, it would henceforth be necessary to identify not one governing law, but three, even though the damage results from a single act of the defendant. This could create real difficulties. It may be extremely difficult to determine the extent of a party's loss in each state where he allegedly suffers damage. Moreover, a defendant who makes a misstatement or misrepresentation may find that it is detrimentally relied upon by different claimants in State A, State B and State C. Each of these states' respective laws will govern a claim in relation to direct damage suffered in that state. The result may be that the defendant is liable by, for example, the law of State A, but not liable by the laws of State B and C. It also means that the defendant will have to comply with the laws of each and every state in which he might conceivably cause some damage to a claimant.

2. EXCEPTIONS

Parties have the Same Habitual Residence

17.169 Article 3(2) states that: 'However, where the person claimed to be liable and the person sustaining damage both have their habitual residence[344] in the same country when the damage occurs, the non-contractual obligation shall be governed by the law of that country'. The Commission justifies this provision on the basis that: 'It reflects the legitimate expectations of the parties'.[345] However, the UK Government had pointed out that there is no obvious reason why the 'general' governing law should be displaced wherever the parties are habitually resident in the same state.[346] Personal connecting factors are not normally used in connection with tortious

---

[342] Save for the torts of defamation: *Berezovsky v Michaels* [2000] 1 WLR 1004. See also the Report of the UK House of Lords European Union Committee, n 336 above, para 120.

[343] Explanatory notes to Art 3(1) of the Draft Regulation.

[344] The meaning of 'habitual residence' is given in Art 19. For companies, it is normally the place where its 'principal establishment' is located. For individuals acting in the course of business, it is the place where the individual is established.

[345] Explanatory notes to Art 3(2) of the Draft Regulation.

[346] www.lcd.gov.uk/consult/general/eurocom.htm; para 10 of the UK Government's response.

liability. It would have been possible to have included the habitual residence of the parties as a material factor under a provision of general exception to the choice of law rule in Article 3(1). As it is, the habitual residence of the parties is given greater precedence than the law governing a pre-existing relationship between the parties, which, as we shall see, is simply a relevant factor in the court's consideration of the exception to the general choice of law rules in Article 3(1) and (2).[347]

A General Exception

There is then a more general exception to the rules stated above, capable **17.170** of displacing both the general rule in Article 3(1), which applies the law of the place of where the damage arises, and the provision in Article 3(2), which applies if the parties have the same state of habitual residence. Article 3(3) provides that:

Notwithstanding paragraphs 1 and 2, where it is clear from all the circumstances of the case that the non-contractual obligation is manifestly more closely connected with another country, the law of that other country shall apply. A manifestly closer connection with another country may be based in particular on a pre-existing relationship between the parties, such as a contract that is closely connected with the non-contractual obligation in question.

The exception clearly has echoes of s 12 of the 1995 Act in providing for the displacement of the governing law where the obligation is 'manifestly more closely connected' to another state.[348] Here, unlike s 12 of the 1995 Act, no list of relevant factors to which one might have regard in applying the Article 3(3) test is given.

In practice, the high threshold for the disapplication of the general rules **17.171** suggests that this provision is likely to be used rarely. Indeed, whereas the Rome Convention contains a series of presumptions as to the law governing the contract in the absence of choice[349] followed by an

---

[347] The draft report of the European Parliament Committee on Legal Affairs and the Internal Market, n 336 above, proposes merging Art 3(2) and Art 3(3), so that there is simply one flexible exception to the choice of law in Art 3(1) which may be triggered by a range of specified factors, one of which is the habitual residence of the parties. However, the Report of the UK House of Lords European Union Committee, n 336 above, para 177, questions whether this will lead to excessive uncertainty and promote litigation.

[348] The Preliminary Draft Regulation had also required that there be '... no significant connection between the non-contractual obligation and the country whose law would be the applicable law under paragraphs 1 and 2'. However, it is difficult to see how there can be *no* significant connection to the state where the claimant suffered immediate damage. If both parties are habitually resident in the same state, it is even harder to see how this can be shown. This clause was wisely dropped from the Commission Proposal.

[349] Arts 4(2), (3) and (4) of the Rome Convention; see above, paras 13.114–126.

exception,[350] the Commission deliberately set out the provisions of Articles 3(1) and (2) of the Draft Regulation as rules, not presumptions, so as to emphasize the exceptional nature of Article 3(3). Such an approach has the merit of providing enhanced legal certainty.

17.172   In principle, Article 3(3) allows the court to look at the law governing the contract in determining whether to apply the exception. 'By having the same law apply to all their relationships, this solution respects the parties' legitimate expectations and meets the need for sound administration of justice.'[351] The extent to which the law applicable to the contract may be a relevant factor in determining the application of the s 12 exception in the 1995 Act was considered above.[352] There, it was suggested that the applicable law of the contract should be of significance[353] where the claim in tort involves the parties to the sales contract. However, it should not normally[354] be important where the claim in tort is brought by or against a third party to the contract.

3. A RIGHT TO CHOOSE THE GOVERNING LAW OF A TORT

17.173   Article 10 is one of the most radical provisions of the Draft Regulation. Article 10(1) permits the parties expressly or impliedly to choose[355] the law applicable to a claim in tort.[356]

The parties may agree, by an agreement entered into after their dispute arose,[357] to submit non-contractual obligations ...[358] to the law of their choice. The choice must be expressed or demonstrated with reasonable certainty by the circumstances of the case. It may not affect the rights of third parties.

This is a fundamental departure from the traditional approach of English law. However, it appears to be one which the UK Government welcomes.[359] In so far as the parties' choice of law extends, on its true

---

[350]   ibid, Art 4(5); see above, paras 13.127–140.

[351]   Explanatory notes to Art 3(3) of the Draft Regulation.

[352]   At 17.76–84, 17.120–121, 17.145, 17.156.   [353]   Although not decisive.

[354]   The possible exception may be a claim for inducement of a breach of contract. The claimant and defendant might both reasonably expect that the law applicable to the contract might determine the defendant's liability in tort for inducing that breach.

[355]   The Commission's Explanatory notes to Art 10(1) comment that this is in line with recent legislative reform in Member States. The examples are given of s 6 of the Dutch Act of 11 April 2001 and s 42 of the German EGBGB.

[356]   Or to a claim in restitution; see below, para 19.100.

[357]   'Since the proposed Regulation does not allow an *ex ante* choice, there is no need for special provisions to protect a weaker party': Commission's Explanatory notes to Art 10(1).

[358]   Other than the obligations to which Art 8 applies. Art 8 is concerned with the infringement of intellectual property rights and is not relevant in the present context.

[359]   See the UK Government's position, para 22.

construction,[360] to claims in tort and is concluded after the dispute has arisen, the chosen law should govern the tortious claim. If the same law governs a party to a contract's liability both in contract and in tort, characterization problems are minimized, and, more importantly, the parties need only comply with one state's law. As such, this provision should be welcomed.

The worst excesses of choice of law shopping are curbed by Article 10(2), **17.174** which is in similar terms to Article 3(3) of the Rome Convention. It states that where the parties choose the law of State X to govern the tort, and all the other elements of the situation are located in State Y at the time when the loss is sustained,[361] the choice of State X's law stands, but is subject to the domestic[362] mandatory rules of State Y. The choice will also be subject to 'the application of provisions of Community law where the other elements of the situation were located in one of the Member States of the European Community at the time when the loss was sustained'.[363] The phrase 'the other elements of the situation' leads to uncertainty. It is not clear what constitutes an element of the situation, nor, more importantly, whether one, some, most or all elements of the situation must be located in a Member State in order for this provision to be triggered. Moreover, Article 3(3) refers to the other elements being located in *one* of the Member States.[364] It is not clear what should happen if the parties choose the law of a non-Member State to govern the tort claim and the situation is otherwise objectively connected to more than one Member State. The result is an unacceptable lack of clarity.

4. MANDATORY RULES AND PUBLIC POLICY

There is also a general right under the Commission Proposal for the **17.175** court to continue to apply the international mandatory rules of the

---

[360] The choice of law may be contained in a contract between the parties and may purport to specify the applicable law both for claims in contract and in tort. If so, and if there is a doubt as to whether the clause extends on its true construction to claims in tort, it could be argued that this is a matter for the applicable law of the tort to determine. However, since it is a term of a contract, it is arguable that its construction and scope should be determined by the applicable law of the contract, pursuant to Art 10(1)(a) of the Rome Convention.

[361] It is not clear why the phrase 'the loss is sustained' is used here, when the general rule in Art 3(1) refers to the where 'the damage arises'. It would have been preferable to use the same phrase in both contexts.

[362] The difference between domestic and international mandatory rules is explained above, paras 13.274–281.

[363] Art 10(3). Again, it is not clear why the phrase 'the loss is sustained' is used rather than 'the damage arises'.

[364] The matter is complicated significantly by the Commission's perplexing comment on this Article that it '. . . applies where all the elements of the case apart from the choice of law are located *in two or more Member States*': Commission's Explanatory notes to Art 10(3) (emphasis added). Art 10(3) expressly refers to the other elements being located in *one* of the Member States.

forum[365] and a residual right to disapply any law specified under the Proposal if it is manifestly contrary to the public policy of the forum to apply that law.[366]

17.176 More controversially, Article 12(1) states that:

> Where the law of a specific third country is applicable by virtue of this Regulation, effect may be given to the mandatory rules of another country with which the situation is closely connected, if and in so far as, under the law of the latter country, those rules must be applied whatever the law applicable to the non-contractual obligation. In considering whether to give effect to these mandatory rules, regard shall be had to their nature and purpose and to the consequences of their application or non-application.

This provision, which was not contained in the earlier Preliminary Draft Proposal, is similar in terms to Article 7(1) of the Rome Convention, in that it allows for the discretionary application of the international mandatory rules of a third state which is neither the forum nor the state whose law governs the claim. Unlike Article 7(1) of the Rome Convention, the present provision contains no right of opt-out.[367] If adopted, it could lead to great uncertainty in tort claims. It would be necessary to determine what factors are relevant and sufficient to create a close connection to a third state. Moreover, it would be necessary to determine whether to give effect to that state's rule, which may generate highly controversial questions in a subject such as tort, where issues relating to the parties' civil liberties may be raised. Given the United Kingdom's objections to applying a third state's international mandatory rules in contract, it is very difficult to see how these could be readily accepted in tort.[368]

5. Conclusion

17.177 This summary suggests that the Commission Proposal is a mixed blessing for choice of law in tort.[369] The place of immediate damage rule may be clearer than the rule in s 11(2)(c) of the 1995 Act, which makes reference only to the most significant element or elements of the events. Against this, the Commission's approach entails the potential application of a different law to each state where the claimant suffers damage from an act of

---

[365] Art 12(2).   [366] Art 22.

[367] The Commission offers little justification for this position. It merely comments that 'the Commission like most of the contributors during the written consultations sees no reason to exclude this possibility [of giving effect to the international mandatory rules of a third state of close connection] since references to foreign mandatory rules have been perfectly exceptional hitherto' (Explanatory Commentary to Art 12(1) of the Draft Regulation).

[368] See the Report of the UK House of Lords European Union Committee, n 336 above, para 146.

[369] On its application to e-commerce, see paras 21.203–210.

the defendant, rather than treating a single act of the defendant as giving rise to a single liability in tort to the claimant that is governed by one law. This may result in considerable complexity in determining where damage occurs, in unpredictable and inconsistent liability for the defendant and in selective framing of actions by the claimant. Moreover, the rule is somewhat claimant friendly, since the place where damage arises will often be the state where the claimant is habitually resident.

The habitual residence exception in Article 3(2) has some attraction, as it **17.178** points to a law which should provide a degree of enduring connection to a claim where other enduring connections may be absent. However, the law of the parties' habitual residence may have no real connection with the *events* which give rise to a claim in tort. Again, the parties may not even be aware that they share the same habitual residence.

The general exception in Article 3(3) is drafted in less detail than s 12 **17.179** of the 1995 Act and the relevant factors not elucidated. However, its explicit reference to the relevance of the applicable law of the contract may provide enhanced legal certainty.

The right to choose the applicable law provides a substantial counter- **17.180** weight to the arguably somewhat 'claimant friendly' nature of the general rule in Article 3(1)[370] and may provide predictability for both parties. However, this may be reduced somewhat by the need for the governing law to be agreed after the dispute has arisen. The result is a set of choice of law rules which continue to make planning as to which law might apply to the parties' potential liability in tort difficult.

It is perhaps the provision allowing for the application of a third state's **17.181** international mandatory rules which will lead to the greatest controversy and uncertainty. The connections that might exist with a third state will be difficult for both parties to determine. The prospect of applying a third state's mandatory rules in tort is not one that the United Kingdom can be expected to relish.

Overall, it is suggested that the Commission Proposal, in so far as it gives **17.182** a greater role to party autonomy than the 1995 Act, will in some respects lead to rules which are more pragmatic. Moreover, there is a virtue in harmonizing choice of law rules. This helps to prevent forum shopping for choice of law advantages. Unfortunately this is counterbalanced by the restrictions on the application of that law, the separate torts approach and the role given to third states' mandatory rules, all of which may lead

---

[370] In that the state where damage arises will often be the state where the claimant is resident.

to excessive unpredictability. Taken as a package, it is doubtful that the Draft Proposal will improve the overall state of choice of law in tort in England.[371]

V. CONCLUDING REMARKS

17.183 The above account has considered how the rules of the 1995 Act may be applied to specific torts that might be relevant to the sale of goods contract. Of course, there is a dearth of authority on these issues, so that the suggested approaches are by necessity speculative. Nevertheless, some general points emerge from the discussion. First, even where a tort claim arises between the parties to a contract, the legally distinct nature of the tort claim must be respected. Second, in determining the most significant element of the events for the purposes of s 11(2)(c), the primary focus should be on the acts of the defendant which are sufficient to expose him to liability in tort, rather than on the damage to the claimant. Third, once the applicable law has been determined by s 11, it should normally hold sway. In particular, the general rule should not be displaced under s 12 solely[372] because the contract is governed by a different law to that which governs the action in tort. Nor should personal connecting factors relating to the parties be given great weight under s 12 for claims which concern damage to property or pure financial loss. However, it must be recognized that it may sometimes be very difficult to ascertain the applicable law under s 11(2). It is also possible, especially where s 11(2)(a) or (b) applies, that this law will have a rather tenuous connection to the tort and that application of another law might be substantially more appropriate under s 12. In particular in the sales context, where the claim is brought in respect to damage to goods, s 11(2)(b) leads to the application of the law of the place where property is when it is damaged. However, this place may be largely arbitrary and, if so, the place where the defendant's act giving rise to potential liability in tort took place may be given considerable weight under s 12.[373]

---

[371] Compare the conclusions of the Report of the UK House of Lords European Union Committee, n 336 above, paras 184–204.

[372] Although this may be a material factor in the decision whether to invoke s 12: see above, paras 17.76–84, 17.120–121, 17.145, 17.156.

[373] At least where it is possible clearly to determine that place and where there is an enduring connection between the claim in tort and that state.

18

Property and Title: Choice of Law

I. INTRODUCTION

18.01 This chapter deals with property rights arising under and in connection with sales transactions.[1] The word 'property' is here used to connote the nature of those rights and not their object, namely, the goods[2] themselves. Sale is one example of a transaction giving rise to an individual transfer of property rights and, so far as it is individual in character, bears certain resemblances to other forms of individual transfer such as gift, presenting

---

[1] See generally Benjamin, Ch 25, esp 25–114 to 25–146; Cheshire and North, Chs 28 and 30; Dicey and Morris, Vol II, Chs 22 and 24.

[2] Although choice of law rules in property matters deal with movables and immovables, and do not follow domestic English law categories of real and personal property, choses in possession and choses in action, etc., it is both convenient and necessary whenever possible to refer to the subject-matter of the sale of goods contract as 'goods'.

also marked differences with universal transfers that arise in the case of death, bankruptcy and, in some countries, marriage. As a broad rule of thumb, an individual transfer is voluntary and partial in character, concerning only some of an individual's assets; a universal assignment, on the other hand, is involuntary and concerns the whole. In contrast with gift, a simpler transaction, the subject of sale deals not just with the transfer of property rights but also, as will be explained, with their creation. Furthermore, those property rights are varied in nature.

II. PROPERTY ISSUES IN SALE OF GOODS TRANSACTIONS

1. PROPERTY TERMINOLOGY

Property issues in sales law command a great deal of attention: the subject **18.02** of sale of goods is indeed a hybrid of contract and property law. Before its constituent parts are considered, a brief note on the terminology used in the Sale of Goods Act 1979 is in order.[3] First, the Act is concerned with the 'sale' of 'goods'. Goods are defined in the usual inclusive way so as to embrace tangible physical things and exclude land,[4] fixtures and documentary intangibles. Sale is defined as the transfer of the 'property' in goods from seller to buyer in return for a money consideration called the price. Property is defined in the Act as the general property as opposed to the special property of a bailee or a pledgee.[5] Hence, property corresponds to ownership, or is the nearest equivalent to absolute ownership in the personal property world of relativity of right[6] where 'title' is not deduced on the occasion of goods being sold.

The Sale of Goods Act is not concerned only with the passing of property. **18.03** As between buyer and seller, it deals also with certain rights of a possessory character, such as the unpaid seller's lien for the price and the right of stoppage in transit against an insolvent buyer.[7] The Act also makes mention of the unpaid seller's right of resale[8] which, when exercised, will certainly have proprietary consequences.

---

[3] See generally Bridge, *The Sale of Goods*, 35–45.
[4] Considerable difficulties, not often of great practical import, are caused by the natural and cultivated produce of the land: see) ibid, 22–26.
[5] Sale of Goods Act 1979, s 61(1).
[6] See *Costello v Chief Constable of Derbyshire* [2001] EWCA Civ 381, [2001] 2 Lloyd's Rep 216 (Auld LJ).
[7] Sale of Goods Act 1979, ss 38–46. [8] ibid, s 48.

2. Contractual Obligation and Property

18.04   The passing of property from seller to buyer is to be distinguished from the warranted strength of proprietary right that the seller undertakes to transfer to the buyer,[9] clearly a matter of contract law. To the extent that the seller is in breach of the statutory condition that he has a right to sell the goods,[10] the buyer has the usual right to elect between rejecting the goods and terminating the contract or retaining the goods and affirming the contract,[11] together with a claim for damages in both cases, the extent of which will depend upon which of these two elective actions is taken.

18.05   The Sale of Goods Act 1979 does not in fact lay an implied obligation on the seller actually to transfer the property in the goods to the buyer. The Act defers to the intention of the parties in determining when property passes[12] and lays down a series of presumptive rules in case the parties do not disclose their intention.[13] These rules presuppose the joint intention of the parties as applicable to the matter. Nevertheless, the Act does not say expressly *when*, or even *whether*, the seller comes under an obligation actually to transfer the property to the buyer. Nor, since it would seem that the buyer's acquiescence in the matter is necessary, does it make any corresponding provision for the buyer to accept a transfer of the property. Rather, once the seller expressly undertakes to 'sell' the goods to the buyer, this express undertaking will be treated as importing an obligation on the part of the seller, not merely to deliver the goods to the buyer against payment of the price, but also to transfer to the buyer the general property, the timing of which is then determined by the parties' intention.[14] The 'contract of sale' will mature into a 'sale' as and when the passing of property, that is, the conveyance, actually does takes place.[15] In this sense, therefore, a contracting party contracts as seller when he undertakes to transfer the totality of his property rights to a party who can correspondingly be called the buyer, and he gives that undertaking when the contract contains the key language of 'buy' or 'sale' or 'seller' or 'buyer'.

3. Movable and Immovable Property

18.06   Terminology is of importance too in the selection of a conflict rule to settle issues concerning property. Instead of the distinction that is drawn

---

[9] ibid, s 12(1).   [10] ibid.   [11] ibid, s 11(2), (4).
[12] ibid, ss 17–19.   [13] ibid, s 18.
[14] Save when the goods are unascertained (s 16) and even then subject to s 20A, which permits an undivided share in an identified bulk to pass to the buyer in accordance with a presumptive intention that is commensurate with the buyer's payment of the price.
[15] Sale of Goods Act 1979, s 1.

between real and personal property in domestic law, English conflict rules, broadly following civilian systems of law in this respect, differentiate in a similar but by no means identical way between movables and immovables.[16] In matters of property transfer, nevertheless, this shift of dichotomy is of no great significance in view of the powerful hold in both cases of the law of the *situs* principle. Goods will, it is submitted, for almost all practical purposes be movables.[17]

4. IMPORTANCE OF PROPERTY AND TITLE

In Chapter 7, it was seen that the most important feature of the passing of **18.07** property lay in the insolvency distribution to be made in the event of the seller or the buyer, as the case may be, becoming bankrupt or entering into an insolvent winding-up. Note was also taken of the importance within the Sale of Goods Act of property in matters relating to the recoverability of the price[18] and the incidence of risk.[19] The relationship between the passing of property and the existence of the right to immediate possession needed by a claimant to maintain an action in the tort of conversion was also considered.

As earlier stated too, the use of the word 'title' was best retained, as the **18.08** Sale of Goods Act itself did so, for dealing with trilateral issues arising where a seller or buyer, in possession of goods though not their owner, was able to pass title to a good faith purchaser free of the rights of the true owner. Treating A as the owner of goods, B as the person in possession of goods, whether by means lawful or unlawful, and C as the good faith purchaser, the question that always arises in title cases is which of two innocent parties is to prevail in a dispute over the goods resulting from B's dishonesty. Is it A, the true owner, or C, the good faith purchaser?

So stated, the proprietary disputes that arise out of the A-B-C relationship **18.09** have no necessary connection with the subject of sale of goods but should be seen instead as anchored in personal property law. Nevertheless, to the extent that transfer of title issues fall within the Sale of Goods Act and related legislation,[20] it is because there is a contract of sale either between A and B or between B and C, or indeed between A and B and B and C. B may agree to buy the goods from A and sell them on to C before paying

---

[16] *Freke v Carbery* (1873) LR 16 Eq 461; *Re Berchtold* [1923] 1 Ch 192; *Re Hoyles* [1911] 1 Ch 179.

[17] A possible exception is crops or other natural produce of the land to be severed. See Bridge, *The Sale of Goods*, 21–31. Unless otherwise stated, references to goods later in this chapter will be to movables for choice of law purposes.

[18] s 49.   [19] s 20.   [20] Sale of Goods Act 1979, ss 21–26; Factors Act 1889.

for the goods and acquiring the property in them from A. Or B may agree to buy in the same way before pledging the goods with C. Or B may acquire possession of the goods by means other than sale, in the capacity of a mercantile agent or possibly by theft, and then contract to sell them to C.

5. Transfer of Title in Substantive Law

18.10 Transfer of title issues arising in connection with sale, in the way described above, concern the circumstances in which the property rights of A, the original owner, are overridden in favour of C, the subsequent transferee, as a result of the actions of another party, B, intervening between the two of them. In English law, the basic rule is that the original owner prevails against the transferee—*nemo dat quod non habet*[21] —but there are nevertheless exceptional cases where a good faith transferee obtains from his counterparty, B, a title that defeats the title of the original owner. Other systems of law possess radically different rules of title transfer.[22] They also protect ownership rights in a quite different way. Whereas the common law invokes the property torts, notably conversion, in the protection of property rights—which compels a fused reference to tort and property conflict rules—other legal systems protect ownership rights through the medium of a proprietary vindication action.[23]

6. Bilateral (Property) and Trilateral (Title) Issues

18.11 It is useful to do as the Sale of Goods Act does and differentiate bilateral (two-party) and trilateral (three-party) issues by using the language of passing of property for the former and the language of transfer of title for the latter. Yet, as clear as the above distinction between bilateral and trilateral property issues might appear to be, it may in some cases be difficult to draw the line between the two. To take one example, suppose that a transaction is carried out in State A, where a sale and resale is recognized by that country's law as being valid on its face and as not giving rise to a security that has to be registered if the financier's interest in the goods is to be protected against third parties and against the insolvency representatives of the seller. The effect of the transaction is that the financier, who buys and then resells the goods to the original seller, under the terms of the resale leg of the agreement with the debtor, the original seller, reserves title to the goods until an enhanced price is

---

[21] ibid, s 21(1).   [22] e.g. the French Code civil in Art 2279.
[23] See above, paras 6.39–41.

paid. The goods are then removed to State B which, not differentiating between transactions entered into in State B or in some other country, requires sale and resale transactions to be registered as security agreements if the financier's reservation of title is to be successfully asserted against third party transferees from the debtor and against general creditors of the debtor.[24] No registration is effected. Under State B's law, the goods are available for distribution to the insolvent debtor's creditors. If the debtor, who under such agreements remains in possession of the goods, had sold those goods to a third party in State B, who then brought the goods into England, a trilateral title issue would have arisen, but this would seem not to be the case where a simple bankruptcy distribution takes place.

7. RESERVATION OF TITLE

Included within the subject of passing of property, however, is that of so-called reservation (or retention) of title clauses, whether in their simple or extended versions. It is useful to divide such clauses informally into two types—simple and complex reservation of title clauses. A simple reservation would apply only to the original goods supplied, though it might extend beyond payment of the price due for those goods to all moneys owed to the seller by the buyer. Complex reservation clauses are more extensive in their reach. To the extent that they go beyond the original goods themselves and treat the money proceeds of the goods in the buyer's hands the subject of a reservation of title, such clauses are not dealing with the subject-matter of the sale as such and indeed are venturing into personal property law. To a lesser extent, the same might be said for clauses vesting new goods, manufactured with the seller's goods, in the seller. It is right to deal with complex clauses in this chapter, nevertheless, because of their close contextual link with contracts of sale. **18.12**

8. ANCILLARY PROPERTY ISSUES IN SALE OF GOODS

Apart from the passing of property between seller and buyer, other proprietary matters arising under the Sale of Goods Act include the exercise of a seller's so-called real remedies, in the event of a buyer's non-payment, the availability to the seller of an action for the price in those cases where the property has passed and the availability of specific performance as a **18.13**

---

[24] For the position where goods are then brought into England and Wales, see the discussion below, paras 18.35–36.

remedy in lieu of damages.[25] There are also property issues between buyer
and seller with which the Sale of Goods Act does not deal at all. One is
the effect of rejection of the goods and termination of the contract on the
location of the property in the goods, in particular its revesting in
the seller,[26] whether it is the seller or the buyer who is terminating the
contract. This issue is closely connected in English law to the unpaid
seller's right of resale. Another issue is whether the terminating buyer
has a right to exercise a lien over the rejected goods as security for the
repayment of the price.[27]

18.14 Property issues that are capable of causing acute concern in the conflict of
laws include the practice of separate dealings with goods and documents.
Their physical separation means that they might be dealt with separately
and simultaneously in an adverse way so as to generate title conflicts.
Similarly, the practice of issuing multiple original copies of bills of lading
poses a risk of similarly inconsistent dealings. The Sale of Goods Act is
somewhat lacking in detail on documents representing the goods.

18.15 Property matters connected with sale but not disposed of in detail in the
Sale of Goods Act include the powers of insolvency office-holders, such as
a liquidator or trustee-in-bankruptcy, to dispose of goods in the bankrupt's possession,[28] and the powers of enforcement officers, such as bail-
iffs, to dispose of goods in execution of judgment. In these various
instances, disputes may arise concerning the rights of the true owner, if
this person is not the bankrupt, the company in liquidation or the judgment debtor. One of the questions presented in such cases is whether a
transferee, taking from the office-holder, acquires a good title at the
expense of the true owner.

9. Artificial Sale Transactions

18.16 In some instances, the characterization of a sale transaction will have an
important bearing on the passing of property. For example, suppose that
goods are made the subject of a sale by A to B with an immediate leaseback from B to A, or with a resale of the goods by B to A at an agreed
interval, thus being the subject of what appears to be a double sale. The
purpose of a transaction of this type is not to convey goods to B for the
latter's use and enjoyment, but rather to use the form of sale as a means of

---

[25] Sale of Goods Act 1979, ss 38–49 and 52.
[26] See *RV Ward Ltd v Bignall* [1967] 1 QB 534.
[27] This is not recognized in English law (see *Kwei Tek Chao v British Traders Shippers* [1954] 2
QB 459) but is recognized under Art 2–713(3) ('security interest') of the US Uniform
Commercial Code.
[28] Bridge, *The Sale of Goods*, 484–485.

raising finance for A that will not appear on A's balance sheet and will not be registrable as a company charge or individual security bill of sale. To the extent that such a two-limbed transaction is open to re-characterization as a charge or security bill of sale,[29] issues may arise as to the governing law.

The question of re-characterization is most likely to arise in the course of **18.17** insolvency proceedings. Insolvency is capable of affecting sales transactions in other ways too. This will happen where goods are sold at an alleged undervalue in the period preceding bankruptcy or company liquidation. To the extent that the buyer has received goods at an undervalue within the scope of the relevant insolvency legislation, or is the beneficiary of a fraudulent conveyance, the buyer is liable to be expropriated in favour of the seller's creditors.[30] An order might be made for goods received to be returned. The same consequence may arise under similar legislation dealing with fraudulent conveyances.

III. CHOICE OF LAW THEORIES

Over the centuries, a range of possible rules have been canvassed in **18.18** English law and in continental European systems for dealing with property issues concerning movables.[31] The reasoning employed in many of the English cases is often unsatisfactory, which is particularly troublesome given the lack of a critical mass of case law. In particular, it is a feature of English cases that courts have, from an abundance of caution, been keener to amass connecting factors in support of the application of a particular country's law than to choose among them.[32] This may do something to reinforce the chosen law in a particular case but it does nothing for the coherent development of the conflict of laws. Sometimes, foreign law has not been pleaded in cases where light might have been shed on

---

[29] See *Re Curtain Dream plc* [1990] BCLC 925.

[30] Insolvency Act 1986, ss 238–240, 339–341.

[31] English choice of law rules adopt a distinction between movables and immovables that is largely but not entirely coterminous with the domestic law distinction between real and personal property. For practical purposes, the categories of tangible personalty and tangible movables are the same. See Cheshire and North, Ch 28.

[32] See P Lalive, *The Transfer of Chattels in the Conflict of Laws* (Oxford: Clarendon, 1955) 76–77. This approach may be fostered by the litigants themselves in the process of amassing arguments in favour of their preferred law. See, e.g. Millett J in *Macmillan Inc v Bishopsgate Investment Trust plc (No 3)* [1995] 1 WLR 978, 999, where he cites Macmillan's reliance upon a number of connecting factors as cumulatively favouring New York law. In considering the English mortgage of a ship, Page Wood V-C in *Simpson v Fogo* (1863) 1 H & M 195, 71 ER 85, felt no need to differentiate among the law of the domicile of the owner, the law of the place of the contract where the mortgage was granted and the law of the *situs* since they were one and the same.

the issue of the governing law.[33] No choice of law conclusions can be drawn from such cases. Over the centuries, three principal choice of law rules have been canvassed in English law: namely, the personal law of the owner; the law of the transfer (or of the place of the transfer, so far as it may be different from the law of the transfer); and the law of the *situs*. These will now be considered in turn.

1. The Owner's Personal Law

18.19 In English law, the personal law of the owner is the law of his domicile. This rule goes back to the mediaeval Italian statutists and has exercised a long attraction in England. Its influence in the field of property reached its zenith in Lord Loughborough's well-known dictum that it was a 'clear proposition' of English law, as well as of any other system of law having 'the semblance of science', that personal property, having 'no visible locality', is subject to the personal law of the owner. In Lord Loughborough's view, this rule applied to both successions as to 'transmission . . . by the act of party'.[34] This rule had the considerable support of Story[35] and of Pothier[36] but has received only limited support in other cases dealing with individual transfers of property.[37]

18.20 A case that is sometimes advanced as supporting the personal law[38] is the difficult Scottish House of Lords decision in *North Western Bank v Poynter Son and MacDonalds*.[39] The court held that English law was the governing law but, because it had not been pleaded and proved, Scots law was applied on the familiar ground that it was deemed to be the same as English law. The facts of the case are not entirely clear but there was a pledge of shipping documents between a Liverpool merchant and a Liverpool bank. The goods were in transit to a Scottish port but it seems they had not arrived at the time of the pledge. It seems too that the goods had been shipped in Liverpool. Under the terms of a trust receipt, the bill of lading had been released to the pledgor merchant that he might take delivery and deal with the goods on their arrival in Glasgow. In English

---

[33] e.g. *Badische Anilin und Soda Fabrik v Basle Chemical Works Bindschedler* [1898] AC 200; *Kursell v Timber Operators & Contractors Ltd* [1927] 1 KB 299.

[34] *Sill v Worswick* (1791) 1 H Bl 665, 690.

[35] *Commentaries on the Conflict of Laws* (Bigelow (ed), 8th edn, Boston: Little and Brown, 1883), 537: 'A transfer of personal property, good by the law of the owner's domicile, is valid wherever else the property may be situate'.

[36] *Des Choses*, §3.

[37] *Liverpool Marine Credit Co v Hunter* (1868) LR 3 Ch App 479, 483. See also the authorities listed by M Wolff, *Private International Law* (2nd edn, Oxford: Clarendon, 1950) 508–509. It receives very qualified support from Channell J in *Dulaney v Merry* [1901] 1 QB 536.

[38] Lalive, n 32 above, 43; Wolff, n 37 above, 509.   [39] [1895] AC 56.

law, such a temporary release takes effect as a deemed continuing pledge of the bill of lading, with the pledgee acquiring upon the surrender to the ship a proprietary interest in the goods themselves as well as in the proceeds of any dealings with them.[40]

In the Scottish equivalent of interpleader proceedings, the court had to **18.21** deal with competing claims of the pledgee and of a Scottish creditor who, as the Scottish equivalent of a garnishor, claimed an interest in a debt that represented the proceeds of the goods. The outcome turned upon whether the pledgee had a prior property right in that debt; the court held that it did. In the course of reaching this conclusion, Lord Watson was of the view that English law applied because the case turned upon whether a fund, namely the debt, was owned by one or other of two Englishmen, namely the Liverpool merchant (pledgor) or the Liverpool bank (pledgee). This reasoning is equivocal, as, to a greater extent, is the proposition of Lord Herschell that English law should govern because the pledge transaction concerned a merchant and a bank in England.[41] This latter statement is more consistent with the application of the law of the place of the transfer than with the application of the personal law.

2. PROBLEMS WITH THE PERSONAL LAW

Reasons for not adopting the law of the domicile include its lack of trans- **18.22** parency, a particularly pointed criticism in view of the technical features of domicile in English law that differentiate it from the more visible habitual residence. In addition, there is the further inconvenience that an application the of law of the owner's domicile may compel a reference to another law if the ownership of the transferor himself is disputed. There is, moreover, for transferees, the not inconsiderable problem of discovering the content of the owner's domiciliary law. The rule therefore discourages commerce.[42] Suppose also that the separate undivided parts of a bulk are disposed of by their various owners, each with a different personal law. Given the complexity of the multilateral proprietary relationship of the various owners of an undivided bulk, the impracticability of applying these different personal laws is manifest.[43] On the other side of the balance sheet, the practical merits of the law of the domicile rule are hard to discern. Its main support comes from maxims that are more

---

[40] *North Western Bank Ltd v Poynter* [1895] AC 56; *Lloyds Bank v Bank of America National Trust* [1938] 2 KB 146; *Re David Allester Ltd* [1922] 2 Ch 211.

[41] The third member of the House of Lords, Lord Macnaghten, simply concurred.

[42] G Zaphiriou, *The Transfer of Chattels in Private International Law: A Comparative Study* (London: Athlone Press/University of London, 1956) 24; Wolff, n 37 above, at 510.

[43] See *Glencore International AG v Metro Trading Inc (No 2)* [2001] 1 Lloyd's Rep 284.

resonant than reasoned, such as *mobilia sequuntur personam*[44] and *mobilia ossibus inhaerent*.[45] The former maxim may have some limited claim to represent reality in the case of an itinerant's immediate personal effects, while the latter maxim has been derided as apt for dealing with a set of false teeth (rarely the subject-matter of a conflicts question).[46] Support for the law of the domicile, however, comes in a dictum concerning the vital national interests of a trading nation whose citizens employ their capital abroad.[47] None of this, however, amounts to very much.

3. Merits of the Personal Law

18.23 The personal law, however, is not without its merits. Perhaps the strongest reason for favouring the personal law is inherent in that category of case where the law of the domicile still governs, namely, universal assignments.[48] Because a bankrupt or a deceased may have or leave personal property located in more than one country, it is convenient to have a single rule that embraces the whole assignment, to the trustee-in-bankruptcy or executors of the will as the case may be. This same reasoning might justify an extension of the rule to those cases where a business is sold by means of a transfer not of the shares but of the business assets themselves. The assets of the target company may be located in a number of jurisdictions, so that compliance with all of these laws might be most inconvenient when the alternative method of selling the business, by disposing of the shareholding, would suffer no such drawback. Since it would present undue complications to differentiate on the facts cases where personal property is sufficiently dispersed for the personal law to be applied and cases where it is too concentrated for this to be done,[49] convenience favours the application of the personal law in all cases of universal assignments. There is no likelihood, however, that the approach adopted for universal assignments will be used for business asset sales.

4. The Law of the Transfer

18.24 A weightier contender for the role of governing law, which has attracted a substantial measure of support, is the law of the transfer. As originally proposed, this is the law of the place where a transaction takes place.

---

[44] Movables follow the person.
[45] Movables are attached to the body or (more poetically) movables are rooted in one's bones.
[46] Wolff, n 37 above, at 510.
[47] *Philips v Hunter* (1795) 2 H Bl 402, 406, cited in Wolff, n 37 above, at 510.
[48] For recognition of the law of the domicile in such cases, see *Bank voor Handel en Scheepvaart NV v Slatford* [1953] 1 QB 248, 257.
[49] Where the personal law and the law of the *situs* are likely to be one and the same in any case.

Nevertheless, just as the law of the place of contracting has fallen out of favour in modern times as the law governing a contract, so too the law of the transfer has emerged on the ground that the law that is the closest, or is chosen by the parties to apply, to a transfer has a stronger claim than the law of the place of the transfer. The law of the transfer, in the case of a sale transaction, will be almost certainly the law applicable to the contract of sale. There is the additional factor that the law of the *place* of a transfer is artificial and hard to discover, at least in those cases where the transfer itself is abstract and consensual.[50] In the English law of sale, it is the locking together of the consents of seller and buyer that brings about the passing of property[51] rather than any physical act of delivery of the goods, though the latter will in many cases evidence the intention of the parties.[52]

This point emerges in a different context in *Henry Kendall & Sons v William* **18.25** *Lillico & Sons Ltd*[53] where the House of Lords considered the application to a CIF contract of a statute importing, '[o]n the sale for use as food for cattle or poultry of [a scheduled] article', a warranty that it be suitable for such use.[54] It had been decided in an earlier case[55] that the statute did not apply where the property in the goods passed at a time when the goods were outside the territorial limits of the United Kingdom. Following this case in the court below in *Kendall*,[56] Diplock LJ stated that all sales of goods take place where the goods are located at the time when the property in them passes from seller to buyer.[57] He rejected the argument that the sale took place at the point where shipping documents, including the bill of lading, were taken up by the buyer.[58] In the House of Lords,

---

[50] Where the parties are situated in different countries, the offer and acceptance problems that surfaced in the contract formation case of *Benaim & Co v Debono* [1924] AC 514 would equally render it difficult to determine the place of the act (*locus actus*). This would be a particular problem now 'with the explosion of communications technology': Aldous LJ in *Macmillan Inc v Bishopsgate Investment Trust plc (No 3)* [1996] 1 WLR 387, 425.

[51] Sale of Goods Act 1979, ss 17–19.

[52] By virtue, for example, of the presumptive rule, in s 18 *Rule 5* of the Sale of Goods Act 1979 that, where the parties have not otherwise expressed their intention, the property in unascertained goods passes when the goods are unconditionally appropriated to the contract by one party with the assent of the other, conventionally interpreted in the case law as occurring on delivery (see *Carlos Federspiel & Co SA v Charles Twigg & Co Ltd* [1957] 1 Lloyd's Rep 240), with a statutory presumption to that same effect when delivery is made to a carrier (*Rule 5(ii)*).

[53] [1969] 2 AC 31.   [54] Fertilisers and Feeding Stuffs Act, s 2(2).

[55] *CEB Draper & Son Ltd v Edward Turner & Son Ltd* [1965] 1 QB 424.

[56] sub nom *Hardwick Game Farm v Suffolk Agricultural & Poultry Producers Association Ltd* [1966] 1 WLR 287.

[57] ibid, at 328.

[58] In reaching this conclusion, Diplock LJ gave the example of specific goods the property in which could not pass at the contract date, in accordance with the English rule in s 18 *Rule 1*, if the goods were situate in Germany and German law required delivery for the property to pass. In his Lordship's view: 'This can only be because the property passes at the place where the goods themselves are': ibid, at 330.

Lord Morris was clearly of the view that a sale took place in London if the shipping documents were exchanged there against the price,[59] though he conceded that, if the goods were located in a foreign country at the time, 'there might be questions whether there were provisions of the local law which would affect the passing of property'.[60] This view, it should be noted, is consistent with the bill of lading standing in for the goods (subject to the concession that the law of the *situs* of the goods might still have a part to play). It does not go so far as to recognize that a sale might occur in the country where the consenting seller and buyer happen to be if this differs from the country where the goods are situate. This further step, however, is taken by Lord Pearce, who gives the example of two Englishmen, a seller and a buyer, dealing with goods owned by the seller and located abroad. In Lord Pearce's view, the sale takes place in England 'where the contract takes effect and the property passes from vendor to purchaser'.[61] *Kendall* was a case concerning the territorial application of an English statute. Whilst it may afford assistance in identifying the law of the place of the transfer, it does not directly support the application of that law in property matters.

5. Judicial Support for the Law of the Transfer

18.26   Treating, for the remainder of this section, the law of the transfer and law of the place of the transfer as one and the same, there is nevertheless a substantial measure of judicial support elsewhere for this rule. In *Alcock v Smith*, Kay LJ, when rejecting the claims of the law of the domicile, stated that the governing law is 'the law of the place where the transfer takes place'.[62] Although he was speaking in general terms of 'personal chattels', however, the case concerned a bill of exchange where the place of transfer and the *situs* of the bill are necessarily the same since transfer consists of indorsement (if the bill is not in bearer form) coupled with delivery.[63] The strength of support for the law of the place of the transfer will always be hard to evaluate in those cases where that law is the same as the law of the *situs*.[64] This was the position in *Hooper*

---

[59] In accordance, no doubt, with the intention of the parties that the property pass at that time.

[60] [1969] 2 AC 31, 101.   [61] ibid, at 119.

[62] [1892] 1 Ch 238, 267. To the same effect is Vaughan Williams LJ in *Embiricos v Anglo-Austrian Bank* [1905] 1 KB 677, 683, which, like *Alcock v Smith*, is a case dealing with bills of exchange and not tangible movables. See also *Lee v Abdy* (1886) 17 QBD 309, 312 (assignment of a life insurance policy).

[63] This is physical delivery and not the notional delivery associated with the making of a deed.

[64] The two, according to Staughton LJ in *Macmillan Inc v Bishopsgate Investment Trust plc (No 3)* [1996] 1 WLR 387, 399, will 'almost invariably be the same'.

v Gumm,[65] where a ship mortgaged in the United States was sent to be England to be sold. The rights of the purchaser against the mortgagee fell to be determined by English law as the law of the country where 'the contract was made and completed'.[66] Support for the law of the place of the transfer is also to be found, as seen above, in *North Western Bank v Poynter Son and MacDonalds* and (less clearly) in a dictum of Lord Parker where, in relation to intention and the passing of property, he states the applicability of the law 'with reference to which the parties enter into the particular transaction'.[67]

A case that is consistent with the application of the law of the place of the **18.27** transfer is *Inglis v Usherwood*,[68] where goods had been loaded in Russia on board a vessel chartered to an English buyer, the effect of which was that the unpaid seller had no right of stoppage in transit under English law. Such a right, however, was recognized in Russian law. When the buyer failed, the court recognized the unpaid seller had validly exercised his right of stoppage by a notice given to the ship's master in London prior to his releasing the goods to the buyer.[69] Now, this case can be also be seen as favouring the law of the *situs*, but only if the right of stoppage is seen as crystallizing at the place where a voyage commences and as not being determined according to the law of the place where the unpaid seller actually exercises the right. Indeed, Grose J remarks that, had English law applied, the delivery to the ship chartered by the buyer would have been tantamount to delivery to the buyer himself. Delivery, however, occurred in Russia under whose law the goods were still to be considered in transit.[70] On the other hand, if the transaction is seen as having been concluded in Russia, as Lord Kenyon CJ remarks,[71] this supports the application of Russian law as the law of the place of the transfer. The case, therefore, is inconclusive on the identity of the choice of law rule but probably inclines more to the law of the place of the transfer.

---

[65] (1867) LR 2 Ch App 282.

[66] ibid, at 289 (Turner LJ). To similar effect is Lord Chelmsford LC at 286.

[67] *The Parchim* [1918] AC 157, 161. See also a dictum of Scrutton LJ in *Republic de Guatemala v Nunez* [1927] 1 KB 669, 689, which seems (but not at all clearly) to prefer the law of the place of the transfer to the law of the *situs* in relation to a transaction valid by the former law and invalid by the latter: 'I have not been able to find . . . any clear statement of the principles governing the question whether a transaction in personal property . . . invalid by the law of the country where the transaction takes place may be valid by the law of the place where the property is situate'. But Scrutton LJ may be referring to a case where the contract falls away under its governing law but the passing of property is governed by a different law under which the contract is treated as valid.

[68] (1801) 1 East 515, 102 ER 198.

[69] The seller had taken the additional precaution of having the goods consigned under bills of lading to his own order.

[70] (1801) 1 East 515, 524, 102 ER 198, 202.

[71] ibid. To the same effect is Lawrence J: (1801) 1 East 515, 525, 102 ER 198, 202.

18.28 Until recently, authority favouring the law of the place of the transfer
seemed scarcely any greater than authority for the law of the domicile but
in *Macmillan Inc v Bishopsgate Investment Trust plc (No 3)*,[72] a case involving
various pledges of shares by a nominee holder in breach of trust, the
claims of the law of the place of the transfer were presented by Millett J. He
first of all treated as a self-evident proposition[73] the applicability in property matters of the law with the closest and most real connection with the
transaction. So far, this would not eliminate the law of the *situs*, since that
law might in many cases be the law thus identified, but rather would
indicate that the law of the *situs* might have to compete with other laws. In
Millett J's opinion, questions of priority between the beneficial owner of
the shares and the pledgees fell to be determined by the law of the place of
the transfer ('the law of the place where the transaction took place on
which the later assignee relies for priority over the claim of the original
owner'). This was because it was 'appropriate in principle that the policy
rules adopted by a particular system of law should be applied to all transactions taking place within its territory, but not elsewhere'.[74] Nevertheless,
he accepted that the law of the *situs* was entrenched in the case of movables,[75] possibly with good reason, and that in a case involving a pledge of
share certificates, like the present, the law of the place of the transfer and
the law of the *situs* would be one and the same.[76] Millett J was seeking,
above all, to avoid the application of the law of the place of incorporation
of the company.[77] His judgment would therefore appear to do little to
assert the claims of the law of the place of the transfer in the case of
movables, except in so far as it might justify a departure from the law of
the *situs* in some, perhaps rare, cases where that law did not have the
closest connection to the transaction disposing of the property interest.

6. THE LAW OF THE *SITUS*

18.29 In the modern law, the law of the *situs* is overwhelmingly favoured as the
governing law.[78] This is not to say, however, that the law of the *situs*

---

[72] [1995] 1 WLR 978, 1008.

[73] ibid, at 991 ('It is impossible to quarrel with the contention . . .').   [74] ibid, at 994.

[75] A conclusion borne out also by the judgments in the Court of Appeal: [1996] 1 WLR 387.

[76] [1995] 1 WLR 978, 995. This was because he took the *situs* from the location of the share
certificates themselves.

[77] The law of the place of incorporation (or possibly of the place where the register of
shares was kept according to Auld LJ at [1996] 1 WLR 387, 411) was applied in the Court of
Appeal as the law of the *situs* of the shares.

[78] It has been described as a rule 'long established beyond challenge': *Air Foyle Ltd v Centre
Capital Ltd* [2002] EWHC 2535 at [42], [2003] 2 Lloyd's Rep 753. It is said by Lord Nicholls and
Lord Hoffmann to be the rule that is 'normally' applied to the transfer of tangible movable
property in *Kuwait Airways Corp v Iraqi Airways Co (Nos 4 and 5)* [2002] UKHL 19 at [13] and
[161], [2002] 2 AC 883 at 1077, 1115.

should reflexively apply to all aspects of property transfer or that it should apply to all types of property right. Before the application of the law of the *situs* is critically evaluated, the cases supporting it will first be considered. There are recognized exceptions to the law of the *situs*: these will be discussed below.

In *Cammell v Sewell*,[79] a Prussian ship carrying a cargo from the Russian **18.30** port of Onega to Hull struck certain rocks off the Norwegian coast. The consignees of the cargo gave notice of abandonment to their underwriters, who paid as for a total loss, so that they personally acquired title to the cargo. Despite the protests of the underwriters, the deals were then sold at auction in Norway by the ship's master pursuant to Norwegian judicial proceedings. By Norwegian law, the sale by the master passed a good title to the purchaser. By English law, there was no necessity justifying the sale with the result that title remained in the underwriters.

In a title dispute between the purchaser and the underwriters, the **18.31** Court of Exchequer Chamber ruled in favour of the purchaser. First, it was for Norwegian law, the law of the *situs* of the goods at the time of the sale to the purchaser, to determine whether title passed to him. Apart from its rejection of the law of the domicile of the owner as the governing law, *Cammell v Sewell* also rejected the personal law of the consignee. In the case of a general ship with consignees in different countries, purchasers in the country where the sale takes place could be assured of no secure title if a cargo were sold and different laws had to be consulted to determine the proprietary effect of the transfer as it related to different parts of that cargo. The law of the ship's flag was also rejected.[80] Furthermore, it made no difference that the presence of the goods in Norway was accidental and not consented to by the owner. Although much of the discussion of Norwegian law centred on the question whether the master had authority to sell the cargo despite the absence of necessity, the majority of the court clearly concluded that title passed under Norwegian law to the purchaser on the judicial sale.[81]

---

[79] (1858) 3 H & N 617, aff'd (1860) 5 H & N 728 (Cam Sc). Cf *Freeman v East India Company* (1822) 5 B & Ald 617, 106 ER 1316, where, in a similar case involving the sale of the remaining cargo of a wrecked ship by its master, the court with one exception (Best J) made no reference to the law of the place (the Cape of Good Hope) where the cargo was sold.

[80] (1860) 5 H & N 728, 747 (Cockburn CJ).

[81] ibid, at 746 (Crompton J and Cockburn CJ). Of the six members of the court, Byles J dissented.

18.32 It followed from the acquisition by the purchaser of a good title under Norwegian law that the purchaser's property was not divested when the goods were brought subsequently into England. This is but a corollary to the first proposition but it testifies to the court's sense of comity. There was a keen awareness that the transfer of title to property arising out of a domestic sale in England, whether because that sale took place in market overt or was conducted by a landlord pursuant to a distress, could have an expropriating effect on the true owner just as much as the Norwegian sale in the present case. Subject to one reservation, *Cammell v Sewell* is strong authority for the proposition that title can pass under the law of the *situs* of movables so as to defeat the title of the true owner, even though the presence of the movables in the *situs* country is accidental, and that this title will be recognized in England. The case makes no claims for the private international rules of other states. The reservation expressed in the case concerns the good faith of the purchaser who, it was assumed, did not know that the sale was carried out by the master without the owner's authority.[82]

18.33 The decision in *Cammell v Sewell* was approved by the House of Lords in *Castrique v Imrie*,[83] which concerned the *in rem* effect of a French judgment directing the sale of British a ship lying in a French port. The title acquired by the buyer was held to be good in England against the original owner. The ship was in the lawful control of the French State and the court had acted within its jurisdiction in ordering the sale.[84] In Lord Blackburn's

---

[82] ibid, at 743 (Crompton J).   [83] (1869–70) LR 4 HL 441.

[84] cf *Simpson v Fogo* (1863) 1 H & M 195, 71 ER 85, where the court refused to recognize the title of the buyer of a ship, sold under the order of a Louisiana court, as against a prior mortgagee of the ship under a mortgage governed by English law. In refusing to recognize the validity of the English mortgage as against Louisiana creditors, because it was a non-possessory form of security, the Louisiana court had been guilty of a 'perverse and deliberate refusal to recognize' (at 247 and 107) English law under which the mortgagee's title had been validly created. According to Page Wood V-C, 'our own citizens must be protected from the loss of their property' (at 243 and 106). The court sought to distinguish *Castrique v Imrie* (at an earlier stage in its proceedings) on the ground that the sale in that case flowed from an in rem decree of the foreign court whereas the sale in *Simpson* flowed from the execution of a writ of *fieri facias*. In most cases, it will not matter whether title is claimed in England directly under a foreign judgment in rem or pursuant to a transaction sanctioned by a court in the country of the *situs*. In the latter case, an English court will recognize the title under the law of the *situs* principle. But a distinction between the two might become relevant if it were necessary for a claimant (the first claimant) to rely upon a *res judicata*, issuing out of an *in rem* judgment, against another (the second claimant) who claims title pursuant to later proceedings in another jurisdiction and then seeks to have that title recognized in England (see generally *Air Foyle Ltd v Centre Capital Ltd* [2002] EWHC 2535, [2003] 2 Lloyd's Rep 753). If the second claimant was bound in respect of the first, *in rem* judgment by *res judicata* in an English court, then the effect of proceedings in the second jurisdiction, even if the movables were at that time situate in the second jurisdiction, ought not, despite the law of the *situs* principle, to be recognized in England. See further above, paras 18.51–54.

view, the recognition of the French judgment in rem 'is in truth a branch of that more general principle' laid down in *Cammell v Sewell*.[85]

7. MODERN AUTHORITIES

In more recent times, *Cammell v Sewell* was followed in *Winkworth v* **18.34**
Christie Manson & Woods Ltd.[86] Certain Japanese works of art, stolen in England, were sold in Italy to the second defendant before being brought back to England. The plaintiff sought a declaration that the works of art had at all times been his property, which depended upon whether he could demonstrate a right to their immediate possession. This in turn prompted the trial of a preliminary issue, namely, whether English domestic law or Italian domestic law applied to the sale in Italy. By English law, the second defendant would probably not have acquired title to the works of art. For the purpose of the present proceedings, the court was prepared to assume that under Italian law he would have done so.

The plaintiff's attempt to distinguish *Cammell v Sewell* centred on the **18.35**
argument that it should not be applied to goods removed from country A and returned to A after a divesting transaction in country B. Whilst the application of the law of the *situs* might be justified by its effective control over movables when they remain in the country of the *situs*, this principle of effectiveness had no part to play in a case like the present where the movables had been brought back to England. The plaintiff further argued that the principle of security of titles demanded an exception to the application of the law of the *situs* so that country A could protect title recognized under its own laws.[87] The court regarded this as the plaintiff's strongest point but nevertheless concluded that security of title was just as

---

[85] The same approach is taken, though at greater length, by Gross J in *Air Foyle Ltd v Centre Capital Ltd* [2002] EWHC 2535 at [44], [2003] 2 Lloyd's Rep 753.

[86] [1980] Ch 496. A case where the court in fact applied the law of the *situs* (though the reasoning of Lord Blackburn is also consistent with the application of the law of the place of the transfer) to an unauthorized pledge of a bill of lading is *City Bank v Barrow* (1880) 5 App Cas 664. *Inglis v Robertson* [1898] AC 616, a decision of the House of Lords on a Scottish appeal (discussed below because it raises issues concerning documents of title), is consistent with the law of the *situs* rule. In *Re Anziani* [1930] 1 Ch 407, 420, a case on the assignment of choses in action, there is a strong dictum of Maugham J favouring the application of the law of the *situs* to goods. The same approach was also taken in the Scots case of *Todd v Armour* (1882) 9 R (Ct of Session) 901 (title to goods, stolen in Ireland and acquired by a purchaser in Ireland, could not have been acquired under similar circumstances under Scots law). In *City of Gotha v Sotheby's (No 2)* The Times, 8 October 1998, it was agreed between the parties that the transfer of title to a painting was governed by the law of the *situs* at the time of the transfer (subject to five exceptions, discussed below, none of which was relevant on the facts).

[87] Logically, there is little reason to distinguish this case from the following: goods are removed from country A, taken to country B, where the purchaser acquires an overriding title, and then brought to country C, neither A nor C in their domestic laws recognizing an overriding title in these circumstances.

important to the innocent purchaser in country B and stated in strong terms that commercial convenience demanded the application of the law of the *situs* rule to proprietary rights in movables. The original presence of the movables in country A might be unknown and unknowable to the purchaser in country B, so that the purchaser could not protect himself by making the necessary enquiries. Commercial certainty would be sacrificed if qualifying factors of the type mentioned by the plaintiff were to be added to the law of the *situs* rule.

18.36 On its facts, *Winkworth* is barely distinguishable from *Cammell v Sewell* but the application of law of the *situs* even to the sale of a stolen painting returned to the country (England) from which it had been stolen, shows the strength of commitment to the law of the *situs*. The absence of a voluntary act on the part of the owner to connect the goods to country B, even the 'surreptitious' removal by someone else of the goods to country B, was no reason to depart from *Cammell v Sewell*. The court in *Winkworth* was unwilling to introduce an uncertain public policy exception to the law of the *situs* rule. British subjects were not entitled to special treatment and English title transfer rules had no claim to superiority over the corresponding Italian rules.

18.37 In the lengthy and systematic judgment of Moore-Bick J in *Glencore International AG v Metro Trading Inc (No 2)*,[88] the law of the *situs* received further strong support. The case concerned the first tranche of complex litigation (phase 1) following the insolvent collapse of MTI, which carried on the dual business of storing oil in its vessels and of selling oil. The proceedings concerned a group of claimants that had delivered oil for storage to MTI, the oil later being sold on by MTI to certain purchasers. For the purposes of the litigation, it was assumed that the claimants all had title to the oil immediately prior to its delivery to MTI's vessels in Fujairah territorial waters, that these vessels remained at all times in Fujairah territorial waters and that the sale and delivery to the purchasers took place in Fujairah. As the law of the *situs*, Fujairah law would therefore apply to two principal property questions: first, whether the claimants lost title to their oil when it was commingled in MTI's vessels and, second, whether the purchasers acquired title to the oil when purchasing it from MTI under the contracts of sale.

8. The Law of the *Situs* and Property and Title Issues

18.38 In the judgment of Moore-Bick J, Fujairah law applied to both property questions. Having recited the general arguments in favour of the law of

---

[88] [2001] 1 Lloyd's Rep 284.

the *situs*,[89] the learned judge stated categorically that no distinction should be drawn, for present purposes, between bilateral property matters, such as the passing of property between seller and buyer, and trilateral matters, such as disputes between an owner and a transferee when an intermediate party in possession of the owner's goods unlawfully sells them to the transferee. To do so would be 'highly anomalous' since '[c]onsistency of principle' requires that the same law be applied to both bilateral and trilateral property matters. Moore-Bick J acknowledged that the leading authorities did not deal with bilateral property matters but observed that his view of bilateral property transfers had also been taken (in an *obiter* passage) by Diplock LJ in the *Hardwick Game Farm* case.[90] In that case, Diplock LJ gave the example of a contract for the sale of specific goods made in England and governed by English law, the goods being situate in Germany whose law requires there to be delivery in order for the seller's ownership to pass to the buyer. According to his Lordship, the provision in s 18 *Rule 1* of the Sale of Goods Act, that the property in specific goods passes at the contract date, could not apply to those goods situate in Germany for it was a matter for German law, the law of the *situs*, to determine when the property in them could pass.

9. CRITICISM OF THE LAW OF THE *SITUS* FOR PASSING OF PROPERTY

It is submitted that, despite the force of the above passage in *Hardwick* **18.39** *Game Farm*, together with the detailed conclusions of Moore-Bick J, the door has not been finally closed on an attempt to differentiate bilateral and trilateral property matters (though it will take a higher court to reopen the distinction).[91] First, to say that a difference would be 'highly anomalous' is a bare conclusion and not a reason. The passing of property in English law is framed as a contractual matter dependent upon the consent of the parties,[92] apart from the case where that consent cannot be effectuated because the goods are unascertained.[93] The transfer of title, in matters involving third parties, obviously cannot be modelled upon bilateral consent. Furthermore, as regards '[c]onsistency of principle', there is no logical reason why a law chosen by the seller and the buyer should not determine *when* property passes between them, with a different law, the law of the *situs*, determining the strength of the buyer's title against third parties. The two property issues are quite different.

---

[89] Discussed below, paras 18.51–54.
[90] *Hardwick Game Farm v Suffolk Agricultural Poultry Producers Association* [1966] 1 WLR 287, 330.
[91] But see above, paras 13.220–222.   [92] Sale of Goods Act 1979, ss 17–19.
[93] ibid, s 16.

18.40 In the *Glencore International AG* case,[94] Moore-Bick J added the further observation that, in a bilateral case, the rights and duties of the parties could be settled as a matter of contract instead of property between them. That is undoubtedly true, as far as it goes, which is as far as the seller's insolvency if the buyer has paid or the buyer's insolvency if the seller has delivered. Insolvent liquidation or bankruptcy is the event that tests the proposition whether, in a bilateral setting, the parties ought to be free to stipulate for the application of a law to the proprietary transfer that is not the law of the *situs*. According to English domestic law, which should assist in shaping English choice of law rules unless a clear reason to the contrary can be demonstrated,[95] a vesting of the bankrupt's assets in the trustee-in-bankruptcy (or the surrender of an insolvent company's assets to the control of its liquidator) is not to be equated with a transfer of assets involving a third party.[96] The trustee or liquidator stands in the shoes of the insolvent party[97] and indeed represents that party. Moreover, arguments in favour of facilitating the security of a transferee's title have no application in this case: any assignment is involuntary and universal, in contrast with the particular and voluntary transfer that arises in the trilateral cases discussed above.

18.41 Insolvency is quite possibly the most important event in defining the magnitude of transaction risk. Any choice of law rule that assists in the calculation of that risk will facilitate productive exchanges. The present rule, which denies autonomy to the parties in determining the law governing property matters arising *inter se*, threatens to inhibit such transactions and therefore invites reappraisal by a higher court.[98]

18.42 Furthermore, the subjection of property matters arising between seller and buyer to the law of the *situs* creates some difficulty in defining the boundary between contract and property in those cases where the contract and the property rules lead to different systems of law. Defining the sphere of property in generous terms could be disruptive of those sale

---

[94] [2001] 1 Lloyd's Rep 284.

[95] As (presumably) was done when proprietary choice of law rules were subjected to the civilian distinction between movables and immovables rather than to the domestic English distinction between real and personal property.

[96] Moore-Bick J in *Glencore International AG v Metro Trading Inc (No 2)* [2001] 1 Lloyd's Rep 284 at [34] meets this point by stating that it is for the law of the *situs* to determine whether a transaction affecting title takes place.

[97] *Madell v Thomas* [1891] 1 QB 230 (Kay LJ).

[98] For the importance of autonomy in bilateral cases, see M Whincop and M Keyes, *Policy and Pragmatism in the Conflict of Laws* (Aldershot: Ashgate, 2001) 110–112 (supporting the parties' right to choose the law applicable to the transfer), though the authors note that autonomy is also served by the law of the *situs* since, subject to transaction costs, the parties are free to move the goods to a friendly *situs* and thereby opt into 'efficient property rights' ('The property's mobility enables the parties to choose the desired law of the *situs*, even where there are constraints on party autonomy on choice of law').

transactions where there is no third party interest in sight. For example, where the seller is not paid prior to or upon delivery as required by the contract, there seems every reason to leave it to the law applicable to the contract to determine whether the seller may exercise a lien or right of retention and not to complicate matters by a search for the content of the law of the *situs*.

This outcome—that the law of the contract and not the law of the *situs* **18.43** should apply—can be achieved in an indirect way by classifying the seller's behaviour not as the exercise of a property right but as a contractual non-delivery of the goods to which the buyer's failure to pay amounts to a defence for the seller.[99] In English law, payment and delivery are presumptively mutual and concurrent conditions under s 28 of the Sale of Goods Act 1979, which expresses in alternative contractual language the effect of a seller's lien.[100] The same expedient, however, is not possible for the unpaid seller's right of stoppage, since delivery has occurred (to the carrier as the agent of the buyer)[101] and the right permits the seller unilaterally to reverse that delivery. Some recognition that the law applicable to the contract, or other law chosen by the parties to apply to property matters *inter se*, may sensibly apply to some extent, at least in bilateral cases involving goods, is evident in the coverage of the Vienna Convention 1980. The Convention, as a uniform law on the international sale of goods which explicitly excludes property matters from its scope,[102] nevertheless permits an unpaid seller, where appropriate, to decline delivery and to exercise the right of stoppage in transit.[103]

In a similar vein, there is much in the proposal that the characterization of **18.44** an issue as proprietary or contractual should not be carried out *a priori* in an abstract way when dealing with liens and other 'special claims'. Instead, the court should make 'empirical decisions' about the desired outcome of the characterization process, which ought to lead to the law applicable to the contract giving rise to the special claim rather than to the law of the *situs*.[104]

---

[99] See also above, paras 13.217–222.
[100] M Chesterman, 'Choice of Law Aspects of Liens and Similar Claims in International Sale of Goods' (1973) 22 ICLQ 213, 224.
[101] Sale of Goods Act 1979, s 32(1).   [102] Art 4(b). See Ch 16.
[103] Arts 30 (the seller is bound to deliver 'as required by the contract') and 71(2) (stoppage arising out of the right to suspend contractual performance).
[104] Chesterman, n 100 above, at 221–223. Chesterman, drawing on Zaphiriou, n 42 above, cites the example of an FOB Hamburg contract on English law terms. The seller's lien is classified as proprietary in English law (and so subject to German law as the law of the *situs*), but as contractual law by German law (and therefore governed by English law). The result, supposedly, would be that the seller could not exercise a lien at all. But surely an English court would apply German law without regard to how German law would classify the seller's right and would give practical effect to the recognition in German law of the seller's lien.

10. Problems with the Law of the *Situs* in Hybrid Cases

18.45 The reference to stoppage in transit[105] above brings up another point in
favour of subjecting at least some bilateral property issues to the law
applicable to the contract. Consider a case where goods are delivered to a
carrier at a loading port in State X in circumstances where the seller's right
of stoppage in transit may be exercised upon the appropriate conditions
being satisfied. When the goods arrive in the destination port in State Y,
the seller issues a stop notice to the carrier. Under the law of State Y, the
delivery to the carrier at the loading port took place in circumstances that
deprived the seller of the right of stoppage. This, of course, is the case of
Inglis v Usherwood[106] where, as seen above, England was State Y and the
exercise by the seller of the right of stoppage conferred by Russian law
was held to be effective.

18.46 A similar issue would arise if, under the laws of State X, but not of State Y,
an unpaid seller were given a right to rescind the contract for non-
payment, the effect of which was to revest in the seller any property right
transferred to the buyer. If property rights are seen as having revested in
the seller,[107] despite the goods at the time of rescission being in State Y, this
conclusion too would be inconsistent with a law of the *situs* rule. Now, the
virtue of subjecting such issues to the law applicable to the contract is that
it avoids a territorial problem which would or should arise under a law of
the *situs* rule.[108] Rights of rescission of the contract with a revesting effect
and rights of stoppage are alike in that both the creation of the right and
its exercise must be considered. If the creation occurs in State X and the
exercise in State Y, this dispersal of creation and exercise gives rise to an
incompletely constituted law of the *situs*. It is not for State X to determine
whether the right has been validly exercised in State Y, just as it is not for
State Y to determine whether the right was validly created in State X.[109]
The law of the *situs* rule, so far as it is recognized in English law, does not
accommodate a hybrid reference to two laws.[110]

---

[105] See also above, paras 13.227–229.   [106] (1801) 1 East 515.
[107] As it was in *Re Hudson Fashion Shoppe* [1926] 1 DLR 199 (Ont) with which cf *Re
Satisfaction Stores* [1929] 2 DLR 435 (Nova Scotia).
[108] See further the discussion of rescission above, paras 13.230–232, and below, paras
19.57–61.
[109] In practical terms, this difficulty can be avoided if the law of the later (not the earlier)
state, State Y, applies extra-territorially to the creation of the right in State X: see the discussion below, paras 18.112–118, of conditional sales.
[110] But compare the approach in the Hague Trust Convention, which distinguishes
between the constitution of the trust (a matter for the law of the *situs*, since matters of
constitution are excluded from the scope of the Convention) and the operation of the
trust (which is governed by the settlor's chosen law: Art 6). See J Harris, *The Hague Trusts
Convention*, (Oxford, Hart, 2002).

11. PASSING OF PROPERTY IN SUBSTANTIVE LAWS

18.47 A final argument in favour of a more sophisticated approach, separating bilateral and trilateral matters, concerns the relationship between the substantive rules of a legal system and its choice of law rules. In respect of rules for the passing of property in sales and similar transactions, national legal systems may broadly be classified as belonging to one or other of two types: those that allow property to pass in accordance with intention, a group to which English and French law belong, and those, like German law, that take as their starting point the requirement of delivery.[111] The difference between these types is nevertheless diminished by exceptions. English law, for example, treats delivery (in effect) as the event upon which property passes as a matter of presumed intention in those cases where the parties have not otherwise expressed their intention.[112] German law recognizes a number of exceptions to its delivery rule, including the constructive delivery that occurs when a seller declares that it is holding goods for the buyer. The existence of consensual and mixed systems of proprietary transfer tends against a rigid choice of law rule based on the law of the *situs*, given the lack of harmony between substantive law and the proffered choice of law rule favouring the law of the *situs*.

18.48 The great merit of the law of the *situs* rule is its supposed practicality, which is based upon its effectiveness.[113] Yet it is capable of producing problems that would not arise if the governing law were, for example, the law applicable to the contract. An example, not dissimilar to the above examples of stoppage in transit and rescission of the contract, concerns goods the subject of a contract of sale that at the date of the contract are in Germany, which applies a delivery rule, but are to be delivered by the seller to the buyer in France, which applies a contract date rule.[114] Once again, the problem of territorial dispersal presents itself. French law cannot apply to the goods so long as they remain in Germany and German law does not apply once the goods arrive in France. On the face of it, there is a vacuum, with no single law of the *situs* in complete command of the situation and no possibility of a hybrid law of the *situs*.

12. LAW OF THE *SITUS*: FURTHER PROBLEMS

18.49 This is by no means the last of the problems presented in bilateral matters by the law of the *situs*. To return to the conjunction of property

---

[111] See Zaphiriou, n 42 above Ch II.   [112] Sale of Goods Act 1979, ss 17–18.
[113] See below, paras 18.51–52.
[114] See F Hellendall, 'The Res in Transitu and Similar Problems in the Conflict of Laws' (1939) 17 Canadian Bar Rev 7 (Part I) and 105 (Part II).

and contract discussed above, an acute problem is created where a contract is valid according to its applicable law but the proprietary transfer is void under the law of the *situs* which, operating a pure consensual mode of property transfer, treats ownership in identified goods as passing to the buyer at the contract date. In consequence, under that law, the voidness of the contract leads automatically to the voidness of the proprietary transfer.[115] For example, suppose that a contract of sale is governed by English law but the goods are situate in France. The contract fails to stipulate the price, but an English court would infer a duty to pay a reasonable price, while a French court would treat the contract on that account as a nullity. If French law were to apply as the law of the *situs* so as to invalidate the proprietary transfer, then the expansive operation of French property law would come at the expense of English law as the law applicable to the contract. At first sight, if the effective control of the law of the *situs* is as strong a consideration as the authorities suggest, this expansive effect may have to be tolerated. On the other hand, the French courts are bound by a network of treaty and similar obligations[116] to give full effect to the choice of an applicable law in contract. These obligations should therefore prise apart contract and property in a way that does not happen in purely domestic French transactions. On balance, it is submitted, an English court would be justified in regarding the French law of proprietary transfer as *pro tanto* modified by these treaty obligations,[117] with the result that, the contract being valid according to its applicable law, the proprietary transfer would be regarded as taking place at the contract date in accordance with French law.

18.50 Difficulties of this kind would be avoided if bilateral property issues were disposed of according to the law applicable to the contract (in our example, English law).[118] This approach appears broadly to be supported by the Hague Sales Convention 1986 which refers to the law applicable to the contract issues concerning the validity and effect as between the

---

[115] This is not the case in English sale of goods law. See *Singh v Ali* [1960] AC 167; *Westdeutsche Landesbank Girozentrale v Islington London Borough Council* [1996] AC 669.

[116] The Rome Convention on the Law Applicable to Contractual Obligations 1980 and the Hague Sales Convention 1955.

[117] The process is similar to renvoi, discussed below, paras 18.68–70.

[118] If it were thought undesirable to bring in, by way of the contract approach, the artificial presumption in the absence of choice in favour of the law of the place of business of the characteristic performer in the Rome Convention (Art 4(2)), an alternative approach would be to explode the property rule so that the law of the *situs* were confined to trilateral matters. In the case of bilateral matters, resort could be had to the law of the transfer, which, in the absence of a choice by the parties, could be the law of the place where the goods are situate at the time of the purported transfer.

contracting parties of reservation of title clauses, the consequences of non-performance of the contract and the consequences of contractual nullity and invalidity.[119] The consequences of non-performance could, for example, include the revesting in the seller of the property in the goods. In conclusion, if English law followed through from its intention-based approach in domestic sale transactions, it might allow intention to play a part in determining the choice of law rule governing the passing of property between seller and buyer. Driven by its fundamental commitment to freedom of contract, English law has long recognized that same freedom in permitting parties to choose the applicable law in contract matters. Consequently, such a development would be true to the basic principles of English law. A distinction between the bilateral conveyance and the trilateral effect of a conveyance is also to be seen in the American Restatement on Conflict of Laws.[120] For a bilateral conveyance, the governing law is the local law of the state with the closest connection to the parties, the chattel and the conveyance, with freedom given to the parties to select that law.[121] In many cases, this law will in fact be the law of the *situs*. In the case of trilateral issues, the governing law is 'usually' the law that would be applied by the law of the place where the chattel was situate at the time of conveyance,[122] a formulation that would allow exceptions to the English rule of the law of the *situs* to be incorporated in the main body of the rule.

13. ASSESSING THE CASE FOR THE LAW OF THE *SITUS*

Apart from any distinction that might be drawn between bilateral and **18.51** trilateral matters, the strength of the arguments in favour of the law of the *situs* has to be assessed. Those arguments are conventionally reduced to two. First, taking what appears to be the strongest argument in favour of the law of the *situs*, it is said that the 'practical realities of control' favour the law of the *situs*.[123] Hence, any disposition of property issues by another law would be ineffectual in the face of adamantine opposition from the law of the *situs*. Carried to its logical conclusions, this argument would require a court to take judicial notice of a foreign law of the *situs* and apply that law whether the parties pleaded it or not. There is no support for such an approach in the case law. Furthermore, in terms of the control exercised by the law of the *situs*, its grip is clearly stronger in the

---

[119] Art 12(e), (f) and (h); see above, paras 15.109–121.   [120] §§ 244–45.   [121] § 244.
[122] § 245. For renvoi, see below, paras 18.68–70.
[123] Moore-Bick J in *Glencore International AG v Metro Trading Inc (No 2)* [2001] 1 Lloyd's Rep 284, 294, echoing Lalive, n 32 above, at 104–105 ('effective control', 'actual control').

case of immovables than it is in the case of movables. The latter are fugitive, especially where they have no national strategic value and are not subject to export quotas or licences. In English domestic law, it is very rare for an *in rem* judgment to be given in respect of goods; the conventional remedy is an award of damages which may not at all need to be enforced in the *situs* state.

18.52 In addition, the continuing grip of the law of the *situs* cannot be justified in terms of efficacy where the movables in question have been moved from the country where the relevant transaction occurred and are at the time of the suit located in another country, for example in the forum state. Any control once exercised by the law of the *situs* is a thing of the past by the time that movable property is removed to another country. To continue to apply the law of the *situs* on the ground that it once exercised control only begs the question: if continuing effect is ascribed to an historical control, once the movables have been removed from the *situs*, it is only because the law of the forum freely accepts the governance of the law of the *situs*, rather than fatalistically acceding to it on the ground that there is no practical alternative. If the practical realities of control had any absolute meaning, the choice of law rule would be that the governing law is the law of the *situs* of the goods at the date of the proceedings. This would encourage forum shopping with the goods in hand and is not a plausible rule.[124] It is also inconsistent with leading authorities where, in addition, that later law of the *situs* was the English law of the forum.[125] There is something almost undeveloped about the *situs* rule, particularly when it is expansively applied. A world-wide judgments convention, to a lesser extent a regional regime like the Brussels I Regulation,[126] might encourage a more nuanced approach to choice of law in property matters since a state's obligation to recognize foreign judgments would do a great deal to reduce the tyranny of the law of the *situs*. Without applying a *situs* rule, the concerns of the law of the *situs* could be addressed by a provision, akin to Article 7(1) of the Rome Convention, that defers to the essential concerns of a closely connected law like the law of the *situs*.

18.53 The second argument is that security of title favours the law of the *situs*, in that a purchaser of goods may rest content with a transaction that is effective under the local law of the *situs* to confer title upon him without his having to investigate other laws, which would require 'extensive and

---

[124] See, however, the 1958 Hague Convention on the Transfer of Property, discussed below, paras 18.71–73.

[125] *Cammell v Sewell* (1860) 5 H & N 728, 157 ER 1377; *Winkworth v Christie Manson & Woods Ltd* [1980] Ch 496.

[126] Council Regulation (EC) 44/2001 [2001] OJ L12/1.

probably fruitless enquiries into the provenance of the goods'.[127] This latter observation seems *germane* only to trilateral property matters and not to the bilateral relations of buyer and seller, where the security of the buyer's title against third parties does not arise.[128] The bilateral question focuses only upon when the seller's property rights, however strong they may be when measured against the world, are transferred to the buyer. Yet the strength of this second law of the *situs* argument depends upon the extent to which it frees purchasers from the need to make extensive enquiries into the provenance of the goods. If the current law of the *situs* does not contain a rule equivalent to the 'possession vaut titre' principle of French law, and requires instead a study of the circumstances whereby the seller acquired the goods in the first place, which is the case with English law and those systems of law built upon it, the buyer's yearning for a secure title will not be satisfied by a reference just to the current law of the *situs* but will demand an enquiry into the provenance of the goods that the law of the *situs* rule is supposed to obviate.

In addition to these arguments, which most recently were relied upon by **18.54** Moore-Bick J in *Glencore International AG*,[129] there are others. A third argument in favour of the law of the *situs* is based upon the notion of clarity and certainty: the *situs* of goods is visible and hence the law of the *situs* is usually easy to identify. That may be so, yet the same could be said of a clear choice by the parties of a law of the transfer or even a default choice of law rule based, for example, upon the residence of the characteristic performer[130] (who would surely be the transferor).[131] If certainty is needed, there are alternatives to the law of the *situs*. A fourth argument is that the law of the *situs* should apply on the ground that the owner has submitted to the jurisdiction where the movable is situate.[132] This may in fact be true in some cases but in others it appears fanciful, and in some is

---

[127] Moore-Bick J in *Glencore International AG v Metro Trading Inc (No 2)* [2001] 1 Lloyd's Rep 284, 294. See also P North 'Reform, but Not Revolution' (1990) 22 Receuil des Cours 13, 265: 'If the rule were otherwise, every international sale contract would be additionally complex. A buyer would not only need to investigate the title of the vendor to the goods under the law of the country where they were situated, but he would also have to trace the history of the goods, perhaps into their component parts, and investigate the foreign title to those goods.'

[128] In so far as it does arise in English law as between seller and buyer, it arises as an aspect of contract. An implied condition of the contract requires the seller to have a right to sell the goods: s 12(1) of the Sale of Goods Act 1979.

[129] [2001] 1 Lloyd's Rep 284.

[130] By analogy with the presumption in Art 4(2) of the Rome Convention 1980.

[131] This rule is discussed by Whincop and Keyes, n 98 above, at 110–112, but rejected on the ground that it lacks the flexibility of the law of the *situs* rule: it is easier to move goods than to change the residence of a company.

[132] Hellendall, n 114 above, citing Savigny.

plainly inapplicable, as where transactions involve goods stolen from
another jurisdiction. It therefore does not support the current English rule
and receives no support from English authorities.

14. Exceptions to the Law of the *Situs*: Casual Location

18.55 The *Winkworth* case[133] is significant for the gathering together of a number
of exceptions to the law of the *situs* rule, none of which applied on the
facts of the case. The court stated that the rule laid down in *Cammell v
Sewell*[134] was 'not likely to be applied' in any of five exceptional cases
mentioned in the course of the proceedings.[135] These five cases appear by
implication to be a comprehensive list. In the order they appear, they are
as follows. First, the goods are in transit and their *situs* is either 'casual' or
'not known'.[136] Now, 'casual' cannot mean 'accidental' or else it would
absorb the case of *Cammell v Sewell* itself, where it was never in anyone's
contemplation that the goods would end up in Norway after a ship-
wreck.[137] It might mean that the goods are just passing through a jurisdiction without ever coming to rest, in which case the difficulty of knowing
where the goods might be at a given time in the course of a complex
transit would be a further reason for describing their *situs* as casual, so
that 'casual' and 'not known' may be seen in some instances as amounting
to the same thing. The *situs* of goods might also be casual if in their
history they have had a very mobile existence, so that they have never
acquired an affiliation to a particular place. Conceivably, it might embrace
a transaction between parties who are not in the country of the law of the
situs at the time of the transaction and who do not order their affairs by
reference to or in reliance upon the law of the *situs*. These parties, moreover, may be dealing in goods not in the immediate possession of the
seller but held instead by a third party bailee.

15. Exceptions to the Law of the *Situs*: Bad Faith and Public Policy

18.56 The second exceptional case, apt for dealing with trilateral matters, concerns a purchaser who has not acted in good faith when acquiring the

---

[133] [1980] Ch 496.   [134] (1860) 5 H & N 728, 157 ER 1371.
[135] In the *Glencore International AG* case ([2001] 1 Lloyd's Rep 284), the bilateral passing of
property in a contract of sale was presented (unsuccessfully) as a further exception.
[136] Applying an exception put forward in Dicey and Morris (Morris (ed), 9th edn, 1973)
539.
[137] 'And we do not think that it makes any difference that the goods were wrecked, and
not intended to be sent to the country where they were sold' (Crompton J in *Cammell v Sewell*
(1860) 5 H & N 728, 745, 157 ER 1371, 1378; cited in *Winkworth* [1980] Ch 496, 504).

goods. For this case to be worth extensive consideration, there would have to be a significant number of legal systems whose laws were indifferent to the acquisition of title in bad faith, which to say the least would be an unusual finding. In *Glencore International AG*, Moore-Bick J was all for leaving the absence of good faith to the law of the *situs*. Moreover, if the purchaser acquires good title under the law of the *situs*, it is difficult to see any reason for permitting an exception along these lines, if the case falls short of the limited scope given to English public policy,[138] which is the third exception listed in *Winkworth*. Of public policy, it is enough to say that an English court rarely gives expression to public policy as an overriding factor.[139] The court in *Winkworth* did not apply public policy so as to defeat the innocent purchaser's title acquired in Italy, even though, for the art market in particular, the availability in certain countries, whose laws are more generous to purchasers than English law, of title laundering possibilities for highly mobile and valuable goods creates positive incentives for an international market in stolen art.[140] Public policy was however invoked by the House of Lords to defeat a proprietary transfer in a case where an Iraqi authority, the Revolutionary Command Council, set up in Kuwait in consequence of the latter country's invasion, procured the passing of a resolution dissolving a Kuwait company and transferring aircraft owned by it to an Iraqi company.[141]

---

[138] Something in the order of a 'monstrous' law of the *situs* would be called for, in the light of the court's reference to Crompton J's judgment in *Cammell v Sewell* (1860) 5 H & N 728, 157 ER 1371. Cf the much-criticized case of *Simpson v Fogo* (1863) 1 H & M 195, 71 ER 85 and the court's commitment to protecting English property rights.

[139] This exception ought to catch the type of rare case that Crompton J referred to in *Cammell v Sewell* of a law of the *situs* that is 'monstrous or barbarous': (1860) 5 H & N 728, 743, 157 ER 1371, 1377.

[140] The provisions of the Return of Cultural Objects Regulations 1994, SI 1994/501, as amended by the Return of Cultural Objects (Amendment) Regulations 1997, SI 1997/1719, which transpose an EEC Directive (93/7) as amended by another Directive (96/100), will have an effect on dealings of this kind. The Secretary of State is empowered to take into his possession cultural objects unlawfully removed from another Member State and to turn over the object to a person or institution designated in a court order. Furthermore, the Member State from which the cultural object has been removed may take proceedings in this country against the possessor of such objects and recover them, paying such compensation 'as the court deems fair according to the circumstances of the case'. These regulations can therefore serve to divest titles otherwise lawfully acquired pursuant to the law of the *situs* principle.

[141] *Kuwait Airways Corp v Iraqi Airways Co (Nos 4 and 5)* [2002] UKHL 19, [2002] 2 AC 883. See Lord Nicholls at [18], referring to 'a residual power, to be exercised exceptionally and with the greatest circumspection' and citing Lord Cross in *Oppenheimer v Cattermole* [1976] AC 249, 277–278. Lord Steyn invokes the notion of 'flagrant breaches of public international law' to inform the public policy exception, though he noted that not every breach of public international law would justify the public policy exception: [2002] 2 AC 883 at [114]. Lord Hoffmann states that 'a legislative act by a foreign state which is in flagrant breach of clearly established rules of international law ought' not to be recognized by the courts of this country as forming part of the *lex situs* of that state': ibid, at [148]. See further above, paras 17.44–46.

16. Remaining Exceptions to the Law of the *Situs*

18.57 The fourth exceptional case in *Winkworth* concerned statutory provisions of the forum state that are expressed to apply in terms that depart from the forum's own choice of law rules, a necessary qualification to any authoritative statement of choice of law rules. A wilful legislature is not known for its deep understanding of the underlying common (or civil) law. Fifth, there were special rules dealing with general assignments of movables arising on bankruptcy or succession.[142] In such cases, there are factors at stake other than the inconvenience of having multiple laws of the *situs*, which in itself may be a reason for departing from the law of the *situs* in the case of complex voluntary and *inter vivos* transfers of movables.[143]

18.58 To the extent that the law of the *situs* rule is made the subject of exceptions, and especially to the extent that they eat into the rationalization of that rule as resting on the effective control of the law of the *situs* over the goods, the gap between the law of the *situs* rule and a law of the transfer rule is diminished. The gap comes close to disappearing altogether if there are numerous exceptions to the law of the *situs* rule and hence only a presumption, albeit a strong one, that the law of the transfer will in the ordinary case be the law of the *situs*.[144] All that is left between the two approaches is the autonomy of the parties to the transaction in selecting a law to govern the proprietary transfer.

17. Governing Law where Exceptions Apply

18.59 The recognition of various exceptions to the law of the *situs* is not an end of the matter, since in some instances that recognition does not as such identify the law governing the transfer. In the case of goods whose *situs* is 'casual' or 'not known', according to Wolff: 'It seems impossible to set up a single and comprehensive formula indicating the appropriate law'.[145] The author considers and rejects the application of the law of destination of the goods and (for goods whose *situs* is unknown) the law of the last place where the goods were known to be located at the time of the transfer.[146] The place of destination, where the transit ends, may not be the

---

[142] Discussed above, para 18.23.

[143] See above (the sale of a company by means of a sale of all its business assets).

[144] See J Morris 'The Transfer of Chattels in the Conflict of Laws' (1945) 22 British Ybk of Intl Law 232, 247 (see Conclusions 1–3); E Sykes and M Pryles, *Australian Private International Law* (3rd edn, Sydney: Law Book Co, 1991), 666–673.

[145] Wolff, n 37 above, at 520.   [146] ibid (discussing the ideas of Niboyet and Zitelmann).

place where the goods finally come to rest, and the application of the last known *situs* could lead to the law of a country which, because the goods have passed through it in the course of transit, has only a slight connection with the goods and the transaction.[147] The argument supporting the law of the transfer in this case is a powerful one but, in practice, the matter is likely to be resolved by reference to the principles governing dealings not in goods but in shipping documents representing the goods.[148]

In the case of the public policy (and good faith) exception, the choice **18.60** appears to lie between the law of the transfer and the law of the forum. If only because, under English law at least, the application of public policy will be essentially negative, in that the interest of the forum state lies only in avoiding the intolerable effects produced by the application of the law of the *situs*, it is submitted that the claims of the forum state to deal with the transfer will be spent by the time that the law of the *situs* has been excluded. The way therefore seems open to applying the law of the transfer with a default reference to the law of the forum if the law of the transfer also offends public policy[149] or turns out to be the law of the *situs* under another name.

18. Foreign Judgments

Finally, though not listed in the *Winkworth* case as an exception to the law **18.61** of the *situs* rule, comes the effect of a foreign judgment relating to movables.[150] When *Cammell v Sewell*[151] was discussed above, it was seen that there was no appreciable difference between the case of a buyer acquiring title, pursuant to the law of the *situs*, under a contract of sale and the buyer acquiring title under a judgment *in rem* given by a *situs* court, where the judgment directed a sale of the movables.[152] A foreign judgment will not be recognized in England as having an *in rem* effect where the movables in question are not situate in the judgment state at the relevant

---

[147] The 1958 Hague Convention on the Transfer of Property (discussed below) would apply the law of the place from which the goods were sent (expédition) as the deemed law of the *situs* in the case of goods in transit (Art 6). It would not always be easy to identify such a country. If goods sold FOB a port in State Y were first transported by the seller to that port from State X, then the law of State Y, it is submitted, should apply. State Y is defined by the parties as the state of commencement of the contractual adventure and, moreover, the buyer may not be aware that the goods started their journey in State X.

[148] Discussed below, paras 18.78–92.

[149] Which would cover a case like *Kuwait Airways Corp v Iraqi Airways Co (Nos 4 and 5)* [2002] UKHL 19, [2002] 2 AC 883.

[150] See above, paras 11.65–69.   [151] (1860) 5 H & N 728, 157 ER 1371.

[152] See also Dicey and Morris, 509 ('[The buyer] is, in other words, relying on the foreign judgment *qua* an assignment rather than *qua* a judgment').

time.[153] So, if an Italian buyer acquired title to movables pursuant to Italian law (the law of the *situs*) and at the expense of the original Russian owner, but, prior to their removal to this country, a judgment in Russia was handed down in favour of the original Russian owner, that judgment should not be recognized in England as having an in rem effect if the movables were not in Russia at the time of the judgment.

18.62 Nevertheless, suppose that the Italian buyer defended those Russian proceedings and that the Russian court, for whatever reason, adjudged the Italian buyer not to have acquired a good title. If an English court were to conclude that the Italian buyer was bound by a *res judicata* estoppel, then the Italian buyer would be precluded from asserting in England that it had acquired a valid title under the Italian transaction. It is clear that *res judicata* has the capacity to make inroads into the rule of the law of the *situs* and it is therefore not surprising that the court in *Air Foyle Ltd v Centre Capital Ltd*[154] gave a restrictive reading to the estoppel. First, it accepted that there could be a general exception, where the foreign judgment was 'perverse, in the sense that it is at variance with generally accepted doctrines of private international law'.[155] Second, it took a conservative view of the subject-matter of the foreign proceedings. In *Air Foyle*, Russian proceedings had earlier taken place between the claimant and defendant in the present English proceedings. These proceedings led to a Russian judgment, given at a time when the aircraft in question was not actually situate in Russia but was deemed under Russian law to be there situate as a Russian immovable, since Russia was the country of registration. The Russian judgment recognized the title acquired pursuant to Russian law (the law applicable to the contract) by the present defendant. In giving its judgment, the Russian court declined to recognize the effect of an earlier Dutch judgment, handed down at a time when the aircraft was situate in Holland and directing the holding of an auction, where the present claimant had purchased it. There was no treaty providing for the recognition of Dutch judgments in Russia. Crucially, however, the Russian court did not hold that the present claimant had failed to acquire a valid title under the Dutch contract of sale, with the result that Gross J was able to conclude that there was no *res judicata* estoppel between the parties. The claimant's Dutch title prevailed over the defendant's Russian title, since Russia was at no relevant time the *situs* of the aircraft.[156]

---

[153] ibid, Rule 40(1).

[154] [2002] EWHC 2535, [2003] 2 Lloyd's Rep 753. See also above, para 11.65.

[155] ibid, at [36], relying upon *Simpson v Fogo* (1863) 1 H & M 195, 71 ER 85 and *Carl Zeiss Stiftung v Rayner & Keeler Ltd (No 2)* [1967] 1 AC 853, 917–918, 922.

[156] The English court declined to treat Russia as the *situs* of the aircraft for reasons given below.

19. Transfer of Title and Passing of Property in Dispersed Transactions

The application of the law of the *situs* was discussed above in relation to a **18.63** transaction concerning goods situate in State Y that was recognized in the forum state as conferring title to the goods on the disponee pursuant to the law of State Y, even though this transaction overrode an owner's title recognized[157] by the law of an earlier *situs*, State X. This section concerns more complex transactions where the elements of the transaction completed in State Y are dispersed between State Y and another state, usually but not necessarily State X. Taking a simple example of a type familiar to English sale of goods lawyers, suppose that goods are entrusted by their owner, A, to a mercantile agent, B, in State X with a limited authority to receive offers to purchase the goods and refer them to A for acceptance. B crosses the frontier into State Y and there sells the goods to C. Taking the simple case of States X and Y both having a basic title transfer rule of *nemo dat quod non habet* and a mercantile agency exception to that rule of identical scope, is C prevented from acquiring a title that overrides A's title on the ground that the mercantile agency exception is not fully consummated in a single state, whether it is X or Y? This example has some similarity to the example above concerning conditional sale goods removed from one state to another, both states having registration provisions.

The sparse English law favours the view that the cross-border elements of **18.64** a *nemo dat* exception can be cumulated. In *Janesich v George Attenborough and Son*,[158] the plaintiff owners of a necklace entrusted it in Paris to Baron Goldschmidt, conferring on him an authority to sell it at a minimum price. Nothing indicated that the authority was confined to France. In breach of his authority, the baron pledged it in England in circumstances that

---

[157] Whether or not the transaction by which the owner acquired title took place in State A or in an earlier *situs* state.

[158] (1908) 102 LT 605 (Hamilton J). A similar-looking case (*Mehta v Sutton* (1913) 108 LT 214) on closer inspection is distinguishable. An agent, entrusted in France with precious stones for the purpose of referring offers of purchase to the plaintiff owner, in breach of his authority and outside the ordinary course of business of a mercantile agent, pawned them with a Government pawnbroker and then pledged the pawn ticket with the defendant's Paris office. This office then redeemed the pawn and remitted the stones to England. In so far as all the elements of the pledge occurred in France, the matter should have been governed by French law since the unauthorized pledge was complete either when the stones were pawned and the pawn ticket passed into the defendant's hands, or when the pawn ticket itself was pledged in Paris. Both of these events occurred in France. Applying both English and French law, the court found in favour of the plaintiff on the ground that the defendant's agent had not acted in good faith. The case should simply have been disposed of according to French law as the law of the *situs*.

accorded with his acting in the ordinary course of business of a mercantile agent. The court held that the 'validity'[159] of the pledge fell to be determined by English law since the defendant pledgees acquired the necklace in England. This approach would seem to subsume all of the elements of the mercantile agency exception,[160] regardless of where they occurred, to English law on the ground that England was the *situs* of the transaction concluded by the mercantile agent with the third party. Had the entrustment occurred in England, with the pledge then taking place in France, then for the sake of consistency French law ought to have been applicable. It is the unauthorized pledge or other transaction that has the divesting effect as far as the owner is concerned and not the initial entrustment. It is consequently the law of the *situs* of the unauthorized transaction that applies. The same approach would be adopted with other exceptions to the rule of *nemo dat*, such as the resale by the seller in possession,[161] the sale by the buyer in possession[162] and the resale by someone with a voidable title.[163]

18.65 An issue of dispersal can also arise in the case of passing of property. Suppose for example that a conditional sale contract is concluded in State X and the goods subsequently removed to State Y. As the buyer pays the instalments falling due, the law of State X recognizes, regardless of the terms of the contract, that the buyer acquires incrementally a property interest in the goods. This principle, however, is not accepted by the law of State Y. Alternatively, the principle of incremental property may be accepted by the law of State Y but not of State X. In the former case, it is submitted that the incremental property interest acquired in State X is preserved despite the removal of the goods to State Y, though it is not supplemented in respect of payments in State Y. Similarly, in the latter case, the buyer starts to acquire an incremental property interest as and when the goods are removed to State Y but cannot build upon earlier payments made when the goods were in State X. Whether, in either case, a defaulting buyer might, in the event of contractual termination by the seller, yet be entitled to relief against the forfeiture of his property interest in the goods ought, it is submitted, to be a matter for the law of the goods at the time of contractual termination,[164] since the question concerns the divesting of the conditional buyer's property interest.

---

[159] That is, its opposability to the plaintiff owners of the necklace.

[160] These would include the status of Baron Goldschmidt as a mercantile agent and his receipt of the necklace in his capacity as a mercantile agent.

[161] Sale of Goods Act 1979, s 24, Factors Act 1889, s 8.

[162] ibid, s 25 and Factors Act 1889, s 9.   [163] ibid, s 23.

[164] The alternative approach would be to submit the issue to the law governing the contract, but this runs against the grain of modern authority favouring the law of the *situs* in bilateral property matters.

IV. SITUS

In contrast with intangible movables, the *situs* of movables presents very **18.66** few problems.[165] Movables are clearly situate in the place where they are physically to be found.[166] If their location is uncertain, then it is likely to be the case that the exception to the rule of the law of the *situs* based upon the casual location of the goods applies, in which case the need to identify the *situs* is avoided. It may be that problems might arise in the case of movables that are representative of a larger whole, as where a seller makes delivery of a china collection by handing over to the buyer a part of it. If a representative *situs* of the whole were to be recognized in such a case, this would come close to allowing the parties to contract directly in favour of the law that they would prefer to govern the propri- etary consequences of their transaction. And if, moreover, such behaviour were not recognized in the *situs* of the balance of the collection, the effi- cacy principle underlying the *situs* rule would compel an English court to decline to recognize a representative *situs*. It is therefore submitted that a representative *situs* should not be recognized unless it were also recog- nized by the *situs* of the balance.[167] This leaves unexplained the position of the law of the *situs* of the representative part. It is submitted that, so long as that law recognizes the proprietary effect of the transaction as it bears on the representative part, there should be no need to consider whether it views the part as representative of the whole.

An exception to the physical *situs* of movables that has been canvassed **18.67** concerns items such as ships and aircraft that are entered upon registers. According to Dicey and Morris, a merchant ship 'may at some times be deemed situate at her port of registry'.[168] It is hard to formulate a proposition of law more tentative than this one and, indeed, the artificial registry *situs* is marked out by the editors as 'convenient and sound in principle' only where the vessel is on the high seas.[169] This is tantamount to ships being subject to the law of the *situs* except in those cases where there is no relevant law of the *situs* or the *situs* is casual, a case that can be accommodated with ease under the rule in *Cammell v Sewell*[170] together with its exceptions. This dispenses with any need for an artificial *situs*. The same tentative exception to the physical *situs* rule is also formulated

---

[165] For the *situs* of digitized products (such as software on a web-server) see Chs 10 and 21.
[166] The *situs* is to be ascertained according to English law as the law of the forum: *Air Foyle Ltd v Centre Capital Ltd* [2002] EWHC 2535, [2003] 2 Lloyd's Rep 753.
[167] Which may be seen as a form of renvoi.
[168] Dicey and Morris, Exception 1 to Rule 112.   [169] ibid, at 936–937.
[170] (1860) 5 H & N 728, 157 ER 1371.

by Dicey and Morris for civil aircraft and the country of their registration.[171] This exception was however rejected in *Air Foyle Ltd v Centre
Capital Ltd*[172] for (unstated) 'overwhelming reasons'.[173] In that case, the
application of a law of the *situs* rule based firmly upon an artificial
registration *situs* would have led to the English court recognizing the
later title of the Russian buyer as overreaching the earlier title of the
Dutch buyer. In the tentative terms favoured by Dicey and Morris, however, the artificial Russian *situs* would have yielded to the identifiable
physical *situs* where the aircraft was grounded at the relevant time.
Given the significance generally attached to the place of registration of
ships and aircraft,[174] the argument that they are situate in the country of
registration merits closer examination than it received in the *Air Foyle*
case.

V. RENVOI

18.68 Where the law of the *situs* is being applied in the case of immovables, it
seems uncontroversial that the renvoi doctrine should be applied,[175] in
that renvoi, especially in its foreign court manifestation, is a concession to
the power over the immovable property exercised by the law of the *situs*.
The case for applying renvoi to movable property is less powerful,[176]
especially where the movables are no longer present in the *situs* state. Of
the various arguments in favour of the law of the *situs* rule, the only one
that supports also the use of renvoi is the effective control of the law of
the *situs* over the movables. The attribute of certainty is far from being
served by renvoi, so that here control and certainty pull in opposite
directions.

18.69 Renvoi was not mentioned in the leading case of *Cammell v Sewell*,[177]
which, given the date of the decision, was understandable. It was
excluded under the terms of the preliminary issue disposed of by the
court in the *Winkworth* case, though Slade J considered that it was 'open to
the plaintiff to argue that English law should apply' if, as was 'theoretically possible', the courts of the *situs* state (Italy) would themselves have

---

[171] Dicey and Morris, Exception 2 to Rule 112.
[172] [2002] EWHC 2535, [2003] 2 Lloyd's Rep 753.   [173] ibid, at [40].
[174] A factor which has much to do with the exclusion of contracts of sale of ships and
aircraft from the Vienna Convention 1980 (see Art 2(e)).
[175] Dicey and Morris, 959 (to the extent that English domestic law should be applied
where the land is situate in England).
[176] In those cases where the law of the *situs* applies under the 1958 Hague Convention on
the Transfer of Property, renvoi is excluded (see Arts 3–5).
[177] (1860) 5 H & N 728, 157 ER 1371.

applied English law on the present facts.[178] The application of renvoi was also left open in *Glencore International AG*,[179] though Moore-Bick J recognized the force of the practical control of the *situs* state over movables still located in that state. In *Macmillan Inc v Bishopsgate Investment Trust plc (No 3)*,[180] which involved intangible movables (shares), akin to tangible movables for present purposes, Millett J declined to apply renvoi, which he referred to as 'largely discredited'.[181] One approach, therefore, would be to apply renvoi only if the movables are still located in the *situs* state. Yet, if the movables are by now in the forum state, the logic of continuing to apply the law of the *situs* applies equally to the conflicts rules of the law of the *situs*. On balance, this presents a case, albeit not a particularly strong one, for the application of renvoi.[182]

Now, supposing renvoi to be applicable, a further question turns upon the **18.70** frequency of its application so as to lead to the domestic law of a state other than the *situs* state. To the extent that a law of the *situs* rule is adopted by systems other than English law, then renvoi will simply lead back to the domestic law of the *situs* state. The more commonplace a law of the *situs* choice of law rule is in legal systems, the more frequent will be the remission to the domestic law of the *situs* state and the less likely it will be for litigating parties to plead and prove the choice of law rules of the *situs* state.[183] The international primacy of the law of the *situs* rule will therefore undercut any need to invoke arguments in favour of renvoi and consign the doctrine to the sidelines.

VI. THE 1958 HAGUE CONVENTION ON THE TRANSFER OF PROPERTY

The Hague Convention on the Transfer of Property,[184] which deals with **18.71** the transfer of proprietary rights in tangible movables by way of sale,

---

[178] [1980] Ch 496, 514.   [179] [2001] 1 Lloyd's Rep 284.   [180] [1995] 1 WLR 978, 1008.

[181] In the Court of Appeal in the same case, Staughton LJ also expressed his opposition to renvoi in the particular case of dealings in shares: [1996] 1 WLR 387, 405.

[182] Just as the American Restatement Second on Conflict of Laws differentiates between bilateral and trilateral issues, so, in approximating bilateral conveyances to contracts it proscribes renvoi in the same way as it does with contract: § 244(1). Where trilateral issues are raised, renvoi is admitted: § 245(1).

[183] Similarly, in the Restatement Second on Conflict of Laws, in respect of trilateral property matters, renvoi is admitted before the following, most odd descriptive and non-normative provision: 'These courts [of the *situs*] would usually apply their own local law in determining such questions' (§ 245(2)).

[184] *Convention sur la loi applicable au transfert de la propriété en cas de vente à caractère international d'objets mobiliers corporels* of 15 April 1958. See L Frédéricq, 'La Vente en Droit International Privé (Quelques Conventions Récentes)' (1958) 93 Receuil des Cours 1.

must be accounted a failure because it received very little support and never came into force.[185] This must be due, in part at least, to its elliptical and obscure character. Nevertheless, its approach is worthy of analysis, distinguishing as it does between the bilateral and trilateral transfer issues.[186] The Convention applies to the sale of movable, tangible things, excluding sales of ships and shares but including documentary sales.[187]

18.72 The Convention identifies the law applicable to the contract of sale as the law for determining when the property in the goods passes from seller to buyer. It does this by indirect and laconical means. According to Article 2, the law applicable to the contract of sale determines the moment when the seller surrenders his right to the products and fruits of the thing sold. It also determines the validity of reservation of title clauses. In Article 3, as regards all parties other than the parties to the contract,[188] the law of the *situs* of the goods at the time a claim is made[189] is identified as the law governing the transfer. The hole in this no doubt 'elegant' scheme is a clear provision that the law applicable to the contract determines when the property passes to the buyer (though it ought to be conceded that this scheme has the merit of avoiding any difficulty of defining what is meant by property). Yet this provision is clearly to be inferred from the Convention, especially when it goes on to provide, by way of exception to this unexpressed rule, that the unpaid seller's rights, in particular those arising under a reservation of title clause or a rescission of the contract, are opposable against creditors of the buyer only to the extent permitted by the law of the *situs* at the time the first claim or execution is made.[190] Similarly, the buyer's rights are subject to the proprietary rights of third parties if so provided by the law of the *situs* at the time of the third party claim,[191] subject to any rights already acquired by the buyer under the law of the *situs* at the time when (and if) the buyer was put in possession of the goods.[192]

18.73 Apart from its obscurity and its failure to define key expressions like third party,[193] the most notable features of the 1958 Convention are its separation of bilateral and trilateral property issues, and its adoption of a sort of roving law of the *situs*, which varies from the place where the buyer first took possession of the goods to the place where the goods were

---

[185] Only Greece and Italy signed the Convention and only the latter acceded to it.
[186] Arts 2–3.
[187] It also excludes sales in furtherance of executions and court orders.
[188] '[A] l'égard de toutes personnes autres que les parties au contrat de vente'.
[189] '[A]u moment où se produit une réclamation les concernant'.
[190] Art 4.   [191] Art 5.   [192] ibid.
[193] 'Tiers'. Does it include a trustee-in-bankruptcy?

situate at the time of third party claims. As an exercise in ineffectual lawmaking, the Convention and its subsequent failure speak for themselves. That should not, however, be treated as a rebuttal of the distinction drawn in this chapter between bilateral and trilateral property issues.

VII. THE CONTROL EXERCISED BY THE GOVERNING LAW

1. ESSENTIAL REQUIREMENTS

According to Falconbridge, the law of the *situs* (or *lex rei sitae*) rule **18.74** 'necessarily applies to any essential requirements of the *lex rei sitae* as to formalities of conveyance as well as any questions of the intrinsic validity of the conveyance'.[194] This assumes the applicability of the law of the *situs* to bilateral property matters and takes no account of trilateral matters. It is noteworthy that the American Restatement Second, in dealing with the bilateral conveyance, whilst adopting a closest connection approach in place of an ironclad law of the *situs* rule, takes an altogether different approach in applying the closest connection test to individual matters such as validity, formalities and capacity.[195] In other words, the Restatement introduces dépeçage into the governing law without requiring such a splitting of the issues to be based upon the parties' express choice.

2. TRILATERAL RELATIONS

In the case of trilateral relations, the issues arising that are disposed of by **18.75** the law of the *situs* are principally the following. There is first of all the question of what is required if the ownership rights of an owner (A) are, as a result of a transaction entered into by an intermediate party (B) with a third party transferee (C), to be overridden in favour of C. When *Winkworth v Christie Manson & Woods Ltd*[196] was discussed, we saw that Italian law, as the law of the *situs* at the time of the transaction between B and C, determined whether C acquired a title that overrode the original title of A. Second, there are the proprietary consequences, as they affect third parties, of a transaction having been avoided as infringing principles of insolvency law. For example, A may have sold goods to B at an under-value[197] and B may have sold those same goods on to C. The avoidance of

---

[194] J Falconbridge, *Conflict of Laws* (2nd edn, Canada Law Book Co, 1954) 443.
[195] American Restatement Second on Conflict of Laws (1971), § 244.
[196] [1980] Ch 496. See above, paras 18.34–36.   [197] Insolvency Act 1986, ss 238, 339.

the A-B sale may affect the property rights of C. In a similar way, the proprietary effectiveness of the B-C transfer is a matter for the law of the *situs* at the time of the transfer. So far as the transaction between B and C is in *proprietary* terms effective unless and until challenged by A's insolvency representative, the issue becomes more difficult. The goods may have been moved by C prior to the making of the challenge. It is submitted that in this case, and in the case also of other types of voidable transaction,[198] the governing law should be the law of the *situs* where the goods are to be found at the time of that representative's challenge. In such a case, that challenge, if effective, would have a divesting effect which makes the law of the later *situs* a more suitable choice.

3. BILATERAL RELATIONS

18.76 Taking now the relations of buyer and seller *inter se*, a broader range of property matters might arise between the parties. First, there are formalities and the capacity of the parties. Second, there are the requirements that have to be met for the seller's ownership to be transferred to the buyer. These requirements may be found in the general law or else, as with retention of title clauses, in the express terms of the contract. Third, there are matters that, apart from the transfer of ownership, concern other property rights retained by the seller or acquired by the buyer. The seller may, for example, have delivered the goods to the buyer, perhaps even have transferred ownership to the buyer, and yet may have rights, possessory or non-possessory, over the goods pending payment in full by the buyer.[199] The seller may also have property rights consequent upon the rejection of the goods and termination of the contract by the buyer.[200] The buyer may, for example, have paid for the goods prior to the transfer of ownership. Hence, the question will be whether such a buyer has acquired property rights, perhaps of an equitable character or by way of tenancy in common in an identified bulk. Or the question may be whether the buyer, having rejected the goods, has a lien over them until the price is repaid. Fourth, there are matters concerning the interests of a connected state. These may include the question whether goods of a certain type, works of art for example, may be freely sold or sold only subject to

---

[198] e.g. Sale of Goods Act 1979, s 23.

[199] Such as a right of resale in the event of termination of the contract (Sale of Goods Act 1979, s 48) or, in French and Quebec law, the right ('privilège') of an unpaid seller to revendicate goods that remain in the hands of the buyer who has not paid for them: Code civil, Art 2102–4° (France—within eight days of delivery); Civil Code of Quebec, Arts 1998–99 (also eight days but 30 days in the case of an insolvent trader).

[200] *RV Ward Ltd v Bignall* [1967] 1 QB 534; *Kwei Tek Chao v British Traders & Shippers Ltd* [1954] 2 QB 459.

conditions that must first be satisfied. Again, a connected state may recharacterize a transaction that takes the form of a sale. A sale and lease-back, for example, might be recharacterized as a charge that has to be registered for perfection purposes. Similarly, a conditional sale may be recharacterized as a mortgage in a way that affects the property rights *inter se* of buyer and seller in the event of the former's failure to pay in full. A defaulting mortgagor may be treated differently from a defaulting conditional buyer.[201] Leaving aside for the moment capacity and formalities, so far as the governing law is the law of the *situs*, all of the above matters are proprietary and are therefore governed by that law.

4. Capacity and Formalities

As for capacity and formalities, a concession to the power of the law of the **18.77** *situs* should leave that law in control of these issues. Nevertheless, the extent of the domain of the law of the *situs* has been called into question.[202] Referring to capacity, Wolff asserts that this issue is '(probably) governed by the rules developed . . . for contracts',[203] so that the governing law is the law of the domicile, though he concedes the absence of supporting authority. The weakness of the power principle in the case of movable property has already been noted, so there is much to be said for treating capacity here as it is treated for contract. The issue of capacity does not go to the interests of the law of the *situs* in regulating proprietary transfers but rather is concerned with the person of either or both of transferor and transferee. In a similar way, Wolff regards formalities as a matter for the law applicable to contractual formalities,[204] though the case he makes here appears to be a weaker one because formalities in the case of proprietary transfers are significantly more important than they are in

---

[201] See J Ziegel, 'Conditional Sales and the Conflict of Laws' (1967) 45 Canadian Bar Rev 284, 329.

[202] In the unhelpful cases of *Republic of Guatemala v Nunez* [1927] 1 KB 669 and also *Re Anziani* [1930] 1 Ch 407, which concerned the transfer of intangible property, a variety of opinions were expressed as to the law dealing with capacity and form ranging across the law of the *situs* and the law of the place of transfer. See the discussion in Lalive, n 32 above, at 121–129.

[203] Wolff, n 37 above, at 523. Cf Lalive, n 32 above, at 124–125: '[O]ther legal systems must accept the fact that the law of the *situs* has the power to consider a transfer invalid for incapacity, or to consider it as made by a person of full capacity and valid, whatever the personal law of the assignor, or assignee, may declare'. To similar effect is Zaphiriou, n 12 above, at 74–75 (arguing that there has been a tendency to assimilate immovables and tangible movables, the latter having a real *situs* as opposed to the artificial *situs* of intangible movables).

[204] Wolff, n 38 above, at 523. Though the Rome Convention would not in its own terms apply to transfer formalities, an English court would probably be guided by its expansive provisions in fashioning a formalities rule distinct from the application of the law of the *situs*.

the case of contracts.[205] For reasons of transparency or public record, the law of the *situs* may for example require transfers to be executed before a notary.[206] Furthermore, it is peculiarly difficult to mark out the difference between the essential validity of a transfer and its formal validity.[207] The better view, therefore, is to subject the issue of formal validity to the law of the *situs*.[208]

VIII. DEALINGS IN DOCUMENTS

1. DOCUMENTARY SALES

18.78 Goods in transit may be dealt with between contracting parties by means of a negotiable bill of lading, which is a versatile document that, amongst other things, represents, in the sense of stands in for, the goods in transit. In English law, it is a document of title to the goods as long as the transit lasts:[209] this means that the lawful holder may demand delivery of the goods from the carrier when the transit is ended. Neither the original consignor of the goods nor the carrier itself may resist that claim.[210] The holder of the bill of lading therefore constructively possesses the goods covered by the bill of lading. The status of the bill of lading as a document of title does not mean that the transfer of the bill of lading by seller to buyer is a prerequisite in English law to the passing of property in the goods to the buyer, though in practice it would be most unusual for this to occur without the transfer of the bill of lading.

18.79 In sale of goods and factors legislation in English law, and in Commonwealth systems that have adopted similar legislation, bills of lading (along with certain other, named documents) are also significant in connection with the various, limited exceptions to the *nemo dat* rule of title transfer.[211] In this connection, possession of the bill of lading plays a role

---

[205] In *Dulaney v Merry* [1901] 1 QB 536, 541, Channell J stated that a failure to comply with the formal requirements of the owner's domiciliary law would not invalidate 'a transfer of movables here [in England] good by our law'.

[206] Compare the liberal rules on formal validity of contracts in Art 9 of the Rome Convention (but note the provision on contracts concerning a right in immovable property in Art 9(6)). See above, paras 13.256–260.

[207] See Zaphiriou, n 42 above, at 80, referring to the requirement of delivery for a gift as a matter of formal validity.

[208] See ibid, at 80—'the only possible solution'.

[209] See discussion below, paras 18.83–85.

[210] In particular, the carrier may not insist that the contract of carriage is with the consignor to whom alone the goods are to be delivered. The carrier does however have a common law lien on the goods for any unpaid freight.

[211] The relevant exceptions are the seller and buyer in possession (ss 8–9 of the Factors Act 1889 and 24–25 Sale of Goods Act 1979) and the mercantile agent in possession (s 2 of the Factors Act 1889).

in title transfer because possession of the bill is treated as 'proof of the possession' of the underlying goods. In stated circumstances, the transfer by an owner of possession of goods is seen as sufficiently indicative of ownership or of an authority to deal as to empower (but not to authorize) the party in possession to transfer a title that overrides the title of the person transferring possession to him.[212] One of the *nemo dat* exceptions referred to above is the buyer in possession of goods or of documents of title to goods where the property has not yet passed to the buyer under the contract of sale. The buyer's receipt of goods, or of documents of title to goods, from the seller empowers the buyer to transfer title to the goods to a good faith purchaser clear of the seller's property rights.[213]

In the United States, the disposing power of the holder of a bill of lading **18.80** in favour of a good faith purchaser is somewhat greater. It helps first to know that, in the case of the goods themselves, any entrustment to a merchant who deals in goods of the same kind empowers that merchant to transfer a good title to a good faith purchaser. This goes a little further than the various statutory exceptions to the *nemo dat* rule in English law.[214] Where, however, a document of title is transferred, the new holder acquires a title to both the goods and the document of title,[215] with certain exceptions,[216] regardless of the status of the person to whom the document of title is transferred.[217] The transfer of a document of title under the Uniform Commercial Code is inherently more pregnant with proprietary consequences than is the case in English law. This is because the process of transfer of a document of title under the Code is more

---

[212] s 1(4) of the Factors Act 1889: 'The expression "document of title" shall include any bill of lading, dock warrant, warehouse-keeper's certificate, and warrant or order for the delivery of goods, and any other document used in the ordinary course of business as proof of the possession or control of goods, or authorising or purporting to authorize, either by endorsement or by delivery, the possessor of the document to transfer or receive goods thereby represented'. The provision may not refer to apparent ownership as such but that notion is congruent with and complementary to apparent authority.

[213] Sale of Goods Act 1979, s 25 and Factors Act 1889, s 8.

[214] The reason is that the American merchant need not receive the goods in the capacity of a merchant dealing in goods of the same kind: cf Uniform Commercial Code, Art 2–403(2).

[215] In English law, the title acquired by the new holder is dependent upon the intention of the transferor: *Sewell v Burdick* (1884) 10 App Cas 74, a qualification not present in the relevant provisions of the Uniform Commercial Code.

[216] The issuance of a document of title does not override any legal interest of a person who did not deliver the goods to the person who surrendered them to a bailee in return for the issuance of a document of title or who acquiesced in the process by: Uniform Commercial Code, Art 7–503(1).

[217] Uniform Commercial Code, Art 7–502(1)(a)–(b): '[A] holder to whom a negotiable document of title has been duly negotiated acquires thereby: (a) title to the document; (b) title to the goods; . . . (d) the direct obligation of the issuer to hold or deliver the goods according to the terms of the document . . .'.

closely approximated than it is in English law to a process of negotiation.[218] The way in which different systems of law analyze the attributes
of a document of title may well have implications for the choice of law
rule, contractual or proprietary, that they employ to deal with conflicts
issues presented by the document.

2. Issues Presented by Documents

18.81 For choice of law purposes, therefore, a number of issues are presented by
documents. First, it is important to know which law determines whether a
given document is a document of title, carrying with it constructive possession of the goods it represents, and whether the transferor of the
document has done what is required to dispose of a property interest in
the underlying goods. A document of title in this sense is one that gives
the holder the right to demand delivery of the goods by the carrier and a
right of action against the carrier who either refuses to deliver or delivers
to the wrong person. Second, going one step beyond this, it is also important to identify the law that determines whether a particular document,
falling short of the status of a document of title, is yet sufficient evidence
of an authority to deal or of ownership of the underlying goods that its
holder is empowered to transfer a proprietary interest in those goods
greater than the one he himself enjoys in them. Third, it may also be
important to know which law is qualified to determine whether the transfer of a bill of lading is essential to pass the property in goods from seller
to buyer (which we have seen is not the case in English domestic law
but which might be the case under other laws). A related question
concerns the law that determines whether dispositions of the goods themselves may take place without reference to a document of title when that
document remains current.

18.82 The above questions involve relations between buyer and seller and
between the holder of a document and the carrier or other person in
possession of goods issuing a document in respect of them. When it comes
to competing proprietary claims arising out of dealings in documents,
stemming from the practice of issuing bills of lading in sets of more than
one original document, it has to be determined which law decides
whether the holder of a document is empowered to transfer property
rights greater than those vested in him and in what circumstances that
power might be effectively exercised. Supposing for the moment that the

---

[218] See G Treitel, 'The Legal Status of Straight Bills of Lading' (2003) 119 LQR 608 (dealing
with *MacWilliam (JI) Co Inc v Mediterranean Shipping Co SA (The Rafaela S)* [2003] EWCA Civ
556 [2004] 2 WLR 283, CA).

above property matters, or some of them, in respect of movables, bilateral and trilateral, are governed by the law of the *situs*, there arises the further question whether the effect of a documentary transfer is to be determined according to the law of the place of the document or of the place of the goods in those cases where the two laws are different and provide for different outcomes. Cutting across these various questions is a time factor problem. Is the potentiality of a document of title to play a part either in the passing of property between a seller and a buyer, or in the transfer of title from a non-owner to a good faith purchaser, to be measured at the time the document is issued or at the time when it is transferred?

3. A Document of Title

The question whether a document such as a bill of lading is a document **18.83** of title and therefore gives constructive possession to the underlying goods appears on its face to be a proprietary question. This appearance arises to a degree from the importance attached in English domestic law to possession in property matters. In English law, two principal consequences flow from whether a document has this effect. The first of these is whether the carrier is bound to surrender the goods to the lawful holder of the document and the second is whether the lawful holder may build upon his constructive possession in maintaining an action in conversion against a tortfeasor, whether this be the carrier or some other wrongdoer.

The first of these questions, on closer examination, contains both con- **18.84** tractual and proprietary features. The effect of the constructive possession rule, against the carrier, is that the carrier may not plead that its obligation to deliver is owed only to the shipper under the original contract of carriage. In English law, this aspect of the relations between carrier and holder has been regarded as quite distinct from the terms and conditions of the carriage contract.[219] This is why legislation was needed to give the holder rights under the contract of carriage that could be exercised against the carrier,[220] even though it had been settled towards the end of the eighteenth century that an on-board, negotiable bill of lading was a document of title in giving the holder the right to demand the surrender of the goods from the carrier.[221] So far as the transfer of the bill of lading confers upon the buyer rights under the contract of carriage, then it should be seen, in a way akin to the case of

[219] *Thompson v Dominy* (1845) 14 M & W 403.
[220] First, the Bills of Lading Act 1855 and then the Carriage of Goods by Sea Act 1992.
[221] *Lickbarrow v Mason* (1787) 2 TR 63, (1790) 1 H Bl 357.

assignment,[222] as governed by the law applicable to the contract of carriage.[223] It is not as such a matter of assignment since the transfer of a bill of lading serves not merely to transfer contractual rights; it may also be instrumental in transferring contractual duties to the new holder.[224] The overall effect of the transfer of the bill of lading on the relations of carrier, transferor of the bill and transferee is similar to a novation but is probably best regarded as being *sui generis*.[225] Nevertheless, whether the matter is looked at in terms of assignment of rights under the contract of carriage to the transferee, or more fully in terms of a novation of the contract of carriage or a *sui generis* matter, the law applicable to the relations of carrier and transferee should,[226] it is

---

[222] It is a matter of no small difficulty to determine what precisely happens when the transfer of a bill of lading from consignee to indorsee, or a broader range of events including the transfer, serves to transfer to the indorsee both rights and duties under the original contract of carriage. In English law, the best analysis, it is submitted, is that under the terms of the Carriage of Goods by Sea Act 1992 a sui generis transfer occurs, which shares certain characteristics with both assignment and novation. See above, paras 5.22 and 14.49–56, and n 225 below.

[223] This is consistent with Art 12(1) of the Rome Convention. See above, para 14.54.

[224] Carriage of Goods by Sea Act 1992, s 3. In the ordinary course of events, the transferor will drop out of the picture when the transferee deals with the bill of lading (see *Borealis AB v Stargas Ltd (The Berge Sisar)* [2002] 2 AC 205), but it is also most likely that, by that time, all duties owed under the contract of carriage to the carrier will have been performed.

[225] In English law, the statutory scheme for the transfer of rights and liabilities to transferees of bills of lading (laid down first in the Bills of Lading Act 1855 and latterly in the Carriage of Goods by Sea Act 1992) bears certain similarities to novation, though, falling short of a full novation, is treated in this work as *sui generis*, neither full novation nor assignment. So far as the approach to novation might serve as an analogy for this *sui generis* transfer, it is instructive to observe that English law treats novation as a two-stage event. First, there is the discharge of the contract between, in this case, the carrier and the transferor, and second, there is the concomitant creation of a new contract between the carrier and the transferee of the bill of lading. In English law, therefore, there might conceivably be two applicable laws—the law applicable to the original contract, which determines whether it has been discharged, and the law applicable to the new contract, which determines whether it has been validly concluded: see *Wight v Eckhardt GmbH* [2003] UKPC 37 [2004] 1 AC 147. It is however unlikely, even on this analysis, that separate laws would be found to govern the rescission of the first and the creation of the second contract. A further complication arising out of the scheme of the Carriage of Goods by Sea Act 1992 is that the transfer of rights and liabilities under the bill of lading contract occur at different times (ss 2–3) and the shipper remains liable on the contract. This strengthens the link between true novation and the *sui generis* statutory transfer. In some civil law systems, novation is seen as dealing with a continuing contract in which one party is replaced by another. Nothing in the Rome Convention would appear to determine which is the proper way to deal with novation (still less a *sui generis* transfer akin to it), with the result that a common law and a civil law country might conceivably, applying the same choice of law previsions in the Rome Convention, arrive at different conclusions as to the applicable law. See further above, paras 14.49–56.

[226] But subject to the further requirement that the 'contract' between the carrier and the transferee is also valid (in terms of both formal and essential validity) between those parties and that the transferee consents to a choice of law clause contained in the bill of lading. See above, para 14.54.

submitted, be the law applicable to the contract of carriage between carrier and transferor.[227]

Furthermore, it is by no means artificial to treat the bill of lading, in its **18.85** characterization as a document of title, as embodying an attornment (or undertaking) by the carrier to whoever might be the holder of the bill of lading from time to time. Similarly, it is only the accident of history that prevents the bill of lading from being seen as containing a unilateral offer to deliver on the part of the carrier, capable of maturing into a contract when it meets an impliedly requested act,[228] whether it be the acceptance of the bill from the transferor or some other act. To treat the holder's constructive possession as tantamount to holding the carrier bound to deliver pursuant to the original contract of carriage, and hence an aspect of that contract, is not at all implausible.[229] Thus seen, the transfer of the bill of lading could be seen as effecting also a transfer of the contractual right to demand delivery from the carrier. The applicable law, in respect of the carrier's duty to deliver to the lawful holder of the bill of lading, would therefore be the law applicable to the contract of carriage and not the law of the place where the bill of lading was issued or the law of the place where from time to time it is transferred. The problem with adopting the latter approach is that it would create a sort of roving governing law, following the bill of lading from place to place, thus varying the contractual risk of the carrier. It would also be hard to reconcile with the domestic rule of English law that the bill of lading, as between carrier and subsequent transferee, is not merely evidence of the contract of carriage but *is* the contract of carriage.[230] Additional support for applying the law of the contract of carriage to the carrier's delivery duty is the fact that the place of transfer of the bill of lading, which in English law turns upon indorsement and delivery, may be a matter of accident.

---

[227] Although reference is here made to the transferor, in the case of a sales string it all goes back to the contract made with the carrier by the shipper, who will also be the transferor (except in those cases where the shipper is not the consignee). For the sake of convenience, the submission made in the text is made even where there are parol provisions in the original contract of carriage that do not transfer to subsequent holders of the bill of lading (see *Leduc & Co v Ward* (1888) 20 QBD 475).

[228] cf *The Future Express* [1992] 2 Lloyd's Rep 79, aff'd [1993] 2 Lloyd's Rep 542.

[229] In *MacWilliam (JI) Co Inc v Mediterranean Shipping Co SA (The Rafaela S)* [2003] EWCA Civ 556, [2004] 2 WLR 283 a straight consigned bill of lading, under which the carrier's duty was to deliver to the named consignee on presentation of the bill, that consignee being unable to transfer the bill to any subsequent holder, was held, for the purpose of the Carriage of Goods by Sea Act 1971, incorporating the Hague-Visby Rules on the liability of carriers, to be a document of title. The bill had been issued in Durban, the contract appeared to be governed by English law and no mention was made of the law of South Africa as the law of the *situs*.

[230] *Leduc & Co v Ward* (1888) 20 QBD 475; *The Ardennes* [1951] 1 KB 55.

4. DELIVERY DUTY AND CONTRACTUAL DUTIES

18.86 Furthermore, given that the carrier's obligation to deliver the goods is its most basic obligation, it would be entirely artificial to allocate that duty to deliver, as expressed in the bill of lading, to the law governing the transfer of proprietary interests in the goods when a different law, the law governing the contract, determined further details of the carrier's obligations, relating for example to the condition of the ship and its navigation. Although dépeçage is recognized in the conflict of laws,[231] it introduces an element of complexity that should not lightly be accepted. It is therefore submitted that all of the carrier's obligations, as expressed in the bill of lading, should be governed by the law applicable to the contract of carriage. That same law should determine whether the bill of lading is a transferable document in the first place and also whether it remains as a 'current, living instrument'.[232] The law applicable to the contract should therefore determine whether the bill of lading has lapsed and whether the carrier is released from its delivery obligation to the lawful holder once it has delivered to the holder of one of the original bills.[233]

5. BILLS OF LADING IN SETS

18.87 A complication arising out of the issue of bills of lading in sets of more than the original[234] is present where original bills have been transferred to different and successive transferees, each claiming an entitlement to receive delivery from the carrier and each holding an original bill of lading. The issue here is one of priority in respect of different dealings involving different versions of an original document. This arose in the domestic case of *Barber v Meyerstein*,[235] where a contest between different transferees, a pledgee bank and a buyer, was resolved by interpreting the language of the bill of lading itself, which stated that the ship's master 'affirmed to three bills of lading, all of the same time and date, one of which being accomplished,[236] the others to stand void'. The first transferee prevailed over the other transferee despite the latter being the first to

---

[231] Rome Convention, Art 3(1).

[232] *Enichem Anic SpA v Ampelos Shipping Co Ltd (The Delfini)* [1990] 1 Lloyd's Rep 252; *Barclays Bank Ltd v Commissioners of Customs & Excise* [1963] 1 Lloyd's Rep 81.

[233] *Glyn Mills, Currie & Co v East and West India Dock Co* (1882) 7 App Cas 591.

[234] Original bills, for historical reasons, are usually issued in sets of three (sometimes four) originals. This gives rise to a significant risk of fraud by the transferor if the transferee does not insist on receiving the full set from the transferor.

[235] (1870) LR 4 HL 317.

[236] The outcome of *Barber v Meyerstein*, ibid, turned on the meaning of this word, which was interpreted by the House of Lords as meaning transferred and not as meaning surrendered to the carrier.

notify the carrier since the accomplishment of the bill dated from the transfer of the first original copy and not from the presentation of the first original copy to the carrier. A similar conflict might arise where the holder of a delivery warrant representing goods in store seeks to pledge or hypothecate the warrant with a creditor whilst at the same time selling the goods themselves to a buyer. It is one thing if the two transactions take place in the same jurisdiction; the issue should be resolved by reference to the temporal priority rules of that jurisdiction. Suppose, however, that in two different jurisdictions a CIF seller first pledges one bill of lading from the original set with a bank and secondly transfers another to a buyer against payment, the contractual intent being that the bank obtains a special property in the underlying goods and the buyer obtains the general property.[237] Now, if one of the governing laws dates priority according to the first transaction, whilst the other dates it according to the order of presentation of the bill of lading to the carrier, then the spectre is presented of two governing laws of the *situs* reaching opposite outcomes.[238] The preferred solution is therefore to abandon the law of the *situs* of the bill of lading at the time of transfer and to apply instead either the law of the forum or the law of the contract of carriage. The former option is somewhat unprincipled so the latter, which governs certain issues involving carriers, is therefore preferable.

6. AN UNSATISFACTORY AUTHORITY

The somewhat unsatisfactory and unclear decision of the House of Lords **18.88** in *Inglis v Robertson*,[239] however, does not provide support for the application of the law of the contract of carriage to some or all of the above issues. In that case, a quantity of whisky in a Glasgow warehouse in the name of Goldsmith was the subject of a hypothecation (or pledge) entered into by Goldsmith in England with a creditor, Inglis. Goldsmith indorsed and delivered to Inglis certain delivery warrants for the whisky issued by the warehouse-keeper and stating that the whisky was 'held to the order of . . . Goldsmith or assigns by indorsement hereon . . .'. Inglis's title to the whisky was contested by certain Scottish creditors who had later caused the whisky to be arrested in the hands of warehouse-keeper. It was their

---

[237] As occurred in *Barber v Meyerstein*, ibid.

[238] In the case of accounts receivable (book debts), the solution adopted by the UN Convention on the Assignment of Receivables in International Trade (Art 22) is to refer the issue of priority, where the receivable is assigned on more than one occasion, to the law of the assignor's location. The CIF equivalent where one original bill of lading is pledged with a bank and the other transferred to the buyer would be to apply the law of the seller's residence.

[239] [1898] AC 616.

contention that they prevailed over Inglis on the ground that he did not have a pledge interest in the whisky because he had not given notice of the hypothecation to the warehouse-keeper, which they asserted was necessary under Scots law.

18.89   The outcome was in favour of the Scottish creditors but the reasoning is somewhat sparse and unhelpful. First, the House of Lords, treating the hypothecation as a pledge, considered the effect of the Factors Act 1889 on this transaction, that Act also being applicable in Scotland.[240] Since the hypothecation preceded the arrest, the Factors Act provisions ought not to have been in issue for they apply to cases where a pledge overrides prior property interests and do not respond to the question whether a transaction within its scope is in turn overridden by a subsequent transaction or action to which it does not apply.[241] The House of Lords ruled that the Factors Act indeed did not apply, but for different reasons. In consequence, the issue now facing the court was whether, as between Goldsmith and Inglis, the whisky itself had been effectively pledged upon the transfer of the delivery warrants. Certainly, as a matter of English law[242] then and now, this would turn upon whether the ordinary requirement— that a pledge of goods which are held by a third party requires the third party bailee to attorn to the supposed pledgee[243]—had been set aside on the ground that the delivery warrants were documents of title whose transfer could perfect the pledge even without the bailee's attornment. In English law, delivery warrants have never been documents of title in this sense. *Inglis v Robertson* in effect held that they were not documents of title under Scots law either, since Scots law was the law applied by the court.

18.90   The one safe conclusion that can be drawn from the case is that the law of the country of transfer, of a document claimed to be a document of title, does not determine the status of that document where the underlying goods are located in a different country. The law of the country of transfer may well govern the pledge of the documents themselves but does not go further and extend the pledge of the documents to the underlying goods when the goods are in another country.[244] That leaves for discussion the reason why Scots law was applied. Lord Watson, the only member of the court to address the central issue, bases his judgment on the *situs*

---

[240]   By the Factors (Scotland) Act 1890.
[241]   Lord Watson, however, was at pains to stress that the provisions of the Factors Act 1889, so far as they might be applicable to pledges of goods by documentary means by mercantile agents, did not go further and alter the Scots law of pledge in general: [1898] AC 616, 628.
[242]   The House of Lords appears to have treated Scots law as the same.
[243]   That is, undertakes to the pledgee to hold the goods at the disposition of the pledgee.
[244]   [1898] AC 616, 625–626 (Lord Watson).

of the goods in Scotland, though he made it plain that he would not apply, to dealings in a bill of lading as representing goods, the law of the country where the ship carrying the goods was to discharge them.[245] Since the fundamental question is whether the warehouse-keeper would have been bound without more ado to deliver the whisky to Inglis, it is submitted that the better approach would be to apply the law governing the warehousing contract. On the facts, that would almost certainly have been Scots law.

7. Misdelivery and the Holder's Options

On the assumption that the above analysis is correct, suppose now that **18.91** the carrier is guilty of misdelivery by handing over the goods to someone who is not the lawful holder of the bill of lading.[246] The lawful holder may elect to sue the carrier for breach of contract. Alternatively, the holder may wish to sue the carrier in the tort of conversion on the basis of misdelivery,[247] which would then be a matter for the law governing the tort. The holder's claim would, in English law at least, be based upon the right to immediate possession of the goods[248] represented by holding a common law document of title to them. The existence of a right to immediate possession arising out of a contract is, in English law, a matter for the law applicable to the contract.[249] As in domestic English law,[250] the holder should have the right to elect between contract and tort in framing his action. Suppose instead or in addition that the holder's action is in tort against a third party tortfeasor, for example a party obtaining delivery of the goods from a carrier without producing the bill of lading and without having the status of the lawful holder of the bill of lading. The holder's right to immediate possession, needed to ground the action against the third party, arising out of the contract of carriage ought again to be determined by the law applicable to the contract. It should not matter that the third party wrongdoer is not a party to that contract. It would be odd if the choice of law rules for conversion of the cargo should be

---

[245] ibid, at 627.

[246] This is a risk frequently run by carriers, against a suitable indemnity, when the bill of lading is not available for presentation at the end of the voyage and appears to be an almost invariable feature of the discharge of bulk oil cargoes.

[247] *Devereux v Barclay* (1819) 2 B & Ald 702.   [248] *Fenn v Bittleston* (1851) 7 Ex 152.

[249] See *Kahler v Midland Bank* [1950] AC 24 and *Zivnostenska Banka v Frankman* [1950] AC 57, as discussed in *Glencore International AG v Metro Trading Inc (No 2)* [2001] 1 Lloyd's Rep 284 at [25]-[27]. It would however be a matter for the law of the *situs* to determine whether a right to immediate possession was relevant for the purpose of maintaining an action to protect a property right: see the discussion of the incidental question below, paras 18.119–121.

[250] *Henderson v Merrett Syndicates* [1995] 2 AC 145.

different according to whether the carrier or the third party was being sued, especially if the two of them are being sued at the same time by the lawful holder.[251]

8. Passing of Property Issues to be Resolved

18.92 There remain for resolution a number of passing of property questions set out above. The law applicable to the contract of carriage has much to commend it when goods and documents are separated and located in different jurisdictions. On this view, that law should determine whether the property in goods can pass without a transfer of the underlying bill of lading. The alternative view is that this is a matter of formal validity and is therefore determined by the law of the *situs* of the goods. On balance, however, the latter law is closer to orthodoxy and so is to be preferred. The next question concerns the law that should determine whether the transfer of a bill of lading or other document of title passes only such property interest as the transferor intends or some other broader interest. The law governing the contract of carriage, it is submitted, is best qualified to deal with this question. Another question concerns the formal requirements that must be satisfied if a document of title is to be transferred (for example, indorsement and delivery). This, it is submitted, should be a matter for the law of the place where the document was issued (*lex rei cartae*). A person to whom the document is subsequently presented or transferred may reasonably not know where the document was previously transferred and should not be put upon inquiry to find out. The final question concerns the possession of documents that give evidence of ownership or of an authority to deal in goods. It may be that the documents are issued in one country, the goods are situate in another and the dealing in the documents takes place in a third. The most practical solution in this case is to remit the question to the law of the *situs* of the goods themselves.

IX. RESERVATION OF TITLE CLAUSES[252]

18.93 The effect of a simple retention of title clause[253] is that the seller retains his property in the goods notwithstanding the delivery to the buyer or the performance of any other act which, but for the clause, would have served

---

[251] See also the discussion of conversion above, paras 17.53–54.

[252] C Morse, 'Reservation of Title in English Private International Law' [1993] JBL 168.

[253] Defined for present purposes as a clause dealing with the original goods, whether or not the clause is an 'all moneys' clause that prevents the property in goods supplied from passing to the buyer until all debts due from the buyer have been paid.

to transfer ownership to the buyer. In more complex cases, sellers have been driven by commercial imperatives to bring within the scope of such clauses a right to new goods manufactured by the buyer with the seller's goods and a right to the money proceeds of the seller's goods or of these new goods. The position regarding simple clauses will be discussed before attention is turned to more complex cases. There have been a number of Irish and Scottish cases but the matter has not come before the English courts. A further matter to consider is the effect of a provision dealing with retention of title in the EC Late Payment Directive.[254]

1. SIMPLE RESERVATION OF TITLE

The position taken in this book is that, in English law, the law applicable **18.94** to the contract determines the validity of a reservation of title clause but the law applicable to property matters determines its effect in proprietary terms.[255] The argument advanced earlier in this chapter was that the law applicable to the contract was more apt to deal with bilateral matters than the law of the *situs*,[256] though the little authority that there is did not support a distinction being drawn between bilateral and trilateral matters. Subject to the identification of the choice of law rule, if a seller effectively under the governing law reserves title to goods delivered to the buyer then that reservation should be recognized once those goods are brought into England.[257] If the goods are in the meantime taken into another country, and if that country's law does not recognize the effect of the seller's reservation, still the reservation will be recognized when the goods are subsequently brought into England. This proposition is subject to the absence of any transfer occurring in that intervening country,[258] for, if such a transfer does take place, the recognition of the law of the *situs* as the governing law necessarily entails the superseding effect of an earlier by a later law of the *situs*.[259]

Supposing that the law of the *situs* is the governing law, then there is **18.95** some difficulty applying it, because *where* the reservation occurs depends

---

[254] Directive on Combating Late Payment in Commercial Transactions (EC) 2000/35 [2000] OJ L200/35.

[255] See above, paras 13.221 and 15.112–115, and below, paras 19.60–61.

[256] Reservation of title as between the contracting parties, both as to validity and effect, is treated by the Hague Convention 1986 (Art 12(e)) as a matter for the law applicable to the contract. See further above, paras 15.112–115.

[257] *Winkworth v Christie Manson & Woods Ltd* [1980] Ch 496.

[258] If the law applied by the English court is the law of the *situs*. If it is the law applicable to the contract, then an intervening transfer, to be effective, must be effective under that law.

[259] This issue is dealt with below in the context of conditional sales. An intervening transfer occurring after the reservation of title by the seller gives rise to a tripartite conflict involving the reserving seller and the third party dealing with the buyer.

upon *when* it occurs. This in turn will depend on the terms upon which delivery took place. The following discussion of FOB and CIF contracts is based upon the applicability of English law to these matters, which, as will be explained below, should not be taken for granted.

18.96 Section 19(1) of the Sale of Goods Act allows the seller to reserve the right of disposal 'by the terms of the contract or appropriation'. A reservation of title upon the appropriation of the goods to the contract would occur, for example, when a German seller delivers goods to a carrier under an FOB Hamburg contract and takes a bill of lading naming himself as consignee, the vessel in question being bound for Southampton where the goods will be discharged. The reservation of title should in principle be effective even if the seller's behaviour is not sanctioned by the contract.[260] The reservation takes place in Germany at the point of delivery to the carrier and it is submitted that reservation is an act, rather than a process that continues as long as the buyer is denied the property in the goods and that has to be justified every time the goods cross national borders.

2. Time of Reservation of Title

18.97 Where the contract itself contains a reservation of title clause, it by no means follows under the law of the *situs* approach that the reservation takes place at the contract date. First, in the great bulk of cases where goods have to be transported to the buyer, they will first have to be ascertained before the property in them can pass.[261] Second, it is only in the case of specific goods that a (weak)[262] presumption arises that the property passes at the contract date.[263] The reservation of title, it is submitted, occurs in English domestic law when, but for the reservation, the property in the goods would pass to the buyer.[264] In the FOB example above, the property would have passed upon delivery to the carrier.[265]

18.98 The position in CIF contracts is a little more difficult. In cases where the particular goods have been identified to the contract before shipment, it

---

[260] There is no authority on this point but it follows from (a) the disjunctive language of s 19(1) ('contract or appropriation'), and (b) from the treatment of the passing of property as a consensual act based upon the consent of both parties (see, eg, s 18 *Rule 5* and its requirement of unconditional appropriation by one party with the assent of the other). A seller acting in breach of contract may yet frustrate the passing of property to the buyer. See J Bradgate, 'The Post-Contractual Reservation of Title' [1988] JBL 477.

[261] Sale of Goods Act 1979, s 16. This is subject to the rules governing the acquisition of an undivided interest in an identified bulk (ss 20A-B) which permit the acquisition of such an interest upon payment. Sections 20A-B are more likely to affect CIF than FOB contracts.

[262] *RV Ward Ltd v Bignall* [1967] 1 QB 534, 545 (Diplock J).

[263] Sale of Goods Act 1979, s 18 *Rule 1*.   [264] ibid, s 18.

[265] ibid, s 18 *Rule 5*; *Carlos Federspiel & Co SA v Charles Twigg & Co Ltd* [1957] 1 Lloyd's Rep 240.

might be thought that the law is the same as for FOB contracts. But the CIF seller does not in the normal case contract with the carrier as the buyer's agent,[266] with the result that delivery to the carrier is not delivery to the buyer. Furthermore, the CIF seller's delivery duty is not a duty to deliver the goods themselves to the buyer or to the buyer's agent. Instead, delivery will take place in the form of documents when these are transferred to the buyer against payment.[267] In this common, even conventional, case, there is no reservation of title at all because in effect payment takes place on documentary delivery. If, however, payment were to be deferred and the seller were to reserve title notwithstanding the transfer of the shipping documents, there would be the added difficulty of knowing where the documentary delivery occurred in those cases where banks become involved in documentary collections. The likely view is that the bank releasing the documents to the buyer—an act that may take place in the buyer's country but may not—is acting as the seller's agent or sub-agent[268] in doing so. On that analysis, the reservation of title would occur at the point of release. Where the goods have not been identified to the contract before shipment, there is the further point that the property cannot pass until a notice of appropriation is given identifying a particular cargo to the contract.[269] As for goods that are dispatched from the seller's country on terms that physical delivery is to be made in the buyer's country,[270] the reservation of title will take effect in the buyer's country, whose law will therefore rule upon the effectiveness of the clause.

3. TIME OF RESERVATION AND FOREIGN LAW

So far, English domestic law has been considered in determining when, **18.99** and thus where, the reservation occurs. In the case of a foreign law of the *situs*, it is not at all self-evident that this is the correct approach to adopt. Furthermore, there are differences in the substantive laws of various countries that invest this issue with some practical significance. Although consent is built into the passing of property in English law, in practice the passing of property hinges in most cases upon delivery in those cases where no reservation of title occurs.[271] Consequently, English law differs

---

[266] The requirement in ibid, s 32(2) that the seller enter into a reasonable contract with the carrier 'on behalf of the buyer', while extending to CIF contracts should not mean that the seller is the buyer's agent: see *Houlder Bros & Co Ltd v Commissioner of Public Works* [1908] AC 276, 290.

[267] *Comptoir d'Achat et du Boerenbond Belge S/A v Luis de Ridder (The Julia)* [1949] AC 293; *Congimex Cia Geral SARL v Tradax Export SA* [1983] 1 Lloyd's Rep 250.

[268] The bank releasing the documents may do so under a mandate conferred by the seller's bank.

[269] Bridge, *The International Sale of Goods*, 167–180.

[270] e.g. DES (delivery ex ship, the Incoterms 2000 equivalent of ex ship contracts).

[271] Bridge, *The Sale of Goods*, Ch 3.

less than might be supposed from systems of law, like German law, that accord to delivery a more formal role in the passing of property.[272] French law, on the other hand, subscribes more fully to the consent rule than English law, and it may be that, under a DES Southampton contract, subject to English law, where shipment has occurred in Le Havre, a French court would consider the reservation to have occurred either at the contract date or when the goods were sufficiently identified to the contract ('individualisé'), perhaps upon shipment or preparation for shipment in France.

18.100 This latter case poses sharply the question whether the time and place that reservation occurs should be determined according to English law or according to French law. To answer this question, one should first ask whether reservation of title is governed by the law of the contract (English law) or by the law of the *situs*.[273] As stated above, English law comes down in favour of the law of the *situs*. The next question is whether that law is the law of the *situs* at the date and place of delivery (English law), or the law of the *situs* at the date of the contract and where the goods are located at that time (French law). The identification of the correct law of the *situs* is no easy matter. English domestic law is on balance biased towards delivery as the pivotal event for the passing of property,[274] while French law is biased towards consent.[275] The possibilities are various. Either the law of the forum could build upon its domestic assumptions, and locate and time the law of the *situs* accordingly. Or it could list the various *situses* of the goods during the life of the contract, and identify the first possible law of the *situs* as the governing law for property matters. Or, in accordance with the power dynamics of the law of the *situs*, the forum could apply the law of that *situs* where the goods are located at the point where the seller loses physical control. (In all three cases, the law of the forum might invoke the choice of law rules of the selected law of the *situs*.) If the last approach is favoured, it would lead to the further complication of considering in detail complex transits involving more than one carrier as well as the details of the various contracts, looking to the transferability of any shipping documents, the identity of

---

[272] BGB §929(1) (delivery is required as well as an agreement that ownership should pass).

[273] The law of the forum (English law) has no claim for consideration except in the case of default of argument.

[274] See *Carlos Federspiel & Co SA v Charles Twigg & Co Ltd* [1957] 1 Lloyd's Rep 240 and Sale of Goods Act 1979, s 18 *Rule 5(ii)*. The presumptive rule that the property in specific goods passes at the contract date (s 18 *Rule 5(i)*) is regarded as quite easily displaced: *RV Ward Ltd v Bignall* [1967] 1 QB 534.

[275] Code civil, Art 1583 (a sale is complete between the parties as soon as the price and the goods are agreed upon ('convenu'), even though delivery and payment have not yet been carried out).

the consignee and the amenability of the carrier to further orders from the seller while goods are being carried.

The fractured nature of the law of the *situs* brings out the point that, if the **18.101** law of the contract were instead the governing law for reservation of title—and in this area above all it is difficult to separate contractual and proprietary issues—it would have the merit of being easier to apply than the law of the *situs*. There would be no need to determine when the reservation takes effect. Furthermore, difficult issues that might arise when the goods themselves and documents of title are both in circulation—which would complicate yet further an already difficult commitment to the law of the *situs*—would be avoided. The preference expressed in the admittedly exiguous authority for the law of the *situs*,[276] nevertheless, compels a further examination of its possibilities according to first principles. Of the possible approaches canvassed above to the law of the *situs*, it is submitted that the law of the *situs* to apply to determine whether the seller's reservation of title is effective is the law of the *situs* at the time of delivery. Delivery, moreover, should be defined in accordance with the law of the forum. The advantage of delivery, at least in the case of English law, is that the test for it is concrete and relatively straightforward. Delivery consists of the voluntary transfer of possession.[277] The occurrence of reservation of title, as seen above, need not be based upon a contractual right to reserve. The application of the law of the *situs* at the time and place of delivery would therefore unify all cases of reservation.

4. RESERVATION OF TITLE AND SUBSEQUENT SITUSES

The examples considered above were based upon the recognition of res- **18.102** ervation of title by the law of the *situs*. Suppose however that the law of the *situs* does not recognize the seller's reservation, whether for technical reasons or not at all. Suppose, further, that the goods are later brought into a jurisdiction, whether England or some other country, that on the same facts would have recognized the seller's reservation. In this case, the effect of the earlier law would have been to allow the property to pass to the buyer despite the seller's efforts to prevent this from happening. It follows that a commitment to the law of the *situs* involves treating the buyer as having the general property in the goods. Unlike the law of the *situs*, the law of the contract does not change so that this question does not arise in the first place. In the event that delivery actually takes place under a

---

[276] See *Glencore International AG v Metro Trading Inc (No 2)* [2001] 1 Lloyd's Rep 284; *Hardwick Game Farm v Suffolk Agricultural & Poultry Producers Association Ltd* [1966] 1 WLR 287, 328 (Diplock LJ).
[277] Sale of Goods Act 1979, s 61(1).

second law of the *situs*, a law that unlike the first does recognize the seller's reservation, then English law, it is submitted, should recognize the effect of the second law of the *situs* even though it means overriding the title acquired by the buyer under the first law of the *situs*. It would, however, be open to an English court to apply the choice of law rules of the second law of the *situs* to determine if that law would have recognized the rights acquired by the buyer under the first law of the *situs*.

18.103 Scottish decisions on simple reservation of title clauses have been complicated by the difficulty that Scottish courts have had in recognizing a simple reservation of title clause taking the form of an all moneys clause. Prior to the decision of the House of Lords, reversing the Inner House of the Court of Session, in *Armour v Thyssen Edelstahlwerke AG*,[278] it was considered that such clauses were not true reservations of title at all but rather impermissible attempts to take a non-possessory security over movable property.[279] Apart from that, the cases support the view that a reservation effective by the law applicable to the contract will be effective in Scotland. The reasoning in the cases is elliptical and it could well be that the law applicable to the contract was also the law of the *situs*. Otherwise, in the case of sale contracts governed by English law, the Scottish court would have applied English law had it not been for the parties' failure to plead and prove it.[280] Some support for the application of the law of the contract comes from the decision of the Outer House in *Zahnrad Fabrik Passau GmbH v Terex Ltd*,[281] which concerned a sale of vehicle components by a German seller to a Scottish buyer in circumstances where the buyer pleaded that the components had been irrevocably attached to certain earth-moving equipment.[282] It may be that Lord Davidson's judgment is limited to cases of attachment (or accession), but the following observation has a more general currency: 'If, as s.17 of the Sale of Goods Act provides, the parties to a contract are entitled to agree when property is to pass, then I think it is wrong to regard the lex *situs* as an inflexible corpus of law'.[283]

---

[278] [1991] 2 AC 339.

[279] *Hammer and Sohne v HWT Realisations Ltd* 1985 SLT 21, Sh Ct; *Emerald Stainless Steel Ltd v South Side Distribution Ltd* 1983 SLT 162, Outer House; *Deutz Engines Ltd v Terex Ltd* 1984 SLT 273, Outer House.

[280] *Emerald Stainless Steel Ltd v South Side Distribution Ltd*, ibid, and *Deutz Engines Ltd v Terex Ltd*, ibid.

[281] 1986 SLT 84. Irish case law on the subject is inconclusive. See *Re Interview Ltd* [1975] IR 382 and *Kruppstahl AG v Quitmann Products Ltd* [1982] ILRM 51. The cases appear to stand for the proposition that the determination between the German seller and the Irish buyer, under a contract governed by German law, of the location of the property in the goods according to German law is without prejudice to the proprietary effect of a transaction concluded in Ireland between the Irish buyer and third parties. So stated, the cases give some support for the application of the law of the contract.

[282] Accession is discussed below.   [283] 1986 SLT 84.

5. LATE PAYMENT DIRECTIVE

Article 4(1) of the EC Late Payment Directive,[284] which has not been the **18.104** subject of a specific transposition into English law, provides as follows:

Member States shall provide in conformity with the applicable national provisions designated by private international law that the seller retains title to goods until they are fully paid for if a retention of title clause has been expressly agreed between the buyer and the seller before the delivery of the goods.

This provision, absent from earlier drafts of the Directive, is far from straightforward.[285] To begin with, it is not in its terms specifically confined to simple reservation of title clauses. Nevertheless, the Directive speaks of the *retention* of title to goods and to payment for these goods: the seller cannot retain title to goods that the seller himself never supplied and the buyer (obviously) does not pay the seller for goods made by the buyer himself with the seller's raw materials. As for the meaning of Article 4(1), this is very difficult to discern and a number of avenues to understanding open up. First, the provision does not require Member States to recognize reservation of title in their own domestic laws. Had it done so, then it might have seemed that there would be no need at all to refer to rules of private international law since reservation of title would have been recognized in all states' laws, thus rendering the choice of law process immaterial. If the words 'designated by private international law' had been absent from Article 4(1), then this is precisely the way the provision could have been interpreted. Nevertheless, even if all Member States recognize reservation of title within their own domestic legal systems, the domestic law of each is territorially limited. Consequently, it does not follow that any one or more of these Member States' laws will recognize a reservation of title clause affecting goods at a time when the goods were outside their individual jurisdictions. It cannot therefore be said that the reference to private international law in Article 4(1) is mere surplusage.

Second, one possible interpretation of Article 4(1) builds upon the **18.105** assumption that the governing law might not recognize the principle of reservation of title. In that case, the forum in the Member State should apply an alternative rule that leads to the recognition of the seller's reservation of title. The insuperable problem with this interpretation is that the

---

[284] See above, n 254. See G McCormack, 'Retention of Title and the EC Late Payment Directive' (2001) 1 J of Corporate L Studies 501.

[285] But see McCormack, ibid, who says at 505: 'The simplest, most straightforward interpretation would be to say that if passing of property questions under a contract are governed by the law of a member state, then the member state must recognize a simple retention of title clause contained in that contract'.

Member State is not required to select a choice of law rule that validates the reservation of title, so as to choose for example the law of the forum as opposed to a hostile law of the *situs* (or law of the contract). Rather, the Member State has to provide for recognition by means of 'national provisions', a vague expression that, used by way of differentiation from private international law, must mean domestic law. If the reference to national provisions had been absent from Article 4(1), then the provision could have been read as requiring the Member State to select a rule of private international law that would have validated the reservation of title. But that awkward reference to national provisions is there and the stubborn fact is that a Member State can create only its own national law.

18.106 Third, Article 4(1) cannot be interpreted with any ease as itself laying down a choice of law rule. It refers to the 'express' agreement of the parties over the reservation clause, but does not state that the validity of this agreement depends upon the law of the contract. It requires that express agreement to be in place before delivery but does not state that its validity depends upon the law of the *situs* at the time of delivery. The Directive, in its recitals,[286] contemplates the portability of a reservation of title clause, so it may be that, once the reservation has been recognized by whichever law may be the governing law, the obligation of Member States is just to continue recognizing the reservation regardless of where the goods are subsequently taken. The problem with this interpretation is that, in the case of goods located in Germany at the time of the agreed reservation clause and then brought to England, Article 4(1) would require of the UK Government no more than that, if English law *does* recognize reservation of title in these circumstances, then it *should* recognize reservation of title.

18.107 Fourth, Article 4(1) might possibly mean that, if a Member State's law is designated by other Member States' private international law rules as applicable to the validity of reservation of title clauses (How many? And what if these rules are different?), then it should so arrange its domestic law that it recognizes the right of sellers to reserve title. Short of disregarding Article 4(1) altogether, it may be that for want of anything better it can be given this rather curious interpretation, which means that Member States already recognizing reservation of title need take no further action.[287] This range of divergent interpretative possibilities may not arise in the case of Westminster statutes but the legislation of the European Community is of an altogether different type and quality.

---

[286] See Recital (21).
[287] This may explain why the UK has taken no active steps to transpose Art 4(1).

6. COMPLEX RESERVATION OF TITLE

The question here is whether a seller's reservation of title survives not- **18.108** withstanding the attachment of the contract goods to other goods (*accessio* or accession), or the mixture of those goods with other goods (*confusio* or *commixtio*), or the processing or treatment of those goods so that they lose their identity and are subsumed under new goods (*specificatio* or specification).[288] A related question is whether a seller's purported reservation of title is recharacterized as having a different legal effect. In English domestic law, accession and specification are alike in that the process leads to the liquidation of the property that is lost. The irrevocable attachment of subsidiary goods to dominant goods means that there no longer exist subsidiary goods capable of being acquired, owned, possessed and alienated. As for specification, the manufacture of new goods can only be at the expense of one or more quantities of existing goods (admixed with labour) supplied to or possessed by the maker of the new goods. This process of liquidating existing goods, by irrevocable attachment or by specification, can only satisfactorily be dealt with by the law of the *situs*.[289] A law of the contract approach cannot work, if only because goods might come from different contractual streams to feed the accession or specification, and moreover the applicable contract laws may produce inconsistent results. Similarly, the law of the *situs* of the goods at the time and place where they are delivered to the buyer is unworkable. The position in the case of mixtures is not so pronounced as, in English domestic law again, ownership rights in respect of the different ingredients in the mixture are capable of surviving in the mixture in the transformed state of tenancies in common. Nevertheless, different contract laws (and *situs* laws) could ascribe different incidents to such shared interests, which also makes a case for applying the law of the *situs* where the mixture occurs.[290]

The issue of accession was considered by the Outer House in *Zahnrad* **18.109** *Fabrik Passau GmbH v Terex Ltd*,[291] where its resolution was complicated by various points of pleading.[292] The reservation of title clause in the contract provided: 'If [the] goods have become an integral part of other plant or machinery ownership shall be transferred to us according to §947(1) BGB

---

[288] On the issues raised by tracing and choice of law, see below, paras 19.8–97. See also J Harris, 'Tracing and the Conflict of Laws' (2002) 73 British Ybk of Intl Law 65.

[289] See *Glencore International AG v Metro Trading Inc (No 2)* [2001] 1 Lloyd's Rep 284, at [35].

[290] See ibid, at [32]. Mixtures are slightly more complex than accession and specification in so far as the components of the mixture might change and the mixture itself might move and attract different treatment as it passes across national borders.

[291] 1986 SLT 84.

[292] The case is strangely reminiscent of a nineteenth century decision of the Court of Exchequer in the heyday of Baron Parke.

(German Civil Law) and the customer will be appointed as custodian'. This clause, in other words, did not seek to negative the process leading to accession but rather to regulate its proprietary consequences. It could have been interpreted as imposing only a contractual obligation to transfer the amalgamated goods to the seller, though this did not fit with the approach of the German Civil Code, reference to which was made in the same clause.[293] The buyer contended that, even if German law was the proper law of the contract, still the matter of property rights was governed by the law of the *situs*, which was Scots law. The judgment of the court was that the buyer had failed to establish that an irrevocable attachment amounting to accession had taken place in accordance with Scots law. The consequence of this failure was that the original reservation of title—'the goods shall remain our property until payment has been made in full'—continued to operate unimpeded.[294] Nevertheless, the court continued, if the buyer had established that the test for accession laid down in Scots law had been satisfied, the contractual conditions posing a 'stiffer test'[295] for accession than Scots law should prevail if they did not oppose any 'fundamental principle of the law of Scotland'.[296] Moreover, Scots law was not fundamentally opposed to the notion of shared ownership arising out of an accession. As a matter of conflict of laws, the court's position seems hard to fathom but, it is submitted, the court does not submit issues of accession to the law of the contract or to the law of the original *situs*. Rather, it is administering the new *situs* law, Scots law, in a way that is flexible and that permits the parties by contract to vary the incidents of its application.[297]

7. Complex Reservation and Recharacterization

18.110 It remains to be considered which law determines whether a complex reservation of title clause is truly a reservation clause or whether it should be recharacterized as something else, such as—to take an example from English domestic law—a charge operating as security for payment by the buyer. Suppose that a German seller supplies raw materials, under the terms of a complex reservation of title clause, to an English buyer who adds further materials and labour by way of specification to manufacture new goods. Is it the law of the *situs* where the goods are situate at the time

---

[293] BGB §947(1) treats the original owners of the goods prior to the accession process as co-owners of the amalgamated goods.

[294] 1986 SLT 84, 86. Which might have been justified—but was not—on the ground that German law was the law of the contract or was the law of the *situs* at the time of the reservation.

[295] ibid, at 88.   [296] ibid, at 88.

[297] See *Glencore International AG v Metro Trading Inc (No 2)* [2001] 1 Lloyd's Rep 284 at [23].

of the contract, or the law of the place where the goods are delivered that determines whether this clause should be recharacterized, or is it rather the law of the *situs* where the work is carried out to make new goods? Or is it even the law of the place where the debtor is resident or where principal insolvency proceedings are conducted on the ground that the issue at stake is the relations among the debtor's various creditors? It is submitted that a commitment to the law of the *situs* based upon the power of that law must direct the application of the law of the *situs* at the time and place where the events occur that, allegedly, lead to the loss of identity of the original goods supplied by the seller, whether this take place by accession or by specification.

Complex reservation of title can also be in issue when a reservation of title **18.111** clause in a contract purports to give the seller rights to the proceeds of sale in the buyer's hands. The clause may, for example, deem the buyer to be reselling the goods as the agent of the seller. Alternatively, even in the absence of a complex reservation of title clause in the contract, the question may arise as to whether the buyer holds the proceeds of sale as a fiduciary so that the seller is entitled to trace the proceeds of the original goods into their substituted monetary in the buyer's hands.[298] In making a proprietary claim to the money proceeds, the seller's claim may be at the expense of the buyer's general creditors (who may be represented by an insolvency office holder) or it may be in competition with the rights of a secured creditor maintaining a claim over assets in the hands of the buyer. The approach taken in Dicey and Morris to restitutionary actions, namely, that the proper law of the obligation applies to actions for the reversal of an enrichment, fails to distinguish between personal and proprietary restitutionary claims.[299] For reasons given elsewhere in this work, it is submitted that the proper law of the obligation is not appropriate to determine whether there lies a proprietary action, brought by the seller claiming the money proceeds in the buyer's hands. Instead, like other proprietary matters, it should be the law of the *situs* that deals with this question.[300]

X. CONDITIONAL SALES

An issue that has arisen within federal countries,[301] but is by no means **18.112** confined to states of this type, concerns goods the subject of a conditional

---

[298] See below, paras 19.88–89; see also Harris, n 288 above.
[299] Rule 200. See below, para 19.70.   [300] See below, para 19.72.
[301] Especially the US and Canada. See Ziegel, n 201 above; J Davis, 'Conditional Sales and Chattel Mortgages in the Conflict of Laws' (1964) 13 ICLQ 53. These issues have not yet arisen in English law.

sale agreement. Suppose that the conditional seller is A (the property to remain with A until payment in full is made), the conditional buyer is B, and C is an innocent purchaser who acquires the goods from B, without notice of A's reserved property. The contract between A and B is concluded in State X and the goods are delivered there before being subsequently removed by B to State Y where they are sold to C. Suppose further that the laws of State X and State Y both contain the following registration rule. If a conditional seller fails to register the transaction, its property rights will be overridden on the sale of the goods by a conditional buyer to a good faith sub-buyer.[302] Registration, therefore, goes to perfection and not priority, which means that any right of priority accorded by the general law is lost or diminished if there has been no compliance with the registration requirement. The possibilities listed below present themselves.

1. FAILURE TO REGISTER

18.113 First, A fails to register the conditional sale agreement in State X and has not registered it in State Y by the time that B sells the goods to C. The goods are now in England where a title dispute between A and C is the subject of proceedings. The English court, it is submitted, should first consider the impact of the legislation of State X on the conditional sale transaction. In interpreting that legislation, the English court may conclude that it is not designed to have extraterritorial effect but rather protects innocent purchasers like C only when they purchase the goods in State X. Turning now to the law of State Y, the English court, in applying the law of State Y to the B-C transaction, must first determine the territorial scope of State Y's legislation. If it transpires that that law does not apply its registration rule where a conditional sale contract is concluded and the goods are delivered to the conditional buyer in another state, the English court should conclude that A's title has not been overridden by the transaction taking place in State Y.[303] If, however, the law of State Y

---

[302] The conditional sale problem can also arise if one or other or both of State X and State Y has a personal property security statute based upon Art 9 of the US Uniform Commercial Code so that a conditional sale is deemed to be a (non-specific) security agreement and a failure to file notice of a security agreement subordinates the secured creditor to purchasers of the collateral. It can also arise if the transaction between A and B is a chattel mortgage (or, in English parlance, a security bill of sale).

[303] This is consistent with the Canadian cases of *Jones v Twohey* (1908) 1 Alta LR 267; *Russell v Cline* (1909) 10 WLR 666; *McAloney & McInnis v General Motors Acceptance Corp* (1955) 37 MPR 131; *Rennie's Car Sales v Union Acceptance Corp* [1955] 4 DLR 822. Cf *Hannah v Pearlman* [1954] 1 DLR 282. For an early American case supporting the majority Canadian view, see *Marvin Safe Co v Norton* (1886) 7 A 418 (NJ).

does accord itself extraterritorial effect with regard to the transaction taking place between A and B in a *previous situs*, then, in so far as that effect is factored into the transaction between B and C taking place in State Y, an English court implementing the law of the *situs* rule should recognize this application of the law of State Y.[304]

Now, if the English court did conclude that the law of State X was **18.114** designed to have extraterritorial effect with regard to legal activity in a *subsequent situs* of the goods, its commitment to the law of the *situs* rule should lead it to refuse to give effect to that law so far as it sought to apply itself to a transaction occurring in State Y. Suppose, however, that the law of State X provides that, if a conditional sale contract is not registered in State X, then, notwithstanding the provisions of the contract, the property in the goods will pass to B. In such a case, the English court should recognize that the property has passed under the A-B transaction and should then apply the law of State Y as far as it concerns a B-C transaction where B is an unchallenged owner. A more difficult case is where the law of State X deems B to be the owner if the conditional sale contract is not registered within a stated period, say 21 days, after the contract is concluded, but the goods are removed to State Y before that period has expired. Here, the English court should disregard the divesting effect of the law of State X since it purports to apply to goods that are in another state. If, however, the law of State X provides that B is deemed to be the owner of the goods unless and until a conditional sale agreement is registered in State X, then an English court should recognize, pursuant to the law of State X, that A remains the owner of the goods at the time that B enters into State Y and sells them to C.

Returning now to the standard case where A remains the owner because **18.115** neither the registration rule of State X nor that of State Y applies, and the law of State Y does not have the extraterritorial effect described above, the result is undoubtedly odd. This is because the A-B transaction takes place in State X and the B-C transaction in State Y when, if both transactions occurred in either State X or in State Y, C would prevail in a title conflict with A. Yet this is the inevitable result of a law of the *situs* conflict rule. In federal states, one solution to the problem would be to have a national system of registration (or linked state systems of registration), so that a search by C in State Y would reveal a transaction registered in State X and

---

[304] It would be different if the law of State Y merely failed to recognize the proprietary effect of a transaction carried out in State X and recognized by the law of State X. An English court would not take account of the law of State Y merely because the goods subsequently passed through State Y: *Glencore International AG v Metro Trading Inc (No 2)* [2001] 1 Lloyd's Rep 284, at [34].

non-compliance with the registration requirement in State X would be tantamount to non-compliance in all other federal states. Another solution would be to modify the law of State Y so that, even in respect of conditional sale contracts concluded in another state, the conditional seller would be able to assert its rights in State Y only if it registered the conditional sale contract in State Y within a stated period of the goods being brought into State Y.[305]

18.116   In the case referred to above, the A-B conditional sale was concluded in State X and the B-C sub-sale in State Y. Suppose, however, that the goods are taken into State Y but are then subsequently removed to England where the B-C transaction is concluded. If the law of State Y provides that conditional sale contracts should be registered in State Y in the case of all goods brought into State Y, then an English court should decline to recognize the effect of that state's law so far as it sought to have extraterritorial effect on the A-B transaction.[306] There is no transaction taking place within State Y that can legitimize the application of the law of State Y as the law of the *situs*.[307] Suppose, further, in this same case that there has been a failure to register in State X but a subsequent registration in State Y. If, under the law of State X, the effect of non-registration is that title is deemed to be vested in B at a time when the goods are still situate in State X, an English court should recognize the effect of the law of State X as the law of the *situs*. There is no transaction occurring in State Y legitimizing the application of that state's law as the law of the *situs*.

18.117   So far, it has been assumed that both State X and State Y require the registration of conditional sales. If there is no such requirement in one or other of State X or State Y, the principles discussed above would continue to apply. In particular, if State X does not require registration of a conditional seller's title, and State Y's requirement of registration is not extraterritorially applied, then an English court should not regard C as prevailing over A because of the latter's failure to register.[308] On the other

---

[305] This solution requires a delicate balance to be established between the competing merits of A and C: the more time that A is given, the longer C is at risk and any requirement that A know of the removal of the goods into State Y would be prejudicial to C. For the purpose of this solution, it should not matter whether A has or has not first registered in State X. Such legislation in State Y might on its interpretation apply only in restricted circumstances. For example, the requirement might extend only to State Y residents or domiciliaries who enter into conditional sale contracts in another state and who then bring the goods back into State Y, and not to residents of other states who then bring the goods into State Y: *Industrial Acceptance Corp Ltd v La Flamme* [1950] 2 DLR 822.

[306] *Glencore International AG v Metro Trading Inc (No 2)* [2001] 1 Lloyd's Rep 284 at [34].

[307] But it will be for the law of State Y, as the law of the *situs*, to determine whether a title transaction has occurred in State Y: ibid, at [34].

[308] See *Goetschius v Brightman* (1927) 245 NY 186 (where State Y was the forum state).

hand, a transaction in State Y recognizing the title of C because of A's failure to register, even though the law of State Y purports to have extra-territorial effect on the A-B transaction, should similarly be recognized in England since the law of State Y is the law of the *situs* as far as the B-C transaction is concerned. If there is a registration requirement in State X, and A has failed to register there, but no registration requirement in State Y, then the effect of the law of State X on the A-B transaction will be recognized in an English court. That effect, however, may be very limited where the B-C transaction takes place in a later state since an English court will not give extraterritorial effect to the legislation of State X in relation to transactions in a *subsequent situs* state. It remains to add that, if the goods are removed from State X to State Y but no transaction takes place in the latter state, then the law of that state will be irrelevant in an English court in proceedings between A and C.

2. Registration of Conditional Sales and Priority Issues

Suppose, now, that registration is not a perfection point but rather a prior- **18.118** ity point, in that the registration of a conditional sale agreement (whether by constructive notice or otherwise) serves to rank the conditional seller ahead of anyone purchasing the goods from a conditional buyer. If the conditional sale is registered in State X but the goods are then brought into State Y, which has no comparable priority rule, the effect of a sale by B to C in State Y should be determined by the law of State Y and not by the law of State X.[309] This is a conventional application of the law of the *situs* rule. If the law of State Y were satisfied with registration in State X, then, in so far as the effect of the B-C transaction taking place in State Y is dealt with in the English courts, the law of State Y should apply to that transaction as the law of the *situs* despite its extraterritorial recognition of registration in State X.

XI. THE INCIDENTAL QUESTION

In the previous section, where successive dealings in the same goods were **18.119** discussed as they took place first in State X and then subsequently in State Y, it was stated that an English court applying the law of the forum would apply the law of State X, so far as it concerned transactions respecting the

---

[309] See *Century Credit Corp v Richard* (1962) 34 DLR (2d) 291; *Traders Finance Corp Ltd v Dawson Implements Ltd* (1958) 15 DLR (2d) 515. The same result applies *a fortiori* if the conditional sale is not registered in State X: *Re Fuhrmann* (1977) 78 DLR (3d) 284.

goods whilst they remained in State X, and the law of State Y, so far as it concerned transactions respecting the goods in State Y. An application of the law of the *situs* based upon the factual power of that law could lead to no other plausible solution. In particular, it was asserted, the law of State Y would be applied even if it gave itself an extraterritorial application to events occurring in State X. In that event, State Y would not itself be applying the *situs* principle.

18.120   The above discussion, therefore, assumes a conclusion to an intractable debate concerning the so-called incidental question.[310] So far as the transactions that are dealt with in this chapter are concerned, the incidental question can be summarized in the following abstract way: A, the seller of goods, reserves title to them under the law of State X, which is the law of the *situs*. The buyer, B, then removes the goods into State Y and sells them to C. According to the law of State Y, C acquires title to the goods, but C does so only because that law impugns A's reservation of title so far as it was effectively accomplished at a time when the goods were situate in State X. It may be that the law of State Y does not recognize reservation of title clauses at all, in a simple sale of goods case, or that the law of State Y, in a financed conditional sale, does not recognize A's (the seller's) title if it was not registered, regardless of whether the law of State X dispenses with the registration of conditional sale agreements.

18.121   As far as English law as the law of the forum is concerned, should it rule in favour of C, in a dispute between A and C, on the ground that the law of the second *situs*, State Y, gave C a title that overrode A's title? Or should it separate the validity of A's reservation of title and, treating it as an incidental question, apply to it the law of State X? If this latter course were adopted, the English court would delimit the law of State Y so that it applied in favour of C only in the case where A's title had not been validly reserved, which would not be the case on this approach. There is no clear answer in the modern law to whether the incidental question (the prior validity of A's reservation of title) should be dealt with by its own choice of law rule or by the choice of law rule dealing with the main question (the title conflict between A and C). Nevertheless, a refusal to treat the incidental question separately has the considerable authority of Dicey and Morris[311] on the ground that it leads to greater certainty.

---

[310] On which, see Dicey and Morris, 45–52; Cheshire and North, Ch 4.

[311] para 24–043 (criticising *Simpson v Fogo* (863) 1 H & M 195, 71 ER 85). See also A Briggs, *The Conflict of Laws* (Oxford: Clarendon, 2002) 19–20.

XII. THE INSOLVENCY REGULATION

The EC Regulation on Insolvency Proceedings[312] regulates judicial insolv- **10.122**
ency proceedings[313] within the European Community. In so doing, it contains provisions dealing with reservation of title and rights *in rem*, an
expression broad enough to embrace the rights of a conditional seller if
these are not already included within reservation of title. The Regulation
ascribes competence to the conduct of insolvency proceedings within the
European Community in those cases where the centre of a debtor's main
interests lies within the Community,[314] and seeks in the process to co-
ordinate the various measures dealing with a debtor's assets.[315] The Regulation provides for the opening of the main insolvency proceedings within
the Member State where the centre of the debtor's main interests lies,[316]
and for the opening of secondary insolvency proceedings in other Member
States where the debtor has an establishment, such secondary proceedings
being winding-up proceedings[317] and limited to assets of the debtor within
the territory of that Member State.[318] This scission of insolvency proceedings is based on the realization that it is impossible to have insolvency
proceedings of universal scope, especially in light of the widely differing
laws on security interests to be found in the Community.[319]

1. CONDUCT OF INSOLVENCY PROCEEDINGS

The Regulation lays down uniform conflict rules, but for the most part only **18.123**
with regard to the conduct of the proceedings.[320] Unless otherwise stated,
this law governing the conduct of the proceedings (the *lex concursus* or
the law of the insolvency proceedings)[321] is the law of the Member State
where the main and secondary proceedings are opened, as the case may

---

[312] No 1346/2000 of 29 May 2000 [2000] OJ L160/1. See G Moss, S Isaacs and I Fletcher
(eds), *The EC Regulation on Insolvency Proceedings* (Oxford: OUP, 2002). On the interpretation
of the Regulation, see the Virgos-Schmit Report of 8 July 1996 on the Convention of [*sic*]
Insolvency Proceedings.
[313] The expression 'insolvency proceedings' is to be given a broad meaning and is not
confined to cases where a judicial authority intervenes: see recital (10) of the Regulation. For
example, it includes the English process of administration (see Annex A), a process that can
now be instigated out of court by certain secured creditors (Insolvency Act 1986, Sch B1 as
added by the Enterprise Act 2002).
[314] Recital (14) of the Regulation.   [315] Recital (3) of the Regulation.   [316] Art 3(1).
[317] If opened after the opening of the main proceedings.   [318] Art 3(2), (3).
[319] Recital (11) of the Regulation.   [320] Recital (23) of the Regulation.
[321] As used in the Regulation, the *lex concursus* refers to the law of the state where the
insolvency proceedings are opened. In the literature, the expression is sometimes more fully
rendered as *lex fori concursus*, which reveals the elision in the expression *lex concursus* as it
captures two meanings: (a) the law of the state where the proceedings are opened; and (b)
the application of that state's law to the proceedings. The law of the insolvency proceedings
is here used in translation of *lex concursus*, especially to pick up this second matter.

be.[322] The Regulation is quite specific that there should be a divergence from the law of the insolvency proceedings in the case of 'rights *in rem*',[323] where the law of the *situs* applies to the 'basis, validity and extent of such a right'.[324] The proprietor of the right *in rem* 'should therefore be able to assert his right to segregation or separate settlement of the collateral security'.[325] It is also provided that the Regulation does not affect the rights *in rem* of creditors to, *inter alia*, tangible movable assets belonging to the debtor and situate in other Member States.[326] These rights include, for example, the right to dispose of assets and obtain satisfaction from the proceeds, particularly by way of mortgage or lien.[327] A similar provision deals with reservation of title over assets situate in another Member State.[328] Subject to this, the law of the insolvency proceedings determines 'the assets which form part of the main estate'.[329]

2. A SUBSTANTIVE CHOICE OF LAW RULE

18.124   Although it is generally true to say that the choice of law provisions in the Regulation are confined to the conduct of proceedings, Article 7(2) goes further and states a substantive choice of law rule. According to this rule, the opening of a seller's insolvency proceedings shall not constitute grounds for rescinding or terminating the sale and shall not prevent the buyer from acquiring title in those cases where the asset is situate in another Member State of the Community.[330] The language is broad enough to go beyond a rule of insolvency law of the state where the insolvency proceedings are opened. It would seem also to catch any attempt (albeit an unlikely prospect) by contracting parties to provide that the opening of insolvency proceedings shall have the proscribed effect on the contract.

18.125   It can therefore be seen that the law of the insolvency proceedings is limited in its effect as regards proprietary rights over tangible movables located in other Member States. The Regulation is silent as to tangible movables located in non-Member States; this subject is left to the choice of law rules of the Member State. It is also silent as to the role of the law of the

---

[322] ibid. In the case of ships and aircraft entered on a register, the applicable law is the law of the Member State where the register is kept: Art 11. That law also determines the rights of purchasers of the registered asset if the disposal takes place after the opening of insolvency proceedings in another Member State: Art 14.

[323] An expression that is not defined.

[324] Recital (25) of the Regulation.   [325] ibid.

[326] Art 5(1). The Regulation's silence with regard to assets in other states is because it is confined to intra-EC insolvency activity.

[327] Art 5(2).   [328] Art 7(1).   [329] Art 4(2)(b).

[330] Again, the Regulation is silent about other states because it is confined to intra-EC insolvency activity.

situs with regard to the creation of proprietary rights, whether by way of reservation of title or otherwise, over tangible movables that during the course of insolvency proceedings are located in the country of the law of the insolvency proceedings. Again, the choice of law rules of the law of the insolvency proceedings determine the extent to which those proprietary rights are to be recognized in the course of insolvency proceedings. The remaining question, therefore, is how far the law of the insolvency proceedings is limited in the scope of any action it may take concerning tangible movables situate in other Member States. The question may be more specifically posed by considering the restrictions imposed by the Insolvency Act 1986 on reservation of title rights where a company goes into administration.[331] Once an administrator has been appointed, no steps may be taken to repossess hire purchase goods except with the consent of the administrator or the permission of the court.[332] For present purposes, hire purchase includes conditional sale contracts and reservation of title agreements.[333] If English law as the law of the insolvency proceedings sought to impose these restrictions on tangible movables situate in another Member State, this, it is submitted, would be in breach of the Regulation. Although such restrictions do not as such amount to a denial of reservation of title and similar rights, the Regulation makes it clear that the 'basis, validity and extent' of *in rem* rights are a matter for the law of the *situs*, so that the party with such rights should 'be able to continue to assert his right to segregation or separate settlement of the collateral security'.[334] It is within the spirit of the Regulation to apply these words to reservation of title and not to limit them to security properly so called.

XIII. THE CAPE TOWN CONVENTION

Conditional sale contracts also arise for discussion under the terms of the **18.126** Cape Town Convention on International Interests in Mobile Equipment 2001, an initiative sponsored by Unidroit (the Rome-based International Institute for the Unification of Private Law).[335] The central feature of this

---

[331] As amended by the Enterprise Act 2002, Sch B1 (the principal effect of which is to extend these restrictions to cases where an administrator is appointed by a creditor out of court where formerly that creditor would have procured the appointment of an administrative receiver).

[332] Sch B1, para 43(3).   [333] Sch B1, para 111(1) (as well as chattel leasing contracts).

[334] Recital (25) of the Regulation.

[335] R Cuming, 'The draft UNIDROIT Convention on International Interests in Mobile Equipment' (1998) 30 Uniform Commercial Code LJ 365; R Cuming, 'The Characterisation of Interests and Transactions under the Convention on International Interests in Mobile Equipment 2001' in I Davies (ed), *Security Interests in Mobile Equipment* (Aldershot: Ashgate Dartmouth, 2002) 377; R Cuming, 'Overview of the Convention on International Interests in

Convention is not the enforcement of national security and similar interests in other jurisdictions but the creation of genuine international security, title reservation and leasing interests, together designated as international interests under the Convention, enforceable in Contracting States. Like any other measure of uniform substantive law, it therefore cuts across the normal choice of law process.[336] The Convention itself contains the general provisions of the scheme and there are specific protocols, at different stages of completion, that deal with aircraft equipment,[337] railway rolling stock and space assets.[338] The Convention cannot work alone without one or more of the protocols,[339] the purpose of the latter being to make necessary adaptations to the Convention for the subject-matter of the particular protocol.

18.127 The relevance of the Convention for sale is primarily that a conditional sale contract is a title reservation agreement under another name.[340] The bundling of security, title reservation and leasing together under the Convention is not quite tantamount to the functional definition of security under Article 9 of the Uniform Commercial Code in the United States and the laws of those other countries with modern personal property security statutes modelled upon Article 9. Unlike Article 9, the remedies of the creditor under the Convention depend upon whether the interest arises under a security agreement, on the one hand, or a title reservation agreement or leasing agreement on the other.[341] So, for a conditional sale, default on the part of the debtor entitles the creditor to terminate the

Mobile Equipment 2001' (2002) 35 Uniform Commercial Code LJ 73; R Goode 'Transcending the Boundaries of Earth and Space: the Preliminary Draft Unidroit Convention on International Interests in Mobile Equipment' (1998) 3 Uniform L Rev 52; R Goode 'The Cape Town Convention on International Interests in Mobile Equipment: a Driving Force for International Asset-Based Financing' (2002) 7 Uniform L Rev 3; R Goode, *Convention on International Interests in Mobile Equipment and Protocol Thereto on Matters Specific to Aircraft Equipment—Official Commentary* (Unidroit, 2002); R Goode, 'The UNIDROIT Mobile Equipment Convention' in M Bridge and R Stevens (eds), *Cross-Border Security and Insolvency* (Oxford: OUP, 2001), 225; Symposium on a New International Regimen Governing the Taking of Security in High-Value Mobile Assets: the Legal and Economic Implications (1999) 4 Uniform L Rev—Part 2. As of 28 May 2003, 26 states had signed the Convention and the Protocol on Aircraft Equipment, which will come into force on the first day of the month following the expiration of three months after the date of the deposit of the third instrument of ratification, acceptance, approval or accession (Art 49.1).

[336] Like the Vienna Convention 1980, however, the Cape Town Convention permits a reference to the applicable law, identified through the choice of law rules of the forum state, to deal with issues governed by the Convention but not expressly settled by it, in the event that general principles on which the Convention is based cannot provide an answer to the question raised (Art 7).

[337] Airframes, aircraft engines and helicopters (Art 2(3)).

[338] The protocols dealing with the last two items are still in draft form.

[339] The Convention and protocol have to be read together as a single instrument (Art 6).

[340] Art 1(ll).

[341] Arts 8, 10. In the case of aircraft, further remedies are given by the protocol in Art IX.

conditional sale agreement and take possession of the equipment or apply to the court for an order to the same effect.[342]

1. APPLICATION OF CONVENTION

The Convention applies when the debtor is situated[343] in a Contracting **18.128** State, the location of the creditor being immaterial.[344] The protocol on 'Matters Specific to Aircraft Equipment' extends the Convention, beyond cases of debtor residence, to cases where a helicopter or airframe is in the aircraft register of a Contracting State.[345] Otherwise, the *situs* of an object is not relevant for the scope of the Convention. The Convention makes provision for a register of international interests for each of the three types of 'object'.[346] The word 'object' is a term of art that apples only to the three types of equipment dealt with in the Convention.[347] The registry is significant for priority purposes, with earlier registrations ranking ahead of later registrations, registered interests ranking ahead of unregistered interests and buyers ranking ahead of unregistered interest but after prior registered interests.[348] An international interest is defined, not by reference to the location or movement of equipment, but simply by reference to its status as 'a uniquely identifiable object' and to its type as aircraft equipment, railway rolling stock or space asset.[349] It is inherent in the nature of such equipment that it can move or be moved across national frontiers, though there is no requirement in a given case that it actually do so. The classification of the agreement as security, title reservation or leasing agreement, significant for remedial purposes, is a matter for the 'applicable law',[350] which is undefined but should refer to the law applicable to the contract in question since it is a question of differentiating among contract types. That law does not provide the remedies—which removes a potential point of friction with the law of the *situs*—since the remedies are provided by the Convention itself. Another choice of law issue concerns attachments since the Convention provides that rights in an item, which is not itself an object but which is installed on an object, will survive that installation if this is provided for by the governing law.[351]

---

[342] Art 10.   [343] For the meaning of this, see Art 4.   [344] Art 3.
[345] Art IV.   [346] Art 16.   [347] Art 1(u).
[348] Art 29. For a modification of these rules in the case of an aircraft object, see Art XIV of the aircraft protocol.

[349] Art 2. The interest, for definitional and priority purposes, extends to the proceeds of equipment: Arts 2(5) and 29(6).

[350] Art 2(4).

[351] Art 29(7)(a). The question of the law that determines whether an irrevocable attachment occurs is for the sake of convenience considered along with reservation of title clauses.

2. THE CONVENTION AND THE LAW OF THE *SITUS*

18.129 The relations between the Convention and the law of the *situs* are not straightforward. As stated above, the remedies available to the creditor are defined by the Convention and not by the law of the *situs*. Again, the formal requirements for an agreement giving rise to an international interest are laid down in the Convention and are not taken from the law of the *situs*.[352] Nevertheless, the reference to the governing law in the case of rights surviving in an installed item permits the forum state to defer to the law of the *situs* of item and object at the date of installation to determine whether rights in the item are extinguished. It is nevertheless, a noticeable feature of the Convention that it functions on the basis of the debtor's residence and not at all on the *situs* of the object, whether at the date of the agreement or at any other time. If the factual control of the law of the *situs* means anything, it is hard to see how the Convention can be enforced in the case, for example, of a priority dispute arising under a conditional sale when the object is located in a state that is not party to the Convention and that would prescribe a different priority outcome.[353]

18.130 The practical limits of an international interest under the Convention in the face of an unaccommodating law of the *situs* are however recognized to a limited degree in the provisions on insolvency in Article 30. First, the Convention does not detract from 'any rules of law applicable in insolvency proceedings relating to the avoidance of a transaction as a preference or as a transfer in fraud of creditors . . .'.[354] This formula is broad enough to catch not just the domestic insolvency rules of a (Contracting) forum state but also its choice of law rules. Second, nevertheless, the Convention provides that a registered international interest is effective in insolvency proceedings.[355] Consequently, a failure by a conditional seller, for example, to conform to any registration requirements laid down by the law of the *situs* would be cured before the courts of the forum state if the conditional seller had registered under the Convention instead. It need hardly be said that this provision would be ineffective if the insolvency proceedings were taking place in a non-Contracting *situs* State. Third, there is a provision that Article 30 does not impair 'the effectiveness of an

---

[352] Art 7.
[353] The Convention also permits Contracting States to make a declaration setting out categories of non-consensual right or interest that prevail over a registered international interest (Art 39), but a state making such a declaration is at liberty to recognize or depart from the priority ranking of the law of the *situs*.
[354] Art 30(3)(a). It is submitted that this provision should be given a broad reading so as to include, for example, English rules on undervalue transactions.
[355] Art 30(1). For further provision, see Art XI of the aircraft protocol.

international interest in insolvency proceedings where that interest is effective under the applicable law'.[356] Hence, even if an international interest is not registered under the Convention, it shall nevertheless be effective in insolvency proceedings if such is the case according to the governing law.[357] Given that this provision like all others in the Convention is addressed to the courts of a Contracting state, it must mean that that state may maintain its existing choice of law rules in relation to agreements and interests governed by the Convention. Suppose, for example, that an international interest arises under a conditional sale agreement with respect to an object that is located in a Non-Contracting State and that interest is not registered under the Convention. If the Contracting forum state adheres to a law of the *situs* rule in property matters, then, as long as the seller's interest is effective under the law of the *situs*, as it will be if it conforms to any registration requirements laid down by that law, it will be recognized as effective in the forum state.

3. SALE OF EQUIPMENT

Lastly, the Convention permits its provisions to be applied to the 'sale and **18.131** prospective sale' of an object to the extent laid down in the relevant protocol.[358] The protocol on 'Matters Specific to Aircraft Equipment' takes up the invitation[359] and, with appropriate adaptations, applies, to sales and prospective sales, certain Convention provisions on the scope of application of the Convention,[360] registration,[361] and the effect of insolvency,[362] together with a number of other, general provisions in the Convention.[363] The protocol also, without reference to the law of the *situs*, permits seller and buyer to determine when the seller's interest is transferred to the buyer[364] and permits the buyer to take an interest clear of interests over which a registered international interest takes priority in Article 29.[365]

XIV. RISK

Risk is commonly thought of as a proprietary matter though in actuality **18.132** this is not the case.[366] It is, in the English law tradition, associated with the

---

[356] Art 30(2).
[357] An unregistered international interest could otherwise only be impaired by Art 30 if para (1) were read as containing an implied provision that such an interest would *not* be effective in insolvency proceedings.
[358] Art 41.   [359] See Art III.   [360] Arts 3–4 (debtor's residence).
[361] Arts 19(4), 20(1) and 25(2).   [362] Art 30.   [363] See the list in Art III.
[364] Art V(2). The protocol also permits buyer and seller to select the law applicable to their contract: Art VIII(2) (if the Contracting State makes a declaration to this effect: Art VIII(1)).
[365] Art X(4).   [366] See the discussion above, paras 13.196–200.

passing of property[367] and so merits some treatment in a chapter dealing with choice of law. The transfer of risk, nevertheless, is in sale of goods a contractual matter because the significance of its transfer is that the buyer, notwithstanding the occurrence of the event falling within the area of risk, is bound to pay the price or may not recover the price if it has already been paid (as the case may be). The failure of the seller to deliver goods of the agreed contractual quality and fitness, or even to deliver at all, would normally have various adverse consequences for the seller. In the event of non-delivery, the buyer could refuse to pay[368] or recover payment, and could also terminate the contract, as from the agreed delivery date in those cases where time is of the essence of the contract.[369] In the case of goods damaged as a result of the risk event, the buyer could not complain of a breach of the implied conditions relating to description, satisfactory quality and fitness for purpose. The significance of the transfer of risk is that what would otherwise amount to a breach of contract—non-delivery or non-conforming delivery by the seller—is not a breach of contract at all. Moreover, for the purpose of the seller's entitlement to the price, the seller in effect is deemed to have performed all conditions necessary for the recovery of the price. For these reasons, the transfer of risk should be regarded as a matter for the law applicable to the contract.[370]

18.133 Where English law, for example, is the law of the contract, an incidental question that could arise in some cases where the seller is suing for the price, or for an action for damages for non-acceptance, is whether the property in the goods has passed to the buyer. In systems where the transfer of risk hinges upon delivery,[371] the question will instead be whether delivery or the transfer of possession has been made. Any identification of one question as the main one and the other as incidental is impressionistic, but there is little room for doubt in the case of risk that, so far as its incidence turns upon proprietary notions like property and possession, these notions are part of the incidental question. Although English case law is short of a coherent and developed treatment of the incidental question,[372] the conventional view is that the choice of law rules governing the main question will also choose the law that governs the

---

[367] Sale of Goods Act 1979, s 20 (risk is transferred presumptively at the time that the property passes).
[368] ibid, s 28 (presumptively, delivery and payment are mutual and concurrent conditions). The Vienna Convention leaves the relationship of payment and delivery to the contract and takes no position on the order of payment and delivery: see Arts 30 and 53.
[369] See Bridge, *The Sale of Goods*, 214–219.
[370] This is the position adopted by the Hague Sales Convention 1986, Art 12(d); see above, para 15.110.
[371] See, e.g. Uniform Commercial Code, Art 2–509.
[372] See the above discussion on reservation of title.

incidental question.[373] Hence, if according to English rules French law is the law of the contract, the fact that at all material times the goods are situate in a third country will not prevent French law disposing of the incidental question.

This conclusion, nevertheless, is not overwhelming, for two reasons. First, **18.134** it overrides the power of the law of the *situs*, which is one of the primary forces behind its selection as the governing law for property matters. So far, nevertheless, as French law, in the above example, were to subscribe to the law of the *situs*, then that power would be recognized, displaced at one remove from English to French choice of law rules. Second, the force of subordinating the incidental to the main question is lessened in those cases where the solutions to main and incidental questions can be reconciled. Taking the case of a contract governed by English law where the goods are located in France at all material times, the English view that the transfer of risk goes presumptively with the passing of property can accommodate any rule governing the passing of property. There is no reason to suppose that it must be a passing of property rule in the Sale of Goods Act. In consequence, the governance of proprietary questions raised under the heading of risk must be considered as remaining open.

---

[373] Briggs, n 311 above, at 20.

19

Restitution and the International Sale of Goods: Choice of Law

I. SYNOPSIS

19.01 The nature and scope of the law of restitution has been the subject of a great deal of discussion. Whilst the subject has advanced enormously, its boundaries remain a subject of controversy. When one moves to discussion of restitution's role in private international law, the waters become murkier still. There is precious little judicial authority as to the classification of matters as restitutionary for choice of law purposes, although the subject has in recent years attracted the attention of academic authors.[1] Moreover, it remains very unclear what the choice of law rules for restitutionary obligations are, and, indeed, what they ought to be.

19.02 It is not the intention of this chapter to explore these questions in detail. That would take a book in its own right. Rather, the function of this

---

[1] See Dicey and Morris, Ch 34; *Cheshire and North*, Ch 20; F Rose (ed), *Restitution and the Conflict of Laws* (Oxford: Mansfield Press, 1995); G Panagopoulos, *Restitution in Private International Law* (Oxford: Hart, 2000).

chapter is to consider certain typical restitutionary claims which might arise in connection with a sale of goods contract.[2] We will then briefly consider the state of judicial and academic opinion as to the choice of law rules which might be applied to such claims. By necessity, any conclusions reached can only be tentative at this still embryonic stage of the development of the law.

II. RESTITUTION AND SALE OF GOODS CONTRACTS

Claims in unjust enrichment may arise if a contract is breached, frus- **19.03** trated, or rescinded for misrepresentation, or a mistake occurs, or the contract was induced by duress or undue influence. A seller may seek to recover goods, or their value, where a contract has been declared void[3] or voidable *ab initio*. A buyer might seek to recover the value of payments already made under the contract. Again, the buyer might have mistakenly overpaid and seek restitution on the grounds of mistake. It might also be that following a breach of contract, a claimant seeks to obtain the value of a benefit obtained by the other party from the breach. For example, a seller might be induced to breach his contract with the buyer by a third party, so that he can sell the goods to that third party for a higher price. The buyer might wish to obtain the value of the enrichment received by the seller.[4] In the situation where a seller is in breach of contract, the buyer might rather choose to treat the contract as discharged by the breach and seek to recover payments made on the basis of a total failure of consideration.[5]

III. CLASSIFICATION

The boundaries of the law of restitution are much debated, and remain **19.04** highly controversial, even in domestic law. 'Within restitution, a state of continual intellectual revolution appears to prevail, and domestic law causes of action are regarded and disregarded as restitutionary with unsettling rapidity.'[6] It is not essential that the same classifications be adopted for substantive law purposes and for choice of law purposes,

---

[2] Or purported contract—restitutionary obligations may frequently arise where the contract turns out to be void or voidable.

[3] Compare, in the jurisdiction context, *Kleinwort Benson Ltd v Glasgow City Council (No 2)* [1999] 1 AC 153, HL, discussed above, paras 8.13–15, 8.32–33.

[4] See, in the jurisdiction context, *Eddie v Alpa Srl* 2000 SLT 1062, Scottish Outer House, discussed above, para 8.16; see also paras 8.91–105.

[5] Compare Art 81 of the Vienna Convention. Alternatively, of course, he may affirm the contract and seek contractual damages for breach of contract.

[6] A Briggs, *The Conflict of Laws* (Oxford: Clarendon 2002) 191.

although one would expect some conceptual harmony between the two.[7] It is clear that issues of classification are capable of giving rise to very complex questions beyond the scope of this chapter.[8] However, in a general sense, we can reach an understanding of the types of claim which fall within the restitution choice of law rules. It has been suggested that 'restitution is identified by a receipt which unjustly enriches the defendant at the expense of the claimant: the cause of action focuses on the enrichment or gain rather than any measure of loss . . .'.[9] So, claims which are brought to recover payments made, or benefits conferred, pursuant to a void, rescinded, or discharged contract should be regarded as restitutionary, and not contractual claims.[10]

19.05 Fortunately, in the sale of goods context, it will be suggested that detailed discussion of the characterization process for choice of law purposes can be side stepped.[11] This is because, if the Rule in Dicey and Morris is accepted to be correct,[12] then most claims arising in connection with a contract will be governed by the law applicable, or putatively applicable, to the contract, however they might be classified. It is not a particular problem if the classification of restitution in private international law overlaps with other classification categories, if the choice of law rules to be applied will be the same, however the claim is classified.[13]

19.06 It would appear to follow that claims which arise pursuant to what was a valid contract should be determined by the same rules as apply to contractual issues. So, 'the consequences of the termination of obligations created by a valid contract, or arising from the mistaken performance of a valid contract, are almost certainly within the Rome Convention'.[14] This is not to deny in any way that these claims are restitutionary in nature; it merely suggests that the most appropriate choice of law rule to apply to such claims is the law applicable to the 'contract'.

---

[7] See Dicey and Morris, 1487.

[8] See also *Macmillan Inc v Bishopsgate Investment Trust plc (No 3)* [1996] 1 WLR 387, CA. Auld LJ stressed that the court must look beyond the framing of the cause of action and identify the real issue or issues raised. It is these issues which fall to be classified.

[9] Briggs, n 6 above, 193.

[10] However, the classification process can be a very complex one: see the discussion of how claims are classified for the purposes of jurisdiction, above, paras 8.13–27, 8.32–33, 8.36–50, 8.64–84, 8.86–88, 8.91–105.

[11] See Cheshire and North, 672–676 for discussion of some of the classification problems that may arise in restitution.

[12] As, with some refinements, it is suggested that it is: see Rule 200, discussed below, paras 19.07–34.

[13] Briggs, n 6 above, 193.

[14] Dicey and Morris, 1487.

IV. THE CHOICE OF LAW RULE FOR RESTITUTIONARY CLAIMS: GENERAL RULE; DICEY AND MORRIS, RULE 200(1)

As has been said, it is impossible definitively to state the choice of law rule **19.07** for all claims where restitution is sought. This is partly because of the number of different circumstances in which such claims might arise (and the fact that some are concerned with reversal of unjust enrichment by subtraction and some with restitution for wrongdoing). However, it is especially so because there is precious little certainty as to what these choice of law rules are and numerous different opinions of what they should be.[15] Where a claim is brought in respect of an unjust enrichment,[16] there are those who support the use of a single connecting factor, such as the law of the forum,[17] the personal law of one of the parties,[18] the law of the place of enrichment,[19] the proper law of the obligation,[20] the law governing the underlying relationship between the parties[21] and the law of the *situs*.[22] There are those who argue for a series of connecting factors to cover different situations.[23] There are those who favour rules of law without an exception,[24] or rules of law with an exception[25] and those who prefer a fluid test of identifying the most significant relationship.[26]

Within the confines of this chapter, it is sensible to examine what is argu- **19.08** ably the most widely accepted assessment of the current choice of law rules, namely the Rule in Dicey and Morris. Rule 200(1)[27] states that:

The obligation to restore the benefit of an enrichment obtained at another person's expense is governed by the proper law of the obligation.

---

[15] For a detailed survey of possible choice of law rules, see Cheshire and North, Ch 20. See also Panagopoulos, n 1 above).

[16] See generally Cheshire and North, 676–685.

[17] e.g. A Ehrenzweig, 'Restitution in the Conflict of Laws' (1961) 36 New York U L Rev 1298.

[18] For argument in support, see J Blaikie, 'Unjust Enrichment in the Conflict of Laws' [1984] Juridical Rev 112, 118.

[19] e.g. H Gutteridge and K Lipstein, 'Conflicts of Law in Matters of Unjustifiable Enrichment' (1939) 7 CLJ 80.

[20] e.g. the *Restatement of the Conflict of Laws, Second*, §221(2).

[21] e.g. Briggs, n 6 above, 196–8.

[22] At least in some contexts, this is favoured by J Bird, 'Choice of Law', Ch 3 in Rose (ed), n 1 above, 116, 119.

[23] e.g. R Stevens, 'The Choice of Law Rules for Restitutionary Obligations', in Rose (ed), n 1 above, 219–220; Panagopoulos, n 1 above, Ch 8, argues for what he terms 'the essential element of the unjust factor'.

[24] Dicey and Morris, Rule 200 contains no express exception.

[25] For discussion, see Cheshire and North, 683.

[26] Blaikie, n 18 above, at 125–126.   [27] Dicey and Morris, 1485.

As the authors accept, the authorities which have expressly accepted this rule are relatively few.[28] They point out that it was implicitly accepted in other cases[29] and that 'certainly no English decision has held the Rule to be wrong'.[30] That said, a Scottish case has expressly departed from one of the sub-Rules,[31] and authority in its favour in England is far from overwhelming.

19.09 Dicey and Morris explain that the general rule should be used to determine the existence of an obligation, as well as its scope and content.[32]

V. APPLICATION OF THE RESTITUTION CHOICE OF LAW RULE TO SPECIFIC CLAIMS ARISING IN CONNECTION WITH A SALE OF GOODS CONTRACT

1. DICEY AND MORRIS, RULE 200(2)(A)

19.10 The general Rule, in itself, is not particularly enlightening. It is difficult to see how Rule 200(1) can be regarded as wrong, couched as it is in such general terms. However, Rule 200(2)[33] goes on to suggest what the proper law of the obligation might be in particular cases:[34]

The proper law of the obligation is (*semble*) determined as follows:

(a) If the obligation arises in connection with a contract, its proper law is the law applicable to the contract;[35]

---

[28] ibid, at 1486. *Arab Monetary Fund v Hashim (No 9)* [1993] 1 Lloyd's Rep 543, QBD (Comm); rev'd (on different grounds) [1994] 2 All ER 685, CA; *Re Jogia (a Bankrupt)* [1988] 1 WLR 484, Ch D; *Hong Kong and Shanghai Banking Corp Ltd v United Overseas Bank Ltd* [1992] 2 Sing LR 495, High Court of Singapore; *Thahir v Pertamina* [1994] 3 Sing LR 257, Court of Appeal of Singapore.

[29] *Macmillan v Bishopsgate Investment Trust plc (No 3)* [1996] 1 WLR 387, CA.

[30] Dicey and Morris, 1486.

[31] See the decision of the Outer House of the Scottish Court of Session in *Baring Bros & Co Ltd v Cunninghame District Council* [1997] CLC 108, refusing to apply Rule 200(2)(a) (considered below, paras 19.11–13).

[32] Dicey and Morris, 1492–1493.

[33] ibid, at 1485. For criticism, see Cheshire and North, 682–683. Compare the *Second Restatement of the Conflict of Laws*, para 221(2), discussed in Cheshire and North, 681. See also the Commission Proposal for a Regulation of the European Parliament and the Council on the Law Applicable to Non-Contractual Obligations ('Rome II'), COM/2003/0427 Final, published on 22 July 2003, available at http://europa.eu.int/eur-lex/pri/en/lip/latest/doc/2003/com2003_0427en01.doc. See in particular Arts 9 and 10 of the Proposal. These provisions are discussed below, paras 19.98–100. The proposed Rome II Regulation is considered at greater length above, paras 17.165–182. See also below paras 21.203–221.

[34] At this point, there is much greater scope of disagreement as to whether the sub-Rules are correct. See Bird, n 22 above.

[35] But see Cheshire and North, p 685–686. Compare Art 10(1) of the proposed Rome II Regulation, n 33 above, considered below, paras 19.100.

(b) If it arises in connection with a transaction concerning an immovable (land), its proper law is the law of the country where the immovable is situated (*lex situs*);

(c) If it arises in any other circumstances, its proper law is the law of the country where the enrichment[36] occurs.[37]

Clearly, of most importance for present purposes is Rule 200(2)(a), which suggests that the law which is applicable to the contract of sale would apply to restitutionary claims which might arise 'in connection with' the sales contract.[38] As Dicey and Morris note: 'Although the obligation to restore an unjust enrichment does not arise *from* a contract, it may, and very frequently does, arise in connection with a contract'.[39]

2. EVALUATION

If the parties have chosen a law to govern the contract, it seems that this **19.11** law may be the law applied to the unjust enrichment claim.[40] This is

[36] This is a reference to the place of *immediate* enrichment: Dicey and Morris, 1501–1502. However, the authors regard Rule 200(2)(c) as a 'starting point' (at 1501) which is capable of being displaced if another law is more closely connected with the cause of action. They give the example of a payment made at the Paris branch of a English bank to be credited to the account of X at the London office of the same bank as one where it may be appropriate to apply the law of the place of ultimate enrichment, England, rather than the law of the place of immediate enrichment, France.

[37] For criticism, see Briggs, n 6 above, 196; Cheshire and North, 686–687. For support, see Gutteridge and Lipstein, n 19 above, at 89–90. See also the *First Restatement of the Conflict of Laws*, para 453.

[38] See *Thahir v Pertamina* [1994] 3 Sing LR 257, Court of Appeal of Singapore. But see the criticisms in *Barings Bros & Co Ltd v Cunninghame District Council* [1997] CLC 108, by Lord Penrose in the Outer House of the Scottish Court of Session.

[39] Dicey and Morris, 1493. See also Cheshire and North, 678–679; R Brereton, 'Restitution and Contract', Ch 4 in Rose (ed), n 1 above, 156–161; Bird, n 22 above 119–30. Bird's preferred sub-Rule is that a claim in unjust enrichment should be governed by 'the governing law of the contract, when there is or was a contractual relationship between the parties, or both parties were under the mistaken assumption that there was such a relationship between them, and the enrichment would not have occurred but for that real or supposed contract' (at 135).

[40] A view which may be supported by *Dimskal Shipping Co SA v International Transport Workers' Federation* [1992] 2 AC 152, HL and by Evans J in *Arab Monetary Fund v Hashim (No 9)* [1993] 1 Lloyd's Rep 543, 566, QBD (Comm). See also *Lloyd v Guibert* (1865) 6 B & S 100, Court of Exchequer Chamber. But see Gutteridge and Lipstein, n 19 above, at 90; Blaikie, n 18 above, at 123; P North, *Essays in Private International Law* (Oxford: Clarendon Press, 1993) 43. Cheshire and North (at 685) reject the view of Dicey and Morris: 'The obligation to make restoration is imposed by law and cannot be a matter for the wishes of the parties'. Art 10(1) of the Rome II Proposal, n 33 above allows the parties to choose the law applicable to an unjust enrichment claim. The choice may be express or demonstrated with reasonable certainty from the circumstances of the case. It must be made after the dispute has arisen. The choice is subject to: (i) the mandatory rules of another state with which the situation is entirely connected objectively (Art 9(2)); and (ii) to the provisions of Community law, where the other elements of the situation are located in a Member State (Art 9(3)). See the discussion below, paras 19.98–100. See also J Bird, 'Choice of Law and Restitution of Benefits Conferred under a Void Contract' [1997] LMCLQ 182, 187–188; Brereton, n 39 above, at 691.

notwithstanding the possible objection that restitutionary claims are independent of contractual obligations and that it could be argued that the Rule subordinates such claims to the contractual choice of law rule.[41] This objection weighed upon the minds of the Scottish Court of Session in *Barings Bros & Co Ltd v Cunninghame District Council*.[42] In that case, the claimant had lent money to a local authority pursuant to what turned out to be an *ultra vires* contract. The contract was stated to be governed by English law. Lord Penrose rejected the application of Rule 200(2)(a) to the ensuing claim in unjust enrichment. He stated that the sub-Rule was 'wholly without judicial support'.[43] He was concerned that this Rule gave insufficient weight to the independence of the unjust enrichment claim, and found that the contract, being void *ab initio*, had no legal effect. He went on to say that the law which governed the contract should be but one material factor in determining the law of closest connection to the unjust enrichment claim.

19.12 However, as Dicey and Morris rightly point out, this objection carries relatively little weight. 'It will be an error to suppose that if the proper law of the obligation to make restitution is held to be the same as the law which governed the anterior relationship, this has denied the integrity or independence of the proper law of the restitutionary obligation.'[44] In other words, it is simply that the law applicable to the contract is also very often the most suitable law to be applied to a claim in unjust enrichment arising in connection with an ineffective contract.[45] Application of the law applicable to the contract to the claim in unjust enrichment is justified 'not because the restitutionary obligation is

---

[41] It should be noted that Cheshire and North, Ch 20, do not support Rule 200(2)(a) and prefer a more flexible approach.

[42] [1997] CLC 108, Outer House. See also *Arab Monetary Fund v Hashim (No 9)* [1993] 1 Lloyd's Rep 543, QBD (Comm), aff'd [1996] 1 Lloyd's Rep 589, CA.

[43] [1997] CLC 108, 121. Cheshire and North convincingly endorse this view. They point out (at 686–687) that the authorities cited by Dicey and Morris in favour of the sub-Rule are weak. In *Fibrosa Spolka Akcyjna v Fairbairn Lawson Combe Barbour Ltd* [1943] AC 32, HL, there was no discussion of why English law was applied to the restitutionary claim. In *Dimskal Shipping Co SA v International Transport Workers' Federation* [1992] 2 AC 152, HL, the parties conceded that the applicable law of the contract should apply to the claim for restitution and the point was not argued in the House of Lords. In *Etler v Kersetz* (1960) 26 DLR (2d) 209, Court of Appeal of Ontario, it was by no means clear that the applicable law of the contract was used to determine the claim in unjust enrichment.

[44] Dicey and Morris, 1490. See also *ibid*, 1496, and K Zweigert and D Müller-Gindullis, 'Quasi-Contract', Ch 30 in K Lipstein (ed), *International Encyclopaedia of Comparative Law* (Leiden: Martinus Nijhoff), Vol III, 12.

[45] *Fibrosa Spolka Acyjna v Fairbairn Lawson Combe Barbour Ltd* [1943] 2 AC 32, HL; *Arab Monetary Fund v Hashim (No 9)* [1993] 1 Lloyd's Rep 543, 563–566, QBD (Comm), aff'd [1996] 1 Lloyd's Rep 589, 597; *Thahir v Pertamina* [1994] 3 Sing LR 257, Court of Appeal of Singapore; *Barings Bros & Co Ltd v Cunninghame District Council* [1997] CLC 108, Outer House, Scottish Court of Session.

itself contractual . . .—it is plainly [not] . . .—but because it arises from and by reason of a prior relationship which is the *causa sine qua non* of the present claim, and because it is simply unreal to regard the consequential obligation as free-floating, independent of and uncoloured by its history'.[46] Indeed, if pragmatism and protection of party expectations are reasons for subjecting claims in unjust enrichment arising in connection with a contract to the law governing the contract, there seems little sense in using a law other than that which *actually did*[47] govern the contract.[48] It is important that choice of law rules are readily intelligible and accessible by litigants.[49]

3. Limited Exception

Dicey and Morris do not regard their rule as wholly inflexible.[50] In a case where the claim in unjust enrichment is clearly more closely connected to a law other than that which governed the contract, that law of closest connection might instead be applied. This was recognized in *Arab Monetary Fund v Hashim (No 9)*.[51] An employer sought to recover bribes accepted by an employee. The court did not invoke Rule 200(2)(a), although the claim arose in connection with an employment contract and Evans J accepted that the claim was, in principle, caught by this sub-Rule. However, he preferred to rest his decision 'on wider grounds'[52] and reached the same conclusion as he would have done had Rule 200(2)(a) been applied. Dicey and Morris suggest that this flexibility may partly meet the concerns expressed in the *Barings Bros* case.[53]

19.13

4. Scope of Rule 200(2)(A)

In principle, the sub-Rule extends to claims arising where a contract is frustrated, to claims arising in the aftermath of rescission of the contract

19.14

---

[46] Briggs, n 6 above, 197.   [47] Or, in the case of a void contract, putatively did.
[48] But contrast the view of Lord Penrose in *Barings Bros & Co Ltd v Cunninghame District Council* [1997] CLC 108.
[49] 'At some point it has to be recognized that the law needs to provide a reasonable solution to litigants' claims, not a construct of unimpeachable theoretical perfection': Briggs, n 6 above, at 197–198. See also A Briggs, 'On Drafting Agreements on Choice of Law' [2003] LMCLQ 389, 393.
[50] Dicey and Morris, 1496.
[51] [1993] 1 Lloyd's Rep 543, QBD (Comm); appeal allowed in part, but not on this issue [1996] 1 Lloyd's Rep 589, CA. See also *Thahir v Pertamina* [1994] 3 Sing LR 257, Court of Appeal of Singapore.
[52] ibid, at 566.
[53] Dicey and Morris, 1497. But for a different view of the case (which supports the decision in *Barings Bros*), see Cheshire and North, 689–690.

and also to claims arising where a contract is found to be void.[54] 'Thus stated, the choice of law rule for dealing with the consequences of a contract being void, or being avoided, or being discharged for frustration, will be the law which governed the real or supposed contract and pursuant to which the avoidance or discharge was brought about.'[55] This is notwithstanding the additional logistical objection that if a contract is void, then it does not have a governing law; and if it does not have a governing law, then that law cannot be applied to a cause of action in unjust enrichment.[56] However, this may be logically justifiable, if the choice of law clause is treated as logically separable from the contract as a whole, and if it is capable of surviving the invalidity of the contract. 'This . . . will require close attention to be paid to the basis for the invalidity of the contract as a source of obligation and the efficacy of the agreement on choice of law as unaffected by such invalidity.'[57]

5. How is the Governing Law of the 'Contract' Determined?

19.15 It is true that the claim in unjust enrichment falls outside the scope of the Rome Convention. For this reason, it could be argued that the choice of law rules to be used to determine the law applicable to the contract, or the putative contract, should be those of the common law and not those of the Convention. Undoubtedly, this is correct in principle. Indeed, use of the Rome Convention might be thought to run counter to the exclusion of Article 10(1)(e) of the Rome Convention in the United Kingdom.[58] However, it would somewhat defeat the point of application of the law governing the actual or putative contract to a claim in unjust enrichment, if the common law considered this to be a law other than that which governs the contract under the Rome Convention.[59] Cheshire and North, who oppose a straightforward application of the law of the contract to claims arising in unjust enrichment, nonetheless accept that 'the same case may involve both a claim in contract and one for unjust enrichment. It

---

[54] Dicey and Morris, 1497, n 35, where the authors speak of a contract being 'ineffective . . . in the sense that the contract which the parties appeared to make, or supposed they had concluded, is held to be ineffective to create legal rights'. For comment, see Cheshire and North, 691.

[55] Dicey and Morris, 1493.

[56] Gutteridge and Lipstein, n 19 above, at 86; contrast Cheshire and North, 679; Bird, n 40 above, at 187.

[57] Dicey and Morris, 1492.   [58] s 2(2) of the Contracts (Applicable Law) Act 1990.

[59] As might well be the case in the absence of choice, since the Convention applies a presumption that would lead to the habitual residence or place of business of the seller, whereas the common law will look for the law of the state of closest connection. See above, paras 13.114–123.

would be very odd, having ascertained the law governing the contract using the Rome Convention, to switch to the proper law of the contract, which may identify a different law as governing the contract, when ascertaining the law governing the obligation to make restoration.'[60] It is suggested that the common law should accordingly adopt the rules of the Rome Convention and apply them to a claim in restitution arising in connection with a contract.[61]

6. Contract Invalidated by a Law other than that which Governed it

Of course, the contract may be invalidated by a law other than that which **19.16** governs the contract, as, for example, where a party to the contract lacks capacity. Dicey and Morris suggest[62] that the law which imposes the invalidity might be used to determine what consequences follow from the invalidity.[63] However, they do not offer an opinion as to whether they endorse this argument. It is suggested that it should be rejected.[64] The parties to a contract are unlikely to expect a law other than the governing law of a contract to determine the aftermath of the contract's invalidity. Moreover, the nature of the cause of action in unjust enrichment is not affected by the particular ground which invalidated the contract, be it lack of capacity, formal validity, or some other reason.

VI. JUSTIFICATION FOR USE OF THE LAW GOVERNING THE CONTRACT

1. General Remarks

Thus far, it has been argued that application of the law applicable to the **19.17** contract does not undermine the independence of a restitutionary claim. If that is the law which is most appropriate to apply to a restitutionary claim, then protestations as to the independence of the claim should not prevent us from seeing the wood for the trees.

The fact that a claim in restitution may arise in connection with, or as a **19.18** direct result of, a vitiating factor relating to the contract should not be

---

[60] Cheshire and North, 692.

[61] Provided of course, that the contract itself falls within the ambit of the Rome Convention: Cheshire and North, 692, n 3.

[62] Dicey and Morris, 1496.

[63] See also *Baring Bros & Co Ltd v Cunninghame District Council* [1997] CLC 108.

[64] Briggs, n 6 above, 195 also rejects such a view.

ignored in formulating a choice of law rule for the unjust enrichment claim. Often, it is the law applicable to the contract which will be the legal forerunner to the claim, and cannot be dismissed as mere factual background.

19.19 Broadly speaking, it is suggested that the arguments in favour of the law governing the contract may hinge upon two possible justifications. The first is that it may be possible to offer a logical justification for the application of the law which governed an ineffective contract to determine a claim in restitution arising in the aftermath of the contract. Second, and more positively, there are pragmatic reasons to justify application of the law of the contract to a claim in restitution arising out of the contract. These arguments will now be considered.

2. Logicistical Objections—the Independence of the Choice of Law Clause

The Objection that the Choice of Law Clause Fails if the Contract Itself Fails

19.20 If we are to apply the law governing the contract to a claim in restitution, a logical objection must be addressed. Where a contract is ineffective, it follows that the terms of the contract are equally ineffective. If a choice of law clause is regarded as just another term of the contract, then it can be argued that it too fails when the contract fails. If so, there is little sense in using the law which governed the 'contract' in respect of a restitutionary claim arising out of the contract. However, a number of points can be made in response to this.

Objection not Present in all Cases

19.21 For one thing, it may be noted that some restitutionary claims do not depend upon the contract being ineffective. As such, the logical objection[65] to the use of the governing law of the contract is not present. Such claims may logically be governed by the applicable law. An example is where a buyer seeks to recover an overpayment made to the seller. There is no suggestion that the contract of sale is void, voidable or discharged. Other claims depend upon the discharge of a contract which clearly did exist and was validly subject to a given law. An example is a claim brought in the aftermath of frustration. The contract may have been

---

[65] Of course, some might still object that this is not a suitable choice of law rule to apply in restitution and undermines the legal independence of the subject; but it cannot be argued that there is no contract, and thus no governing law of the contract.

discharged, but the claim clearly arises against the factual backdrop of a contract which was valid and which was subject to a governing law.

Contract is Rescinded *Ab Initio*

More difficult are contracts which are void or rescinded *ab initio*. As to the **19.22** latter, where a contract has been rescinded *ab initio*, it could be argued that it was potentially valid had it not been avoided and would have been subject to a valid choice of law. If the factor which rendered the contract voidable does not appear to vitiate the parties' consent to the choice of law clause, it could be argued that the clause should survive. However, if the contract really is rescinded *ab initio*, then it is not obviously possible to choose which terms are or are not affected by the vitiating factor. The contract, once avoided, is no longer in being. The best that can be said is that application of the law of the contract to a restitutionary obligation makes slightly more sense in the case of voidable contracts, on the basis that the contract was at least in force and subject to a governing law until avoided.

The Problem of Void Contracts

Void contracts present perhaps the greatest logical hurdle. There are, in **19.23** fact, two logical contradictions possible. First, if a contract is void by its governing law, then there is a paradox; for if the contract never existed, it did not have a governing law; and if it did not have a governing law, it is not obvious that that law should ever have been used to determine the validity of the contract.[66] Second, it seems difficult in logic to defend the application of the law of a 'contract' which never actually existed to a claim which is in any event not contractual, but restitutionary.

In short, then, it appears that there are formidable legal objections to use **19.24** of the law governing the 'contract' to claims arising from contracts which are void *ab initio* and to contracts which are voidable and are rescinded *ab initio*.

Surmounting the Logical Objection: Can the Choice of Law Clause be Regarded as Separate to the Contract Itself?

However, these logical objections may be largely met if the choice of law **19.25** clause can be regarded as logically separable from the contract itself. If so, then it is possible to say that although the contract itself has failed, the choice of law clause has survived. That makes it much more defensible to

---

[66] This is the bootstraps objection to Art 8(1) of the Rome Convention (discussed above, paras 13.143–149).

use that law, which is the product of the parties' autonomy, for all claims which might arise from the aftermath of the ineffective contract.

19.26 The view that a choice of law clause may stand separate from the contract itself has recently been favoured by Nygh. He points out that as far as arbitration clauses are concerned, the principle of severability is enshrined in England in s 7 of the Arbitration Act 1996, which states that:

> unless otherwise agreed by the parties, an arbitration agreement which forms or was intended to form part of another agreement (whether or not in writing) shall not be regarded as invalid, non-existent or ineffective because that other agreement is invalid, or did not come into existence or has become ineffective, and it shall for that purpose be treated as a distinct agreement.[67]

Nygh also regards the choice of law clause as independent of the contract.[68]

19.27 The consequence of this approach would be that the clause could logically be used to determine whether the 'main' contract was valid, without falling foul of the bootstraps objection that the law applicable to a non-existent contract cannot be used to test the validity of that contract. Moreover, if the clause still exists, it is logically possible for it also to determine a claim in restitution arising from the contract.

19.28 Unfortunately, it is suggested that, whilst the principle of severability can be accepted in principle, its unconditional acceptance must be rejected. Certainly, where the existence of a contract is in issue, but both parties accept that, if it is valid, so too is the choice of law clause, little harm can be caused by subjecting a claim in restitution arising out of the contract to the law specified by the choice of law clause. At the other extreme, however, a 'contract' tainted with illegality cannot necessarily be divorced from the choice of law clause which relates to it. As Hoffmann LJ put it in relation to an arbitration clause in *Harbour Assurance Ltd v Kansas Ltd*:[69]

> it is particularly necessary to have regard to the purpose and policy of the rule which invalidates the contract and to ask . . . whether the rule strikes down the arbitration clause as well . . . . Thus, saying that arbitration clauses because separable, are never affected by the illegality of the principal contract is as much a case of false logic as saying that they must be.

Why the agreement on choice of law should be treated other than as a disputed part of a contract is not obvious, where it too is contested. It is

---

[67] P Nygh, *Autonomy in International Contracts* (Oxford Monographs in Private International Law: Clarendon Press, 1999), 75.

[68] ibid, at 84.　　　　　　　　　　　　　　　　　　　　[69] [1993] QB 701, CA.

even less so when the law identified as putatively applicable regards the clause as part of the main contract. Moreover, even if severability is accepted, it is arguable that the choice of law agreement is dependent upon the main contract.

In the present authors' view, it is not sensible to try to determine, for all **19.29** purposes, whether the choice of law clause is independent of the contract. Rather, it is suggested that the validity of the choice of law clause is a matter for the law governing the contract. It should be that governing law which determines *whether the choice of law clause is separate from the contract and capable of surviving the invalidity of the contract itself.*[70] If the answer is 'no', then it must be admitted that the logical justification for application of the law of the contract to a claim in restitution does not exist. Applica- tion of this law can then only be justified on the pragmatic ground con- sidered below. But if the applicable law *does* consider that the clause is capable of surviving a contract being rescinded, or declared void *ab initio*, then the logical objection to use of that law diminishes.

The Governing Law of the Contract should Determine if a Choice of Law Clause Survives the Contract's Invalidity

The fact that the applicable law of the contract holds that the choice of law **19.30** clause *is capable* of surviving the invalidity of the contract itself does not mean that it inevitably will. For the applicable law of the contract should then be used to determine whether the clause *actually does survive*. For example, where a contract is void on the ground of mistake, the mistake may relate to the subject-matter of the contract; but the choice of law clause may not have been the subject of a mistake at all. If so, then it may legitimately be used in respect of a claim in restitution arising from the mistake. However, if the contract is set aside as the product of duress, it may be that the choice of law clause itself was also a product of duress and was 'infected' by it. If that is the case, then there should be no question of the law specified by the clause being used in respect of any restitutionary claim.

Conclusion

It follows that the key distinction to be drawn on this analysis is not **19.31** between contracts which are void, voidable or discharged. Rather, the key questions are:

(1) According to the law which (putatively) governs the 'contract', is the

---

[70] This is consistent with Arts 3(4) and 8(1) of the Rome Convention.

choice of law clause separate from the contract itself, so that it is capable of surviving the invalidity of the contract itself? If the answer is 'no', then the clause cannot logically survive the invalidity of the contract; but if the answer is 'yes', there should be a second question:

(2) Is the choice of law clause still valid according to the law specified in that clause? In answering this, the question will arise whether the factor which led to the invalidity of the contract itself also 'infects' and invalidates the choice of law clause. If it does 'infect' the clause,[71] then the clause cannot logically survive. But if it does not, then the clause, logically separable from the contract and not rendered invalid, therefore still stands. If so, it may logically be used to determine a claim in restitution arising out of the contract.

3. Pragmatism—Predictability and Uniformity

The Pragmatic Argument

19.32 Even if the law specified in the contract is not logically capable of surviving the contract's invalidity on the basis of the above analysis, there is the second, pragmatic justification which may nonetheless be sufficient to justify use of the law specified in the choice of law clause. This pragmatic justification is extremely important in a commercial area such as the international sale of goods. The law specified in the clause is likely to be the one which the parties to a sales contract will expect[72] to govern any unjust enrichment claims that might arise from it. Moreover, if the law applicable to a contract determines that it is frustrated, or that the buyer may rescind the contract, it is neither desirable nor commercially sensible for a different law then to be applied to determine the restitutionary consequences of this event. Suppose that an English buyer contracts with a seller resident in State X under a contract of sale governed by English law. The buyer pays the purchase price to the seller in State X, prior to the seller passing the goods to the buyer. The goods perish before the risk passes to the buyer and English law holds that the contract is frustrated on the facts.[73] Imagine that the law of State X, the place of enrichment of the seller, was used to determine a claim in unjust enrichment brought by the buyer to seek restitution of money paid. The law of State X might, hypothetically, hold on the facts that the contract is not frustrated, and so

---

[71] Examples are given below of when this might or might not be the case: paras 19.35–68.
[72] In so far as they have considered the matter.
[73] If they are specific goods, s 7 of the Sale of Goods Act 1979 applies, if its conditions are met.

consider there to be no recovery in unjust enrichment in the instant case. If this is overlooked, and we simply ask 'assuming that the contract is frustrated, does the law of State X allow a claim in unjust enrichment on the facts', then the question is somewhat artificial and results in the application of the law of State X in a way in which a court in State X would itself not apply it.[74]

Cases where the Pragmatic Justification does not Exist

The pragmatic justification exists in the great majority of cases. However, **19.33** it is possible in rare cases that the logical justification will exist, but the pragmatic one will not. The classic example would be where the contract and/or the choice of law clause were not freely agreed upon, but are the product of duress, undue influence, or where the clause cannot be accepted, if the whole contract is set aside for illegality.

The Vienna Convention

Finally, it should be noted that the Vienna Convention contains certain **19.34** provisions that deal with the law of restitution.[75] For example, Article 81(2) states that: 'A party who has performed the contract either wholly or in part may claim restitution from the other party of whatever the first party has supplied or paid under the contract. If both parties are bound to make restitution, they must do so concurrently.' Further provisions can be found in Article 84(2).[76] These provisions lend support to the argument for subjecting such restitutionary claims to the same law which governs the contract.

VII. APPLICATION OF THE CHOICE OF LAW RULES IN RESTITUTION TO PARTICULAR ISSUES ARISING IN THE INTERNATIONAL SALE OF GOODS

1. (THE AFTERMATH OF) VOID CONTRACTS

It might be argued that application of the law governing the contract may **19.35** be defended in the case of a voidable contract, or one which is discharged for frustration. In contrast, it may appear that the application of the law

---

[74] Which, in turn, raises the prospect of forum shopping.
[75] Even though the Convention applies only to 'contracts of sale of goods': Art 1(1).
[76] Which deals with the seller's duty to account for all benefits which he has derived from the goods.

which governed the 'contract' to a claim in unjust enrichment is logically indefensible, if that 'contract' is void *ab initio*.[77] However, it was argued above that the choice of law clause may be capable of surviving the contract's voidness. Even if it cannot survive, there may still be said to be strong pragmatic reasons for using the law which would have governed the contract had it been valid. This law may well best reflect the expectations of the parties.

19.36 It is true that the United Kingdom did not enact Article 10(1)(e) of the Rome Convention, which would have subjected the consequences of nullity of a contract to the law which governed that 'contract'.[78] The United Kingdom did not regard such claims as concerning 'contractual obligations'[79] but rather as part of the law of unjust enrichment.[80] However, there is no reason why the common law may not adopt the law of the 'contract' as a choice of law rule in unjust enrichment cases arising in connection with a 'contract'.[81] In so far as the application of the law governing the 'contract' can be defended upon the logical and pragmatic grounds described above, the case for its application remains potent. So, if a seller supplies goods to the buyer in Japan, pursuant to a contract expressly stated to be governed by English law and the contract is void on the ground of mistake, it is suggested that English law should still be used to determine the seller's claim to recover the value of the goods from the buyer.

2. RESTITUTION FOR WRONGDOING[82]

Breach of Contract

19.37 We are concerned here with cases where the defendant makes a profit through a breach of contract. A claimant might seek restitutionary damages in respect of a breach of contract.[83] An example would be where a

---

[77] In *Mackender v Feldia AG* [1967] 2 QB 590, CA, in the context of a jurisdiction clause, Lord Denning MR remarked (at 598) that 'I can well see that if the issue was whether there ever had been a contract at all, as, for instance, if there was a plea of *non est factum*, then the foreign jurisdiction clause might not apply at all'. See also the remarks of Diplock LJ (at 602–603).

[78] Pursuant to s 2(2) of the Contracts (Applicable Law) Act 1990.

[79] Within the meaning of Art 1 of the Rome Convention.

[80] Giuliano and Lagarde Report [1980] OJ C282/1, 56.

[81] See Brereton, n 39 above, at 175.

[82] See Cheshire and North, 693–696 for a discussion of the various possible choice of law rules for restitution for wrongdoing.

[83] Brereton, n 39 above, at 148. See *Attorney-General v Blake* [2001] 1 AC 268, HL; *Satnam Investments Ltd v Dunlop Heywood & Co Ltd* [1999] 3 All ER 652, CA; *Experience Hendrix v PPX Enterprises Inc* [2003] EWCA Civ 323, [2003] 1 All ER (Comm) 830.

seller agrees to sell specific goods to a buyer for £50,000. The seller breaks his contract with the buyer and instead sells the same goods to X for a higher price, say £75,000. The buyer might seek restitutionary damages to the value of £25,000, being the value of the profit made by the seller from breaking his contract with the original buyer.[84] Such a claim may be viewed as one seeking restitution for wrongdoing.

A number of cases concerning restitution of bribes taken by an agent or **19.38** employee have applied the Rule in Dicey and Morris on restitution.[85] It may be argued that even if the claim is classified as restitutionary, the appropriate rule to adopt in claims for restitution for breach of contract is to apply the governing law of the contract. The claim arises from a breach of contract, and the governing law of the contract decides if there has been a breach. 'The law which says there is a wrong should also dictate the nature of damages available for that wrong.'[86]

However, there is a strong argument that the claim should simply be **19.39** classified as contractual for choice of law purposes. Dicey and Morris expressly state that Rule 200(2)(a) dealing with unjust enrichment claims arising in connection with contracts does not apply 'where the contract has been broken and damages are claimed for the breach but assessed in a restitutionary measure'.[87] A contractual classification would again lead to the conclusion that the law applicable to the contract should apply. A claim arising for restitution following a breach of contract is a consequence of the breach of contract. 'One would have thought that those who recoil at the suggestion that unjust enrichment issues should be characterized as contractual would feel less hesitant about characterising a claim for restitution for breach of contract as contractual.'[88] Article 10(1)(c) of the Rome Convention appears to cover such cases. The only doubt is that Article 1 of the Rome Convention states that the Convention applies only to 'contractual obligations' and it could be argued that an obligation to make restitution following a breach is not a contractual but a

---

[84] Another example might be where the seller withholds the goods from the buyer once the latter has become entitled to them. The goods were valued at £50,000. The goods rise in value whilst they are in the hands of the seller to £65,000. If the goods are never delivered by the seller, the buyer might seek restitutionary damages equivalent to the present value of the goods of £65,000.

[85] Brereton, n 39 above, at 148 cites *Arab Monetary Fund v Hashim (No 9)* [1993] 1 Lloyd's Rep 543, QBD (Comm); *Hong Kong and Shanghai Banking Corp Ltd v United Overseas Bank Ltd* [1992] 2 SLR 495, High Court of Singapore; *Sumitomo Bank Ltd v Kartika Ratna Thahir* [1993] 1 Sing LR 735, High Court of Singapore; *Thahir v PT Permtambangan Minyak Dan Gas Bumi Negara (Pertamina)* [1994] 3 Sing LR 257, Court of Appeal of Singapore.

[86] Brereton, n 39 above, at 178.

[87] Dicey and Morris, 1495, n 63.

[88] Brereton, n 39 above, at 177.

restitutionary obligation. Nevertheless, convenience certainly dictates that the law which governs a contract should determine the range of remedies available in the event of breach. The advantage of the Rule in Dicey and Morris is that it allows the same law to be applied whichever classification is adopted.

Tortious Wrongdoing

19.40 A claim for restitution for tortious wrongdoing might arise in respect of the tort of conversion, if a party, Y, wrongfully sells goods belonging to X. Rather than claiming for the loss caused to him, X might prefer to claim the value of the sale made by Y. This will obviously be attractive if Y has struck a good bargain, so that the value of the sale proceeds is greater than the loss suffered to the claimant.

19.41 Whatever the nature of the claim in domestic law,[89] it is suggested that such a claim should, in the private international law context, be governed by the choice of law rules in tort. A number of arguments support this. First, the claim arises from a prior relationship which is the genesis of the present claim.[90] Second, since the basis of the claim is clearly the tort itself, whether the claimant seeks compensation for loss or restitution of a gain made by the defendant is essentially a remedial matter and remedies are not normally the subject of their own choice of law rules. Third, the Private International Law (Miscellaneous Provisions) Act 1995, Part III applies to 'issues *relating* to tort'.[91] Even if one does not regard the claim as one *in* tort, it is very hard to dispute that it *relates* to tort. After all, the tortious wrongdoing is the very basis of the claim itself.

3. DISCHARGE BY FRUSTRATION

19.42 In the common law case of *Fibrosa Spolka Akcyjna v Fairbairn Lawson Combe Barbour Ltd,*[92] an English company had agreed in 1939 to deliver machinery to a Polish company in Gdynia. The Polish company made part payment for the machinery. The contract was frustrated by the German occupation of Gdynia two months later. The Polish company successfully recovered the payments that it had made. The court applied English law to the claim. Dicey and Morris explain the case as one where English law was presumably applied because it was the law which governed the frustrated contract. However, the case is of limited use, since no

---

[89] See the discussion above, paras 8.89–98.
[91] s 9(1), emphasis added.
[90] Briggs, n 6 above, at, 197.
[92] [1943] AC 52, HL.

foreign law was pleaded and there was not even a discussion of which law governed the contract.[93]

Support for application of the applicable law of the contract may be found **19.43** in the Law Reform (Frustrated Contracts) Act 1943. This allows for the recovery of benefits conferred under a frustrated contract. It applies only where the contract is governed by English law.[94] In other words, where the applicable law of the contract is English, English law is applied to the aftermath of frustration. Nor is there any provision in the Act to say that it shall not apply where English law governs the contract only by virtue of a choice of that law by the parties.

It should be noted that the 1943 Act does not apply to the sale of specific **19.44** goods which have perished.[95] However, it should also be pointed out that most commodity sales are likely to be of unascertained goods. A seller who undertakes to supply commodities will normally do so in generic terms with a subsequent appropriation from an identified bulk (for example, a contract of sale of 10,000 tonnes US-origin soya beans shipment Gulf of Mexico port(s)). The 1943 Act applies to such claims. In those cases where the 1943 Act does not apply, s 7 of the Sale of Goods Act 1979 is the operative provision. However, there is no reason in principle to suppose that this provision is of general application[96] other than when the contract itself is governed by English law.

In principle, it may be thought desirable that the law which determines **19.45** whether a contract is frustrated is also used to determine the consequences of frustration. Today, it is possible that Article 10(1)(d) of the Rome Convention may be applied, as the matter may be said to relate to the extinction of obligations. If so, the issue would be treated as contractual and subject to the law applicable to the contract.

However, this is uncertain, since it may be argued that this provision only **19.46** expressly deals with the question *whether* the contract is extinguished and has nothing to say as to the aftermath of extinction. Indeed, it may be argued that a claim arising in the aftermath is not a 'contractual obligation' within the meaning of Article 1, so that the Rome Convention does not apply.

Nonetheless, it is suggested that even if the claim is classified as one in **19.47** unjust enrichment, this should nonetheless lead to the application of the

---

[93] Cheshire and North, 686.
[94] s 1(1) of the Law Reform (Frustrated Contracts) Act 1943.   [95] ibid, s 2(5)(c).
[96] Indeed, s 7 of the Sale of Goods Act 1979 does not even apply to a contract governed by the law of a part of the UK, if that law applies only by virtue of a choice by the parties: s 27(1) of the Unfair Contract Terms Act 1977. See further paras 13.309–314.

law applicable to the contract.[97] It is clear that the contract was initially valid and is not discharged *ab initio*. That being so, it is logically possible to use the law of a contract which did enter into force and was subject to a governing law validly chosen by the parties. After all, it is hard to see how the event which leads to frustration could affect the parties' consent to the choice of law clause in the contract. Moreover, application of the law which governed the contract to the extinction of that contract, and the consequences thereof, is likely to reflect the expectations of the parties and will lead to a harmonized result, in that the finding that a contract is discharged and the consequences of discharge will be subject to a single law. As Brereton points out,[98] in *Government of Gibraltar v Kennedy*,[99] Sellers J applied an arbitration clause to a claim under the 1943 Act. The clause survived the frustration of the contract and also extended to the claim in unjust enrichment. It may be that the same analysis can be applied to a choice of law clause and that 'a proper construction may require that it can be applied in respect of restitution following discharge'.[100]

4. Discharge by Acceptance of Repudiation

19.48   A claimant may be entitled to repudiate a contract in the event of a breach by the seller. The law applicable to the contract will determine this matter.[101] The claimant may then seek to recover payments or benefits advanced pursuant to the contract on the basis of a total failure of consideration. As Brereton notes, the case of *Dies v British and International Mining and Finance Corp*[102] lends support to use of the applicable law of the contract for the restitutionary claim. A claimant made an advanced payment under a contract. Subsequently, he refused to take delivery and the defendant repudiated the contract. The claimant recovered the contract payment. Stable J applied the law governing the contract, English law, to the claim to recover the advanced payment. This seems eminently sensible, since: 'The contract explains the enrichment and is critical in determining whether the enrichment is unjust . . . The law governing the contract is the only law which the parties could reasonably have expected

---

[97]   A view shared by Benjamin, 25–169 (see also the cases that they cite: *Fibrosa Spolka Akcyjna v Fairbairn Lawson Combe Barbour Ltd* [1943] AC 52, HL; *Arab Bank Ltd v Barclays Bank (Dominion, Colonial and Overseas)* [1953] 2 QB 527, 572, CA; *Etler v Kersetz* (1960) 26 DLR (2d) 209, Court of Appeal of Ontario, in support). See also R Plender and M Wilderspin, *The European Contracts Convention* (2nd edn, London: Sweet & Maxwell, 2001) 221–223.
[98]   Brereton, n 39 above, at 164.
[99]   [1956] 2 QB 410.
[100]   Brereton, n 39 above, at 165.
[101]   Art 10(1)(c) and (d) of the Rome Convention.
[102]   [1939] 1 KB 724; Brereton, n 39 above, at 165.

to be applied.'[103] Moreover, the claim to recover the payment made may be regarded as one of the 'consequences of breach' of contract. If so, it arguably[104] falls within Article 10(1)(c) of the Rome Convention. For all these reasons, it is argued that the claim in unjust enrichment should be determined by the law applicable to the contract.

5. MISTAKE

The fact that a contract is void or voidable for mistake by its governing[105]   **19.49** law may or may not mean that the law which governed that 'contract' should apply to any ensuing claims in unjust enrichment. The key question is whether the choice of law clause can logically survive the impugning of the contract for mistake.[106] This depends upon whether the clause may be regarded as separate to the contract itself. This, it was argued above,[107] is a matter for the applicable law of the contract to determine. If it is not treated by that law as separate to the contract, then it logically fails as well. But if it is treated as logically separate, then it can survive and the question is whether the mistake also 'infects' the choice of law clause. This issue should also be determined by the governing law of the contract. The mistake may well not 'infect' the choice of law clause. As Dicey and Morris explain: 'The parties may have been clear in their intention that Ruritanian law should govern the contract and any consequences of its invalidity, even though they were mistaken as to the existence of the subject-matter of the contract'.[108] In such a case, the chosen law may logically be applied to the unjust enrichment claim. There is then clearly a strong pragmatic reason for applying that law to the unjust enrichment claim, as it is the law which the parties will have expected to be applied to such claims.

6. ILLEGALITY

It seems that restitutionary claims may be governed by the law of a con-   **19.50** tract which is declared to be illegal. Dicey and Morris[109] cite the Ontario Court of Appeal's decision in *Etler v Kertesz*.[110] In that case, the authors

---

[103] ibid, 166.
[104] Arguably, because it could be countered that the Rome Convention applies only to contractual obligations and that this is not a contractual obligation. Even if this is so, it is suggested that the common law should reach the same conclusion as to the law applicable to the restitutionary claim.
[105] Or, in the case of void contracts, its putative governing law.
[106] Bird, n 40 above, at 187.   [107] At paras 19.25–30.
[108] Dicey and Morris, 1495; see also A Dickinson, 'Restitution and Incapacity: a Choice of Law Solution?' (1997) 5 Restitution L Rev 66, 68.
[109] Dicey and Morris, 1494.
[110] (1960) 26 DLR (2d) 209, 223–224, Court of Appeal of Ontario.

argue that the court applied Austrian law to a claim to recover money paid under a contract governed by Austrian law, but by whose law the contract was illegal. However, Cheshire and North note that the court did not actually say that Austrian law governed the restitutionary claim.[111] Moreover, the court applied the law of the forum, to the extent that this provided that money paid pursuant to an illegal contract could not be recovered.

19.51 In *Arab Bank Ltd v Barclays Bank (Dominion, Colonial and Overseas)*,[112] a contract was governed by Israeli law, by which law it was said to be illegal. Although the court decided that the contract was not void, Jenkins LJ remarked obiter that 'if the cancellation of the contractual debt was brought about by Israeli law, it would be at least logical to look to Israeli law for the consequences of such cancellation'.[113] One reason for this, as Brereton points out, is that 'one might expect some relationship between failure under Israeli law and the consequences of failure, which may be upset by the application of any law other than Israeli law to the question of restitution'.[114]

19.52 Ultimately, it is suggested that the key question is whether the law which governs the contract is itself tainted with illegality. It may well not be. In *Mackender v Feldia AG*,[115] the question arose as to whether a jurisdiction clause might survive if the contract to which it related was void or voidable. Diplock LJ remarked that: 'A claim that a contract is void for illegality does not raise any issue as to whether or not the parties in fact agreed to the terms of the policy including those in the foreign jurisdiction . . . It thus raises no dispute about the consensus *ad idem* of the parties as to the exclusive jurisdiction of the . . . court . . .'[116] In such a case, application of the law applicable to the contract might be thought best to reflect the reasonable expectations of the parties.[117]

7. DURESS

19.53 Where a contract is void or voidable for duress by its governing[118] law, it is suggested that there is a stronger case for rejecting use of the law

---

[111] Cheshire and North, 686.
[112] [1953] 2 QB 527, CA. See also *Boissevain v Weil* [1949] 1 KB 482, CA.
[113] [1953] 2 QB 527, 572, CA   [114] Brereton, n 39 above, at 168.
[115] [1967] 2 QB 590, 602–603, CA.   [116] ibid, at 602.
[117] But see Brereton, n 39 above, at 160 for discussion of whether where a contract is illegal by some law other than that which governs the contract, such as the law of the forum, that law should apply to a claim in unjust enrichment. See also *Boissevain v Weil* [1949] 1 KB 482, CA.
[118] Or, its putative governing law.

applicable to that 'contract' for determining any restitutionary claims which might ensue.[119] This is because there is a serious risk that any choice of law clause contained in the contract is itself the product of duress.

In the common law case of *Dimskal Shipping Co SA v International Transport* **19.54** *Workers' Federation*,[120] a contract governed by English law was allegedly the product of duress.[121] The court applied English law to decide whether the contract was void or voidable. Today, Article 8(1) of the Rome Convention would lead to the same conclusion. However, the House of Lords did not have to determine the governing law for any consequential unjust enrichment claim. Accordingly, the case is of little use in the present context.[122]

It is suggested that the law applicable to the contract should determine **19.55** what constitutes duress, the effects of duress upon a contract and whether the choice of law clause can survive the duress,[123] even if the contract as a whole does not. If application of that law leads unreasonably to the conclusion that the clause is valid, Article 8(2) of the Rome Convention might be invoked by a contracting party, to show that, by the law of his habitual residence, he did not consent to the clause. If this still leads to a conclusion, in the eyes of English law, that is unreasonable or even oppressive, then the English court can regard the clause as infringing English public policy. But the point is that it is *contractual* doctrines which should determine whether the choice of law clause survives. If it does, then it seems acceptable to apply the governing law of the 'contract' to restitutionary claims arising in the aftermath of duress.[124]

---

[119] In the case of undue influence, it could be argued that the claim arises in equity and that a different choice of law rule might apply: Bird, n 22 above, at 77. However, it would seem wholly unsatisfactory for the classification of the matter in English domestic law to affect the choice of law rule applied to cross-border cases. A category of equitable claims does not exist in most legal systems of the world, and so would be likely to lead to a choice of law rule out of line with that applied in foreign courts. Moreover, undue influence may clearly *affect* the validity or operation of a contract, and it would be somewhat anomalous for it to be subject to a wholly different choice of law rule to other factors which might vitiate the contract. Rather, it is suggested that the same choice of law rule should apply to claims for rescission on the basis of undue influence as applies to duress. See also ibid, at 78. See further T Yeo, *Choice of Law for Equitable Doctrines* (Oxford: OUP, 2004).

[120] [1992] 2 AC 152, HL. See also J Cooke, T Young, A Taylor, J Kimball, D Martowski and L Lambert, *Voyage Charters* (2nd edn, London: LLP, 2001) 1.94. See further *Royal Boskalis v Mountain* [1999] QB 674, CA.

[121] Brereton, n 39 above, at 170–171.

[122] Cheshire and North, 686.

[123] Compare *IFR Ltd v Federal Trade SpA* (19 September 2001, QBD), where Colman J ruled that a jurisdiction clause was capable of surviving, even if the contract itself to which it related was voidable on the grounds of duress. See also *Mackender v Feldia AG* [1967] 2 QB 590, CA.

[124] See also Dicey and Morris, 1495, n 61, on whether a claimant must establish that the defendant has committed the tort of duress before he may proceed to bring a restitutionary claim.

19.56   If the choice of law clause does not survive, then there can be no question of that law applying. Instead, Dicey and Morris suggest that the law with which the contract had its closest connection should be applied.[125] However, it is suggested that this approach should not be followed. If the contract itself is the product of duress, then its terms will be likewise be 'infected' by the duress. The choice of law clause might be said to be a special case, capable of surviving the contract's invalidity in some circumstances; but it is not easy to see how other terms which are clearly inseparable from the contract may survive. These might include such terms as the place of delivery, the currency of payment or the place of payment. If so, it is undesirable to apply what would have been the law of closest connection to the contract, had the contract been valid. Rather, it is suggested that Rule 200(2)(c) should apply where the choice of law clause is also impugned by duress and the proper law of the restitutionary claim will normally be the law of the place of enrichment. For example, suppose that a buyer, acting under the duress of the seller, enters into a contract of sale, pursuant to which he pays the purchase price to the seller in Japan. The contract was stated to be governed by English law. However, English law holds that the contract should be impugned for duress and that this duress also invalidates the choice of law clause. If the buyer seeks to reclaim the purchase price from the seller, it is submitted that Japanese law should apply, as the law of the place of enrichment of the seller.

8. The Aftermath of Rescission for Misrepresentation

19.57   It is suggested that the question of whether a contract may be rescinded is a matter relating to the availability of a contractual remedy.[126] Article 10(1)(c) of the Rome Convention should determine whether the remedy is, *in principle*, available. If the answer is 'no', then there is, of course, no question of rescission being available. However, if the answer is 'yes', then the claimant may proceed to seek recovery of money or benefits conferred under the contract. He might seek either personal or proprietary restitution. In either case, this might be said to be a matter which is properly governed by distinct choice of law rules for unjust enrichment, and not by contractual choice of law rules.[127]

---

[125] ibid, 1495, n 65.

[126] Any suggestion that the matter should be classified as procedural, because providing a remedy rather than conferring a right, cannot be credible today. The remedy is awarded pursuant to a contract and it would be most unsatisfactory for the law of the forum to determine whether a contract governed by a foreign law may be rescinded. See Bird, n 22 above, at 84.

[127] See ibid, 76–77.

Personal Claims for Restitutionary Damages

At least where the claim is a personal one for damages, it would be **19.58** undesirable to apply different laws to the questions of whether the contract is rescinded and to restitutionary claims arising in the aftermath of rescission. It is a recipe for artifice if the law applicable to the contract should determine whether the remedy of rescission is available in principle, and another law should determine whether rescission should lead to the payment of a sum to the claimant. As Dicey and Morris cogently put it, '. . . the undesirability of seeking to separate these [claims to repayment] from the contractual right to rescind and to subject them to different laws is plain; and they should therefore be governed by the law which governed the contract, whether classified as contractual or restitutionary in nature'.[128]

It may be otherwise if the misrepresentation also affected the choice of **19.59** law clause, so that there was no true meeting of minds of the parties as to the governing law.[129] If so, then it is suggested that the claim in restitution should be governed by the law which governed the contract in the absence of choice (since it is desirable that the law which governed the contract should also determine the aftermath of rescission). However, in determining that law of closest connection, it will be necessary to disregard those terms which were themselves the product of the misrepresentation and upon which there was no meeting of minds. If the misrepresentation is such that there appears to be no meeting of minds upon any term of the contract, then the law governing the unjust enrichment claim should be determined in accordance with Dicey and Morris, Rule 200(2)(c).[130]

Rescission of the Transfer Itself

Matters are much less clear where the claimant seeks not damages, but **19.60** to assert or to recover property in the payment or goods transferred under the contract.[131] Any right of rescission of the transfer itself

---

[128] Dicey and Morris, 1487, n 17.   [129] Bird, n 40 above, at 187.

[130] On which, see above, para 19.10. Compare the discussion of duress above, where it is argued that almost by definition, where a 'contract' and its choice of law clause are the product of duress, so too will be the other 'terms' of the 'contract'. In that case, it is argued that the law of the place of enrichment should apply to the restitutionary aftermath.

[131] See the Canadian cases cited in Benjamin, 25–176, n 54. See, in particular *Rhode Island Locomotive Works v South Eastern Ry Co* (1886) 31 LCJ 86; *Re Hudson Fashion Shoppe Ltd* (1926) 1 DLR 199; *Re Viscount Supply Co Ltd* (1963) 40 DLR (2d) 501; *Re Modern Fashions Ltd* (1969) 8 DLR (3d) 590; *Re Satisfaction Stores* [1929] 2 DLR 435; *Re Farley and Grant* [1936] 1 DLR 57.

should[132] be classified either as a restitutionary[133] or proprietary matter.[134] There may be complex questions as to whether the claimant seeks to vindicate a continuing property right, or seeks to revest property which has passed to the defendant. The former claim looks to be properly subject to the choice of law rules in property; the latter to the rules in restitution.

19.61 If Rule 200 in Dicey and Morris is correct,[135] then the same law applies to a claim that is classified as one in unjust enrichment, whether the remedy sought is personal or proprietary in nature. This may be defended on the basis that the cause of action and unjust factor are the same in either case, and the law applicable to the cause of action should determine what remedies are available to reverse the unjust enrichment. However, this approach creates profound problems of classification where proprietary remedies are sought, since one law will apply if the claim is treated as one to vindicate a continuing property right (the law of the *situs*) and another if the claim is to regarded as one to reverse unjust enrichment (the law applicable to the contract). Yet, where a proprietary remedy is sought, it is suggested that the expending of a great deal of effort by a court in classifying a claim as one in property or unjust enrichment risks missing the wood for the trees. As will be argued below,[136] much of the justification for application of the law of the *situs* to property claims is pragmatic: the law of the *situs* is said to be the law which has effective control over assets within its jurisdiction and any order made in an English court needs to be effective in the courts of the *situs*. That argument applies whether the nature of the claim is technically proprietary or restitutionary. In other words, it is the *remedy* which justifies application of the law of the *situs*. For this reason, it is suggested that the Rule in Dicey and Morris should *not* be accepted in relation to claims where a proprietary right is asserted. Rather, a claim for rescission of the transfer of property in goods or payments made upon the contract of sale should be subject to the law of the

---

[132] It could be argued that this matter should be determined by the applicable law of the contract. The Vienna Convention deals with this matter, even though the Convention excludes property matters (Art 4(b)). Moreover, revesting upon contractual termination is regarded in English law as a matter of implied contractual terms—*Ward v Bignall* [1967] 1 QB 534, CA. However, the question clearly relates to the effect of rescission on property in the goods themselves and so should not be regarded as a contractual matter for choice of law purposes.

[133] Arts 81(2) and 84(2) of the Vienna Convention lend some support to this approach.

[134] Compare Benjamin, 25–177 and 25–178. But see Case 518/99 *Gaillard v Chekili* [2001] ECR I-2771, in which the ECJ ruled that a claim by a seller for rescission of a contract for the sale of land did not have as its object rights *in rem* in immovable property for the purposes of Art 16(1) of the Brussels Convention.

[135] See above, paras 19.10–16.

[136] See the discussion of claim asserting a proprietary interest below, paras 19.69–73.

situs.[137] This principle should apply whether the claim for rescission of the transfer involved is between the buyer and the seller only,[138] or whether it involves the assertion of a proprietary interest against a third party. In either case, the judgment will result in a decision as to the allocation of property rights; and it is on this matter that the law of the *situs* should hold sway.

9. OVERPAYMENTS OF MONEY

In the situation where a buyer seeks restitution of money overpaid to **19.62** the seller, Dicey and Morris suggest that Article 10(1)(b) of the Rome Convention should apply, as the question relates to performance of the contract.[139] This is questionable.[140] The matter relates only to performance in the sense that the correct price to be paid by the buyer needs to be ascertained in order to substantiate the claim. However, the claim itself can only loosely be described as concerning performance under the contract. The claim is based upon unjust enrichment.[141] The contract is a factual background to the claim, but the claim itself is legally independent of it. Indeed, the nature of the claim would be essentially the same if there had been no contract between the parties and the buyer sought to recover a payment mistakenly made by gift, or made to the wrong party.

That said, in the context of overpayments made by a buyer to a seller of **19.63** goods, there is a strong argument for the law which determines the obligations of the parties, and, in the event of a dispute, what the agreed purchase price was or how it was to be calculated, also to determine

---

[137] The authors of Benjamin, 25–177 and 25–178, appear to suggest that the law of the *situs* may have some say in the matter. However, it is not wholly clear precisely what role they envisage for this law.

[138] But see Benjamin, 25–177, where the authors appear to favour application of the law of the contract 'as between seller and buyer alone'. It is suggested that this approach must be rejected on the present state of authorities. A finding that property in the goods or payment is in one party or the other has implications for parties other than those to the litigation. In a different context, it was stressed in *Glencore International AG v Metro Trading International Inc (No 2)* [2001] 1 Lloyd's Rep 284, QBD (Comm) that a property claim remains a property claim, and the law of the *situs* must be applied to it, notwithstanding that the only parties to the litigation are the buyer and seller under a contract. However, on the argument as to whether the applicable law of the contract should, in principle, determine proprietary issues arising between the buyer and seller, see above, paras 18.37–54.

[139] Dicey and Morris, 1487, n 16.

[140] And is doubted by Brereton, n 39 above, at 176. He nonetheless argues that the law which governs the contract under the Convention rules should be applied to what he calls 'restitution within contract'.

[141] Compare, in the jurisdiction context, *Eddie v Alpa Srl* 2000 SLT 1062, Scottish Outer House.

whether the claimant may recover an excess payment. Indeed, since the contract will not be void, voidable or discharged, this is perhaps a relatively clear case where the law applicable to a contract should be used for a claim in unjust enrichment.[142]

10. Oversupply by the Seller

19.64 Similar arguments apply if the seller erroneously oversupplies goods to the buyer. The seller may seek to recover payment for such excess goods retained by the buyer. Under English law, such a claim may arise pursuant to s 30 of the Sale of Goods Act 1979. This provides that where a seller supplies a larger quantity of goods than he contracted to sell, the buyer may reject the excess goods.[143] A buyer who does not deal as a consumer may also reject the whole of the goods supplied, unless the seller can show[144] that the excess quantity supplied 'is so slight that it would be unreasonable for [the buyer] . . . to do so'.[145]

19.65 If the buyer accepts the excess quantity supplied, the seller's claim to obtain payment for these goods may be seen as a case of implied contract. The buyer has *accepted* the excess goods. The converse case of the buyer who accepts the shortfall tender[146] would perforce be treated as an implied variation of the original contract.

19.66 The same approach should be taken even if the seller's claim to obtain payment for excess goods accepted by the buyer is seen as one in unjust enrichment. It is the law applicable to the contract which determines what quantity of goods is to be supplied, and, therefore, whether there has been an oversupply to the buyer. The contract itself, though in one sense only the factual background to the claim by the seller, supplies the framework pursuant to which the seller supplied the goods to the buyer. The contract itself remains intact and the parties' expectations are likely to be furthered by application of the law governing the contract to the claim for payment for the excess goods supplied by the seller to the buyer. Indeed, it does not seem desirable for the seller's claim to obtain payment for goods falling within the contractual specification to be subject to the governing law of the contract, but for the claim in respect of the excess goods to be governed by some other law.

---

[142] Brereton, n 39 above, at 174–176, describes this as 'restitution within contract'. See also *Lloyd v Guibert* (1865) 6 B & S 100, Court of Exchequer Chamber.
[143] s 30(2) of the Sale of Goods Act 1979.
[144] The seller has the burden of proof: ibid, s 30(2)(B).
[145] ibid, s 30(2)(A).
[146] ibid, s 30(1).

11. Delivery or Payment to the Wrong Person

Of course, there will be cases where the buyer or seller seeks to obtain **19.67**
restitutionary damages from a party with whom he is not in a pre-existing
contractual relationship. A seller might, for example, deliver the goods to
the wrong person. If so, he may simply seek to recover his property, by
invoking the law of the *situs*. However, if the recipient has dissipated the
property, or the property has perished or fallen in value, the claimant
might instead seek to claim damages equivalent to the value of the goods
received by the defendant. In such a case, there seems no reason to apply
the law applicable to the contract of sale to this claim in unjust enrichment.
It would be unacceptable for the recipient to be subject to this law, when it
was agreed upon in a contract to which he was not party. Rather, it is
suggested that Rule 200(2)(c) should apply. This means that the law of the
place of enrichment will be applied. This is likely to be construed as the
place of immediate benefit, namely the place of misdelivery, rather than
any other place where the defendant might subsequently use those goods
to his benefit.[147] So, if a seller erroneously delivers goods to a recipient in
England, English law should apply to a claim for restitutionary damages,
notwithstanding that the recipient has his principal place of business
elsewhere, or has subsequently sold the goods in another jurisdiction.

Likewise, if the buyer erroneously pays the purchase price to the wrong **19.68**
person, it is suggested that a claim to recover the value of that payment
from its recipient should be subject to Rule 200(2)(c). This means that the
law of the place of enrichment will be applied. This is likely to be the place
of immediate enrichment, i.e. the place where the payment was made to
the defendant, rather than any place where the recipient might subsequently transfer the funds paid. So, if the buyer erroneously pays a
recipient in England, English law should apply to a claim for restitutionary damages, notwithstanding that the recipient has now moved those
funds to an account in, say, Switzerland.

VIII. CLAIMS ASSERTING A PROPRIETARY INTEREST

1. Proprietary Interests in Goods or Payments

Frequently, the seller or buyer will be seeking restitutionary damages. **19.69**
In other words, the remedy sought will be personal. It may, however,
happen that the claimant asserts a proprietary interest. An example

---

[147] Compare s 128(2) of the Swiss Private International Law Statute: see Cheshire and
North, 679, n 16.

would be where the buyer pays for goods and accepts the bill of lading, in circumstances where it is intended that property will pass conditionally to the buyer. The buyer subsequently rejects the goods. An action to obtain the goods by the seller might be classified as one in unjust enrichment. It may be argued that the seller asserts not that the property was and is still his, but that it should revest in him. Another example might arise where a seller has not been paid, but has, unusually, already vested title in the buyer. The seller might then seek to have the property revested in himself. Normally, of course, the unpaid seller will not have passed property in the goods and any claim will simply be a vindication of his property rights and governed by the law of the *situs*. Again, in the event that a contract is declared void, the buyer might claim not merely restitutionary damages in respect of payment already made under the supposed contract, but that the money paid to the seller remains the buyer's property, or that the property becomes revested in the buyer. In the event of rescission, a party might wish to claim his property back, rather than being content with a claim in damages.[148]

19.70   Rule 200[149] in Dicey and Morris does not distinguish between claims affecting goods[150] which seek personal restitution and claims which seek proprietary restitution. At first sight, this has the doctrinal advantage that it classifies the cause of action, and not the remedy sought. However, it has the unfortunate effect that it makes it vital to distinguish between claims which are classified as property law claims and claims which seek proprietary restitution to reverse unjust enrichment. In principle, it is suggested that the essential difference to be drawn is between claims to vindicate a *continuing* property right and claims that property should *revest* in the claimant.[151] The former claim is a property one and the property choice of law rules should be applied to determine whether the claimant can assert a continuing title to goods. This would lead to the application of the law of the *situs*. The latter claim is a claim in unjust enrichment, and the choice of law rules applicable to restitution should be applied.[152] If Rule 200 in Dicey and Morris is applied, this will lead to the application of the law applicable to the actual or putative contract where a claim arises in the aftermath of a failed contract.

---

[148]   See S Worthington, 'The Proprietary Consequences of Rescission' (2002) 10 Restitution L Rev 28.

[149]   On which, see above, paras 19.10–16.

[150]   They envisage a special rule where the restitutionary obligation arises in connection with land: Rule 200(2)(b).

[151]   See A Burrows, *The Law of Restitution* (2nd edn, Craydon: Butterworths, 2002) 60–75. But see Bird, n 22 above, at 79–83 for a discussion of the various points of view.

[152]   But see the views of G Virgo, *The Principles of the Law of Restitution* (Oxford: OUP, 1999) Ch 20.

This is capable of giving rise to acute problems of classification as to **19.71** whether the claim should be regarded as proprietary or restitutionary in nature.[153] For example, a seller may seek the return of goods, if the buyer fails to pay the purchase price. Different legal systems might legitimately disagree as to whether the buyer's claim is a property law claim to assert a continuing property right, which should be governed by the law of the *situs*, or to have the property revested in him, which should be determined by the choice of law rule for unjust enrichment claims. In such a case, we cannot classify by the governing law of the claim; for the very point is that until the English court has determined whether the claim is proprietary or restitutionary, it will not know what the governing law is. So, characterization is a matter for the law of the forum. Yet this creates an intractable problem, since the relationship between the law of property and the law of restitution is extremely uncertain even in domestic law. Such complexity can only be intensified when a classification is made for choice of law purposes, since different legal systems may disagree as to the nature of the claimant's action.

In part because of the complexities of characterization which arise, it is **19.72** suggested that Rule 200 in Dicey and Morris should be rejected where proprietary rights in goods[154] are at stake. More significantly, it is apparent that the law which is most appropriate to apply to a claim asserting an interest in property is the law of the *situs*.[155] This fact should not be obscured by the refinements of the classification process. The principal reasons proffered for application of the law of the *situs* to 'ordinary' property claims concerning inter vivos transfers of tangible movables are result orientated. The law of the *situs* is the law of the state which has the greatest control over the assets in question. Any English order may need enforcement in that state; and any English judgment concerning property rights in that asset may be unenforceable in the courts of the *situs* if the latter courts take a different view as to the parties' property rights. Moreover, application of the law of the *situs* is usually clear cut[156] and unlikely to defeat the expectations of the parties.[157] This is because any party familiar with the basics of choice of law will know that the law specified in a contract will not normally be effective to determine property rights in the goods concerned and that the law of the *situs* determines this matter.[158]

---

[153] See also above, paras 8.106–117, 8.121–127.   [154] Or any tangible movable property.

[155] A view shared by Stevens, n 23 above, at 180, 183.

[156] At least where the goods are not in transit when property in them allegedly passes.

[157] Including the expectations of third parties who may be affected by a decision as to property rights in the goods.

[158] See the remarks of Staughton LJ in *Macmillan Inc v Bishopsgate Investment Trust plc (No 3)* [1996] 1 WLR 387, 400, CA.

19.73 In short, application of the law of the *situs* to property claims is justified both on the basis of party expectation and on the basis of the practical *consequences* of any order affecting property rights, which may need enforcement in the courts of the *situs*. Whether a claim is technically one in property law or for proprietary restitution is not the most important question. In either case, property rights are ultimately in issue. For this reason, it is suggested that where a party claims an interest in property, the law of the *situs* should be applied, whether the claim is technically one in property or in restitution. So if, for example, a seller seeks to recover goods transferred pursuant to a rescinded contract governed by English law, and those goods had been transferred to the buyer in Japan, it is suggested that Japanese law, being the law of the place where the last purported transaction in the property occurred, should be applied to determine the seller's claim. As indicated above, this also has the considerable advantage that problems of classification are minimized, since the same law will be applied however the claim is classified.

2. Interests Under a Trust

General Principles

19.74 In English law, matters are more complicated where property rights are in issue. A party might claim not that he is, or should be made, outright owner of goods or payments made pursuant to an actual or supposed contract, but that the recipient of that property holds it on constructive trust for the claimant. Such claims bring into play the rules concerning trusts. For example, where a buyer contracts to buy unique goods from the seller not freely available on the open market, he may argue that, from the moment of conclusion of the contract, the seller holds the goods on constructive trust for the buyer.[159] Again, imagine that a buyer pays the purchase price to the seller. The seller fails to pass title to the buyer. The buyer might seek to hold the seller liable to account in damages to him. But what if the seller claims beneficial *ownership* of the sum representing the purchase price, on the basis that the seller holds the money on trust for him, as he might wish to do if, for example, the sum has been reinvested and increased in value? The extent to which trusts might arise pursuant to an actual or void contract is a matter of considerable conjecture in domestic

---

[159] Or subject to an equitable lien. The language of constructive trusts is not normally used in sale of goods cases and that of the equitable lien is preferred: see, e.g. *Re Wait* [1927] 1 Ch 606, CA.

law.[160] But, for choice of law purposes, it is possible to state the general principles which will determine which law decides whether such trusts arise.

The authors of Dicey and Morris favour application of the restitution **19.75** choice of law rules to determine whether a defendant has an obligation to restore a benefit to the claimant and argue 'more tentatively' that 'that law will provide the legal concept by which the obligation to restore the benefit is secured'.[161] In other words, the law applicable to the cause of action will also determine whether the claimant is entitled to a personal or a proprietary remedy. So, if the nature of the claim is one in unjust enrichment, the law designated by the restitution choice of law rules would determine whether the claimant holds on constructive trust. 'It follows that an English court should recognize and give effect to a constructive trust . . . in circumstances where . . . [it would not] exist in English law.'[162]

Application of the Hague Trusts Convention

It is very curious that the authors of Dicey and Morris do not consider the **19.76** application of the Hague Convention on the Law Applicable to Trusts and on their Recognition (hereafter, 'the Hague Trusts Convention')[163] to constructive trusts. It is equally curious that the Hague Trusts Convention has barely been cited in judicial decisions where it has been alleged that the defendant holds on constructive trust.[164] In *Arab Monetary Fund v Hashim (No 11)*,[165] Chadwick J remarked that:

[I]n cases involving a foreign element in which an English court is asked to treat a defendant as a constructive trustee of assets which he has acquired through

---

[160] Particular controversy has surrounded the question of whether a resulting trust might arise where a contract is void. See *Westdeutsche Landesbank Girozentral v Islington London Borough Council* [1996] AC 669, HL. See also, e.g. P Birks, 'Restitution and Resulting Trusts' in S Goldstein (ed), *Equity: Contemporary Legal Developments* (Jerusalem: Hebrew University of Jerusalem, 1992); P Birks, 'Trusts Raised to Reverse Unjust Enrichment: the *Westdeutsche* Case' (1996) 4 Restitution L Rev 3; A Burrows, 'Swaps and the Friction between Common Law and Equity' (1995) 3 Restitution L Rev 15; R Chambers, *Resulting Trusts* (Oxford: OUP, 1997), esp 93–219; W Swadling, 'A new role for resulting trusts?' (1996) 16 LS 110; S Worthington, 'The Proprietary Consequences of Contract Failure' in F Rose (ed) *Failure of Contracts: Contractual, Restitutionary and Proprietary Consequences* (Oxford: Hart, 1997), ch 5.

[161] Dicey and Morris, 1503. [162] ibid.

[163] The text is contained in the *Proceedings of the Fifteenth Session of the Hague Conference on Private International Law 1984, Book II—Trusts, Applicable Law and Recognition*, 361.

[164] e.g. *El Ajou v Dollar Land Holdings plc* [1993] 3 All ER 717, Ch D (rev'd on different grounds: [1994] 2 All ER 685, CA); *Arab Monetary Fund v Hashim (No 11)* The Times, 11 October 1994, QBD (Comm); *Trustor AB v Smallbone* (9 May 2000, CA); *Kuwait Oil Tanker v Al Bader (No 3)* [2000] 2 All ER (Comm) 271, CA (and see G Virgo, 'Interest, Constructive Trusts and the Conflict of Laws' (2000) 8 Restitution L Rev 122); *Grupo Torras v Al-Sabah (No 5)* [2001] Lloyd's Rep Bank 36, CA (noted by Garton (2001) 15 Trust L Intl 93).

[165] The Times, 11 October 1994, QBD (Comm).

misuses of his powers, the relevant questions are: (i) what is the proper law which governs the relationship between the defendant and the person for whose benefit those powers have been conferred; (ii) what, under that law, are the duties to which the defendant is subject in relation to those powers; (iii) is the nature of those duties such that they would be regarded by an English court as fiduciary duties; and (iv) if so, is it unconscionable for the defendant to retain those assets?

This curious examination of the governing law in its context, so that the law of the forum can decide whether to treat the relationship as fiduciary and whether to impose a constructive trust, makes no reference to the Hague Trusts Convention.

19.77   Yet the scope of the Convention in the United Kingdom has been extended by s 1(2) of the Recognition of Trusts Act 1987 in such a way that it clearly means that most resulting and constructive trusts are caught by the Convention's choice of law rules. Accordingly, where it is alleged that a defendant holds on constructive trust, it is to the Convention,[166] that we should first look for the law which will determine whether that trust exists.[167]

19.78   We must now, therefore, briefly study the key provisions of the Hague Trusts Convention that are relevant to the present discussion. Starting with its scope, Article 3 of the Convention states that it applies to trusts 'created voluntarily and evidenced in writing'. Section 1(2) of the Recognition of Trusts Act 1987 applies the Convention 'not only in relation to the trusts described in Articles 2 and 3 of the Convention but also in relation to any other trusts of property arising under the law of any part of the United Kingdom or by virtue of a judicial decision whether in the United Kingdom or elsewhere'. This seems to mean that the vast majority of trusts will fall within the scope of the Convention. This is the case whether the trust is express, resulting or constructive in nature.[168]

19.79   Article 6 of the Convention allows the settlor expressly or impliedly to choose the law applicable to the trust. Suppose that a contract of sale is alleged to give rise to a specifically enforceable obligation, so that a

---

[166] As extended in the UK by the Recognition of Trusts Act 1987.

[167] Or should be imposed by the court.

[168] Although it is arguable that trusts imposed regardless of the will of the parties, and which arise institutionally from a set of facts, rather than being imposed by a court decision, fall outside the Act if the trust is not governed by the law of a part of the UK: see J Harris, *The Hague Trusts Convention* (Oxford: Hart, 2002) 145–150. Contrast G Miller, J Mowbray, L Tucker, N Le Poidevin and E Simpson, *Lewin on Trusts* (17th edn, London: Sweet and Maxwell, 2000) 288.

constructive trust arises. It is very likely that a court will find that the law chosen to govern the contract of sale itself will also govern the trust thereby generated.

However, in the case of most resulting and constructive trusts, the applic- **19.80** able law will usually be determined in the absence of choice.[169] Article 7 states that the law of closest connection to the trust will apply. It then lays down an implicitly hierarchical,[170] but non-exhaustive[171] list of factors to which regard should be had in determining the law of closest connection. Article 7(2) states that:

In ascertaining the law with which a trust is most closely connected reference shall be made in particular to—

(a) the place of administration of the trust designated by the settlor;
(b) the *situs* of the assets of the trust;
(c) the place of residence or business of the trustee;
(d) the objects of the trust and the places where they are to be fulfilled.

Some of these factors do not seem terribly relevant to resulting and constructive trusts. Factor (a) does not seem relevant and nor does factor (d). Moreover, where the trust arises as a response to a vitiating factor affecting a contract, it seems reasonable to suppose that considerable importance should be attached to the law which governed the contract itself. But the point is that the Convention will determine whether a resulting or constructive trust of property exists; and in determining this issue, it is the law of objective closest connection to the (putative) trust which should be applied.

The Trust in Operation: Retention of Title Clauses and the Proceeds of Sale

Goods sold with the permission of the seller

A case where a trust might arise in the sale of goods context is where a **19.81** buyer is subject to a retention of title clause in favour of the unpaid seller,

---

[169] On the law applicable to a trust in the absence of choice, see Art 7 of the Hague Trusts Convention; Harris, n 168 above, at 215–232, esp 232. See also *Chellaram v Chellaram (No 2)* [2002] 3 All ER 17, Ch D.

[170] *The Explanatory Report on the Convention on the Law Applicable to Trusts and on their Recognition by Professor M Alfred Von Overbeck, Proceedings of the Fifteenth Session of the Hague Conference on Private International Law 1984, Book II—Trusts, Applicable Law and Recognition,* (hereafter 'the von Overbeck Report'), comments at para 77 that: 'The delegations of the civil law countries also agreed that the second paragraph, by the order in which the criteria were set forth, comprised an implicit hierarchy which would satisfy the needs of practice'.

[171] 'But the text will also allow the judges of the common law countries to take into account, as they have the habit of doing, all factors at the same time': ibid.

but has permission[172] to enter into a sub-sale and is able to pass good title to a third party. In English domestic law, the *Romalpa*[173] decision held that any proceeds of sale were held by the buyer on constructive trust for the seller. However, the *Romalpa* conclusion was reached because of the buyer's concession that the bailment under which the goods were supplied gave rise to a fiduciary relationship, which subsequent cases have denied.[174] Hence, in English law there may be only a personal action for money had and received. However, more generally, the question arises as to which law should be used in an international context to determine whether a constructive trust arises?

19.82   It could be argued that the alleged trust is created voluntarily. This will be the case if the contract itself expressly specifies that the proceeds of sale are to be held on trust for the seller.[175] Even if this is not stated in the contract, the buyer may be taken to have agreed that if he exercises his power to sell, he must hold the proceeds on trust for the seller. If the retention of title clause is also evidenced in writing,[176] one might conclude that it satisfies the requirements of Article 3 of the Hague Trusts Convention.[177] However, it is not necessary to reach a conclusion on this point, since the trust is in any event likely to be caught by the statutory extension of the Convention in the United Kingdom by s 1(2) of the Recognition of Trusts Act 1987.[178] If so, the law that will apply will be the law chosen by the parties. Arguably, they could be said impliedly to have chosen the law applicable to the contract. If this is not accepted, then the law of closest connection must be ascertained under Article 7 in the absence of choice.

19.83   The seller might alternatively seek a personal remedy for damages equivalent to the value of the proceeds received. This obligation arises in unjust enrichment. However, it is equally clear that it arises pursuant to a sale authorized by the original contract between buyer and seller. It might be said to relate to the performance of a contractual right of the buyer to sell the goods. If so, Article 10(1)(b) of the Rome Convention would lead

---

[172] According to the law applicable to the contract.

[173] *Aluminium Industrie Vaassen BV v Romalpa Aluminium Ltd* [1976] 1 WLR 676, CA.

[174] See, e.g. *Clough Mill v Martin* [1985] 1 WLR 111, CA; *Hendy Lennox (Industrial Engines) v Grahame Puttick* [1984] 1 WLR 485, QBD.

[175] As Benjamin, 25–138, correctly notes, the fact that a contractual term expressly stipulates that the proceeds should be held on trust does not make the issue a contractual one, since 'it purports to give the seller proprietary rights'. See also *United States Surgical Corp v Hospital Products International Pty Ltd* [1983] 2 NSWLR 157, 192, New South Wales Court of Appeal, (1984) 156 CLR 41, HC of Australia.

[176] It could be argued that a written contract containing a reservation of title clause is itself sufficient evidence that a trust will arise in favour of the seller in respect of the proceeds of sale.

[177] On which, see Harris, n 168 above, at 123–139.   [178] See above, para 19.78.

to the application of the applicable law of the contract to the question of whether the buyer was liable to account in damages. Moreover, it was argued above that even if the obligation is seen as an independent one in unjust enrichment (and outside the ambit of Article 1 of the Rome Convention), the law applicable to the contract is still the most appropriate law to be applied to the obligation in unjust enrichment.

Goods sold without the permission of the seller

Would matters differ if the buyer subject to a retention of title clause did **19.84** *not* have permission to sell the goods?[179] Which law should then determine if the buyer is liable to account for the proceeds of sale? On the one hand, the liability of the buyer to account may be seen as an equitable obligation, but one which responds to the wrongdoing of the buyer by forcing him to disgorge the enrichment made from the sale. On the other hand, if the buyer subject to a retention of title clause does not have permission to sell the goods, the obligation to account for the proceeds might be viewed as a remedy for breach of that contract.

It is suggested that the law to be applied should depend upon whether the **19.85** seller is claiming beneficial *ownership* of the proceeds or just seeking to render the buyer personally liable to account for the value of the proceeds. In the former case, it is suggested that the law applicable to the (putative) trust should be applied,[180] as determined by Article 7 of the Hague Trusts Convention. It is true that Article 3 of the Convention states that the Convention applies to trusts created voluntarily and that this trust is imposed *against* the will of the buyer. However, it must be recalled that s 1(2) of the Recognition of Trusts Act 1987 extends the Convention to '. . . any other trusts of property arising under the law of any part of the United Kingdom or by virtue of a judicial decision whether in the United Kingdom or elsewhere'. This suggests that constructive trusts are covered by the Convention's choice of law rules even if they are imposed against the will of the 'trustee'.[181]

If, however, the remedy sought by the seller is to render the buyer *person-* **19.86** *ally* liable it is suggested that the availability of restitutionary damages might be seen as a consequence of the breach and determined by the applicable law of the contract, in accordance with Article 10(1)(c) of the Rome Convention. Alternatively, it may be argued that the Rome Convention does not apply to what is in substance a restitutionary obligation.

---

[179] This should be determined according to the applicable law of the contract.
[180] If the claim is that the seller is *outright* owner of the proceeds, the law of the *situs* should be used.
[181] But see Harris, n 168 above, at 122–50 (esp 145–150).

However, even if this is so, on the basis of the arguments made above, it is suggested that the applicable law of the contract is still the most appropriate law to be applied to this restitutionary obligation.

19.87 In short then, this leads to the application of the same choice of law rules in respect of the liability of the buyer in respect of the proceeds of sale, regardless of whether the sale was with the permission of the original seller. In either case, the following choice of law rules are suggested:

(1) The question of whether a buyer subject to a retention of title clause must hold the proceeds of sale on trust for the seller is a matter for the law putatively applicable to that trust. This is the law of closest connection to the trust, as determined by Article 7 of the Hague Trusts Convention.

(2) The question of whether a buyer subject to a retention of title clause is subject to a personal liability to the seller to the value of the proceeds of sale should be determined by the law applicable to the contract of sale.[182]

3. TRACING

General Remarks

19.88 Tracing is the process which determines whether a party can identify assets in the hands of another person which represent his original property. This may be because the assets are a substitute for the original owner's property, or because his original property has been mixed with the property of another person. Suppose that a seller seeks to recover from the buyer goods subject to a retention of title clause. Without permission, the buyer sells the goods. The seller might seek to establish that, since he owned the original goods, he also owns the proceeds of sale. Alternatively, the goods may have become mixed with the buyer's own goods. For example, the seller may have supplied oil to the buyer, who has blended it with the buyer's own oil. The seller may wish to establish a proprietary interest in the blended oil.

19.89 Great uncertainty surrounds the nature of tracing in domestic law. In private international law, there is very little discussion of the classification of tracing and of the choice of law rules to be applied to it.[183] Although a

---

[182] But contrast Benjamin, 25–139. Its authors prefer to determine a single law applicable to the question of whether the buyer is liable to account for the proceeds of sale. They would then let that law determine whether the appropriate remedy is a personal one, or whether the buyer is required to hold the proceeds on trust for the seller.

[183] G Panagopoulos, 'Cross Border Tracing; Conflict of Laws Issues' (1998) 6 Restitution L Rev 73; J Harris, 'Tracing and the Conflict of Laws' (2002) 73 British Ybk of Intl Law 65.

full discussion of this subject is beyond the scope of this chapter, some relatively brief comments can be made.[184] First, although tracing is a process of identification of value, it should not be classified as procedural for private international law purposes.[185] The whole process has evolved to identify property rights. Second, if tracing is a substantive issue, then the question arises as to which law governs the tracing process. In particular, is the issue whether a party can successfully trace the subject of a choice of law rule in its own right, or should whichever law governs the claimant's (primary) cause of action also determine the (incidental) tracing issue?

Tracing and the Hague Trusts Convention

Analysis: meaning and effect of Article 11(3)(d) of the Convention

It is necessary to distinguish those claims which fall within the ambit of **19.90** the Hague Trusts Convention, as extended in the United Kingdom by the Recognition of Trusts Act 1987, from those which do not. Article 11(3)(d), which states that recognition shall imply *in so far as the law applicable to the trust requires or provides* 'that the trust assets may be recovered when the trustee, in breach of trust, has mingled trust assets with his own property or has alienated trust assets'.[186] This provision covers both recovery of the trust property itself and the mixing of trust property with the trustee's own property. This is a very clear preference for the law governing the original trust, a law which may have been expressly chosen by the settlor.[187]

However, Article 11(3)(d) goes on severely to limit the role of the law **19.91** applicable to the trust. It mentions expressly only the mixing of trust assets with the trustee's own property; it does not expressly deal with the mixing of the trust assets with a third party's assets. Although it does also deal with the alienation of trust assets (presumably covering the following[188] of them into the hands of a third party), it does not make clear what should happen if those trust assets are subsequently mixed by a third

---

[184] See also the discussion of complex reservation of title clauses above, paras 18.108–111.

[185] *Chase Manhattan Bank NA v Israel-British Bank (London) Ltd* [1981] Ch 105, Ch D; *El Ajou v Dollar Land Holdings plc* [1993] 3 All ER 717, Ch D (rev'd on different grounds: [1994] 2 All ER 685, CA).

[186] It may be doubted whether Panagopoulos affords sufficient consideration to Art 11(3)(d) in his discussion of the choice of law rules applicable to tracing trust property. See Harris, n 183 above, 93–99.

[187] Art 6.

[188] Following is the process of locating property which has not changed its form, either through mixture or substitution. Tracing is the process of identifying and locating property which has changed its form through mixture and/or substitution.

party with his own assets, or if a clean substitution for the trust property is made.[189]

The rights of third parties to the trust

19.92   More importantly, in the situation where the property or its value is to be recovered from a third party holder of the assets, that third party's rights and obligations 'shall remain subject to the law determined by the choice of law rules of the forum'.[190] This provision originated from concerns to provide adequate protection to banks which received trust property, although the provision is applicable to all third party holders.[191] Nor is the provision expressly confined to purchases by third parties.

19.93   That said, there is a strong argument that the final sentence of Article 11(3)(d) should only be invoked in England where the issue concerns acquisition by the third party and whether, as a *bona fide* purchaser, he takes free of a subsisting equitable interest. It would not be relevant to the question whether the trust assets or their value could be traced into the third party's hands, which is determined under the first sentence of Article 11(3)(d) by the law applicable to the trust. Properly considered, in other words, the final sentence of Article 11(3)(d) is not a tracing provision; it is a provision preserving property defences which might avail a third party holding assets traceable from the original trust property.

19.94   The final sentence of Article 11(3)(d) refers only to the 'rights and obligations' of third party holders. Tracing does not determine either rights or obligations, even if it is a key step to the assertion of rights. Accordingly, it may be that the second sentence of Article 11(3)(d) has no application to the 'mere' process of identifying value in a mixed fund held by a third party. It is argued that, in England at least, the only matter which should 'remain subject to the law determined by the choice of law rules of the forum' is whether a third party purchaser in good faith has taken free of the interest under the trust, even if the law applicable to the trust states that trust assets or their value can be traced into the third party's hands. From the third party's perspective, a purchase of trust property is an 'ordinary' property acquisition and the *lex situs* should determine whether he takes free of the beneficial interest under the trust.

---

[189] The recognition of the clean substitution of trust assets is not expressly provided for in the Convention, but it would fatally undermine the Convention if recognition was not required in this case. Moreover, M Koppenol-Laforce, *Het Haagse Trustverdrag* (Deventer: Kluwer, 1997) 269 concludes that: 'Most countries recognize in their own law the possibility of substitution if it concerns a fund with a specific purpose. Therefore, recognition will not be a problem, although it is not completely clear where the basis for this can be found in the Convention.'

[190] Art 11(3)(d), second sentence.

[191] See further the von Overbeck Report, paras 113–117.

Conclusion

Accordingly, it is suggested that a two stage test operates in relation to the **19.95** tracing and claiming of trust assets from a third party under the Hague Trusts Convention:

(1) The law governing the trust determines whether the assets or their value can be followed or traced into the hands of the third party.[192] If they may not be, then they cannot be recovered from the third party.

(2) If they can be, the law of the *situs* shall determine whether a third party has taken free of the beneficial interest under the trust by virtue of purchasing it or its value in good faith.[193] If he has, the assets or their value cannot be recovered; if he has not, then the assets or their value can be recovered.

Tracing where the Hague Trusts Convention does not Apply

Outside this context, the choice of law rule applicable to tracing[194] is not **19.96** well settled. It is perhaps most likely that tracing will simply be determined by the law which governs the original cause of action. This is the view of Dicey and Morris[195] and also of Panagopoulos.[196] This may be justified on the basis that tracing itself is a process of identification. It does not itself confer rights and it may be thought inappropriate for it to be subject to its own choice of law rule. Rather, it may be treated as a form of incidental question that is subordinate to the law governing the claimant's cause of action. If this is correct, it means that if the basis of the seller's claim to the original goods is vindication of an undestroyed property right, then the law of the *situs* of that original property at the time of the last transaction in it will determine whether the seller can demonstrate a proprietary interest in it. The same law will determine whether the assets in the defendant's hands are the traceable proceeds of those assets. If, by contrast, the foundation of the seller's claim to the original property is on the basis of unjust enrichment, then the choice of law rules which determine whether proprietary restitution[197] of the original

---

[192] And, indeed, whether they can be traced into the hands of the original trustee.

[193] But the law of the *situs* should not be applied to determine whether the third party has taken free of the beneficiary's interest for any other reason, such as if that law does not consider the assets held by the defendant to be the traceable proceeds of the trust property, or it does not know the concept of the trust.

[194] In English domestic law, there must also be a pre-existing fiduciary relationship in order that the claimant can trace and successfully claim property in equity. On the choice of law questions that this raises, see Harris, n 183 above, at 87–88.

[195] Dicey and Morris, 1502.   [196] Panagopoulos, n 183 above.

[197] Although it is argued above that the same choice of law rule should apply where proprietary restitution is sought as where a claim is brought to vindicate an undestroyed property right: see paras 19.69–73.

property is, in principle, available to the claimant will determine whether the claimant can assert a proprietary interest in the mixed or substituted property.[198]

4. Proprietary Defences to Restitutionary Claims

19.97   Finally, it should be noted that even if the claimant can assert a claim in unjust enrichment to assets in another's hands, that party may have subsequently sold the goods in question to a third party purchaser. If the claimant seeks to claim the property from that third party, the latter may allege that he is a *bona fide* purchaser of the legal estate in that property and that he takes free of any interest of the claimant. This is clearly a matter of property law and it is the law of the *situs* which should determine whether this defence can succeed.[199]

IX. THE PROPOSED EUROPEAN REGULATION ON CHOICE OF LAW FOR NON-CONTRACTUAL OBLIGATIONS (THE 'ROME II' REGULATION)

19.98   The European Commission has issued a Proposal for a Regulation of the European Parliament and the Council on the Law Applicable to Non-Contractual Obligations.[200] Most of the choice of law rules in the Proposal are common to tort and to other non-contractual obligations, such as those arising in restitution. The key provisions of the Proposal are analysed in Chapter 17 on choice of law in tort, to which the reader is referred.[201]

19.99   Article 9 of the Proposal is the only Article that is specific to non-

---

[198]   But for a different view, see Harris, n 183 above.

[199]   *Macmillan Inc v Bishopsgate Investment Trust plc (No 3)* [1996] 1 WLR 387, CA.

[200]   COM/2003/0427 Final, of 22 July 2003, available at http://europa.eu.int/eur-lex/ pri/en/lip/latest/doc/2003/com2003_0427en01.doc. See also the Report of the UK House of Lords European Union Committee, available at www.publications.parliament.uk/pa/ ld200304/ldselect/ldeucom/660/6602.htm. On 3 May 2002, the European Commission had issued a Consultation on a Preliminary Draft Proposal for a Council Regulation on the Law Applicable to Non-Contractual Obligations: see http://europa.eu.int/comm/ dgs/justice_home/index_en.htm. See also the 'Follow-up of the Consultation on a Preliminary Draft Proposal for a Council Regulation on the Law Applicable to Non-Contractual Obligations' available at: http://europa.eu.int/comm/justice_home/unit/ civil/consultation/contributions_en.htm. On the UK Government's position on the Preliminary Draft Rome II Regulation, see http://www.lcd.gov.uk/consult/general/ eurocom.htm.

[201]   Above, paras 17.165–182. See also below, paras 21.203–210.

contractual obligations arising out of an act other than a tort or delict.[202] Article 9(1) states that:

If a non-contractual obligation arising out of an act other than a tort or delict concerns a relationship previously existing between the parties, such as a contract closely connected with the non-contractual obligation, it shall be governed by the law that governs that relationship.[203]

In other words, if a claim in restitution arises in connection with a contractual relationship between the parties, that claim will be governed by the applicable law of the contract. This provision supports the approach advocated in this chapter. It is true that the provision is qualified to some extent by Article 9(5), which states that '. . . where it is clear from all the circumstances of the case that the non-contractual obligation is manifestly more closely connected with another country, the law of that other country shall apply'. However, the forceful wording of this provision makes it clear that it will be applied only where there is a very clear case for applying a law other than that to which Article 9(1) points.[204]

Furthermore, Article 10(1) of the Proposal allows the parties directly to choose the law applicable to a claim in restitution. It states that: **19.100**

The parties may agree, by an agreement entered into after their dispute arose, to submit non-contractual obligations other than the obligations to which Article 8 applies to the law of their choice. The choice must be expressed or demonstrated

---

[202] It is not welcomed by the Report of the UK House of Lords European Union Committee, n 200 above. It comments (at para 144) that: 'We note the very serious doubts expressed as to whether it is sensible for the Regulation to deal with non-contractual obligations other than tort or delict given the rather embryonic state of the development of the law in this area . . . [L]iabilities in tort and, for example, restitution are conceptually quite distinct. For the Regulation to extend to and to provide sufficiently clear rules to deal with all "non-contractual obligations" is far too ambitious.' The Report urges that Art 9 be deleted, or that, if it is retained, its scope is clarified: ibid. The draft report of the European Parliament Committee on Legal Affairs and the Internal Market (Rapporteur Diana Wallis MEP), available at www.aig.org/r2g/downloads/dw_romeii_draftreport_090304.pdf, proposes the removal of Art 9, so that restitutionary claims are governed by the same rules as claims in tort (in particular, the rules in Art 3, discussed above, paras 17.165–172). However, the Report of the UK House of Lords European Union Committee, para 182, rightly points out the implications of such an approach need far more analysis before such a solution can be endorsed.

[203] Where there is no pre-existing relationship between the parties, Art 9(3) states that, '. . . a non contractual obligation arising out of unjust enrichment shall be governed by the law of the country in which the enrichment takes place'. This is subject to Art 9(2), which states that 'where the parties have their habitual residence in the same country when the event giving rise to the damage occurs, the law applicable to the non-contractual obligation shall be the law of that country'. Art 9(2) is again only relevant where there is no pre-existing relationship between the parties. Both Arts 9(2) and (3) may be displaced by the general exception in Art 9(5).

[204] Compare Art 3(3), discussed above, paras 17.170–172.

with reasonable certainty by the circumstances of the case. It may not affect the rights of third parties.[205]

Although this provision is concerned with a direct choice of the law applicable to the non-contractual claim, and must be affirmed after the dispute arose, it represents a triumph of party autonomy. Where the parties have chosen a law to govern a contract between them, it might even be argued that it can be 'demonstrated with reasonable certainty' that the parties intended[206] the same law to govern a claim in restitution arising in connection with that actual or purported contract. At the very least, Article 10(1) undermines the argument that claims in restitution arise as a matter of law and, as such, are not the proper subject of party autonomy for choice of law purposes.

X. CONCLUSION

19.101   The conclusions reached in this chapter in no way seek to undermine the importance, or autonomy, of the law of restitution, either domestically or for private international law purposes. However, it is argued that where claims for restitutionary damages arise in relation to an actual or supposed contract, the law applicable to that 'contract' is the most appropriate law to apply to the claim. It has been suggested that this view is, in many cases, logically defensible, even where the contract itself is void *ab initio*. It has also been suggested that it is desirable that the law which determines whether a contract is void, voidable or discharged should also determine the consequences thereof, especially as this is most likely to protect the expectations of the parties.

19.102   Nevertheless, it is suggested that this party autonomy should not extend to claims where interests in property in the goods, or payments made under the 'contract' are in issue. This is consistent with the fact that parties are not generally[207] at liberty to specify the law applicable to matters of property law. It has also been suggested that the law to govern such claims should not depend upon whether the claim is technically classified

---

[205] This is subject to the limitations in Art 10(2) and (3). The chosen law will prevail, save that: (i) if all the other objective elements of the claim are located in a country other than that whose law is chosen, the chosen law will be subject to the mandatory rules of the state of close connection (Art 10(2)); and (ii) where all the other elements of the claim are located in a Member State, the choice of law shall not debar the application of provisions of Community law (Art 10(3)). See further above, paras 17.173–174.

[206] With the proviso that that intention has to be reaffirmed by the parties after the dispute has arisen.

[207] Although they might choose the governing law where a trust is concerned: Art 6 of the Hague Trusts Convention.

as one in property, or one in restitution. In either case, the reasons for the application of the law of the *situs* are similar and are justified by concerns of predictability and enforceability.

A significant benefit of the conclusions reached in this chapter is that **19.103** problems of classification are minimized. It means that courts need spend less time on the classification of a personal claim as a matter of contract or restitution; and of a claim asserting a proprietary interest as one of property or restitution. In a minefield such as the private international law of restitution, this is a considerable benefit.

20

Concurrent Claims: Choice of Law

I. INTRODUCTION

20.01 There are a number of circumstances in which an act or omission by a defendant might give rise to liability in more than one branch of the law. A claimant may, for example, have claims available to him in contract and in tort; in contract and in restitution; or in tort and restitution. These claims may arise as alternatives to one another, or as distinct causes of action; or a single act or omission might generate parallel claims resting essentially upon the same basis. Some examples of such claims which might be relevant in the international sales context will be considered in this chapter. However, the primary function of this chapter is not exhaustively to identify all those situations in which there may be concurrent liability on the part of a buyer or seller. Rather, the purpose is to seek to elucidate a coherent private international law approach to the availability of concurrent claims which is capable of more general application.

20.02 Concurrent claims raise particular difficulties in private international law. Different states might disagree as to whether the claimant has more than one cause of action available to him. This raises difficulties for the classification process. States might also adopt different positions on the question of whether the claimant may pursue either claim at his election, or should be forced to pursue one claim to the exclusion of the other. A coherent approach to dealing with concurrent claims is needed which is capable of consistent, predictable application, but which does not distort the content of foreign law.

II. MULTIPLE CLAIMS WHICH MIGHT ARISE FROM A SALES CONTRACT

1. DISTINCT CAUSES OF ACTION

20.03 The fact that a claimant has more than one potential cause of action available to him does not mean that the claims in question are necessary legally connected. For example, if a seller is induced to breach the contract of sale by a third party, the buyer might bring a claim for breach of contract against the seller. He might also bring a claim in tort against the third party. However, the claims are quite distinct and each can be brought pursuant to the choice of law rules in contract and tort respectively.[1]

---

[1] Although the law applicable to either claim might preclude double recovery in respect of the same loss. In any event, it is likely that the law of the forum would regard double recovery as contrary to its public policy.

2. Related but Separate Claims

There may be claims which, although similar to each other, are not identi- **20.04** cal. In *Viskase Ltd v Paul Kiefel (GmbH)*,[2] the plaintiffs sought damages for breach of contract on the ground that the machines supplied were not fit for purpose. It was also claimed that the defendant had misrepresented that the machines were able to process certain types of film. These claims, though all relating to the supply of machinery, were not grounded on the same facts. Although counsel for the plaintiffs did not pursue the claim in tort, Chadwick LJ clearly regarded it as a separate claim to the one for breach of contract. At the choice of law stage, there is little doubt that a claimant should be permitted to pursue both claims, since they do not seek recovery on the same basis.[3]

3. Alternative, Mutually Exclusive Claims Arising from the Same Facts

An example of this scenario would be where a buyer pays part of the **20.05** purchase price of goods in advance and the seller fails to deliver. The buyer may seek to obtain rescission of the contract and the return of the payment made. The buyer might combine such a claim with an alternative one for damages for breach of contract, if the court refuses to allow rescission. This latter claim could only arise on the basis that the contract remains in force. Again, a buyer might sue for breach of contract on the basis that the seller has failed to pass good title to him and seek specific performance of this obligation. He might claim in the alternative that title has already passed to him under the contract. A further example is provided by the case of *Tesam Distribution Ltd v Schuh Mode Team GmbH and Commerzbank AG*.[4] The buyer sued a bank for breach of contract. The alleged breach in question was a failure to deliver shoes to the buyer. The buyer alleged that the bank was the owner of the shoes, or had a charge over them, and was party to the sales contract. The buyer also brought an alternative claim in tort on the basis that if the bank was not party to the sales contract, it had nonetheless induced the seller to breach that contract. Clearly the two claims were distinct and success in one precluded success in the other. Such claims are not problematic in the sense that the claimant seeks not to bring the claims concurrently, but to bring a primary claim and, if that fails, then to pursue another (single) cause of action.[5]

---

[2] [1999] 1 WLR 1305, CA. See further above, paras 3.111, 3.181, 3.211, 3.265–269.
[3] See also *Raiffeisen Zentralbank Osterreich AG v National Bank of Greece SA ('RZB v NGB')* [1999] 1 Lloyd's Rep 408, QBD (Comm).
[4] [1990] IL Pr 149, CA.
[5] See also *Domicrest v Swiss Bank Corp* [1999] QB 548, esp at 561.

4. CONSECUTIVE CLAIMS

20.06 Suppose that a buyer claims that a contract has been frustrated. The cause of action is in contract and the rules of the Rome Convention will be applied.[6] However, once he has established this, he may then seek to recover the value of payments made under the contract. This claim may be classified as one in unjust enrichment. It is clear that it is contingent upon the contractual claim first succeeding. However, there is no difficulty in principle in the claim to establish that the contract is frustrated being subject to contract choice of law rules, and the claim to recover payments made being governed by restitutionary choice of law rules.[7] There is no concurrence of causes of action. Rather, there is merely the application to separate legal issues of different choice of laws rules.

5. PARALLEL CLAIMS ARISING FROM A SINGLE ACT

20.07 It is possible that the same act may give rise to causes of action in more than one branch of the law of obligations. In English domestic law, an example would be a claim by the buyer against the seller in respect of a misrepresentation about the goods which induced the buyer to contract. A claim for negligent misstatement under the *Hedley Byrne*[8] line of authority in tort might co-exist with a claim for breach of the contractual duty to take care. In such a case, the claimant has a choice how to pursue his case.[9] Moreover, a claim under s 2(1) of the Misrepresentation Act 1967[10] for damages may be brought alongside a claim for breach of warranty.[11] It might be that a seller who negligently certifies that the goods are of a satisfactory quality may render himself potentially liable both in tort and in contract for his assertion.[12] In *Source Ltd v TUV Rheinland Holding AG*,[13]

---

  [6] Specifically, Art 10(1)(d) of the Rome Convention, discussed above, paras 15.240–246, esp 15.241–242.
  [7] Although it is argued above, paras 19.07–34 and 19.42–47, that the law applicable to the actual or putative contract should in fact be used to determine restitutionary claims arising from the 'contract'.
  [8] *Hedley Byrne & Co Ltd v Heller & Partners Ltd* [1964] AC 465, HL.
  [9] *Henderson v Merrett Syndicates Ltd* [1995] 2 AC 149, HL. See also *Base Metal Trading Ltd v Ruslan Borisovich Shamurin* [2002] CLC 322, QBD (Comm); noted A Briggs, 'Decisions of British Courts During 2000: Private International Law' (2002) 73 British Ybk of Intl Law 453, 481–487. See further the Court of Appeal's decision [2004] EWCA (Civ) 1316.
  [10] On which, see above, paras 6.67–71.   [11] s 1(1) of the Misrepresentation Act 1967.
  [12] *Source Ltd v TUV Rheinland* [1998] QB 54, CA, discussed above, paras 3.72 and 3.75, and considered also below, paras 20.29–34 and 20.38.
  [13] ibid.

it was alleged that the defendants were in breach of contract and that they had breached the duty of care in the preparation and supply of reports as to the quality of the goods bought by the claimants.[14]

A recent example of concurrent claims arising in contract and for the tort **20.08** of negligence arose in *Ennstone Building Products Ltd v Stanger Ltd.*[15] The claimants alleged that the defendant, a company with its principal place of business in England, was in breach of contract and liable in tort for failing adequately to investigate the staining of stonework on a building situated in Scotland.[16]

Concurrent claims may also arise from the fraudulent conduct of one of **20.09** the contracting parties. For example, in *Re an Italian Cargo of Adulterated Wine*,[17] a contract had been concluded between a German buyer and an Italian seller for the delivery of wine. The wine was found by customs to have been diluted. The German buyer sued the seller in respect of the breach of contract committed and also in tort in respect of the seller's alleged act of deception.

Although not our primary concern, it may also be noted that parallel **20.10** claims in contract and tort may arise in connection with the carriage of goods. For example, in English domestic law, when determining a consignee's right to sue a charterer or owner of a ship, one needs to determine who is the other party to the contract. A consignee's right to sue in contract depends upon the terms of s 2 of the Carriage of Goods by Sea Act 1992.[18] The Act does not deal with claims in tort and does not prevent these being pursued solely because the claimant has a contractual claim.[19]

Parallel claims raise complex private international law questions and **20.11** this chapter will focus primarily on such cases. They give rise to questions of classification, and of the extent to which a party can elect which

---

[14] Although both claims were held to be 'matters relating to contract' for the purposes of Art 5(1) of the Brussels Convention.

[15] [2002] 1 WLR 3059, CA; noted J Perkins, 'Identifying the Locus of the Tort' [2003] CLJ 274.

[16] See also the decision of the German Bundesgerichtshof in *Re a Consignment of Italian Wine* [1988] ECC 159, where the claimants argued that the defendants were in breach of contract in failing to provide goods in conformity with the contract and that they had negligently infringed wine regulations on minimum alcohol content.

[17] Decision of the Oberlandesgericht of Koblenz [1991] IL Pr 473.

[18] Considered above, paras 5.01, 5.08, 5.22, and paras 14.03–05, 14.40–56.

[19] Although there is little benefit in such a claim, because the same defences and limitations of liability contained in the Hague-Visby Rules still apply.

claim to pursue, or is forced to pursue a certain claim to the exclusion of another.

6. Parallel Claims Arising Solely by Virtue of Different Private International Law Classifications of a Single Domestic Cause of Action

20.12 It is theoretically possible that a claimant may have a single cause of action in domestic law, but that he might nonetheless be able to choose how to frame his claim in an English court for the purposes of private international law. In other words, a claimant might have more than one cause of action not because *domestic* law recognizes a plurality of claims, but because a single cause of action in domestic law might be placed in more than one category by an English court *for private international law purposes*. For example, suppose that the seller installs goods supplied to the buyer. The obligation to install the goods is not contained in the contract itself, but is freely undertaken by the seller. The installation is faulty and the goods are damaged. Suppose that the contract of sale is governed by the law of State X, by which the claim by the buyer is considered to be solely a contractual one. However, the act of installation occurred in State Y, by which law the claim is considered to be solely a tortious one. In other words, although the two states' laws disagree as to the nature of the claim, they agree that the claimant does *not* have more than one cause of action. However, if the buyer brings an action on the basis of the faulty installation, there is a question as to whether, for *private international law* purposes, an English court should classify the claim as one in contract, in tort, or, conceivably, both.

20.13 This issue is discussed in Chapter 17 on torts and choice of law, to which the reader is referred.[20] However, to summarize, the issue essentially is whether there is mutual exclusivity of classification for choice of law purposes. Since the definition of 'contractual obligations' in Article 1 of the Rome Convention is a European autonomous one and the definition of 'tort' for the purposes of s 9(2) of the Private International Law (Miscellaneous Provisions) Act 1995 is an English private international law one, it is possible that they are not mutually exclusive.[21] However, the most practical solution for an English court to adopt is to ask first whether the claim falls within the scope of Article 1 of the Rome Convention as a contractual obligation. If so, then that Article states that the rules of the Convention 'shall apply'. It could be said that this means shall apply *to the exclusion of*

---

[20] At paras 17.20–22; see also para 17.97.   [21] See Briggs, n 9 above, at 486–487.

any other choice of law rules.[22] In other words, the same claim could not also be classified as tortious for choice of law purposes. One would first determine whether the claim was caught by the contractual regime; and claims in tort could only be made in respect of matters *not* caught by that regime and the Rome Convention.[23] This suggests that private international law will strive to ensure that it does classify a single claim in domestic law within one, and only one, private international law category.[24]

III. CONCURRENT CLAIMS: EXAMPLES FROM DIFFERENT BRANCHES OF LAW

1. Concurrent Claims in Contract and Tort

A simple example of potential concurrent liability in contract and tort is **20.14** where a misrepresentation by the seller is incorporated as a term of the contract. Another example is illustrated by the case of *Empresa Exportadora de Azúcar v Industria Azucarera Nacional SA, (The Playa Larga and Marble Islands).*[25] In that case, the buyer had paid for goods which the seller failed to deliver. The goods were diverted to another location. The buyer brought an action in respect of the breach of a contractual warranty of quiet possession of goods alongside a claim for conversion. Again, concurrent claims might arise in the case of a term of the contract that the seller should install the goods supplied to the buyer. If he does so unsatisfactorily, the buyer might have claims in both contract and for the tort of negligence against the seller.

---

[22] But see *Thierry Morin v Bonhams* [2003] EWCA Civ 1802, [2004] IL Pr 24, where the Court of Appeal applied the choice of law rules in tort in the Private International Law (Miscellaneous Provisions) Act 1995 and held that the law of Monaco applied to claims for misrepresentation and negligent misstatement. It did this notwithstanding that there was evidence that the latter claim would be treated as contractual by the law of Monaco. The parties did not dispute the classification of the claims and the court did not even consider whether it was bound to determine nonetheless whether either or both claims were within the scope of the Rome Convention.

[23] But see *Base Metal Trading Ltd v Ruslan Borisovich Shamurin* [2002] CLC 322, QBD (Comm), noted Briggs, n 9 above, at 481–487, where Moore-Bick J took the view that the Rome Convention does not seek to address the problem of cumulative obligations. However, this was in the context of a discussion of where the claimant has more than one cause of action. Our present concern is where the claimant has a single cause of action and the question is whether this may be classified for choice of law purposes as both contractual and tortious. See further the Court of Appeal's decision [2004] EWCA (Civ) 1316.

[24] This must be distinguished from the discussion below of a mutually exclusive approach to classification where the claimant argues that he has more than one cause of action in domestic law. It is argued below, paras 20.28–52, that in such a case an English court must recognize the separate nature of the claims and classify them separately, rather than striving for mutual exclusivity.

[25] [1983] 2 Lloyd's Rep 171, CA.

2. Concurrent Claims in Contract and Restitution

20.15 An example of alternative claims in contract and restitution would be where the buyer seeks rescission of a contract and the return from the seller of payments made by him in advance. If the claim is unsuccessful, the buyer might, in the alternative, claim damages for breach of contract.[26] There may also be concurrent liability in contract and restitution. Such liability might arise if, for example, the seller is induced by a third party to breach his contract with the buyer and instead to sell the goods to the third party. The buyer might seek to claim damages for breach of contract or he might seek restitutionary damages equivalent to the value of the sum paid for the goods by the third party to the seller.[27]

3. Concurrent Claims in Contract and in Property or Trusts

20.16 An unpaid seller might allege that the buyer has not acquired title to the goods, or that title should be revested in the seller. If he fails in such a claim, he might claim damages for breach of contract. If a seller has sold goods to a third party without the consent of the buyer, the buyer might claim alternatively that the seller holds the proceeds of sale on trust for the buyer, or seek to claim damages for breach of contract, or for the tort of conversion.

4. Concurrent Claims in Property and Tort

20.17 In *Glencore International AG v Metro Trading International Inc (No 2)*,[28] a number of claimants argued that oil sold by the Metro Oil Corporation to third party purchasers was the property of the claimants and had been sold without their consent. They brought claims against, *inter alia*, the third party purchasers to recover the property and also for the tort of conversion.[29]

---

[26] See further the discussion above, paras 19.35–68, for examples of restitutionary claims which might arise in connection with a contract of sale. See also G Panagopoulos, *Restitution in Private International Law* (Oxford: Hart, 2000), 48–53; S Smith, 'Concurrent Liability in Contract and Unjust Enrichment: the Fundamental Breach Requirement' (1999) 115 LQR 245.

[27] A Briggs, *The Conflict of Laws* (Oxford: Clarendon, 2002), observes that: 'The existence of overlapping causes of action in contract and tort is permissible and not uncommon . . .; and it is contrary to common law principle to suppose that this is not also reflected in the relationship between restitution and other common law causes of action': at 192, n 1.

[28] [2001] 1 Lloyd's Rep 284, QBD (Comm).

[29] See also *Kuwait Airways Corp v Iraqi Airways Co (Nos 4 and 5)* [2002] 2 AC 883, HL.

5. CONCURRENT CLAIMS IN TORT AND RESTITUTION

In *Arab Monetary Fund v Hashim (No 9)*,[30] the claimant, AMF, alleged that **20.18** its former President, Dr Hashim, had taken bribes from an employee in order to improve its prospects of successfully bidding for a tender for the construction of the claimant's new headquarters. The claimant alleged that it was entitled to restitution of the bribe. It also claimed that the defendants were liable in tort on the basis that the claimant had suffered loss from the defendants' actions.[31] As Dicey and Morris note, '... concurrent claims in tort and restitution appear to have been approved in principle' by the Court of Appeal.[32]

IV. ARE THE OBLIGATIONS OF A PARTY TO THE SALES CONTRACT CONTRACTUAL? IF SO, DOES THE CONTRACTUAL CLAIM EXTINGUISH THE NON-CONTRACTUAL CLAIM?

Of course, it may sometimes be difficult in the sales context to determine **20.19** whether the defendant's obligations are contractual or non-contractual. An example might be where the seller is alleged to have failed to inspect the goods properly before certifying that they are of a satisfactory quality. The question may arise whether the obligation to inspect the goods properly was incorporated into the contract. That must be a question for the applicable law of the contract.[33]

However, the fact that the obligation is contractual does not, of course, **20.20** necessarily mean that there may not be concurrent liability in tort. The applicable law of the contract cannot be allowed to determine whether the claimant has a cause of action in tort. This is because contractual choice of law rules have no application to a claim which is, *ex hypothesi*, non-contractual. Rather, the effect of the contractual claim on any non-contractual cause of action is, of course, a matter for English private international law rules to determine. In the instant case, this means that the law applicable to the tort should determine whether the fact that the claimant's obligation is contained in the contract has the effect that a claim in tort is unavailable. It may be that it will hold that the claim in tort is still available. However, if that is so, one possible solution, where concurrent

---

[30] [1996] 1 Lloyd's Rep 589, CA. See also the Dutch judgment of 27 March 1979, *Bombardieri v Esta Trust Reg* Aae 1981, 193, Note: De Boer; NJ 1980, No 512; D Series I-5.1.2—B 24.
[31] It was also found that Dr Hashim was in breach of contract.
[32] Dicey and Morris, 1495, n 61.   [33] Art 8(1) of the Rome Convention.

actions are in principle available, is for the English court to force the claimant to sue in contract rather than in tort.[34]

V. EFFECT OF A CHOICE OF LAW CLAUSE WHERE CONCURRENT ACTIONS ARE BROUGHT[35]

1. Application of Choice of Law Clauses to Non-contractual Claims

20.21 One way to minimize the difficulties raised by concurrent claims is if the same law applies to each claim.[36] One particularly relevant issue in this context is whether a choice of law clause contained in a contract is capable of extending to a non-contractual claim.

2. Tort

20.22 The relevance of the law applicable to the contract is considered in Chapter 17 on tort claims.[37] It could be argued that it is simply a matter of construction of the choice of law clause to see whether it was intended by the parties that it should also govern a claim in tort.[38] In many cases, this will have been the parties' intention. 'In the commercial context, it seems improbable that parties really intend that a chosen law apply to some sorts of foreseeable claim but that others, equally foreseeable, are not, and are instead to be left to the expensive lottery of choice of law rules.'[39] However, the choice of law rules in tort do not permit the parties to choose a governing law. 'A choice of law clause has nothing to do with the events constituting the tort.'[40] At most,[41] the fact that the parties intended

---

[34] This is considered below, paras 20.37–40.

[35] See A Briggs, 'On Drafting Agreements on Choice of Law' [2003] LMCLQ 389.

[36] See *Johnson v Coventry Churchill International Ltd* [1992] 3 All ER 14, QBD; but see *Base Metal Trading Ltd v Ruslan Borisovich Shamurin* [2002] CLC 322, QBD (Comm), [2004] EWCA (Civ) 1316, CA.

[37] See, in particular, the discussion of conversion, above, paras 17.76–84; and see paras 17.120–121, 17.145, 17.156. See also *Empresa Exportadora de Azúcar v Industria Azucarera Nacional SA (The Playa Larga and Marble Islands)* [1983] 2 Lloyd's Rep 171, CA; *Kitechnology BV v Unicor GmbH Rahn Plastmaschinen* [1994] IL Pr 560, Ch D 568, CA (examined above, paras 6.02–05); and see the Scottish decision of the Outer House in *Compagnie Commercial André SA v Artibell Shipping Co Ltd* 1999 SLT 1051.

[38] See the remarks of Evans LJ in *Kitechnology*, ibid, at 575. See also the discussion above, paras 6.02–05, on the question whether a jurisdiction clause applies in relation to a tort claim.

[39] Briggs, n 35 above, at 392.

[40] *Thierry Morin v Bonhams & Brooks Ltd* [2003] IL Pr 25 at 443 [33] *per* Hirst QC (sitting as a Deputy Judge of the High Court). See also the decision of the Court of Appeal, [2003] EWCA Civ 1802, [2004] IL Pr 24.

[41] Although A Briggs, 'Choice of Choice of Law?' [2003] LMCLQ 12, 35 points out that even this is rather difficult to accommodate within the exception, which refers to the connections to a particular *country*, rather than to a particular *law*.

a law stipulated in the contract to govern a claim in tort may be taken into account when the court determines whether to invoke an exception to the general rule contained in s 11 of the Private International Law (Miscellaneous Provisions) Act 1995.[42]

Case law indicates differing attitudes of the courts to the relevance of the **20.23** law applicable to the contract to a claim in tort. In *Empresa Exportadora de Azúcar v Industria Azucarera Nacional SA (The Playa Larga and Marble Islands)*,[43] the buyer brought an action in respect of a breach of a contractual warranty of quiet possession of goods alongside an action in tort for conversion. The contract stated that: 'Any controversy that might arise from this contract is . . . submitted to "The Sugar Association of London" for its solution in accordance with the Rules on Arbitration of said Association'. Rule 401 of that Association provided for the competence of the Sugar Association of London as arbitrator. The Court of Appeal held that the conversion claim was sufficiently closely connected to the contractual claim that it was caught by the arbitration clause contained in the contract.[44] The court appeared to regard the matter as one of construction of the arbitration clause. It could be argued likewise that if a choice of *law* clause is intended on a true construction[45] also to extend to a claim in tort, the chosen law should govern the tort claim.[46] However, matters cannot be stated so confidently. For one thing, a major concern in relation to arbitration clauses is that multiplication of fora should be avoided. It would be undesirable for a claim in contract to be heard by arbitration and a claim in tort to be heard in court, perhaps in another jurisdiction. That concern does not apply to choice of law. Furthermore, the choice of law rules in tort do not expressly allow the parties to stipulate a law applicable to claims in tort.

In *Re Claim by a Polish Producer of Zinc and Copper Products*,[47] a Polish **20.24** claimant company and a German defendant company had concluded a contract subject to Polish law and to the jurisdiction of the Polish courts.

---

[42] s 11 of the Private International Law (Miscellaneous Provisions) Act 1995 lays down the general rule; s 12 creates a limited exception. See *Thierry Morin v Bonhams & Brooks Ltd* [2003] IL Pr 25 at [33] and [36], where Hirst QC suggested that the law chosen by the parties might be a relevant factor under s 12, although he preferred not to offer a final view on this issue. Mance LJ commented to similar effect in the Court of Appeal, although he too expressly left the point open: [2003] EWCA Civ 1802 at [23], [2004] IL Pr 24 at 398.

[43] [1983] 2 Lloyd's Rep 171, CA. See also *The Pioneer Container* [1994] 2 AC 324, PC; *Donohue v Armco Inc* [2002] 1 Lloyd's Rep 425, HL. Compare also s 46 of the Arbitration Act 1996.

[44] *The Playa Larga* [1983] 2 Lloyd's Rep 171, 182–183, CA.

[45] The law which putatively governs the contract, as stated in that clause, should itself determine the construction of that clause: Arts 3(4), 8(1) and 10(1)(a) of the Rome Convention.

[46] Contrast the German Oberlandesgericht of Cologne's decision in *Re a Claim by a Polish Producer of Zinc and Copper Products* [1998] IL Pr 727.

[47] ibid.

The Polish claimant sued the defendants in the Oberlandesgericht Cologne. Its claim was that one of its directors had acted dishonestly, as a result of which the German defendant had received and retained money owed to the claimants from the sale of its products. The court held that since the claim was not contractual, but rather alleged that the defendant had caused damage to the claimant in collusion with the claimant's former director, the jurisdiction and choice of law clause did not apply.

20.25 Against this, the court in *Glencore International AG v Metro Trading International Inc (No 2)*[48] invoked s 12 of the Private International Law (Miscellaneous Provisions) Act 1995 in respect of a claim in tort for wrongful interference with goods, where the claim involved the parties to the sales contract. This was on the basis that the claim arose from the relationship created between the parties by the sales contract and was closely related to it.[49] This may indirectly allow the same law to be applied to the claim in contract and in tort.[50] If so, then the problem of concurrent claims is largely removed, since both the claim in contract and in tort will be subject to the same law. This means that legally irreconcilable results will not be reached and that this law is very unlikely to permit the claimant to recover twice over.

20.26 Indeed, it seems that a court will strive to ensure that concurrent claims involving the same parties[51] in contract and tort which arise from the same act or omission will be governed by the same law where this is feasible. In *Ennstone Building Products Ltd v Stanger Ltd*,[52] the claimant, EBP, brought actions against the defendant, Stanger, a company with its principal place of business in England, alleging that it had breached its

---

[48] [2001] 1 Lloyd's Rep 284, QBD (Comm).   [49] See also Briggs, n 41 above, at 33.

[50] But see Briggs, n 9 above at 394, who doubts whether this approach is valid. He points out that, strictly speaking, s 12 of the Private International Law (Miscellaneous Provisions) Act 1995 may be invoked where there is a *country* whose law it is substantially more appropriate to apply than that of the country where the tort occurred. This suggests that only territorial connections to another state are relevant. The fact that another *law* governs the contract would not accordingly be relevant. He suggests (at 393) that the position was different under the common law choice of law rules in tort, which were more flexible in nature and able to take into account the law applicable to the contract. However, Mance LJ in *Thierry Morin v Bonhams & Brooks Ltd* [2003] EWCA Civ 1802 at [23], [2004] IL Pr 24 at 398, addressed the argument of Briggs and suggested that a choice of law clause would be a relevant factor under s 12. He remarked that: 'The law of a country is after all a feature of the country'. However, he expressly left open the issue of the effect of a choice of law clause under s 12 of the 1995 Act.

[51] But not if the parties are not the same, as *Glencore* itself illustrates. The court ruled that the law applicable to the contract of sale should be given little or no weight when determining the law applicable to a claim for conversion against a third party purchaser of the goods. See the discussion of the case above, paras 17.76–84; and see paras 17.82, 17.120–121, 17.145, 17.156.

[52] [2002] 1 WLR 3059, CA; noted Perkins, n 15 above.

duty when investigating the staining of stonework on a building situated in Scotland. The Court of Appeal first found that the law applicable to the contract was English law, being the law of the principal place of business of Stanger, the characteristic performer.[53] There was no compelling case to rebut this presumption.[54] It then held that the law of the place of the tort was also England, as the advice was received at EBP's office in England.[55] However, it also held that even if the tort had occurred in Scotland, English law would still have governed the tort claim. The court would have been willing to invoke an exception[56] and to disapply the law of the place of the tort rule. This would have been on the basis that the claim arose from advice given in England by one English company to another.

3. RESTITUTION

Similarly, it is argued in Chapter 19 dealing with restitution and choice of **20.27** law that claims arising in relation to an actual, voidable or void contract should be governed by the applicable law of the 'contract'.[57] This should be the case regardless of whether the applicable law of the contract was determined by the choice of the parties or in the absence of choice. That being so, the problem of concurrent claims and the approach to be taken to them for conflicts purposes does not arise in this context. The law applicable to the contract should determine whether both a claim in contract and one in restitution may be brought and whether the claimant must pursue one to the exclusion of the other.

VI. POSSIBLE APPROACHES TO PARALLEL CLAIMS

1. THE OPTIONS[58]

In the case of parallel actions, Nygh notes that a number of private **20.28** international law approaches are possible[59] including: mutually exclusive classification, so as to remove the danger of overlap; preferring the

---

[53] Art 4(2) of the Rome Convention.   [54] Pursuant to Art 4(5).

[55] Pursuant to the common law choice of law rules in tort; on which, see paras 17.03–09 above.

[56] The case was concerned with the common law choice of law rules in tort. Accordingly, the exception discussed was that contained in *Boys v Chaplin* [1971] AC 356 and refined in *Red Sea Insurance v Bouygues* [1995] 1 AC 190. See above, paras 17.04–05.

[57] See above, paras 19.07–68.

[58] See P North, 'Choice in Choice of Law' (1992) King's College LJ 29; Briggs, n 41 above.

[59] P Nygh, *Autonomy in International Contracts* (Oxford Monographs in Private International Law: Clarendon Press, 1999) 238–240.

contractual choice of law;[60] preferring the tort rules; or adopting a *sui generis* solution.[61]

2. MUTUALLY EXCLUSIVE CLASSIFICATION

20.29 For the purposes of the Brussels I Regulation, a mutually exclusive approach to the meanings of 'matters relating to contract' and 'matters relating to tort' has been adopted by the European Court of Justice. In *Kalfelis v Schroder, Munchmayer, Hengst and Co*,[62] the European Court of Justice indicated that a 'matter relating to tort' for the purposes of Article 5(3) of the Brussels Convention is one which seeks to determine the defendant's liability and which is not *'related* to a "contract" ' within the meaning of Article 5(1).[63] An example of the application of this rule in English courts is provided by the Court of Appeal decision in *Source Ltd v TUV Rheinland*,[64] where claims were brought for breach of contract and breach of a duty of care in failing to exercise reasonable skill and care in the preparation and supply of reports as to the quality of goods purchased by the plaintiffs. The Court of Appeal ruled that for the purposes of jurisdiction under Article 5(1) of the Brussels Convention, both claims were 'matters relating to contract'. It followed that neither claim was a 'matter relating to tort' within the meaning of Article 5(3) of the Brussels Convention, since the application of that provision is residual and Articles 5(1) and 5(3) are mutually exclusive.[65]

20.30 Briggs and Rees note that in English domestic law, parallel claims are permissible against a party who has negligently performed professional services.[66] In the sales context, such services might include faulty installation or inspection of goods by the seller. However, they argue that, for the purposes of the Brussels I Regulation, it is likely that the claims would be regarded solely as a matters 'relating to contract' within the meaning of Article 5(1). '[T]here is only one obligation, namely to exercise reasonable care and skill, and that obligation is one which arises out of (or is imposed upon the defendants by and because of) the agreement between the parties, which agreement was itself freely entered into.'[67]

---

[60] As the majority in *Sayers v International Drilling Co NV* [1971] 1 WLR 1176 appears to do.
[61] See the judgment of Lord Denning in *Sayers*, ibid.
[62] Case 189/87 [1988] ECR 5565, 5585, para 17 of the judgment.
[63] See above, paras 6.10–13.   [64] [1998] QB 54, CA.
[65] The decision is criticized above, paras 3.72, 3.75.
[66] Briggs and Rees, 127; citing *Henderson v Merrett Syndicates Ltd* [1995] 2 AC 145. See also *Base Metal Trading Ltd v Ruslan Borisovich Shamurin* [2002] CLC 322, QBD (Comm), [2003] EWHC 2419 (Comm), [2004] IL Pr 5, [2004] EWCA Civ 1316, CA.
[67] Briggs and Rees, 127. See also *Domicrest Ltd v Swiss Bank Corp* [1999] QB 548.

However, the fact that a mutually exclusive classification is adopted for **20.31** jurisdictional purposes under the European regime[68] does not mean that the same approach need be taken for choice of law purposes.[69] In English domestic law, Staughton LJ noted in *Source* that the claimant might sue for breach of contract or in tort.[70] Moreover, in *Base Metal Trading Ltd v Ruslan Borisovich Shamurin*, Moore-Bick J took the view that the Rome Convention does not seek to address the problem of cumulative obligations that might arise in contract and in tort.[71] Briggs notes that: 'There is no real authority to require the answer that the claimant's freedom . . . has been curtailed by the Rome Convention'.[72] If there is no mutual exclusivity, it would appear to follow that the claimant might sometimes be free to choose whether to bring his claim in contract or in tort.

That said, the virtues of simplicity, predictability and, arguably, not hand- **20.32** ing an excessive choice to the claimant to the detriment of the defendant[73] all point in favour of a similar approach to parallel claims for choice of law purposes as that adopted in *Source* for jurisdiction purposes. There is a coherent argument that the issue of concurrent actions can be resolved most directly by mutually exclusive characterization.[74] It has even been questioned whether 'so one-sided a right to accumulate causes of action and to select between them according to private advantage offends the principle of a "fair" trial . . . for the purposes of [Article 6 of] the Human Rights Act 1998'.[75] Moreover, Article 18 of the Rome Convention requires a court to have regard to the uniform international character of the rules of the Convention when interpreting and applying them. One might argue

[68] i.e. the Brussels I Regulation, the Brussels Convention and the Lugano Convention.
[69] But see Briggs, n 41 above, at 25–31.
[70] *Source Ltd v TUV Rheinland* [1998] QB 5, 60. He remarked that the case was pleaded in contract and tort and that this 'happens not infrequently in English law'.
[71] [2002] CLC 322, QBD (Comm); see also the Court of Appeal's decision [2004] EWCA (Civ) 1316. See Briggs, n 9 above, at 481–487. See also R Plender and M Wilderspin, *The European Contracts Convention* (2nd edn, London: Sweet & Maxwell, 2001) 176. This situation must be distinguished from the one where the claimant has only a single cause of action and the question arises whether, for private international law purposes, that cause of action must be classified as either contractual or tortious, but not both; see above, paras 20.12–13.
[72] Briggs, n 41 above, at 26.
[73] Briggs, ibid, 13 comments that: 'If the vice of forum shopping has been substantially eliminated from the common law of civil jurisdiction . . . this has not been accompanied by any significant examination of its counterpart in choice of law'.
[74] A view supported by the judgment of Mance LJ in *Raiffeisen Zentralbank Osterreich AG v Five Star General Trading LLC* [2001] QB 825, CA, where his Lordship suggested that the approach to classification should be viewed in the light of the ultimate question of whether it leads to the application of the most appropriate law. Briggs, n 41 above, at 37 comments that: 'If one asks which law is the most appropriate law to be applied, aiming to construct a doctrine of characterization which serves it best, the answer is likely to place predictability high on the list of desiderata'.
[75] Briggs, ibid, 15.

that this requirement will not best be fulfilled if an English court applies its own common law doctrines which permit the choice between causes of action. This may lead to the result that a claimant will sidestep the application of the Rome Convention in an English court in circumstances where the Convention would be applied in another Contracting State.[76]

20.33   Nevertheless, there must be doubt as to whether such an approach will prevail. The fact that English domestic law recognizes in principle the availability of concurrent claims tends to suggest that it will likewise permit a concurrence of causes of action at the choice of law stage.[77] In *Coupland v Arabian Gulf Oil*, Robert Goff LJ had to deal with the argument that a claim in contract relying on contractual choice of law rules precluded a claim in tort relying upon tortious choice of law rules. He commented that: 'The plaintiff can advance his claim as he wishes, either in contract of in tort and no doubt he will, acting on advice, advance the claim on the basis of what is most advantageous to him'.[78]

20.34   It is suggested that this approach is correct in principle.[79] Suppose that the buyer argues that he has distinct claims in contract and tort against the seller who has carried out an inadequate inspection of the goods. The basis of the former claim is that this amounts to a breach of a term of the contract; the basis of the second claim is that irrespective of the legal existence of a contract, the seller took upon himself a duty of care which gives rise to a non-contractual obligation to compensate for loss to the buyer. These claims may be parallel to each other and arise *factually* from a single act of the seller, but *legally* they are distinct. To classify them both as contractual obligations for choice of law purposes is to fail to respect the separate legal nature of the claims. In such a case, it is contended that an English court should classify the claims for choice of law purposes respectively as one in contract and one in tort. Accordingly, it is suggested that the mutual exclusivity approach to classification should be rejected in the case of parallel claims.[80] *A fortiori*, such an approach is not possible where the claims are distinct.[81]

---

[76] See also Briggs, ibid, at 27–28.

[77] See also Plender and Wilderspin, n 71 above, at 176–177.

[78] [1983] 1 WLR 1136, 1152, CA. See also *Base Metal Trading Ltd v Shamurin* [2004] EWCA (Civ) 1316.

[79] But see Briggs, n 41 above, at 23.

[80] This must be distinguished from the discussion above of where what is a single claim in domestic law might fall within more than one private international law category. It was argued above that such an approach should be avoided by an English court if at all possible.

[81] As in, eg, *Viskase Ltd v Paul Kiefel (GmbH)* [1999] 1 WLR 1305, CA, above, para 20.04; see also paras 3.111, 3.181, 3.211, 3.265–269.

3. The Claimant is Permitted to Choose but to Pursue One Cause of Action Only

If the classification process leads to the conclusion that the claimant has, **20.35** in principle, more than one cause of action, then there is arguably no coherent reason for forcing the claimant to pursue one claim to the exclusion of the other. This suggests that the claimant should be permitted to choose how to frame his case. However, this should be subject to an overriding principle of English public policy which should prevent the claimant from recovering in respect of the same loss more than once.[82]

The difficulty with the free choice approach is that it may distort foreign **20.36** law. If the law applicable to the contractual claim does not let the claimant choose, and the law applicable to the non-contractual claim is to the same effect, then the claimant is handed a choice not available in either putatively applicable legal system. In such a case, it is not obvious that the English courts should offer the claimant a free choice. If it were to do so, this would distort foreign law and risk attracting forum shoppers.

4. Force Claimant to Pursue Contractual Claim

It could be argued that even if the claimant has concurrent claims which **20.37** fall to be classified differently for private international law purposes, the claimant should not be permitted to choose which claim to bring. In particular, it could be said that if the claimant has a non-contractual claim, this provides the 'general' law which is intended to apply if, but only if, there has been no express voluntary agreement between the parties as to their rights and duties. But where the parties have made such an arrangement, there is a tenable argument that the claimant should be forced to pursue the claim in contract: the general claim gives way to the specific one. This would correspond with the *non-cumul* doctrine of French law which generally requires a claimant to pursue a contractual claim to the exclusion of a delictual one, where the claims are parallel.[83] Of course, a similar rule to the *non-cumul* doctrine does not exist in English domestic law.[84]

---

[82] See A Burrows, 'Solving the Problem of Concurrent Liability' (1995) 48 CLP 103; J Stevens, 'Contract, Unjustified Enrichment and Concurrent Liability: a Scots Perspective—a Comment', Ch 15 in F Rose (ed), *Failure of Contracts: Contractual, Restitutionary and Proprietary Consequences* (Oxford: Hart, 1997) 225. In relation to alternative measures of recovery, see *Tang Min Sit v Capacious Investments* [1996] AC 514, PC; P Birks, 'Inconsistency between Compensation and Restitution' (1996) 112 LQR 375.

[83] See the discussion above, paras 6.72–73 (the position in Germany is also discussed at para 6.74).

[84] *Henderson v Merrett Syndicates Ltd* [1995] AC 145; *Bristol & West Building Society v Mothew* [1998] Ch 1, 20, CA; *Base Metal Trading Ltd v Ruslan Borisovich Shamurin* [2002] CLC 322, QBD (Comm); [2004] EWCA (Civ) 1316.

20.38 It was stated above that the court in *Source Ltd v TUV Rheinland*[85] ruled that claims arising from faulty inspection of goods for breach of contract and for failure to take due care were both matters relating to contract for the purposes of Article 5(1) of the Brussels Convention. However, Staughton LJ also appeared to suggest that even if one claim had been classified as relating to contract and the other as relating to tort, the claimant would be forced to pursue the former claim to the exclusion of the latter.[86]

20.39 More generally, the European Court of Justice's approach in *Kalfelis v Schroder, Munchmayer, Hengst and Co*,[87] which defined 'matters relating to tort' for the purposes of Article 5(3) of the Brussels Convention as those which seek to determine the defendant's liability and which are not '*related* to a "contract" ' within the meaning of Article 5(1) was motivated partly by 'the civilian doctrine against the accumulation of remedies; in French law, if a claim falls within the area of contract, there is no legal possibility of a parallel remedy in delict'.[88]

20.40 The contractual solution finds some support in German law: 'it proceeds on the principle that where a specific relationship exists between the parties regulating their rights and obligations towards each other (such as one based on contract or marriage), and in the course of carrying out the obligations of that relationship an obligation based on the general law (such as one arising out of the law of delict) is infringed, the claims arising out the breadth of the general duty should be subject to the same law as that which governs their existing relationship'.[89] This approach, equally capable of application to unjust enrichment claims, 'promotes unity of applicable law, certainty and predictability and meets the reasonable expectations of the parties. It avoids the jockeying for advantage which is inherent in the Anglo-Commonwealth system.'[90] Nygh points out that this is not so where no choice of law was made and that, where a choice has been made, this approach may tend to favour the economically stronger party. More fundamentally, however, it is not obvious why duties imposed by the 'general' law, which, in the absence of a contract would involuntarily create rights and duties, should be subordinated to

---

[85] [1998] QB 54, CA; above, para 20.29. See also paras 3.72 and 3.75. See also the discussion of the boundaries of sale in the Vienna Convention, above, paras 16.91–94.

[86] At 64, citing Dicey and Morris (12th edn, 1993), 362 and Briggs and Rees (2nd edn, 1997) 95. To similar effect is the decision of the Oberlandesgericht, Koblenz in *Re An Italian Cargo of Adulterated Wine* [1991] IL Pr 473.

[87] Case 189/87 [1988] ECR 5565, 5585, para 17 of the judgment.

[88] Briggs and Rees, 149.

[89] Nygh, n 59 above, at 240, basing his definition on that of M Keller and K Siehr, *Allgemeine Lehren des Internationalen Privatrechts* (Schulthess, 1986) 285.

[90] Nygh, ibid, at 241.

private agreements. To put it another way, one might say that tortious duties are in their nature mandatory.

5. FORCE CLAIMANT TO PURSUE NON-CONTRACTUAL CLAIM

Every legal system recognizes that even if the claimant and defendant are **20.41** in a contractual relationship, the claimant might, on the facts, only have a claim in tort. We have seen that French law does not permit cumulative claims in contract and in tort. However, in *Max Mara SA v Galerie Kleber SA*,[91] the French Cour de cassation was faced with a claim by a French buyer who had contracted with French and Italian suppliers. The buyer sought compensation for the suppliers' refusal to sell it a particular line of goods. The suppliers argued that the buyer had a claim in contract and must pursue this to the exclusion of the delictual claim. The court disagreed. The refusal to sell raised an issue solely of delictual liability and the buyer was entitled to pursue it. Moreover, the *non-cumul* doctrine does not apply to pre-contractual liability which exists outside the contract, as in the case of, for example, fraud, or the abusive withdrawal of a contractual offer.[92] So, the availability to the claimant of the remedy of avoidance of the contract on the basis of fraud does not prevent him bringing a delictual claim in respect of fraudulent behaviour under Article 1382 of the Code civil.[93]

However, our present concern is with the situation where a claimant *does* **20.42** have concurrent claims available to him. Two questions arise: (i) should the claimant be *permitted* to pursue a claim in tort to the exclusion of a claim in contract and (ii) should he be *forced* to pursue the claim in tort to the exclusion of the contractual claim?

As to the first question, it is possible that a claimant might choose to **20.43** ignore a possible claim in contract and to pursue a claim solely in tort. In French law, such a choice is not permitted and the claimant must pursue the contract claim to the exclusion of the tort claim. However, we need not dwell on this question at present, since it goes to the issue considered above as to whether a claimant should be permitted to choose how to frame his action. We shall return to this question below.[94]

As to the second question, there is little support for forcing the claimant to **20.44** proceed in tort. The main argument in its favour is that tort is a branch of

---

[91] [1996] IL Pr 629, French Cour de cassation.
[92] J Carbonnier, *Droit Civil, Tome 4, Les Obligations* (19th edn, Presses Universitaires de France, 1995) 458, considered above, para 6.73.
[93] Decision of the Cour de cassation, Com 18 October 1994.
[94] See below, paras 20.48–52.

law concerned with 'general' obligations of one party towards another. These are non-consensual obligations and it could be argued that they should not be subordinated to a particular arrangement that the parties have made by contract. However, much of the law of tort is concerned with obligations arising because the parties *choose* to place themselves in a particular factual position. So, for example, a seller who inspects goods and negligently asserts that they are satisfactory has consented so to act. Another way of saying this is that although *legal* liability is created without the consent of the parties, it often only arises because the parties consensually place themselves in a given *factual* situation. If the parties freely choose to make their own arrangements as to their rights and obligations by contract, it would seem curious to deny them the right to assert their rights under the contract.

6. PERMIT CLAIMANT TO PURSUE MULTIPLE CAUSES OF ACTION

20.45 In *Ennstone Building Products Ltd v Stanger Ltd*,[95] a claimant brought claims in contract and in tort in respect of the defendant's alleged breach of duty in failing properly to investigate the staining of stonework on a building in Edinburgh. The Court of Appeal determined separately the law applicable to the claim in contract and in tort, suggesting that the claimant might be permitted to pursue both claims.

20.46 More generally, it may be said that where the classification process leads to the conclusion that the claimant has causes of action in more than one branch of the law, he should be permitted to choose how to frame his action. There does not seem to be a principled reason for favouring the contractual claim over the non-contractual claim, or vice versa. There is no first amongst equals.

20.47 On the other hand, there is one serious drawback to this approach. If neither the law applicable to the contractual nor the non-contractual claim would permit the claimant to pursue either claim at his election, then English law might be said to be distorting foreign law by permitting the claimant to make such a choice. That, in turn, creates incentives for the claimant to forum shop in an English court.[96]

7. A COHERENT APPROACH—REJECTION OF ALL OF THE ABOVE OPTIONS IN FAVOUR OF A MORE FLEXIBLE SOLUTION

20.48 Where the claimant does have causes of action which fall within different private international law categories, the simplest approach is to permit

---

[95] [2002] 1 WLR 3059, CA; noted Perkins, n 15 above.
[96] This point is developed below, paras 20.48–51.

him to pursue either claim at his option. However, this might lead to distortion of the application of foreign law. Suppose, for example, that English law were to allow concurrent claims wherever the causes of action fell within different private international law categories. The law applicable to the contract might not allow the claimant to choose how to frame his claim, or to pursue more than one cause of action. The law applicable to the non-contractual action might concur. If so, if an English court nonetheless lets the claimant choose how to frame his cause of action, it will apply foreign law in such a way as it would be applied neither in the courts of the state whose law applies to the contractual claim nor in the courts of the state whose law applies to the non-contractual claim.

Against this, if an English court were always to force a claimant to pursue **20.49** the contractual claim to the exclusion of a non-contractual claim, this might be unacceptable if both the applicable law of the contractual and non-contractual claim allowed the claimant to choose how to frame his claim, or even allowed the claimant to sue in both.[97] The claimant would have to bring his claim in contract in an English court even though he would not be required to do so in the courts of the state whose law applies to the contractual claim.

In order not to distort the foreign law, one approach would be to examine **20.50** what the applicable law of each potential claim would be. If each law concurs as to whether the claimant may choose how to frame his claim, or each law forces him to pursue a particular action (say, in contract) to the exclusion of the other, it would seem obvious that the English court should take the same approach.

This will leave the 'hard' case of where the two foreign laws disagree as to **20.51** how the claimant might proceed. In such a case, any solution that the English court will adopt may be said to involve some distortion of foreign law. At this point, it is suggested that an English court's own domestic law leanings on the issue of concurrent claims should prevail. That will almost certainly mean that where the claimant seeks to bring distinct claims

---

[97] But contrast the approach of Briggs, n 41 above, at 31. He argues that, in principle, an English court should characterize in such a way as to ensure that a single governing law is identified by the English court. He then contends that the law identified should decide whether the claimant may accumulate causes of action. This must be determined by the domestic law principles of accumulation of that state, rather than its choice of law rules. Otherwise, this would be tantamount to the application of the doctrine of renvoi. However, the disadvantage of this approach is that it effectively delegates the decision of whether actions may be accumulated to the *domestic* law of a *foreign* state. Yet the situation will also be a conflicts case in the foreign state whose law is identified. To that extent, it may be something of a distortion of the foreign law to apply its rules on accumulation designed purely for the domestic context. See also *Base Metal Trading Ltd v Ruslan Borisovich Shamurin* [2003] EWHC 2419 (Comm), [2004] IL Pr 5 at [45], *per* Tomlinson J; and see the views of the Court of Appeal [2004] EWCA (Civ) 1316.

based upon the same facts against different parties (for example, against the seller for breach of contract and a third party for inducing the seller to breach his contract), the claimant will not be able to recover twice over, but will be able to choose which claim to pursue. In the case of alternative claims, such as claims for damages for breach of contract or for rescission of the transfer of goods, the claimant will, of course, be able to pursue the claims in the alternative. In the case of parallel claims arising from the same set of facts, such as a failure of the seller's duty to inspect goods properly when certifying that they are of satisfactory quality, matters are more complex. It is suggested that in so far as the obligation falls to be classified for the purposes of private international law as both contractual and tortious, the claimant must be permitted to sue and recover damages on either basis. However, if the claimant chooses to sue in contract, it will almost certainly be said to be contrary to the public policy of the forum to permit the claimant also to recover damages in tort[98] and vice versa.[99]

VII. CONCLUSIONS ON PARALLEL CLAIMS

20.52 (1) An English court should first classify the claimant's cause(s) of action for the purposes of private international law.

(2) This may lead to the claimant having a cause of action in more than one branch of the law. This may be because the claims are distinct or alternative claims. It may also be because a single act gives rise to parallel claims.

(3) Where the claimant has parallel claims available to him, the English court should examine the law applicable to each claim. If both laws concur as to whether the claimant must pursue one particular action to the exclusion of another, or as to whether the claimant may choose how to frame his case, then an English court should respect that position and adopt the same approach.[100]

(4) If the foreign laws do not concur, English law has to seek another solution. It is suggested that English law should *not* autonomously decide that the claimant must pursue one cause of action to the exclusion of the other. There is no principled reason for doing so. In so far as the process of classification leads to the claimant having more than one cause of action, then this must be respected. It should follow that the claimant should be permitted to choose how to frame his claim.

---

[98] Pursuant to s 14(3)(a)(i)of the Private International Law (Miscellaneous Provisions) Act 1995.

[99] Pursuant to Art 16 of the Rome Convention.

[100] See Burrows, n 82 above; but see *Base Metal Trading Ltd v Shamurin* [2004] EWCA (Civ) 1316.

(5) However, English law is likely to regard it as a rule of public policy that a claimant should not be able to recover more than once in respect of the same act or omission.[101] Accordingly, where a single act gives rise to more than one cause of action, English law is likely autonomously to decree that once the claimant has recovered successfully in one, he will be prohibited from recovering in any other. This will not, of course, apply if the two damages claims are distinct from each other, so that there is no question of the claimant recovering twice over.

VIII. CONTRACTUAL CLAUSES PURPORTING TO EXCLUDE OR LIMIT A PARTY'S LIABILITY IN TORT

1. A COHERENT SOLUTION

A related issue concerns the effect of a contractual exclusion or limitation **20.53** clause on a party's non-contractual liability.[102] The leading case is *Sayers v International Drilling Co NV*.[103] An English employee of a Dutch company was employed to work on an oil rig in Nigerian waters. He was allegedly injured by the negligence of his fellow employees. The employment contract contained an exemption clause which was valid by Dutch law, but not English law under the Law Reform (Personal Injuries) Act 1948. The validity of this term[104] was pleaded as a defence to the tortious action. The majority seemed to treat the issue as purely contractual.[105] However, North has pointed out that the *claim* was in tort, seeking damages for personal injury, even if the *defence* arose in a contract.[106] This means that the question of what effect the clause had on the tortious action should have been governed by the choice of law in tort rules; whether the clause was valid would then be a matter for the applicable law of the contract. Nygh notes that this is logical, but impractical.[107] It would be 'easier' for the validity and effect of the clause to be determined entirely by the

---

[101] A view shared by Briggs, n 41 above, at 14, n 11.

[102] See *Amiri Flight Authority v BAE Systems plc* [2003] EWCA Civ 1447.

[103] [1971] 1 WLR 1176, CA. See also *Canadian Pacific Rail Co v Parent* [1917] AC 195, PC; *Coupland v Arabian Gulf Co* [1983] 1 WLR 1136, CA; *Chiron Corp v Organon Teknika (No 2)* [1993] FSR 567, CA; *Ennstone Building Products Ltd v Stanger Ltd* [2002] 1 WLR 3059, CA; *Brodin v A/R Seljan* 1973 SC 13, Scottish Court of Session, Outer House.

[104] Briggs, n 41 above, at 33, argues that such a term does not constitute a *defence* to an accrued liability but a provision which seeks to modify the terms of liability itself, citing in support *Photo Production Ltd v Securicor Transport Ltd* [1980] AC 827, HL, esp the remarks of Lord Diplock, 850–851.

[105] Lord Denning MR sought to apply a single law to the whole claim, namely the law with which the entire matter was most closely connected.

[106] P North, 'Contract as a Tort Defence in the Conflict of Laws' (1977) 26 ICLQ 914.

[107] Nygh, n 59 above, at 252.

applicable law of the contract.[108] However, it is suggested that this is not a case where pragmatism should prevail. This is not a dispute as to the correct classification of the claim itself. A claim which is in nature tortious does not cease to be so by virtue of the conduct of the parties. If an English court were not to apply the tortious choice of law rules, this would distort the coherence of the characterization and choice of law process. But whether the contractual clause is in fact valid ought naturally to be answered by the law applicable to the contract, just as other questions relating to the validity of contractual terms would be.

2. Contractual Exclusion of Liability in Negligence and the Unfair Contract Terms Act 1977

20.54 In English law, s 2 of the Unfair Contract Terms Act 1977 states that:

(1) A person cannot by reference to any contract term or to a notice given to persons generally or to particular persons exclude or restrict his liability for death or personal injury resulting from negligence.

(2) In the case of other loss or damage, a person cannot so exclude or restrict his liability for negligence except in so far as the term or notice satisfies the requirement of reasonableness.

(3) Where a contract term or notice purports to exclude or restrict liability for negligence a person's agreement to or awareness of it is not of itself to be taken as indicating his voluntary acceptance of any risk.

A question might arise as to whether these provisions should be seen as rules of contract or tort law. For example, do these restrictions on contractual exclusion or limitation of negligence liability apply if the law applicable to the contract is English law, but the law applicable to the tort claim is the law of State X? What if the law applicable to the contract is that of State X, but the law applicable to the tort claim is English law?

20.55 It is suggested that the answer should be that the rules partake of a contractual and a tortious character.[109] On the one hand, they lay down

---

[108] In the US case of *Delta Air Line Inc v McDonnell Douglas Corp* [1975] 1 Lloyd's Rep 205, US Court of Appeals Fifth Circuit, the plaintiffs bought an aircraft from the defendant manufacturers. The contract contained a clause which purported to exclude the defendant's liability in negligence. One question which arose was whether this infringed the public policy of the law of the forum, Georgia, or of the law which the parties chose to govern the contract, California. The court found that it infringed neither. It then concluded that the clause was, on its true construction, intended to extend to the defendant's liability in tort and that it was effective to do so. It appeared to regard the matter solely as one as to the validity and effectiveness of a contract term. See also *Greenman v Yuba Power Products Inc* 59 Cal 2d 57, 27 Cal Rptr 697, 377 P2d 897 (1963).

[109] s 2 catches both the tort of negligence and negligent breach of contract. Cf s 15A of the Limitations Act 1980, which does not extend time in the case of negligent breaches of contract.

the circumstances in which tortious liability may be restricted or excluded and s 2 is headed 'negligence liability'.[110] On the other hand, these provisions go to the effectiveness of a term of the contract.

When, then, do the restrictions in s 2 apply? In some cases, the Act **20.56** requires their application. This means that they will apply where the contract is governed by English law, unless the exclusion in relation to international supply contracts contained in s 26 applies.[111] If it does not, then s 2 must be satisfied where English law governs the contract, unless the restriction on the scope of the Act contained in s 27(1) applies. That sub-section is triggered in circumstances where English law is applicable solely by virtue of the choice of the parties.[112] Conversely, if the contract is not caught by the international supply exclusion and the parties choose a foreign law to govern it, the provisions of s 2 still apply if the provisions of s 27(2) operate.[113] It is suggested that the rules stated in this paragraph must apply even if a foreign law applies to the claim in tort.

This leaves the scenario where the Act does not *require* its application, but **20.57** where the law applicable to the claim in tort is English law. Suppose, for example, that the claimant sues in tort in respect of the seller's failure properly to inspect the goods in England. This means that the law applicable to the claim in tort is English law. The contract itself is governed by English law by virtue of the choice of the parties. However, both parties have their places of business in State X, and the contract itself is otherwise wholly objectively connected to State X. The contract is not caught by the international supply contracts exclusion in s 26 of the Unfair Contract Terms Act 1977, because the parties are not based in different states.[114] However, because English law governs the contract solely by virtue of the parties' choice, s 27(1) of the Unfair Contract Terms Act 1977 has the effect that the provisions of s 2 'do not operate *as part of the law applicable to the contract*'.[115] What the 1977 Act does not say is whether the provisions of s 2 may nonetheless operate on the facts *as part of the law of the place of the tort*.

In the authors' view, the answer to this question should be 'yes'. It is **20.58** suggested that the question of whether liability in tort may be excluded or restricted by a contractual clause is a matter for the law applicable to the tort. This accords with the North analysis considered above. It is dubious

---

[110] Indeed, the provisions on notice in s 2(3) appear to be designed only for the tort relationship.
[111] See above, paras 13.302–308. See also *Amiri Flight Authority v BAE Systems plc* [2003] EWCA Civ 1447, [2003] 2 Lloyd's Rep 767, CA.
[112] See above, paras 13.309–314.   [113] See above, paras 13.315–320.
[114] s 26(3)(b) of the Unfair Contract Terms Act 1977.   [115] Emphasis added.

whether an English court would be happy to see liability in negligence excluded or restricted by an unreasonable contractual clause,[116] where the act of negligence occurred in England.[117] Moreover, one would not necessarily have expected the 1977 Act to have made special provision for situations where the tort occurs in England, since at the time English law applied routinely to all claims in tort as part of the double actionability rule.[118] Accordingly, in the above example, it is suggested that the rules of s 2 of the Unfair Contract Terms Act 1977 should operate and that, where English law governs a claim in tort pursuant to the Private International Law (Miscellaneous Provisions) Act 1995, Part III, a contractual clause excluding liability in negligence for death or personal injury should be ineffective, and subject to a reasonableness requirement in respect of any other loss or damage.

---

[116] Or to see liability for death or personal injury excluded or restricted *at all.*
[117] Especially when English law also governs the contract.
[118] See the discussion of common law choice of law rules above, paras 17.02–05.

21

Electronic Commerce: Choice of Law

I. INTRODUCTION

21.01 'With the growth of the internet, everyone now has the possibility of communicating internationally, as material placed on the world wide web may be accessed in any country in the world. People with little knowledge of foreign laws are faced with a wide range of potential liabilities.'[1]

---

[1] Law Commission, *Defamation and the Internet: a Preliminary Investigation*, Scoping Study No 2, December 2002, para 1.8. See also ibid, paras 4.1 and 4.2. See further *Godfrey v Demon Internet Ltd* [2001] QB 201 at 204–205; the US case of *Zippo Manufacturing Co v Zippo Dot Com, Inc* 952 F Supp 1119 at 1123–1124 (W D Pa 1997); the Canadian decision in *Braintech Inc v Kostiuk* (1999) 171 DLR (4th) 46 and the decisions of *League Against Racism and Antisemitism v Yahoo! Inc* (County Court of Paris, 20 November 2000 *per* Gomez DJ; Judgment No 4741, Italian Court of Cassation, 27 December 2000 *per* Calabrese J). These cases (and others) are cited by Kirby J in the High Court of Australia's decision in *Dow Jones & Company Inc v Gutnick* 210 CLR 575, HC of Australia; [2002] HCA 56, judgment of 10 December 2002, para 78. See also M Burnstein 'Conflicts on the Net: Choice of Law in Transnational Cyberspace' (1996) 29 Vanderbilt J of Transnational Law 75, 78–87.

The exponential growth of electronic commerce[2] has posed a range of new challenges to private international lawyers. Many of the generic challenges are considered in Chapter 10 on e-commerce and jurisdiction and are not repeated here in any detail.[3]

We are concerned in this chapter with international sales contracts con- **21.02** cluded online or by email. We are also concerned with international sales[4] contracts which are to be performed online or by email involving digitized products. However, our concern is wider than this and also includes use of email or the internet to carry on commercial activities, even if the contract was not negotiated or concluded online or by email, and even if it involves the sale of 'traditional' goods.

The application of existing rules of choice of law to this area is scarcely less **21.03** problematic than the application of the rules of jurisdiction. Choice of law rules which place relevance upon the localization of events and obligations are placed under considerable strain by the delocalized nature of e-commerce. After all, the internet 'is ubiquitous, borderless, global and ambient in its nature'.[5] For example, where a contract concluded by electronic means contains no choice of law clause, it may be necessary to consider, in determining the applicable law, such factors as where a contract was concluded, where the parties were resident (a factor which may be difficult for a contracting party to determine at the time of conclusion of the contract),[6] where their computers were, where the company providing

---

[2] See the definition of 'information society services' in Recital 18 of the E-Commerce Directive, [2000] OJ L178/1: 'Information society services span a wide range of economic activities which take place online; these activities can, in particular, consist of selling goods online; activities such as the delivery of goods as such or the provision of services off-line are not covered; information society services are not solely restricted to services giving rise to online contracting but also, in so far as they represent an economic activity, extend to services which are not remunerated by those who receive them, such as those offering online information or commercial communications, or those providing tools allowing for search, access and retrieval of data; information society services also include services consisting of the transmission of information via a communication network, in providing access to a communication network or in hosting information provided by a recipient of the service . . . [S]ervices which are transmitted point to point, such as video-on-demand or the provision of commercial communications by electronic mail are information society services; the use of electronic mail or equivalent individual communications for instance by natural persons acting outside their trade, business or profession including their use for the conclusion of contracts between such persons is not an information society service . . .'

[3] See above, paras 10.01–23.

[4] On whether such transactions are 'sales' contracts, see above, paras 10.44–53; and see below, paras 21.113–118.

[5] *Dow Jones & Company Inc v Gutnick*, 210 CLR 575, HC of Australia; [2002] HCA 56, para 79, *per* Kirby J.

[6] Although s 6(1) of the Electronic Commerce (EC Directive) Regulations 2002, SI 2013/2002, imposes a duty upon information service providers established in a Member State to supply the recipient with their name and place of establishment.

access to the internet was located, where tangible goods were to be delivered or digitized products were transferred to, or payment (which may be by the buyer or recipient providing credit card details over the internet) is to take place. All of these factors may be difficult to determine, or difficult to foresee at the time that the parties contract with one another.

21.04   In some ways, the problems raised by the law of tort are still more formidable. Identification of the law of the place where a tort occurs can be problematic enough where business is conducted by 'traditional' means. However, localization of a tort where the key events take place over the internet, which is an inherently borderless means of communication, is an unenviable task, where whichever choice is made is likely to be somewhat artificial.[7] There are credible cases for treating the residence of either party, the state where the service provider is when he uploads the information, the state of downloading and the location of the server as the place of the tort.[8] It may also be that the place of the tort should be determined differently depending upon the tort in question. Moreover, given the 'arbitrary' nature of the place of the tort in e-commerce cases, English courts may come to place increased reliance upon the exception to the general rule and identification of the state with which the matter has its closest connection.[9] However, this might give rise to an unacceptable element of uncertainty in cross-border electronic commerce.

21.05   It should be noted that if a dispute arises as to property in digitized products, it may be necessary to determine where those products are located. Whenever one ascribes a situs to an intangible product, there is bound to be an air of artifice about the process. There may also be problems in applying the unjust enrichment choice of law rules where the enrichment consists in the delivery of digitized products by electronic means, or the provision of credit or debit card details by electronic means.

21.06   There are also particular complexities raised by the uncertain interrelationship between the E-Commerce Directive[10] and the existing rules of private international law. It is unclear whether the Directive lays down

---

[7] However, C Reed, *Internet Law: Text and Materials* (London: Butterworths, 2000) 188 refers to the cyberspace 'fallacy': 'The problem with cyberspace is that its constituent elements, the human and corporate actors and the computing and communications equipment through which the transaction is effected, all have a real-world existence and are located in one or more physical world legal jurisdictions. These corporeal elements of cyberspace are sufficient to give national jurisdictions a justification for . . . the applicability of the their laws to . . . an Internet transaction.'

[8] Or, more precisely, as the most significant element of the events for the purposes of s 11(2)(c) of the Private International Law (Miscellaneous Provisions) Act 1995.

[9] Pursuant to s 12 of the 1995 Act.

[10] Directive (EC) 2000/31 of the European Parliament and Council, 8 June 2000, on Certain Legal Aspects of Information Society Services, in particular Electronic Commerce ('the E-Commerce Directive') [2000] OJ L178/1.

choice of law rules. It is also uncertain whether the substantive, harmonized rules of the Directive must be applied even where existing choice of law rules provide for the application of the law of a state with no such substantive rules.

The chapter will consider the application of the existing rules of private **21.07** international law in contract, tort, restitution and property law to disputes which might arise in the context of commercial international sales. It will also consider the impact of the E-Commerce Directive. We shall then consider briefly whether electronic commerce can satisfactorily be accommodated within existing choice of law rules and possible reform of the law.

II. THE ELECTRONIC COMMERCE DIRECTIVE

1. General Remarks

The main provisions of the E-Commerce Directive[11] have been analyzed **21.08** in Chapter 10 on e-commerce and jurisdiction claims, to which the reader is referred.[12] No attempt is made to repeat that information here. Rather, the focus of this section is on the complex question of the inter-relationship between choice of law rules and the rules contained in the Directive, and in the United Kingdom's enacting provisions.[13]

One of the purposes of the E-Commerce Directive is to reduce uncertainty **21.09** as to the laws which must be satisfied where a party established in a Member State of the European Union pursues an 'information society service'.[14] However, as will become all too evident, the impact of the E-Commerce Directive on choice of law is complex and obscure.

2. Types of Rule Contained in the Directive: Uniform Law and the Country of Origin Principle

The Directive contains what may be described as a mix of substantive, **21.10** uniform laws which must be applied in all Member States and the 'country of origin' principle which requires the application of the rules of the state where the information service provider is established. The former type of rule appears, at least at first sight, to harmonize, and override,

---

[11] ibid

[12] Above, paras 10.25–33. See also G Smith, *Internet Law and Regulation* (London: Sweet and Maxwell, 2002) 266–277 (esp 276–277); M Anassutzi, 'The E-Commerce Directive 00/31', [2002] ICCLR 337.

[13] Contained in the Electronic Commerce (EC Directive) Regulations 2002, SI 2002/2013. The Regulations entered into force on 21 August 2002. On the Regulations, see K Sandford, 'Analysis of the UK Regulations', (2002) 4(3) E-Commerce Law and Policy 7.

[14] *Defamation and the Internet: a Preliminary Investigation*, n 1 above, para 4.49.

rules of private international law. The latter type of rule itself looks something like a choice of law rule, since it lays down the state's law to be applied within the 'coordinated field' of activity covered by the Directive.

3. Uniform Laws

21.11 The uniform laws category contains a number of examples, of which just two will be mentioned here.[15] Article 5 requires Member States to ensure that an information service provider[16] shall render to the recipient[17] certain general information, including the name and address of the provider and his email address.[18] Article 6 requires Member States to ensure that 'commercial communications'[19] which are part of an information society service are clearly identifiable as such and contain certain information.[20] It seems best to describe these as *uniform* substantive laws, rather than choice of law rules. They are rules which a state must apply[21] to an information service provider established in that state, or in any other Member State. In that sense, they could be described as territorially limited *mandatory rules*. They are mandatory in the sense that a Member State *must* apply them to a service provider established in that state and is responsible for doing so. Moreover, since these rules apply throughout the European Union, they should also be applied to an information service provider established in another Member State, even if the ultimate responsibility for ensuring compliance with the provisions rests with that other Member State. It seems that these provisions must be applied to an information service provider established in the United Kingdom *even if the contract of sale itself is governed by the law of a non-Member State*. As such, they are international mandatory rules of the forum. This also shows that it is simply not true to say that the Directive has no effect on the rules of private international law applicable in England.

21.12 However, it does not seem that these provisions would need to be applied to an information service provider established outside the European

---

[15] Others are mentioned above, paras 10.27–33.

[16] Art 2(a) of the E-Commerce Directive states that this term has the meaning given to it in Art 1(2) of Directive (EC) 98/34 of the European Parliament and the Council of 22 June 1998 laying down a procedure for the provision of information in the field of technical standards and regulation, as amended by Directive (EC) 98/48. It 'covers any service normally provided for remuneration, at a distance, by a means of electronic equipment for the processing (including digital compression) and storage of data, and at the individual request of a recipient of a service' (Recital 17 to the E-Commerce Directive). See also SI 2002/2013, reg 2.

[17] This word is defined in Art 2(d) of the E-Commerce Directive. See also Recital 20 and SI 2002/2013, reg 2.

[18] SI 2002/2013/reg 6.   [19] Defined in Art 2(f) and in SI 2002/2013, reg 2.

[20] SI 2002/2013, reg 7.

[21] Save where an exception or derogation is contained in the Directive itself.

Union. Accordingly, they are mandatory where the Directive calls for their application, but limited in territorial scope. Furthermore, it is uncertain whether the rules must be applied to a contract governed by the law of England, if the service provider is established in a non-Member State. It is true that the provisions of the Directive, as enacted in the Regulations, *are* part of English law. However, they are part of English law *only where the service provider is established in England*. If it is not, then they do not form part of English law. For this reason, it is suggested that they do not apply in this scenario. Likewise, an English court should not apply the Directive requirements to an information service provider established outside the European Union if the contract is governed by the law of another Member State, such as France.

It should be noted that for an English court to give effect to the rules of the **21.13** Directive only within their territorial scope does not amount to application of the doctrine of renvoi in contract law.[22] There is no attempt to have regard to another state's choice of law rules. Rather, we are simply determining the scope of a state's domestic law and whether, on given facts, the uniform rules of the Directive apply as a part of that state's domestic law.

4. The Meaning of 'Established'

The Directive places great importance upon the place of establishment of **21.14** the service provider. It is, accordingly, important to consider the meaning of this word a little further. One of the Recitals to the E-Commerce Directive comments thus:

The place at which a service provider is established should be determined in conformity with the case-law of the Court of Justice according to which the concept of establishment involves the actual pursuit of an economic activity through a fixed establishment for an indefinite period; this requirement is also fulfilled where a company is constituted for a given period; the place of establishment of a company providing services via an Internet website is not the place at which the technology supporting its website is located or the place at which its website is accessible but the place where it pursues its economic activity; in cases where a provider has several places of establishment it is important to determine from which place of establishment the service concerned is provided; in cases where it is difficult to determine from which of several places of establishment a given service is provided, this is the place where the provider has the centre of his activities relating to this particular service.[23]

---

[22] Which is prohibited: Art 15 of the Rome Convention.
[23] Recital 19. See also the shorter, formal definition of 'established service provider' in Art 2(c). A longer definition, which takes in the matters referred to in Recital 19 and Art 2(c), can be found in SI 2002/2013, reg 2. The Regulation also stresses that a service provider must be a national of a Member State or a company or firm as mentioned in Art 48 of the EC Treaty.

5. The Country of Origin Rule

A Choice of Law Rule?

21.15 The Directive is certainly not wholly concerned with laying down provisions of uniform law. It contains the 'country of origin' rule enshrined in Article 3(1), applicable to business to business contracts only.[24] This states that:

> Each Member State shall ensure that the information society services provided by a service provider established on its territory comply with the national provisions applicable in the Member State in question which fall within the coordinated field.[25]

This avoids the problem within the 'coordinated field'[26] of an information service provider who conducts dealings throughout the European Union otherwise having to comply with the national laws of each and every Member State, which would be a powerful disincentive to free trade. Furthermore, Recital 22 to the Directive suggests that: 'information society services should be supervised at the source of the activity, in order to ensure an effective protection of public interest objectives'. In other words, the law of England should be applied to an information services provider established in England, even if the service is provided to another Member State. English law must, of course, include the substantive uniform requirements of the Directive, but, subject to this requirement, it is the domestic law of England that will hold sway.

21.16 It seems that English law should be applied, *even if the choice of law rules in contract (or in tort) point to the application of another legal system.* In that sense, it is very difficult to see how it is other than a choice of law rule.[27] Yet, Article 1(4) states that 'this Directive does not establish additional rules on private international law . . .'. This provision gives rise to enormous uncertainty. This uncertainty is only worsened by a look at the Recitals to the Directive. Recital 23 of the Directive states that, '[i]t neither aims to establish additional rules on private international law relating to conflicts of law nor does it deal with the jurisdiction of Courts'. However, it then continues within the same sentence apparently directly to contra-

---

[24] This is stated in Annex 3, which states that Art 3 does not apply to contractual obligations concerning consumer contracts.

[25] Member States may take proportionate measures to derogate from this principle in certain circumstances detailed in Art 3(4), including public policy, protection of public health, public security and the protection of consumers. See also SI 2002/2013, reg 5.

[26] On which, see below, para 21.19.

[27] See also A Thünken, 'Multi-State Advertising over the Internet and the Private International Law of Unfair Competition' (2002) 51 ICLQ 909, 940.

dict itself: 'provisions of the applicable law designated by rules of private international law must not restrict the freedom to provide information society services'. As the Law Commission has rightly observed: 'It is difficult to understand how one could introduce country-of-origin regulation and prevent such restrictions without making at least some changes to rules about applicable law'.[28]

The United Kingdom's Enacting Regulations

This state of confusion led the drafters of the enacting Regulations in the **21.17** United Kingdom effectively to hedge their bets and omit reference to whether the Regulations affects rules of private international law. In a very useful paragraph,[29] the Law Commission comments thus:

The Department of Trade and Industry has commented that 'the Directive as a whole does not make clear whether the role of private international law is retained or superseded'.[30] Initially, the DTI took the view that the Directive was *not* intended to affect the way that private international law provisions affected civil claims against ISPs. Thus their draft Regulations, published in March 2002, explicitly stated that they did not change the rules on private international law or the jurisdiction of the courts. During consultation, however, many respondents argued that this was inconsistent with the idea of country-of-origin regulation. The final Regulations therefore removed this exclusion, and appear to have wide ranging effects on civil claims.

There is no doubt that this confusion and reservation was justified. For the Directive leaves the inter-relationship between its provisions and private international law unacceptably vague. Nevertheless, we must endeavour to make some sense of the inter-relationship in the following paragraphs.

The country of origin principle appears in the United Kingdom's enacting **21.18** Regulation 4. Regulation 4(1) states that: 'Any requirement[31] which falls within the coordinated field shall apply to all information service providers established in the UK, regardless of whether the service was provided in the UK or another Member State'. Regulation 4(3) states that any requirement[32] should not be applied to a provider that is established in another Member State, if such a requirement would restrict that provider's freedom to provide information society services in the United Kingdom.

---

[28] *Defamation and the Internet: a Preliminary Investigation*, n 1 above, para 4.39, n 36.
[29] ibid, para 4.40.
[30] The Law Commission cite 'Department of Trade and Industry, A Guide for Business to the Electronic Commerce (EC Directive) Regulations 2002' July 2002, para 4.8. The DTI Report can be obtained from www.dti.gov.uk/publications.
[31] The drafting could perhaps be better here, Presumably, what is meant is 'any requirement of English, or, as appropriate, Scots law'.
[32] Again, the drafting would have been clearer if reference had been made to 'any requirement of English, or, as appropriate, Scots law'.

The 'Coordinated Field'

21.19 The country of origin principle should be applied only to activities within what the Directive describes as 'the coordinated field' of activity. This effectively regulates the process of pre-contractual activity online and the process of contracting itself online. However, there is absolutely no question of the rules of the Directive being applied to the rights and duties of the parties under the contract itself, once that contract has been properly formed (and the information specified in the Directive provided to the recipient). So, Recital 21 states that:

> . . . the coordinated field covers only requirements relating to online activities such as online information, online advertising, online shopping, online contracting and does not concern Member States' legal requirements relating to goods such as safety standards, labelling obligations, or liability for goods, or Member States' requirements relating to the delivery or the transport of goods, including the distribution of medicinal products; the coordinated field does not cover the exercise of rights of pre-emption by public authorities concerning certain goods such as works of art.

Later, Article 2(h)(ii) emphasizes that the co-ordinated field does not cover 'requirements applicable to goods as such'; and 'requirement applicable to the delivery of goods'. It should make no difference in this respect that the products are digitized. The same distinction between the contracting process and the substantive requirements of the contract itself should be made.[33]

Consumer Contracts and the Country of Origin Rule

21.20 It is important to distinguish between business-to-business contracts and business-to-consumer contracts.[34] There can be no question of the Directive laying down rules of private international law for consumer contracts.[35] Recital 55 specifically states that the Directive 'does not affect the law applicable to contractual obligations relating to consumer contracts; accordingly, this Directive cannot have the result of depriving the consumer of the protection afforded to him by the mandatory rules relating to contractual obligations of the law of the Member State in which he has his habitual residence'. Hence, the rules of Article 5 of the Rome Convention will continue to hold sway.

---

[33] See also SI 2002/2013, reg 2, which adopts the same definition.
[34] We are not concerned with the details of consumer contracts in this book. It may, however, be important to determine whether a particular contract is a commercial or a consumer contract.
[35] A consumer is defined in Art 2(e) as 'any natural person who is acting for purposes which are outside his or her trade, business of profession'.

Outside this context, the effect of the Directive on rules of private inter- **21.21**
national law is less clear.

6. The Effect of the Directive on the Parties' Freedom to Choose the Governing Law of a Contract

Effect upon the Country of Origin Principle

Annex 3 of the Directive states that the provisions of Article 3 do not **21.22**
apply to 'the freedom of the parties to choose the law applicable to their
contract'. It is very difficult to understand this Annex provision. It suggests that if an information service provider is established in England, but
the law chosen to apply to a contract concluded by it is, say, Texan law, the
country of origin rule does not, after all, apply. The law of Texas should be
applied to the full extent that the rules of the Rome Convention decree,
and the law of England should not be applied to matters within the
'coordinated field'.

Curiously, although the United Kingdom's E-Commerce Regulations do **21.23**
not state whether they affect rules of private international law, they *do* say
that the country of origin principle shall not apply to 'the freedom of
parties to a contract to choose the applicable law'.[36] Hence whilst it is
arguable that there may be instances where the Directive affects private
international law rules, the country of origin principle is not one of them,
at least where a law is chosen by the parties.[37]

Effect upon the Uniform Law Provisions

It could still be the case that the *uniform* law provisions contained elsewhere **21.24**
in the Directive must be applied where a service provider is established in
the United Kingdom, even if the law of Texas is chosen by the parties to
govern the contract of sale. Annex 3 only states that the country of origin

---

[36] SI 2002/2013, Sch s 3.

[37] But contrast Art 23(2) of the European Commission's Proposal for a Regulation of
the European Parliament and the Council on the Law Applicable to Non-Contractual
Obligations COM/2003/0427 Final, of 22 July 2003, (the 'Rome II' Regulation) available at
http://europa.eu.int/eur-lex/pri/en/lip/latest/doc/2003/com2003_0427en01.doc. This
states that: 'This regulation shall not prejudice the application of Community instruments
which, in relation to particular matters and in areas coordinated by such instruments, subject
the supply of services or goods to the laws of the Member State where the service-provider is
established and, in the area coordinated, allow restrictions on freedom to provide services or
goods originating in another Member State only in limited circumstances'. In other words,
where they coincide, the choice of law rules of the proposed Rome II Regulation would give
way to the country of origin principle in the E-Commerce Directive. See also the discussion
of the proposed Rome II Regulation below, paras 21.203–210; and above, paras 17.165–182.

principle in Article 3 does not derogate from the parties' freedom to choose the applicable law. It does not deal with the uniform law provisions.

21.25 It is true that the Directive is said not to affect rules of private international law. Against this, these *substantive* rules should arguably take precedence over the rules of the Rome Convention. Indeed, Article 20 of the Rome Convention states that a court is required to give precedence to any rules of Community law. It is difficult to believe that a service provider established in England and a business customer established in Germany might avoid the substantive rules of the Directive by choosing, say, the law of Texas to govern the contract.

7. The Application of the E-Commerce Directive where the Law Applicable to a Contract is Determined in the Absence of Choice

Nature of the Problem

21.26 There is then a further problem. What if the contract contains *no* choice of law, either express or implied, so that its applicable law is ascertained in the absence of choice? In that scenario, the Annex does not exclude the country of origin principle in relation to business to business contracts. Article 4(2) of the Rome Convention will normally lead to the happy conclusion that the applicable law is that of the place of the service provider's establishment. This avoids the 'conflict', because if the service provider is established in England and the contract is governed by English law, there can be no doubt that the Directive applies. It is likewise if the service provider is established in Germany and the contract governed by German law. Equally clearly, the Convention does not apply if the service provider is established in Texas and Texan law applies.

21.27 The 'hard' case is where the place of establishment of the service provider and the applicable law of the contract in the absence of choice do not coincide. For example, suppose that a service provider established in England contracts by electronic means with a business established in Texas. The contract requires payment in US dollars to a Dallas bank, and delivery of the tangible goods is to be made to Dallas. It is highly arguable that the applicable law in the absence of choice is Texan law, on the basis that, pursuant to Article 4(5) of the Rome Convention, 'it appears from the circumstances as a whole that the contract is more closely connected with another country'. If that is so, does the E-commerce Directive apply and, if so, to what extent? This gives rise to two specific issues: does the country of origin rule still apply; and do the uniform rules contained elsewhere in the Directive apply?

Does the Country of Origin Rule Still Apply?

If the 'country of origin' principle in Article 3 were applied in the given **21.28** example, this would mean that the provisions of English law should be applied to a contract governed, in the absence of choice, by Texan law. The arguments as to whether the country of origin rule should be applied are finely balanced. On the one hand, Annex 3 states that the rule in Article 3 is excluded where the parties have chosen the applicable law of the contract. By strong implication, it is *not* excluded where they did not. On the other hand, the Directive states that the rules of private international law are not affected by the Directive and, as suggested above, it cannot seriously be questioned that the country of origin rule *is* a rule of private international law, nor that it does affect and differ from the existing choice of law rules applicable in contract (and, for that matter, tort). Then again, the UK Regulations do not contain a provision stating that the Directive does not apply to rules of private international law and it could be argued that there is nothing in them to suggest that the country of origin rule should not apply to a service provider established in England, even where a foreign law applies in the absence of choice. Furthermore, it is difficult to understand the point of a country of origin rule, if that rule does not apply wherever the applicable law of the contract is not the law of that state. It is tantamount to saying that 'the requirements of English law must be satisfied if English law governs the contract'. That seems trite and self-evident.

Nevertheless, the intention of the Directive not to affect rules of private **21.29** international law is clear and, since the United Kingdom would be in breach of its obligations if it were to fail to give effect to the Directive, it should be concluded that the country of origin rule does *not* operate where the applicable law of the contract points to a different law. Moreover, it would be bordering on perverse if the country of origin rule were excluded where the parties *chose* a foreign law to govern a contract (which law may have no real connection to the contract), but does apply where the applicable law in the absence of choice points to a foreign law (which, almost by definition, will have a substantial connection to the contract).

Do the Uniform Rules of the Directive Still Apply?

As to the question whether the uniform rules apply, the answer is not **21.30** straightforward. On the one hand, it could be argued that the Directive does not affect rules of private international law and that, if precedence is given to these substantive rules, the unbounded scope of the Rome Convention is restricted. Texan law would *not* be applied in an unqualified manner. Against this, it can be argued that application of the Directive's rules *is* consistent with the Rome Convention, which expressly states that it is subject to relevant provisions of Community law.[38] Moreover, the E-Commerce Regulations do not state that they operate without prejudice to the rules of private international law, tacitly acknowledging the fact that they may well prejudice such rules. On balance, it is suggested that the substantive rules of the Directive *should* be applied in the given example. In essence, it is suggested that the substantive rules must *always* be satisfied where the service provider is established in England, no matter what law governs the contract and irrespective of whether that law was determined by the parties or in the absence of choice. This approach is also consistent with the fact that the Regulations are not generally stated to be without prejudice to rules of private international law.

21.31 Accordingly, it is concluded that the uniform, substantive rules of the Directive should be applied where a service provider is established in a Member State, no matter what law governs the contract. In contrast, the country of origin rule should be applied only where the service provider is established in a Member State and that State's law governs the contract.

8. CONCLUSION

21.32 One can only agree with the conclusion of the Law Commission that: 'The Regulations, as drafted, have not succeeded in their avowed aim of reducing the legal uncertainty over which national rules apply to ISPs. Confusion remains about how far they prevent an ISP based in another member state from being held liable under English law . . .'.[39]

21.33 Perhaps the one small saving grace is that there is express provision both in the Directive and the Regulation that the country of origin rule does not impair the freedom of the parties to choose a governing law. Furthermore, in the absence of choice, the law applicable to a contract under the Rome Convention will normally be that of the service provider's principal place of business,[40] which will usually coincide with the law of the place of the service provider's establishment, specified by the Directive. This means questions as to the precise impact of the Directive on contractual choice of law rules may be minimized.[41]

---

[38] Art 20 of the Rome Convention.
[39] *Defamation and the Internet: a Preliminary Investigation*, n 1 above, para 4.49.
[40] Art 4(2) of the Rome Convention.
[41] The same cannot, however, be said in tort. It is likely that the law of the place of the tort will point to a law other than the country of origin. In such a case, the impact of the country of origin rule is obscure.

Although we cannot be sure how the inter-relationship between rules **21.34** of private international law and the Directive will be interpreted, the following conclusions are suggested:

(1) The substantive, uniform rules of the Directive must be applied to an information service provider established in a Member State, save where the Directive provides an exception or derogation.

(2) Those uniform rules should be applied to an information service provider established in a Member State, even if the parties choose a different law to govern the contract, such as the law of a non-Member State. The uniform rules should also apply where the applicable law of the contract is determined in the absence of choice and points to the law of a non-Member State.

(3) The 'country of origin' principle suggests that where an information service provider is established in England, English law should be applied to activities within the 'coordinated field'. Conversely, English law should not be applied within the 'coordinated field' where an information service provider is established in another Member State, even though he directs his activities to England, in so far as this would restrict the service provider's ability to provide the service.

(4) The 'co-ordinated field' deals with the pre-contractual negotiations and the process of contracting itself. It does not affect the substantive law of sale as such. In particular, it does not apply to questions relating to the goods themselves and the delivery of the goods.

(5) The 'country of origin' principle does not affect the operation of the choice of law rules applicable to consumer contracts.

(6) The 'country of origin' principle does not affect the application of the law chosen by the parties to govern a contract.

(7) Nor should the 'country of origin' principle be applied where the applicable law in the absence of choice, as determined by the Rome Convention, points to a different law.

III. CHOICE OF LAW IN CONTRACT

1. INTRODUCTION; THE DOMINANCE OF THE LAW EXPRESSLY CHOSEN BY THE PARTIES

It will be demonstrated that the choice of law rules in contract present **21.35** relatively few problems in respect of business to business sales transactions by electronic means. In particular, the predominance of the law expressly chosen by the parties[42] means that less importance is attached to

---

[42] Art 3(1) of the Rome Convention.

territorial factors, which can be difficult to locate in an e-commerce context. The primary concern is to ensure that a choice of law clause contained on an internet site, or included in an email, was sufficiently visible and actually represents the bilateral consent of the parties.

2. CONSENT TO A CHOICE OF LAW CLAUSE: CLAUSE TOO SMALL, NOT VISIBLE ON SCREEN ETC.

21.36 There appear to be no widespread problems in determining the parties' consent to a choice of law clause in a contract concluded over the internet.[43] A choice of choice of law clause may be inserted into a contract if the owner of a website sets up an interactive 'click wrap agreement'.[44] This requires a customer to agree to the terms of the contract by clicking on an acceptance button on the website. If the customer does not do this the website will not accept the customer's order.

21.37 However, a question might sometimes arise as to whether the parties consented to a choice of law clause in a contract concluded by electronic means. In particular, what if one party alleges that a choice of law clause contained upon the service provider's[45] website was not visible on screen and could only be seen if one were to scroll down the screen, or click on a separate link?[46]

21.38 A question arises here as to whether the issue in question is to be classified as one of form or of substance. The argument for the former is that the issue goes to the *manner* in which the choice of law clause should appear on screen and requires it to be presented in a clear and easily visible way. However, it is suggested that the issue is in fact one of substance. It does not go to the question whether the method of communication is adequate, nor to the question of whether anything more than the consent of the parties to the clause must be shown to exist. Rather, it simply goes to the

[43] Compare the views expressed in relation to jurisdiction clauses at the expert meeting on Electronic Commerce and International Jurisdiction organized by the Hague Conference on Private International Law held in Ottawa from 28 February to 1 March 2000, Summary of Discussions, 4. See also the earlier Geneva Round Table see the Report of Commission III set out in Prel Doc No 7 of April 2000, entitled Electronic Data Interchange, Internet and Electronic Commerce by Kessedjian for the attention of the Special Commission of May 2000 on general affairs and policy of the Hague Conference on Private International Law, 22–23). These documents can be accessed at http://hcch.e-vision.nl/index_en.php?act= progress.listing&cat=9.

[44] *Stomp Inc v NeatO* 61 F Supp 2d 1074 at 1080–1081 (CD Cal 1999).

[45] The term 'service provider' is used in this chapter as it is understood in Art 2(a) of the E-Commerce Directive and SI 2002/2013, reg. 2(1). This definition includes parties who sell goods online.

[46] Compare the decision in *Rudder v Microsoft Corp* 1999 Carswell Ont 3195, Ontario Superior Court of Justice, where a similar argument was raised and rejected in connection with a jurisdiction clause.

question of whether the parties agreed to the term or not. Such a question falls within the parameters of Article 3(4) of the Rome Convention. This means that the law which would govern the choice of law clause if it were valid should determine whether the parties have indeed consented to a clause which can only be viewed by scrolling down a web page or clicking on a new link. If the choice of law clause specifies, for example, Japanese law, then it is the law of Japan that shall determine if that clause was agreed upon.

Similar arguments apply if a party alleges that the choice of law clause **21.39** was too small, or if it was illegible. These go not to the formalities needed to conclude the contract, but to the question whether the party could be said to consent to a clause which he cannot properly read. Once again, the putative applicable law should determine whether the clause was agreed upon.[47]

3. Choice of a Law with No Objective Connection to the Contract—Article 3(3)

At first sight, this provision raises no specific issues related to **21.40** e-commerce. It will be recalled that the provision states that if the parties choose[48] the law of State X to govern a contract, but all the other elements relevant to the situation point to the law of State Y, then the mandatory rules of State Y should be superimposed onto the contract. These are the rules of state Y from which the parties could not have derogated *if State Y's law had been the governing law*.

The real question in this context is what constitutes an element 'relevant **21.41** to the situation.'[49] Benjamin convincingly suggests that Article 3(3) will apply to an English buyer of tangible goods contracting with an English seller, even if the contract is concluded through the seller's website on the internet, if the only foreign connection aside from a choice of law is that the website is hosted in a foreign state. This does not seem materially relevant to the 'situation' of the contract.[50] It has no bearing on the negotiation, conclusion or execution of the contract itself. Moreover, the point of Article 3(3) is to prevent a party from avoiding the application of the

---

[47] Subject to the limited exception in Art 8(2) of the Rome Convention, which allows a party to rely upon the law of his habitual residence to show that he did not consent to a contract or any of its terms, if it would not be reasonable for the court to determine this matter entirely by the putative applicable law. See further above, paras 13.150–153.

[48] Expressly or impliedly.

[49] The Rapporteur at the Geneva Round Table comments in Prel Doc No 7, n 43 above, 23, n 60 that 'some members of the Commission were opposed to defining internationality for the online environment, which they regard as being international in the nature of things'.

[50] Benjamin 25–038. See also Recital 19 of the E-Commerce Directive.

mandatory rules of the law of closest connection by choice of another law of no objective connection. It would make little sense if the mandatory rules of the law of closest connection could be sidestepped by the service provider setting up a website hosted in a particular state of no connection to the contract. That just allows him to avoid the anti-avoidance measure in Article 3(3).

21.42 The Geneva Round Table meeting suggested that a choice of law clause should not be regarded as truly 'international' unless 'the parties are habitually resident in the same state *and* this fact is known or clearly identified at the time when the contract is concluded'.[51] If an English service recipient and an English service provider conclude a contract governed by a foreign law, and neither party was aware of the other's habitual residence, the contract cannot be said to have been motivated by avoidance tactics. There is a strong argument for saying that if both parties genuinely and reasonably believed that they were concluding an 'international' contract, the contract should be so treated. As such, the chosen law would be applied without being subject to the mandatory rules of the law with which the contract is entirely objectively connected.

21.43 The place of conclusion of the contract is, it is suggested, not a factor 'relevant to the situation'. This state may be very difficult to determine where, for example, a contract is concluded by exchange of emails and may well be arbitrary, especially if the email account of one or both parties is registered in a state other than that where they are resident, or if some of the negotiations take place whilst one or both of the parties are overseas on business. It is argued that the place of conclusion has no material connection in its own right with the contract and no legitimate 'interest' in the contract. As such, if the parties choose the law of State Y to govern a contract concluded by electronic means in State Y, but all other elements of the contract point to State X, it is suggested that Article 3(3) should still apply and that the mandatory rules of that law must still be satisfied.

21.44 The place of dispatch and receipt of information should likewise not in themselves be considered relevant elements in relation to sales of 'traditional' goods. They may be arbitrary, capable of being manipulated and have no bearing on the subsequent execution of the contract. However, if there are digitized products, the matter is different. The place of dispatch[52] and receipt[53] are equivalent to the places of discharge of goods and

---

[51] Prel Doc No 7, n 43 above, at 23.

[52] That is, the state where the server is located to which the information is uploaded by the service provider: see above, paras 10.60, 10.66–67.

[53] Which is likely to be the state where the recipient downloads the information.

delivery/receipt of those goods. It cannot sensibly be denied that these are relevant to the contract itself. In such circumstances, Article 3(3) should not be triggered, even if all objective factors point to State X, save that the place of dispatch or of receipt is in State Y.

The place of performance is obviously a highly important element where **21.45** a contract concerns tangible goods. This is so regardless of whether the contract was negotiated or concluded online. What, however, if the contract itself involves the delivery of digitized products to the recipient? Is the place of performance still a relevant element of the contract for the purposes of Article 3(3)? The meeting of the Geneva Round Table concluded that '. . . if the contract is performed electronically, the place of performance cannot be taken into consideration for the purpose of deciding the international nature of the clause'.[54] Although this remark was made in connection with jurisdiction clauses, one might wonder whether the same is true for choice of law purposes. It can be very difficult to determine the place of performance of a contract for the provision of digitized products by electronic means and that place may well be arbitrary.[55] If the place of performance is taken to be the place where the recipient downloads the product, then this may have little real connection to the contract. A recipient resident in State Y may happen to download the information whilst on a short business trip to State Z. However, the fact remains that the service provider does discharge the essential obligation to transfer information in that state. Moreover, this is the performance which is 'characteristic' of the contract.[56] As such, it seems very unlikely that it can be disregarded as an irrelevant element of a digitized contract for the purposes of Article 3(3). Accordingly, it is suggested that where digitized products are sold to the recipient and performance is to be effected by electronic means, the place of performance should considered a relevant element for the purposes of Article 3(3).

4. IMPLIED CHOICE OF LAW

The E-Commerce Regulations 2002, Regulation 9(1)(d)[57] requires the pro- **21.46** vider of an information service to state the languages offered for the conclusion of the contract. It may be that the language, once ascertained and agreed upon by the parties, can be said to be equivalent to a term which refers to a particular legal system, at least if it points to only one system.

---

[54] Prel Doc No 7, n 43 above, at 22
[55] See the discussion of Art 5(1) of the Brussels I Regulation above, paras 10.56–75, 10.78–80.
[56] See Art 4(2) of the Rome Convention.   [57] Art 10(1)(d) of the E-Commerce Directive.

So, if one party to a contract is resident in England and the other in Sweden and there are no factors pointing to any other state, a contract concluded in Swedish might give rise to an inference that Swedish law was chosen by the parties to govern the contract.

21.47 A court might infer that English law should govern a contract that is concluded in English. However, this should be rather less conclusive, given that contracts are often concluded in English and that this does not point to *one* particular legal system. If the parties were an English and a Texan resident and the contract was in English, it would be impossible to infer anything from the language used as to the governing law.[58]

21.48 What if the parties have a previous course of dealings which was subjected to a choice of law clause, but which was concluded other than by electronic means? Is it a legitimate inference that the parties intended a later contract concluded by electronic means to be governed by the same law, if they are silent on the matter? It could be argued that the fact that the parties employ a new method of communication does not alter the nature of the contract itself, and that an inference as to the governing law can be drawn. In essence, one needs to look at the contract as a whole and see whether other material terms have been altered, or whether the contract is in substance identical. If the terms have been altered, it may be argued that the omission to specify a governing law is material and, indeed, might even tend to indicate that the parties did *not* want the same law to apply as that which governed preceding contracts. However, if the contract is, in all material respects, identical, then an inference may readily be drawn that the law which governed previous contracts between the parties should also govern the present contract.[59]

5. APPLICABLE LAW IN THE ABSENCE OF CHOICE: ARTICLE 4(2)

General Principle

21.49 Article 4(1) provides that the law of the country with which the contract has its closest connection applies in the absence of a choice of law.[60] It will

---

[58] If a standard form is used in a contract, no internet specific issues arise. The contract and its terms must, of course, represent the genuine consent of the parties. This is a matter for the putative applicable law of that contract to determine, pursuant to Art 8(1) of the Rome Convention.

[59] See also C Gringras, *The Law of the Internet*, (2nd edn, London: Butterworths, 2003) 62–63.

[60] Burnstein, n 1 above, at 96 comments that this is 'unhelpful' in the e-commerce context. However, this is unfair, as he wholly omits to mention the presumption in Art 4(2), which, it will be argued, provides a clear and sensible solution in e-commerce cases. See also U Kohl, 'Eggs, Jurisdiction and the Internet' (2002) 51 ICLQ 555, 569, who, equally unfairly, describes Art 4 as 'a perfect discouraging example' of a broad and vague test unsuited to the demands of finding a clear, efficient approach to e-commerce and private international law.

be recalled that Article 4(2) lays does a presumption as to which law will apply. It introduces the idea of characteristic performance, which is the performance for which payment is due.[61] The characteristic performer in a sales contract is the seller. Equally, where a person pays to access a service provider's website and download a digitized product, the characteristic performer is the service provider.

Article 4(2) states that where the characteristic performer concludes a **21.50** contract in the course of business, the relevant law is the state in which its principal place of business is situated,[62] or, if performance is to be conducted through a different place of business, the place where that other business is located. A question arises as to whether a business with its central administration in State X which does business via the internet using a website located in State Y[63] (with no further connections to that State) may be regarded as effecting performance through a place of business in State Y.[64] The mere fact that the service provider uses a website to promote its goods or digitized products does not itself create a place of business.[65] However, if the service provider has its own server located in State Y, from which it concludes contracts of sale, would matters be different? There is now an enduring connection with State Y. If the website is an interactive one which allows customers to contract online, rather than a passive channel of communication, then there is a case to say that the company has a place of business in State Y. Nevertheless, it is clear that the website is still a business tool for the company itself, which is and remains entirely located in State X. The website has no independent business identity and, as such, it is suggested that Article 4(2) must still point to the law of State X.[66]

---

[61] Giuliano and Lagarde Report, [1980] OJ C282/10 at 20.

[62] On which, see *Owners of Cargo Lately Laden on Board the Rewia v Caribbean Liners (Caribtainer) Ltd (The Rewia)* [1991] 2 Lloyd's Rep 325.

[63] If the website is located in State Y, there can surely be no question of the company being deemed to have a place of business elsewhere simply because that website is accessible throughout the world. See also Case 33/78 *Somafer v Saar-Ferngas* [1978] ECR 2183. Nor can the mere exchange of emails give rise to a suggestion of a place of business in the state where the email account of the company happens to be located. See further Reed, n 7 above, at 200–210.

[64] See also the discussion of whether activity over the internet may constitute the use of a branch, above, paras 10.81–87, 10.89–97. See further *Matchnet v Blair* [2002] EWHC 2128 (Ch), [2003] 2 BCLC 195.

[65] See the expert meeting Summary of Discussions, n 43 above, at 9. See also the Giuliano and Lagarde Report, 20–21.

[66] See the Nygh and Pocar Report on the Draft Convention on Jurisdiction and Foreign Judgments in Civil and Commercial Matters (the Hague Judgments Convention), Prel Doc No 11, at 57; expert meeting Summary of Discussions, n 43 above, at 9. See also P Bolger, 'Making Contracts over the Internet', (1999) 3(3) Irish Intellectual Property Rev 20; Gringras, n 59 above, at 70–71.

21.51 A related case is where a company based in State X uses the website of another company which is based in State Y and has its server located in State Y. It may be unlikely that the company in State Y could be said to be under the control of the company in State X in any meaningful way. The State Y company is likely to be free to conduct its own independent business. Even if the website provides for the online auction of goods, it is difficult to say that the State X company has a place of business in State Y. The website is entirely concerned with promoting the business of the company, and that company is entirely based in State X. Moreover, the website itself is likely to be accessed across the world, so that it is not particularly aimed at conducting business activity in State Y. That being so, it would seem curious for the law of State Y to apply under Article 4(2), where the company is neither based there nor particularly conducting its business there. This would lead to the application of a law of little connection to the contract and contrary to the parties' expectations.

21.52 Even if, contrary to what is argued above, a website could constitute a place of business, Article 4(2) also requires that performance is to be effected through that place of business. This will often be impossible to demonstrate. In most cases, performance will involve the sale and, frequently, delivery of tangible goods. Even if the contract was concluded online, the performance itself will emphatically be rendered by the company. It would be different if the 'performance' consisted of the transfer of digitized products downloaded from the service provider's website. In such a case, if the website itself could be deemed to be a place of business, then one would surely conclude that the performance was rendered though that website.

21.53 In conclusion, it is suggested that where a company has its principal place of business in State X and no other physical place of business in another state, the fact that it has, or uses, a server in State Y should not constitute a place of business in State Y. It is to the law of State X that Article 4(2) points.

The Attraction of Article 4(2) and the Possibility of Rebutting the Presumption that the Law of the Place where the Characteristic Performer has its Central Administration will Apply: Article 4(5)

21.54 Article 4(2) leads to the happy coincidence that the law which governs a contract in the absence of choice will usually also be the law which falls to be applied within the 'coordinated field' in the E-Commerce Directive, namely the law of the place of the information service provider's central administration.[67] That reason alone might lead to reluctance on a court's part to displace the presumption in Article 4(2) in favour of another law pursuant to Article 4(5).

The Strength of the Presumption in Article 4(2)—Relevance of the Habitual Residence or Place of Business of the Parties

The relevance of the residence or place of business of the parties to a **21.55** contract concluded by electronic means is unclear. The primary argument against weighing the factor significantly is that parties at arm's length might conclude a contract via a website with almost no knowledge of each other, still less of the other's state of residence or place of business. If the applicable law of the contract were to be affected by such a factor, this might be wholly contrary to the parties' expectations. To that, however, there are a number of retorts. First, the applicable law in the absence of choice is not concerned particularly with protecting party expectations. Parties who wish to have their expectations protected should make provision as to the governing law. If they do not, then Article 4 moves to a territorial approach which seeks to determine the state of closest connection. Second, many of the connections identified by a contract concluded by electronic means may be highly transient and of little obvious significance. Such factors as the place of conclusion of the contract, the place of uploading,[68] the location of the service provider at the time of uploading and the place to which the product is downloaded provide little by way of enduring connection. In contrast, the residence of a party provides a relatively enduring and strong connection with that state. It is also likely that litigation involving the parties will take place in the state where one or other is resident and it is expeditious that the state hearing the case should be able to apply the law of the forum. Third, it is more likely that the recipient will know the service provider's place of business or residence than vice versa. For information service providers established in a Member State of the European Union, the E-Commerce Directive stipulates that they must provide certain basic information, including their place of business.[69] Since the service provider will normally be the characteristic performer under Article 4(2), the recipient should be aware of the information which will enable him to determine which law will apply in the absence of choice. More generally, one could also argue that the presumption in Article 4(2) may be stronger for a corporate service provider than

---

[67] Art 3 of the E-Commerce Directive refers to the place of establishment of the information service provider.

[68] That is, the location of the server to which the product is uploaded.

[69] Art 5(1) of the Directive; SI 2002/2013, reg 6(1).

an individual service provider. The place of business of the company is likely to be stated on its website, or any email communication, and so be clear to the recipient.

21.56 Of course, there is nothing to prevent a service provider from lying as to his place of residence or business. However, it is suggested that if he is proven to have done so, a court is likely to be much more willing to displace the presumption in Article 4(2).

21.57 In conclusion, one might say that the lure of the service provider's residence or place of business may be especially strong in an e-commerce case. As such, it is relatively unlikely to be displaced under Article 4(5). Furthermore, the law of the recipient's residence may be accorded rather less significance under Article 4(5), both because his performance is not characteristic of the contract and because it is more likely that his habitual residence or place of business will be unknown to the service provider than the converse.[70]

The Exception in Article 4(5)

21.58 In considering the exception in Article 4(5), a question arises as to the importance to be attached to various connecting factors where a contract of sale is negotiated and/or concluded electronically. Where the contract concerns the sale of tangible goods, the importance of such factors as the place of delivery, currency and other matters relating to performance itself under the contract do not vary just because the contract was negotiated in a particular manner. Our present concern is rather with factors whose importance might alter where a contract is negotiated and/or concluded electronically, or concerns the transfer of digitized products.

The Exception in Article 4(5): which Law Determines where a Sales[71] Contract Involving Electronic Commerce was Concluded and to be Performed?

21.59 Before we consider the importance of various connecting factors which might lead to the displacement of Article 4(2), a preliminary question arises as to whether such matters as the place of delivery, transfer, payment and of conclusion of the contract should be determined by English law alone, or should instead be determined by the law putatively applicable to the contract under Article 4(5). This may be a particularly

---

[70] See the discussion below, paras 21.69–70.
[71] On the question whether a contract to be performed by electronic means is one of 'sale', see above, paras 10.44–53. See also below, paras 21.113–118.

important issue in the e-commerce context, where the place of conclusion of a contract concluded by electronic means, or the place of transfer of digitized products or payment by provision of credit card details over the internet may be less than clear cut, and something upon which different legal systems might disagree.

The argument in favour of the applicable law is that matters such as the **21.60** place of delivery are terms of the contract. Article 8(1) subjects the validity of those terms to the applicable law of the contract. Article 10(1) indicates that such matters as the interpretation and performance[72] of the contract are to be determined by the applicable law. Moreover, it could be said to be curious and undesirable for an English court to apply the law of the forum to determine these matters and to decide that, on this basis, the presumption of characteristic performance is displaced, if the law which is then deemed applicable holds that the place of delivery, conclusion etc, is in fact in a different state.

Against this, there is the obvious logical objection that the present exercise **21.61** is concerned with ascertaining the applicable law. Until that law is determined, it makes little sense to determine the existence of connecting factors other than by the law of the forum. Moreover, since the law of different states might disagree as to where, for example, a contract formed over the internet was concluded, or where digitized products were trans-ferred, it may be impossible coherently to identify a law which is puta-tively applicable. One could argue that the law specified under Article 4(2) should accordingly be applied to determine the place of payment, delivery, transfer, conclusion etc, on the basis that it is *putatively* applic-able, unless and until displaced under Article 4(5). However, since the very process of Article 4(5) is to determine whether Article 4(2) should be displaced, it is questionable whether the law to which Article 4(2) points should be used effectively to determine this process.

Furthermore, it may be argued that the identification of the law of closest **21.62** connection is a process of drawing together various connecting factors. It is the law of the forum which determines the applicable law and which gives it its lifeblood. Only *after* that process has been resolved finally does the applicable law 'take over.' The law of the state of closest connection is determined by the terms of the contract. Since it is a matter for the law of the forum to determine the law of the state of closest connection, it must also be for the law of the forum to decide what the terms of the contract appear to be, in order to make that decision. Of course, the English court

---

[72] Though, in the case of performance, this is subject to the provision on manner of performance in Art 10(2).

cannot be certain at this stage what the terms of the contract may be. All it can do is to ask whether it is satisfied, to its civil standard of proof, that the term in question is part of the contract.[73]

21.63 At this point, a practical observation is that if such matters as the place of transfer of digitized products, the place of conclusion of a contract formed via the internet or by email, or the place of payment over the internet by credit card cannot easily be determined as a matter of fact, it seems very unlikely that they would be accorded any real weight when applying Article 4(5). Once the issue arises as to which law should determine these matters, it seems the case almost by definition that they do not point decisively to a single state. In a flexible system such as Article 4(5), one would not want the answer to such a technical question to determine the applicable law. As such, it is suggested that undue complexity should be avoided. The place of delivery, transfer, conclusion and payment should be regarded as connecting factors and determined by the law of the forum. Once they have been ascertained, their weight should be assessed. However, they are fairly unlikely to affect the determination of the applicable law in the absence of choice.

Assessing the Relevance of Certain Connecting Factors for the Purposes of Article 4(5)[74]

The law of the forum

21.64 It could be argued that the law of the forum is relevant here, on the basis that it may be difficult in an e-commerce case to find an enduring connection to a particular state. However, this cannot have any bearing on the application of Article 4(5). The fact that certain connecting factors may be difficult to ascertain in an e-commerce case is not an argument for increased use of the law of the forum. This is not a case where *no* foreign law can be ascertained. Article 4(2) provides a workable choice of law rule and, in deciding whether to rebut that presumption, the fact that English law is the law of the forum should have absolutely no relevance.

Place of transfer of digitized products

21.65 We are not concerned here with contracts concluded by electronic means requiring the delivery of tangible goods. The relevance of the place of

---

[73] In England, this should mean the balance of probabilities. Any lower standard would be unfair to one of the parties, where the terms of the contract are themselves disputed. The burden of proof would need also to be allocated. In principle, the person alleging that a term forms part of the contract should have the burden of proving that does.

[74] See also the discussion of the application of the forum conveniens test to electronic contracts, above, paras 10.109–133.

delivery is unaffected in such a case by the means of communication. Rather, our focus is on the transfer of digitized products.[75]

We saw in Chapter 10 on e-commerce and jurisdiction that it can be an **21.66** extremely complex question where digitized products are to be transferred.[76] The pros and cons of the place of dispatch,[77] the place of receipt and where either party has a specified connecting factor were considered in detail. Most of these are equally relevant in the choice of law context and are not repeated here.[78]

It was argued above that the place of delivery or transfer should be **21.67** determined by the law of the forum for the purposes of Article 4. At this stage, the applicable law of the contract is unknown. We saw in Chapter 10 on e-commerce and jurisdiction that the arguments as between the place of dispatch and the place of receipt are very finely balanced.[79] It could be argued that the place where the recipient is when he receives[80] the information should be regarded by an English court as the place of transfer for these purposes.[81] It is at the point that the products are received that the recipient will have received all that he bargained for.[82] Against this, the place of dispatch[83] of digitized products could be said to be at least as important under Article 4(5) as the place of receipt. The service provider will normally dispatch the information from a single state.[84] In contrast, the place of receipt will vary from customer to customer and may be said to have less significant connection to the contract

---

[75] Whether this is technically a contract of sale, or of service, or neither, is a moot point. The issue is discussed in more detail in connection with Art 5(1) of the Brussels I Regulation, above, paras 10.44–53. It is also considered in connection with the discussion of mandatory rules and public policy in contract below, paras 21.113–118. See also the expert meeting, Summary of Discussions, n 43 above, at 5, which favours the view that where a contract is to be performed online, it is best regarded as similar to a contract for the provision of services.

[76] Above, paras 10.54–74.

[77] In the case of internet transactions, this will be the place where the information is placed on a web-server and is accessed by the customer. If a digitized product is transferred by an email attachment, the place of dispatch is more difficult to identify. See above, paras 10.60, 10.66–67.

[78] See above, paras 10.54–74. See also Reed, n 7 above, at 193–195.

[79] Above, paras 10.66–69.

[80] Technically, one could argue that where transfer is by email, the relevant place is that where the mailbox is located. Compare s 14 of the Australian Electronic Communications Act 1999.

[81] This is likely to be the place of downloading of the digitized product by the recipient. See above, paras 10.68–69.

[82] But Reed, n 7 above, at 195 suggests that where the products are downloaded from a website, 'there is a strong argument that delivery occurs at that website'. He draws an analogy to FOB contracts, in that the 'seller' makes the 'goods' available and the 'buyer' is responsible for arranging the 'collection' of the 'goods' for himself.

[83] That is, the state where the web-server is located to which the product was uploaded: see above, paras 10.60, 10.66–67.

[84] Save where the product is uploaded to mirror sites located in different jurisdictions.

than that place of dispatch. Moreover, where the service provider's website is located in his home state, the place of dispatch will usually coincide with the law to which Article 4(2) points. There are also arguments in favour of the place where the recipient has a specified personal connecting factor as the place of transfer of digitized products.[85]

21.68 It is precisely because, in the case of digitized products, there may be no clear place of transfer, and no enduring or substantial connection with that place, that we need not detain ourselves unduly with determining where the place of transfer is.[86] Overall, whereas in the context of 'ordinary' goods, the fact that the characteristic performer is to effect performance in a state other than his 'home' state is one of the strongest reasons for invoking Article 4(5), it is extremely unlikely that this factor would, in itself, displace the presumption in Article 4(2) where digitized products are concerned.

Recipient's place of residence or business

21.69 It was suggested in Chapter 10 that this connecting factor should be regarded as the place where services are provided or goods delivered for the purposes of Article 5(1)(b) of the Brussels I Regulation.[87] However, this was considered in the context of a specific provision of the Brussels I Regulation which requires the court to attribute a place of performance to a contractual obligation.

21.70 The matter is different in respect of the Rome Convention.[88] It is not essential to rely upon any one connecting factor when considering the application of Article 4(5). Accordingly, the relevance of the recipient's place of residence or business should be determined in its own right. This was discussed above when we considered the importance of the residence or place of business of the parties. It was suggested that this factor is unlikely to be given strong weight. The recipient is not the characteristic performer under the contract and the service provider may be unable to determine the place of residence of business of the recipient at the time of the conclusion of the contract. Moreover, the E-Commerce Directive adopts a country of origin principle which points to the law of the place where the service provider, not the recipient, is established.[89]

---

[85] See below, paras 21.69–70.
[86] Compare the views of the Geneva Round Table, Prel Doc No 7, n 43 above, at 19.
[87] Above, paras 10.72–74.
[88] See also the discussion of forum non conveniens above, paras 10.109–133, esp para 10.131.
[89] See above, paras 10.26 and 21.15–21. See further above, paras 21.55–57.

Place of payment

For the reasons given above,[90] it is suggested that, when working out the **21.71** governing law, the place of payment should be determined by the law of the forum. In practice, this is only likely to be a problem where payment is made over the internet by credit or debit card. In such a case, the place of payment may well be difficult to determine[91] and unlikely to have an enduring connection to any particular state. There is no indication that the place of payment is a particularly weighty factor for 'ordinary' contracts under Article 4(5). It is likely to be substantially less important where that place cannot readily be determined and where, even if it can, it provides no real objective connection to the contract.

Location of the computers used by each party; place where service provider is located at the time of dispatch and place where recipient is located when it downloads the product

It is suggested that little importance is to be attached to the physical **21.72** location of the parties at the point at which they negotiate or conclude a contract by electronic means.[92] It may be very difficult for either party to determine the location of the other's computer. Moreover, a party might simply lie as to the location of the computer. More significantly still, if the contract relates to the delivery of 'ordinary' goods to be paid for by 'conventional' means, the fact that it was negotiated and/or concluded by electronic means seems of substantially less importance to the centre of gravity of the contract than the performance of the obligations under the contract. Even if both computers are located in a single state, this may be fortuitous, in that the parties may be at arm's length and know nothing of this and have concluded the contract on the basis that it was genuinely international in nature. It is also possible that the location of the computers was fortuitous. One or both parties may happen to have logged into a computer in an overseas state whilst abroad on business. If they are indeed both resident in the state where the computers are located, or have their principal place of business in that state, this might provide a more enduring connection. However, that is an argument for the importance of the residence of the parties as a connecting factor, not the location of the computers.[93]

---

[90] At paras 21.59–63.

[91] See the discussion of forum non conveniens above, paras 10.106–108, 10.124–125. See also the discussion of the place of enrichment in the analysis of restitution and e-commerce below, paras 21.241–245.

[92] But see *Rudder v Microsoft Corp* 1999 Carswell Ont 3195, Ontario Superior Court of Justice.

[93] And since Art 4(2) leads to the law of the seller or service provider's residence or place of business in any event, there would be no case for invoking Art 4(5).

21.73 Even where a transfer of digitized products is concerned, it is argued that the same approach should be adopted. The recipient may be unaware of the state in which the service provider's computer was located at the time that it dispatched the product to a web-server. The location of the service provider's computer can also be manipulated and may have no connection with where the service provider carries out its internet business activity or where it has its place of business. Moreover, the product may consist of regularly updated information which has been uploaded by the service provider whilst it is physically located in more than one state.

21.74 As for the place where the recipient is at the time of downloading of the product, it is true that there is an analogy to the place where conventional goods are ultimately supplied to the buyer. But the place of downloading is unlikely to be a stipulated term of the contract. It may be equally difficult for the service provider to predict, especially if the product is downloaded when, for example, the recipient is away from his home state on business. It is also capable of manipulation. Moreover, this connecting factor will be particularly insignificant where the recipient downloads the product in more than one state, as where it purchases statistical information over the internet by a yearly subscription and can access this as the recipient wants over the year.[94] The recipient may download the information at different times in different states.

The place of conclusion of the contract

21.75 There seems little case for attaching importance to this factor. Where a contract is concluded by conventional means, this factor may be difficult to determine, arbitrary and have little connection with the performance of the contract itself. Where a contract is concluded by electronic means, these reservations apply a fortiori.[95] The law of the forum[96] will have to identify the place of conclusion of the contract.[97] In many cases, that it is likely to be a highly complex question. The mere fact that it is not a clear cut matter tends to demonstrate that the state identified will have no real enduring connection with the contract solely because it is the place of conclusion. It is hard to see this factor having any real weight at all under Article 4(5).

Place of breach

21.76 The place of breach will, of course, be irrelevant. The applicable law must be determined at the time of conclusion of the contract, not at the time of any later breach.

---

[94] This may be seen as a contract of service: see above, para 10.50. See also *1st Mover APS v Direct Hedge SA* [2003] IL Pr 31, Eastern Court of Appeal, Denmark.
[95] A view shared by the Geneva Round Table, Prel Doc No 7, n 43 above, at 19.
[96] See above, paras 21.59–63.
[97] On which, see 'E-commerce—the Legal Aspects' 23(7) The Buyer, 1, 2.

Place where property in the goods or digitized products is to pass

The place where property in the goods or digitized products is to pass[98] **21.77** should, in cases of doubt, be determined by the law of the situs. It is true that this is a connecting factor used for the purposes of identifying the applicable law of the contract in the absence of choice, and that it has generally been suggested that such connecting factors should be determined by the law of the forum. However, the place where property is to pass raises a property law question. If the law putatively applicable to the transfer of property is itself apparent, there is no reason not to apply that law to this question.

It could be argued that this factor is of no relevance, since it concerns a **21.78** matter of property law and not contract law. However, this overlooks the fact that the obligation to pass property is one of the key *contractual* obligations of a sales[99] contract. That said, in the case of 'conventional' goods, the place where property is to pass should be accorded no special significance merely because the contract is concluded by electronic means. It is likely to be one factor, but rather less important than the place of delivery of the goods. The law of the place where the goods are to be delivered may be said to have a greater connection with, and interest in, the law applicable to the contract, as the goods will be located in that jurisdiction. The precise point along that journey at which property in them passes seems rather less significant.

In the case of digitized products, it may be less clear whether,[100] and if so **21.79** where, property is to pass. This may depend upon the place of downloading of the product, which may be arbitrary and difficult to predict. As such, this factor is very unlikely to be given any real weight under Article 4(5).

The place of dispatch of the product; location of the server to which the product is uploaded

The location of the seller's website is unlikely to be significant where a **21.80** contract is concluded or negotiated by electronic means, but involves the delivery of tangible goods by conventional means. It is not central to the performance of the contract.

Matters are more complex where a digitized product is transferred via the **21.81** internet. We saw in Chapter 10 that the place of dispatch of digitized

---

[98] If, indeed, property is to pass at all; see the discussion of the nature of contracts to be performed by electronic means, above, paras 10.44–53, and below, paras 21.113–118. See also below, paras 21.211–238, on the application of choice of law rules in property to e-commerce.
[99] But see ibid on whether a contract performed by electronic means is a 'sales' contract.
[100] ibid.

products is best regarded as being the location of the server to which the service provider uploads the product.[101] The location of the service provider's website may be the state where a contract is concluded by the parties. It is also argued below that this state is probably the situs of digitized products at the time at which they are made available to the recipient for transfer.[102]

21.82 Despite this, it is unlikely to provide an enduring connection to the contract.[103] Indeed, where the service provider uploads a product to a series of 'mirror' sites, this may fail to point to a single state in any event. Moreover, the service provider may locate his website in a state with no other connection to the contract. If neither party is established in that state, and neither party is to perform his obligations in that state, then there is no reason why the law of the place where a website is based should apply.

21.83 Of course, a digitized product might be transferred by email attachment, rather than being downloaded by the recipient from the service provider's website. In such a case, even if the service provider does have a website, its location is unlikely to be of any real relevance when a court is determining whether to invoke Article 4(5) of the Rome Convention.

Location of the party providing access to the internet

21.84 The party providing access to the internet is the 'passport' to the internet. At least where both parties use the same party to provide internet access, or different providers established in the same state, it could be argued that this is a relevant factor in ascertaining the law of the state of closest connection.

21.85 However, it is suggested that the location of the party providing access to the internet is unlikely to be materially relevant under Article 4(5). Neither party may be aware of which party the other was using to obtain access to the internet. As such, even if they use the same provider of internet access, or different internet access providers established in the same state, this may be mere coincidence. More to the point, it is difficult to see how this state could be said to be of enduring connection to the contract.[104] A contract of sale is connected with the parties, with the

---

[101] At paras 10.60, 10.66–67.

[102] See the section on the choice of law rules in property applicable in e-commerce cases, below, paras 21.211–238.

[103] Contrast the position in relation to choice of law in tort, below, paras 21.151–154; and in relation to choice of law in property, paras 21.224–228, 21.238.

[104] But contrast Burnstein, n 1 above, at 96–97, who argues that users 'might be considered "citizens" of their access provider' and that, in this way, 'it is possible to assign a "cyber-domicile" to each user'. He later contends that cyberspace has similarities with Admiralty law and that the state where one's access provider is located is functionally similar to the law of the flag (ibid, 104). It is difficult to imagine that any English court would adopt this approach.

negotiation and conclusion of the contract and with the obligations under the contract. The party used to provide access to the internet to the parties bears no significant relationship to the contract of sale itself.[105]

Sales through another party's website (including auction sales)—the location of the website and the website owner's place of business

A service provider may make use of another party's website to sell his **21.86** goods and digitized products. In such a case, it may be important to distinguish cases where the goods or digitized products[106] are clearly sold by the service provider in his own right from cases where the goods or digitized products are sold by using the website owner as an intermediary.

Where the service provider is clearly selling his own goods or digitized **21.87** products[107] in his own right, and merely makes use of a website 'hosted' by another party, it is suggested that the location of the website and the host's place of business should be of little significance. The location of the website itself is unlikely to provide any enduring connection to the contract. Moreover, since the contract is clearly between service provider and recipient, the place of business of a web host which acts as a mere channel of communication has no enduring connection to the contract of sale itself.

Suppose, however, that the goods or digitized products are themselves **21.88** sold through the website of another party in circumstances where it is not clear to the recipient who the original service provider is. This may occur if a service provider sells his goods or digitized products by use of an online auctioneer. Should the location of that website or the website owner itself be a material factor? It is suggested that the answer should be 'yes', if the website is located in the same state as the website owner's place of business. It may be said that the recipient might expect that a contract to purchase goods or digitized products online through an auctioneer company may be governed by the law of that auctioneer, in the absence of any further stipulation. Much is likely to depend upon how clearly the identity of the auctioneer, and of the original service provider, is stated on the website. If the identity and principal place of the auctioneer is clearly stated on the website, but little or no information is given as

---

[105] See also the criticisms made by H Kronke, 'Applicable Law in Torts and Contracts in Cyberspace', in K Boele-Woelki and C Kessedjian (eds), *Internet: Which Court Decides? Which Law Applies?* (The Hague: Kluwer, 1998) 65, at 85–86.
[106] In which case, the contract may not be one of 'sale'; see above, paras 10.44–53; and see below, paras 21.113–118.
[107] He may be merely providing recipients with a licence to use information: ibid.

to the identity of the original service provider, this ought to marginalize the importance of the latter's home law. As such, it is an argument for rebutting the presumption of Article 4(2). Both service provider and recipient might be said reasonably to contemplate that the law of the auctioneer's place of business should instead apply.

21.89 However, if the website is located in a state other than that where the website owner has its place of business, it is very unlikely that either party will contemplate that the law of the state where the website was located would govern the contract. Moreover, there is no reason to suppose that that law will have any real connection with the contract.

Conclusion on the Applicable Law in the Absence of Choice

21.90 If anything, Article 4(2) provides a more satisfactory result in the case of contracts concluded by electronic means than contracts concluded by conventional means. The one law that is likely to have an enduring connection with the contract is that of the service provider's place of business. Furthermore, this law is likely to be known to the recipient in most cases, as it will normally be disclosed on the service provider's website or email message. In contrast, a number of other objective factors seem no more relevant, and in some ways less relevant, where a contract is negotiated and/or concluded by electronic means. Moreover, where the products are themselves digitized, the nature of connections other than the parties' places of business is likely to be difficult to determine and often ephemeral and insignificant. The place of 'delivery' by the service provider, which may be a material factor in relation to 'conventional' goods becomes difficult to determine and of a much less significant territorial connection where digitized products are concerned. On the whole, the net effect is likely to be that Article 4(5) will be invoked rarely in e-sales. The law of the service provider's place of business is likely to hold sway. This has the added advantage of harmonizing with the 'country of origin' principle in the E-Commerce Directive.

6. Performance and Remedies

Article 10(1)(c) of the Rome Convention and the E-Commerce Regulations: Rescission for Lack of Opportunity to Correct Input Errors

21.91 A peculiar complexity caused by the E-Commerce Directive in relation to remedies for breach of contract should be mentioned here. One would expect the contractual remedies available for breach of contract to be determined by the applicable law of the contract. Article 10(1)(c) of the

Rome Convention so states. However, the UK enacting Regulations mirror those of the E-Commerce Directive in stating that where a recipient of a service places his order by electronic means, the service provider must acknowledge receipt of that order without undue delay by electronic means.[108] This rule applies 'unless parties who are not consumers have agreed otherwise'.[109] Moreover, the Regulations state that the service provider must make available to the recipient appropriate and accessible technical means to enable him to identify and correct input errors by technical means prior to placing the order.[110] The Regulations state that these rules do not apply where a contract is concluded solely by exchange of emails or similar individual communications.[111]

Article 15 of the Regulations then goes on cryptically to provide a right of **21.92** rescission to the recipient of the contract where he has not been granted by the service provider the means to identify and correct input errors.[112] This right of rescission exists 'unless any court having jurisdiction in relation to the contract in question orders otherwise on the application of the service provider'.[113] It is less than clear whether this provides a right of rescission in an English court regardless of the applicable law of the contract. It amounts to saying that rescission should be allowed unless the court decides, on the application of the service provider, that it should not be allowed. Nevertheless, the tone of the Regulations suggest that an English court would, in principle, grant rescission on this basis even if the applicable law did not permit it. The service provider might convince the court that it should not grant rescission on the facts. However, the ultimate decision seems to be that of the English court, effectively applying the law of the forum. That being so, reg 15 appears to override Article 10(1)(c) of the Rome Convention in this area.

Article 10(2)—Relevance of 'Manner of Performance' and the Law of the Place of Performance

It will be recalled that Article 10(1)(b) of the Rome Convention subjects **21.93** questions concerning performance to the applicable law of the contract. However, in respect of the manner of performance, Article 10(2) states

---

[108] reg 11; Art 11 of the Directive. reg 11(2)(b) states that where the service is an information society service, the provision of the service is itself sufficient to constitute the acknowledgment of receipt.

[109] reg 11(1).　　　　　　　　　　　　　　[110] reg 11(1)(b); Art 11(2) of the Directive.

[111] reg 11(3); Art 11(3) of the Directive.

[112] NB but not where the service provider has failed to acknowledge receipt (although, of course, if he has not done so, there may be no opportunity for the recipient to correct input errors).

[113] reg 15.

that 'regard shall be had' to the law of the place of performance.[114] A question might arise as to the application of this provision where the contract is for the provision of digitized products and payment is to be made by the recipient providing his credit or debit details by electronic means to the service provider.

21.94 A preliminary issue is the ascertainment of the place of performance. Where the transfer of digitized products is concerned, this may be no easy matter.[115] It was suggested above that the place of performance should be determined by the law of the forum when considering the applicable law in the absence of choice under Article 4.[116] This was because, at that stage, the applicable law is not known. However, when Article 10 comes to be applied, the applicable law will already have been determined. Since the place of performance is a term of the contract, that place should be determined, in cases of doubt, by the applicable law of the contract.

21.95 There might also be a question of what performance entails. For example, suppose that the parties conclude a contract for the provision of access to a digitized product which the customer will download. Kronke points out that performance could be the making of the data *accessible* to the customer. Alternatively, it could be the provision of guidance to the customer to ensure that he does actually receive a legible copy of the data.[117] Ultimately, this is a question of how the contractual obligation is to be performed and should, as such, be resolved by the applicable law of the contract.

21.96 It could be argued that given the delocalized nature of transfers of digitized products, it would be inappropriate to give effect to the law of the place of performance under Article 10(2) with respect to questions concerning the manner of performance. That state has a much weaker territorial connection to the contract than it would have where 'conventional' goods are to be delivered there. However, much depends upon the strength of the views of the place of performance. Suppose that the applicable law finds that the place of performance is the place of downloading[118] by the recipient of a digitized product. It may be that the downloading of the product in question is contrary to the law of the place of downloading. This might be because the material contained in

---

[114] See further above, paras 13.160–166.

[115] Kronke, n 105 above, at 79 makes the point that this will be especially complex when parties in different countries are co-operating on a project and are jointly responsible for performance.

[116] At paras 21.59–63.   [117] Kronke, n 105 above, at 79.

[118] Or, in the case of an email attachment, the place of receipt of the email.

the programme is considered to be, for example, subversive or immoral. There may be problems in requiring the service provider to perform the contract in that state, who may fear that he might fall foul of the law of the place of performance.[119] If the service provider attempts to refuse to provide the product once the contract is concluded or, once the product is transferred, the customer refuses to pay for it, it could be argued that the law of the place of performance should be applied to determine the consequences of such refusal. Put differently, if the downloading of the product in question is contrary to the mandatory rules of the state of performance, then there is a strong case for permitting application of that law under Article 10(2).

7. FORMALITIES FOR THE CONCLUSION OF A CONTRACT BY ELECTRONIC MEANS

Introduction

At first sight, it is not obvious that the choice of law rules on formalities **21.97** for the conclusion of a contract are affected by the sale being concluded by electronic means. However, it becomes apparent that there are certain complexities in applying the formality rules of Article 9 of the Rome Convention. More importantly, there are European Community instruments which appear to impose harmonized rules as to the formalities permitted where a contract is concluded by electronic means and the service provider is established in a Member State.[120]

Article 9 of the Rome Convention: where is the Place of Conclusion of a Contract?

Article 9 places importance on determining the place of conclusion of a **21.98** contract. If both parties were in the same state at the time of conclusion, that state's law or that of the applicable law must be satisfied on questions of formalities.[121] If the parties were in different states at the time of conclusion, the formality requirements of the law of the state where either party was, or of the applicable law must be satisfied.[122] However, 'Article 9 was thought up before contracts concluded by email had become common practice. But how is the place of conclusion to be determined for each

---

[119] Although, of course, the service provider may make no active decision on this. A party who enters his credit card details on the service provider's website may be able to download the product without any moderation by the service provider.

[120] See H Beale and L Griffiths, 'Electronic Commerce: Formal Requirements in Commercial Transaction' [2002] LMCLQ 467, esp the discussion of sale of goods at 478–479.

[121] Art 9(1) of the Rome Convention.   [122] ibid, Art 9(2).

party, this being one of the branches of the alternative proposed, when offer and acceptance are done by a simple exchange of emails?'[123]

21.99 This problem might have arisen in the past where the parties had allegedly concluded a contract by an exchange of fax. It could be argued that the problem is no more acute in the case of an exchange of emails. In most cases, even if the parties disagree as to the precise moment when the contract was concluded, they are likely each to have been in one state throughout the process of negotiation, so that it should be clear whether they were or were not both in the same state at the time of conclusion. The difficult case would be, for example, where A is based in State X and B in State Y and the process of negotiation takes place by email. What if A then travels to State Y on business and, whilst there, sends an email which is alleged to have been the act which concluded the contract between the parties?

21.100 It is suggested that the law applicable to the contract should determine when and where the parties concluded the contract. This is consistent with Articles 8(1) and 10 of the Rome Convention. Admittedly, it could be argued that the place of conclusion of the contract in Article 9 is a connecting factor, and connecting factors are normally determined by the law of the forum. However, this could lead to different states reaching differing conclusions as to the point of conclusion and, accordingly, whether the parties were in the same state at the time of conclusion. In an extreme case, that could lead to the formal validity of the contract 'limping', depending upon the views of the law of a particular forum. In our earlier example, suppose that the contract were governed by the law of State Z, by which it were formally invalid, and that it was also formally invalid by the law of State Y. It is formally valid by the law of State X. If the law of the forum is applied, one state might find that the contract was concluded when both parties were in State Y. Article 9(1) would then lead to the conclusion that the contract was invalid. However, if the law of another forum found that the contract had already been concluded when one party was in State X and the other in State Y, Article 9(2) would apply.

---

[123] See the European Commission's 'Green Paper on the Conversion of the Rome Convention of 1980 on the Law Applicable to Contractual Obligations into a Community Instrument and its Modernisation' COM/2002/0654 Final, para 3.2.12.2. One option mentioned in the Green Paper (para 3.2.12.3) would be that in a case where the place of conclusion could not be determined, the law of the state of habitual residence of the party that communicates acceptance of the contract could be added as an additional possible law which could be satisfied as to formalities. However, that law may be difficult for the other party to know or to foresee and may be said scarcely to help in the search for commercial certainty. Moreover, it is not obvious why the law of the party communicating its acceptance should be preferred to the law of the offeror.

Since that provision requires only the formality rules of *one* of States X, Y and Z to be satisfied, the contract would be formally valid.

Rather, the place of conclusion is a term of the contract and, as such, **21.101** should be determined by the applicable law of the contract. It is true that it was argued above, in the context of Article 4(5), that it may be necessary to apply the law of the forum to determine such factors as the place of conclusion, payment, delivery, etc.[124] However, the difference is that there the process is geared to *finding* the applicable law of the contract. Here, the applicable law will already have been determined and so it is quite logical for it to be used to determine the place of conclusion.

The Brussels I Regulation Contrasted: a Special Provision on E-Commerce and Choice of Court Clauses

Unlike the Rome Convention, the Brussels I Regulation lays down **21.102** autonomous formal requirements for the validity of a choice of court clause for a Member State. The Brussels Convention had stated that one of these alternative requirements was that the clause be in writing or evidenced in writing.[125] When this provision was re-enacted in the Brussels I Regulation,[126] a new provision was added. Article 23(2) of the Brussels I Regulation states: 'Any communication by electronic means which provides a durable record of the agreement shall be equivalent to "writing" '.[127] It may be that a similar provision will be adopted for choice of law clauses if and when the Rome Convention is converted into a Regulation.

The Content of a State's Formality Rules on E-Commerce

Of course, each state will have its own formality requirements for deal- **21.103** ings by electronic commerce, the detail of which is beyond the scope of this work.[128] However, the pressure for each state to have flexible, modern

---

[124] At paras 21.59–63. [125] Art 17(1) of the Brussels Convention.
[126] Art 23(1) of the Brussels I Regulation.
[127] This provision is discussed further above, paras 10.36–39.
[128] In England, see the Advice from the Law Commission on 'Electronic Commerce: Formal Requirements in Commercial Transactions', December 2001. This considers the formality requirements existing in various branches of commercial law and whether a requirement for 'writing', a 'signature' or 'document' might be satisfied by various modes of electronic communication (see para 1.5 of the Advice). The application of formality rules in the English sale of goods to electronic commerce is considered in Part 5 of the Advice. However, this is essentially concerned with the passing of property. See also the Judicial Studies Board's *Digital Signatures: Guidelines on the Creation and Use of Digital Signatures*: www.jsboard.co.uk/publications/digisigs.

rules which have adapted to the demands of e-commerce is intense. In England, the Law Commission has observed of the question whether formality rules may be met by means of electronic communication, that: 'If UK law does not keep up to date it may put UK companies at a competitive disadvantage, make the UK a less attractive place to do business, and mean that English law loses its status as the choice of law governing many international contracts'.[129]

EC Directive on a Community Framework for Electronic Signatures

21.104 A number of other uniform law provisions have been introduced by the European institutions to deal with the demands of electronic commerce which have an impact upon the choice of law process. One important source of such rules is Directive (EC) 1999/93 of the European Parliament and of the Council on a Community Framework for Electronic Signatures.[130] Its provisions have been given effect in the United Kingdom by the Electronic Communications Act 2000 and the Electronic Signatures Regulations 2002.[131] Section 7 of the Electronic Communications Act 2000 is of especial relevance for present purposes. It does not lay down formality rules as such. What it does do is state the effects that an electronic signature must be given in a Member State. It provides for the admissibility of electronic signatures to determine the authenticity of data. Section 7 reads thus:

(1) In any legal proceedings—
  (a) an electronic signature incorporated into or logically associated with a particular electronic communication or particular electronic data; and
  (b) the certification by any person of such a signature,
  shall each be admissible in evidence in relation to any question as to the authenticity of the communication or data or as to the integrity of the communication or data.
(2) For the purposes of this section an electronic signature is so much of anything in electronic form as—
  (a) is incorporated into or otherwise logically associated with any electronic communication or electronic data; and
  (b) purports to be so incorporated or associated for the purpose of being used in establishing the authenticity of the communication or data, the integrity of the communication or data, or both.
(3) For the purposes of this section an electronic signature incorporated into or associated with a particular electronic communication or particular electronic data is certified by any person if that person (whether before or after the making of the communication) has made a statement confirming that—

---

[129] Advice from the Law Commission, para 1.3.   [130] [2000] OJ L13/12.
[131] SI 2002/318.

(a) the signature,
(b) a means of producing, communicating or verifying the signature, or
(c) a procedure applied to the signature,
is (either alone or in combination with other factors) a valid means of establishing the authenticity of the communication or data, the integrity of the communication or data, or both.

Although matters of evidence and procedure fall outside the Rome Convention by Article 1(2)(h), this provision makes clear that a state cannot refuse to accept e-signatures as evidence of the *authenticity or integrity* of a communication. That seems to stop short of actually saying that such a signature shall be deemed to satisfy the formality rules of a particular state. For example, it would be possible to accept the authenticity of an electronic signature, but still to require the signature to have been created in the presence of two other witnesses.

The E-Commerce Directive: the Conclusion of Contracts by Electronic Means

The E-Commerce Directive comes the closest to laying down formality **21.105** rules as such for Member States. Recital 34 states that:

Each Member State is to amend its legislation containing requirements, and in particular requirements as to form, which are likely to curb the use of contracts by electronic means; the examination of the legislation requiring such adjustment should be systematic and should cover all the necessary stages and acts of the contractual process, including the filing of the contract; the result of this amendment should be to make contracts concluded electronically workable ... the acknowledgement of receipt by a service provider may take the form of the online provision of the service paid for.

Although this stops short of saying *positively* that conclusion of a contract by electronic commerce must be deemed to satisfy the formality requirements in the United Kingdom in every case, it does state *negatively* that the United Kingdom must not maintain formality rules which are likely to restrict e-commerce.

Article 9(1) of the Directive itself is phrased in more positive terms. It **21.106** specifically requires[132] that Member States shall ensure that their legal system allows contracts to be concluded by electronic means. Member States shall, in particular, ensure that the legal requirements applicable to the contractual process neither create obstacles to the use of electronic contracts nor result in such contracts being deprived of legal effectiveness and validity on account of their having been made by electronic means.

---

[132] Subject to the exceptions contained in Art 9(2).

This comes very close to an autonomous Community formality rule. If a Member State wishes to impose formality rules on the conclusion of a contract by e-commerce, they must not have the effect of impeding the flow of electronic communications.

21.107 More significantly, the provisions of the E-Commerce Directive apply to a service provider established in the United Kingdom. They can thus be said to *override* Article 9 to a certain extent. Indeed, it was argued in the discussion of the E-Commerce Directive above that the uniform rules must apply to a service provider established in a Member State and to that extent oust the existing choice of law rules specified by the Rome Convention. Suppose that a service provider based in England concludes a contract with a customer whilst both are in State X and that the contract is governed by the law of State X. By the law of State X, a contract of sale must be concluded in writing and, for this purpose, an electronic signature is not accepted as writing. Article 9(1) of the Rome Convention suggests that the contract is formally invalid. However, Article 9 of the E-Commerce Directive would suggest that this constitutes an impediment to the contractual process. As such, it *overrides* Article 9(1) of the Rome Convention and the contract should still be valid as to form.[133]

The E-Commerce Directive: Permission to Pursue Activities as an Information Service Provider

21.108 It should be noted that a Member State may not impose a formality requirement that an information service provider needs to obtain prior permission before pursuing such activities. Article 4(1) of the E-Commerce Directive states that:

Member States shall ensure that the taking up and pursuit of the activity of an information society service provider may not be made subject to prior authorisation or any other requirement having equivalent effect.

Again, this is a uniform rule which overrides the formality rules stipulated in Article 9 of the Rome Convention. It must be applied to a service provider established in a Member State.

Conclusion

21.109 The following conclusions are suggested:

(1) In principle, the rules of Article 9 of the Rome Convention apply to

---

[133] This is consistent with Art 20 of the Rome Convention, which expressly states that it is subject to relevant provisions of Community law.

contracts concluded by electronic commerce as they apply to other contracts.

(2) However, in practice, the E-Commerce Directive requires that Member States allow contracts to be concluded by electronic means. Moreover, their formality rules must not impede the operation of e-commerce. These rules apply where the service provider is established in a Member State. As such, they override any choice of law rules stipulated by Article 9 of the Rome Convention. In particular, if Article 9 of the Rome Convention leads to the conclusion that a contract is formally invalid by virtue of a formality rule which impedes the operation of e-commerce, the contract shall nevertheless be treated as valid as to form if the service provider is established in a Member State.

(3) The same applies if Article 9 of the Rome Convention leads to the conclusion that a contract is formally invalid because a service provider established in a Member State has not obtained prior authorization to engage in such activities.

(4) Where s 7 of the Electronic Communications Act 2000 is applicable, a UK court must accept electronic signatures as admissible evidence of the authenticity or integrity of an electronic communication.

(5) Where a service provider is not established in a Member State, the 'general' rules of Article 9 of the Rome Convention continue to apply. In such a case, the law applicable to the contract should determine the point at which the contract was concluded. If Article 9 of the Rome Convention leads to the conclusion that the contract is formally invalid because concluded by electronic means and the service provider is not established in a Member State, that conclusion shall be allowed to stand in an English court.

8. MANDATORY RULES AND PUBLIC POLICY

E-Commerce Directive

The general principles[134] governing mandatory rules[135] and public policy **21.110** are equally applicable to e-commerce sales. However, one specific point concerns the inter-relationship of the E-Commerce Directive and the Rome Convention. It was argued above[136] that although the E-Commerce

---

[134] See above, paras 13.271–294.

[135] See *People of the State of New York v World Interactive Gaming Corp* 714 NYS 2d 844 (NY County Sup Ct 1999); considered in Y Lim, *Cyberspace Law: Commentaries and Materials* (Oxford: OUP, 2002) 25–32. In that case, the Supreme Court of the State of New York County applied certain statutory provisions of New York law to an internet casino located in Antigua. See also Reed, n 7 above, at 199–223.

[136] At paras 21.15–23, 21.26–29, 21.32–34.

Directive lays down a 'country of origin' principle, this operates without prejudice to the application of the Rome Convention. Suppose that a service provider established in the United Kingdom concludes a contract which is stated to be governed by the law of State X. The law of State X will apply notwithstanding the country of origin principle. However, the contract will still be subject to the uniform rules laid down in the E-Commerce Directive.[137] These are, in effect, mandatory rules which override the governing law of the contract.[138]

21.111 More generally, an English court may be more willing to disapply the governing law in whole or in part where a service provider is established in England. English law is likely to have an enhanced interest in regulating the activities of those established in its own territory and in 'policing' their contracts.

Where the E-Commerce Directive is Inapplicable

21.112 The E-Commerce Directive does not apply where the information service provider is not established in a Member State. But suppose that an information service provider is established in State X, a non-Member State, by which law the contract is governed. Suppose that the law of State X prevents or seriously restricts the ability of a service provider to negotiate or contract by electronic means. Although the uniform rules of the E-Commerce Directive do not apply, it is likely that the English court would consider such restrictions as unacceptably restrictive of free trade. Accordingly, there is a strong possibility that it would disapply such provisions of State X which unduly restrict electronic commerce on public policy grounds.[139]

The Unfair Contract Terms Act 1977

21.113 One particular problem concerns the application of the Unfair Contract Terms Act 1977 to contracts relating to digitized products. It will be recalled that s 26 of the Act states that the Act does not apply to a contract for the sale of goods, or one pursuant to which possession or ownership of

---

[137] Art 20 of the Rome Convention establishes that: 'The Convention shall not affect the application of provisions which, in relation to particular matters, lay down choice of law rules relating to contractual obligations and which are or will be contained in acts of the institutions of the European Communities or in national laws harmonized in implementation of such acts'.

[138] Case C-381/98 *Ingmar CB LH v Eaton Leonard Technologies Inc* [2000] ECR I-9305.

[139] Pursuant to Art 16 of the Rome Convention.

goods passes.[140] There is some doubt[141] whether a contract whereby a party pays for the right to download[142] digitized products is a contract of sale[143] or a contract of service,[144] or neither.[145]

In the typical case, the customer is actually paying money in order to **21.114** obtain the right to use information.[146] A business to business contract for the transfer of digitized information will frequently take the form of a licensing agreement with ownership remaining with the licensor. As such, it cannot be described as a contract of sale.[147]

Nor is the contract easily described as one pursuant to which possession **21.115** or ownership passes. This is the view of Gringras, who argues that there is no passing of property in the information and no *physical* possession.[148] Indeed, it is difficult to argue that possession passes in a digitized product, where an indefinite number of 'copies' of that product can be downloaded from a web-server of the provider.

Accordingly, even in a business to business contract, the contract will be **21.116** potentially subject to the provisions of the Unfair Contract Terms Act 1977,[149] regardless of the law which otherwise governs it. However, it must be recalled that the Act will apply to a contract governed by a foreign law only if the term appears to the court to have been imposed in

---

[140] s 26(3)(a). This is subject to the provisos that the parties have their places of business or habitual residences in different states and that one of the further conditions in s 26(4) is met. See above, paras 13.302–308.

[141] See expert meeting Summary of Discussions, n 43 above, at 151.

[142] Or receive the product by email attachment.

[143] The sale of software has been treated as a sale of goods under the Vienna Convention: see Oberlandesgericht Kolenz of 17 September 1993 (translated at http://cisgw3.law.pace.edu/cases/930917gi.html); Landgericht Munich of 8 February 1995 (translated at http://cisgw3.law.pace.edu/cases/950208g4.html); Handelsgericht Zurich of 17 February 2000 (translated at http://cisgw3.law.pace.edu/cases/000217s1.html).

[144] See the ABA Cyberspace Report, 5. It will be recalled that the E-Commerce Directive speaks of a person marketing online as an information *service* provider and describes the other party as an information *service* recipient. In *1st Mover APS v Direct Hedge SA* [2003] IL Pr 31, the Eastern Court of Appeal, Denmark treated the design of a website for a customer as the provision of a service for the purposes of the Rome Convention.

[145] See above, paras 10.44–53.

[146] See expert meeting Summary of Discussions, n 43 above, at 5.

[147] *St Alban's City and District Council v International Computers Ltd* [1997] FSR 251, 265 (*per* Sir Iain Glidewell), CA; *Unisys Canada Inc v Imperial Optical Co* 44 BLR (2d) 311, aff'd 2 BLR (3d) 172, Ont CA. See generally RT Nimmer, 'Through the Looking Glass: What Courts and UCITA say about the Scope of Contract Law in the Information Age' (2000) 38 Duquesne L Rev 255. See further above, para 10.45.

[148] Gringras, n 59 above, at 45; and see ibid, at 64–66. See also the view of Sir Iain Glidewell in *St Alban's City and District Council v International Computers Ltd* [1997] FSR 251, 265, CA.

[149] Subject to s 27(1). It will be recalled that the Act does not apply if the contract is governed by the law of a part of the UK only by choice of the parties and would, but for that choice, be governed by a foreign law.

order to enable the person imposing it to evade the application of the Act.[150]

21.117 More difficult are cases where property is intended to pass in the computer software or some other intangible product. The example given in Chapter 10 on e-commerce and jurisdiction is of a bank that wishes to own bespoke software developed for the banking industry rather than having a licence for a fixed period.[151] Although there appears to be a 'sale', it is less clear whether what are sold are 'goods'.[152] The recipient does not purchase tangible property, but rather an intangible product, namely information.[153] The English Court of Appeal held in *St Alban's City and District Council v International Computers Ltd*[154] that computer programs are not 'goods' for the purposes of the Sale of Goods Act 1979. However, it has been suggested that software transferred online constitutes 'goods' for the purposes of the Vienna Convention.[155] Furthermore, the District Court of Munich has held that a computer software program that has been delivered and installed by the supplier constitutes 'goods' for the purposes of the Vienna Convention.[156] However, the definition adopted for the purposes of the Vienna Convention by overseas courts cannot be regarded as being decisive on this matter. The present question concerns the construction of a UK statute. It is highly likely that the *St Alban's* line of reasoning will be followed by an English court when construing s 26 of the Unfair Contract Terms Act 1977. Accordingly, it is suggested that a sale of a bespoke digitized product is not a sale of *goods*. If this is correct, it means that the exclusion in s 26 will not apply to such contracts.

21.118 This leaves the case where a digitized product, such as software, takes the form of a disk packaged in a box which is to be sent to the purchaser. This involves the delivery of tangible goods,[157] which may be bought via the internet but would have to be delivered by traditional means, such as by

---

[150] s 27(2)(a), discussed above, paras 13.314–319.   [151] At para 10.46.

[152] See above, paras 10.46–49, 10.53.

[153] See expert meeting Summary of Discussions, n 43 above, at 5.

[154] [1997] FSR 251, 265, CA.   [155] Schlechtriem, 23.

[156] Landgericht Munich of 8 February 1995 (translated at http://cisg3.law.pace.edu/cases/950208g4.html). But see the decision of the Court of Appeal, Cologne, Oberlandesgericht Köln of 26 August 1994 (translated at http://cisg3.law.pace.edu/cases/940826g1.html), where the development of software for an individual client was treated as a contract for the provision of services.

[157] One could argue that the disk is simply the container for an intangible product. However, the disk is a *tangible* and functional form of property upon which the information is stored and there can be no doubt that the disk itself is tangible. One cannot disentangle the disk itself and the information, since the recipient acquires both under the contract. As the recipient acquires tangible property in the form of the disk, which he uses to access the information, it is suggested that the whole contract is a 'sale of goods' for the purposes of s26 of the 1977 Act.

post. Although the purchaser requires the disk in order to access the information contained upon it, there is a transfer of tangible property involved. Accordingly, the contract may be described as a 'contract of sale of goods or . . . one under or in pursuance of which the possession or ownership of goods passes' within the meaning of s 26(3)(a) of the 1977 Act.[158]

9. CAPACITY

In principle, the law of capacity raises no particular problems with regard **21.119** to e-commerce.[159] However, Benjamin[160] points out that where the parties conclude a contract online and are both in the same country, the service provider is very unlikely to be aware of an incapacity of the recipient under another law. This means, pursuant to Article 11, that it will be rare that the service provider will be able to invoke his common law incapacity, unless of course, that incapacity arises by the same law as that of the place where the parties concluded the contract.

IV. CHOICE OF LAW IN TORT

1. INTRODUCTION

The choice of law rules in tort can in some ways raise still more extensive **21.120** challenges for e-commerce than the choice of law rules in contract. This is largely because they emphasize territorial and event-based considerations. It is necessary to determine where a tort took place.[161] However, where the tort in question was allegedly committed by electronic means of communication, which are in their nature somewhat delocalized, it can become very difficult to determine where the place of the tort should be.[162] Indeed, it has been argued that: 'If injury occurs in cyberspace. . . . the place of the wrong is cyberspace itself'.[163]

---

[158] The position is less clear where the software purchased is contained on a disk but this is not delivered to the recipient. The service provider might send round an employee to the recipient who brings the disk with him, installs the information on the recipient's computer and leaves with the disk. In such a case there is no transfer of the disk itself, which is tangible property, to the recipient and the contract may not be regarded as one for the ' . . . sale of *goods* or . . . one under or in pursuance of which the possession or ownership of *goods* passes' within the meaning of s 26(3)(a) of the 1977 Act (emphasis added). See further above, paras 10.51 and 10.53.

[159] The rules are discussed in detail above, paras 13.23–29.   [160] Benjamin, 25–084.

[161] Or, more accurately, the most significant element or elements of the events for the purposes of s 11(2)(c) of the Private International Law (Miscellaneous Provisions) Act 1995.

[162] See Thünken, n 27 above.   [163] Burnstein, n 1 above, at 93.

2. A Special Set of Rules for E-Commerce Torts?

21.121 An important policy consideration is whether the law of the place of the tort should, in e-commerce cases, be determined differently to where a tort is committed by 'normal' means of committing a tort.[164] In *Dow Jones & Company Inc v Gutnick*,[165] Kirby J referred to the comment of Lord Bingham in the context of the law of defamation that the internet will require 'almost every concept and rule in the field . . . to be reconsidered in the light of this unique medium of instant worldwide communication'.[166] In the same case, Gleeson CJ, McHugh, Gummow and Hayne JJ referred to the evidence of an expert witness called by Dow Jones, who observed that the internet was unlike any preceding communications technology, in that it 'enables inter-communication using multiple data-formats . . . among an unprecedented number of people using an unprecedented number of devices [and] among people and devices without geographic limitation'.[167]

21.122 Normally, one would expect the applicable law to be determined by the nature of the tort in question, not by the means of communication involved. 'It is not the task of private international law to pave the way for new factual (economic, sociological, technological) developments. Rather, new facts have to come to terms with existing rules of law unless society and legislators decide otherwise, and shape the rules accordingly.'[168] If e-commerce were to be subject to a special approach when ascertaining the governing law, then it would need to be demonstrated that it is a means of communication so fundamentally different to others developed in the past as to merit a distinct approach. However, it is doubtful whether this is the case. The point was well put by Kirby J in *Dow*:

Whilst the Internet does indeed present many novel technological features, it also shares many characteristics with earlier technologies that have rapidly expanded the speed and quantity of information distribution throughout the world. I refer

---

[164] See M Dogauchi, 'Law Applicable to Torts and Copyright Infringement through the Internet' in J Basedow and T Kono (eds), *Legal Aspects of Globalization: Conflict of Laws, Internet, Capital Markets and Insolvency in a Global Economy* (The Hague: Kluwer, 2000) 49.

[165] 210 CLR 575, HC of Australia; [2002] HCA 56, judgment of 10 December 2002, HC of Australia. See A Briggs, 'The Duke of Brunswick and Defamation by Internet' (2003) 119 LQR 210; U Kohl, 'Defamation on the Internet- Nice Decision, Shame about the Reasoning: *Dow Jones & Co v Gutnick*' (2003) 52 ICLQ 1049.

[166] *Dow Jones*, para 66, citing the Foreword to M Collins, *The Law of Defamation and the Internet* (Oxford: OUP, 2001) v.

[167] *Dow Jones*, para 14.

[168] Kronke, n 105 above, at 69–70.

to newspapers distributed (and sometimes printed) internationally; syndicated telegraph and wire reports of news and opinion; newsreels and film distributed internationally; newspaper articles and photographs reproduced instantaneously by international telefacsimile; radio, including shortwave radio; syndicated television programmes; motion pictures; videos and digitalized images; television transmission; and cable television and satellite broadcasting. Generally speaking, it is undesirable to express a rule of the common law in terms of a particular technology. Doing so presents problems where that technology is itself overtaken by fresh developments. It can scarcely be supposed that the full potential of the Internet has yet been realized. The next phase in the global distribution of information cannot be predicted. A legal rule expressed in terms of the Internet might very soon be out of date.[169]

It is suggested that we should seek to apply existing choice of law **21.123** principles in tort to those torts which are committed by electronic means. Choice of law rules are formulated with a view to identifying the most appropriate law to apply to a legal *cause of action or issue*. The nature of that cause of action or issue does not itself change merely because the tort in question is allegedly committed by electronic means. As such, it is suggested that it would be inappropriate to adopt separate choice of law rules for torts committed in such a manner. However, one must recognize that identification of traditional connecting factors, such as the place of the tort, can be especially problematic in relation to a method of communication that is in its nature delocalized. Accordingly, careful consideration has to be given as to the application of *existing* connecting factors to *new* forms of technology. It is to this issue of determining the place of the tort in an e-commerce case that we now turn.

3. The Place of the Tort: Place of Acting, Place of Damage, or Some Other State?

A further key issue is whether the law of the place of the tort should **21.124** normally involve reference to the place of acting by the service provider or to the place where the damage[170] is inflicted on the recipient.[171] The prime advantage of the former approach is that any other approach risks

---

[169] *Dow Jones*, para 125.

[170] Or, as in the case of a misstatement or misrepresentation, the communication to the recipient of the advice upon which he then relies detrimentally.

[171] See the Hague Conference on Private International Law, Prel Doc No 17 February 2002 entitled 'The Impact of the Internet on the Judgments Project: Thoughts for the Future', submitted by A Haines, esp 7–17. The document is accessible at http://hcch.e-vision.nl/index_en.php?act=progress.listing&cat=4.

paralyzing e-commerce.[172] A service provider could be potentially subject to tortious liability by the law of any state in which the recipient suffers damage.[173] It may be impossible to foresee which law of tort might be applied to determine the service provider's liability and, as such, seriously discourage the recipient from making use of electronic means of communication. Against this, a place of acting rule may be equally disadvantageous to the recipient. He may be powerless to prevent the service provider from engaging in activities legal by the place of acting but giving rise to tortious liability in the state where the recipient suffers damage. Moreover, if the essence of the tort in question is the communication of a statement to the recipient rather than the making of the statement itself, it would seem curious nonetheless to find that the tort occurred in the place where the action giving rise to the claim was committed.

4. A CASE STUDY: *DOW JONES & COMPANY INC V GUTNICK*

The Decision

21.125   A detailed consideration of the difficulty of ascertaining the place where a tort committed over the internet takes place was conducted by the High Court of Australia[174] in the jurisdiction case of *Dow Jones & Company Inc v Gutnick*,[175] a case which concerned cross-border libel. Many of the observations made in that case may be considered to be of general relevance to the choice of law process and to typical torts which might arise in the international sales context.[176]

21.126   The appellant, Dow Jones, printed and published the magazine *Barron's*.

---

[172] See the comment, in ibid, para 8, in connection with the law of jurisdiction: 'A "country of origin" approach is generally favoured by business interests and other Internet users who are concerned that they will be forced to defend themselves against actions in a multitude or jurisdictions with no ability to narrow the scope of such expansive jurisdiction claims since a website is globally transmitted and it is virtually impossible to determine where a customer is located with certainty'.

[173] Or, alternatively, any state in which the recipient accesses the information upon which he then relies detrimentally.

[174] For a consideration of other relevant Australian cases on the internet and jurisdiction, see Lim, n 135 above, Ch 2, esp 33–51.

[175] 210 CLR 575, HC of Australia; [2002] HCA 56, judgment of 10 December 2002, HC of Australia. See Briggs, n 165 above Kohl, n 165 above. See also A Joyce, 'Consequences of Publication on the Internet' (2003) 17 Corp Brief 5; N Shanmuganathan and L Caddy, 'Liability of Online Publishers following *Gutnick*' (2003) 153 NLJ 383. See further the discussion above, paras 10.111, 10.115, 10.142, 10.169, 10.171, 10.221, 10.249.

[176] Compare, in England, *Godfrey v Demon Internet* [2001] QB 201, QB; *Loutchansky v Times Newspapers Ltd* [2002] 2 WLR 640; *Harrods v Dow Jones* [2003] EWHC 1162, QB; *King v Lewis* [2004] EWHC 168, QB, affirmed [2004] EWCA (Civ) 1329.

It also offered *Barron's Online*, a subscription[177] service on the World Wide Web. One edition of *Barron's Online* in October 2000 contained an article containing references to a Mr Gutnick. Mr Gutnick alleged that these references to him were libellous and sued Dow Jones in the Supreme Court of Victoria in respect of the harm to his reputation in that state. Mr Gutnick was a Victorian resident with his business headquarters in that state, albeit with business interests elsewhere, including the United States. The question of the court's jurisdiction, and whether the proceedings in Victoria should be stayed, arose and eventually reached the High Court of Australia. One relevant question in determining whether to stay proceedings was whether the Victorian Court would have to apply a foreign law on the merits, or whether it would apply the law of the forum. In this way, a choice of law question was raised. The answer to that question was in turn to be found by determining where the allegedly defamatory material was published. This was no easy question. Dow Jones had its editorial offices in New York,[178] where the material was prepared on computers; however, the six servers onto which the relevant article was loaded were located in New Jersey. It was the law of New Jersey which Dow Jones alleged should apply to any libel action. Moreover, only a modest number of all the persons who paid for the internet subscription service had an Australian address. Yet, it was in respect only of the publication in Victoria and his loss of reputation in that state that Gutnick sued.

The 'policy' argument of Dow Jones was that a single law should govern **21.127** the conduct of a person who makes material available over the World Wide Web. That law should be the place of uploading,[179] at least where that place was not merely opportunistic.[180] 'The alternative, so the argument went, was that a publisher would be bound to take account of the law of every country on earth, for there were no boundaries which

---

[177] Kohl, n 165 above, at 1051, 1056, criticizes the judgment in *Dow Jones* for failing to distinguish between subscription sites and freely accessible sites. She comments (at 1051) that: 'The difference between subscription websites and freely accessible sites is that the publisher of a subscription site clearly has control over who accesses the site. This makes exposure to the laws of the subscribers clearly foreseeable and allows the publisher to exclude subscribers in legally inhospitable jurisdictions- an option inherently unavailable to freely accessible sites.' She goes on to note (ibid) that a publisher of a fee-paying subscription website profits from subscriptions to the site and that with the benefit of that profit should arguably go the burden of having to defend himself in the state of the subscriber. See also *Re The Maritim Trademark* (Case 416 0294/00) [2003] IL Pr 17, Landgericht (District Court), Hamburg.

[178] But was a Delaware corporation.

[179] i.e. the place where the web-server was located which stored the material. See further above, paras 10.60, 10.66–67.

[180] A word which would raise a whole set of further problems: see para 21 of *Dow Jones*.

a publisher could effectively draw to prevent anyone, anywhere, downloading the information it put on its web-server.'[181]

21.128 Against this, it could be retorted that whilst a service provider should be able to foresee which law will be applied to a tortious claim that might arise over the internet:

> . . . certainty does not necessarily mean singularity. What is important is that publishers can act with confidence, not that they be able to act according to a single legal system, even if that system might, in some sense, be described as their 'home' legal system. Activities that have effects beyond the jurisdiction in which they are done may properly be the concern of the legal systems in each place.[182]

Those who make information available on the internet know that the information will ordinarily be accessible worldwide.[183] It could be argued that with the benefit of global reach via the internet goes the burden of potential liability in a recipient's home state according. The point was made neatly by Callinan J in *Dow*:

> Some brands of motor cars are ubiquitous but their manufacturers, if they wish to sell them in different jurisdictions, must comply with the laws and standards of those jurisdictions. There is nothing unique about multinational business, and it is in that that this appellant chooses to be engaged. If people wish to do business in, or indeed travel to, or live in, or utilize the infrastructure of different countries, they can hardly expect to be absolved from compliance with the laws of those countries.[184]

21.129 Furthermore, 'the spectre of "global" liability should not be exaggerated. Apart from anything else, the costs and practicalities of bringing proceedings against a foreign publisher will usually be a sufficient impediment to discourage even the most intrepid of litigants.'[185] A service provider with no connections with a particular foreign state might simply ignore proceedings in that state, confident that it will be able to resist enforcement of any foreign judgment in its home state.[186]

21.130 In the event, the Court noted that the essence of the tort of libel is that it focuses on the damage to reputation. That damage does not occur unless and until material is published in comprehensible form, which in turn happens when downloaded[187] by a user from the web-server.[188] That pointed towards the place of downloading, Victoria, rather than the place

---

[181] para 20. See also para 117.   [182] para 24.   [183] para 39.
[184] para 186.   [185] para 165.   [186] ibid.
[187] On the possible relevance of the plaintiff's habitual residence, see Briggs, n 165 above, at 213.
[188] para 44.

of uploading, New Jersey, as the applicable law.[189] It took the view that rules of private international law should be affected by the nature of the tort in question, not by developments in the world of communications. After all, 'the problem of widely disseminated communications is much older than the Internet and the World Wide Web'.[190]

What can We Learn from *Dow* for Other Torts?

The decision in *Dow* demonstrates that the need to protect free trade and **21.131** predictability does not necessarily entail that the service provider must be subject to the law of his home state, or the state of uploading,[191] or the state where the service provider is when he uploads the information.[192] It is reasonably foreseeable that information posted on the internet may be accessed worldwide. If the service provider wishes to make clear that its website is aimed at a particular market in a particular state, it should do so expressly. Otherwise, it may be said that with the opening of a global market to the service provider comes the risk of being subject to the law of tort of a foreign state.

Dow also suggests that we should be seeking to apply established prece- **21.132** dents to determine the place of the tort in e-commerce cases. We should not be seeking special choice of law rules for torts committed over the internet. Choice of law rules are dictated by causes of action and by legal issues, not by forms of communication.

5. THE GOVERNING LAW—IS THERE A NEED FOR A SEPARATE APPROACH
FOR EACH TORT?

Dow Jones also shows that we cannot adopt a general rule as to where a **21.133** tort occurs which is capable of application to all torts. Different torts have differing constituent elements and it may not be appropriate to focus on the same connecting factor for all of them.

Attempts to apply a single rule of location (such as a rule that intentional torts are committed where the tortfeasor acts, or that torts are committed in the place where the last event necessary to make the actor liable has taken place) have proved unsatisfactory if only because the rules pay insufficient regard to the different kinds of tortious claims that may be made ... In the end the question is 'where in substance did this cause of action arise'?[193]

---

[189] See paras 24–28. Nor was the Court prepared to alter the longstanding rule that each act of publication constitutes a separate defamatory act in favour of a single publication rule which treated the activities of Dow Jones as a single actionable wrong and sought to ascertain where in substance that wrong took place.

[190] para 38.　　　　　　　　　　　　[191] That is, the place where the web-server is located.

[192] Or, in the case of email, the place where he is when he dispatches the message.

[193] para 43, *per* Gleeson CJ, McHugh, Gummow and Hayne JJ, citing *Distillers Co (Biochemicals) Ltd v Thompson* [1971] AC 458 at 468, PC; (Australia); *Voth v Manildra Flour Mills Pty Ltd* (1990) 171 CLR 538 at 567, HC of Australia.

Later, in the same case, Kirby J stated that:

> I agree that no single overly-generalized criterion such as the place of injury or damage, or the place where the defendant acted would be appropriate for identifying the place of the wrong in all actions of tort. Rather, the place of the wrong needs to be ascertained in a principled fashion, based on an analysis of the relevant legal issues in view of the rights, interests and legitimate expectations of the parties.[194]

21.134   Accordingly, we must ask what the constituent ingredients of an alleged tort are. We may then determine where the key element of the tort took place. In libel, established precedent tells us that each publication of material in each state gives rise to a separate tort in the place of publication. However, it will be different in an action based upon cross-border misstatement or misrepresentation. A negligent misstatement, negligent or fraudulent misrepresentation made by a service provider in England using a website located in France, which is communicated to a recipient in Germany and relied upon by him in Italy and Spain gives rise to a *single* potential tort and it will be necessary to determine where that one tort occurred.[195] Again, in a libel action, the material must be produced, but no potential claim will arise unless the defendant publishes the material. In a negligent misstatement, negligent or fraudulent misrepresentation action, the misstatement or misrepresentation must be made, but the service provider cannot expose itself to potential liability until it communicates the misstatement or misrepresentation to the recipient.[196] Even then, of course, the recipient will have no cause of action unless and until he relies upon that misstatement or misrepresentation to his detriment.

6. Section 11(1)—the Applicable Law of the Tort where All the Elements of the Events Occur in a Single State

21.135   It will be recalled that s 11 of the Private International Law (Miscellaneous Provisions) Act 1995, Part III states that if all the elements of the events occur in a single state, the applicable law is the law of the state in which the events constituting the tort occur.[197] A question arises here as to what are the relevant elements of the events constituting a tort. Suppose, for example, that a service provider resident in England makes

---

[194] *Dow Jones*, para 150.

[195] Or, more accurately, what the most significant element or elements of the events are for the purposes of s 11(2)(c) of the Private International Law (Miscellaneous Provisions) Act 1995.

[196] The Court in *Dow Jones* also suggested that more relevance might be placed upon the actions of the defendant for torts where the defendant's state of mind is relevant, such as negligence.

[197] See above, para 17.26.

a representation via the internet using a server located in England. The representation is viewed by a customer in France, who relies upon that misrepresentation. There can be little doubt that the relevant elements do not occur in a single state. But what if the representation were made by a service provider resident in England to a customer also resident in England who relies upon the representation in England, but the service provider had used a website or email domain located in France? Does this mean that the elements constituting the tort occur in more than one state, with the result that s 11(1) does not apply? Again, what if the English customer had happened to receive the representation when he had downloaded it to a computer whilst on a business trip to France?

In essence, the question is whether events such as the place of upload- **21.136** ing[198] and the place of downloading can be said to be elements of the tort itself. It is suggested that the answer in relation to these should be 'yes'. After all, s 11(1) does not indicate that only 'substantial' elements of the events, or ones which do not seem arbitrary, may be considered relevant. In a misstatement or misrepresentation action, the making of the statement or representation will be a key event. It is arguable that the statement or representation is made available by the uploading of the material and its storing on a web-page located on a particular server. Equally, the recipient will have no cause of action unless and until he views the representation. It is difficult to see how the place where this occurs could not be described as one of the events constituting the tort. Accordingly, it is suggested that where any elements of the chain of events giving rise to the tort occurs in different states, s 11(1) should not apply and s 11(2) should instead be applied.

In contrast, the place where the service provider is located at the time **21.137** that it uploads the information[199] cannot be described as an event.[200] Accordingly, if a service provider is located in France when it uploads information to a web-server located in England and it is downloaded and detrimentally relied upon by the recipient in England,[201] it is suggested that s 11(1), rather than s 11(2) is applicable, since all the elements of the *events* occur in one state, namely England.

---

[198] That is, the location of the server which stores the information. In *Dow Jones*, this was New Jersey, where the server which stored the information was located.

[199] In *Dow Jones*, much of the information was prepared in New York before being uploaded to a server in New Jersey. In that scenario, 'the place where the service provider is located when it uploads the information' refers to New York.

[200] The same is true of the residence of the parties.

[201] Causing loss which is entirely felt by the recipient in England.

7. Section 11(2)—The Applicable Law of the Tort where Elements of the Events Occur in More than One State

Personal Injury

21.138 It will be recalled that where elements of the events constituting the tort occur in different states, s 11(2) applies, and that the sub-rule applicable depends upon the nature of the damage claimed. It is possible that the goods complained of could give rise to personal injury. For example, suppose that a buyer purchases machinery over the internet from the seller, which the seller agrees to install for the buyer. If the installation is defective, it may cause personal injury to the buyer. It is possible that he may wish to sue the seller for negligence. However, this raises no internet specific issue, since the damage itself is not inflicted by electronic means. The applicable law under s 11(2)(a) is the place where the injury was sustained by the claimant.

Damage to Property

Damage to the claimant's computer

21.139 Usually, the damage complained of in the sales[202] context will be either damage to the property itself, or economic loss. In relation to the former, s 11(2)(b) clearly points to the place where the property was when it was damaged. This will not create any particular difficulty in the e-commerce context where the goods are tangible in nature.

21.140 It must also be the case that where software is ordered via the internet, but is physically delivered to the purchaser upon a disk, there is a transfer of property. If the disk does not work properly, it may be described as

---

[202] Of course, the recipient may wish to sue the manufacturer of a digitized product which simply fails to run when downloaded by the recipient because it is in some way corrupted. In the case of a product liability claim arising from the transfer of a bespoke product by electronic means, where is the property when it is damaged? It is true that the property is designed for use on the recipient's computer. However, one might also say that the digitized products either are or are not 'damaged' at the point when the manufacturer places them on the market. That place of damage may be said to the state where the manufacturer makes the products available to the service provider. Even then, it is still not clear to which state this refers. It is certainly unlikely that the recipient will be able to foresee where this state might be. A preferable approach may be to say that the products are manufactured for ultimate transfer to a recipient transfer. Without the transfer to the recipient, that party has no claim in tort. Accordingly, the products should be free from defect at the time when they are made available to the recipient. One might argue that they are made available to the recipient on the server from which they may be downloaded. This is consistent with the argument made below, paras 21.211–238, esp paras 21.224–228, that the situs of digitized products is the location of the server onto which the product is uploaded.

damaged and s 11(2)(b) will again apply. However, the application of s 11(2)(b) raises no e-commerce specific question in this context.

What, though, if the product in question is digitized and is downloaded **21.141** by the recipient? One might wonder whether a downloaded programme is in fact 'property', since it may exist on a server and be capable of replicating itself an indefinite number of times by any person who wishes to pay to download it. It could simply be described as information that is not properly supplied. One might argue that the act of downloading does not give the recipient property rights in the product, but merely the licence to access and use that product. If that licence is personal to the recipient and cannot endure against third parties, it does not have the character of a property right. If so, s 11(2)(b) of the 1995 Act will not apply.[203]

However, where a bespoke digitized product is ordered by a customer **21.142** that wishes to own that product rather than having a licence for a fixed period, it is argued above[204] that there is a sale of that product and property will pass to the purchaser when the product is transferred by electronic means. It is a moot point whether this can be described as a sale of 'goods'. However, it seems clear that it involves a transfer of 'property' rights. As such, s 11(2)(b) will apply if that property is in some way 'damaged'.

Suppose that a service provider resident in State A contracts with a recipi- **21.143** ent resident in State B for the transfer of a computer program. The service provider happens to be located in State C when it uploads the program onto a server located in State D. It is then downloaded by the recipient in State E. Suppose that the product contains a virus which does serious damage to the recipient's computer, or that the service provider mis-represented whether the product was compatible with the operating system used on the recipient's computer. The recipient may wish to bring a negligence action against the service provider in respect of the damage caused to his computer[205] by the downloading of the purchased product.

---

[203] See Gringras, n 59 above, at 45 and 159; Sir Iain Glidewell in *St Alban's City and District Council v International Computers Ltd* [1997] FSR 251, 265. See further above, paras 10.45 and 10.53, and the discussion, above, paras 21.114–116, of the Unfair Contract Terms Act 1977.

[204] At paras 10.46–49, 10.53 and 21.117.

[205] In such a case, the recipient may effectively have a choice whether to sue in respect of the damage to the digitized products (which may be in the state where the server is located onto which they have been uploaded and are stored), or the damage to the computer itself. He is likely to sue in respect of the latter where the damage to the computer also results in consequential financial loss, or simply where the extent of the damage to the computer exceeds the amount of compensation which could be recovered for the damage to the product itself.

Two questions arise: is the computer 'damaged'; and where does the 'damage' occur? It seems difficult to dispute that the computer itself is damaged. It may or may not be possible to eliminate the virus from the computer's hard drive. However, the operation of the computer itself will be compromised by the virus. It may also result in the loss of information contained on the computer, the compromising of the computer's security, and the possible slowing down or paralysis of the workings of the computer.

21.144 It must be the case that this damage to property occurs at the place where the computer is located at the time at which the product is downloaded which infects it with a virus. So if a recipient, habitually resident in State B, happens to download the 'infected' digitized product to his laptop computer whilst on a short business trip to State E, the latter is the place where the computer is 'damaged' for the purposes of s 11(2)(b). If it is retorted that this may result in a degree of choice of law shopping,[206] and a certain degree of arbitrariness as to the law of the place where the property is damaged, then there are two responses. First, that s 11(2)(b) uses the connecting factor of the place where the property is damaged, and, in e-commerce cases, this is often likely to produce a somewhat arbitrary conclusion, given the de-localized nature of the transaction. Second, in so far as the other party can show that the factors which connect the tort to another state render it substantially more appropriate for that other state's law to govern the claim, the general choice of law rule in s 11(2)(b) may be displaced by that other law pursuant to s 12.

Damage to the claimant's computer and consequent economic loss

21.145 It is true that the recipient may not wish to sue solely for the damage to the computer itself. He may also wish to sue for economic loss caused by the damage to his computer. He may, for example, lose several months worth of work, or a confidential business plan or design stored on the computer. It could be argued that the law which governs this part of the claim is not covered by s 11(2)(b), which deals only with damage to property. However, it is suggested that the *basis* of the action is still damage to the computer itself. Any claim for economic loss is contingent upon the damage to the property in the first place. As such, it is suggested that the entire claim should be governed by the law of the place where the property was at the time of damage, pursuant to s 11(2)(b).

---

[206] In the sense that the English courts might apply a different law to that of other states elsewhere.

Economic Loss

It is particularly difficult in e-commerce cases to determine which law **21.146** should apply where the damage is economic in nature.[207] Section 11(2) refers to the place where the most significant element or elements of the events occur. Where those events occur over the internet or by email, it is unclear what significance should be attached to the various connecting factors. Although it is clear that, at the present state of the law, separate choice of law rules are not to be adopted for e-commerce torts, s 11(2)(c) determines the applicable law of the tort, in cases other than personal injury or damage to property, as being that where the most significant elements of the events occur. This is a flexible test. That necessarily raises the question of which event or events are the most significant where the tort involves electronic communication.

Of course, s 11(2)(c) does allow a court to look at more than one element of **21.147** the events before determining the applicable law. This means that it need not treat any one element as decisive. Indeed, in *Protea Leasing Ltd v Royal Air Cambodge Ltd*[208] and in *Thierry Morin v Bonhams & Brooks Ltd*,[209] the court emphasized that s 11(2)(c) does not place reliance upon a single connecting factor. Rather, the whole pattern of the events must be examined. As such, one cannot generalize, even for a particular tort, as to which law will govern.

Nevertheless, in order to achieve a measure of certainty, it is suggested **21.148** that it would be preferable for English courts habitually to regard a particular connecting factor as the most significant one for determining the governing law of the tort in e-commerce cases falling within the scope of s 11(2)(c). If a party then argues that another state is substantially more closely connected to the dispute on the facts, that argument can be made pursuant to s 12 of the Act and the rule of displacement. In that way, something resembling a rebuttable presumption of the applicable law can be obtained, which enables the parties to foresee, without going to court, which law might apply. At the same time, such an approach is sufficiently flexible to give way in appropriate cases. Accordingly, we will now consider the merits and demerits of the principal connecting factors which might exist in an e-commerce tort case.

---

[207] But see the Geneva Round Table, Prel Doc No 7, n 43 above, at, 22.
[208] [2002] EWHC 2731, The Times, 13 January 2003, QBD (Comm).
[209] [2003] IL Pr 25, at 431, *per* Hirst QC (sitting as a Deputy Judge of the High Court); aff'd in the Court of Appeal by Mance LJ, [2003] EWCA Civ 1802 at [18], [2004] IL Pr 24 at 396–397.

21.149 Many of the pros and cons of the connecting factors considered below were considered at length in Chapter 10 on jurisdiction[210] and e-commerce and are equally relevant here. For example, the generic comments there about the possibility of manipulation, arbitrariness or the unforeseeable nature of a particular connecting factor, are equally relevant here. For this reason, the reader is referred to that earlier discussion[211] and rather briefer comment about the connecting factors is offered here.

8. Ascertainment of the Applicable Law of the Tort for the Purposes of s 11(2)(C)

Law of the Forum

21.150 The argument for the law of the forum is based on the view that it may be very difficult to ascertain the most significant element of the events in e-commerce cases. As such, the law of the forum applies in default. However, this view must be rejected.[212] It is true that it may be difficult to select between different laws, each of which has a connection to the events. Nevertheless, a principled basis must be found for selecting between them. To apply the law of the forum would be the worst option. It may lead to a law of no connection to the tort. It would also create a forum shopper's paradise, if English courts were to apply a law other than that which would be applied in any other state worldwide. From the service provider's point of view, it may render him liable to a law which is wholly unpredictable.

The Place of Uploading

21.151 The pros and cons of this connecting factor have been considered elsewhere.[213] For present purposes, we should note that, arguably, the place of uploading[214] provides the most significant, enduring connection to a tort committed by electronic means. Uploading is clearly an 'event', and the

---

[210] On the question of whether the place of the tort should be determined in the same manner for the purposes of common law jurisdiction and choice of law, see *David Syme & Co Ltd v Grey* (1992) 38 FCR 303 at 314 (Australia). In that case, Gummow J said that there was no clear reason why they should be. See also *Dow Jones v Gutnick* 210 CLR 575, HC of Australia; [2002] HCA 56, para 145, Kirby J. It should be noted that, strictly speaking, s 11(2)(c) of the 1995 test is based upon the most significant element or elements of the events, rather than upon the place of the tort.

[211] Above, paras 10.138–161, 10.167–172.

[212] Surprisingly, there was some support for the law of the forum at the Geneva Round Table: see Prel Doc No 7, n 43 above, at 22.

[213] See the discussion above, paras 10.60, 10.66–67, 10.141–150, 10.164, 10.171–172; and see the discussion in relation to choice of law in contract, above, paras 21.80–83.

[214] That is, the state where the server is located to which the product is uploaded.

focus of the choice of law rules[215] is on events, not the location of people involved in those events. The location of the server to which the information is uploaded is foreseeable to the service provider and does not force him to comply with a plethora of tort laws. The act of uploading will also be a key stage in any tort action deriving from a misrepresentation or negligent piece of advice uploaded onto a website.

An obvious problem is that the location of the server to which the infor- **21.152** mation is uploaded is too easy for the service provider to manipulate. By using or locating his server in a certain state, the service provider might avoid being subject to rigorous tortious liability. Moreover, as the High Court of Australia pointed out in *Dow*, any attempt to say that this law should not be applied where it appears that the location of the server was manipulated by the service provider creates more problems than it solves as to what constitutes manipulation and builds in a further layer of uncertainty. Nor will this connecting factor inevitably point to a single state. Where the service provider uses a series of mirror sites, there may be more than one place of uploading. Callinan J pointed out in *Dow* that: 'Matter may be stored on more than one web-server, and with different web-servers at different times. Different parts of a single web page may be stored on different web-servers in different jurisdictions.'[216]

It is true that the uploading of material by the service provider onto a **21.153** server is a key element of the events giving rise to a claim. However, it does not seem to be a cause of loss in itself. Without the downloading of the relevant material by the recipient, there is no cause of action in tort. The focus of the choice of law rules in s 11 of the 1995 Act is principally on the causing of immediate damage to the recipient,[217] rather than the place where the events that gave rise to that damage began.

A practical consequence of use of the law of the place of uploading is that **21.154** it will lead to a marked and, arguably, unattractive increase in use of the law of a state of the United States in English courts. This is because a disproportionate number of servers are located in the United States.[218] This law may be applied to the detriment of the law of the England,[219]

---

[215] And s 11(2)(c) in particular, which is our present concern.

[216] *Dow Jones*, para 199.

[217] It is true that s 11(2)(c) does not say this, but s 11(1) and 11(2)(a) and (b) support the view that this is the general philosophy of the provisions. See also the UK's position on the Preliminary Draft 'Rome II' Regulation, (www.lcd.gov.uk/consult/general/eurocom.htm), para 5, where the UK expresses its support that 'the law of the place of the tort should apply and this should be the place where the direct damage or injury was sustained and not the place where the conduct leading to the tort occurred'.

[218] See *Defamation And The Internet: a Preliminary Investigation*, n 1 above, para 4.24. See also D Rolph, 'The Message, Not the Medium: Defamation, Publication and the Internet in *Dow Jones & Co Inc v Gutnick*' (2002) 24 Sydney L Rev 262, (cited by the Law Commission at 273).

[219] Or, of course, on appropriate facts, to the detriment of another law.

even though one or both parties to the sales contact might be resident in England, or the recipient may have downloaded the relevant information in England.[220]

The Place where the Service Provider is Located when it Uploads the Information

21.155 Although the act of uploading is clearly an event, the place where the service provider is located when it uploads the information cannot be said to be an 'event'. To the question 'what happened?', a sensible answer is not 'the service provider was located in New York'.

21.156 There are further serious disadvantages to use of this law to govern a tort. The place where the service provider is located at the time when it uploads to a server may be entirely unpredictable from the recipient's point of view, especially if it does not coincide with the place of establishment or residence of the service provider, or the location of the server on to which the information is uploaded. Again, it is capable of manipulation not just to avoid the clutches of the service provider's home law, but of *any* law which the service provider does not wish to satisfy. It is suggested that this connecting factor should not be regarded as significant for the purposes of s 11(2)(c).

The Place where the Recipient is when he Downloads the Information

21.157 If one were to apply a place of downloading rule, it is necessary to define what one means by this. It could be argued that if the receipt is by email, the relevant law is that of the server on which the recipient's mailbox is stored, rather than the place where the recipient physically was when he downloaded the information. Section 14(3)(a) of the Australian Electronic Communications Act 1999 states that if the addressee of an electronic communication has designated an information system for the purpose of receiving electronic communications, the time of receipt is, unless otherwise agreed, when the communication enters that information system. The downloading to that information system gives the recipient the means of access to the information. However, it is not the *means* of access to the information, but the *transmission* of that information to the recipient which gives rise to the claim. As such, it is suggested that it is preferable to regard the state where the recipient is located at the time of downloading as the place of downloading.[221]

---

[220] Although, of course, the general rule can be displaced under s 12 in appropriate cases. However, this would not operate unless it were 'substantially more appropriate' to apply another law.

[221] See further Reed, n 7 above, at 193–195.

There may be a problem if a person downloads information to his com- **21.158**
puter using the internet whilst in State A, but does not read it until he
reaches State B. In such a case, it is suggested that the relevant law is still
that of State A. Once the information is downloaded in State A, the recipient has the means of access to it and all relevant steps have been taken for
its communication to him. The reading by him of the information in
another state is not a material step in the bilateral act of communication of
the information by the sender to the recipient.

There is much to be said for a rule based upon the place where the recipi- **21.159**
ent was when he downloaded the information. The downloading of
material will usually be an essential element of a tort claim where the tort
is committed by electronic means. Its focus on the defendant's actions
seems more in keeping with the general approach, both at common law
and under the Act, than does use of the place where the act giving rise to
the damage occurred.

It is true that the place of downloading may be unpredictable from the **21.160**
service provider's point of view, since 'there is presently no effective way
for a website operator to determine, in every case, the geographic origin of
the Internet user seeking access to the website'.[222] Accordingly, the service
provider may be forced potentially to comply with the tort laws of every
state in the world. It is also true that the party downloading information
might successfully mask its identity and/or location.[223] There again, if a
service provider places material on a website, without stating that it is
intended for parties downloading the information in a certain state, then
the service provider stands to benefit from the conclusion of contracts
worldwide and it is reasonably foreseeable that he may be exposing himself to liability in the state of downloading by any recipient. Furthermore,
it is possible to exaggerate the likelihood of the service provider being
exposed in practice to a plethora of different tort laws and liabilities. It
might expressly state to whom a representation is made. Moreover, the Law
Commission has pointed out that the theoretical possibility of multiple,
insubstantial claims being brought in England from a series of 'trivial'
torts said to have occurred around the globe is minimized in the United
Kingdom by the ability to strike out a case as an abuse of process.[224]

One might object that a cause of action may not be generated unless **21.161**
and until the recipient detrimentally relies on, say, a misstatement or

---

[222] *per* Kirby J in *Dow Jones*, para 84.

[223] '[T]he Internet has recently witnessed a rapid growth of technologies ('anonymising
technologies') that enable Internet users to mask their identities (and locations). In the case
of a buyer or recipient, one cannot rely on his credit card details, as a UK resident might, for
example, obtain a credit card from a US bank' (ibid, para 86).

[224] See *Defamation and the Internet: a Preliminary Investigation*, n 1 above, esp paras
4.19–4.20.

misrepresentation on the service provider's website that he has down-loaded. However, the essence of the tort might be said to be the making and communication of a misstatement or misrepresentation. Once this has been done, the question whether the recipient might choose detri-mentally to rely on that statement or representation is wholly outside the service provider's control and the place of detrimental reliance even more difficult potentially to predict than the place of downloading.[225]

21.162 There is also the theoretical risk that the place of downloading will be manipulated by the recipient for its own ends. However, it would be easy to overstate the likelihood of a party choice of law shopping in such a calculated way. Moreover, s 11(2) points only to a general rule. In circum-stances where the place of downloading has little connection to the tort, this law is likely to give way under the rule of displacement in s 12.

The Place where the Service Provider is Established or Habitually Resident

21.163 A number of things can be said in favour of this connecting factor.[226] First, it is very difficult for the service provider to manipulate this law. Second, this law necessarily provides a significant connection to a particular state, whereas, in contrast, the place of uploading, downloading or location of the service provider at the time of uploading may be arbitrary. The Geneva Round Table gathering concluded that in tort 'it is difficult to depart from one of the two connecting factors: defendant's or victim's habitual residence'.[227] Third, it harmonizes with the philosophy of the E-Commerce Directive, which establishes a 'country of origin principle' that an information service provider established in a Member State is required to comply with the law of that state, and only that state, for matters within the 'co-ordinated field'.[228] Fourth, it also harmonizes with the approach taken to ascertaining the applicable law of a contract in the

---

[225] See further below, paras 21.175–182.

[226] See above, paras 10.70–71, 10.119, 10.151–159; see also the discussion in relation to choice of law in contract, above, paras 21.50–57. This connecting factor also attracts the support of the Geneva Round Table, Prel Doc No 7, n 43 above, at, 21–22. See further s 14(5)(b) of the Australian Electronic Communications Act 1999, which states that unless otherwise agreed, an electronic communication is deemed to have been received at the place where the addressee has its place of business.

[227] Press Release on the Geneva Round Table on Electronic Commerce and Private Inter-national Law, available at http://hcch.e-vision.nl/upload/wop/press01e.html, Recommenda-tion No 8. The remark was made in connection with the law of jurisdiction, but may be equally applicable to choice of law.

[228] Thünken, n 27 above, at 941 favours an interpretation of s 11(2)(c) of the Act that leads to the application of the law of the place where the service provider is established. This is partly on the basis that such an approach harmonizes with the country of origin principle in the E-Commerce Directive.

absence of choice under Article 4 of the Rome Convention, where Article 4(2) leads to a rebuttable presumption in favour of the law of the principal place of business of the seller or service provider. This, in turn, reduces certain classification problems[229] where it is unclear if, for example, a claim based upon a negligent misstatement or misrepresentation is to be characterized as contractual or tortious. Fifth, in the case of a corporate service provider, the place of establishment of the service provider may very well be known to the recipient. The place of business of the service provider is likely to be stated on the service provider's website, or at the bottom of its email communications. Sixth, this law avoids the potentially stifling effect on free trade of subjecting the service provider to the laws of any state where the material which he makes available happens to be accessed.

However, a number of things can be said against regarding the place **21.164** where the service provider is established or habitually resident as a significant connecting factor. First, English courts ascertain the applicable law of a tort by looking at the events which constitute it.[230] It cannot be said that the residence or place of establishment of the service provider is an 'event'. It is true that one could circumvent this problem by saying that we are still looking for the most significant element of the events, and it is simply that, in e-commerce torts, the most significant event is presumed to take place in the state of the service provider's establishment. This, though, is little more than a legal fiction. If it is sought to apply the law of the service provider's place of establishment, we should arguably do so directly. Since this would need a special provision to be written into the Private International Law (Miscellaneous Provisions) Act 1995, it is suggested that, at present, this connecting factor cannot and should not be regarded as the most significant element of the events for the purposes of s 11(2)(c). Second, whilst it is true that the place of the service provider's establishment may be known to the recipient, this may be much less likely if the service provider is a sole trader or private individual. In that case, the law of that party's habitual residence may not be discernible on his website and application of the law of that residence may defeat the expectations of the recipient. Third, we saw in the *Dow* case that the fear of stifling e-commerce if the law of the recipient's home state, or the law of the place of downloading, is applied is somewhat exaggerated. Moreover, there is a legitimate argument that with the benefit of reaching a wider audience via the internet goes the risk of being subjected to the law of a foreign state. Fourth, the law of the service provider's place of

---

[229] Though only, of course, where there is no express or implied choice of law to govern the 'contract'.

[230] Especially where s 11(2)(c) of the 1995 Act is applicable.

establishment is effectively a notional place where the act giving rise to the damage takes place. We have already seen that English law typically does not regard this place as that where a tort occurs, but instead tends to focus on the infliction of the loss itself.[231]

21.165 On balance, it is fair to say that the law of the service provider's place of establishment does have a potentially significant connection to e-commerce torts, one which is arguably greater than the law of the place where the service provider is located at the time that it uploads material. However, the place of establishment should not be considered as a relevant connecting factor for the purposes of s 11 of the 1995 Act. Rather, it is suggested that this is a factor to which significant weight should be given when considering the application of the rule of displacement in s 12 of the Act.

The Place where the Recipient is Established or Habitually Resident

21.166 The advantage of this law is that it focuses on the person upon whom damage is inflicted. This appears broadly consistent with the 'general' approach in the English conflict of laws to determining the law applicable to a tort. Furthermore, this law has a substantially more enduring connection to a particular jurisdiction than the place of downloading might have. The latter may be arbitrary, if the material is downloaded in a particular state whilst the recipient is temporarily located overseas and logs into a computer in that overseas state. Again, the place of residence or establishment is very difficult to manipulate, in contrast to the place of uploading, downloading or the location of the service provider at the time of uploading. Moreover, the concern that application of the law of the recipient might stifle electronic communications may be exaggerated. It may also be said that a service provider who makes material available by electronic means may obtain the benefit of business with recipients worldwide. Furthermore, the recipient might reasonably expect that his 'home' law would apply to a tort claim arising from dealings with a service provider who publishes material freely available by electronic means.

21.167 In the context of internet libel, the law of the recipient's residence has attracted some support in *Dow* from Kirby J, who commented that:

> At least in the case of the publication of materials potentially damaging to the reputation and honour of an individual, it does not seem unreasonable, in principle, to oblige a publisher to consider the law of the jurisdiction of that person's

---

[231] Compare s 11(2)(a) and (b) of the 1995 Act. See also above, paras 17.27–32.

habitual residence.. In its . . . report on choice of law, the ALRC concluded that 'residence is the best option for a choice of law rule for defamation'.[232]

Kirby J went on to point out that this provides an objective criterion, which would tend to give effect to the expectations of the parties and will usually be the place where the recipient suffers the most harm.[233]

Against this, the UK Law Commission expressed disapproval of this con- **21.168** necting factor. Its 1990 Report observed that:

> A final possibility would be to limit the claimant's choice to the law of their home jurisdiction. During consultation, this received relatively little discussion. It was felt to be an uncomfortable halfway house. Publishers would still be required to be familiar with the law of every domicile of every person discussed, expressly or by implication. On the other hand, claimants whose reputations genuinely crossed boundaries would be caught by technicalities of the law of the country in which they were said to be habitually resident.[234]

It may also be objected that s 11(2) focuses on events, and that the place of **21.169** habitual residence or establishment is not an event. To this, it may be retorted that, in e-commerce torts, the place of the recipient's habitual residence is *deemed* to be the place where the most significant element of the events occurs.[235] This, however, is something of a legal fiction and is tantamount to applying a new connecting factor, the residence of the recipient, as the governing law of a tort. That might be said to be effectively a new choice of law rule for e-commerce torts; and we have already seen that the 1995 Act does not envisage that choice of law rules are determined by the particular means of communication used.

Finally, one might observe that the place of business or residence of the **21.170** recipient may be difficult for the service provider to determine. Unless it asks the recipient for this information,[236] the service provider might find itself subject to a law whose application it could not have foreseen. In contrast, the place of business of the service provider will normally be stated on its website or email correspondence.

---

[232] *Dow Jones*, para 134. See Australian Law Reform Commission, *Choice of Law*, Report No 58 (1992) at 58; see also the earlier Australian Law Reform Commission, Unfair Publication: Defamation and Privacy, Report No 11 (1979) at 191. See further *Australian Broadcasting Corp v Waterhouse* (1991) 25 NSWLR 519.

[233] *Dow Jones*, paras 165–167, relying upon the judgment of Samuels JA in *Australian Broadcasting Corp v Waterhouse* (1991) 25 NSWLR 519, 539. In the latter case, the judge indicated that application of this law would also discourage forum shopping. However, it is hard to see why; indeed, application by a court of the recipient claimant's home law would seem to encourage him to forum shop there.

[234] *Defamation and the Internet: a Preliminary Investigation*, n 1 above, para 4.35; considering Law Com No 193; Scot Law Com No 124, para 3.29.

[235] For the purposes of s 11(2)(c).

[236] Even then, there is a risk of the customer lying about this. See expert meeting Summary of Discussions, n 43 above, at 5–6.

21.171 On balance, it is suggested that this law should *not* be regarded as significant under s 11(2). Rather, it may be a material factor when it comes to the application of the rule of displacement under s 12.

Conclusion: A Preference for the Law of the Place where the Recipient is when he Downloads the Information as the most Significant Element of the Events Constituting the Tort

21.172 It is self evident that the need to identify the governing law of a tort committed by electronic means will be no easy matter and, where the elements of the events are scattered across different states, the process may appear somewhat arbitrary. There are serious pros and cons to each of the possible connecting factors which one might use to identify the governing law. However, it is suggested that, on balance, the law of the place of downloading fits best with the approach usually taken by English courts to ascertaining the applicable law of the tort, based as it is on the immediate cause of harm to the claimant.

21.173 If the law of the state of downloading is accepted generally to be the most significant element of the events, it could be argued that this rule should not apply where the recipient has taken reasonable steps to avoid doing business in that state, such as where a service provider's website is in a language not widely spoken.[237] However, this may lead to more uncertainty as to when such a reasonable attempt has been made.[238] Less uncertainty would arguably be caused by maintaining the view that the most significant element of the events occurs in the state of downloading under s 11(2)(c). When consideration is given to whether it is substantially more appropriate for some other law to apply under s 12, the fact that the service provider does not direct his activities to the state of downloading or seek to do business there should be a relevant, but not decisive, factor.

21.174 That said, precisely because this law may be unforeseeable to the service provider, potentially arbitrary or capable of manipulation, it may be easier to displace this law under s 12 in relation to e-commerce torts than it would be to displace s 11(2)(c) in relation to torts committed by other means. This will be so where the place of downloading has little other objective connection to the tort and where several other elements, such as

---

[237] Compare Art 10(1)(b) of the draft Hague Judgments Convention of June 2001 (now superseded by a further draft Convention of much more limited scope). That provision stated that a claimant might sue in the courts of the state 'in which the injury arose, unless the defendant establishes that the person claimed to be responsible could not reasonably foresee that the act or omission could result in an injury of the same nature in that State'. See http://hcch.e-vision.nl/index_en.php?act=progress.listing&cat=4.
[238] See ABA Cyberspace Report, 30.

the place of establishment or residence of the parties, point towards another state, whose law it may be substantially more appropriate to apply on the facts.

9. SPECIFIC TORTS

Negligent Misstatement, Negligent and Fraudulent Misrepresentation

In Chapter 17 on torts and choice of law, we saw that the courts do not **21.175** view any one particular connecting factor as the most important indicator of the governing law under s 11(2)(c) of the 1995 Act.[239] As such, one simply cannot generalize as to which connecting factor will be regarded as the most important; everything hinges on the facts of the case. However, it was argued that such an approach creates an atmosphere of excessive uncertainty and that it is preferable to regard a particular factor as being of especial significance when ascertaining the governing law. Moreover, common law cases suggest that the place of receipt and detrimental reliance, not the place from which the misstatement of misrepresentation is sent, is of paramount importance where the means of communication is instantaneous.[240] This would clearly cover a statement or representation contained on a website or sent by email. Accordingly, s 11(2)(c) of the Act should generally be taken as referring to the place of receipt and reliance upon a misstatement or misrepresentation.

Where receipt and reliance do not occur in the same state, it was sug- **21.176** gested the law of the place of receipt should normally be treated as the most significant element of the events. After all, without communication of the misstatement or misrepresentation to the recipient, no liability can accrue. It is true that the recipient will have no cause of action unless and until he detrimentally relies upon the misstatement or misrepresentation. However, this is a matter outside the control of the service provider. Once it has made and communicated the misstatement or misrepresentation, it has performed all the actions necessary on its part potentially to expose it to tortious liability. The communication itself is the immediate action by the service provider which renders it liable in tort for any damage inflicted by it upon the recipient.

It was argued above that the approach to determining the applicable law **21.177** should not be determined by the form of communication in issue, but

---

[239] At paras 17.28–30, 17.102–118.

[240] See *Diamond v Bank of London and Montreal* [1979] 1 QB 333, CA; *Bastone & Firminger Ltd v Nasima Enterprises (Nigeria) Ltd* [1996] CLC 190, Rix J. However, there is some doubt as to how important common law jurisdiction cases on the place of the tort are for choice of law purposes: see *David Syme & Co Ltd v Grey* (1992) 38 FCR 303 at 314 (Australia).

rather by the type of tort in question. This suggests that the place of receipt should be equally significant where a misstatement or misrepresentation is made by email or via the internet. Where, though, is the place of receipt? Is it the place where the information is uploaded, the place where the service provider who uploads the information is located, or resident, the place of downloading by the recipient, the residence of the recipient, or some other state?

21.178 If the essence of the tort is the communication of a misstatement or misrepresentation, it is true that the service provider makes the information available by uploading it. This is the place at which the service provider has done everything within its power to make the information available. At this stage, its tortious liability rests upon the acts of the recipient in downloading the information and relying upon it to his detriment. Moreover, this is a law whose application can be foreseen by the party making the statement or representation. However, it is difficult to say that the information is *communicated* to the recipient at that point. The state of uploading may be viewed as equivalent to the state from which a fax is sent; unless and until the information reaches the recipient in accessible form, there is no potential liability. If the material is not downloaded by the recipient, there is no information upon which he might detrimentally rely. Moreover, before the recipient downloads the information, the other party may, of course, remove the information from the server, or issue a correction.

21.179 A fortiori, the state where the service provider is located at the time that it uploads the misstatement or misstatement is not of significance. This state may be arbitrary and unforeseeable to the recipient. Moreover, unless and until the material is downloaded by the recipient, there can be no detrimental reliance upon it. Furthermore, it is very difficult to describe the location of the service provider at the time of uploading as an 'event'. Accordingly, it is suggested that this connecting factor should be rejected.[241]

21.180 The residence of the recipient is another connecting factor which might be used to ascertain the place of receipt of a misstatement or misrepresentation. Use of the law of the recipient's residence might seem precluded by s 11(2)(c), which clearly refers to 'events'. The recipient's residence or place of establishment is not an 'event'. However, this might not be conclusive. In the absence of other suitable candidates, it would be possible to argue that this *event* should be deemed to have taken place in the state of

---

[241] Equally clearly, the law of the service provider's place of business or habitual residence must be rejected. Moreover, it is difficult to describe the place of business or residence of the defendant as an 'event'.

the recipient's residence. That law may have a more enduring connection with the tort than other candidates and it substantially reduces the risk of evasive tactics by a recipient who chooses to view the service provider's material whilst temporarily based overseas, or uses an email address not located in his home state. Nevertheless, it is suggested that this connecting factor should be rejected. A party resident in State A, who downloads information whilst in State B, cannot be said to receive the information in State A. Any attempt to say that he does is artificial and distorts the choice of law rule contained in s 11(2)(c).

This leaves the place where the recipient is located when he downloads **21.181** the misstatement or misrepresentation as the place of receipt. It is only at this stage that the information can accurately be said to have been communicated to him. It will not be intelligible to the recipient until he downloads the information. Whether the recipient chooses detrimentally to rely on that information, and so have a possible cause of action, is beyond the control of the party making the misstatement or misrepresentation.

It is true that the place of downloading could be arbitrary, as where the **21.182** recipient accesses his email, or logs onto the service provider's website, whilst on a short business trip overseas. It is also true that the place of downloading may be difficult or impossible for the service provider to foresee. As such, a court might consider the place of receipt not to be the most significant element of the events. Nevertheless, the place of receipt arguably best encapsulates the essence of the tort, and of the key stage of *communication* passing from defendant to claimant. More importantly, it must be remembered that s 11(2)(c) provides only a general rule. If another law is substantially more closely connected to the claim on the facts, then that law may displace the law of the place of downloading under s 12.[242] Where the place of receipt is indeed arbitrary, and where there are substantial connections to another law, such as where the statement or representation is sent by the service provider from State A, received in State B, but detrimentally relied upon by the recipient in State A, it is likely that the general rule would indeed be displaced. Equally, if it is alleged that the recipient has chosen to download the information in a certain state in order to evade the law otherwise applicable, it is likely that the allegation can only be made out where the state of downloading has little connection to the claim and another law is substantially more closely

---

[242] Alternatively, the court may say that the most significant elements of the events do not occur in the place of receipt under s 11(2)(c). This is arguably more in line with the approach that English courts have taken thus far to the Act. It may, however, generate substantial uncertainty as to which law applies under the general rule in s 11, forcing the parties to litigate to determine this question.

connected to it.[243] Such cases may likewise be dealt with by the exception in s 12.

Conversion

21.183 It is possible for a party to commit the tort of conversion, or otherwise wrongfully to interfere with tangible goods in the possession of another, by electronic means. A simple example would be where a party offers for sale by email or on a website goods which belong to another person. It might also cover the infliction of damage upon digitized products, for example, by infecting them with a virus.

21.184 In principle, it is suggested that these torts should not be treated any differently when they occur by electronic means. Accordingly, s 11(2)(c) should be applied to an action in conversion. However, it may be difficult to generalize as to the most significant element of the events. It is important to recall that the act of conversion can be committed in numerous ways.[244] It may include: buying and taking delivery from a person without title; use of goods; a disposition to a third party; or a refusal to deliver to the true owner.

21.185 If a party uses electronic means to sell tangible goods belonging to another, one might still say that the immediate action on the part of the 'seller' which gives rise to tortious liability is not the procuring of the contract of sale, but the delivery of the product to the new 'buyer'. It is at this point that the rights of possession and ownership of the claimant are interfered with in a way which the law deems actionable. If the act complained of is the 'buyer' ordering tangible goods by electronic means from a person without title and taking delivery of them, it is suggested that the same is true. The essence of the infringement of the claimant's property rights is not the conclusion of a contract between the 'seller' and the 'buyer'; rather, it is the taking delivery of the goods which are owned and/or possessed by the claimant. Accordingly, s 11(2)(c) should still point to the law of the place where the 'buyer' took delivery.

21.186 Matters may be more complex where the act complained of is the refusal to deliver tangible goods to the true owner. If the refusal is communicated by email, where does the refusal take place? The arguments are balanced. On the one hand, it could be argued that the refusal is *communicated* to the

---

[243] Whether the fact that the recipient acted in bad faith is itself relevant under s 12 is a moot point. The test appears simply to be an objective one of closest connection.

[244] Moreover, a defendant is capable of committing the tort multiply and sequentially. It is conversion to contract to sell the goods of another; and conversion to deliver to another person, and so forth.

true owner, and as such takes place in the state where the true owner accesses the relevant email. On the other hand, a party can commit the tort of conversion by refusing to deliver goods, without expressly telling the true owner that he does not intend to deliver. The electronic communication is not an essential part of the claim. Accordingly, it could be argued that the refusal takes place in the state of the service provider's residence. In any event, it was argued in Chapter 17 on torts and choice of law that the essence of the claim is still the refusal to hand the goods to the true owner at the state where they were to be delivered, or where one would expect them to be delivered in the ordinary course of events.[245] It is this law to which s 11(2)(c) should point. As such, the fact that a refusal took place by electronic means should not change the position.

A more difficult case is where there are digitized products stored upon **21.187** a web-server. There is a question as to whether the tort of conversion may be committed in respect of digitized products.[246] However, there is Canadian[247] and New Zealand[248] authority to the effect that computer software can be the subject of conversion. We shall therefore proceed on the basis that digitized products may be the subject of conversion.

Suppose that the service provider agrees to sell a bespoke[249] computer **21.188** program to a customer.[250] The service provider then arranges to sell the same program to another person, X, and makes the software available to X to download, which X duly does. Suppose that the service provider uploads the product to a server located in State A. X downloads the product in State B. The original customer is resident in State C, where he had expected to download the product. The original customer claims that by a particular law he has the right to possession of the digitized product and that X and the service provider have wrongfully interfered with this right.

With respect to the liability of the service provider, the question arises **21.189** whether the foundation of the alleged tort is the making available of the product to X, the downloading of the digitized product by X, or the failure to transfer the product to the original customer. This may make a difference in determining the governing law. The last view would tend to point

---

[245] Above, paras 17.71–72. [246] See above, paras 10.189–190.

[247] *Unisys Canada Inc v Imperial Optical Co* 44 BLR (2d) 311, aff'd 2 BLR (3d) 172, Ont CA.

[248] *Pacific Software Technology Ltd v Perry Group Ltd* [2004] 1 NZLR 164.

[249] Conversion must be to the exclusion of others. In most cases, the converter will only obtain a copy of the product and so this requirement will not be satisfied; see above, paras 10.46–49, 10.190 and 21.117.

[250] See above, paras 10.44–53, 10.190 and 21.113–118. It is not certain whether the act of conversion can be committed in respect of a bespoke 'product', which is not classified as 'goods'. See also *Unisys Canada Inc v Imperial Optical Co* 44 BLR (2d) 311, aff'd 2 BLR (3d) 172, Ont CA.

to the law of State C, the state where the products were, in the ordinary course of dealings, to be downloaded by the original customer. One could argue that even if the service provider had not delivered to X, the original customer might still have maintained a claim against the service provider for failing to deliver the product. However, it may be countered that the primary basis of the instant claim is that the product was delivered to X, in violation of the original customer's interest.[251] The second view points to the law of State B. It focuses directly upon the transfer to X and the point at which X may make use of the digitized product. However, from the service provider's point of view, this place may be arbitrary and beyond his control. If the first view is correct, it would tend to point to the law of State A, the place where the server is located where the product is made available to X. This may be justified on the basis that the focus of the choice of law rules in tort should be upon the actions of the defendant which are sufficient to render him liable. Once the service provider makes the product available to X for downloading, it has done everything required of it potentially to be liable in tort. Whether X then downloads the product is not within the service provider's control.[252] It is accordingly suggested that it is the law of State A which should apply to the claim pursuant to s 11(2)(c).

21.190 With respect to the liability of X, it is suggested that the relevant act of conversion is the receiving of the product. This occurs at the point where X downloads the product. Accordingly, s 11(2)(c) should point to the law of State B.

Failure to Sell

21.191 This civilian tort, which exists in French law, was examined in the chapters on jurisdiction[253] and choice of law in tort.[254] It was argued in the latter chapter that the essence of the tort for choice of law purposes is the refusal itself, which occurs where the decision to refuse to sell is made, rather than the place where this refusal was communicated to the 'buyer'. The 'seller' renders himself potentially liable in tort by failing to sell, regardless of whether he communicates his intention not to sell to the 'buyer'. Moreover, this law is preferable to the state of intended resale of the

---

[251] Moreover, if the product had also been made available to the original customer, the service provider would still have been in breach of its obligations to supply the product exclusively to the original customer.

[252] At least if the service provider does not take positive steps to remove the product from the server, or block access to it by X.

[253] See above, paras 6.115–128.   [254] See above, paras 17.122–134.

goods, since the 'seller' might not intend to resell the goods at all, and, in any event, the essence of the claim focuses on the *failure* to sell to the 'buyer', not upon an incompatible sale to some other party.

If the failure to sell occurs by pure omission, then the law of the 'seller's' **21.192** place of business should apply. Of course, it makes no difference at all that the parties have previously communicated by electronic means. However, suppose that the 'seller' sends an email to the 'buyer' indicating his refusal to sell. In such a case, it is suggested that the relevant state is the place where the act of refusal occurred. This will be the state where the 'seller' was when he sent the email. If it so happens that this state has little connection with the matter, on the basis that a seller with its place of business in State A happened to send the email whilst on a short business trip in State B, it is, of course, possible that the latter law will displace the former law.[255]

Inducement of Breach of Contract

The tort of inducing a breach of contract may occur by electronic means. A **21.193** defendant might use electronic mail to persuade a service provider to breach his contract of sale with a customer. Again, the defendant might conclude a contract with the service provider by electronic means which is inconsistent with the service provider's contractual obligations to a customer, as where he agrees to buy a product already the subject of a contract of sale between the original customer and the service provider.

What is the most significant element of the events where the tort of **21.194** inducement of breach of contract occurs in an e-commerce case? This may depend upon the precise inducement and breach that is alleged. If the defendant used electronic mail to persuade the service provider not to carry out his obligation to deliver tangible goods to the customer, but did not himself conclude a contract with the service provider inconsistent with the terms of the original contract, it may be said that the defendant had done everything within his power to induce a breach at the point of communication of the email to the service provider. This probably points to the state where the email was communicated to the service provider, namely where the service provider downloaded the email.

However, this is not a tort in respect of which the last act of the defendant **21.195** can be determinative.[256] The tort focuses on the inducement leading to a

---

[255] Either under s 11(2)(c) of the 1995 Act, or under s 12, on the basis that it is substantially more appropriate for the law of State B to apply,

[256] Contrast the position in respect to misstatement or misrepresentation, where it is argued that the communication to the recipient is the key act. See above, paras 21.175–182.

breach of contract. In *Metall und Rohstoff AG v Donaldson Lufkin & Jenrette Inc*,[257] the Court of Appeal held that the tort of inducement of breach of contract took place not in New York, the place where the acts of inducement took place, but in London, where the breach of contract itself was committed and where the defendant suffered the resulting damage. The same approach should be adopted where the tort is committed by electronic means. The essence of the tort is not the act of inducement per se, but the fact that it results in a breach of contract. This suggests that one should focus on the breach itself. The key breach in this example is the failure to transfer the product itself to the recipient. It is suggested that the law of the place where the product should have been transferred pursuant to the contract should accordingly apply.

21.196 Would it make a difference if the defendant had used electronic mail to conclude a contract with the service provider incompatible with the latter's contractual obligations to the customer? In such a case, it is unclear whether the essence of the tort is the service provider's *failure* to meet his obligations to the customer, especially that of transfer, or the *positive* act of concluding an inconsistent contract with the defendant. It is suggested that, on balance, the former approach should be adopted. From the customer's point of view, the essence of the tort is that the service provider has not met his contractual obligations *to him*. The particular person with whom he has concluded an incompatible sales contract is less material, and the state where that incompatible contract is concluded is, from the point of view of the original customer, wholly unpredictable and potentially arbitrary. Moreover, the decision in *Metall* suggests that both the breach of contract and the consequent harm that it causes to the claimant are the material elements of the tort. The harm to the claimant largely flows from the failure to transfer the product to him. Accordingly, it is suggested that the law of the state to which the product should have been transferred to the claimant should again be applied, pursuant to s 11(2)(c) of the 1995 Act.

21.197 The tort might also be committed by the defendant preventing a party from performing his contractual obligations. This might occur, if, for example, there are digitized products and the contract states that the products should be available for downloading from an internet site by the customer. The defendant might host a server used by the service provider. He might make the server unavailable for a prolonged period of time, in order to upgrade it. This may have the effect of making it impossible for the service provider to transfer the product to the customer.[258] In such a

---

[257] [1990] 1 QB 391.   [258] A fact of which the defendant may be aware.

case, the material act of the defendant which grounds his liability is the failure to provide a properly functioning server in the state where that server is located. However, it is suggested that in such a case, as with the above examples, it is important to focus not upon the activities of the defendant which give rise to tortious liability, but on the breach itself to which this gives rise. Here, the breach is the failure of the service provider to transfer to the customer. It is the law of the place where the breach occurs which should apply. If one accepts that transfer of digitized products should ordinarily occur in the state where they would, in the normal course of events, be downloaded, then this law should apply. The place of downloading in the ordinary course of events will usually be the state where the recipient is resident or has its principal place of business.[259]

Negligence

It is possible that a claim in negligence may arise in the context of **21.198** e-commerce transactions. This may be most likely in the context of digitized products. One example would be where the service provider fails to warn the recipient of a problem with the product which comes to light after transfer, such as a virus, a security problem or incompatibility with other software. The recipient might seek to sue the service provider for damage to the computer itself and possibly also for consequent economic loss caused by the digitized product. Another example would be where the service provider uses a server hosted by a third party, X. Suppose that the recipient downloads the digitized product from the server, which contains a virus that damages the recipient's computer. The recipient might wish to sue X for damage to the computer itself and possibly also for consequent economic loss. A third example would be where the server hosted by X is unavailable for a prolonged period, preventing the customer from downloading the product which he has purchased. The customer might sue X for economic loss arising from the delay in being able to access and use the digitized product.

The first two examples relate to *damage* to the recipient's computer result- **21.199** ing from the negligent act of the defendant. Accordingly, the law of the place where the recipient's computer was at the time that it was damaged applies, pursuant to s 11(2)(b). It was argued above that this state should be deemed to be the place where the recipient's computer was at the time when the product was downloaded.[260] This should equally be the case

---

[259] Technically, one could argue that the applicable law of the contract should determine where the breach took place. This is because the place of transfer is a term of the contract.
[260] See the earlier discussion of s 11(2)(b), above, para 21.144.

if the recipient also claims for consequent economic loss, as where the digitized product infects the recipient's computer, causing him to lose work.[261] The cause of action itself is based upon damage to property and the economic loss is contingent upon that claim.

21.200 The third example considered above, that of the server host, X, preventing the customer from accessing the digitized product promptly, is somewhat different in nature. In that case, the claim does not relate to 'damage' to the product, but the late transfer of it. It is likely that the claimant's case will be based upon economic loss, if, for example, the digitized product was a computer program intended for use by the recipient in the course of business. It is necessary to apply s 11(2)(c) of the 1995 and to determine where the most significant element or elements of the events occurred. Arguably, the immediate harm caused to the recipient occurs in the state where the computer is located onto which the product would have been downloaded for use. Against this, the basis of the claim is that the defendant, X, negligently failed *in the state where the server was located*, to make the digitized product available for downloading. On balance, it is suggested that the law of the place of uploading should apply under s 11(2)(c). After all, the defendant is responsible for maintaining the server in the state where it is located and can reasonably be expected to meet the standards of care expected in that state. The defendant's negligence occurs in that state. Any loss which the recipient suffers is consequent upon that negligence.[262]

10. MANDATORY RULES[263] AND PUBLIC POLICY

21.201 If the place of downloading is normally taken to be the place where the most significant element of the events constituting a tort occurs, there is a serious risk that a service provider established in the United Kingdom will be subjected in an English court to the law of a foreign state. In other words, e-commerce increases the likelihood that a service provider will be exposed to the application of foreign law. The service provider may also be exposed to the law of a far flung corner of the world where, for

---

[261] See above, para 21.145.

[262] See also *Dow Jones v Gutnick*, 210 CLR 575, HC of Australia; [2002] HCA 56, paras 43–44.

[263] For an example of the application of New York law to an internet casino located in Antigua, see *People of the State of New York v World Interactive Gaming Corp* 714 NYS 2d 844 (NY County Sup Ct 1999); considered in Lim, n 135 above, at 25–32. In that case, the bet was transmitted from New York and the casino actively targeted New York customers. Contrast *Bensusan Restaurant Corp v King* 937 F Supp 295 (SDNY 1996), where the New York Court of Appeals did not consider that New York law applied to the acts of a Florida defendant who did not urge New York residents to use his website and did not conduct business himself in New York (discussed by Lim at 30–33).

example, its misrepresentations are read and detrimentally relied upon, even though it never contemplated dealing with parties in that state. Given these risks, there is, perhaps, a correspondingly increased possibility that the English courts will need to have recourse to public policy.[264] This would allow them to disapply the applicable law of the tort, where, for example, it exposes the service provider to excessively onerous liability. To some extent, this is a by-product of the ease with which parties may now communicate with one another across the globe. Increased transnational activity leads to greater scope for the more frequent application of foreign laws, and for the application of previously rarely encountered foreign laws. Any choice of law rule which points to the law of the place of the tort[265] 'would need to respect the entitlement of each legal regime not to enforce foreign legal rules contrary to binding local law or important elements of local public policy.'[266] However, it does lead to the unfortunate consequence that in a world where borders are being broken down and international relations are ever more important, an English court may more frequently have to comment *negatively* upon a foreign law, and refuse to apply it in whole or in part.[267]

It will be recalled that s 14(3)(a)(i) of the 1995 Act does not explicitly limit **21.202** itself to the application of *English* public policy. In theory, this leaves open the possibility of the application of the public policy of a third state of close connection. In an e-commerce case, there may well be one or more states with a substantial connection to the claim other than the governing law. However, it was suggested in Chapter 17 on torts and choice of law that it is very unlikely that an English court will allow this section to be used to give effect to a third state's public policy.[268]

11. The Proposed European Regulation on Choice of Law for Non-contractual Obligations (The 'Rome II' Regulation)

Proposed Choice of Law Rule

The European Commission has issued a Proposal for a Regulation of **21.203** the European Parliament and the Council on the Law Applicable to

---

[264] Pursuant to s 14(3)(a)(i) of the 1995 Act.

[265] Or, in the case of s 11(2)(c), the law of the place where the most significant element or elements of the tort took place.

[266] *Dow Jones*, para 119, *per* Kirby J, citing *Attorney-General (UK) v Heinemann Publishers Australia Pty Ltd* (1988) 165 CLR 30, HC of Australia.

[267] Something which would not have been necessary under the old double actionability rule of the common law, where it was necessary to demonstrate that the act complained of gave rise to liability by the English domestic law of tort.

[268] Above, para 17.46.

Non-Contractual Obligations.[269] This is discussed in Chapter 17 on tort and choice of law,[270] to which the reader is referred. However, it is worth considering briefly how the proposed Regulation would apply to e-commerce.[271] It will be recalled that Article 3(1) lays down the general choice of law rule in tort that the applicable law is that of the state in which the damage arises, or is likely to arise. If a negligent misstatement, negligent or fraudulent misrepresentation is sent by electronic mail from France to England, and detrimentally relied upon by the recipient to invest in German companies, Germany would be the state whose law is applicable to the tort. In the context of e-commerce, the place of immediate damage may be substantially easier to foresee than the state where the recipient received the advice. If, for example, the defendant had posted the misstatement or misrepresentation on its website, it may be impossible to determine who might access that website and 'receive' the misstatement or misrepresentation. However, if the misstatement or misrepresentation related to the financial affairs of a German company, then it is reasonably foreseeable to both claimant and defendant that the claimant might detrimentally rely on the misstatement or misrepresentation to invest in Germany, and suffer direct damage in the form of financial loss in Germany.

21.204 Against this, the direct place of damage rule fits uncomfortably with the country of origin principle in the E-Commerce Directive,[272] which requires an information service provider established in a Member State to comply with the laws of his state of establishment within the 'coordinated field'.[273] Far from applying the law of the defendant's place of establishment, the direct place of damage rule will frequently lead to the application of the law of the state where the claimant is resident.

21.205 The commentary to the Draft Regulation comments that '. . . where damage is sustained in several countries, . . . the laws of all the countries

---

[269] COM/2003/0427 Final, of 22 July 2003, available at http://europa.eu.int/eur-lex/pri/ en/lip/latest/doc/2003/com2003_0427en01.doc. See also the Report of the UK House of Lords European Union Committee, available at www.publications.parliament.uk/pa/ ld200304/ldselect/ldeucom/66/6602.htm.

[270] Above, paras 17.165–182. It is further discussed in Ch 19 on restitution and choice of law, paras 19.98–100.

[271] Compare the views of Report of the UK House of Lords European Union Committee, n 269 above, paras 117–119, 157–162.

[272] ibid, paras 157–162.

[273] Although it appears that in so far as there is a conflict between the Draft Regulation and the E-Commerce Directive, the latter prevails. Art 23(2) of the Draft Regulation states that: 'This regulation shall not prejudice the application of Community instruments which, in relation to particular matters and in areas coordinated by such instruments, subject the supply of services or goods to the laws of the Member State where the service-provider is established and, in the area coordinated, allow restrictions on freedom to provide services or goods originating in another Member State only in limited circumstances'. See the Report of the UK House of Lords European Union Committee, n 269 above, para 162.

concerned will have to be applied on a distributive basis . . . .'.[274] This could create real difficulties,[275] particularly in relation to e-commerce. A defendant who makes a misrepresentation on a website may find that it is detrimentally relied upon by a claimant in State A, State B and State C. The defendant will have to comply with the laws of each and every state in which he might cause some damage to a potential claimant.

Exceptions

Parties have the same habitual residence

It will be recalled that Article 3(2) provides that: 'However, where the **21.206** person claimed to be liable and the person sustaining damage both have their habitual residence in the same country when the damage occurs, the non-contractual obligation shall be governed by the law of that country.' Although some reservations were expressed in Chapter 17 on this provision,[276] in the e-commerce context, one might observe that the rule makes reasonable sense, as the residence of the parties provides what may be the only enduring territorial connection to a tort claim. Against this, where parties are dealing at arm's length, neither party might actually be aware of the other's habitual residence.[277] That being the case, automatic application of that law might actually defeat the parties' expectations.

A general exception

Article 3(3) lays down a general exception to Articles 3(1) and (2). This **21.207** states that 'where it is clear from all the circumstances of the case that the non-contractual obligation is manifestly more closely connected with another country, the law of that other country shall apply.' The high threshold for the disapplication of the general rules suggests that this provision may be used infrequently. However, in electronic commerce cases, where the place of the tort may well not be the state with which the tort has the closest connection, it is not clear that such an inflexible exception is desirable.

A Right to Choose the Governing Law of a Tort[278]

Article 10(1) allows the parties expressly or impliedly to choose the law **21.208** applicable to a claim in tort or claim in restitution, provided that the

---

[274] Explanatory notes to Art 3(1) of the Draft Regulation.
[275] See above, para 17.168. [276] At para 17.169.
[277] Although Art 5(1) of the E-Commerce Directive requires an information service provider established in a Member State to disclose his name and place of establishment to the recipient. This provision is enacted in the UK by SI 2002/2013, reg 6(1).
[278] Or a claim in restitution.

agreement is entered into after their dispute arose. In a minefield such as electronic commerce, where the governing law of the tort is so difficult to determine and for the parties to foresee, there is eminent practical sense in removing that uncertainty at a stroke by permitting the parties to choose the applicable law of the tort.

Mandatory Rules and Public Policy

21.209 It will be recalled that one of the most controversial provisions of the Proposal is Article 12(1), which states that '. . . effect may be given to the mandatory rules of another country with which the situation is closely connected . . .'. The uncertainty which this provision may generate is only magnified in e-commerce cases. It would be necessary to determine what factors are relevant and sufficient to create a close connection to a third state. Would these include, for example, that it was the state of uploading or downloading, or the place where the service provider was located at the time of uploading? The place of uploading or location of the service provider may be unknown to the claimant, and the place of downloading unknown to the defendant. It would also be necessary to determine the nature and purpose of the third state's rule.[279]

Conclusion

21.210 In so far as the Commission Proposal gives the parties the freedom to choose the law applicable to a non-contractual claim, it will be suited to the demands of e-commerce, since it will relieve much of the complexity of ascertaining the governing law. However, the separate torts approach and the role given to third states' mandatory rules may lead to particular complexity in e-commerce cases. It is doubtful whether the Proposal will improve the choice of law rules in tort in general, and in their application to e-commerce in particular.[280]

V. *INTER VIVOS* PROPERTY TRANSFERS OF DIGITIZED PRODUCTS

1. The Difficulty of Determining where Digitized Products are Located

21.211 A question might arise as to whether property in a digitized product has passed pursuant to a contract of sale. Very often, there will be no question

---

[279] Which may be a particularly complex matter if the third state's law was itself not enacted with the concerns of e-commerce in mind.
[280] See also Gringras, n 59 above, at 159.

of property passing. The customer will download information from a server for his use; but there is no attempt to pass property.[281] It is argued above that this constitutes a licence to use the information.[282] However, there may be a question of the passing of property[283] if the customer purchases a bespoke product, such as a single available copy of a computer program.

If a property law question does arise, it is no easy matter to determine the **21.212** situs of the property. It could, for example, be said to be 'located' at the place of uploading, the place of downloading, the place where the service provider is located when it uploads the product, or the place of residence of the recipient or service provider.

It is true that intangible property is, by its nature, not physically located in **21.213** a particular state. However, with respect to other forms of intangible property, the law does not shy away from attributing a situs to the property. For example, shares have their situs in the country where they may be dealt with between shareholder and company. So, if shares are only transferable by entry on the register, they are situated in the country where the register is kept.[284] If the company has a register in two countries, and the transfer may be registered in either, the *situs* is the place where in the ordinary course of business the transfer would be registered.[285] A debt due under a contract is generally regarded as having its *situs* where the debtor resides,[286] because that is where it generally needs to be enforced. If he has more than one residence, it is where the creditor stipulates for the debt to be paid[287] and in the absence of such a stipulation, where it is payable in the normal course of business.[288]

It must be remembered that the law looks to the *situs* of property *at the* **21.214** *time of the last actual or purported transaction.* Accordingly, the fact that a party has downloaded digitized products onto his computer, so that they are located on his hard drive, does not mean that the relevant *situs* is the

---

[281] In which case, it is not in any case accurate to describe this as a contract of 'sale'.

[282] See above, para 10.45; see also the discussion above, paras 21.114–116. See further *St Alban's City and District Council v International Computers Ltd* [1997] FSR 251, 265 CA (*per* Sir Iain Glidewell).

[283] The information itself may be viewed as intangible property.

[284] See eg *Brassard v Smith* [1925] AC 371, PC (Canada); *Eric Beach Co v Attorney-General for Ontario* [1930] AC 161; *R v Williams* [1942] AC 541, PC (Canada); *Macmillan Inc v Bishopsgate Trust plc (No 3)* [1996] 1 WLR 387, CA.

[285] *Treasurer of Ontario v Blonde* [1948] AC 24, PC (Canada); *Standard Chartered Bank Ltd v IRC* [1978] 1 WLR 1160, Ch D.

[286] *New York Life Insurance Co v Public Trustee* [1924] 2 Ch 101, CA.

[287] *Kwok Chi Leung Karl v Estate Duty Commissioners* [1988] 1 WLR 1035.

[288] *Power Curber International Ltd v National Bank of Kuwait SAK* [1981] 1 WLR 1233, CA.

place where the computer is presently located. Rather, we must consider the more complex question of where digitized products were located *at the time of the purported dealing with them.*

21.215 It could be objected that it is artificial to attribute a *situs* to intangible property.[289] However, the rules for ascertaining the *situs* of property provide a ready way to locate intangible property and hence provide a straightforward choice of law rule. Indeed, the *situs* of a debt, contingent as it is upon the residence of the debtor, may well be less likely to change than the situs of tangible movables.

2. The *Situs* of Digitized Products: the Possibilities

General Remarks

21.216 If it is accepted that a *situs* needs to be attributed to digitized products, the question is where they might be said to be located. There are a number of candidates. In particular, suppose that a contract is concluded between a service provider with its business in State A and a recipient with its place of business in State B for the sale[290] of a digitized product. The service provider is located in State C when it uploads the product to a server located in State D. The recipient accesses the server and downloads the digitized product to his computer whilst in State E. Each of these laws has a case for being the *situs* of the digitized product. A further possibility would be not to rely upon any one connecting factor, but to apply the law with which the transaction has its closest connection as the general rule. We will now consider the strength of each case in turn.

Habitual Residence or Principal Place of Business of the Recipient

21.217 The habitual residence or principal place of business of the recipient does not seem an appropriate *situs*. Only in the most artificial sense can digitized products be said to be located where the recipient is resident, when they are in fact stored on a computer server and access is obtained to them by downloading the products that have been uploaded by the service provider. A chain of *events* leads to a *transfer*; and the residence of the recipient is not an event. Moreover, it would be impossible for the service provider to foresee which law might apply. Even if the service provider attempts to restrict access by, for example, using the German language

---

[289] For criticism in relation to debts, see P Rogerson 'The Situs of Debts in the Conflict of Laws-Illogical, Artificial and Misleading' [1990] CLJ 441. See also M Moshinsky, 'The Assignment of Debts in the Conflict of Laws' (1992) 108 LQR 591.

[290] As opposed to the provision of a licence to use the product.

on his website, it is possible that a fluent German speaker, or German national, may have taken up habitual residence in England, from where he downloads the product.[291] Moreover, this connecting factor would mean that two customers, X (resident in France) and Y (resident in Japan) would have their property law disputes with the service provider resolved by different laws. This could lead to differing judgments in respect of what are, to all intents and purposes,[292] the same products. It would also mean that the service provider is potentially subject to the property law of each and every state in the world, with worrying consequences for the stifling of international trade.

Habitual Residence or Principal Place of Business of the Service Provider

The service provider's habitual residence or principal place of business **21.218** has more promise as a connecting factor. It leads to a single law which must be satisfied. This law can be foreseen by the service provider and will not discourage it from selling digitized products by electronic means. Moreover, at least where the service provider is a company, it will usually be apparent to the recipient from the service provider's website or email where its principal place of business is. Of course, digitized products cannot in any meaningful sense be regarded as located in this state. They are uploaded onto a server, stored there and downloaded by the recipient. There again, it could equally be said that a debt is not in a meaningful sense located in the state of the debtor's residence. However, the law *attributes* the *situs* to this state, on pragmatic grounds. These grounds rest ultimately on the need to enforce a debt if the debtor defaults and the fact that the debt will ordinarily be payable in the debtor's home state. One might also argue that if the service provider is alleged to have failed to transfer property in digitized products to the recipient, it is in the state of the service provider's habitual residence that the obligation might most naturally be enforced.

Against this, a debt can be owned, but it must be *recovered*. Products, **21.219** when digitized, are uploaded to a server, from the state where the service

---

[291] Kirby J commented in *Dow* that 'the nature of Internet technology itself makes it virtually impossible, or prohibitively difficult, cumbersome and costly, to prevent the content of a given website from being accessed in specific legal jurisdictions when an Internet user in such jurisdictions seeks to do so. In effect, once information is posted on the Internet, it is usually accessible to all Internet users everywhere in the world. Even if the correct jurisdiction of an Internet user could be ascertained accurately, there is presently no adequate technology that would enable non-subscription content providers to isolate and exclude all access to all users in specified jurisdictions.'

[292] Although they must be bespoke products for each customer, if the customer is to acquire property in the product.

provider is located at the time of uploading, and may be downloaded by the recipient. It seems difficult to argue that they are not located in *any* of these states. Moreover, debts are essentially a legal construct; it follows that any attempt to locate them will have an air of artifice. In contrast, digitized products are a clearly defined, albeit intangible, form of property, which, being available for uploading, storage and downloading, can legitimately be said to be located in any particular state, without falling back on a rule of residence.

The Place of Downloading

21.220 The place of downloading[293] has a strong case for being treated as the *situs*. After all, the sales[294] contract will involve an agreement for the transfer of a product to the recipient. Indeed, the product cannot be used by the recipient unless and until he has downloaded it. It is true that property in the product will not necessarily be transferred to the recipient at the point of downloading. Nevertheless, the property must be transferred to the recipient and it is arguably most appropriate to say that transfer occurs in the state where the digitized product is downloaded.[295] If the product is to be delivered to this state, there is some sense in saying that this is the *situs*. The state where the products are downloaded might be said to have some notional 'control' over the product, and questions as to whether property has properly vested in the recipient might frequently be litigated in the courts of this state, which could then apply its 'home' law.

21.221 However, there are serious disadvantages to this solution. The service provider may meet his contractual obligations to the recipient by uploading digitized products onto a server ready for downloading. Furthermore, to focus on the place of downloading is to look at an act of the claimant recipient. However, this sits uncomfortably with the law relating to debts, where it is the defendant debtor, and the need to enforce a property right against him, which is considered critical in attributing a situs. Again, the place of downloading may be manipulated. Nor is it obvious that the state of downloading exercises any meaningful form of control over digitized products. For example, a recipient may download a product to his laptop when on business in France, but actually use the product when he returns to the state of his habitual residence, Italy. Another disadvantage of this

---

[293] In the case of email, this is likely to correspond to the place of receipt.
[294] Assuming that it is a contract of sale, rather than the provision of a licence to use the product: see above, paras 10.44–53 and 21.113–118.
[295] See the discussion of the place of delivery with respect to Art 5(1)(b) of the Brussels I Regulation above, paras 10.56–74, 10.78–80.

law is that different recipients might download digitized products in different states. That means that the property rights of X to a digitized product downloaded in France would be governed by French law, whilst the property rights of Y to what is, in all material respects,[296] an identical product downloaded in Japan would be governed by Japanese law. There is a real risk that the two laws may differ, if a dispute arises as to the nature and quality of the property rights passed to the recipient, or, indeed, as to whether property has passed to him at all. Finally, it will be almost impossible for the service provider to foresee where digitized products are downloaded. Even if the service provider seeks to appeal to a particular market, there is no guarantee of predictability. For example, if the website is in the German language, the service provider is appealing to German speakers first and foremost. Nevertheless, it is quite possible that a German recipient might download the product in England, where he is either temporarily or permanently based.

The Place where the Service Provider is Located when it Uploads the Information

The place where the service provider is located when it uploads the **21.222** products has a certain attraction. Since it is the place where the service provider takes the first substantial steps to made the digitized products available, it has a more realistic claim to be the situs than the more artificial residence of one of the parties. It also provides a single law which will apply wherever the recipient resides or downloads the product. This will not discourage the service provider to conduct business over the internet in digitized products.

Against this, the digitized products are uploaded by the service provider **21.223** *to* a server where they may be accessed and transferred. Until that point, no transaction in them will take place. That being the case, it is difficult to describe the location of the service provider when he begins the process of uploading as the *situs* at the time of transfer to the recipient. In addition, it may be impossible for the recipient to determine the location of the service provider at the time that it uploads the product and be contrary both to his expectations and the expectations of third parties if this law is applied.

---

[296] Although it is suggested above, paras 10.45 and 21.114–116, that in this scenario the customer will obtain a licence to use the product, rather than acquiring property rights in it. However, the service provider might provide bespoke products to different customers which are very similar in nature to each other; or if two different parties purport to purchase a single, bespoke digitized product, a property question could arise as to who has the prior claim to the property.

The Place of Uploading

21.224 That leaves us with the law of the place of uploading[297] as the last credible candidate. Of course, there are downsides to the application of this law. The server may be selected by the service provider, or it may use another party's server, in order to subject the transaction to a particular law. However, one might make a similar point in relation to tangible movable property, whose situs could, in principle, be manipulated by the seller at the time of transfer. In practice, a service provider is likely to select the location of its server on a number of criteria, including the cost and space and speed of the server, and the convenience and freedom offered in the state where it is located. One could overstate how likely any given service provider is to choose the location of a server in order to secure the application of favourable conflicts rules.

21.225 A potentially more serious problem arises where the service provider uses a series of 'mirror sites', each located on a different server in a different state. This may allow the service provider to choose where to 'locate' particular digitized products. Perhaps more disturbingly, it will mean that if X accesses a server in France to obtain the digitized products, and Y accesses a server in Japan to obtain what are, in substance,[298] the same products, their property rights in those products will be subject to different laws. Finally, the place of uploading cannot be used where a transfer is made by email and it would be necessary to rely on some other connecting factor.[299]

21.226 Despite these reservations, it is suggested that the law of the place of uploading still represents the most appropriate connecting factor for the purpose of determining the *situs* of digitized products. Products are most naturally 'located' where they are stored available for transfer. It is true that the recipient will not have the benefit of those products unless and until he downloads them. However, the focus of property choice of law rules is not on the act of transfer itself, but on the location of the products at the time of a purported transfer. An analogy may be drawn with tangible goods. Suppose that a seller agrees to sell a cargo of tangible goods located in State A to a buyer. The goods are to be delivered to the buyer's home state, State B. The *situs* at the time of the

---

[297] That is, the place where the server upon which the digitized product is available is located.

[298] Although it is suggested above that where information is available to transfer to multiple parties, this should be viewed as a creating a licence to use the information, rather than being seen as a transfer of property. However, where two different parties purport to purchase a single, bespoke digitized product, a property question could arise as to who has the prior claim to the property.

[299] Such as the place of dispatch of the email.

transaction is State A. State B is equivalent to the state of downloading of a digitized product. It is the place to which the goods will be sent. However, it is clearly *not* the state where the goods are located when a transaction with respect to them takes place. State A is equivalent to the place of uploading. It is not the place of ultimate destination. It is, however, the place where the goods are located at the time that they are made available to the purchaser for sale. In the case of digitized products, the transaction will be completed by the service provider securing a means of payment from the recipient, which will usually take the form of the recipient entering his credit or debit card details on the service provider's website.[300] Thereafter, the service provider makes the product *available* to the recipient on the server to which the product has been uploaded, so that he can them download it to whichever state he happens to be in. Moreover, the argument that the place of uploading may not be foreseeable to the recipient cannot be fatal. In the case of tangible goods, the buyer may not know where they are located at the time of the transaction, especially if they are, for example, stored in bulk in a warehouse.[301]

If the place of uploading is accepted as the *situs*, a question arises whether **21.227** this law should be disapplied where it appears that the server has been selected by the service provider solely to manipulate the applicable choice of law rules in property. However, as the court in *Dow Jones* noted, an anti-manipulation test simply gives rise to a host of additional problems and uncertainties. When is the selection of a particular server motivated by legitimate, commercial incentives and the legitimate desire not to expose oneself to unduly unfavourable law and when does it constitute unwarranted manipulation? How readily would the law of the place of uploading give way in the face of such evidence? Which law would be substituted in its place? It is suggested that, on balance, no special rule should apply to deal with cases of manipulation. A seller is able to manipulate the *situs* of tangible goods. Moreover, it is not just the service provider who may manipulate the *situs* of a digitized product. The recipient may equally be capable of manipulating the *situs*, where the product is located on more than one server in different states, by choosing[302] to access a server in State X rather than in State Y.[303] In any event, an English court will, on general principles, disapply the law of the *situs* if its application

---

[300] Payment might also be made by means of electronic money: see above, para 10.108.

[301] Compare *Inglis v Robertson* [1898] AC 616.

[302] Assuming, of course, that he is aware that there are different servers, that they are located in different states and that he knows which states these are.

[303] Although one must concede that there is an element of 'two wrongs do not make a right' about this argument that both parties might be able to manipulate the *situs*.

would be contrary to English public policy.[304] There seems no reason to make special provision for digitized product *situs* 'manipulation'.

21.228 Where the product is located on a number of servers in different states, the relevant law is that of the state where the server from which the recipient accessed the product is located. However, if the service provider fails to make the provider available *at all* from *any* server, it may be difficult to determine the *situs* of the product. In such a case, it is suggested that the exception considered below should apply, and the law of closest connection should be determined.

The Law of Closest Connection

21.229 It could be argued that no one connecting factor should be conclusive when determining the *situs* of digitized products and that we should instead simply apply the law with which the transaction has its closest connection[305] as the general rule. However, intolerable uncertainty would arise at two levels.

21.230 First, it would be impossible for either party to foresee which law might be applied at the time of transfer. The same would be true of, indeed, any third party who might acquire an interest in those products. In an area such as property law, commercial certainty is of paramount importance, in order to promote the alienability and security of title and because an interest in property affects not just the parties to the litigation, but third parties as well.[306] It is true that if the law of the place of uploading is treated as the *situs*, the recipient may not be able to foresee where the digitized products are located. However, he could, of course, make enquiry of the service provider. Moreover, it is suggested below that in cases where the law of the location of the server looks to have little connection with the matter, the recipient might argue for the displacement of the general rule by the law of closest connection. Nevertheless, it is suggested that it is preferable to adopt a general rule that the law of the place where the server is situated applies, subject to a limited exception, rather than to leave the whole matter to the vagaries of the objective proper law.

21.231 Second, a general rule based upon the law of closest connection would also create uncertainty at the time when any dispute between the parties

---

[304] See the observations of Slade J in *Winkworth v Christie* [1980] Ch 496, Ch D. See also *Kuwait Airways v Iraqi Airways (Nos 4 and 5)* [2002] AC 883, HL.

[305] Or the law of the state with which the transaction has its closest connection.

[306] *Glencore International AG v Metro Trading International Inc (No 2)* [2001] 1 Lloyd's Rep 284, QBD (Comm). The third party argument may be less important in the e-commerce context, since software can be supplied multiply to different persons without prior recipients being prejudiced. However, this is not the case where a bespoke product is supplied in which the recipient alone has property.

arises. It may be impossible for the parties to settle that dispute, if it is wholly unclear which is the law of the *situs*. The only way to resolve the matter conclusively would be through litigation. In contrast, a general rule with a limited exception provides a clear starting point for the resolution of disputes, albeit one with an element of flexibility.

3. Preferred Solution: A General Rule in Favour of the Place of Uploading Coupled with an Exception

As with the choice of law rules in tort or contract, what is needed is a **21.232** general rule as to what constitutes the applicable law for *inter vivos* transfers of digitized products. Like in those areas, there needs also to be an exception which recognizes that in certain cases, another law[307] may be substantially more connected to the transaction than the one identified by the general rule. It is suggested that this exception might be modelled on s 12 of the Private International Law (Miscellaneous Provisions) Act 1995. In other words, one should examine the factors which connect the transaction to the law identified by the general rule, the place of uploading. One should then compare the factors which point to another law. If the person seeking to rely on the exception can demonstrate that it is substantially more appropriate to apply the latter law, then the general rule should cede to this law of closest connection.

Relevant 'factors' will include the place of residence or business of the **21.233** recipient and service provider, the place where the service provider is located at the time that it uploads the product and the place of downloading. In weighing up the 'factors', it is likely that the pros and cons of the connecting factors considered above will be taken into account. For example, the law of the service provider's place of business was stated not to be suitable as a general rule. However, it may well be important when applying the exception. This is a law which provides an enduring connection to a particular state. It is a law which will not paralyze transactions involving digitized products, because it requires the service provider only to satisfy a single law. Moreover, it is relatively unlikely to defeat the expectations of the parties. The service provider will normally state its place of business on its website, or in email correspondence. If it does not, this may be a reason to give this connecting factor less weight than if it does state this.

The recipient's place of business also provides an enduring connection to **21.234** a certain state. Moreover, wherever a recipient downloads the product, it is likely that he will habitually use it in the state where his place of

---

[307] Or another state.

business or residence is. However, it will be much harder for the service provider to foresee this law. Moreover, there is the concern that giving significant weight to this law means that the service provider may potentially have to satisfy the property laws of every state where the digitized product might be downloaded, with damaging effects on free trade.[308] This suggests that this factor might tend to be given slightly less weight than the place of the service provider's business.

21.235 The place where the service provider is located at the time that it uploads the product will provide a single[309] point of contact[310] which will be clear and favourable[311] to the service provider. Nevertheless, there may be no way of the recipient knowing where this place is. Moreover, the products are not available for transactions unless and until they are *accessible* to the recipient, which occurs where they are to be found on a server. This suggests that the place where the service provider is located at the time that it uploads the product may generally be given rather little weight under the exception.

21.236 Finally, there is the place of downloading. This may be given more weight than the place of uploading. After all, the product is of no real use to the recipient unless and until he has downloaded it. If and when he does so, it could be argued that this state exercises a form of control over the product. Moreover, the place of downloading may be said to be equivalent to the place of transfer of the product to the recipient. At least in the contract sphere, this is a factor to which considerable weight is accorded. Where the transaction involves a dispute about the nature and quality of property in the product itself, there is reason equally to treat this as an important connecting factor. Against this, the fact that this law may be wholly unforeseeable to the service provider, and that it might force him to satisfy the property laws of any state in the world,[312] may suggest that it will usually be a less important factor than, say, the place of the service provider's business.

21.237 It could be objected that the suggested general rule plus exception is tantamount to a special rule for e-commerce and the law of property. It

---

[308] But this fear may be greatly exaggerated. It has been suggested above, paras 10.44–53 and 21.113–118, that property passes in a digitized product only where a bespoke program is transferred; otherwise, the recipient simply obtains a licence to use the product.

[309] At least if the service provider is located in only one state during the process of uploading the products.

[310] Whereas the place of uploading may cause difficulties in the case of uploading to mirror sites located in different jurisdictions.

[311] Save in the unlikely event that it uploads the product whilst in a state whose property laws are unfavourable to the service provider.

[312] But again, this argument should be kept in proportion. Property will only pass in a bespoke product: see above, paras 10.46–49 and 21.117.

was argued above that choice of law rules should attach to the type of claim in question, not to the form of communication in issue. However, the point is that digitized products involve not just a new form of communication, but a new form of *property*. Where intangible property is concerned, it is necessary to determine a suitable choice of law rule. If one balances the range of connecting factors and the need for a level of certainty, a reasonable conclusion is that a general rule based upon the location of the server should apply, subject to a rule of displacement.

4. Conclusion

In summary, the following choice of law rule is suggested for *inter vivos* **21.238** transfers of digitized products:

(1) Where an *inter vivos* transaction, or purported transaction, in a digitized product takes place, questions concerning property rights in that digitized product, or an interest in that product, shall be determined by the law of the state where the server is situated onto which the product is uploaded.[313]

(2) However, where having regard to the factors which connect the transaction as a whole to the law of that state specified in rule (1) above and the factors which connect the transaction as a whole to the law of another state, it is substantially more appropriate for the latter law to govern the transaction, the general rule in (1) shall be displaced. In such circumstances, the law of the state with which the transaction has its closest connection shall instead be applied.[314]

VI. RESTITUTION[315]

1. Personal Claims

Cases where it may be Necessary to Determine the Place of Enrichment

It was argued in Chapter 19 on restitution and choice of law that the law **21.239** applicable to the 'contract' should generally apply to unjust enrichment

---

[313] If the service provider uses mirror sites located in different states, the relevant *situs* is the server from which the recipient downloads the digitized product.

[314] This law should also apply where the product is located on a number of servers, but the service provider fails to provide the recipient with access to the product for the purposes of downloading from any server. In such a case, it is not possible meaningfully to determine the *situs* of the product.

[315] See also the discussion of the possible impact of the proposed Rome II Regulation on e-commerce above, paras 21.203–210; see also paras 19.98–100 and 17.165–182.

claims arising from an actual or supposed contract.[316] Accordingly, there are few specific problems raised by electronic commerce in this area. However, it was suggested that there may be cases where the factor which rendered the contract void or voidable also 'infects' the choice of law clause contained in the contract. An example may be a contract which is the product of duress. If the duress meant that the choice of law clause was not the result of genuine bilateral consent, then it was argued that the law of the place where the enrichment was received should instead be applied.[317] Other examples would be where a buyer erroneously makes payment to a party other than the seller and seeks restitution of the payment, or where the seller erroneously delivers the goods to someone other than the buyer. In such cases, the law applicable to a contract between buyer and seller should not be applied to a claim against a third party not bound by the terms of the contract of sale. Rather, the law of the place of enrichment should apply.

21.240 This leads on to the question of what happens if the enrichment itself is conferred by electronic means. A recipient might pay for products over the internet by supplying credit card details under duress to the service provider, or supply them to the wrong person. A service provider might make available digitized products to a person other than the recipient. In such cases, the place of enrichment is not entirely obvious.

Payment of Money: the Provision of Credit or Debit Card Details by Electronic Means

21.241 Where the enrichment takes the form of a payment of money using the internet, is the enrichment obtained at the place where the payer sends the information, the place where the payee downloads the information, the place of residence or business of the payer or of the payee, the place of business of the credit card operator, the place where the payee's bank account is located into which the money is paid, or in some other state? The question is not easy to answer.

21.242 The unjust factor upon which the cause of action is based is likely to impinge upon the payer in his home state. In the case of a mistaken payment, the mistake naturally takes place where the payer is located; in a duress case, the duress will normally operate upon the payer in that state.

21.243 Against this, there is no enrichment of the payee until he has the means of access to the payer's credit card. He will not have this until the credit

---

[316] At paras 19.07–34.   [317] See Dicey and Morris, Rule 200(2)(c).

card details are *communicated* to him, which will occur in the place where he downloads the information and might suggest that this law should apply.

There again, the credit card details and the mandate to seek payment **21.244** from the credit card company provide no enrichment in themselves. It is the enforcement of these rights which gives rise to enrichment of the payee. Where payment is made by credit card, the payee will normally enforce his rights in the state where the credit card company has its place of business, or in the case of a multinational company, in the state where the branch of the company which issued the buyer's credit card is located. A debtor/creditor relationship exists between the credit card company and the payee. The *situs* of the debt created is, consistent with general principle, the place where the debtor has its place of business.[318]

However, the fact that the debt is located in the state of the credit card **21.245** company's place of business does not mean that the payee is immediately enriched in that state. The immediate enrichment is not the right to enforce a debt. That is a secondary right which becomes important only where the debtor defaults. The primary enrichment is the payment of the money to the payee. It is suggested that if money is paid by a French credit card company into the payee's bank account in Germany, the latter is the state of immediate enrichment. This remains the case even if the payee is resident in England. Any enrichment that he receives in England is indirect and consequent on the payment made in Germany.

Transfer of Digitized Products

Where the claim is brought by a service provider who supplies digitized **21.246** products to the wrong person, it is suggested that matters are somewhat simpler. Suppose that the products are uploaded by the service provider whilst it is located in State A, to a server in State B and downloaded by the recipient in State C. One might say that the cause of action rests upon the activities of the service provider in mistakenly making the product available for downloading by the recipient *from the server in State B*. This is the immediate cause of the opportunity of the recipient to obtain access to the product. However, the choice of law rules focus not on the immediate actions which enable the recipient to obtain enrichment, but on the

---

[318] *New York Life Insurance Co v Public Trustee* [1924] 2 Ch 101, CA; *Kwok Chi Leung Karl v Estate Duty Commissioners* [1988] 1 WLR 1035; *Power Curber International Ltd v National Bank of Kuwait SAK* [1988] 1 WLR 1035, CA.

immediate enrichment itself. Unless and until the recipient does obtain access to the digitized product, there is no basis for a claim against him. He obtains access to the product when it is available for his use. This occurs in the state where he downloads them. It is the law of this state, State C, which should be deemed to be the state of immediate enrichment.

Conclusion

21.247 Accordingly, it is suggested that where it is necessary[319] to determine for choice of law rules the place of enrichment of the defendant, the following rules should apply:

> (1) Where the enrichment consists of the payment of money to the payee which is made available by the claimant providing his debit or credit card details to the payee, the place of enrichment is the state where the account is located into which the money is paid.
>
> (2) Where the enrichment consists of the service provider making available a digitized product to the recipient, the place of enrichment is that state in which the product is downloaded.

2. Proprietary Restitution

21.248 Would it make any difference if the claimant sought not personal, restitutionary damages, but to assert or obtain a proprietary interest in the payment made by an internet credit card transaction, or the digitized product made available to the defendant? It was argued in Chapter 19 on restitution and choice of law that regardless of whether such claims are classified as proprietary or restitutionary, the law of the *situs* at the time of the last actual or purported transaction should apply.[320]

21.249 Suppose that a bespoke digitized product is uploaded by the service provider whilst it is located in State A. The place of uploading is State B.[321] It is downloaded by the recipient in State C and is now located on the recipient's computer, which is kept in his state of residence, State D. Which is the relevant law if a claim is brought that the product is vested in the original service provider or a third party, or that it should revest in that party? It is true that the product is now located in State D. However, if one draws an analogy to the transfer of tangible movable property, the

---

[319] On which, see above, paras 21.239–240 and 19.30, 19.33, 19.53–56, 19.67–68.
[320] At paras 19.96–73.
[321] That is, the place where the web-server is located to which the product is uploaded.

relevant property choice of law rule points to the place where the property was located at the time of the last actual or purported transaction in it.[322] It was argued above that digitized products are located in the state where the server to which the products are uploaded is situated. Accordingly, it is suggested that this claim should be governed by the law of State B.[323]

A similar approach should be taken to claims to assert a property inter- **21.250** est[324] in money paid pursuant to an internet credit card transaction. If the money is paid into the payee's account in State A, and the payee has since moved the money to another bank account located in State B,[325] the relevant situs is State A. The money may now be located in State B; however, there has been no actual or purported transfer in that State. State A is the place where the last transaction occurred.

VII. EVALUATION AND OPTIONS FOR REFORM

1. Options for Reform

In Chapter 10 on e-commerce and jurisdiction, three principal options for **21.251** reform were considered: leaving the courts to evolve suitable principles; reform of existing legislation to make special provision, where appropriate, for e-commerce; and having a wholly separate legislative regime for e-commerce.[326] The same options are, of course, available in respect of e-commerce and choice of law.

At the heart of the matter is the question of whether email and the internet **21.252** are just the latest in a long line of communications breakthroughs, or are so fundamentally different in nature to all other developments as to merit new rules altogether.[327] Certainly, it is undeniable that the rules of

---

[322] *Cammell v Sewell* (1858) H & N 617; *Winkworth v Christie* [1980] Ch 496, Ch D. See further Dicey and Morris, 963–977; Cheshire and North, Ch 30.

[323] If it is alleged that the product is held on trust for the claimant, the law which determines whether a trust arises and, if so, which law governs it, will probably be determined by the Hague Trusts Convention. Art 7 thereof states that the law of closest connection to the trust will apply to it, in the absence of an express or implied choice of law. See the discussion above, paras 19.74–87, esp para 19.80.

[324] If it is argued that the payment is held on trust for the claimant, the principles stated in the preceding footnote apply.

[325] In which case, it may be necessary to trace the money into a mixed fund in State B: see the discussion of tracing above, paras 19.88–96.

[326] At paras 10.242–258.

[327] Briggs, n 165 above, at 212, comments that: 'The view that the law had taken radio and television in its stride and would assimilate and digest the internet with equal ease may not be altogether convincing, but in the absence of legislation it probably has to be believed in'.

private international law currently in force were not designed to deal with e-commerce. At times, they might appear difficult to apply to this technology. In the context of the multiple publications rule in libel, Kirkby J pointedly remarked that, 'the Internet is global. As such, it knows no geographic boundaries. Its basic lack of locality suggests the need for a formulation of new legal rules to address the absence of congruence between cyberspace and the boundaries and laws of any given jurisdiction.'[328] On the other hand, it has been argued that the case for a separate e-commerce regime is unproven. 'That the conflict of laws is more relevant to transactions over the Internet should not suggest that the Internet demands any legal novelties in this area. After all, the principles in the conflict of laws exist for the very reason that multi-jurisdictional contracts can be made'.[329]

21.253 We shall now consider the possible options for reform, and the case for adopting them, a little further.

2. Leaving Reform to the Courts

General Comment

21.254 If reform were left to the courts, this would not resolve defects inherent in the legislative choice of law rules. Of course, the application of choice of law rules to e-commerce awaits clarification in the English courts. It is likely that it will take a considerable period of time before such a body of law emerges and, in the meantime, there will inevitably be a degree of uncertainty. Moreover, leaving the matter to judges will inevitably constrain the extent to which the law might evolve in this area.[330] This would not resolve any defects inherent in the legislative choice of law rules.

No Real Case for any Reform of Choice of Law in Contract Rules

21.255 That said, it has been shown that the choice of law rules in contract are generally suited to application to e-commerce disputes. In most cases, the contract will simply contain a choice of law clause.[331] Where it does not, the presumption in Article 4(2) of the Rome Convention works well, as it points to the law of the service provider's place of business. That is

---

[328] *Dow Jones*, para 113.   [329] Gringras, *The Law of the Internet*, (1st edn, 1997) 45.
[330] *Dow Jones*, para 138.
[331] 'In business-to business electronic transactions, party autonomy should be the leading principle both as regards applicable law and jurisdiction': Press Release, Geneva Round Table on Electronic Commerce and Private International Law, available at http://hcch.e-vision.nl/upload/wop/press01e.html, Recommendation No. 4.

a law which will normally be clear to the recipient, as it will be stated on the service provider's website or email communication; and the E-Commerce Directive imposes an obligation on the service provider to inform the recipient of, *inter alia*, his name and place of establishment.[332] The application of this law is also consistent with the 'country of origin' principle in the E-Commerce Directive. Again, this is the state where the service provider will usually will have its assets. Even in an e-commerce case, enforcement of an English judgment overseas may be an important issue. There are likely to be fewer problems if an English court has applied the same law that a judge in the state of enforcement would have applied. Applying the same law to e-commerce cases as for other cases also avoids the difficulty of deciding in some cases if a contract is an e-commerce transaction or not, as where some negotiations took place by email but the contract itself was concluded by other means.

Of course, the general rule may be rebutted under Article 4(5) if the con- **21.256** tract as a whole is more closely connected to another state. It is true that it may be difficult to localize certain factors in an e-commerce case. However, rather than attempting to do so, one might conclude that this very difficulty indicates a lack of an enduring or significant connection to that state. The consequence is that Article 4(5) may be used rarely. Legal certainty will actually be enhanced if the presumption in Article 4(2) is difficult to displace in an e-commerce case. Accordingly, it is suggested that no reform is needed of the choice of law rules in contract, as they apply to commercial transactions.

Clarification by the Courts of the Applicable Law in the Case of E-Commerce Torts and the *Situs* of Digitized Products

In tort, the existing choice of law rules work slightly less well in e- **21.257** commerce cases because there is some difficulty in determining the most significant element or elements of the tort and where they occur.[333] However, it would be possible for the courts to develop, over time, clear statements as to the law specified by s 11 of the 1995 Act in e-commerce cases. They may likewise put beyond doubt the *situs* of digitized products for the purposes of applying the property choice of law rule.

---

[332] See SI 2002/2013, reg 6(1)(a) and (b), implementing Art 5(1) of the E-Commerce Directive.
[333] For the purposes of s 11(2)(c) of the 1995 Act. There may also be difficulties with determining whether a claim is in respect of damage to property and, if so, where the property is when it is damaged, for the purposes of s 11(2)(b).

3. LEGISLATIVE REFORM: LIMITED PROVISIONS FOR E-COMMERCE CASES
WITHIN A GENERAL LEGISLATIVE FRAMEWORK

**Clarification by Legislative Provision of the Applicable Law in the Case
of E-Commerce Torts**

21.258 Another option would be to modify existing legislation, in order to
accommodate any specific concerns raised by e-commerce within the
general choice of law framework. The legislature will have a greater freedom to lay down a specific provision for e-commerce than the courts, who
should naturally be wary of over-zealous judicial creativity in adopting
an e-commerce specific interpretation of existing legislation.

21.259 It may be that the Rome Convention, if and when transformed into a
Regulation, will adopt such an approach.[334] In the jurisdiction context, it is
one that has found favour under the Brussels I Regulation[335] and during
the negotiation of the proposed Hague Judgments Convention.[336]

21.260 This approach has the advantage of allowing measured reflection as to
what special rules might be necessitated by e-commerce, without departing from the overarching aims of the choice of law rules in a given area. It
recognizes the doctrinal unity of choice of law in tort and the fact that
there is no compelling case for entirely separate choice of law rules for
e-commerce cases. It would also bring welcome clarity.

21.261 There is some case for such an approach in tort. The event based nature
of the choice of law rules in tort does create problems in the case of
e-commerce. It is necessary to locate events, notwithstanding that
e-commerce is inherently delocalized.

21.262 One option would be to lay down a legislative presumption that a tort
takes place in either the state of the claimant's or defendant's place of
business or residence.[337] This would provide an enduring connection in
tort, which may be notably lacking if one focuses on the 'events' which

---

[334] The Green Paper raises this issue, and suggests that this may be a particularly import-
ant issue in relation to consumer contracts. See 'Green Paper on the Conversion of the Rome
Convention of 1980 on the Law Applicable to Contractual Obligations into a Community
Instrument and its Modernisation' COM/2002/0654 Final.

[335] See above, paras 10.36–39, 10.239. See also paras 3.19 and 3.22. See, in particular, Art
23(2). See also Art 15(1)(c), which is concerned with consumer contracts.

[336] See the conclusions of Commission I on General Affairs and Policy of the Nineteenth
Diplomatic Session of the Hague Conference meeting held on 22 to 24 April 2002; Reflection Paper to Assist in the Preparation of a Convention on Jurisdiction and Recognition
and Enforcement of Foreign Judgments in Civil and Commercial Matters, by Schulz,
Enforcement of Judgments Prel Doc No 19 August 2002.

[337] Compare s 14 of the Australian Electronic Communications Act 1999.

give rise to a cause of action, such as the place of uploading, the place where the service provider is located at the time it uploads the information, or the place of downloading. A test based upon residence or place or business would be very difficult for the parties to manipulate. The law of the service provider would be consistent with the country of origin principle in the E-Commerce Directive and also with the law which is presumed to apply in contract law where the parties have made no express or implied choice of law.[338] The law of the recipient ensures that the state where the claimant is most likely to feel the effects of the tort applies.

However, the application of the law of the place of business or habitual **21.263** residence of either party would amount to the adoption of a new choice law rule for e-commerce, which uses a 'personal' connecting factor rather than an event based connecting factor. The case for such a change is unproven. The fact that the most significant element[339] of the events constituting the tort is hard to determine is not a reason to adopt a new choice of law rule altogether. The problem of torts which are difficult to localize in a single state existed before email and the internet, as where a misrepresentation was sent by fax from State A to State B[340] and detrimentally relied upon in State C. Nor is it true to say that torts committed by electronic means are entirely delocalized. It will be possible to determine the state of uploading and downloading of information, and of detrimental reliance. We have seen that it is then possible to determine where the most significant element or elements of the events constituting the tort occurred.[341] The fact that the general choice of law rule might lead to the application of the law of a state with little enduring connection to the tort is precisely why there is an exception in s 12 of the 1995 Act. In short, torts committed by electronic means can and should be accommodated within existing choice of law principles.

Harmonization of Choice of Law Rules

In order to protect the position of the parties, and not to expose the service **21.264** provider to liability by a range of laws in different states of the world, there is a case for international legislative harmonization in areas where it

---

[338] Art 4(2) of the Rome Convention. This, in turn, would reduce classification difficulties, at least where the 'contract' contains no express or implied choice of law.

[339] Or elements.

[340] Moreover, the defendant need not, of course, be resident in State A and the claimant need not be resident in State B. They might be resident in States D and E respectively.

[341] For the purposes of s 11(2)(c) of the 1995 Act.

does not exist, such as tort.[342] However, any such harmonization would not be e-commerce specific, but would apply generally to torts. At most, it might contain one or two e-commerce specific provisions within a unified doctrinal framework for torts.

4. Legislative Reform: Specific Legislation for E-Commerce

21.265 The most radical option is to introduce a special legislative regime for e-commerce.[343] Traditional choice of law rules, particularly in tort and property, emphasize territorial connections which may be inappropriate to delocalized means of communication such as the internet and email, where territorial connections may appear tenuous.[344]

21.266 However, at least in the commercial sales context, we have seen that the fact that a contract is negotiated and/or concluded by electronic means, or has been induced by a misrepresentation contained on a website or in an email, does not mean that there are not enduring territorial connections. The location of the products themselves and the place to which they are to be transferred provide no less powerful connecting factors than if entirely 'traditional' means of communication had been used. Choice of law rules are determined by the nature of the cause of action and the issue in question. They are not determined by the means of communication used. This suggests that a separate set of choice of law rules is not appropriate for communication over the internet[345] or by email[346] Accordingly, the case for e-commerce specific legislative reform is rather less than overwhelming.[347]

21.267 More importantly, the study in this chapter has shown that the existing rules are far from unsatisfactory and that the case for such a radical solution is simply not established.[348] A new regime would also raise

---

[342] A Rome II Regulation on choice of law in tort and unjust enrichment would provide a harmonized set of choice of law rules in these areas. However, this would be the case whether or not it contained e-commerce specific choice of law rules.

[343] Compare Burnstein, n 1 above, at 82. For a suggestion as to appropriate choice of law rules in relation to e-commerce cases involving consumer contracts, see R Schu, 'Consumer Protection and Private International Law in Internet Contracts' (1997) 5 Intl J of Law and Information Technology 192, esp 227–229.

[344] Indeed, in the context of internet defamation and the conflict of laws, the Law Commission's Preliminary Investigation concluded that: '. . . any solution would require an international treaty, accompanied by greater harmonisation of the substantive law of defamation. We do not think that the problem can be solved within the short to medium term. We do not therefore recommend reform in this area at the present time.' See *Defamation and the Internet: a Preliminary Investigation*, n 1 above para 4.54.

[345] *Dow Jones v Gutnick* 210 CLR 575, HC of Australia; [2002] HCA 56.

[346] Compare *Internet Doorway Inc v Parks* 138 F Supp 2d 773 (SD Miss 2001).

[347] Compare the approach in the US: ABA Cyberspace Report, 32–92.

[348] Such a view was expressed in relation to the law of jurisdiction at the Geneva Round Table Commission I, Prel Doc No 7, n 43 above.

definition problems as to what is meant by electronic commerce[349] and what special choice of law rules should apply.[350]

VIII. CONCLUSION

That electronic commerce has changed the shape of the business world **21.268** can barely be disputed. However, it has been demonstrated that existing choice of law rules applicable to commercial activity can cope with electronic commerce within their existing frameworks. There is a serious risk that a move to electronic commerce specific rules would create an unfortunate schism within doctrinally coherent areas of law. There would also be complex questions of defining the scope of these rules and their content. On balance, it is argued that the adoption of electronic commerce specific choice of law rules would do more harm than good.

---

[349] Burnstein, n 1 above, at 90 suggests a definition based upon how the line is drawn in the US between Admiralty cases and other cases, which asks whether there is a 'significant connection to traditional maritime activity'. However, it is difficult to see how this takes us forward. It seems to introduce a further tier of uncertainty and unpredictability. Moreover, it is less than obvious that 'the high seas are conceptually very similar to cyberspace' (ibid, at 103). Events upon the high seas may lack a territorial connection; however, in e-commerce disputes, there *will* be a series of connections to different states, such as the state of uploading, downloading and of detrimental reliance. Moreover, e-commerce raises the problem of ease of access and the possibility of exposure, through a single act, to liability by any law of the world. See also the US Supreme Court's decision in *Lauritzen v Larsen* 345 US 57 (1953).

[350] See Burnstein, ibid, at 102, where the author argues for a *lex mercatoria* for cyberspace. However, he offers little suggestion as to the content of this law; see also D Johnson and D Post, 'Laws and Borders-the Rise of Law in Cyberspace' (1996) 48 Stanford L Rev 1367. Compare the ABA Cyberspace Report, 20–23. But see Reed, n 7 above Ch 7, esp 188.

distribution problems as to what is meant by electronic commerce, and what special choice-of-law rules should apply.

VIII. CONCLUSION

That electronic commerce has changed the shape of the business world 21.268 can hardly be disputed. However, it has been demonstrated that existing choice of law rules applicable to commercial delivery can cope with electronic commerce within their existing frameworks. There is a serious risk that a move to electronic commerce specific rules would create an unfortunate schism within currently coherent areas of law. There would also be complex questions of defining the scope of these rules and their content. On balance it is argued that the adoption of electronic commerce specific choice of law rules would do more harm than good.

Bibliography

Books and Chapters in Books

Anton, AE and PR Beaumont, *Private International Law* (2nd edn, Edinburgh: Green, 1990)

Baatz, Y, 'The Impact of the EC Conventions and Directives on Governing Law and Jurisdiction in Marine Insurance and Reinsurance Contracts', Ch 10 in D Rhidian Thomas (ed), *The Modern Law of Marine Insurance* (London: LLP, 1996)

Barcelo, JJ and KM Clermont (eds), *A Global Law of Jurisdiction and Judgments: Lessons from the Hague* (The Hague/London: Kluwer Law, 2002)

Basedow, J and T Kono (eds), *Legal Aspects of Globalization: Conflict of Laws, Internet, Capital Markets and Insolvency in a Global Economy* (The Hague: Kluwer, 2000)

Beatson, J, *The Use and Abuse of Unjust Enrichment* (Oxford: Clarendon, 1991)

Beaumont, P, 'The Brussels Convention becomes a Regulation: Implications for Legal Basis, External Competence, and Contract Jurisdiction', Ch 1 in J Fawcett (ed), *Reform and Development of Private International Law* (Oxford: OUP, 2002)

Bell, A, *Forum Shopping and Venue in Transnational Litigation* (Oxford: OUP, 2003)

Bell, J, S Boyron and S Whittaker, *Principles of French Law* (Oxford: Clarendon, 1998)

Benatti, F, *La Responsibilità Precontracttuale* (Milan: 1963)

Bennett, H, *The Law of Marine Insurance* (Oxford: Clarendon, 1996)

Berliri, M, 'Jurisdiction and the Internet, and European Regulation 44 of 2001' in D Campbell and S Woodley (eds), *E-Commerce: Law and Jurisdiction: The Comparative Law Yearbook of International Business—Special Issue 2002* (Aspen, 2002)

Bird, J, 'Choice of Law', Ch 3 in F Rose (ed), *Restitution and the Conflict of Laws* (Oxford: Mansfield, 1995)

Birks, P, 'Restitution and Resulting Trusts' in S Goldstein (ed), *Equity: Contemporary Legal Developments* (Jerusalem: Hebrew University of Jerusalem, 1992)

—— *An Introduction to the Law of Restitution* (Oxford: Clarendon, 1995)

—— *Restitution: The Future* (Annandale, NSW: Federation, 1992)

Boele-Woelki, K, 'Convention sur la Loi Applicable aux Ventes à Caractère International d'Objets Mobiliers Corporels, du 15 Juin 1955' in M Sumampouw (ed), *Les Nouvelles Conventions de la Haye* (Dordrecht: Martinus Nijhoff, 1984)

Bowtle, G and K McGuiness, *The Law of Ship Mortgages* (London: LLP, 2001)

Boyd, S, A Burrows and D Foxton, *Scrutton on Charterparties and Bills of Lading* (20th edn, London: Sweet & Maxwell, 1996)

Brazier, MR (ed), *Clerk and Lindsell on Torts* (17th edn, London: Sweet & Maxwell, 1995)

Brereton, R, 'Restitution and Contract', Ch 4 in F Rose (ed), *Restitution and the Conflict of Laws* (Oxford: Mansfield, 1995)

Bridge, M, *The Sale of Goods* (Oxford: Clarendon, 1997)

——, *The International Sale of Goods: Law and Practice* (Oxford: OUP, 1999)

——, *Personal Property Law* (3rd edn, Oxford: OUP, 2002)

——, 'English Conflicts Rules for Transfers of Movables: A Contract-based Approach?', Ch 7 in M Bridge and R Stevens, *Cross-Border Security and Insolvency* (Oxford: OUP, 2001)

Briggs, A, *The Conflict of Laws* (Oxford: Clarendon, 2002)

—— and P Rees, *Civil Jurisdiction and Judgments* (3rd edn, London: LLP, 2002)

Burrows, A, *The Law of Restitution* (2nd edn, Croydon: Butterworths, 2002)

Campbell, D and S Woodley (eds), *E-Commerce: Law and Jurisdiction: The Comparative Law Yearbook of International Business—Special Issue 2002* (Aspen, 2002)

Carbonnier, J, *Droit Civil, Tome 3, Les biens (Monnaie, immeubles, meubles)* (16th edn, Presses Universitaires de France, 1995)

——, *Droit Civil, Tome 4, Les obligations* (19th edn, Presses Universitaires de France, 1995)

Chambers, R, *Resulting Trusts* (Oxford: OUP, 1997)

Collins, L et al (eds), *Dicey and Morris on the Conflict of Laws* (13th edn, London: Sweet & Maxwell, 1999)

Collins, M, *The Law of Defamation and the Internet* (Oxford: OUP, 2001)

Cooke, J, T Young, A Taylor, J Kimball, D Martowski and L Lambert, *Voyage Charters* (2nd edn, London: LLP, 2001)

Cornish, W, R Nolan, J O'Sullivan and G Virgo (eds), *Restitution: Past, Present and Future* (Oxford: Hart, 1998)

Cuming, R, 'The Characterisation of Interests and Transactions under the Convention on International Interests in Mobile Equipment 2001' in I Davies (ed), *Security Interests in Mobile Equipment* (Aldershot: Ashgate Dartmouth, 2002)

Dannemann, G, 'The "Battle of the Forms" and the Conflict of Laws', Ch 11 in F Rose (ed), *Lex Mercatoria—Essays on International Commercial Law in Honour of Francis Reynolds* (London: LLP, 2000)

Davies, I (ed), *Security Interests in Mobile Equipment* (Aldershot: Ashgate Dartmouth, 2002)

Dogauchi, M, 'Law Applicable to Torts and Copyright Infringement through the Internet' in J Basedow and T Kono (eds), *Legal Aspects of Globalization: Conflict of Laws, Internet, Capital Markets and Insolvency in a Global Economy* (The Hague: Kluwer, 2000)

Dugdale, AM (ed), *Clerk and Lindsell on Torts* (18th edn, London: Sweet & Maxwell, 2000)

Edwards, L and C Waelde, *Law and the Internet: Regulating Cyberspace* (Oxford: Hart, 1997)

Eörsi, G, 'General Provisions' in NM Galston and H Smit, *International Sales: The United Nations Convention on Contracts for the International Sale of Goods* (Parker School of Comparative Law, 1984)

Falconbridge, J, *Conflict of Laws* (2nd edn, Canada Law Book Co, 1954)

Fawcett, J, *Declining Jurisdiction in Private International Law* (Oxford: Clarendon Press, 1995)

—— 'Jurisdiction', Ch 6 in A Grubb and G Howells (eds), *The Law of Product Liability* (London: Butterworths, 2000)

—— (ed), *Reform and Development of Private International Law* (Oxford: OUP, 2002)

—— and Torremans, *Intellectual Property and Private International Law* (Oxford: OUP, 1998)

Fentiman, R, *Foreign Law in English Courts* (Oxford: OUP, 1998)

Forner Delaygua, JJ, 'Internet Jurisdiction in "Business to Business" On-Line Performed Contracts: Lessons From the Hague?' in JJ Barcelo and KM Clermont (eds), *A Global Law of Jurisdiction and Judgments: Lessons from the Hague* (The Hague/London: Kluwer Law, 2002)

Fridman, G, *The Law of Torts in Canada* (Toronto: Carswell, 1989)

Galston, NM and H Smit, *International Sales: The United Nations Convention on Contracts for the International Sale of Goods* (Parker School of Comparative Law, 1984)

Gaskell, N, R Asariotis and Y Baatz, *Bills of Lading: Law and Contracts* (London: LLP, 2000)

Goldstein, S (ed), *Equity: Contemporary Legal Developments* (Jerusalem: Hebrew University of Jerusalem, 1992)

Goode, R, 'The UNIDROIT Mobile Equipment Convention' in M Bridge and R Stevens, *Cross-Border Security and Insolvency* (Oxford: OUP, 2001)

Gringras, C, *The Law of the Internet* (1st edn, London: Butterworths, 1997)

——, —— (2nd edn, London: Butterworths, 2003)

Grubb, A and G Howells (eds), *The Law of Product Liability* (London: Butterworths, 2000)

Guest, A (ed), *Benjamin's Sale of Goods* (6th edn, London: Sweet & Maxwell, 2002)

Harris, J, 'Launching the Rocket: Capacity and the Creation of *Inter Vivos* Trusts', Ch C2 in J Glasson, *International Trust Laws* (Bristol: Jordans, looseleaf)

—— 'Consumer Protection in Private International Law', Ch 11 in F Meisel and P Cook (eds), *Property and Protection: Essays in Honour of Brian Harvey* (Oxford: Hart Publishing, 2000)

—— *The Hague Trusts Convention* (Oxford: Hart, 2002)

Hill, J, *The Law Relating to International Commercial Disputes* (2nd edn, London: LLP, 1998)

Hondius, E, *Precontractual Liability* (Deventer: Kluwer, 1991)

Honnold, J, *Documentary History of the Uniform Law for International Sales* (Deventer: Kluwer, 1989)

——, *Uniform Law for International Sales under the 1980 United Nations Convention* (2nd edn, Deventer: Kluwer, 1990)

——, —— (3rd edn, Deventer: Kluwer, 1999)

Horn, N, H Kötz and HG Leser (trans Weir), *German Private and Commercial Law: An Introduction (Oxford: Clarendon, 1982)*

Keller, M and K Siehr, *Allgemeine Lehren des Internationalen Privatrechts* (Schulthess, 1986)

Koppenol-Laforce, M, *Het Haagse Trustverdrag* (Deventer: Kluwer, 1997)

Kronke, H, 'Applicable Law in Torts and Contracts in Cyberspace' in K Boele-Woelki and C Kessedjian (eds), *Internet: Which Court Decides? Which Law Applies?* (The Hague: Kluwer, 1998)

Lalive, P, *The Transfer of Chattels in the Conflict of Laws* (Oxford: Clarendon, 1955)

Lim, Y, *Cyberspace Law: Commentaries and Materials* (Oxford: OUP, 2002)

Lipstein, K (ed), *International Encyclopaedia of Comparative Law* (Leiden: Martinus Nijhoff)

Mandaraka-Shepherd, A, *Modern Admiralty Law* (London: Cavendish, 2001)

Markesinis, B, *The German Law of Obligations, Volume II The Law of Torts: A Comparative Introduction* (3rd edn, Oxford: Clarendon, 1994)

——, W Lorenz and G Danneman, *The German Law of Obligations, Volume I, The Law of Contracts and Restitution: A Comparative Introduction* (Oxford: Clarendon, 1997)

—— and H Unberath, *The German Law of Torts* (4th edn, Oxford: Hart, 2002)

Matic, Z, 'The Hague Convention on the Law Applicable to Contracts for the International Sale of Goods—Rules on the Applicable Law', Ch 4 in P Sarcevic (ed), *International Contracts and Conflicts of Laws: a Collection of Essays* (London: Graham & Trotman, 1990)

Merkin, R and A Rodger, *EC Insurance Law* (London: Longman, 1997)

Miller, G, J Mowbray, L Tucker, N Le Poidevin and E Simpson, *Lewin on Trusts* (17th edn, London: Sweet & Maxwell, 2000)

Moss, G, S Isaacs and I Fletcher, *The EC Regulation on Insolvency Proceedings* (Oxford: OUP, 2002)

Moura Ramos, R, 'The New EC Rules on Jurisdiction and the Recognition and Enforcement of Judgments' in J Nafziger and S Symeonides (eds), *Law and Justice in a Multistate World: Essays in Honor of Arthur T von Mehren* (New York: Transnational Publishers Inc, 2002)

Nafziger, J, and S Symeonides (eds), *Law and Justice in a Multistate World: Essays in Honor of Arthur T von Mehren* (New York: Transnational Publishers Inc, 2002)

North, P, *Essays in Private International Law* (Oxford: Clarendon, 1993)

—— and J Fawcett (eds), *Cheshire and North's Private International Law* (13th edn, London: Butterworths, 1999)

Nygh, P, *Autonomy in International Contracts* (Oxford Monographs in Private International Law: Clarendon Press, 1999)

O'Malley, S and A Layton, *European Civil Practice* (London: Sweet & Maxwell, 1989)

Panagopoulos, G, *Restitution in Private International Law* (Oxford: Hart, 2000)

Peel, E, 'Conflict of Laws', Ch 15 in E McKendrick (ed), *Sale of Goods* (London: LLP, 2000)

Peel, E, 'Jurisdiction under the Brussels Convention', Ch 1 in F Rose (ed), *Restitution and the Conflict of Laws* (Oxford: Mansfield, 1995)

Plender, R and M Wilderspin, *The European Contracts Convention* (2nd edn, London: Sweet & Maxwell, 2001)

Reed, C, *Internet Law: Text and Materials* (London: Butterworths, 2000)

Rhidian Thomas, D (ed), *The Modern Law of Marine Insurance* (London: LLP, 1996)

Rogers, WVH, (ed), *Winfield and Jolowicz on Tort* (16th edn, London: Sweet & Maxwell, 2002)

Rose, F (ed), *Restitution and the Conflict of Laws* (Oxford: Mansfield, 1995)

—— (ed), *Failure of Contracts: Contractual, Restitutionary and Proprietary Consequences* (Oxford: Hart, 1997)

Rubino-Sammartano, M and C Morse, *Public Policy in Transnational Relationships* (The Hague: Kluwer, 1992)

Sarcevic, P, *International Contracts and Conflicts of Laws: A Collection of Essays* (London: Graham & Trotman, 1990)

Sassoon, D, *C.i.f. and F.o.b. Contracts* (4th edn, London: Sweet & Maxwell, 1995)

Schlechtriem, P, *Uniform Sale Law—The UN Convention on the International Sale of Goods* (Vienna: 1986)

—— (ed) (trans Thomas), *Commentary on the UN Convention on the International Sale of Goods* (2nd edn, Oxford: Clarendon, 1998)

Seatzu, F, *Insurance in Private International Law: A European Perspective* (Oxford: Hart Publishing, 2003)

Simmons and Simmons, *E-Commerce Law* (2001)

Smith, G, *Internet Law and Regulation* (London: Sweet & Maxwell, 2002)

Sono, K, 'The Vienna Sale Convention: History and Perspective' in P Volken and P Sarcevic, *International Sale of Goods: Dubrovnik Lectures* (New York: Oceana, 1986)

Stevens, J, 'Contract, Unjustified Enrichment and Concurrent Liability: a Scots Perspective—a Comment', Ch 15 in F Rose (ed), *Failure of Contracts: Contractual, Restitutionary and Proprietary Consequences* (Oxford: Hart, 1997)

Stevens, R, 'The Choice of Law Rules for Restitutionary Obligations' in F Rose (ed), *Restitution and the Conflict of Laws* (Oxford: Mansfield, 1995)

Story, J, *Commentaries on the Conflict of Laws* (Bigelow (ed), 8th edn, Boston: Little and Brown, 1883)

Sykes, E and M Pryles, *Australian Private International Law* (3rd edn, Sydney: Law Book Co, 1991)

Todd, P, *Bills of Lading and Bankers' Documentary Credits* (3rd edn, London: LLP, 1998)

Todd, S, *The Law of Torts in New Zealand* (3rd edn, Wellington: Brookers, 2001)

Virgo, G, *The Principles of the Law of Restitution* (Oxford: OUP, 1999)

Volken, P and P Sarcevic, *International Sale of Goods: Dubrovnik Lectures* (New York: Oceana, 1986)

Whincop, M and M Keyes, *Policy and Pragmatism in the Conflict of Laws* (Aldershot: Ashgate, 2001)

Wilford, M, T Coghlin and J Kimball, *Time Charters* (5th edn, London: LLP, 2003)

Wilson, J, *Carriage of Goods by Sea* (4th edn, Harlow: Longman, 2001)

Wolff, M, *Private International Law* (2nd edn, Oxford: Clarendon, 1950)

Worthington, S, 'The Proprietary Consequences of Contract Failure', Ch 5 in F Rose (ed), *Failure of Contracts: Contractual, Restitutionary and Proprietary Consequences* (Oxford: Hart, 1997)

Yeo, T, *Choice of Law for Equitable Doctrines* (Oxford: OUP, 2004)

Zaphiriou, G, *The Transfer of Chattels in Private International Law: A Comparative Study* (London: Athlone Press/University of London, 1956)

Zweigert, K and H Kötz, *An Introduction to Comparative Law* (2nd edn, Oxford: Clarendon, 1987)

—— and D Müller-Gindullis, 'Quasi-Contract', Ch 30 in K Lipstein (ed), *International Encyclopaedia of Comparative Law* (Leiden: Martinus Nijhoff)

Journal articles

Anassutzi, M, 'The E-Commerce Directive 00/31' [2002] ICCLR 337

Ancel, B, 'The Brussels I Regulation: Comment' (2001) III Ybk of Private Intl Law 101

Asariotis, R, 'Implications of a "British" Jurisdiction Clause' [1992] JBL 321

Atrill, S, 'Choice of Law in Contract: the Missing Pieces of the Article 4 Jigsaw?' (2004) 53 ICLQ 549

Bagert, S, '*South Central Bell v. Barthelemy*. The Louisiana Supreme Court determines that computer software is tangible personal property' (1995) 69 Tulane L Rev 1367

Beale, H and L Griffiths, 'Electronic Commerce: Formal Requirements in Commercial Transaction' [2002] LMCLQ 467

Beatson, J and J Cooper, 'Rights of Suit in Respect of Carriage of Goods by Sea' [1991] LMCLQ 196

Beaumont, P, 'European Court of Justice and Jurisdiction and Enforcement of Judgments in Civil and Commercial Matters' (1999) 48 ICLQ 225

Beck, A, 'Floating Choice of Law Clauses' [1987] LMCLQ 523

Bird, J, 'Choice of Law and Restitution of Benefits Conferred under a Void Contract' [1997] LMCLQ 182

Birks, P, 'Trusts Raised to Reverse Unjust Enrichment: the *Westdeutsche* Case' (1996) 4 Restitution L Rev 3

—— 'Inconsistency between Compensation and Restitution' (1996) 112 LQR 375

Blaikie, J, 'Unjust Enrichment in the Conflict of Laws' [1984] Juridical Rev 112

Boele-Woelki, K, 'The Limitation of Rights and Actions in the International Sale of Goods' (1999) IV(3) Uniform L Rev 621

Bolger, P, 'Making Contracts over the Internet' (1999) 3(3) Irish Intellectual Property Rev 20

Bonell, MJ, 'The UNIDROIT Principles as a Means of Interpreting and Supplementing International Law' (2002) 13 ICC International Court of Arbitration Bulletin (Special Supplement) 29

Borchers, PJ, 'Tort and Contract Jurisdiction via the Internet: The "Minimum Contacts" Test and the Brussels Regulation Compared' [2003] Netherlands Intl L Rev 401

Bradgate, J, 'The Post-Contractual Reservation of Title' [1988] JBL 477

Bradgate, R and F White, 'The Carriage of Goods by Sea Act 1992' (1993) 56 MLR 188

Bridge, M, 'The Carriage of Goods by Sea Act 1992' [1993] JBL 379

Briggs, A, 'The Validity of "Floating" Choice of Law and Jurisdiction Clauses' [1986] LMCLQ 508

—— 'The Formation of International Contracts' [1990] LMCLQ 192

—— 'The International Dimension to Claims for Contribution' [1995] LMCLQ 437

—— 'Choice of Law in Tort and Delict' [1995] LMCLQ 519

—— 'Decisions of British Courts During 2000: Private International Law' (2002) 73 British Ybk of Intl Law 453

—— 'Public Policy in the Conflict of Laws: a Sword and a Shield?' (2002) 6 Singapore J of Intl and Comparative Law 953

—— 'Choice of Choice of Law?' [2003] LMCLQ 12

—— 'On Drafting Agreements on Choice of Law' [2003] LMCLQ 389

—— 'The Duke of Brunswick and Defamation by Internet' (2003) 119 LQR 210

Brodsky, W, 'Surfin' the Stream of Commerce: *Compuserve v. Patterson*' (1997) 70 Temple L Rev 825

Burnstein, M, 'Conflicts on the Net: Choice of Law in Transnational Cyberspace' (1996) 29 Vanderbilt J of Transnational Law 75

Burrows, A, 'Swaps and the Friction between Common Law and Equity' (1995) 3 Restitution L Rev 15

—— 'Solving the Problem of Concurrent Liability' (1995) 48 CLP 103

Carruthers, J, 'Substance and Procedure in the Conflict of Laws: a Continuing Debate in Relation to Damages' (2004) 53 ICLQ 691

—— and E Crawford, 'Kuwait Airways Corporation v Iraqi Airways Company' (2003) 52 ICLQ 761

Carter, P, 'Rejection of Foreign Law: Some Private International Law Inhibitions' (1984) 55 British Ybk of Intl Law 111

—— 'The Role of Public Policy in English Private International Law' (1993) 42 ICLQ 1

—— 'The Private International Law (Miscellaneous Provisions) Act 1995' (1996) 112 LQR 190

Castel, J, 'The Internet in Light of Traditional Public and Private International Law Principles and Rules Applied in Canada' [2001] Canadian Ybk of Intl Law 3

Chesterman, M, 'Choice of Law Aspects of Liens and Similar Claims in International Sale of Goods' (1973) 22 ICLQ 213

Cohen, D and B Ughetto, 'La Nouvelle Convention de La Haye Relative à la Loi Applicable aux Ventes Internationales de Marchandises' (1986) 20 Recueil Dalloz 149 (continued in (1987) 21 Recueil Dalloz 157)

Collins, L, 'Forum Non Conveniens and the Brussels Convention' (1990) 106 LQR 535

Cuming, R, 'The draft UNIDROIT Convention on International Interests in Mobile Equipment (1998) 30 Uniform Commercial Code LJ 365

—— 'Overview of the Convention on International Interests in Mobile Equipment 2001' (2002) 35 Uniform Commercial Code LJ 73

Curwen, N, 'Title to Sue in Conversion' [2004] Conveyancer and Property Lawyer 308

Davis, J, 'Conditional Sales and Chattel Mortgages in the Conflict of Laws' (1964) 13 ICLQ 53

Diamond, A, 'Harmonisation of Private International Law Relating to Contractual Obligations' (1986–IV) 199 Hague Recueil 233

Dickinson, A, 'Restitution and Incapacity: a Choice of Law Solution?' (1997) 5 Restitution L Rev 66

D'Oliveira, J, 'Characteristic Obligation in the draft EEC Obligation Convention' (1977) 25 AJCL 303

Dore, I, 'Choice of Law under the International Sales Convention: a US Perspective' [1983] American J of Intl Law 521

Droz, G, 'Entrée en Vigueur de la Convention sur la Loi Applicable aux Ventes à Caractère International d'Objets Mobiliers Corporels' [1964] Revue Critique de Droit International Privé 663

—— '_Delendum est forum contractus?_ (vingt ans après les arrêts _De Bloos_ et _Tessili_ interprétant l'article 5.1 de la Convention de Bruxelles du 27 septembre 1968)' [1997] Recueil Dalloz 351

Dutson, S, 'The Conflict of Laws and Statutes: the International Operation of Legislation Dealing with Matters of Civil Law in the United Kingdom and Australia' (1997) 60 MLR 668

Ehrenzweig, A, 'Restitution in the Conflict of Laws' (1969) 36 New York U L Rev 1298

Enonchong, N, 'Public Policy in the Conflict of Laws: a Chinese Wall around Little England?' (1996) 45 ICLQ 633

Fawcett, J, 'A New Approach to Jurisdiction over Companies in Private International Law' (1988) 37 ICLQ 645

—— 'Multi-party Litigation in Private International Law' (1995) 44 ICLQ 744

—— 'Cross-Fertilisation in Private International Law' [2000] CLP 303

—— 'Non-exclusive Jurisdiction Agreements in Private International Law' [2001] LMCLQ 234

Fentiman, R, 'Commercial Expectations and the Rome Convention' (2002) 61 CLJ 50

Ferrari, F, ' "Forum Shopping" Despite International Uniform Contract Law Conventions' (2002) 51 ICLQ 689

Forner, J-J, 'Special Jurisdiction in Commercial Contracts: From the 1968 Brussels Convention to Brussels-One Regulation' [2002] ICCLR 131

Forsyth, C and P Moser, 'The Impact of the Applicable Law of Contract on the Law of Jurisdiction under the European Conventions' (1996) 45 ICLQ 190

Foyer, J, 'La Convention de La Haye du 15 Juin 1955' [1990] Revue Critique de Droit International Privé 712

Frédéricq, L, 'La Vente en Droit International Privé (Quelques Conventions Récentes)' (1958) 93-I Recueil des Cours de l'Académie de droit international de La Haye 1

Garton, J, (2001) 15 Trust L Intl 93

Giliker, P, 'A Role for Tort in Pre-Contractual Negotiations? An Examination of English, French and Canadian Law' (2003) 52 ICLQ 969

Gillies, L, 'A Review of the New Jurisdiction Rules for Electronic Consumer Contracts within the European Union' [2001] J of Information, Law & Technology 1

Gilmore, M, 'Hague Conference on the Law Applicable to Contracts for the International Sale of Goods' (1987) 28 Harvard Intl LJ 526

Girvin, S, 'Contracting Carriers, Himalaya Clauses and Tort in the House of Lords' [2003] LMCLQ 311

Goldring, J, 'Jurisdiction and Applicable Law in the Carriage of Goods by Sea' (2000) 5 Uniform L Rev 348

Goode, R, 'Transcending the Boundaries of Earth and Space: the Preliminary Draft Unidroit Convention on International Interests in Mobile Equipment' (1998) 3 Uniform L Rev 52

—— 'The Cape Town Convention on International Interests in Mobile Equipment: a Driving Force for International Asset-Based Financing' (2002) 7 Uniform L Rev 3

Grodecki, J, 'Conflict of Laws in Time' (1959) 35 British Ybk of Intl Law 58

Gutteridge, H and K Lipstein, 'Conflicts of Law in Matters of Unjustifiable Enrichment' (1939) 7 CLJ 80

Harris, J, 'Related Actions and the Brussels Convention' [1998] LMCLQ 145

—— 'Choice of Law in Tort—Blending in with the Landscape of the Conflict of Laws?' (1998) 61 MLR 33

—— 'Contractual Freedom in the Conflict of Laws' (2000) 20 OJLS 247

—— 'Tracing and the Conflict of Laws' (2002) 73 British Ybk of Intl Law 65

—— and F Meisel, 'Public Policy and the Enforcement of International Arbitration Awards: Controlling the Unruly Horse' [1998] LMCLQ 568

Hellendall, F, 'The Res in Transitu and Similar Problems in the Conflict of Laws' (1939) 17 Canadian Bar Rev 7 (Part I) and 105 (Part II)

Hill, J, 'Jurisdiction in Matters Relating to a Contract under the Brussels Convention' [1995] ICLQ 591

—— 'Choice of Law in Contract under the Rome Convention: the Approach of the UK Courts' (2004) 53 ICLQ 325

Hogan, G, 'Contracting Out of the Rome Convention' (1992) 108 LQR 12

Hogan-Doran, J, 'Jurisdiction in cyberspace: The when and where of online contracts' (2003) Australian LJ 377

Jacobson, D, 'The International Sale of Goods' (1954) 3 ICLQ 659

Jaffey, A, 'Essential Validity of Contracts in the English Conflict of Laws' (1974) 23 ICLQ 1

—— 'Offer and Acceptance and Related Questions in the English Conflict of Laws' (1975) 24 ICLQ 603

—— 'The English Proper Law Doctrine and the EEC Convention' (1984) 33 ICLQ 531

Johnson, D and D Post, 'Law and Borders: The Rise of Law in Cyberspace' (1996) 48 Stanford L Rev 1367

Joyce, A, 'Consequences of Publication on the Internet' (2003) 17 Corp Brief 5

Kahn, P, 'La Convention de La Haye sur la Loi Applicable aux Ventes à Caractère International d'Objets Mobiliers Corporels' [1966] Journal du Droit International 301

Kalow, G, 'Note, From the Internet to Court: Exercising Jurisdiction over World Wide Web Communications' (1997) 65 Fordham L Rev 2241

Kennett, W, 'Place of Performance and Predictability' [1995] Ybk of European Law 193

Kimball, J and S Harter, 'Choice of Law Issues in Contracts for the International Sale of Goods: Getting What You Bargained for in the United States' (1997) 1 Intl Trade LQ 28

Kohl, U, 'Eggs, Jurisdiction and the Internet' (2002) 51 ICLQ 555

—— 'Defamation on the Internet—Nice Decision, Shame about the Reasoning: *Dow Jones & Co v Gutnick*' (2003) 52 ICLQ 1049

Koneru, P, 'The International Interpretation of the UN Convention on Contracts for the International Sale of Goods: An Approach Based on General Principles' (1997) 6 Minnesota J of World Trade 105

Lagarde, P, 'The European Convention on the Law Applicable to Contractual Obligations: an Apologia' (1981) 22 Virginia J of Intl Law 91

—— 'La Nouvelle Convention de La Haye sur la Loi Applicable aux Contrats de Vente Internationale de Marchandises' in Journées de la Société de Législation Comparée (1985) 7 Revue Internationale de Droit Comparé 327

—— 'Le Nouveau Droit International Privé des Contrats' (1991) 80 Revue Critique de Droit International Privé 287

Lando, O, 'The EEC Convention on the Law Applicable to Contractual Obligations' [1987] CML Rev 159

—— 'The 1985 Hague Convention on the Law Applicable to Sales' [1987] Rabels Zeitschrift für Ausländisches und Internationales Privatrecht 60

—— 'The 1955 and 1985 Hague Conventions on the Law Applicable to the International Sale of Goods' [1993] 1/2 Rabels Zeitschrift für Ausländisches und Internationales Privatrecht 155

Leslie, R, 'The Relevance of Public Policy in Legal issues Involving Other Countries and their Laws' (1995) 6 Juridical Rev 477

Libling, D, 'Formation of International Contracts' (1979) 42 MLR 169

Loos, MBM, 'Towards a European Law of Service Contracts' (2001) 9 European Rev of Private Law

Loussouarn, Y, 'La Convention de La Haye d'Octobre 1985 sur la Loi Applicable aux Contrats de Vente Internationale de Marchandises' [1986] Revue Critique de Droit International Privé 271

Magnus, U, 'General Principles of UN-Sales Law' (1997) 3 Intl Trade and Business L Annual 33

Mann, F, 'The Time Element in the Conflict of Laws' (1954) 32 British Ybk of Intl Law 217

—— 'Statutes and the Conflict of Laws' (1972–3) 46 British Ybk of Intl Law 117

—— 'The Proper Law of the Contract—an Obituary' (1991) 107 LQR 353

Martin-Clark, D, 'Where are you leading us, Ranger?' (2002) 2 Shipping and Trade Law 1

McCormack, G, 'Retention of Title and the EC Late Payment Directive' (2001) 1 J of Corporate L Studies 501

McLachlan, C, 'The New Hague Sales Convention and the Limits of the Choice of Law Process' (1986) 102 LQR 591

Morris, J, 'The Transfer of Chattels in the Conflict of Laws' (1945) 22 British Ybk of Intl Law 232

—— 'The Time Factor in the Conflict of Laws' (1966) 15 ICLQ 422

Morse, C, 'Consumer Contracts, Employment Contracts and the Rome Convention' (1992) 41 ICLQ 1

—— 'Reservation of Title in English Private International Law' [1993] JBL 168

—— 'Torts in Private International Law: A New Statutory Framework' (1996) 45 ICLQ 888

Moshinsky, M, 'The Assignment of Debts in the Conflict of Laws' (1992) 108 LQR 591

Nimmer, RT, 'Through the Looking Glass: What Courts and UCITA say about the Scope of Contract Law in the Information Age' (2000) 38 Duquesne L Rev 255

North, P, 'Contract as a Tort Defence in the Conflict of Laws' (1977) 26 ICLQ 914

—— 'Reform, but not Revolution' (1990-I) 220 Recueil des Cours 9

—— 'Choice in Choice of Law' (1992) King's College LJ 29

O'Keefe, R, 'English Public Policy Internationalized—and Conversion Clarified Too' (2002) 61 CLJ 499

Oren, J, 'International Jurisdiction Over Consumer Contracts in E-Europe' (2003) 52 ICLQ 665

Panagopoulos, G, 'Cross Border Tracing; Conflict of Laws Issues' (1998) 6 Restitution L Rev 73

Peel, E, 'The Scope of Double Actionability and Public Policy' (2003) 119 LQR 1

—— 'Actual Carriers and the Hague Rules' (2004) 120 LQR 11

Pelichet, M, 'La Vente Internationale de Marchandises et le Conflit de Lois' (1987) 201-I Recueil des Cours de l'Académie de droit international de La Haye 9

Perkins, J, 'Identifying the Locus of the Tort' [2003] CLJ 274

Pierce, D, 'Post-Formation Choice of Law in Contract' (1987) 50 MLR 176

Réczei, L, 'The Area of Operation of the International Sale Conventions' (1981) 29 American J of Comparative Law 513

Reed, A, 'The Private International Law (Miscellaneous Provisions) Act 1995 and the Need for Escape Devices' (1996) 15 CJQ 305

—— and TP Kennedy, 'International Torts and *Shevill*: The Ghost of Forum-Shopping Yet to Come' [1996] LMCLQ 108.

Reynolds, F, 'Proper Law of a Brandt v Liverpool Contract' [1985] LMCLQ 188

—— '*Vita Food* Resurgent' (1992) 108 LQR 395

—— 'The Carriage of Goods by Sea Act 1992' [1993] LMCLQ 436

Rogerson, P, 'The Situs of Debts in the Conflict of Laws—Illogical, Artificial and Misleading' [1990] CLJ 441

—— '*Kuwait Airways Corp v Iraqi Airways Corp*: the Territoriality Principle in Private International Law—Vice or Virtue?' (2003) 56 CLP 265

Rolph, D, 'The Message, Not the Medium: Defamation, Publication and the Internet in *Dow Jones & Co Inc v Gutnick*' (2002) 24 Sydney L Rev 262

Rosett, A, 'UNIDROIT Principles and Harmonization of International Commercial Law: Focus on Chapter 7' (1997) 2 Uniform L Rev (NS) 441

Sandford, K, 'Analysis of the UK Regulations' (2002) 4(3) E-Commerce Law and Policy 7

Schmidt, J, 'The Invalidity of Certain Choices of Law Clauses under German Law' [1995] JBL 308

Schu, R, 'Consumer Protection and Private International Law in Internet Contracts' (1997) 5 Intl J of Law & Information Technology 192

Shanmuganathan, N and L Caddy, 'Liability of Online Publishers following *Gutnick*' (2003) 153 NLJ 383

Sing, T, 'Conflict of Laws Implications of the Carriage of Goods by Sea Act 1992' [1994] LMCLQ 280

Smith, S, 'Concurrent Liability in Contract and Unjust Enrichment: the Fundamental Breach Requirement' (1999) 115 LQR 245

Spiro, E, 'The Incidence of Time in the Conflict of Laws' (1969) 19 ICLQ 357

Staniland, H, 'The Himalaya Clause in South Africa' [1992] LMCLQ 317

Staudenmayer, D, 'The Directive on the Sale of Consumer Goods and Associated Guarantees—A Milestone in European Consumer and Private Law' (2000) 8 European Rev of Private Law 547

Stevens, R, 'The Contracts (Rights of Third Parties) Act 1999' (2004) 120 LQR 292

Struycken, T, 'Some Dutch Judicial Reflections on the Rome Convention Art.4(5)' [1996] LMCLQ 18

Swadling, W, 'A new role for resulting trusts?' (1996) 16 LS 110

Takahashi, K, 'Jurisdiction in Matters Relating to Contract: Article 5(1) of the Brussels Convention and Regulation' [2002] ELR 530

Thomson, A, 'A Different Approach to Choice of Law in Contract' (1980) 43 MLR 650

Thünken, A, 'Multi-State Advertising over the Internet and the Private International Law of Unfair Competition' (2002) 51 ICLQ 909

Treitel, G, 'The Legal Status of Straight Bills of Lading' (2003) 119 LQR 608

Vilkova, N, 'The Unification of Conflict of Laws Rules in the CIS Countries' (2000) 26 Rev of Eastern European Law 75

Virgo, G, 'Interest, Constructive Trusts and the Conflict of Laws' (2000) 8 Restitution L Rev 122

Weatherill, S, 'Consumer Guarantees' (1994) 110 LQR 545

Webb, PRH, and North, PM, 'The Place of Commission of a Tort in Private International Law' (1965) 14 ICLQ 1314

White, R, 'Enforcement of Foreign Judgments in Equity' (1982) 11 Sydney L Rev 631

Winship, P, 'Private International Law and the U.N. Sales Convention' [1988] Cornell Intl LJ 487

Withers, C, 'Jurisdiction Clauses and the Unfair Terms in Consumer Contracts Regulations' [2002] LMCLQ 56

Worthington, S, 'The Proprietary Consequences of Rescission' (2002) 10 Restitution L Rev 28

Ziegel, J, 'Conditional Sales and the Conflict of Laws' (1967) 45 Canadian Bar Rev 284

INDEX